Lecture Notes in Computer Science   9088

Commenced Publication in 1973
Founding and Former Series Editors:
Gerhard Goos, Juris Hartmanis, and Jan van Leeuwen

Editorial Board

More information about this series at http://www.springer.com/series/7409

Fabien Gandon · Marta Sabou
Harald Sack · Claudia d'Amato
Philippe Cudré-Mauroux
Antoine Zimmermann (Eds.)

The Semantic Web

Latest Advances and New Domains

12th European Semantic Web Conference, ESWC 2015
Portoroz, Slovenia, May 31 – June 4, 2015
Proceedings

Editors
Fabien Gandon
Inria
Sophia Antipolis
France

Claudia d'Amato
Università degli Studi di Bari "Aldo Moro"
Bari
Italy

Marta Sabou
Technische Universität Wien
Wien
Austria

Philippe Cudré-Mauroux
University of Fribourg
Fribourg
Switzerland

Harald Sack
Hasso-Plattner-Institut
Potsdam
Germany

Antoine Zimmermann
École des Mines de Saint-Étienne
Saint-Étienne
France

ISSN 0302-9743   ISSN 1611-3349   (electronic)
Lecture Notes in Computer Science
ISBN 978-3-319-18817-1   ISBN 978-3-319-18818-8   (eBook)
DOI 10.1007/978-3-319-18818-8

Library of Congress Control Number: 2015938439

LNCS Sublibrary: SL3 – Information Systems and Applications, incl. Internet/Web and HCI

Springer Cham Heidelberg New York Dordrecht London

Printed on acid-free paper

Springer International Publishing AG Switzerland is part of Springer Science+Business Media
(www.springer.com)

Preface

For several years now, the Web has exceeded its initial instantiation of being a document-centric space. Following its many evolutions, it has become a virtual place where people and software can cooperate within mixed communities. It supports a hybrid society where humans and Web robots interact in particular through shared metadata. These large-scale interactions create many problems, and in particular the ongoing need to reconcile the formal semantics of computer science (logics, ontologies, typing systems, etc.) on which the Web architecture is built, with the soft semantics of people (posts, tags, status, and so on) through which Web content is created.

As the Web becomes a ubiquitous infrastructure reflecting all the objects of our world, we witness ever-increasing frictions between formal semantics and social semantics. This trend is also amplified by the growing number of datasets published, interlinked, and reused on the Web. This expanding Web of data, together with the schemas, ontologies, and vocabularies used to structure and link it, forms a formal Semantic Web with which we have to design new interaction means to support the next generation of Web applications.

Another perspective on the above can be found by considering how the initial graph of linked pages of the Web has been joined by a growing number of other graphs including: sociograms capturing social network structures, workflows specifying decision paths to be followed, browsing logs capturing trails of navigation, automata of service compositions specifying distributed processing, linked open data from distant datasets, etc.

Moreover, these graphs are distributed over many different sources with very different characteristics. Some subgraphs are public (e.g. DBpedia), while others are private (e.g. semantic intraWebs). Some subgraphs are small and local (e.g., a user's profile on a device), and some are huge and hosted on clusters (e.g., Wikipedia). Some are largely stable (e.g., a thesaurus for Latin), some change several times per second (e.g., sensor data in a city), etc. And each type of graph of the Web is not an isolated island. Graphs interact with each other: the networks of communities influence the message flows, their subjects and types, the semantic links between terms interact with the links between sites and vice versa, the small changing graphs of sensors are joined to the large stable geographical graphs that position them, etc. Not only do we need the methods to represent and analyze each kind of graph, we also require the means to combine them and to perform multi-criteria analyzes on their combinations.

As soon as we want to analyze and combine these many facets of one Web, we face the general challenge of the Web. If it is true that the Web architecture is designed through standards, its participatory nature makes the Web emerge as an openly co-constructed global object. The "world-wide way" of deploying the Web everywhere and for everything implies that, as the Web is spreading into the world, the world is spreading into the Web. The resulting world "wild" Web that is being created and is evolving every day is contaminated by the complexity of our world. This complexity implies that a huge challenge for Web development is its need for large-scale multi-disciplinary cooperation: the three 'W's of the World Wide Web call for the three 'M's of a Massively Multidisciplinary Methodology, and the Semantic Web is no exception to this. The diversity of linked data within the Semantic Web is an asset to address the diversity of resources identified on the Web. But for the Semantic Web to reach its full potential, it needs in return to embrace the multidisciplinary needs of the Web. ESWC 2015 embeds the above, being a truly interdisciplinary event.

The ESWC Conference is now established as a yearly major venue for discussing the latest scientific results and technology innovations related to the Semantic Web. This 12th edition took place from May 31st to June 4th 2015 in Portoroz, Slovenia. Besides having a main focus on advances in Semantic Web research and technologies, we, the Chairs of ESWC 2015, decided to broaden the scope to span other relevant research areas. The core tracks of the research conference were complemented with new tracks focusing on linking machine and human computation at Web scale (Cognition and Semantic Web, Human Computation and Crowdsourcing).

This choice also resulted in three exciting invited keynotes. Lise Getoor (University of California) explained how to combine statistics and semantics to turn data into knowledge, building on state-of-the-art optimization methods in a distributed implementation to solve large-scale knowledge graph extraction problems. Viktor Mayer-Schönberger (Oxford Internet Institute/Oxford University) discussed why Big Data really matters a lot and why we need to be cautious and well aware of its limitations. Massimo Poesio (University of Essex) showed what crowdsourcing tells us about cognition taking the special case of a game-with-a-purpose designed to collect data about anaphora.

The main scientific program of the conference comprised of 42 papers: 33 research papers and 9 in-use, selected out of 164 submissions, which corresponds to an acceptance rate of 23% for the 145 research papers submitted, and of 47% for the 19 in-use papers submitted. This program was completed by a demonstration and poster session, in which researchers had the chance to present their latest results and advances in the form of live demos. In addition, the PhD Symposium program included 12 contributions, selected out of 16 submissions.

To have an open, multidisciplinary, and cross-fertilizing event, we complemented the conference program with 21 workshops, 9 tutorials, as well as 5 challenges and the EU Project Networking session. This year, an open call for challenges allowed us to select and support 5 challenges.

As General and Program Committee chairs, we would like to thank the many people that were involved in making ESWC 2015 a success.

First of all, our thanks go to the 24 track chairs and 427 reviewers including 107 external reviewers for ensuring a rigorous blind review process that led to an excellent scientific program and an average number of 4.75 reviews per article. This was also completed by an inspiring selection of posters and demos chaired by Serena Villata and Christophe Guéret.

Special thanks go to the PhD Symposium Chairs, Claudia d'Amato and Philippe Cudré-Mauroux, who proposed and managed a very constructive organization ensuring a real mentoring to all the brilliant students who participated.

We had a great selection of workshops and tutorials thanks to the dynamism of our Workshop Chairs Catherine Faron and John Breslin and Tutorial Chairs Elena Simperl and Antoine Isaac.

Thanks to our EU Project Networking Session Chairs Frédérique Segond, Jun Zhao, Erik Mannens, and Sergio Consoli we had the opportunity to arrange meetings and exciting discussions between the contributors of the leading research projects.

Thanks to the work of Elena Cabrio and Milan Stankovic and all the Challenges Chairs, we successfully established a challenge track with an open call leading to a very useful comparison of the latest solutions for five challenge areas.

Thanks to STI International for supporting the conference organization, to Ioan Toma (from STI) for taking care of the budget. Of course we warmly thank our local organizers, in particular Marko Grobelnik, Špela Sitar, and Monika Kropej from the Jožef Stefan Institute Ljubljana. youvivo GmbH and in particular Martina Hartl deserves special thanks for the professional support of the conference organization.

We are very grateful to Mauro Dragoni, our Publicity Chair who kept our community informed at every stage and Serge Tymaniuk, who administered the Website.

Our Sponsor Chair Blaž Fortuna played an extremely important role in collecting sponsorships for the conference, the awards and the grants. And of course we also thank our sponsors listed in the next pages, for their vital support to this edition of ESWC.

We also want to stress the huge work achieved by the Semantic Technologies coordinators Anna Lisa Gentile, Andrea Giovanni Nuzzolese, Luca Costabello, Lionel Medini, and Fuqi Song who developed a new version of our "ESWC Conference Live" mobile app.

Special thanks also to our Proceedings Chair Antoine Zimmermann, who did a remarkable job in preparing this volume with the kind support of Springer.

March 2015

Fabien Gandon
Marta Sabou
Harald Sack

Organization

Organizing Committee

General Chair

Fabien Gandon   Inria, France

Program Chairs

Marta Sabou   Vienna University of Technology, Austria
Harald Sack   Hasso-Plattner-Institute for IT Systems
                Engineering, University of Potsdam, Germany

Local Chair

Marko Grobelnik   Jožef Stefan Institute Ljubljana, Slovenia

Workshops Chairs

John Breslin   NUI Galway, Ireland
Catherine Faron   University of Nice Sophia Antipolis, France

Poster and Demo Chairs

Christophe Guéret   Data Archiving and Networked Services,
                      The Netherlands
Serena Villata   Inria, Sophia Antipolis, France

Tutorials Chairs

Elena Simperl   University of Southampton, UK
Antoine Isaac   Vrije Universiteit Amsterdam, The Netherlands

PhD Symposium Chairs

Claudia d'Amato   Università degli Studi di Bari, Italy
Philippe Cudré-Mauroux   University of Fribourg, Switzerland

Challenge Chairs

Elena Cabrio   Inria, Sophia Antipolis, France
Milan Stankovic   Sépage & STIH, Université Paris-Sorbonne, France

Semantic Technologies Coordinators

Andrea Giovanni Nuzzolese   University of Bologna/STLab ISTC-CNR, Italy
Luca Costabello   Fujitsu, Galway, Ireland

Lionel Medini	University of Lyon, France
Fuqi Song	Inria, Sophia Antipolis, France
Anna Lisa Gentile	University of Sheffield, UK

EU Project Networking Session Chairs

Frédérique Segond	Viseo, Grenoble, France
Jun Zhao	Lancaster University, UK
Erik Mannens	Multimedia Lab - iMinds - Ghent University, Belgium
Sergio Consoli	STLab ISTC-CNR, Italy

Publicity Chair

Mauro Dragoni   Fondazione Bruno Kessler, Italy

Sponsor Chair

Blaž Fortuna   Ghent University, Belgium

Web Presence

Serge Tymaniuk   STI International, Austria

Proceedings Chair

Antoine Zimmermann   Ecole nationale supérieure des mines de Saint-Étienne, France

Treasurer

Ioan Toma   STI International, Austria

Local Organization and Conference Administration

Špela Sitar	Jožef Stefan Institute Ljubljana, Slovenia
Monika Kropej	Jožef Stefan Institute Ljubljana, Slovenia

Program Committee

Program Chairs

Marta Sabou	Vienna University of Technology, Austria
Harald Sack	Hasso-Plattner-Institute for IT Systems Engineering, University of Potsdam, Germany

Track Chairs

Silvio Peroni	University of Bologna, Italy and National Research Council, Italy
Pavel Shvaiko	Informatica Trentina SpA, Italy
Pascal Hitzler	Wright State University, USA
Stefan Schlobach	Vrije Universiteit Amsterdam, The Netherlands

Sören Auer	University of Bonn, Germany
Stefan Dietze	L3S Research Center, Germany
Miriam Fernandez	Knowledge Media Institute, The Open University, UK
Markus Strohmaier	GESIS and University of Koblenz-Landau, Germany
Olivier Curé	Université Pierre et Marie Curie, France
Axel Polleres	Vienna University of Economics and Business, Austria
Kalina Bontcheva	University of Sheffield, UK
Simone Paolo Ponzetto	University of Mannheim, Germany
Bettina Berendt	Katholieke Universiteit Leuven, Belgium
Heiko Paulheim	University of Mannheim, Germany
Alasdair Gray	Heriot-Watt University, UK
Terry Payne	University of Liverpool, UK
Carlos Pedrinaci	Knowledge Media Institute, The Open University, UK
Aba-Sah Dadzie	The HCI Centre, The University of Birmingham, UK
Andreas Nürnberger	Otto-von-Guericke University Magdeburg, Germany
Lora Aroyo	Vrije Universiteit Amsterdam, The Netherlands
Gianluca Demartini	University of Sheffield, UK
Vanessa Lopez	IBM Research, Ireland
Giovanni Tumarello	SindiceTech/Fondazione Bruno Kessler, Italy

Members (All Tracks)

Karl Aberer	Peter Bloem
Maribel Acosta	Eva Blomqvist
Guadalupe Aguado-De-Cea	Fernando Bobillo
Harith Alani	Kalina Bontcheva
Bernd Amann	Stefano Borgo
Kemafor Anyanwu	Johan Bos
Lora Aroyo	Gosse Bouma
Manuel Atencia	Paolo Bouquet
Martin Atzmueller	Alessandro Bozzon
Sören Auer	Paul Buitelaar
Nathalie Aussenac-Gilles	Liliana Cabral
Claudio Baldassarre	Elena Cabrio
Michele Barbera	Jean-Paul Calbimonte
Payam Barnaghi	Nicoletta Calzolari
Pierpaolo Basile	Erik Cambria
Zohra Bellahsene	Amparo E. Cano
Bettina Berendt	Iván Cantador
Chris Biemann	David Carral
Antonis Bikakis	Marco Antonio Casanova

Michele Catasta
Irene Celino
Pierre-Antoine Champin
Jean Charlet
Vinay Chaudhri
Paolo Ciccarese
Marco Combetto
Mariano Consens
Bonaventura Coppola
Oscar Corcho
Gianluca Correndo
David Corsar
Fabio Cozman
Danilo Croce
Philippe Cudré-Mauroux
Olivier Curé
Claudia d'Amato
Mathieu d'Aquin
Aba-Sah Dadzie
Danica Damljanovic
Jérôme David
Joseph Davis
Anna De Liddo
Ernesto William De Luca
Gerard de Melo
Thierry Declerck
Luciano Del Corro
Emanuele Della Valle
Gianluca Demartini
Elena Demidova
Leon Derczynski
Tommaso Di Noia
Stefan Dietze
Djellel Eddine Difallah
Dejing Dou
Mauro Dragoni
Anca Dumitrache
Esra Erdem
Vadim Ermolayev
Jérôme Euzenat
Federico Michele Facca
Nicola Fanizzi
Miriam Fernandez
Besnik Fetahu
Fabian Flöck
Blaž Fortuna

Flavius Frasincar
Fred Freitas
Johannes Fürnkranz
Fabien Gandon
Aldo Gangemi
Roberto Garcia
José María García
Nuria García Santa
Raúl García-Castro
Daniel Garijo
Dragan Gasevic
Anna Lisa Gentile
Chiara Ghidini
Alain Giboin
Fausto Giunchiglia
François Goasdoué
John Goodwin
Thomas Gottron
Jorge Gracia
Michael Granitzer
Alasdair Gray
Gunnar Aastrand Grimnes
Gerd Groener
Paul Groth
Tudor Groza
Alessio Gugliotta
Giancarlo Guizzardi
Asunción Gómez-Pérez
Peter Haase
Ollivier Haemmerlé
Harry Halpin
Siegfried Handschuh
Andreas Harth
Olaf Hartig
Oktie Hassanzadeh
Yulan He
Benjamin Heitmann
Sebastian Hellmann
Martin Hepp
Pascal Hitzler
Aidan Hogan
Laura Hollink
Matthew Horridge
Katja Hose
Veronique Hoste
Geert-Jan Houben

Guilin Qi
Yuzhong Qu
Achim Rettinger
Chantal Reynaud
Mikko Rinne
Carlos R. Rivero
Giuseppe Rizzo
Mariano Rodriguez-Muro
Víctor Rodríguez Doncel
Haggai Roitman
Dumitru Roman
Camille Roth
Marie-Christine Rousset
Matthew Rowe
Edna Ruckhaus
Marta Sabou
Harald Sack
Hassan Saif
Cristina Sarasua
Felix Sasaki
Marco Luca Sbodio
Ansgar Scherp
Stefan Schlobach
Thomas Schneider
Stefan Schulte
Juan F. Sequeda
Luciano Serafini
Baris Sertkaya
Amit Sheth
Pavel Shvaiko
Gerardo Simari
Kiril Simov
Elena Simperl
Philipp Singer
Monika Solanki
Steffen Staab
Steffen Stadtmüller
Milan Stankovic
Yannis Stavrakas
Thomas Steiner
Armando Stellato
Giorgos Stoilos
Umberto Straccia
Markus Strohmaier
Heiner Stuckenschmidt
Gerd Stumme
Fabian Suchanek

Vojtech Svátek
Marcin Sydow
Pedro Szekely
Valentina Tamma
Ke Tao
Kerry Taylor
Jeni Tennison
Martin Theobald
Thanassis Tiropanis
Ioan Toma
Alessandra Toninelli
Farouk Toumani
Thanh Tran
Volker Tresp
Raphaël Troncy
Tania Tudorache
Giovanni Tumarello
Anni-Yasmin Turhan
Jürgen Umbrich
Christina Unger
Alejandro A. Vaisman
Herbert Van De Sompel
Willem Robert Van Hage
Frank Van Harmelen
Pierre-Yves Vandenbussche
Joaquin Vanschoren
Paola Velardi
Ruben Verborgh
Maria Esther Vidal
Evelyne Viegas
Boris Villazón-Terrazas
Johanna Völker
Holger Wache
Claudia Wagner
Haofen Wang
Kewen Wang
Shenghui Wang
Erik Wilde
Cord Wiljes
Gregory Todd Williams
Gerhard Wohlgenannt
Stuart Wrigley
Josiane Xavier Parreira
Fouad Zablith
Ondrej Zamazal
Ziqi Zhang
Antoine Zimmermann

Additional Reviewers

Azad Abad
Markus Ackermann
Xavier Aimé
Muhammad Intizar Ali
Pramod Anantharam
Mario Arias Gallego
Isabelle Augenstein
Stefan Baier
Fredah Banda
Maria Bermudez-Edo
Shreyansh Bhatt
Georgeta Bordea
Stefano Bortoli
Julia Bosque-Gil
Martin Brümmer
Jose Camacho Collados
Vinay Chaudhri
Catherine Chavula
Long Cheng
Evangelia Daskalaki
Brian Davis
Jeremy Debattista
Chiara Di Francescomarino
Zlatan Dragisic
Mauro Dragoni
Steffen Eger
Basil Ell
Cristobal Esteban
Daniel Faria
Tiziano Flati
Andre Freitas
Natalja Friesen
Irini Fundulaki
Michael Färber
Jhonatan Garcia
Andrés García
Kalpa Gunaratna
Yingjie Hu
Luis Ibanez
Natalya Keberle
Felix Leif Keppmann
Robin Keskisärkkä
Sarah Kohail

Sefki Kolozali
Spyros Kotoulas
Denis Krompass
Tobias Käfer
Benedikt Kämpgen
Sarasi Lalithsena
Maxime Lefrançois
Tatiana Lesnikova
Angela Locoro
Michael Luggen
Fadi Maali
Robert Meusel
Florian Michahelles
Pasquale Minervini
Aditya Mogadala
Gabriela Montoya
Andrea Moro
Raghava Mutharaju
Hai Nguyen
Phuong Nguyen
Quoc Viet Hung Nguyen
Nikolay Nikolov
Samuel Okure
Niklas Petersen
Riccardo Porrini
Jędrzej Potoniec
Valentina Presutti
Freddy Priyatna
Roman Prokofyev
Iuliia Proskurnia
Daniel Puschmann
Behrang Qasemizadeh
Gianluca Quercini
Giseli Rabello Lopes
Sonja Radenkovic
David Ratcliffe
Steffen Remus
Yuan Ren
Ryan Ribeiro De Azevedo
Petar Ristoski
Giuseppe Rizzo
Cleyton Rodrigues
Jessica Rosati

Tong Ruan
Eugen Ruppert
Adam Sanchez Ayte
Emilio Sanfilippo
Marco Luca Sbodio
Jörg Schlötterer
Michael Schmidt
Kunal Sengupta
Kostas Stefanidis
Simone Tallevi-Diotallevi
Paolo Tomeo
Pierpaolo Tommasi

Georgia Troullinou
Kateryna Tymoshenko
Jürgen Umbrich
Tim vor der Brück
Joerg Waitelonis
Xin Wang
Zhe Wang
Christian Wirth
Jiewen Wu
Tianxing Wu
Marcin Wylot
Zhang, Wei Emma

PhD Symposium Program Committee

Chairs

Claudia d'Amato	Università degli Studi di Bari, Italy
Philippe Cudré-Mauroux	University of Fribourg, Switzerland

Members

Abraham Bernstein	University of Zurich, Switzerland
Eva Blomqvist	Linköping University, Sweden
Philippe Cudré-Mauroux	University of Fribourg, Switzerland
Olivier Curé	Université Paris-Est LIGM, France
Claudia d'Amato	Università degli Studi di Bari, Italy
Mathieu d'Aquin	Knowledge Media Institute, The Open University, UK
John Domingue	The Open University, UK
Nicola Fanizzi	Università degli studi di Bari, Italy
Aldo Gangemi	Université Paris 13 and CNR-ISTC, Italy
Chiara Ghidini	FBK-IRST, Italy
Siegfried Handschuh	University of Passau, Germany
Krzysztof Janowicz	University of California, Santa Barbara, USA
Freddy Lecue	IBM Research, Ireland
Enrico Motta	Knowledge Media Institute, The Open University, UK
Natasha Noy	Google, USA
Bijan Parsia	University of Manchester, UK
Valentina Presutti	STLab ISTC-CNR, Italy
Sebastian Rudolph	Technische Universität Dresden, Germany
Uli Sattler	University of Manchester, UK
Stefan Schlobach	Vrije Universiteit Amsterdam, The Netherlands
Luciano Serafini	Fondazione Bruno Kessler, Italy
Gerardo Simari	Universidad Nacional del Sur and CONICET, Argentina

Elena Simperl	University of Southampton, UK
Steffen Staab	University of Koblenz-Landau, Germany
Heiner Stuckenschmidt	University of Mannheim, Germany
Vojtěch Svátek	University of Economics, Prague, Czech Republic
Valentina Tamma	University of Liverpool, UK
Matthias Thimm	University of Koblenz-Landau, Germany
Tania Tudorache	Stanford University, USA
Jürgen Umbrich	Vienna University of Economics and Business, Austria

Steering Committee

Chair

| John Domingue | The Open University, UK and STI International, Austria |

Members

Claudia d'Amato	Università degli Studi di Bari, Italy
Grigoris Antoniou	FORTH, Greece
Philipp Cimiano	Bielefeld University, Germany
Oscar Corcho	Universidad Politécnica de Madrid, Spain
Marko Grobelnik	Jožef Stefan Institute Ljubljana, Slovenia
Axel Polleres	Vienna University of Economics and Business, Austria
Valentina Presutti	STLab (ISTC-CNR), Italy
Elena Simperl	University of Southampton, UK

Sponsoring Institutions

Combining Statistics and Semantics to Turn Data into Knowledge

Lise Getoor

University of California, USA

Abstract. Addressing inherent uncertainty and exploiting structure are fundamental to turning data into knowledge. Statistical relational learning (SRL) builds on principles from probability theory and statistics to address uncertainty while incorporating tools from logic to represent structure. In this talk I will overview our recent work on probabilistic soft logic (PSL), an SRL framework for collective, probabilistic reasoning in relational domains. PSL is able to reason holistically about both entity attributes and relationships among the entities, along with ontological constraints. The underlying mathematical framework supports extremely efficient inference. Our recent results show that by building on state-of-the-art optimization methods in a distributed implementation, we can solve large-scale knowledge graph extraction problems with millions of random variables orders of magnitude faster than existing approaches.

Why Big Data Matters - A Lot

Viktor Mayer-Schönberger

Oxford University, UK

Abstract. Much has been made of "big data", our ability to gain novel insights from a comprehensive set of data points, but a lot of it is hype, and marketing-speak to sell more tools and consulting. In this talk, I will explain what Big Data really is, why it isnt just a marketing fad or the tool du jour, but a new way of making sense of the world around us, and consequently why Big Data matters a great deal, in particular also in the context of semantic technologies. But I will also mention why we need to be cautious and well aware of Big Data limitations when utilizing it.

What Crowdsourcing Tells Us about Cognition: The Case of Anaphora

Massimo Poesio

University of Essex, UK

Abstract. Crowdsourcing is usually seen primarily as an inexpensive and quick way of creating large resources for a variety of Artificial Intelligence tasks. However, our work with Phrase Detectives, a game-with-a-purpose designed to collect data about anaphora, suggests that collecting large numbers of judgments about very large amounts of data also tells us a lot about the extent to which human subjects agree or disagree about the interpretation of such data. In the talk I will introduce Phrase Detectives and discuss our results and their implications.

Contents

Machine Learning

Mobile Web, Internet of Things and Semantic Streams

Services, Web APIs, and the Web of Things

Cognition and Semantic Web

Human Computation and Crowdsourcing

In-Use and Industrial Track

PhD Symposium

XXVIII   Contents

Vocabularies, Schemas, Ontologies

Requirements for and Evaluation of User Support for Large-Scale Ontology Alignment

Valentina Ivanova[1,2], Patrick Lambrix[1,2(✉)], and Johan Åberg[1]

[1] Department of Computer and Information Science,
Linköping University, 581 83 Linköping, Sweden
patrick.lambrix@liu.se
[2] The Swedish e-Science Research Centre, Linköping University,
581 83 Linköping, Sweden

Abstract. Currently one of the challenges for the ontology alignment community is the user involvement in the alignment process. At the same time, the focus of the community has shifted towards large-scale matching which introduces an additional dimension to this issue. This paper aims to provide a set of requirements that foster the user involvement for large-scale ontology alignment tasks. Further, we present and discuss the results of a literature study for 7 ontology alignments systems as well as a heuristic evaluation and an observational user study for 3 ontology alignment systems to reveal the coverage of the requirements in the systems and the support for the requirements in the user interfaces.

1 Motivation

The growth of the ontology alignment area in the past ten years has led to the development of many ontology alignment tools. The progress in the field has been accelerated by the Ontology Alignment Evaluation Initiative (OAEI) which has provided a discussion forum for developers and a platform for an annual evaluation of their tools. The number of participants in the OAEI increases each year, yet few provide a user interface and even fewer navigational aids or complex visualization techniques. Some systems provide scalable ontology alignment algorithms. However, for achieving high-quality alignments user involvement during the process is indispensable.

Nearly half of the challenges identified in [29] are directly related to user involvement. These include *explanation of matching results* to users, fostering the *user involvement* in the matching process and *social and collaborative matching*. Another challenge aims at supporting users' collaboration by providing *infrastructure and support* during all phases of the alignment process. All these challenges can be addressed by providing user interfaces in combination with suitable visualization techniques.

The demand for user involvement has been recognized by the alignment community and resulted in the introduction of the OAEI Interactive track in 2013. Quality measures for evaluation of interactive ontology alignment tools have been proposed in [25]. The results from the first two editions of the track show

© Springer International Publishing Switzerland 2015
F. Gandon et al. (Eds.): ESWC 2015, LNCS 9088, pp. 3–20, 2015.
DOI: 10.1007/978-3-319-18818-8_1

the benefits from introducing user interactions (in comparison with the systems' non-interactive modes). In the first edition the precision for all (five) participants and the recall for three was raised. For the second edition three (out of four) systems increased their precision and two their recall. The test cases presented in [13] show that simulating user interactions with 30 % error rate during the alignment process has led to the same results as a non-interactive matching.

With the development of the ontology engineering field the size and complexity of the ontologies, the alignments and, consequently, the matching problems increase as emphasized in [29] by the *large-scale matching evaluation* challenge. This trend is demanding scalable and (perhaps) novel user interfaces and interactions which is going to impose even stricter scalability requirements towards the algorithms in order to provide timely response to the users. Scalability, not only in terms of computation, but also in terms of interaction is one of the crucial features for the ontology alignment systems as stated in [13]. According to [27] user interactions are essential (in the context of large ontologies) for configuring the matching process, incremental matching and providing feedback to the system regarding the generated mapping suggestions.

This paper provides requirements for ontology alignment tools that encourage user involvement for large-scale ontology alignment tasks (Sect. 2). We also present the results from a literature study (Sect. 3) and two user interface evaluations (Sect. 4) to reveal the coverage of the requirements in current ontology alignment systems and the support for the requirements in their user interfaces. Section 5 concludes the paper.

2 Requirements for User Support in Large-Scale Ontology Alignment

This section presents requirements for ontology alignment systems meant to foster user engagement for large-scale ontology alignment problems. We extend the requirements in [8] which address the cognitive support that should be provided by an alignment system to a user during the alignment process. While they are essential for every alignment system, their influence becomes more pressing with increasing ontology size and complexity. Further, the focus in the community has shifted towards large-scale matching since the time they have been developed. Thus other requirements (not necessary related to the user interface) to assist the user in managing larger and more complex ontologies and alignments are in demand. They are extracted from existing works and systems and from the authors' personal experience from developing ontology alignment and debugging systems [16–18]. These requirements contribute to the development of a complete infrastructure that supports the users during large-scale alignment tasks and may pose additional visualization and interface requirements. We note that the requirements in [10] and [7] may also be seen as subsets of the requirements in this paper.

The requirements identified in [8] are based on research in the area of cognitive theories. They are grouped in four conceptual dimensions (Table 1). The *Analysis*

Table 1. Cognitive support requirements adapted from [8].

Dimensions	Requirements
Analysis and Generation Dimension	#3.1: automatic discovery of some mappings;
	#3.2: test mappings by automatically transforming instances between ontologies;
	#3.3: support potential interruptions by saving and returning users to given state;
	#3.4: support identification and guidance for resolving conflicts;
Representation Dimension	#4.1: visual representation of the source and target ontology; (I)
	#4.2: representation of a potential mapping describing why it was suggested, where the terms are in the ontologies, and their context; (I,E)
	#4.3: representation of the verified mappings that describe why the mapping was accepted, where the terms are in the ontologies, and their context; (I,E)
	#4.4: identify visually candidate-heavy regions; (I)
	#4.5: indicate possible start points for the user; (E)
	#4.6: progress feedback on the overall mapping process; (E)
	#4.7: feedback explaining how the tool determined a potential mapping; (E)
Analysis and Decision Making Dimension	#1.1: ontology exploration and manual creation of mappings; (I,M) tooling for the creation of temporary mappings; (M)
	#1.2: method for the user to accept/reject a suggested mapping; (M)
	#1.3: access to full definitions of ontology terms; (I)
	#1.4: show the context of a term when a user is inspecting a suggestion; (I)
Interaction Dimension	#2.1: interactive access to source and target ontologies; (I)
	#2.2: interactive navigation and allow the user to accept/reject suggestions; (I,M)
	#2.3: interactive navigation and removal of verified mappings; (I,M)
	#2.4: searching and filtering the ontologies and mappings; (I)
	#2.5: adding details on verified mappings and manually create mappings; (M)

and Generation dimension includes functions for automatic computation and trial execution of mapping suggestions (potential mappings), inconsistency detection/ resolution and services for interrupting/resuming the alignment process. The mappings and mapping suggestions together with explanations why/how they are suggested/accepted are visualized by services in the *Representation* dimension. Other functions include interactions for overview and exploration of the ontologies and alignments and feedback for the state of the process. The *Analysis and Decision Making* dimension considers the users' internal decision making processes and involves exploration of the ontology terms and their context during the process of discovering and creating (temporary) mappings, and validating mapping suggestions. The requirements in this dimension can be considered to utilize the functionalities represented by the requirements in the *Interaction* dimension—during which the user interacts with the system through its exploration, filtering and searching services in order to materialize his/her decisions by creating mappings and accepting/rejecting mapping suggestions.

The requirements provided by the *Representation* and *Interaction* dimensions are involved in the human-system interaction and can be roughly separated in the following three subcategories of the user interface category (shown in Table 2)—manipulation (M), inspection (I) and explanatory (E) requirements. Those in the first category include actions for transforming the mapping suggestions in an alignment—accept/reject mapping suggestions, add metadata and manually create mappings, etc. Similar functionalities are needed for the ontologies (#5.0), as well, since the user may need to, for instance, introduce a concept in order to provide more accurate mappings, as described in [20] as well. Those in the second category cover a broad set of actions for inspecting the ontologies and alignments—exploring the ontologies, mappings and mapping suggestions, search and filter by various criteria, zoom, overview, etc. The third category includes services for presenting information to the user, for instance, reasons to suggest/ accept a mapping suggestion, how the tool has calculated it, hinting at possible starting points and showing the current state of the process.

Various requirements arise from the tendency of increasing the size and complexity of the ontologies, alignments and alignment problems. They are grouped in the infrastructure and algorithms category in Table 2. We do not discuss techniques for large-scale matching [27] or matching with background knowledge despite they affect the interactivity of the systems and thus indirectly influence the user involvement.

Aligning large and complex ontologies cannot be handled on a single occasion. Thus the user should be able to suspend the process, preserve its state and resume it at another point in time (#3.3). Such **interruptions of the alignment process (#5.1)** may take place during different stages, for instance, during the computation of mapping suggestions, during their validation, etc. At the time of interruption the system may provide partial results which can be reused when the alignment process has been resumed. SAMBO [17] implements this by introducing interruptible computation, validation and recommendation sessions.

Table 2. Requirements to support user involvement in large-scale matching tasks. (supported (✓); partly supported (+); special case, details in the text (*); not supported (-))

		Requirements	AlViz	SAMBO	PROMPT	CogZ	RepOSE	AML	COMA
large-scale	user interface — manipulate	#2.5;1.1 create mapping manually	✓(*)	✓	✓	✓	+	-	✓(*)
		#2.2;1.2 accept/reject suggestion	✓(*)	✓	✓	✓	✓	-	✓(*)
		#2.5 add metadata to mapping	-	✓	✓	✓	-	-	-
		#2.3 move a mapping to list	-	✓	✓	✓	+	-	-
		#5.0 ontology	✓	-	✓	✓	-	-	-
	user interface — inspect	#2.2;1.4 mapping suggestions	✓(*)	✓	✓	✓	+	-	✓(*)
		#2.3 mappings	✓(*)	✓	✓	✓	✓	✓	✓(*)
		#4.4 heavy-regions	✓	-	-	✓	-	-	+
		#2.4 filter/search	-/✓	-/✓	-/-	✓/✓	-/-	+/✓	-/✓
		#4.1/2/3;2.1;1.1/3 ontologies	✓	✓	✓	✓	✓	+	✓
	explain	#4.2/7;5.8 why/how suggested	+	+	✓	✓	+	+	+
		#4.3 why accepted	-	✓	✓	✓	-	-	-
		#4.5 starting point	+	-	-	+	✓	-	+
		#4.6 process state	✓	+	+	✓	+	-	+
	infrastructure & algorithms	#5.1;3.3 sessions	+	✓	+	+	+	-	✓
		#5.2 clustering	✓	+	-	✓	✓	✓	✓
		#5.3 reduce user interventions	-	+	+	-	-	-	-
		#5.4 collaboration	-	-	-	-	-	-	-
		#5.5 environment	-	+	+	-	-	+	+
		#5.6 recommend/rank	-	✓	+	+	✓	-	✓
		#5.7;3.4 debugging	-	✓	✓	✓	✓	✓	-
		#5.8;4.2/7 matchers configuration	-	✓	+	+	✓	✓	✓
		#5.9.1;3.2 trial execution	-	-	-	-	-	-	-
		#5.9.2;1.1 temporary decisions	✓	+	+	✓	-	-	-

Another strategy to deal with large-scale tasks is to **divide** them **into smaller tasks (#5.2)**. This can be achieved by clustering algorithms or grouping heuristics. Smaller problems can be more easily managed by single users and devices with limited resources. The authors of AlViz [19] highlight that clustering the graph improves the interactivity of the program. Clustering of the ontologies and alignments will allow reusing visualization techniques that work for smaller problems. A fragment-based strategy is implemented in [6] where the authors also note that not all fragments in one schema would have corresponding fragments in another.

In the context of large-scale matching it is not feasible for a user to validate all mapping suggestions generated by a system, i.e., tool developers should aim at **reducing unnecessary user interventions (#5.3)**. The authors in [25] define a measure for evaluating interactive matching tools based on the number and type of user interventions in connection with the achieved F-measure. LogMap2 [13] only requires user validation for problematic suggestions. In [17] the authors demonstrate that the session-based approach can reduce the unnecessary user interventions by utilizing the knowledge from previously validated suggestions. GOMMA [15] can reuse mappings between older ontology versions in order to match their newer versions. PROMPT [23] logs the operations performed for merging/aligning two ontologies and can automatically reapply them if needed. Reducing the user interventions, but at the same time effectively combining manual validation with automatic computations are two of the challenges identified in [24]. The authors in [5] and [28] discuss criteria for selecting mapping suggestions that are shown to the user and strategies for user feedback propagation in order to reduce the user-system interactions. The same issues in a multi-user context are presented in [4]. A dialectical approach reusing partial alignment to map portions of two ontologies without exposing them is evaluated in [26].

Matching large ontologies is a lengthy and demanding task for a single user. It can be relaxed by involving several users who can discuss together and decide on problematic mappings in a collaborative environment. The **social and collaborative matching (#5.4)** is still a challenge for the alignment community [29].

Another challenge insufficiently addressed [29] by the alignment community is related to the **environment (#5.5)** where such collaboration could happen. Apart from aligning ontologies it should also support a variety of functions for managing alignments as explained in [7]. The environment should support communication services between its members as well—discussion lists, wikis, messages, annotations, etc.

Providing **recommendations (#5.6)** is another approach to support the user during the decision making process. They can be based on external resources, previous user actions, etc. and can be present at each point user intervention is needed—choosing an initial matcher configuration [1,17], validating mapping suggestions [16] etc.

The outcome of the applications that consume alignments is directly dependent on the quality of the alignments. A direct step towards improving the quality of the alignments and, consequently, the results from such applications is the introduction of **a debugging step during the alignment process (#5.7)**. It was shown in [11] that a domain expert has changed his decisions regarding mappings he had manually created, after an interaction with a debugging system. Most of the alignments produced in the Anatomy, LargeBio and even Conference (which deals with medium size ontologies) tracks in OAEI 2013 are incoherent which questions the quality of the results of the semantically-enabled applications utilizing them. According to [13] *reasoning-based error diagnosis* is one of the three essential features for alignment systems. Almost half of the quality aspects for ontology alignment in [20] address lack of correctness in the alignment in terms of *syntactic, semantic* and *taxonomic* aspects. The increasing size and complexity of the alignment problem demands debugging techniques thus a debugging module should be present in every alignment system. The authors in [14] show that repairing alignments is feasible at runtime and improves their logical coherence when (approximate) mapping repairing techniques are applied. Since ontology debugging presents considerable cognitive complexity (due to the, potentially, long chains of entailments) adequate visual support is a necessity.

In the field of ontology debugging there is already ongoing work that addresses explanation of defects. These techniques could be borrowed and applied to ontology alignment to address the challenge for **explaining the matching results** to the users (#4.2, #4.7). The authors in [24] specify generating human under-standable explanations for the mappings as a challenge as well. The authors in [1] implement advanced interfaces for **configuring** the **matching process** (**#5.8**) which provide the users with insights of the process and contribute to the understanding of the matching results.

Trial execution of mappings (#5.9.1) (what-if) will be of even greater help during the debugging and alignment by aiding the user understanding the consequences of his/her actions. Additionally **support for temporary decisions (#5.9.2)**, including temporary mappings (#1.1), list of performed actions and undo/redo actions, will help the user to explore the effects of his/her actions (and reduce the cognitive load).

3   Literature Study

A literature study was performed on a number of systems (presented in [12]). The systems were selected because they have mature interfaces, often appear in user interface evaluations and accommodate features addressing the alignment of large ontologies. Table 2 shows the systems support for the requirements identified in Sect. 2. The manipulation and inspection requirements are almost entirely supported by the first four systems. However to be able to draw conclusions for the level of usability of the different visualization approaches, a user study is needed. It is worth noting that COMA++ and AlViz do not distinguish between mappings and mapping suggestions ($\checkmark$(*)), a functionality that may help the users to keep track which correspondences have been already visited. The least supported category from the requirements in [8] is the one that assists the users most in understanding the reasons for suggesting/accepting mapping suggestions. While PROMPT and CogZ provide a textual description to explain the origin of mapping suggestions, the other tools only present a confidence value (which may (not) be enough depending on how familiar the domain expert already is with the ontology alignment field). Other requirements in this category include providing a starting point and a state of the process. Even though rarely supported they can often be observed by the number/status of the verified suggestions. Some systems limit the amount of data presented to the user by using sessions and clustering. Only two systems preserve the state of the process during interruptions. The others partially address the session requirement by save/load (ontologies and alignments) functions but without preserving the already computed suggestions. Almost all of the tools support clustering of the content presented to the user (not necessary for all views/modes) to avoid cluttering of the display. Clustering during the computations is also often supported.

4   User Interface Evaluations

As a further step in our study, we conducted a usability evaluation to reveal to what level the requirements are supported. We applied a multiple method approach by conducting an observational study and a heuristic evaluation to address the three aspects of the ISO 9241-11 standard for usability: efficiency, effectiveness, satisfaction. We selected three ontology alignment systems (CogZ, COMA 3.0 and SAMBO), from those in the literature study, that support as many as possible of the requirements in the user interface category; were freely available to us and that could be used without the installation of additional software packages. Details for their configurations are available in [12]. We evaluated the user interfaces using a heuristic evaluation (effectiveness) by an expert user as well as through an observational study (efficiency, effectiveness) using novice users. The satisfaction aspect is addressed by the SUS questionaire [2].

4.1 Heuristic Evaluation

Our first evaluation is a heuristic evaluation. We present its most important findings here, the entire evaluation is available in [12]. It aims to reveal usability issues by comparing the systems' interfaces to a set of accepted usability heuristics. This evaluation considers Nielsen's ten heuristics defined in [22] and presented briefly below. We note that these heuristics are not related in any way to the requirements in Table 2.

a. *Simple and Natural Dialog*—provide only absolutely necessary information, any extra information competes for the users' attention; group relevant information together and follow gestalt principles;
b. *Speak the Users' Language*—use users' familiar terminology and follow the natural information workflow; use metaphors with caution;
c. *Minimize the Users' Memory Load*—pick from a list rather than recall from the memory; use commonly recognizable graphic elements;
d. *Consistency*—the same things are at the same place and perform the same function; follow accepted graphical/platform/etc. conventions;
e. *Feedback*—provide timely feedback for all actions and task progress information;
f. *Clearly Marked Exits*—provide components to revoke or reverse actions;
g. *Shortcuts*—design the system proactively rather than reactively, provide accelerators for (experienced) users or default configurations for novice users;
h. *Good Error Messages*—meaningful error messages showing the problem in users' language and possible recovery actions instead of system codes;
i. *Prevent Errors*—provide confirmation dialogs for irreversible actions;
j. *Help and Documentation*—provide documentation for different type of users.

SAMBO provides two separate modes—*Suggestion Align* and *Align Manually*—to validate and create mappings. The system is web-based and the navigation between the modes is performed with a button, however, a link would be a more intuitive choice {d}. Both modes provide minimalistic design but they also contain elements that are not necessary for the tasks and take vertical space on the screen—the logo and the email address at the bottom {a}. The browser window in the *Suggestion Align* mode is divided into two parts by a thick gray line but the buttons above and below are very close to it, {a}, and thus the components may be perceived as one instead of different units. The information belonging to a concept is grouped together and enclosed in a box in the upper and central parts {a}. All mappings for a concept are presented as a list. The user can annotate and rename a mapping using the text fields below. Each mapping can be accepted as equivalence or subsumption mapping or rejected by the corresponding buttons. Their labels clearly explain their function, however, the buttons' color matches the background color, they are glued together and slightly change their appearance on hover. Since they perform the most important function in this mode they can be designed such that they stand out among the other elements {a}. The bottom part of the screen encloses several elements with various functions {a}—the button for navigation between the modes is aligned together with the undo button, a button that automatically aligns the remaining potential mappings and a label that provides information for them. This label is actually a link which lists all remaining suggestions but it does not look clickable {d}. Below is the history label with the same issues and a warning box next to it shows a message relevant to the previous action. The window is divided similarly in the *Align Manually* mode. The top and central parts contain both ontologies represented as unmodifiable indented trees, the comment box is below them together with a search field. The buttons for creating mappings are aligned with the undo button (placed on the other side of the screen) and their labels look differently than in the other mode {d}. The search function has several issues—it is case sensitive, accepts only exact input (no autocomplete or correction) and it should be activated by the search button next to the text field. The search reloads both trees and loses the current selection. It does not jump to hit and highlights only the first match in the hierarchy.

COMA 3.0 is a desktop system which provides one view during the alignment process [21]. Most of the screen space is occupied by the two ontologies which are placed side-by-side. Several labels below each ontology show statistical information regarding its structure which is not directly related to the ontology alignment task {a}. As a concept is selected the labels are updated to show the concept name and path to it in the hierarchy. The labels for both ontologies are connected through small colored squares. Their colors resemble mappings color-coding but no explanation what they represent is given {a}. Search boxes are available for each of the ontologies. Selected functions from the toolbar menus are available through the buttons in the resizable left side of the screen {c}. The ontologies are represented as unmodifiable indented trees where explicit guiding lines connect a concept with its parent. The mappings are depicted with color-coded lines in the red-green spectrum depending on their confidence values. There is no explicit distinction between validated and potential mappings as there is in the other two systems {c}. In our opinion the list with calculated mappings in COMA 3.0 is closer to (and thus considered as) mapping suggestions, since the users go through it and choose which of them (not) to keep in the final alignment. If a concept in a mapping is selected the system automatically shows the other concept in the mapping if it is under a unfolded branch {g}. The user cannot select a mapping. All actions for a mapping are available through its concepts' context menus {d}. To achieve more intuitive interaction the mappings should be selectable and the corresponding actions should be available in the mappings context menu {d}. Actions available for a single mapping include *Create Correspondence*, *Delete Correspondence* and *Set Highest Similarity Value*. The last action is only available for mappings computed by the system and carries the 'validate mapping' semantics, i.e., the user wants to preserve this correspondence in the final alignment. However its phrasing significantly differs from the phrasing of the other two {b, d}. The search function has several issues—the scroll bar shows pink markers where the results appear but there is no jump to hit. Only concepts under expanded branches are considered during the search.

CogZ has a more complex interface than those of the other two systems. The screen is divided into two major resizable views—each side of the upper part contains an ontology represented as a unmodifiable indented tree; the space between them is occupied by their mappings; the bottom part contains three tabs. The mappings can be selected and have a tooltip but do not have a context menu {d}. Several buttons above the mappings are used to apply different functions to them. The mark as mapped/temporary and (m^-) buttons apply actions on potential mappings while (m^+), (m^-) and (t^+) are used to add, delete and add temporary mappings. (m^-) is placed in group with (m^+) and (t^+) and at a distance from mark as mapped/temporary (it also looks differently from them) {d}. Four buttons are aligned with these above and apply different filters on the mappings. They have different icons but two of them have the same tooltip. There is a search box above each ontology and a red-green progress bar which shows the state of the process {e}, i.e., what portion of the mappings for each ontology are validated. Next to the progress bar a toggle button filters the ontologies according to the different mappings.

The first tab in the bottom part contains a table with all potential mappings. When a potential mapping is selected it is also highlighted in the upper view (if it is not filtered) {g}. A search strip on top of the table is activated on a key press {g}. Four buttons on top of the search strip and at the far right corner apply actions on a single potential mapping. They are almost unnoticeable due to their distance, color, unfamiliar icons and tooltips (view/create/remove operation) {a}. A double click on a potential mapping opens the same dialog as the view/create operation buttons. At the same time there is a *Create Mapping* button at the very bottom of the window which is much more visible than these four; it does not show the same dialog as them. The three operation buttons could be moved down to the *Create Mapping* button or in a potential mapping context menu (currently not existing) {d}. The *Create Mapping* button attracts attention even when the user is working at the upper part of the screen. This is due to its size, the size of the buttons (smaller) at the top of the upper view and probably because of the unclear separation of both views. In short the system provides several buttons with different appearance and tooltips which look like they are meant for the same two actions, i.e., validate and create a mapping {c, d}. The reason why the system has calculated the mapping is shown at the bottom {c, e}. The second tab shows the completed mappings and is synchronized with the upper view {c, d, g}. The third tab contains two parts, each showing (as a graph) the neighborhood of the selected concept in each ontology.

The system provides carefully designed search functionality—it filters away the concepts which do not match the search criteria and jumps to the first hit {g}. The concept names consisting of more than a word and including space are enclosed in a single quote ('). When searching for those the users have to use the same character at the beginning of the input or '*' which replaces an arbitrary number of characters.

4.2 Observational User Study

We conducted an observational user study in order to achieve better understanding of how the systems support the requirements in the manipulation, inspection and explanation categories. We describe the study design, the participants and show its results.

Procedure and Participants. 8 participants took part in the study—3 master and 5 PhD students (7 male, 1 female). All had Computer Science background and acquired basic ontology engineering knowledge as part of ongoing or past university courses. Each participant performed between 11 and 17 tasks with the systems (since not all of the systems supported all of the requirements). The study was scheduled for 2 sessions, which lasted for 2 h (with a break after 1 h) and 1 h, respectively. It was expected that the user would work with each system for approximately 1 h. To prevent carry-over effects (learning) between the systems we changed the order in which they were presented to the users. We also used a different order of the input ontologies.

We used the two ontologies from the Anatomy track from the OAEI 2014— AMA (2,737 concepts, 1,807 asserted is-a relations) and NCI-A (3,298 concepts, 3,761 asserted is-a relations) as representatives of the smallest use cases in a large-scale setting.

The study was conducted as follows. Each participant was presented with a project introduction and a tutorial during the first session. The tutorial provided basic knowledge about ontologies and ontology alignment and ended with several small tasks in order to ensure that all participants possessed the same level of understanding. After that the participants started solving the tasks with a particular system. Before the first task with each system the participants received the same hints on how to use search (since there are issues in all three systems). They were observed by one of the authors who took notes regarding their actions and their comments after each task and regarding the systems. The observer provided the right answer if a participant gave a wrong one.

Tasks Design. The tasks in the study were developed to include as many of the requirements in the user interface category as possible. Most of the requirements in the infrastructure and algorithms category were not covered due to their limited support in the systems and since they would require significantly longer sessions and domain knowledge. A brief description of the tasks and the corresponding requirements are listed in Table 3. Some tasks were performed

Table 3. User study tasks.

Task	Requirement
A. Discard following potential mapping.	#2.2, 1.2
B. Count mapping suggestions for X in A and Y in B.	#2.2
C. Find ONE parent and child for X in A and Y in B.	#2.1/4, 1.1/4, 4.1/2/3
D. Keep following potential mapping.	#2.2, 1.2
E. Create following mapping.	#2.5, 1.1
F. Count ALL parents and children of X in A and Y in B.	#2.1/4, 1.1/4, 4.1/2/3
G. Find in the system why/how it has suggested potential mapping between X in A and Y in B.	#4.2, 4.7
H. Set up the system to display ALL concepts in potential mappings.	#2.4
I. Find a concept that has nearby children and/or parents with more than 10 potential mappings.	#4.4
J. Give estimation of the validated mappings.	#4.6
K. Write in the system your arguments to decide there is a mapping between X in A and Y in B.	#2.5
L. Record in the system the mapping between X in A and Y in B is correct, such that you can change your current decision.	#1.1, 5.9.2
M. Give estimation of the potential mappings for validation.	#4.6
N. Set up the system to display ALL concepts in verified mappings.	#2.4
O. Find in the system why the mapping X in A and Y in B was created/accepted.	#4.3
P. Show in the system ALL concepts for which you may change your decision.	#2.4

twice since we were interested in their subsequent execution times. Task success and task times were collected for each task. The participants filled in the System Usability Scale (SUS) [2] questionnaire after all tasks with one system were completed. They were asked to provide at most three things that they like and dislike after working with each system as well.

Results. Table 4 shows the number of participants that successfully completed each of the tasks per system. Although we collected time per task and task success for task G (*) in COMA 3.0 we use this to understand how the users perceive the similarity value. COMA 3.0 does not provide explicit explanation why it has suggested a potential mapping. It provides the similarity value on top of the link however it was not directly perceived as an explanation by the users.

Table 4. Number of participants (max 8) successfully completed a task. / Average task time per system in seconds. (details in the text (*); not applicable (-))

System/Task	A	B	C	D	E	F	G	H	I	J	K	L	M	D	A	N	O	E	P
SAMBO	8/30*	1/254	5/191	6/76	7/149	4/265	-	-	7/118	5/28	8/6	-	8/1	6/21	8/9*	-	6/47	7/67	-
COMA 3.0	2/174	2/183	7/99	2*/93	8/41	4/243	*	-	6/64	-	-	-	-	8/34	8/31	-	-	8/25	-
CogZ	7/167*	4/87	8/97	8/44	3/128	4/108	7/40	5/37	8/64	8/6	-	4/105	8/102	8/29	7/17	8/11	-	7/38	8/5

Several were looking for an explicit explanation. Three of the participants stated that if they would know the matching algorithm they would know the reason.

The first 6 tasks were solved with varying success by the participants. Most (4 out of 6) who did not complete task A in COMA 3.0 chose a wrong option to reject the mapping—instead of deleting a mapping using *Delete Correspondence* they used the 'X' button which deletes the entire alignment. The participant who did not solve task A in CogZ could not find the mapping but after help from the observer he was able to solve it. The success in task B varied due to different reasons. For SAMBO most users (4 out of 7) could not find where the mapping suggestions are listed. They had to open a separate link, however the link looks like a label. For COMA 3.0 the users provided wrong numbers due to not realizing that a concept may exist in several places in the tree and as a consequence several lines represent a mapping between the same two concepts. For CogZ 2 participants did not understand the task and 2 gave wrong numbers since they were counting the suggestions between the two ontologies while one of the ontologies was filtered because of previous search. Most of the users that did not solve task F (all systems) did not realize that a concept may appear several times in the hierarchy although this was hinted in the task description and a similar situation appeared in task B. Task E in CogZ was not solved since 2 participants had problems finding one of the concepts, 1 participant did not realize that it is not a mapping suggestion and looked at the mapping suggestions list (after help from the observer he still had problems finding it). As mentioned earlier there is no explicit separation between mappings and mapping suggestions in COMA 3.0. Thus the way task D (*) is interpreted is that the user keeps the mapping if he chooses *Sets Highest Similarity Value*. In 3 out of 6 cases the participants selected *Retain only Fragment Correspondences*.

Table 4 also shows the average time per task per system. The task times for task A (*) in SAMBO are not directly comparable with the other systems due to the system's design and study scenario. While the user has to search for a mapping suggestion in COMA 3.0 and CogZ and then delete/remove it in SAMBO the suggestion was presented to the user (due to the system design). Task A (*) in CogZ took much longer for one of the participants. The average time for this task is 1:35 min if we exclude his time from the results. The task success and time improved significantly for the subsequent execution of tasks A, D and E. Figure 1 shows the results of the SUS questionnaire.

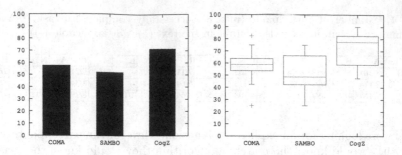

Fig. 1. SUS questionnaire scores. (average (left) and boxplot of the dataset (right))

4.3 Discussion

In [12] we discuss the results of the user study and heuristic evaluation in connection with the requirements from Table 2. Here we present additional important findings.

Several issues became noticeable while observing the users performing the tasks and in their comments after each task. In several cases the users could not complete a task or gave a wrong answer because they could not find the concept they were looking for because of the visualization. Although COMA 3.0 provides guiding lines 3 users counted a sibling concept as a parent, while for others the guiding lines were very helpful. One participant counted one parent twice in CogZ. In SAMBO two had problems aligning parents and children in the trees, two others used a pen to align the concepts.

Another issue appeared around the tree representation of the ontologies. The participants had to consider multiple inheritance, i.e., the same concept appears several times under different parents (and thus places) in an ontology, for task B (COMA 3.0) and F (all three). An example of multiple inheritance was given in the tutorial as well. Two participants did not experience difficulties with that but only one of them managed to solve all F tasks correctly. All other participants did not think of searching for more than a single occurrence of a concept. While some of them did not make the same mistake again others did it in the B and after that in the F tasks with the same system.

As commented in the heuristic evaluation the search functionality was tricky and due to it several tasks were not successfully completed. In three cases that happened with SAMBO. 5 participants complained about the search functionality in COMA 3.0 as well. Although CogZ provided the best search functionality among the three systems two users did not solve task E due to search problems as well.

Another issue that constantly appeared across all systems was the terminology (also covered by the second Nielsen heuristic in Subsect. 4.1). While it should be noted that the participants are not regular ontology alignment systems users all of them have had an ontology engineering course. Thus the terminology is not completely new for them. SAMBO uses the term *mapping suggestions* for potential mappings, *Suggestion Align* for the mode where potential mappings are validated and *Remaining Suggestions* for the mappings left for validation. Two users were unsure what *Suggestion Align* means/does and two others complained about the other two terms. The term *correspondence* denotes a mapping in COMA 3.0 and *Match Result*—the alignment. Two users were unsure for the meanings of the options in the context menu. It was observed that the users hesitated to press *Set Highest Similarity Value*. The terminology issue in CogZ had another aspect—the users were not confident in choosing actions. As said earlier CogZ has *Mark as mapped, (m^+), Create Mapping, View operation, Create operation* and a *View operation* dialog which opens on double click on a potential mapping. The users were unsure of using *Mark as mapped* in at least four cases. One user was not sure what *Remove operation* does and three others said they were wondering which button to use.

We list briefly comments that appeared in the like/dislike section and other observations for each system. One of the most appreciated features in SAMBO was the *Suggestion Align* view. *Remaining suggestions* and *History* were also explicitly mentioned although lists with potential/completed mappings are presented in CogZ as well. Apart from the search and terminology the users also disliked that the potential mappings were not shown in the *Align Manually* mode. In COMA 3.0 the users liked the mapping representation—color-coded lines between the trees. Many of the users tried to select a mapping by clicking on it and were also looking for a context menu. One disliked that the mapping context menu actually appeared for a concept. This comment can be juxtaposed to heuristic {d} in Subsect. 4.1 which suggests that common conventions should be followed. The *Neighborhood View* appeared as one of CogZ advantages. The users expected a context menu in the table with potential mappings as well. During the first task several users were confused because it was not clear which ontology is presented on which side of the screen. One user stated that the button *Create Mapping* draws attention and the two views are not well separated. Comparing the three systems CogZ was most unstable in the sense that it was not clear if an action took place.

It comes at no surprise that most of the tasks are supported in CogZ since they are based on the requirements in the manipulation, inspection and explanation categories which are based on [8]. As shown in Tables 2, 3 and 4 SAMBO and COMA 3.0 cover fewer requirements. The explanation category is the least supported. As it can be seen from the task success and time the users showed varying performance at the beginning which improved in terms of success and decreased in time to the last tasks. CogZ achieved the highest SUS score from the three (Fig. 1) which falls at the border between *OK* and *GOOD* in the adjective rating scale in [3]. COMA 3.0 scored a bit higher at SUS than SAMBO, both at the beginning of the *OK* interval. *OK* should not be perceived as satisfactory but rather that improvements are needed. SUS provides a good assessment of the perceived usability of a system with a small sample as in our case and SUS scores have "modest correlation with task performance" [3]. As take away issues from this study we would pinpoint the search and filter functionality especially in large-scale context, explicit explanation of the matching results (reduces the users cognitive load) and the *Suggestion Align* mode which was appreciated by the users.

5   Conclusions and Future Work

We have developed and presented requirements to foster user involvement in large-scale ontology alignment and have conducted a user study to reveal to what extent the requirements in the user interface category are supported in three selected systems. A heuristic evaluation was conducted by one of the authors as well to provide additional critique to the systems interfaces and cover aspects slightly or not mentioned in the user study (e.g., positioning of the elements on the screen). We also showed that the heuristic evaluation can provide quick yet valuable feedback for the user interface design.

The literature study showed that the requirements in the infrastructure and algorithms category are supported to a varying degree and more research and support is needed in, e.g., sessions, reducing user intervention, collaboration and trial execution. The explanation category, which assists the users most in understanding the reasons for suggesting/accepting mapping suggestions, is the least supported from the first three categories. The user interface evaluations show that state-of-the-art ontology alignment systems still have many weaknesses from a usability point of view. The study highlighted the importance of seemingly trivial issues like search and issues like ontology visualization which become crucial in a large-scale setting. Regarding our study, one limitation, that needs to be addressed in future work, is that all systems in the interface evaluations represent ontologies as trees. It was shown in [9] that a graph representation may be more suitable when dealing with multiple inheritance.

Acknowledgments. We thank the National Graduate School in Computer Science (CUGS) and the Swedish e-Science Research Centre (SeRC) for financial support.

References

1. Aumüller, D., Do, H.H., Maßmann, S., Rahm, E.: Schema and ontology matching with COMA++. In: SIGMOD, pp. 906–908 (2005)
2. Brooke, J.: SUS: a quick and dirty usability scale. In: Jordan, P.W., Thomas, B., Weerdmeester, B.A., McClelland, I.L. (eds.) Usability Evaluation in Industry, pp. 189–194. Taylor and Francis, London (1996)
3. Brooke, J.: SUS: a retrospective. J. Usability Stud. **8**(2), 29–40 (2013)
4. Cruz, I.F., Loprete, F., Palmonari, M., Stroe, C., Taheri, A.: Pay-As-You-Go multi-user feedback model for ontology matching. In: Janowicz, K., Schlobach, S., Lambrix, P., Hyvönen, E. (eds.) EKAW 2014. LNCS, vol. 8876, pp. 80–96. Springer, Heidelberg (2014)
5. Cruz, I.F., Stroe, C., Palmonari, M.: Interactive user feedback in ontology matching using signature vectors. In: ICDE, pp. 1321–1324 (2012)
6. Do, H.H.: Schema matching and mapping-based data integration. Ph.D. Thesis (2005)
7. Euzenat, J., Shvaiko, P.: User involvement. In: Ontology Matching, pp. 353–375. Springer, Heidelberg (2013)

8. Falconer, S.M., Storey, M.-A.: A cognitive support framework for ontology mapping. In: Aberer, K., et al. (eds.) ASWC 2007 and ISWC 2007. LNCS, vol. 4825, pp. 114–127. Springer, Heidelberg (2007)

9. Fu, B., Noy, N.F., Storey, M.-A.: Indented tree or graph? A usability study of ontology visualization techniques in the context of class mapping evaluation. In: Alani, H., et al. (eds.) ISWC 2013, Part I. LNCS, vol. 8218, pp. 117–134. Springer, Heidelberg (2013)

10. Granitzer, M., Sabol, V., Onn, K.W., et al.: Ontology alignment-a survey with focus on visually supported semi-automatic techniques. Future Internet **2**, 238–258 (2010)

11. Ivanova, V., Bergman, J.L., Hammerling, U., Lambrix, P.: Debugging taxonomies and their alignments: the ToxOntology-MeSH use case. In: WoDOOM, pp. 25–36 (2012)

12. Ivanova, V., Lambrix, P., Åberg, J.: Extended version of this paper. http://www.ida.liu.se/~patla/publications/ESWC15/

13. Jiménez-Ruiz, E., Grau, B.C., Zhou, Y., Horrocks, I.: Large-scale interactive ontology matching: algorithms and implementation. In: ECAI, pp. 444–449 (2012)

14. Jiménez-Ruiz, E., Meilicke, C., Grau, B.C., Horrocks, I.: Evaluating mapping repair systems with large biomedical ontologies. In: Description Logics, pp. 246–257 (2013)

15. Kirsten, T., Gross, A., et al.: GOMMA: a component-based infrastructure for managing and analyzing life science ontologies and their evolution. J. Biomed. Semant. **2**, 6 (2011)

16. Lambrix, P., Ivanova, V.: A unified approach for debugging is-a structure and mappings in networked taxonomies. J. Biomed. Semant. **4**, 10 (2013)

17. Lambrix, P., Kaliyaperumal, R.: A session-based approach for aligning large ontologies. In: Cimiano, P., Corcho, O., Presutti, V., Hollink, L., Rudolph, S. (eds.) ESWC 2013. LNCS, vol. 7882, pp. 46–60. Springer, Heidelberg (2013)

18. Lambrix, P., Tan, H.: SAMBO - a system for aligning and merging biomedical ontologies. J. Web Semant. **4**(3), 196–206 (2006)

19. Lanzenberger, M., Sampson, J., Rester, M.: Ontology visualization: Tools and techniques for visual representation of semi-structured meta-data. J. UCS **16**(7), 1036–1054 (2010)

20. Lanzenberger, M., Sampson, J., Rester, M., Naudet, Y., Latour, T.: Visual ontology alignment for knowledge sharing and reuse. J. Knowl. Manag. **12**(6), 102–120 (2008)

21. Massmann, S., Raunich, S., Aumüller, D., Arnold, P., Rahm, E.: Evolution of the COMA match system. In: OM, pp. 49–60 (2011)

22. Nielsen, J.: Usability Engineering. Morgan Kaufmann Publishers Inc., San Francisco (1993)

23. Noy, N.F., Musen, M.A.: Algorithm and tool for automated ontology merging and alignment. In: AAAI, pp. 450–455 (2000)

24. Otero-Cerdeira, L., Rodríguez-Martínez, F.J., Gómez-Rodríguez, A.: Ontology matching: a literature review. Expert Syst. Appl. **42**(2), 949–971 (2015)

25. Paulheim, H., Hertling, S., Ritze, D.: Towards evaluating interactive ontology matching tools. In: Cimiano, P., Corcho, O., Presutti, V., Hollink, L., Rudolph, S. (eds.) ESWC 2013. LNCS, vol. 7882, pp. 31–45. Springer, Heidelberg (2013)

26. Payne, T.R., Tamma, V.: A dialectical approach to selectively reusing ontological correspondences. In: Janowicz, K., Schlobach, S., Lambrix, P., Hyvönen, E. (eds.) EKAW 2014. LNCS, vol. 8876, pp. 397–412. Springer, Heidelberg (2014)

27. Rahm, E.: Towards large-scale schema and ontology matching. In: Bellahsene, Z., et al. (eds.) Schema Matching and Mapping, pp. 3–27. Springer, Heidelberg (2011)
28. Shi, F., Li, J., Tang, J., Xie, G., Li, H.: Actively learning ontology matching via user interaction. In: Bernstein, A., Karger, D.R., Heath, T., Feigenbaum, L., Maynard, D., Motta, E., Thirunarayan, K. (eds.) ISWC 2009. LNCS, vol. 5823, pp. 585–600. Springer, Heidelberg (2009)
29. Shvaiko, P., Euzenat, J.: Ontology matching: state of the art and future challenges. Knowl. Data Eng. **25**(1), 158–176 (2013)

RODI: A Benchmark for Automatic Mapping Generation in Relational-to-Ontology Data Integration

Christoph Pinkel[1]([✉]), Carsten Binnig[2,3], Ernesto Jiménez-Ruiz[4],
Wolfgang May[5], Dominique Ritze[6], Martin G. Skjæveland[7],
Alessandro Solimando[8], and Evgeny Kharlamov[4]

[1] Fluid Operations AG, Walldorf, Germany
christoph.pinkel@fluidops.com
[2] Brown University, Providence, RI, USA
carsten_binnig@brown.edu
[3] Baden-Wuerttemberg Cooperative State University, Mannheim, Germany
[4] University of Oxford, Oxford, UK
{Ernesto.Jimenez-Ruiz,evgeny.kharlamov}@cs.ox.ac.uk
[5] Göttingen University, Lower Saxony, Germany
may@informatik.uni-goettingen.de
[6] University of Mannheim, Mannheim, Germany
dominique@informatik.uni-mannheim.de
[7] University of Oslo, Oslo, Norway
martige@ifi.uio.no
[8] Università di Genova, Genoa, Italy
alessandro.solimando@unige.it

Abstract. A major challenge in information management today is the integration of huge amounts of data distributed across multiple data sources. A suggested approach to this problem is ontology-based data integration where legacy data systems are integrated via a common ontology that represents a unified global view over all data sources. However, data is often not natively born using these ontologies. Instead, much data resides in legacy relational databases. Therefore, mappings that relate the legacy relational data sources to the ontology need to be constructed. Recent techniques and systems that automatically construct such mappings have been developed. The quality metrics of these systems are, however, often only based on self-designed benchmarks. This paper introduces a new publicly available benchmarking suite called *RODI*, which is designed to cover a wide range of mapping challenges in *R*elational-to-*O*ntology *D*ata *I*ntegration scenarios. *RODI* provides a set of different relational data sources and ontologies (representing a wide range of mapping challenges) as well as a scoring function with which the performance of relational-to-ontology mapping construction systems may be evaluated.

© Springer International Publishing Switzerland 2015
F. Gandon et al. (Eds.): ESWC 2015, LNCS 9088, pp. 21–37, 2015.
DOI: 10.1007/978-3-319-18818-8_2

1   Introduction

Data integration is a big challenge in industry, life sciences, and the web, where data has not only reached large volumes, but also comes in a variety of formats. Integration increases the utility of data, it provides a unified access point to several databases and allows to analyse them, e.g., by correlating their data and identifying important patterns [3,5].

One of the major challenges in the integration task is to address the heterogeneity of data. A promising recent approach to address this challenge is to use ontologies, semantically rich conceptual models [12], to provide a conceptual integration and access layer on top of databases [27]. The ontology is 'connected' to databases with the help of *mappings* that are declarative specifications describing the relationship between the ontological vocabulary and the elements of the database schema.

Ontologies are already available in many domains, and many of them can naturally be employed to support integration scenarios. For example, in biology there is the Gene Ontology and in medicine [7] there is the International Classification of Diseases (ICD) ontology. Another recent example is *schema.org*, an ontology to mark up data on the web with schema information. Industrial examples include NPD FactPages ontology [17,30] created for petroleum domain and Siemens ontology [15] created for the energy sector.

Mappings, however, cannot easily be reused since they are typically specific for each source database. Thus, they usually need to be developed from scratch. Creating and curating relational-to-ontology mappings manually is a process that often involves an immense amount of human effort [25]. In order to address this challenge, a number of techniques and systems [10,13,18,22,24,28,32] have been recently developed to assist in the relational-to-ontology data integration problem, either in a semi-automatic fashion or by bootstrapping initial mappings. However, claims about the quality of the created mappings are only based on self-designed benchmarks, which make comparisons difficult. While there already exist some standardized benchmarks or testbeds for data integration scenarios in data warehousing [26] or for ontology alignment [21], these benchmarks do not include the mapping challenges that arise from relational-to-ontology mappings.

In this paper we present a systematic overview of different types of mapping challenges that arise in relational-to-ontology data integration scenarios. Based on these types of mapping challenges, we selected existing ontologies and created corresponding relational databases for our benchmark to have a good coverage of all types. Moreover, the benchmark queries have been designed such that each query targets different mapping challenges. That way, the results of the scoring function for the individual queries can be used to draw inferences on how good different types of structural heterogeneity are supported by a certain integration system.

As the main contribution this paper introduces a new publicly available benchmarking suite[1] called *RODI* which is designed for *R*elational-to-*O*ntology *D*ata *I*ntegration Scenarios. *RODI* provides researchers with a set of different relational data sources (schema and data) and ontologies (only schema) that model data of research conferences (e.g., sessions, talks, authors, etc.). The challenge of the benchmark is to map the schema elements of the relational database to the schema elements of the ontology in order to instantiate the ontology. In addition, the benchmark provides a set of query pairs (i.e., a query over parts of the database and an equivalent query over the ontology). The idea is that each of the query pairs targets schema elements that represent different types of mapping challenges. Moreover, the benchmark also provides a scoring function to evaluate the quality of the mappings created by a certain tool. For covering other forms of heterogeneity, our benchmark provides extension points that allow users to integrate other relational databases, ontologies and test queries.

Thus, *RODI* is an end-to-end integration benchmark to test different mapping challenges. We decided to design an end-to-end integration benchmark instead of evaluating individual artifacts of the data integration process (i.e., correspondences, mappings, ...) since existing systems implement a wide range of different integration approaches that do not allow a good way of comparison. For example, a major difference is that some integration systems directly map relational databases to ontologies (e.g., IncMap [24]) while other tools first translate the relational database into an ontology and then apply an ontology alignment technique (e.g., BootOX [10]) resulting in different artifacts during the integration process.

The outline of our paper is the following. Section 2 provides a classification of the different types of mapping challenges. Section 3 gives an overview of our benchmark and describes the details about the ontologies and relational databases as well as the benchmarking queries and the evaluation procedure. Section 4 illustrates the initial use of our benchmark suite by evaluating four mapping generation systems. Finally, Sect. 5 summarizes related work and Sect. 6 concludes the paper.

2   Mapping Challenges

In the following we present our classification of different types of mapping challenges in relational-to-ontology mapping. As top level of the classification, we use the standard classification for data integration described by Batini et al. [2]: naming conflicts, structural heterogeneity, and semantic heterogeneity.

2.1   Naming Conflicts

Typically, relational database schemata and ontologies use different conventions to name their artifacts even when they model the same domain and thus should

---

[1] Download at: http://www.fluidops.com/downloads/collateral/rodi1.0-2.zip.

use a similar terminology. While database schemata tend to use short identifiers for tables and attributes that often include technical artifacts (e.g. for tagging primary keys and for foreign keys), ontologies typically use long "speaking" names. Moreover, names in ontologies include IRIs with prefixes (that refer to a namespace). Thus, the main challenge is to be able to find similar names despite the different naming patterns.

Other model differences include the use of plural vs. singular form for entities, common tokenization schemes, use of synonyms etc. that are not present in other data integration scenarios (e.g., relational-to-relational or ontology alignment).

2.2   Structural Heterogeneity

The most important differences in relational-to-ontology integration scenarios compared to other integration scenarios are structural heterogeneities. We discuss the different types of structural heterogeneity covered by *RODI*.

Type Conflicts: Relational schemata and ontologies represent the same artifacts by using different modeling constructs. While relational schemata use tables, attributes, as well as constraints, ontologies use modeling elements such as classes and subclasses (to model class hierarchies), data and object properties, restrictions, etc. Clearly there exist direct (i.e., naive) mappings from relational schemata to ontologies for some of the artifacts (e.g., classes map to tables). However, most real-world relational schemata and corresponding ontologies do not follow any naive mapping. Instead, the mapping rules are much more complex and there exist big differences (i.e., type conflicts) in the way how the same concepts are modeled. One reason is that relational schemata are often optimized towards a given workload (e.g., they are normalized for update-intensive workloads or denormalized for read-intensive workloads) while ontologies model a domain on the conceptual level. Another reason is that some modeling elements have no direct translation (e.g., class hierarchies in ontologies can be mapped to relational schemata in different ways). In the following, we list the different type conflicts covered by *RODI*:

1. *Normalization Artifacts:* Often properties that belong to a class in an ontology are spread over different tables in the relational schema as a consequence of normalization.
2. *Denormalization Artifacts:* For read-intensive workloads, tables are often denormalized. Thus, properties of different classes in the ontology might map to attributes in the same table.
3. *Class Hierarchies:* Ontologies typically make use of explicit class hierarchies. Relational models implement class hierarchies implicitly, typically using one of three different common modeling patterns (c.f., [8, Chap. 3]). In the following we describe those patterns (see Fig. 1): (1) In one common variant the relational schema materializes several subclasses in the same table and uses additional attributes to indicate the subclass of each individual. Those additional attributes can take the shape of a numeric type column for disjoint

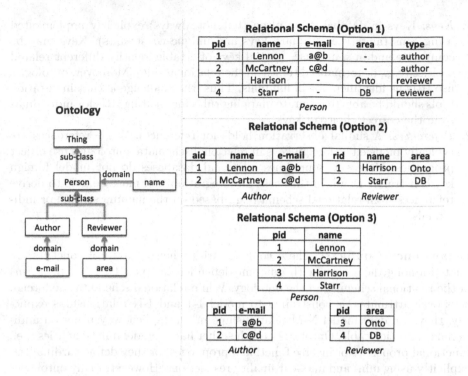

Fig. 1. Class hierarchies – ontology vs. relational schema

subclasses and/or a combination of several type or role flags for non-disjoint subclasses. In this case, several classes need to be mapped to the same table and can be told apart only by secondary features in the data, such as the value in a type column. (2) Another common way is to use one table per most specific class in the class hierarchy and to materialize the inherited attributes in each table separately. Thus, the same property of the ontology must be mapped to several tables. (3) A third variant uses one table for each class in the hierarchy, including for possibly abstract superclasses. Tables then use the same primary key to indicate the subclass relationship. This variant has a closer resemblance to ontology design patterns. However, it is also rarely used in practice, as it is more difficult to design, harder to query, impractical to update and usually considered unnecessary.

Thus, the main challenge is that integration tools should be capable to resolve different levels of (de-)normalization and different patterns implementing class hierarchies in a relational schema when mapping a schema to an ontology.

Key Conflicts: In ontologies and relational schemata, keys and references (to keys) are represented in different ways. In the following, we list the different key conflicts covered by *RODI*:

1. *Keys:* Keys in databases are often (but not always) explicitly implemented using constraints (i.e., primary keys and unique constraints). Keys may be composite and in some cases partial keys of a table identify different related entities (e.g., denormalized tables on the relational side). Moreover, ontologies use IRIs as identifiers for individuals. Thus, the challenge is that integration tools should be able to generate mapping rules for creating IRIs for individuals from the correct choice of keys.

2. *References:* A similar observation holds for references. While references are typically modeled as foreign keys in relational schemata, ontologies use object properties. Moreover, sometimes relational databases do not model foreign key constraints at all. In that case an integration tool must be able to derive references from relational schema (e.g., based on the naming scheme or individuals).

Dependency Conflicts: These conflicts arise when a group of concepts are related among themselves with different dependencies (i.e., $1 : 1, 1 : n, n : m$) in the relational schema and the ontology. While relational schemata use foreign keys over attributes as constraints to model 1-1 and 1-N relationships explicitly, they can only model N-M relationships in an implicit way using an additional connection table. Ontologies, on the other hand, model functionalities (i.e., functional properties or inverse functional properties) or they define cardinalities explicitly using min- and max-cardinality restrictions. However, many ontologies do not make use of these constraints and thus are often underspecified.

2.3 Semantic Heterogeneity

Besides the usual semantic differences between any two conceptual models of the same domain, two additional factors apply in relational-to-ontology data integration: (1) the *impedance mismatch* between the closed-world assumption (CWA) in databases and the open-world assumption (OWA) in ontologies;[2] and (2) the difference in semantic expressiveness, i.e., databases may model some concepts or data explicitly where they are derived logically in ontologies. The challenge is thus to bridge the model gap. In general, this challenge is inherent to all relational-to-ontology mapping problems.

3   *RODI* Benchmark Suite

In the following, we present the details of our *RODI* benchmark: we first give an overview, then we discuss the details of the data sets (relational schema and ontologies) as well as the queries, and finally we present our scoring function to evaluate the benchmark results.

---

[2] Other notions of impedance mismatch exist (e.g., modeling of values vs. objects). The OWA/CWA notion is most relevant w.r.t. specific mapping challenges.

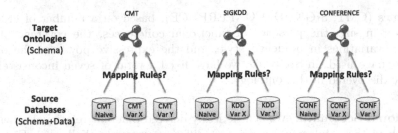

Fig. 2. Overview of the *RODI* benchmark

3.1   Overview

Figure 2 gives an overview of our benchmark. In its basic version, the benchmark provides three target ontologies (T-Box only) and different relational source databases for each ontology (schema and data) varying in the types of mapping challenges that are covered.

As the primary domain for testing, we chose the conference domain: it is well understood, comprehensible even for non-domain experts but still complex enough for realistic testing and it has been successfully used as the domain of choice in other benchmarks before (e.g., by the OAEI [21]). For each ontology, we provide different variants of corresponding databases, each focusing on different types of mapping challenges.

The benchmark asks systems to create mapping rules from the different source databases to their corresponding target ontologies. We call each such combination of a database and an ontology a *benchmark scenario*. For evaluation, we provide query pairs for each scenario to test a range of mapping challenges. Query pairs are evaluated against the instantiated ontology and the provided databases, respectively. Results are compared for each query pair and aggregated in the light of different mapping challenges using our scoring function.

In order to be open for other data sets and different domains, our benchmark can be easily extended to include scenarios with real-world ontologies and databases. In our initial version, we already provide one such extension from a real-world application of the oil and gas domain.

3.2   Data Sources

In the following, we discuss the data sources (i.e., ontologies and relational schemata) as well as the combinations used as mapping scenarios for the benchmark in more details.

Conference Ontologies. The conference ontologies in this benchmark are provided by the Ontology Alignment Evaluation Initiative (OAEI) [21] and were originally developed by the OntoFarm project.[3] We selected three particular

---

[3] http://nb.vse.cz/~svatek/ontofarm.html.

ontologies (CMT, SIGKDD, CONFERENCE), based on a number of criteria: variation in size, the presence of functional coherences, the coverage of the domain, variations in modeling style, and the expressive power of the ontology language used. In SIGKDD, we have fixed a total of seven inconsistencies that we discovered in this ontology.

Relational Schemata. We synthetically derived different relational schemata for each of the ontologies, focusing on different mapping challenges. First, for each ontology we derived a relational schema that can be mapped to the ontology using a naive mapping as described in [11]. The algorithm works by extracting an entity-relationship (ER) model from an OWL DL ontology. It then translates this ER model into a relational schema according to text book rules (e.g., [8]). We extended this algorithm to consider ontology instance data to derive more proper functionalities (rather than just looking at the T-Box as the existing algorithm did). Otherwise, the generated naive relational schemata would have contained an unrealistically high number of $n : m$-relationship tables. The naively translated schemata of the algorithm are guaranteed to be in fourth normal form (4NF), fulfilling normalization requirements of standard design practices. Thus, the naive schemata already include various normalization artifacts as mapping challenges. Also, all scenarios reflect the kind of semantic heterogeneity that is inherent to relational-to-ontology mappings.

From each naively translated schema, we systematically created different variants by introducing different aspects on how a real-world schema may differ from a naive translation and thus to test different mapping challenges:

1. *Adjusted Naming:* As described in Sect. 2.1, ontology designers typically consider other naming schemes than database architects do, even when implementing the same (verbal) specification. Those differences include longer vs. shorter names, "speaking" prefixes, human-readable property IRIs vs. technical abbreviations (e.g., "hasRole" vs. "RID"), camel case vs. underscore tokenization, preferred use of singular vs. plural, and others. For each naively translated schema we automatically generate a variant with identifier names changed accordingly.
2. *Varying Hierarchies:* The most critical structural challenge comes with different relational design patterns to model class hierarchies more or less implicitly, as we have discussed in Sect. 2.2. We automatically derive variants of all naively translated schemata where different hierarchy design patterns are presented.
3. *Combined Case:* In the real world, both of the previous cases (i.e., adjusted naming and hierarchies) would usually apply at the same time. To find out how tools cope with such a situation, we also built scenarios where both are combined.
4. *Removing Foreign Keys:* Although it is considered as bad style, databases without foreign keys are not uncommon in real-world applications.
   The mapping challenge is that mapping tools must guess the join paths to connect tables of different entities. Therefore, we have created one dedicated

Table 1. Scenario combinations

	CMT	CONFERENCE	SIGKDD
Naive	($\checkmark$)	($\checkmark$)	($\checkmark$)
Adjusted naming	$\checkmark$	$\checkmark$	$\checkmark$
Cleaned hierarchies	$\checkmark$	$\checkmark$	$\checkmark$
Combined case	($\checkmark$)	($\checkmark$)	$\checkmark$
Missing FKs	-	$\checkmark$	-
Denormalized	$\checkmark$	-	-

scenario to test this challenge with the CONFERENCE ontology and based it on the schema variant with cleaned hierarchies.

5. *Partial Denormalization:* In many cases, schemata get partially denormalized to optimize for a certain read-mostly workload. Denormalization essentially means that correlated (yet separated) information is jointly stored in the same table and partially redundant. We provide one such scenario for the CMT ontology.

Mapping Scenarios. For each of our three main ontologies, CMT, CONFERENCE, and SIGKDD, the benchmark includes five scenarios, each with a different variant of the database schema (discussed before). Table 1 lists the different versions. All scenarios cover the main semantic challenges and to some degree also the structural challenges. Renamed scenarios cover the naming conflicts challenge. Scenarios with cleaned hierarchies and advanced cases mostly address structural heterogeneity but also stress the challenge of semantic differences more than other scenarios. To keep the number of scenarios small for the default setup, we differentiate between default scenarios and non-default scenarios. While the default scenarios are mandatory to cover all mapping challenges, the non-default scenarios are optional (i.e., users could decide to run them in order to gain additional insights). Non-default scenarios are put in parentheses in Table 1. Similarly, we include scenarios that require mappings of schemata to one of the other ontologies (e.g., mapping a CMT database schema variant to the SIGKDD ontology), but do not consider them as default scenarios either. They represent more advanced scenarios.

Data. In *RODI*, we provide data to fill both the databases and ontologies, as all ontologies are provided as empty T-Boxes, only. All data are first generated as A-Box facts for the different ontologies, and then translated into the corresponding relational data. Actually, for the evaluation it would not be necessary to generate data for the ontologies. However, this design simplifies the evaluation since all databases can be automatically derived from the given ontologies as described before. Our conference data generator deterministically produces a scalable amount of synthetic facts around key concepts in the ontologies, such as conferences, papers, authors, reviewers, and others. In total, we generate data for 23 classes, 66 object properties (including inverse properties) and 11 datatype properties (some of which apply to several classes).

3.3 Queries

We test each mapping scenario with a series of *query pairs*, consisting of semantically equivalent queries against the instantiated ontology and the provided databases, respectively.

Each query pair is based on one SPARQL query, which we then translated into equivalent SQL for each corresponding schema using the same translation mechanism as used for schema translation. To double-check that queries in each pair are in fact equivalent, we manually checked result sets on both ends. Queries are manually curated and designed to test different mapping challenges.

To this end, all query pairs are tagged with categories, relating them to different mapping challenges. All scenarios draw on the same pool of 56 query pairs, accordingly translated for each ontology and schema. However, the same query may face different challenges in different scenarios, e.g., a simple 1 : 1 mapping between a class and table in a naive scenario can turn into a complicated $n : 1$ mapping problem in a scenario with cleaned hierarchies. Also, not all query pairs are applicable on all ontologies (and thus, on their derived schemata).

3.4 Evaluation Criteria

It is our aim to measure the practical usefulness of mappings. We are therefore interested in the correctness (precision) and completeness (recall) of query results, rather than comparing mappings directly to a reference mapping set. This is important because a number of different mappings might effectively produce the same data w.r.t. a specific input database. Also, the mere number of facts is no indicator of their semantic importance for answering queries (e.g., the overall number of conferences is much smaller than the number of paper submission dates, yet are at least as important in a query about the same papers).

We therefore define precision and recall locally for each individual test (i.e., for each query pair) and use a simple scoring function to calculate averages for different subsets of tests, i.e., for tests relating to a specific mapping challenge.

Unfortunately, precision and recall cannot be measured immediately by naively checking results of query pairs tuple by tuple for equality, as different mappings typically generate different IRIs to denote the same entities. Instead, we define an equivalence measure that is agnostic of entity IRIs.

In the following, we define tuple set equivalence based on a more general equivalence of query results (i.e., tuple sets):

Definition 1 (Structural Tuple Set Equivalence). *Let $V = IRI \cup Lit \cup Blank$ be the set of all IRIs, literals and blank nodes, $T = V \times ... \times V$ the set of all n-tuples of V. Then two tuple sets $t_1, t_2 \in \mathcal{P}(T)$ are* structurally equivalent *if there is an isomorphism $\phi : (IRI \cap t_1) \rightarrow (IRI \cap t_2)$.*

For instance, {(urn:p-1, 'John Doe')} and {(http://my#john, 'John Doe')} are structurally equivalent. On this basis, we can easily define the equivalence of query results w.r.t. a mapping target ontology:

Definition 2 (Tuple Set Equivalence w.r.t. Ontology $(\sim_O)$). *Let O be a target ontology of a mapping, $I \subset IRI$ the set of IRIs used in O and $t_1, t_2 \in \mathcal{P}(T)$ result sets of queries q_1 and q_2 evaluated on a superset of O (i.e., over O plus A-Box facts added by a mapping).*

Then, $t_1 \sim_O t_2$ (are structurally equivalent w.r.t. O) iff t_1 and t_2 are structurally equivalent and $\forall i \in I : \phi(i) = i$.

For instance, {(urn:p-1, 'John Doe')} and {(http://my#john, 'John Doe')} are structurally equivalent, *iff* http://my#john is *not* already defined in the target ontology. Finally, we can define precision and recall:

Definition 3 (Precision and Recall under Tuple Set Equivalence). *Let $t_r \in \mathcal{P}(T)$ be a reference tuple set, $t_t \in \mathcal{P}(T)$ a test tuple set and $t_{rsub}, t_{tsub} \in \mathcal{P}(T)$ be maximal subsets of t_r and t_t, s.t., $t_{rsub} \sim_O t_{tsub}$.*

Then the precision of the test set t_t is $P = \frac{|t_{tsub}|}{|t_t|}$ and recall is $R = \frac{|t_{rsub}|}{|t_r|}$.

Table 2. Example results from a query pair asking for author names (simplified)

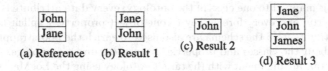

(a) Reference   (b) Result 1   (c) Result 2   (d) Result 3

We observe precision and recall locally on each query test, i.e., based on how many of the result tuples of each query are structurally equivalent to a reference query result set. Table 2 shows an example with a query test that asks for the names of all authors. The corresponding query pair here would be:

```
SQL:     SELECT name FROM persons WHERE person_type = 2.
SPARQL:  SELECT ?name WHERE {?p a :Author; foaf:name ?name}).
```

Result set 1 is structurally equivalent to the reference result set, i.e., it has found all authors and did not return anything else, so both precision and recall are 1.0. Result set 2 is equivalent with only a subset of the reference result (e.g., it did not include those authors who are also reviewers). Here, precision is still 1.0, but recall is only 0.5. In case of result set 3, all expected authors are included, but also another person, James. Here, precision is only 0.66, but recall is 1.0.

To aggregate results of individual query pairs, a scoring function calculates the averages of per query numbers for each scenario and for each challenge category. For instance, we calculate averages of all queries testing $1 : n$ mappings.

3.5   Extension Scenarios

Our benchmark suite is designed to be extensible, i.e., additional scenarios can be easily added. The primary aim of supporting such extensions is to allow actual real-world mapping challenges to be tested on a realistic query workload alongside our more controlled default scenarios.

To demonstrate the feasibility of extension scenarios we added and evaluated one example of an extension scenario in our benchmark suite, based on the data, ontology and queries from *The Norwegian Petroleum Directorate (NPD) FactPages* [30]. The test set contains a small relational database ($\approx$40 MB), but with a relatively complex structure (70 tables, $\approx$1000 columns and $\approx$100 foreign keys), an ontology covering the domain of the database (with $\approx$300 classes and $\approx$350 properties), and 17 query pairs. The database and ontology are constructed from a publicly available dataset containing reference data about past and ongoing activities in the Norwegian petroleum industry, and the queries in the test set are built from real information needs collected from end-users of the NPD FactPages.

4   Benchmark Results

Setup: In order to show the usability of our benchmark and the usefulness and significance of its results, we have performed an initial evaluation with four systems: *BootOX* [9,16], *IncMap* [23,24], *morph/MIRROR*[4] and *ontop* [29].

(1) *BootOX* (*Boot*strapper of *Ox*ford) is based on the approach called 'direct mapping' by the W3C:[5], i.e., every table in the database (except for those representing $n : m$ relationships) is mapped to one class in the ontology; every data attribute is mapped to one data property; and every foreign key to one object property. Explicit and implicit database constraints from the schema are also used to enrich the bootstrapped ontology with axioms about the classes and properties from these direct mappings. Afterwards, *BootOX* performs an alignment with the target ontology using the LogMap system [31]. (2) *IncMap* maps an available ontology directly to the relational schema. *IncMap* represents both the ontology and schema uniformly, using a structure-preserving metagraph for both. (3) *morph/MIRROR* (*M*app*I*ngs for *R*db to *R*df generat*OR*) is a tool for generating an ontology and R2RML direct mappings automatically from an RDB schema. *morph/MIRROR* has been implemented as a module of the RDB2RDF engine *morph-RDB* [28]. (4) *ontop* is an ontology-based data access system that also includes a module to automatically compute direct mappings and a simple ontology with the vocabulary used in the mappings. For the last step of aligning to the target ontology we have coupled both *morph/MIRROR* and *ontop* with LogMap in a similar setup to the one used in *BootOX* .

Results: For each of those systems we were running the default scenarios of our benchmark (as discussed in Sect. 3). We mainly report overall aggregates but also highlight some of the most interesting findings in more detail.

Table 3 shows precision, recall and f-measure averaged over all tests for each scenario. What becomes immediately apparent is that measured quality is relatively modest. Another surprising observation is that for each system, precision, recall and f-measure are always the same per scenario. A manual analysis of results has shown,

---

[4] https://github.com/oeg-upm/MIRROR.
[5] http://www.w3.org/TR/rdb-direct-mapping/.

that the reason for this behavior is linked to the relatively low overall quality: systems did only solve some of the simpler query tests and those tend to result in atomic answers, which may be either correct or incorrect, but nothing in-between. For instance, if a query asks for the number of author instances, the result in either correct ($p = r = f = 1.0$) or incorrect ($p = r = f = 0.0$). Systems did surprisingly well on some tests of medium difficulty, e.g., author names (where, e.g., some other persons could be mistaken for authors) and scored $p = r = f = 1.0$ in all cases where they submitted any results at all. For the most complex queries, where results could be likely in $]0; 1[$, systems failed the query tests completely. We expect this behavior to change as systems improve in general and overall scores go up.

Best numbers are generally reached for "adjusted naming" scenarios, which are close to the naive ontology translation and thus schemata resemble their corresponding ontologies most closely. Besides the generic model gap and those, these scenarios only test the challenges of naming conflicts and normalization artifacts. Quality drops rapidly for almost all other types of scenarios, i.e., whenever we introduce additional challenges that are specific to the relational-to-ontology modeling gap. With a few exceptions, *BootOX* and *ontop* perform better than the others. Where differences appear between the two of them, *ontop* surprisingly outperforms *BootOX*. Note that those two similar setups differ mostly in that *ontop* only produces a very simple ontology while *BootOX* tries to additionally include some knowledge encoded in the database structure. Results hint that this additional knowledge may be noisy. For CMT, *IncMap* outperforms other systems both adjusted names and cleaned hierarchies. This is interesting, as *IncMap* has been designed to work on typical databases and CMT differs from the other ontologies insofar as it contains relatively flat class hierarchies and results in a somewhat more realistic relational database even when translated naively. The generally low numbers of *morph/MIRROR* come as a surprise. We had expected it to perform similarly to or somewhat better than *BootOX* as it follows the same idea of leveraging knowledge from the database schema to build a better ontology, but does so more systematically. The effect of noise seems to be insufficient as an explanation in this case. As *morph/MIRROR* is still under development, we assume that some of the effects may be related to technical issues that we could not isolate and identify as such.

The drop in accuracy between "adjusted names" and "cleaned hierarchies" is mostly due to the $n : 1$ mapping challenge, introduced by one of the relational patterns to represent class hierarchies which groups data for several subclasses in a single table. Neither of the systems managed to solve even a single test on this challenge.

In the most advanced cases, all systems lose on the additional challenges, although to different degrees. For instance, all systems failed to solve any of the tests specifically targeted to the challenge of denormalization artifacts. (For *BootOX* and *ontop*, there is no difference to the "cleaned hierarchies" scenario as the systems failed the relevant queries already on that simpler scenario.) While *BootOX* stands up relatively well in those most advanced scenarios, *IncMap* records significant further drops. *ontop* failed to produce mappings for the advanced scenario involving missing foreign keys.

All systems struggle with identifying properties, as Table 4 shows. A close look shows that this is in part due to the challenge of normalization artifacts, with no system succeeding in detecting any properties that map to multi-hop join paths in the tables. Here, *IncMap* shows its stronger suit, mapping datatype properties with an average f-measure of up to 0.5. It has however to be noted that we test properties only in the context of their domains and ranges, i.e., to succeed in a property test, a correct mapping at least for its domain class is a precondition, making those tests generally harder.

On NPD FactPages, our extension scenario with real-world data and queries, all four tested systems fail to answer any of the 17 query tests correctly. Given the previous

Table 3. Average results of all tests per scenarios. Precision, Recall and F-measure are all equal as systems fail the more complex tasks while simpler ones are atomic.

Scenario	BootOX			IncMap			MIRROR			ontop		
	P	R	F	P	R	F	P	R	F	P	R	F
Adjusted naming												
CMT	0.33	0.33	0.33	**0.5**	**0.5**	**0.5**	0.28	0.28	0.28	0.39	0.39	0.39
CONFERENCE	0.33	0.33	0.33	0.26	0.26	0.26	0.27	0.27	0.27	**0.37**	**0.37**	**0.37**
SIGKDD	**0.45**	**0.45**	**0.45**	0.21	0.21	0.21	0.3	0.3	0.3	**0.45**	**0.45**	**0.45**
Cleaned hierarchies												
CMT	0.28	0.28	0.28	**0.44**	**0.44**	**0.44**	0.17	0.17	0.17	0.28	0.28	0.28
CONFERENCE	0.23	0.23	0.23	0.16	0.16	0.16	0.23	0.23	0.23	**0.3**	**0.3**	**0.3**
SIGKDD	**0.16**	**0.16**	**0.16**	0.11	0.11	0.11	0.11	0.11	0.11	**0.16**	**0.16**	**0.16**
Combined case												
SIGKDD	**0.16**	**0.16**	**0.16**	0.05	0.05	0.05	0.11	0.11	0.11	**0.16**	**0.16**	**0.16**
Missing FKs												
CONFERENCE	**0.17**	**0.17**	**0.17**	0.03	0.03	0.03	**0.17**	**0.17**	**0.17**	-	-	-
Denormalized												
CMT	**0.28**	**0.28**	**0.28**	0.22	0.22	0.22	0.22	0.22	0.22	**0.28**	**0.28**	**0.28**

Table 4. Average F-measure results for the adjusted naming scenarios. 'C' stands for queries about classes, 'D' stands for queries involving data properties and 'O' stands for queries involving object properties

Adjusted naming	BootOX			IncMap			MIRROR			ontop		
	C	D	O	C	D	O	C	D	O	C	D	O
CMT	0.67	0.0	0.0	0.67	**0.50**	0.0	0.56	0.0	0.0	**0.78**	0.0	0.0
CONFERENCE	0.67	0.0	0.0	0.42	**0.24**	0.0	0.53	0.0	0.0	**0.73**	0.0	0.0
SIGKDD	**0.69**	0.0	0.0	0.34	0.0	0.0	0.46	0.0	0.0	**0.69**	0.0	0.0

results from the default scenarios, this was to be expected. The query tests in NPD FactPages consist of real-world queries, only. Just as systems failed the most complex queries in the (generally still simpler) default scenarios, they also failed all queries in the extension scenario.

5   Related Work

Mappings between ontologies are usually evaluated only on the basis of their underlying correspondences (usually referred to as ontology *alignments*). The Ontology Alignment Evaluation Initiative [21] provides tests and benchmarks of those alignments that can be considered as de-facto standard. Mappings between relational databases are typically not evaluated by a common benchmark. Instead, authors compare their tools to an industry standard system (e.g., [1,6]) in a scenario of their choice. A novel TPC benchmark [26] was created only recently.

Similarly, evaluations of relational-to-ontology mapping generating systems were based on one or several data sets deemed appropriate by the authors and are therefore not comparable. In one of the most comprehensive evaluations so far, QODI [32] was evaluated on several real-world data sets, though some of the reference mappings were rather simple. IncMap [24] was evaluated on real-world mapping problems based on data from two different domains. Such domain-specific mapping problems could be easily integrated in our benchmark through our extension mechanism.

A number of papers discuss different quality aspects of such mappings in general. Console and Lenzerini have devised a series of theoretical quality checks w.r.t. consistency [4]. In another benchmark, Impraliou et al. generate synthetic queries to measure the correctness and completeness of OBDA query rewriting [14]. The presence of complete and correct mappings is a prerequisite to their approach. Mora and Corcho discuss issues and possible solutions to benchmark the query rewriting step in OBDA systems [20]. Mappings are supposed to be given as immutable input. The NPD benchmark [19] measures performance of OBDA query evaluation. Neither of these papers, however, address the issue of systematically measuring mapping quality.

6   Conclusion

We have presented *RODI*, a benchmark suite for testing the quality of generated relational-to-ontology mappings. *RODI* tests a wide range of relational-to-ontology mapping challenges, which we discussed of the paper.

Initial results on four systems demonstrate that existing tools can cope with simpler mapping challenges to varying degrees. However, all tested tools fail on more advanced challenges and are still a long way from solving actual real-world problems. In particular, results show that mapping accuracy degrades massively when relational schemata use design patterns that differ greatly from the corresponding ontologies (e.g., in scenarios with "cleaned hierarchies"). We also gave detailed feedback about specific shortcomings to the authors of several of the tested systems, which has already lead to adjustments in one case and will lead to improvements in others.

As the main avenue of future work, we plan to conduct a both broader and deeper evaluation, also involving a greater number of systems. Another interesting aspect would be the addition of further extension scenarios to cover data from a number of application domains out of the box.

Acknowledgements. This research is funded by the Seventh Framework Program (FP7) of the European Commission under Grant Agreement 318338, "Optique". Ernesto Jiménez-Ruiz and Evgeny Kharlamov were also supported by the EPSRC projects MaSI^3, Score! and DBOnto.

References

1. Aumueller, D., Do, H.H., Massmann, S., Rahm, E.: Schema and ontology matching with COMA++. In: SIGMOD (2005)
2. Batini, C., Lenzerini, M., Navathe, S.B.: A comparative analysis of methodologies for database schema integration. ACM Comput. Surv. **18**(4), 323–364 (1986)
3. Bhardwaj, A.P. et al.: DataHub: Collaborative data science and dataset version management at scale. In: CIDR (2015)
4. Console, M., Lenzerini, M.: Data quality in ontology-based data access: The case of consistency. In: AAAI (2014)

5. Dong, X.L., Srivastava, D.: Big data integration. In: PVLDB, vol. **6**(11), pp. 1188–1189 (2013)
6. Fagin, R., et al.: Clio: Schema mapping creation and data exchange. In: Borgida, A.T., Chaudhri, V.K., Giorgini, P., Yu, E.S. (eds.) Conceptual Modeling: Foundations and Applications. LNCS, vol. 5600, pp. 198–236. Springer, Heidelberg (2009)
7. Freitas, F., Schulz, S.: Survey of current terminologies and ontologies in biology and medicine. RECIIS Elect. J. Commun. Inf. Innov. Health **3**, 7–18 (2009)
8. Garcia-Molina, H., Ullman, J.D., Widom, J.: Database Systems—The Complete Book. 2nd edn. Prentice Hall, Englewood Cliffs (2008)
9. Giese, M. et al.: Optique Zooming In on Big Data Access. IEEE Computer (in press) (2015)
10. Haase, P. et al.: Optique system: Towards ontology and mapping management in OBDA solutions. In: WoDOOM (2013)
11. Hornung, T., May, W.: Experiences from a TBox reasoning application: Deriving a relational model by OWL schema analysis. In: OWLED Workshop (2013)
12. Horrocks, I.: What are ontologies good for? In: Evolution of Semantic Systems, pp. 175–188. Springer (2013)
13. Hu, W., Qu, Y.: Discovering simple mappings between relational database schemas and ontologies. In: Aberer, K., Choi, K.-S., Noy, N., Allemang, D., Lee, K.-I., Nixon, L.J.B., Golbeck, J., Mika, P., Maynard, D., Mizoguchi, R., Schreiber, G., Cudré-Mauroux, P. (eds.) ASWC 2007 and ISWC 2007. LNCS, vol. 4825, pp. 225–238. Springer, Heidelberg (2007)
14. Impraliou, M., Stoilos, G., Cuenca Grau, B.: Benchmarking ontology-based query rewriting systems. In: AAAI (2013)
15. Kharlamov, E., Solomakhina, N., Özçep, Ö.L., Zheleznyakov, D., Hubauer, T., Lamparter, S., Roshchin, M., Soylu, A., Watson, S.: How semantic technologies can enhance data access at siemens energy. In: Mika, P., Tudorache, T., Bernstein, A., Welty, C., Knoblock, C., Vrandečić, D., Groth, P., Noy, N., Janowicz, K., Goble, C. (eds.) ISWC 2014, Part I. LNCS, vol. 8796, pp. 601–619. Springer, Heidelberg (2014)
16. Kharlamov, E. et al.: Optique 1.0: Semantic access to big data – The case of norwegian petroleum directorates FactPages. In: ISWC (Posters and Demos) (2013)
17. Kharlamov, E., et al.: Optique: Towards OBDA systems for industry. In: Cimiano, P., Fernández, M., Lopez, V., Schlobach, S., Völker, J. (eds.) ESWC 2013. LNCS, vol. 7955, pp. 125–140. Springer, Heidelberg (2013)
18. Knoblock, C.A., et al.: Semi-automatically mapping structured sources into the semantic web. In: Simperl, E., Cimiano, P., Polleres, A., Corcho, O., Presutti, V. (eds.) ESWC 2012. LNCS, vol. 7295, pp. 375–390. Springer, Heidelberg (2012)
19. Lanti, D., Rezk, M., Slusnys, M., Xiao, G., Calvanese, D.: The NPD benchmark for OBDA systems. In: SSWS (2014)
20. Mora, J., Corcho, O.: Towards a systematic benchmarking of ontology-based query rewriting systems. In: ISWC (2014)
21. Ontology Alignment Evaluation Initiative. http://oaei.ontologymatching.org
22. Papapanagiotou, P. et al.: Ronto: Relational to Ontology Schema Matching. AIS SIGSEMIS BULLETIN (2006)
23. Pinkel, C., Binnig, C., Kharlamov, E., Haase, P.: Pay as you go matching of relational schemata to OWL ontologies with incmap. In: ISWC, pp. 225–228 (2013)
24. Pinkel, C., Binnig, C., Kharlamov, E., Haase, P.: IncMap: Pay-as-you-go matching of relational schemata to OWL ontologies. In: OM (2013)

25. Pinkel, C., et al.: How to best find a partner? An evaluation of editing approaches to construct R2RML mappings. In: Presutti, V., d'Amato, C., Gandon, F., d'Aquin, M., Staab, S., Tordai, A. (eds.) ESWC 2014. LNCS, vol. 8465, pp. 675–690. Springer, Heidelberg (2014)
26. Poess, M., Rabl, T., Caufield, B.: TPC-DI: the first industry benchmark for data integration. PVLDB **7**(13), 1367–1378 (2014)
27. Poggi, A., Lembo, D., Calvanese, D., De Giacomo, G., Lenzerini, M., Rosati, R.: Linking data to ontologies. J. Data Semant. **10**, 133–173 (2008)
28. Priyatna, F., Corcho, O., Sequeda, J.: Formalisation and experiences of R2RML-based SPARQL to SQL query translation using morph. In: WWW (2014)
29. Rodriguez-Muro, M. et al.: Efficient SPARQL-to-SQL with R2RML mappings. J. Web Semant. (in press) (2015)
30. Skjæveland, M.G., Lian, E.H., Horrocks, I.: Publishing the norwegian petroleum directorate's FactPages as semantic web data. In: Alani, H., Kagal, L., Fokoue, A., Groth, P., Biemann, C., Parreira, J.X., Aroyo, L., Noy, N., Welty, C., Janowicz, K. (eds.) ISWC 2013, Part II. LNCS, vol. 8219, pp. 162–177. Springer, Heidelberg (2013)
31. Solimando, A., Jiménez-Ruiz, E., Guerrini, G.: Detecting and correcting conservativity principle violations in ontology-to-ontology mappings. In: Mika, P., Tudorache, T., Bernstein, A., Welty, C., Knoblock, C., Vrandečić, D., Groth, P., Noy, N., Janowicz, K., Goble, C. (eds.) ISWC 2014, Part II. LNCS, vol. 8797, pp. 1–16. Springer, Heidelberg (2014)
32. Tian, A., Sequeda, J.F., Miranker, D.P.: QODI: Query as context in automatic data integration. In: Alani, H., Kagal, L., Fokoue, A., Groth, P., Biemann, C., Parreira, J.X., Aroyo, L., Noy, N., Welty, C., Janowicz, K. (eds.) ISWC 2013, Part I. LNCS, vol. 8218, pp. 624–639. Springer, Heidelberg (2013)

VocBench: A Web Application
for Collaborative Development
of Multilingual Thesauri

Armando Stellato[1(✉)], Sachit Rajbhandari[2], Andrea Turbati[1],
Manuel Fiorelli[1], Caterina Caracciolo[2], Tiziano Lorenzetti[1],
Johannes Keizer[2], and Maria Teresa Pazienza[1]

[1] ART Group, Department of Enterprise Engineering,
University of Rome, Tor Vergata, Via del Politecnico 1, 00133 Rome, Italy
{stellato, turbati, fiorelli, lorenzetti,
pazienza}@info.uniroma2.it
[2] The Food and Agricultural Organization of UN (FAO),
Viale delle Terme di Caracalla, 00153 Rome, Italy
{sachit.rajbhandari, caterina.caracciolo,
johannes.keizer}@fao.org

Abstract. We introduce VocBench, an open source web application for editing thesauri complying with the SKOS and SKOS-XL standards. VocBench has a strong focus on collaboration, supported by workflow management for content validation and publication. Dedicated user roles provide a clean separation of competences, addressing different specificities ranging from management aspects to vertical competences on content editing, such as conceptualization versus terminology editing. Extensive support for scheme management allows editors to fully exploit the possibilities of the SKOS model, as well as to fulfill its integrity constraints. We discuss thoroughly the main features of VocBench, detail its architecture, and evaluate it under both a functional and user-appreciation ground, through a comparison with state-of-the-art and user questionnaires analysis, respectively. Finally, we provide insights on future developments.

Keywords: Collaborative thesaurus management · SKOS · SKOS-XL

1 Introduction

SKOS [1] provided public institutions and other organizations with a fast path toward the Semantic Web [2], by allowing them to represent in RDF thesauri and other *knowledge organization systems* (KOSs) [3] traditionally adopted for tasks such as resource indexing, query expansion and faceted search. SKOS proves advantageous [4] for representing concept-based KOSs on the Semantic Web and the Linked Data [5], as it fosters interoperability of resources and the development of distributed applications. Additionally, SKOS-XL [6] provides an extension for describing terms, through lexical relationships and various metadata, concerning aspects such as history notes, editorial workflows and publication status. The SKOS specification is intentionally loose in defining the semantics of the provided modeling, in order to accommodate the variety

© Springer International Publishing Switzerland 2015
F. Gandon et al. (Eds.): ESWC 2015, LNCS 9088, pp. 38–53, 2015.
DOI: 10.1007/978-3-319-18818-8_3

of existing practices and guidelines for the compilation of KOSs. Furthermore, many of the constraints that are part of the SKOS specification are not expressed through OWL axioms: verifying the logical consistency of a KOS through OWL-compliant systems is thus insufficient for validating it. *Dedicated editors* should then ensure the consistent use of SKOS (possibly adopting dedicated validators [7, 8]), while at same time implementing useful abstractions over raw data. The maintenance of a SKOS dataset is often beyond the possibility of a single developer, since thesauri tend to be heavy-weight (i.e., composed of many concepts and labels). Moreover, the normative nature of thesauri requires them to be "[...] developed, managed and endorsed by *practice of communities*" [9]. As such, thesaurus development should be a collaborative effort, rather than a top-down process independent from the communities that the thesaurus aims to serve.

In this paper, we present VocBench, a collaborative Web-based multilingual thesaurus editor, which complies with SKOS and its extension SKOS-XL. VocBench allows for collaborative management of the overall editorial workflow, by introducing different roles with specific competencies.

2 Motivations and Requirements

In 2008, the AIMS group of the Food and Agriculture Organization of the United Nations (FAO, http://www.fao.org/) fostered the development of a collaborative platform for managing the Agrovoc thesaurus [10]: the "Agrovoc Workbench". The rising interest in such a platform from other FAO departments and several other organizations motivated its reengineering into a more general thesauri management system: Voc-Bench. Its latest incarnation – VocBench 2, the system presented here – has been developed in collaboration between FAO and the ART group of the University of Tor Vergata in Rome (http://art.uniroma2.it). VocBench 2 has been rethought as a fully-fledged collaborative platform for thesauri management, available free-of-use and open source, offering native RDF support for SKOS-XL thesauri, while retaining from its original version the focus on multilingualism, collaboration and on a structured content validation & publication workflow.

VocBench is meant to satisfy the needs of large institutions and organizations (though may be adopted in smaller settings as well), by matching an assortment of requirements:

R1. Multilingualism. Properly characterizing the data in different natural languages is fundamental, especially for thesauri, due to their use in Information Retrieval.

R2. Controlled Collaboration. Opening up to communities is important, though the development of authoritative resources demands for the presence of some control to be exerted over the resource lifecycle.

R3. Data Interoperability and Consistency. Interoperability of several resources – which is at the basis of SKOS adoption – critically depends on data integrity and conformance to representation standards. However, the flexibility of SKOS translates to

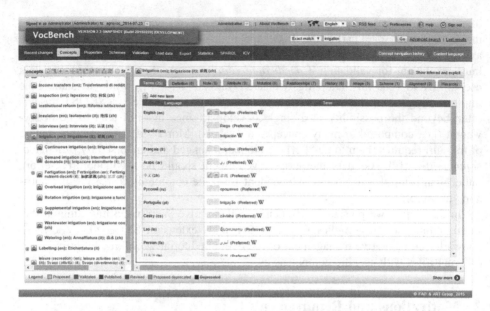

Fig. 1. VocBench user interface showing a fragment of the AGROVOC thesaurus

an underspecified model, at the same time exhibiting formal constraints that are even beyond the expressiveness of OWL. It is thus important that VocBench enforces a consistent use of SKOS, by preventing the editors from generating invalid data. Properly covering the whole family of RDF modeling languages is also part of this requirement, as SKOS actually sits on top of OWL and may benefit from the reuse of OWL vocabularies adding additional domain properties or specific modeling axioms. Finally, support for alignment to other datasets is also a must for the Linked Data World.

R4. Software Interoperability/Extensibility. The system should be able to interact with (possibly interchangeable) standard technologies in the RDF/Linked Data world.

R5. Scalability. The system must deal with (relatively) large amount of data, still offering a friendly environment. User Interface must take that into account.

R6. Under-the-hood data access/modification. While a friendly UI for content managers/domain experts is important, knowledge engineers need to access raw data beyond the usual front-ends, as well as to benefit from mass editing/refactoring facilities.

R7. Ease-of-use for both users and system administrators. This was a particularly important requirement in migrating from the first VocBench (adopted in a close, though large, community) to its second version, released as an open-source free-of-use system.

3   The New VocBench 2

VocBench (also abbreviated as VB) has been conceived as a web application accessible through any modern browser, therefore disburdening end users from software installation and configuration. Many of the limitations of VB1 with respect to the requirements described in the previous section were related to the lack of a real RDF backend. While VB1 was based on the API of Protégé 3 OWL (a non-native OWL wrapper around the legacy Protégé 3 frame-based model), VB2 has been re-designed to rely on the capabilities of Semantic Turkey [11], an RDF management platform already developed and currently maintained by University of Tor Vergata. Semantic Turkey (ST from now on) offers an OSGi service-based layer for designing and developing OWL ontologies and SKOS/SKOS-XL thesauri. A lightweight Firefox interface is available for use as a desktop tool, now complemented by VB, which mainly differentiates for its collaborative nature (and the focus on thesauri).The insight on usability of real thesaurus publishers informed the development. Specially, FAO and its partners provided great support for shaping user interaction and collaboration capabilities, therefore ensuring that VocBench was indeed functioning and meeting its user requirements.

In the rest of this section, we discuss the main characteristics of the software.

User Interface (UI). The user interface consists of multiple tabs, each one associated with specific information and functionalities. A quick exploration of the available tabs is sufficient to discover most of the VocBench functionalities, at least at the user level.

Figure 1 offers a typical view of VocBench, with the concept tree on the left, and the description of the selected concept on the right, centered on the term tab, listing all terms in the different languages available for the resource. Concepts in the tree may be shown through their labels in all of the selected languages for visualization. An option allows to toggle between preferred labels and all labels. Also the multilingual characteristics (requisite R1) of VB are not limited to content management, as the UI is itself localized in different languages, currently: English, Spanish, Dutch and Thailandese.

Controlled Collaborative Editing through Role-based Access Control. A single installation of VocBench may handle multiple independent thesauri. Upon registration, users indicate the thesauri they are interested in and the roles they want to cover; at any time, the administrator may grant additional permissions. VocBench promotes the separation of responsibilities through a role-based access control mechanism, checking user privileges for requested functionalities through the role they assume (req. R2). A completely customizable access policy specifies roles and their assigned privileges. New roles can be created, and existing ones can be modified. The default policy recognizes typical roles and their acknowledged responsibilities: *Administrators*, *Ontology editors*, *Term editors* (Terminologists), *Validators* and *Publishers*.

Formal Workflow and Recent Changes. Collaboration is essential for distributing effort and reaching consensus on the thesaurus being developed. To facilitate collaboration, VocBench provides an editorial workflow in which editors' changes are tracked and stored for approval by content validators. This workflow management is supported by role-based access control, by providing users with different roles so to enforce the separation between their responsibilities. In a collaborative environment, where users may proactively edit a shared resource, it is important to have means for monitoring the situation. Regarding this aspect, the ability to control recent changes to the thesaurus is useful for detecting hot sections and coordinating with other editors. In VocBench, users can see recent changes both in the Web user interface and as an RSS feed.

Advanced Scheme Management. The definition of scheme in SKOS is blurred, as the SKOS reference [1] neutrally defines the scheme as an "aggregation of concepts" while SKOS primer [12] promotes schemes as identifiers for thesauri themselves, though reporting that several issues exist: #secskoscontainment. VocBench allows to manage thesauri organized around multiple concept schemes. Users can switch across schemes by selecting them through the relevant *Schemes* tab in the user interface. The Concepts tab shows the concept hierarchy and filters out concepts not belonging to the selected scheme. Concepts may belong to more than one scheme but must be in at least one, otherwise they are *dangling*, as they cannot be seen in any scheme view. VocBench functionalities are well-behaved with respect to schemes, as actions that would generate dangling concepts are forbidden, detailing the cause of the impediment to the users. In any case, since data can be loaded from pre-existing sources developed outside of VocBench, a fixing utility for dangling concepts is available through the UI. This will be part of a larger section dedicated to Integrity Constraints Validation, providing issue detection and repair actions (thus meeting requirements R3), which is currently available in ST and its Firefox UI and will ported to the UI of VB in the forthcoming VB2.4.

Vocabulary Import and Data Import/Export. The SKOS standard defines a very general, domain-agnostic, meta-model for the representation of KOSes. VocBench allows to import ontology vocabularies (from the web, file system or even a dedicated local mirror), providing additional shared descriptors (e.g. additional properties, which reflect specific conceptual and lexical relations for the domain of interest) for modeling the thesaurus. Data import/export is available for all notable RDF serialization formats. **Metrics & SPARQL Querying**. VocBench supports the computation of several metrics concerning the thesaurus itself and the collaborative workflow. These metrics are grouped with respect to common themes: distribution of labels across different languages, structure of the thesaurus, vocabulary use and workflow statistics. Structural metrics are helpful in assessing the granularity (hierarchy depth) of the thesaurus, its scope (hierarchy width) and its level of uniformity (variance of metrics). Statistics about the use of vocabulary properties help in understanding the completeness of the resource. Finally, workflow statistics support management of the entire editing process.

In addition to statistics and visualizations provided by VocBench, users may formulate SPARQL 1.1 queries to select information precisely, or to perform analytical tasks. The query editor is based on the open source project Flint SPARQL Editor (https://github.com/TSO-Openup/FlintSparqlEditor), which provides syntax highlighting and completion. The Flint syntax completion has been customized to be fed with information (e.g. the adopted namespaces and their chosen prefixes) originating from the edited thesaurus. Availability of SPARQL updates completes the above in order to fulfill requirement R6.

Alignment. From version 2.3 (latest stable version at the time of writing), VocBench features a dedicated tab in the concept description area, showing alignments to other thesauri. Currently, the creation of alignments can either be performed manually, by inserting URIs as values of the various SKOS mapping properties, or be assisted in case of mappings to other thesauri managed by the same instance of VocBench. In the latter case, a concept-tree browser with advanced search interfaces (which can be manually prompted or automatically populated with the lexicalizations of the local concept) facilitates the identification of the best matching concepts from the targeted datasets.

4 Architecture

VocBench has a layered architecture (Fig. 2) consisting of a presentation and multi-user management layer, a service layer and a data management layer. The first layer is implemented as a Web application, powered by GWT (Google Web Toolkit, http://www.gwtproject.org/). The other layers coincide with the Semantic Turkey RDF management platform, equipped with an extension providing additional services expressly developed for VocBench. VocBench is also in charge of user and workflow management, since these aspects are not covered by Semantic Turkey. User accounts and tracked changes are stored in a relational database accessed through a JDBC connector. The ST backend manages the data and implements all the required editing functionalities. The interface between the frontend and backend consists of a series of lightweight Web services in the spirit of the Web API movement. Semantic Turkey provides core services related to project management, OWL and RDFS ontologies, SPARQL, etc. Furthermore, the adoption of OSGi allows for dynamic plugging of extensions: in particular, other than realizing additional services, different connectors for specific RDF middleware and triple storage technologies can be provided (req. R4). VocBench is currently shipped with a connector for Sesame2 [13], supporting all of its storage/connection possibilities: in memory, native, remote connection and their respective configurations. The remote connection is particularly useful, as it allows VocBench to connect to Sesame2 compliant triple stores (e.g. GraphDB [14]) without need for a dedicated connector. VocBench RDF API are based on OWL ART (http://art.uniroma2.it/owlart/), an abstraction layer supporting access to different triple stores. Different connectors can be implemented from scratch in terms of those API, or by reusing middleware already bridged through other existing connectors. For instance, the Virtuoso triplestore [15] is compatible with the Sesame API, but requires a dedicated client library: it thus needs to be introduced by a specific connector, though its implementation may be largely realized as an extension of the already existing Sesame connector.

Particular attention has been paid to system scalability (req. R5), both on performance and maintenance aspects. To this end, information is provided to the frontend as much as possible in an incremental fashion (e.g., each level of the concept hierarchy, as

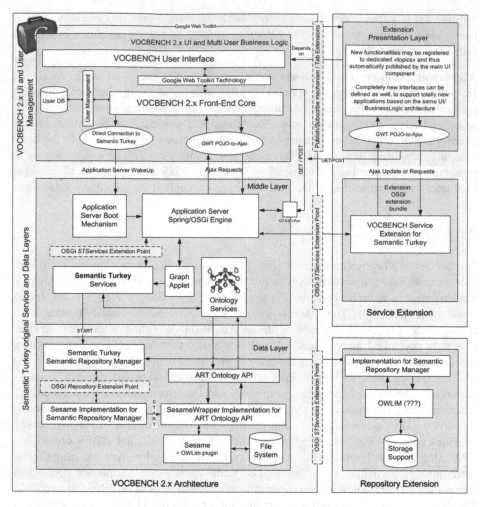

Fig. 2. VocBench 2 extensible architecture

nodes are expanded). Also, though we tried to maintain a meaningful core set of RDF services, many functionalities (especially in the user interface) require the composition of several calls. We thus provided both per-service ad hoc solutions (heavy weight single services realizing specific functionalities) and general development facilities for the injection of additional information into common API calls (e.g. the rendering of RDF resources is available as an extension point, with different implementations being dynamically injectable into the SPARQL queries of several services).

A continuous check-on-start life cycle satisfies requirement R7: VB technically never recognizes itself as installed/deployed, rather at each application startup it checks that the complete set of pre-requisites for a correct start is satisfied. Whenever a new VB version is installed, if new features have been introduced, or mandatory configuration options added, or the database requires update batches, the system will identify these needs and react accordingly, eventually interacting with the user upon necessity.

5 Related Tools

In this section, we survey other thesaurus editors that we will later compare to Voc-Bench. We analyzed the latest versions of the systems (unless differently reported, as in the case of SKOSed) by asking evaluation licenses when necessary, as in the case of proprietary tools. Even though our survey is certainly incomplete with respect to existing tools (e.g. we have never received the license we requested for Topbraid EVN, http://www.topquadrant.com/products/topbraid-enterprise-vocabulary-net/), we believe our sample is representative of existing technologies.

WebProtégé, http://webprotege.stanford.edu/ [16] is an open source web based system for collaborative ontology development. Unfortunately, WebProtégé has not a dedicated support for SKOS (it covers editing of OWL/OBO), however it has been included in the survey due to extensive support to collaboration, which is an important aspect in our review. WebProtégé is available as a locally installable web application, also offered as a free service via a public portal. It has a clean user interface, organized in a collection of tabs, which in turn contain widgets showing different types of information. The user interface is completely configurable: users (even at runtime) can add, remove or reposition the widgets within a tab as well as add/remove tabs themselves.

WebProtégé relies on the collaboration plugin for Protégé 3 [17], providing change tracking, inline discussions and notifications. It also features an access control mechanism for user groups, based on configurable policies enforced at various granularities. It has a plugin architecture, which supports the development and deployment of additional functionalities. Integration with other applications is also possible through the API provided by the service and backend layers.

PoolParty, http://www.poolparty.biz/ [18] is a proprietary Web based editor for thesauri utilizing Linked Data. It exists in different editions, possibly bundled with other tools supporting semantic tagging and semantic search. Buying options include both on-premises installation and hosted solutions. For our analysis, we obtained a free evaluation account for PoolParty Advanced Server version 4.5.1 (rev 5429).

PoolParty supports by default SKOS and has an optional add-on for SKOS-XL. SKOS compliance includes concept lists and collections; PoolParty does not explicitly attach concepts to schemes, but the sole connection with a scheme lies in the reachability from one of its top concepts (this is in contrast with the specification of non-entailment of scheme containment along concept hierarchies, specified in Sect. 4.6.4 of the SKOS Reference [1]). PoolParty supports custom modelling vocabularies expressed in RDFS or OWL, either locally edited or imported from external sources.

Version Tracking is supported, as the system performs access control to some extent. An add-on further enables an approval workflow based on the existing role based access control mechanism. Editing history is shown both at project level and at entity level.

PoolParty supports the lookup over resources published as LOD, either to gather additional information or to create mappings. Similarly, different projects can be linked together, for instance, to enable concept mapping. Additionally, PoolParty publishes a SPARQL endpoint, dereferenceable URIs, and a wiki with limited editing capabilities.

Depending on the specific settings, quality criteria are enforced interactively (i.e., illegal operations are blocked), or violations are simply recorded in a quality report.

PoolParty uses Sesame2 as an abstraction layer over different RDF triple stores, possibly supporting inference. APIs for integration with other applications are available, ranging from basic synchronization up to text mining and indexing applications.

TemaTres, http://www.vocabularyserver.com/, is an open source web application for the management, publication and sharing of controlled vocabularies. TemaTres adopts a term-based meta-model for the representation of thesauri and controlled vocabularies in general. While vocabularies are inherently monolingual, a form of multilingualism is supported through alignments between vocabularies (on the same instance of TemaTres, or remotely accessible through a dedicated web service interface). It is possible to export the data in several formats as well as to import from SKOS and tabular representations. Due to the term-based nature of the model, the export to SKOS is often confusing as, for instance, two terms bound as synonyms are actually exported as two different skos:Concepts. Each vocabulary is associated to a single skos: ConceptScheme.

TemaTres has a rigid access control mechanism based on user roles (administrator, editor, guest). It also features workflow management, which is based on the transition of terms from the candidate status to either accepted or rejected. Editing of a term changes the last modification date, but it is not subjected to further approval. In other words, once a term is approved, changing it does not revert its status from accepted.

Facilities for data quality include metrics and a flexible reporting generator.

TemaTres exposes an API for integration with other systems, such as a thesaurus publishing interface, and a WordPress plugin. A TemaTres add-on, TemaTres Keywords Distiller, supports the automatic categorization of unstructured content.

SKOSEd, https://code.google.com/p/skoseditor/ [19]. An open source plugin for Protégé 4.x for editing SKOS thesauri, SKOSEd represents an exception in our survey as, differently from the aforementioned systems, it is not a web application but a desktop tool, which however we consider worth being mentioned. Being embedded into an ontology editor, SKOSEd allows interweaving SKOS and OWL constructs, and inherits from the hosting environment various capabilities: reasoning, usage search and various rendering options (enhanced through SKOS labelling properties).

We have evaluated version 1.0-alpha(build04) on Protégé 4.1 as, unfortunately, the more recent version 2.0-alpha has a bug related to scheme management: once a scheme has been created, it is no longer possible to create new concepts.

SKOSEd adds to Protégé a dedicated tab, offering tree visualization of concept hierarchies, as well as an input form tailored to the SKOS model. However, the system adopts the same form for concepts and concept schemes; consequently, a user can easily assert that a concept scheme is a top concept of another concept scheme. The hosting environment allows creation and import of additional RDFS and OWL vocabularies. Despite this overall flexibility, the SKOS view is somewhat rigid, since the widget for asserting related concept is not aware of possible refinement provided by additional vocabularies. In fact, these properties are only accessible as other properties.

SKOSEd supports plugging of external reasoners to determine whether the thesaurus being edited is consistent with respect to the OWL definition of the SKOS model.

As for PoolParty, the concept tree visualization is only based on the membership of topconcepts to a given scheme, not filtering out narrower concepts not belonging to it.

Being an extension of Protégé 4.x, SKOSEd may not be used in conjunction with the collaboration framework developed for Protégé 3.x.

6 Functional Evaluation

In this section, we compare VocBench to the previously reviewed tools with respect to dimensions expressing interesting and useful features (Table 1).

The first consideration is that VocBench is open source and free to use. This fact is particularly unique among the most accredited thesaurus editors (e.g. PoolParty or Topbraid EVN), which are typically proprietary. The open source nature is advantageous, since it allows wide customizability for specific uses, as well as the possibility to add features to the mainstream distribution. TemaTres seems to depend on a term-based representation of thesauri, which can be exported to many formats, including SKOS. The downside of this approach is the somewhat approximated and limited support to SKOS constructs. VocBench is the only editor natively supporting the SKOS-XL specification (followed by PoolParty with its dedicated SKOS-XL addon).

Support for concept schemes is practically inexistent in TemaTres (each thesaurus is a scheme), while PoolParty and SKOSEd suffer from the same issue with improper entailment of scheme membership inherited from topConcepts. Conversely, VocBench fits better the intended semantics of concept schemes in SKOS with its Advanced Scheme Management features.

The grounding of SKOS in a specific domain/application or editorial environment is realized by the adoption of other RDF vocabularies. SKOSEd is the most advanced with respect to the creation capability, as it is embedded in the ontology editor Protégé. The downside of this power is lesser control on the data being edited/created. VocBench, on the other hand, though not providing the full OWL editing capabilities of Protégé, still allows limited property editing and supports owl:importing external OWL vocabularies.

Obviously, all the systems support import/export of the edited thesaurus. TemaTres has an extensive support for different formats, not limited to RDF. PoolParty and TemaTres are also able to import data from tabular representations, such as spreadsheets, based on a set of statically defined conventions for their format. VocBench has not such a built-in feature in its User Interface. However, we have already developed a highly flexible converter, Sheet2RDF (http://art.uniroma2.it/sheet2rdf/), and made it available for the Firefox interface of Semantic Turkey. It is possible to use the Firefox UI over the same ST instance that is backing VocBench, thus making the whole

Table 1. Comparison of thesaurus management tools

Name	VocBench	PoolParty	WebProtégé	TemaTres	SKOSEd
License	GNU GPL v3 (web application), Mozilla Public License MPL (Semantic Turkey)	Proprietary	Mozilla Public License (MPL)	GNU General Public License version 2.0 (GPLv2)	GNU Lesser GPL
Free to use	Yes	No	Yes	Yes	Yes
Deployment	Web application	Web application	Web application	Web application	Desktop application
Data Models	SKOS-XL, SKOS through offline scaling tool	SKOS SKOS-XL add-on	OWL 2, OBO	Term based thesaurus organization	SKOS
Import/Export	SKOS(-XL), versatile spreadsheet import (through ST Firefox UI)	SKOS(-XL), static spreadsheet import	OWL	MADS, SKOS-Core, Zthes, Others Import from: Skos-Core, tabulated or tagged text file	SKOS
Scheme Management	Yes	Only top concepts	Not applicable	One scheme per vocabulary	Only top concepts
Custom Relations	Import, use	Creation, use	Creation, use	Creation, use	Creation, use
Reasoner	Depends on triple store	Depends on triple store	No, external reasoning possible	No	Depends on available plugins
Data quality	Metrics	Metrics Validation rules	Metrics	Metrics, Reports	KB consistency
Extendibility / Interoperability	API, shared backend, pluggable	REST API	API, shared backend, pluggable	API	Pluggable
ACL	Yes	Yes	Yes	Yes; limited	No
Workflow Management	Yes	Yes (add-on)	No	Yes; limited	No
Collaboration, Content Validation	Change feed, validation	History, versioning, validation	Discussion, watching, changes feed	Limited validation	No
RDF Middleware	OWL ART API (connectors to others: Sesame2 bundled)	Sesame SAIL API	OWL API	No RDF Middleware, SKOS RDF/XML available only as an export	OWL API (used by Protégé 4)
RDF Backend	provided by Sesame2, or other connectors	provided by Sesame2	provided by Protégé 3	Relational database (MySQL by default)	provided by Protégé 4 (OWL API)
SPARQL Querying	Yes	Yes	No	Not native, no realtime, can export data to a SPARQL endpoint through ARC2 (RDF library for PHP)	Yes (inherited from Protégé 4)
Semantic Integration	assisted (browse&search) linking of resources from other projects / manual linking of LOD resources. Extensions for RDF lifting from unstructured content	Linking Text Mining & Entity Extraction, Search function	linking to BioPortal	Linking between vocabularies, Entity Extraction (via addon)	N/A

process require no export/import nor adaptation of data. Sheet2RDF integration inside VocBench UI is also under development.

The RDF framework supports the automatic inference of implicit facts from the explicitly represented knowledge. Reasoning might be useful to materialize redundant information in SKOS thesauri, e.g. skos:broader/narrower relationships, or their transitive closure through skos:broader/narrowerTransitive, or even more elaborated facts determined by axioms defined in the domain vocabularies. VocBench and PoolParty exploit the reasoning capabilities provided by the implementations of the knowledge base, while SKOSed and WebProtégé generally assume that reasoning is performed not in real-time, but by an external component connecting to the backend holding the data.

In traditional ontology development, reasoning is important to formally validate the ontology, by verifying its logical consistency: this is not the case for SKOS thesauri, since most assumptions about the use of SKOS are not explicitly encoded as formal OWL axioms. Therefore, assessing and improving the quality of SKOS thesauri requires dedicated solutions. PoolParty supports different sets of validation rules, which can be enforced during editing or used to generate quality reports. VocBench enforces the consistent use of SKOS constructs, such as the already described constraints on concept scheme management or the uniqueness of preferred labels in a given language, by providing both in line validation and fixing utilities for ingested non-orthodox data.

Another feature relevant for data quality is the possibility to compute metrics and generate various types of reports. Tools differ from each other in terms of the metrics they are able to calculate.

WebProtégé stands up for its support to coordination, by providing history, watching and discussion facilities. VocBench and PoolParty do support history as well, and in addition they support change validation, with VocBench distinguishing more life cycle states than PoolParty. TemaTres has an even more limited set of states, and, as said, once a term has been accepted, subsequent editing does not cause revert the state back from accepted. In both VocBench and PoolParty, validation leverages the role-based access control mechanism. PoolParty has a couple of roles, while VocBench has a more fine-grained and flexible mechanism, which is based on primitive permissions associated with specific actions. Then, specific roles are defined as an assignment of these permissions. VocBench provides by default roles commonly found in thesaurus development processes; nonetheless, it is possible to create new roles as desired. Thus, VocBench allows matching each role to a specific set of competences and duties.

Most of the tools, including VocBench, offers great flexibility for the connection to RDF semantic stores targeting different tradeoffs between requirements. Similarly, these tools tend to support the development of extensions and the integration with other systems. In VocBench, this is achieved by a pluggable architecture and APIs offered to clients. Even the RSS feed can be seen as API to support coordination with other tools, since it contains all the relevant information about each change. Individual editors may subscribe to this RSS feed to be warned of thesaurus changes, which can be considered as a form of watching.

Finally, in some of these tools the aforementioned extendibility supports complex features related to semantic integration beyond thesaurus editing. PoolParty may be integrated with unstructured content analysis systems, as well as with semantic search systems. TemaTres supports the federation of different vocabularies, in order to establish links between them. VocBench has been equipped with ontology alignment capabilities, currently either by manual data entry or by assisted browsing of other projects internally managed by the application.

7 User Community and Evaluation

VocBench 2.0 was released in November 2013. Thanks to word-of-mouth about the previous VocBench 1.x, and to the insights about the new features and larger flexibility the new version would have brought, it has immediately gathered the interest of a discrete number of organizations (http://aims.fao.org/tools/vocbench/partners).

The current version of the system is VB2.3, released March 2015.

Table 2. USE values

	Usefulness	Ease of use	Ease of learning	Satisfaction
Global	5,34	4,49	5,11	4,93
Experienced	5,58	4,66	5,18	5,02
Inexperienced	4,97	4,19	5,00	4,79

VocBench has a public Web site: http://vocbench.uniroma2.it/. Two mailing lists have been made available to support users (http://groups.google.com/group/vocbench-user) and developers (http://groups.google.com/group/vocbench-developer). To evaluate the appreciation of VocBench among its users, we administered an online questionnaire to the mailing subscribers. We received 11 anonymous responses which have been made publicly available (http://vocbench.uniroma2.it/purl/VocBench-User-Questionnaire_2014-10.zip). The questionnaire is composed of three sections: user profiling, a usability evaluation and features evaluation.

The respondents considered themselves quietly proficient with thesaurus editing, as well as with languages of the RDF family, although in the latter case the answers were more scattered. Users experiences with other tools confirmed our belief in the representativeness of our survey of thesaurus editors.

We adopted the USE questionnaire (http://hcibib.org/perlman/question.cgi?form=USE) to evaluate how VocBench users perceive its usability along four dimensions: usefulness, ease of use, ease of learning and satisfaction. Each dimension is evaluated through a set of Likert-items (with scores ranging from 1 to 7). Table 2 reports the average score regarding each dimension.

The first row of the table represents the average over the entire sample. All averages represent an encouraging result, especially if considering that the highest value was given to Usefulness: this means that users believe that using this tool aids them in their work despite they consider it not very easy to use and to be learned.

We divided the respondents into two disjoint groups based on whether they reported to have adopted other related tools (64 %) or not (36 %). The usability metrics on the experienced group are consistently (and uniformly) higher than those obtained from the inexperienced one. This is a good indicator as somewhat reflects a good positioning with respect to the state of the art.

The last part of the questionnaire was aimed at surveying the perceived value of some of the most important features of VocBench, in terms of interestingness, effectiveness and easiness of use. For each dimension, a 7-point scale was used. Table 3 shows the average agreement on each dimension and the rows are ordered in decreasing order of how they are perceived as interesting by the users.

Unsurprisingly, collaboration related features are the top rated characteristics. The only negative value in that table (below 4) is the easiness of the triple store connectivity, which is, though, an intrinsically complex feature, negatively affected by the still scarce standardization of triple store connectivity. Users are however interested (average score: 5) in the possibility to plug different stores or even RDF middleware.

Table 3. Feature evaluation

	It's easy to use	It's effective	It's interesting
History	5,38	5,50	6,33
SPARQL querying	4,00	5,40	6,29
Publication workflow Management	5,50	5,63	6,22
Collaborative management	5,75	5,88	6,11
Scheme management	4,83	5,17	5,57
Role-based access control	5,33	5,22	5,40
Reasoning	4,29	4,43	5,38
Triple store connectivity	3,67	4,50	5,00

8 Conclusion and Future Work

VocBench addressed the need of an open-source general-purpose editor of SKOS-XL thesauri supporting a formalized editorial workflow. In this paper, we discussed the features of VocBench and its architecture. Then, we surveyed a representative sample of related tools, to identify important features, and to show that VocBench mostly covers them and in some cases surpasses the state-of-the-art.

A vibrant user community[1] grew around VocBench initially inside various departments of FAO, and later spread across other organizations with analogous needs. Continuous user feedback allowed us to spot bugs and to improve the usability of VocBench.

The most important improvement we are working on consists in a more extensive and uniform access to internal and external resources (such as Linked Open Data). This will be particularly useful for improving the alignment user experience, with users browsing both local and LOD resources from within the VocBench interface, performing alignments in a seamless way. Another improvement is towards more complete extensibility: as we previously mentioned, Semantic Turkey has already support

---

[1] See http://vocbench.uniroma2.it/support/ and the related community and mailing lists links.

for extensions, however when it comes to the UI extensions, the GWT framework is rather limited due to its java → javascript compilation phase. We will explore how to overcome this limitation. By following the user evaluation results, we will also add more data connectors for covering the most notable middlewares and triple stores.

Acknowledgments. This research has been partially supported by the EU funded projects SemaGrow (http://www.semagrow.eu/) under grant agreement no: 318497, and AgInfra (http://aginfra.eu/) under grant agreement: RI- 283770.

References

1. World Wide Web Consortium (W3C): SKOS Simple Knowledge Organization System Reference. In: World Wide Web Consortium (W3C). http://www.w3.org/TR/skos-reference/. Accessed 18 August 2009
2. Berners-Lee, T., Hendler, J., Lassila, O.: The semantic web: a new form of web content that is meaningful to computers will unleash a revolution of new possibilities. Sci. Am. **279**(5), 34–43 (2001)
3. Hodge, G.: Systems of Knowledge Organization for Digital Libraries: Beyond Traditional Authority Files. Council on Library and Information Resources, Washington, DC (April 2000)
4. Pastor–Sanchez, J.A., Martinez–Mendez, F.J., Rodríguez–Muñoz, J.V.: Advantages of thesaurus representation using the simple knowledge organization system (SKOS) compared with proposed alternatives. Inf. Res. **14**(4), 10 (2009)
5. Heath, T., Bizer, C.: Linked data: evolving the web into a global data space. Synth. Lect. Semant. Web Theory Technol. **1**(1), 1–136 (2011)
6. World Wide Web Consortium (W3C): SKOS Simple Knowledge Organization System eXtension for Labels (SKOS-XL). In: World Wide Web Consortium (W3C). http://www.w3.org/TR/skos-reference/skos-xl.html. Accessed 18 August 2009
7. Mader, C., Haslhofer, B., Isaac, A.: Finding quality issues in SKOS vocabularies. In: Zaphiris, P., Buchanan, G., Rasmussen, E., Loizides, F. (eds.) Theory and Practice of Digital Libraries 7489, pp. 222–233. Springer, Heidelberg (2012)
8. Suominen, O., Hyvönen, E.: Improving the quality of SKOS vocabularies with Skosify. In: ten Teije, A., Völker, J., Handschuh, S., Stuckenschmidt, H., d'Acquin, M., Nikolov, A., Aussenac-Gilles, N., Hernandez, N. (eds.) Knowledge Engineering and Knowledge Management. LNCS, vol. 7603, pp. 383–397. Springer, Heidelberg (2012)
9. Shadbolt, N., Berners-Lee, T., Hall, W.: The semantic web revisited. IEEE Intell. Syst. **21**(3), 96–101 (2006)
10. Caracciolo, C., Stellato, A., Morshed, A., Johannsen, G., Rajbhandari, S., Jaques, Y., Keizer, J.: The AGROVOC linked dataset. Semant. Web J. **4**(3), 341–348 (2013)
11. Pazienza, M., Scarpato, N., Stellato, A., Turbati, A.: Semantic Turkey: a browser-integrated environment for knowledge acquisition and management. Semant. Web J. **3**(3), 279–292 (2012)
12. World Wide Web Consortium (W3C): SKOS Simple Knowledge Organization System Primer. In: World Wide Web Consortium (W3C). http://www.w3.org/TR/skos-primer. Accessed 18 August 2009

13. Broekstra, J., Kampman, A., van Harmelen, F.: Sesame: a generic architecture for storing and querying RDF and RDF schema. In: Horrocks, I., Hendler, J. (eds.) ISWC 2002. LNCS, vol. 2342, pp. 54–68. Springer, Heidelberg (2002)
14. Kiryakov, A., Ognyanov, D., Manov, D.: OWLIM – a pragmatic semantic repository for OWL. In: International Workshop on Scalable Semantic Web Knowledge Base Systems (SSWS 2005), WISE 2005, New York City, USA, 20 November 2005
15. Erling, O., Mikhailov, I.: RDF support in the virtuoso DBMS. In: Pellegrini, T., Auer, S., Tochterman, K., Schaffert, S. (eds.) Networked Knowledge - Networked Media. Studies in Computational Intelligence, vol. 221, pp. 7–24. Springer, Berlin Heidelberg (2009)
16. Tudorache, T., Nyulas, C., Noy, N., Musen, M.: WebProtégé: a collaborative ontology editor and knowledge acquisition tool for the web. Semant. Web 4(1), 89–99 (2013)
17. Tudorache, T., Noy, N., Tu, S., Musen, M.: Supporting collaborative ontology development in protégé. In: Sheth, A., Staab, S., Dean, M., Paolucci, M., Maynard, D., Finin, T., Thirunarayan, K. (eds.) The Semantic Web - ISWC 2008 5318, pp. 17–32. Springer, Heidelberg (2008)
18. Schandl, T., Blumauer, A.: PoolParty: SKOS thesaurus management utilizing linked data. In: Aroyo, L., Antoniou, G., Hyvönen, E., Teije, A., Stuckenschmidt, H., Cabral, L., Tudorache, T. (eds.) The Semantic Web: Research and Applications 6089, pp. 421–425. Springer, Heidelberg (2010)
19. Jupp, S., Bechhofer, S., Stevens, R.: A flexible API and editor for SKOS. In: Aroyo, L., Traverso, P., Ciravegna, F., Cimiano, P., Heath, T., Hyvönen, E., Mizoguchi, R., Oren, E., Sabou, M., Simperl, E. (eds.) The Semantic Web: Research and Applications 5554, pp. 506–520. Springer, Heidelberg (2009)

Leveraging and Balancing Heterogeneous Sources of Evidence in Ontology Learning

Gerhard Wohlgenannt$^{(\boxtimes)}$

Vienna University of Economics and Business,
Welthandelsplatz 1, 1200 Vienna, Austria
gerhard.wohlgenannt@wu.ac.at
http://www.wu.ac.at

Abstract. Ontology learning (OL) aims at the (semi-)automatic acquisition of ontologies from sources of evidence, typically domain text. Recently, there has been a trend towards the application of multiple and heterogeneous evidence sources in OL. Heterogeneous sources provide benefits, such as higher accuracy by exploiting redundancy across evidence sources, and including complementary information. When using evidence sources which are heterogeneous in quality, amount of data provided and type, then a number of questions arise, for example: How many sources are needed to see significant benefits from heterogeneity, what is an appropriate number of evidences per source, is balancing the number of evidences per source important, and to what degree can the integration of multiple sources overcome low quality input of individual sources? This research presents an extensive evaluation based on an existing OL system. It gives answers and insights on the research questions posed for the OL task of concept detection, and provides further hints from experience made. Among other things, our results suggest that a moderate number of evidences per source as well as a moderate number of sources resulting in a few thousand data instances are sufficient to exploit the benefits of heterogeneous evidence integration.

Keywords: Heterogeneous evidence sources · Ontology learning · Evidence integration · Spreading activation

1 Introduction

Ontologies are a cornerstone technology and backbone for the Semantic Web, but the manual creation of ontologies is cumbersome and expensive, therefore there have been many efforts towards (semi-)automatic ontology generation in order to assist ontology engineers.

The process of ontology learning (typically from text) in a first step extracts facts (lexical entries) and patterns (evidence) from text, and then turns them into shareable high-level constructs. This includes the identification of domain concepts, which is an ontology learning (OL) task building on term extraction and the detection of synonyms [2].

© Springer International Publishing Switzerland 2015
F. Gandon et al. (Eds.): ESWC 2015, LNCS 9088, pp. 54–68, 2015.
DOI: 10.1007/978-3-319-18818-8_4

OL evolved from working on static domain text to Web sources, and more recently there are a few approaches that make use of multiple and heterogeneous data sources (see next section for more details). The introduction of heterogeneous sources into the learning process offers the potential for higher levels of accuracy, on the other hand there are challenges regarding the meaningful integration and balancing (of the impact) of sources. Manzano-Macho et al. [6] list some of the reasons for increased accuracy when using heterogeneous evidence sources: (i) redundancy of information in different sources represents a measure of relevance and trust, and (ii) additional sources can provide complementary data and valuable information that the other sources did not detect.

The question arising is to quantify the gains in accuracy in various OL tasks when using heterogeneous evidence sources. In this paper we take a detailed look on gains in the concept detection task. So, the research question is: How does the number and the characteristics of heterogeneous evidence sources affect accuracy (i.e. the ratio of relevant concept candidates) in concept detection? In other words, the problem is as follows: We start with an OL system that includes a number of (heterogeneous) evidence acquisition methods, which basically provide terminology (heterogeneous lists of terms). These are the input, the output of concept detection are a number of domain concept candidates. In the evaluation section we study the impact of the (i) number of evidence sources, (ii) number of evidences per source, (iii) heterogeneity and quality of sources and (iv) the balance between sources on the accuracy of concept detection.

The evidence used in the OL system is heterogeneous in various respects. It originates from different sources such as Web documents, social Web APIs, and structured sources, and from different extraction methods applied. This leads to heterogeneity regarding the quality of evidence, the vocabulary used, the number of evidences and the dynamics of the source (see Sect. 4).

The experiments are conducted with an OL system (see Sect. 3) that generates lightweight ontologies using the spreading activation algorithm [5] to integrate evidence. Lightweight ontologies typically only contain concepts, taxonomic relations and unlabeled non-taxonomic relations, and are applied in many areas, e.g. to fuel everyday applications like Web search and enabling intelligent systems [19]. For the experiments, the architecture generated lightweight ontologies in two different domains ("climate change" and "tennis") in monthly intervals from scratch. As spreading activation is a simple and intuitive way to integrate heterogeneous evidence, the results can largely be generalized to other OL systems and integration logics for heterogeneous evidence which use a similar approach.

The outline of the paper is as follows: After presenting related work in Sects. 2 and 3 introduces the OL system used in the experiments. Section 4 provides details about the heterogeneous sources of evidence. Results of the extensive experiments are found in Sects. 5 and 6 concludes with a summary, the main contributions, and future work.

2   Related Work

Most OL systems learn ontologies from only one source, typically domain text, e.g. Text2Onto [4] or OntoLearn Reloaded [14]. Some authors, e.g. Sanchez and Moreno [12], combine corpus-based methods with Web statistics for ontology learning tasks. Others exploit structured data present in the current Semantic Web, e.g. Alani [1], who proposes a method for ontology building by cutting and pasting segments from online ontologies. More recently, some systems start to make use of heterogeneous evidence sources in OL. Using only one evidence source typically results in modest levels of accuracy [6], the combination of several sources may partially overcome this problem.

Manzano-Macho et al. [6] present an architecture which learns from multiple sources using a number of methods. In the acquisition layer the system learns hypotheses about candidate elements (the core terminology of the domain) which include a probability of relevance and relations to other candidate elements. Acquisition uses statistical methods as well as NLP tools and visual (HTML layout-based) methods. Furthermore, the system filters for domain relevance, detects domain concepts and taxonomic relations, and evaluates the resulting ontology against a pre-selected reference ontology. OntoElect [13] is methodology for ontology engineering, which applies term extraction to papers by domain experts. They also describe termhood saturation experienced when extending the collection of papers. Among the few papers which focus on OL from heterogeneous sources is also an approach by Cimiano et al. [3] to learn taxonomic relations. This method converts evidence into first order logic features, and then uses standard classifiers (supervised machine learning) on the integrated data to find good combinations of input sources. The input sources include data from lexico-syntactical pattern matching, head matching and subsumption heuristics applied to domain text. Völker et al. [15] propose a similar approach which uses the confidence scores of several heterogeneous methods as features in a classifier, aiming to enrich existing ontologies with disjointness axioms. Manzano-Macho et al. [6] focus on small corpora of high quality domain text, our system however uses noisy and evolving data from the Web and also includes more diverse sources such as APIs from social media Websites and a linked data source (DBpedia). In terms of evaluation, we employ user-based evaluation with domain experts (see below), whereas Manzano-Macho et al. [6] compare their results against a reference ontology. Gacitua and Sawyer [8] present a quantitative comparison of technique combinations for concept extraction. Although the goal is similar to our work, they investigate which process pipeline of NLP techniques is most helpful for term extraction from a domain corpus, whereas we study the balancing of term lists stemming from heterogeneous evidence sources.

As mentioned, the skillful combination and balancing of evidence sources is a crucial factor to leverage the potential of heterogeneous sources. Spreading activation, which is a method for searching semantic networks and neural networks, is the key tool to integrate evidence sources in our framework. Spreading activation is also frequently used in information retrieval. In his survey Crestani [5] concludes that spreading activation is capable of providing good results in associative information retrieval.

3   The Ontology Learning Framework

As each ontology is generated from scratch, it is straightforward to measure and compare results obtained by using different settings (regarding the evidence from heterogeneous input sources). The experiments discussed in this paper were conducted with an OL system first published by Liu et al. [11]. The generated ontologies are lightweight [18], most OL systems aim at learning ontologies which make little or no use of axioms (lightweight ontologies) [19].

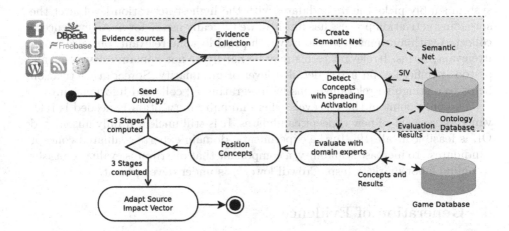

Fig. 1. The Ontology learning framework.

As the basic OL framework has been presented before, its description will be kept to a minimum. This section focuses on the new components and elements necessary to understand the evidence integration processes.

The basic workflow of the system, shown in Fig. 1, is as follows:

1. The OL starts from a small *seed ontology* – typically only a few concepts, for example [global_warming subClassOf climate_change.] in the domain of climate change, in the tennis domain it is [tennis_match subClassOf tennis.].
2. *Collection of evidence* for all seed concepts from the evidence sources (details on the sources of evidence are found in the next section).
3. Integrate the evidence in a so-called *semantic network.*
4. Transform the semantic network into a spreading activation network.
5. The *spreading activation* algorithm yields new concept candidates (concept detection phase).
6. Domain experts *rate* concept candidates as either relevant to the domain or non-relevant.
7. Relation detection and *positioning* of new (relevant) concepts in the ontology.
8. Start over with step one, using the extended ontology as seed ontology in the next iteration. Thereby the ontology gets bigger and more granular.
9. Finally, after a predefined number of extension iterations: Stop.

The parts of Fig. 1 highlighted light-gray are the most interesting regarding the evaluation of the system. These parts are either covered in more detail in the upcoming section (evidence sources), or in the remainder of this section.

The neural network technique of spreading activation is a crucial algorithm in the system, used for the selection of new candidate concepts and also in concept positioning. Spreading activation typically activates a number of seed nodes, the algorithm then propagates the activation energy through the network according to link weights. In the iterative process a decay factor D is used to diminish activation propagation farther away from the seed nodes. In concept selection the system simply picks the n candidates with the highest activation level after the spreading activation process has finished, we typically use 25 for n. All evidence is collected with automated methods, which provide some relevant, but also many irrelevant, terms. Irrelevant terms may be hardly or not domain-relevant at all, or too specific, i.e. on a too detailed level of granularity. Spreading activation helps to distinguish relevant terms by integrating all collected information.

The only point in the OL cycle where human intervention is needed is relevance assessment of new concept candidates. It is still unclear if fully automated OL is feasible at all [19]. In the experiments, domain experts evaluated concept candidates. To increase scalability, a component that distributes evaluation tasks to online labor markets (esp. CrowdFlower[1]) is under development.

4   Generation of Evidence

To understand the characteristics of evidence sources, it is necessary to understand the data sources we use, and the methods to extract evidence from these data sources. The evidence sources (listed in Sect. 4.3) emerge from the application of extraction methods to data sources.

4.1   Heterogeneous Data Sources

In this paper we distinguish between evidence and data sources. Data sources refer to the *raw* resources, they include domain text from various origins, structured data (WordNet, DBpedia), and calls to social media APIs.

Figure 2 provides an overview of the data sources used. Most importantly, the data sources include (i) **Domain text corpora**. Using the webLyzard suite of Web mining tools[2] the framework generates corpora from news media (segregated by geo-location), social media (public postings on Facebook, Youtube, Twitter, etc.) and other sites such as NGO's Websites and the Fortune 1000. Web content typically needs content extraction (boilerplate removal), we apply the approach discussed in [10]. A domain detection tool yields domain-specific documents in the given time interval (month). Domain-detection is only applied for the *climate change* domain, in the *tennis* domain the system uses general

---

[1] crowdflower.com.
[2] www.weblyzard.com.

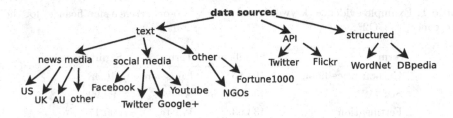

Fig. 2. Heterogeneous data sources used.

(news) media corpora. Furthermore, the system uses **structured sources**, that is WordNet and the DBpedia dataset. And finally, we execute (iii) **API calls** to (social) Web services.

4.2 Extraction Methods

The OL system applies a variety of methods to extract terminology from the data sources – depending on their type. For all text-based sources, we currently use: (i) Computation of keywords for a seed concept (represented by its label). The keyword service (see [11] for details) detects significant phrases and applies co-occurrence statistics to generate a list of keywords ordered by χ^2 significance. The keywords appear in the same *page (document)* or *sentence* as the concept. For short documents (tweets, Facebook postings) we only compute page-level keywords. (ii) Hearst patterns [9], which are lexical patterns to find common phrases that link hypo-/hypernym pairs.

Table 1 includes example data for term extraction, it presents a short snippet of page-level keywords generated for the seed concept "CO2" from UK news media text (evidence source no. 4) in July 2013. This demonstrates the typical characteristics of evidence acquisition: some terms are relevant to the *climate change* domain, some are not relevant, some are too specific. A full listing of evidence for a seed term ("CO2") and examples of ontology run results is found at https://ai.wu.ac.at/~wohlg/conf_data. A demo portal of the underlying OL system is available at http://hugo.ai.wu.ac.at:5050.

Social Web APIs (Twitter, Flickr) which directly provide related terms (or "tags") are simply queried with a seed concept label as input to extract terminology. These APIs typically provide very recent terminology and are helpful to collect terms complementary to text sources. Example data for social sources is found in Weichselbraun et al. [16].

Finally, regarding structured sources, from WordNet [7] the system extracts hyponyms, hypernyms, and synonyms for an input term, see Liu et al. [11] for details and examples. We also query the DBpedia SPARQL endpoint[3] with *dbpedia:acronyms*, *dcterms:subject* and *dbpedia:othernames* predicates to get related terms to a seed term. For our example of term "CO2", *dcterms:subject* suggests

---

[3] dbpedia.org/sparql.

Table 1. Example evidence (keywords and their χ^2 co-occurrence significance) for the seed concept "CO2".

Term	Significance	Term	Significance
Carbon price floor	164.85	Emission	110.48
Sec	135.54	Air	99.99
Fertilisation	133.63	Waste	90.17
PM10	123.45	0–62 mph	89.12
Environment committee	121.27	Flame	86.74
Member state	114.62	Carbon tax	78.53

Table 2. The 26 evidences sources used in the ontology learning process based on domain text. The data is collected from the Web to create corpora in monthly intervals.

	Method		
Data sources			
Domain text from	Keywords/page	Keywords/sentence	Hearst patterns
US news media	1	2	3
UK news media	4	5	6
AU/NZ news media	7	8	9
Other news media	10	11	12
Social media: Twitter	13	-	14
Social media: Youtube	15	-	16
Social media: Facebook	17	-	18
Social media: Google+	19	-	20
NGOs Websites	21	22	23
Fortune 1000 Websites	24	25	26

the following terms from DBpedia: "Acid anhydrides", "Acidic oxides", "Carbon dioxide", "Coolants", "Fire suppression agents", "Greenhouse gases", etc.

4.3   Evidence Sources

This section primarily gives an overview about all 32 heterogeneous sources of evidence used in the experiments with an OL system. As already mentioned, evidence sources arise from the application of extraction methods on data sources. Table 2 presents the 26 evidence sources originating from using the keyword and Hearst pattern techniques on domain text data sources.

Every line in Table 2 represents a data source. Each text data source (except the ones with very short documents), yields three evidence sources, namely keywords on page (document) level, keywords on sentence level, and relations (and terms) extracted with Hearst patterns [9]. 26 of 32 evidence sources extract terminology from text, making domain text corpora an important input to the system.

Table 3. The remaining 6 evidence sources, which are based on WordNet, Social Media APIs, and DBpedia.

Data source	Method				
	Hypernyms	Hyponyms	Synonyms	API	SPARQL
WordNet	27	28	29	-	-
DBpedia	-	-	-	-	30
Twitter	-	-	-	31	-
Flickr	-	-	-	32	-

The remaining 6 evidence sources extract terms from WordNet and DBpedia, or with social Web API queries as shown in Table 3.

Obviously, the 32 sources are heterogeneous in type and number of results, we use spreading activation to integrate evidence (see Sect. 3) and parameters to balance and limit the number of evidences per source (see below).

5   Evaluation

This section includes evaluation results of ontology learning (OL) experiments conducted between July 2013 and December 2014. Starting from the seed ontology the system generated 75 concept candidates (3 runs of 25 concepts each) per ontology – this fixed number of 75 concept candidates per ontology was used in all upcoming experiments, irrespective of the number of evidence sources used. After Sect. 5.1 provides details about the evidence (term lists) used, Sect. 5.2 describes the experiments for integrating heterogeneous evidence. Section 5.3 discusses concept relevance assessment.

5.1   Characteristics of Evidence Sources

In order to get a meaningful interpretation of evidence balancing and integration, first the characteristics of the underlying input data need to be investigated. Two properties greatly vary between evidence sources: the number of evidences provided (for a seed concept), and the average term quality per evidence acquisition method. Term quality was measured as the ratio of terms supplied by the respectively method which label a relevant domain concept. A domain expert manually evaluated sufficiently large term lists for different seed concepts and methods – resulting in a few thousand terms – to assess term quality.

Table 4 gives an overview of these characteristics. It lists the methods described in Sect. 4, and gives the rough average numbers of evidences per seed concept which the evidence sources provide (*Avg. Num. of Evid.*). Furthermore, the table includes term quality in the remaining columns. Only co-occurrence statistics-based terms (*keywords*) have a significance value assigned (and are thereby ordered), for these we evaluated the top 25, top 100, and top 500 most significant terms. For all other sources we evaluated all terms supplied. Table 4

Table 4. Average number of evidence and evidence quality per extraction method.

Method	Avg. Num. of Evid.	Term quality		
		Top 25	Top 100	Top 500
Keywords/page	400	0.31	0.26	0.12
Keywords/sentence	200	0.27	0.19	0.10
Hearst Patterns	18	0.15		
API Twitter	70	0.10		
API Flickr	16	0.18		
WordNet (Hypernyms)	15	0.24		
WordNet (Hyponyms)	17	0.21		
DBpedia	13	0.27		

shows (i) that the average number of evidences greatly differs between sources, and also that term quality varies to a large extent. Term quality is high for the 25 most significant keywords per seed concept, and also for terms provided by Word-Net and DBpedia. Keywords of low significance, and social sources (esp. Twitter) yield low quality terms on average. Hearst patterns generate rather sparse results which are of moderate quality.

One aspect of using heterogeneous sources is that they provide **complementary input** to better cover the domain of interest. In our system, corpus-based techniques (mostly keywords) account for the base layer of evidence. Apart from text-based input, social sources add very recent and emotional terminology, helpful to improve results and capture dynamic aspects of the domain [16], but also include a large share of noise, typos, etc. WordNet typically offers general and high quality input, which also helps to build the taxonomic backbone, but does not reflect dynamic aspects of domain evolution. The current version of SPARQL queries against DBpedia returns specific and technical terms, but also many terms which are too specific or not relevant to the domain.

Balancing the Number of Evidences. As seen in Table 4, if not limited, the number of evidences (terms) supplied strongly varies between evidence sources. Whereas the number of keywords for a concept sometimes exceeds 1000 terms, other sources provide comparably few results. In the upcoming section we present experiments where the number of evidences per source is either not limited, or limited to a maximum number of evidences per source to (i) balance the influence of sources on the resulting ontology and (ii) study which impact the amount of evidence has on the quality of concept candidates suggested by the OL system.

5.2   Leveraging and Balancing Sources and Evidences

As stated in Sect. 1, the goal of this research is to provide hints and insights on the combination and integration of heterogeneous evidence sources in OL (specifically for the concept detection phase) which can be generalized.

$$Accuracy = \frac{Relevant\ concept\ candidates\ generated}{All\ concept\ candidates\ generated} \qquad (1)$$

In this section, we measured the accuracy of the system by the ratio of relevant concept candidates resulting from the OL system, see Eq. 1. Other aspects, such as the positioning of new concepts in the ontology and the detection and labeling of relations are not part of this study, some of these points are covered in [17].

The Number of Evidences per Source. The first question to address is the impact of the number of evidences per source on the quality of concept candidates. Table 5 summarizes experiments where every of the 32 evidence sources was limited to suggest only 5, 10, etc. evidences per seed concept. As discussed in the previous section, some sources like WordNet or DBpedia typically provide very few evidence, whereas keyword-based sources produce up to 1000 terms per source. Obviously, limiting all sources to (for example) 10 evidences per seed concept, will reduce the impact of keyword-based sources. Using limits (i) balances to number of evidence between sources, (ii) saves computation time, but also (iii) removes data which might be helpful in the spreading activation (ie. evidence integration) process. We use two domains in the experiments, *climate change* and *tennis*. The *climate change* ontologies were generated from scratch in every month between July 2013 and November 2014, the *tennis* ontologies between July 2014 and November 2014. The accuracy numbers in Table 5 are based on 17 ontologies computed per respective setting for *climate change*, which leads to 1275 (75 ∗ 17) concept candidates per setting. In the *tennis* domain, we have 5 ontologies per setting with 375 concept candidates. If not stated otherwise, these numbers also apply to upcoming tables later in this section.

With very few evidences per source (*limit=5*), the benefits of redundancy and integration of heterogeneous sources are small (poor accuracy), although using only the best (most significant) keywords. Only in interactive systems where runtime is a very critical issue such a setting should be considered. On the other hand, in our experiments with a limit of 200 or more evidences per seed concept, the number of evidences per source is unbalanced, and more and more keywords with low significance are added to the spreading algorithm network, negative effects exceed the benefits of additional evidence data. Accuracy is lower in the *tennis* domain, we attribute this to the underlying data used, which are general domain-agnostic (news) media corpora, whereas for *climate change* the system uses domain-specific corpora.

In contrast to our initial expectations that more evidence is always better regarding resulting ontology quality (although it will be computationally expensive), even low numbers (*limit=10*) allow high accuracy if evidence is ranked by expected quality. In our system keywords are ranked by their significance value. Our experiments suggest that in the range of 20 to 50 terms per evidence source very good or even best results can be expected. However, this is only true while using a sufficient number of evidence sources (see below). A remark: the differences in accuracy in Table 5 are statistically significant, eg. with $p = 0.009$ between accuracy of *limit=10* and *limit=20*.

Table 5. Accuracy of concept detection (percentage of relevant concept candidates) for the domains of *climate change* (CC) and *tennis* depending on the number of evidences per source, with default and random selection of keyword evidence.

No. of evidences	Acc. CC	Acc. tennis	Acc. Random Keyw. CC
limit=5	56.44	46.80	52.72
limit=10	64.05	55.53	56.51
limit=20	67.57	60.27	60.98
limit=50	68.68	59.87	61.64
limit=100	67.79	58.27	62.73
limit=200	67.87	58.53	65.13
limit=500	66.39	57.88	66.01
no limit	66.29	57.34	66.29

A more detailed look at the ontologies exhibits a more frequent occurrence of specific and exotic (but still relevant) concepts when using a low limit (such as *limit=5*), while a high limit promotes more general terms. This fact, which is in favor of high *limit* settings is not reflected by the data in Table 5.

Out of curiosity we also experimented with choosing keywords randomly from the list of all keywords (instead using of the most significant), see column *Acc. Random Keyw. CC* in Table 5. As expected this lowers the accuracy with low *limits*, and gives a more realistic picture for systems where evidence per source is not ordered. Therefore, in a machine learning environment where the expected quality of evidence is unknown and there is no explicit grading, it is advisable to use more evidence per source to fully benefit from redundancy. Another experiment, in which the keyword significance (as yielded by co-occurrence statistics) was not used at all, gave very poor results. This confirms that the quality of sources is important, and that low-quality evidence cannot be compensated by using multiple sources entirely.

In summary, it is important to have enough data to benefit from redundancy and aggregation. Additional evidence beyond this point can even have a negative impact if the balance between sources is lost, or the quality of additional evidence is not sufficient.

The Number of Evidence Sources Used. Not only the number of evidences per source is important, also the influence of the number of heterogeneous sources on the learning algorithm has to be taken into consideration. We evaluated the impact of using (i) only one source which yields rather low quality terms (*1 Twitter*), (ii) only one source with high quality input (page-level keywords from UK media – *1 UK-KW-page*), (iii) five random sources (*5 sources*), (iv) *15 sources*, (v) all sources (*32 sources*). Table 6 presents the results for these five variants, it shows the outcome for limit settings with the number of evidences (terms) not exceeding 50 and 200, respectively.

Table 6. Accuracy (percentage of relevant concept candidates) of concept detection regarding the number of evidence sources ("srcs") used – for two limit-settings, in the domains of *climate change* and *tennis*.

%Relevant	1 (Twitter)	1 (UK-KW-page)	5 srcs	15 srcs	32 srcs
CC limit=50	16.54	48.80	59.52	68.28	68.84
CC limit=200	19.85	49.78	57.48	67.73	67.64
Tennis limit=50	21.15	50.67	52.25	56.88	57.87
Tennis limit=200	23.17	52.78	54.33	57.74	58.33

When relying on a single source, the quality of evidence of that source is essential, obviously – see *1 Twitter* and *1 UK-KW-Page*. In our experiments, *5 sources* of mixed quality are sufficient to see the benefits of using multiple sources. Around *15 sources* can be enough to gain the full advantage of heterogeneous evidence integration and redundancy. This means that a small and computationally efficient spreading activation network with a sum of a few thousand terms (suggested by 10–15 sources) can be quite enough to get best results. The difference between 5 and 15 evidence sources is statistically significant e.g. for the *climate change* domain as confirmed with a binomial test ($p \approx 0.0006$ for both *limit* settings).

The know-how regarding the minimal number of sources necessary can be helpful in various situations: (i) when setting up a new system, (ii) when there is need to scale down an existing system that is too slow or consumes too many resources, (iii) when there is need to use only a subset of evidence sources for a particular application. For example, we plan ontology evolution and trend detection experiments in which we will only use sources which are highly dynamic, and omit more static sources such as WordNet.

The Number of Seed Concepts. Finally, we investigated the impact of the type and number of seed concepts for which evidence is collected. Our system learns ontologies in 3 iterations of extension. In the first iteration (*Stage1*) there are only very few seed concepts (in the climate domain: "climate change" and "global warming"), which are obviously very relevant to the domain. The seed concepts in *Stage2* are the expert confirmed concepts learned in *Stage1*, in *Stage3* the system uses the concepts acquired in *Stage2*. The concepts in *Stage2* are typically more general than in *Stage3*, in which the ontology gets more granular. Table 7 presents the ratio of relevant concepts suggested regarding the stage (the number and granularity of seed concepts) and the number of evidences used.

A combination of a low number of seed concepts in *Stage1* and low number of evidences (*limit=5*) does not provide spreading activation with enough data to produce good results. Such a setting creates a network with only a few hundred evidences (2 SC * 32 sources * 5 evidences per source). This is well below the critical number of evidences of a few thousand (according to our experiments) which is needed for high accuracy. On the other hand, when the number of

Table 7. Accuracy depending on seed concepts (SC) and evidence limit applied.

	Stage1 – 2 SC	Stage2 – ca. 18 SC	Stage3 – ca. 35 SC
limit=5	54.67	61.87	56.53
limit=50	80.30	69.96	55.56
limit=200	78.83	68.33	56.22

seed concepts is high, then a high number of evidences per seed concept offers no additional benefit, accuracy for *limit=50* and *limit=200* is very similar. The best results are achieved in *Stage1*, which uses domain concepts of high relevance and generality, and enough evidence to exploit redundancy (limit $\geq$ 50). The accuracy in Stages 2 and 3 is diminishing, because the seed concepts tend to get less domain-relevant with increasing distance from the initial seed ontology.

Observations. A list of key observations and hints concludes this section: (i) It is critical to ensure having enough evidence to benefit from redundancy at every step of the learning cycle. In our system enough evidence corresponds to at least a few thousand pieces of evidence (terms). Additional evidence beyond this points only slows the system down while providing little use. (ii) When there is no order (regarding quality) in evidence data, then more evidence will be needed to get the best results. (iii) Using our evidence integration method and settings, around 10–15 sources of heterogeneous evidence are sufficient to gain the full effect of evidence integration. (iv) Balancing input from evidence sources is typically more important than the raw number of evidence per source.

And interesting strain of future work will be the attempt to optimize the source impact vector (SIV), which controls the influence of a particular source on the learning process. In this research we use a uniform source impact for all evidence sources as the goal is to study the balancing of evidence. In future work we will try to find an (almost) optimal configuration of impact of evidence sources in the spreading activation network. Preliminary studies show that this will lead to a significantly higher accuracy of the system.

5.3   Relevance Assessment

This section, which concludes the evaluation, takes an alternative view at the judgments on concept relevance made by the domain experts, especially on concept candidates rated *non-relevant*. When rating concept candidates, domain experts had only two choices: *relevant* or *non-relevant* to the domain at the given level of granularity. We took a more detailed look at concept candidates that were rated as *non-relevant*. From 100 candidates rated *non-relevant* to the domain of *climate change*, 61 % were in fact at least partly relevant to the domain, but very generic or too specific. Only the remaining 39 % were not relevant at all, but according to the domain experts not relevant for this level of granularity. For this reason, depending on point of view and granularity, the accuracy of the OL system is higher than stated in the evaluation data. Among the 61 % of candidates partly relevant to the domain of *climate change* are mostly terms that are too generic (for example: "impact", "mitigation", "issue", "policy", etc.). The 39 % of clearly non-relevant terms include fragments from the phrase detection algorithm such as "change conference" or candidates simply unrelated ("century", "level", "wave").

6 Conclusions

The integration of heterogeneous evidence sources can improve accuracy in ontology learning and other areas which use similar machine learning techniques and multiple evidence sources. In this paper we study how a system needs to be set up to gain the desired results, and give hints and insights on the impact on accuracy of the number of evidences per source, the number of evidence sources, of quality per evidence source, etc. Among the key findings and contributions is the surprising fact that a limited number of evidences – a few thousand terms from heterogeneous sources – provides results of similar quality compared to using much higher numbers. In addition, in our experiments around 10–15 evidence sources were sufficient to gain full benefits of redundancy and evidence aggregation. Heterogeneous sources of evidence not only help to raise accuracy, but also offer complementary vocabulary to cover the domain.

Future work will apply the presented experiments to similar systems. We expect similar results as the basic characteristics of evidence integration do not change. Furthermore, we will further optimize the system using the source impact vector (SIV) by (i) adapting the SIV over time according to the quality of concept candidates suggested by the source to increase the impact of sources that consistently suggest a high ratio of relevant concepts, and (ii) conducting optimization experiments of find an optimal configuration for the SIV.

Acknowledgments. The work presented was developed within project uComp, which receives the funding support of EPSRC EP/K017896/1, FWF 1097-N23, and ANR-12-CHRI-0003-03, in the framework of the CHIST-ERA ERA-NET programme.

References

1. Alani, H.: Position paper: ontology construction from online ontologies. In: Carr, L., Roure, D.D., Iyengar, A., Goble, C.A., Dahlin, M. (eds.) WWW 2006, Edinburgh, Scotland, May 23–26, pp. 491–495. ACM (2006)
2. Buitelaar, P., Cimiano, P., Magnini, B.: Ontology learning from text: an overview. In: Buitelaar, P., Cimiano, P., Magnini, B. (eds.) Ontology Learning from Text: Methods, Evaluation and Applications. Frontiers in Artificial Intelligence and Applications, vol. 123, pp. 3–12. IOS Press, Amsterdam (2005)
3. Cimiano, P., Pivk, A., Schmidt-Thieme, L., Staab, S.: Ontology Learning from Text, Chapter Learning Taxonomic Relations from Heterogeneous Sources of Evidence, pp. 59–76. IOS Press, Amsterdam (2005)
4. Cimiano, P., Völker, J.: Text2Onto. In: Montoyo, A., Muñoz, R., Métais, E. (eds.) NLDB 2005. LNCS, vol. 3513, pp. 227–238. Springer, Heidelberg (2005)

5. Crestani, F.: Application of spreading activation techniques in information retrieval. Artif. Intell. Rev. **11**(6), 453–482 (1997)
6. Manzano-Macho, D., Gómez-Pérez, A., Borrajo, D.: Unsupervised and domain independent ontology learning: combining heterogeneous sources of evidence. In: Calzolari, N., Choukri, K., et al. (eds.) Proceedings of LREC 2008. European Language Resources Association (ELRA), Marrakech, Morocco, May 2008
7. Fellbaum, C.: Wordnet an electronic lexical database. Comput. Linguist. **25**(2), 292–296 (1998)
8. Gacitua, R., Sawyer, P.: Ensemble methods for ontology learning - an empirical experiment to evaluate combinations of concept acquisition techniques. In: ICIS 2008, pp. 328–333. IEEE Publishing, May 2008
9. Hearst, M.A.: Automatic acquisition of hyponyms from large text corpora. In: COLING 1992, Nantes, France, pp. 539–545 (1992)
10. Lang, H.P., Wohlgenannt, G., Weichselbraun, A.: Textsweeper - a system for content extraction and overview page detection. In: International Conference on Information Resources Management (Conf-IRM), pp. 17–22. AIS, Vienna (2012)
11. Liu, W., Weichselbraun, A., Scharl, A., Chang, E.: Semi-automatic ontology extension using spreading activation. JUKM **1**, 50–58 (2005)
12. Sanchez, D., Moreno, A.: Learning non-taxonomic relationships from Web documents for a domain ontology construction. DKE **64**(3), 600–623 (2008)
13. Tatarintseva, O., Ermolayev, V., Keller, B., Matzke, W.-E.: quantifying ontology fitness in OntoElect using saturation- and vote-based metrics. In: Ermolayev, V., Mayr, H.C., Nikitchenko, M., Spivakovsky, A., Zholtkevych, G. (eds.) ICTERI 2013. CCIS, vol. 412, pp. 136–162. Springer, Heidelberg (2013)
14. Velardi, P., Faralli, S., Navigli, R.: OntoLearn reloaded: a graph-based algorithm for taxonomy induction. Comput. Linguist. **39**(3), 665–707 (2013)
15. Völker, J., Vrandečić, D., Sure, Y., Hotho, A.: Learning disjointness. In: Franconi, E., Kifer, M., May, W. (eds.) ESWC 2007. LNCS, vol. 4519, pp. 175–189. Springer, Heidelberg (2007)
16. Weichselbraun, A., Wohlgenannt, G., Scharl, A.: Augmenting lightweight domain ontologies with social evidence sources. In: Tjoa, A.M., Wagner, R.R. (eds.) DEXA 2010, pp. 193–197. IEEE, Bilbao, August 2010
17. Weichselbraun, A., Wohlgenannt, G., Scharl, A.: Refining non-taxonomic relation labels with external structured data to support ontology learning. Data Knowl. Eng. **69**(8), 763–778 (2010)
18. Wohlgenannt, G., Weichselbraun, A., Scharl, A., Sabou, M.: Confidence management for learning ontologies from dynamic Web sources. In: KEOD 2012, pp. 172–177. SciTePress, Barcelona, October 2012
19. Wong, W., Liu, W., Bennamoun, M.: Ontology learning from text: a look back and into the future. ACM Comput. Surv. **44**(4), 20:1–20:36 (2012)

Reasoning

A Context-Based Semantics for SPARQL Property Paths Over the Web

Olaf Hartig[1](✉) and Giuseppe Pirrò[2]

[1] University of Waterloo, Ontario, Canada
ohartig@uwaterloo.ca
[2] Institute for High Performance Computing and Networking, ICAR-CNR,
Rende, Italy
pirro@icar.cnr.it

Abstract. As of today, there exists no standard language for querying Linked Data *on the Web*, where navigation across distributed data
sources is a key feature. A natural candidate seems to be SPARQL,
which recently has been enhanced with navigational capabilities thanks
to the introduction of *property paths* (PPs). However, the semantics of
SPARQL restricts the scope of navigation via PPs to *single* RDF graphs.
This restriction limits the applicability of PPs on the Web. To fill this
gap, in this paper we provide formal foundations for evaluating PPs on
the Web, thus contributing to the definition of a query language for
Linked Data. In particular, we introduce a query semantics for PPs that
couples navigation at the data level with navigation on the Web graph.
Given this semantics we find that for some PP-based SPARQL queries
a complete evaluation on the Web is not feasible. To enable systems to
identify queries that can be evaluated completely, we establish a decidable syntactic property of such queries.

1 Introduction

The increasing trend in sharing and interlinking pieces of structured data on the
World Wide Web (WWW) is evolving the classical Web—which is focused on
hypertext documents and syntactic links among them—into a Web of Linked
Data. The Linked Data principles [4] present an approach to extend the scope
of Uniform Resource Identifiers (URIs) to new types of resources (e.g., people,
places) and represent their descriptions and interlinks by using the Resource
Description Framework (RDF) [16] as standard data format. RDF adopts a
graph-based data model, which can be queried upon by using the SPARQL query
language [12]. When it comes to Linked Data on the WWW, the common way
to provide query-based access is via SPARQL endpoints, that is, services that
usually answer SPARQL queries over a single dataset. Recently, the original core
of SPARQL has been extended with features supporting query federation; it is

This project has been partially funded by the project "Cybersecurity - P2
(PON03PE_00032_2), financed by the Italian Ministry of Education, University and
Research (MIUR) within the PON Project - Research and Competitiveness.

© Springer International Publishing Switzerland 2015
F. Gandon et al. (Eds.): ESWC 2015, LNCS 9088, pp. 71–87, 2015.
DOI: 10.1007/978-3-319-18818-8_5

now possible, within a single query, to target multiple endpoints (via the SERVICE operator). However, such an extension is not enough to cope with an unbounded and a priori unknown space of data sources such as the WWW. Moreover, not all Linked Data on the WWW is accessible via SPARQL endpoints. Hence, as of today, there exists no standard query language for Linked Data on the WWW, although SPARQL is clearly a candidate.

While earlier research on using SPARQL for Linked Data is limited to fragments of the first version of the language [5,13,14,25], the more recent version 1.1 introduces a feature that is particularly interesting in the context of queries over a graph-like environment such as Linked Data on the WWW. This feature is called *property paths* (PPs) and equips SPARQL with navigational capabilities [12]. However, the standard definition of PPs is limited to single, centralized RDF graphs and, thus, not directly applicable to Linked Data that is distributed over the WWW. Therefore, toward the definition of a language for accessing Linked Data live on the WWW, the following questions emerge naturally: *"How can PPs be defined over the WWW?"* and *"What are the implications of such a definition?"* Answering these questions is the broad objective of this paper. To this end, we make the following main contributions:

1. We formalize a query semantics for PP-based SPARQL queries that are meant to be evaluated over Linked Data on the WWW. This semantics is *context-based*; it intertwines Web graph navigation with navigation at the level of data.
2. We study the feasibility of evaluating queries under this semantics. We assume that query engines do not have complete information about the queried Web of Linked Data (as it is the case for the WWW). Our study shows that there exist cases in which query evaluation under the context-based semantics is not feasible.
3. We provide a decidable syntactic property of queries for which an evaluation under the context-based semantics is feasible.

The remainder of the paper is organized as follows. Section 2 provides an overview on related work. Section 3 introduces the formal framework for this paper, including a data model that captures a notion of Linked Data. In Sect. 4 we focus on PPs, independently from other SPARQL operators. In Sect. 5 we broaden our view to study PP-based SPARQL graph patterns; we characterize a class of *Web-safe* patterns and prove their feasibility. Finally, in Sect. 6 we conclude and sketch future work.

2   Related Work

The idea of querying the WWW as a database is not new (see Florescu et al.'s survey [11]). Perhaps the most notable early works in this context are by Konopnicki and Shmueli [18], Abiteboul and Vianu [1], and Mendelzon et al. [20], all of which tackled the problem of evaluating SQL-like queries on the traditional hypertext Web. While such queries included navigational features, the focus was on retrieving specific Web pages, particular attributes of specific pages, or content within them.

From a graph-oriented perspective, languages for the *navigation and specification* of vertices in graphs have a long tradition (see Wood's survey [26]). In the RDF world, extensions of SPARQL such as PSPARQL [2], nSPARQL [21], and SPARQLeR [17] introduced navigational features since those were missing in the first version of SPARQL. Only recently, with the addition of *property paths* (PPs) in version 1.1 [12], SPARQL has been enhanced officially with such features. The final definition of PPs has been influenced by research that studied the computational complexity of an early draft version of PPs [3,19], and there also already exists a proposal to extend PPs with more expressive power [9]. However, the main assumption of all these navigational extensions of SPARQL is to work on a single, centralized RDF graph. Our departure point is different: *We aim at defining semantics of SPARQL queries (including property paths) over Linked Data on the WWW*, which involves dealing with two graphs of different types; namely, an RDF graph that is distributed over documents on the WWW and the Web graph of how these documents are interlinked with each other.

To express queries over Linked Data on the WWW, two main strands of research can be identified. The first studies how to extend the scope of SPARQL queries to the WWW , with existing work focusing on basic graph patterns [5, 13,25] or a more expressive fragment that includes AND, OPT, UNION and FILTER [14]. The second strand focuses on navigational languages such as NautiLOD [8,10]. These two strands have different departure points. The former employs navigation over the WWW to collect data for answering a given SPARQL query; here navigation is a means to discover query-relevant data. The latter provides explicit navigational features and uses querying capabilities to filter data sources of interest; here navigation (not querying) is the main focus. The context-based query semantics proposed in this paper combines both approaches. We believe that the outcome of this research can be a starting point toward the definition of a language for querying and navigating over Linked Data on the WWW.

3   Formal Framework

This section provides a formal framework for studying semantics of PPs over Linked Data. We first recall the definition of PPs as per the SPARQL standard [12]. Thereafter, we introduce a data model that captures the notion of Linked Data on the WWW.

3.1   Preliminaries

Assume four pairwise disjoint, countably infinite sets $\mathcal{I}$ (IRIs), $\mathcal{B}$ (blank nodes), $\mathcal{L}$ (literals), and $\mathcal{V}$ (variables). An *RDF triple* (or simply *triple*) is a tuple from the set $\mathcal{T} = (\mathcal{I} \cup \mathcal{B}) \times \mathcal{I} \times (\mathcal{I} \cup \mathcal{B} \cup \mathcal{L})$. For any triple $t \in \mathcal{T}$ we write iris(t) to denote the set of IRIs in that triple. A set of triples is called an *RDF graph*.

A *property path pattern* (or *PP pattern* for short) is a tuple $P = \langle \alpha, \mathtt{path}, \beta \rangle$ such that $\alpha, \beta \in (\mathcal{I} \cup \mathcal{L} \cup \mathcal{V})$ and $\mathtt{path}$ is a *property path expression* (*PP expression*) defined by the following grammar (where $u, u_1, \ldots, u_n \in \mathcal{I}$):

$$\mathtt{path} = u \mid !(u_1 \mid \ldots \mid u_n) \mid {}^{\wedge}\mathtt{path} \mid \mathtt{path}/\mathtt{path} \mid (\mathtt{path}\mid\mathtt{path}) \mid (\mathtt{path})^*$$

Note that the SPARQL standard introduces additional types of PP expressions [12]. Since these are merely syntactic sugar (they are defined in terms of expressions covered by the grammar given above), we ignore them in this paper. As another slight deviation from the standard, we do not permit blank nodes in PP patterns (i.e., $\alpha, \beta \notin \mathcal{B}$). However, standard PP patterns with blank nodes can be simulated using fresh variables.

Example 1. *An example of a PP pattern is* $\langle \mathsf{Tim}, (\mathsf{knows})^*/\mathsf{name}, ?n \rangle$, *which retrieves the names of persons that can be reached from* Tim *by an arbitrarily long path of* knows *relationships (which includes* Tim*). Another example are the two PP patterns* $\langle ?p, \mathsf{knows}, \mathsf{Tim} \rangle$ *and* $\langle \mathsf{Tim}, {}^{\wedge}\mathsf{knows}, ?p \rangle$, *both of which retrieve persons that know* Tim.

The (standard) query semantics of PP patterns is defined by an evaluation function that returns multisets of *solution mappings* where a solution mapping μ is a partial function $\mu : \mathcal{V} \rightarrow (\mathcal{I} \cup \mathcal{B} \cup \mathcal{L})$. Given a solution mapping μ and a PP pattern P, we write $\mu[P]$ to denote the PP pattern obtained by replacing the variables in P according to μ (unbound variables must not be replaced). Two solution mappings, say μ_1 and μ_2, are *compatible*, denoted by $\mu_1 \sim \mu_2$, if $\mu_1(?v) = \mu_2(?v)$ for all variables $?v \in \big(\mathrm{dom}(\mu_1) \cap \mathrm{dom}(\mu_2)\big)$.

We represent a *multiset* of solution mappings by a pair $M = \langle \Omega, card \rangle$ where Ω is the underlying set (of solution mappings) and $card : \Omega \rightarrow \{1, 2, \ldots\}$ is the corresponding *cardinality function*. By abusing notation slightly, we write $\mu \in M$ for all $\mu \in \Omega$. Furthermore, we introduce a family of special (parameterized) cardinality functions that shall simplify the definition of any multiset whose solution mappings all have a cardinality of 1. That is, for any set of solution mappings Ω, let $\mathsf{card1}^{(\Omega)} : \Omega \rightarrow \{1, 2, \ldots\}$ be the *constant-1 cardinality function* that is defined by $\mathsf{card1}^{(\Omega)}(\mu) = 1$ for all $\mu \in \Omega$.

To define the aforementioned evaluation function we also need to introduce several SPARQL algebra operators. Let $M_1 = \langle \Omega_1, card_1 \rangle$ and $M_2 = \langle \Omega_2, card_2 \rangle$ be multisets of solution mappings and let $V \subseteq \mathcal{V}$ be a finite set of variables. Then:

$M_1 \sqcup M_2 = \langle \Omega, card \rangle$ where $\Omega = \Omega_1 \cup \Omega_2$ and (i) $card(\mu) = card_1(\mu)$ for all solution mappings $\mu \in \Omega \setminus \Omega_2$, (ii) $card(\mu) = card_2(\mu)$ for all $\mu \in \Omega \setminus \Omega_1$, and (iii) $card(\mu) = card_1(\mu) + card_2(\mu)$ for all $\mu \in \Omega_1 \cap \Omega_2$.

$M_1 \bowtie M_2 = \langle \Omega, card \rangle$ where $\Omega = \big\{ \mu_1 \cup \mu_2 \mid (\mu_1, \mu_2) \in \Omega_1 \times \Omega_2 \text{ and } \mu_1 \sim \mu_2 \big\}$ and, for every $\mu \in \Omega$, $card(\mu) = \sum_{(\mu_1,\mu_2) \in \Omega_1 \times \Omega_2 \text{ s.t. } \mu = \mu_1 \cup \mu_2} card(\mu_1) \cdot card(\mu_2)$.

$M_1 \setminus M_2 = \langle \Omega, card \rangle$ where $\Omega = \big\{ \mu_1 \in \Omega_1 \mid \mu_1 \not\sim \mu_2 \text{ for all } \mu_2 \in \Omega_2 \big\}$ and, for every $\mu \in \Omega$, $card(\mu) = card_1(\mu)$.

Function ALP1(γ, path, G)

Input: $\gamma \in (\mathcal{I} \cup \mathcal{B} \cup \mathcal{L})$,
  path is a PP expression,
  G is an RDF graph.

1: *Visited* $:= \emptyset$
2: ALP2$(\gamma, \text{path}, \textit{Visited}, G)$
3: **return** *Visited*

Function ALP2$(\gamma, \text{path}, \textit{Visited}, G)$

Input: $\gamma \in (\mathcal{I} \cup \mathcal{B} \cup \mathcal{L})$, path is a PP expression,
  Visited $\subseteq (\mathcal{I} \cup \mathcal{B} \cup \mathcal{L})$, G is an RDF graph.

4: **if** $\gamma \notin$ *Visited* **then**
5:   add γ to *Visited*
6:   **for all** $\mu \in [\![\langle ?x, \text{path}, ?y\rangle]\!]_G$ s.t. $\mu(?x) = \gamma$ **do**
7:     ALP2$(\mu(?y), \text{path}, \textit{Visited}, G)$ // $?x, ?y \in \mathcal{V}$

Fig. 1. Auxiliary functions for defining the semantics of PP expressions of the form path*.

$$\pi_V(M_1) = \langle \Omega, card\rangle \text{ where } \Omega = \{\mu \mid \exists \mu' \in \Omega_1 : \mu \sim \mu' \text{ and } \text{dom}(\mu) = V \cap \text{dom}(\mu')\} \text{ and, for every } \mu \in \Omega, card(\mu) = \sum_{\mu' \in \Omega_1 \text{ s.t. } \mu \sim \mu'} card_1(\mu').$$

In addition to these algebra operators, the SPARQL standard introduces auxiliary functions to define the semantics of PP patterns of the form $\langle \alpha, \text{path}^*, \beta\rangle$. Figure 1 provides these functions—which we call ALP1 and ALP2—adapted to our formalism.[1] We are now ready to define the standard query semantics of PP patterns.

Definition 1. *The evaluation of a PP pattern P over an RDF graph G, denoted by $[\![P]\!]_G$, is a multiset of solution mappings $\langle \Omega, card\rangle$ that is defined recursively as given in Fig. 2 where $\alpha, \beta \in (\mathcal{I} \cup \mathcal{L} \cup \mathcal{V})$, $x_L, x_R \in (\mathcal{I} \cup \mathcal{L})$, $?v_L, ?v_R \in \mathcal{V}$, $u, u_1, ..., u_n \in \mathcal{I}$, $?v \in \mathcal{V}$ is a fresh variable, and $\mu_\emptyset$ denotes the empty solution mapping $(\text{dom}(\mu_\emptyset) = \emptyset)$.*

3.2 Data Model

The standard SPARQL evaluation function for PP patterns (cf. Sect. 3.1) defines the expected result of the evaluation of a pattern over a single RDF graph. Since the WWW is not an RDF graph, the standard definition is insufficient as a formal foundation for evaluating PP patterns over Linked Data on the WWW. To provide a suitable definition we need a data model that captures the notion of a Web of Linked Data. To this end, we adopt the data model proposed in our earlier work [14]. Here, a *Web of Linked Data* (*WoLD*) is a tuple $W = \langle D, data, adoc\rangle$ consisting of (i) a set D of so called *Linked Data documents* (*documents*), (ii) a mapping $data : D \to 2^{\mathcal{T}}$ that maps each document to a finite set of RDF triples (representing the data that can be obtained from the document), and (iii) a partial mapping $adoc : \mathcal{I} \to D$ that maps (some) IRIs to a document and, thus, captures a IRI-based retrieval of documents. In this paper we assume that the set of documents D in any WoLD $W = \langle D, data, adoc\rangle$ is finite, in which case we say W is *finite* (for a discussion of infiniteness refer to our earlier work [14]).

---

[1] Variable $?x$ in line 6 is necessary since PP patterns in our formalism do not have blank nodes.

$$[\![\langle \alpha, u, \beta \rangle]\!]_G = \Big\langle \{ \mu \mid \mathrm{dom}(\mu) = (\{\alpha, \beta\} \cap \mathcal{V}) \text{ and } \mu[\langle \alpha, u, \beta \rangle] \in G \}, \, \mathrm{card1}^{(\Omega)} \Big\rangle$$

$$[\![\langle \alpha, !(u_1 \mid \cdots \mid u_n), \beta \rangle]\!]_G = \Big\langle \{ \mu \mid \mathrm{dom}(\mu) = (\{\alpha, \beta\} \cap \mathcal{V}) \text{ and }$$
$$\exists \mu[\langle \alpha, u, \beta \rangle] \in G : u \in (\mathcal{I} \setminus \{u_1, \ldots, u_n\}) \}, \, \mathrm{card1}^{(\Omega)} \Big\rangle$$

$$[\![\langle \alpha, {}^{\wedge}\mathrm{path}, \beta \rangle]\!]_G = [\![\langle \beta, \mathrm{path}, \alpha \rangle]\!]_G$$

$$[\![\langle \alpha, \mathrm{path}_1/\mathrm{path}_2, \beta \rangle]\!]_G = \pi_{\{\alpha, \beta\} \cap \mathcal{V}} \Big([\![\langle \alpha, \mathrm{path}_1, ?v \rangle]\!]_G \Join [\![\langle ?v, \mathrm{path}_2, \beta \rangle]\!]_G \Big)$$

$$[\![\langle \alpha, (\mathrm{path}_1 \mid \mathrm{path}_2), \beta \rangle]\!]_G = [\![\langle \alpha, \mathrm{path}_1, \beta \rangle]\!]_G \sqcup [\![\langle \alpha, \mathrm{path}_2, \beta \rangle]\!]_G$$

$$[\![\langle x_{\mathrm{L}}, (\mathrm{path})^*, ?v_{\mathrm{R}} \rangle]\!]_G = \Big\langle \{ \mu \mid \mathrm{dom}(\mu) = \{?v_{\mathrm{R}}\} \text{ and } \mu(?v_{\mathrm{R}}) \in \mathtt{ALP1}(x_{\mathrm{L}}, \mathrm{path}, G) \}, \, \mathrm{card1}^{(\Omega)} \Big\rangle$$

$$[\![\langle ?v_{\mathrm{L}}, (\mathrm{path})^*, ?v_{\mathrm{R}} \rangle]\!]_G = \Big\langle \{ \mu \mid \mathrm{dom}(\mu) = \{?v_{\mathrm{L}}, ?v_{\mathrm{R}}\} \text{ and } \mu(?v_{\mathrm{L}}) \in \mathrm{terms}(G) \text{ and }$$
$$\mu(?v_{\mathrm{R}}) \in \mathtt{ALP1}(\mu(?v_{\mathrm{L}}), \mathrm{path}, G) \}, \, \mathrm{card1}^{(\Omega)} \Big\rangle$$

$$[\![\langle ?v_{\mathrm{L}}, (\mathrm{path})^*, x_{\mathrm{R}} \rangle]\!]_G = [\![\langle x_{\mathrm{R}}, ({}^{\wedge}\mathrm{path})^*, ?v_{\mathrm{L}} \rangle]\!]_G$$

$$[\![\langle x_{\mathrm{L}}, (\mathrm{path})^*, x_{\mathrm{R}} \rangle]\!]_G = \Big\langle \begin{cases} \{\mu_\emptyset\} & \text{if } \exists \mu \in [\![\langle x_{\mathrm{L}}, (\mathrm{path})^*, ?v \rangle]\!]_G : \mu(?v) = x_{\mathrm{R}} \\ \emptyset & \text{else} \end{cases}, \, \mathrm{card1}^{(\Omega)} \Big\rangle$$

Fig. 2. SPARQL 1.1 W3C property paths semantics.

A few other concepts are needed for the subsequent discussion. For any two documents $d, d' \in D$ in a WoLD $W = \langle D, data, adoc \rangle$, document d has a *data link* to d' if the data of d mentions an IRI $u \in \mathcal{I}$ (i.e., there exists a triple $\langle s, p, o \rangle \in data(d)$ with $u \in \{s, p, o\}$) that can be used to retrieve d' (i.e., $adoc(u) = d'$). Such data links establish the *link graph* of the WoLD W, that is, a directed graph $\langle D, E \rangle$ in which the edges E are all pairs $\langle d, d' \rangle \in D \times D$ for which d has a data link to d'. Note that this graph, as well as the tuple $\langle D, data, adoc \rangle$ typically are not available directly to systems that aim to compute queries over the Web captured by W. For instance, the complete domain of the partial mapping $adoc$ (i.e., all IRIs that can be used to retrieve some document) is unknown to such systems and can only be disclosed partially (by trying to look up IRIs). Also note that the link graph of a WoLD is a different type of graph than the RDF "graph" whose triples are distributed over the documents in the WoLD.

4 Web-Aware Query Semantics for Property Paths

We are now ready to introduce our framework, which does not deal with syntactic aspects of PPs but aims at defining query semantics that provide a formal foundation for using PP patterns as queries over a WoLD (and, thus, over Linked Data on the WWW).

4.1 Full-Web Query Semantics

As a first approach we may assume a full-Web query semantics that is based on the standard evaluation function (as introduced in Sect. 3.1) and defines an expected query result for any PP pattern in terms of *all data* on the queried WoLD. Formally:

Definition 2. *Let P be a PP pattern, let $W = \langle D, data, adoc \rangle$ be a WoLD, and let G^* be an RDF graph such that $G^* = \bigcup_{d \in D} data(d)$, then the evaluation of P over W under* full-Web *semantics, denoted by $[\![P]\!]_W^{fw}$, is defined by $[\![P]\!]_W^{fw} = [\![P]\!]_{G^*}$.*

We emphasize that the full-Web query semantics is mostly of theoretical interest. In practice, that is, for a WoLD W that represents the "real" WWW (as it runs on the Internet), there cannot exist a system that guarantees to compute the given evaluation function $[\![\cdot]\!]^{fw}$. over W using an algorithm that both terminates and returns complete query results. In earlier work, we showed such a limitation for evaluating other types of SPARQL graph patterns—including triple patterns—under a corresponding full-Web query semantics defined for these patterns [14]. This result readily carries over to the full-Web query semantics for PP patterns because any PP pattern $P = \langle \alpha, \texttt{path}, \beta \rangle$ with PP expression $\texttt{path}$ being an IRI $u \in \mathcal{I}$ is, in fact, a triple pattern $\langle \alpha, u, \beta \rangle$. Informally, we explain this negative result by the fact that the three structures D, $data$, and $adoc$ that capture the queried Web formally, are not available in practice. Consequently, to enumerate the set of all triples on the Web (i.e., the RDF graph G^* in Definition 2), a query execution system would have to enumerate all documents (the set D); given that such a system has limited access to mapping $adoc$ (in particular, $\text{dom}(adoc)$—the set of all IRIs whose lookup retrieves a document—is, at best, partially known), the only guarantee to discover all documents is to look up any possible (HTTP-scheme) IRI. Since these are infinitely many [7], the enumeration process cannot terminate.

4.2 Context-Based Query Semantics

Given the limited practical applicability of full-Web query semantics for PPs, we propose an alternative query semantics that interprets PP patterns as a language for navigation over Linked Data on the Web (i.e., along the lines of earlier navigational languages for Linked Data such as NautiLOD [8]). We refer to this semantics as *context-based*.

The main idea behind this query semantics is to restrict the scope of searching for any next triple of a potentially matching path to specific data within specific documents on the queried WoLD. As a basis for formalizing these restrictions we introduce the notion of a *context selector*. Informally, for each IRI that can be used to retrieve a document, the context selector returns a specific subset of the data within that document; this subset contains only those RDF triples that have the given IRI as their subject (such a set of triples resembles Harth and Speiser's notion of subject authoritative triples [13]). Formally, for any WoLD $W = \langle D, data, adoc \rangle$, the context selector of W is a function $\mathrm{C}^W \colon \mathcal{I} \cup \mathcal{B} \cup \mathcal{L} \cup \mathcal{V} \to 2^{\mathcal{T}}$ that, for each $\gamma \in (\mathcal{I} \cup \mathcal{B} \cup \mathcal{L} \cup \mathcal{V})$, is defined as follows:[2]

---

[2] To simplify the following formalization of context-based semantics, context selectors are defined not only over IRIs, but also over blank nodes, literals, and variables.

$$C^W(\gamma) = \begin{cases} \{\, \langle s,p,o\rangle \in data(adoc(\gamma)) \mid \gamma = s \,\} & \text{if } \gamma \in \mathcal{I} \text{ and } \gamma \in \mathrm{dom}(adoc), \\ \emptyset & \text{otherwise.} \end{cases}$$

Informally, we explain how a context selector restricts the scope of PP patterns over a WoLD as follows. Suppose a sequence of triples $\langle s_1,p_1,o_1\rangle, \ldots, \langle s_k,p_k,o_k\rangle$ presents a path that already matches a sub-expression of a given PP expression. Under the previously defined full-Web query semantics (cf. Sect. 4.1), the next triple for such a path can be searched for in an arbitrary document in the queried WoLD W. By contrast, under the context-based query semantics, the next triple has to be searched for only in $C^W(o_k)$. Given these preliminaries, we now define context-based semantics:

Definition 3. *Let P be a PP pattern and let $W = \langle D, data, adoc\rangle$ be a WoLD. The evaluation of P over W under context-based semantics, denoted by $[\![P]\!]_W^{ctx}$, returns a multiset of solution mappings $\langle \Omega, card\rangle$ defined recursively as given in Fig. 3, where $u, .., u_n \in \mathcal{I}$; $x_L, x_R \in (\mathcal{I} \cup \mathcal{L})$; $?v_L, ?v_R \in \mathcal{V}$; $\mu_\emptyset$ is the empty solution mapping (i.e., $\mathrm{dom}(\mu_\emptyset) = \emptyset$); function ALPW1 is given in Fig. 4; and $?v \in \mathcal{V}$ is a fresh variable.*

There are three points worth mentioning w.r.t. Definition 3: First, note how the context selector restricts the data that has to be searched to find matching

$$[\![\langle u_L, p, \beta\rangle]\!]_W^{ctx} = \Big\langle \{\, \mu \mid \mathrm{dom}(\mu) = (\{\beta\} \cap \mathcal{V}) \text{ and } \mu[\langle u_L, p, \beta\rangle] \in C^W(u_L) \,\} , \mathrm{card1}^{(\Omega)} \Big\rangle$$

$$[\![\langle l_L, p, \beta\rangle]\!]_W^{ctx} = \Big\langle \emptyset, \mathrm{card1}^{(\emptyset)} \Big\rangle$$

$$[\![\langle ?v_L, p, \beta\rangle]\!]_W^{ctx} = \Big\langle \{\, \mu \mid \mathrm{dom}(\mu) = (\{?v_L, \beta\} \cap \mathcal{V}) \text{ and } \mu[\langle ?v_L, p, \beta\rangle] \in \bigcup_{u \in \mathcal{I}} C^W(u) \,\} , \mathrm{card1}^{(\Omega)} \Big\rangle$$

$$[\![\langle u_L, !(u_1 \mid \cdots \mid u_n), \beta\rangle]\!]_W^{ctx} = \Big\langle \{\, \mu \mid \mathrm{dom}(\mu) = (\{\beta\} \cap \mathcal{V}) \text{ and } \exists \mu[\langle u_L, p, \beta\rangle] \in C^W(u_L) : p \notin \{u_1, \ldots, u_n\} \,\} , \mathrm{card1}^{(\Omega)} \Big\rangle$$

$$[\![\langle l_L, !(u_1 \mid \cdots \mid u_n), \beta\rangle]\!]_W^{ctx} = \Big\langle \emptyset, \mathrm{card1}^{(\emptyset)} \Big\rangle$$

$$[\![\langle ?v_L, !(u_1 \mid \cdots \mid u_n), \beta\rangle]\!]_W^{ctx} = \Big\langle \{\, \mu \mid \mathrm{dom}(\mu) = (\{?v_L, \beta\} \cap \mathcal{V}) \text{ and } \exists \mu[\langle ?v_L, p, \beta\rangle] \in \bigcup_{u \in \mathcal{I}} C^W(u) : p \notin \{u_1, \ldots, u_n\} \,\} , \mathrm{card1}^{(\Omega)} \Big\rangle$$

$$[\![\langle \alpha, {}^\wedge\mathrm{path}, \beta\rangle]\!]_W^{ctx} = [\![\langle \beta, \mathrm{path}, \alpha\rangle]\!]_W^{ctx}$$

$$[\![\langle \alpha, \mathrm{path}_1/\mathrm{path}_2, \beta\rangle]\!]_W^{ctx} = \pi_{\{\alpha,\beta\}\cap\mathcal{V}}\Big([\![\langle \alpha, \mathrm{path}_1, ?v\rangle]\!]_W^{ctx} \bowtie [\![\langle ?v, \mathrm{path}_2, \beta\rangle]\!]_W^{ctx} \Big)$$

$$[\![\langle \alpha, \mathrm{path}_1 \mid \mathrm{path}_2, \beta\rangle]\!]_W^{ctx} = [\![\langle \alpha, \mathrm{path}_1, \beta\rangle]\!]_W^{ctx} \sqcup [\![\langle \alpha, \mathrm{path}_2, \beta\rangle]\!]_W^{ctx}$$

$$[\![\langle x_L, (\mathrm{path})^*, ?v_R\rangle]\!]_W^{ctx} = \Big\langle \{\, \mu \mid \mathrm{dom}(\mu) = \{?v_R\} \text{ and } \mu(?v_R) \in \mathrm{ALPW1}(x_L, \mathrm{path}, W) \,\} , \mathrm{card1}^{(\Omega)} \Big\rangle$$

$$[\![\langle ?v_L, (\mathrm{path})^*, ?v_R\rangle]\!]_W^{ctx} = \Big\langle \{\, \mu \mid \mathrm{dom}(\mu) = \{?v_L, ?v_R\} \text{ and } \mu(?v_L) \in \mathrm{terms}(W) \text{ and } \mu(?v_R) \in \mathrm{ALPW1}(\mu(?v_L), \mathrm{path}, W) \,\} , \mathrm{card1}^{(\Omega)} \Big\rangle$$

$$[\![\langle ?v_L, (\mathrm{path})^*, x_R\rangle]\!]_W^{ctx} = [\![\langle x_R, ({}^\wedge\mathrm{path})^*, ?v_L\rangle]\!]_W^{ctx}$$

$$[\![\langle x_L, (\mathrm{path})^*, x_R\rangle]\!]_W^{ctx} = \Big\langle \begin{cases} \{\mu_\emptyset\} & \text{if } \exists \mu \in [\![\langle x_L, (\mathrm{path})^*, ?v\rangle]\!]_W^{ctx} : \mu(?v) = x_R, \\ \emptyset & \text{else} \end{cases} , \mathrm{card1}^{(\Omega)} \Big\rangle$$

Fig. 3. Context-based query semantics for SPARQL property paths over the web.

Function ALPW1(γ, path, W)

Input: $\gamma \in (\mathcal{I} \cup \mathcal{B} \cup \mathcal{L})$,
      path is a PP expression,
      W is a WoLD.
1:   *Visited* := $\emptyset$
2:   ALPW2$(\gamma, \text{path}, \textit{Visited}, W)$
3:   **return** *Visited*

Function ALPW2$(\gamma, \text{path}, \textit{Visited}, W)$

Input: $\gamma \in (\mathcal{I} \cup \mathcal{B} \cup \mathcal{L})$,   path is a PP expression,
     Visited $\subseteq (\mathcal{I} \cup \mathcal{B} \cup \mathcal{L})$, W is a WoLD.
4:   **if** $\gamma \notin$ *Visited* **then**
5:      add γ to *Visited*
6:      **for all** $\mu \in [\![\langle ?x, \text{path}, ?y \rangle]\!]_W^{\text{ctx}}$ s.t. $\mu(?x) = \gamma$ **do**
7:          ALPW2$(\mu(?y), \text{path}, \textit{Visited}, W)$ // $?x, ?y \in \mathcal{V}$

Fig. 4. Auxiliary functions used for defining context-based query semantics.

triples (e.g., consider the first line in Fig. 3). Second, we emphasize that context-based query semantics is defined such that it resembles the standard semantics of PP patterns as close as possible (cf. Sect. 3.1). Therefore, for the part of our definition that covers PP patterns of the form $\langle \alpha, \text{path}^*, \beta \rangle$, we also use auxiliary functions— ALPW1 and ALPW2 (cf. Fig. 4).

These functions evaluate the sub-expression path recursively over the queried WoLD(instead of using a fixed RDF graph as done in the standard semantics in Fig. 1). Third, the two base cases with a variable in the subject position (i.e., the third and the sixth line in Fig. 3) require an enumeration of all IRIs. Such a requirement is necessary to preserve consistency with the standard semantics, as well as to preserve commutativity of operators that can be defined on top of PP patterns (such as the ANDoperator in SPARQL; cf. Sect. 5). However, due to this requirement there exist PP patterns whose (complete) evaluation under context-based semantics is infeasible when querying the WWW. The following example describes such a case.

Example 2. *Consider the PP pattern* $P_{E_2} = \langle ?v, \text{knows}, \text{Tim} \rangle$, *which asks for the IRIs of people that know Tim. Under context-based semantics, any IRI* u' *can be used to generate a correct solution mapping for the pattern as long as a lookup of that IRI results in retrieving a document whose data includes the triple* $\langle u', \text{knows}, \text{Tim} \rangle$. *While, for any WoLD that is finite, there exists only a finite number of such IRIs, determining these IRIs and guaranteeing completeness requires to enumerate the infinite set of all IRIs and to check each of them (unless one knows the complete—and finite—subset of all IRIs that can be used to retrieve some document, which, due to the infiniteness of possible HTTP IRIs, cannot be achieved for the WWW).*

It is not difficult to see that the issue illustrated in the example exists for any triple pattern that has a variable in the subject position. On the other hand, triple patterns whose subject is an IRI do not have this issue. However, having an IRI in the subject position is not a sufficient condition in general. For instance, the PP pattern $\langle \text{Tim}, {}^{\wedge}\text{knows}, ?v \rangle$ has the same issue as the pattern in Example 2 (in fact, both patterns are semantically equivalent under context-based semantics). A question that arises is whether there exists a property of PP patterns that can be used to distinguish between patterns that do not have this issue (i.e., evaluating them over any WoLD is feasible) and those that do. We shall discuss this question for the more general case of PP-based SPARQL queries.

5   SPARQL with Property Paths on the Web

After considering PP patterns in separation, we now turn to a more expressive fragment of SPARQL that embeds PP patterns as the basic building block and uses additional operators on top. We define the resulting PP-based SPARQL queries, discuss the feasibility of evaluating these queries over the Web, and introduce a syntactic property to identify queries for which an evaluation under context-based semantics is feasible.

5.1   Definition

By using the algebraic syntax of SPARQL [22], we define a *graph pattern* recursively as follows: (i) Any PP pattern $\langle \alpha, \texttt{path}, \beta \rangle$ is a graph pattern; and (ii) if P_1 and P_2 are graph patterns, then $(P_1\texttt{AND}P_2)$, $(P_1\texttt{UNION}P_2)$, and $(P_1\texttt{OPT}P_2)$ are graph patterns.[3] For any graph pattern P, we write $\texttt{V}(P)$ to denote the set of *all variables* in P.

By using PP patterns as the basic building block of graph patterns, we can readily carry over our context-based semantics to graph patterns: For any graph pattern P and any WoLD W, the *evaluation* of P over W under context-based semantics is a multiset of solution mappings, denoted by $[\![P]\!]_W^{\texttt{ctx}}$, that is defined recursively as follows:[4]

- If P is a PP pattern, then $[\![P]\!]_W^{\texttt{ctx}}$ is defined in Definition 3.
- If P is $(P_1 \texttt{ AND } P_2)$, then $[\![P]\!]_W^{\texttt{ctx}} = [\![P_1]\!]_W^{\texttt{ctx}} \bowtie [\![P_2]\!]_W^{\texttt{ctx}}$.
- If P is $(P_1 \texttt{ UNION } P_2)$, then $[\![P]\!]_W^{\texttt{ctx}} = [\![P_1]\!]_W^{\texttt{ctx}} \sqcup [\![P_2]\!]_W^{\texttt{ctx}}$.
- If P is $(P_1 \texttt{ OPT } P_2)$, then $[\![P]\!]_W^{\texttt{ctx}} = \left([\![P_1]\!]_W^{\texttt{ctx}} \bowtie [\![P_2]\!]_W^{\texttt{ctx}} \right) \sqcup \left([\![P_1]\!]_W^{\texttt{ctx}} \setminus [\![P_2]\!]_W^{\texttt{ctx}} \right)$.

5.2   Discussion

Given a query semantics for evaluating PP-based graph patterns over a WoLD, we now discuss the feasibility of such evaluation. To this end, we introduce the notion of *Web-safeness* of graph patterns. Informally, graph patterns are Web-safe if evaluating them completely under context-based semantics is possible. Formally:

Definition 4. *A graph pattern P is* Web-safe *if there exists an algorithm that, for any finite WoLD $W = \langle D, data, adoc \rangle$, computes $[\![P]\!]_W^{\texttt{ctx}}$ by looking up only a finite number of IRIs without assuming direct access to the sets D and $\mathrm{dom}(adoc)$.*

---

[3] For this paper we leave out other types of SPARQL graph patterns such as filters. Adding them is an exercise that would not have any significant implication on the following discussion.

[4] Note that the definition uses the algebra operators introduced in Sect. 3.1.

Example 3. *Consider graph pattern* $P_{\mathsf{E}_3} = (\langle \mathsf{Bob}, \mathsf{knows}, ?v \rangle \, \mathsf{AND} \langle ?v, \mathsf{knows}, \mathsf{Tim} \rangle)$. *The right sub-pattern* $P_{\mathsf{E}_2} = \langle ?v, \mathsf{knows}, \mathsf{Tim} \rangle$ *is not Web-safe because evaluating it completely over the WWW is not feasible under context-based semantics (cf. Example 2). However, the larger pattern* P_{E_3} *is Web-safe; it can be evaluated completely under context-based semantics. For instance, a possible algorithm may first evaluate the left sub-pattern, which is feasible because it requires the lookup of a single IRI only (the IRI* Bob*). Thereafter, the evaluation of the right sub-pattern* P_{E_2} *can be reduced to looking up a finite number of IRIs only, namely the IRIs bound to variable* $?v$ *in solution mappings obtained for the left sub-pattern. Although any other IRI* u^* *might also be used to discover matching triples for* P_{E_2}*, each of these triples has IRI* u^* *as its subject (which is a consequence of restricting retrieved data based on the context selector introduced in Sect. 4.2). Therefore, the solution mappings resulting from such matching triples cannot be compatible with any solution for the left sub-pattern and, thus, do not satisfy the join condition established by the semantics of* AND *in pattern* P_{E_3}*.*

The example illustrates that some graph patterns are Web-safe even if some of their sub-patterns are not. Consequently, we are interested in a *decidable* property that enables to identify Web-safe patterns, including those whose sub-patterns are not Web-safe.

Buil-Aranda et al. study a similar problem in the context of SPARQL federation where graph patterns of the form $P_S = (\mathsf{SERVICE} ?v \, P)$ are allowed [6]. Here, variable $?v$ ranges over a possibly large set of IRIs, each of which represents the address of a (remote) SPARQL service that needs to be called to assemble the complete result of P_S. However, many service calls may be avoided if P_S is embedded in a larger graph pattern that allows for an evaluation during which $?v$ can be bound before evaluating P_S. To tackle this problem, Buil-Aranda et al. introduce a notion of *strong boundedness* of variables in graph patterns and use it to show a notion of safeness for the evaluation of patterns like P_S within larger graph patterns. The set of *strongly bound variables* in a graph pattern P, denoted by $\mathrm{SBV}(P)$, is defined recursively as follows:

- If P is a PP pattern, then $\mathrm{SBV}(P) = \mathrm{V}(P)$ (where $\mathrm{V}(P)$ are all variables in P).
- If P is of the form $(P_1 \, \mathsf{AND} \, P_2)$, then $\mathrm{SBV}(P) = \mathrm{SBV}(P_1) \cup \mathrm{SBV}(P_2)$.
- If P is of the form $(P_1 \, \mathsf{UNION} \, P_2)$, then $\mathrm{SBV}(P) = \mathrm{SBV}(P_1) \cap \mathrm{SBV}(P_2)$.
- If P is of the form $(P_1 \, \mathsf{OPT} \, P_2)$, then $\mathrm{SBV}(P) = \mathrm{SBV}(P_1)$.

The idea behind the notion of strongly bound variables has already been used in earlier work (e.g., *"certain variables"* [23], *"output variables"* [24]), and it is tempting to adopt it for our problem. However, we note that one cannot identify Web-safe graph patterns by using strong boundedness in a manner similar to its use in Buil-Aranda et al.'s work alone. For instance, consider graph pattern P_{E_3} from Example 3. We know that (i) P_{E_3} is Web-safe and that (ii) $\mathrm{V}(P_{\mathsf{E}_3}) = \{?v\}$ and also $\mathrm{SBV}(P_{\mathsf{E}_3}) = \{?v\}$. Then, one might hypothesize that for every graph pattern P, if $\mathrm{SBV}(P) = \mathrm{V}(P)$, then P is Web-safe. However, the PP pattern $P_{\mathsf{E}_2} = \langle ?v, \mathsf{knows}, \mathsf{Tim} \rangle$ disproves such a hypothesis because, even if $\mathrm{SBV}(P_{\mathsf{E}_2}) = \mathrm{V}(P_{\mathsf{E}_2})$, pattern P_{E_2} is not Web-safe (cf. Example 2).

We conjecture the following reason why strong boundedness cannot be used directly for our problem. For complex patterns (i.e., patterns that are not PP patterns), the sets of strongly bound variables of all sub-patterns are defined *independent* from each other, whereas the algorithm outlined in Example 3 leverages a specific relationship between sub-patterns. More precisely, the algorithm leverages the fact that the same variable that is the subject of the right sub-pattern is also the object of the left sub-pattern.

Based on this observation, we introduce the notion of *conditionally Web-bounded variables*, the definition of which, for complex graph patterns, is based on specific relationships between sub-patterns. This notion shall turn out to be suitable for our case.

Definition 5. *The* conditionally Web-bounded variables *of a graph pattern P w.r.t. a set of variables X is the subset $CBV(P \mid X) \subseteq V(P)$ that is defined recursively as follows:*

If P is:		then $CBV(P \mid X)$ is:
1) $\langle \alpha, u, \beta \rangle$ or $\langle \alpha, !(u_1 \mid \dots \mid u_n), \beta \rangle$	such that $\alpha \in (\mathcal{I} \cup \mathcal{L})$ or $\alpha \in X$	$V(P)$
2) $\langle \alpha, u, \beta \rangle$ or $\langle \alpha, !(u_1 \mid \dots \mid u_n), \beta \rangle$	such that $\alpha \notin (\mathcal{I} \cup \mathcal{L})$ and $\alpha \notin X$	$\emptyset$
3) $\langle \alpha, (path)^*, \beta \rangle$ s.t. $\alpha \in V$ and $\beta \notin V$		$CBV(\langle \beta, (\char`\^ path)^*, \alpha \rangle \mid X)$
4) $\langle \alpha, (path)^*, \beta \rangle$ s.t. (i) $\alpha \notin V$ or $\beta \in V$, and (ii) for any two variables $?x, ?y \in V$	it holds that $CBV(\langle ?x, path, ?y \rangle \mid \{?x\}) = \{?x, ?y\}$	$CBV(\langle \alpha, path, \beta \rangle \mid X)$
5) $\langle \alpha, (path)^*, \beta \rangle$ such that none of the above		$\emptyset$
6) $\langle \alpha, \char`\^ path, \beta \rangle$ with $P' = \langle \beta, path, \alpha \rangle$		$CBV(P' \mid X)$
7) $\langle \alpha, (path_1 \mid path_2), \beta \rangle$ with $P' = (\langle \alpha, path_1, \beta \rangle \text{ UNION } \langle \alpha, path_2, \beta \rangle)$		$CBV(P' \mid X)$
8) $\langle \alpha, path_1 / path_2, \beta \rangle$ s.t., for any $?v \in V \setminus (X \cup \{\alpha, \beta\})$, $?v \in CBV(P' \mid X)$	where $P' = (\langle \alpha, path_1, ?v \rangle \text{ AND } \langle ?v, path_2, \beta \rangle)$	$CBV(P' \mid X) \setminus \{?v\}$
9) $\langle \alpha, path_1 / path_2, \beta \rangle$ such that none of the above		$\emptyset$
10) $(P_1 \text{ AND } P_2)$ s.t. $CBV(P_1 \mid X) = V(P_1)$ and $CBV(P_2 \mid X) = V(P_2)$		$V(P)$
11) $(P_1 \text{ AND } P_2)$ s.t. $CBV(P_1 \mid X) = V(P_1)$ and $CBV(P_2 \mid X \cup SBV(P_1)) = V(P_2)$		$V(P)$
12) $(P_1 \text{ AND } P_2)$ s.t. $CBV(P_2 \mid X) = V(P_2)$ and $CBV(P_1 \mid X \cup SBV(P_2)) = V(P_1)$		$V(P)$
13) $(P_1 \text{ AND } P_2)$ such that none of the above		$\emptyset$
14) $(P_1 \text{ UNION } P_2)$		$CBV(P_1 \mid X) \cap CBV(P_2 \mid X)$
15) $(P_1 \text{ OPT } P_2)$ s.t. $CBV(P_1 \mid X) = V(P_1)$ and $CBV(P_2 \mid X) = V(P_2)$		$V(P)$
16) $(P_1 \text{ OPT } P_2)$ s.t. $CBV(P_1 \mid X) = V(P_1)$ and $CBV(P_2 \mid X \cup SBV(P_1)) = V(P_2)$		$V(P)$
17) $(P_1 \text{ OPT } P_2)$ such that none of the above		$\emptyset$

Example 4. *For the PP pattern $P_{E_2} = \langle ?v, \text{knows}, \text{Tim} \rangle$—which is not Web-safe (as discussed in Example 2)—if we use the set $\{?v\}$ as condition, then, by line 1 in Definition 5, it holds that $CBV(P_{E_2} \mid \{?v\}) = \{?v\}$. However, if we use the empty set instead, we obtain $CBV(P_{E_2} \mid \emptyset) = \emptyset$ (cf. line 2 in Definition 5).*

While for the non-Web-safe pattern P_{E_2} we thus observe $CBV(P_{E_2} \mid \emptyset) \neq V(P_{E_2})$, for graph pattern $P_{E_3} = (\langle \text{Bob}, \text{knows}, ?v \rangle \text{ AND } \langle ?v, \text{knows}, \text{Tim} \rangle)$—which is Web-safe (cf. Example 3)—we have $CBV(P_{E_3} \mid \emptyset) = V(P_{E_3})$. The fact that $CBV(P_{E_3} \mid \emptyset) = \{?v\}$ follows from (i) $CBV(\langle \text{Bob}, \text{knows}, ?v \rangle \mid \emptyset) = \{?v\}$, (ii) $SBV(\langle \text{Bob}, \text{knows}, ?v \rangle) = \{?v\}$, (iii) $CBV(\langle ?v, \text{knows}, \text{Tim} \rangle \mid \{?v\}) = \{?v\}$, and (iv) line 11 in Definition 5.

The example seems to suggest that, if *all* variables of a graph pattern are conditionally Web-bounded w.r.t. the empty set of variables, then the graph pattern is Web-safe. The following result verifies this hypothesis.

Theorem 1. *A graph pattern P is Web-safe if $CBV(P \mid \emptyset) = V(P)$.*

Note 1. *Due to the recursive nature of Definition 5, the condition $CBV(P \mid \emptyset) = V(P)$ (as used in Theorem 1) is decidable for any graph pattern P.*

We prove Theorem 1 based on an algorithm that evaluates graph patterns recursively by passing (intermediate) solution mappings to recursive calls. To capture the desired results of each recursive call formally, we introduce a special evaluation function for a graph pattern P over a WoLD W that takes a solution mapping μ as input and returns only the solutions for P over W that are compatible with μ.

Definition 6. *Let P be a graph pattern, let W be a WoLD, and let $\langle \Omega, card \rangle = [\![P]\!]_W^{ctx}$. Given a solution mapping μ, the μ-restricted evaluation of P over W under* context-based semantics, *denoted by $[\![P \mid \mu]\!]_W^{ctx}$, is the multiset of solution mappings $\langle \Omega', card' \rangle$ with $\Omega' = \{\mu' \in \Omega \mid \mu' \sim \mu\}$ and $card'(\mu') = card(\mu')$ for all $\mu' \in \Omega'$.*

The following lemma shows the existence of the aforementioned recursive algorithm.

Lemma 1. *Let P be a graph pattern and let μ_{in} be a solution mapping. If it holds that $CBV(P \mid \mathrm{dom}(\mu_{in})) = V(P)$, there exists an algorithm that, for any finite WoLD W, computes $[\![P \mid \mu_{in}]\!]_W^{ctx}$ by looking up a finite number of IRIs only.*

Before providing the proof of the lemma (and of Theorem 1), we point out two important properties of Definition 6. First, it is easily seen that, for any graph pattern P and WoLD W, $[\![P \mid \mu_\emptyset]\!]_W^{ctx} = [\![P]\!]_W^{ctx}$, where $\mu_\emptyset$ is the empty solution mapping (i.e., $\mathrm{dom}(\mu_\emptyset) = \emptyset$). Consequently, given an algorithm, say A, that has the properties of the algorithm described by Lemma 1, a trivial algorithm that can be used to prove Theorem 1 may simply call algorithm A with the empty solution mapping and return the result of this call (we shall elaborate more on this approach in the proof of Theorem 1 below). Second, for any PP pattern $\langle \alpha, \mathtt{path}, \beta \rangle$ and WoLD W, if α is a variable and $\mathtt{path}$ is a base PP expression (i.e., one of the first two cases in the grammar in Sect. 3.1), then $[\![P \mid \mu]\!]_W^{ctx}$ is empty for every solution mapping μ that binds (variable) α to a literal or a blank node. Formally, we show the latter as follows.

Lemma 2. *Let P be a PP pattern of the form $\langle ?v, u, \beta \rangle$ or $\langle ?v, !(u_1 \mid \cdots \mid u_n), \beta \rangle$ with $?v \in V$ and $u, u_1, \ldots, u_n \in I$, and let μ be a solution mapping. If $?v \in \mathrm{dom}(\mu)$ and $\mu(?v) \in (B \cup L)$, then, for any WoLD W, $[\![P \mid \mu]\!]_W^{ctx}$ is the empty multiset.*

Proof (Lemma 2). Recall that, for any IRI u and any WoLD W, context $C^W(u)$ contains only triples that have IRI u as their subject. As a consequence, for any WoLD W, every solution mapping $\mu' \in [\![P]\!]_W^{ctx}$ binds variable $?v$ to some IRI (and never to a literal or blank node); i.e., $\mu'(?v) \in I$. Therefore, if $?v \in \mathrm{dom}(\mu)$ and $\mu(?v) \in (B \cup L)$, then μ cannot be compatible with any $\mu' \in [\![P]\!]_W^{ctx}$ and, thus, $[\![P \mid \mu]\!]_W^{ctx}$ is empty. $\qquad \square$

We use Lemma 2 to prove Lemma 1 as follows.

Proof idea (Lemma 1). We prove the lemma by induction on the possible structure of graph pattern P. For the proof, we provide Algorithm 1 and show that this (recursive) algorithm has the desired properties for any possible graph pattern (i.e., any case of the induction, including the base case). Due to space limitations, in this paper we only present a fragment of the algorithm and highlight essential properties thereof. The given fragment covers the base case (lines 1–11) and one pivotal case of the induction step, namely, graph patterns of the form $(P_1 \text{AND} P_2)$ (lines 57–72). The complete version of the algorithm and the full proof can be found in an extended version of this paper [15].

For the base case, Algorithm 1 looks up at most one IRI (cf. lines 2–5). The crux of showing that the returned result is sound and complete is Lemma 2 and the fact that the only possible *context* in which a triple $\langle s, p, o \rangle$ with $s \in \mathcal{I}$ can be found is $C^W(s)$.

For PP patterns of the form $(P_1 \text{AND} P_2)$ consider lines 57–72. By using Definition 5, we show $\text{CBV}(P_i \mid \text{dom}(\mu_{\text{in}})) = \text{V}(P_i)$ and $\text{CBV}(P_j \mid \text{dom}(\mu_{\text{in}}) \cup \text{dom}(\mu)) = \text{V}(P_j)$ for all $\mu \in \Omega^{P_i}$. Therefore, by induction, all recursive calls (lines 60 and 62) look up a finite number of IRIs and return correct results; i.e., $\langle \Omega^{P_i}, card^{P_i} \rangle = [\![P_i \mid \mu_{\text{in}}]\!]_W^{\text{ctx}}$ and $\langle \Omega^{\mu}, card^{\mu} \rangle = [\![P_j \mid \mu_{\text{in}} \cup \mu]\!]_W^{\text{ctx}}$ for all $\mu \in \Omega^{P_i}$. Then, since each $\mu \in \Omega^{P_i}$ is compatible with all $\mu' \in \Omega^{\mu}$ and all processed solution mappings are compatible with μ_{in}, it is easily verified that the computed result is $[\![(P_1 \text{AND} P_2) \mid \mu_{\text{in}}]\!]_W^{\text{ctx}}$. □

We are now ready to prove Theorem 1, for which we use Lemma 1, or more precisely the algorithm that we introduce in the proof of the lemma.

Proof (Theorem 1). Let P be a graph pattern s.t. $\text{CBV}(P \mid \emptyset) = \text{V}(P)$. Then, given the empty solution mapping $\mu_\emptyset$ with $\text{dom}(\mu_\emptyset) = \emptyset$, we have $\text{CBV}(P \mid \text{dom}(\mu_\emptyset)) = \text{V}(P)$. Therefore, by our proof of Lemma 1 we know that, for any finite WoLD W, Algorithm 1 computes $[\![P \mid \mu_\emptyset]\!]_W^{\text{ctx}}$ by looking up a finite number of IRIs. We also know that the empty solution mapping is compatible with any solution mapping. Consequently, by Definition 6, $[\![P \mid \mu_\emptyset]\!]_W^{\text{ctx}} = [\![P]\!]_W^{\text{ctx}}$ for any WoLD W. Hence, by passing the empty solution mapping to it, Algorithm 1 can be used to compute $[\![P]\!]_W^{\text{ctx}}$ for any finite WoLD W, and during this computation the algorithm looks up a finite number of IRIs only. □

While the condition in Theorem 1 is sufficient to identify Web-safe graph patterns, the question that remains is whether it is a necessary condition (in which case it could be used to decide Web-safeness of *all* graph patterns). Unfortunately, the answer is no.

Example 5. *Consider the graph pattern $P = (P_1 \text{ UNION } P_2)$ with $P_1 = \langle u_1, p_1, ?x \rangle$ and $P_2 = \langle u_2, p_2, ?y \rangle$. We note that $\text{CBV}(P_1 \mid \emptyset) = \{?x\}$ and $\text{CBV}(P_2 \mid \emptyset) = \{?y\}$, and, thus, $\text{CBV}(P \mid \emptyset) = \emptyset$. Hence, the pattern does not satisfy the condition in Theorem 1. Nonetheless, it is easy to see that there exists a (sound and complete) algorithm that, for any WoLD W, computes $[\![P]\!]_W^{\text{ctx}}$ by looking up*

Algorithm 1. $EvalCtxBased(P, \mu_{in})$, which computes $[\![P \,|\, \mu_{in}]\!]_W^{ctx}$.

1: **if** P is of the form $\langle \alpha, u, \beta \rangle$ or P is of the form $\langle \alpha, !(u_1 \,|\, \cdots \,|\, u_n), \beta \rangle$ **then**
2:   **if** $\alpha \in \mathcal{I}$ **then** $u' := \alpha$
3:   **else if** $\alpha \in \mathcal{V}$ **and** $\alpha \in \mathrm{dom}(\mu_{in})$ **and** $\mu_{in}(\alpha) \in \mathcal{I}$ **then** $u' := \mu_{in}(\alpha)$
4:   **else** $u' := \texttt{null}$

5:   **if** u' is an IRI and looking it up results in retrieving a document, say d **then**
6:     $G :=$ the set of triples in d (use a fresh set of blank node identifiers when parsing d)
7:     $G' := \{ \langle s, p, o \rangle \in G \,|\, s = u' \}$
8:     $\langle \Omega, card \rangle := [\![P]\!]_{G'}$ ($[\![P]\!]_{G'}$ can be computed by using any algorithm that implements the standard SPARQL evaluation function)
9:     **return** a new multiset $\langle \Omega', card' \rangle$ with $\Omega' = \{ \mu' \in \Omega \,|\, \mu' \sim \mu_{in} \}$ and
$$card'(\mu') = card(\mu') \text{ for all } \mu' \in \Omega'$$
10:   **else**
11:     **return** a new empty multiset $\langle \Omega, card \rangle$ with $\Omega = \emptyset$ and $\mathrm{dom}(card) = \emptyset$
     $\ldots$

57: **else if** P is of the form $(P_1 \mathrm{AND} P_2)$ **then**
58:   **if** $\mathrm{CBV}(P_1 \,|\, \mathrm{dom}(\mu_{in})) = \mathrm{V}(P_1)$ **then** $i := 1; j := 2$ **else** $i := 2; j := 1$
59:   Create a new empty multiset $M = \langle \Omega, card \rangle$ with $\Omega = \emptyset$ and $\mathrm{dom}(card) = \emptyset$
60:   $\langle \Omega^{P_i}, card^{P_i} \rangle := EvalCtxBased(P_i, \mu_{in})$
61:   **for all** $\mu \in \Omega^{P_i}$ **do**
62:     $\langle \Omega^{\mu}, card^{\mu} \rangle := EvalCtxBased(P_j, \mu_{in} \cup \mu)$
63:     **for all** $\mu' \in \Omega^{\mu}$ **do**
64:       $\mu^* := \mu \cup \mu'$
65:       $k := card^{P_i}(\mu) \cdot card^{\mu}(\mu')$
66:       **if** $\mu^* \in \Omega$ **then**
67:         $old := card(\mu^*)$
68:         Adjust $card$ such that $card(\mu^*) = k + old$
69:       **else**
70:         Adjust $card$ such that $card(\mu^*) = k$
71:         Add μ^* to Ω
72:   **return** M

---

a finite number of IRIs only. For instance, such an algorithm, say A, may first use two other algorithms that compute $[\![P_1]\!]_W^{ctx}$ and $[\![P_2]\!]_W^{ctx}$ by looking up a finite number of IRIs, respectively. Such algorithms exist by Theorem 1, because $\mathrm{CBV}(P_1 \,|\, \emptyset) = \mathrm{V}(P_1)$ and $\mathrm{CBV}(P_2 \,|\, \emptyset) = \mathrm{V}(P_2)$. Finally, algorithm A can generate the (sound and complete) query result $[\![P]\!]_W^{ctx}$ by computing the multiset union $[\![P_1]\!]_W^{ctx} \sqcup [\![P_2]\!]_W^{ctx}$, which requires no additional IRI lookups.

Remark 1. The example illustrates that "only if" cannot be shown in Theorem 1. It remains an open question whether there exists an alternative condition for Web-safeness that is both sufficient and necessary (and decidable).

6   Concluding Remarks and Future Work

This paper studies the problem of extending the scope of SPARQL property paths to query Linked Data that is distributed on the WWW. We have proposed a context-based query semantics and analyzed its peculiarities. Our perhaps most interesting finding is that there exist queries whose evaluation over the WWW is not feasible. We studied this aspect and introduced a decidable syntactic property for identifying feasible queries.

We believe that the presented work provides valuable input to a wider discussion about defining a language for accessing Linked Data on the WWW. In this context, there are several directions for future research such as the following three. First, studying a more expressive navigational core for property paths over the Web; e.g., along the lines of other navigational languages such as nSPARQL [21] or NautiLOD [8]. Second, investigating relationships between navigational queries and SPARQL federation. Third, while the aim of this paper was to introduce a formal foundation for answering SPARQL queries with PPs over Linked Data on the WWW, an investigation of how systems may implement efficiently the machinery developed in this paper is certainly interesting.

References

1. Abiteboul, S., Vianu, V.: Queries and computation on the web. Theor. Comput. Sci. **239**(2), 231–255 (2000)
2. Alkhateeb, F., Baget, J.F., Euzenat, J.: Extending SPARQL with regular expression patterns (for querying RDF). J. Web Sem. **7**(2), 57–73 (2009)
3. Arenas, M., Conca, S., Pérez, J.: Counting beyond a yottabyte, or how SPARQL 1.1 property paths will prevent adoption of the standard. In: Proceedings of the 21st International Conference on World Wide Web (2012)
4. Berners-Lee, T.: Design issues: Linked Data, July 2006
5. Bouquet, P., Ghidini, C., Serafini, L.: Querying the web of data: a formal approach. In: Gómez-Pérez, A., Yu, Y., Ding, Y. (eds.) ASWC 2009. LNCS, vol. 5926, pp. 291–305. Springer, Heidelberg (2009)
6. Buil-Aranda, C., Arenas, M., Corcho, O., Polleres, A.: Federating queries in SPARQL1.1: syntax, semantics and evaluation. J. Web Semant. **18**(1), 1–17 (2013)
7. Fielding, R., Gettys, J., Mogul, J.C., Frystyk, H., Masinter, L., Leach, P.J., Berners-Lee, T.: Hypertext Transfer Protocol - HTTP/1.1. RFC 2616, June 1999
8. Fionda, V., Gutierrez, C., Pirrò, G.: Semantic navigation on the web of data: specification of routes, web fragments and actions. In: Proceedings of the 21st International Conference on the World Wide Web (2012)
9. Fionda, V., Pirrò, G., Consens, M.: Extended property paths: writing more SPARQL queries in a succinct way. In: Proceedings of the 28th AAAI Conference on Artificial Intelligence (AAAI) (2015)
10. Fionda, V., Pirrò, G., Gutierrez, C.: NautiLOD: a formal language for the web of data graph. ACM Trans. Web **9**(1), 1–43 (2015)
11. Florescu, D., Levy, A., Mendelzon, A.: Database techniques for the World-Wide Web: a survey. SIGMOD Rec. **27**, 59–74 (1998)
12. Harris, S., Seaborne, A.: SPARQL 1.1 query language. W3C Reccomendation (2013)

13. Harth, A., Speiser, S.: On completeness classes for query evaluation on linked data. In: Proceedings of the 26th AAAI Conference (2012)
14. Hartig, O.: SPARQL for a web of linked data: semantics and computability. In: Simperl, E., Cimiano, P., Polleres, A., Corcho, O., Presutti, V. (eds.) ESWC 2012. LNCS, vol. 7295, pp. 8–23. Springer, Heidelberg (2012)
15. Hartig, O., Pirrò, G.: A context-based semantics for sparql property paths over the web (extended version) (2015). http://arxiv.org/abs/1503.04831, CoRR abs/1503.04831
16. Klyne, G., Carroll, J.J.: Resource Description Framework (RDF): Concepts and Abstract Syntax (2006)
17. Kochut, K.J., Janik, M.: SPARQLeR: extended SPARQL for semantic association discovery. In: Franconi, E., Kifer, M., May, W. (eds.) ESWC 2007. LNCS, vol. 4519, pp. 145–159. Springer, Heidelberg (2007)
18. Konopnicki, D., Shmueli, O.: Information gathering in the World-Wide Web: The W3QL query language and the W3QS system. ACM Trans. database Syst. 23(4), 369–410 (1998)
19. Loseman, K., Martens, W.: The complexity of evaluating path expressions in SPARQL. In: Proceedings of the 31st ACM Symposium on Principles of Database Systems (2012)
20. Mendelzon, A.O., Mihaila, G.A., Milo, T.: Querying the World Wide Web. Int. J. Digit. Libr. 1, 54–97 (1997)
21. Pérez, J., Arenas, M., Gutierrez, C.: nSPARQL: a navigational language for RDF. J. Web Semant. 8(4), 255–270 (2010)
22. Pérez, J., Arenas, M., Gutierrez, C.: Semantics and complexity of SPARQL. ACM Trans. Database Syst. (TODS) 34(3), 1–45 (2009)
23. Schmidt, M., Meier, M., Lausen, G.: Foundations of SPARQL query optimization. In: Proceedings of the 13th International Conference on Database Theory (2010)
24. Toman, D., Weddell, G.E.: Fundamentals of Physical Design and Query Compilation. Synthesis Lectures on Data Management. Morgan & Claypool Publishers, San Rafael (2011)
25. Umbrich, J., Hogan, A., Polleres, A., Decker, S.: Link traversal querying for a diverse web of data. Semant. Web J. (2014)
26. Wood, P.T.: Query languages for graph databases. SIGMOD Rec. 41(1), 50–60 (2012)

Distributed and Scalable OWL EL Reasoning

Raghava Mutharaju[1]([⊠]), Pascal Hitzler[1], Prabhaker Mateti[1],
and Freddy Lécué[2]

[1] Wright State University, OH, USA
{mutharaju.2,pascal.hitzler,prabhaker.mateti}@wright.edu
[2] Smarter Cities Technology Centre, IBM Research, Dublin, Ireland
freddy.lecue@ie.ibm.com

Abstract. OWL 2 EL is one of the tractable profiles of the Web Ontology Language (OWL) which is a W3C-recommended standard. OWL 2 EL provides sufficient expressivity to model large biomedical ontologies as well as streaming data such as traffic, while at the same time allows for efficient reasoning services. Existing reasoners for OWL 2 EL, however, use only a single machine and are thus constrained by memory and computational power. At the same time, the automated generation of ontological information from streaming data and text can lead to very large ontologies which can exceed the capacities of these reasoners. We thus describe a distributed reasoning system that scales well using a cluster of commodity machines. We also apply our system to a use case on city traffic data and show that it can handle volumes which cannot be handled by current single machine reasoners.

1 Introduction

We predict that ontology-based knowledge bases will continue to grow to sizes beyond the capability of single machines to keep their representations in main memory. Manually constructed knowledge bases will most likely remain considerably smaller, but the automated generation of ABox and TBox axioms from e.g. data streams [10] or texts [12] will likely go beyond the capabilities of current single-machine systems in terms of memory and computational power required for deductive reasoning. Also, for some reasoning tasks the output is several times larger than the input. For such cases, distributed memory reasoning will be required.

In this paper, we consider knowledge bases (ontologies) which fall into the tractable OWL 2 EL profile [13]. In particular, our distributed reasoner, DistEL, supports almost all of $\mathcal{EL}^{++}$ which is the description logic underlying OWL 2 EL. The following are our main contributions.

1. We describe our distributed algorithms along with the data distribution and load balancing scheme. To the best of our knowledge, this is the first such work for the $\mathcal{EL}^{++}$ description logic.
2. We demonstrate that DistEL scales well and also achieves reasonable speedup through parallelization. It can handle ontologies much larger than what current other reasoners are capable of.

© Springer International Publishing Switzerland 2015
F. Gandon et al. (Eds.): ESWC 2015, LNCS 9088, pp. 88–103, 2015.
DOI: 10.1007/978-3-319-18818-8_6

3. `DistEL` is GPL open-sourced at https://github.com/raghavam/DistEL. Its usage and build are fully documented and it works on publicly available ontologies.

The paper is structured as follows. After recalling preliminaries on OWL EL (Sect. 2), we describe the algorithms for `DistEL` (Sect. 3) and discuss some specific optimizations we have used (Sect. 4). We close with a performance evaluation (Sect. 5), related work (Sect. 6), and a conclusion (Sect. 7).

2 Preliminaries

We will work with a large fragment of the description logic $\mathcal{EL}^{++}$ [2] which underlies OWL 2 EL. We briefly recall notation, terminology, and key definitions, primarily taken from [2] which serves as general reference. We define only the fragment which we use through this paper, and for convenience we call it EL^*.

The underlying language of our logic consists of three mutually disjoint sets of atomic concept names N_C, atomic role names N_R and individuals N_I. An (EL^*-)axiom can have one of the following forms. (i) General concept inclusions of the form $C \sqsubseteq D$, where C and D are *classes* defined by the following grammar (with $A \in N_C$, $r \in N_R$, $a \in N_I$):

$$C ::= A \mid \top \mid \bot \mid C \sqcap C \mid \exists r.C \mid \{a\}$$
$$D ::= A \mid \top \mid \bot \mid D \sqcap D \mid \exists r.D \mid \exists r.\{a\}$$

(ii) Role inclusions of the form $r_1 \circ \cdots \circ r_n \sqsubseteq r$, where $r, r_i \in N_R$.

An (EL^*-)ontology consists of a finite set of EL^*-axioms. Axioms of the form $\{a\} \sqsubseteq A$ and $\{a\} \sqsubseteq \exists r.\{b\}$ are called *ABox* axioms, and they are sometimes written as $A(a)$ and $R(a, b)$ respectively.

The primary omissions from $\mathcal{EL}^{++}$ are concrete domains and that we limit the use of *nominals*, which are classes of the form $\{a\}$, to the inclusion of ABox axioms as described above.[1] In particular, `DistEL` does not support concept inclusions of the form $C \sqsubseteq \{a\}$.

The model-theoretic semantics for EL^* follows the standard definition, which we will not repeat here. For this and other background see [7].

We recall from [2] that every EL^* ontology can be normalized in such a way that all concept inclusions have one of the forms $A_1 \sqsubseteq B$, $A_1 \sqcap \cdots \sqcap A_n \sqsubseteq B$, $A_1 \sqsubseteq \exists r.A_2$, $\exists r.A_1 \sqsubseteq B$ and that all role inclusions are in the form of either $r \sqsubseteq s$ or $r_1 \circ r_2 \sqsubseteq r_3$, where $A_i \in BC_{\mathcal{O}} = N_C \cup \{\top\}$ (for all i) and $B \in BC_{\mathcal{O}}^{\perp} = N_C \cup \{\bot\}$.

In rest of the paper, we assume that all ontologies are normalized.

The reasoning task that is of interest to us (and which is considered the main reasoning task for $\mathcal{EL}^{++}$) is that of *classification*, which is the computation of the complete subsumption hierarchy, i.e. of all logical consequences of the form $A \sqsubseteq B$ involving all concept names and nominals A and B. Other tasks such

---

[1] Domain axioms can be expressed directly, and allowed range axioms can be rewritten into EL^* as shown in [3].

Table 1. Completion rules and key value pairs

Rn	Input	Action	Key: Value
R1	$A \sqsubseteq B$	$U[B] \ \cup= \ U[A]$	$A_{R1} : B$
R2	$A_1 \sqcap \cdots \sqcap A_n \sqsubseteq B$	$U[B] \ \cup= \ U[A_1] \cap \cdots \cap U[A_n]$	$(A_1, \ldots, A_n)_{R2} : B$
R3	$A \sqsubseteq \exists r.B$	$R[r] \ \cup= \ \{(X, B) \mid X \in U[A]\}$	$A_{R3} : (B, r)$
R4	$\exists r.A \sqsubseteq B$	$Q[r] \ \cup= \ \{(Y, B) \mid Y \in U[A]\}$	$A_{R4} : (B, r)$
R5	$R[r], Q[r]$	$U[B] \ \cup= \ \{X \mid (X, Y) \in R[r]$ and $(Y, B) \in Q[r]\}$	⟨none⟩
R6	$R[r]$	$U[\bot] \ \cup= \ \{X \mid (X, Y) \in R[r]$ and $B \in U[\bot]\}$	⟨none⟩
R7	$r \sqsubseteq s$	$R[s] \ \cup= \ R[r]$	$r_{R7} : s$
R8	$r \circ s \sqsubseteq t$	$R[t] \ \cup= \ \{(X, Z) \mid (X, Y) \in R[r]$ and $(Y, Z) \in R[s]\}$	$r_{R8a} : (s, t)$
			$s_{R8b} : (r, t)$
		$U[X] = \{A, B, \ldots\}$	$X_U : \{A, B, \ldots\}$
		$R[r] = \{(X, Y), \ldots\}$	$(Y, r)_{RY} : X; \ldots$
			$(X, r)_{RX} : Y; \ldots$
		$Q[r] = \{(X, Y), \ldots\}$	$(Y, r)_Q : X; \ldots$

as concept satisfiability and consistency checking are reducible to classification. Note that ABox reasoning (also known as *instance retrieval*) can be reduced to classification in our logic.

To classify an ontology, we use the completion rules given in Table 1 (left of the vertical line). These rules make use of three mappings $U : BC_{\bar{O}}^{\bot} \to 2^{BC_{\bar{O}}^{\bot}}$, $R : N_R \to 2^{BC_O \times BC_O}$ and $Q : N_R \to 2^{BC_O \times BC_{\bar{O}}^{\bot}}$ which encode certain derived consequences. More precisely, $X \in U[A]$ stands for $X \sqsubseteq A$, while $(A, B) \in R[r]$ stands for $A \sqsubseteq \exists r.B$ and $(A, B) \in Q[r]$ stands for $\exists r.A \sqsubseteq B$. For each concept $X \in BC_{\bar{O}}^{\bot}$, $U[X]$ is initialized to $\{X, \bot\}$, and for each role r, $R[r]$ and $Q[r]$ are initialized to $\emptyset$. The operator $\cup=$ adds elements of the set on the right-hand side to the set on the left-hand side.

The rules in Table 1 are applied as follows. Given a (normalized) input ontology, first initialize the $U[X]$, $R[r]$ and $Q[r]$ as indicated. Each axiom in the input knowledge base is of one of the forms given in the Table 1 *Input* column, and thus gives rise to the corresponding action given in the table. R5 and R6 are exceptions as they do not correspond to any input axiom types, but instead they take $Q[r]$, $R[r]$ as input and trigger the corresponding action.

To compute the completion, we non-deterministically and iteratively execute all actions corresponding to all of the rules. We do this to exhaustion, i.e., until none of the actions resulting from any of the axioms causes any change to any of the $U[X]$, $R[r]$ or $Q[r]$. Since there are only finitely many concept names, role names, and individuals occurring in the input knowledge base, the computation will indeed terminate at some stage.

The rules in Table 1 are from [2], except for rules R4 and R5, which is combined into one rule in [2]. Using two rules instead of one helps in the division and distribution of work in our reasoner; conceptually, we only have to store intermediate results (using Q, and this is the only use of Q we make), and otherwise there is no difference. We also use the function U instead of a function S which is used in [2], where $A \in S[X]$ is used to stand for $X \sqsubseteq A$. The difference is really notational only. Our rules (and corresponding algorithm) are really just a minor syntactic variation of the original rules, and the original correctness proofs carry over trivially. In Sect. 4 we will comment further on the reasons we have for using U instead of S: while it is only a notational variant, it is actually helpful for algorithm performance.

In DistEL, we use key:value pairs to encode both the input knowldge base and the output resulting from rule actions. In turn, these key:value pairs are also used to control the (then deterministic) parallel and sequential execution of rules, and we will discuss this in detail in the next section.

3   Algorithms of DistEL

In the algorithm descriptions in this section, we use a few CSP [1] inspired notations. The expression P ! tag(e) ? v, occurring in a process Q, denotes that the message tag(e) is sent to a process named P and the response received from P is assigned to v. If P is not ready to receive tag(e), Q blocks until P is ready. After this message is sent, Q waits for a response from P which it will save in v. P may take a while to compute this response. But when it sends this reply, Q is ready (since it has been waiting). So P does not block when replying. The corresponding expression Q ? tag(u) occurring in process P denotes receiving a message tag(e) from process Q and the body of the message is assigned to variable u local to P. The expression P ! tag(e) occurring in a process Q simply sends a message tag(e) to process P.

A process might receive many messages, and in order to distinguish between them and provide the right service to the requester, *tag* is used. These tags are descriptive names of the service that ought to be provided.

The **on** statements stand for an event processing mechanism that is ever ready but asleep until triggered by a request, and the corresponding response is shown on the rhs of the **do**.

Table 1 lists six unique axiom forms (excluding R5 and R6). R5 and R6 depend on the sets, $Q[r]$ and $R[r]$, for each role r. $Q[r]$ and $R[r]$ are set representations of axioms. For simplicity, we consider these two sets also as two separate axiom forms. This gets the total axiom forms to eight and now the input ontology $\mathcal{O}$ can be partitioned into eight mutually disjoint ontologies, $\mathcal{O} = \mathcal{O}_1 \cup \cdots \cup \mathcal{O}_8$, based on the axiom forms. Ontology $\mathcal{O}_i$ is assigned to a subcluster (subset of machines in the cluster) SC_i. Rule Ri, and no other, must be applied on $\mathcal{O}_i$. DistEL creates eight subclusters, one for each rule, from the available machines. For example (Fig. 1) axioms that belong to SC_4 are divided among its three nodes. Note that, axioms in $\mathcal{O}_i$ are further divided among the machines in SC_i and are not duplicated.

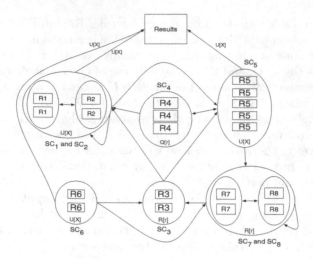

Fig. 1. Node assignment to rules and dependency among the completion rules. A rectangle represents a node in the cluster and inner ovals represent subclusters. Outer ovals enclosing SC_1/SC_2, and SC_7/SC_8 show their tighter input-output relationships. The set (U[X], R[r], or Q[r]) affected by the rule is shown within the enclosing oval. For simplicity, only one node is shown to hold results.

$K_1 := x := 0;$
forall the $A \sqsubseteq B \in \mathcal{O}_1$ **do**
$\quad$ UN ! update(B_U, A) ? $x;$
$\quad K_1 {+} = x;$

Algorithm 1. R1: $A \sqsubseteq B \Rightarrow$ $U[B] \sqsubseteq U[A]$

$K_2 := x := 0;$
forall the $A_1 \sqcap \cdots \sqcap A_n \sqsubseteq B \in \mathcal{O}_2$
do
$\quad$ UN ! $\sqcap(B_U, \{A_1, \ldots, A_n\})$? $x;$
$\quad K_2 {+} = x;$

Algorithm 2. R2: $A_1 \sqcap \cdots \sqcap A_n \sqsubseteq B \Rightarrow$ $U[B] \sqcup= U[A_1] \cap \cdots \cap U[A_n]$

Ontology partitioning should be done in such a way, so as to reduce internode communication. By following the described partitioning strategy, this goal is achieved since most of the data required for the rule application is available locally on each node. Other partitioning strategies such as MapReduce based data partitioning where spatial locality is followed (data in contiguous locations are assigned to one mapper) and hash partitioning (axiom key is hashed) did not yield good results [15].

Rule Processes. This section presents the bodies of each of the rules of Table 1. These bodies are wrapped and repeatedly executed by the rule processes; this wrapper code is discussed in the termination section further below.

The service process UN is described as Algorithm 9, and RN as Algorithm 10, further below. Note that, there can be any number of processes of a particular type (R1, ..., R8, UN, RN). In all the algorithms, immediately following the **forall the** keywords is the retrieval of axioms, discussed further below. Given a key such as $(Y, r)_Q$, it is fairly easy to i) extract individual values from it

$K_3 := x := 0;$
forall the $A \sqsubseteq \exists r.B \in \mathcal{O}_3$ **do**
$\quad s := \text{timeOf}(A_U);$
$\quad \text{UN ! queryTS}(A_U, s) \ ? \ M;$
$\quad$ **forall the** $X \in M$ **do**
$\quad\quad \text{RN ! update}((B, r)_{RY}, X) \ ? \ x;$
$\quad\quad K_3 {+} = x;$

Algorithm 3. R3: $A \sqsubseteq \exists r.B \Rightarrow$ $R[r] \ \sqcup= \ \{(X, B) \mid X \in U[A]\}$

$K_4 := x := 0;$
forall the $\exists r.A \sqsubseteq B \in \mathcal{O}_4$ **do**
$\quad s := \text{timeOf}(A_U);$
$\quad \text{UN ! queryTS}(A_U, s) \ ? \ M;$
$\quad$ **forall the** $Y \in M$ **do**
$\quad\quad \text{R5 ! new}((Y, r)_Q, B) \ ? \ x;$
$\quad\quad K_4 {+} = x;$

Algorithm 4. R4: $\exists r.A \sqsubseteq B \Rightarrow$ $Q[r] \ \sqcup= \ \{(Y, B) \mid Y \in U[A]\}$

$K_5 := x := 0;$
on R4 ? $\text{new}((Y, r)_Q, B)$ **do**
$\{ \ \text{R4 !} \ (Q[(Y, r)_Q] \ \sqcup= \ \{B\}) \#;$
$s := \text{timeOf}((Y, r)_{RY});$
$\text{RN ! queryTS}((Y, r)_{RY}, s) \ ? \ T;$
forall the $X \in T$ **do**
$\quad \text{UN ! update}(B_U, X) \ ? \ x;$
$\quad K_5 \ {+}= \ x;$
$\};$
on RN ? $\text{rpair}((Y, r)_{RY}, X)$ **do**
$\{ \ s := \text{timeOf}((Y, r)_Q);$
$T := \text{range}(Q[(Y, r)_Q], s, \infty);$
forall the $B \in T$ **do**
$\quad \text{UN ! update}(B_U, X) \ ? \ x;$
$\quad K_5 \ {+}= \ x;$
$\}$

Algorithm 5. R5: $(X, Y) \in R[r] \wedge$ $(Y, B) \in Q[r] \Rightarrow U[B] \ \sqcup= \ \{X\}$

$K_6 := x := 0;$
on RN ? $\text{yxpair}(Y_{R6}, X)$ **do**
$\{ \ \text{UN ! isMember}(\bot_U, Y_{R6}) \ ? \ b;$
if b **then**
$\quad \text{UN ! update}(\bot_U, X) \ ? \ x;$
$\quad K_6 \ {+}= \ x;$
$\}$

Algorithm 6. R6: $X \sqsubseteq \exists r.Y \Rightarrow$ $U[\bot] \ \sqcup= \ \{X \mid Y \in U[\bot]\}$

$K_7 := x := 0;$
on RN ? $\text{rpair}((Y, r)_{RY}, X)$ **do**
forall the s $\quad (\text{with } r \sqsubseteq s \in \mathcal{O}_7)$
do
$\quad \text{RN ! update}((Y, s)_{RY}, X) \ ? \ x;$
$\quad K_7 \ {+}= \ x;$

Algorithm 7. R7: $r \sqsubseteq s \Rightarrow$ $R[s] \ \sqcup= \ R[r]$

(such as Y and r) and ii) convert to key of different type but same values, such as $(Y, r)_{RY}$. This conversion, though not explicitly stated in all the algorithms listed here, is implicitly assumed.

Algorithms 1 and 2 follow directly from rules R1 and R2 respectively. Here (and in subsequently described algorithms), keys such as B_U correspond to those listed in Table 1; see also the discussion of axiom retrieval further below. K_1 (and more generally the K_i in subsequently described algorithms) are used for termination handling, as detailed towards the end of this section.

In Algorithms 3, 4 and 5, timeOf(X) returns the access timestamp up to which the values of the key A_U have been read previously. Only the subsequently added values are considered.

In the first **on** statement of Algorithm 5, the rule process R5 receives values for $(Y, r)_Q$ and B from R4. The expression R4 ! $(Q[(Y, r)_Q] \ \sqcup= \ \{B\}) \#$ shall mean that $\{B\}$ is added to $Q[(Y, r)_Q]$ and that either 1 or 0 (the latter if B was already in $Q[(Y, r)_Q]$) is returned to R4. In the second **on** statement, R5 receives values for $(Y, r)_{RY}$ and X from RN. R5 gets triggered either when an axiom $\exists r.Y \sqsubseteq B$ is newly generated by R4 or a new (X, Y) is added to $R[r]$,

$K_8 := x = 0;$
on RN **?** rpair($(Y,r)_{RY}, X$) **do** {
    forall the s, t (*with* $r \circ s \sqsubseteq t \in \mathcal{O}_8$) **do**
    | RN **!** queryX($(Y,s)_{RX}$) **?** T;
    | **forall the** $Z \in T$ **do**
    | | RN **!** update($(Z,t)_{RY}, X$) **?** x;
    | | K_8 += x;

    forall the s, t (*with* $s \circ r \sqsubseteq t \in \mathcal{O}_8$) **do**
    | RN **!** queryY($(X,s)_{RY}$) **?** T;
    | **forall the** $Z \in T$ **do**
    | | RN **!** update($(Y,t)_{RY}, Z$) **?** x;
    | | K_8 += x;

}
on RN **?** isOnLHS2(s_{R8b}) **do** { $b :=$ exists(s_{R8b}); RN **!** b };
Algorithm 8. R8: $r \circ s \sqsubseteq t \Rightarrow R[t]$ $\cup=$ $\{(X,Z) \mid (X,Y) \in R[r], (Y,Z) \in R[s]\}$

on pid **?** queryTS(X_U, ts) **do** { $T :=$ range($U[X]$, ts, ∞); pid **!** T };
on pid **?** update($X_U, \{A_1, \ldots, A_n\}$) **do** pid **!** ($U[X]$ $\cup=$ $\{A_1, \ldots, A_n\}$)#;
on R6 **?** isMember(X_U, Y) **do** R6 **!** ($Y \in U[X]$);
on R2 **?** $\sqcap(B_U, \{A_1, \ldots, A_n\})$ **do** R2 **!** ($U[B]$ $\cup=$ $U[A_1] \cap \cdots \cap U[A_n]$)#;
Algorithm 9. Process UN maintains $U[X]$, for all X.

which is what these two **on** statements represent. range($Q[(Y,r)_Q], s, \infty$) is a range operation on the set $Q[(Y,r)_Q]$ in which elements starting at timestamp s and going up to the maximum available timestamp are returned. The $Q[r]$ sets, for all roles r, are maintained by rule R5 since it is the only rule process that uses them.

In Algorithm 6 for rule process R6, a set membership request is made to UN which returns a boolean value that is stored in b. Algorithm 7 straightforwardly follows from rule R7.

In Algorithm 8 for rule process R8, whenever a new role pair (X,Y) is added to $R[r]$, it is checked whether this particular role r is part of any role chain axiom, say $p \circ q \sqsubseteq t$. The two possible cases are i) r equals p or ii) r equals q. Based on the case, the corresponding matching role pair is retrieved from RN.

Service Processes UN and RN. Each $U[X]$ is a set and the process UN handles the operations over each of the $U[X]$, for any X. There can be several such UN processes which allows them to share the load. UN associates with the elements e of set $U[X]$ a timestamp indicating when e was added to that set.

UN handles four kinds of requests, see Algorithm 9 – the first two from any arbitrary process (here named pid), the third one from R6 and the fourth from R2. The expression ($U[X]$ $\cup=$ $setS$)# stands for updating $U[X]$ and returning the number of new items added. The first type is a request from a process named pid asking for a range of elements newly added to $U[X]$ since its last such request made at time ts. It is the responsibility of the client to keep track of the previous

on R5 ? queryTS($(Y,r)_{RY}$, ts) **do** $\{T := \text{range}(R[(Y,r)_{RY}], \text{ts}, \infty); \text{R5 ! } T\};$
on R8 ? queryX($(X,r)_{RX}$) **do** R8 ! $(R[(X,r)_{RX}]);$
on R8 ? queryY($(Y,r)_{RY}$) **do** R8 ! $(R[(Y,r)_{RY}]);$
on pid ? update($(Y,r)_{RY}$, X) **do** {
    pid ! $(R[(Y,r)_{RY}] \; \cup= \; \{X\})\#;$
    R5 ! rpair($(Y,r)_{RY}$, X);
    R6 ! yxpair(Y_{R6}, X);
    R7 ! rpair($(Y,r)_{RY}$, X);
    R8 ! rpair($(Y,r)_{RY}$, X);
    R8 ! isOnLHS2(r_{R8b}) ? b;
    if b **then**
        $R[(X,r)_{RX}] \; \cup= \; \{Y\};$
}

Algorithm 10. Node RN maintains $R[r]$ sets

timestamp up to which it has read from a particular $U[X]$. The second one is a request of the form update(X_U, D) from pid. This updates U as in $U[X] \; \cup= \; D$. Elements of D are added to $U[X]$. The size increase of $U[X]$ is replied back. The third one is a membership request from R6 asking whether a particular element Y is in $U[X]$. A true or false value is given as a response. The fourth is a request from R2 to retrieve the intersection of a group of $U[A_1], \ldots, U[A_n]$.

Analogous to UN, there is an RN process that handles operations over each of the $R[r]$, for any role r, and there can be several such RN processes sharing the load. RN handles four kinds of requests, see Algorithm 10, with most of them similar to the requests handled by UN. The time stamp ts is sent in by the requester. Whenever RN receives an update message with a new role pair $((Y,r)_{RY}, X)$, it notifies the processes (R5, R6, R7, R8) that depend on $R[r]$ values. A new role pair is duplicated on the rule process R8 for further processing. This is done because it is more efficient than separate retrieval of the right role pair using a key. However, this duplication is not required in all cases: If, for a particular role r, this r does *not* appear in the second position of the chain, (e.g., in the position of q as in $p \circ q \sqsubseteq t$), then this particular $R[r]$ is *not* duplicated.

The expression $(R[(Y,r)_{RY}] \; \cup= \; \{X\})\#$ stands for updating $(R[(Y,r)_{RY}]$ and returning the number of new items, zero or one, added.

Retrieval of Axioms from the Key Value Store. We use key-value stores [5] to keep the eight parts of the ontology including the $U[X]$, the $R[r]$ and the $Q[r]$, for all concepts X and roles r. Each of these is maintained by separate service processes. The O_i processes are co-located with the R_i rule processes. We retrieve axioms from the O_i services in the **forall the ... do** statements.

Concepts and roles are mnemonic strings of the ontology and we encode them as integers. E.g., 032560 represents a concept (indicated by the last 0) whose ID is 256. The length of the ID is given in the first two positions (03 in this case).

Table 1 shows the keys and their corresponding values for axioms in the ontology. Axioms have a left hand side and a right hand side with respect to $\sqsubseteq$. In most cases, the left hand sides becomes the key and right hand side the

```
repeat
  │  Kᵢ := apply Ri on 𝒪ᵢ once;
  │  broadcast(Kᵢ);
  │  nUpdates := barrier-sum-of
  │  Kᵢ;
until nUpdates = 0;
```
Algorithm 11. Wrapper for Ri

```
repeat
  │  nUpdates :=
  │  barrier-sum-of Kᵢ;
until nUpdates = 0;
```
Algorithm 12. Wrapper for
UN and RN

value, both encoded as unsigned 64-bit integers. The paired expressions yield an integer from which the paired items can be peeled off. The hash of the concepts is used in encoding them as keys.

The choice of key is not straightforward. For example, for axioms of type $A \sqsubseteq \exists r.B$ (R3), making r as the key would lead to load imbalance since there are generally only a few roles in an ontology and comparatively many axioms of type $A \sqsubseteq \exists r.B$. On the other hand, making A as key leads to better load distribution, thus allowing several machines to work on $R[r]$.

R8 gets triggered when there is a change to either $R[r]$ or $R[s]$. In order to retrieve the exact match, i.e., given (X, Y) of $R[r]$, get (Y, Z) of $R[s]$ or vice versa, the $R[r]$ sets, for any r, have two keys $(Y, r)_{RY}$ and $(X, r)_{RX}$. The $R[r]$ sets are selectively duplicated. For the same reason, there are two keys for the role chain axioms as well.

Termination. Algorithm 11 invokes the rule process Ri on the axioms in $\mathcal{O}_i$ once i.e., Ri is applied on the axioms one time and the updates made to the $U[X]$ and $R[r]$ sets are collected in K_i (this could be 0). Notice that a K_i is associated with each Ri in Algorithms 1–3. This value is broadcast to all the other rule processes. Then it waits for similar update messages to be received from other rule processes. Barrier synchronization [1] is used in waiting for K_i from all Ri (indicated by the barrier-sum statement). If no rule process made an update, they quit; otherwise, they continue with another iteration. The same termination condition is used for processes handling $U[X]$ and $R[r]$ sets (Algorithm 12). Algorithms 11 and 12 act as wrappers around the other processes Ri, UN, RN.

This termination condition is easy to check on a single machine. But in a distributed system, termination is no longer obvious. For example, just when the process working on rule R1 is done and quits, the next moment, a process working on rule R5 might add a new B to $U[X]$. Although barrier synchronization simplifies the termination detection, it also makes several nodes wait idly. This idleness is reduced in our system using a work stealing mechanism, which is detailed in Sect. 4.

4   Optimizations

We discuss some of the efficiency optimizations we have realized in our approach.

U[X] instead of S[X]. $S[X]$ defined as $A \in S[X]$ iff $X \sqsubseteq A$ is used in the original formulation of the algorithm in [2]. We recast this as $U[X]$ defined as $A \in U[X]$ iff $A \sqsubseteq X$. Use of $U[X]$ instead of $S[X]$ makes the check $A \in S[X]$, which is required in several rules, a single read call, and thus significantly more efficient.

For example, assume that there are five concepts in the ontology, K, L, M, N and P. Suppose $K \sqcap L \sqcap M \sqsubseteq N \in \mathcal{O}$. During some iteration of the classification assume $S(K) = \{K, L, N, \top\}$, $S(L) = \{L, P, M, \top\}$, $S(M) = \{M, N, K, \top\}$, $S(N) = \{N, \top\}$, and $S(P) = \{P, K, L, M, \top\}$. Now, according to rule R2 in [2], we have to check for the presence of K, L and M in each of the five $S(X)$, where $X = K, L, M, N, P$. Since only $S(P)$ has K, L, M, we have to add N to $S(P)$.

On the other hand, we use instead $U[K] = \{K, M, P\}$, $U[L] = \{L, K, P\}$, $U[M] = \{M, L, P\}$, $U[N] = \{N, K, M, P\}$, $U[P] = \{P, L\}$. In this case, instead of checking all $U[X]$, we can compute the intersection of $U[K], U[L], U[M]$, which is $\{P\}$. So, $P \sqsubseteq N$ which is represented as $U[N] \cup= \{P\}$. In large ontologies, the number of concepts could be in the millions, but the number of conjuncts in axioms like $A_1 \sqcap \cdots \sqcap A_n \sqsubseteq B$ would be very low. So the performance is better by using $U[X]$ since set intersection needs to be performed only on a very small number of sets.

Rule Dependencies. Say rule R3 just finished processing axiom $\alpha = A \sqsubseteq \exists r.B$. If none of R1, R2, R5 or R6 make any changes to $U[A]$, R3 need not be triggered again to consider α. If and when R3 gets triggered again, it resumes from entries in $U[A]$ with a later timestamp. Thus, we reduce the number of axioms to work on in subsequent iterations.

Dynamic Load Balancing. Processing time for each of the rules, R1 to R8, varies due to the number and type of axioms. This can lead to improper load balancing where there are busy and idle nodes. We apply the well known work stealing mechanism [11], where idle nodes take (steal) work from busy nodes, thus reducing their load. Although this is a well known idea, to the best of our knowledge, there is no freely available distributed work stealing library. Although work stealing increases the communication cost, performance improvement outweighs it.

5 Evaluation

We believe that it is possible to distribute computation of the completion of OWL EL ontologies in such a way that the distributed approach ...

[(**Claim 1**)] scales to very large ontologies to finish the classification task and
[(**Claim 2**)] shows reasonable speedup in the number of nodes.

We verified these claims by implementing a prototype in Java, called DistEL, downloadable from http://github.com/raghavam/DistEL. We used Redis[2], a

---

[2] http://redis.io.

Table 2. Number of axioms, before and after classification, in ontologies.

	GO	SNOMED	SNOMEDx2	SNOMEDx3	SNOMEDx5	Traffic
Before	87,137	1,038,481	2,076,962	3,115,443	5,192,405	7,151,328
After	868,996	14,796,555	29,593,106	44,389,657	73,982,759	21,840,440

Table 3. Classification times in seconds.

Ontology	ELK	jCEL	Snorocket	Pellet	HermiT	FaCT++
GO	23.5	57.4	40.3	231.4	91.7	367.89
SNOMED	31.8	126.6	52.34	620.46	1273.7	1350.5
SNOMEDx2	77.3	OOM[a]	OOM[a]	OOM[a]	OOM[a]	OOM[a]
SNOMEDx3	OOM[a]	OOM[a]	OOM[a]	OOM[a]	OOM[a]	OOM[a]
SNOMEDx5	OOM[a]	OOM[a]	OOM[a]	OOM[a]	OOM[a]	OOM[a]
Traffic	OOM[b]	OOM[c]	OOM[c]	OOM[b]	OOM[b]	OOM[c]

OOM[a]: reasoner runs out of memory.
OOM[b]: reasoner runs out of memory during incremental classification.
OOM[c]: ontology too big for OWL API to load in memory.

key-value store, as our database. Redis was selected because it provides excellent read/write speed along with built-in support for set operations, database sharding, transactions and server-side scripting.

Since one of the use cases is *streaming* traffic data, DistEL also has support for incremental classification. It is *inherently supported*, since, in each iteration of the classification procedure, only the newly added axioms are considered and appropriate rules are applied.

We used Amazon's Elastic Cloud Compute (EC2) to run our experiments. Specifically, we used m3.xlarge instances which have 4 cores, 15 GB RAM and SSD hard disk. 5 GB was given to the JVM on each node, for all the experiments. These settings and the m3.xlarge instances were selected so as to evaluate our system on a cluster of machines with commodity hardware.

Our test data (see Table 2) comprises of biomedical ontologies GO,[3] SNOMED CT[4] and traffic data of the city of Dublin, Ireland.[5] We also duplicated 2x, 3x and 5x copies of SNOMED CT in order to test the scalability.

Traffic data reasoning is used in the diagnosis and prediction of road traffic congestions [9,10]. These tasks depend on (i) classifying any new individual from the ontology stream, and (ii) identifying their causal relationships and correlation with other streams such as city events. There is no bound on the

---

[3] http://code.google.com/p/elk-reasoner/wiki/TestOntologies.

[4] http://www.ihtsdo.org.

[5] Raw data of the traffic ontology is from http://dublinked.ie/datastore/datasets/dataset-215.php. This data is converted to $\mathcal{EL}^{++}$ ABox statements as described in [10]. The TBox statements (base ontology), along with two samples of ABox statements, are available from http://www.dropbox.com/sh/9jnutinqjl88heu/AAAi-5ot8A5fStz69Bd0VyGCa.

Table 4. Classification time (in seconds) of DistEL

Ontology	8 nodes	16 nodes	24 nodes	32 nodes	64 nodes
GO	134.49	114.66	109.46	156.04	137.31
SNOMED	544.38	435.79	407.38	386.00	444.19
SNOMEDx2	954.17	750.81	717.41	673.08	799.07
SNOMEDx3	1362.88	1007.16	960.46	928.41	1051.80
SNOMEDx5	2182.16	1537.63	1489.34	1445.30	1799.13
Traffic	60004.54	41729.54	39719.84	38696.48	34200.17

number of axioms since it is a continuous stream of traffic data. In this scenario, existing reasoners were not able to cope with the increasing velocity and volume of data. Here, we considered traffic data of *only one single day*. Data is collected every 20 seconds and we have 1441 such bursts.

Results. Table 3 has the classification times for ELK 0.4.1, jCEL 0.19.1, Snorocket 2.4.3, Pellet 2.3.0, HermiT 1.3.8 and FaCT++ 1.6.2. All the reasoners are invoked through the OWL API and ontology loading time is excluded wherever applicable.

All the reasoners ran out of memory on the SNOMEDx3, SNOMEDx5 and Traffic. On traffic data, incremental classification has been used by the reasoners that support it (ELK, Pellet, HermiT). This experiment with single machine reasoners demonstrates that a scalable solution is required to handle large ontologies.

Table 4 shows the classification times of our system as we added nodes. The cluster size need not be in multiples of 8. DistEL is able to classify all the ontologies including the largest one having close to 74 million axioms. This validates Claim 1 of our hypothesis.

Table 6 shows the speedup achieved by DistEL on SNOMED CT with increasing number of nodes. As can be seen, there is a steady increase in the speedup with increase in the number of nodes. This validates Claim 2 of our hypothesis.

Excluding GO (a small ontology), for all the other large ontologies, classification time decreases as we increase the number of nodes. On 64 nodes, we notice an increase in the runtime for all but the largest of the ontologies. This indicates that beyond a point, the advantages of the distributed approach are overshadowed by the distribution and communication overhead. However, this is not the case for largest ontology, traffic data. We believe this is also due to the axiom composition in traffic data. 75 % of traffic data axioms are in the form of $A \sqsubseteq \exists r.B$ (R3). The output of R3 serves as input to R5, R6, R7 and R8 i.e., 63 % of nodes are always busy, i.e. there are more busy nodes than idle nodes. This is not the case as such for the other ontologies.

Table 5 shows the memory (RAM) taken by Redis in MB on each of the 8 nodes for traffic data. In this case, only one node is used to collect the results

Table 5. Memory taken by **redis** on each node for traffic data

Node	MB
R1	186.72
R2	0.81
R3	257.47
R4	0.79
R5	1970
R6	380.61
R7	0.79
R8	1470.00
Result	654.53
Total	4921.72

Table 6. Speedup achieved by DistEL on SNOMED CT

Nodes	Runtime	Speedup
8	544.38	1.00
16	435.79	1.24
24	407.38	1.33
32	386.00	1.41
64	444.19	1.22

Table 7. Speed (in seconds) for simple read, write operations of 1,000,000 items using RAM and **redis**

Operation	RAM	redis
Read	0.0861	3.719
Write	0.1833	4.688

Table 8. Speedup achieved by ELK, with all the threads on one 8-core machine, on SNOMED CT

Threads	Runtime	Speedup
1	31.80	1.00
2	19.37	1.64
3	16.29	1.95
4	14.91	2.13
5	13.99	2.27
6	14.16	2.24
7	13.17	2.41
8	13.36	2.38

$(U[X]$ sets). $R[r]$ sets are spread across other nodes. As can be seen, each node takes very little memory. But on single machine reasoners, this quickly adds up for large ontologies and current reasoners hit their limit in terms of memory (see Table 3) and computational power.

Discussion. We believe DistEL is the first distributed reasoner for EL ontologies and so we cannot do a like-for-like comparison. At the risk of being skewed, the following are our observations in comparison to ELK, which is the fastest reasoner among the ones we tested on (see Table 3).

Table 8 shows the speedup of ELK on SNOMED on an 8 core machine. For DistEL, 8 nodes was the starting point. Considering that ELK is a shared memory system with all the threads on one machine, the speedup achieved by DistEL (Table 6) is very reasonable in comparison. On this basis, we can say that our design and optimization decisions (Sects. 3 and 4) are justified.

DistEL on 8 nodes for SNOMED takes 544 seconds whereas ELK takes 32 seconds. Classification is not "embarrassingly parallel", so linear speedup cannot be achieved. Since axioms are distributed across many nodes, communication is necessary. Another contributing factor is the mismatch in the speed of in-memory and Redis operations (Table 7). This is a simple experiment where 1 million integers are read and written to a Java HashMap. Similar operations were performed on a Redis hash data structure.[6] Although this is a rather simple experiment, the difference in read/write speeds in the case of RAM and Redis is quite obvious.

---

[6] The code used for this experiment is available at https://gist.github.com/raghavam/2be48a98cae31c418678.

These experiments suggest that a distributed approach should be used only on very large ontologies where the size/complexity of ontologies simply overwhelms current reasoners. Thus a distributed approach has potential benefits which are quite complementary to single machine reasoners.

6 Related Work

There is very little work implemented, evaluated and published on distributed approaches to OWL 2 EL reasoning. Three approaches to distributed reasoning were tried in [15]. Among them, two approaches – MapReduce [16] and a distributed queue version of the corresponding sequential algorithm from [4] turned out to be inefficient. In the MapReduce approach, axioms are reassigned to the machines in the cluster in each iteration. Communication between mappers and reducers cannot be finely controlled and the sort phase is not required here. In the distributed queue approach, distribution of axioms in the cluster happens randomly and hence batch processing of reads/writes from/to the database cannot be done unlike in the approach presented here. The work discussed here is an extension of the most promising one among the three approaches. Initial results of this approach were presented in [14]. Our current work expands on this in several ways, such as, support for nominals, incremental reasoning, static and dynamic load balancing, its application and evaluation over traffic data.

A distributed resolution technique for $\mathcal{EL}^+$ classification is presented in [18] without evaluation. Though not distributed, parallelization of OWL 2 EL classification has been studied in [8,17]. Classifying EL ontologies on a single machine using a database has been tried in [6].

7 Conclusion

We described DistEL, an open source distributed reasoner and presented a traffic data application where ontologies are generated from streaming data. We show that existing reasoners were not able to classify traffic data and other large ontologies. Our system on the other hand handles these large ontologies and shows good speedup with increase in the number of machines in the cluster.

Ontologies continue to grow and to hope to keep their representations in the main memory of single machines, no matter how powerful and expensive, is hardly realistic. Large farms of commodity inexpensive machines will push the field of ontology reasoning.

Next, we plan to further explore approaches to efficiently manage communication overhead, including other ontology partitioning strategies as well as alternate classification approaches and rule sets such as the one from ELK. We also plan to do performance modeling and fine-grained analysis on larger datasets, with higher number of nodes in the cluster. Alternatives to the usage of Redis including developing custom storage and data structure solutions can also be looked into.

Acknowledgement. The first two authors acknowledge support by the National Science Foundation under award 1017225 "III: Small: TROn – Tractable Reasoning with Ontologies."

References

1. Andrews, G.R.: Concurrent Programming: Principles and Practice. Benjamin/ Cummings Publishing Company (1991)
2. Baader, F., Brandt, S., Lutz, C.: Pushing the EL envelope. In: Kaelbling, L.P., Saffiotti, A. (eds.) IJCAI-05, Proceedings of the Nineteenth International Joint Conference on Artificial Intelligence, Edinburgh, Scotland, UK, July 30-August 5, 2005, pp. 364–369. AAAI (2005)
3. Baader, F., Brandt, S., Lutz, C.: Pushing the EL envelope further. In: Proceedings of the OWLED DC Workshop on OWL (2008)
4. Baader, F., Lutz, C., Suntisrivaraporn, B.: Is tractable reasoning in extensions of the description logic EL useful in practice? In: Proceedings of the 2005 International Workshop on Methods for Modalities (M4M–05) (2005)
5. Cattell, R.: Scalable SQL and NoSQL data stores. ACM SIGMOD Record **39**(4), 12–27 (2011)
6. Delaitre, V., Kazakov, Y.: Classifying ELH ontologies in SQL databases. In: Proceedings of the 5th International Workshop on OWL: Experiences and Directions (OWLED 2009), Chantilly, VA, United States, October 23–24, 2009. CEUR Workshop Proceedings, vol. 529 (2009). CEUR-WS.org
7. Hitzler, P., Krötzsch, M., Rudolph, S.: Foundations of semantic web technologies. Chapman & Hall/CRC (2010)
8. Kazakov, Y., Krötzsch, M., Simančík, F.: Concurrent classification of EL ontologies. In: Aroyo, L., Welty, C., Alani, H., Taylor, J., Bernstein, A., Kagal, L., Noy, N., Blomqvist, E. (eds.) ISWC 2011, Part I. LNCS, vol. 7031, pp. 305–320. Springer, Heidelberg (2011)
9. Lécué, F., Schumann, A., Sbodio, M.L.: Applying semantic web technologies for diagnosing road traffic congestions. In: Cudré-Mauroux, P., Heflin, J., Sirin, E., Tudorache, T., Euzenat, J., Hauswirth, M., Parreira, J.X., Hendler, J., Schreiber, G., Bernstein, A., Blomqvist, E. (eds.) ISWC 2012, Part II. LNCS, vol. 7650, pp. 114–130. Springer, Heidelberg (2012)
10. Lécué, F., Tucker, R., Bicer, V., Tommasi, P., Tallevi-Diotallevi, S., Sbodio, M.: Predicting severity of road traffic congestion using semantic web technologies. In: Presutti, V., d'Amato, C., Gandon, F., d'Aquin, M., Staab, S., Tordai, A. (eds.) ESWC 2014. LNCS, vol. 8465, pp. 611–627. Springer, Heidelberg (2014)
11. Lifflander, J., Krishnamoorthy, S., Kalé, L.V.: Work stealing and persistence-based load balancers for iterative overdecomposed applications. In: Proceedings of the 21st International Symposium on High-Performance Parallel and Distributed Computing, HPDC 2012, pp. 137–148. ACM, Delft, Netherlands (2012)
12. Ma, Y., Syamsiyah, A.: A hybrid approach to learn description logic ontology from texts. In: Posters & Demonstrations Track of the 13th International Semantic Web Conference, ISWC 2014, Riva del Garda, Italy, October 21, 2014. CEUR Workshop Proceedings, vol. 1272, pp. 421–424 (2014)
13. Motik, B., Grau, B.C., Horrocks, I., Wu, Z., Fokoue, A., Lutz, C. (eds.): OWL 2 Web ontology language profiles. In: W3C Recommendation (2012). Available at http://www.w3.org/TR/owl2-profiles/

14. Mutharaju, R., Hitzler, P., Mateti, P.: DistEL: A distributed EL+ ontology classifier. In: Liebig, T., Fokoue, A. (eds.) Proceedings of the 9th International Workshop on Scalable Semantic Web Knowledge Base Systems, Sydney, Australia. CEUR Workshop Proceedings, vol. 1046, pp. 17–32 (2013). CEUR-WS.org
15. Mutharaju, R., Hitzler, P., Mateti, P.: Distributed OWL EL reasoning: the story so far. In: Proceedings of the 10th International Workshop on Scalable Semantic Web Knowledge Base Systems, Riva Del Garda, Italy. CEUR Workshop Proceedings, vol. 1261, pp. 61–76 (2014). CEUR-WS.org
16. Mutharaju, R., Maier, F., Hitzler, P.: A MapReduce algorithm for EL+. In: Haarslev, V., Toman, D., Weddell, G. (eds.) Proceedings of the 23rd International Workshop on Description Logics (DL2010), Waterloo, Canada. CEUR Workshop Proceedings, vol. 573, pp. 464–485 (2010). CEUR-WS.org
17. Ren, Y., Pan, J.Z., Lee, K.: Parallel ABox reasoning of EL ontologies. In: Pan, J.Z., Chen, H., Kim, H.-G., Li, J., Wu, Z., Horrocks, I., Mizoguchi, R., Wu, Z. (eds.) JIST 2011. LNCS, vol. 7185, pp. 17–32. Springer, Heidelberg (2012)
18. Schlicht, A., Stuckenschmidt, H.: MapResolve. In: Rudolph, S., Gutierrez, C. (eds.) RR 2011. LNCS, vol. 6902, pp. 294–299. Springer, Heidelberg (2011)

Large Scale Rule-Based Reasoning Using a Laptop

Martin Peters[1]($\boxtimes$), Sabine Sachweh[1], and Albert Zündorf[2]

[1] Department of Computer Science, University of Applied Sciences Dortmund,
Dortmund, Germany
{martin.peters,sabine.sachweh}@fh-dortmund.de
[2] Software Engineering Research Group, Department of Computer Science
and Electrical Engineering, University of Kassel, Kassel, Germany
zuendorf@cs.uni-kassel.de

Abstract. Although recent developments have shown that it is possible to reason over large RDF datasets with billions of triples in a scalable way, the reasoning process can still be a challenging task with respect to the growing amount of available semantic data. By now, reasoner implementations that are able to process large scale datasets usually use a MapReduce based implementation that runs on a cluster of computing nodes. In this paper we address this circumstance by identifying the resource consuming parts of a reasoner process and providing a solution for a more efficient implementation in terms of memory consumption. As a basis we use a rule-based reasoner concept from our previous work. In detail, we are going to introduce an approach for a memory efficient RETE algorithm implementation. Furthermore, we introduce a compressed triple-index structure that can be used to identify duplicate triples and only needs a few bytes to represent a triple. Based on these concepts we show that it is possible to apply all RDFS rules to more than 1 billion triples on a single laptop reaching a throughput, that is comparable or even higher than state of the art MapReduce based reasoner. Thus, we show that the resources needed for large scale lightweight reasoning can massively be reduced.

Keywords: Large scale reasoning · Rule-based reasoning · GPU · RETE algorithm · Memory efficient · Triple compression

1 Introduction

Semantic data and ontologies are used in a wide area of application like biomedical applications, smart environments and of course the Semantic Web. To be able to fully explore the existing data and for example to ensure a complete result set for queries, reasoners are used to derive facts that are implicitly given by the existing data. Thus, the reasoning process is one key feature when using semantic technologies. Nevertheless, with respect to the growing amount of data we face the challenge to provide a fast, scalable and efficient reasoning process.

© Springer International Publishing Switzerland 2015
F. Gandon et al. (Eds.): ESWC 2015, LNCS 9088, pp. 104–118, 2015.
DOI: 10.1007/978-3-319-18818-8_7

This problem was already addressed by different approaches, where most of them use a MapReduce based implementation to distribute the workload to a cluster of computing nodes [1–3].

While MapReduce based reasoners have turned out to be highly scaleable and efficient when using an adequate number of computing nodes, they are also complex and costly to deploy. On the other side, most of the real world datasets that are used in the scientific community have a size varying from a few million statements to up to a few billion statements. For example the Bio2RDF[1] portal provides different biomedical datasets with a size varying from less than 100 k statements to about 5 billion statements. One other often used semantic datasets is DBpedia [4], which is derived from Wikipedia and contains about 400 million statements in the English version. The real need resulting from these observations is to be able to process datasets with up to a few billion triples on a simple and affordable hardware like a well equipped laptop or a single workstation.

In our previous work [5,6] we introduced a rule-based reasoner that makes use of the massively parallel hardware of graphic cards (GPUs). The work is based on the RETE algorithm [7], which was introduced by Charles Forgy and is a widely used algorithm to implement production systems. Unlike most of the related work in the area of fast and scalable reasoning, which implements a static semantics (the semantics describes which implicit given facts shall be derived by the reasoner), the use of the RETE algorithm allows to define the semantics using simple rules that are provided by a rule-file and thus can easily be edited. In [6] we showed that our approach scales in a linear way for simple rulesets like RDFS on datasets with up to one billion triples on a single computing node. Nevertheless, the RETE algorithm and thus our implementation was quite memory consuming which is why we had to use a server with 192 GB of memory to be able to process one billion triples. This means that even a dataset with a few hundreds of millions of statements can easily exceed the capabilities of simple hardware like a laptop.

In this paper we address the aforementioned problems and introduce new concepts for an efficient reasoning process using the GPU on limited hardware[2] in terms of available memory. In detail we provide solutions to reduce the memory consumption of the RETE algorithm as well as of the data structures that are needed to efficiently identify duplicate triples. Furthermore, for an efficient execution, we introduce an approach that generates the source code executed on the GPU during runtime with respect to the given set of rules. After a short introduction of the RETE algorithm in Sect. 2 we start with an evaluation of the memory critical parts for a reasoner implementation. We are going to point out the aforementioned aspects in more detail and give examples on how much memory is actually needed to process different datasets. Based on these findings we introduce an adapted use of the RETE algorithm in Sect. 3, which allows to make heavy use of the hard disk instead of using the main memory. Section 4

---

[1] http://bio2rdf.org/.

[2] Limited hardware in this paper is understood as single computers like laptops or workstations.

finally addresses the need to hold all triples in main memory for a fast identification of duplicate triples that get inferred during the reasoning process. To reduce the memory consumption for deduplication, a memory efficient triple representation based on different approaches like differential encoding and variable byte coding is introduced.

2   Using RETE for a Reasoner Implementation

The RETE algorithm [7] is a pattern matching algorithm which can be used to implement production systems. Because the semantics that defines which implicit given facts should be materialized during the reasoning process can often be expressed in a rule-based way, like RDF Schema (RDFS) and pD* [8], the RETE algorithm can also be used to implement a reasoner. This not only results in a semantics independent implementation, but also allows to apply application specific rules.

2.1   Basic Concept

To introduce the RETE algorithm, we use two rules from the RDFS semantics that build the ruleset for an example:

$$(?x \ ?p \ ?y) \rightarrow (?p \ \text{rdf:type} \ \text{rdf:Property}) \tag{R1}$$

$$(?x \ ?p \ ?y) \ (?p \ \text{rdfs:domain} \ ?c) \rightarrow (?x \ \text{rdf:type} \ ?c) \tag{R2}$$

The first step of the algorithm is to build a RETE network. The network consists of different nodes $n \in N$, which can be alpha or beta nodes. Each unique rule term is mapped to one alpha node. A beta node in turn always has exactly two parent nodes (which can be alpha or beta) and may connect for example the two alpha nodes that are created from the two rule terms of R_2. The resulting RETE network from R_1 and R_2 is depicted in Fig. 1.

After the network was created, the matching process starts by applying the alpha matching. This means that all input triples are matched against all alpha nodes to check if a given triple matches the condition of the alpha node. For α_1 in Fig. 1 every triple will match, because the whole rule term consists of variables

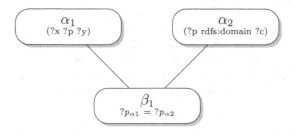

Fig. 1. RETE network of R_1 and R_2

(marked with a "?"). For α_2 a matching triple needs to have a predicate equal to "rdfs:domain". For every node in the network a working memory W is created that stores a reference to all matching triples. Based on the working memories of the alpha nodes, the beta matching can be performed. For β_1 this means that all matches that are stored in the working memory of α_1 are combined with all matches of α_2 to check if the combination of both is a match of β_1. That is the case, if the predicate of the α_1 match is equal to the subject of the α_2 match (or in other words if the elements of both matches marked with the variable ?p are equal).

Following up on the matching process, the rules can be fired to create new facts. For R_1 the working memory of α_1 is used as a fact basis because α_1 is the *terminal node* of R_1 and completely maps to the rule. Accordingly, for rule R_2, which consists of two rule terms, the working memory of β_1 is used to fire the rule. Using the new inferred facts the process starts again by iterating the new facts through the network (alpha and beta matching) and firing the rules, until no new triples are derived. For a more detailed description of how to use the RETE algorithm to infer new RDF facts we refer to [5] and [6].

2.2 Memory Consumption

After the short introduction of the RETE algorithm, next we are going to make some observations about the memory consumption of a RETE-based reasoner implementation. The following subsections introduce the major data structures that are necessary for such a reasoner implementation, while the last subsection gives a detailed overview about the particular memory consumption. We further assume that the triples are dictionary encoded, which means that each string is replaced by a numerical representation, where two identical strings are mapped to the same value. Thus, the dictionary encoding can be seen as a preprocessing of the input data which finally allows to operate on the data using more efficient numerical operations.

Triples. First of all the dictionary encoded triples need to be stored in memory for a reasoner implementation like described in [6]. The triples need to be stored in an array like data structure, where each triple can be addressed using a simple index, because this index is stored as a reference by the working memories of the RETE algorithm. Accordingly, using 8 byte datatypes for the numerical representation of one triple term, the memory footprint of the triple array is $n * 24$ byte, where n is the number of triples.

Working Memories. The second data structure is responsible to store all working memories W for the RETE algorithm. The size of the working memories highly depends on the used data- and ruleset. Furthermore, a single match in a working memory may take a single reference (the index of the referenced triple) like for alpha nodes, or multiple entries for beta nodes which always refer to multiple triples.

Table 1. Approximated memory consumption of triples and working memories for ρdf and RDFS assuming a load factor of 0.7 for the triple HashSet

Dataset	Ruleset	Total triples (n)	Triple size	Triple HashSet	Matches	References	Size of W	Total size
LUBM2000	ρdf	333.7 M	8009 MB	3814 MB	287.5 M	1022.5 M	8180 MB	20.0 GB
LUBM2000	RDFS	377.1 M	9050 MB	4310 MB	629.1 M	2119.1 M	16953 MB	30.3 GB
DBpedia	ρdf	400.6 M	9614 MB	4578 MB	123.1 M	446.7 M	3574 MB	17.8 GB
DBpedia	RDFS	475.1 M	11402 MB	5430 MB	554.1 M	1978.5 M	15828 MB	32.7 GB

Triple HashSet. Finally, a third data structure is needed that can be used to efficiently identify duplicate triples that may get inferred during the rule-firing of the reasoning process. These triples need to be rejected and should not be added to the triple list. As a minimal implementation this could be achieved by using a HashSet, where the value of the set stores the position of a triple in the triples-array. To check for a duplicate, the hash code of a new triple would be calculated to find the corresponding position in the HashSet and thus in the triple array. This would allow to check for a duplicate by one simple lookup in the HashSet and one more lookup in the triples-array (in case of hash collisions multiple lookups might be necessary). Because a HashSet should only be filled up to a specific load factor f (like 0.7) to reduce the number of collisions, an additional overhead of at least $(\frac{n}{f} - n)$ entries is necessary.

Total Memory Consumption. Table 1 gives a detailed overview of the size of the different data structures for different datasets that were processed with the ρdf [9] and RDFS ruleset. ρdf is a simplified version of the RDFS vocabulary and contains all RDFS rules with at least two rule terms. For the evaluation we used the Lehigh University Benchmark (LUBM) [10], which is an often used synthetic benchmark dataset that can easily be scaled to different sizes by defining the number of universities that shall be generated. To show the memory consumption, we generated 2000 universities which is why the dataset is called LUBM2000. Furthermore, we used DBpedia [4] (version 3.9) including all datasets of the English language as a real world dataset.

The size of the triples is directly calculated by the number of total triples (parsed and inferred). The number of matches and references are derived by an execution of the RETE algorithm using the given data- and ruleset. Note that the total memory consumption is only an approximation. Using Java, further overheads for example resulting from instantiating objects, may occur. Nevertheless, it can be seen that the total memory consumption for datasets with an input size of 270 M (LUBM2000) to 400 M (DBpedia) triples easily exceeds 17.8 to 32.7 GB, depending on the dataset and ruleset that was applied. In consequence, an adequate hardware like a workstation or server providing a large memory is necessary to be able to process datasets with the given size.

3   RETE on the GPU with an Adapted Working-Memory Concept

Modern GPUs provide a massively parallel hardware that may have much more computing power than modern CPUs if they are used in an appropriate way and are faced with a problem that can be highly parallelized. Thus, the challenge is to parallelize a problem in a way such that an optimal performance can be achieved when executed on a GPU.

The parallelization of the RETE algorithm for a rule-based reasoner implementation was already introduced in [5] and [6]. For alpha matching this means to create a thread on the GPU for every input triple (a thread or *work item* on the GPU is much more lightweight than on a CPU). Each thread is responsible for one triple and checks the match condition for every alpha node. If the triple does match an alpha node, it creates an entry in the corresponding working memory. During beta matching, all matches of one parent node ($m_{parent1} \in W_{parent1}$) need to be matched against all matches of the second parent node ($m_{parent2} \in W_{parent2}$). Therefore, a thread for every entry in $W_{parent1}$ is created that iterates through all matches in $W_{parent2}$ and checks if the combination of both matches meet the conditions of the beta node. This operation is performed for every beta node in the RETE network.

One disadvantage of the RETE algorithm is the high memory usage, which is caused by maintaining the working memories. Considering large datasets, a working memory can easily contain millions of entries (in the case of beta nodes the number of entries in a working memory can easily exceed the number of triples within the input dataset) that are references to the actual data. One way to reduce the amount of used memory would be to swap the working memories to the hard disk. Because the working memories are only accessed in bulks and no access to single entries is required, this would not cause much overhead in terms of load time. Nevertheless, this approach would still require to hold all triples in the main memory to be able to resolve the references contained in the working memories before the data can be processed. This is because for processing not only the references, but also the triples itself are needed.

Based on the previous considerations and in contrast to our previous work, an approach is needed that allows to fully swap the matches to the hard disk without the need to hold any additional data like the triples in main memory. To achieve this, we extend the use of the working memories to not hold a reference to the corresponding triples, but the matching elements of the triples itself. For α_2 from Fig. 1 for example the working memory would contain all values that correspond to the variables $?p$ and $?c$ from the matching triples. The working memory of β_1 in turn would hold four elements, which correspond to $?x, ?p, ?y$ and $?c$. Note that neither static elements of matches (like the rdfs:domain of α_2) nor double elements like the $?p$ in W_{β_1} are stored. A comparison of both approaches using working memories storing references and using working memories storing the actual data is depicted in Fig. 2.

While the resulting working memories will need more storage space than working memories storing only references, they can completely be swapped to

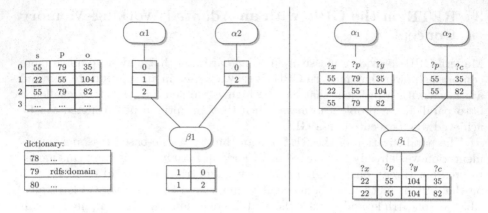

Fig. 2. RETE network with working memories using references (left) and RETE network with working memories using the full data excluding static data or recurring variables (right), for a dictionary encoded dataset

the hard disk. For a further processing, they can be read in blocks and directly be handed over to the corresponding task without the need to resolve any references. This allows to further minimize the usage of the main memory.

4   Compressed Triple-Index Structure

In the previous section we showed how the memory usage of the RETE algorithm can significantly be reduced by reorganizing the working memories and making use of the hard disk. One more problem that needs to be addressed is the memory consumption of the HashSet that is used in combination with the triples array to identify duplicate triples. To underline the importance of an efficient duplicate-lookup, Table 2 gives an overview of the number of triples that get inferred including the duplicates for the already known datasets. As can be seen, many of the derived triples are duplicates (up to 98.8 %). To be able to handle such an amount of lookups in an efficient way (more than 2 billion for DBpedia and RDFS), an in memory solution is necessary. To be able to reduce the memory

Table 2. Number of interred triples

Dataset	Ruleset	Derived triples	Unique triples	Duplicate triples	Percentage of duplicates
LUBM2000	ρdf	529.9 M	66.7 M	463.2 M	87.4 %
LUBM2000	RDFS	1813.6 M	110.1 M	1703.5 M	93.9 %
DBpedia	ρdf	580.1 M	7.0 M	573.1 M	98.8 %
DBpedia	RDFS	2263.6 M	81.5 M	2182.1 M	96.4 %

usage and to apply a compression to the triples needed for deduplication, one
has to consider that each triple must only be compressed separately from other
triples. This is necessary to be able to access the compressed version of each
triple without decompressing other triples.

For triple compression we propose an index structure that stores the existing
triples without loss of precision but with a much lower memory footprint. To
do so, we make use of *vertical partitioning* [11], which is based on the fact that
many datasets are only described by a few predicates. For each predicate in a
dataset, a two column table is created that stores the subjects in the first column
and the objects in the second column. Considering that the LUBM dataset only
uses 32 predicates, this already results in a reduction of memory consumption
of about 33 % (neglecting the overhead that is created by organizing the triples
in 32 two-column tables instead of one three-column table).

For a further compression, we apply different well known techniques to the
remaining two numerical values of a triple. First of all we try to reduce the
amount of information to be encoded by checking if applying differential encoding
could preserve memory. Differential encoding means for example to not store
(s, o), but $(s, s - o)$. Making sure that $(s > o)$ and $((s - o) < o)$, the resulting
value can be compressed more efficiently in the following steps. To avoid negative
values resulting from differential encoding, we also have to make sure that the
smaller value is subtracted from the bigger one. Finally, we map the subject as
well as the object to a left value v_l and right value v_r in a way that the right
value is always the smaller one, independently of the fact if differential encoding
was applied or not. The calculation of v_l and v_r is described in Algorithm 1.

Algorithm 1. Calculation of v_l and v_r

    Data: subject: s, object: o
    Result: value left: v_l, value right: v_r
    $v_l = s$;
    $v_r = o$;
    if *(s > o)* then
        if *((s - o) < o)* then
            $v_r = $ s - o;
    else
        if *((o - s) < s)* then
            $v_r = $ o - s;
            $v_l = $ o;
        else
            $v_l = $ o;
            $v_r = $ s;

The reason why we may reorder the subject and object in a way that the
smaller value always becomes v_r is because we use variable byte encoding to

store v_r. Variable byte encoding means to encode the data in units of bytes, where the lower-order seven bits are used to store the data and the eighth bit is used as an indicator of the end of a data value [12]: In particular the eighth bit is equal to 1 if the end of a data value is reached and 0 otherwise. The values $[0, 2^7)$ for example can be encoded using a single byte, where the first seven bits store the binary representation of the value and the eighth bit is equal to 1 to indicate the end of the value. Accordingly, the values in $[2^7, 2^{14})$ can be stored using two bytes, where the eighth bit of the first byte is equal to 0 and the eighth bit of the second byte is set to 1. The remaining 14 bits are used to encode the actual data.

Because we only store two numerical values in a row, we only have to encode v_r like described before. After reading a 1 at the eighth position of a byte, the start of the second value can explicitly be identified while the end of that value is defined by the remaining bytes. Thus, both values v_l and v_r can be encoded together in a single byte array that is explicitly sized to the amount of data that is needed to encode both values. To ensure that the encoded order of s and o is preserved as well as the fact if differential encoding was applied, two more bits are used, which are the most significant bits in the byte array.

For an example consider $s = 622$ and $o = 35$. Because $((s-o) > o)$, we do not apply differential encoding and get $v_l = s = 622$ and $v_r = o = 35$. The binary representation of 35 is 0010 0011, which results in 1010 0011 after applying variable byte encoding (the first bit was set to 1). The binary representation of 622 is 0000 0010 0110 1110, where the two most significant bits are used to point out if differential encoding was applied and if the order of the encoding of the subject as a left value and the object as a right value was preserved. Because we did not apply differential encoding, the most significant bit remains 0 and because we preserved the order of the s and o, the second most significant bit remains 0, too. Finally we can concatenate both binary values to

$$00 \underbrace{00\ 0010\ 0110\ 1110}_{v_l}\ 1\underbrace{010\ 0011}_{v_r}$$

which can be encoded using three bytes. Assuming we are using 8 byte data types to dictionary encode the triple terms and we apply the aforementioned compression of vertical partitioning, differential encoding and variable byte encoding, we are able to reduce the amount of used data for the triple from the previous example from 24 byte to 3 byte without loss of precision. Nevertheless, the compression rate depends on the efficiency of vertical partitioning for a given dataset as well as on the respective value for s and o.

Based on the introduced triple-compression, a fast and memory efficient triple-index structure can be build to identify duplicate triples, which will be the only data structure that needs be be kept in memory during the reasoning process. For every predicate a HashSet can be created that stores the compressed value of s and o instead of storing for example two 8 byte values. This solution still allows to efficiently search for a duplicate triple by using hashing, but uses much less memory than the approach described in Sect. 2.2. Detailed information about the compression rate for different datasets is given in the next section.

5   Evaluation

In the following section we are going to evaluate the proposed concepts of an adapted working-memory for the RETE algorithm as well as the compressed index structure and give a detailed view on different aspects. Finally we are going to show how the concepts perform together in our reasoner implementation on different datasets.

5.1   Implementation

To evaluate our concepts, we used the reasoner implementation presented in [6] and adapted it to the new concepts and requirements. The reasoner is implemented in Java and uses OpenCL[3], the open standard for parallel programming of heterogeneous systems. It allows to program heterogeneous devices like GPUs and supports a wide range of parallelism. Furthermore, we use the jocl-library[4] as OpenCL Java bindings.

To allow an efficient execution of application code on the GPU, it is important to minimize memory access as well as to minimize the use of control flow structures like loops and if-then-else statements. To achieve these requirements, we also integrated a novel approach that generates the source code that is executed on the GPU during runtime. Based on the rule file that is given as an input when the reasoner execution is started, we generate the code that is executed on the GPU specific to the rules. This allows us to provide dedicated methods for example for each beta node that can be adapted to explicitly meet the needs of a single beta node and ensures to only load the data from memory that is needed. Furthermore, dictionary encoded values can directly be embedded to the code. This allows for example to check a triple to meet the conditions from α_2 in Fig. 1 (a triple predicate needs to be equal to "rdfs:domain") by directly compare a predicate to the numerical value of 79 instead of a variable (in Fig. 2 the dictionary encoded value for "rdfs:domain" is 79).

5.2   Datasets and Environment

Basically we use three different datasets. The Lehigh University Benchmark (LUBM) [10] was already mentioned before. It is widely used for reasoner evaluation and thus gives a good reference for a comparison. We generate datasets ranging from 1000 universities up to 8000 universities, which consist of more than 1 billion triples. In addition to the synthetic dataset, we also use the complete English version of DBpedia (version 3.9) as well as the real world Comparative Toxicogenomics Database (CTD) [13], which describes cross-species chemical-gene/protein interactions and chemical- and gene-disease relationships. All three datasets are used with the complete RDFS ruleset as it is defined by the W3C[5] as well as with the RDFS subset ρdf [9].

---

[3] http://www.khronos.org/opencl/.

[4] http://www.jocl.org/.

[5] http://www.w3.org/TR/2004/REC-rdf-mt-20040210/#RDFSRules.

Table 3. Reasoning results for ρdf and RDFS on a laptop

Dataset	Input triples	ρdf total triples	ρdf reasoning	ρdf throughput	RDFS total triples	RDFS reasoning	RDFS throughput
LUBM1000	134 M	167 M	41.6 s	4017 ktps	189 M	114.1 s	1653 ktps
LUBM2000	267 M	334 M	98.4 s	3391 ktps	377 M	287.6 s	1312 ktps
LUBM4000	534 M	668 M	296.9 s	2249 ktps	754 M	758.3 s	996 ktps
LUBM8000	1068 M	1335 M	716.7 s	1863 ktps	1509 M	1824.8 s	827 ktps
DBPedia	394 M	401 M	409.9 s	1154 ktps	475 M	2886.6 s	165 ktps
CTD	335 M	358 M	70.2 s	5104 ktps	358 M	306.8 s	1176 ktps

The evaluation is performed using an Apple MacBook Retina laptop from 2012 equipped with 16GB of memory, a 2.3 GHz Intel Core i7 processor, a 256GB SSD hard disk and a NVIDIA GeForce GT 650M graphic card with 1024MB of memory. All tests were performed five times and the average time of the whole reasoning process including materialization and deduplication is given.

5.3 Reasoning

The reasoning results in Table 3 show a decreasing throughput for both rulesets on the LUBM datasets. The highest throughput of 4017 kilo triples per second (ktps) is reached for LUBM1000 and the ρdf ruleset, which decreases to 1863 ktps for LUBM8000. The decrease is caused by different factors. First of all, we noticed that with a growing number of triples also the Java virtual machine garbage collector activity increases, which causes delays in the reasoner execution. Furthermore, the complexity of the beta-calculation of the RETE algorithm may grow in an exponential way for some rules, depending on the dataset. With respect to the used hardware, this further reduced the throughput.

Compared to ρdf, RDFS is not more complex, but causes more alpha nodes to be created during the RETE execution and materializes much more triples. This results in a more computation intensive execution and a lower throughput. Nevertheless, for RDFS we were able to reach a throughput ranging from 165 ktps (DBpedia) to 1653 ktps (LUBM1000). Furthermore, the full RDFS ruleset was successfully applied to more than 1 billion triples resulting in a total of 1.5 billion unique statements on a single laptop.

The memory consumption caused by the triple-index structure that is necessary to allow an efficient deduplication during the reasoning process is given in Table 4. It can be seen that the memory consumption per triple is between 5.94 and 7.45 byte, depending on the dataset. Thus, in comparison to a 24 byte triple representation we reached a compression of up to 75 %, which finally enables us to reason on large scale datasets like LUBM8000 on a hardware with only 16GB of memory. Because the triple information are kept in a hash structure, Table 4 gives also the used bytes per triple with overhead, which also considers the used memory for free entries in the HashSets. Depending on the reached density of values in the HashSets the overhead may differ in size.

Table 4. Memory usage of the triple-index structure after applying ρdf reasoning

Dataset	Predicates	Byte/triple	Byte/triple with overhead	Total memory
LUBM1000	32	6.04	9.71	1620 MB
LUBM2000	32	6.11	9.29	3098 MB
LUBM4000	32	5.69	8.26	5513 MB
LUBM8000	32	6.16	8.80	11748 MB
DBpedia	53139	7.45	12.81	5129 MB
CTD	43	5.94	9.36	3137 MB

Furthermore, Table 4 gives the number of predicates that are used within a dataset. As can be seen, for LUBM as well as for CTD the number of predicates is quite small such that the overhead when the vertical partitioning is applied is infinitesimal small. Even for DBpedia, where the number of predicates is much higher, the overhead that is caused by about 53k predicates is less than 8 MB for vertical partitioning, assuming that a single predicate causes an overhead of about 150 byte in our implementation.

Overall, the proposed concepts including the adapted RETE algorithm, which allows to completely swap the working memories to the hard disk, allow to reduce the main-memory consumption by more than 84 %. While using the naive approach for storing triple information we approximately used 20.0 GB of memory for applying ρdf Reasoning on LUBM2000. Using the new concepts, we only need about 3.1 GB for the compressed triple-index structure.

6   Related Work and Discussion

RDF compression has been investigated in the related work under several aspects. In [14] and [15] a binary representations for RDF graphs is used for a fast and memory efficient query answering. While query answering is not the purpose of the introduced triple-index structure, our goal was to efficiently identify duplicate triples, which can be done by checking the existence of a single (and unique) value. An OWL2 RL reasoner called RDFox that completely works in main memory is proposed in [16]. While the parallelization is applied similar to our work by creating multiple threads (one for each CPU core) that handle all triples one after the other, they report a memory consumption of at most 80 bytes per triple for creating the necessary index structures, which is about 10 times more than our implementation needs, but also serves a different purpose.

Large scale reasoning has recently been addressed in several works. While they may differ in the ontology language they implement, most of them have in common that they use a MapReduce implementation to handle the large amount of data and to be able to scale the architecture [1–3,17]. In [17] the authors introduce WebPie, a MapReduce based implementation for RDFS and pD* reasoning.

They show that their architecture is highly scalable and is able to reason over 100 billion (LUBM) triples. On 64 computing nodes they reach a throughput of 481 ktps for 1 billion triples and a maximum throughput of 2125 ktps for 20 billion triples. The lower throughput for the smaller datasets is founded in the overhead that is introduced by the platform. While our implementation is not able to scale like WebPie, it is still able to reason over 1 billion triples and reaches a throughput of 1863 ktps on a laptop, which is nearly 4 times faster than WebPie for the same dataset. For smaller datasets our approach even reaches a throughput of 4017 ktps, which is almost twice as much as the maximum throughput reported in [17]. In [18] a parallel reasoner implementation is proposed that does not use MapReduce, but also distributes the workload to multiple computing nodes. The largest dataset used in [18] was a LUBM10000/4 (10.000 universities were generated, but only every fourth instance triple was used) with about 350M triples. The dataset was processed on 64 computing nodes each running four processes (each process was running on its own processor core). They reached a throughput of 1185 ktps (of input triples), but did not apply any deduplication.

A reasoner implementation that uses only a single computing node is described in [19]. The authors also use the massively parallel architecture of a GPU to apply the ρdf ruleset. Unlike our implementation, the work in [19] does not support user defined rules and is only able to process datasets that fit into the main memory of a single GPU. A high throughput for reasoning with the ρdf rules on a single machine is also reported for DynamiTE [20], which is a stream reasoner that was also evaluated by applying a full materialization. The reasoner makes use of multicore processors and reaches an input processing ratio of about 227 ktps for the LUBM8000 benchmark.

In comparison to our previous work [6] (using 192 GB memory and two GPUs reaching a maximum throughput of 2700 ktps for LUBM1000 and the ρdf rules), we were able to reduce the required hardware resources and increase the throughput at the same time. This was mainly possible by eliminating the need to resolve the references of working memories and by providing a faster implementation of the code that gets executed on the GPU by generating the code based on the given rules, leading to an overall increased throughput.

The presented concepts in this paper provide a holistic approach for large scale reasoning on limited hardware. Even though the hardware can be scaled in terms of using multiple GPUs, our approach does not allow to scale like a MapReduce based implementation mainly because the main memory is still a limiting factor. The throughput that is achieved depends on the structure of the dataset as well as on the ruleset and is particular high if the number of beta-matches that need to be computed is small. Thus, using more expressive and complex semantics, a MapReduce based approach can be more efficient due to the higher computation power. While we used only a single GPU from a laptop, the influence of these factors can be further reduced when multiple and more powerful GPUs are used, like described in [6]. Nevertheless, using lightweight ontology languages or appropriate user-defined rules, the proposed approach allows to reason on large datasets achieving a throughput that is comparable or even higher than state of the art reasoner reach on a cluster of computing nodes.

7   Conclusion

To the best of our knowledge, this work is the first one that shows a reasoner implementation that is able to apply the RDFS rules to a dataset with more than 1 billion triples using only a single laptop. This is possible by using a massively parallel execution in combination with a substantially reduction of the memory consumption of the whole reasoner process. To do so, we first introduced a concept to adapt the RETE algorithm by changing the way, working memories are used. Using the new concept, working memories can completely be stored to the hard disk without the need to hold all triples in memory. An efficient execution of the algorithm based on the new concepts was achieved by generating the source code that gets executed on the massively parallel hardware of a GPU based on the provided rules during runtime. This novel concept of applying a generative approach for the execution on parallel hardware allows to apply optimizations like reducing control flow structures and reducing memory access.

Furthermore, we introduced a compressed triple-index structure that allows to efficiently identify duplicate triples that get inferred during the reasoning process. The new triple-index structure has a memory footprint of about 25 % of the original dictionary encoded triple representation, which allows to keep much more triples for deduplication in memory. To achieve this, we used the vertical partitioning approach known from triple compression and combined it with different methods of integer compression and adapted them to our needs. Finally, we were able to process large scale datasets on a simple hardware without the need of a costly and time consuming setup of multiple computing nodes running in a cluster. While we did the evaluation using a laptop, a workstation equipped with more memory and a more powerful GPU (or even multiple GPUs) should be able to process even larger datasets.

After showing that GPUs are suitable to perform massively parallel reasoning on large datasets, our future work will include the investigation of adapting our approach to not only perform reasoning on static data, but also on data streams. Furthermore, an extension of the expressiveness that is supported by our rule-based reasoner will be part of the future work.

References

1. Urbani, J., Kotoulas, S., Massen, J., van Harmelen, F., Bal, H.: WebPIE: A web-scale parallel inference engine using MapReduce. Science, Services and Agents on the World Wide Web, Web Semantics (2012)
2. Liu, C., Qi, G., Wang, H., Yu, Y.: Reasoning with large scale ontologies in fuzzy pD* using MapReduce. Comput. Intell. Mag. **7**(2), 54–66 (2012)
3. Zhou, Z., Qi, G., Liu, C., Hitzler, P., Mutharaju, R.: Reasoning with Fuzzy-EL+ ontologies using MapReduce. In: Proceedings of the 20th European Conference on Artificial Intelligence, pp. 933–934. ECAI (2012)
4. Lehmann, J., Isele, R., Jakob, M., Jentzsch, A., Kontokostas, D., Mendes, P.N., Hellmann, S., Morsey, M., van Kleef, P., Auer, S., Bizer, C.: DBpedia - A Large-scale. Multilingual Knowledge Base Extracted from Wikipedia, Semantic Web Journal (2014)

5. Peters, M., Brink, C., Sachweh, S., Zündorf, A.: Rule-based reasoning on massively parallel hardware. In: 9th International Workshop on Scalable Semantic Web Knowledge Base Systems, pp. 33–49 (2013)
6. Peters, M., Brink, C., Sachweh, S., Zündorf, A.: scaling parallel rule-based reasoning. In: Presutti, V., d'Amato, C., Gandon, F., d'Aquin, M., Staab, S., Tordai, A. (eds.) ESWC 2014. LNCS, vol. 8465, pp. 270–285. Springer, Heidelberg (2014)
7. Forgy, C.L.: Rete: A fast algorithm for the many pattern/many object pattern match problem. In: Expert Systems, pp. 324–341 (1990)
8. ter Horst, H.J.: Completeness, decidability and complexity of entailment for RDF Schema and a semantic extension involving the OWL vocabulary. Web Semant. Sci. Serv. Agents World Wide Web 3(2–3), 79–115 (2005)
9. Muñoz, S., Pérez, J., Gutierrez, C.: Minimal deductive systems for RDF. In: Franconi, E., Kifer, M., May, W. (eds.) ESWC 2007. LNCS, vol. 4519, pp. 53–67. Springer, Heidelberg (2007)
10. Guo, Y., Pan, Z., Heflin, J.: LUBM: A benchmark for OWL knowledge base systems. Web Semant. 3(2–3), 158–182 (2005)
11. Abadi, D.J., Marcus, A., Madden, S.R., Hollenbach, K.: Scalable semantic web data management using vertical partitioning. In: Proceedings of the 33rd International Conference on Very Large Data Bases, pp. 411–422. VLDB Endowment (2007)
12. Lemire, D., Boytsov, L.: Decoding billions of integers per second through vectorization. In: Practice and Experience, Software (2013)
13. Mattingly, C.J., Rosenstein, M.C., Davis, A.P.P., Colby, G.T., Forrest, J.N., Boyer, J.L.: The comparative toxicogenomics database: a cross-species resource for building chemical-gene interaction networks. Toxicol. Sci.: Off. J Soc. Toxicol. 92(2), 587–595 (2006)
14. Álvarez-García, S., Brisaboa, N.R., Fernández, J.D., Martínez-Prieto, M.A.: Compressed k2-triples for Full-In-Memory RDF engines. In: Association for Information Systems Conference (AMCIS) (2011)
15. Atre, M., Chaoji, V., Zaki, M.J., Hendler, J.A.: Matrix "bit" loaded: A scalable lightweight join query processor for RDF data. In: Proceedings of the 19th International Conference on World Wide Web, pp. 41–50. ACM (2010)
16. Motik, B., Nenov, Y., Piro, R., Horrocks, I., Olteanu, D.: Parallel OWL 2 RL materialisation in centralised, Main-Memory RDF systems. In: Informal Proceedings of the 27th International Workshop on Description, pp. 311–323 (2014)
17. Urbani, J., Kotoulas, S., Maassen, J., van Harmelen, F., Bal, H.: OWL Reasoning with WebPIE: Calculating the Closure of 100 Billion Triples. In: Aroyo, L., Antoniou, G., Hyvönen, E., ten Teije, A., Stuckenschmidt, H., Cabral, L., Tudorache, T. (eds.) ESWC 2010, Part I. LNCS, vol. 6088, pp. 213–227. Springer, Heidelberg (2010)
18. Weaver, J., Hendler, J.A.: Parallel materialization of the finite RDFS closure for hundreds of millions of triples. In: Bernstein, A., Karger, D.R., Heath, T., Feigenbaum, L., Maynard, D., Motta, E., Thirunarayan, K. (eds.) ISWC 2009. LNCS, vol. 5823, pp. 682–697. Springer, Heidelberg (2009)
19. Heino, N., Pan, J.Z.: RDFS reasoning on massively parallel hardware. In: Cudré-Mauroux, P., Heflin, J., Sirin, E., Tudorache, T., Euzenat, J., Hauswirth, M., Parreira, J.X., Hendler, J., Schreiber, G., Bernstein, A., Blomqvist, E. (eds.) ISWC 2012, Part I. LNCS, vol. 7649, pp. 133–148. Springer, Heidelberg (2012)
20. Urbani, J., Margara, A., Jacobs, C., van Harmelen, F., Bal, H.: DynamiTE: parallel materialization of dynamic RDF data. In: Alani, H., Kagal, L., Fokoue, A., Groth, P., Biemann, C., Parreira, J.X., Aroyo, L., Noy, N., Welty, C., Janowicz, K. (eds.) ISWC 2013, Part I. LNCS, vol. 8218, pp. 657–672. Springer, Heidelberg (2013)

RDF Digest: Efficient Summarization
of RDF/S KBs

Georgia Troullinou$^{(\boxtimes)}$, Haridimos Kondylakis, Evangelia Daskalaki,
and Dimitris Plexousakis

Institute of Computer Science, FORTH, N. Plastira 100, Heraklion, Greece
{troulin,kondylak,eva,dp}@ics.forth.gr

Abstract. The exponential growth of the web and the extended use of semantic web technologies has brought to the fore the need for quick understanding, flexible exploration and selection of complex web documents and schemas. To this direction, ontology summarization aspires to produce an abridged version of the original ontology that highlights its most representative concepts. In this paper, we present *RDF Digest*, a novel platform that automatically produces summaries of RDF/S Knowledge Bases (KBs). A summary is a valid RDFS document/graph that includes the most representative concepts of the schema adapted to the corresponding instances. To construct this graph, our algorithm exploits the semantics and the structure of the schema and the distribution of the corresponding data/instances. The performed preliminary evaluation demonstrates the benefits of our approach and the considerable advantages gained.

Keywords: Semantic summaries · RDF/S documents/graphs · Schema summary

1 Introduction

The vision of Semantic Web is the creation of a common framework that allows data to be shared and reused across application, enterprise, and community boundaries. Ontologies are playing an important role in the development and deployment of the Semantic Web since they model the structure of knowledge and try to organize information for enhancing the understanding of the contextual meaning of data. Lately, ontologies have been used in database integration [1], obtaining promising results, for example in the fields of biomedicine and bioinformatics, but also as means for publishing large volumes of interlinked data from which we can retrieve abundant knowledge. The Linked Open Data cloud for example contains more than 62 billion triples (as of January 2014).

Given the explosive growth in both data size and schema complexity, data sources are becoming increasingly difficult to understand and use. They often have extremely complex schemas which are difficult to comprehend, limiting the exploration and the exploitation potential of the information they contain. Moreover, regarding ontology engineering, ontology understanding is a key element for further development and reuse. For example, a user/ontology engineer, in order to formulate queries, has to examine carefully the entire schema in order to identify the interesting elements.

© Springer International Publishing Switzerland 2015
F. Gandon et al. (Eds.): ESWC 2015, LNCS 9088, pp. 119–134, 2015.
DOI: 10.1007/978-3-319-18818-8_8

Besides schema, the data contained in the different sources should also drive the identification of the relevant items. Currently, an efficient and effective way to understand the content of each source without examining all data is still a blind spot.

As a result, there is now, more than ever, an increasing need to develop methods and tools in order to facilitate the understanding and exploration of various data sources. Approaches for ontology modularization [2] and partitioning [3] try to minimize and partition ontologies for better understanding but without preserving the important information. Other works focus on providing overviews on the aforementioned ontologies [5–8, 13] maintaining however the more important ontology elements. Such an overview can also be provided by means of an ontology summary. Ontology summarization [7] is defined as the process of *distilling knowledge from an ontology in order to produce an abridged version*. While summaries are useful, creating a "good" summary is a non-trivial task. A summary should be concise, yet it needs to convey enough information to enable a decent understanding of the original schema. Moreover, the summarization should be coherent and provide an extensive coverage of the entire ontology (multiple subjects of the ontology). So far, although a reasonable number of research works tried to address the problem of summarization from different angles, a solution that simultaneously exploits the semantics provided by the schemas and the data instances is still missing.

In this paper, we focus on RDF/S ontologies and demonstrate an efficient and effective method to automatically create high-quality summaries. A summary constitutes a "valid" sub-schema providing an overview of the original schema considering also the available data. Specifically the contributions of this paper are the following:

- We present RDF Digest, a novel platform that automatically produces RDF schema summaries that highlight the most representative concepts of the schema adapted to the corresponding data instances.
- In order to construct these summarized graphs our system exploits (a) the *semantics* of the schema, (b) the *structure* of the RDFS graph and (c) the *distribution* of the corresponding *data/instances* in order to identify and select the most important and representative elements of the ontology.
- To identify the most important nodes we define the notion of *relevance* based on the *relative cardinality* and the *in/out degree centrality* of a node. Moreover, to ensure that our summary selects the most representative nodes of the entire schema we use the notion of *coverage*. Those two notions are combined in an algorithm that finally produces a "valid" summary schema out of the original schema.
- Finally, our experimental evaluation show the feasibility of our approach and the considerable advantages gained.

To our knowledge, this is the first approach that, in the context of ontology, combines both schema and data instance information to produce a high-quality summary graph.

The rest of the paper is organized as follows. Section 2 introduces the formal framework of our solution and Sect. 3 describes the metrics used in our algorithms to determine the nodes and paths to be included in the summary. Section 4 presents our algorithm and Sect. 5 describes the evaluation conducted. Section 6 presents related work and finally, Sect. 7 concludes the paper.

2 Preliminaries

Schema summarization aims to highlight the most representative concepts of a schema, preserving "important" information and reducing the size and the complexity of the schema [8]. Despite the significance of the problem there is still no universally accepted measurement on the importance of nodes in an RDF/S graph. In our approach, we try to elicit this information from (a) the *structure* of the graph, (b) the *semantics* of the schema and (c) the *distribution* of the corresponding *data*. Our goal is to produce a simple and expressive graph that presents an overview of the schema and also provides an intuition about the corresponding stored data.

Specifically, in this paper we focus on RDF/S KBs, as RDF/S is the de facto standard for publishing and representing data on the web [9]. The representation of knowledge in RDF is based on triples of the form of *(subject predicate object)*. RDF datasets have attached semantics through RDF Schemas [10]. RDF Schema is a vocabulary description language that includes a set of inference rules used to generate new, implicit triples from explicit ones. Note that in our case the inference is implemented only at the RDF schema level to avoid overloading the super-classes with instances. Each RDF schema S defines a finite set of class names C and property names P. Properties are defined using class names or literal types, so that, for each property p, the domain of property p, i.e. *domain(p)*, is a class and the range of p, i.e. *range(p)*, is either a class or a literal. The classes and the properties of a schema are uniquely identified by the names in $N = C \cup P$ (possibly using namespace URIs for disambiguation). Moreover, we denote by $H = (N, \prec)$, a hierarchy of class and property names. H is well-formed if $\prec$ is a smallest partial ordering such that: if $p1$, $p2 \in P$ and $p1 \prec p2$, then *domain(p1)* $\prec$ *domain(p2)* and *range(p1)* $\prec$ *range(p2)*. In this paper, we ignore unnamed resources, also called blank nodes. Moreover, for the representation of the RDF/S documents we will use a graph data model first introduced by Karvounarakis et al. [11]. Formally, we define an RDF schema graph as:

Definition 1 (RDF schema graph): An *RDF schema graph* S is a labeled directed graph $S = (V, E, \lambda_c, \lambda_p, H)$ depicting a collection of triples $T_S = (s, p, o) = URIs$ x $URIs$ x $URIs$ where:

- V represents a set of nodes.
- E represents a set of edges of the form $e(v_i, v_j)$ with $v_i, v_j \in V$ and direction from v_i to v_j. Given that, e, v_i, v_j correspond to a property p, the *domain(p)* and the *range(p)*, respectively. The label of e is $\lambda_P(e) = p$, where $p \in P$.
- H is a well-formed hierarchy of a class and property names $H = (N, \prec)$
- λ_c: is a value function that assigns to each node $v \in V$ in S a class name (URI) from C. Such as $\lambda_c(v) = c, c \in C$.
- λ_p: is a value function that assigns to each edge $e \in E$ in S one property name from P. Such as $\lambda_p(e) = p, p \in P$.

Moreover, we assume a function κ_P that characterizes the type of a property p among the *standard RDF properties* (e.g. "rdfs:subClassOf", "rdfs:label") and the *user defined properties*. RDF schema provides also *inference semantics*, which is of two types, namely *structural inference* (provided mainly by the transitivity of subsumption relations) and *type inference* (provided by the typing system, e.g., if p is a property, the triple $\{p, type, property\}$ can be inferred). The RDF schema, which contains all triples that are either explicit or can be inferred from explicit triples in an RDF graph S (using *both* types of inference), is called the *closure* of S and is denoted by $Cl(S)$. An *RDFS KB S* is an RDF schema graph, which is closed with respect to *type inference*, i.e., it contains all the triples that can be inferred from S using type inference. We also assume that the RDF/S KBs are *valid*. The validity constraints that we consider concern *type uniqueness,* i.e., each resource has a unique type, the *acyclicity* of the *subClassOf* and *subPropertyOf* relations and that the subject and object of the instance of some property should be correctly classified under the domain and range of the property, respectively. The full list of the validity constraints we adopt is contained in [12]. Those constraints are enforced to enable unique and non-ambiguous detection of the summary. Next, we define an RDF instance graph.

Definition 2 (RDF instance graph): *An RDF instance graph I*, is a labeled directed graph $I = (N, R, \tau_v, \tau_c, \tau_p)$, depicting a collection of triples $T_I = (s, p, o) = URIs \times URIs \times (URIs \cup Literals)$ where:

- N is a finite set of nodes.
- R is a finite set of directed edges between nodes, $r(n_i, n_j)$ with $n_i, n_j \in N$ and direction from n_i to n_j.
- τ_v: is a value function that assigns to each node $n \in N$ in I a *URI* or a *literal*.
- τ_p: is a value function that correlates edges of S to edges of I. (such that $\tau_p(r) = \lambda_p(e)$). For each edge r in R going from a node n_i to a node n_j, τ_p returns a property name $p \in P$, where values n_i and n_j belongs to the interpretation of p: $domain(p) = \lambda_c(v_i) = \tau_c(n_i)$, $range(p) = \lambda_c(v_j) = \tau_c(n_j)$
- τ_c: is a labeling function that captures *rdfs:type* declarations, linking the RDF instance graph I with the RDF schema graph S. The τ_c returns either the name of a class $c \in C$ or the value of the container type (literal). Based on terms of RDFS, the $n \in N$ is an instance of class $\lambda_c(v)$ (or the n is type class $\lambda_c(v)$), where $v \in V$.

Now, as an example, consider the CIDOC-CRM[1] ontology part shown in Fig. 1 used to describe the process of information acquisition and the involved actors in cultural heritage. Although this is only a short example, we have 27 classes and many properties that need to be examined in order to understand the schema. In blue color, we can see the summarized graph as it is produced by our method. Obviously, it is easier to understand schema content using only the summary graph since it contains the most important nodes out of the initial graph.

3 Assessment Measures

In this section, we present the properties that a sub-graph of our schema is required to have in order to be considered a high-quality summary. Specifically, we are interested in important schema nodes that can describe efficiently the whole schema and reflect the distribution of the data instances at the same time. To capture these properties, we

---

[1] http://www.cidoc-crm.org/official_release_cidoc.html.

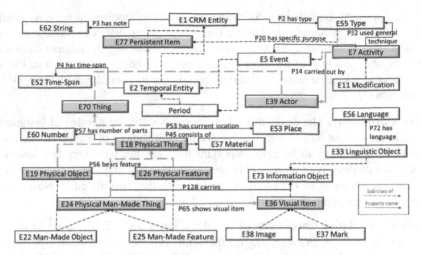

Fig. 1. Example of RDFS knowledge base and the corresponding summary graph (in blue) (Color figure online)

use the notions of *relevance* and *coverage* which are further analyzed below. Relevance is used for identifying the most important nodes and coverage is used for extracting nodes/paths, which cover the whole spectrum of the RDF/S document.

3.1 Relevance

Importance has a broad range of meanings and this has led to many different algorithms that try to identify it. Originating from the analysis of social graphs, in the domain of Semantic Web, algorithms adapting the well-known PageRank [4, 5] have been proposed to determine the importance of elements in an XML document. For RDF/S, other approaches use measures such as the *degree centrality*, the *between-ness* and the eigenvector centrality *(weighted Page Rank and HITS)* [7], adjusting them to the specific features of RDF/S or they try to adapt *the degree* centrality and *the closeness* [8] to calculate the relevance of a node.

In our case, we believe that the importance of a node should describe how well a node could represent a part of a KB (its area) giving an intuition about its neighborhood. Intuitively, nodes with many connections in a schema graph will have a high importance. However, since RDF/S KBs might contain huge amounts of data, the latter data should also be involved when trying to estimate a node's importance.

Consider for example the node *"E37 Mark"* and the node *"E38 Image"* in the schema graph of Fig. 1. The two nodes have the same number of connections and they are connected to the same node *"E18 Physical Thing"*. Now assume that the node *"E38 Image"* has the double number of instances. Due to the same number of connections, the two nodes may be considered equal but essentially the *"E38 Image"* is more important for the specific RDF/S KB, due to the higher number of instances it contains. Obviously, the number of instances of the class - that a node corresponds to - is a valuable piece of information for identifying its importance.

In our approach, initially, we determine how central/important a node is, judging from the instances it contains (*relative cardinality*). After that, we estimate the centrality of a node in the entire KB (*in/out centrality*), combining the relative cardinality with the number and type of the incoming and outgoing edges in the schema. Finally, the *relevance* of a schema node is defined by comparing its centrality with the centrality of its neighbors.

Relative Cardinality. The cardinality of a schema node is the number of instances it contains in the current RDF/S KB. If there are many instances of a specific class, then that class is more likely to be more important than another with very few instances. Similarly, the cardinality of an edge between two nodes in a graph is the number of the corresponding instances of the nodes connected with that specific edge. Now we can formally define the relative cardinality of an edge.

Definition 3 (Relative Cardinality of an edge). Let $S = (V, E, \lambda_c, \lambda_p, H)$ be an RDF schema graph and $I = (N, R, \tau_v, \tau_c, \tau_p)$ the RDF instance graph of S. The *relative cardinality* of an edge $e(v_i, v_j)$ in S, where $e \in E$ and $v_i, v_j \in V$, i.e. the $RC(e(v_i, v_j))$, (remember that $\lambda_p(e) = p$) is the following:

- *In case of available instances*: The number of specific instance connections $r(n_i, n_j)$ $\in R$, $n_i, n_j \in N$, where $\tau_p(r) = \lambda_p(e)$, $\tau_c(n_i) = \lambda_c(v_i)$ and $\tau_c(n_j) = \lambda_c(v_j)$, divided by the total number of the connections ($r_k (n_i, n_a)$, $r_t (n_b, n_j) \in R$, where $n_a, n_b \in N$) of the instances of these two nodes v_i, v_j. A constant value a is added to this number.
- *In case of no available instances*: A constant value a.

$$RC\big(e\big(v_i, v_j\big)\big) = \begin{cases} \alpha + \frac{\left|\left\{r_m\left(n_i, n_j\right)\right\}\right|}{\left|\{r_k(n_i, n_a)\}\right| + \left|\left\{r_t\left(n_b, n_j\right)\right\}\right|}, & r_m\left(n_i, n_j\right) \in R \\ \alpha & r_m\left(n_i, n_j\right) \notin R \end{cases} \tag{1}$$

The constant value a has the value 1/#*connections* where #*connections* is the number of connections $e(v_i, v_j)$ that exist in the schema. Our algorithm is flexible enough to focus on the available instances when they exist, and if they are not available, it only exploits the semantics and the structure of the schema.

In/Out Centrality. In order to combine the notion of centrality in the schema and the distribution of the corresponding dataset, we define the *in/out centrality*, exploiting also the relative cardinality of nodes and edges. The *in/out* centrality is an adaptation of *the degree centrality* [7]. In an undirected graph, the *degree centrality* is defined as the number of links incident upon a node. In a directed graph however, as in our case, the degree centrality is distinguished to the *in-degree centrality* and the *out-degree centrality*.

The *in-centrality* of a schema node v, i.e. $C_{in}(v)$, is the sum of the weighted relative cardinalities of the incoming edges. The weights, that are used, are experimentally defined and depend on the types of the properties as they are identified by the function κ_P. As already mentioned, there are two types of properties, the standard RDF types (for example "rdfs:subClassOf", "rdfs:label", "rdfs:comment") and the user defined properties (for example the "P45 consists of", "P128 carries" shown in Fig. 1). We would like to consider as more important the latter, whereas the former are not considered to be equally important. This is partly because the user-defined properties correlate classes, each exposing the connectivity of the entire schema, in contrast to the hierarchical RDF/S properties.

Definition 4 (in(out)-centrality of a node). Let S be an RDF schema graph and m be the number of the incoming (outgoing) edges $e(v_i, v)$ $(e(v, v_i))$ of a node v in S. The $C_{in}(v)$ $(C_{out}(v))$ of v *is the sum of the relative cardinality* of the edges $e(v_i, v)$ ($e(v, v_i)$), multiplied by a weight w_p according to the type of edge.

$$C_{in}(v) = \sum_1^m RC(v_i, v) * w_p \quad C_{out}(v) = \sum_1^m RC(v, v_i) * w_p \tag{2}$$

Relevance. The notion of centrality, as defined previously, is a measure that can give us an intuition about how central a schema node in an RDF/S KB is. However, its importance should be determined considering also the centrality of the other nodes as well. Consider for example, the nodes *"E60 Number"* and *"E56 Language"* shown in Fig. 1. They have the same number of incoming and outgoing edges and assume that they have the same number of instances as well. However the *"E60 Number"* is connected to more important elements compared to the *"E56 Language"*. For example, the node *"E18 Physical Thing"* is directly connected to the *"E60 Number"* and has many other connections and instances. Since the *"E18 Physical Thing"* is obviously a very important node, the *"E60 Number"* is a less appropriate node to represent this area in a summary. On the other hand, the *"E56 Language"* is more relevant than the *"E60 Number"* to represent the specific part of the graph since its neighbors do not have such a high relevance.

To achieve the aforementioned goal, the *relevance* of a node is affected by its surrounding neighbors and more specifically by the number and the connections of its adjacent nodes. To be more precise, the formula estimates the (number of) connections of a node and this number is compared to the connections of its neighbors.

Definition 5 (Relevance of a node). Let S be an RDF schema graph, np_{in} be the number of incoming nodes v_i connected to v with $e_a(v_i, v)$, and the np_{out} be the number of outgoing nodes v_j connected to v with $e_b(v, v_j)$. The *relevance* of v, i.e. *Relevance(v)*, is the sum of *in* and *out centrality* of v multiplied by the corresponding number of nodes, divided by the sum of *out-centrality* of the incoming nodes v_i and the *in-centrality* of the outgoing nodes v_j.

$$Relevance(v) = \frac{C_{in}(v) * np_{in} + C_{out}(v) * np_{out}}{\sum_1^{np_{in}} (C_{out}(v_i)) + \sum_1^{np_{out}} (C_{in}(v_j))} \tag{3}$$

Obviously, the relevance of a schema node in an RDF/S KB is determined by both its connectivity in the schema and the cardinality of the instances. Thus, the number of instances of a node is of vital importance in the assessment procedure. When the data distribution significantly changes, the focus of the entire data source is shifted as well, and as a result, the relevance of the nodes changes. In addition, the importance of each node is compared to the other nodes in the specific area/neighborhood in order to identify the most relevant nodes that can represent all the concepts of a graph.

3.2   Coverage

After having estimated the relevance of each node in the schema graph, it is now time to focus on the paths that exist in a schema graph. The idea behind this is that we are not interested in extracting isolated nodes, but most importantly we want to produce valid sub-schema graphs. So the chosen paths should be selected having in mind to collect the more relevant nodes by minimizing the overlaps.

Definition 6 (Path $v_s \longrightarrow v_i$). A *path* from v_s to v_i, i.e. $v_s \longrightarrow v_i$, is the finite sequence of edges, which connect a sequence of nodes, starting from the node v_s and ending in the node v_i.

As a consequence, the relative cardinality of a path is the sum of relative cardinalities of the individual edges. Moreover, the length of a path, i.e. $d_{v_s \longrightarrow v_i}$, is the number of the edges that exist in that path.

In our running example of Fig. 1, the nodes *"E53 Place"* and *"E57 Material"* are directly connected to the node *"E18 Physical Thing"* and have similar connectivity in the graph. The node *"E18 Physical Thing"* has a high relevance in the graph and as a consequence a great probability to be included in the summary. However, although the *"E18 Physical Thing"* can be located only in one *"E53 Place"*, it might consist of many *"E57 Material"*. As a consequence, the relative cardinality of the path from the *"E18 Physical Thing"* to the *"E57 Material"* (*RC(e("E18 Physical Thing", "E57 Material")))* will be higher than the relative cardinality of the path form *"E18 Physical Thing"* to *"E53 Place"*. This means that the path from *"E18 Physical Thing"* to *"E57 Material"* is more representative to be included in the summary than the path from *"E18 Physical Thing"* to *"E53 Place"*. This is because the *"E18 Physical Thing"* already covers the *"E53 Place"* - a physical thing is located only in one place.

In the above example, we dealt with paths of length one. However, the paths included in the summary should contain the most relevant schema nodes which represent the remaining nodes, achieving the digest of the entire content of the RDF/S KB. As a consequence, the main criteria to estimate the level of coverage of a specific path are: (a) the relevance of each node contained in the path, (b) its relevant instances in the dataset and (c) the length of the path. As a result, similar to the approach of Yu et al. [5], we define the notion of *coverage* as follows:

Definition 7 (Coverage of a path). Let S be an RDF schema graph and I be an instance of S. The *coverage* of a path $v_s \longrightarrow v_i$, i.e. the *Coverage*$(v_s \longrightarrow v_i)$, is derived by the sum of the *Relevance* of the sequential nodes v_j contained between the nodes v_s and v_i, multiplied by the *relative cardinality* of each edge $e(v_{j-1}, v_j)$ contained in the path. The result is divided by the length of the path in order to penalize the longer paths.

$$Coverage(v_s \rightarrow v_i) = \frac{1}{d_{n_s \rightarrow n_i}} * \sum_{j=2}^{d_{n_s \rightarrow n_i}} \left(Relevance(v_j) * RC\left(e\left(v_{j-1}, v_j\right)\right)\right) \qquad (4)$$

The above formula assesses a path and provides a metric to identify the degree of the contained relevant nodes and how this path can represent (a part of) the original graph without overlapping issues. Our goal is to select the schema nodes that are more relevant while avoiding having nodes (or paths) in the summary which cover one another. The highest the coverage of a path, the more relevant this path is considered in representing the original graph or part of it.

4   Construction of RDF Summary

Now that we have explained all formulas required in order to calculate the relevance and the coverage of the elements of an RDF/S KB, we can describe the algorithm for constructing the RDF schema summary, shown in Fig. 2. Below we explain in more detail each of the steps of the algorithm.

Algorithm 1. *ComputeRDFSchemaSummary(B, n)*
Input: An RDF/S Knowledge Base *B*, *n* the number of the requested nodes
Output: An RDF Schema Summary *S*
  1. Let *V* be the set of nodes in *B*
  2. *for each* node $v_i \in V$
  3. $r_i := calculate\_relevance(B, v_i)$
  4. *TOP* := *select_top_nodes(B, r, n)*
  5. *ADJ* := *identify_adjacent_nodes(TOP)*
  6. *S* := *construct_subgraph(ADJ)*
  7. if *ADJ* <> TOP *then*
  8.   *for each* node $v_i \in$ TOP/ADJ
  9.   *ADJ* := *ADJ* - v_i
 10.   *TOP* := *TOP* $\cup v_i$
 11.   S := S $\cup$ *identify_path_with_max_coverage(B, S, v_i)*
 12. Return *S*

Fig. 2. The algorithm for computing the RDF Schema Summary

In the beginning (lines 2–3) the relevance of each schema node is assessed. Specifically, a value is assigned to each node in the RDF graph according to the *Relevance* measure (calculated using the Definition 5). Having calculated the relevance of each node we would like to get the *n* most important ones to be further elaborated (line 4). Usually *n* is defined by the user. However, if it is left blank this function automatically retrieves a specific percentage of the nodes in the schema (usually 30–40 %). The schema nodes in *TOP* are the structural components to build the schema summary. However, these nodes might not be directly connected in the RDF schema. Since our goal is to create a valid summary schema, we should find the appropriate paths that connect the non-adjacent nodes of the selected collection (lines 5–6). If all nodes are adjacent then the schema summary S is the connected subgraph containing these nodes produced using the *construct_subgraph* function. Usually however, the nodes included in the *TOP* set are not adjacent. Nevertheless, they should also be included in the produced summary. The goal is to find paths, which connect these nodes with the already connected ones (lines 7–11). However, we are not looking for random paths but the ones maximizing the coverage. In other words, we select the paths which contain the most relevant nodes according to the coverage measure as described in the previous section. Note that the selection of the nodes to complete the subgraph is done out of the initial RDF schema graph, since the summary should be coherent with the original schema. Moreover, in this selection, other nodes might be also included in the summary in order to connect the most important ones.

When the algorithm finishes its execution, the selected sub-graph S, according to the previous steps, will be the RDF schema summary. In addition, the result of our algorithm for a specific input is unique. If the data distribution changes, the summary is also changed in order to provide an updated view on the corresponding schema and the updated data instances.

5   Evaluation

The algorithm described in this paper was implemented in the RDF Digest prototype. We developed the RDF Digest using JAVA and a beta version of the platform is currently available as a service online.[2] A user can upload the RDF/S document, he would like to be summarized and he is optionally able to define the expected length of the summary as well. When the input is submitted, the RDF/S document is preprocessed by computing the corresponding RDF/S KB. The result is stored in a Virtuoso Instance (http://virtuoso.openlinksw.com/) which enables efficient data access. Then, the algorithm described in Sect. 4 runs and the results are presented to the user.

To evaluate our system, we selected four ontologies: the BIOSPHERE ontology,[3] the Financial ontology,[4] the Aktors Portal ontology[5] and the CIDOC-CRM[6] ontology. BIOSPHERE (87 classes, 3 properties) models information in the domain of bioinformatics, the Financial ontology (188 classes, 4 properties) incudes classes and properties in the financial domain and the Aktors Portal ontology (247 classes, 327 properties) describes an academic computer science community. Finally, the CIDOC-CRM (82 classes, 539 properties) provides definitions and a formal structure for cultural heritage documentation. The first three ontologies have been previously used to evaluate relevant works on RDF/S summarization, so we can compare our results with

---

[2] http://www.ics.forth.gr/isl/rdf-digest.

[3] http://www.aiai.ed.ac.uk/project/biosphere/downloads.html.

[4] http://www.larflast.bas.bg/ontology.

[5] http://www.daml.org/ontologies/322.

[6] http://www.cidoc-crm.org/official_release_cidoc.html.

these works. More specifically our algorithms are compared to the algorithms proposed by Peroni et al. [13] and by Queiroz-Sousa et al. [8]. Peroni et al. automatically define the key concepts in an ontology, combining cognitive principles, lexical and topological measurements. Queiroz-Sousa et al. on the other hand propose an algorithm that produces an ontology summary in two manners: automatically using relevance measures and semi-automatically, using the users' opinion in addition. Moreover, we tried but could not get access to [7] to perform the same experiments.

Note that in order to compare our results with the aforementioned works we used only the RDF schema graph of each ontology since the other approaches do not consider instances. To demonstrate a scenario where instances are available we evaluated our algorithms using CIDOC-CRM with instances as well. Those instances are real instances retrieving from a real database. Thus, the evaluation is more objective rather than the creation of synthetic data which may not correspond to a real situation. To proceed with the evaluation of the first three ontologies, summaries were generated by eight human experts. These human experts had a good experience in ontology engineering [13] and were familiar with the aforementioned ontologies. The experts were requested to select up to 20 concepts which were considered as the most representative of each ontology. The generated reference summaries were also used by Queiroz-Sousa et al. [8] in their evaluation. The level of agreement among experts for the three ontologies had a mean value of 74 % [13] meaning that the experts did not entirely agree on their selections. For CIDOC-CRM, the CIDOC Core[7] ontology was proposed by experts as the core subset of the ontology aimed to represent the basic concepts of CIDOC-CRM into a simple ontology of 29 classes. We used this subset as the reference summary of CIDOC-CRM.

Metrics like precision, recall and F-measure, used by the previous works [8, 13–15], are limited in exhibiting the added value of a summarization system because of the "disagreement due to synonymy" [16] meaning that they fail to identify closeness with the ideal result when the results are not exactly the same with the reference ones. On the other hand, content based metrics compute the similarity between two summaries in a more reliable way [7]. In the same spirit, Maedche et al. [17] argue that ontologies can be compared at two different levels: lexical and conceptual. At the lexical level, the classes and the properties of the ontology are compared lexicographically, whereas at the conceptual level the taxonomic structures and the relations in the ontology are compared. To this direction, we use the following similarity metric $Sim(S, A)$ in order to define the level of agreement between an automatically produced summary S and a reference summary A.

$$Sim(S,A) = \frac{|K_{match}| + 0.6 * \sum_{1}^{|Ksub|} \frac{1}{depth} + 0.3 * \sum_{1}^{|K\,super|} \frac{1}{depth}}{|K|} \quad (5)$$

More precisely, K is set of classes contained in A, $K_{match} \subseteq K$, is the set of classes appearing also in S, $K_{sub} \subseteq K - K_{match} / K_{super} \subseteq K - K_{match}$ (where $K_{sub} \cap K_{super} = \varnothing$) is

---

[7] http://www.cidoc-crm.org/technical_papers.html.

the set of classes having sub-classes/super-classes in K and *depth* is the distance between the ideal class and the class identified by the summary. Note that the above formalism assesses the existence of sub-classes and the super-classes of S in A with a different percentage. The idea behind that is that the super-classes, since they generalize their sub-classes, are assessed to have a higher weight than the sub-classes. Consequently, the effectiveness of a summarization system is calculated by the average number of the similarity values between the summaries produced by the system and the set of the corresponding experts' summaries. In our case, each summary contains approximately the same number of classes according to the experts' selections, 20 classes for the BIOSPHERE, the Financial, and the Aktros Portal ontologies, and 29 classes for the CIDOC-CRM ontology. Our evaluation compares the similarity – as defined previously- between the summaries produced by our algorithm and the reference summaries used by the other works and the results are shown in Fig. 3.

As we can observe, the summaries generated by our system appear to be quite similar to what experts have produced, in most of the cases showing better results than other similar systems. Specifically, the summary of the CIDOC-CRM ontology presents the highest similarity. On the other hand, the results of our system have a good similarity with the experts in the cases of the BIOSPHERE, the Financial, and the Aktros Portal ontologies. We have to note that whereas the reference summaries on these three ontologies contain only isolated classes in the case of CIDOC-CRM the CIDOC Core contains an entire sub-ontology similar to the result we get from our system. This is also the reason for the better results that appear for CIDOC-CRM. Obviously, when instances are used the similarity of the result summary highly increases and in our case we reach a similarity level of 0.965 which demonstrates the added value of our approach.

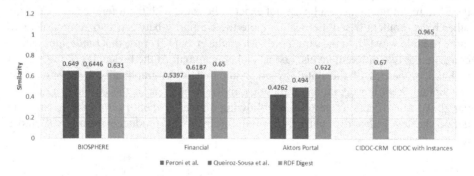

Fig. 3. A comparative result of ontology summarization methods

Moreover, our system seems to react better when it deals with dense schemas, which are confirmed also by the results shown in Fig. 3. As we can see in the image the Aktors Portal and the CIDOC-CRM ontologies have better results compared to the BIOSPHERE and the Financial ontologies which contain only hierarchical relationships. However, this observation is to be further verified with more experiments.

Furthermore, during our experiments, we observed that as the ontology size and as a consequence the complexity increases, the similarity of the summaries produced by the RDF Digest is improved. This is also depicted in Fig. 4 showing that the similarity increases as the number of properties and classes in the ontology increases as well.

Finally, to test the efficiency of our system, we measured the average time to produce the summaries using the aforementioned ontologies. We have to note that the experiments run on a 64 bit Windows 8.1 system with 4 GB of main memory and a Core i5 Intel CPU running at 1.6 GHz. The results are shown in Fig. 5. As we can observe, our algorithms produce the requested summary quite fast and require at most 33 sec. Moreover, it is obvious that the larger and the more complex the ontology, the more time it requires to calculate the corresponding RDF schema summary which is reasonable as it has to calculate the relevance for more nodes and has to perform more path constructions for calculating the coverage.

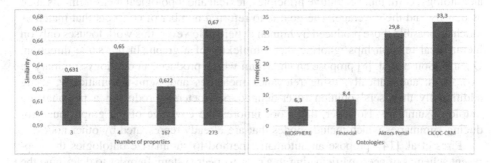

Fig. 4. The similarity as the number of properties increase (CIDOC-CRM)

Fig. 5. Execution times for producing the RDF schema summary

6 Related Work

As already stated, various techniques have been developed for the identification of summaries over different types of schemas and data. The first works on schema summarization focused on conceptual [18] and XML schemas [4, 5]. Yu et al. [5] affirm that, while schema structure is of vital importance in summarization, data distribution often provides important knowledge that improves the summary quality. Another work [4] on XML Schemas derives a summary of the schema and then transforms the instances through summary functions. Other works focus on summarizing meta-data and large graphs. For example, Hasan [15] proposes a method to summarize the explanation of the related metadata over a set of Linked Data, based on user specified filtering criteria and producing rankings of explanation statements. One of the latest approaches that deals with graph summaries [19] examines only the structure of an undirected graph, neglecting any additional information (such as semantics). The goal of this work is to generate a summary graph that minimizes the loss of information out of the original graph. However, our system differs from the above in terms of both goals and techniques. Although we reuse interesting ideas from these works, our approach is focused towards RDF/S KBs expressing richer semantics than conceptual schemas and XML.

More closely related works to our data model and approach are [7, 8, 13]. Zhang et al. [7] propose a method for ontology summarization based on the RDF Sentence Graph. The notion of RDF Sentence is the basic unit for the summarization and corresponds to a combination of a set of RDF statements. The creation of a sentence graph is customized by the domain experts who provide as input the length of the summary and their navigation preferences to create the RDF Sentence graph. The importance of each RDF sentence is assessed by determining its centrality in the graph. In addition, the authors compare five different centrality measures (degree, between-ness, PageRank, HITS), showing that weighted in-degree centrality and some eigen-vector-based centralities are better. However, in this approach, the coverage of the entire graph is not considered and many important nodes may be left out.

On the other hand, Peroni et al. [13] try to identify automatically the key concepts in an ontology, combining cognitive principles, lexical and topological measurements such as density and the coverage. The goal is to return a number of concepts that match as much as possible those produced by human experts. However, this work focuses only on hierarchical relationships ignoring the complexity of a graph. In the same direction, Queiroz-Sousa et al. [8] propose an algorithm which produces an ontology summary in two ways: automatically, using relevance measures and, semi-automatically, using additionally the users' opinion (user-defined parameters), producing a personalized ontology summary. However, this work ignores the coverage of the graph thus pro-ducing summaries which include nodes that are already represented by other nodes.

Pires et al. [14], propose an automatic method to summarize ontologies that rep-resent schemas of peers participating in a peer-to-peer system. In order to determine the relevance of a concept, a combination two measures, *centrality* and *frequency* is used.

Although in most of works the importance of each node is calculated considering each node in isolation, in our work, we assess its importance in comparison with its neighbors, producing a better result. Moreover, many of these works (such as [8, 15]) do not consider the coverage of each node and end up collecting nodes already rep-resented by other nodes. In addition, some of these works (e.g. [8, 13]) provide a list of the more important nodes, whereas others [7, 8, 14] and our approach, create a valid summary schema. Finally, other approaches try to navigate on the Linked Data Cloud using summaries of interlinked datasets [20]. However, our work is the only one that automatically produces a summary graph, exploiting the data instances and essentially provides an overview of the entire KB (both schema and instances).

7   Conclusions and Future Work

In this paper, we present a novel method that automatically produces summaries of RDF/S KBs. To achieve that, our algorithm exploits the semantics and structure of the schema and the distribution of the data by combining all these information using the relevance and the coverage properties. The performed evaluation verifies the feasibility of our solution and demonstrates the advantages gained by efficiently producing good summaries. Compared to other similar systems, our approach produces better results, further improved by exploiting knowledge about the instance distribution. Moreover, although most of the systems just select nodes or paths as the result summary, our result is a valid RDFS graph/document out of the initial RDF schema graph and can be used for query answering as well.

We plan to extend our implementation in order to produce the schema summary of large schemas in the Linked Data Cloud. Instead of relying on reference summaries for the evaluation of the automatically produced summaries, an interesting idea is to check if these summaries are able to answer the most common queries formulated by the users. Another interesting topic would be to extend our approach for OWL ontologies. As the size and the complexity of schemas and data increase, ontology summarization is becoming more and more important and several challenges arise.

Acknowledgments. This work was partially supported by the EU projects DIACHRON (FP7-601043), iManageCancer (H2020-643529), MyHealthAvatar (FP7-600929) and EURECA (FP7-288048).

References

1. Calvanese, D., De Giacomo, G., Lembo, D., Lenzerini, M., Poggi, A., Rodriguez-Muro, M., Rosati, R.: Ontologies and databases: the *DL-Lite* Approach. In: Tessaris, S., Franconi, E., Eiter, T., Gutierrez, C., Handschuh, S., Rousset, M.-C., Schmidt, R.A. (eds.) Reasoning Web 2009. LNCS, vol. 5689, pp. 255–356. Springer, Heidelberg (2009)
2. Stuckenschmidt, H., Parent, C., Spaccapietra, S. (eds.): Modular Ontologies. LNCS, vol. 5445. Springer, Heidelberg (2009)
3. Stuckenschmidt, H., Klein, M.: structure-based partitioning of large concept hierarchies. In: McIlraith, S.A., Plexousakis, D., van Harmelen, F. (eds.) ISWC 2004. LNCS, vol. 3298, pp. 289–303. Springer, Heidelberg (2004)
4. Marciniak, J.: XML schema and data summarization. In: Rutkowski, L., Scherer, R., Tadeusiewicz, R., Zadeh, L.A., Zurada, J.M. (eds.) ICAISC 2010, Part II. LNCS, vol. 6114, pp. 556–565. Springer, Heidelberg (2010)
5. Yu, C., Jagadish, H.V.: Schema summarization. In: VLDB, pp. 319–330 (2006)
6. Graves, A., Adali, S., Hendler, J.: A method to rank nodes in an RDF graph. In: ISWC (2008)
7. Zhang, X., Cheng, G., Qu, Y.: Ontology summarization based on RDF sentence graph. In: WWW, pp. 707–716 (2007)
8. Queiroz-Sousa, P.O., Salgado, A.C., Pires, C.E.: A method for building personalized ontology summaries. J. Inf. Data Manage. **4**(3), 236 (2013)
9. Schmachtenberg, M., Bizer, C., Paulheim H.: State of the LOD Cloud, November 2014. http://linkeddatacatalog.dws.informatik.uni-mannheim.de/state/
10. RDF Schema 1.1, November 2014. http://www.w3.org/TR/rdf-schema/
11. Karvounarakis, G., Alexaki, S., Christophides, V., Plexousakis, D., Scholl, M.: RQL: a declarative query language for RDF. In: WWW, pp. 592–603 (2002)
12. Serfiotis, G., Koffina, I., Christophides, V., Tannen, V.: Containment and minimization of RDF/S query patterns. In: ISWC, pp. 607–623 (2005)
13. Peroni, S., Motta, E., d'Aquin, M.: Identifying key concepts in an ontology, through the integration of cognitive principles with statistical and topological measures. In: Domingue, J., Anutariya, C. (eds.) ASWC 2008. LNCS, vol. 5367, pp. 242–256. Springer, Heidelberg (2008)

14. Pires, C.E., Sousa, P., Kedad, Z., Salgado, A.C.: Summarizing ontology-based schemas in PDMS. In: Data Engineering Workshops (ICDEW), pp. 239–244 (2010)
15. Hasan, R.: Generating and summarizing explanations for linked data. In: ESWC, pp. 473–487 (2014)
16. Donaway, R.L., Drummey, K.W., Mather, L.A.: A comparison of rankings produced by summarization evaluation measures. In: NAACL-ANLP Workshop, pp. 69–78 (2000)
17. Maedche, A., Staab, S.: Measuring similarity between ontologies. In: Gómez-Pérez, A., Benjamins, V. (eds.) EKAW 2002. LNCS (LNAI), vol. 2473, pp. 251–263. Springer, Heidelberg (2002)
18. Castano, S., De Antonellis, V., Fugini, M.G., Pernici, B.: Conceptual schema analysis: techniques and applications. TODS **23**(3), 286–333 (1998)
19. Liu, X., Tian, Y., He, Q., Lee, W.C., McPherson, J.: Distributed graph summarization. In: CIKM, pp. 799–808 (2014)
20. Khatchadourian, S., Consens, M.P.: ExpLOD: summary-based exploration of interlinking and RDF Usage in the linked open data cloud. In: Aroyo, L., Antoniou, G., Hyvönen, E., ten Teije, A., Stuckenschmidt, H., Cabral, L., Tudorache, T. (eds.) ESWC 2010, Part II. LNCS, vol. 6089, pp. 272–287. Springer, Heidelberg (2010)

Linked Data

A Comparison of Data Structures to Manage URIs on the Web of Data

Ruslan Mavlyutov, Marcin Wylot(✉), and Philippe Cudré-Mauroux

eXascale Infolab, University of Fribourg, Fribourg, Switzerland
{ruslan.mavlyutov,marcin.wylot,philippe.cudre-mauroux}@unifr.ch

Abstract. Uniform Resource Identifiers (URIs) are one of the corner stones of the Web; They are also exceedingly important on the Web of data, since RDF graphs and Linked Data both heavily rely on URIs to uniquely identify and connect entities. Due to their hierarchical structure and their string serialization, sets of related URIs typically contain a high degree of redundant information and are systematically dictionary-compressed or encoded at the back-end (e.g., in the triple store). The paper represents, to the best of our knowledge, the first systematic comparison of the most common data structures used to encode URI data. We evaluate a series of data structures in term of their read/write performance and memory consumption.

1 Introduction

Uniform Resource Identifiers (URIs) are essential on the Web of data, since RDF graphs heavily rely on them to uniquely identify and connect online entities. Due to their hierarchical structure and serialization, sets of related URIs typically contain a high degree of redundant information and are very often dictionary-compressed or encoded at the back-end (e.g., in the triple store). In our own Diplodocus system [18–20], for instance, every URI is encoded as an integer number during the loading phase, and almost all subsequent operations are applied on the fixed-size, compact, and encoded version rather than on the variable-size original string. After resolving a query, though, we have to translate those ID back to their original values to display results to the client.

Working on Diplodocus, we observed that a significant part of query execution times can be consumed by encoding and decoding IDs assigned to URIS back and forth. For this reason, we present in the following and to the best of our knowledge the first systematic comparison of the most common data structures and hash functions used to encode URI data. Although related studies on data structures or hash-tables were already performed [15][1,2], they were not using the very large sets of URIs we typically operate on in the context of Semantic Web applications. Semantic Web URIs, for instance, are not standard strings, since

---

[1] http://attractivechaos.wordpress.com/2008/08/28/comparison-of-hash-table-libraries/.

[2] http://incise.org/hash-table-benchmarks.html.

© Springer International Publishing Switzerland 2015
F. Gandon et al. (Eds.): ESWC 2015, LNCS 9088, pp. 137–151, 2015.
DOI: 10.1007/978-3-319-18818-8_9

they exhibit some very unique properties including longer lengths, high overlaps between related URIs, and hierarchical structures. Also, previous studies focused mostly on a few specific operations (like insertion, random updates or deletions), without giving a clear picture of the most important operations on URIs in our context (e.g., repeated look-ups or memory impact, etc.).

This paper analyzes the performance of various data structures from a pragmatic point of view. Therefore we formulate the following research question: **Which data structure performs best when encoding a URI dictionary for a triplestore?** In our analysis we take various factors into account like data size, data type (synthetic or real world data), and specific use-cases, e.g., read-mostly or read/write workloads.

The rest of this paper is structured as follows: We start by briefly reviewing the related work below in Sect. 2. We introduce the generic data structures and system-specific structures we benchmark in Sect. 3. We describe our experimental setup, the datasets we use, and our experimental results in Sect. 4, before concluding in Sect. 6.

2 Related Work

Most of the triplestores and RDF data management systems today include some component to encode the URIs appearing the RDF triples. We only cite a handful of approaches below, that are directly used in our performance evaluation hereafter. We refer the reader to recent surveys of the field (such as [8,9,11] or [13]) for a more comprehensive coverage of RDF systems and of the methods they use to encode data.

In RDF-3X [17], Neumann et al. use standard B+-tree to translate strings into IDs. Instead of using a similar approach to perform translations back (from IDs to literals after query processing as ended), they implement a direct mapping index [7]. This solution is tuned for id lookups, which helps them achieve a better cache-hit ratio.

Several pieces of work including [1] or [3] implement dictionary-mapping schemes. Typically, these systems implement two independent structures to handle two-way encoding/decoding (id to value, and value to id). For the value to id mapping, many approaches use disk-resident solutions. To perform the id to value mapping, approaches typically use auxiliary constant-time direct access structures.

In [14], Martinez-Prieto et al. describe advanced techniques for effectively building RDF dictionaries and propose a working prototype implementing their techniques. In their approach, values are grouped by the roles they play in the dataset such that all resulting encodings are organized by their position in the triples (e.g., subject, predicate, or object). Hence, the client has to specify the role of the desired piece of data when retrieving it.

3   Evaluated Methods

Reflecting on the approaches and systems described above, we decided to focus our evaluation on a set of generic data structures and to include in addition a few popular systems and approaches that were designed specifically to handle Semantic Web data. We present a series of generic data structures in Sect. 3.1, and a set of approaches we borrowed from Semantic Web systems in Sect. 3.2 below.

Our goal is primarily to analyze the performance of different paradigms (tries, hash tables, search trees) on RDF data (specifically, URIs). We compare different implementations of the same paradigm to see how the implementation might affect the performance and provide factual information to the community. We found that implementations matter: our results (see Sect. 5) show striking performance differences between various implementations. Our goal is not to show the superiority one given data structure, but to empirically measure and analyze the tradeoffs between different paradigms and implementations.

3.1   Generic Data Structures

We describe below the various data structures we decided to evaluate.

Hash Table (STL):[3] std::unordered_map is an unordered associative container that contains key-value pairs with unique keys. It organizes data in unsorted buckets using hashes. Hence, search, insertion and deletion all have a constant-time complexity.

Google Sparse Hash Map:[4] Google Sparse Hash is a hashed, unique associative container that associates objects of type Key with objects of type Data. Although it is efficient, due to its intricate memory management it can be slower than other hash maps. An interesting feature worth mentioning is its ability to save and restore the structure to and from disk.

Google Dense Hash Map:[5] google::dense_hash_map distinguishes itself from other hash-map implementations by its speed and by its ability to save and restore contents to and from disk. On the other hand, this hash-map implementation can use significantly more space than other hash-map implementations.

Hash Table (Boost):[6] this is the unordered_map version provided by the Boost library; It implements the container described in C++11, with some deviations from the standard in order to work with non-C++11 compilers and libraries.

Binary Search Tree (STL):[7] std map is a popular ordered and associative container which contains key-value pairs with unique keys. Search, removal,

---

[3] http://en.cppreference.com/w/cpp/container/unordered_map.
[4] https://code.google.com/p/sparsehash/.
[5] https://code.google.com/p/sparsehash/.
[6] http://www.boost.org/doc/libs/1_55_0/doc/html/unordered.html.
[7] http://en.cppreference.com/w/cpp/container/map.

and insertion operations all have logarithmic complexity. It is implemented as a red-black tree (self-balancing binary search tree).

B+ Tree:[8] STX B+ Tree is designed as a drop-in replacement for the STL containers set, map, multiset and multimap, STX B+ Tree follows their interfaces very closely. By packing multiple value-pairs into each node of the tree, the B+ tree reduces the fragmentation of the heap and utilizes cache-lines more effectively than the standard red-black binary tree.

ART Tree: Adaptive radix tree (trie) [12] is designed to be space efficient and to solve the problem of excessive worst-case space consumption, which plagues most radix trees, by adaptively choosing compact and efficient data structures for internal nodes.

Lexicographic Tree: Lexicographic Tree is an implementation of a prefix tree, where URIs are broken based on their common parts such that every substring is stored only once. An auto-incremented identifier is stored in the leaf level. The specific implementation we benchmark was initially designed for our own Diplodocus [18,20] system.

HAT-trie: HAT-trie [2] represents a recent combination of different data structures. It is a cache-conscious data structure which combines a trie with a hash table. It takes the idea of the burst trie and replaces linked-lists bucket containers there with cache-conscious hash tables.

3.2 Data Structures from RDF Systems

We describe below the two specific URI encoding subsystems that we directly borrowed from popular Semantic Web systems.

RDF-3X: As triples may contain long strings, RDF-3X [17] adopts the approach of replacing all literals by IDs using a mapping dictionary (see, e.g., [5]) to get more efficient query processing, at the cost of maintaining two dictionary indexes. During query translation, the literals occurring in the query are translated into their dictionary IDs, which is performed using an optimized B+-tree to map strings onto IDs. For our experiments, we extracted the dictionary structure from the presented system. We also maintained the entire dictionary in main memory to avoid expensive I/O operations[9].

HDT: HDT [14] follows the last approach described above in our Related Work section; Data is stored in HDT in four dictionaries containing: (i) common subjects and objects (ii) subjects (iii) objects and finally (iv) predicates. When benchmarking this data structure, we followed exactly the same scenario as for the previous one, i.e. we extracted the dictionary structure from the system and then fitted the data in main memory. Similarly, the structure is available on our web page.

---

[8] https://panthema.net/2007/stx-btree/.
[9] See http://exascale.info/uriencoding.

4   Experimental Setup

We give below some details on the dataset, the hardware platform, and the methodology we used for our tests. Then, we present the results of our performance evaluation. All the datasets and pieces of code we used, as well as the full set of graphs that we generated from our tests, are available on our project webpage: http://exascale.info/uriencoding.

4.1   Datasets

We extracted URIs and literal values from well-known RDF benchmarks. To get additional insight into the various datasets, we compressed them with a standard tools (bzip2 [4]) and analyzed the structure of their URIs. Along with the descriptions of the datasets below, we present the compression ratios we obtained with bzip2 (denoted as CR), the number of levels in a radix trie (#L) built on top of each dataset, and the average number of children per level in the top-3 levels of the trie (L1, L2, L3).

DS1: 26,288,829 distinct URIs (1.6 GB) were extracted from the dataset generated by the Lehigh University Benchmark (LUBM) [10] for 800 universities. LUBM is one of the oldest and most popular benchmarks for the Semantic Web. It provides an ontology describing universities together with a data generator producing well-structured datasets. [CR 42:1, #L 15, L1 7.5, L2 5.9, L3 4.9]. The URIs in this dataset are highly regular and mostly keep entities labels of around 50 classes ("Department", "University", "Professor", etc.). The entities are organized as a forest with universities as root nodes of each tree.

DS2: 64,626,232 distinct URIs (3.3 GB) were extracted from the dataset generated by the DBpedia SPARQL Benchmark [16], with a scale factors of 200 %. [CR 10:1, #L 59, L1 58, L2 50.8, L3 15.4]. It is a real dataset, with distinct entity names, such that there is no distinct recurring pattern in them. Properties may be strings, numbers (real and integer), dates, URIs (http, ftp) and links to other entities. Labels and properties may have a language suffix (2 character string). Properties may have a property type suffix which is a URI from a set of around 250 URIs.

DS3: 24,214,968 distinct URIs (2.1 GB) were extracted from the dataset generated by the Berlin SPARQL Benchmark (BSBM)[10], with a scale factor 439,712. [CR 72:1, #L 17, L1 33, L2 14.8, L3 10]. This dataset describes entities and properties in a e-commerce use-case. The way of identifying entities is similar to LUBM. Entities have however a rich set of properties (around 50 % of all elements in the dataset).

DS4: 36,776,098 distinct URIs (3.2 GB) were extracted from a dataset generated by BowlognaBench [6] for 160 departments. [CR 49:1, #L 17, L1 22.5, L2 2.5, L3 1.6]. The dataset is almost fully constituted by entities labels. The way of creating these entities is similar to LUBM.

---

[10] http://wifo5-03.informatik.uni-mannheim.de/bizer/berlinsparqlbenchmark/.

DS5: 52,616,588 distinct URIs (3.2 GB) were extracted from the dataset generated by the Lehigh University Benchmark [10] for 1,600 universities. We
generated this data set to work with a larger number of elements in order to
evaluate scalability. [CR 42:1, #L 15, L1 7.5, L2 5.9, L3 4.5].

DS6: 229,969,855 distinct URIs (14 GB) were extracted from dataset generated
by the Lehigh University Benchmark [10] for 7,000 Universities. This is the
biggest dataset we considered. [CR 42:1, #L 15, L1 7, L2 6.2, L3 5.8].

Due to the space limitations, only a subset of the results, mostly from DS2
and DS6, are presented below. After conducting the experiments and carefully
analyzing the results we noticed that those two datasets represent the most
interesting scenarios. DS6 is the biggest dataset we use and can show how data
structures scale with the data size. DS2 is a real dataset and is especially interesting given the heterogeneity of its URIs (length, subpath, special characters,
etc.). The full experimental results are available on our project webpage: http://
exascale.info/uriencoding.

4.2 Experimental Platform

All experiments were run on a HP ProLiant DL385 G7 server with two Twelve-
Core AMD Opteron Processor 6180 SE, 64 GB of DDR3 RAM, running Linux
Ubuntu 12.04.1 LTS. All data were stored on a recent 2.7TB Serial ATA disk.

4.3 Experimental Methodology

We built a custom framework for working with the various data structures, in
order to measure the time taken to insert data, as well as the memory used and
the look-up time. The framework covers URI-to-ID mappings and URI look-ups.

When measuring time, we retrieve the system time the process consumes to
perform the operation (e.g., loading data, retrieving results) and exclude the
time spent on loading data from disk in order to eliminate any I/O overhead.
We also retrieve the memory consumed by the actual data by extracting the
amount of resident memory used by the process.

As is typical for benchmarking database systems (e.g., for tpc-x[11]), we run
all the benchmark ten times and we report the average value of the ten runs.

During our experiments, we noticed significant differences in performance
when working with ordered and unordered URIs, thus we additionally tested all
data structures for both of those cases. Finally, in order to avoid the artifacts
created by memory swapping, we had to limit DS6 to 100M elements when
benchmarking the data structures.

Figure 1 gives an overview of our test procedure for the data structures and
subsystems. First, we load all URIs available from a file into an in-memory array
to avoid any I/O overhead during the benchmarking process. Then, we iteratively
insert and query for URIs by batches of 100 k: At each step, we first measure

---

[11] http://www.tpc.org/.

the time it takes to load 100 k URIs, and then do 100 k random look-ups on the elements inserted so far, until all URIs are inserted. In summary, we report the following for the data structures:

- total insertion time [s];
- incremental insertion time by steps of 100 k inserted URIs [s];
- relative memory consumption, which is the ratio between the dictionary memory consumption and the total size of the inserted URIs;
- lookup time by steps of 100 k inserted URIs [s].

As noted above, our goal is to compare the various structures from a pragmatic perspective. For each structure, we investigate its performance on bulk load (total insertion time) and on dynamically incoming data (incremental insertion time). Using the relative memory consumption, we show if the data structure performs any compression or if it introduces any space overhead. Finally, we investigate how fast it performs URI lookups w.r.t. the size of the data structure (number of URIs loaded).

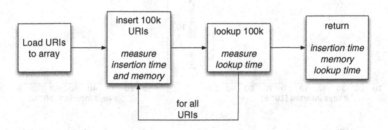

Fig. 1. Overview of our test procedure for the data structures

5 Experimental Results

5.1 Results for Generic Structures

Figures 2 and 3 show the insertion time for DS2 and DS6, respectively for a varying number of keys and for the full dataset. We observe that for synthetic data all the tree-like structures preform slightly better. As the data is more regular, it is easier to decompose URIs in that case.

We observe that for inserts, hash tables work equally well for ordered and unordered data (as they anyway hash the value before inserting it), which is not the case for other data structures. In addition, hash tables are on average faster than their alternatives. The only exception is Google Sparse Hash Map, which was 5 times slower than the other hash tables.

Tries and search trees are very sensitive to the key ordering. Shuffled datasets were taking 3–4 times more time to be inserted than the same datasets with sorted keys. On the other hand, in case of sorted datasets, they are as fast as

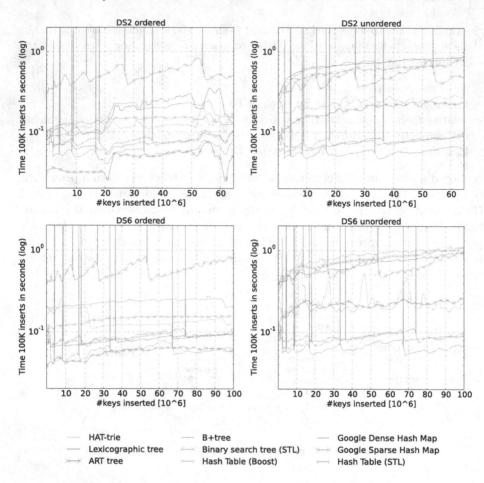

Fig. 2. Insertion time as a function of dictionary size for DS2, DS6

hash tables. ART-Tree is clearly more efficient in that context than the other data structures.

The average insert time—given as a function of the data structure size (see Fig. 2)—stays nearly constant for all structures. We know that it is actually logarithmic to the size of a dictionary for tries and search trees, though the curves are reaching their flatter part quite early.

Figure 2 is also showing a very prominent drawback of hash tables: timeouts when inserting data caused by regular hash table resize (the size of the underlying structure is typically doubled every time the table is filled up to a certain percent). The timeouts might last for several seconds. The other data structures do not exhibit such a behavior.

Figure 4 shows the relative memory consumption of the data structures under consideration. Most of the structures consume 2–3 times more memory than the original datasets. However, the optimized tries (ART-tree and HAT-Trie) show

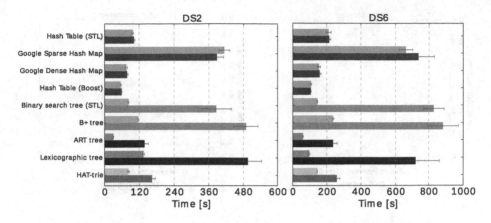

Fig. 3. Total time for fill a dictionary (DS2, DS6)

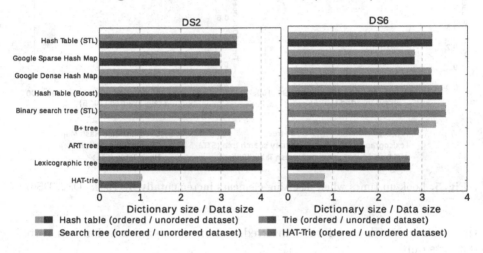

Fig. 4. Relative memory consumption (DS2, DS6)

outstanding results. ART-TRee consumes about 1.5x more memory than the size of DS6. HAT-Trie takes less memory than the original data (90 % of DS6). So, it can actually compress the data while encoding it. We connect this feature to the fact that tries (prefix trees) can efficiently leverage the structure of rdf URIs, which are characterized by repetitive prefixes (domains and subdomains of sets of entities).

Figure 5 reports the look-up times for 100 K random records after inserting 100 K records incrementally for ordered and unordered datasets. As for the loading times, the regularity of the data positively influences the look-ups. Regular and synthetic data is easier to handle and the performance is closer to linear, especially when the URIs are ordered. We observe a strong impact on performance for the prefix and the search trees, while hash tables stay indifferent to

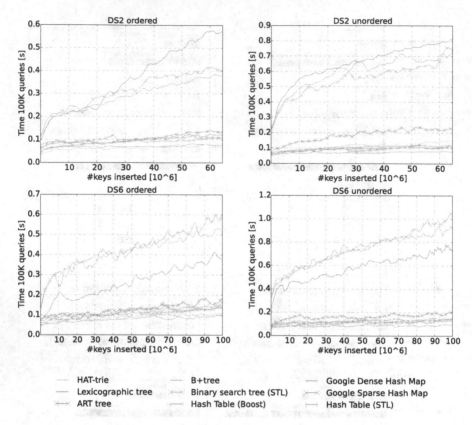

Fig. 5. Look-up times when inserting elements incrementally by 100 k (DS2, DS6)

the order in which the data is inserted. Further analyzes are done on sorted datasets only.

Search trees (B+tree and STL Map) and Lexicographic tree look-up times grow logarithmically with the size of the dictionary. In general, they are 3–6 times slower than the fastest data structures. All the others included hash tables, the HAT-Trie and ART-Trie are showing similar results, and can handle 100 K queries in approximately 0.1 s regardless of the size of the dictionary.

The aforementioned features make hash tables an excellent option for dynamic or intermediate dictionaries, which are crucial for many data processing steps. They are fast in inserts and queries and do not require the keys to be sorted. For RDF archival or static dictionaries, a better option would be a modern data structure like the ART-tree or HAT-trie. They are as fast as hash tables for queries and consume much less memory (HAT-trie actually compresses the data). The sensitivity to the key's order is not crucial for a static case, since data can be pre-sorted.

5.2   Results for RDF Subsystems

Dictionary structures from RDF systems behave very differently, since they represent very polarized ways of dealing with the problem of storing triples. HDT is an in-memory compressed and complex set of structures to manage URIs. RDF-3X on the other hand represents a disk-oriented structure (that is then partially mapped into main-memory) based on B+tree.

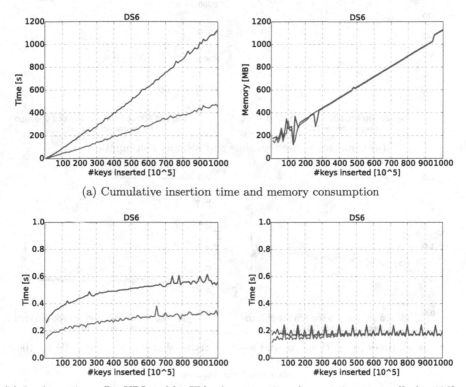

(a) Cumulative insertion time and memory consumption

(b) Look-up times (by URI and by ID) when inserting elements incrementally by 100k on unordered data

■ ordered ■ unordered

Fig. 6. Results for HDT (DS6)

Figure 6a shows the cumulative time and memory consumption during insertion for HDT. To insert all elements of DS6, it takes about 450 s for ordered values and 1100 s for unordered, consuming about 1.1 GB of memory in both cases. Loading elements is linear in time. Memory consumption increases linearly also.

We benchmarked look-ups both by URI and by ID (Fig. 6b). Unsurprisingly, retrieving data by string elements is more expensive than by integers, about 3 times for unordered elements. However, for ordered elements the difference is not that large, i.e., less than 2x. URIs look-ups are close to being constant in time, though we can observe some negative influence from growing amounts of data. Retrieving values by ID does not depend on the order of the elements and performs in constant time, without much influence from the data size.

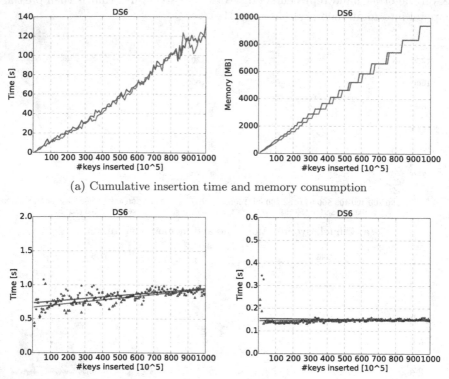

(a) Cumulative insertion time and memory consumption

(b) Look-up times (by URI and by ID) when inserting elements incrementally by 100k on unordered data

ordered   unordered

Fig. 7. Results for RDF-3X (DS6)

The RDF-3X dictionary needs about 120 s to load all elements of DS6, consuming at the same time more than 9 GB of memory (Fig. 7a). The insertion costs are independent of the order of the elements in the dataset. We can also observe here a difference between look-ups by URI and ID (Fig. 7b), however for RDF-3X the difference is significantly bigger; it is more that 5 times slower to retrieve string values than integers. The string look-up time here is also less sensitive to the order of values. Retrieving values by ID performs in linear time when increasing the data size.

6   Conclusions

URI encoding is an important aspect of the Web of data, as URIs are omnipresent in Semantic Web and LOD settings. Most RDF systems use their own encoding scheme, making it difficult to have a clear idea on how different methods compare in practice. In this paper, we presented, to the best of our knowledge, the first systematic comparison of the most common data structures used to manage URI data. We evaluated a series of data structures (such as sparse hash maps or lexicographic trees) and RDF subsystems in terms of their read/write performance and memory consumption. Beyond the selection of graphs presented in this paper, all the datasets and pieces of code we used, as well as the full set of graphs that we generated from our tests, are available online[12].

We make a series of observations from the results obtained through our performance evaluation:

1. Data loading times can widely vary for different index structures; Google's dense map, the Hash Tables from STL and boost, ART tree, and HAT-trie are one order of magnitude faster than Google's sparse map, Binary Search Tree, and the B+ and lexicographic trees implementations we benchmarked for reasonably big datasets.
2. Data loading times for more sophisticated structures from RDF-3X or HDT are considerably slower; RDF-3X is typically one to two orders of magnitude slower than the standard data structures. HDT is even slower, as it is almost one order of magnitude worse than RDF-3x.
3. Memory consumption also exhibits dramatic differences between the structures; most of the usual data structures are in the same ballpark (differences of about 20 % for big datasets), with HAT-trie significantly outperforming other generic data structures (three times less memory consumed comparing to the average). RDF-3X is also very effective in that context, requiring 30 to 40 % less memory than any of the standard data structures. The clear winner in terms of resulting data size is however HDT, requiring one order of magnitude less space than the other structures (which confirms the validity of the compression mechanisms used for that project).
4. The time taken to retrieve data from the structures also vary widely; Google's dense map, ART tree, HAT-trie, and the Hash Tables from STL and boost are here also one order of magnitude faster than the other structures.
5. Look-up performance for more sophisticated structures borrowed from RDF systems are competitive; HDT is a few times slower than the best hash-tables for look-ups, while RDF-3X is around 5 to 10 times slower.
6. Cache-aware algorithms (e.g., HAT-trie) perform better than others since they take advantage of the structure of the cache hierarchy of modern hardware architectures.
7. Finally, the order of inserted elements matters for most of the data structures. Ordered elements are typically inserted faster and look-ups are executed more efficiently, though they consume slightly more memory for the B+tree.

---

[12] http://exascale.info/uriencoding.

Overall, the HAT-trie appears to be a good comprise taking into account all aspects, i.e., memory consumption, loading time, and look-ups. ART also appears as an appealing structure, since it maintains the data in sorted order, which enables additional operations like range scans and prefix lookups, and since it still remains time and memory efficient.

We believe that the above points highlight key differences and will help the community to make more sensible choices when picking up hashes and data structures for the Web of Data. As a concrete example, we decided to change the structures used in our own Diplodocus system following those results. As we need in our context to favor fast insertions (both for ordered and unordered datasets), fast look-ups and relatively compact structures with no collision, we decided to replace our prefix tree (LexicographicTree) with the HAT-trie. We gained both in terms of memory consumption and efficient look-ups compared to our previous structure; We believe that this new choice will considerably speed-query execution times and improve the scalability of our system.

Our benchmarking framework can easily be extended to handle further data structures. In the future, we also plan to run experiments on new dataset such as Wikidata and bioinformatics use-cases.

Acknowledgement. This work was funded in part by the Swiss National Science Foundation under grant numbers PP00P2_128459 and 200021_143649.

References

1. Abadi, D.J., Marcus, A., Madden, S.R., Hollenbach, K.: Scalable semantic web data management using vertical partitioning. In: Proceedings of the 33rd International Conference on Very Large Data Bases, pp. 411–422. VLDB Endowment (2007)
2. Askitis, N., Sinha, R.: Hat-trie: a cache-conscious trie-based data structure for strings. In: Proceedings of the Thirtieth Australasian Conference on Computer Science, vol. 62, pp. 97–105. Australian Computer Society Inc. (2007)
3. Broekstra, J., Kampman, A., van Harmelen, F.: Sesame: a generic architecture for storing and querying RDF and RDF schema. In: Horrocks, I., Hendler, J. (eds.) ISWC 2002. LNCS, vol. 2342, pp. 54–68. Springer, Heidelberg (2002)
4. Burrows, M., Wheeler, D.J.: A block-sorting lossless data compression algorithm (1994)
5. Chong, E.I., Das, S., Eadon, G., Srinivasan, J.: An efficient SQL-based RDF querying scheme. In: Proceedings of the 31st International Conference on Very Large Data Bases, pp. 1216–1227. VLDB Endowment (2005)
6. Demartini, G., Enchev, I., Wylot, M., Gapany, J., Cudré-Mauroux, P.: BowlognaBench—Benchmarking RDF analytics. In: Aberer, K., Damiani, E., Dillon,T. (eds.) SIMPDA 2011. LNBIP, vol. 116, pp. 82–102. Springer, Heidelberg (2012)
7. Eickler, A., Gerlhof, C.A., Kossmann, D.: A performance evaluation of oid mapping techniques. Fakultät für Mathematik und Informatik, Universität Passau (1995)
8. Faye, D., Cure, O., Blin, G.: A survey of RDF storage approaches. ARIMA J. **15**, 11–35 (2012)

9. Guo, Y., Pan, Z., Heflin, J.: An evaluation of knowledge base systems for large OWL datasets. In: McIlraith, S.A., Plexousakis, D., van Harmelen, F. (eds.) ISWC 2004. LNCS, vol. 3298, pp. 274–288. Springer, Heidelberg (2004)
10. Guo, Y., Pan, Z., Heflin, J.: LUBM: a benchmark for OWL knowledge base systems. Web Semant. Sci. Serv. Agents World Wide Web **3**(2–3), 158–182 (2005)
11. Haslhofer, B., Roochi, E.M., Schandl, B., Zander, S.: Europeana RDF Store Report. University of Vienna, Technical report (2011). http://eprints.cs.univie.ac.at/2833/1/europeana_ts_report.pdf
12. Leis, V., Kemper, A., Neumann, T.: The adaptive radix tree: ARTful indexing for main-memory databases. In: 2013 IEEE 29th International Conference on Data Engineering (ICDE), pp. 38–49. IEEE (2013)
13. Liu, B., Hu, B.: An evaluation of RDF storage systems for large data applications. In: First International Conference on Semantics, Knowledge and Grid, SKG 2005, p. 59, November 2005
14. Martínez-Prieto, M.A., Fernández, J.D., Cánovas, R.: Compression of RDF dictionaries. In: Proceedings of the 27th Annual ACM Symposium on Applied Computing, pp. 340–347. ACM (2012)
15. Maurer, W.D., Lewis, T.G.: Hash table methods. ACM Comput. Surv. **7**(1), 5–19 (1975)
16. Morsey, M., Lehmann, J., Auer, S., Ngonga Ngomo, A.-C.: DBpedia SPARQL benchmark – performance assessment with real queries on real data. In: Aroyo, L., Welty, C., Alani, H., Taylor, J., Bernstein, A., Kagal, L., Noy, N., Blomqvist, E. (eds.) ISWC 2011, Part I. LNCS, vol. 7031, pp. 454–469. Springer, Heidelberg (2011)
17. Neumann, T., Weikum, G.: Rdf-3x: a risc-style engine for RDF. Proc. VLDB Endow. **1**(1), 647–659 (2008)
18. Wylot, M., Cudre-Mauroux, P., Groth, P.: Tripleprov: efficient processing of lineage queries in a native RDF store. In: Proceedings of the 23rd International Conference on World Wide Web, WWW 2014, pp. 455–466. International World Wide Web Conferences Steering Committee (2014)
19. Wylot, M., Cudré-Mauroux, P., Groth, P.: Executing provenance-enabled queries over web data. In: Proceedings of the 24rd International Conference on World Wide Web, WWW 2015, Republic and Canton of Geneva, Switzerland. International World Wide Web Conferences Steering Committee (2015)
20. Wylot, M., Pont, J., Wisniewski, M., Cudré-Mauroux, P.: dipLODocus[RDF]—short and long-tail RDF analytics for massive webs of data. In: Aroyo, L., Welty, C., Alani, H., Taylor, J., Bernstein, A., Kagal, L., Noy, N., Blomqvist, E. (eds.) ISWC 2011, Part I. LNCS, vol. 7031, pp. 778–793. Springer, Heidelberg (2011)

Heuristics for Fixing Common Errors in Deployed *schema.org* Microdata

Robert Meusel[(✉)] and Heiko Paulheim

Research Group Data and Web Science,
University of Mannheim, Mannheim, Germany
{robert,heiko}@dwslab.de

Abstract. Being promoted by major search engines such as Google, Yahoo!, Bing, and Yandex, Microdata embedded in web pages, especially using *schema.org*, has become one of the most important markup languages for the Web. However, deployed Microdata is most often not free from errors, which limits its practical use. In this paper, we use the WebDataCommons corpus of Microdata extracted from more than 250 million web pages for a quantitative analysis of common mistakes in Microdata provision. Since it is unrealistic that *data providers* will provide clean and correct data, we discuss a set of heuristics that can be applied on the *data consumer* side to fix many of those mistakes in a post-processing step. We apply those heuristics to provide an improved knowledge base constructed from the raw Microdata extraction.

Keywords: Microdata · schema.org · Data quality · Knowledge base construction

1 Introduction

In the recent years, languages for incorporating structured knowledge into HTML web pages, such as RDFa, Microformats, and Microdata, have been proposed. Out of those, the latter shows the widest adoption [11], in particular due to the *Schema.org* initiative driven by major web search engines such as Google, Bing, Yahoo!, and Yandex.[1]

The main motivation for web site providers to include Microdata is an improved displaying of results by major search engines and by this a improved awareness of their page to the user. Search engines display richer results for web sites described with Microdata. Furthermore, the extraction of a large-scale knowledge base is possible by harvesting data from different sites. One such knowledge base is the Web Data Commons Microdata corpus[2] [11].

In order to fully exploit such capabilities, it is necessary that web site providers adhere to the standards defined by schema.org. For example, a product offer will only appear on an aggregate search site if it uses the correct schema.org classes

---

[1] http://schema.org.

[2] http://webdatacommons.org/structureddata/.

© Springer International Publishing Switzerland 2015
F. Gandon et al. (Eds.): ESWC 2015, LNCS 9088, pp. 152–168, 2015.
DOI: 10.1007/978-3-319-18818-8_10

and properties to annotate the relevant information. Furthermore, a knowledge base extracted from Microdata will be of higher utility the more strictly the given schema is followed.

In this paper, we analyze common mistakes made in the adoption of schema.org for Microdata. Using the *WebDataCommons* Microdata corpus extracted from the web corpora provided by the Common Crawl Foundation,[3] we perform a quantitative analysis of those mistakes, and we compare the findings to similar analyses carried out on Linked Open Data (LOD). For many of those mistakes, we discuss heuristics to fix them, and apply the fixes to the recent WebDataCommons Microdata corpus. That cleaned corpus contains data that is both syntactically and semantically corrected, and thus represents a more valuable knowledge base. Each heuristic applied is evaluated with respect to its quantitative impact.

The rest of this paper is structured as follows. Section 2 gives an overview of related work. Section 3 shows the quantitative analysis of common mistakes observed in deployed Microdata, and Sect. 4 discusses heuristics for fixing many of those mistakes, as well as the construction of a cleaned up Microdata corpus. We close with a summary and an outlook on future work.

2   Related Work

In [14], the definition of schema.org and its mapping to RDF triples and OWL has been reviewed from a model-theoretic perspective. While that work is rather top-down, starting from the schema definition, we follow a bottom-up approach, making quantitative statements about the actually deployed data – a task named as future work in [14].

Only few works have analyzed the current deployment of RDFa, Microdata, and Microformats in the Web. Mika et al. have presented the first statistics of deployment of the three markup languages in 2011 [12] and 2012 [13], using a non-public web crawl owned by Yahoo!. Bizer et al. [4] present a broader analysis of the current deployment using the public web crawls of the Common Crawl Foundation. They report a strong deployment of markup to describe companies, persons, products, and events, but also note a rather flat usage of properties to describe those items. All those works solely perform an empiric analysis on the current deployment of the different markups and schemas, without a discussion the deviation between the schema definition(s) and the actual usage.

The problem of flatly described items is analyzed in-depth for the class s:Product[4] [15]. The authors propose to use regular expressions for extracting features from the title and the description of products marked with Microdata.

A study on validation problems with HTML pages has been done by Chen et al. [5]. They found that only 5 % of all web pages are valid according to HTML standards, and analyzed the major problems leading to this invalidity.

---

[3] http://commoncrawl.org.

[4] In this paper, we use s:Foo as a shorthand notation for http://schema.org/Foo.

For Linked Open Data (LOD), similar works have been carried out [18]. While many of the metrics applied for LOD are rather LOD-specific (such as the presence and correctness of dataset interlinks), some of the typical mistakes apply to both LOD and Microdata, mainly in the categories of *validity* and *consistency*. In the following, we cite some works which perform similar analyses as the one presented in this paper on LOD. Similar to our work for Microdata described in this paper, *LOD Laundromat* project provides cleaned versions of LOD datasets with syntax errors removed [3].

One of the closest works is the work on the *Pedantic Web* [8]. The authors identify four categories of mistakes in Linked Open Data, i.e., *incomplete, incoherent, hijack*, and *inconsistent*. An updated study on a more recent crawl of LOD has been discussed in [17]. Similar to those papers, *Prolod++* [1], among others, can search for typical modeling problems such as data properties with inconsistent data values (e.g., mixing numbers and dates). The work by Ziawasch et al. [2] even goes one step further. Using the deployment of Linked Open Data, their work aims to check whether properties are attached to the "right level" within the hierarchy or if certain properties should be redefined.

In this paper, we specifically analyze to which extent the *schema definition* of schema.org is followed. Similar works also exist for Linked Open Data, e.g., the *DataBugger* framework, which is based on user-formulated tests run against SPARQL endpoints [9] and examines the adherence of instance data to a schema and additional, user-defined constraints. Similarly, *SWIQA* uses patterns and rules, e.g., for defining legal ranges of literals [6]. On the schema level, tools like *OOPS!* [16] search for common violations of modeling best practices.

3   A Quantitative Analysis of Common Errors in Schema.org Microdata

For our analysis, we use the most recent Microdata corpus[5] from WebDataCommons [11]. That original corpus includes over 8.7 billion triples originating from 463 539 pay-level domains (PLDs), where we focus on the large majority of PLDs which make use of the *schema.org* vocabulary (see Sect. 3.1).[6]

To avoid misleading results which are artifacts due to the selection strategy of the underlying web crawl (not all PLDs are fully crawled), we mainly report numbers aggregated to PLDs instead of triples. This leads to more representative numbers, assuming that an institution (with one or more web masters) is responsible to maintain the pages of a PLD, and that this institution will always apply the same patterns for markup, i.e., they will also repeat the same set of mistakes. Moreover, many websites are generated from databases, and the markup of the information follows a global algorithm, i.e., values from the same

---

[5] http://webdatacommons.org/structureddata/2013-11/.

[6] Only 0.1 % of all PLDs deploying RDFa use schema.org, and only 2.4 % of all LOD sources [11,17]. Hence, we restrict ourselves to Microdata, where we see a large-scale adoption of schema.org.

database field are always marked up in the same way for one PLD. Different aggregations are only used for making comparisons to other research works.[7]

For the schema description of schema.org, we use the RDF description of schema.org, using version 1.91.[8]

From the *Pedantic Web* paper [8] (see above), we have selected those mistakes that can also occur in Microdata. However, since we base our analysis on an extracted corpus of structured data, not the original embedding web pages, we have no data for some of the categories reported in their paper, such as syntax errors preventing a correct parsing of the contents. Furthermore, some of the categories, such as the misuse of constructs that exist in OWL, but not schema.org, are not applicable to our use case.

3.1 Usage of Wrong Namespaces and Identification of Relevant PLDs

In this paper, we are primarily interested in *schema.org* Microdata. Hence, we first identify all PLDs from the Microdata corpus which deploy such data by looking at the *namespaces* used. To extract the namespaces from the types within our corpus, we worked with a known namespace list, which includes the most common namespaces as done by Bizer et al. [4].

In our case, the two namespaces for *data-vocabulary.org* and *schema.org* are mostly deployed. For all non-fitting namespaces, we consider the substring until the last non-trailing slash as a namespace.[9]

As a result of this extraction, we could identify over 15 K different namespaces within the whole Microdata corpus. At a first glance, besides the two major namespaces (*data-vocabulary.org* and *schema.org*), we identified obvious typos of those two major namespaces, and a large number of website specific namespaces.

As proposed by [11], and since we are mostly interested in the most common errors, we filtered out all namespaces occurring solely in one PLD. This results in 361 different namespaces, including the two major namespaces. By manually inspecting this set, we could identify 162 namespaces, used by 398 542 PLDs, which obviously were meant to be *schema.org*, but did not use the correct namespace. 149 of those included the substring `schema.org`. The remaining 13 were well-formed URIs[10] whose protocol and authority is within an edit distance of 1 to http://schema.org.

Inspecting the most common errors we found that 102 namespaces include a leading `www.`, 19 use the `https` protocol, 11 have missing slashes within the namespace, and four used a wrong capitalization (e.g., `SChema.org`). Despite this

---

[7] Although the comparisons should be handled with care, since they might be biased by different crawling strategies underlying the corpora at hand.

[8] http://schema.rdfs.org/.

[9] Note that this might lead to a larger amount of different namespaces in the case of wrong written namespaces or the use of the schema.org extension mechanism, as defined by http://schema.org/docs/extension.html.

[10] Based on http://www.ietf.org/rfc/rfc2396.txt.

large variety, overall only 4 909 (1.23 %) from 398 542 pay-level domains deploy a wrong namespace meant to be http://schema.org.

In the following sections, we will only use those triples which at least include the substring `schema.org` within the namespace. Those 398 542 PLDs, originating from 217 018 636 different URLs, contain 6.4 billion triples describing 1.4 billion different instances (identified by a class), which corresponds to 86.0 % of the complete Microdata corpus.

The problem of wrong namespaces in schema.org Microdata is a subproblem of the *dereferencability issues* in [8], although only for schema elements, not for instances (a schema element with a wrong namespace will not be derefencable, but a non-derefencable one may still have a correct namespace). Still, we can compare it to the analysis of *dereferencability of vocabulary elements* for LOD provided in [17]. According to that paper, 80 % of all LOD datasets use at least one schema element which is not de-referenceable, which is a much larger fraction than for schema.org Microdata.[11]

3.2 Usage of Undefined Types

Using the definitions from the schema.org website, we identified 24 227 (6.07 %) PLDs which make use of undefined types by simply selecting the *type*-triple for each entity and searching its value in this definition. Table 1 lists the ten most common used schema.org types, which are not defined by the official schema. Inspecting a larger fraction of the list of undefined types manually, we could identify three major different types of errors:

Missing Slashes: As already mentioned in the section above, some data providers did not set the slashes correctly, which results in unknown types when parsing the page (e.g. http://schema.orgStore on 6 236 different PLDs).

Capitalization: We orientated our analysis on the formal definition given on the web page of schema.org, including the capitalization. Miscapitalization (e.g. `s:localbusiness`) is also a major source of errors, observed for 1 169 PLDs.

Empty Types: A third mistake, according to our observation, are empty or missing types. We identified 228 PLDs, which did not set a type for at least one item on their page. Furthermore, 3 506 PLDs left the type empty within the markup on the HTML page.

Reference [8] reports that for LOD, 38.8 % of all documents use undefined types, as opposed to 5.82 % of all documents in our corpus.

3.3 Usage of Undefined Properties

Again using the definitions on the *schema.org* website, we could identify 15 597 (3.92 %) PLDs which use at least one undefined property. Table 2 shows the most

---

[11] Even if we pessimistically assume that all other namespaces we observe are wrong.

Table 1. Most common used undefined types within schema.org, ordered by number of pay-level domains.

	Type	# PLDs		Class	# PLDs
1	http://schema.orgStore	6 236	6	http://schema.orgApartmentComplex	767
2	http://schema.org	3 507	7	http://schema.org/product	566
3	http://schema.orgAggregateRating	1 931	8	http://schema.orgClothingStore	404
4	http://schema.orgPerson	1 738	9	http://schema.org/Postaladdress	368
5	http://schema.org/localbusiness	1 169	10	http://schema.orgPostalAddress	325

Table 2. Most common used undefined properties by type within schema.org, ordered by number of PLDs.

	Type	Property	#PLDs	Comment
1	s:ImageObject	s:contentURL	5 904	typo: s:contentUrl
2	s:Article	s:type	2 393	not defined
3	s:BlogPosting	s:postId	1 574	not defined
4	s:BlogPosting	s:blogId	1 572	not defined
5	s:BlogPosting	s:image_url	1 509	not defined
6	s:LocalBusiness	s:URL	1 365	typo: s:url
7	s:VideoObject	s:embedURL	1 299	typo: s:embedUrl
8	s:SoftwareApplication	s:operatingSystems	529	typo: s:operatingSystem
9	s:VideoObject	s:thumbnailURL	464	close: s:thumbnail
10	s:Offer	s:currency	442	close: s:priceCurrency
11	s:LocalBusiness	s:rating	394	close: s:aggregatedRating
12	s:PostalAddress	s:AddressLocality	387	typo: s:addressLocality
13	s:VideoObject	s:contentURL	382	typo: s:contentUrl
14	s:LocalBusiness	s:fax	302	not defined
15	s:SoftwareApplication	s:SoftwareApplicationCategory	295	close: s:applicationCategory
16	s:SoftwareApplication	s:softwareApplicationCategory	274	close: s:applicationCategory
17	s:PostalAddress	s:postalcode	255	typo: s:postalCode
18	s:Person	s:jobtitle	201	typo: s:jobTitle
19	s:Review	s:itemreviewed	193	typo: s:itemReviewed
20	s:Product	s:identifier	173	close:s:productID

20 common used properties which are not defined in schema.org, together with the type they are to be used with. In this list, we can identify different types of errors. One main source of errors are spelling mistakes, as in s:contentURL, which is only defined as s:contentUrl. This error applies to eight out of the top 20 mistakes. Besides completely not defined properties like s:postId and s:blogId, we also find we also find properties where there is a close match, e.g., s:priceCurrency for s:priceCurrency.

The prevalence of undefined properties in LOD has also been investigated in [8], where the authors report that 72.4 % of all documents use undefined properties, while in our corpus, there are 9.69 % of all documents. In [17], it is reported that 80.75 % of all documents use non-dereferencable vocabulary elements, i.e., either undefined properties or types.

Table 3. Most common ObjectProperties used with a literal.

	Domain	Property	#PLDs	Actual Domain
1	s:PostalAddress	s:addressCountry	10 249	s:Country
2	s:Product	s:manufacturer	7 933	s:Organization
3	s:Review	s:author	7 807	s:Organization, s:Person
4	s:BlogPosting	s:author	7 089	s:Organization, s:Person
5	s:Article	s:author	5 491	s:Organization, s:Person
6	s:WebPage	s:mainContentOfPage	5 441	s:WebPageElement
7	s:Article	s:creator	4 567	s:Organization, s:Person
8	s:Product	s:brand	4 402	s:Brand, s:Organization
9	s:AutoDealer	s:address	2 437	s:PostalAddress
10	s:Recipe	s:author	2 392	s:Organization, s:Person
11	s:ImageObject	s:thumbnail	2 233	s:ImageObject
12	s:Review	s:itemReviewed	1 564	s:Thing
13	s:Organization	s:address	1 284	s:PostalAddress
14	s:AggregateRating	s:itemReviewed	1 177	s:Thing
15	s:Blog	s:author	1 171	s:Organization, s:Person
16	s:Event	s:location	1 086	s:Place, s:PostalAddress
17	s:WebPage	s:author	991	s:Organization, s:Person
18	s:Offer	s:seller	845	s:Organization, s:Person
19	s:VideoObject	s:thumbnail	818	s:ImageObject
20	s:Book	s:author	619	s:Organization, s:Person

3.4   Confusion of ObjectProperties and DatatypeProperties

In our corpus (using only types and properties which are defined by the website) 163 404 PLDs make use of ObjectProperties. Over half of those sites, namely 92 449 (56.58 %) use those properties with a literal value at least once. This percentage is large in comparison to LOD where only 8 % of all documents use object properties with literal objects [8], as opposed to 24.35 % of all documents in our corpus.

Table 3 lists the 20 most commonly misused ObjectProperties by the number of PLDs making use of them.[12] Within this list, literals are mostly used to describe objects of the types s:Organization, s:Person, and s:PostalAddress.

The reverse case is neglectable. While 356 274 PLDs of the corpus use Datatype-Properties, only 810 (0.2 %) of those sites use an instance and not a literal for at least one datatype property. This number is low compared to the numbers reported by [8] for LOD, i.e., 2.2 % of all documents use datatype properties with non-literal objects, as opposed to 0.56 % of the documents in our corpus.

---

[12] We have excluded all properties which are also used with literals in the examples provided at http://schema.org.

3.5 Datatype Range Violations

For DatatypeProperties, eight different datatypes are defined in schema.org: `Text` (the most general type), `URL` for all kinds of links, `Boolean` for binominal values, `Date`, `DateTime`, and `Time` for temporal values, and `Number` and `Integer` for numeric values. It is notable that, in some cases, more than one datatype is allowed. For example, the property `s:discount` expects either a `Number` or a `Text` as value. For the given values of each datatype property within our corpus, we tried to parse them into one of the defined datatypes (e.g. for the property `s:deathDate`, we tried to parse the literal into a date) using the type guessing code from the *Mannheim Search Join Engine* for parsing web tables [10]. The type guesser uses defensive heuristics, e.g., for URL, we only checked if the literal starts with something like `http`, `www`, `ftp`, or `sftp`, and even includes more possible types for dates than the proposed ISO 8601 standard.

From the 356 274 PLDs using datatype properties, the parser was not able to parse the literal to one of the defined datatypes on at least one property in 34 324 (9.63 %) PLDs. Table 4 shows the top 20 properties with non-parseable literals.

Table 4. Most common datatype property values with non-parseable values, sorted by number of PLDs.

	Domain	Property	#PLDs	Expected Datatype
1	s:BlogPosting	s:datePublished	7 890	s:Date
2	s:Event	s:startDate	4 877	s:Date
3	s:Article	s:dateCreated	4 807	s:Date
4	s:Review	s:datePublished	2 691	s:Date
5	s:Event	s:endDate	2 422	s:Date
6	s:Article	s:datePublished	2 247	s:Date
7	s:ImageObject	s:uploadDate	2 097	s:Date
8	s:AggregateRating	s:reviewCount	1 644	s:Number
9	s:Product	s:url	926	s:URL
10	s:NewsArticle	s:datePublished	750	s:Date
11	s:Article	s:dateModified	610	s:Date
12	s:AggregateRating	s:ratingCount	552	s:Number
13	s:VideoObject	s:uploadDate	481	s:Date
14	s:Person	s:url	409	s:URL
15	s:UserComments	s:commentTime	401	s:Date
16	s:Organization	s:url	390	s:URL
17	s:JobPosting	s:datePosted	369	s:Date
18	s:Person	s:birthDate	321	s:Date
19	s:OpeningHoursSpecification	s:opens	295	s:Time
20	s:OpeningHoursSpecification	s:closes	271	s:Time

Obviously, most difficulties exist for dates: when investigating the data manually, we found various strings that were interpretable as dates for human beings, but which did not follow a known standard. Also for some PLDs, we could not parse the values for s:reviewCount properly. Here, not only a number was given in the literal, but also the unit, e.g. "10 votes".

A similar analysis was presented in [8] for LOD. Here, the authors examined whether the lexical syntax of literals matched the lexical form. They report that 4.6 % of all literals have a mismatch between their declared type and their lexical form, as opposed to 12.06 % of all documents in our corpus. Here, the most dominant source of problems were also dates, with prominently 26.6 % of all xsd:dateTime literals being malformed.

3.6   Property Domain Violations

For each property, *schema.org* defines a domain and a range. It is important to note that the semantics for schema.org are different than for LOD. Schema.org uses s:domainIncludes and s:rangeIncludes to define *disjunctive*, not *conjunctive* enumerations of domains and ranges as in RDFS and OWL [14]. We assume the enumerations of possible domains and ranges to be *complete*, and count each typed subject or object as a mistake if it has a type which is not contained in the domain or range enumeration (or an rdfs:subclassOf thereof), respectively, although disjointness is not explicitly defined in schema.org.

In total, 15 949 PLDs (4.0 %) expose domain violations. Table 5 lists the 20 most common domain violations. Column four shows the types the property was actually defined for. Inspecting this list, we found that most of the properties which are used actually have s:PostalAddress, s:Offer, and s:Rating as their domain. Looking at the types these properties are used with, we can find a unique direct link between the defined and the used type. In most cases, those types are needed to describe the original item further (e.g. Offer to describe prices, availability of a Product). It seems that the data providers used a "shortcut", without modeling the in-between instance, as defined by the schema. For example, the triple[13]

1. _:1 s:ratingValue ''5'' .

is used for an s:Article instead of the set of triples

1. _:1 s:aggregateRating _:2 .
2. _:2 a s:AggregateRating .
3. _:2 s:ratingValue ''5'' .

3.7   ObjectProperty Range Violations

We used the schema given at the website to gather a list of all ObjectProperties and their ranges, including all the subtypes and supertypes. This means, e.g. for

---

[13] Following [7], we use blank nodes for instances extracted from Microdata.

Table 5. Most common used defined properties with a domain violation, ordered by number of PLDs.

	Class	Property	#PLDs	Is property of type
1	s:Product	s:price	2 480	s:Offer
2	s:LocalBusiness	s:addressLocality	1 437	s:PostalAddress
3	s:LocalBusiness	s:addressRegion	1 143	s:PostalAddress
4	s:Product	s:availability	1 163	s:Offer
5	s:Product	s:video	1 032	s:CreativeWork
6	s:Article	s:ratingValue	983	s:Rating
7	s:Article	s:ratingCount	943	s:Rating
8	s:WebPage	s:title	868	s:JobPosting
9	s:LocalBusiness	s:streetAddress	766	s:PostalAddress
10	s:Event	s:price	731	s:Offer
11	s:LocalBusiness	s:postalCode	687	s:PostalAddress
12	s:Event	s:telephone	565	s:Person, s:Organization, s:Place
13	s:WebPage	s:location	550	s:PostalAddress
14	s:Place	s:startDate	545	s:Event, s:Role, s:Season, s:Series
15	s:Event	s:email	510	s:Person, s:Organization
16	s:Product	s:category	508	s:Offer
17	s:Place	s:endDate	489	s:Event, s:Role, s:Season, s:Series
18	s:Product	s:priceCurrency	390	s:PostalAddress
19	s:Review	s:ratingValue	344	s:Rating
20	s:Blog	s:breadcrumb	336	s:WebPage

the property s:bloodSupply expecting an object of type s:Vessel, we recursively included all subtypes (e.g. s:Artery and s:Vein), as well as all supertypes (s:AnatomicalStructure, s:MedicalEntity, and s:Thing) of this object. An instance of any of those types in the object position, respectively, was counted as correctly typed.

From the 163 404 PLDs making use of ObjectProperties, 14 089 (8.62 %) PLDs violate the defined range of at least one object property on their pages. Table 6 lists the 20 most common range violations. This list does only include those PLDs which use the object properties with an object as range, and not with a literal, as those mistakes are covered in Sect. 3.4.

The most common *mistake* is made for the property s:mainContentOfPage for the type s:WebPage, expecting an object of type s:WebPageElement. Here webmasters in 92.5 % of the cases maintain an object of type s:Blog as value. Semantically, this might make sense, as the Blog is part of the web page, but based on the schema, s:Blog is a subtype of s:CreativeWork and by that no subtype of s:WebPageElement. For the property s:aggregateRating of type s:Article, we found that the major reason for the range violation results from undefined types, resulting from spelling mistakes, e.g. s:aggregatedrating.

Table 6. Most common type, object property range violation ordered by number of PLDs.

	Domain	Property	#PLDs		Domain	Property	#PLDs
1	s:WebPage	s:mainContentOfPage	6 230	11	s:Review	s:reviewRating	179
2	s:Article	s:aggregateRating	1 696	12	s:JobPosting	s:jobLocation	173
3	s:BlogPosting	s:author	1 460	13	s:JobPosting	s:address	151
4	s:Product	s:offers	405	14	s:Product	s:review	131
5	s:Place	s:address	396	15	s:Recipe	s:reviews	108
6	s:Review	s:aggregateRating	298	16	s:Article	s:author	103
7	s:LocalBusiness	s:address	283	17	s:Dentist	s:address	95
8	s:Product	s:aggregateRating	259	18	s:Movie	s:director	76
9	s:Place	s:geo	257	19	s:Event	s:location	66
10	s:Organization	s:address	219	20	s:SoftwareApplication	s:aggregateRating	63

In [8], a similar analysis has been carried out for LOD, using reasoning to find inconsistencies between a type assigned to an instance, and the expected type according to the domain/range of its properties. On average, 2.4 % of all LOD documents are reported to show one such inconsistency, as opposed to 3.2 % of the document in our corpus.

3.8 Hybrid Properties

Last, we have a look at properties which are defined as DatatypeProperties as well as ObjectProperties in schema.org. In comparison to LOD, where this phenomenon is only rarely applied [8], 24 such properties exist in schema.org, e.g. s:category, s:citation, s:defaultValue, s:image, s:option, and s:query to name just a few.[14] While those are not a mistake w.r.t. schema.org, they lead to an unclean knowledge base when applying RDFS/OWL semantics.

Table 7 lists all of the hybrid properties which are deployed within our corpus with the number of PLDs making use of them at least once. From the 24 available hybrid properties, only 10 are present within our corpus. The most common used property is s:image, whose range can be an URL or an s:ImageObject, the same holds for s:logo. The third most common used hybrid property is s:model, where the schema expects a textual description of an item of type s:ProductModel. A still broadly used property is s:category. The schema allows a textual description, as well as a s:Thing and more specific a s:Physical ActivityCategory.

For those 10 properties, we again used our datatype guesser (see Sect. 3.5) to find out what kind of value is mostly used for those properties. Table 8 lists for each of the properties the percentage of value types used by PLDs for this property. Whenever it was not possible to find a more specific datatype, the datatype s:Text was guessed. The table reveals that most of the cases, objects are not the dominantly deployed value types for those properties. Among the

---

[14] The complete list of properties can be found at http://webdatacommons.org/structureddata/2013-11/stats/fixing_common_errors.html.

Table 7. List of all deployed hybrid properties, ordered by the number of pay-level domains using them at least once.

	Property	#PLDs		Property	#PLDs
1	s:image	133 819	6	s:citation	24
2	s:logo	10 929	7	s:license	13
3	s:model	2 231	8	s:eligibleRegion	12
4	s:category	825	9	s:toLocation	1
5	s:screenshot	305	10	s:fromLocation	1

Table 8. Distribution of deployed object or datatypes for hybrid properties by percentage of PLDs making use of those values. Most outstanding values are marked bold. The table lists only properties used by more than one PLD.

Property	# Different PLDs	Object	Text	URL	Number	Date
s:image	133 819	0.08 %	15.22 %	**84.68 %**	0.01 %	0.00 %
s:logo	10 929	1.59 %	3.41 %	**95.00 %**	0.00 %	0.00 %
s:model	2 231	0.14 %	**76.82 %**	0.82 %	14.27 %	7.94 %
s:category	825	0.12 %	**98.32 %**	1.20 %	0.24 %	0.12 %
s:screenshot	305	3.25 %	5.84 %	**90.91 %**	0.00 %	0.00 %
s:citation	24	14.29 %	50.00 %	32.14 %	3.57 %	0.00 %
s:license	13	0.00 %	**76.92 %**	23.08 %	0.00 %	0.00 %
s:eligibleRegion	12	0.00 %	**100.00 %**	0.00 %	0.00 %	0.00 %

properties, `s:citation` stands out. Here, we cannot define the major used value type, as beside `s:CreativeWork` and `s:Text` (as defined by the schema), 32 % of the PLDs use a URL as value.

4 Heuristics for Fixing Deployed Schema.org Microdata

Since we cannot rely that data *providers* will fix their Microdata, we follow the approach of repairing the data on the *consumer* side. In the following, we introduce a set of simple heuristics for fixing schema.org Microdata, and quantify their coverage. With those heuristics, many of the mistakes discussed above can be fixed rather easily.

4.1 Identifying and Fixing Wrong Namespaces

According to our observation from the previous section, we identified a set of heuristics to fix the most common namespace mistakes:

1. Removal of the leading `www.` before `schema.org`
2. Replacement of `https://` by `http://`

3. Conversion of the whole domain name to lower case
4. Removal of any additional sequence between `http://` and `schema.org`
5. Addition of an extra slash after `schema.org`, if none is present.

Using these rules in the given order, we are able to fix 147 out of 148 of wrongly spelled `schema.org` namespaces. The remaining namespace had a duplication of the top-level domain `.org` and could not be fixed by these heuristics.

4.2   Handling Undefined Types and Properties

Apart from mistakes resulting from errors within the namespace and missing slashes, our analysis in Sect. 3.2 and 3.3 has revealed that a large number of undefined types and properties are caused by spelling errors, in particular wrong capitalization (e.g. `s:contentURL` and `s:jobtitle`). Thus, whenever parsing Microdata entities from web pages, we suggest to not take capitalization into account, and replace each schema element with the properly capitalized version. This approach has also been proposed for consuming LOD in [8].

Applying this heuristic (together with the fixing of namespaces as above) to the undefined/unknown types, it is possible to replace them by correct types for 17 192 (71.0 %) of all PLDs using undefined types. Likewise, we can replace undefined properties on 10 281 (65.92 %) of the PLDs exposing that problem. However, we can observe a long tail distribution here, i.e., the remaining 29.0 % (34.08 %) PLDs account for 73.89 % (91.82 %) of all undefined types (properties, resp.). Those long-tail errors are typically hard-to-detect typos or types and properties that have been made up freely.

4.3   Handling ObjectProperties with a Literal Value

As shown in Sect. 3.4, the main objects which are modeled by the webmasters as literals are `s:Organization`, `s:Person`, and `s:PostalAddress`. Thus, we randomly inspected 715 such property value for the properties `s:author`, `s:creator`, and `s:address`, to get a better understanding. From this analysis, we saw that the majority of literals for `s:Person` and `s:Organization` are person and organization names or URLs, while `s:PostalAddress` is usually represented by a textual representation of the address.

From this observation, we derive the following strategy for fixing literal valued ObjectProperties: Given a triple

1. `_:1 s:op l .,`

where `s:op` is an ObjectProperty, and `l` is a literal, replace the triple by

1. `_:1 s:op _:2 .`
2. `_:2 a s:t .`
3. `_:2 (s:name|s:url) l .`

Here, `s:t` is the range of `s:op`, or the least abstract common supertype of all ranges, if there are more than one. If `l` is a valid URL, then it is set as the `s:url` of the newly created instance, otherwise, it is used as its `s:name`.[15]

With this heuristic, we are able to replace *all* misused `ObjectProperties` on 92 449 PLDs with a semantically correct set of triples. Note that using this heuristic might change the overall distribution of types within the corpus, as it will create a larger number of new entities (e.g., of type `s:PostalAddress`). For example, mapping all `s:address` literal values to a new `s:PostalAddress` would create around 14 million new entities of this type, which would be an increase of 11 %. Inspecting this shift more closely will be subject to future work.

4.4 Handling Property Domain Violations

As discussed in Sect. 3.3, properties used on objects that they are not defined on are often caused by "shortcuts" taken by the data provider. Picking up the example above, the data provider used the triple

1. `_:1 s:ratingValue ''5'' .`

instead of the set of triples

1. `_:1 s:aggregateRating _:2 .`
2. `_:2 a s:AggregateRating .`
3. `_:2 s:ratingValue ''5'' .`

where `_:1` is of type `s:Article`. In order to expand the wrong triple to the correct set of triples, we need to guess what the data provider meant. To that end, we use the following approach: Given two triples

1. `foo:x s:r foo:y .`
2. `foo:x a s:t .`

where `s:t` is *not* the domain of `s:r`, we try to find a relation R and a type T within schema.org such that one of the following two patterns is fulfilled:

1. `R s:domainIncludes s:t .`   1. `R s:rangeIncludes s:t .`
2. `R s:rangeIncludes` T`.`   2. `R s:domainIncludes` T `.`
3. `s:r s:domainIncludes` T `.`   3. `s:r s:domainIncludes` T`.`

If there is *one unique* solution for *only one of the two* pattern, we replace the erroneous triple with the solution we found. In a second step, we unify all newly created entities of one type into one entity. Thus, given that in the above example, there was also a `s:ratingCount` defined, we would end up with only instance of *s:AggregateRating* with both the `s:ratingValue` and the `s:ratingCount` properties from the original `s:Article`.

With that heuristic, we could replace 1 098 out of 3 767 properties used with types they are not defined for, which corresponds to 5 011 (31.42 %) of all PLDs. In 986 cases, no solution could be found for any of the two patterns; in the remaining 1 683 cases, the solution found was not unique.

---

[15] Note that `s:name` is more generic than, e.g., the name of a person. It is comparable to `rdfs:label` in RDF.

5   Conclusion and Outlook

In this paper, we have identified the most common mistakes made by providers of *schema.org* Microdata. Beside more obvious mistakes as spellings errors within namespaces, types or property names, we have identified various confusions within the usage of values of ObjectProperties and DatatypeProperties, and the violation of domain and range constraints defined for schema.org. Additionally, we have investigated the parseability of values, e.g., numbers or dates.

For the issues identified, we have performed a quantitative analysis and compared the numbers to similar analyses carried out on Linked Open Data. The comparison shows that Microdata is cleaner than LOD w.r.t. simple errors such as the usage of undefined types or properties, while schema conformance (such as respecting domain/range restrictions) is higher for LOD.

One main finding is that the majority of information marked-up using Microdata with *schema.org* can be parsed following the recommended schema. We have proposed a set of simple heuristics that can be applied by data consumers to fix a large fraction of wrong markup in a post-processing step. With those heuristics, we were able to curate an improved, cleaned up version of the WebDataCommons Microdata corpus, which corrects many of the syntactic and semantic errors made on the data providers' side. This new corpus is a higher quality knowledge base, derived from Microdata deployed on the web, and fixing data provided at tens of thousands of PLDs.[16]

Many of our heuristics are still simple, and there is a room for improvement. For example, we are currently not trying to guess matching properties for misspelled ones beyond capitalization errors. Furthermore, our method for creating new objects for literal-valued ObjectProperties is rather simple. In particular for complex objects, such as addresses, it could be strongly improved by training extractors that decompose the given literal into a street, a city, ZIP code, etc. Furthermore, our heuristic for domain violation so far only works if there is a *unique* solution, but a more relaxed version looking for *likely* solutions (e.g., patterns that are more commonly deployed than others) could fix even more mistakes. Similar solutions could be applied for fixing ObjectProperty range violations, which are currently not addressed by our approach.

Another interesting observation we made was that some classes and properties – such as s:Game – were already widely used in the corpus *before* they became a standard. With our methods, we can identify such widely used cases and provide quantitative evidence to discussions on missing classes and properties in the data schema.

While in this paper, we have taken a *synchronic* approach, looking only at the state of the data deployment at the current time, we aim at extending our analysis with a *diachronic* perspective, looking at the changes over time. This would reveal insights data quality change over time, as well as on the pace at which changes in the data schema (such as deprecations) are adopted.

---

[16] The corpus is available for download at http://webdatacommons.org/structured-data/2013-11/stats/fixing_common_errors.html.

References

1. Abedjan, Z., Gruetze, T., Jentzsch, A., Naumann, F.: Profiling and mining rdf data with prolod++. In: 2014 IEEE 30th International Conference on Data Engineering (ICDE), pp. 1198–1201. IEEE (2014)
2. Abedjan, Z., Lorey, J., Naumann, F.: Reconciling ontologies and the web of data. In: Proceedings of the 21st International Conference on Information and Knowledge Management (CIKM), Maui, Hawaii, USA, pp. 1532–1536 (2012)
3. Beek, W., Rietveld, L., Bazoobandi, H.R., Wielemaker, J., Schlobach, S.: LOD laundromat: a uniform way of publishing other people's dirty data. In: Mika, P., Tudorache, T., Bernstein, A., Welty, C., Knoblock, C., Vrandečić, D., Groth, P., Noy, N., Janowicz, K., Goble, C. (eds.) ISWC 2014, Part I. LNCS, vol. 8796, pp. 213–228. Springer, Heidelberg (2014)
4. Bizer, C., Eckert, K., Meusel, R., Mühleisen, H., Schuhmacher, M., Völker, J.: Deployment of RDFa, microdata, and microformats on the web – a quantitative analysis. In: Alani, H., et al. (eds.) ISWC 2013, Part II. LNCS, vol. 8219, pp. 17–32. Springer, Heidelberg (2013)
5. Chen, S., Hong, D., Shen, V.: An experimental study on validation problems with existing html webpages. In: Proceedings of the 2005 International Conference on Internet Computing, ICOMP 2005 (2005)
6. Fürber, C., Hepp, M.: Swiqa-a semantic web information quality assessment framework. In: ECIS (2011)
7. Hickson, I., Kellogg, G., Tennison, J., Herman, I.: Microdata to rdf - second edition (2014). http://www.w3.org/TR/microdata-rdf/
8. Hogan, A., Harth, A., Passant, A., Decker, S., Polleres, A.: Weaving the pedantic web. In: Linked Data on the Web (2010)
9. Kontokostas, D., Westphal, P., Auer, S., Hellmann, S., Lehmann, J., Cornelissen, R., Zaveri, A.: Test-driven evaluation of linked data quality. In: Proceedings of the 23rd International Conference on World Wide Web, pp. 747–758 (2014)
10. Lehmberg, O., Ritze, D., Ristoski, P., Eckert, K., Paulheim, H., Bizer, C.: Extending tables with data from over a million websites. In: Semantic Web Challenge (2014)
11. Meusel, R., Petrovski, P., Bizer, C.: The webdatacommons microdata, RDFa and microformat dataset series. In: Mika, P., et al. (eds.) ISWC 2014, Part I. LNCS, vol. 8796, pp. 277–292. Springer, Heidelberg (2014)
12. Mika, P.: Microformats and RDFa deployment across the web (2011). http://tripletalk.wordpress.com/2011/01/25/rdfa-deployment-across-the-web/
13. Mika, P., Potter, T.: Metadata statistics for a large web corpus. In: LDOW 2012: Linked Data on the Web. CEUR Workshop Proceedings, vol. 937. CEUR-ws.org (2012). http://ceur-ws.org/Vol-937/
14. Patel-Schneider, P.F.: Analyzing Schema.org (2014)
15. Petrovski, P., Bryl, V., Bizer, C.: Integrating product data from websites offering microdata markup. In: 4th Workshop on Data Extraction and Object Search (DEOS2014) @ WWW (2014)
16. Poveda-Villalón, M., Gómez-Pérez, A., Suárez-Figueroa, M.C.: Oops!(ontology pitfall scanner!): An on-line tool for ontology evaluation. Int. J. Semant. Web Inf. Syst. (IJSWIS) **10**(2), 7–34 (2014)

17. Schmachtenberg, M., Bizer, C., Paulheim, H.: Adoption of the linked data best practices in different topical domains. In: Mika, P., Tudorache, T., Bernstein, A., Welty, C., Knoblock, C., Vrandečić, D., Groth, P., Noy, N., Janowicz, K., Goble, C. (eds.) ISWC 2014, Part I. LNCS, vol. 8796, pp. 245–260. Springer, Heidelberg (2014)
18. Zaveri, A., Rula, A., Maurino, A., Pietrobon, R., Lehmann, J., Auer, S., Hitzler, P.: Quality assessment methodologies for linked open data. Submitted Semant. Web J. (2013)

Semantic Web and Web Science

Scientific Web and Web Science

Using @Twitter Conventions to Improve #LOD-Based Named Entity Disambiguation

Genevieve Gorrell[✉], Johann Petrak, and Kalina Bontcheva

Department of Computer Science, University of Sheffield,
211 Portobello, Sheffield, UK
{G.Gorrell,Johann.Petrak,K.Bontcheva}@sheffield.ac.uk

Abstract. State-of-the-art named entity disambiguation approaches tend to perform poorly on social media content, and microblogs in particular. Tweets are processed individually and the richer, microblog-specific context is largely ignored. This paper focuses specifically on quantifying the impact on entity disambiguation performance when readily available contextual information is included from URL content, hash tag definitions, and Twitter user profiles. In particular, including URL content significantly improves performance. Similarly, user profile information for @mentions improves recall by over 10 % with no adverse impact on precision. We also share a new corpus of tweets, which have been hand-annotated with DBpedia URIs, with high inter-annotator agreement.

1 Introduction

A large body of research has focused on Linked Open Data-based Named Entity Disambiguation (NED), where names mentioned in text are linked to URIs in Linked Open Data (LOD) resources (e.g., [11,18]).

State-of-the-art LOD-based NED approaches (see Sect. 2) have been developed and evaluated predominantly on news articles and other carefully written, longer texts [5,23]. As discussed in Sect. 2, very few microblog corpora annotated with LOD URIs exist and they are also small and incomplete.

Moreover, where researchers have evaluated microblog NED, e.g. [8], state-of-the-art approaches have shown poor performance, due the limited context, linguistic noise, and use of emoticons, abbreviations and hashtags. Each microblog post is treated in isolation, without taking into account the wider available context. In particular, only tweet text tends to be processed, even though the complete tweet JSON object also includes author profile data (full name, optional location, profile text, and web page). Around 26 % of all tweets also contain URLs [4], 16.6 % – hashtags, and 54.8 % – at least one user name mention.

Our novel contribution lies in systematically investigating the impact that such additional context has on LOD-based entity disambiguation in tweets (see Sect. 6). In particular, in the case of hashtags, tweet content is enriched with hashtag definitions, which are retrieved automatically from the web. Similarly, tweets containing @mentions are enriched with the textual information from that Twitter profile. In the case of URLs, the corresponding web content is included

© Springer International Publishing Switzerland 2015
F. Gandon et al. (Eds.): ESWC 2015, LNCS 9088, pp. 171–186, 2015.
DOI: 10.1007/978-3-319-18818-8_11

as context. Disambiguation performance is measured both when such context expansion is performed *individually* (i.e. only hashtags, only URLs, etc.), as well as when all this contextual information is used *jointly*.

A new corpus of around 800 tweets is made available, annotated with DBpedia URIs, by multiple experts (Sect. 3). The tweets contain hashtags, URLs, and user mentions, including many with corresponding DBpedia URIs (e.g. @eonenergyuk). The resulting dataset[1] is split into equally sized training and evaluation parts.

2 Related Work

There are a number of openly available, state-of-the-art LOD-based NED systems (for a complete list see [5]), including DBpedia Spotlight [18], AIDA [11], and, most recently, AGDISTIS [27]. Another notable example is TagMe, which was designed specifically for annotating short texts with respect to Wikipedia [9]. A comparative evaluation of all openly available state-of-the-art approaches, except the most recent AGDISTIS, is reported in [5], using several available news datasets, which however exhibit very different characteristics to social media.

Microblog named entity disambiguation is a relatively new, under-explored task. Recent tweet-focused evaluations uncovered problems in using state-of-the-art NED approaches in this genre [1,8], largely due to the brevity of tweets (140 characters). There has been limited research on analysing Twitter hashtags and annotating them with DBpedia entries, to assist semantic search over microblog content, e.g. [16]. NER systems targeted at microblog text don't commonly utilize these cues, for example treating hashtags as common words, e.g. [15,21] or not considering them, as in TwiNER [14]. Shen et al. [26] use additional tweets from a user's timeline to find user-specific topics and use those to improve the disambiguation. Huang et al. [13] present an extension of graph-based disambiguation which introduces "Meta Paths" that represent context from other tweets through shared hash tags, authors, or mentions. Gattani et al. [10] make use of URL expansion and use context derived from tweets by the same author and containing the same hashtag, but don't evaluate the contribution of this context to end performance, and don't make use of hashtag definitions or user biographies.

Microblog corpora created specifically for LOD-based entity disambiguation are very limited. Some, e.g. Ritter's [24], contain only entity types, whereas those from the MSM challenges [3,25] have anonymised the URLs and user name mentions, which makes them unsuitable for our experiments. Corpora created for semantic linking, such as Meij [17], are not well suited for evaluating named entity disambiguation, since annotations in those corpora include entities which are not mentioned explicitly, as well as generic concepts (e.g. art).

3 The Annotated Tweet Corpus

A set of 794 tweets were collected. 400 of those were tweets from 2013 coming from financial institutions and news outlets, which were chosen due to the

---

[1] Available from https://gate.ac.uk/applications/yodie.html.

relatively high frequency of named entities within. They are challenging for entity recognition and disambiguation, since capitalisation is not informative (all words have initial capital), but on the other hand, they are quite grammatical.

The rest are random tweets collected in 2014, as part of the DecarboNet project on analysing online climate change debates [22]. Keywords such as "climate change", "earth hour", "energy", and "fracking" were used and the 394 tweets were chosen as a representative sample, containing sufficient named entities, without significant repetition.

The 794 tweets (see Table 1) were annotated manually by a team of 10 NLP researchers, using a CrowdFlower interface. Each tweet was tagged by three annotators, chosen at random by CrowdFlower amongst these ten. Annotations for which no clear decision was made were adjudicated by a fourth expert, who had not previously seen the tweets. Unanimous inter-annotator agreement occurred for 89 % of entities, which can be used as the upper bound on performance attainable by an automatic method on this dataset and task.

While others [12] have used automatic named entity recognition tools to identify entities and only then carry out manual disambiguation, we avoided bias by first asking annotators to manually tag all tweets with named entities. Then entity disambiguation annotation was carried out in a second manual annotation round, where annotators had to choose amongst one of the candidate URIs or NIL (no target entity), when no target entity exists in DBpedia. The latter case is quite frequent in tweets, where people often refer to friends and family.

Highly ambiguous entity mentions (e.g. Paris), however, can have tens or even over a hundred possible candidate DBpedia URIs. Since showing so many options to a human annotator is not feasible, instead, during data preparation, candidate entity URIs were ranked according to their Wikipedia commonness score [19] and only the top 8 were shown, in addition to "none of the above" and "not an entity" (to allow for errors in the entity tagging stage).

Table 1. Corpus statistics

	Tweets	Total NEs	URLs	Hashtags	@mentions
Total	794	681	504 (236)	359 (188)	334 (316)
Training	397	257	242 (112)	172 (88)	167 (157)
Test	397	424	262 (124)	187 (100)	167 (159)

The resulting corpus contains 252 person annotations, 309 location annotations, 347 organization annotations and 218 nil annotations. With respect to URLs, user mentions, and hashtags, Table 1 shows the statistics of their availability in the corpus. The number in brackets shows how frequently expanded context can be obtained for them. It is evident that whilst URLs appear frequently in the data, only around half of them are successfully retrieved. This is due to both web pages becoming outdated and also URLs often being truncated in re-tweets where tweet character limits are often exceeded. Similar to the findings of earlier studies, hashtags are less frequent, and again, we are able to retrieve their definitions from the web automatically in only half of the cases. @mentions are the least frequent; however, we were able to obtain the corresponding Twitter user profiles for most of them, with variable quality.

4   The NED Framework

In order to experiment with the effects of tweet expansion on NED performance, and in particular, on how additional contextual information impacts different semantic similarity metrics (see Sect. 5), we make use of a NED framework built on top of GATE [6], called YODIE[2]. It combines GATE's existing ANNIE NER system with a number of widely used URI candidate selection strategies, similarity metrics, and a machine learning model for entity disambiguation, which determines the best candidate URI.

In this section, we provide a brief overview of YODIE, focusing in particular on the similarity metrics investigated in the tweet expansion experiments in this paper, and the final disambiguation stage, since these are the parts that are influenced by tweet expansion. For a complete description, including more information about candidate selection and the features used for disambiguation see [2]. We conclude the section with a comparison positioning YODIE with respect to other state-of-the-art NED systems, which demonstrates that YODIE is a representative framework in performance terms in which to conduct our experiments.

4.1   Scoring and Feature Creation

At each NE location and for every candidate, YODIE calculates a number of normalized scores, which reflect the semantic similarity between the entity referred to by the candidate and the context of its mention:

- *Relatedness Score*: introduced in [20], uses the proportion of incoming links that overlap in the Wikipedia graph to favour congruent candidate choices.
- *LOD-based Similarity Score*: similar to above but based on the number of relations between each pair of URIs in the DBpedia graph (introduced next).
- *Text-based Similarity Scores*: measure the similarity between the textual context of the mentioned named entity and text associated with each candidate URI for that mention (see below).

LOD-based Similarity Scores: LOD-based similarity scores are calculated as the number of direct or indirect relations between each candidate URI of an ambiguous named entity and the URIs of candidates for other named entities within a given context window. All relations present in DBpedia are considered for this calculation. We calculate several separate scores, for the number of direct relations ($a \rightarrow b, a \leftarrow b$) between URIs a and b, and for the indirect relations between a and b that involve one other node x ($a \leftarrow x \rightarrow b$, $a \rightarrow x \leftarrow b$, $a \rightarrow x \rightarrow b$, $a \leftarrow x \leftarrow b$).

---

[2] https://gate.ac.uk/applications/yodie.html.

For example, if the document mentions both *Paris* and *France*, a direct relations score is assigned to db:Paris, as the two are connected directly via the db:country property. On the other hand, if *Paris* appears in the context of *USA*, a higher indirect score for db:Paris,_Texas will be assigned by combining the DBpedia knowledge that Paris, Texas is related to Texas and the additional knowledge that Texas is a US state.

Since any NE mention can have several candidate URIs, and each of the other entities in the context can have several candidates too, YODIE calculates the value of each score as the sum over all pairs for each candidate, divided by the distance in characters between the candidate locations [2]. This means that where a relationship is found, both candidates in question will benefit. The combined LOD-based similarity score is a sum of scores for all relation types each weighted by the inverse square of the degrees of separation, i.e., indirect relations receive a quarter weighting compared with direct relationships. The context for the calculation of these scores and the relatedness score is set to 100 characters to the left and 100 to the right of each location, rounded down to the nearest whole word, as a heuristic designed to make the calculation quickly achievable by reducing the number of neighbours.

Text-based Similarity Scores: YODIE's text-based similarity scores evaluate candidate URIs on the basis of how well the surrounding context matches representative text associated with the candidate URI. Three approaches to text-based similarity are supported, as follows:

1. Text from the URI's DBpedia abstract, limited to the words within the first 5000 characters, again, as a heuristic to avoid very variable computation times due to unexpectedly large documents.
2. The abstract text as above, plus the literals from all datatype properties for the URI.
3. All previous words, plus the literals from all datatype properties of directly linked other URIs.

The entire tweet is used as context, subject to stop word removal and lower-casing. The three textual similarity scores for each candidate URI are calculated as the cosine similarities between the context vector and the vector of the respective text for the candidate. Cosine was chosen for its wide popularity.

4.2   Disambiguation

As described above, YODIE generates a number of similarity scores, each providing different information about the fit of each candidate URI to the entity mention. The process of deciding how to combine these scores to select the best candidate URI is non-trivial. YODIE uses LibSVM[3] to select the best candidate. A probabilistic SVM is used, in order to make use of the classification probability estimates in selecting a candidate. Default parameters are used, since tuning failed to improve performance.

---

[3] http://www.csie.ntu.edu.tw/~cjlin/libsvm/.

Training data for the model consists of one training instance for each candidate generated by the system on the training corpus. Each instance receives a target of `true` if the candidate is the correct disambiguation target and `false` otherwise. The values of the various similarity metrics are used as features (see [2] for details). This means that at application time, the model assigns to each candidate a class of true or false, along with a probability. This classification is independent of the other candidates on that entity, but ranking of the candidate list is able to be performed on the basis of the probability. The most probable URI is thus assigned as the target disambiguation for this entity, unless its probability is below a given confidence threshold, in which case "nil" is assigned. We trained on TAC KBP data from 2009 to 2013, excluding the 2010 set[4], along with the AIDA training set [11], and the tweet training set introduced in Sect. 3.

4.3   Comparison to Other NED Systems

In order to validate YODIE as a framework suitable for performing the tweet expansion experiments, we compare performance with other available state-of-the-art NED approaches. Results are reported on the widely used "Test B" part of the Aida/CoNLL corpus [11] (see Table 2). This corpus contains 231 documents with 4485 target annotations.

The results shown in Table 2 for AGDISTIS (the most recent NED system) are those reported in [27]. AIDA [11], Spotlight [7,18], and TagMe [9] results are as reported in [5] (this AIDA result is indicated with a "2013" suffix in the table). The latter paper also includes a detailed comparison against the Illinois Wikifier and Wikipedia Miner. However, due to space limitations here, these worse performing systems are excluded. The results for the latest Aida algorithm in 2014 [12] are also included, based on a local installation of the 2014-08-02 version of the system (as recommended on the AIDA web page) and the 2014-01-02v2 version of the dataset[5]. Results for several other widely used NED services are also included (default parameter settings are used), namely Lupedia[6], TextRazor[7] and Zemanta[8].

As can be seen in Table 2, on this news dataset, YODIE performs second best. The latest AIDA system outperforms others by some margin on the AIDA dataset, but amongst others, YODIE compares favourably. The rest of the paper will focus on more in-depth experiments and analysis of the various tweet expansion techniques and their impact on NED precision and recall.

5   Expansions Studied

This section describes our methodology for retrieving and utilizing expanded context from hashtags, user mentions, and URLs.

---

[4] http://www.nist.gov/tac/2013/KBP/.

[5] http://www.mpi-inf.mpg.de/departments/databases-and-information-systems/research/yago-naga/aida/downloads/.

[6] http://lupedia.ontotext.com/.

[7] https://www.textrazor.com/.

[8] http://www.zemanta.com/.

Table 2. AIDA B evaluation

System	Prec.	Recall	F1
YODIE	0.62	0.65	0.64
Aida/2013	**0.74**	0.34	0.47
Aida/2014	0.70	**0.74**	**0.72**
Spotlight	0.31	0.40	0.35
TagMe	0.61	0.56	0.58
AGDISTIS	0.64	0.56	0.60
Lupedia	0.58	0.31	0.40
TextRazor	0.35	0.58	0.34
Zemanta	0.51	0.29	0.37

5.1   Performing Tweet Context Expansion

In the YODIE NED framework, each individual tweet is represented as a separate document. Context expansion is performed by temporarily including additional text about each @mention, hashtag and URL link. Subsequent stages then process the original tweet text together with each individual context section. This approach makes use of the flexible way in which GATE models arbitrary text spans in documents, through stand-off annotations. In other words, processing can be restricted to just those parts of the expanded tweet which are of interest, e.g. the original tweet text and the context created from all definitions of all hashtags present in the tweet. Metadata features on the annotations are also used to establish the link between the original hashtag, @mention, or URL in the tweet and their corresponding expansion text. Since documents in GATE are dynamically editable, all additional content is removed, after NED processing is completed and before evaluation.

Figure 1 illustrates an expanded tweet (yellow highlighted text in the main pane); "KAGAWA will be allowed to rejoin Borussia Dortmund in January in a swap deal which would see defender @NSubotic4 join #MUFC http://tiny.cc/4t19ux". The tweet includes a hashtag, #MUFC, highlighted in blue, a user ID, "NSubotic4" in pink and a URL in green. Each of these items is expanded into the longer section of correspondingly coloured text included below, in the order they appear in the tweet. Entities are indicated in a darker shade.

Expansion of Hashtags: Hashtags are a Twitter convention, which makes it easy for users to find all tweets on a given topic or event, e.g. a name (#obama), an abbreviation (#gop), concatenations of several words (#foodporn). Some hashtags are also ambiguous, i.e. can have different meanings at different times. Since many hashtags contain entity mentions, which are often missed by state-of-the-art NED systems, we experimented with expanding tweets with hashtag definitions, provided by the web site https://tagdef.com.

Tagdef hashtag definitions are crowdsourced. Since anyone is free to enter any definition, there is plenty of noise, for example in the expansions for Manchester

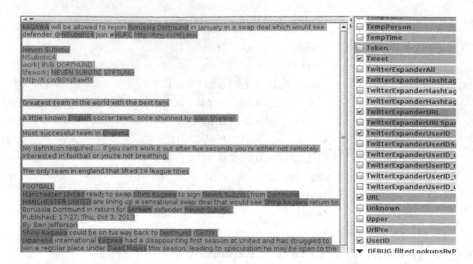

Fig. 1. A screenshot showing tweet expansions and entities found in them (Color figure online).

United Football Club in our screenshot example, the expansions are humorous and opinionated rather than informative. The website offers an API that returns up to 6 definitions, which are all added as additional context to the original tweet document. TagDef does not have definitions for all hashtags: in the 794 documents there are 359 hashtags of which 171 have no definitions.

Expansion of @Mentions: For each @mention, tweets are enriched with the following user profile textual information: `name`, `screen_name`, `location`, `description`, and `url`. The latter are not expanded with more content recursively. GATE annotations are added which identify from which of these fields the text originates. Not all @mentions found in a tweet can be expanded since the user may have deleted their account or an account may have been suspended. There are 334 @mentions in our corpus, of which 18 could not be resolved.

Expansion of URLs: For each URL in the tweet, the content of the corresponding web page is retrieved and added to the document. Since many web pages contains boilerplate text (e.g. navigational menus), this is filtered automatically and only the core text is added as additional context. Images are currently ignored. Since many people post images in their tweets, this is one of the reasons why URL expansion is not always possible. In addition, the target page may no longer exist or may not be accessible at retrieval time. In our corpus there are 504 URLs, of which 236 could not be expanded.

5.2   Making Use of the Expanded Content

As discussed above, for each candidate URI YODIE calculates a number of similarity scores, which are then used as features in the entity disambiguation model. Our experiments in tweet enrichment focus on its influence via the three introduced earlier, as well as the possibility of adding new candidates via back-projection of entities, as outlined below.

Contextual Similarity and Expansion: Contextual similarity uses the additional information in the expanded tweets, in order to calculate more reliable textual similarity scores. It treats the newly expanded text as though it were collocated with the original hashtag, user mention, or URL. Thus, if an item of expandable content appears within the context window, the entire, corresponding expanded content is included. Where multiple expansions apply, these are simply added in, since the context vectors are bag-of-words based. In the screenshot example, all of Neven Subotic's twitter profile, all of the hashtag expansions for Manchester United Football Club and the entire content of the URL are included as context for the entities in the tweet.

LOD-based and Relatedness Similarity Scores and Expansion: Since semantic relations between two candidate URIs are often sparse, we experimented also with using entities from the expanded context, in order to overcome this. As before, the entire expanded content is treated as though it were collocated with the item it is an expansion of. This means that relation-based similarities are calculated not only between candidates for the target entity and other candidate entities in the context window, but also between the target candidates and candidates for entities in the expanded content. In the screenshot example, we can see for example that "Alan Shearer" appears as an entity in the hashtag expansion, so in calculating a LOD-based similarity score for Borussia Dortmund's candidates, we consider whether they are related to candidates for Alan Shearer.

Back-Projection of Entities: In addition, we experiment with *improving entity disambiguation recall*, based on @mention expansions. This is motivated by the fact that an @mention may directly represent an entity which should be linked to the knowledge base, e.g. in our example, `@NSubotic4`. However, the concrete user name often does not get recognized as a named entity and therefore no candidate URIs are generated for it. Nevertheless, textual user names from the tweet author profiles often get recognized as named entities. In the example, the name "Neven Subotic" appears twice as a recognized entity in the expansion.

Therefore, we experiment with projecting the information from the named entity recognized in the expanded user profile, back on to the original @mention, thus potentially finding entity candidates which would not have been identified otherwise. In effect, this assigns the full list of candidate URIs from the named entity onto the user mention. This new candidate list is then used by YODIE for context-based disambiguation.

6   Experimental Results

This section presents the experimental results that demonstrate the impact of the three tweet expansion techniques on the semantic similarity scores discussed above. Statistics are presented on the entire tweet corpus, since scoring takes place before the ML-based disambiguation. This allows us to evaluate how the scores change without reserving training data for ML. Using a larger corpus maximizes the reliability and informativeness of the results. We present evaluation on the conditions outlined below, chosen for their interest and informativeness, since the full set of combinations would be large.

- **Base** The baseline condition includes no tweet expansion at all. Where machine learning is used, no tweet expansion was used in the training data.
- **Id** @mention expansions are used only. Where machine learning is used, only @mention expansions are included in the training data.
- **Url** URL expansions are used only. Where machine learning is used, only text from URL content is included in the training data.
- **Hash** Hashtag expansions only are used. Where machine learning is used, only hashtag expansions are included in the training data.
- **Id+Proj** @mention expansions are used along with back-projection of entities found in the expansion to create an entity on the @mention where previously there was none. Back-projection without @mention expansion doesn't make sense, hence these conditions must be evaluated together. This type of expansion is used only in the machine learning training data.
- **All** This experiment includes all expansions.
- **Id+Proj+Url** We explicitly evaluate the combination of Id+Proj and URL expansions without hashtags for reasons that become apparent in Sect. 6.2.

Finally, having considered how Twitter expansions affect the LOD-based and contextual similarity scores separately, we consider the impact on the entire system, i.e. including the ML-based disambiguation stage. See Sect. 6.2 for final system performances in comparison to other state-of-the-art systems. The results are reported on the test corpus, the training corpus having been used along with the TAC and AIDA corpora to train the support vector machine disambiguation model.

6.1   Impact of Tweet Expansion on Individual Similarity Features

There are several ways in which tweet expansions can influence YODIE's performance; via their influence on each of the of scores, and via the creation of new candidates via back-projection from @mentions. These also influence the decisions made by the disambiguation SVM model, hence impact of tweet expansion on the similarity scores is investigated first here, independent of the particular disambiguation algorithm.

In order to give an idea of the contribution of each score, results are reported for precision, recall and F1, obtained where the best candidate is selected on the basis of that individual score alone. It should be noted that naturally results obtained from such individual scores are comparatively low, since overall performance is made possible only by several features being used in combination by the ML model.

Table 3. LOD-based sim. score

	Prec.	Recall	F1
Base	**0.416**	0.267	0.326
Id	0.399	**0.276**	0.326
Url	0.414	0.272	**0.328**
Hash	0.385	0.253	0.305
Id+Proj	0.318	0.266	0.313
Id+Proj+Url	0.373	0.269	0.312
All	0.373	0.260	0.306

Table 4. Relatedness score

	Prec.	Recall	F1
Base	0.236	0.244	0.240
Id	**0.253**	0.272	**0.262**
Url	0.236	0.242	0.239
Hash	0.235	0.241	0.238
Id+Proj	0.244	0.269	0.256
Id+Proj+Url	0.249	**0.276**	**0.262**
All	0.250	0.266	0.258

Therefore, to put these individual scores in context, consider that if we select, for each entity, a URI from the candidate list at random, an F1 measure of 0.229 is achieved on the test tweet corpus. If we select the best ranked candidate URI based on URI frequencies in Wikipedia, this achieves an F1 of 0.521. URI frequency in Wikipedia, intuitively, indicates how important an entity target is in general world knowledge. This turns out to be a very hard baseline to beat, since not only is the most common candidate more likely to be correct by definition, but also it is more likely to be mentioned in the corpus. These two scores therefore demonstrate the range of performance realistically achievable by a metric, giving a lower (F1=0.229) and upper bound (F1=0.521). The performance of the three individual similarity metrics examined here, as expected, falls within this range.

As can be seen in Tables 3 and 4, the Wikipedia relatedness score and the LOD-based similarity score respond slightly differently to the inclusion of tweet expansion information. In particular, the expansion of user ids benefits recall for LOD-based similarity (Table 3), but also decreases precision. The best overall F1 is achieved with URL expansion only, but even then the score is not much higher than the F1 = 0.326 without any expansion. Results where back projection and @mention expansions are performed are substantially worse.

In contrast, the relatedness similarity score (Table 4) does benefit substantially from the additional textual information. @mention expansions, in particular, lead to improvements in both precision and recall, whereas hashtag and URL expansions have relatively little impact.

For text-based similarity on DBpedia abstracts alone, Table 5 shows that @mention expansion and entity projection lead to improved precision and recall, with hashtag and URL expansions bringing limited benefit only.

When other textual fields from DBpedia are used in addition to abstracts, as context for comparison of each candidate, then tweet expansion leads to even higher performance gains (see Table 6). In this case, URL and hashtag expansions both lead to improved results, with further gains brought by back projection and @mention expansion. The best overall result is when all expansions are combined.

6.2 Impact on Overall Disambiguation Performance

The full impact of tweet expansion on NED performance was also evaluated. Table 7 shows the results, where the three similarity features discussed

Table 5. Text: abstracts only			
	Prec.	Recall	F1
Base	0.201	0.421	0.272
Id	0.208	0.436	0.282
Url	0.194	0.407	0.263
Hash	0.204	0.427	0.276
Id+Proj	**0.217**	**0.463**	**0.295**
Id+Proj+Url	0.212	0.454	0.289
All	0.216	0.461	0.294

Table 6. Text: abstracts plus			
	Prec.	Recall	F1
Base	0.221	0.379	0.279
Id	0.226	0.389	0.286
Url	0.234	0.402	0.296
Hash	0.234	0.401	0.295
Id+Proj	0.235	0.414	0.300
Id+Proj+Url	0.247	0.434	0.315
All	**0.253**	**0.446**	**0.323**

individually in the previous section are now used in combination by the SVM disambiguation model. All other YODIE features and parameters remain unchanged.

We can see that in terms of F1, the biggest improvement comes from @mention expansions including also back-projection of entities. Compared with the baseline, the difference in accuracy is significant to $p < 0.0001$, as established using the McNemar Sign Test. The contribution of @mention expansion alone is not significantly better than the baseline. Hashtags, however, do produce a significant improvement in accuracy ($p = 0.046$), as do URLs ($p = 0.021$).

The confidence threshold on the disambiguation probability produced by the SVM is tuned on the dataset where all expansions are carried out. This leads to the levelling effect across precision and recall that we see in the final result. When compared against the other models, using all tweet expansion strategies leads to a slightly lower recall, but higher precision. Ultimately, this leads to the best overall performance in terms of F1 score.

Since hashtags contribute only marginally, we also examine whether this expansion could be excluded without impact on overall performance. Therefore, results were calculated using @mention with back-projection and URL expansion only (see row "Id+Proj+Url"). This leads to higher accuracy, compared to the system that includes all expansions. F1, however, is higher where hashtag expansion is included. The improvement in disambiguation accuracy is significant at $p = 0.004$; however, depending on the application, a higher F1 might be preferable. The difference in F1 can not be assessed for significance using a paired test.

We also evaluated whether hashtag and URL expansion could be excluded, since the difference in accuracy between all three expansion strategies versus including only @mention expansion with back-projection ("Id+Proj") is not statistically significant ($p = 0.1441$). However, when overall disambiguation accuracy with added URL expansion ("Id+Proj+Url") is compared against "Id+Proj" alone, the latter is indeed significantly worse ($p = 0.011$). Coupled with the fact that F1 also decreases, the conclusion is that URL expansion helps, when used in combination with the two @mention expansion strategies.

Table 7. Overall result

	Prec.	Recall	F1	Acc
Base	0.442	0.550	0.490	0.550
Id	0.444	0.557	0.494	0.557
Id+Proj	0.444	0.642	0.525	0.642
Url	0.452	0.568	0.504	0.568
Hash	0.446	0.559	0.496	0.559
Id+Pr+Url	0.452	**0.660**	0.536	**0.660**
All	**0.495**	0.623	**0.552**	0.623

Table 8. Tweet comparison

System	Prec.	Recall	F1
YODIE (Base)	0.44	0.55	0.49
YODIE (Exp)	0.50	0.62	**0.55**
Aida 2014	**0.59**	0.38	0.46
Lupedia	0.50	0.24	0.32
Spotlight	0.09	0.51	0.15
TagMe	0.10	**0.67**	0.17
TextRazor	0.19	0.44	0.26
Zemanta	0.48	0.56	0.52

The relative contribution of the three types of context expansion cannot be predicted easily for a different corpus, since the distribution of hashtags, user mentions, and URLs can vary from one tweet dataset to another. Nevertheless, extrapolating on the basis that if accuracy improvement due to an expansion type is x, and we had n successful expansions of that type in the corpus, then the improvement per successful expansion is x/n. Therefore, for a hypothetical corpus of 397 documents containing one single successful @mention expansion per document, we might see an accuracy improvement of 0.23; for URL expansions, 0.06; and for hashtag expansions, 0.04. The actual value in real terms, however, depends on the likelihood of those expansion types occuring in an actual corpus and the likelihood that expanded contextual information will be available at disambiguation time.

6.3 Contextualizing Potential Performance Gain

In order to contextualize the magnitude of improvement obtained within results obtained by state-of-the-art NED methods, YODIE's performance with and without tweet expansion is compared on the evaluation part of the tweet corpus described in Sect. 3. The best performing systems obtain F1 scores in the range of 0.46 to 0.52, as Table 8 shows, so the six point gain in F1 that we have shown to be possible through the use of tweet expansion is substantial, and sufficient to reposition a system in comparison with others.

7   Conclusions and Future Work

This paper investigated the impact on named entity disambiguation in tweets, when the original tweet text is enriched with additional contextual information from URLs, hashtags, and @mentions. The tweet expansion approaches investigated here can easily be incorporated within other LOD-based NED approaches, through the integration of the relatedness, textual similarity, and LOD-based similarity scores.

Our experiments demonstrated that tweet expansions lead to significantly improved NED performance on microblog content. In particular, overall accuracy improves by 7.3 percentage points, an improvement of 13.3 % compared with the baseline. Performance gain is slightly lower for F1 – an improvement of 6.2 percentage points (11.3 % over the baseline).

The main gains arise from the ability to disambiguate @mentions in which the tweet-text only baseline fails to identify their DBpedia referent. The dominant contribution in this case, therefore, is in terms of recall. It should also be noted that even without mention expansions, URL and hashtag expansions also lead to statistically significant improvements.

Limitations to the work include its dependence on the particular candidate scoring metrics and final disambiguation strategy used, since these constitute the channels through which tweet expansion can impact on performance. Future work will involve evaluating tweet expansion in the context of other systems in order to further investigate this interaction.

Acknowledgements. The authors wish to thank all volunteers from the NLP research group in Sheffield, who annotated the tweet corpus. This work was partially supported by the European Union under grant agreements No. 287863 TrendMiner and No. 610829 DecarboNet, as well as UK EPSRC grant No. EP/I004327/1.

References

1. Abel, F., Gao, Q., Houben, G.-J., Tao, K.: Semantic enrichment of Twitter posts for user profile construction on the social web. In: Antoniou, G., Grobelnik, M., Simperl, E., Parsia, B., Plexousakis, D., De Leenheer, P., Pan, J. (eds.) ESWC 2011, Part II. LNCS, vol. 6644, pp. 375–389. Springer, Heidelberg (2011)
2. Aswani, N., Gorrell, G., Bontcheva, K., Petrak, J.: Multilingual, ontology-based information extraction from stream media - v2. Technical report D2.3.2, TrendMiner Project Deliverable (2013). http://www.trendminer-project.eu/images/d2.3.2_final.pdf
3. Basave, A.E.C., Rizzo, G., Varga, A., Rowe, M., Stankovic, M., Dadzie, A.S.: Making sense of microposts (#microposts2014) named entity extraction & linking challenge. In: 4th Workshop on Making Sense of Microposts (#Microposts2014) (2014)
4. Carter, S., Weerkamp, W., Tsagkias, E.: Microblog language identification: Overcoming the limitations of short, unedited and idiomatic text. Lang. Resour. Eval. J. **47**, 195–215 (2013)
5. Cornolti, M., Ferragina, P., Ciaramita, M.: A framework for benchmarking entity-annotation systems. In: Proceedings of the 22nd International Conference on World Wide Web, WWW 2013, pp. 249–260 (2013)
6. Cunningham, H., Tablan, V., Roberts, A., Bontcheva, K.: Getting more out of biomedical documents with GATE's full lifecycle open source text analytics. PLoS Comput. Biol. **9**(2) (2013)
7. Daiber, J., Jakob, M., Hokamp, C., Mendes, P.N.: Improving efficiency and accuracy in multilingual entity extraction. In: Proceedings of the 9th International Conference on Semantic Systems, I-SEMANTICS 2013, New York, NY, USA, pp. 121–124 (2013)

8. Derczynski, L., Maynard, D., Rizzo, G., van Erp, M., Gorrell, G., Troncy, R., Bontcheva, K.: Analysis of named entity recognition and linking for tweets. Inf. Process. Manag. **51**, 32–49 (2015)
9. Ferragina, P., Scaiella, U.: Fast and accurate annotation of short texts with Wikipedia pages. IEEE Softw. **29**(1), 70–75 (2012)
10. Gattani, A., Lamba, D.S., Garera, N., Tiwari, M., Chai, X., Das, S., Subramaniam, S., Rajaraman, A., Harinarayan, V., Doan, A.: Entity extraction, linking, classification, and tagging for social media: a Wikipedia-based approach. Proceed. VLDB Endow. **6**(11), 1126–1137 (2013)
11. Hoffart, J., Yosef, M.A., Bordino, I., Furstenau, H., Pinkal, M., Spaniol, M., Taneva, B., Thater, S., Weikum, G.: Robust disambiguation of named entities in text. In: Conference on Empirical Methods in Natural Language Processing, pp. 782–792 (2011)
12. Hoffart, J., Altun, Y., Weikum, G.: Discovering emerging entities with ambiguous names. In: Proceedings of the 23rd International Conference on World Wide Web, pp. 385–396 (2014)
13. Huang, H., Cao, Y., Huang, X., Ji, H., Lin, C.Y.: Collective tweet wikification based on semi-supervised graph regularization. In: Proceedings of the 52nd Annual Meeting of the Association for Computational Linguistics, pp. 380–390 (2014)
14. Li, C., Weng, J., He, Q., Yao, Y., Datta, A., Sun, A., Lee, B.S.: Twiner: named entity recognition in targeted Twitter stream. In: Proceedings of the 35th International ACM SIGIR Conference on Research and Development in Information Retrieval, pp. 721–730. ACM (2012)
15. Liu, X., Zhang, S., Wei, F., Zhou, M.: Recognizing named entities in tweets. In: Proceedings of the 49th Annual Meeting of the Association for Computational Linguistics: Human Language Technologies, pp. 359–367 (2011)
16. Lösch, U., Müller, D.: Mapping microblog posts to encyclopedia articles. Lect. Notes Inform. **192**(150) (2011)
17. Meij, E., Weerkamp, W., de Rijke, M.: Adding semantics to microblog posts. In: Proceedings of the Fifth International Conference on Web Search and Data Mining (WSDM) (2012)
18. Mendes, P.N., Jakob, M., García-Silva, A., Bizer, C.: DBpedia Spotlight: shedding light on the web of documents. In: Proceedings of I-SEMANTICS, pp. 1–8 (2011)
19. Milne, D., Witten, I.H.: Learning to link with Wikipedia. In: Proceedings of the 17th Conference on Information and Knowledge Management (CIKM), pp. 509–518 (2008)
20. Milne, D., Witten, I.H.: An effective, low-cost measure of semantic relatedness obtained from Wikipedia links. In: Proceedings of AAAI 2008 (2008)
21. Murnane, E.L., Haslhofer, B., Lagoze, C.: Reslve: leveraging user interest to improve entity disambiguation on short text. In: Proceedings of the 22nd International Conference on World Wide Web Companion, pp. 1275–1284. International World Wide Web Conferences Steering Committee (2013)
22. Piccolo, L.S.G., Alani, H., De Liddo, A., Baranauskas, C.: Motivating online engagement and debates on energy consumption. In: Proceedings of the 2014 ACM Conference on Web Science (2014)
23. Rao, D., McNamee, P., Dredze, M.: Entity linking: finding extracted entities in a knowledge base. In: Poibeau, T., Saggion, H., Piskorski, J., Yangarber, R. (eds.) Multi-Source, Multi-Lingual Information Extraction and Summarization, pp. 93–115. Springer, Heidelberg (2013)
24. Ritter, A., Clark, S., Mausam, Etzioni, O.: Named entity recognition in tweets: an experimental study. In: Proceedings of EMNLP (2011)

25. Rowe, M., Stankovic, M., Dadzie, A., Nunes, B., Cano, A.: Making sense of microposts (#msm2013): big things come in small packages. In: Proceedings of the WWW Conference - Workshops (2013)
26. Shen, W., Wang, J., Luo, P., Wang, M.: Linking named entities in tweets with knowledge base via user interest modeling. In: Proceedings of the 19th ACM SIGKDD International Conference on Knowledge Discovery and Data Mining, pp. 68–76. ACM (2013)
27. Usbeck, R., Ngonga Ngomo, A.-C., Röder, M., Gerber, D., Coelho, S.A., Auer, S., Both, A.: AGDISTIS - graph-based disambiguation of named entities using linked data. In: Mika, P. (ed.) ISWC 2014, Part I. LNCS, vol. 8796, pp. 457–471. Springer, Heidelberg (2014)

Knowledge Enabled Approach to Predict the Location of Twitter Users

Revathy Krishnamurthy, Pavan Kapanipathi$^{(\boxtimes)}$, Amit P. Sheth, and Krishnaprasad Thirunarayan

Kno.e.sis Center, Wright State University, Dayton, USA
{revathy,pavan,amit,tkprasad}@knoesis.org

Abstract. Knowledge bases have been used to improve performance in applications ranging from web search and event detection to entity recognition and disambiguation. More recently, knowledge bases have been used to analyze social data. A key challenge in social data analysis has been the identification of the geographic location of online users in a social network such as Twitter. Existing approaches to predict the location of users, based on their tweets, rely solely on social media features or probabilistic language models. These approaches are supervised and require large training dataset of geo-tagged tweets to build their models. As most Twitter users are reluctant to publish their location, the collection of geo-tagged tweets is a time intensive process. To address this issue, we present an alternative, knowledge-based approach to predict a Twitter user's location at the city level. Our approach utilizes Wikipedia as a source of knowledge base by exploiting its hyperlink structure. Our experiments, on a publicly available dataset demonstrate comparable performance to the state of the art techniques.

Keywords: Wikipedia · Twitter · Location prediction · Semantics · Social data · Knowledge graphs

1 Introduction

Location of Twitter users is a prominent attribute for many applications such as emergency management and disaster response [15], trend prediction [1], and event detection [24]. Twitter users can choose to publish their location information by way of (1) geo-tagging their tweets, or (2) specifying it in the location

This material is complemented in part based upon work supported by the National Institute of Health under Grant No. 1R01DA039454-01 and National Science Foundation under Grant No. IIS-1111182. Any opinions, findings, and conclusions or recommendations expressed in this material are those of the author(s) and do not necessarily reflect the views of the employer or funding organization. We would like to thank: (1) Zemanta for their support; (2) Derek Doran, Lu Chen, and Wenbo Wang for their invaluable feedback.
R. Krishnamurthy and P. Kapanipathi—Joint first authors.

© Springer International Publishing Switzerland 2015
F. Gandon et al. (Eds.): ESWC 2015, LNCS 9088, pp. 187–201, 2015.
DOI: 10.1007/978-3-319-18818-8_12

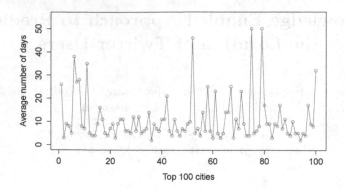

Fig. 1. Estimates of average number of days to collect geo-tagged tweets for top 100 cities in the training dataset of [5]

field of their Twitter profile. However, recent studies have shown that less than 4 % of tweets are geo-tagged [13,19]. Also, while many users choose to leave the location field of their profile empty or enter invalid information, others specify location at different granularity such as city, state, and country. Thus, most of the information entered in this field cannot be reverse geocoded to a city. For instance, Cheng et al. [5] found that, in their dataset comprising of 1 million Twitter users, only 26 % of the users shared their location at the city level.

Existing approaches to predict the location of Twitter users, based on their tweets, use supervised learning techniques [4,5,17]. They are built on the hypothesis that the geographic location of users influences the content of their tweets. These approaches are data-driven and require large training dataset of geo-tagged tweets to build statistical models that predict a user's location. Cheng et al. [5] created a training dataset comprising of 4,124,960 geo-tagged tweets from 130,689 users in continental United States. The collection of this dataset was time intensive and done over a period of 5 months from September 2009 to January 2010. However, in the recent times we have seen a rapid growth of Twitter. Hence, we examined the effort required to create a similar data set in the present day. We selected the top 100 cities with the maximum count of tweets in the dataset of [5] and collected geo-tagged tweets from these cities over a period of 5 days. Based on the tweets collected in this duration, Fig. 1 shows the average number of days required to collect tweets comparable in volume to [5]. We see that for some cities it would take up to 50 days for creating a high quality training data set. This makes it a time intensive process; consequently, making the approach challenging to adapt to newer cities. We address this weakness by proposing a knowledge based solution.

Knowledge bases have been used to either propose alternatives to learning approaches [11,12] or in combination with learning approaches to improve their performance [8,25]. This work falls in the former category. Our approach can be organized into three steps: (1) First, the *Creation of a Location Specific Knowledge base*, which exploits the hyperlink structure of Wikipedia to build a knowledge base of location specific entities. Additionally, we weight each entity by its ability to discriminate between locations. (2) Second, *User Profile Generation*, which creates a semantic profile of a Twitter user whose location is to be determined. The user profile consists of wikipedia entities found in their tweets and are weighted to reflect their importance to the user. (3) Finally, we use the overlap between the entities in the tweets of a user and the location specific knowledge base to predict the user location in the *Location Prediction* step. Concretely, we make the following contributions:

- We propose a novel knowledge based approach to predict the location of a Twitter user at the city level.
- We introduce the concept of *local entities* which are entities that can discriminate between geographic locations.
- We evaluate our approach using a benchmark dataset published by Cheng et al. [5] and show that our approach, which does not rely on a training dataset, performs comparable to the state of the art approaches.

The rest of the paper is organized as follows. Section 2 describes the creation of a location specific knowledge base. Section 3 describes our approach to predict the location of a user using the location specific knowledge base. Section 4 describes the evaluation and results of our approach. In Sect. 5, we explain the related work on location prediction. Finally, Sect. 6 concludes with suggestions for future work.

2 Creation of Location Specific Knowledge Base

To create a location specific knowledge base, we (1) identify the local entities of a city, and (2) compute their localness measure with respect to the city.

2.1 Local Entities

Previous research that address the problem of location prediction of Twitter users, have established that the content of a user's posts reflects his/her location. Cheng et al. [5] introduced the idea of *local words* which are words that convey a strong sense of location. For example, they found that the word *rockets* is local to Houston whereas words such as *world* and *peace* are more generic and do not exhibit an association to any particular location. Using the same intuition, we introduce the concept of *local entities*. Local entities are wikipedia entities that can distinguish between locations.

We leverage Wikipedia to identify the local entities for each city. While there are many knowledge bases, such as Yago[1], DMOZ[2], and Geo Names[3], we choose Wikipedia because (1) it is comprehensive, (2) it contains dedicated pages for

---

[1] http://www.mpi-inf.mpg.de/yago-naga/yago.

[2] http://www.dmoz.org.

[3] http://download.geonames.org/export/dump/.

cities, and (3) it has a hyperlink structure that can be exploited for our purposes. A wikipedia page comprises of links to other wikipedia pages. These links are referred to as *internal links*[4] of the wikipedia page and are semantically related to the page (or a portion of it) [21]. Consequently, we consider the entities represented by internal links in the wikipedia page of a city as local entities of that city. For example, the wikipedia page of *San Francisco* contains a link to the wikipedia page of *Golden Gate Bridge*. Thus, we consider *Golden Gate Bridge* as a local entity with respect to *San Francisco*. Note that while a wikipedia page does not contain link to itself, we consider the city as a local entity to itself because location names in tweets provide important cues towards the actual location of the user.

2.2   Localness Measures

All the local entities of a city are not equally local with respect to the city. For example, consider *San Francisco Giants* and *Major League Baseball* that are local entities of the city *San Francisco*[5]. While the *San Francisco Giants* are a baseball team based out of San Francisco, *Major League Baseball* is a professional baseball organization in North America. Intuitively, the entity *San Francisco Giants* has a higher potential than *Major League Baseball* to distinguish *San Francisco* from other cities in United States. Therefore, we introduce the concept of localness measure for each local entity such that the localness score reflects the distinguishing ability of the local entity with respect to a city. We experiment with four measures to determine the localness of an entity. These measures can be classified into three categories: (1) association based measure, (2) graph based measure, and (3) semantic overlap based measures.

Association Based Measure. In information theory, pointwise mutual information is a standard measure of association. It is used to determine association between terms based on the probability of their co-occurrence. The intuitive basis for using an association measure to establish localness of an entity is that, higher the co-occurrence of a local entity with the city in wikipedia pages, higher is the localness of the entity with respect to the city. In order to determine the association between a local entity and a city, we utilize the whole Wikipedia corpus. We define the PMI of a city and its local entity as:

$$PMI(le, c) = \log_2 \frac{P(le, c)}{P(le)P(c)} \tag{1}$$

where c is the city and le is a local entity of the city.

We compute the joint probability of occurrence, $P(le, c)$ as the fraction of the wikipedia pages that contain links to the Wikipedia pages of both the city and the entity. Additionally, the individual probabilities of the city $P(c)$ and the local entity $P(le)$ are computed as the fraction of the wikipedia pages that contain links to the wikipedia page of the city and the local entity alone respectively.

---

[4] http://en.wikipedia.org/wiki/Help:Link#Wikilinks.
[5] http://en.wikipedia.org/wiki/San_Francisco.

Graph Based Measure. The Wikipedia hyperlink structure can also be represented as a directed graph whose vertices are the wikipedia pages. An edge in this graph represents a link from the wikipedia page of the source node to the wikipedia page of the target node. Since the hyperlink structure of Wikipedia allows us to represent a city and its local entities as a graph, we use a graph theoretic measure to compute the localness of the local entities.

To construct the graph of local entities for a city, we prune the Wikipedia hyperlink graph by selecting only those edges that connect the local entities of the city. For instance, *San Francisco Giants* and *Major League Baseball* are nodes in the graph of local entities of San Francisco. A directed edge from *San Francisco Giants* to *Major League Baseball* represents the link from the wikipedia page of *San Francisco Giants* to the wikipedia page of *Major League Baseball*.

Betweenness centrality has been used extensively to find influential nodes in a network. Our hypothesis is that, the relative importance of a node in the graph of local entities, reflects the localness of the local entity with respect to the city. It is defined as follows:

$$C_B(le,c) = \sum_{le_i \neq le \neq le_j} \frac{\sigma_{le_i le_j}(le)}{\sigma_{le_i le_j}} \tag{2}$$

where c is a city, le, le_i, le_j are local entities of c, $\sigma_{le_i le_j}$ represents the total number of shortest paths from le_i to le_j and $\sigma_{le_i le_j}(le)$ is the number of shortest paths from le_i to le_j through le. We normalize the measure by dividing C_B by $(n-1)(n-2)$ where n is the number of nodes in the directed graph.

Semantic Overlap Measure. Halaschek et al. [10] measure the relatedness between concepts using the idea that related concepts are connected to similar entities. Similarly, we measure the localness of an entity with respect to a city as the overlap between the internal links of the entity and the internal links of the city. To compute this semantic overlap, we use the following set based measures: (1) Jaccard Index, and (2) Tversky Index.

Jaccard Index is a symmetric measure of overlap between two sets and is normalized for their sizes. Jaccard Index for a city c and its local entity le is defined as follows:

$$jaccard(le,c) = \frac{|IL(c) \cap IL(le)|}{|IL(c) \cup IL(le)|} \tag{3}$$

where $IL(c)$ and $IL(le)$ are the internal links found in the wikipedia page of city c and local entity le respectively.

Tversky Index is an asymmetric measure of overlap of two sets [26]. While the Jaccard Index determines the overlap between a city and a local entity, a local entity generally represents a part of the city. For example, consider the local entity *Boston Red Sox*[6] of the city *Boston*. Its internal links may not symmetrically overlap with that of *Boston* because internal links of *Boston* are from different categories such as *Climate*, *Geography* and *History*. Hence, we

---

[6] Boston Red Sox is the baseball team of Boston.

adapt Tversky Index to measure unidirectional overlap of the local entity le to the city c as follows:

$$ti(le, c) = \frac{|IL(c) \cap IL(le)|}{|IL(c) \cap IL(le)| + \alpha|IL(c) - IL(le)| + \beta|IL(le) - IL(c)|} \tag{4}$$

where we choose $\alpha = 0$ and $\beta = 1$ to penalize the local entity, for every internal link in its page not found in the wikipedia page of the city.

3   Knowledge Enabled Location Prediction

In Sect. 2, we created a location specific knowledge base comprising of local entities and their localness measures. Now, we describe our algorithm to predict the location of a Twitter user using the location specific knowledge base.

3.1   User Profile Generation

Our approach is based exclusively on the content of a user's tweets. We create a semantic profile of the user whose location is to be predicted. It comprises of wikipedia entities mentioned in their tweets. From this profile, entities that are local entities of a city are used to predict the location of the user. The *User Profile Generation* can be explained in two steps: (1) Entity Recognition from user's tweets; (2) Entity Scoring to measure the extent of the usage of the entity by the Twitter user.

Entity Recognition. Entity recognition is the process of recognizing information like people, organization, location, and numeric expressions[7]. To perform this task on tweets, we utilize existing APIs since the focus of this paper is to predict a Twitter user's location. We opted for Zemanta because of the following reasons: (1) It has been shown to be superior to others as evaluated against other entity recognition and linking services, by Derczynski et al. [6]; (2) Zemanta's web service[8] also links entities from the tweets to their wikipedia pages. This allows an easy mapping between the Zemanta annotations and our knowledge base extracted from Wikipedia; and (3) It provides co-reference resolution for the entities.[9]

Entity Weighting. We weight each entity with the frequency of its occurrence in a user's tweets. Frequency of mentions of an entity indicates the significance of the entity to the user.

3.2   Location Prediction

To predict the location of a user, we compute a score for each city whose local entities are found in the profile of the user, defined as follows:

---

[7] More details on entity recognition can be found in [20].
[8] http://developer.zemanta.com/docs/suggest/.
[9] We thank Zemanta for their support.

$$locScore(u, c) = \sum_{e \in LE_{cu}} locl(e, c) \times s_e \tag{5}$$

where LE_{cu} is the set of local entities of c found in the profile of user u, $locl(e, c)$ is the localness measure of the entity e with respect to the city c and s_e is the weight of the local entity in the user profile. The location of the user is determined by ranking the cities in the descending order of $locScore(u, c)$.

4 Evaluation

First, we compare our approach with the four localness measures explained in Sect. 2.2. Then, we use the best performing measure to evaluate against the state of the art content based location prediction algorithms.

4.1 Dataset

For a fair comparison of our approach against the existing approaches, we use the dataset published by Cheng et al. [5]. The dataset contains 5119 users, from the continental United States, with approximately 1000 tweets of each user. These users have published their location in their profile in the form of latitude and longitude coordinates. These locations are considered to be the ground truth. Spammers and bots are filtered out from this dataset using Lee et al.'s [16] work.

To create the location specific knowledge base, we consider all the cities of United States with population greater than 5000, as published in the census estimates of 2012. Accordingly, our location specific knowledge base comprises of 4,661 cities with 500,714 local entities.

4.2 Evaluation-Metrics

We adopt the following four evaluation measures used by the existing location prediction approaches [5]:

- *Accuracy* (ACC): The percentage of users identified within 100 miles of their actual location.
- *Average Error Distance* (AED): The average of the error distance across all users. *Error distance* is the distance between the actual location of the user and the estimated location by our algorithm.
- *Accuracy@k* (ACC@k): The percentage of users whose actual locations are within the *top-k* predicted locations of the user, with an error distance of 100 miles.
- *Average Error Distance@k* (AED@k): The Average of error distance, between the closest predicted location at *top-k* to the actual location, across all the users in the dataset.

4.3 Baseline

We implement a baseline system which considers all the entities of a city to be equally local to the city. To predict the location of a user, we compute the score for each city by aggregating the count of local entities of the city found in the user's tweets and selecting the city with the maximum score. In other words, the localness score (*locl*) of each entity in Eq. 5 is 1.

4.4 Results

Table 1 reports the results for location prediction using the (1) Baseline, (2) Pointwise Mutual Information (PMI), (3) Betweenness Centrality (BC), (4) Semantic Overlap Measures - Jaccard Index (JC), and (5) Semantic Overlap Measures - Tversky Index (TI). We see that Tversky Index is the best performing localness measure with approximately 55 % ACC and 429 miles of AED. The ACC is doubled compared to the baseline. However, compared to Jaccard Index, there is only a slight improvement in ACC from 53.21 % to 54.48 % and decrease in AED from 433 to 429 miles.

Table 1. Location prediction using different localness measures

Method	ACC	AvgErrDist (in Miles)	ACC@2	ACC@3	ACC@5
Baseline	25.21	632.56	38.01	42.78	47.95
PMI	38.48	599.408	49.85	56.06	64.15
BC	47.91	478.14	57.39	62.18	66.98
JC	53.21	433.62	67.41	73.56	78.84
TI	**54.48**	**429.00**	**68.72**	**74.68**	**79.99**

The top k cities for a user are determined by ordering the aggregate score for each city (defined in Eq. 5). As shown in Fig. 2, the ACC of our approach increases with k. At $k = 5$, using Tversky Index as the localness measure, we are able to predict the exact location of approximately 80 % of the users. Similarly, as shown in Fig. 3, the AED decreases as k increases. Figure 4 shows the accuracy of prediction within increasing radius (in miles). As seen in the graph, we can predict approximately 46 % of the users within 30 miles of the actual location of the user.

Performance of Localness Measures. Table 1, Figs. 2 and 3 have compared the results of our approach using the localness measures described in Sect. 2.2. In this section, we discuss our findings and analysis on why some localness measures performed better than others in the location prediction task.

Pointwise mutual information measure is sensitive to low frequency data [3]. This led to high absolute PMI scores for the local entities of a city like *Glen Rock, New Jersey* as compared to that of *San Francisco* due to the low occurrence of

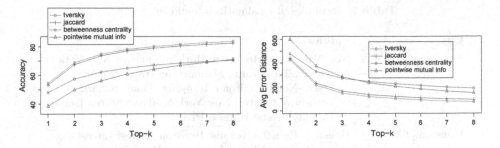

Fig. 2. Top-k accuracy   **Fig. 3.** Top-k average error distance

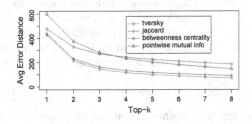

Fig. 4. Accuracy of prediction at increasing miles of radius

the former as compared to the latter in the wikipedia corpus. Nevertheless, the prediction results using PMI show a significant improvement over the baseline.

Betweenness centrality, as a localness measure, performs better than PMI. Although, betweenness centrality addresses the sensitivity to low frequency, it weights certain generic entities higher than more specific entities. For example, in our knowledge base, *United States* is a local entity with respect to the city *San Francisco*. We found that there are multiple shortest paths through *United States* in the graph of local entities of *San Francisco*, thus increasing its importance. However, the entity *United States* is fairly generic and cannot discriminate between the cities in our knowledge base.

The semantic overlap measures overcome the disadvantages of both betweenness centrality and PMI. The primary distinction between the two semantic overlap measures is that Jaccard Index is symmetric while Tversky Index is assymmetric. Jaccard Index is biased against local entities that have less internal links. For example, consider the two entities *Eureka Valley, San Francisco* and *California*. Both are local entities of the city *San Francisco*. Intuitively, we would expect *Eureka Valley, San Francisco* (a residential neighbourhood in San Francisco) to be more local than *California* with respect to the city *San Francisco* but with Jaccard Index the result is opposite. This problem motivated the use of an asymmetric measure. Using the Tversky Index, the localness measure of an entity is the highest when all its internal links are subsumed by those in the wikipedia page of the city. Furthermore, the local entity is penalized for only the internal links in its page not present in the city. Therefore, in the above

Table 2. Examples of local entities found in tweets

City	Entities
New York City, NY	New York City; Brooklyn; Harlem; Queens; New York Knicks; The Bronx; Manhattan; Train station; Metro-North Railroad; Rapping; Times Square; Broadway theatre; New York Yankees; Staten Island; Brooklyn Nets; Hudson River;
Houston, TX	Houston; Houston Texans; Houston Astros; Interstate 45; Houston Chronicle; Greater Houston; Harris County, Texas; Galveston, Texas; Downtown Houston; Houston Rockets;
Nashville, TN	Nashville, Tennessee;Belmont University; Frist Center for the Visual Arts; Southeastern Conference; Centennial Park (Nashville); Gaylord Opryland Resort & Convention Center; Nashville Symphony; Cheekwood Botanical Garden and Museum of Art;

example it is able to assign a higher degree of localness to *Eureka Valley, San Francisco* than *California* with respect to the city *San Francisco*. This approach to weighting the local entities performs better than Jaccard's index with improved accuracy and lower average error distance. Table 2 shows examples of local entities extracted from the tweets of users. These examples illustrate that local entities of various types such as sports teams, landmarks, organizations, local television networks and famous people are used to predict the location of a user.

Comparison with Existing Approaches. For the location prediction task based on user's tweets, the state of the art approaches require a training dataset of geo tagged tweets. Their models are trained using a dataset of 4.1 million tweets collected over 5 months between 2009 and 2010. From Fig. 1, we can see that the collection of geo-tagged tweets for the *top-100* cities (ranked based on the number of geo-tagged tweets from the cities used to train the models [4,5]) in 2015 can take up to 50 days[10]. On the other hand, our approach requires a pre-processing step of creating an index of the wikipedia links (or Dbpedia wikilinks that can be easily downloaded from DBpedia[11]).

We compare the existing approaches against our approach with the best performing localness measure, i.e. Tversky Index (see Table 3). For a fair comparison in the results, we have evaluated our approach on the same test dataset as Cheng et al. [5], Chang et al. [4] and Jalal et al. [17]. As reported in Table 3, our approach performs comparable to the state of the art approaches.

---

[10] This experiment was performed keeping in mind the extensive growth of Twitter from 2009 to 2015.

[11] http://wiki.dbpedia.org/Downloads2014.

Table 3. Location prediction results compared to existing approaches

Method	ACC
Cheng et al. 2010 [5]	51.00
Chang et al. 2012 [4]	49.9
Jalal et al. 2014 [17]	**55.00**
Our approach with TI	54.48

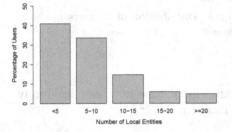

Fig. 5. Percentage of users with the count of distinct local entities from the predicted city

Fig. 6. Predictions corresponding to the count of distinct local entities in users' tweets (Tversky Index)

Impact of Local Entities on Prediction Accuracy. Twitter users have varying frequency of mentioning local entities of their city in tweets. From the test dataset of 5119 users (with approximately 1000 tweets per user), Fig. 5 shows the percentage of users against the frequency of *distinct local entity* mentions. While 40 % of users have mentioned less than 5 distinct local entities, 25 % of the users have more than 10 distinct local entities in their tweets. The impact in determining the location of users based on this varying frequency of local entity mentions is shown in Fig. 6. The accuracy of prediction increases with increase in the number of distinct local entities in the tweets of a user. The accuracy of prediction is 66 % for users who mention more than 10 local entities in their tweets.

Geographic Distribution of Predictions. The count of local entities for the cities in our knowledge base ranges from 11 (for *Island Lake, Illinois*) to 1095 (for *Chicago*). This reflects the information available on wikipedia about the city. The first thought is that, these variations can impact the performance of our approach. In order to analyze this issue, we performed experiments to check if any bias exists towards specific cities as a result of the number of local entities of the city. Hence, we plotted the distribution of our accurate predictions on a map of United States (Fig. 7) and the distribution of test users in the dataset as shown in Fig. 8. We can see that despite the variation in the amount of information available for each city, our algorithm was able to predict locations

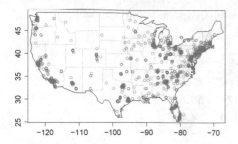

Fig. 7. Distribution of users predicted within 100 miles of their location

Fig. 8. Distribution of all users in the dataset

of users from all over United States. The knowledge base for these accurately predicted cities ranged between 40 to 1095 local entities.[12]

5   Related Work

Geo-locating twitter users has gained a lot of traction due to its potential applications. Existing approaches to solve this problem can be grouped in to classes: (1) content based location prediction, and (2) network based location prediction.

Content-based location prediction approaches are grounded on the premise that the online content of a user is influenced by their geographical location. It relies on a significantly large training dataset to build a statistical model that identifies words with a local geographic scope. Cheng et al. [5] proposed a probabilistic framework for estimating a Twitter user's city-level location based on the content of approximately 1000 tweets of each user. They formulated the task of identifying local words as a decision problem. They used the model of spatial variation proposed by [2] to train a decision tree classifier using a hand-curated list of 19,178 words. Their approach on a test dataset of 5119 users, could locate 51 % of the users within 100 miles with an average error distance of 535 miles. The disadvantage of this approach was the assumption that a "term" is spatially significant to or characteristic of only one location/city. This challenge was addressed by Chang et al. [4] by modeling the variations as a Gaussian mixture model. While this approach still required a training dataset of geo-tagged tweets, it did not need a labeled set of seed words. Their tests on the same dataset showed an accuracy (within 100 miles) of 49.9 % with 509.3 miles of average error distance. Eisenstein et al. [7] proposed cascading topic models to identify lexical variation across geographic locations. Using the regional distribution of words, determined from these models, they predicted the locations of twitter users. Their dataset comprised of users from United States. Their

---

[12] Further information on the evaluation, datasets and code can be found at the Wiki page of this project http://wiki.knoesis.org/index.php/Location_Prediction_of_Twitter_Users.

accuracy at the region and state level was 58 % and 27 % respectively. Kinsella et al. [14] addressed two problems, namely, (1) predicting the location of an individual tweet and (2) predicting the location of a user. They created language models for each location at different granularity levels of country, state, city and zipcode, by estimating a distribution of terms associated with the location. Jalal et al. [17] used an ensemble of statistical and heuristic classifiers. These classifiers used words, hashtags, and location names as features. A low level classifier, that predicts location at the city level, needs to discriminate among many locations. To alleviate that, they propose an ensemble of hierarchical classifiers that predict the location at time zone, state and city level. However, their approach is also supervised and relies on a training dataset.

Network based solutions are grounded in the assumption that the locations of the people in a user's network and their online interaction with the user can be used to predict his/her location. McGee et al. [18] used the interaction between users in a network to train a Decision Tree to distinguish between pairs of users likely to live close by. They reported an accuracy of 64 % (within 25 miles). Rout et al. [23] formulated this task as a classification task and trained an SVM classifier with features based on the information of users' followers-followees who have their location information available. They tested their approach on a random sample of 1000 users and reported 50.08 % accuracy at the city level. However, a network based approach can only be used to determine the location of users who have other users in their network whose location is already known.

In the Twitter domain, Wikipedia has been leveraged for many tasks. Osborne et al. [22] have shown that Wikipedia can enhance the performance of first story detection on Twitter. The graph structure of Wikipedia has been utilized by Genc et al. [9] to classify tweets. Also, the Wikipedia graph has been leveraged by Kapanipathi et al. [12], with an adaptation of spreading activation theory to determine the hierarchical interests of users based on their tweets.

6   Conclusion and Future Work

In this paper, we presented a novel knowledge based approach that uses Wikipedia to predict the location of Twitter users. We introduced the concept of local entities for each city and demonstrated the results of different measures to compute the localness of the entities with respect to a city. Without any training dataset, our approach performs comparable to the state of the art content based approaches. Furthermore, our approach can expand the knowledge base to include other cities which is remarkably less laborious than creating and modeling a training dataset.

In future, we will explore the use of semantic types of the Wikipedia entities to improve the accuracy of the location prediction and decrease the average error distance. We also plan to augment our knowledge base with location information from other knowledge bases such as Geo Names and Wikitravel. Additionally, we will examine how to adapt our approach to predict the location of a user at a finer granularity level like the neighborhoods in a city.

References

1. Achrekar, H., Gandhe, A., Lazarus, R., Yu, S.-H., Liu, B.: Predicting flu trends using twitter data. In: 2011 IEEE Conference on Computer Communications Workshops (INFOCOM WKSHPS), pp. 702–707. IEEE (2011)
2. Backstrom, L., Kleinberg, J., Kumar, R., Novak, J.: Spatial variation in search engine queries. In: Proceedings of the 17th International Conference on World Wide Web, pp. 357–366. ACM (2008)
3. Bouma, G.: Normalized (pointwise) mutual information in collocation extraction. In: Proceedings of the Biennial GSCL Conference (2009)
4. Chang, H.-W., Lee, D., Eltaher, M., Lee, J.: @ Phillies tweeting from philly? predicting twitter user locations with spatial word usage. In: ASONAM 2012 (2012)
5. Cheng, Z., Caverlee, J., Lee, K.: You are where you tweet: a content-based approach to geo-locating twitter users. In: Proceedings of the 19th ACM International Conference on Information and Knowledge Management, pp 759–768. ACM (2010)
6. Derczynski, L., Maynard, D., Aswani, N., Bontcheva, K.: Microblog-genre noise and impact on semantic annotation accuracy. In: Proceedings of the 24th ACM Conference on Hypertext and Social Media, pp 21–30. ACM (2013)
7. Eisenstein, J., O'Connor, B., Smith, N.A., Xing, E.P.: A latent variable model for geographic lexical variation. In: Proceedings of the 2010 Conference on Empirical Methods in Natural Language Processing, pp. 1277–1287. Association for Computational Linguistics (2010)
8. Gabrilovich, E., Markovitch, S.: Overcoming the brittleness bottleneck using wikipedia: enhancing text categorization with encyclopedic knowledge. In: AAAI, vol. 6, pp. 1301–1306 (2006)
9. Genc, Y., Sakamoto, Y., Nickerson, J.V.: Discovering context: classifying tweets through a semantic transform based on wikipedia. In: Schmorrow, D.D., Fidopiastis, C.M. (eds.) FAC 2011. LNCS, vol. 6780, pp. 484–492. Springer, Heidelberg(2011)
10. Halaschek, C., Aleman-Meza, B., Arpinar, I.B., Sheth, A.P.: Discovering and ranking semantic associations over a large rdf metabase. In: Proceedings of the Thirtieth International Conference on Very Large Data Bases, vol. 30, pp. 1317–1320. VLDB Endowment (2004)
11. Hu, X., Zhang, X., Lu, C., Park, E.K, Zhou, X.: Exploiting wikipedia as external knowledge for document clustering. In: Proceedings of the 15th ACM SIGKDD International Conference on Knowledge Discovery and Data Mining, pp. 389–396. ACM (2009)
12. Kapanipathi, P., Jain, P., Venkataramani, C., Sheth, A.: User interests identification on twitter using a hierarchical knowledge base. In: Presutti, V., d'Amato, C., Gandon, F., d'Aquin, M., Staab, S., Tordai, A. (eds.) ESWC 2014. LNCS, vol. 8465, pp. 99–113. Springer, Heidelberg (2014)
13. Khanwalkar, S., Seldin, M., Srivastava, A., Kumar, A., Colbath, S.: Content-based geo-location detection for placing tweets pertaining to trending news on map. In: The Fourth International Workshop on Mining Ubiquitous and Social Environments, p. 37 (2013)
14. Kinsella, S., Murdock, V., O'Hare, N.: I'm eating a sandwich in glasgow: modeling locations with tweets. In: Proceedings of the 3rd International Workshop on Search and Mining User-Generated Contents, pp. 61–68. ACM (2011)
15. Kireyev, K., Palen, L., Anderson, K.: Applications of topics models to analysis of disaster-related twitter data. In: NIPS Workshop on Applications for Topic Models: Text and Beyond, vol. 1 (2009)

16. Lee, K., Caverlee, J., Webb, S.: Uncovering social spammers: social honeypots+ machine learning. In: Proceedings of the 33rd International ACM SIGIR Conference on Research and Development in Information Retrieval (2010)
17. Mahmud, J., Nichols, J., Drews, C.: Home location identification of twitter users. ACM Trans. Intell. Syst. Technol. (TIST) **5**, 47 (2014)
18. McGee, J., Caverlee, J., Cheng, Z.: Location prediction in social media based on tie strength. In: Proceedings of the 22nd ACM International Conference on Information & Knowledge Management, pp. 459–468. ACM (2013)
19. Morstatter, F., Pfeffer, J., Liu, H., Carley, K.M.: Is the sample good enough? comparing data from twitters streaming api with twitters firehose. In: Proceedings of ICWSM (2013)
20. Nadeau, D., Sekine, S.: A survey of named entity recognition and classification. Lingvisticae Investigationes **30**(1), 3–26 (2007)
21. Nuzzolese, A.G., Gangemi, A., Presutti, V., Ciancarini, P.: Encyclopedic knowledge patterns from wikipedia links. In: Aroyo, L., Welty, C., Alani, H., Taylor, J., Bernstein, A., Kagal, L., Noy, N., Blomqvist, E. (eds.) ISWC 2011, Part I. LNCS, vol. 7031, pp. 520–536. Springer, Heidelberg (2011)
22. Osborne, M., Petrovic, S., McCreadie, R., Macdonald, C., Ounis, I.: Bieber no more: first story detection using twitter and wikipedia. In: Proceedings of the Workshop on Time-aware Information Access, TAIA, vol. 12 (2012)
23. Rout, D., Bontcheva, K., Preoţiuc-Pietro, D., Cohn, T.: Where's @wally?: a classification approach to geolocating users based on their social ties. In: HT (2013)
24. Sakaki, T., Okazaki, M., Matsuo, Y.: Earthquake shakes twitter users: real-time event detection by social sensors. In: Proceedings of the 19th International Conference on World Wide Web, pp. 851–860. ACM (2010)
25. Song, Y., Wang, H., Wang, Z., Li, H., Chen, W.: Short text conceptualization using a probabilistic knowledgebase. In: Proceedings of the Twenty-Second International Joint Conference on Artificial Intelligence-Volume Volume Three, pp. 2330–2336. AAAI Press (2011)
26. Tversky, A.: Features of similarity. Psychol. Rev. **84**(4), 327 (1977)

Semantic Data Management, Big Data, Scalability

A Compact In-Memory Dictionary
for RDF Data

Hamid R. Bazoobandi[1]([⊠]), Steven de Rooij[1,2], Jacopo Urbani[1,3],
Annette ten Teije[1], Frank van Harmelen[1], and Henri Bal[1]

[1] Department of Computer Science, VU University Amsterdam,
Amsterdam, The Netherlands
h.bazoubandi@vu.nl, {jacopo,annette,frank.van.harmelen,bal}@cs.vu.nl
[2] Department of Computer Science, University of Amsterdam,
Amsterdam, The Netherlands
s.deRooij@uva.nl
[3] Max Planck Institute for Informatics, Saarbrücken, Germany

Abstract. While almost all dictionary compression techniques focus on
static RDF data, we present a compact in-memory RDF dictionary for
dynamic and streaming data. To do so, we analysed the structure of
terms in real-world datasets and observed a high degree of common prefixes. We studied the applicability of Trie data structures on RDF data
to reduce the memory occupied by common prefixes and discovered that
all existing Trie implementations lead to either poor performance, or an
excessive memory wastage.

In our approach, we address the existing limitations of Tries for RDF
data, and propose a new variant of Trie which contains some optimizations explicitly designed to improve the performance on RDF data. Furthermore, we show how we use this Trie as an in-memory dictionary by
using as numerical ID a memory address instead of an integer counter.
This design removes the need for an additional decoding data structure,
and further reduces the occupied memory. An empirical analysis on real-
world datasets shows that with a reasonable overhead our technique uses
50–59% less memory than a conventional uncompressed dictionary.

1 Introduction

Dictionary encoding is a simple compression method used by a wide range of
RDF [17] applications to reduce the memory footprint of the program. A dictionary encoder usually provides two basic operations: one for replacing strings
with short numerical IDs (encoding), and one for translating IDs back to the
original strings (decoding). This technique effectively reduces the memory footprint, because numerical values are typically much smaller than string terms. It
also boosts the general performance since comparing or copying numerical values
is more efficient than the corresponding operations on strings.

Dictionary encoding relies on a bi-directional map, which we call a dictionary, to store the associations between the numeric and textual IDs. If the input

© Springer International Publishing Switzerland 2015
F. Gandon et al. (Eds.): ESWC 2015, LNCS 9088, pp. 205–220, 2015.
DOI: 10.1007/978-3-319-18818-8_13

contains many unique tokens, then the size of the dictionary can saturate main memory and start hampering the functioning of the program. Given the increasing size of RDF datasets, this is becoming a frequent scenario, e.g. [19] reports cases where the size of the dictionary becomes even larger than the resulting encoded data. This becomes particularly problematic for applications that need to keep the dictionary in memory while processing the data.

An additional challenge comes from the dynamic nature of the Web, which demands that the application access and/or updates the dictionary with high frequency (for example when processing high velocity streams of RDF data). This requirement precludes the usage of most existing dictionary compression techniques (e.g. [10,19]) since these sacrifice update performance in order to maximize compression, which was the rational trade-off when processing static RDF data. To the best of our knowledge, there is no method to store dictionaries of RDF data that is space-efficient and allows frequent updates.

The goal of this paper is to fill this gap by proposing a novel approach, called RDFVault, to maintain a large RDF dictionary in main memory. RDF-Vault design contains *two main novelties*: First, it exploits the high degree of similarity between RDF terms [9] and compresses the common prefixes with a novel variation of a Trie [11]. Tries are often used for this type of problems, but standard implementations are memory inefficient when loaded with skewed data [13], as is the case with RDF [16]. To address this last issue, we present a Trie variation based on a List Trie [7], which addresses the well-known limitations of List Tries with a number of optimizations that exploit characteristics of RDF data.

Second, inspired by symbol tables in compilers, our approach unifies the two independent tables that are normally used for encoding and decoding into a single table. Our unified approach maps the strings not to a counter ID (as is usually the case), but to a memory address from where the string can be reconstructed again. The advantage of this design is that it removes the need of an additional mapping from IDs back to strings.

To support our contribution, we present an empirical analysis of the performance and memory consumption of RDFVault over realistic datasets. Our experiments show that our technique saves 50–59% memory compared to uncompressed hash-based dictionary while maintaining competitive encoding speed and up to 2.5 times slower decoding performance. Given that decoding in a conventional hash-based dictionary is very fast (a single hash table look up), we believe that the decoding speed of RDFVault is still reasonably good, and that in many cases this is a fair price to pay for better memory consumption.

The rest of this paper is organized as follows: In Sect. 2 we report some initial experiments that illustrate the potential saving that we can obtain with redundancy-aware techniques. In Sect. 3 we overview related work on the structure of existing dictionaries, and briefly discuss some of the existing efforts to reduce their memory consumption. In this section we also introduce the Trie data structure which will be the basis of our method. In Sect. 4 we focus on a number of existing Trie variants and analyze their strengths and weaknesses when applied to RDF data. Then, we present our method in Sect. 5 and an empirical evaluation of its performance in Sect. 6. Finally, Sect. 7 concludes the paper and discusses possible directions for future work.

2 String Redundancy in RDF: An Empirical Analysis

It is well known that the hierarchical organization of IRIs produces a large amount of string redundancy in a typical RDF dataset [9]. However, the scale of such redundancy has never been exactly quantified. Therefore, we selected a random subset of four realistic datasets (Table 1 shows more details on each dataset), and for each of them we computed the collective amount of common prefixes of any length.

Table 1. Number and type of terms in examined datasets

Datasets	#Terms (M)			#Unique Terms (M)			Triples (M)
	IRI	Literal	All	IRI	Literal	All	
BioPortal [22]	112.17	17.80	130	3.32	4.11	7.44	43.33
Freebase [12]	237.59	60.50	300	19.06	10.48	29.77	100
BTC2014 [14]	228.33	20.79	300	11.47	3.42	17.97	100
DBPedia (EN) [3]	280.07	19.22	300	50.01	1.85	51.87	100

Figure 1(a) reports (divided by type of terms) the results of our experiment. Although we expected some degree of redundancy in RDF data, this level of redundancy was beyond our expectations. We observed that 74–84% of the total space required by all unique strings is occupied by prefixes that appear more than once. Furthermore, the chart also shows that the redundancy is not confined to IRIs, but extends to literals as well (e.g. in Freebase [12] about 80 % of the space is occupied by repeated prefixes of different lengths).

In addition, we calculated the average length of the common prefixes and observed that common prefixes are between 20 to 30 characters long depending on the dataset. Such observations support the idea that minimizing the storage of common prefixes has the potential of effectively reducing the total memory consumption. These findings motivated our research to design an efficient dictionary encoder that exploits these redundancies in RDF strings to reduce the space occupied by the dictionary. The remainder of this paper describes our efforts towards this goal.

3 Existing Approaches

Related work. Dictionary encoding is a popular technique in real-world applications.(e.g. RDF-3x [21], or Virtuoso [8]). In general the systems that apply dictionary encoding construct the dictionary with two independent data structures,

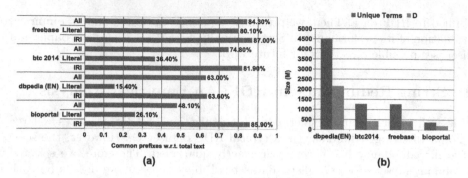

Fig. 1. (a) The collective amount of common prefixes of any length categorized by type of terms. (b) The disk space occupied by HDT dictionary versus unique string terms.

one for mapping strings to IDs, and one for mapping IDs to their corresponding strings. The method proposed by [25] tries to alleviate the overhead of common prefixes in IRIs by splitting them based on the last occurrence of '/' character and storing the prefix only once in a separate hash table for all IRIs that share that prefix. The problem with this approach is that in RDF data, common prefixes have a variable lengths. Therefore many common prefixes will be still stored more than once. In addition, our analytical study (see Sect. 2) shows that common prefixes do not occur only in IRIs, but also in literals, which are outside the scope of this optimization.

There are also approaches that offer dictionary compression over static datasets, e.g. HDT [10] applies PPM [6] to compress its D (dictionary) part (*FourSectionDictionary*)[1]. Our experiments presented in Fig. 1(b) compare the disk space occupied by unique strings in datasets presented in Table 1 versus that of HDT dictionary. The Figure clearly shows that in almost all cases, the whole HDT dictionary (strings and IDs) occupies more than 50 % less space than uncompressed strings. Another similar approach [19] is a compact dictionary which partly relies on partitioning terms based on the role they play in the datasets to achieve a dictionary compression level of 20–64%. Although both approaches effectively compact the dictionary, they require the whole dataset to be available at compression time, and they both function under this assumption that the data rarely changes after the dictionary creation. As a result, they support relatively efficient decoding (order of micro seconds in our experiments) but support no new encoding after the dictionary is created. Thus, these techniques are great if the data is static, but inapplicable for dynamic and streaming data sources used in many real-time usecases such as stream RDF processing.

Reference [4] proposes an order preserving in-memory dictionary based on a single data structure that supports dynamic updates, however the approach is vulnerable to memory wastage for highly skewed data with many duplicates (like

---
[1] https://code.google.com/p/hdt-java/.

RDF data). References [5,24] propose approaches that address the scalability issue of massive RDF compression by resorting to distributed approaches.

Trie. If we look at the data structures that are normally used inside the dictionary, then we notice that often B^+-trees are chosen if the dictionary is stored on disk, while arrays, hash tables, or memory mapped files are normally preferred if the dictionary is supposed to reside in main memory [19]. Regardless of the data structure, in general existing approaches do not attempt to minimize the storage of common prefixes, and therefore consume significant space.

A Trie [11] (also known as radix or prefix tree) is special multi-way tree that was initially proposed as an alternative to binary trees [15] for indexing strings of variable length. In a Trie, each node represents the string that is spelled out by concatenating the edge labels on the path from the root. The string stored in a Trie is represented by the terminal node, while each internal node represents a string prefix. The children of a node are identified by the character on their edge labels; So, the fastest Trie implementation stores an array of $|\Sigma|$ child pointers in each node, where Σ is the alphabet. For instance, if a Trie should store ASCII strings, then the arrays would need to have 128 entries.

To better illustrate the functioning of a Trie, we show in Fig. 2(a) a small example of a standard Trie that supports uppercase English alphabet and contains three simple keys ("ABCZ", "ABCA", and "XYZ"). The example shows that no node in the Trie stores the key associated with that node. Instead, it is the position of the node in the Trie that determine the key associated with that node. In other words, the indices followed to reach a node, determines the key associated with that node. In this example we also see that the strings "ABCZ", and "ABCA" share the part of the Trie that represents the common prefix. Because of this, Tries have the following desirable properties:

- All strings that share the same prefix will be stored using the same nodes. Therefore common prefixes are stored only once;
- Keys can be quickly reconstructed via a bottom up traversal of the Trie;
- Time complexity of insertions, and lookups are proportional only to the *length of the key*, and not to the number of elements in the Trie.

Our experiments in Sect. 2 show that a storage strategy that minimizes string redundancy has the potential of being very effective in terms of resource consumption. Therefore, Tries can potentially be an ideal data structure for the compression of RDF terms in memory. Unfortunately, the most serious drawback of Tries is that if the input is skewed, and the alphabet is large, the Trie nodes become sparse [13] and cause low memory efficiency. In last years, this limitation has received considerable attention, and a number of papers have proposed some interesting solutions. In the next section we discuss the most prominent ones and analyze how they perform in our specific usecase.

4 Towards an Optimal Trie Implementation for RDF

Compact Trie. In a standard Trie (Fig. 2(a)), each edge represents a single character of the key, and thus all characters of all input strings are represented

Input: ABCZ, ABCA, XYZ

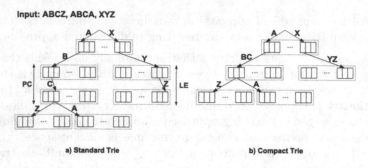

a) Standard Trie   b) Compact Trie

Fig. 2. Lazy expansion and path compression optimizations

by pointers between nodes. If the strings represent natural language text, then standard Tries are extremely vulnerable to memory wastage when nodes become sparse [13]. To mitigate this issue, the two following optimizations [20,23] are particularly effective:

Lazy Expansion. Chains of single descendant (child) nodes that lead to a terminal node (leaf) are omitted and the eliminated characters are usually stored in the leaf.

Path Compression. Single descendent nodes that do not lead to leaves are omitted and the skipped characters are either stored in the (multi-descendant) nodes, or only the numbers of characters is stored in the nodes, and the entire string is stored in the leaves to ensure correctness.

We call a Trie that implements both optimizations a *Compact Trie*. Figure 2(b) shows nodes that are affected by path compression (PC) and lazy expansion (LE) optimizations. Unfortunately, even with these optimizations in place, our experiments (the second column of Table 2) show that still more than 98 % of entries in the pointer arrays of a compact Trie remain unused when we store RDF data. This shows us that even though these two optimizations are useful in the general case, they do not help turn the data structure into a memory-efficient data structure for RDF.

Table 2. Percentage of used node pointers in a compact trie and ART when loaded with realistic RDF data.

Dataset	Compact trie	ART
BioPortal	1.58 %	47.90 %
DBPedia (EN)	1.19 %	46.60 %
Freebase	1.91 %	48.03 %
BTC2014	1.23 %	44.79 %

Burst Trie and HAT Trie. A Burst Trie [13] is a hybrid data structure comprised of a standard Trie called *access Trie* whose leaves are *containers* that can be any data structure (linked lists by default). HAT-Trie [2] improves performance by using hash tables instead of linked lists. Initially strings are only organized in containers, but once the algorithm detects a container is inefficient, it bursts the container into a Trie node, with multiple smaller containers as its leaves.

An advantage of this hybrid design is that it is more resistant to memory wastage for skewed data. However, this data structure is not attractive for saving common prefixes because (a) it does not minimize the storage of all common prefixes, but only those that are in the access Trie b) the burst Trie does not apply path compression and lazy expansion optimizations, therefore the access Trie can become very inefficient for long strings.

Adaptive Radix Trie. Adaptive Radix Tree (ART) [18] further improves memory efficiency, not only by applying the lazy expansion and path compression optimizations, but also by adaptively changing the size of the pointer array in nodes to minimize the number of unused pointers. To this end, ART uses nodes with variable length which grow in size where there is not enough space in their arrays. We measured the effect of this new optimization for RDF data, and report the results in the third column of Table 2. As we can see from the table, the adaptive node policy significantly boosts the memory efficiency compared to the Compact Trie. Nevertheless, still more than half of the pointer array entries are left unused. Therefore, for large Tries with many nodes, the memory efficiency is still unacceptably high.

List Trie. The last type of Trie that we considered is the List Trie [7]. This Trie organizes the children pointers of each node in linked lists instead of arrays. The advantage is that, unlike arrays, linked lists are not vulnerable to sparsity. However, the price to pay is that linked lists do not support random accesses. Therefore, in generic cases the performance of a List Trie is significantly lower than other Trie variants. Our experiments (not shown because of space limitations) show that a Standard Trie is more than two times faster than a List Trie in storing English words in a dictionary, though a List Trie consumes 6.3 times less memory than a Standard Trie to do so.

5   RDFVault: An In-Memory Dictionary Optimized for RDF Data

In the previous section we analyzed the existing Trie variants and showed why none of them is ideal for RDF. In fact, while Tries remove the problem of string redundancy, array-based tries are still memory inefficient because of the excessive number of unused pointers (Table 2), and list-based Tries cannot guarantee a good performance in generic cases.

To address these limitations, we propose a new variant of a List Trie and use it as an optimized in-memory dictionary named RDFVault for dynamic and streaming RDF data. There are three important factors that differentiate our solution from existing methods. *First*, our Trie variant uses linked lists (despite their general suboptimality) and improves the performance by introducing a move-to-front policy. *Second*, our dictionary encoding approach removes the need for a dedicated decoding data structure by using as ID the memory location of the Trie node that represents the string. Finally, it further optimizes memory usage by using two different types of nodes in the construction of the Trie. The remainder of this section describe each of these points in more detail.

Move-to-front policy. To support our decision to use linked lists, we run an experiment that calculates the distribution of used pointers in a Compact Trie (8-bit characters) loaded with RDF terms of some real-world datasets (Table 1). The results reported in Fig. 3 show that nodes with fewer than four used pointers (out of 256) are the majority. This observation plays in favor of using a list instead of array to keep track of children, because even with $O(n)$ lookup time complexity, when the n is small, the overall cost is reasonably low.

However, using a list is not enough. In fact, the plot shows that there are nodes with more than a dozen children. These nodes, although not many, can constitute a significant performance bottleneck if they appear on frequent paths. For example, if such popular nodes appear during the encoding of a term in the RDF vocabulary, then the overall performance will be severely affected.

Nevertheless, the high skewness and similarities among RDF terms suggest that some nodes in the lists are looked up much more than others. Therefore, to overcome the performance degradation introduced by popular long lists, we introduced a *move-to-front* policy which moves the last accessed child to the beginning of the list. In this way, the popular nodes will tend to move to the front of the list, while the least accessed nodes will automatically drift to the rear. This allows us to have a very compact data structure with no string redundancy, no memory wastage due to unused pointers, and still reasonably fast.

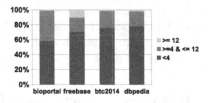

Fig. 3. Children distribution of nodes in Tries loaded with RDF data

Trie as a Dictionary. The most common approach for dictionary encoding is to assign an ID taken from an internal counter to every distinct term in the input. This requires the dictionary to maintain two maps, one for mapping strings to IDs, and one for inverse operation. In our approach, we improve this by using as ID, the memory address of the Trie node that represents the string. We make this design decision to remove the need for a second decoding data structure, and by doing so, we are actually reducing the implementation of a dictionary from two maps to a single set which we implement using our memory efficiency Trie. This is possible thanks to this interesting property of Tries (explained in Sect. 3) that offers the reconstruction of strings via a bottom-up traversal in a time complexity proportional to the length of string.

A downside of this choice is that we must add a pointer from every child to its parent to make the upward traversal possible. However, this extra cost is negligible compared to maintaining a whole second data structure in memory.

The main disadvantage of using the memory location as ID is that we are no longer allowed neither to relocate nor to reuse nodes that are associated with strings. This option has a limited impact on deletion operations (we assume that if a string is removed from the dictionary, then the ID assigned to that string is recyclable[2]) but it obliged us to adapt the original insertion algorithm to ensure that this condition is always observed.

In more details, we needed to address two cases: the first is when the insertion of a new string causes branching in a node whose address is already assigned as ID to a string. For example, Fig. 4(a) shows a scenario in which the address of a node (highlighted with bold lines) is associated with string "AB", and then the insertion of string "AC" requires a reorganization of nodes. Since both strings share the prefix "A", our algorithm adds a parent node (highlighted with dashed lines) which holds the prefix, and another node which holds "C" (the remainder of the new string) and the address of this new node is assigned to string "AC". The node which already contained string "AB" is now the child of the new node that contains the prefix "A", therefore, the content of this node is changed to "B" so that still a bottom-up traversal returns back the string "AB".

A second but less frequent case happens when an already inserted string is the prefix of a new string. Figure 4(b) illustrates such a scenario where the address of a node (highlighted with bold lines) is associated with string "AB", but the insertion of string "ABC" requires a new organization of nodes. In this case, the whole string "AB" is a prefix of string "ABC". Therefore, our algorithm adds a new parent node (highlighted with dashed line) which hold the string "AB", and then add the new node "C" (highlighted with dashed line) as its child. The node which previously hosted string "AB" keeps the null string now (highlighted with bold line) so that its memory location is intact, and still a bottom up traversal will reconstruct the original string "AB".

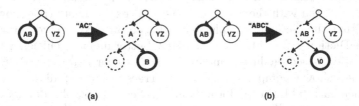

(a)   (b)

Fig. 4. Preserving memory locations already assigned as IDs

---

[2] This assumption holds in all dictionary encoding implementations we are aware of.

Differentiating Internal Nodes from Terminal Nodes. In our implementation, each node contains four fields: *parent*, which is a pointer to the parent node; *string*, which contains the portion of the string that results from path compression and lazy expansion optimizations; *children*, which refers to the first child in the linked list of children, and *sibling*, which links to the next node in the list. Thus, the first child of a node is accessed by first following its *children* link, and the other children are then obtained by following *sibling* links.

The field *children* is used only on the internal nodes. Therefore, we use two different data structures to represent the nodes: one with the field "children" if the node is internal, or without otherwise. This optimization has significant impact on memory efficiency because *any* tree without unary nodes contains more terminal than internal nodes, and this difference is especially more prominent on multiway trees. For instance, on a 64-bit machine, each *children* field occupies at least 8 bytes in memory, and given that the insertion of each unique string will add one leaf to the Trie, for a dataset with 300 M unique terms, we can save 2.2 G of memory only via this optimization.

Notice that we can add this optimization only because our insertion algorithm preserves the constraint on the fixed memory location. Without it, we were unable to change data structure whenever a terminal node becomes an internal one, without breaking the constraint.

6 Evaluation

We implemented RDFVault in the Java programming language, and released the source code online[3]. Our implementation stores RDF terms as Java character arrays, therefore it supports an alphabet of 16-bit characters.

As mentioned in Sect. 3, all existing dictionary compression techniques only target static data and thus do not support efficient updates. Hence, we chose an uncompressed conventional dictionary that consists of two hash tables as the baseline (as mentioned in Sect. 3, this is the most popular dictionary implementation that supports fast updates).

For the implementation of this conventional dictionary, we used the GNU Trove Hash Table library (with the default configurations) which is a robust and very memory efficient open-addressing hash implementation. Trove hash allows strings to be directly stored as character arrays which removes the substantial overhead associated with the String objects. Our experiments (not shown here) estimated that the dictionary implemented based on GNU Trove library (hereafter Trove Dictionary) yields more than 20 % better memory efficiency than the implementation based on Java standard HashMap over real-world RDF data.

We do not show a comparison against B^+ trees because if all data is in main memory then hash tables outperform them significantly. We also did not compare our work against other Trie variants, because we showed in Sect. 4 that they are very memory inefficient for the construction of an RDF dictionary.

---

[3] https://github.com/bazoohr/RDFVault.git

To evaluate our approach, we used the four real-world datasets that were considered throughout the previous sections (see Table 1). All experiments were run on a machine equipped with a 32 cores Intel(R) Xeon(R) CPU E5-2650 v2 @ 2.60 GHz, and 256 G of memory. The system runs Ubuntu 14.04 and we used Java 1.8.0 with 128 GB of maximum heap space.

To measure the memory consumption, we developed a technique which we were able to validate against existing Java libraries [1]. To measure the performance, we ran each experiment 10 times and report the average value to minimize the overhead of garbage collection on the comparability of our results.

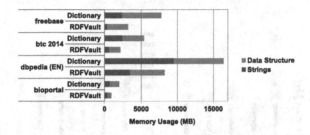

Fig. 5. Memory consumption results.

6.1 Memory Consumption

Overall Space Consumption. Figure 5 shows that RDFVault consumes 50–59% less memory than the conventional dictionary. It is interesting to see that in case of DBPedia (EN), and BTC2014 datasets, the whole memory consumption of RDFVault is less than the memory merely occupied by strings in the conventional dictionary. This clearly shows that RDFVault can successfully exploit the common prefixes of RDF terms to build a highly compact dictionary in memory.

By comparing the results in Fig. 5, with Fig. 1(b), we see that HDT dictionary is considerably smaller than RDFVault, but as we mentioned before this compression is achieved by sacrificing updatability.

Data Structure Overhead. Figure 5(a) shows that in all cases the overhead of RDFVault is less than that in conventional dictionary. It also shows that due to the string compression in RDFVault, sometimes strings consume much less space than the data structure (compared to the conventional dictionary). This means that in some cases the data structure becomes the main source of memory consumption in RDFVault. This is the observation that motivated our last optimizations to introduce different data structures to implement the nodes. Further optimization in this direction might be very effective in reducing the overall compression.

Note that although most existing dictionaries consist of two tables, it may also be possible to confine a conventional dictionary into a single hash table. Nonetheless, because strings are shared between the two tables, omitting one table at best can only reduce the data structure overhead to half, but the memory consumption of strings remains intact. Thus, RDFVault still offers better memory efficiency in all cases (see Figs. 5 and 6).

IRIs and Literals Compression. To evaluate the effect of compression on IRIs and literals, we first performed the encoding only on IRIs, and then only on the literals. The results reported in Fig. 6 confirm that eliminating common prefixes is an effective compression technique for IRIs, since it always significantly outperforms the baseline. On the other hand, our technique is less effective in compressing the literals, even though also in this case our method always outperforms the baseline.

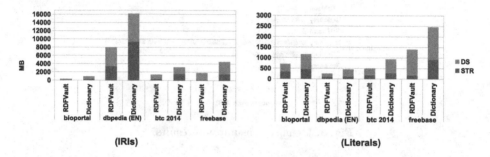

Fig. 6. Memory usage considering both IRIs and Literals (DS represents the space occupied by the data structure, while STR is the one taken for strings.

6.2   Encoding/Decoding Runtime

We now focus our attention on the impact of our method during encoding and decoding. To this end, we measure the time necessary to encode and decode all terms in the datasets in the order they appear in the publicly available serialization of data (hereafter input order). To be more specific, we also run the same experiment once on IRIs, and once on Literals. Terms were encoded and decoded one after another, and the average encoding/decoding runtime per term is reported in Fig. 7.

As we can see from the left graph, in the worst case it takes about 650ns to encode a term, and about 450ns to decode it. In general, the encoding performance of our approach is comparable to the one of the Trove hash map, and in two cases (BioPortal, BTC 2014) the runtimes are even better. The figure shows that encoding literals is often more expensive both in the conventional dictionary and RDFVault. This suggests that the lower encoding performance of literals could be because they are longer than IRIs. Similar reasons can be given for the slow encoding speed of IRIs in case of DBPedia (EN) dataset, namely because this dataset uses long IRIs, both the conventional dictionary and RDFVault present slower encoding performance than average.

The right graph of Fig. 7 presents the average decoding runtime of RDF terms. The results show that a hash map performs up to 2.5 times better decoding performance, even though in some cases the margin with RDFVault is minimal. In theory the time complexity of both approaches is proportional to the length of string (hash code calculation for conventional dictionary, and string reconstruction in RDFVault), but in practice RDFVault needs to follow multiple references for the bottom up traversal and concatenate the substrings to reconstruct the original one. Therefore, it usually needs to execute more instructions than the conventional dictionary. The positive result is that strings do not have (on average) an excessive length. Therefore, the price that we pay for compressing our input in terms of decoding speed remains rather limited.

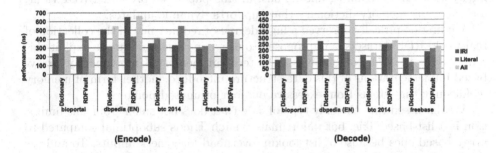

Fig. 7. Encoding and decoding runtime of our approach against the baseline.

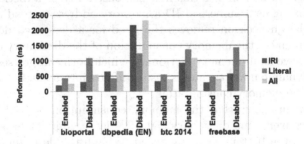

Fig. 8. Effect of Move to front policy on encoding performance

6.3 Move-to-front Policy Effectiveness

In this experiment, we evaluate the performance gain of applying move-to-front policy on children lists. To that end, we measure the encoding performance of RDFVault over the datasets Table 1 presents with and without move-to-front policy and report the results in Fig. 8.

Results clearly show that the move-to-front policy can effectively achieve up to 3.5 times performance improvement compared to when this optimization is disabled. It is interesting to see that the effectiveness of the move-to-front policy is not limited to IRIs, and literal terms benefit from this optimization as well.

7 Conclusions and Future Work

Dictionary encoding is widely used in semantic web applications, however, recent studies [19] show that sometimes the size of dictionaries becomes even larger than the encoded data. Hence, some efforts (e.g. HDT, and [19]) propose dictionary compression methods that considerably reduce the dictionary size for static datasets. Nonetheless, to the best of our knowledge there is no such technique for dynamic and streaming data. Thus, in this paper, we presented RDFVault, a compact in-memory dictionary that supports dynamic updates.

We first empirically observed a high degree of redundancy in the collection of real-world RDF datasets, and proposed to use Trie data structure to exploit this redundancy in order to compress RDF term in memory. Unfortunately, array-based implementations of this data structure introduce another form of memory inefficiency that stems from excessive number of unused pointers.

We discussed that the only type of Trie that does not suffer from this limitation is a list-based Trie, but unfortunately such Trie is suboptimal compared to array-based ones because of list lookup overhead for generic inputs. To address this last limitation, we introduced a novel list-based Trie that leverages the high degree of similarities and skewness among RDF terms to apply a move-to-front policy in order to reduce the list lookup overhead.

Then, we showed how we use this new list-based Trie as a dictionary named RDFVault, by using as a numerical ID a memory address instead of an integer counter. This design decision removes the need for a dedicated decoding data structure and enhances the memory consumption of the dictionary even further. As a result, we have an in-memory dictionary which both compresses the strings, and supports dynamic updates, and is also confined into a single data structure which reduces the memory consumption.

Our experiments show that the memory consumption of RDFVault is less than half of a conventional dictionary (50–59% less) while it offers comparable (and sometimes even better) encoding speed, though the decoding performance is degraded up to 2.5 times. Given that the decoding in a conventional dictionary is very fast (requires only a single table lookup), we believe that this is still a fairly good performance and a reasonable price to pay for higher compactness level, especially for applications that require frequent encoding or decoding such as stream processing frameworks.

For the future work we intend to extend this study further by exploring the possibilities of multiple concurrent dictionary updates in RDFVault.

Acknowledgment. This project was partially funded by the COMMIT project, and by the NWO VENI project 639.021.335.

References

1. java.sizeof. http://sizeof.sourceforge.net/
2. Askitis, N., Sinha, R.: Hat-trie: a cache-conscious trie-based data structure for strings. In: Proceedings of the Thirtieth Australasian Conference on Computer Science, vol. 62, pp. 97–105. Australian Computer Society Inc (2007)
3. Auer, S., Bizer, C., Kobilarov, G., Lehmann, J., Cyganiak, R., Ives, Z.G.: DBpedia: a nucleus for a web of open data. In: Aberer, K., Choi, K.-S., Noy, N., Allemang, D., Lee, K.-I., Nixon, L.J.B., Golbeck, J., Mika, P., Maynard, D., Mizoguchi, R., Schreiber, G., Cudré-Mauroux, P. (eds.) ASWC 2007 and ISWC 2007. LNCS, vol. 4825, pp. 722–735. Springer, Heidelberg (2007)
4. Binnig, C., Hildenbrand, S., Färber, F.: Dictionary-based order-preserving string compression for main memory column stores. In: SIGMOD. ACM (2009)
5. Cheng, L., Malik, A., Kotoulas, S., Ward, T.E., Theodoropoulos, G.: Efficient parallel dictionary encoding for RDF data
6. Cleary, J.G., Witten, I.: Data compression using adaptive coding and partial string matching. IEEE Trans. Commun. **32**(4), 396–402 (1984)
7. De La Briandais, R.: File searching using variable length keys. In: Papers Presented at the 3–5 March 1959, Western Joint Computer Conference. ACM (1959)
8. Erling, O., Mikhailov, I.: RDF support in the Virtuoso DBMS. In: Networked Knowledge-Networked Media, pp. 7–24. Springer (2009)
9. Fernández, J.D., Gutierrez, C., Martínez-Prieto, M.A.: RDF compression: basic approaches. In: WWW, pp. 1091–1092. ACM (2010)
10. Fernández, J.D., Martínez-Prieto, M.A., Gutierrez, C.: Compact representation of large RDF data sets for publishing and exchange. In: Patel-Schneider, P.F., Pan, Y., Hitzler, P., Mika, P., Zhang, L., Pan, J.Z., Horrocks, I., Glimm, B. (eds.) ISWC 2010, Part I. LNCS, vol. 6496, pp. 193–208. Springer, Heidelberg (2010)
11. Fredkin, E.: Trie memory. Commun. ACM **3**(9), 490–499 (1960)
12. Google. Freebase data dumps. http://download.freebase.com/datadumps
13. Heinz, S., Zobel, J., Williams, H.E.: Burst tries: a fast, efficient data structure for string keys. ACM TOIS **20**(2), 192–223 (2002)
14. Käfer, T., Harth, A.: Billion triples challenge data set (2014). Downloaded from http://km.aifb.kit.edu/projects/btc-2014/
15. Knuth, D.E.: The Art of Computer Programming, Volume 3: Sorting and Searching. International Monetary Fund (1998)
16. Kotoulas, S., Oren, E., Van Harmelen, F.: Mind the data skew: distributed inferencing by speeddating in elastic regions. In: WWW. ACM (2010)
17. Lassila, O., Swick, R.R.: Resource description framework (RDF) model and syntax specification (1999)
18. Leis, V., Kemper, A., Neumann, T.: The adaptive radix tree: ARTful indexing for main-memory databases. In: 2013 IEEE 29th International Conference on ICDE, pp. 38–49. IEEE (2013)
19. Martínez-Prieto, M.A., Fernández, J.D., Cánovas, R.: Querying RDF dictionaries in compressed space. ACM SIGAPP **12**(2), 64–77 (2012)
20. Morrison, D.R.: PATRICIA-practical algorithm to retrieve information coded in alphanumeric. JACM **15**(4), 514–534 (1968)
21. Neumann, T., Weikum, G.: RDF-3X: a RISC-style engine for RDF. VLDB **1**(1), 647–659 (2008)
22. Noy, N.F., Shah, N.H., Whetzel, P.L., Dai, B., Dorf, M., Griffith, N., Jonquet, C., Rubin, D.L., Storey, M.-A., Chute, C.G., et al.: Bioportal: ontologies and integrated data resources at the click of a mouse. Nucleic Acids Res. **37**, W170–W173 (2009)

23. Sussenguth Jr., E.H.: Use of tree structures for processing files. Commun. ACM **6**(5), 272–279 (1963)
24. Urbani, J., Maassen, J., Bal, H.: Massive semantic web data compression with MapReduce. In: HPDC, pp. 795–802. ACM (2010)
25. Yuan, P., Liu, P., Wu, B., Jin, H., Zhang, W., Liu, L.: TripleBit: a fast and compact system for large scale RDF data. VLDB **6**(7), 517–528 (2013)

Quality Assessment of Linked Datasets Using Probabilistic Approximation

Jeremy Debattista$^{(\boxtimes)}$, Santiago Londoño, Christoph Lange, and Sören Auer

University of Bonn and Fraunhofer IAIS, Bonn, Germany
{debattis,londono,langec,auer}@cs.uni-bonn.de

Abstract. With the increasing application of Linked Open Data, assessing the quality of datasets by computing quality metrics becomes an issue of crucial importance. For large and evolving datasets, an exact, deterministic computation of the quality metrics is too time consuming or expensive. We employ probabilistic techniques such as Reservoir Sampling, Bloom Filters and Clustering Coefficient estimation for implementing a broad set of data quality metrics in an approximate but sufficiently accurate way. Our implementation is integrated in the comprehensive data quality assessment framework Luzzu. We evaluated its performance and accuracy on Linked Open Datasets of broad relevance.

Keywords: Data quality · Linked data · Probabilistic approximation

1 Introduction

The Web of Data is continuously changing with large volumes of data from different sources being added. Inevitably, this causes the data to suffer from inconsistency, both at a semantic level (contradictions) and at a pragmatic level (ambiguity, inaccuracies), thus creating a lot of noise around the data. It also raises the question of how *authoritative* and *reputable* the data sources are. Taking *DBpedia*[1] as an example, data is extracted from a semi-structured source created in a crowdsourcing effort (i.e. Wikipedia). This extracted data might have quality problems because it is either mapped incorrectly or the information itself is incorrect. *Data consumers* increasingly rely on the Web of Data to accomplish tasks such as performing analytics or building applications that answer end user questions. Information overload is a consistent problem that these consumers face daily. Ensuring quality of the data on the Web is of paramount importance for data consumers, since it is infeasible to filter this infobesity manually.

A particular challenging area is the quality analysis of large-scale, evolving Linked Data datasets. In their editorial [9], Hitzler and Janowicz claim that

---

This work is supported by the European Commission under the Seventh Framework Program FP7 grant 601043 (http://diachron-fp7.eu).

[1] http://www.dbpedia.org.

F. Gandon et al. (Eds.): ESWC 2015, LNCS 9088, pp. 221–236, 2015.
DOI: 10.1007/978-3-319-18818-8_14

Linked Data is an ideal pilot to experiment with the 4th paradigm of big data (Veracity). However, Linked Data is frequently overlooked due to its reputation of being of poor quality. The quality of data can usually not be described using a single measure, but commonly requires a large variety of quality measures to be computed. Doing this for large datasets poses a substantial data processing challenge. However, for large datasets meticulously exact quality measures are usually not required. Instead users want to obtain an *approximate* indication of the quality they can expect.

Previous work on Linked Data quality analysis primarily employed deterministic algorithms (cf. the survey by Zaveri et al. [23]). Although such algorithms usually have polynomial complexity they are intractable for large datasets and it is difficult to reach runtimes sufficient for practical applications. The rationale of this paper is to show that we can apply probabilistic techniques to assess Linked Data quality. In particular, we employ three techniques commonly used in big data applications: *Reservoir Sampling*, *Bloom Filters* and *Clustering Coefficient estimation*. We develop strategies how these techniques can be applied to boost quality metric computations. We also thoroughly evaluate the quality metrics to tweak the required parameters for more accurate results yet keeping the running time acceptable. All implemented quality metrics are part of a large quality assessment framework, *Luzzu*^{2} [5].

The rest of this paper is organised as follows. Section 2 looks at the state of the art. Section 3 provides preliminaries. Section 4 details the Linked Data quality metrics under discussion. Section 5 discusses the implementation of the big data techniques and metrics. Section 6 reports our evaluation results. Final remarks and conclusions are presented in Section 7.

2   State of the Art

In a recent article, Dan O'Brien [17] discusses how big data, which is now being applied in many companies and applications, challenges data governance, including data quality. This section overviews the state of the art in relation to the probabilistic approximation techniques that can be applied to assess data quality in Linked Open Datasets. To our knowledge, there is currently no concrete use of such techniques to assess linked dataset quality.

Since their inception, *Bloom Filters* have been used in different scenarios, including dictionaries and spell-checkers, databases (for faster join operations and keeping track of changes), caching, and other network related scenarios [3]. Recently, this technique was also used to tackle the detection of duplicate data in streams in a variety of scenarios [1,6,11,14]. Such applications included the detection of duplicate clicks on pay-per-click adverts, fraud detection, URI crawling, and identification of distinct users on platforms. Metwally et al. [14] designed a Bloom Filter that applies the "window" principle: sliding windows (finding duplicates related to the last observed part of the stream), landmark windows

---

^{2} Luzzu is open source and available to download from http://eis-bonn.github.io/Luzzu.

(maintaining specific parts of the stream for de-duplication), and jumping windows (a trade-off between the latter two window types). Deng and Rafiei [6] go a step further than [14] and propose the Stable Bloom Filter, guaranteeing good and constant performance of filters over large streams, independent of the streams' size. Bera et al. [1] present a novel algorithm modifying Bloom Filters using *reservoir sampling* techniques, claiming that their approach not only provides a lower *false negative rate* but is also more stable than the method suggested in [6].

Random sampling, in different forms, is often used as an alternative to complex algorithms to provide a quick yet good approximation of results [20]. Sample-based approaches such as the latter were used to assess the quality of Geographic Information System data [18,21]. Xie et al. [21] describe different sampling methods for assessing geographical data. In their approach, Saberi and Ghadiri [18] sampled the original base geographical data periodically. The authors in [12] propose how data quality metrics can be designed to enable (1) the assessment of data quality and (2) analyse the economic consequences after executing data quality metrics. They suggest sampling the dataset attributes to get an estimate measure for the quality of the real-world data.

Lately, various efforts have been made to estimate values within big networks, such as *estimating the clustering coefficient* [8] or calculating the average degree of a network [4]. Hardiman et al. [8] provide an estimator to measure the network size and two clustering coefficient estimators: the network average (local) clustering coefficient and the global clustering coefficient. These measures were applied on public datasets such as DBLP, LiveJournal, Flickr and Orkut. Similarly, Dasgupta et al. [4] calculate the average degree of a network using similar public domain datasets. As Guèret et al. pointed out in [7], network measures can be exploited to assess Linked Data with regard to quality, as Linked Data uses the graph-based RDF data model.

3   Preliminaries

The LOD Cloud[3] comprises datasets having less than 10 K triples, and others having more than 1 billion triples. Deterministically computing quality metrics on these datasets might take from some seconds to days. This section introduces three probabilistic techniques commonly used in big data applications; they combine with a high probability near-to-accurate results with a low running time.

Reservoir Sampling. Reservoir sampling is a statistics-based technique that facilitates the sampling of evenly distributed items. The sampling process randomly selects k elements ($\leq n$) from a source list, possibly of an unknown size n, such that each element in the source list has a k/n probability of being chosen [20]. The reservoir sampling technique is part of the *randomised algorithms* family. Randomised algorithms offer simple and fast solutions for time-consuming counterparts by implementing a degree of randomness. Vitter [20]

---

[3] http://lod-cloud.net.

introduces an algorithm for selecting a random sample of k elements from a bigger list of n elements, in one pass. The author discusses that by using a *rejection-acceptance technique* the running time for the sampling algorithm improves. The main parameter that affects the tradeoff between fast computation and an accurate result is the reservoir size (k). The sample should be *large enough* such that the law of large numbers[4] can be applied.

Bloom Filters. A Bloom Filter [2] is a fast and space efficient bit vector data structure commonly used to query for elements in a set ("is element A in the set?"). The size of the bit vector plays an important role with regard to the precision of the result. A set of hash functions is used to map each item added to be compared, to a corresponding set of bits in the array filter. The main drawback of a Bloom Filter is that they can produce *false positives*, therefore being possible to identify an item as existing in the filter when it is not, but this happens with a very low probability. The trade-off of having a fast computation yet a very close estimate of the result depends on the size of the bit vector. With some modifications, Bloom Filters are useful for detecting duplicates in data streams [1].

Clustering Coefficient Estimation. The clustering coefficient algorithm measures the neighbourhood's density of a node. The clustering coefficient is measured by dividing the number of edges of a node and the number of possible connections the neighbouring nodes can have. The time complexity for this algorithm is $\mathcal{O}(n^3)$, where n is the number of nodes in the network. Hardiman and Katzir [8] present an algorithm that estimates the clustering coefficient of a node in a network using *random walks*. A *random walk* is a process where some object jumps from one connected node to another with some probability of ending in a particular node. A random walker stops when the *mixing time* is reached. In a Markov model, mixing time refers to the time until the chain is close to its steady state distribution, i.e. the total number of steps the random walker should take until it retires. Given the right *mixing time*, the value is proved to be a close approximate of the actual value. The authors' suggested measure computes in $\mathcal{O}(r) + \mathcal{O}(rd_{\max})$ time, where r is the total number of steps in the random walk and $d_{\max}$ is the node with the highest degree[5].

4   Linked Data Metrics

Zaveri et al. present a comprehensive survey [23] of quality metrics for linked open datasets. Most of the quality metrics discussed are *deterministic* and computable within *polynomial time*. On the other hand, once these metrics are exposed to large datasets, the metrics' upper bound grows and as a result, the computational time becomes intractable. In this section we discuss some metrics that are known to suffer from the big data phenomenon.

---

[4] http://mathworld.wolfram.com/LawofLargeNumbers.html.
[5] The number of in-links plus out-links of a node.

Dereferenceability. HTTP URIs should be dereferenceable, i.e. HTTP clients should be able to retrieve the resources identified by the URI. A typical web URI resource would return a 200 OK code indicating that a request is successful and a 4xx or 5xx code if the request is unsuccessful. In Linked Data, a successful request should return an RDF document containing triples that describe the requested resource. Resources should either be *hash* URIs or respond with a 303 Redirect code [19]. The dereferenceability metric assesses a dataset by counting the number of valid dereferenceable URIs (according to these LOD principles) divided by the total number of URIs. Yang et al. [22] describe a mechanism[6] to identify the dereferenceability process of a Linked Data resource.

A naïve approach for this metric is to dereference all URI resources appearing in the subject and the object of all triples. In this metric we assume that all predicates are dereferenceable. This means that the metric performs at worst $2n$ HTTP requests, where n is the number of triples. It is not possible to perform such a large number of HTTP requests in an acceptable time.

Existence of Links to External Data Providers. This metric measures the degree to which a resource is linked to external data providers. Ideally, datasets have a high degree of linkage with external data providers, since interlinking is one of the main principles of Linked Data [10].

The simplest approach for this metric is to compare the subject's resource pay-level domain (PLD) against the object's resource PLD[7]. Although this metric is not considered to be computationally expensive ($\mathcal{O}(n)$, where n represents the number of triples), it is also a good candidate for an estimation.

Extensional Conciseness. At the data level, a linked dataset is concise if there are no redundant instances [13]. This metric measures the number of unique instances found in the dataset. The uniqueness of instances is determined from their properties and values. An instance is unique if no other instance (in the same dataset) exists with the same set of properties and corresponding values.

The most straightforward approach is to compare each resource with every other resource in the dataset to check for uniqueness. This gives us a time complexity of $\mathcal{O}(i^2 t)$, where i is the number of instances in the datasets and t is the number of triples. The major challenge for this algorithm is the number of triples in a dataset, since each triple (predicate and object) is compared with every other triple streamed from the dataset.

Clustering Coefficient of a Network. The clustering coefficient metric is proposed as part of a set of network measures to assess the quality of data mappings in linked datasets [7]. This metric aims at identifying how well resources are

---

[6] Also used in the Semantic Web URI Validator Hyperthing (http://www.hyperthing.org).

[7] "PLDs allow us to identify a realm, where a single user or organization is likely to be in control." [16]. For example the PLD for http://dbpedia.org/resource/Malta is dbpedia.org.

Table 1. Mapping probabilistic approximation techniques with Linked Data quality metrics

Probabilistic Approximation Technique	Linked Data Metric
Reservoir Sampling	Dereferenceability
	Links to External Data Providers
Bloom Filters	Extensional Conciseness
Clustering Coefficient Estimation	Clustering Coefficient of a Network

connected, by measuring the density of the resource neighbourhood. A network has a high clustering cohesion when a node has a large number of neighbouring nodes, all of which are connected to each other. This means that links may end up being meaningless [7].

When assessing the clustering coefficient of a network, a graph is built where the *subject* and *object* of a triple (either URI resources or blank nodes) are represented as vertices in the graph, whilst the *predicate* is the edge between them. As this ignores triples with literal objects, there is no direct correlation between the number of triples in a dataset and number of vertices. Calculating this measure on a network takes $\mathcal{O}(n^3)$, especially for large datasets. This is because each vertex in the network has to be considered: for each vertex v in the graph, we identify the number of links between the neighbours of v (i.e. how many of v's neighbours are connected together) and divide it by the number of possible links.

5 Implementation

Based on the probabilistic techniques described in Sect. 3, we analyse how they can help in assessing quality in linked datasets. These metrics are implemented as an extensible package for *Luzzu*. Luzzu [5] is a Linked Data quality assessment framework that provides an integrated platform which: (1) assesses Linked Data quality using a library of generic and user-provided domain specific quality metrics in a scalable manner; (2) adds queryable quality metadata to the assessed datasets; and (3) assembles detailed quality reports on assessed datasets. Datasets are assessed using a sequential streaming approach. Table 1 shows which approximation can be used for each respective metric.

5.1 Reservoir Sampling

Our implementation is based on the *rejection-acceptance* technique [20]. The trade-off parameter is the definition of the maximum number of items (k) that can be stored. Various factors are taken to define k, such as the rough estimation of the size of the dataset and available memory, since this reservoir is stored in-memory.

When attempting to add an *item* to the reservoir sampler, an item counter (n) is incremented. This increment is required to calculate the *replacement probability*, since the exact size of the source (in our case the dataset) is unknown. The *item* can be (i) *added* to the reservoir, (ii) become a *candidate* to replace another item, or (iii) be *discarded*. The first possible operation is straightforward. If the reservoir sampler has free locations ($n < k$), the *item* is added. On the other hand, when the reservoir is full, the *item* can either replace another item in the list, or rejected. The decision is made by generating a random number (p) between 0 and n. If p lies in the range of the reservoir list length (i.e. $p < k$), then the new *item* replaces the current item stored in that position of the reservoir, else it is rejected. This simulates the k/n *replacement probability* for all items.

Estimated Dereferenceability Metric. Each resource URI is split into two parts: (1) the pay-level Domain (PLD), and (2) the path to the resource. For this metric we employ a "global" reservoir sampler for the PLDs. Furthermore, for each PLD we employ another reservoir sampler holding an evenly distributed sample list of resources to be dereferenced. If the pay-level domain returns a 4xx/5xx code upon an HTTP request, then all other sampled resources in that reservoir are automatically deemed as non-dereferenceable. Envisaging the possibility of multiple HTTP requests to same domain or resource, we make use of the Luzzu's caching mechanism, to store HTTP requests. The metric value is calculated as a ratio of the total number of dereferenced URIs against the total number of sampled URIs.

Estimated Links to External Data Providers Metric. In order to measure the use of external data providers, the metric must first identify the base URI of the dataset that is being assessed. As each triple is streamed to the metric processor, a heuristic mechanism identifies the base URI. For this, we apply one of the two heuristics, listed in order of priority:

1. Extract the base URI from a triple having the *predicate* rdf:type and *object* void:Dataset or owl:Ontology.
2. The URI (PLD) with the maximum number of occurrences in the *subject* of the assessed dataset.

Each triple's *object* in the dataset is then used to estimate the value of this metric, by first extracting its PLD and attempting to add it to the metric's reservoir. The value of this metric is defined as the ratio of the number of PLDs in the sampler that are not the same as the base URI, against the total number of URIs in the sampler.

5.2 Bloom Filters

Linked datasets might suffer from instance duplication. Bera et al. [1] introduced some modifications to the mechanics of Bloom Filters to enable the detection

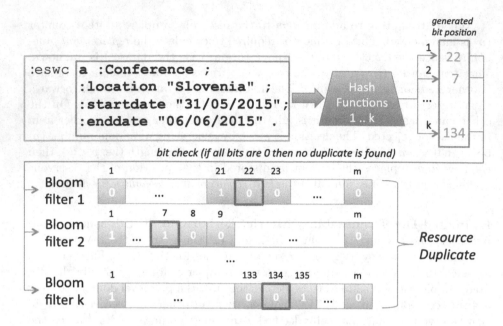

Fig. 1. Illustrating bloom filters with an example

of duplicate elements in data streams. These modifications allow items to be inserted indefinitely by probabilistically resetting bits in the filter arrays when they are close to getting overloaded. The Randomised Load Balanced Biased Sampling based Bloom Filter (RLBSBF) is used to implement the detection of duplicate instances. The authors show that this approach is efficient and generates a low *false positive* rate.

An RLBSBF algorithm is initialised with (1) the total memory used by filter arrays in bits (M); and (2) a threshold value (t_{FPR}) for the false positive rate. The bit vector is initialised with k Bloom Filters. Each bloom filter has a size of M/k and a hash function is mapped to it. The authors in [1] suggest that k is calculated using the threshold value t_{FPR}. A high threshold value means faster computation but less accurate results.

Whenever a new element is processed, the Bloom Filter sets all k bit positions using the hash functions mapped to them. If the bit positions were previously set in the bit vector, it means that a duplicate was detected. Otherwise, the probabilistic resetting of bits is performed before the new element is added to the bit vector. Our implementation uses 128-bit Murmur3[8] hashing functions. Figure 1 illustrates how Bloom Filters help to identify a Linked Data resource that already exists in a dataset.

Estimated Extensional Conciseness Metric. When triples are streamed to the metric processor, the *predicate* and *object* are extracted and serialised as a

---

[8] https://code.google.com/p/smhasher/wiki/MurmurHash3.

string. The latter string is stored in a sorted set. This process is repeated until a triple with a different *subject* identifier is processed. The sorted set is then flattened to a string and added to the Bloom Filter, discovering any possible duplicates. The set is then initialised again for the new resource identifier and the process is repeated until no more triples are streamed.

The main drawback of our proposed algorithm is that a dataset must be sorted by *subject*, such that all triples pertaining to the same instance are streamed one after another. Although it is common practice to publish datasets sorted by subject (e.g. DBpedia), this cannot be guaranteed in the general case. In our experiments we pre-process RDF dumps by converting them to the N-Triples serialisation, which can be sorted by subject in a straightforward way.

5.3   Clustering Coefficient Estimation

In [8], the authors propose an approach for estimating a social network's clustering coefficient by creating a random walk. In their proposed algorithm, Hardiman and Katzir use $\log^2 n$[9] as the base *mixing time*, i.e. the number of steps a random walker takes until it converges to a steady-state distribution. However, different network characteristics lead to different *mixing times*, where well-connected networks have a small (fast) mixing time [15].

To calculate an estimate of the clustering coefficient given a random walk $R = \{x_1, x_2, \ldots, x_r\}$, Hardiman and Katzir propose the Estimator 1:

Estimator 1

$$\Phi_l = \frac{1}{r-2} \sum_{r-1}^{k=2} \phi_k \frac{1}{d_{x_k} - 1}$$

$$\Psi_l = \frac{1}{r} \sum_{r}^{k=1} \frac{1}{d_{x_k}}$$

$$\hat{c}_l \triangleq \frac{\Phi_l}{\Psi_l}$$

where r is the total number of steps in the random walk R, x_k is the index of the kth node in the random walk, d_{x_k} is the degree of node x_k and ϕ_k represents the value in the adjacency matrix A in position $A_{x_{k-1}, x_{k+1}}$.

Estimated Clustering Coefficient Metric. When triples are streamed into the metric, the vertices are created by extracting the *subject* and the *object*, whilst the *predicate* acts as a directed edge between the two nodes. We use URI resources and blank nodes to create the network vertices. To calculate the estimated clustering coefficient value, a random walk is performed on the graph.

---

[9] The square of $\log n$.

Similarly to the approach in [8], we view the graph as undirected. The idea is that if the random walker ends up in a dead-end (i.e. cannot move forward), it can go back to continue crawling the network. Our mixing time parameter is $m \log^2 n$. Since linked open data advocates interlinking and re-use of resources, we expect[10] that such datasets have a low mixing time. The multiplier factor m thus enables us to increase or decrease the mixing time as required. The reason behind this is to enable a parameter modifier to the base mixing time ($\log^2 n$), since it is difficult to find a one size fits all mixing time. Estimator 1 is used to obtain a close estimate of the dataset's clustering coefficient. Finally, the estimated value is normalised as described in [7].

6   Metric Analysis and Experiments

Having implemented the metrics using probabilistic approximation techniques, we measure the computed quality metric values and runtime for the approximate metrics and compare them with the actual metrics. For each approximate metric, we experimented with different parameter settings to identify the best parameter values. All tests are run on a Unix virtual machine with an Intel Xeon 3.00 GHz, with 3 cores and a total memory of 3.8 GB. We used a number of datasets of varying sizes and covering different application domains. We found them on Datahub, looking for datasets tagged with the *lod* tag. These are:

- Learning Analytics and Knowledge (LAK) Dataset $\approx$ 75 K triples;
- Lower Layer Super Output Areas (LSOA) $\approx$ 280 K triples;
- Southampton ECS E-Prints Dataset $\approx$ 1 M triples;
- WordNet 2.0 (W3C) Dataset $\approx$ 2 M triples;
- Sweto DBLP Dataset $\approx$ 15 M triples;
- Semantic XBRL $\approx$ 100 M triples;

Parameter Setting. In order to maximise accuracy, the parameters of the algorithms have to be tweaked. Therefore, we experimented with different parameter values and analysed the metric results. Parameter settings were obtained by observing the algorithm's parameters in correlation with the datasets and metrics. The rationale behind this experiment is to identify a single parameter that, when used in a metric, gives acceptable results within reasonable time. This experiment was not performed on all datasets, since in certain cases the actual metric does not complete its computation.

The *Dereferenceability* metric was implemented using reservoir sampling. Table 2 shows the time taken (in seconds) and the approximate value for different parameter settings. The biggest time factor in this metric is the network access time, i.e. the time an HTTP request takes to respond. The parameter settings employed for this experiment are: (P1) global reservoir size: 10, PLD reservoir size: 1000; (P2) global reservoir size: 50, PLD reservoir size: 100; (P3) global

---

[10] We are currently performing research on the mixing time of the linked datasets available in the LOD Cloud.

Table 2. Dereferenceability metric with different parameter settings

	Time (s)	Value		Time (s)	Value
Actual (LAK)	1423.33	0.045533	**Actual (LSOA)**	3189.819	0
P1	842.082	0.345548	P1	149.913	0
P2	426.892	0.162581	P2	80.748	0
P3	618.761	0.057866	P3	388.522	0
P4	480.972	0.262936	P4	316.862	0

Table 3. Existence of links to external data providers metric with different parameter settings

	Time(s)	Value		Time(s)	Value
Actual (LAK)	2.271	0.000156	**Actual (LSOA)**	3.529	3.272144×10^6
P1	0.578	0.000156	P1	1.287	3.272144×10^6
P2	0.481	0.000156	P2	1.182	3.272144×10^6
P3	0.466	0.000156	P3	1.153	3.272144×10^6
P4	0.444	0.000156	P4	1.124	3.272144×10^6

	Time(s)	Value		Time(s)	Value
Actual (S'OTON)	23.872	6.166189×10^6	**Actual (WN)**	33.82	0
P1	20.693	6.166189×10^6	P1	7.362	0
P2	20.008	6.166189×10^6	P2	7.779	0
P3	20.4	6.166189×10^6	P3	7.557	0
P4	20.589	6.166189×10^6	P4	7.258	0

reservoir size: 50, PLD reservoir size: 10000; (P4) global reservoir size: 100, PLD reservoir size: 1000. Whilst the approximate metrics completed the computation for all datasets, the exact computation was only ready for the LAK and LSOA datasets. Based on the available results from the datasets, we can conclude that the optimal parameter for this metric is close to the P3 settings. The results for the LSOA dataset are 0 due to the fact that all resources returned a **4xx/5xx** error. This was verified manually.

Another application of the Reservoir Sampling was the *Existence of Links to External Data Providers*. Table 3 shows the time taken (in seconds) and the estimated value for different parameter settings. The parameter settings used to initialise the sampler were: (P1) 5,000; (P2) 10,000; (P3) 20,000; (P4) 50,000. The results show that the approximation technique did not record any major difference up to 2 M, but the technique fares better with very big datasets (c.f. Fig. 2). One possible reason for this is that since the actual metric is not expected to fit in-memory, our implementation uses $MapDB^{11}$, a pure Java database that stores memory data structures such as hash maps on disk. It is also worth noting that all estimates gave the same value as the actual. The reason for this is that the number of object PLDs fits in the smallest reservoir. Therefore, since the runtime between different parameters varies a little, setting a higher or lower reservoir sampler in this case is a matter of available memory space. If all PLDs fit in the reservoir sampler, the result is 100 % accurate.

---

[11] http://www.mapdb.org.

Table 4. Extensional conciseness metric with different parameter settings

	Time(s)	Value		Time(s)	Value
Actual (LAK)	81.334	0.994860	**Actual (LSOA)**	375.873	1
P1	1.348	0.621315	P1	1.043	0.617729
P2	1.377	0.962249	P2	1.328	0.966795
P3	1.67	0.993946	P3	1.807	0.999240
P4	2.212	0.994593	P4	2.98	1

	Time(s)	Value		Time(s)	Value
Actual (S'OTON)	7366.225	0.737523	**Actual (WN)**	96511.334	0.948
P1	24.304	0.512887	P1	7.407	0.570991
P2	20.217	0.782946	P2	11.502	0.885790
P3	17.512	0.783529	P3	17.653	0.900407
P4	20.275	0.660193	P4	35.381	0.844733

Table 5. Clustering coefficient metric with different parameter settings

	Time(s)	Value		Time(s)	Value
Actual (LAK)	42.729	0.961040	**Actual (LSOA)**	62.618	1
Mixing time 0.1	4.595	0.978220	Mixing time 0.1	7.657	0.999995
Mixing time 0.5	4.595	0.997945	Mixing time 0.5	6.829	0.999999
Mixing time 0.7	4.766	0.998665	Mixing time 0.7	6.561	0.999503
Mixing time 1.0	4.832	0.998974	Mixing time 1.0	6.528	0.999999

	Time(s)	Value		Time(s)	Value
Actual (S'OTON)	408.358	0.933590	**Actual (WN)**	9012.454	0.759257
Mixing time 0.1	46.373	0.993067	Mixing time 0.1	243.009	0.810405
Mixing time 0.5	46.362	0.997634	Mixing time 0.5	248.925	0.999919
Mixing time 0.7	46.238	0.997939	Mixing time 0.7	251.396	0.999917
Mixing time 1.0	46.225	0.998312	Mixing time 1.0	252.522	0.999967

The *Extensional Conciseness* metric was implemented using Bloom Filters. Table 4 shows the time taken (in seconds) and the estimated value for different parameter settings. We applied 4 different settings for experimentation: (P1) 2 filters (k) with a size (M) of 1,000; (P2) 5 filters with a size of 10,000; (P3) 10 filters with a size of 100,000; (P4) 15 filters with a size of 10,000,000. This technique showed a lot of potential in the de-duplication process. The time taken in the approximate algorithms are lower than the actual, with results being almost as accurate. Based on the Bloom Filter trade-off, a setting between P3–P4 would exploit the potential of this technique in assessing the quality of linked datasets with regard to duplication problems.

For the *clustering coefficient* metric we multiplied the base mixing time of $\log^2 n$ with 0.1, 0.5, 0.7 and 1.0 respectively to test with fast mixing time. Table 5 shows the time taken (in seconds) and the estimated value for different parameter settings. The results show that for the assessed datasets the $\log^2 n$ mixing time is not ideal. This is due to the fact that the smallest multiplier setting, i.e. 0.1, proved to be the closest to the actual result in all cases. Determining a more accurate average mixing time, and hence a more accurate estimate (cf. Sect. 3), requires the evaluation (such as in [15]) of all datasets in the LOD Cloud.

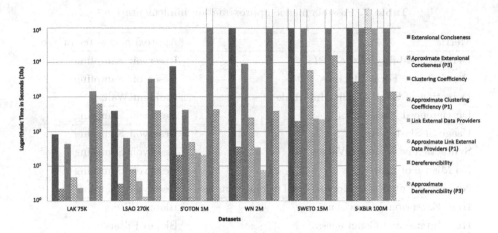

Fig. 2. Runtime of Metrics vs. Datasets

Table 6. Metric value (actual and approximate) per dataset

	LAK 75K	LSOA 270K	S'OTON 1M	WN 2M	SWETO 15M	S-XBLR 100M
Extensional Conciseness	0.9948	1	0.7375	0.948	0,000370	N/A
Approx. Extensional Conciseness	0.9945	1	0.6601	0.8447	0.9998	0.1097
Clustering Coefficiency	0.9610	1	0.9335	0.7592	N/A	N/A
Approx. Clustering Coefficiency	0.9782	0.9999	0.9930	0.8104	1	0
Link External Data Providers	0.01569×10^{-6}	3.2721×10^{-6}	6.1661×10^{-6}	0	N/A	N/A
Approx. Link External Data Prov.	0.01569×10^{-6}	3.2721×10^{-6}	6.1661×10^{-6}	0	0.000370	$4,9557 \times 10^{-8}$
Dereferencibility	0.0455	0	N/A	N/A	N/A	N/A
Approx. Dereferencibility	0.0578	0	0.4122	0.9681	0	$0,0955 \times 10^{-8}$

Evaluation Discussion. Our experiments gave promising results towards the use and acceptance of probabilistic approximation for estimating the quality of linked open datasets. Figure 2 shows the time taken in all implemented metrics (actual and approximated) against the evaluated datasets. The graph clearly shows that all approximate metrics have a lower runtime than their equivalent actual metric. Whilst the approximate metrics for *link external data providers*, *dereferenceability*, and *extensional conciseness* computed all metrics, the approximate *clustering coefficient* and the actual *link external data providers* managed to compute 5 datasets within a reasonable time. The actual *dereferenceability*

Table 7. Possible metric approximation implementation

Metric	Approximation technique
Dereferenceability of the URI	Reservoir Sampling
Dereferenced Forward-Links	Reservoir Sampling
Detection of Good Quality Interlinks	Random Walk
Dereferenced Back-Links	Reservoir Sampling
Usage of Slash-URIs	Reservoir Sampling
Syntactically Accurate Values	Reservoir Sampling
No Misuse of Properties	Reservoir Sampling
No Use of Entities as Members of Disjoint Classes	Reservoir Sampling
High Extensional Conciseness	Bloom Filters
High Intensional Conciseness	Bloom Filters
Duplicate Instance	Bloom Filters
Relevant Terms Within Meta-Information Attributes	Page Rank
Coverage	Reservoir Sampling

metric managed only to compute two datasets, while the other two actual metrics computed up to the WordNet dataset. Table 6 shows the metric (actual and estimated) values for the datasets. The approximate results are in most cases very close to the actual results. However, approximate measures are calculated in an acceptable time unlike their actual counterparts. As part of a larger effort to implement scalable LOD quality assessment metrics, we assessed the metrics identified in [23] and assigned to them possible approximation techniques discussed in this article (cf. Table 7).

Overall, given that the results were obtained on yet small datasets (the chosen ones might not be considered to be big enough) due to limited infrastructure, this paper contributes towards invaluable results that can be the basis for further studies. These results show that with probabilistic approximation techniques:

1. Runtime decreases considerably – for larger datasets easily by more than an order of magnitude;
2. Loss of precision is acceptable in most cases with less than 10% deviation from actual values;
3. Large linked datasets can be assessed for quality even within very limited computational capabilities, such as a personal notebook.

7   Conclusion

In this article, we have demonstrated how the three approximate techniques reservoir sampling, Bloom Filters and clustering coefficient estimation can be successfully applied for Linked Data quality assessment. Our comprehensive experiments have shown that we can reduce runtime in most cases by more than an order of magnitude, while keeping the precision of results reasonable for most practical applications. All in all, we have demonstrated that using these approximation techniques enables data publishers to assess their datasets in a convenient and efficient manner without the need of having a large infrastructure for computing quality metrics. Therefore, data publishers are encouraged to assess their data before publishing it to the Web, thus ensuring that data consumers receive quality data at their end.

In terms of Linked Data quality assessment we aim to extend our work both in terms of used big data techniques and metric coverage. Regarding probabilistic approximation techniques, we aim to assess other probabilistic data structures such as quotient filters or random trees. A further interesting avenue of research is to investigate how such techniques can be easily employed for domain specific data quality metrics.

References

1. Bera, S.K., Dutta, S., Narang, A., Bhattacherjee, S.: Advanced Bloom filter based algorithms for efficient approximate data de-duplication in streams (2012)
2. Bloom, B.H.: Space/time trade-offs in hash coding with allowable errors. Commun. ACM **13**(7), 422–426 (1970)
3. Broder, A.Z., Mitzenmacher, M.: Network applications of Bloom filters: a survey. Internet Math. **1**, 485–509 (2004)
4. Dasgupta, A., Kumar, R., Sarlos, T.: On estimating the average degree. In: WWW, pp. 795–806. ACM, New York (2014)
5. Debattista, J., Londoño, S., Lange, C., Auer, S.: LUZZU - a framework for linked data quality assessment (2014). http://arxiv.org/abs/1412.3750
6. Deng, F., Rafiei, D.: Approximately detecting duplicates for streaming data using stable bloom filters. In: ACM SIGMOD 2006, pp. 25–36. ACM (2006)
7. Guéret, C., Groth, P., Stadler, C., Lehmann, J.: Assessing linked data mappings using network measures. In: Simperl, E., Cimiano, P., Polleres, A., Corcho, O., Presutti, V. (eds.) ESWC 2012. LNCS, vol. 7295, pp. 87–102. Springer, Heidelberg (2012)
8. Hardiman, S.J., Katzir, L.: Estimating clustering coefficients and size of social networks via random walk. In: WWW, pp. 539–550. ACM (2013)
9. Hitzler, P., Janowicz, K.: Linked data, big data, and the 4th paradigm. Semant. Web **4**(3), 233–235 (2013)
10. Hogan, A., Umbrich, J., Harth, A., Cyganiak, R., Polleres, A., Decker, S.: An empirical survey of linked data conformance. J. Web Sem. **14**, 14–44 (2012)
11. Jain, N., Dahlin, M., Tewari, R.: Taper: tiered approach for eliminating redundancy in replica synchronization. In: FAST, USENIX (2005)
12. Kaiser, M., Klier, M., Heinrich, B.: How to measure data quality? - a metric-based approach. In: International Conference on Information Systems (ICIS), p. 108 (2007)
13. Mendes, P.N., Mühleisen, H., Bizer, C.: Sieve: linked data quality assessment and fusion. In: 2012 Joint EDBT/ICDT Workshops, pp. 116–123. ACM (2012)
14. Metwally, A., Agrawal, D., Abbadi, A.E.: Duplicate detection in click streams. In: WWW 2005. ACM (2005)

15. Mohaisen, A., Yun, A., Kim, Y.: Measuring the mixing time of social graphs. In: SIGCOMM. IMC 2010, pp. 383–389. ACM (2010)
16. Mühleisen, H.: Vocabulary usage by pay-level domain (2014). http://webdatacommons.org/structureddata/vocabulary-usage-analysis/
17. O'Brien, D.: January 2015. http://insideanalysis.com/2015/01/the-key-to-quality-big-data-analytics/
18. Saberi, B., Ghadiri, N.: A sample-based approach to data quality assessment in spatial databases with application to mobile trajectory nearest-neighbor search (2014)
19. Sauermann, L., Cyganiak, R.: Cool URIs for the semantic web. Interest Group Note, W3C, December 2008. http://www.w3.org/TR/2008/NOTE-cooluris-2008 1203/
20. Vitter, J.S.: Random sampling with a reservoir. ACM Trans. Math. Softw. **11**, 37–57 (1985)
21. Xie, H., Tong, X.H., Jiang, Z.Q.: The quality assessment and sampling model for the geological spatial data in China. In: ISPRS Archives - Volume XXXVII, Part B2. ISPRS 2008, pp. 819–824 (2008)
22. Yang, Y., Che, H., Gibbins, N., Hall, W., Shadbolt, N.: Dereferencing semantic web URIs: what is 200 OK on the semantic web?. https://dl.dropboxusercontent.com/u/4138729/paper/dereference_iswc2011.pdf
23. Zaveri, A., Rula, A., Maurino, A., Pietrobon, R., Lehmann, J., Auer, S.: Quality assessment methodologies for linked open data. Semant. Web J. (2014). http://www.semantic-web-journal.net/content/quality-assessment-linked-data-survey

Cooperative Techniques for SPARQL Query Relaxation in RDF Databases

Géraud Fokou, Stéphane Jean, Allel Hadjali$^{(\boxtimes)}$, and Mickael Baron

LIAS/ISAE-ENSMA - University of Poitiers,
1, Avenue Clement Ader, 86960 Futuroscope Cedex, France
{geraud.fokou,jean,allel.hadjali,baron}@ensma.fr

Abstract. This paper addresses the problem of failing RDF queries. Query relaxation is one of the cooperative techniques that allows providing users with alternative answers instead of an empty result. While previous works on query relaxation over RDF data have focused on defining new relaxation operators, we investigate in this paper techniques to find the parts of an RDF query that are responsible of its failure. Finding such subqueries, named *Minimal Failing Subqueries* (MFSs), is of great interest to efficiently perform the relaxation process. We propose two algorithmic approaches for computing MFSs. The first approach (LBA) intelligently leverages the subquery lattice of the initial RDF query while the second approach (MBA) is based on a particular matrix that improves the performance of LBA. Our approaches also compute a particular kind of relaxed RDF queries, called *Maximal Succeeding Subqueries* (XSSs). XSSs are subqueries with a maximal number of triple patterns of the initial query. To validate our approaches, a set of thorough experiments is conducted on the LUBM benchmark and a comparative study with other approaches is done.

1 Introduction

With the extensive adoption of RDF, specialized databases called RDF databases (or triple-store) have been developed to manage large amounts of RDF data (e.g., Jena [1]). RDF databases are based on a generic representation (a triples table or one of its variants) that can manage a set of diverse RDF data, ranging from structured data to unstructured data. This flexibility makes it difficult for users to correctly formulate RDF queries that return the desired answers. This is why user RDF queries often return an empty result.

Query relaxation is one of the cooperative techniques that allows providing users with alternative answers instead of an empty result. Several works have been proposed to relax queries in the RDF context [2–8]. They mainly focus either on introducing new relaxation operators or on the efficient processing of *top-k* RDF queries. Usually, only some parts of a failing RDF query are responsible of its failure. Finding such subqueries, named *Minimal Failing Subqueries* (MFSs), provides the user with an explanation of the empty result returned and a guide to relax his/her query.

© Springer International Publishing Switzerland 2015
F. Gandon et al. (Eds.): ESWC 2015, LNCS 9088, pp. 237–252, 2015.
DOI: 10.1007/978-3-319-18818-8_15

To the best of our knowledge, no work exists in the literature that addresses the issue of computing MFSs of failing RDF queries. Inspired by some previous works in relational databases [9] and recommendation systems [10], we propose in this paper two algorithmic approaches for searching MFSs of failing RDF queries. The first one is a smart exploration of the subquery lattice of the failing query, while the second one relies on a particular matrix obtained by executing each triple pattern involved in the query. These algorithms also compute a particular kind of relaxed queries, called *Maximal Succeeding Subqueries* (XSSs), that return non-empty answers. Each XSS provides a simple way to relax a query by removing or making optional the set of triple patterns that are not in an XSS. Our contributions are summarized as follows.

1. We propose an adapted and extended variant of Godfrey's approach [9], called LBA, for computing both the MFSs and XSSs of a failing RDF query. Both properties and algorithmic aspects of LBA are investigated.
2. Inspired by the work done in [10], we devise a second approach, called MBA, which only requires n queries over the target RDF database, where n is the number of query triple patterns. The skyline of the matrix on which this approach is based, directly provides the XSSs of a query. This matrix can also improve the performance of LBA.
3. We study the efficiency and effectiveness of the above approaches through a set of experiments conducted on two datasets of the LUBM benchmark. We also compare our propositions with existing similar approaches on the basis of the experimental results obtained.

The paper is structured as follows. Section 2 introduces some basic notions and formalizes the problem we consider. Sections 3 and 4 present our approaches LBA and MBA to find the MFSs and XSSs of a failing RDF query. We present our experimental evaluation in Sect. 5 and conclude in Sect. 6.

2   Preliminaries and Problem Statement

This section formally describes the parts of RDF and SPARQL that are necessary to this paper. We use the notations and definitions given in [11].

Data Model. An RDF *triple* is a triple (subject, predicate, object) $\in (U \cup B) \times U \times (U \cup B \cup L)$ where U is a set of URIs, B is a set of blank nodes and L is a set of literals. We denote by T the union $U \cup B \cup L$. An RDF *database* stores a set of RDF triples in a triples table or one of its variants.

Query. An RDF *triple pattern* t is a triple (subject, predicate, object) $\in (U \cup V) \times (U \cup V) \times (U \cup V \cup L)$, where V is a set of variables disjoint from the sets U, B and L. We denote by $var(t)$ the set of variables occurring in t. We consider RDF *queries* defined as a conjunction of triple patterns: $Q = t_1 \wedge \cdots \wedge t_n$. The number of triple patterns of a query Q is denoted by $|Q|$.

Query Evaluation. A *mapping* μ from V to T is a partial function $\mu : V \to T$. For a triple pattern t, we denote by $\mu(t)$ the triple obtained by replacing the variables in t according to μ. The domain of μ, $dom(\mu)$, is the subset of V where μ is defined. Two mappings μ_1 and μ_2 are *compatible* when for all $x \in dom(\mu_1) \cap dom(\mu_2)$, it is the case that $\mu_1(x) = \mu_2(x)$ i.e., when $\mu_1 \cup \mu_2$ is also a mapping. Let Ω_1 and Ω_2 be sets of mappings, we define the *join* of Ω_1 and Ω_2 as: $\Omega_1 \bowtie \Omega_2 = \{\mu_1 \cup \mu_2 \mid \mu_1 \in \Omega_1, \mu_2 \in \Omega_2 \text{ are compatible mappings}\}$. Let D be an RDF database, t a triple pattern. The evaluation of the triple pattern t over D denoted by $[[t]]_D$ is defined by: $[[t]]_D = \{\mu \mid dom(\mu) = var(t) \wedge \mu(t) \in D\}$. Let Q be a query, the evaluation of Q over D is defined by: $[[Q]]_D = [[t_1]]_D \bowtie \cdots \bowtie [[t_n]]_D$. This evaluation can be done under different entailment regimes as defined in the SPARQL specification. In this paper, the examples as well as our implementation are based on the simple entailment regime. However, the proposed algorithms can be used with any entailment regime.

MFS and XSS. Given a query $Q = t_1 \wedge \cdots \wedge t_n$, a query $Q' = t_i \wedge \cdots \wedge t_j$ is a *subquery* of Q, $Q' \subseteq Q$, iff $\{i, \cdots, j\} \subseteq \{1, \cdots, n\}$. If $\{i, \cdots, j\} \subset \{1, \cdots, n\}$, we say that Q' is a *proper subquery* of Q ($Q' \subset Q$). If a subquery Q' of Q fails, then the query Q fails.

A *Minimal Failing Subquery MFS* of a query Q is defined as follows: $[[MFS]]_D = \emptyset \wedge \nexists Q' \subset MFS$ such that $[[Q']]_D = \emptyset$. The set of all MFSs of a query Q is denoted by $mfs(Q)$. Each MFS is a minimal part of the query that fails.

A *Maximal Succeeding Subquery XSS* of a query Q is defined as follows: $[[XSS]]_D \neq \emptyset \wedge \nexists Q'$ such that $XSS \subset Q' \wedge [[Q']]_D \neq \emptyset$. The set of all XSSs of a query Q is denoted by $xss(Q)$. Each XSS is a maximal (in terms of triple patterns) non-failing subquery viewed as a relaxed query.

Problem Statement. We are concerned with computing the MFSs and XSSs of a failing RDF query over an RDF database efficiently.

3   Lattice-Based Approach (LBA)

LBA is an algorithm to compute simultaneously both the sets $mfs(Q)$ and $xss(Q)$ of a failing RDF query Q. It is a three steps procedure: (1) find an MFS of Q, (2) compute the potential XSSs, i.e., the maximal queries that do not include the MFS previously found and (3) execute potential XSSs; if they return results, they are XSSs, else this process will be applied recursively on failing potential XSSs.

Finding an MFS. This step is performed with the *a_mel_fast* algorithm proposed in [9]. This algorithm is based on the following proposition (proved in [9]). Let $Q = t_1 \wedge \ldots \wedge t_n$ be a failing query and $Q_i = Q - t_i$ a proper subquery of Q. If $[[Q]]_D = \emptyset$ and $[[Q_i]]_D \neq \emptyset$ then any MFS of Q contains t_i.

This property is leveraged in the Algorithm 1 to find an MFS in n steps (i.e., its complexity is then $\mathcal{O}(n)$). The algorithm removes a triple pattern t_i from Q resulting in the proper subquery Q'. If $[[Q']]_D$ is not empty, t_i is part of any MFS (thanks to the previous proposition) and it is added to the result Q^*. Else, Q' has an MFS that does not contain t_i. Then, the algorithm iterates over another triple pattern of Q to find an MFS in $Q' \wedge Q^*$. This process stops when all the triple patterns of Q have been processed.

Algorithm 1. Find an MFS of a failing SPARQL query Q

FindAnMFS(Q, D)
  inputs : A failing query $Q = t_1 \wedge ... \wedge t_n$; an RDF database D
  output: An MFS of Q denoted by Q^*
  $Q^* \leftarrow \emptyset$;
  $Q' \leftarrow Q$;
  foreach *triple pattern* $t_i \in Q$ **do**
    $Q' \leftarrow Q' - t_i$;
    if $[[Q' \wedge Q^*]]_D \neq \emptyset$ **then**
      $Q^* \leftarrow Q^* \wedge t_i$;
  return Q^*;

Figure 1 shows an execution of the Algorithm 1 to compute an MFS of the following query $Q = t_1 \wedge t_2 \wedge t_3 \wedge t_4$:

```
Select ?X ?Y Where {
    ?Y ub:subOrganizationOf <http://www.University8.edu> .     (t₁)
    ?X ub:researchInterest "Research28" .                       (t₂)
    ?X rdf:type ub:Lecturer .                                    (t₃)
    ?X ub:worksFor ?Y }                                          (t₄)
```

The algorithm removes the triple pattern t_1 from Q, resulting in the subquery Q'. As this subquery returns an empty result, the algorithm iterates over the triple pattern t_2 to find an MFS in $t_2 \wedge t_3 \wedge t_4$. The subquery $t_3 \wedge t_4$ is successful, hence t_2 is part of the MFS Q^*. The same result is obtained for t_3, which is added to Q^*. For t_4, the subquery $t_2 \wedge t_3$ returns an empty result and thus t_4 does not belong to Q^*. As all the triple patterns of Q have been processed, the algorithm stops and returns the MFS $Q^* = t_2 \wedge t_3$.

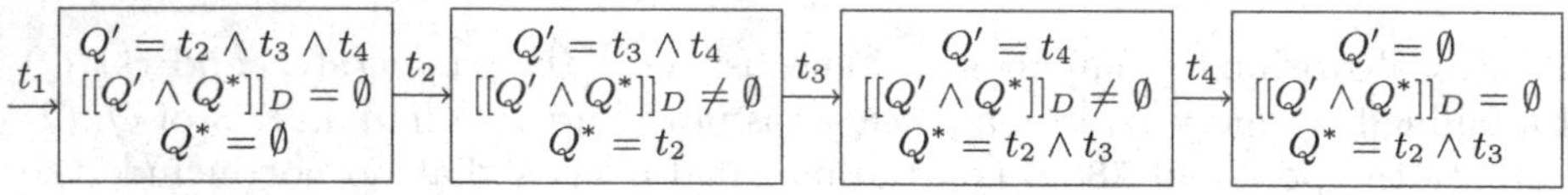

Fig. 1. An execution of Algorithm 1 to find an MFS of Q

Computing Potential XSSs. By definition, all queries that include the MFS Q^*, found in the previous step, return an empty set of answers. Thus, they can be neither MFS nor XSS of Q and they are pruned from the search space. The exploration of the subquery lattice continues with the largest subqueries of Q that do not include Q^*. If these subqueries are successful, they are XSSs of Q. Thus, we call them *potential* XSSs and we denote this set of queries by $pxss(Q, Q^*)$. This set can be computed as follows:

$$pxss(Q, Q^*) = \begin{cases} \emptyset, & \text{if } |Q| = 1. \\ \{Q - t_i \mid t_i \in Q^*\}, & \text{otherwise.} \end{cases}$$

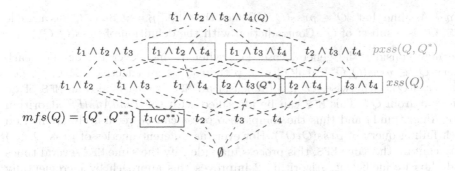

Fig. 2. The lattice of subqueries of Q with its MFSs and XSSs

Indeed, for each triple pattern t_i of Q^*, a subquery of the form $Q_m \leftarrow Q - t_i$ does not include Q^* and, in addition, it is maximal due to its large size, i.e., $|Q_m| = |Q| - 1$. Following the previous definition, $pxss(Q, Q^*)$ is computed with a simple algorithm running in linear time ($\mathcal{O}(n^*)$ where $n^* = |Q^*|$).

Figure 2 illustrates $pxss(Q, Q^*)$ of our running example ($Q = t_1 \wedge t_2 \wedge t_3 \wedge t_4$ and $Q^* = t_2 \wedge t_3$) on the lattice of subqueries. The maximal subqueries of Q that do not contain $t_2 \wedge t_3$ are $t_1 \wedge t_2 \wedge t_4$ and $t_1 \wedge t_3 \wedge t_4$.

Algorithm 2. Find the MFSs and XSSs of a query Q

LBA(Q, D)
    inputs : A failing query $Q = t_1 \wedge ... \wedge t_n$; an RDF database D
    outputs: The MFSs and XSSs of Q
    $Q^* \leftarrow FindAnMFS(Q, D)$;
    $pxss \leftarrow pxss(Q, Q^*)$;
    $mfs(Q) \leftarrow \{Q^*\}$; $xss(Q) \leftarrow \emptyset$;
    while $pxss \neq \emptyset$ **do**
        $Q' \leftarrow pxss.element()$; /* **choose an element of** Q' */
        if $[[Q']]_D \neq \emptyset$ **then** /* Q' **is an XSS** */
            $xss(Q) \leftarrow xss(Q) \cup \{Q'\}$;
            $pxss \leftarrow pxss - \{Q'\}$;
        else /* Q' **contains an MFS** */
            $Q^{**} \leftarrow FindAnMFS(Q', D)$;
            $mfs(Q) \leftarrow mfs(Q) \cup \{Q^{**}\}$;
            foreach $Q'' \in pxss$ such that $Q^{**} \subseteq Q''$ **do**
                $pxss \leftarrow pxss - \{Q''\}$;
                $pxss \leftarrow pxss \cup \{Q_j \in pxss(Q'', Q^{**}) \mid \nexists Q_k \in pxss : Q_j \subseteq Q_k\}$;
    return $\{mfs(Q), xss(Q)\}$;

Finding all XSSs and MFSs (Algorithm 2). If Q has only a single MFS Q^* (which includes the case where Q is itself an MFS), then $xss(Q) = pxss(Q, Q^*)$.

Proof. Assume that $\exists Q' \in pxss(Q, Q^*)$ such that $[[Q']]_D = \emptyset$. Since Q has a single MFS, Q^* is a subset of Q'. Contradiction with the definition of $pxss(Q, Q^*)$.

We now consider the general case, i.e., when Q has several MFSs. For each query $Q' \in pxss(Q, Q^*)$, if $[[Q']]_D \neq \emptyset$ then Q' is an effective XSS of Q, i.e., $Q' \in xss(Q)$. Otherwise, Q' has (at least) an MFS, which is also an MFS of Q, different from Q^*. This MFS can be identified with the *FindAnMFS* algorithm (see Algorithm 1) and thus the complete process can be recursively applied on each failing query of $pxss(Q, Q^*)$. However, as different queries of $pxss(Q, Q^*)$ may contain the same MFS, this process may identify the same MFS several times and thus be inefficient. Algorithm 2 improves this approach by incrementally computing potential XSSs that do not contain the set of identified MFSs. When a second MFS Q^{**} is identified, this algorithm iterates over the previously found potential XSSs *pxss* that contain Q^{**}. To avoid finding again this MFS, the algorithm replaces them by their largest subqueries that do not contain Q^{**} (i.e., their own potential XSSs) and are not included in any query of *pxss* (otherwise they are not the largest potential XSSs of Q).

Figure 3 shows an execution of Algorithm 2 to compute the MFSs and XSSs of our running example: $Q = t_1 \wedge t_2 \wedge t_3 \wedge t_4$, $Q^* = t_2 \wedge t_3$ and $pxss(Q, Q^*) = \{t_1 \wedge t_2 \wedge t_4, t_1 \wedge t_3 \wedge t_4\}$. The algorithm executes the query $t_1 \wedge t_3 \wedge t_4$. As an empty set of answers is obtained, the Algorithm 1 is applied on this query to find a second MFS $Q^{**} = t_1$. The two potential XSSs contain this MFS and thus

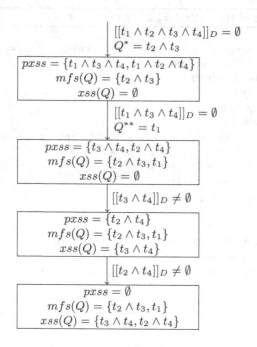

Fig. 3. An execution of Algorithm 2 to find the MFSs and XSSs of Q

they are replaced with their largest subqueries that do not contain Q^{**}, i.e., $t_3 \wedge t_4$ and $t_2 \wedge t_4$. By executing these two queries, the algorithm finds that these potential XSSs are effectively XSSs. The algorithm stops and returns these two XSSs and the MFSs previously found (see Fig. 2).

4 Matrix-Based Approach (MBA)

In the approach proposed in the previous section, the theoretical search space exponentially increases with the number of triple patterns of the original query. Jannach [10] has proposed a solution to avoid this problem in the context of recommender systems. This approach is based on a matrix, called the *relaxed matrix*, computed in a preprocessing step with n queries where n is the number of query atoms. This matrix gives, for each potential solution of a query, the set of query atoms satisfied by this solution. The XSSs of the query can then be obtained from this matrix without the need for further database queries.

In this section, we adapt this approach to RDF databases to compute both the XSSs and MFSs of a query. Compared to [10], the main difficulty is to compute the set of potential solutions of a query. Indeed, in the context of recommender systems, these solutions are already known as they are the set of products described in the product catalog. This is not the case in the context of RDF databases.

The Relaxed Matrix of a Query. We first informally define the notion of relaxed matrix through an example. Figure 4(c) presents the relaxed matrix of the query Q given in Fig. 4(b) when it is executed on the RDF dataset presented in Fig. 4(a). Each row of the matrix is a mapping (as defined in Sect. 2) that

Triples		
s	p	o
p1	type	Prof
p1	advises	s4
p2	type	Prof
p2	advises	s1
s1	age	27
p3	type	AssistantProf
p3	advises	s2
s2	age	25
s3	age	25

(a) RDF triples

	?p	?s	t1	t2	t3
	p1	NULL	1	0	0
	p2	NULL	1	0	0
*	p1	s4	1	1	0
*	p2	s1	1	1	0
*	p3	s2	0	1	1
*	p1	s2	1	0	1
*	p1	s3	1	0	1
*	p2	s2	1	0	1
*	p2	s3	1	0	1
	NULL	s2	0	0	1
	NULL	s3	0	0	1

(c) The relaxed matrix of Q

t1 = (?p type Prof) ^
t2 = (?p advises ?s) ^
t3 = (?s age 25)

(b) The query Q

xss(Q) = { t1^t3, t2^t3, t1^t2 }
mfs(Q) = { t1^t2^t3 }

(d) XSSs and MFSs of Q

Fig. 4. Matrix-based approach

satisfies at least one triple pattern. For example, the first row corresponds to the mapping $\mu : ?p \rightarrow p_1$. A mapping μ has the value 1 in the column t_i, if μ satisfies t_i. Thus the matrix entry that lies in the first row and the t_1 column is set to 1 as p_1 is a professor in the considered RDF dataset.

As we have seen in Sect. 2, the evaluation of a query consists in finding the mappings that satisfy *all its triple patterns* using join operations. The relaxed matrix contains the mappings that satisfy *at least one triple pattern*. Intuitively, one can think of using the OPTIONAL operator of SPARQL to compute these mappings. However, the semantics of this operator is based on the outer join operation [11], which eliminates from its operands the mappings that satisfy the inner join operation [12]. In our case, we need to keep these mappings as they may be compatible with the mappings of another triple pattern. For example, the operation $[[t_1]]_D \bowtie [[t_2]]_D$ eliminates the mapping $\mu : ?p \rightarrow p_1$ from the relaxed matrix in the example presented in Fig. 4. This mapping is needed to find other mappings such as $\mu : ?p \rightarrow p_1 \; ?s \rightarrow s_2$. As a consequence, we have defined an *extended join operation*, which is defined as follows.

Formal Definition of the Relaxed Matrix. Let Ω_1 and Ω_2 be sets of mappings, the *extended join* of Ω_1 and Ω_2 is defined by: $\Omega_1 \bowtie^* \Omega_2 = \Omega_1 \cup (\Omega_1 \bowtie \Omega_2) \cup \Omega_2$. Let Q be a query, the *relaxed evaluation* of Q over D is defined by: $[[Q]]_D^R = [[t_1]]_D \bowtie^* \cdots \bowtie^* [[t_n]]_D$. We define the relaxed matrix M of a query Q over an RDF database D as a two-dimensional table with $|Q|$ columns (one for each triple pattern of the query) and $|[[Q]]_D^R|$ rows (one for each mapping of $[[Q]]_D^R$). For a mapping $\mu \in [[Q]]_D^R$ and a triple pattern $t_i \in Q$, $M[\mu][t_i] = 1 \Leftrightarrow \mu(t_i) \in D, else\; M[\mu][t_i] = 0$.

Computing the Relaxed Matrix. Thus, to obtain the relaxed matrix, we need first to evaluate each triple pattern t_i over D to obtain $[[t_i]]_D$. Then, we compute the extended joins of all the $[[t_i]]_D$ while keeping track of the matched triple patterns to get the matrix values. The Algorithm 3 follows this approach using a nested loop algorithm. This algorithm only requires n queries where n is the number of triple patterns. Yet, our experiments conducted on the LUBM benchmark (see Sect. 5) show that this algorithm can still take a notable amount of time as the size of the matrix can be large for queries over large datasets involving triple patterns that are not selective. Moreover, proper subqueries of the initial query can lead to Cartesian products (the triple patterns do not share any variable), which imply an expensive computation cost as well as a matrix of a large size (see Sect. 5 for details). As a first step to improve this approach, we have specialized this approach for star-shaped queries (i.e., a set of triple patterns with a shared join variable in the subject position) as they are often found in the query logs of real datasets [13].

Optimized Computation for Star-Shaped Queries. The computation of star-shaped queries is simpler than in the general case. First, subqueries of a star-shaped query cannot be Cartesian products. Second, a single variable is used to join all the triple patterns. Thanks to this latter property we can use full outer joins to compute the relaxed matrix as depicted in the Algorithm 4. This algorithm executes one query for each triple pattern. For each result μ of such a

---

Algorithm 3. Computation of the relaxed matrix of a query Q

ComputeMatrix(Q, D)

    inputs : A failing query $Q = t_1 \wedge ... \wedge t_n$; an RDF database D

    output: The relaxed matrix M

    $M \leftarrow \emptyset$;

    foreach *triple pattern* $t_i \in Q$ **do**

        foreach $\mu \in [[t_i]]_D$ **do**

            $isInserted \leftarrow false$;

        foreach $\mu' \in M$ **do**

            if μ *and* μ' *are compatible* **then**

                if $(\mu' \cup \mu) \notin M$ **then**

                    $M \leftarrow M \cup \{\mu' \cup \mu\}$;

                    $M[\mu' \cup \mu][t_k] \leftarrow M[\mu'][t_k]$ for $k \in 1 \cdots n \wedge k \neq i$;

                $M[\mu' \cup \mu][t_i] \leftarrow 1$;

                if $(\mu \cup \mu') = \mu$ **then**

                    $isInserted \leftarrow true$;

        if *not* $isInserted$ **then**

            $M \leftarrow M \cup \{\mu\}$;

            $M[\mu][t_k] \leftarrow 1$ if $k = i$, else 0; $(k \in 1 \cdots n)$

    return M;

---

subquery, the value of the join variable (i.e., the restriction of the function μ to $\{x\}$ denoted by $\mu_{|\{x\}}$) is added to the matrix, if it is not already in it, and the value of this row is set to 1 for the corresponding triple pattern.

The Algorithm 4, called NQ, can be used for any RDF database (implemented on a relational database management system (RDBMS) or not). If we consider an RDF database implemented as a triples table $t(s, p, o)$ in an RDBMS, we can use a single SQL query to compute the relaxed matrix. This query is roughly the translation of the $[[t_1]]_D \bowtie \cdots \bowtie [[t_n]]_D$ expression. Inspired by the work of Cyganiak conducted on the translation of SPARQL queries into SQL [14], we use SQL outer join operators to compute this expression and the *coalesce* function[1] to manage unbound values. In addition, we use the *case* operator to test if a triple pattern is matched and thus to get the matrix values (1 if it is matched, else 0). For example, the SQL query used to compute the relaxed matrix of the query $t_1 \wedge t_2$ (Fig. 4) is:

```
select coalesce(t1.s , t2.s),
       case when t1.s is null then 0 else 1 end as t1,
       case when t2.s is null then 0 else 1 end as t2
from (select distinct s from t where p='type' and o='professor') t1
full join (select distinct s from t where p='advises') t2 on t1.s = t2.s
```

This approach, called *1Q*, has two advantages: (1) a single query is used to compute the relaxed matrix, (2) the RDBMS chooses the adequate join algorithm.

---

[1] The *coalesce* function returns the first non-null expression in the list of parameters.

Algorithm 4. Computation of the matrix for star-shaped queries (NQ)

ComputeMatrixStarQueryNQ(Q, D)

    inputs : A failing star-shaped query $Q = t_1 \wedge \ldots \wedge t_n$ with x as join variable;
            An RDF database D
    output: The relaxed matrix M
    $M \leftarrow \emptyset$;
    foreach *triple pattern* $t_i \in Q$ **do**
        foreach $\mu \in [[t_i]]_D$ **do**
            if $\mu_{|\{x\}} \notin M$ **then**
                $M \leftarrow M \cup \{\mu_{|\{x\}}\}$;
                $M[\mu_{|\{x\}}][t_k] \leftarrow 0$ for $k \in 1 \cdots n \wedge k \neq i$;
            $M[\mu_{|\{x\}}][t_i] \leftarrow 1$;
    return M;

Computing the XSSs from the Relaxed Matrix. Abusing notation, we denote by $xss(\mu)$ the proper subquery of Q that can be executed to retrieve μ. It can be directly obtained from the relaxed matrix: $xss(\mu) = \{t_i \mid M[\mu][t_i] = 1\}$. Finding the XSSs of a query Q can be done in two steps:

1. Computing the skyline SKY of the relaxed matrix: $SKY(M) = \{\mu \in [[Q]]_D^R \mid \nexists \mu' \in [[Q]]_D^R$ *such that* $\mu \prec \mu'\}$ where $\mu \prec \mu'$ if (i) on every triple pattern t_i, $M[\mu][t_i] \leq M[\mu'][t_i]$ and (ii) on at least one triple pattern t_j, $M[\mu][t_j] < M[\mu'][t_j]$. This step can be done by using one of the numerous algorithms defined to efficiently compute the skyline of a table (see [15] for a survey). In Fig. 4(c), all the rows composing the skyline of the relaxed matrix are marked with $*$.
2. Retrieving the distinct proper subqueries of Q that can be executed to retrieve an element of the skyline: $xss(Q) = \{xss(\mu) \mid \mu \in SKY(M)\}$. Each such proper subquery is an XSS. The XSSs of our example are given in Fig. 4(d) and appear in bold in the relaxed matrix.

Using the Relaxed Matrix as an Index for the LBA Approach. In the LBA algorithm, subqueries are executed on the RDF database to find whether they return an empty set of answers or not. Instead of executing a subquery, one can compute the intersection of the matrix columns corresponding to the subquery triple patterns. If the resulting column is empty, the subquery returns an empty set of answers and conversely. Thus, the MBA approach can be seen as an index to improve the performance of the LBA approach. This approach still requires exploring a search space that exponentially increases with the number of triple patterns, but this search space does not require the execution of any database query.

5   Experimental Evaluation

Experimental Setup. We have implemented the proposed algorithms in JAVA 1.7 64 bits on top of Jena TDB. Our implementation is available at http://www. lias-lab.fr/forge/projects/qars. These algorithms take as input a failing SPARQL query and return the set of MFSs and XSSs of this query. We run these algorithms on a Windows 7 Pro system with Intel Core i7 CPU and 8 GB RAM. All times presented in this paper are the average of five runs of the algorithms. The results of algorithms are not shown for queries when they consumed too many resources i.e., when they took more than one hour to execute or when the memory used exceeded the size of the JVM (set to 4 GB in our experiments).

Dataset and Queries. Due to the lack of an RDF query relaxation benchmark, Huang et al. [6] have designed 7 queries based on the LUBM benchmark. These queries cover the main query patterns (star, chain and composite) but they only have between 2 and 5 triple patterns. Yet the study proposed by Arias and al. [13] has shown that real-world SPARQL queries executed on the DBPedia and SWDF datasets range from 1 to 15 triple patterns. As a consequence, we have modified the 7 queries proposed in [6] to reflect this diversity. The modified versions of these queries[2] have respectively 1, 5, 7, 9, 11, 13 and 15 triple patterns. Q1, Q2 are chain, Q3, Q5, Q7 are star and Q4, Q6 are composite query patterns. We used two generated datasets to evaluate the performances of our algorithms on these queries: LUBM20 (3 M triples) and LUBM100 (13 M triples).

Relaxed Matrix Size and Computation Time. The MBA approach relies on the relaxed matrix. To define the data structure of this matrix, we have leveraged the similarity between this matrix and bitmap indexes used in RDBMS. Thus, the matrix is defined as a set of compressed bitmaps, one for each column. We have used the Roaring bitmap library version 0.4.8 for this purpose [16]. As Table 1 shows, this data structure ensures that the matrix size remains small even if the number of matrix rows is large (less than 2 MB for 2 M rows). Table 1 only includes results for star-shaped queries as other queries required too many resources due to Cartesian products.

For the computation of the MBA relaxed matrix, we have tested the two algorithms *1Q* and *NQ* described in Sect. 4. As the *1Q* approach requires an RDF

Table 1. Relaxed matrix properties

	LUBM20			LUBM100		
	Q3	Q5	Q7	Q3	Q5	Q7
Computation time with NQ (in sec)	8.6	8.6	8.6	42.6	43.4	44.6
Computation time with 1Q (in sec)	6.1	6.3	6.8	30.4	34.6	38.5
Size (in KB)	293	400	335	1385	1912	1590
Number of rows (in K)	430	430	430	2149	2149	2149

---

[2] Available at http://www.lias-lab.fr/publications/16873/Report_MFS_XSS.pdf.

database implemented on top of an RDBMS, we have used the Oracle 12c RDBMS to implement the triples table and test this algorithm. As Table 1 shows, the *1Q* algorithm is about 25 % faster than *NQ*. Even with this optimization, which is only possible for specific RDF databases, the computation time of the matrix is important: around 6 s on LUBM20 and 35 s on LUBM100. Despite this important computation time, the MBA approach can still be interesting as the matrix can be precomputed for usual failing queries identified with query logs. Moreover, the next experiment shows that MBA is faster than other algorithms for large queries even if the matrix is computed at runtime.

XSS and MFS Computation Time. We compare the performance of the following algorithms for computing the XSSs and MFSs of the benchmark queries.

- LBA: the algorithm described in Sect. 3.
- MBA+M: this algorithm first computes the relaxed matrix using Algorithm 4 for star-shaped queries and Algorithm 3 for other queries. Then, it computes XSSs and MFSs of the query with the LBA algorithm that uses the relaxed matrix instead of executing queries.
- MBA-M: same as MBA+M but without the computation of the relaxed matrix.
- DFS: a depth-first search algorithm of the subquery lattice that we modified to prune the search space when no more MFSs and XSSs can be found.
- ISHMAEL: the algorithm proposed in [9] that we have tailored to return both the XSSs and MFSs of a query.

Figure 5 shows the performance of each algorithm displayed in logarithmic scale for readability. An algorithm that evaluates most of the subqueries such as DFS can be used for queries with only a few triple patterns (Q1 and Q2). For larger queries, the number of subqueries exponentially increases and thus the performance of DFS quickly decreases.

In this case, the smart exploration of the search space provided by the LBA and ISHMAEL algorithms is more efficient. Their response times are between

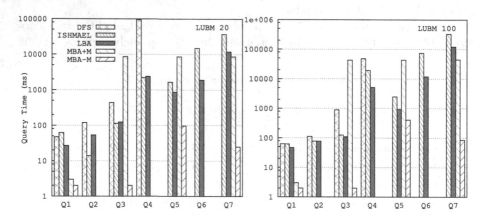

Fig. 5. Performance of the algorithms on LUBM20 and LUBM100

1 and 10 seconds for queries that do not have more than 11 triple patterns (Q1-Q5). The performance of LBA and ISHMAEL are close for queries Q1-Q5 and LBA outperforms ISHMAEL on Q6 and Q7 (recall that the results are presented in logarithmic scale). We have identified that the performance difference is due to the simplified computation of the potential XSSs and to the order in which these potential XSSs are evaluated. Indeed, according to this order, the caching performed by Jena TDB can be more or less efficient. For example, we have found some cases where the same query can be executed with a response time differing by a factor of 2 according to the caching usage. Thus, a perspective is to find the best ordering of the potential XSSs to maximize the cache usage.

Finally, the MBA approach can only be used for star-shaped queries. MBA − M provides response times of some milliseconds even for Q7, which has 15 triple patterns. This is due to the fact that this approach just needs to compute the intersection of bitmaps using bitwise operations instead of executing subqueries. However, this approach makes a strong assumption: the matrix must be precomputed i.e., the query must have been identified as a usual failing query (e.g., using query logs). If the matrix is computed at runtime (MBA + M), this computation time is important (see Table 1) and thus MBA + M is only interesting for queries with a large number of triple patterns or with only selective triple patterns (they can be identified using database statistics). As a consequence, the MBA approach is complementary with an approach such as LBA: it should be used when LBA does not scale anymore.

Performance as the Number of Triple Patterns Scales. The previous experiments show that the number of triple patterns plays an important role in the performance of the proposed algorithms. In order to explore this further, we have decomposed Q7 in 15 subqueries ranging from 1 to 15 triple patterns. The first subquery only includes the first triple pattern of Q7, the second subquery includes the first two triple patterns and so on. The result of this experiment is shown in Fig. 6. This experiment confirms our previous observation. DFS does not scale when a query exceeds 5 triple patterns. LBA and ISHMAEL can be used with a response time between 1 and 10 s for queries with less than 13 triple

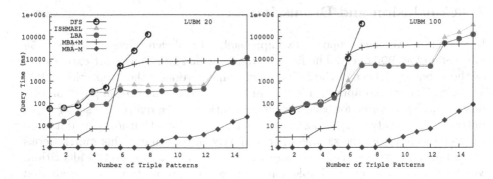

Fig. 6. Query 7 performance as the number of its triple patterns increases

patterns. The MBA − M scales well for star queries even with a large number of triple patterns. The MBA + M is only interesting when the query has more than 13 triple patterns as the cost of computing the matrix is important.

6 Related Work

We review here the closest works related to our proposal done both in the context of RDF and relational databases. In the first setting, Hurtado et al. [5] proposed some rules and operators for relaxing RDF queries. Adding to these rules, Huang et al. [6] specified a method for relaxing SPARQL queries using a semantic similarity measure based on statistics. In our previous work [7], we have proposed a set of primitive relaxation operators and have shown how these operators can be integrated in SPARQL in a simple or combined way. Cali et al. [8] have also extended a fragment of this language with query approximation and relaxation operators. As an alternative to query relaxation, there have been works on *query auto-completion* (e.g., [17]), which check the data during query formulation to avoid empty answers. But, none of the previous works has considered the issue related to the causes of RDF query failure and then the issue of MFS computation.

As for relational databases, many works have been proposed for query relaxation (see Bosc et al. [18] for an overview). In particular, Godfrey [9] has defined the algorithmic complexity of the problem of identifying the MFSs of failing relational query and developed the ISHMAEL algorithm for retrieving them. The LBA approach is inspired by this algorithm. Compared with ISHMAEL, LBA computes both the MFSs and the potential XSSs in one time. Moreover, LBA proposes a simplified computation of the potential XSSs. Bosc et al. [18] and Pivert et al. [19] extended Godfrey's approach to the fuzzy query context. Jannach [10] studied the concept of MFS in the recommendation system setting. The MBA approach is inspired by this approach. Contrary to [10], the computation of the matrix rows is not straightforward in the context of RDF queries. Moreover, in [10], the matrix is only used to retrieve the XSSs of the query while, in our work, we used and stored this matrix as a bitmap index to improve the performance of LBA.

7 Conclusion and Discussion

In this paper we have proposed two approaches to efficiently compute the MFSs and XSSs of an RDF query. The first approach, called LBA, is a smart exploration of the subquery lattice of the failing query that leverages the properties of MFS and XSS. The second approach, called MBA, is based on the precomputation of a matrix, which records, for each potential solution of the query, the set of triple patterns that it satisfies. The XSSs of a query can be found without any database access by computing the skyline of this matrix. Interestingly, this matrix looks like a bitmap index and can also improve the performance of the LBA algorithm. We have done a complete implementation of our propositions and evaluated their performances on two datasets generated with the LUBM benchmark. While a straightforward algorithm does not scale for queries with more than 5 triple patterns, the LBA approach scales up to approximatively 11 triple patterns in our experiments. The MBA approach is only interesting for star-shaped queries. If the matrix is precomputed, which assumes that the query has been identified as a usual failing query, XSSs and MFSs can be found in some milliseconds even for queries with many triple patterns (a maximum of 15 in our experiments). If the matrix is computed at runtime, this approach can still be interesting for large queries as the cost of computing the matrix becomes acceptable in comparison with the optimization of LBA it permits. Optimizing the MBA approach for other kinds of RDF query is part of our future work. We also plan to define query relaxation strategies based on the MFSs and XSSs of a failing RDF query.

References

1. Wilkinson, K.: Jena property table implementation. In: SSWS (2006)
2. Dolog, P., Stuckenschmidt, H., Wache, H., Diederich, J.: Relaxing RDF queries based on user and domain preferences. IJIIS **33**(3), 239–260 (2009)
3. Elbassuoni, S., Ramanath, M., Weikum, G.: Query relaxation for entity-relationship search. In: Antoniou, G., Grobelnik, M., Simperl, E., Parsia, B., Plexousakis, D., De Leenheer, P., Pan, J. (eds.) ESWC 2011, Part II. LNCS, vol. 6644, pp. 62–76. Springer, Heidelberg (2011)
4. Hogan, A., Mellotte, M., Powell, G., Stampouli, D.: Towards fuzzy query-relaxation for RDF. In: Simperl, E., Cimiano, P., Polleres, A., Corcho, O., Presutti, V. (eds.) ESWC 2012. LNCS, vol. 7295, pp. 687–702. Springer, Heidelberg (2012)
5. Hurtado, C.A., Poulovassilis, A., Wood, P.T.: Query relaxation in RDF. In: Spaccapietra, S. (ed.) Journal on Data Semantics X. LNCS, vol. 4900, pp. 31–61. Springer, Heidelberg (2008)
6. Huang, H., Liu, C., Zhou, X.: Approximating query answering on RDF databases. J. World Wide Web **15**(1), 89–114 (2012)
7. Fokou, G., Jean, S., Hadjali, A.: Endowing semantic query languages with advanced relaxation capabilities. In: Andreasen, T., Christiansen, H., Cubero, J.-C., Raś, Z.W. (eds.) ISMIS 2014. LNCS, vol. 8502, pp. 512–517. Springer, Heidelberg (2014)
8. Calí, A., Frosini, R., Poulovassilis, A., Wood, P.T.: Flexible querying for SPARQL. In: Meersman, R., Panetto, H., Dillon, T., Missikoff, M., Liu, L., Pastor, O., Cuzzocrea, A., Sellis, T. (eds.) OTM 2014. LNCS, vol. 8841, pp. 473–490. Springer, Heidelberg (2014)
9. Godfrey, P.: Minimization in cooperative response to failing database queries. Int. J. Coop. Inf. Syst. **6**(2), 95–149 (1997)
10. Jannach, D.: Fast computation of query relaxations for knowledge-based recommenders. AI Commun. **22**(4), 235–248 (2009)
11. Pérez, J., Arenas, M., Gutierrez, C.: Semantics and complexity of SPARQL. ACM Trans. Database Syst. **34**(3), 16:1–16:45 (2009)
12. Galindo-Legaria, C.A.: Algebraic optimization of outerjoin queries. Ph.D thesis, Harvard University, Technical report TR-12-92 (1992)
13. Arias, M., Fernández, J.D., Martínez-Prieto, M.A., de la Fuente, P.: An empirical study of real-world SPARQL queries. In: USEWOD (2011)
14. Cyganiak, R.: A relational algebra for sparql. HP-Labs, HPL-2005-170 (2005)
15. Hose, K., Vlachou, A.: A survey of skyline processing in highly distributed environments. VLDB J. **21**(3), 359–384 (2012)

16. Chambi, S., Lemire, D., Kaser, O., Godin, R.: Better bitmap performance with roaring bitmaps (2014). arXiv preprint arXiv:1402.6407
17. Campinas, S.: Live SPARQL auto-completion. In: ISWC 2014 (Posters & Demos), pp. 477–480 (2014)
18. Bosc, P., Hadjali, A., Pivert, O.: Incremental controlled relaxation of failing flexible queries. JIIS **33**(3), 261–283 (2009)
19. Pivert, O., Smits, G., Hadjali, A., Jaudoin, H.: Efficient detection of minimal failing subqueries in a fuzzy querying context. In: Eder, J., Bielikova, M., Tjoa, A.M. (eds.) ADBIS 2011. LNCS, vol. 6909, pp. 243–256. Springer, Heidelberg (2011)

HDT-MR: A Scalable Solution for RDF Compression with HDT and MapReduce

José M. Giménez-García[1]($\boxtimes$), Javier D. Fernández[2],
and Miguel A. Martínez-Prieto[3]

[1] DataWeb Research, Department of Computer Science, Univ. de Valladolid,
Valladolid, Spain
josemiguel.gimenez@alumnos.uva.es
[2] Vienna University of Economics and Business, Vienna, Austria
jfernand@wu.ac.at
[3] DataWeb Research, Department of Computer Science, Univ. de Valladolid,
Segovia, Spain
migumar2@infor.uva.es

Abstract. HDT a is binary RDF serialization aiming at minimizing the space overheads of traditional RDF formats, while providing retrieval features in compressed space. Several HDT-based applications, such as the recent *Linked Data Fragments* proposal, leverage these features for diverse publication, interchange and consumption purposes. However, scalability issues emerge in HDT construction because the whole RDF dataset must be processed in a memory-consuming task. This is hindering the evolution of novel applications and techniques at Web scale. This paper introduces HDT-MR, a MapReduce-based technique to process huge RDF and build the HDT serialization. HDT-MR performs in linear time with the dataset size and has proven able to serialize datasets up to several billion triples, preserving HDT compression and retrieval features.

1 Introduction

The *Resource Description Framework* (RDF) was originally proposed as a data model for describing resources in the Web [12], and has evolved into a standard for data interchange in the emergent Web of (Linked) Data. RDF has been widely used in the last years, specially under the *Linked Open Data* initiative, where it shows its potential for integrating non-structured and semi-structured data from several sources and many varied fields of knowledge. This flexibility is obtained by structuring information as triples: (i) the *subject* is the resource being described; (ii) the *predicate* gives a property about the resource; and (iii) the *object* sets the value of the description. A set of RDF triples is a labeled directed graph, with subjects and objects as nodes, and predicates as edges.

This "graph view" is a mental model that helps to understand how information is organized in RDF, but triples must be effectively serialized in some way for storage and/or interchange. The World Wide Web Consortium (W3C)

© Springer International Publishing Switzerland 2015
F. Gandon et al. (Eds.): ESWC 2015, LNCS 9088, pp. 253–268, 2015.
DOI: 10.1007/978-3-319-18818-8_16

Working Group addresses this need in the last RDF Primer proposal[1]. The considered RDF serialization formats (JSON-LD, RDF/XML or Turtle-based ones) provide different ways of writing down RDF triples, yet all of them serialize an RDF graph as plain text. This is a double-edged sword. On the one hand, serialization is an easy task with no much processing overhead. On the other hand, the resulting serialized files tend to be voluminous because of the verbosity underlying to these formats. Although any kind of universal compressor (*e.g.* gzip) reduces space requirements for RDF storage and interchange purposes [6], space overheads remain a problem when triples are decompressed for consumption (parsing, searching, etc.). This situation is even more worrying because end-users have, in general, less computational resources than publishers.

HDT (*Header-Dictionary-Triples*) is an effective alternative for RDF serialization. It is a binary format which reorganizes RDF triples in two main components. The *Dictionary* organizes all terms used in triples and maps them to numerical identifiers. This decision allows the original graph to be transformed into a graph of IDs encoded by the *Triples* component. Built-in indexes, in both components, allow RDF triples to be randomly retrieved in compressed space. In other words, HDT outputs more compact files than the aforementioned formats and also enables RDF triples to be efficiently accessed without prior decompression [13]. This fact makes HDT an ideal choice to play as storage engine within semantic applications. *HDT-FoQ* [13] illustrates how HDT can be used for efficient triple pattern and SPARQL join resolution, while *WaterFowl* [4] goes a step further and provides inference on top of *HDT* foundations. This notion of HDT-based store is deployed in applications such as *Linked Data Fragments* [18], the *SemStim* recommendation system [8] or the Android app *HDTourist* [9].

Nevertheless, these achievements are at the price of moving scalability issues to the publishers, or data providers in general. Serializing RDF into HDT is not as simple as with plain formats, given that the whole dataset must be exhaustively processed to obtain the *Dictionary* and *Triples* components. Current HDT implementations demand not negligible amounts of memory, so the HDT serialization lacks of scalability for huge datasets (*e.g.* those having hundreds of millions or billions of triples). Although these datasets are currently uncommon, semantic publication efforts on emerging data-intensive areas (such as biology or astronomy) or integrating several sources into heterogeneous mashups (as RDF excels at linking data from diverse datasets) are starting to face this challenge.

This paper improves the HDT workflow by introducing MapReduce [5] as the computation model for large HDT serialization. MapReduce is a framework for the distributed processing of large amounts of data, and it can be considered as *de facto* standard for Big Data processing. Our MapReduce-based approach, HDT-MR, reduces scalability issues arising to HDT generation, enabling larger datasets to be serialized for end-user consumption. We perform evaluations scaling up to 5.32 billion triples (10 times larger than the largest dataset serialized by the original HDT), reporting linear processing times to the dataset size. This states that HDT-MR provides serialization for RDF datasets of arbitrary size while preserving both the HDT compression and retrieval features [6,13].

---

[1] http://www.w3.org/TR/2014/NOTE-rdf11-primer-20140624.

The rest of the paper is organized as follows. Section 2 summarizes the background required to understand our approach, which is fully described in Sect. 3. Section 4 reports experimental results about HDT-MR. Finally, Sect. 5 concludes about HDT-MR and devises some future work around it.

2   Background

This section provides background to understand our current approach. We give basic notions about MapReduce and explain HDT foundations. Then, we compare HDT to the current state of the art of RDF compression.

2.1   MapReduce

MapReduce [5] is a framework and programming model to process large amounts of data in a distributed way. Its main purpose is to provide efficient parallelization while abstracting the complexity of distributed processing. MapReduce is not schema-dependent; unstructured and semi-structured can be processed, at the price of parsing every item [11]. A MapReduce job comprises two phases. The first phase, map, reads the data as pairs key-value $(k1, v1)$ and outputs another series of pairs key-value of different domain $(k2, v2)$. The second phase, reduce, processes the list of values $v2$, related to each key $k2$, and produces a final list of output values $v2$ pertaining to the same domain. Many tasks are launched on each phase, all of them processing a small piece of the input data. The following scheme illustrates input and output data to be processed in each phase:

$$\text{map:} \quad (k1, v1) \rightarrow list(k2, v2)$$
$$\text{reduce:} \quad (k2, list(v2)) \rightarrow list(v2)$$

MapReduce relies on a master/slave architecture. The *master* initializes the process, distributes the workload among the cluster and manages all bookkeeping information. The *slaves* (or *workers*) run map and reduce tasks. The workers commonly store the data using a distributed filesystem based on the GFS *(Google File System)* model, where data are split in small pieces and stored in different nodes. This allows workers to leverage *data locality* as much as possible, reading data from the same machine where the task runs [5]. MapReduce performs exhaustive I/O operations. The input of every task is read from disk, and the output is also written on disk. It is also intensive in bandwidth usage. The map output must be transferred to reduce nodes and, even if most of the map tasks read their data locally, part of them must be gathered from other nodes.

Apache Hadoop[2] is currently the most used implementation of MapReduce. It is designed to work in heterogeneous clusters of commodity hardware. Hadoop implements HDFS *(Hadoop Distributed File System)*, as distributed filesystem providing data replication. It replicates each split of data in a number of nodes (commonly three), improving data locality and also providing fault tolerance.

---

[2] http://hadoop.apache.org/.

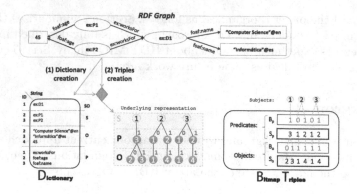

Fig. 1. HDT *Dictionary* and *Triples* configuration for an RDF graph.

2.2 HDT

HDT[3] [6] is a binary serialization format optimized for RDF storage and transmission. Besides, HDT files can be mapped to a configuration of succinct data structures which allows the inner triples to be searched and browsed efficiently.

HDT encodes RDF into three components carefully described to address RDF peculiarities within a *Publication-Interchange-Consumption* workflow. The *Header* (**H**) holds the dataset metadata, including relevant information for discovering and parsing, hence serving as an entry point for consumption. The *Dictionary* (**D**) is a catalogue that encodes all the different terms used in the dataset and maps each of them to a unique identifier: ID. The *Triples* (**T**) component encodes the RDF graph as a graph of IDs, *i.e.* representing tuples of three IDs. Thus, *Dictionary* and *Triples* address the main goal of RDF compactness. Figure 1 shows how the *Dictionary* and *Triples* components are configured for a simple RDF graph. Each component is detailed below.

Dictionary. This component organizes the different terms in the graph according to their role in the dataset. Thus, four sections are considered: the section **SO** manages those terms playing both as subject and object, and maps them to the range [1, |SO|], being |SO| the number of different terms acting as subject and object. Sections **S** and **O** comprise terms that exclusively play subject and object roles respectively. Both sections are mapped from |SO|+1, ranging up to |SO|+|S| and |SO|+|O| respectively, where |S| and |O| are the number of exclusive subjects and objects. Finally, section **P** organizes all predicate terms, which are mapped to the range [1, |P|]. It is worth noting that no ambiguity is possible once we know the role played by the corresponding ID.

Each section of the *Dictionary* is independently encoded to grasp its particular features. This allows important space savings to be achieved by considering that this sort of string dictionaries are highly compressible [14]. Nonetheless,

---

[3] HDT is a *W3C Member Submission*: http://www.w3.org/Submission/HDT/.

efficient encoding of string dictionaries [2] is orthogonal to the current problem, hence it is not addressed in this paper.

Triples. This component encodes the structure of the RDF graph after ID substitution. That is, RDF triples are encoded as groups of three IDs (ID-triples hereinafter): $(id_s\ id_p\ id_o)$, where id_s, id_p, and id_o are respectively the IDs of the corresponding subject, predicate, and object terms in the *Dictionary*. The *Triples* component organizes all triples into a forest of trees, one per different subject: the subject is the root; the middle level comprises the ordered list of predicates reachable from the corresponding subject; and the leaves list the object IDs related to each (subject, predicate) pair. This *underlying representation* (illustrated in Fig. 1) is effectively encoded following the *BitmapTriples* approach [6]. In brief, it comprises *two sequences*: Sp and So, concatenating respectively all predicate IDs in the middle level and all object IDs in the leaves; and *two bitsequences*: Bp and Bo, which are respectively aligned with Sp and So, using a 1-bit to mark the end of each list.

Building HDT. Once *Dictionary* and *Triples* internals have been described, we proceed to summarize how HDT is currently built[4]. Remind that this process is the main scalability bottleneck addressed by our current proposal.

To date, HDT serialization can be seen as a three-stage process:

- **Classifying RDF Terms.** This first stage performs a triple-by-triple parsing (from the input dataset file) to classify each RDF term into the corresponding *Dictionary* section. To do so, it keeps a temporal data structure, consisting of three hash tables storing subject-to-ID, predicate-to-ID, and object-to-ID mappings. For each parsed triple, its subject, predicate, and object are searched in the appropriate hash, obtaining the associated ID if present. Terms not found are inserted and assigned an auto-incremental ID. These IDs are used to obtain the temporal ID-triples $(id_s\ id_p\ id_o)$ representation of each parsed triple, storing all them in a temporary ID-triples array. At the end of the file parsing, subject and object hashes are processed to identify terms playing both roles. These are deleted from their original hash tables and inserted into a fourth hash comprising terms in the SO section.
- **Building HDT *Dictionary*.** Each dictionary section is now sorted lexicographically, because prefix-based encoding is a well-suited choice for compressing string dictionaries [2]. Finally, an auxiliary array coordinates the previous temporal ID and the definitive ID after the *Dictionary* sorting.
- **Building HDT *Triples*.** This final stage scans the temporary array storing ID-triples. For each triple, its three IDs are replaced by their definitive IDs in the newly created *Dictionary*. Once updated, ID-triples are sorted by subject, predicate and object IDs to obtain the *BitmapTriples* streams. In practice, it is a straightforward task which scans the array to sequentially extract the predicates and objects into the Sp and So sequences, and denoting list endings with 1-bits in the bitsequences.

---

[4] HDT implementations are available at http://www.rdfhdt.org/development/.

2.3   Related Work

HDT was designed as a binary serialization format, but the optimized encodings achieved by *Dictionary* and *Triples* components make HDT also excels as RDF compressor. Attending to the taxonomy from [16], HDT is a *syntactic* compressor because it detects redundancy at serialization level. That is, the *Dictionary* reduces symbolic redundancy from the terms used in the dataset, while the *Triples* component leverages structural redundancy from the graph topology.

To the best of our knowledge, the best space savings are reported by syntactic compressors. Among them, k^2-triples [1] is the most effective approach. It performs a predicate-based partition of the dataset into subsets of pairs (subject, object), which are then encoded as sparse binary matrices (providing direct access to the compressed triples). k^2-triples achievements, though, are at the cost of exhaustive time-demanding compression processes that also need large amounts of main memory. On the other hand, *logical* compressors perform discarding triples that can be inferred from others. Thus, they achieve compression because only encode a "primitive" subset of the original dataset. Joshi *et al.* [10] propose a technique which prunes more than 50 % of the triples, but it does not achieve competitive numbers regarding HDT, and its compression process also reports longer times. More recently, Pan, *et al.* [16] propose an hybrid compressor leveraging syntactic and semantic redundancy. Its space numbers slightly improves the less-compressed HDT configurations, but it is far from k^2-triples. It also shows non-negligible compression times for all reported datasets.

Thus, the most prominent RDF compressors experience lack of scalability when compressing large RDF datasets. This issue has already been addressed by using distributed computation. Urbani *et al.* [17] propose an algorithm based on dictionary encoding. They perform a MapReduce job to create the dictionary, where an ID is assigned to each term. The output of this job are key-value pairs, where the key is the ID and the value contains the triple identifier to which the term belongs, and its role on it. Then, another MapReduce job groups by triple and substitutes the terms by their ID. This work makes special emphasis on how RDF skewness can affect MapReduce performance, due to the fact that many terms can be grouped and sent to the same reducer. To avoid this problem, a first job is added, where the input data are sampled and the more popular terms are given their ID before the process starts. Finally, Cheng *et al.* [3] also perform distributed RDF compression on dictionary encoding. They use the parallel language X10, and report competitive results.

3   HDT-MR

This section describes HDT-MR, our MapReduce-based approach to serialize large RDF datasets in HDT. Figure 2 illustrates the HDT-MR workflow, consisting in two stages: *(1) Dictionary Encoding* (top) and *(2) Triples Encoding* (bottom), described in the following subsections. The whole process assumes the original RDF dataset is encoded in N-Triples format (one statement per line).

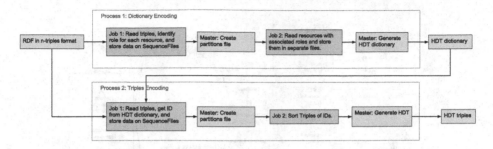

Fig. 2. HDT-MR workflow.

3.1 Process 1: Dictionary Encoding

This first process builds the HDT *Dictionary* from the original N-Triples dataset. It can be seen as a three-task process of (i) identifying the role of each term in the dataset, (ii) obtaining the aforementioned sections (**SO**, **S**, **O**, and **P**) in lexicographic order, and (iii) effectively encoding the *Dictionary* component.

We design HDT-MR to perform these three tasks as two distributed MapReduce jobs and a subsequent local process (performed by the *master* node), as shown in Fig. 2. The first job performs the role identification, while the second is needed to perform a global sort. Finally, the *master* effectively encodes the *Dictionary* component. All these sub-processes are further described below.

Job 1.1: Roles Detection. This job parses the input N-Triples file to detect all roles played by RDF terms in the dataset. First, mappers perform a triple-by-triple parsing and output (key,value) pairs of the form (`RDF term, role`), in which role is S (subject), P (predicate) or O (object), according to the term position in the triple. It is illustrated in Fig. 3, with two processing nodes performing on the RDF used in Fig. 1. For instance, (`ex:P1`,S), (`ex:worksFor`,P), and (`ex:D1`,O) are the pairs obtained for the triple (`ex:P1, ex:worksFor, ex:D1`).

These pairs are partitioned and sorted among the reducers, which group the different roles played by a term. Note that RDF terms including roles S and O, result in pairs (`RDF term`, SO). Thus, this job outputs a number of lexicographically ordered lists (`RDF term, roles`); there will be as many lists as reducers on the cluster. Algorithm 1 shows the pseudo-code of these jobs.

Finally, it is important to mention that a *combiner* function is used at the output of each `map`. This function is executed on each node before the `map` transmits its output to the reducers. In our case, if a mapper emits more than one pair (`RDF term, role`) for a term, all those pairs are grouped into a single one comprising a list of all roles. It allows the bandwidth usage to be decreased by grouping pairs with the same key before transferring them to the reducer.

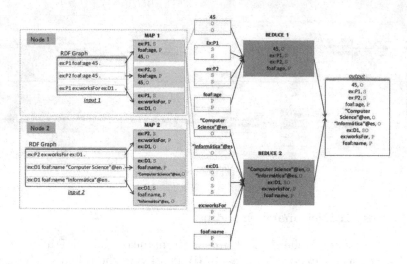

Fig. 3. Example of dictionary encoding: roles detection (Job 1.1).

Algorithm 1. Dictionary Encoding: roles detection (Job 1.1)

```
function MAP(key,value)                    ▷ key: line number (discarded)              ▷ value: triple
    emit(value.subject,"S")
    emit(value.predicate,"P")
    emit(value.object,"O")
end function
function COMBINE/REDUCE(key,values)         ▷ key: RDF term       ▷ value: roles (S, P, and/or O)
    for role in values do
        if role contains "S" then isSubject ← true
        else if role contains "P" then isPredicate ← true
        else if role contains "O" then isObject ← true
        end if
    end for
    roles ← ""
    if isSubject then append(roles,"S")
    else if isPredicate then append(roles,"P")
    else if isObject then append(roles,"O")
    end if
    emit(key, roles)
end function
```

Job 1.2: RDF Terms Sectioning. The previous job outputs several lists of pairs (RDF term, roles), one per reduce of previous phase, each of them sorted lexicographically. However, the construction of each HDT *Dictionary* section requires a unique sorted list. Note that a simple concatenation of the output lists would not fulfill this requirement, because the resulting list would not maintain a global order. The reason behind this behavior is that, although the input of each reducer is sorted before processing, the particular input transmitted to each reducer is autonomously decided by the framework in a process called *partitioning*. By default, Hadoop *hashes* the key and assigns it to a given reducer, promoting to obtain partitions of similar sizes. Thus, this distribution does not respect a global order of the input. While this behavior may be changed to assign the reducers a globally sorted input, this is not straightforward.

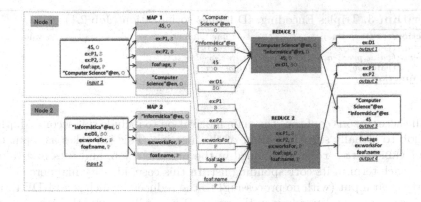

Fig. 4. Example of dictionary encoding: RDF terms sectioning (Job 1.2).

Algorithm 2. Dictionary Encoding: RDF terms sectioning (Job 1.2)

---

function REDUCE(key,value)   ▷ key: RDF term   ▷ value: roles (S, P, and/or O)
    for resource in values **do**
        if resource contains "S" **then** *isSubject* ← *true*
        else if resource contains "P" **then** *isPredicate* ← *true*
        else if resource contains "O" **then** *isObject* ← *true*
        end if
    end for
    output ← ""
    if isSubject &isObject **then** *emit_to_SO*(*key, null*)
    else if *isSubject* **then** *emit_to_S*(*key, null*)
    else if *isPredicate* **then** *emit_to_P*(*key, null*)
    else if *isObject* **then** *emit_to_O*(*key, null*)
    end if
end function

A naïve approach would be to use a single reducer, but this would result extremely inefficient: the whole data had to be processed by a single machine, losing most of the benefits of distributed computing that MapReduce provides. Another approach is to manually create partition groups. For instance, we could send terms beginning with the letters from a to c to the first reducer, terms beginning with the letters from d to f to the second reducer, and so on. However, partitions must be chosen with care, or they could be the root of performance issues: if partitions are of very different size, the job time will be dominated by the slowest reducer (that is, the reducer that receives the largest input). This fact is specially significant for RDF processing because of its skewed features.

HDT-MR relies on the simple but efficient solution of sampling input data to obtain partitions of similar size. To do so, we make use of the *TotalOrder-Partitioner* of Hadoop. It is important to note that this partitioning cannot be performed while processing a job, but needs to be completed prior of a job execution. Note also that the input domain of the reducers needs to be different from the input domain of the job to identify and group the RDF terms (that is, the job receives triples, while the reducers receive individual terms and roles).

Algorithm 3. Triples Encoding: ID-triples serialization (Job 2.1)

```
function MAP(key,value)              ▷ key: line number (discarded)         ▷ value: triple
    emit(value.subject, dictionary.id(value.subject)
    emit(value.predicate, dictionary.id(value.predicate))
    emit(value.object, dictionary.id(value.object))
end function
```

All these reasons conforms the main motivation to include this second MapReduce job to globally sort the output of the first job. This job takes as input the lists of (RDF term, roles) obtained in the precedent job, and uses role values to sort each term in its corresponding list. In this case, identity mappers deliver directly their input (with no processing) to the reducers, which send RDF terms to different outputs depending on their role. Figure 4 illustrates this job. As only the term is needed, a pair (RDF term, *null*) is emitted for each RDF term (*nulls* are omitted on the outputs). We obtain as many role-based lists as reducers in the cluster, but these are finally concatenated to obtain four sorted files, one per *Dictionary* section.The pseudo-code for this job is described in Algorithm 2.

Local Sub-process 1.3: HDT Dictionary Encoding. This final stage performs locally in the *master* node, encoding dictionaries for the four sections obtained from the MapReduce jobs. It means that each section is read line-per-line, and each term is differentially encoded to obtain a Front-Coding dictionary [2], providing term-ID mappings. It is a simple process with no scalability issues.

3.2 Process 2: Triples Encoding

This second process parses the original N-Triples dataset to obtain, in this case, the HDT *Triples* component. The main tasks for such *Triples* encoding are (i) replacing RDF terms by their ID in the *Dictionary*, and (ii) getting the ID-triples encoding sorted by subject, predicate and object IDs. As in the previous process, HDT-MR accomplishes these tasks by two MapReduce jobs and a final local process (see the global overview in Fig. 2), further described below.

Job 2.1: ID-Triples Serialization. This first job replaces each term by its ID. To do so, HDT-MR first transmits and loads the–already compressed and functional–*Dictionary* (encoded in the previous stage) in all nodes of the cluster. Then, mappers parse N-Triples and replace each term by its ID in the *Dictionary*. Identity reducers simply sort incoming data and output a list of pairs (ID-triple, *null*). We can see this process in action in Fig. 5, where the terms of each triple are replaced by the IDs given in the previous example (note that *nulls* are omitted on the outputs). The output of this job is a set of lexicographically ordered lists of ID-Triples; there will be as many lists as reducers on the cluster. The pseudo-code of this job is illustrated in Algorithm 3.

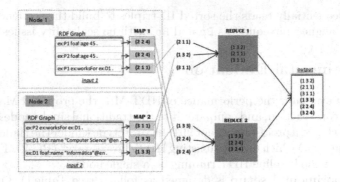

Fig. 5. Example of triples encoding: ID-triples serialization (Job 2.1).

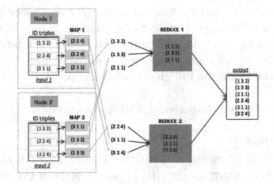

Fig. 6. Example of triples encoding: ID-triples sorting (Job 2.2)

Job 2.2: ID-Triples Sorting. Similarly to the first process, Triples Encoding requires of a second job to sort the outputs. Based on the same premises, HDT-MR makes use of Hadoop *TotalOrderPartitioner* to sample the output data from the first job, creating partitions of a similar size as input for the second job. Then, this job reads the ID-triples representation generated and sorts it by subject, predicate and object ID. This is a very simple job that uses identity mappers and reducers. As in the previous job, ID-triples are contained in the key and the value is set to *null*. In fact, all the logic is performed by the framework in the partitioning phase between map and reduce, generating similar size partitions of globally sorted data. Figure 6 continues with the running example and shows the actions performed by this job after receiving the output of the previous job (note again that *nulls* are omitted on the outputs).

Local Sub-process 2.3: HDT Triples Encoding. This final stage encodes the ID-triples list (generated by the previous job) as HDT *BitmapTriples* [6]. It is performed locally in the *master* node as in the original HDT construction.

That is, it sequentially reads the sorted ID-triples to build the sequences Sp and So, and the aligned bitsequences Bp and Bo, with no scalability issues.

4   Experimental Evaluation

This section evaluates the performance of HDT-MR, the proposed MapReduce-based HDT construction, and compares it to the traditional single-node approach. We have developed a proof-of-concept HDT-MR prototype (under the Hadoop framework: version 1.2.1) which uses the existing HDT-Java library[5] (RC-2). This library is also used for the baseline HDT running on a single node.

The **experimental setup** is designed as follows (see Table 1). On the one hand, we use a powerful computational configuration to implement the role of data provider running HDT on a single node. On the other hand, we deploy HDT-MR using a potent *master* and 10 *slave* nodes running on a more memory-limited configuration. This infrastructure tries to simulate a computational cluster in which further nodes may be plugged to process huge RDF datasets. For a fair comparison, the amount of main memory in the single node is the same as the total memory available for the full cluster of Hadoop.

Table 1. Experimental setup configuration.

MACHINE	CONFIGURATION
Single Node	Intel Xeon E5-2650v2 @ 2.60 GHz (32 cores), 128 GB RAM. Debian 7.8
Master	Intel Xeon X5675 @ 3.07 GHz (4 cores), 48 GB RAM. Ubuntu 12.04.2
Slaves	Intel Xeon X5675 @ 3.07 GHz (4 cores), 8 GB RAM. Debian 7.7

Regarding **datasets**, we consider a varied configuration comprising real-world and synthetic ones. All of them are statistically described in Table 2. Among the real-world ones, we choose them based on their volume and variety, but also attending to their previous uses for benchmarking. *Ike*[6] comprises weather measurements from the Ike hurricane; *LinkedGeoData*[7] is a large geospatial dataset derived from *Open Street Map*; and DBPedia 3.8[8] is the well-known knowledge base extracted from Wikipedia. We also join these real-world datasets in a *mashup* which comprises all data from the three data sources. On the other hand, we use the LUBM [7] data generator to obtain synthetic datasets. We build "small datasets" from 1,000 (0.13 billion triples) to 8,000 universities (1.07 billion triples). From the latter, we build datasets of incremental size (4,000 universities: 0.55 billion triples) up to 40,000 universities (5.32 billion triples).

Table 2 also shows original dataset sizes both in plain NTriples (NT) and compressed with lzo. It is worth noting that HDT-MR uses lzo to compress the

---

[5] http://code.google.com/p/hdt-java/.
[6] http://wiki.knoesis.org/index.php/LinkedSensorData.
[7] http://linkedgeodata.org/Datasets, as for 2013-07-01.
[8] http://wiki.dbpedia.org/Downloads38.

Table 2. Statistical dataset description.

DATASET	TRIPLES	|SO|	|S|	|O|	|P|	NT	NT+lzo	HDT	HDT+gz
							Size (GB)		
LinkedGeoData	0.27BN	41.5M	10.4M	80.3M	18.3K	38.5	4.4	6.4	1.9
DBPedia	0.43BN	22.0M	2.8M	86.9M	58.3K	61.6	8.6	6.4	2.7
Ike	0.51BN	114.5M	0	145.1K	10	100.3	4.9	4.8	0.6
Mashup	1.22BN	178.0M	13.2M	167.2M	76.6K	200.3	18.0	17.1	4.6
LUBM-1000	0.13BN	5.0M	16.7M	11.2M	18	18.0	1.3	0.7	0.2
LUBM-2000	0.27BN	10.0M	33.5M	22.3M	18	36.2	2.7	1.5	0.5
LUBM-3000	0.40BN	14.9M	50.2M	33.5M	18	54.4	4.0	2.3	0.8
LUBM-4000	0.53BN	19.9M	67.0M	44.7M	18	72.7	5.3	3.1	1.0
LUBM-5000	0.67BN	24.9M	83.7M	55.8M	18	90.9	6.6	3.9	1.3
LUBM-6000	0.80BN	29.9M	100.5M	67.0M	18	109.1	8.0	4.7	1.6
LUBM-7000	0.93BN	34.9M	117.2M	78.2M	18	127.3	9.3	5.5	1.9
LUBM-8000	1.07BN	39.8M	134.0M	89.3M	18	145.5	10.6	6.3	2.2
LUBM-12000	1.60BN	59.8M	200.9M	133.9M	18	218.8	15.9	9.6	2.9
LUBM-16000	2.14BN	79.7M	267.8M	178.6M	18	292.4	21.2	12.8	3.8
LUBM-20000	2.67BN	99.6M	334.8M	223.2M	18	366.0	26.6	16.3	5.5
LUBM-24000	3.74BN	119.5M	401.7M	267.8M	18	439.6	31.9	19.6	6.6
LUBM-28000	3.74BN	139.5M	468.7M	312.4M	18	513.2	37.2	22.9	7.7
LUBM-32000	4.27BN	159.4M	535.7M	357.1M	18	586.8	42.5	26.1	8.8
LUBM-36000	4.81BN	179.3M	602.7M	401.8M	18	660.5	47.8	30.0	9.4
LUBM-40000	5.32BN	198.4M	666.7M	444.5M	18	730.9	52.9	33.2	10.4

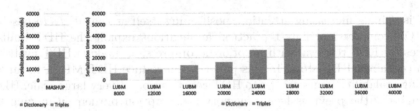

Fig. 7. Serialization times: HDT-Java vs HDT-MR.

Fig. 8. Serialization times: HDT-MR.

datasets before storing them in HDFS. This format allows for compressed data to be split among the reducers, and provides storage and reading speed improvements [15]. As can be seen, our largest dataset uses 730.9 GB in NTriples, and this spaces is reduced up to 52.9 GB with lzo compression.

Figure 7 compares serialization times for HDT-Java and HDT-MR, while Fig. 8 shows HDT-MR serialization times for those datasets where HDT-Java is unable to obtain the serialization. These times are averaged over three independent serialization processes for each dataset. As can be seen, HDT-Java reports an excellent performance on real-world datasets, while our current approach only achieves a comparable time for *Ike*. This is an expected result because HDT-Java runs the whole process in main-memory while HDT-MR relies on I/O operations. However, HDT-Java crashes for the *mashup* because the 128 GB of available RAM are insufficient to process such scale in the single node. The situation is similar for the LUBM datasets: HDT-Java is the best choice for the smallest datasets, but the difference decreases with the dataset size and HDT-MR shows better results from *LUBM-5000* (0.67 billion triples). HDT-Java fails to process datasets from *LUBM-8000* (1.07 billion triples) because of memory requirements. This is the target scenario for HDT-MR, which scales to the *LUBM-40000* without issues. As can be seen in both figures, serialization times increase linearly with the dataset size, and triples encoding remains the most expensive stage.

RDF compression is not the main purpose of this paper, but it is worth emphasizing HDT space numbers, as previous literature does not report compression results for such large datasets. These numbers are also summarized in Table 2. HDT always reports smaller sizes than the original datasets compressed with lzo. For instance, HDT serializes *LUBM-40000* using 19.7 GB less than NT+lzo. The difference increases when compressed with gzip. For *LUBM-40000*, HDT+gz uses 42.5 GB less than NT+lzo. In practice, it means that HDT+gz uses 5 times less space than NT+lzo. Finally, it is worth remembering that HDT-MR obtains the same HDT serialization than a mono-node solution, hence achieving the same compression ratio and enabling the same query functionality. Source code and further details on HDT-MR are available at the HDT-MR project[9].

5 Conclusions and Future Work

HDT is gaining increasing attention, positioning itself as the *de facto* baseline for RDF compression. Latest practical applications exploit the HDT built-in indexes for RDF retrieval with no prior decompression, making HDT evolve to a self-contained RDF store. In this paper we introduce HDT-MR, a technique tackling scalability issues arising to HDT construction at very large scale. HDT-MR lightens the previous heavy memory-consumption burden by moving the construction task to the MapReduce paradigm. We present the HDT-MR distributed workflow, evaluating its performance against the mono-node solution in huge real-world and benchmarking RDF datasets, scaling up to more than 5 billion triples. Results show that HDT-MR is able to scale up to an arbitrary size in commodity clusters, while the mono-node solution fails to process datasets larger than 1 billion triples. Thus, HDT-MR greatly reduces hardware requirements for processing Big Semantic Data.

Our future work focuses on two directions. First, we plan to exploit HDT-MR achievements as these can be directly reused by the HDT community, fostering the development of novel applications working at very large scale. Finally, our

---

[9] http://dataweb.infor.uva.es/projects/hdt-mr/.

research consider to combine HDT and MapReduce foundations to work together on other Big Semantic Data tasks, such as querying and reasoning.

Acknowledgments. This paper is funded by the Spanish Ministry of Economy and Competitiveness: TIN2013-46238-C4-3-R, Austrian Science Fund (FWF): M1720-G11, and ICT COST Action KEYSTONE (IC1302). We thank Javier I. Ramos by his support with the Hadoop cluster, and Jürgen Umbrich for lending us his sever.

References

1. Álvarez-García, S., Brisaboa, N., Fernández, J.D., Martínez-Prieto, M.A., Navarro, G.: Compressed Vertical Partitioning for Efficient RDF Management. Knowl. Inf. Syst. (2014). doi:10.1007/s10115-014-0770-y
2. Brisaboa, N.R., Cánovas, R., Claude, F., Martínez-Prieto, M.A., Navarro, G.: Compressed string dictionaries. In: Pardalos, P.M., Rebennack, S. (eds.) SEA 2011. LNCS, vol. 6630, pp. 136–147. Springer, Heidelberg (2011)
3. Cheng, L., Malik, A., Kotoulas, S., Ward, T.E., Theodoropoulos, G.: Efficient parallel dictionary encoding for RDF data. In: Proceedings of WebDB (2014)
4. Curé, O., Blin, G., Revuz, D., Faye, D.C.: WaterFowl: a compact, self-indexed and inference-enabled immutable RDF store. In: Presutti, V., d'Amato, C., Gandon, F., d'Aquin, M., Staab, S., Tordai, A. (eds.) ESWC 2014. LNCS, vol. 8465, pp. 302–316. Springer, Heidelberg (2014)
5. Dean, J., Ghemawat, S.: MapReduce: simplified data processing on largee clusters. In: Proceedings of OSDI, pp. 137–150 (2004)
6. Fernández, J.D., Martínez-Prieto, M.A., Gutiérrez, C., Polleres, A., Arias, M.: Binary RDF representation for publication and exchange. J. Web Semant. **19**, 22–41 (2013)
7. Guo, Y., Pan, Z., Heflin, J.: LUBM: a benchmark for OWL knowledge base systems. J. Web Semant. **3**(2), 158–182 (2005)
8. Heitmann, B., Hayes, C.: SemStim at the LOD-RecSys 2014 challenge. In: Presutti, V., Stankovic, M., Cambria, E., Cantador, I., Di Iorio, A., Di Noia, T., Lange, C., Reforgiato Recupero, D., Tordai, A. (eds.) SemWebEval 2014. CCIS, vol. 475, pp. 170–175. Springer, Heidelberg (2014)
9. Hervalejo, E., Martínez-Prieto, M.A., Fernández, J.D., Corcho, O.: HDTourist: exploring urban data on android. In: Proceedings of ISWC (Poster and Demos), vol. CEUR-WS 1272, pp. 65–68 (2014)
10. Joshi, A.K., Hitzler, P., Dong, G.: Logical linked data compression. In: Cimiano, P., Corcho, O., Presutti, V., Hollink, L., Rudolph, S. (eds.) ESWC 2013. LNCS, vol. 7882, pp. 170–184. Springer, Heidelberg (2013)
11. Lee, K.-H., Lee, Y.-J., Choi, H., Chung, Y.D., Moon, B.: Parallel data processing with mapreduce: a survey. ACM SIGMOD Rec. **40**(4), 11–20 (2012)
12. Manola, F., Miller, R.: RDF Primer. W3C Recommendation (2004). www.w3.org/TR/rdf-primer/
13. Martínez-Prieto, M.A., Arias Gallego, M., Fernández, J.D.: Exchange and consumption of huge RDF data. In: Simperl, E., Cimiano, P., Polleres, A., Corcho, O., Presutti, V. (eds.) ESWC 2012. LNCS, vol. 7295, pp. 437–452. Springer, Heidelberg (2012)
14. Martínez-Prieto, M.A., Fernández, J.D., Cánovas, R.: Querying RDF dictionaries in compressed space. SIGAPP Appl. Comput. Rev. **12**(2), 64–77 (2012)

15. Mirajkar, N., Bhujbal, S., Deshmukh, A.: Perform wordcount Map-Reduce job in single node apache hadoop cluster and compress data using Lempel-Ziv-Oberhumer (LZO) algorithm (2013). http://arxiv.org/abs/1307.1517
16. Pan, J.Z., Gómez-Pérez, J.M., Ren, Y., Wu, H., Zhu, M.: SSP: compressing RDF data by summarisation, serialisation and predictive encoding. Technical report (2014). http://www.kdrive-project.eu/wp-content/uploads/2014/06/WP3-TR2-2014_SSP.pdf
17. Urbani, J., Maassen, J., Bal, H., Drost, N., Seintra, F., Bal, H.: Scalable RDF data compression with mapreduce. Concurrency Comput. Pract. Experience **25**, 24–39 (2013)
18. Verborgh, R., Hartig, O., De Meester, B., Haesendonck, G., De Vocht, L., Vander Sande, M., Cyganiak, R., Colpaert, P., Mannens, E., Van de Walle, R.: Querying datasets on the web with high availability. In: Mika, P., Tudorache, T., Bernstein, A., Welty, C., Knoblock, C., Vrandečić, D., Groth, P., Noy, N., Janowicz, K., Goble, C. (eds.) ISWC 2014, Part I. LNCS, vol. 8796, pp. 180–196. Springer, Heidelberg (2014)

Processing Aggregate Queries in a Federation of SPARQL Endpoints

Dilshod Ibragimov[1,2] (✉), Katja Hose[2], Torben Bach Pedersen[2], and Esteban Zimányi[1]

[1] Université Libre de Bruxelles, Brussels, Belgium
{dibragim,ezimanyi}@ulb.ac.be
[2] Aalborg University, Aalborg, Denmark
{diib,khose,tbp}@cs.aau.dk

Abstract. More and more RDF data is exposed on the Web via SPARQL endpoints. With the recent SPARQL 1.1 standard, these datasets can be queried in novel and more powerful ways, e.g., complex analysis tasks involving grouping and aggregation, and even data from multiple SPARQL endpoints, can now be formulated in a single query. This enables Business Intelligence applications that access data from federated web sources and can combine it with local data. However, as both aggregate and federated queries have become available only recently, state-of-the-art systems lack sophisticated optimization techniques that facilitate efficient execution of such queries over large datasets. To overcome these shortcomings, we propose a set of query processing strategies and the associated Cost-based Optimizer for Distributed Aggregate queries (CoDA) for executing aggregate SPARQL queries over federations of SPARQL endpoints. Our comprehensive experiments show that CoDA significantly improves performance over current state-of-the-art systems.

1 Introduction

In recent years, we have witnessed the growing popularity of the Semantic Web and the Open Data movement. Nowadays a plethora of data is available in RDF format, published as Linked Open Data [6], accessible free of charge, and often queryable via SPARQL endpoints. Using these data in combination with the SPARQL 1.1 standard [24], organizations can build novel and powerful analytics applications that integrate their private data with web RDF datasets, enabling analyses that were not possible before. For example, a company wants to analyze its revenue in different countries against macro-economic indicators of these countries. Such information is unavailable locally, but can instead be obtained from the World Bank (http://www.worldbank.org/), accessed as Linked Open Data (http://worldbank.270a.info/) and queried via a SPARQL endpoint. Thus, the company has efficient access to up-to-date information without the costs of local maintenance, and as the company is accessing Linked Data, more information (geographical, census, etc.) for further analyses can efficiently be retrieved from linked sources, such as GeoNames [22] and DBpedia [4]. Such analytical

© Springer International Publishing Switzerland 2015
F. Gandon et al. (Eds.): ESWC 2015, LNCS 9088, pp. 269–285, 2015.
DOI: 10.1007/978-3-319-18818-8_17

queries, however, are based on complex queries involving grouping and aggregation as well as subqueries that need to be evaluated at remote sources. Formulating this in a single SPARQL statement has only recently become possible with the SPARQL 1.1 standard, which supports grouping, aggregation, and SERVICE subqueries.

Motivating Example. Analytical queries are not only beneficial for companies, but also in other scenarios. In March 2011, an earthquake in the Pacific triggered a powerful tsunami and led to a huge devastation at the Japanese coast, which eventually caused a nuclear accident (http://goo.gl/AcqLpe). After these events, the Japanese government made daily announcements of radioactivity statistics observed hourly at 47 prefectures. These observations from March 16, 2011 to March 15, 2012 were converted to RDF data by Masahide Kanzaki and made publicly available via a SPARQL endpoint (http://www.kanzaki.com/works/2011/stat/ra/). An example observation in RDF format is given below.

```
#observation                                <http://sws.geonames.org/1852083/>
<http://www.kanzaki.com/works/2011/           vcard:region "Tokyo"@en ;
    stat/ra/20110414/p13/t08>                 vcard:locality "Shinjuku"@en ;
  rdf:value "0.079"^^ms:microsv ;             gn:lat "35.69355" ;
  ev:place <http://sws.geonames.org/          gn:long "139.70352" .
    1852083/> ;                            #dimension - time
  ev:time <http://www.kanzaki.com/          <http://www.kanzaki.com/works/2011/stat
    works/2011/stat/dim/d/                      /dim/d/20110414T08PT1H>
    20110414T08PT1H> ;                       rdfs:label "2011-04-14T08";
  scv:dataset <http://www.kanzaki.com/       tl:at "2011-04-14T08:00:00+09:00"
    works/2011/stat/ra/set/moe> .              ^^xsd:dateTime ;
#dimension - place                           tl:duration "PT1H"^^xsd:duration .
```

The places that the observations were recorded at are represented by a URI from GeoNames. With the observations of radioactivity in multiple geographical locations (cities in our case) and information about their upper administrative divisions (prefectures in Japan) retrievable from GeoNames, interesting analyses become possible. For instance, we can compute the average radioactivity separately for each prefecture in Japan to find out which prefectures were more affected than others. Or we can compute the minimum and maximum radioactivity for each prefecture and hence identify the changes in radioactivity over the one-year observations. Formulating such queries involves grouping and aggregation as well as combining information from two SPARQL endpoints. Listing 1.1 shows an example query that computes the average radioactivity for all prefectures in Japan. This query could be executed at a triple store with information about radioactivity and uses the LOD Cloud Cache SPARQL endpoint (http://lod2.openlinksw.com/sparql) to query GeoNames data remotely.

```
SELECT ?regName (AVG(?radioValue) AS ?average)
WHERE { ?s ev:place ?placeID; ev:time ?time; rdf:value ?radioValue .
  SERVICE <http://lod2.openlinksw.com/sparql> {
    ?placeID gn:parentFeature ?regionID . ?regionID gn:name ?regName . }
} GROUP BY ?regName
```

Listing 1.1. Aggregate query over radioactivity observations

This looks like a simple query but current state-of-the-art triple stores supporting SPARQL 1.1, such as Virtuoso v07.10.3207, Sesame v2.7.11, and Jena Fuseki v1.0.0 (based on ARQ) timed out while trying to answer this query. Inspecting a query execution plan was not possible for Virtuoso, Jena, and Sesame since they do not support a comfortable explain function for SPARQL queries as known from relational database systems, so we used Wireshark (http://www.wireshark.org) to analyze the network traffic. We found out that Virtuoso and Fuseki query the GeoNames endpoint for every single radioactivity observation, while Sesame is trying to download all triples that match the pattern from the remote endpoint. In the first case, a triple store needs to send more than 400,000 requests to answer the query, and in the second case it needs to download more than 7.8 million triples from GeoNames.

The strategies implemented by these state-of-the-art triple stores are obviously insufficient in the scenario we consider in this paper. As the SPARQL 1.1 standard is not yet completely supported by all SPARQL endpoints [9], there is only little research regarding the evaluation of queries involving aggregation and grouping. To the best of our knowledge, this is the first paper to investigate aggregate queries in the context of federations of SPARQL endpoints and their optimization. In summary, the contributions of this paper are:

- the Mediator Join, SemiJoin, and Partial Aggregation query processing strategies for this scenario
- a cost model and techniques for estimating constants and result sizes for triple patterns, joins, grouping and aggregation
- the combination of these with the processing strategies into the Cost-based Optimizer for Distributed Aggregate queries (CoDA) approach for aggregate queries in federated setups that is generally able to choose the best execution strategy among a number of alternatives
- a comprehensive experimental evaluation showing that CoDA is efficient, scalable, and robust over different scenarios, and significantly faster than state-of-the-art triple stores.

The remainder of the paper is structured as follows. Related work is discussed in Sect. 2. Section 3 identifies several alternative strategies for processing aggregated SPARQL queries in a federated setup. Section 4 introduces a cost-based query optimizer for aggregate queries over federations of SPARQL endpoints. The results of our evaluation are presented in Sect. 5; Sect. 6 concludes the paper.

2 Related Work

Federated query processing in database management systems (DBMS) has been a topic of research for several decades. In contrast to well-structured classic data models, federated RDF systems support arbitrary RDF datasets (even without explicit schema) and allow the use of special constructs to perform joins and express bindings (such as VALUES) not present in SQL-based systems.

The literature proposes a number of approaches for querying federated RDF sources. Some of these approaches require the availability of VoID [23] statistics. SPLENDID [15], for instance, uses VoID statistics to select a query execution plan for a federated query. For triple patterns not covered in the VoID statistics, the system requests the information by issuing SPARQL ASK queries. The system makes use of a cost-based model and cardinality estimations for selecting a query plan. However, the SPLENDID system and its cost-model do not cover the combination of grouping, aggregation, and SERVICE subqueries.

FedX [20] uses SPARQL ASK queries for triple patterns in a query to collect basic information that can be used for source selection. It implements bound joins with SPARQL UNION keyword (similar to a semi-join) to group triple patterns related to one source and, thus, reduces the number of queries that are sent. FedX has originally been developed based on the SPARQL 1.0 standard and does not use cost-based query optimization. Hence, it does not provide any particular optimization techniques for our use case and would always use a semi-join based strategy, which is only one of the options our optimizer (CoDA) chooses from.

ANAPSID [1] uses a catalog of endpoint descriptions to decompose a user query into subqueries that can be executed by separate endpoints. The query engine implements a technique based on the symmetric hash join [12] and the XJoin [21] to execute subqueries in a non-blocking fashion. SIHJoin [18] also uses a hash join implementation to enable pipelining in combination with a lightweight cost-model with weight factors calibrated for remote systems. Both approaches were not designed with regard to aggregate queries and use a hash join implementation so that results from a join can already be forwarded to other operators in the query execution tree. However, pipelining is not helpful for analytical queries since the complete result of the query is needed for the aggregation.

Avalanche [5] and WoDQA [2], on the other hand, do not maintain data source registrations. Avalanche depends on third parties such as search engines to find a proper data source for executing a query. Statistics about cardinalities and data distributions are considered for breaking a query into a set of subqueries that in combination provide a full query answer. Then, these subqueries are executed in parallel against several endpoints. WoDQA uses VoID directories such as CKAN (http://ckan.net) and VoIDStore (http://void.rbkexplorer.com) to find possible sources of data. The system uses VoID statistics to group triple patterns into subqueries in a federated form and executes it by Jena ARQ.

An RDF data processing system that supports simple transactional queries as well as complex analytical queries is proposed in [25]. Aggregate queries are efficiently resolved by the system by using special look-up mechanisms. However, the system does not consider aggregate queries in a federated environment.

SPARQL-DQP [7] on the other hand, discusses semantics of the SPARQL 1.1 federation extension on a theoretical level and introduces the notion of well-defined patterns. It focuses on the optimization of federated queries in the presence of OPTIONAL subqueries but it was not designed to optimize and support analytical queries. Different strategies to implement federated queries in SPARQL 1.1 are discussed in [10]. Several limitations that may cause incorrect results and the potential validity restrictions are identified and fixes are proposed.

In summary, only very few approaches consider analytical queries [7,25] but not in the context of a federated setup. Most state-of-the-art approaches for federated query processing are designed with a focus on SPARQL 1.0 [1,2,5, 15,20] and lack full support of the more recent SPARQL 1.1 standard or do not offer support or particular optimizations for analytical queries. In contrast, this paper proposes a cost-based approach to optimize and execute aggregate SPARQL queries over federations of endpoints.

3   Federated Processing of Aggregate Queries

In this section, we will systematically outline several strategies that can be used to evaluate aggregated queries in federations of SPARQL endpoints. Section 4 will then introduce a cost-based approach to choose the best strategy for a query.

For ease of presentation, this section focuses on queries with a single SERVICE subquery. But the discussed principles can be extended to the general case of well-designed patterns with strongly bound variables [8]. The proposed approach can be combined with rule-based rewriting so that subpatterns, and especially joins, are evaluated in a cost-minimizing order. If an endpoint imposes limits on result sizes, then additional techniques, such as pagination [10], are used.

In the following, we use P_{AGG} to represent the original user query and P_e denotes the SERVICE subquery evaluated at SPARQL endpoint e. P_M represents the subquery that is created from the original query P_{AGG} by extracting P_e, adding a join on their common variables $var(P_e) \cap var(P_M)$, and, depending on the strategy, preserving grouping and aggregation. P_M is evaluated on the same endpoint M that P_{AGG} was sent to. Note that this section focuses on the implementation of the joins combining the partial results of the subqueries evaluated by remote endpoints. We do not make any restrictions on the local implementations that the remote endpoints use to evaluate joins contained in the subqueries they receive.

Mediator Join Strategy (MedJoin). The first strategy we describe is based on the mediator join technique that is used by many approaches for federated SPARQL query processing. The mediator/federator is the SPARQL engine that receives a query P_{AGG} from the user. The query optimizer at the mediator M defines P_e and P_M and sends P_e to endpoint e whereas P_M is processed on the endpoint m. Parallelization can be exploited by processing P_M and P_e at the same time. The main principle is to find all solutions to P_e and P_M first and then compute the remaining operations at the mediator, including the join (on ?placeID in the example below) that combines the partial results as well as grouping and aggregation. Listings 1.2 and 1.3 illustrate P_M and P_e for our running example query (Listing 1.1).

```
SELECT ?placeID ?radioValue WHERE {
  ?s ev:place ?placeID; ev:time ?time.
  ?s rdf:value ?radioValue.
}
```

Listing 1.2. MedJoin: query P_M

```
SELECT ?placeID ?regName WHERE {
  ?placeID gn:parentFeature ?regionID.
  ?regionID gn:name ?regName.
}
```

Listing 1.3. MedJoin: query P_e

Note that due to the fact that SPARQL does not remove duplicate results, we do not need to keep all variables in the select clauses of P_e and P_M. If duplicates were removed (like in SQL), we would have to keep all variables in the subqueries to ensure that the number of tuples that form the result are preserved, otherwise the average function in our example query would not return the correct result.

In principle, constructs such as OPTIONAL and FILTER are assigned to the subqueries that their variables refer to. If there is a complex expression, e.g., a FILTER is defined on a condition involving variables from different subqueries (e.g., $?a < ?b$), then the FILTER is evaluated after the partial results are combined at the mediator. The strength of this strategy is that partial queries can be evaluated in parallel. However, it can easily become expensive if the intermediate results are very large or when the datasets are very big.

Semi Join Strategy (SemiJoin). This strategy is based on the bound join or semi-join technique [14,20], which was already available based on UNION or FILTER constructs in SPARQL 1.0. The recent SPARQL 1.1 standard, however, supports the VALUES clause, which allows for a much more elegant solution.

The main principle of this strategy is to execute the subquery with the smallest result first and use the retrieved results as bindings for the join variables in the other subquery. The intuition is that for selective joins, sending a few partial results to an endpoint is much faster than receiving the complete result for the more general subquery. It is then the task of the cost optimizer to identify the most promising order of execution of subqueries. Constructs, such as FILTER and OPTIONAL, can be assigned to subqueries as discussed for MedJoin. Let us consider an example query with a FILTER.

```
SELECT ?regName (AVG(?radioValue) AS ?average) WHERE {
  ?s ev:place ?placeID . ?s ev:time ?time . ?s rdf:value ?radioValue .
  SERVICE <http://lod2.openlinksw.com/sparql>{
    ?placeID gn:parentFeature ?regionID . ?regionID gn:name ?regName .
  } FILTER(?radioValue < 0.08) . } GROUP BY ?regName
```

This query can be evaluated efficiently by evaluating query P_M (Listing 1.4) and then using the obtained bindings for the join variable ?placeID in the VALUES clause of the query P_e (Listing 1.5).

```
SELECT ?placeID ?radioVal            SELECT ?placeID ?regName
WHERE {                              WHERE { ?placeID gn:parentFeature ?rgID.
  ?s rdf:value ?radioVal ;             ?rgID gn:name ?regName.
  ev:place ?placeID; ev:time ?time.    VALUES (?placeID) {
  FILTER (?radioValue < 0.08) . }      <http://sws.geonames.org/1852083/>...} }
```

Listing 1.4. SemiJoin: query P_M **Listing 1.5.** SemiJoin: query P_e

In contrast to MedJoin, this strategy evaluates the subqueries sequentially and is particularly efficient for selective joins. However, as the VALUES clause is not yet widely supported by existing endpoints [9], the SPARQL 1.0 compliant alternatives of UNION (or FILTER) must often be used.

Partial Aggregation Strategy (PartialAgg). For queries where the grouping attributes of the original query contain a subset of the variables of the subquery that is executed first and the aggregate values are contained in the subquery that is evaluated second, further optimization is possible. The Partial Aggregation Strategy (PartialAgg) builds upon MedJoin by extending the subquery executed second with a `GROUP BY` clause and aggregate functions. The goal is to reduce the size of the partial result and compute partial aggregate values early so that P_{AGG} can be evaluated more efficiently.

Using PartialAgg our running example query (Listing 1.1) is decomposed into P_M (below) and P_e (Listing 1.5). First, P_M is computed, the result bindings are fed into the `VALUES` clause of P_e, and P_{AGG} combines the partial results via a join and computes final grouping and aggregation.

```
SELECT ?placeID (SUM(?radioValue) AS ?sum) (COUNT(?radioValue) AS ?count)
WHERE { ?s ev:place ?placeID; ev:time ?time; rdf:value ?radioValue . }
GROUP BY ?placeID
```

Note that P_M here groups by `?placeID` whereas the original query (Listing 1.1) groups by `?regName`, this is because P_M uses the join attributes $var(P_e) \cap var(P_M)$ in the `GROUP BY` clause. Whereas a particular placeID would occur in many results for P_M in the MedJoin strategy, the additional grouping here guarantees that the result set contains only one. Hence, the size of the intermediate result is reduced.

When performing such an optimization, however, we need to take into account whether the aggregate function in the original query is algebraic or distributive [16]. Computing aggregates for distributive functions (SUM, MIN, MAX, COUNT) is straightforward, while for computing AVG we first need to compute both SUM and COUNT in separate and in the final step divide the sum of all intermediate SUMs by the sum of all intermediate COUNTs, i.e., $AVG = \frac{\sum_{i=1}^{N} SUM_i}{\sum_{i=1}^{N} COUNT_i}$.

4 Cost-Based Query Optimization

For each user query, the query optimizer needs to decide which of the strategies that we discussed in the previous section to use. In this section, we present CoDA (**Co**st-based Optimizer for **D**istributed **A**ggregate Queries). A cost-based optimizer, finds the best strategy by computing query execution costs for different alternative query execution plans and choosing the one with minimum costs. In the remainder of this section, we first sketch how the query optimizer works, then we introduce the cost model. Finally, we present details regarding cardinality estimation and processing costs.

Query Optimizer. To find the best query execution plan, we need to systematically examine alternative query execution plans that produce the same result. We first decompose the original query into multiple subqueries as described in Sect. 3. We obtain a query P_M and endpoint queries $P_{e_1}, \ldots, P_{e_n}$. We then optimize the subqueries in separate, e.g., reordering the triple patterns based on a cost model so that the execution costs are minimized. Afterwards, we enumerate all possible plans that combine these subqueries using the strategies introduced in Sect. 3. For each of these alternative plans, we estimate execution costs (as described in the remainder of this section) and choose the plan with the minimum costs for query execution.

4.1 Cost Model

The overall costs of a distributed query execution plan (C_Q) consist of the costs for communication between endpoints and mediator (C_C) and the costs for processing the query on the data endpoint (C_P), i.e.: $C_Q = C_P + C_C$. To simplify the cost model, we estimate the costs for all subqueries in the same way. By calibrating the cost factors for each involved endpoint separately, the cost model can consider different sytem characteristics and estimate subqueries at the mediator and remote subqueries alike.

The cost model estimates C_Q for each subquery in separate and computes the costs of the complete query plan by combining the costs of its subqueries with the additional operators in P_{AGG} that compute the final result. For subqueries that are executed in parallel, as for the MedJoin strategy, the cost model needs to consider parallel execution. As the subquery that takes the longest determines the time when the result is available, we take the maximum time of these parallel subqueries, e.g., $C_Q(S_1, S_2) = \max(C_Q(S_1), C_Q(S_2))$, where $C_Q(S_i)$ denotes the costs of subquery S_i.

The communication costs C_C for a subquery S_i are estimated as: $C_C(S_i) = C_O + c_{S_i} \cdot C_{map}$, where C_O denotes the overhead to establish communication, c_{S_i} denotes the estimated number of transmitted solution mappings contained in the subquery, and C_{map} denotes the costs of transferring a single solution mapping. For SemiJoin $c_{S_i} \cdot C_{map}$ includes the costs for transferring data in both directions.

Processing costs (C_P) are determined by I/O and CPU costs and are very specific to the particular triple store and available indexes, current load, hardware characteristics, implemented algorithms, etc. As such details are not available for endpoints, we estimate processing costs based on the amount of data that the query is evaluated on. We assume, however, that indexes are used to access triples matching a triple pattern efficiently. We obtain $C_P = \sum_{t=1}^{M}(c_{tp} \cdot C_G)$, where c_{tp} is the estimated number of solution mappings selected by triple pattern t contained in the subquery, and C_G denotes the costs of processing a single triple.

Finally, the costs for processing grouping and aggregation costs for P_{AGG} are estimated as $c_{tp_{AGG}} \cdot C_G$, where $c_{tp_{AGG}}$ represents the number of observations involved in aggregation and C_G represents the costs for processing a single observation.

4.2 Estimating Cost Factors

The cost estimation formulas introduced above rely on several system-specific constants, i.e., C_O, C_{map}, and C_G. As each endpoint has different characteristics, we need to obtain estimates for every endpoint involved in a query. CoDA estimates these values based on several probe queries. The estimates are reused for future queries and repeated regularly to account for changes at the endpoints.

C_{map} is estimated using template queries such as: `SELECT * WHERE {?s #p ?o . FILTER(?o=#o)} LIMIT #L`. This query is executed several times with different values for `#L`, `#o` and `#p` and measures the time it takes to receive an answer from the endpoint. Values for `#o` are taken from a query such as `SELECT DISTINCT(?o) WHERE {?s #p ?o} LIMIT #L`. This is done to measure C_{map} on real values present in the dataset. Based on the pairwise difference between the queries' execution times and the number of retrieved results, we estimate the average time for a single result C_{map}.

C_O is estimated based on queries that do not retrieve data from triple stores such as: `SELECT(1 AS ?v){}` or `ASK{}`. Multiple queries are executed to determine an average.

C_G is estimated based on queries such as: `SELECT COUNT(*) WHERE {?s ?p ?o} GROUP BY #g`. Again, multiple queries with different valid values for `#g` and `#c` are used to build an average. By measuring the time it takes to receive the results and substracting the message overhead C_O and the costs of transferring the result based on C_{map}, we can estimate C_G. Note that C_G represents the costs to process a single input triple. Hence, before computing the average over multiple queries, we need to divide by the number of triples that the aggregate query was computed on – this can conveniently be derived from the query result (`COUNT(*)` is the number of input triples for each group).

Note that these estimates might not be perfectly accurate but this is acceptable for our purposes because we do not aim at accurately predicting execution costs but only to find out which execution plan is more efficient than the others.

4.3 Result Size Estimation

Another important part of the cost model is estimating the size of partial results (result cardinality). Similar to [15,17], we base our estimations on VoID statistics [3,23] as this is a standardized format and is most commonly used. Nevertheless, not all SPARQL endpoints offer such statistics. In such cases, we send a series of SPARQL queries with `COUNT` functions to the endpoint to compute the statistics.

VoID statistics can logically be divided into three parts: dataset statistics, property partition, and class partition. The dataset statistics describe the complete dataset: the total number of triples (`void:triples`, c_t), the total number of distinct subjects (`void:distinctSubjects`, c_s), and the total number of distinct objects (`void:distinctObjects`, c_o). The property partition contains such values for each property of the dataset ($c_{p,t}, c_{p,s}, c_{p,o}$). Finally, the class partition shows the number of entities of each class (`void:entities`).

Estimating Result Sizes for Basic Triple Patterns. To estimate result sizes for complex queries, we first need to estimate the result size of basic queries (a single triple pattern and, optionally, a condition expressed by a `FILTER`).

Based on statistics, we estimate the result size c_{res} of a triple patterns as follows: (?s ?p ?o) is directly given by c_t, (s ?p ?o) is estimated as $\frac{c_t}{c_s}$, (?s ?p o) as $\frac{c_t}{c_o}$, and (s ?p o) as $\frac{c_t}{c_s \cdot c_o}$. When the predicate of the triple pattern is specified, (?s p ?o) is given by $c_{p,t}$, (s p ?o) is estimated as $\frac{c_{p,t}}{c_{p,s}}$, (?s p o) as $\frac{c_{p,t}}{c_{p,o}}$, and (s p o) is assumed to be 1. Tighter estimates based on VoID statistics are possible when the property rdf:type is used [17].

We further introduce several optimizations that are often used in relational database systems [13]. As distributions are skewed, we assume a Zipfian distribution of values and multiply c_{res} with the correction coefficient of 1.1 (close to Zipfian ideal). In case a FILTER involves an inequality comparison (e.g. $?x >= 10$), we assume that one third of the triples satisfy the requirements and divide c_t or $c_{p,t}$ in the above formulas by a factor of 3. If a FILTER contains an expression with the inequality operator (e.g. $?x! = 10$), we need to replace $\frac{1}{c_s}$ with $\frac{c_s-1}{c_s}$ because we select all except 1 out of c_s different values. The same consideration holds for c_o, $c_{p,s}$, and $c_{p,o}$.

Estimating Result Sizes for Joins. To estimate the sizes of join results, we need to distinguish between different shapes of joins: (1) star-shaped joins are characterized by multiple triple patterns joining on the same variable (e.g., ?s1 p1 ?o1 . ?s1 p2 ?o2) and (2) path-shaped joins are characterized by multiple triple patterns that join on different variables (e.g., ?s1 p1 ?o1 . ?o1 p2 ?o2).

To estimate the result size, we use the cardinality estimation model proposed in [17]. The model proposes formulas for different types of joins. For example, for queries such as SELECT ?y WHERE { ?x p1 ?y . ?x p2 ?o1 . FILTER(?o1=10) } (star-shaped join) the cardinality is calculated as $c_{res} = \frac{\frac{c_{p2,t}}{c_{p2,o1}} \cdot c_{p1,t}}{max(c_{p2,x}, c_{p1,x})}$, while for queries such as SELECT ?x WHERE { ?x p1 ?y . ?y p2 ?o1 . FILTER(?o1=10) } (path-shaped join) the cardinality is calculated as $c_{res} = \frac{\frac{c_{p2,t}}{c_{p2,o1}} \cdot c_{p1,t}}{max(c_{p1,y}, c_{p2,y})}$.

Estimating Result Sizes for Grouping and Aggregation. The upper bound for the cardinality of grouping and aggregation is the size of the input, i.e., for a non-restrictive grouping we have $c_{res} = c_{in}$. If the GROUP BY clause contains only a subset $(?x_1, \ldots ?x_n)$ of the variables contained in the query, then c_{res} (or more specifically c_{AGG}) is bound by the product of the variables' distinct bindings $\prod_{i=1}^{n} distinct(?x_i)$.

When solution reducers are present in the query, such as FILTER statements and/or triples with literals, that are connected to grouping variables through joins, we assume that the number of distinct values is reduced proportionally: $distinct(?x) = \frac{c_{p_x,x}}{c_{p_y,y} \cdot N}$ where $c_{p_x,x}$ is the number of distinct bindings for variable $?x$, $c_{p_y,y}$ the number of distinct bindings for variable ?y, which is connected to $?x$ through star-shaped or path-shaped joins, and N is the reduction factor, which is equal to 1 in case of a solution reducer with equality, $1/3$ in case of a solution reducer with inequality, and $\frac{c_{p_y,y}-1}{c_{p_y,y}}$ in case of the a solution reducer with negation [13].

5   Evaluation

In this section, we present the results of evaluating the strategies presented in this paper. Our solution uses the .NET Framework 4.0 and dotNetRDF (http://dotnetrdf.org/) to implement a mediator that accepts queries, optimizes their execution using the proposed strategies (SemiJoin, PartialAgg, and MedJoin), and sends subqueries to the SPARQL endpoints, which are using Virtuoso as local triple store.

5.1   Experimental Setup

We evaluate our strategies based on a standard benchmark originally designed to measure the performance of aggregate queries in relational database systems: the Star Schema Benchmark (SSB) [19]. This benchmark is well-known in the database community and was chosen for its simple design (refined decision support benchmark TPC-H [11]) and its well-defined testbed.

RDF Dataset. The data in SSB is generated as relational data. We used different scale factors (1 to 5–6 M to 30 M observations) to generated multiple datasets of different sizes. We translated the datasets into RDF using a vocabulary that strongly resembles the SSB tabular structure. For example, a lineorder tuple is represented as a star-shaped set of triples where the subject (URI) is linked via a property (e.g., `rdfh:lo_orderdate`) to a an object (e.g., `rdfh:lo_orderdate_19931201`) which in turn can be subject of another

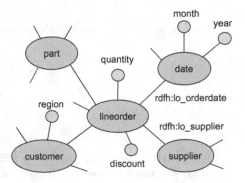

Fig. 1. Simplified description of the SSB dataset

star-shaped graph. Values such as quantity and discount are connected to lineorder entities as literals. A simplified schema of the RDF structure is illustrated in Fig. 1. Converted datasets contain 110,5 M (scale factor 1) to 547,5 M (scale factor 5) triples.

Queries. SSB defines 13 queries. They represent 4 "prototypical" queries with different selectivity factors. A brief description of the queries is given in Table 1. We converted all 13 queries into SPARQL and used the `SERVICE` keyword to query federated endpoints.

Configuration. To test the queries in a federation of SPARQL endpoints, we partitioned the datasets as follows:

- To simulate two endpoints (one endpoint containing main observation data and one `SERVICE` endpoint containing supporting data), we created two partitions: partition 1 (lineorders, parts, customers, and suppliers) and partition 2 (dates).

Table 1. SSB queries

Query prototypes	Query no	Query parameters for various selectivities
Prototype 1. Amount of revenue increase that would have resulted from eliminating certain company-wide discounts.	Q1.1	Discounts 1, 2, and 3 for quantities less than 25 shipped in 1993.
	Q1.2	Discounts 1, 2, and 3 for quantities less than 25 shipped in 01/1993.
	Q1.3	Discounts 5, 6, and 7 for quantities less than 35 shipped in week 6 of 1993.
Prototype 2. Revenue for some product classes, for suppliers in a certain region, grouped by more restrictive product classes and all years.	Q2.1	Revenue for 'MFGR#12' category, for suppliers in America
	Q2.2	Revenue for brands 'MFGR#2221' to 'MFGR#2228', for suppliers in Asia
	Q2.3	Revenue for brand 'MFGR#2239' for suppliers in Europe
Prototype 3. Revenue for some product classes, for suppliers in a certain region, grouped by more restrictive product classes and all years.	Q3.1	For Asian suppliers and customers in 1992-1997
	Q3.2	For US suppliers and customers in 1992-1997
	Q3.3	For specific UK cities suppliers and customers in 1992-1997
	Q3.4	For specific UK cities suppliers and customers in 12/1997
Prototype 4. Aggregate profit, measured by subtracting revenue from supply cost.	Q4.1	For American suppliers and customers for manufacturers 'MFGR#1' or 'MFGR#2' in 1992
	Q4.2	For American suppliers and customers for manufacturers 'MFGR#1' or 'MFGR#2' in 1997-1998
	Q4.3	For American customers and US suppliers for category 'MFGR#14' in 1997-1998

- To simulate three endpoints (two **SERVICE** endpoints containing supporting data), we created three partitions: partition 1 (lineorders, parts, customers), partition 2 (dates), and partition 3 (suppliers).
- To simulate four endpoints (three **SERVICE** endpoints containing supporting data), we created four partitions: partition 1 (lineorders, parts), partition 2 (dates), partition 3 (suppliers), and partition 4 (customers).

All the queries and the datasets used for the experiments are available at http://extbi.cs.aau.dk/coda.

We used four different machines for our experiments depending on the configuration. We used the most powerful machine (CPU Intel(R) Core(TM) i7-950, RAM 24 GB, HDD 1.5 TB RAID5, 1 TB SATA, 600 GB SAS RAID0) for partition 1. We used three identical machines (CPU AMD(R) Opteron(TM) 285 2.6 GHz, RAM 8 GB, HDD 80 GB) for serving data of partitions 2 to 4. 64-bit Ubuntu 14.04 LTS operating system was installed on all computers. As a mediator, we used a virtual machine with one dedicated core of Xeon E3-1240V2 3.4 GHz (2 threads), 10 GB RAM, 100 GB HDD, and 64-bit Windows Server 2008 Service Pack 1 as operating system. All machines were located on the same LAN. All benchmark queries were executed 5 times following a single warm-up run. During this warm-up run, all statistics and system measurements were obtained, stored in the system, and later used for the subsequent query executions. Statistics were gathered with the help of COUNT queries. Statistics collection took between 18 (scale factor 1) to 129 (scale factor 5) seconds. The execution time for each query is measured on the mediator from the time the query is received from a user till the time the complete results are reported back. We used a timeout of 1 h for the experiments.

5.2 Experimental Results

As discussed in Sect. 1, we initially experimented with three systems (Virtuoso, Sesame, and Jena Fuseki). Sesame is always trying to download all triples that match the patterns defined in the SERVICE subquery from the remote endpoint and is timing out even for small datasets. Jena Fuseki and Virtuoso are using the same strategy to evaluate SERVICE subqueries with grouping and aggregation. We chose Virtuoso v07.10.3207 as representative for this strategy in our experiments and include results for a native Virtuoso setup, in which Virtuoso is optimizing the distributed execution of the aggregate query.

In our first line of experiments, we measured the runtime for the benchmark queries in the configuration with one SPARQL endpoint. For the SemiJoin strategy, due to issues with large numbers of bindings in the VALUES clause in existing endpoints [9], we often have to partition the set of bindings that we aim to pass in a VALUES statement into smaller partitions and send a separate messages for each of the partitions.

Table 2 shows the results for scale factors 1 to 5. CoDA clearly chooses the best strategy for all queries. For scale factor 1, the CoDA algorithm selected the SemiJoin strategy for queries with highly selective subqueries (where the number of intermediate subquery results are low) (Q1.1, Q1.2, Q1.3, Q3.1, Q3.4, and Q4.2), the MedJoin strategy for queries with high selectivity (Q2.3), and the PartialAgg strategy for the rest.

CoDA scales well with the increase in the number of triples as the results for scale factors 2 to 5 in Table 2 show. Due to the increased number of triples to process, the strategy for Query 2.3 changes from MedJoin to PatrialAgg. CoDA also changed the strategies for queries 1.1 and 4.1 due to different estimations of C_C and C_P for various scale factors. In general, CoDA chooses the best strategy for all queries (the difference between the CoDA approach and the best approach for query Q3.4 in scale factor 2 is due to the overhead of optimization, which is only 14 ms).

Figure 2 shows the execution times for several queries with high selectivity (Q4.3, Q3.3, Q3.4) and low selectivity (Q2.2, Q3.2, Q2.3) for different strategies and scale factors – due to timeouts in execution, some lines end earlier than others. MedJoin and native Virtuoso do not scale well and some queries time out while SemiJoin and PartialAgg return answers for all the queries. This can be explained by the internal logic behind the strategies. For example, Virtuoso sends SPARQL requests for every aggregated observation, while MedJoin needs to transfer much data to the mediator. Due to the result size restrictions (the maximum result set size for Virtuoso is 1,048,576), the system downloads all data in chunks but still times out. In contrast, SemiJoin and PartialAgg transfer only necessary data and are thus reducing the communication costs.

We also evaluated the influence of the number of endpoints. For this purpose, we chose an example query from our workload (Q4.3) that is complex enough to be rewritten into a query with up to three SERVICE endpoints and selective enough not to require all triples for the calculation (Fig. 3). Going up to three endpoints, only the PartialAgg strategy was able to answer the query. With data coming from two or three endpoints, the number of values that needs to be passed in the SemiJoin strategy increases and system performance quickly degrades (yellow lines in Fig. 3). With the partition of the dataset into more endpoints, MedJoin also needs to load much more data into the mediator site to answer the query and for the scale factors 3 to 5 this leads to timeouts (green lines in Fig. 3). The same reason (the need to send more requests to answer the query) leads to the timeout in the Virtuoso strategy (red lines) for queries with more than one SERVICE endpoint. Therefore, the obvious choice of the CoDA strategy is PartialAgg (blue lines) in these cases.

Table 2. Benchmark results for scale factor 1 to 5, in seconds

	Q1.1	Q1.2	Q1.3	Q2.1	Q2.2	Q2.3	Q3.1	Q3.2	Q3.3	Q3.4	Q4.1	Q4.2	Q4.3
Scale Factor 1													
Virtuoso	T/O	T/O	760	500,3	107,8	21,3	215,8	21,2	1,4	1,4	863	969	7,3
SemiJoin	1,3	0,2	0,1	12,7	13,5	12,6	14,1	11,0	6,5	0,2	4,8	8,1	4,5
PartialAgg	1,6	1,4	0,8	9,4	4,5	3	17,5	2,8	0,5	0,3	4	18,5	1,0
MedJoin	249,5	213,4	82,9	11	5,2	2,9	98,9	3,4	0,8	0,3	26,4	32	1,1
CoDA	1,3	0,2	0,1	9,4	4,5	2,9	14,1	2,8	0,5	0,2	4	8,1	1,0
Scale Factor 2													
Virtuoso	T/O	T/O	T/O	950,9	T/O	462,9	992,2	42,9	1,8	1,9	T/O	1054	46,5
SemiJoin	3,6	0,9	0,5	25,7	102,8	101	15,4	11,1	89,7	0,32	30,6	35,5	20,6
PartialAgg	17,1	16,5	7,3	16,2	9,5	5,9	18,4	5,8	0,8	0,34	77,3	37,4	10,5
MedJoin	T/O	T/O	T/O	T/O	143,7	31,5	612,7	36,7	1,8	1,7	T/O	T/O	246,7
CoDA	3,6	0,9	0,5	16,2	9,5	5,9	15,4	5,8	0,8	0,33	30,6	35,5	10,5
Scale Factor 3													
Virtuoso	T/O	T/O	T/O	1465	T/O	T/O	T/O	63,5	2,8	3,1	T/O	T/O	68,5
SemiJoin	46,3	5,4	2,2	330,7	303,4	344,1	20,2	14,2	250,7	0,6	45,4	105,3	39,8
PartialAgg	18,4	18,8	8,3	29,5	13,2	8,2	23,2	8,6	1,1	0,7	217,4	606	33,9
MedJoin	T/O	T/O	T/O	T/O	205,7	39,5	1312	44,8	2	2,4	T/O	T/O	305,3
CoDA	18,4	5,4	2,2	29,5	13,2	8,2	20,2	8,6	1,1	0,6	45,4	105,3	33,9
Scale Factor 4													
Virtuoso	T/O	T/O	T/O	T/O	T/O	T/O	T/O	86,9	4,7	4,7	T/O	T/O	118,4
SemiJoin	64,2	6.9	2,4	368,5	430,3	455,4	23,7	14,5	275,6	0,7	54,2	116,2	73,5
PartialAgg	33,9	27,6	9,8	146,2	15,2	12,9	27,2	12,5	1,6	0,8	980,8	1017	68,3
MedJoin	T/O	T/O	T/O	T/O	267,5	43,6	T/O	64,5	2,3	3,9	T/O	T/O	T/O
CoDA	33,9	6.9	2,4	146,2	15,2	12,9	23,7	12,5	1,6	0,7	54,2	116,2	68,3
Scale Factor 5													
Virtuoso	T/O	T/O	T/O	T/O	T/O	T/O	T/O	109,2	5,3	5,7	T/O	T/O	143,4
SemiJoin	77,7	8,4	2,9	453,4	460,3	503,6	60,9	15,8	352,9	1,2	59,2	126,8	123,6
PartialAgg	37,7	29,2	18,4	249,5	19,8	14,9	78,5	14,4	2,2	1,7	1565	1577	105,1
MedJoin	T/O	T/O	T/O	T/O	301,2	46,3	T/O	80,4	3,3	5,8	T/O	T/O	T/O
CoDA	37,7	8,4	2,9	249,5	19,8	14,9	60,9	14,4	2,2	1,2	59,2	126,8	105,1

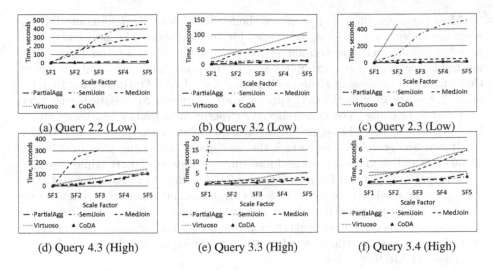

(a) Query 2.2 (Low)   (b) Query 3.2 (Low)   (c) Query 2.3 (Low)

(d) Query 4.3 (High)   (e) Query 3.3 (High)   (f) Query 3.4 (High)

Fig. 2. Execution times for queries with low and high selectivity, one endpoint

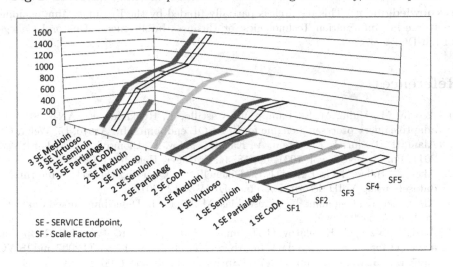

Fig. 3. Execution of query 4.3 over several endpoints (Colour figure online)

In summary, the experimental results show that CoDA is able to select the best strategy and thus executes all queries for RDF data of all tested data sizes.

6 Conclusions and Future Work

Motivated by the increasing availability of RDF data over SPARQL endpoints, the new powerful aggregation functionality in SPARQL 1.1, and the desire to perform ad-hoc analytical queries, this paper investigated the problem of efficiently processing aggregate queries in a federation of SPARQL endpoints.

More precisely, the paper proposed the Mediator Join, SemiJoin, and Partial Aggregation query processing strategies for this scenario. The paper also proposed a cost model, and techniques for estimating constants and result sizes for triple patterns, joins, grouping and aggregation, and the combination of these with the processing strategies into the Cost-based Optimizer for Distributed Aggregate queries (CoDA) approach for aggregate SPARQL queries over endpoint federations. The comprehensive experimental evaluation, based on an RDF version of the widely used Star Schema Benchmark, showed that CoDA is efficient and scalable, able to pick the best query processing plan in different situations, and significantly outperforms current state-of-the art triple stores.

Interesting directions for future work include using more complex statistics with precomputed join result sizes and correlation information to better estimate cardinalities, optimizing the execution of more complex queries (e.g., with optional patterns or complex aggregation functions), and investigating the influence of ontological constraints and inference/reasoning in the context of federated aggregate SPARQL queries.

Acknowledgment. This research is partially funded by the Erasmus Mundus Joint Doctorate in "Information Technologies for Business Intelligence – Doctoral College (IT4BI-DC)".

References

1. Acosta, M., Vidal, M.-E., Lampo, T., Castillo, J., Ruckhaus, E.: ANAPSID: an adaptive query processing engine for SPARQL endpoints. In: Aroyo, L., Welty, C., Alani, H., Taylor, J., Bernstein, A., Kagal, L., Noy, N., Blomqvist, E. (eds.) ISWC 2011, Part I. LNCS, vol. 7031, pp. 18–34. Springer, Heidelberg (2011)
2. Akar, Z., Halaç, T.G., Ekinci, E.E., Dikenelli, O.: Querying the web of interlinked datasets using VoID descriptions. In: LDOW 2012 (2012)
3. Alexander, K., Cyganiak, R., Hausenblas, M., Zhao, J.: Describing linked datasets. In: LDOW 2009 (2009)
4. Auer, S., Bizer, C., Kobilarov, G., Lehmann, J., Cyganiak, R., Ives, Z.G.: DBpedia: a nucleus for a web of open data. In: Aberer, K., et al. (eds.) ASWC 2007 and ISWC 2007. LNCS, vol. 4825, pp. 722–735. Springer, Heidelberg (2007)
5. Basca, C., Bernstein, A.: Avalanche: putting the spirit of the web back into semantic web querying. In: SSWS 2010 (2010)
6. Berners-Lee, T.: Linked data. W3C Design Issues (2006). http://www.w3.org/DesignIssues/LinkedData.html
7. Buil-Aranda, C., Arenas, M., Corcho, O.: Semantics and optimization of the SPARQL 1.1 federation extension. In: Antoniou, G., Grobelnik, M., Simperl, E., Parsia, B., Plexousakis, D., De Leenheer, P., Pan, J. (eds.) ESWC 2011, Part II. LNCS, vol. 6644, pp. 1–15. Springer, Heidelberg (2011)
8. Buil-Aranda, C., Arenas, M., Corcho, O., Polleres, A.: Federating queries in SPARQL 1.1: syntax, semantics and evaluation. Web Semant. **18**(1), 1–17 (2013)
9. Buil-Aranda, C., Hogan, A., Umbrich, J., Vandenbussche, P.-Y.: SPARQL web-querying infrastructure: ready for action? In: Alani, H., et al. (eds.) ISWC 2013, Part II. LNCS, vol. 8219, pp. 277–293. Springer, Heidelberg (2013)

10. Buil-Aranda, C., Polleres, A., Umbrich, J.: Strategies for executing federated queries in SPARQL1.1. In: Mika, P., et al. (eds.) ISWC 2014, Part II. LNCS, vol. 8797, pp. 390–405. Springer, Heidelberg (2014)
11. Transaction Processing Performance Council. TPC Benchmark H - Decision Support. http://www.tpc.org/tpch
12. Deshpande, A., Ives, Z., Raman, V.: Adaptive query processing. Found. Trends Databases 1(1), 1–140 (2007)
13. Garcia-Molina, H., Ullman, J.D., Widom, J.: Database Systems - The Complete Book, 2nd edn. Pearson Prentice Hall, Upper Saddle River (2009)
14. Görlitz, O., Staab, S.: Federated data management and query optimization for linked open data. In: Vakali, A., Jain, L.C. (eds.) New Directions in Web Data Management 1. SCI, vol. 331, pp. 109–137. Springer, Heidelberg (2011)
15. Görlitz, O., Staab, S.: SPLENDID: SPARQL endpoint federation exploiting VoID descriptions. In: COLD 2011 (2011)
16. Gray, J., Bosworth, A., Layman, A., Pirahesh, H.: Data cube: a relational aggregation operator generalizing group-by, cross-tab, and sub-total. In: ICDE 1996, pp. 152–159 (1996)
17. Hagedorn, S., Hose, K., Sattler, K.-U., Umbrich, J.: Resource planning for SPARQL query execution on data sharing platforms. In: COLD 2014 (2014)
18. Ladwig, G., Tran, T.: SIHJoin: querying remote and local linked data. In: Antoniou, G., Grobelnik, M., Simperl, E., Parsia, B., Plexousakis, D., De Leenheer, P., Pan, J. (eds.) ESWC 2011, Part I. LNCS, vol. 6643, pp. 139–153. Springer, Heidelberg (2011)
19. O'Neil, P., O'Neil, E.J., Chen, X.: The star schema benchmark (SSB). Technical report, UMass/Boston, June 2009
20. Schwarte, A., Haase, P., Hose, K., Schenkel, R., Schmidt, M.: FedX: optimization techniques for federated query processing on linked data. In: Aroyo, L., Welty, C., Alani, H., Taylor, J., Bernstein, A., Kagal, L., Noy, N., Blomqvist, E. (eds.) ISWC 2011, Part I. LNCS, vol. 7031, pp. 601–616. Springer, Heidelberg (2011)
21. Urhan, T., Franklin, M.J.: XJoin: a reactively-scheduled pipelined join operator. IEEE Data Eng. Bull. 23(2), 27–33 (2000)
22. Wick, M.: GeoNames geographical database. http://www.geonames.org
23. World Wide Web Consortium. Describing Linked Datasets with the VoID Vocabulary (W3C Interest Group Note 03 March 2011). http://www.w3.org/TR/void/
24. World Wide Web Consortium. SPARQL 1.1 Overview (W3C Recommendation 21 March 2013). http://www.w3.org/TR/sparql11-overview/
25. Wylot, M., Pont, J., Wisniewski, M., Cudré-Mauroux, P.: dipLODocus[RDF]—short and long-tail RDF analytics for massive webs of data. In: Aroyo, L., Welty, C., Alani, H., Taylor, J., Bernstein, A., Kagal, L., Noy, N., Blomqvist, E. (eds.) ISWC 2011, Part I. LNCS, vol. 7031, pp. 778–793. Springer, Heidelberg (2011)

A Survey of HTTP Caching Implementations on the Open Semantic Web

Kjetil Kjernsmo[✉]

Department of Informatics, University of Oslo, Postboks 1080 Blindern,
0316 Oslo, Norway
kjetil@kjernsmo.net

Abstract. Scalability of the data access architecture in the Semantic Web is dependent on the establishment of caching mechanisms to take the load off of servers. Unfortunately, there is a chicken and egg problem here: Research, implementation, and evaluation of caching infrastructure is uninteresting as long as data providers do not publish relevant metadata. And publishing metadata is useless as long as there is no infrastructure that uses it.

We show by means of a survey of live RDF data sources that caching metadata is prevalent enough already to be used in some cases. On the other hand, they are not commonly used even on relatively static data, and when they are given, they are very conservatively set. We point out future directions and give recommendations for the enhanced use of caching in the Semantic Web.

1   Introduction

Caching has been given a prominent place in the foundational documents of the World Wide Web. Out of the 6 documents that make up the HTTP 1.1 standard, RFC7234 [6] is entirely devoted to the topic. RFC7232 [7] defines conditional requests, and is also important when constructing caches. As RFC7234 notes:

> The goal of caching in HTTP/1.1 is to significantly improve performance by reusing a prior response message to satisfy a current request.

Furthermore, caching is discussed throughout the Architecture of the World Wide Web [11], and the definition of the Representational State Transfer (REST) architectural style [8] is partly motivated from the requirement to implement efficient caching. We also note that caching in the Internet infrastructure, through so-called Content Delivery Networks, is both a large business area and could provide great value to the Semantic Web.

If used correctly, caching mechanisms will reduce the need to make HTTP requests, reduce lookups to the backend systems, reduce the need to make repetitive computations, enable sharing of responses in Internet infrastructure, improve uptime and reduce latency since requests may be answered closer to the client.

© Springer International Publishing Switzerland 2015
F. Gandon et al. (Eds.): ESWC 2015, LNCS 9088, pp. 286–301, 2015.
DOI: 10.1007/978-3-319-18818-8_18

In spite of this, we have not seen it in widespread use in the Semantic Web, and therefore we decided to conduct a survey to investigate the actual compliance to RFC7234 and RFC7232. The objectives of this paper are:

1. Understand the actual usage rather than rely on anecdotal conceptions.
2. Encourage the implementation of these mechanisms in Semantic Web infrastructure.
3. Point out future research directions.

The contributions of this paper are to meet these objectives by means of a survey that shows that while the uptake has been moderate, practical benefits may be realized already. Based on this survey as well as practical experience, we point out future research directions as well as some recommendations for deployed implementations.

We note that caching is not only useful for long-living resources, even though that may be the most important use. If a resource is frequently requested, it may make sense to cache it even though it may be fresh for only a very short period.

Caching may be deployed at several different levels: An HTTP cache may be in a reverse proxy close to the server, in which case it may have much in common with a conventional database cache. It may also be anywhere between a server and a client, in which case it may be shared, i.e. it may cache responses from a number of servers to many clients. Another example is an institutional forward proxy, which are close to several users. Finally, the User Agent may implement a private cache for its user at the client side.

1.1 HTTP Caching Standards

As mentioned, the two documents from the HTTP 1.1 standards suite that are relevant for this study are RFC7234, named "Caching", and RFC7232, named "Conditional Requests". The main difference is that the caching standard defines when a response may be reused without any contact to origin server, whereas the conditional requests define how to validate a response by contacting the origin server. The two can be combined: Clients and proxies may use the latter to revalidate a response that has been cached based on the former.

RFC7234 defines two important headers. The first of which is Expires, whose value is a date and time of when the response is considered stale, and therefore should not be used. The second is Cache-Control, which allows detailed control of the cache, including a max-age field, which gives the time in seconds for how long the the response may be used from the time of the request. max-age takes precedence over Expires. In this article, *freshness lifetime* is understood as the number of seconds that the response may be used without contacting the origin server. Ideally, the calculation of the freshness lifetime should be based of the above, we therefore shall refer to this as "standards-compliant caching". It can also be based on heuristics, Sect. 4.2.2 in RFC7234 provides some loose constraints for such practice as well as a suggestion for a useful heuristic. This heuristic is based on a fraction of the time lapsed between the current time and the modification time given in the `Last-Modified` header. This approach still requires the Web server to be cooperative to be successful. Commonly, Web servers can track this, for example if RDF is served from a file system the file modification time is used.

RFC7232, on the other hand, defines a protocol for asking the server if the cached response is still fresh using conditional requests. This doesn't burden the content provider with the task of estimating the freshness lifetime beforehand. However, the server is then required to be able to answer if the resource has changed less expensively than it would be to serve the entire response. Either of two headers must be set by the server to achieve this: `ETag`, which sets an opaque identifier for the response, or `Last-Modified` which gives the time and date of the last modification of the resource. Clients that have obtained these values may use them to validate an earlier response by using `If-None-Match` and/or `If-Modified-Since` respectively in a subsequent request. If the server finds the response has not changed based on this, it will respond with a 304 status code and no body, otherwise it will return the full response. The other headers we recorded are listed in Table 1.

RFC7234 provides detailed control of caching, and caching may also be prohibited by the server, either by setting a non-positive freshness lifetime or explicitly using a `no-store` control field.

In this paper, we study to what extent SPARQL endpoints, vocabulary and data publishers support these standards. Data and code to reproduce this work are available at http://folk.uio.no/kjekje/#cache-survey.

2   Related Work

We are not aware of any surveys of this type. Although the database literature is rich with query cache literature, it is mostly relevant to what would happen within the server or between the server and a reverse proxy, which is opaque to the Internet, and therefore not of our concern. For the same reason, caching that happens within the SPARQL engine is not relevant.

The Dynamic Linked Data Observatory (DyLDO) [12] performed, and continues to do so, monitoring of parts of the Linked Open Data Cloud to determine dynamicity characteristics of Linked Data. Caching is one of their motivations, but they have not published statistics on HTTP headers.

Linked Data Fragments is claimed in [20] to take advantage of caching and contrasts this with the unavailability of SPARQL query caches. They assert that this is an architectural problem. In [9], the authors examine cacheable as one of the desiderata for sustainable data access. They claim, without further justification, that SPARQL isn't cacheable.

In [16] the authors implemented a reverse proxy that controlled the changes to the dataset, and therefore could make sure the proxy had all the information needed to determine freshness. We are interested in the situation where the changes cannot be controlled.

Table 1. Recorded HTTP headers

Header	Reference	Description
Age	RFC7234	When obtaining response from a cache, the number of seconds since validation
Cache-Control	RFC7234	Header used for a variety of directives
Expires	RFC7234	Gives the date/time after which the response is considered stale.
Pragma	RFC7234	Archaic HTTP 1.0 header
Warning	RFC7234	For additional information about possible incorrectness
Content-Type	RFC7231	To select the correct parser
If-None-Match	RFC7232	Request header to check if ETag has changed
If-Modified-Since	RFC7232	Request header to check if Last-Modified has changed
Last-Modified	RFC7232	When the resource was last modified
ETag	RFC7232	An opaque validator to check if the resource has changed
X-Cache		Inserted by some caches to indicate cache status
Date	RFC7231	The time of the message. Used in conditional requests and heuristics
Surrogate-Capability	Edge [17]	Draft to allow fine-grained control for proxies.
Client-Aborted	libwww	Header inserted by User Agent to indicate that it aborted the download
Client-Warning	libwww	Header inserted by User Agent to give details about problems with the download

In [19], the term caching was used in a different sense than we use it. They rather prefetched an entire dataset to a local store and based on heuristics tried to determine which parts of the query should be evaluated remotely and locally. [15] explored when caching had a positive effect on complex SPARQL queries.

In the broader Web literature, [1] analysed the value of caching based anonymized traces of actual Web usage at a major Internet Service Provider. They found that while caching often yields little benefit when content is user-generated, there is still some potential.

While these studies have little overlap with the present paper, they underline the importance of understanding the current deployment and future potential. In some of the related work, it is shown that caching does not necessarily give tangible benefits. Yet, we shall assume that sharing the metadata required for caching outside of the server is desirable, and that it is possible in most cases. We shall see that it most likely will be beneficial in cases that do not benefit from caching today.

3   Methodology

We want to find information resources on the Web, and examine HTTP headers that may allow caching. To do this, we perform GET requests on SPARQL endpoints, vocabularies, dataset descriptions and other resources and record headers recommended by current standards, as well as obsoleted and non-standard headers. Additionally, we examine the triples in the returned information resources to see if there is information that may be used to calculate heuristic freshness.

We made several approaches to ensure that we visited a large and representative section of the open Semantic Web. We took SPARQL Endpoints from the SPARQLES survey [3], vocabularies from Linked Open Vocabularies (LOV) [2] and prefix.cc, and we augmented these data with spidered data from the Billion Triple Challenge (BTC) 2014 [13] dataset. Of these, BTC2014 is by far the largest, the others are small, curated and targeted datasets. However, the size is besides the point, we were only interested in examining as many hosts as possible, and they are still few.

We used SPARQLES survey list of SPARQL endpoints as of 2014-11-17, and filtered out those deemed unresponsive. This resulted in a list of 312 endpoints.

To examine as many different implementations and hosts as possible, we noted that the Billion Triple Challenge 2014 [13] dataset consisted of a 4 GTriple corpus of spidered Web data. This was seeded from datahub.io (aka CKAN), as well as other sources. To compile a list of candidates for further examination, we performed a series of data reduction steps, manually inspecting the result between each step. The details of this process are given in a companion technical report [14].

The end result of this process is a list of 3117 unique hosts, for each several resources would be visited, some several times, as they may host SPARQL endpoints, vocabularies, or other information resources, by a spider also detailed in [14], resulting in 7745 requests, done on 2015-01-02.

This results in an NQuads file per host, which is then loaded into a Virtuoso-based SPARQL endpoint for analysis by using the statistics system R [10] in the following section.

3.1   Challenges to Validity

Key challenges to the validity of the survey are biases that may be introduced by the coverage and then the data reduction. The breadth of the Semantic Web is derived mainly from the BTC2014 crawl. While LODstats[1] has presently seen an order of magnitude more triples, the number of error-free datasets were at the time of this writing 4442. We work under the assumption that cache headers are set mostly on a per-host basis, and if this assumption is valid, sampling a URL per host is sufficient. LODstats do not report per-host statistics, but often one host will host several datasets. Another recent crawl was reported by [18]. It is not clear how many hosts were crawled, but the number of triples is much

---

[1] http://stats.lod2.eu/.

smaller than that of BTC2014. It is therefore a fair assumption that BTC2014 fairly well represents the breadth of the Semantic Web, momentarily at least.

As for the coverage of vocabularies, we have verified that all resolveable vocabularies in LODstats that are found in more than 10 datasets are visited, and it is not far inferior in number to LODstats. The number of SPARQL endpoints found in SPARQLES is larger than LODstats, and we also looked for further endpoints both in the BTC2014 and our own crawl, finding only 18. If endpoints went underdiscovered, then there is a discovery problem that is beyond this survey to rectify.

The data reduction that was subsequently done was mainly done to eliminate errors. We have not investigated biases that may be introduced by discarding momentarily dysfunctional parts of the Semantic Web, but we investigated whether the freshness lifetimes reported in the case of certain errors were distributed differently from those that returned a valid response, see the companion technical report [14]. We found that they were, but we have assumed that this is due to that errors are configured to be cached differently, which we know from experience is common practice. The following analysis is based on valid responses.

4   Analysis

The analysis is focused on finding descriptive statistics to understand how different servers support caching, for how long resources hosted with those that do support caching may be considered fresh, if it is possible to easily compute a heuristic freshness lifetime, and revalidate the response on expiry. Apart from quoting the numbers we aggregated, we do this by presenting summarized data distribution visualizations, to allow for an intuitive understanding of the data. Where appropriate, we also do statistical hypothesis tests, using so-called contingency tables, see [14] for details.

4.1   Different Server Implementations

First, we investigated whether certain server implementations provided better support for caching than others. To do this, we formulated SPARQL queries to examine the `Server` headers of successful responses. We used optional clauses matching the standards-compliant computed freshness lifetime (which is the ideal) as well as whether the response had other indications of caching-related metadata that may assist caching such as modification time, certain predicates, etc.

For each unique `Server` header, we found the ones where *all* responses had a freshness lifetime or other usable metadata. For the former, this amounted to 22 servers, which are listed in Table 2. 70 servers always responded with usable metadata. Inspecting the values we find the well-known Virtuoso and Callimachus servers, as well as the Perl modules RDF::LinkedData and RDF::Endpoint, which are partly developed by and run on a server operated by this author. Apart from those, we see that the they reveal very little about the RDF-specific

Table 2. Server headers for hosts that enabled a freshness lifetime to be computed for *all* requests.

1	DFE/largefile
2	git_frontend
3	nginx/1.3.9
4	thin 1.6.0 codename Greek Yogurt
5	Oracle-Application-Server-10g/10.1.3.4.0 Oracle-HTTP-Server [...]
6	Oracle-Application-Server-10g/10.1.3.4.0 Oracle-HTTP-Server [...]
7	TwistedWeb/8.2.0
8	RDF::Endpoint/0.07
9	Jetty(6.1.26)
10	nginx/1.6.1
11	Jigsaw/2.3.0-beta3
12	Apache/2.2.9 (Win32) PHP/5.2.6
13	Apache/2.4.10 (Unix) mod_fcgid/2.3.9
14	
15	GFE/2.0
16	RDF::LinkedData/0.70
17	Apache/2.2.17 (Unix) mod_wsgi/3.3 Python/2.6.6
18	Virtuoso/07.10.3211 (Linux) i686-generic-linux-glibc212-64 VDB
19	Apache/2.2.24 (Unix) mod_ssl/2.2.24 OpenSSL/0.9.8y
20	Apache/2.2.22 (Fedora)
21	INSEE
22	GitHub.com

parts of the underlying server implementation, e.g. Apache is a very common generic Web server, the others are also generic. A quick inspection of all Server headers confirmed that few reveal any further detail.

For a more systematic approach, we wish to test the hypothesis that some servers are better configured to support caching than others. Using the methodology given in the companion technical report [14], we find in both the cases of standards-compliant freshness lifetime and for the other usable metadata, the test reports p-value = 0.0001. We can conclude that it is highly likely that some servers are better at exposing cache headers than others. Unfortunately, since most Server headers only contain generic values, little can be learnt about these implementations. We note, however, that DBPedia exposes standards-compliant freshness lifetime of 604800 seconds (i.e. 1 week) for both LOD and SPARQL endpoints. DBPedia has historically been updated only a few times a year, but this was probably chosen to avoid making a commitment far into the future. It may provide considerable benefits.

4.2   Other Caching Headers

We also looked for other headers in Table 1. We found `Pragma` (archaic HTTP 1.0 header) in 287 responses, but except for two hosts, where they were superfluous, they were only used to prohibit caching. `Surrogate-Capability` were not observed.

4.3   Distribution of Freshness Lifetime

We obtained a successful response from a total 2965 information resources, either with SPARQL results or RDF data. A successful response is rather strictly defined, not only must there be a successful HTTP response after redirects are resolved, the response must also return a valid RDF media type (unless it is a SPARQL result) and the response must parse into an RDF model. We have given priority to survey many hosts since configuration usually doesn't differ much across a host, especially since it also captures different types of resources. It is therefore acceptable that the number of resources is relatively small.

Since we are interested in the properties of valid response, including examining some of the RDF contained in them, and that web servers may be configured to instruct clients and proxies to cache errors differently, we will study the statistical properties of valid responses.

Standards-Compliant Caching Headers. Of the 2965 resources, 405 returned valid headers, but 114 did so to prohibit caching of the response, and 3 contained conflicting headers, i.e. set a freshness lifetime, but also prohibited caching. In most cases, `Cache-Control` and `Expires` both occurred, but the former is more common than the latter in the cases where only one of them occur. Additionally, 269 resources had a `Cache-Control` header to control other aspects of caching than lifetime, i.e. to say that only private caches may use the response, that the cache must be revalidated, or to prohibit caching. Note that the freshness lifetime is 0 whenever caching is prohibited.

In Fig. 1, there is a barplot where the freshness lifetime is grouped in bins. We see that in these categories, the most common is to prohibit caching. Nevertheless, many also declare a standards compliant freshness lifetime in minutes to days.

In Fig. 2, we have broken this up by the type of resource that was accessed, i.e. SPARQL endpoints, vocabularies, dataset descriptions or unclassified information resources. Firstly, we note that it seems like the distribution of freshness lifetime is quite different for the different types, an observation that is also supported by a similar hypothesis test as above, with a p-value $= 0.00001$ (note, however, that it is more contrived than above, since the bins are like in Fig. 2, which is chosen for intuitive interpretation rather than statistical rigor). Secondly, we note that it is often prohibited to cache dataset descriptions. This is odd, since statistics about datasets is usually costly to compute and should be cached. The VoID specification [4] also notes that the statistics are considered estimates.

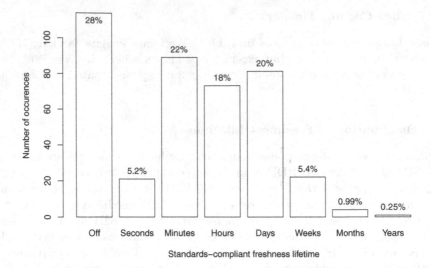

Fig. 1. Barplot counting all standards-compliant freshness lifetimes found, with the percentage of occurrences indicated on the bars. On the horizontal axis, the first bin are the cases where caching is explicitly prohibited. The next bins are for lifetimes, where the values are grouped if they are on the order of seconds, minutes, hours, etc., i.e. the second bin counts the lifetimes in the interval [1,59] seconds, etc. On the vertical axis, the number of times a certain freshness lifetime was found.

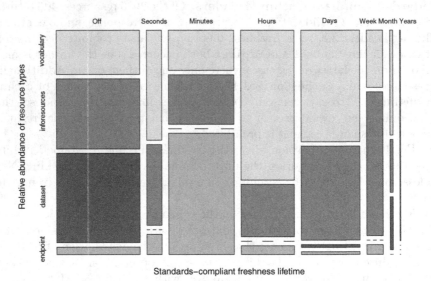

Fig. 2. Mosaic Plot. On the vertical axis, the size of the boxes are determined by the fraction of the types of resources. On the horizontal axis the width of the boxes is proportional to the total counts, using the same bins as in Fig. 1. From bottom to top, light blue boxes denote SPARQL endpoints, dark violet dataset descriptions, orange generic information resources and light orange vocabularies (Color figure online).

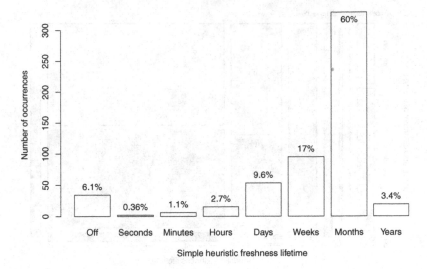

Fig. 3. Barplot counting all simple heuristic freshness lifetimes found. Axes as in Fig. 1.

We also note that prohibition of SPARQL results caching is rare. Amongst the servers that expose caching headers it is common that the result may be cached for some minutes, and closer inspection of the dataset reveals that many of these are due to that RBKExplorer[2] sets an freshness lifetime of 300 s for many endpoints.

Simple Heuristic Freshness Estimates. We next consider the simple heuristic freshness lifetime as suggested in Sect. 4.2.2 in RFC7234 and mentioned in the introduction.

We were able to compute a heuristic lifetime for 554 resources, a larger number than standards-compliant resources. In Fig. 3, we see that the distribution of lifetimes is radically different from the case in Fig. 1. In this case, we may cache many resources for months. Only a handful of resources changed in the last minutes. Since this is based on actual times since last modifications, this suggests that many resources should have had explicit cache headers with very long lifetimes. This is supported by DyLDO [12], which concludes that:

> [...] We found that 62.2 % of documents didn't change over the six months and found that 51.9 % of domains were considered static.

This agrees well with that 60 % of the simple heuristic lifetimes are in the month range.

Moreover, by inspecting Fig. 4, we note that the difference between different types of resources is much smaller. This is confirmed by a hypothesis test that yields p-value = 0.02.

---

[2] http://www.rkbexplorer.com/about/.

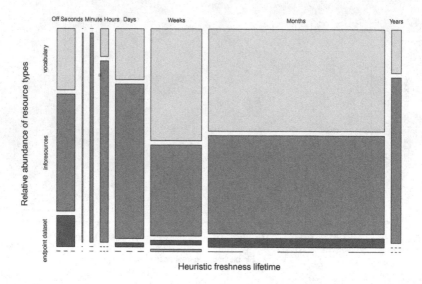

Fig. 4. Mosaic Plot for heuristic freshness lifetime. See caption of Fig. 2 for description.

We find that only one SPARQL endpoint yields a heuristic lifetime, on closer inspection, we find this to be hosted by Dydra[3]. We speculate that this is due to that few underlying DBMS systems help track modification times in a way that can be used on a SPARQL result basis.

Heuristic Freshness from Dublin Core Properties. We noted that the Dublin Core Metadata terms vocabulary has a number of predicates that may become useful in determining heuristic freshness in the future, so we recorded any statements containing the predicates dct:date, dct:accrualPeriodicity, dct:created, dct:issued, dct:modified or dct:valid.

First, we compared dates given in dct:modified to dates given in Last-Modified when both are available for a resource. They were often not the same, but it appeared that dates in the former are further back in time than the latter. We speculated that this may be due to that the web-server tracks semantically insignificant changes through the file system, while authors of RDF only update timestamp when significant changes are made, or it may be that authors forget to update their timestamps.

dct:modified occurred in 2687 triples, but 2487 of these does not have the Request-URI of the information resource as their subject, i.e. it gives the last modification time of some subgraph of the returned RDF. Nevertheless, given its prevalence, it is highly likely that the presence of dct:modified will be useful in determining a heuristic freshness lifetime, as the latest date may be used.

---

[3] http://dydra.com/.

`dct:valid` occurred 21 times, and could be used in lieu of an `Expires` header, but none of these occurrences had a date in the future.

`dct:accrualPeriodicity` occurred only twice, and in neither case contained machine readable data.

`dct:date`, `dct:created` and `dct:issued` were present in 36, 389 and 1475 triples respectively. They correspond roughly to the `Date` header, which is present in all requests, and they are therefore not important, but given their prevalence they could be useful in further analysis.

4.4   Cache Validation

So far, we have considered the case where the client or proxy does not send a HTTP request to the server when a resource that is present in the cache is requested. This is desirable if the client can be sufficiently confident that the response is fresh, either by having a standards-compliant freshness lifetime or a heuristic to determine it. At the end of this period, or if the previous response have no lifetime, due to lack of information, or to that the server has stated so in the `Cache-Control` header, responses must be revalidated. In this case, RFC7232 defines the behaviour, with `ETag` and `Last-Modified` as the relevant response headers.

The BTC had recorded these headers in their data, where 1733 had the `ETag` header and 690 had `Last-Modified` with a great overlap. For the resources where either or both were available, we made our initial request conditional, and 911 responses were verified as still fresh.

In total, 1260 successful initial responses contained an `ETag`, 606 for vocabularies, 117 for datasets, just 12 for endpoints and 525 for unclassified information resources.

To see if the server actually supported conditional requests, and not just merely set the response headers, we made another 1822 requests to the resources that had these headers. Then, we checked if the response code was 200, and the conditional headers had not changed since our initial requests. In 85 cases, conditional requests were not supported according to the standard, no cases for endpoints, 3 for datasets and 23 for vocabularies, 59 for generic information resources.

5   Conclusions and Outlook

We found moderate uptake for HTTP caching and conditional requests in the Semantic Web. We found, in agreement with DyLDO [12], that many resources change at a very slow pace, but also that this is not reflected in the standards-compliant freshness lifetimes advertised by servers.

We found that errors are commonplace, but that they do not usually pertain to the caching headers. We found a small number of self-contradictory `Cache-Control` headers, and some servers that set conditional request response headers, but could not support conditional requests.

It is possible in a substantial number of cases to compute a heuristic freshness lifetime, either from the `Last-Modified` header, or from Dublin Core properties.

For SPARQL endpoints, we found that conditional requests are seldomly supported, but standards-compliant freshness lifetimes have been seen, and since it is supported by DBPedia, benefits from caching may be realised already.

In spite of this, most of the Semantic Web is unhelpful even though it is changing slowly.

5.1   Future Work

In this work, we have only explored the cases where the server is cooperative, in the sense that message data or metadata provides at least a hint of a resource's cacheability. We also noted that the majority of the Semantic Web is unhelpful. Therefore, an interesting direction is to learn the change frequency of resources to use in a heuristic freshness lifetime estimation. However, such work should operate within the loose constraints of Sect. 4.2.2 in RFC7234, and should find its niche when the other techniques described in this paper are unavailable. Once this is done, the correctness of caching headers should be assessed, possibly using contingency tables similar to those in the companion technical report [14].

Investigate whether curated collections such as LOV or SPARQLES contain resources that have different characteristics. Since the different sources we surveyed overlap, this cannot be done with the simple hypothesis test in this paper, but requires more sophisticated statistics.

We found that some implementations are likely better than others, but further understanding of these differences are impeded by the fact that most `Server` headers contained very little information. Future work could seek more sophisticated fingerprinting and understanding of the nature of these differences. With this, it may also be possible to investigate whether expiry times have been set consciously.

Further investigate the suitability of the `dct:modified` property for estimating heuristic freshness lifetime.

Estimating the freshness lifetime is a challenging problem for data owners. It must necessarily include the human users involved in the publishing cycle since they are making a commitment about future changes. Designing user support systems as well as interfaces that fit the publisher's workflow is an important problem.

We believe that [20] and [9] prematurely reject caching in connection to SPARQL. They are correct that currently, query results can only be cached on a per-query basis. Moreover, semantically insignificant changes to a query, such as whitespace or the order of triple patterns in a basic graph pattern, currently causes problems for caches. The latter problem can probably be fixed by developing digest algorithms. Such algorithms exist, but are focused on cryptographical strength, and much simpler algorithms could be used for this problem.

Furthermore, by using similarity measures, like those discussed in [5], shared proxies, e.g. an institutional cache or a Content Delivery Network, can examine queries for frequent subpatterns and proactively prefetch data into a cache to help answer queries on the proxy. A cost model that takes into account several data access methods, those described by [9] as well as the novel work in [20] may be a key ingredient in enabling efficient SPARQL evaluation on the Web.

Even though it is clear that other parts of the Web benefit greatly from caching, and that the potential for HTTP metadata to better reflect actual update practices in the Semantic Web is great, estimating the actual impact of doing so should be a topic for further research.

5.2 Recommendations

It is mainly the objective of this paper to be descriptive, but from the results of this study and on the results of DyLDO, we note that it is highly likely that most cache prohibitions are misguided, and server administrators are advised to turn them off unless they are sure they are required.

Additionally, based in part on the survey, but also on other practical experience, we suggest the following:

In many cases, setting reasonable cache headers is straightforward, and should be done by data owners. Framework authors should make it easy to set the expected lifetime, heeding the metadata association good practice recommendation of [11]. If the author is unable to influence HTTP headers, they should set a `dct:valid` time into the future and make use of `dct:modified`.

To allow generation and validation of `Last-Modified` and `ETag` headers, DBMS authors should make sure it is much cheaper to retrieve the modification time of any subgraph, than to retrieve the subgraph itself. This would be a great improvement for RFC7232-based caching, when revalidation is required. It would also help simple heuristics based caching. Research in that direction has been published in [21].

A change periodicity predicate should be standardized in VoID [4].

All Web cache implementations we have studied have cached responses in the form of a key that identifies a serialized object. For short-term impact, future work should accept this as an architectural constraint.

Acknowledgements. The author would like to thank Jürgen Umbrich and Martin Giese for careful review and critical comments, and Gregory Todd Williams for promptly solving issues in the underlying libraries used in this study, Axel Polleres for encouraging comments and Jonas Smedegaard for proofreading. We also thank the anonymous reviewers for extensive reviews. Finally, many thanks to Helen Murray for linguistic assistance.

References

1. Ager, B., Schneider, F., Kim, J., Feldmann, A.: Revisiting cacheability in times of user generated content. In: INFOCOM IEEE Conference on Computer Communications Workshops, pp. 1–6. IEEE (2010)
2. Baker, T., Vandenbussche, P.-Y., Vatant, B.: Requirements for vocabulary preservation and governance. Libr. Hi Tech **31**(4), 657–668 (2013)

3. Buil-Aranda, C., Hogan, A., Umbrich, J., Vandenbussche, P.-Y.: SPARQL web-querying infrastructure: ready for action? In: Alani, H., Kagal, L., Fokoue, A., Groth, P., Biemann, C., Parreira, J.X., Aroyo, L., Noy, N., Welty, C., Janowicz, K. (eds.) ISWC 2013, Part II. LNCS, vol. 8219, pp. 277–293. Springer, Heidelberg (2013)
4. Cyganiak, R., Zhao, J., Hausenblas, M., Alexander, K.: Describing linked datasets with the VoID vocabulary. W3C note, W3C, March 2011. http://www.w3.org/TR/2011/NOTE-void-20110303/
5. Dividino, R.Q., Gröner, G.: Which of the following sparql queries are similar? why? In: CEUR Workshop Proceedings, vol. 1057 (2013)
6. Fielding, R., Nottingham, M., Reschke, J.: Hypertext transfer protocol (HTTP/1.1): caching. RFC 7234 (Proposed Standard), June 2014
7. Fielding, R., Reschke, J.: Hypertext transfer protocol (HTTP/1.1): conditional requests. RFC 7232 (Proposed Standard), June 2014
8. Fielding, R.T.: Architectural styles and the design of network-based software architectures. Ph.D. thesis, University of California, Irvine (2000)
9. Hogan, A., Gutierrez, C.: Paths towards the sustainable consumption of semantic data on the web. In: AMW. CEUR Workshop Proceedings, vol. 1189 (2014)
10. Ihaka, R., Gentleman, R.: R: A language for data analysis and graphics. J. Comput. Graph. Stat. 5(3), 299–314 (1996)
11. Jacobs, I., Walsh, N.: Architecture of the world wide web, volume one. W3C recommendation, W3C, December 2004. http://www.w3.org/TR/2004/REC-webarch-20041215/
12. Käfer, T., Abdelrahman, A., Umbrich, J., O'Byrne, P., Hogan, A.: Observing linked data dynamics. In: Cimiano, P., Corcho, O., Presutti, V., Hollink, L., Rudolph, S. (eds.) ESWC 2013. LNCS, vol. 7882, pp. 213–227. Springer, Heidelberg (2013)
13. Käfer, T., Harth, A.: Billion triples challenge data set (2014). http://km.aifb.kit.edu/projects/btc-2014/
14. Kjernsmo, K.: Addendum to a survey of HTTP caching on the Semantic Web. Technical report 444, Department of Informatics, University of Oslo, March 2015
15. Lampo, T., Vidal, M.-E., Danilow, J., Ruckhaus, E.: To cache or not to cache: the effects of warming cache in complex SPARQL queries. In: Meersman, R., Dillon, T., Herrero, P., Kumar, A., Reichert, M., Qing, L., Ooi, B.-C., Damiani, E., Schmidt, D.C., White, J., Hauswirth, M., Hitzler, P., Mohania, M. (eds.) OTM 2011, Part II. LNCS, vol. 7045, pp. 716–733. Springer, Heidelberg (2011)
16. Martin, M., Unbehauen, J., Auer, S.: Improving the performance of semantic web applications with SPARQL query caching. In: Aroyo, L., Antoniou, G., Hyvönen, E., ten Teije, A., Stuckenschmidt, H., Cabral, L., Tudorache, T. (eds.) ESWC 2010, Part II. LNCS, vol. 6089, pp. 304–318. Springer, Heidelberg (2010)
17. Nottingham, M., Liu, X.: Edge architecture specification. W3C note, W3C, August 2001. http://www.w3.org/TR/2001/NOTE-edge-arch-20010804
18. Schmachtenberg, M., Bizer, C., Paulheim, H.: Adoption of the linked data best practices in different topical domains. In: Mika, P., Tudorache, T., Bernstein, A., Welty, C., Knoblock, C., Vrandečić, D., Groth, P., Noy, N., Janowicz, K., Goble, C. (eds.) ISWC 2014, Part I. LNCS, vol. 8796, pp. 245–260. Springer, Heidelberg (2014)
19. Parreira, J.X., Umbrich, J., Karnstedt, M., Hogan, A.: Hybrid SPARQL queries: fresh vs. fast results. In: Cudré-Mauroux, P., Heflin, J., Sirin, E., Tudorache, T., Euzenat, J., Hauswirth, M., Parreira, J.X., Hendler, J., Schreiber, G., Bernstein, A., Blomqvist, E. (eds.) ISWC 2012, Part I. LNCS, vol. 7649, pp. 608–624. Springer, Heidelberg (2012)

20. Verborgh, R., Sande, M.V., Colpaert, P., Coppens, S., Mannens, E., de Walle, R.V.: Web-scale querying through linked data fragments. In: Proceedings of the Workshop on Linked Data on the Web Co-Located with the 23rd International World Wide Web Conference (WWW 2014), Seoul, Korea, 8 April 2014
21. Williams, G.T., Weaver, J.: Enabling fine-grained HTTP caching of SPARQL query results. In: Aroyo, L., Welty, C., Alani, H., Taylor, J., Bernstein, A., Kagal, L., Noy, N., Blomqvist, E. (eds.) ISWC 2011, Part I. LNCS, vol. 7031, pp. 762–777. Springer, Heidelberg (2011)

Query Execution Optimization for Clients of Triple Pattern Fragments

Joachim Van Herwegen$^{(\boxtimes)}$, Ruben Verborgh, Erik Mannens,
and Rik Van de Walle

Multimedia Lab – Ghent University – iMinds,
Gaston Crommenlaan 8 Bus 201, 9050 Ledeberg-Ghent, Belgium
joachim.vanherwegen@ugent.be

Abstract. In order to reduce the server-side cost of publishing queryable Linked Data, Triple Pattern Fragments (TPF) were introduced as a simple interface to RDF triples. They allow for SPARQL query execution at low server cost, by partially shifting the load from servers to clients. The previously proposed query execution algorithm uses more HTTP requests than necessary, and only makes partial use of the available metadata. In this paper, we propose a new query execution algorithm for a client communicating with a TPF server. In contrast to a greedy solution, we maintain an overview of the entire query to find the optimal steps for solving a given query. We show multiple cases in which our algorithm reaches solutions with far fewer HTTP requests, without significantly increasing the cost in other cases. This improves the efficiency of common SPARQL queries against TPF interfaces, augmenting their viability compared to the more powerful, but more costly, SPARQL interface.

Keywords: Linked data · SPARQL · Query execution · Query optimization

1 Introduction

In the past few years, there has been a steady increase of available RDF data [10]. If a publisher decides to provide live queryable access to datasets, the default choice is to offer a public SPARQL endpoint. Users can then query this data using the SPARQL query language [5]. The downside of the flexibility of SPARQL is that some queries require significant processing power. Asking a lot of these complex queries can put a heavy load on the server, causing a significant delay or even downtime. Recently, triple pattern fragments (TPF [15]) were introduced as a way to reduce this load on the server by partially offloading query processing to clients. This is done by restricting the TPF server interface to more simple queries. Clients can then obtain answers to complex SPARQL queries by requesting multiple simple queries and combining the results locally. Concretely, a TPF server only replies to requests for a single triple pattern. The response of the server is then a list of matching triples, which can be paged in case the response would be too large. Furthermore, each TPF contains metadata and hypermedia controls to aid clients with query execution.

F. Gandon et al. (Eds.): ESWC 2015, LNCS 9088, pp. 302–318, 2015.
DOI: 10.1007/978-3-319-18818-8_19

The biggest challenge for the client is deciding which triple pattern queries result in the most efficient solution strategy. Since every subquery causes a new HTTP request to the server, minimizing the number of queries reduces the network load and improves the total response time. The algorithm proposed by Verborgh et al. [15] is greedy: at each decision point, clients choose the local optimum by executing the request that has the fewest results. This works fine for certain classes of queries, but others can perform quite badly. In this paper, we therefore propose a new solution that tries to minimize the number of HTTP requests, thus reducing the network traffic, server load, and total response time. We make use of all metadata provided by the TPF server and attempt to predict the optimal query path based on a combination of both metadata and intermediate results.

In Sect. 2, we outline the core concepts of the problem space and relate them to existing work. In Sect. 3, we take a closer look at the problem statement and its necessity. Section 4 introduces our solution for TPF-based query optimization, while an optimized triple store for this algorithm is described in Sect. 5. The results of our work are evaluated in Sect. 6 before concluding in Sect. 7.

2   Core Concepts and Related Work

Since the way queries are executed on the Web depends on the available interfaces on the server side, we first discuss the range of existing interfaces. We then describe different approaches to execute queries over such interfaces.

2.1   RDF Interfaces on the Web

Linked Data Fragments. In order to characterize the many possibilities for publishing Linked Datasets on the Web, *Linked Data Fragments* (LDF [15]) was introduced as a uniform view on all possible Web APIs to Linked Data. The common characteristic of all interfaces is that, in one way or another, they offer specific parts of a dataset. Consequently, by analyzing the parts offered by an interface, we can analyze the interface itself. Each part is called a *Linked Data Fragment*, consisting of:

- **data:** the triples of the dataset that match an interface-specific *selector*;
- **metadata:** triples to describe the fragment itself;
- **controls:** hyperlinks and/or hypermedia forms that lead to other fragments.

The choices made for each of those elements influence the functional and non-functional properties of an interface. This includes the server-side effort to generate fragments, the cacheability of those fragments, the availability and performance of query execution, and the party responsible for executing those queries.

File-Based Datasets. So-called *data dumps* are conceptually the most simple APIs: the *data* consists of all triples in the dataset. They are combined into a (usually compressed) archive and published at a single URL. Sometimes the archive contains *metadata*, but *controls*— with the possible exception of HTTP URIs in RDF triples— are not present. Query execution on these file-based datasets is entirely the responsibility of the client; obtaining up-to-date query results requires re-downloading the entire dataset periodically or upon change.

SPARQL Endpoints. The SPARQL query language [5] allows to express very precise selections of triples in RDF datasets. SPARQL endpoints [4] allow the execution of SPARQL queries on a dataset through HTTP. A SPARQL fragment's *data* consists of triples matching the query (assuming the CONSTRUCT form); the *metadata* and *control* sets are empty. Query execution is performed entirely by the server, and because each client can ask highly individualized requests, the reusability of fragments is low. This, combined with complexity of SPARQL query execution, likely contributes to the low availability of public SPARQL endpoints [3].

Triple Pattern Fragments. The triple pattern fragments API [14] interface has been designed to minimize server-side processing, while at the same time enabling efficient live querying on the client side. A fragment's *data* consists of all triples that match a specific triple pattern, and can possibly be paged. Each fragment page mentions the estimated total number of matches to allow for query planning, and contains hypermedia controls to find all other triple pattern fragments of the same dataset. Since requests are less individualized, fragments are more likely to be reused across clients, which increases the benefit of caching [14]. Because of the decreased complexity, the server does not necessarily require a triple store to generate fragments, which enables less expensive servers.

2.2   Query Execution Approaches

Server-Side Query Processing. The traditional way of executing SPARQL queries is to let the server handle the entire query processing. The server hosts the triple store containing all the data, and is responsible for parsing and executing queries. The client simply pushes a query and receives the results. Several research efforts focus on optimizing how servers execute queries, for example, by using heuristics to predict the optimal join path [13], or by rewriting to produce a less complex query [11]. Quite often, these interfaces are made available through public SPARQL endpoints, with varying success [3]. Another downside is that it is unclear which queries servers can execute, as not all servers support the complete SPARQL standard [3].

Client-Side Query Processing. Hartig [6] surveyed several approaches to client-side query processing, in particular *link-traversal-based querying*. The only assumption for such approaches is the existence of *dereferencing*, i.e., a server-side API such that a request for a URL results in RDF triples that describe the corresponding entity. SPARQL queries are then solved by dereferencing known URLs inside of them, traversing links to obtain more information. While this approach works with a limited server-side API, querying is slow and not all queries can be solved in general.

Hybrid Query Processing. With hybrid query processing approaches, clients and servers each solve a part of a SPARQL query, enabling faster queries than link-traversal-based strategies, yet lower server-side processing cost than that of SPARQL endpoints. One such strategy is necessary when the server offers a triple pattern interface: complex SPARQL queries are decomposed into triple patterns by clients [14]. While this reduces server load, it means that clients must execute more complex queries themselves. In this paper, we devise an optimized algorithm for TPF-based querying.

Federated Query Processing. Executing federated queries requires access to data on multiple servers. The problems pertaining to this include source selection, i.e., finding which servers are necessary to solve a specific query, and executing the query in such a way that network traffic and response time is minimized [7,9,12]. Our approach similarly aims to reduce the number of HTTP requests. The difference is again the type of queries allowed by the interface. While federated systems similarly require splitting up the query depending on the content of the servers, it is still assumed these servers answer to complete SPARQL queries.

3   Problem Statement

As mentioned in Sect. 1, the greedy algorithm to execute SPARQL queries against triple pattern fragments [14] performs badly in several situations. For instance, consider the query in Listing 1.1, taken from the original TPF paper [15].

```
SELECT ?person ?city WHERE {
    ?person a dbpedia-owl:Architect.              # p₁:      ±1,200 triples
    ?person dbpprop:birthplace ?city.             # p₂:    ±430,000 triples
    ?city dc:subject dbpedia:Capitals_in_Europe.  # p₃:         57 triples
}
```

Listing 1.1. SPARQL query to find European architects

The example shows how many matches the server indicates when requesting the first page of each triple pattern. Between different TPF servers, the *page size* (number of triples per request) can vary. Assuming a page size of 100, the results of p_3 fit on the first page. The greedy algorithm would thus start from the triples from p_3, map all of its ?city bindings to p_2 (57 cities with an average of 750 people per city $\approx \pm 430$ calls), then map all ?person bindings to p_1 ($\pm 43,000$ calls). A more efficient solution would be to download all triples from p_1 (12 calls) and join them locally with the values of p_2, thus reducing the total number of calls from $\pm 43,440$ to ± 440.

The problem is that because of the limited information, we cannot know in advance what the optimal solution would be, which means heuristics will be necessary. The algorithm we will propose next tries to find a more efficient solution by looking for a global optimum instead of a local one, and this while emitting results in a streaming way.

4   Client-Side Query Execution Algorithm

To find the optimal queries to ask the server, we need to maximize the utility of all available metadata, which becomes increasingly available as responses arrive. During every iteration, we re-evaluate the choices made based on new data from the server. Decisions are based on estimates, which are updated continuously.

Like typical client-side querying approaches [6], our optimization focuses on Basic Graph Pattern (BGP) queries. Filters, unions, and other non-BGP elements are applied locally to the results of these BGP components. For generality, we assume all triple patterns in the BGP are connected through their variables; if not, Cartesian joins can connect independent parts. The algorithm consists of (1) an initialisation, and an iteration of (2) selection; (3) reading; (4) propagation; (5) termination.

4.1   Initialization

During initialization, we try to use the available information to make our initial assumptions. Information is still sparse at this point: TPFs only contain an estimated match count of each triple pattern. Using these counts, we try to predict which patterns would be best to start. Once the algorithm is iterating, these predictions will be updated based on new data we receive.

Triple Pattern Roles. Our goal is to find all relevant triples for every triple pattern and then join these locally. The algorithm assigns one of two ways to obtain relevant triples for a pattern, called the *role* of a pattern.

Patterns with the *download* role—simply called **download patterns**—are the most straightforward option. To receive download pattern data, we request the corresponding triple pattern from the server. The server replies with a page of initial triples and a link to the next page. By continuously requesting the remaining pages, we obtain all matches. An advantage of this role is that each new HTTP request results in a full page of data, which is the highest possible number of results per request.

In contrast, **bind patterns** are dependent on the results of other patterns. They bind values to one of their variables, hence the name. For each binding that arrives from upstream, the client sends a request to the server for the bound triple pattern (which is then subsequently treated as a download pattern). The total number of HTTP requests needed for this role depends on the number of bound values and on the average number of triples per binding. If the number of bindings is low, the bind role potentially uses significantly less HTTP requests to retrieve all relevant triples. If, on the other hand, the number of bindings is high, using a download pattern would be more efficient.

To clarify these roles, consider the example in Listing 1.1. Assuming we already obtained all the European capitals from p_3, we then have to choose a role for p_2. Choosing the download role amounts to sending the pattern p_2 to the server and requesting its pages. Assuming a page size of 100, this requires $\pm 4,300$ requests. The bind role would bind the variable ?city to the local list of European capitals. We would then send all these bound patterns (e.g., ?person `dbpprop:birthplace dbpedia-owl:Amsterdam, ?person dbpprop:birthplace dbpedia-owl:Athens...`) to the server and request all their pages. In this case, this results in a total of ± 430 calls—10 times less than if we chose the download role.

Initial Role Assignment. The role choice for each pattern has a big influence on the number of HTTP requests. Unfortunately, the initial count metadata provides almost no knowledge about the data properties of each pattern. In general, we can decide *after* having executed the query which solution would have been best. At runtime, we are thus forced to make assumptions for role assignment. Our initial role assignment is purposely simple, as can be seen in Algorithm 1. We make use of the following multiple helper functions and sets.

P A query's BGP, consisting of triple patterns $t_0, \ldots, t_n$.

V All variables in P.

R $\{download\} \cup \{bind_v \mid v \in V\}$

vars(t) $P \to 2^V$ All variables in the given triple pattern

count(t) $P \to \mathbb{N}$ The total match estimate for the given triple pattern

role(t) $P \to R$ The role of a pattern

All $bind_v$ patterns bind their variable v to values found by other patterns. Since not all patterns can depend on each other, we need at least one download pattern. We choose the smallest pattern to be our initial download pattern, which is the best possible choice given the initial knowledge. Each remaining pattern is assigned a $bind_v$ role for a specific v, since bind patterns are often a lot more efficient than download patterns. We will show later how to update roles at runtime in case this assumption is proven wrong.

Supply Graph. A pattern t *supplies* values for a variable v if $v \in$ vars(t) and role$(t) \neq bind_v$. A pattern t is *supplied* by a variable v if role$(t) = bind_v$. If a pattern is supplied by a variable and has no other variables, we say it *filters* that variable. These filter patterns provide no new values; they can only be used to check if the bindings found so far are valid. Using these definitions we can introduce the *supply graph*.

A supply graph visualizes the dependencies between different patterns. The supply graph in Fig. 1 is the result of applying Algorithm 1 to the query in Listing 1.2. These dependencies will be used multiple times by the algorithm.

```
SELECT ?person ?city WHERE {
  ?club a dbpedia-owl:SoccerClub;
        dbpedia-owl:ground ?city.
  ?player dbpedia-owl:team ?club;
          dbpedia-owl:birthPlace ?city.
  ?city dbpedia-owl:country dbpedia:Spain.
}
```

Listing 1.2. SPARQL query: Spanish soccer players

Data: A basic graph pattern $P = \{t_0, \ldots, t_n\}$.
Result: Values for the role function.

1 $t_{min} := \arg\min_{t \in P} \text{count}(t)$
2 $\text{role}(t_{min}) := download$
3 $V_{update} := \text{variables}(t_{min})$
4 $V_{used} := \emptyset$
5 **while** $|V_{update}| > 0$ **do**
6      $v_{update} := $ pop first element of V_{update}
7      $V_{used} := V_{used} \cup \{v_{update}\}$
8   **for** $t \in P$ **do**
9   **if** $v_{update} \in \text{vars}(t) \wedge \text{role}(t)$ is undefined **then**
10             $\text{role}(t) := bind_v$
11             $V_{update} := V_{update} \cup (\text{vars}(t) \setminus V_{used})$
12 **return** role

Algorithm 1. Initial pattern role assignment

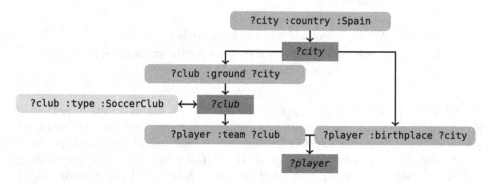

Fig. 1. Supply graph after applying Algorithm 1 to Listing 1.2. The top node is a download pattern; the double-sided arrow indicates a filter pattern.

Extended Initial Role Assignment. The supply graph allows us to improve upon the naive role assignment of Algorithm 1. Therefore, Algorithm 2 extends the initial role assignment algorithm, using this helper function:

$\text{suppliers}(v)$ $V \rightarrow 2^P$ The suppliers for the given variable.

The main purpose of this extended role assignment is to improve our initial assignments. Although suboptimal role assignment would be detected at runtime, this would take some time, increasing the wait until the first results.

The changes are twofold. Firstly, if a pattern has a much lower count than the patterns that supply its bound variable, we change its role to download. The underlying assumption is that even if only 1 in 100 (empirically chosen) bindings can be matched between the suppliers, it would still be more efficient to download this pattern upfront. Secondly, we check whether it would be more efficient to bind a pattern to one of its other variables. If the suppliers of its other variable have a lower count, we assume there will exist fewer bindings for that variable.

Data: P and role from Algorithm 1
Result: An updated role assignment role$'$.
1   role$'$:= role
2   **do**
3   role := role$'$
4   **for** $t \in \{t \in P \mid \text{role}(t) \neq download\}$ **do**
5         $v := v'$ such that $\text{role}(t) = bind_{v'}$
6   **if** $\forall s \in \text{suppliers}(v) : \text{count}(t) < \frac{\text{count}(s)}{100}$ **then**
7   role$'(t) := download$
8   **else**
9             $v_{min} := \arg\min_{v' \in \text{vars}(t)} \min_{s \in \text{suppliers}(v')} \text{count}(s)$
10   role$'(t) := bind_{v_{min}}$
11   **while** role$' \neq$ role
12   **return** role$'$

Algorithm 2. Extended initial pattern role assignment

Pattern Dependencies. During execution, multiple patterns might be bound to the same variable. Binding all known accepted values for that variable to both patterns would be wasteful: there is no need for the second pattern to check a binding rejected by the first. To solve this, we introduce *pattern dependencies*. These are all preceding patterns a value has to "pass through" before it can be used by a pattern. This is done by generating an ordered list of patterns, using the ordering $\prec \subset P \times P$ defined below.

We define $\forall t, t' \in P$:

- $\text{role}(t) = download \land \text{role}(t') \neq download \Rightarrow t \prec t'$
- $\exists v \in V : v \in \text{vars}(t') \land t \in \text{suppliers}(v) \land t' \notin \text{suppliers}(v) \Rightarrow t \prec t'$
- If ordering not implied by previous rules: $\text{count}(t) < \text{count}(t') \Rightarrow t \prec t'$

This ordering gets applied to the output of Algorithm 2. Algorithm 3 then uses this sorted list to generate the dependencies for a bind pattern. We take all patterns from the ordered list preceding the given pattern. Because of the way this list is structured, this includes all patterns that directly or indirectly supply that pattern.

4.2 Selection

This is the first iterative step of the algorithm and assumes we have all the information that was generated during the initialization phase. Every iteration we download triples from a single pattern. The choice of which pattern we download from is obviously quite important: if we only download triples for a single pattern we won't reach results for the full query. Hence we try to estimate which pattern has the highest chance of providing new results with more triples. We do this by first finding local optima: for every variable we find the pattern that would improve the results for that variable the most. Afterwards, we find the global optimum among them, which would provide the best result for the query.

Data: An ordered list of triple patterns P_o.
        A bind pattern $t \in P_o$ with bound variable $v \in V$.
Result: A list of patterns $D(t) \subset P_o$ corresponding to the dependencies of t.
1 $P'_o :=$ the subset of patterns from P_o preceding t.
2 $D(t) :=$ suppliers(v)
3 $D' := D(t)$
4 **do**
5 $\quad$ $D(t) := D'$
6 $\quad$ $V' := \bigcup_{t' \in D(t)} \text{vars}(t')$
7 $\quad$ $D'_{new} := \{t' \in P'_o \setminus D(t) \mid \text{vars}(t') \cap V' \neq \emptyset\}$
8 $\quad$ $D' := D(t) \cup D'_{new}$
9 **while** $D(t) \neq D'$
10 **return** $D(t)$

Algorithm 3. Calculating pattern dependencies

Locally Optimal Patterns. First, we determine for every variable which pattern we need to download triples from to get more bindings for that variable. The reason for this is that as soon as we get more bindings for a variable, we can use these in all other patterns containing that variable, bringing us closer to a solution for the query. We only add a binding to a variable if each of its suppliers and filter patterns have a triple containing that binding. We can only know that these triples exist if we downloaded them previously, which is why it is important to choose the correct pattern to download from.

We go through four steps to find our local optimum:

1. Start with all the suppliers and filter patterns of the variable.
2. Remove patterns that cannot supply new values. These are bind patterns that have no (unused) bindings.
3. If there are still filter patterns remaining, return one of these.
4. If not, return the pattern that has downloaded the least triples so far.

We prioritize filter patterns since having a value for a filter pattern means it already passed all other (non-filter) suppliers. After that, we verify the download count to ensure no supplier is ignored.

Globally Optimal Pattern. Because of the previous step, we now have a single pattern for every variable. First, we filter out any pattern that has a supply path going to any of the other patterns in the list of results, as described in Fig. 1. If there are still multiple patterns remaining, we pick the one with the smallest number of stored triples.

We prioritize patterns on the bottom of the supply graph for the same reason we prioritize filter patterns: if a value reaches that point, it has already passed preceding patterns, increasing the odds of this value leading to a query result.

4.3   Reading

Once we have chosen a triple pattern, we fetch its results through a single HTTP request. For download patterns, this involves downloading the first page of triples we did not encounter yet. For bind patterns, we check if there is a page remaining for the current binding. In that case we download the next page. If not, we bind a new stored value to the bound variable and download the first page of that pattern. These new triples are then stored in a local triple store.

4.4 Propagation

The previous step added new triples to the local triple store. We now want to use these triples to improve our results in the next iteration. For bind patterns, this means finding new values which can be used as bindings. We do this by executing a query on the local triple store per bind pattern, consisting of all the dependencies of the pattern, as described in Algorithm 3.

Cost Estimation. At this point we also want to verify if our pattern role assumptions were correct. Maybe we made a mistake during initialization because of the limited information. To do this we introduce the following functions:

G	The set of ground triples.
triples(t)	$P \to 2^G$ Triples downloaded so far for the given pattern
pagesize(t)	$P \to \mathbb{N}$ The page size for the given pattern
avgTriples(t)	$P \to \mathbb{N}$ Average triple count per binding (detailed later)
valCount(t)	$P \to \mathbb{N}$ Number of bind values found so far for the pattern

Even though the algorithm has already performed several HTTP requests, it might still be more efficient to let a pattern switch roles. To verify this, we need to estimate how many HTTP requests are still required to finish a bind pattern and compare that to the number of requests needed if the pattern were a download pattern $\left(\text{which is } \left\lceil \frac{\text{count}(t)}{\text{pagesize}(t)} \right\rceil\right).$

To estimate the number of requests for a bind pattern, we start by estimating how many values will be bound to its variable. We use the following function to estimate the total number of requests needed for a bind pattern t:

(average pages per binding for t)

$\cdot$(percentage of supplier triples that contain a new binding)

$\cdot$(total number of supplier triples)

We estimate these values with the following functions:

$$\max\left(1, \left\lceil \frac{\text{avgTriples}(t)}{\text{pagesize}(t)} \right\rceil \right) \cdot \max\left\{ \frac{\text{valCount}(t)}{|\text{triples}(t')|} \cdot \text{count}(t') \,\middle|\, t' \in \text{suppliers}(t) \right\}$$

In case we did not find any values yet, we assume the estimate to be ∞, but we do not change the pattern role. This formula looks at the number of values we found compared to the total number of triples downloaded so far. We assume this ratio will be stable for the remaining triples we download. This assumption might be too strong, which is why we re-evaluate it at every iteration. We take the maximum value of these estimates to compensate for the fact that some patterns might have already downloaded more triples than others.

The function avgTriples is an estimate of how many triples are returned per variable binding for this pattern: we need to take into account that a single bound value might have multiple pages that need to be downloaded. This is done by looking at the values we already bound so far. We take the average number of triples for these values and assume this represents the average of future values. Because wrong estimates can substantially skew the results, we only trust the estimate after having acquired multiple counts. We only trust the result if the estimate remains within the margin of error after adding a new value, assuming a Gaussian distribution and a 95 % level of confidence. Similarly as before, if we have no values to estimate, or we do not trust the estimate, we assume it to be ∞ without changing the pattern role.

After these steps, we have an estimate for the number of requests of a bind pattern and can compare it to the number of requests if it was a download pattern. If our estimates indicate that continued use of the bind pattern would require at least 10 % more requests (empirically chosen) than switching to the download role, we change its role and update the supply graph.

Intermediate Results. To find intermediate results to the query, we execute the complete query on our local triple store. This will return all answers to the query that can be found using the triples we have downloaded so far. We do this after every iteration to see if we found new results during that iteration. By using the techniques described in Sect. 5, we minimize the local computation time.

4.5   Termination

Once all download patterns finished retrieving all their pages, and all bind patterns finished all their bindings, the algorithm terminates. All results found so far, which have been emitted in a streaming way, form the response to the query.

5   Local Triple Store

Due to the nature of the algorithm, many similar or even identical queries are executed against a client's local triple store. For example, in the *Intermediate results* step we need to execute the complete query to find new results. During every *Propagation* step we execute a query for each pattern. This query contains the dependencies of the the pattern and is thus a subquery of the complete query. A standard triple store might cache repeated queries, but this does not serve our purpose since the data changes every iteration. We instead want to maximize reuse of previous query results. For repeated queries, this means *storing* the results of intermediate steps. For queries where one is a subquery of the other, this means *sharing* the intermediate steps. At every iteration of the algorithm, we only download new triples for a single triple pattern. This causes the local database, as well as the intermediate query results, to only change slightly. While related work on such specialized caching exists [8], we can cache even more efficiently since we have substantially more information about the queries that will be executed on the store. We introduce helper functions for our local triple store algorithm, explained in depth in the next paragraphs.

C		The set of *cache entries* (described below).
B		The set of *bindings*. A binding maps one or more variables $v \in V$ to a value.
cache(P')	$2^P \to C$	The cache entry corresponding to the patterns, or an empty entry if not used before
patterns(c)	$C \to 2^P$	The patterns in the given cache entry. Inverse of the cache function
bindings(c)	$C \to 2^B$	The bindings stored in the cache entry
tripleCounts(c)	$C \to (P \to \mathbb{N})$	Function that the value of $|triples(t)|$ when the cache entry was last updated
binding$_t(g)$	$G \to B$	Transforms a triple g to a binding based on the given pattern $t \in P$
ids(b)	$B \to (P \to \mathbb{N})$	The indices stored for the given binding
join(B', B'')	$(B \times B) \to B$	Joins the two given sets of bindings

Our triple store consists of two data components: the *cache entries* (C) and the ground *triples* (G). For every pattern, we store the triples in the order they were downloaded, which means we can associate an index with each of them. We will use these indices (ids(b)) to determine which results can be reused. The cache entries represent these intermediate results. Whenever we calculate a set of bindings B' for a set of patterns $P' \subseteq P$, we store them in the cache object cache(P'). Besides the bindings, the cache entry also stores $|triples(t)|$ for every $t \in P'$ (tripleCounts(c)). This allows us to identify which triples have been downloaded since the last time this cache entry was used. When we generate a binding from a triple (binding$_t(x)$), that binding also includes which pattern the triple belongs to and what its index is for that pattern. If we join bindings (join(B', B'')), the indices are also joined.

Algorithm 4 describes the process of executing a query on our local triple store. For clarity, we have used less strict notions of lists and sets, preferring legibility over mathematical rigor. When performing the query, we try to maximize the amount of data we reuse. We also try to order the uncached patterns to minimize the size of the join operations. During the join process we split the triples for the current pattern in two sets G_{old} and G_{new}. G_{old} represents the triples that were already used in a previous iteration to create bindings for the current cache entry. Similarly, we split the bindings from the *previous* cache entry c_{prev} in B'_{used} and B'_{unused}. B'_{unused} contains the bindings that were not used to create the bindings in the *current* cache entry because they did not exist at the time. To do a full join between our results so far and the triples of the current pattern, we would have to calculate $(G_{old} \cup G_{new}) \times (B'_{used} \cup B'_{unused})$. Since we store old results in our

Data: A list of triple patterns P.

Result: All corresponding bindings.

1   $C_{valid} := \{c \in C \mid \forall t \in \text{patterns}(c) : |\text{triples}(t)| = \text{tripleCounts}(c)_t\}$

2   $c_{best} := \arg\max_{c \in C_{valid}} |\text{patterns}(c)|$

3   $P_{uncached} := P \setminus \text{patterns}(c_{best})$

4   Sort the patterns $t \in P_{uncached}$ by $\text{count}(t)$.

5   Move all patterns in $P_{uncached}$ that have changed since the previous iteration to the back, maintaining relative ordering.

6   $V := \bigcup_{t \in \text{patterns}(c_{best})} \text{vars}(t)$

7   **if** $V = \emptyset$ **then**

8 | $V := \text{vars}(\text{head}(P_{uncached}))$.

9   $P'_{uncached} := [\,]$

10 **while** $|P'_{uncached}| < |P_{uncached}|$ **do**

11 | $t_{min} := \text{head}(\{t \in P_{uncached} \setminus P'_{uncached} \mid \text{vars}(t) \cap V \neq \emptyset\})$

12 | $P'_{uncached} := P'_{uncached} \cup [t_{min}]$

13 | $V := V \cup \text{vars}(t_{min})$

14 $c_{prev} := c_{best}$

15 $P' := \text{patterns}(c_{best})$

16 **for** $t \in P'_{uncached}$ **do**

17 | $P' := P' \cup \{t\}$

18 | $c := \text{cache}(P')$

19 | $B'_{unused} := \{b \in \text{bindings}(c_{prev}) \mid \exists t' \in P' : \text{ids}(b)_{t'} > \text{tripleCounts}(c)_{t'}\}$

20 | $G_{old} := \{\text{binding}_t(g_i) \mid g_i \in \text{triples}(t) \wedge i < \text{tripleCounts}(c)_t\}$

21 | $G_{new} := \{\text{binding}_t(g_i) \mid g_i \in \text{triples}(t) \wedge i \geq \text{tripleCounts}(c)_t\}$

22 | $B_{old} := \text{join}(B'_{unused}, G_{old})$

23 | $B_{new} := \text{join}(\text{bindings}(c_{prev}), G_{new})$

24 | $B := \text{bindings}(c) \cup B_{old} \cup B_{new}$

25 | $\text{bindings}(c) := B$

26 | $c_{prev} := c$

27 **return** $\text{bindings}(c_{prev})$

Algorithm 4. Cached triple store algorithm

cache entries, we already have a part of this join: $G_{old} \times B'_{used}$ corresponds to the results stored in cache entry ($= \text{bindings}(c)$). If we also calculate $G_{old} \times B'_{unused}$ ($= B_{old}$) and $G_{new} \times (B'_{used} \cup B'_{unused})$ ($= B_{new}$) we have a full join of these two sets of bindings, while limiting the number of joins that need to be executed.

6   Evaluation

To evaluate our implementation, we executed a set of SPARQL queries using both the original greedy implementation [14] and our proposed algorithm. Since our goal was to reduce execution time by minimizing the number of HTTP requests, we measured both execution time and the number of HTTP requests per query. We also calculated the time and requests until we found the first result. To precisely control network latency, the server and client ran on the same machine (Intel Core i5-3230 M CPU at 2.60 GHz with 8 GB of RAM). To simulate the time

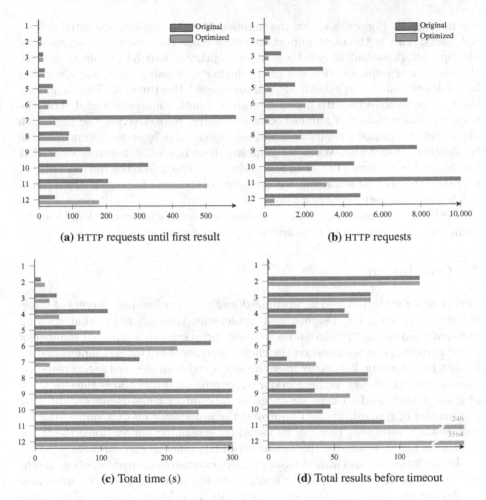

(a) HTTP requests until first result   **(b)** HTTP requests

(c) Total time (s)   **(d)** Total results before timeout

Fig. 2. Results of WatDiv queries, grouped by number of triple patterns in the BGP

it might take a server to respond to a client over the internet, we introduced an artificial delay of 100 ms on the server. We used a query timeout of 5 min and noted how many results (and HTTP requests) were found up to that point.

The WatDiv benchmark was designed to stress test and compare multiple SPARQL query algorithms using only BGP queries [1,2]. This makes WatDiv perfectly suited for our evaluation, since the two algorithms focus on BGP queries. We used a set of ±1,000 queries that were generated for the WatDiv stress test [1] against the WatDiv dataset of 10 million triples. We clustered the queries based on the number of triple patterns in the query, ranging from 1 to 12. The median results can be seen in Fig. 2.

Figure 2a shows how many HTTP requests were executed before a first result was found. This shows that in most of the cases the optimizations of our algorithm focusing on quickly finding results help in reducing the HTTP requests for the first result. Figure 2b shows the number of HTTP requests executed during the query. This is the most important graph since this was the main focus of our optimizations and as can be seen, our optimizations had a big impact on the number of requests. Because of the higher processing time, our algorithm has a lower call count if both algorithms exceed the timeout. This is mostly the case in the queries with a higher pattern count. Figures 2c and d show the total execution time and number of results found respectively. Note that both algorithms guarantee a complete result set; observed differences are entirely due to the timeout of 5 min. When we combine these figures, it becomes clear that our algorithm performs better in the majority of cases. For the queries with 12 patterns, the original algorithm has a median of 0 results because it often timed out before even getting its first result.

Both our evaluation code[1] as our complete evaluation result logs[2] can be found online to repeat the tests and interpret the results.

7   Conclusion

In this paper we introduced an optimized way to query low-cost servers of triple pattern fragments. We designed and implemented an algorithm that uses all metadata present in TPFs to find a solution for queries in a minimal number of HTTP requests. The workload on the client increases, but this is compensated by fewer HTTP requests. Especially in environments with an elevated server response time or network latency, is this a major improvement. It also allows the execution of queries that used to take an excessive amount of time. Besides improving the queries in general, we also improved the amount of effort required until a first result is returned. This can be useful for streaming applications: the faster a result is found, the faster the remainder of the pipeline can continue.

In the future we also want do make a more extensive comparison of our methods and those already existing for generic SPARQL and SQL query optimization.

An obvious possible improvement is parallelism. Multiple parts of the algorithm can be done in parallel. For example, we can download triples for multiple patterns at the same time instead of just a single pattern at a time. The multiple queries we execute on our local database can also be executed in parallel, although care has to be taken when accessing the cache entries. Besides that, the algorithm can still be improved in multiple ways: the local triple store can generate better join trees or have even better caching, the prediction of which pattern to download from can be improved, etc.

A remaining optimization is to detect those cases where a greedy algorithm would provide more results faster (at the cost of more HTTP requests). Furthermore, our algorithm mainly focuses on BGP queries. Other queries constructs are supported, but not optimized. While BGPs are the most essential part of a query, in the future, our algorithm could be extended by taking the other components into account. For example, limits could be incorporated in the estimations of

---

[1] http://github.com/LinkedDataFragments/Client.js/tree/query-optimization.

[2] http://github.com/LinkedDataFragments/QueryOptimizationResults.

total HTTP requests still needed, and pattern-specific filters could be processed early on. Although we have not arrived at a complete TPF solution yet, the algorithm introduced here drastically increases the scope of efficiently supported queries.

References

1. Aluç, G., Hartig, O., Özsu, M.T., Daudjee, K.: Diversified stress testing of RDF data management systems. In: Mika, P., Tudorache, T., Bernstein, A., Welty, C., Knoblock, C., Vrandečić, D., Groth, P., Noy, N., Janowicz, K., Goble, C. (eds.) ISWC 2014, Part I. LNCS, vol. 8796, pp. 197–212. Springer, Heidelberg (2014)
2. Aluç, G., Özsu, M.T., Daudjee, K., Hartig, O.: Chameleon-db: a workload-aware robust RDF data management system. Technical report CS-2013-10, University of Waterloo (2013). https://cs.uwaterloo.ca/~galuc/papers/chameleon-db-research.pdf
3. Buil-Aranda, C., Hogan, A., Umbrich, J., Vandenbussche, P.-Y.: SPARQL web-querying infrastructure: ready for action? In: Alani, H., Kagal, L., Fokoue, A., Groth, P., Biemann, C., Parreira, J.X., Aroyo, L., Noy, N., Welty, C., Janowicz, K. (eds.) ISWC 2013, Part II. LNCS, vol. 8219, pp. 277–293. Springer, Heidelberg (2013)
4. Feigenbaum, L., Williams, G.T., Clark, K.G., Torres, E.: SPARQL 1.1 protocol. Recommendation, World Wide Web Consortium (March 2013). http://www.w3.org/TR/sparql11-protocol/
5. Harris, S., Seaborne, A.: SPARQL 1.1 query language. Recommendation, World Wide Web Consortium (March 2013). http://www.w3.org/TR/sparql11-query/
6. Hartig, O.: An overview on execution strategies for linked data queries. Datenbank-Spektrum 13(2), 89–99 (2013)
7. Hartig, O., Bizer, C., Freytag, J.-C.: Executing SPARQL queries over the web of linked data. In: Bernstein, A., Karger, D.R., Heath, T., Feigenbaum, L., Maynard, D., Motta, E., Thirunarayan, K. (eds.) ISWC 2009. LNCS, vol. 5823, pp. 293–309. Springer, Heidelberg (2009)
8. Martin, M., Unbehauen, J., Auer, S.: Improving the performance of semantic web applications with SPARQL query caching. In: The Semantic Web: Research and Applications (2010)
9. Quilitz, B., Leser, U.: Querying distributed RDF data sources with SPARQL. In: Bechhofer, S., Hauswirth, M., Hoffmann, J., Koubarakis, M. (eds.) ESWC 2008. LNCS, vol. 5021, pp. 524–538. Springer, Heidelberg (2008)
10. Schmachtenberg, M., Bizer, C., Paulheim, H.: Adoption of the linked data best practices in different topical domains. In: Mika, P., Tudorache, T., Bernstein, A., Welty, C., Knoblock, C., Vrandečić, D., Groth, P., Noy, N., Janowicz, K., Goble, C. (eds.) ISWC 2014, Part I. LNCS, vol. 8796, pp. 245–260. Springer, Heidelberg (2014)
11. Schmidt, M., Meier, M., Lausen, G.: Foundations of SPARQL query optimization. In: Proceedings of the 13th International Conference on Database Theory, pp. 4–33. ACM (2010)
12. Schwarte, A., Haase, P., Hose, K., Schenkel, R., Schmidt, M.: FedX: optimization techniques for federated query processing on linked data. In: Aroyo, L., Welty, C., Alani, H., Taylor, J., Bernstein, A., Kagal, L., Noy, N., Blomqvist, E. (eds.) ISWC 2011, Part I. LNCS, vol. 7031, pp. 601–616. Springer, Heidelberg (2011)

13. Stocker, M., Seaborne, A., Bernstein, A., Kiefer, C., Reynolds, D.: SPARQL basic graph pattern optimization using selectivity estimation. In: Proceedings of the 17th International Conference on World Wide Web, pp. 595–604 (2008)
14. Verborgh, R., Hartig, O., De Meester, B., Haesendonck, G., De Vocht, L., Vander Sande, M., Cyganiak, R., Colpaert, P., Mannens, E., Van de Walle, R.: Querying datasets on the web with high availability. In: Mika, P., Tudorache, T., Bernstein, A., Welty, C., Knoblock, C., Vrandečić, D., Groth, P., Noy, N., Janowicz, K., Goble, C. (eds.) ISWC 2014, Part I. LNCS, vol. 8796, pp. 180–196. Springer, Heidelberg (2014)
15. Verborgh, R., Vander Sande, M., Colpaert, P., Coppens, S., Mannens, E., Van de Walle, R.: Web-scale querying through linked data fragments. In: Proceedings of the 7th Workshop on Linked Data on the Web, April 2014

Natural Language Processing and Information Retrieval

LIME: The Metadata Module for OntoLex

Manuel Fiorelli[1], Armando Stellato[1](✉), John P. McCrae[2],
Philipp Cimiano[2], and Maria Teresa Pazienza[1]

[1] ART Research Group, University of Rome "Tor Vergata", Rome, Italy
{fiorelli, stellato, pazienza}@info.uniroma2.it
[2] Cognitive Interaction Technology Center of Excellence,
University of Bielefeld, Bielefeld, Germany
{jmccrae, cimiano}@cit-ec.uni-bielefeld.de

Abstract. The OntoLex W3C Community Group has been working for more than three years on a shared lexicon model for ontologies, called *lemon*. The *lemon* model consists of a core model that is complemented by a number of modules accounting for specific aspects in the modeling of lexical information within ontologies. In many usage scenarios, the discovery and exploitation of linguistically grounded ontologies may benefit from summarizing information about their linguistic expressivity and lexical coverage by means of metadata. That situation is compounded by the fact that *lemon* allows the independent publication of ontologies, lexica and lexicalizations linking them. While the VoID vocabulary already addresses the need for general metadata about inter-linked datasets, it is unable by itself to represent the more specific metadata relevant to *lemon*. To solve this problem, we developed a module of *lemon*, named LIME (Linguistic Metadata), which extends VoID with a vocabulary of metadata about the ontology-lexicon interface.

Keywords: Ontolex · Metadata · Ontologies · Natural language · Discovery

1 Introduction

Ontologies and widely shared vocabularies are the cornerstone of the Semantic Web as they provide the basis for interoperability as well as for reasoning, consistency detection, etc. Yet, the grounding of ontology and vocabulary elements in natural language is crucial to ensure communication with humans [1]. Enriching ontologies and Semantic Web vocabularies with information about how the vocabulary elements are expressed in natural language is crucial to support tasks such as ontology mediation [2] as well as in all tasks in which natural language needs to be interpreted with respect to a formal vocabulary or ontology (e.g. question answering [3, 4], ontology-based information extraction [5], ontology learning [6]) or in which natural language descriptions need to be generated from a given ontology or dataset [7–9].

A number of models have been proposed to enrich ontologies with information about how vocabulary elements are expressed in different natural languages, including the Linguistic Watermark framework [10, 11], LexOnto [12], LingInfo [13], LIR [14], LexInfo [1] and more recently *lemon* [15].

© Springer International Publishing Switzerland 2015
F. Gandon et al. (Eds.): ESWC 2015, LNCS 9088, pp. 321–336, 2015.
DOI: 10.1007/978-3-319-18818-8_20

The OntoLex W3C Community Group[1] has the goal of providing an agreed-upon standard by building on the aforementioned models, the designers of which are all involved in the community group. Additionally, linguists have acknowledged [16] the benefits that the adoption of the Semantic Web technologies could bring to the publication and integration of language resources. As such, the Open Linguistics Working Group[2] of the Open Knowledge Foundation is contributing to the development of a LOD (Linked Open Data) (sub)cloud of linguistic resources.[3]

These complementary efforts by Semantic Web practitioners and linguists are in fact converging, as the ontology lexicon model provides a principled way [17] to encode even notable resources such as the Princeton WordNet [18, 19] and other similar ones (which we will refer to hereafter as wordnets) for other languages.

The *lemon* model envisions an open ecosystem in which ontologies[4] and lexica for them co-exist, both of which are published as data on the Web. It is in line with a many-to-many relationship between: (i) ontologies and ontological vocabularies, (ii) lexicalization datasets and (iii) lexical resources. While an OWL T-Box consists essentially of classes and properties, a lexicon mainly consists of a collection of lexical entries. Lexicalizations in our sense are reifications of the relation between an ontology reference and the lexical entries by which these can be expressed within natural language. *lemon* foresees an ecosystem in which many independently published lexicalizations and lexica for a given ontology co-exist. Within such an ecosystem, it is crucial to support the discovery of lexica and lexicalizations for a given ontology according to a number of criteria. Relevant criteria in choosing a particular lexicalization or lexicon include the following:

- **Vocabulary Coverage:** How many vocabulary elements of a given ontology are covered by at least one lexicalization in the lexicon?
- **Language Coverage:** How many natural languages are covered in the lexicon?
- **Variation:** How many different lexicalizations are there per vocabulary element?
- **Linguistic Model:** Which model is used to express lexicalizations for vocabulary elements (rdfs:label, skos/skosxl:{pref,alt,hidden}Label, *lemon*, LexInfo, etc.?)

When data are immediately accessible, it may be the case that relevant metadata can be computed automatically by statistical profiling. However, its explicit representation through a dedicated vocabulary is still useful for many reasons. Firstly, it promotes architectural clarity, by separating metadata gathering and exploitation. Concerning the latter, available approaches include symbolic manipulation of structured metadata, as well its use in the construction of a feature space for the application of machine learning algorithms. The second advantage of explicit metadata is that metadata can be computed once and be reused multiple times, possibly avoiding computationally

---

[1] http://www.w3.org/community/ontolex/.

[2] http://linguistics.okfn.org/.

[3] http://nlp2rdf.lod2.eu/OWLG/llod/llod.svg.

[4] It would be more appropriate to adopt the term "reference dataset" (including thus also SKOS thesauri and datasets in general), to express data containing the logical symbols for describing a certain domain. In line with the traditional name OntoLex (and thus the ontology-lexicon dualism), we will however often refer to them with the term ontology.

intensive queries over the actual data. In fact, the reuse of pre-computed metadata opens it up the possibility of aggregating metadata in Web accessible repositories that can answer queries expressed through the metadata vocabulary.

In this paper, we introduce LIME (**Li**nguistic **Me**tadata), the metadata vocabulary for the *lemon* model. The paper is structured as follows: in the next Sect. 2 we discuss related work, mainly related to the representation of metadata. Section 3 briefly introduces the Lexicon Model for Ontologies (*lemon*) reflecting the current agreements of the OntoLex community group. Section 4 introduces requirements on the metadata vocabulary, and Sect. 5 presents the actual vocabulary. In Sect. 6, we sketch an application scenario for the model in the context of ontology mediation or alignment. We conclude in Sect. 7.

2 Related Work

Semantic Web practitioners have accepted the necessity of metadata describing the interlinked datasets themselves (e.g. what is it about? [20]), rather than focusing only on the description of entities in the universe of discourse.

VoID (Vocabulary of Interlinked Datasets) [21] satisfied the need for a machine-understandable coarse-grained description of the LOD as a whole, by defining a vocabulary of metadata about datasets and their interconnections, as well as mechanisms to publish, locate and aggregate dataset descriptions. The VoID framework can be extended for different usages. VOAF (Vocabulary of a Friend)[5] is one such extension, supporting the description of OWL ontologies and RDFS schemas. VOAF distinguishes various types of dependencies between vocabularies, supports the categorization of vocabularies, and defines statistical metrics relevant to vocabularies (e.g. number of classes). VOAF can be complemented with modules providing additional metadata (e.g. the preferred prefix). Currently, the LOV (Linked Open Vocabularies)[6] service exploits VOAF metadata to support the navigation and discovery of vocabularies and to understand their relationships. LOV mashes up the data provided by LODStats [22] on the usage of vocabularies in the LOD.

DCAT (Data Catalog Vocabulary) [23] is a related vocabulary for the description of data catalogs on the Semantic Web, aiming at improving their discoverability and supporting federated queries across them. While DCAT is agnostic with respect to data models/formats, it is possible to combine it with other format-specific vocabularies, such as VoID in the case of RDF datasets.

In the field of HLT (Human Language Technology), structured metadata supports the reuse of Language Resources (LRs). The OLAC (Open Language Archives Community) [24] metadata model provides a template for the description of LRs, by extending the Dublin Core Metadata Element Set.[7] Supported metadata includes, among others, provenance metadata, resource typology and language identification.

---

[5] http://purl.org/vocommons/voaf.

[6] http://lov.okfn.org/.

[7] http://dublincore.org/documents/dces.

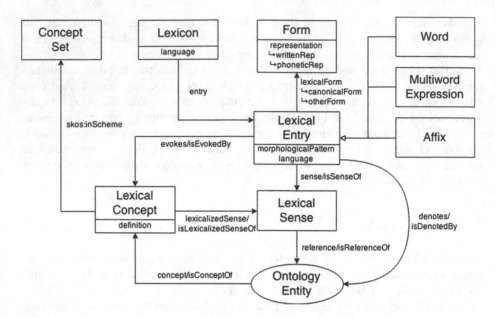

Fig. 1. The Lemon/OntoLex Model as presented in the Ontolex Final Model Specification, and available at: http://www.w3.org/community/ontolex/wiki/Final_Model_Specification. For some properties the inverse is denoted as 'property/inverse property'; only the direction of the first property is indicated in the diagram.

OLAC is intended to specialize the general infrastructure provided by OAI (Open Archives Initiative) [25], which supports the federation of archives and the aggregation of the associated metadata.

While OLAC aims to define a distributed infrastructure for resource sharing, LRE Map [26] is a crowd-sourced catalog of LRs, initially fed by authors submitting papers to LREC Conferences. LRE Map defines numerous resource types and usage applications, whilst OLAC distinguishes only a handful of types. Similar in scope to OLAC, META-SHARE [27] has its own metadata schema. These works commit to a definition of LR that includes both software tools (e.g. part of speech taggers and parsers) and data (e.g. corpora, dictionaries and grammars) expressed in different formats. Because of their broad coverage, these works fail to provide specific metadata for the description of the relationship between ontologies and lexica, which is the core of OntoLex. Moreover, these works are not specifically tailored to the description of Semantic Web datasets, nor do they fit the metadata ecosystem that is being developed on the Semantic Web through initiatives such as VoID and DCAT.

Starting from previous works about metadata for linguistic resources [10], we filled this gap by proposing a standard (LIME) that extends VoID to provide descriptive statistics at the level of the lexicon-ontology interface, in particular for the *lemon* model developed by the OntoLex community group. The model we present here represents a refined version of the initial proposal [28] that was seeded to the community before *lemon* was finalized.

3   The *Lemon*/OntoLex Model

The *lemon* model (see Fig. 1) developed by the OntoLex community group is based on the original *lemon* model, which by now has been adopted by a number of lexica [29–32], and as such was taken as the basis of the OntoLex community group to develop an agreed-upon and widely accepted model. The *lemon* model is based onto the idea of a separation between the lexical and the ontological layer following Buitelaar [33] and Cimiano et al. [34], where the ontology describes the semantics of the domain and the lexicon describes the morphology, syntax and pragmatics of the words used to express the domain in a language. The model thus organizes the lexicon primarily by means of *lexical entries*, which are a word, affix or multiword expression with a single syntactic class (part-of-speech) to which a number of *forms* are attached, such as for example the plural, and each form has a number of *representations* (*string forms*), e.g. written or phonetic representation. Entries in a lexicon can be said to *denote* an entity in an ontology, however normally the link between the lexical entry and the ontology entity is realized by a *lexical sense* object where pragmatic information such as domain or register of the connection may be recorded.

In addition to describing the meaning of a word by reference to the ontology, a lexical entry may be associated with a *lexical concept*. Lexical concepts represent the semantic pole of linguistic units, and are the mentally instantiated abstractions which language users derive from conceptions [35]. Lexical concepts are intended primarily to represent such abstractions when present in existing lexical resources, e.g. synsets for wordnets. An example of a lexical entry lexicalizing the property knows in the FOAF (Friend of a Friend) vocabulary (http://xmlns.com/foaf/spec/) is as follows:

```
:acquainted_with a ontolex:LexicalEntry;
   lexinfo:partOfSpeech lexinfo:adjective;
   ontolex:canonicalForm :acquainted_form;
   synsem:synBehavior :acquainted_adjective_frame;
   ontolex:sense :acquainted_with_sense.

:acquainted_form a ontolex:Form;
   ontolex:writtenRep "acquainted"@en.

:acquainted_adjective_frame a lexinfo:AdjectivePPFrame;
   lexinfo:coplativeArg :acquainted_adjective_arg1;
   lexinfo:prepositionalObj :acquainted_adjective_arg2.

:acquainted_with_sense ontolex:reference foaf:friend;
   synsem:subjOfProp :acquainted_adjective_arg1;
   synsem:objOfProp :acquainted_adjective_arg2.

:acquainted_adjective_arg2 synsem:marker :with;
   synsem:optional "false"^^xsd:boolean .

:with a ontolex:LexicalEntry;
   ontolex:canonicalForm :with_form .

:with_form ontolex:writtenRep "with"@en .
```

The *lemon* model is structured into a core module (ontolex prefix in the example above) and four additional modules. Firstly, the *syntax and semantics* (synsem prefix) module describes the syntactic usage of a frame and furthermore how this syntax can be mapped into logical representations, as well as further conditions that may affect whether a word can be used for a concept in the ontology. This mapping is based on a proven mechanism for representing the meaning of ontological concepts with lexical elements [36]. The second module is concerned with *decomposition* of terms into their component elements, that is either the decomposition of multiword elements into individual words, or of synthetic words into individual lexemes. The next module is the *variation* module that describes how terminological and lexical variants and relations may be stated and in particular how we can represent translations of terms taking into account a meaning of a word in an ontology. The final module is the *metadata* module described in this paper.

4   Requirements for the Metadata Module

The design of LIME has been informed by the following requirements, which express information that is relevant to different use-cases and applications.

R1. *Compatibility with the lemon model.*
R2. *Compatibility with other lexicalization models,* such as RDFS, SKOS (Simple Knowledge Organization System), SKOS-XL (SKOS eXtension for Labels).
R3. *Distributed publication* of each component of the ontology-lexicon interface.
R4. *Encoding.* It must provide metadata describing how content is encoded.
R5. *Content summarization.* It must provide summaries about the dataset content.
R6. *Reuse of existing vocabularies.*

5   The Metadata Vocabulary

The LIME vocabulary (see Fig. 2) we present here, though inspired by the proposal in [28], is in fact very different because of the need for a better alignment with the overall scope of the working group and for accommodating the flexible publication scenario envisaged by *lemon*.

Following the conceptual model of the ontology-lexicon interface defined by *lemon* (see Requirement R1), we distinguish at the metadata level three entities:

1. the ontology (bearing semantic information),
2. the lexicon (bearing linguistic information),
3. the set of lexicalizations (intended as the mere correspondences between logical entities in the ontology and lexical entries in the lexicon).

From the perspective of a metadata vocabulary, LIME focuses on the representation of the relation between these three entities and summaries and descriptive statistics concerning these entities and their relations (see Requirement R5).

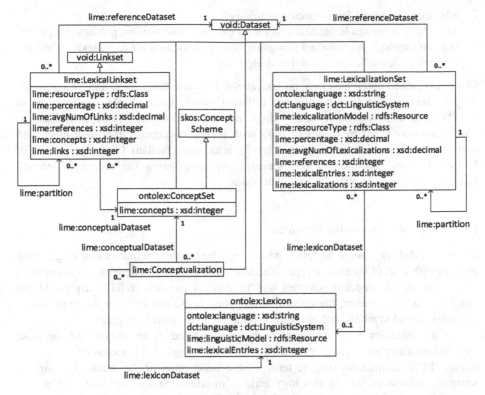

Fig. 2. The LIME Model

The three entities (ontology, lexicon and lexicalization set) are regarded as instances of void:Dataset. While the *lemon* model introduces a subclass of void: Dataset to represent lexica (ontolex:Lexicon), no such subclass exists for lexicalizations. LIME introduces such a subclass, lime:LexicalizationSet, to describe the relation between the lexicon and the ontology in question. A lime: LexicalizationSet object thus holds all the relevant metadata and descriptive statistics about the lexicalizations that relate ontology elements in the ontology to lexical entries (possibly found in a lexicon).

Moving away from our original assumption that lexicalizations are embedded within an ontology, we allow each entity to be published independently or combined with others into a single resource (see Requirement R3). By allowing this freedom, we support the following scenarios:

1. a lexicon is published as a stand-alone resource, independently of any specific ontology. We further distinguish the following two cases:
   (a) an ontology contains a set of lexicalizations by means of entries in the lexicon (thus ontology + lexicalization as a single data source)
   (b) an ontology exists independently of the lexicon, and a third party publishes a lexicalization of the ontology by adopting the above lexicon (thus all the three datasets are separate entities)

2. a lexicon is created for a specific ontology:
   (a) the lexicon and lexicalizations for an existing ontology are published together.
   (b) an ontology is published alongside with its lexicon (ontology, lexicon and the set of lexicalizations published together).

Obviously, since ontologies may be lexicalized for more languages, and as a general-purpose lexicon may be reused across different ontologies, multiple combinations of the above cases may happen for any single resource. Finally, linguistic enrichment of ontologies may occur by means of links with lexical concepts, rather than links with specific lexical entries, as suggested by Pazienza and Stellato [37]. The notion of Lexical Linkset accounts for this scenario, by specializing the notion of void: Linkset to make explicit its linguistic value.

5.1   Describing (Domain) Datasets

From the LIME viewpoint, any RDF dataset may be lexicalized in a natural language or aligned with a set of lexical concepts. The term dataset is meant hereafter to encompass ontologies, SKOS concept schemes and in general any set of RDF triples. In the ontology-lexicon dualism, the dataset corresponds to the ontology, in the sense that it provides formal symbols that need for grounding in a natural language.

At the metadata level, a dataset is then represented as an instance of the class void:Dataset or a more specific subclass, e.g. voaf:Vocabulary for vocabularies. LIME defines no specific term for the description of the dataset bearing the semantic references for the ontology-lexicon interface. Still, it suggests the use of appropriate metadata terms suggested by the VoID specification (see Requirement R6). For instance, in the following excerpt:

```
<http://xmlns.com/foaf/0.1/> a voaf:Vocabulary;
    foaf:homePage <http://xmlns.com/foaf/0.1/>;
    dct:title "The Friend of a Friend (FOAF) Vocabulary"@en;
    void:dataDump <http://xmlns.com/foaf/spec/index.rdf>;
    voaf:classNumber 13;
    voaf:propertyNumber 62 .
```

we declare an instance of voaf:Vocabulary describing the FOAF vocabulary. In the example, we show how to provide the name of the vocabulary, its home page (providing a unique key supporting data aggregation), a download file and the count of classes and properties. In the previous example, we followed LOV when reusing the URI of FOAF to provide additional metadata. This approach requires the publication of metadata via a SPARQL endpoint or some other API (Application Programming Interface). Alternatively, one can create a new URI for the metadata instance, so that it can be dereferenced. Meanwhile, the connection to the vocabulary is established via an owl:sameAs axiom, or some other uniquely identifying property.

5.2   Describing Lexica

A lexicon comprises a collection of lexical entries in a given natural language, and is generally independent from the semantic content of ontologies. The class `ontolex:Lexicon` represents lexica in both the core (data) and metadata levels of the OntoLex specification. This class extends `void:Dataset`, such that recommendations from the VoID specification apply.

Perhaps the most important fact about a lexicon is the language it refers to, an explicit marker for applicability of the resource in given scenarios. This information can be represented either as a literal (according to ISO 639 [38]) through property `ontolex:language` or as a resource (through the property `dct:language`), using any of the vocabularies assigning URIs to languages (e.g. http://www.lexvo.org/, http://www.lingvoj.org/, http://id.loc.gov/). The following example describes an English lexicon:

```
ex:myLexicon a ontolex:Lexicon;
   ontolex:language "en";
   dct:language <http://lexvo.org/id/iso639-3/eng>;
   void:dataDump <http://example.org/lexicon/dump.rdf>;
   void:sparqlEndpoint <http://example.org/lexicon/sparql>;
   void:triples 10000 .
```

The description above contains terms from VoID (see Requirement R6), e.g. to provide a data dump and a SPARQL endpoint. An agent may choose between the available types of access based on various criteria: (i) the suitability of the local triple store for handling the advertised number of triples, (ii) the necessity of specialized processing not provided by the SPARQL endpoint, (iii) the willingness to avoid stressing the data provider with frequent/complex queries.

To support the actual exploitation of a lexicon, LIME supports metadata about the way a lexicon has been encoded (see Requirement R4). The reason is that *lemon* does not commit to a specific catalog of linguistic categories (e.g. part-of-speech), whereas it defers to the user the choice of a specific catalog. The adopted catalog may be indicated as a value of the property `lime:linguisticModel`. This property is defined as a subproperty of `void:vocabulary`, to better qualify the specific association between the lexicon and the ontology providing linguistic categories. For instance, we can say that `ex:myLexicon` uses LexInfo2 as repository of linguistic annotations:

```
ex:myLexicon a ontolex:Lexicon;
   lime:linguisticModel <http://www.lexinfo.net/ontology/2.0/lexinfo>
```

An important metric indicating the usefulness of a lexicon is the number of lexical entries it contains (see Requirement R5):

```
ex:myLexicon lime:lexicalEntries 13 .
```

5.3   Describing Lexicalization Sets

We use the term lexicalization for the reified relation between a lexical entry and the ontological meaning it denotes. A collection of such lexicalizations is modeled by the class lime:LexicalizationSet, which in turn subclasses void:Dataset. For example, the property foaf:knows can be lexicalized as "X is friend of", "X knows Y", "X is acquainted with X" etc., all corresponding to different lexicalizations.

A lime:LexicalizationSet is characterized (as an ontolex:Lexicon) by the natural language it refers, which can be indicated via the properties already used for the same purpose within ontolex:Lexicon. Moreover, a lime:Lexical-izationSet may play an associative function, as it may relate a dataset with a lexicon providing lexical entries. The properties lime:referenceDataset and lime:lexiconDataset point to the dataset and the lexicon, respectively. The presence of explicit links with the dataset and lexicon will allow metadata indexes answering queries that seek, as an example, a lexicalization set in a natural language for a given dataset (see Requirement R3). This is an example of an English lexicalization set for FOAF utilizing an OntoLex lexicon:

```
ex:LexicalizationSet a lime:LexicalizationSet;
   ontolex:language "en";
   dct:language <http://lexvo.org/id/iso639-3/eng>;
   lime:referenceDataset <http://xmlns.com/foaf/0.1/>;
   lime:lexiconDataset ex:myLexicon .
```

The mandatory property lime:referenceDataset tells which dataset the lex-icalization is about. Similarly, the optional property lime:lexiconDataset holds a reference to the lexicon being used. This optionality allows supporting previous lexi-calization models (see Requirement R2) that rely on plain literals (e.g. RDFS and SKOS) or introduce reified labels (e.g. SKOS-XL), but in any case have no separate notion of lexicon. It is thus necessary to introduce the mandatory property lime:lexi-calizationModel, which holds the model used in a specific lexicalization set (see Requirement R4). We may say, for instance, that FOAF has an embedded lexicalization set expressed in RDFS:

```
<http://xmlns.com/foaf/0.1/> void:subset ex:embedLexSet .
ex:embedLexSet a lime:LexicalizationSet;
   ontolex:language "en";
   lime: lexicalizationModel <http://www.w3.org/2000/01/rdf-schema#>
```

Knowing that a dataset is lexicalized in a given natural language does not guarantee that the available linguistic information is useful. In particular, the value of a lexi-calization set may be assessed by means of metrics (see Requirement R5). For instance, in the following excerpt:

```
:myItalianLexicalizationOfFOAF a lime:LexicalizationSet;
   ontolex:language "it";
   lime:referenceDataset <http://xmlns.com/foaf/0.1/>;
   lime:lexicalizationModel ontolex:;
   lime:lexiconDataset :italianWordnet;
   lime:partition [
      lime:resourceType owl:Class;
      lime:percentage 0.75;
```

```
    lime:avgNumOfLexicalizations 3.54;
    lime:references 13;
    lime:lexicalEntries 46;
    lime:lexicalizations 46
].
```

the property `lime:partition` (domain: `lime:LexicalizationSet` ⊔ `lime:LexicalLinkset`) points to a `lime:LexicalizationSet`, which is the subset of the lexicalization set dealing exclusively with instances of the class referenced by `lime:resourceType`. The properties `lime:references` and `lime:lexicalEntries` hold, respectively, the number of entities from the reference dataset and the number of lexical entries from the lexicon that participate in at least one lexicalization, while `lime:lexicalizations` holds the total number of lexicalizations. Additionally, `lime:avgNumOfLexilicazions` gives the average number of lexicalizations per resource, while `lime:percentage` indicates the ratio of resources having at least one lexicalization. There is a certain level of redundancy among these properties, so that it is at the discretion of the publisher to choose a number of properties. For instance, if metadata for the lexicalized ontology is not available, then it is mandatory to provide ratios (such in the above example), whereas clients can combine counts (if available from both the lexicalization and the reference datasets) in order to compute them.

5.4 Describing Lexical Concept Sets

The class `ontolex:ConceptSet` is a subclass of `void:Dataset` that defines a collection of `ontolex:LexicalConcepts`. It holds LIME-specific and other dataset-level metadata. Lexical concepts are instances of `skos:Concept` (as `ontolex:LexicalConcept` is a subclass of `skos:Concept`). In fact, following the pattern already adopted for the lexicon, we combined the concept scheme with the concept set, by making the latter a subclass of the former. It is possible to summarize the content of a concept set (see Requirement R5), by reporting (via the property `lime:concepts`) the total number of lexical concepts in a concept set. Beyond the need for such summarizing information, the rationale for the class `ontolex:ConceptSet` is to support the publication of lexical concepts as a separate dataset (see Requirement R3). This, in turn, allows the independent publication of the linguistic realization of those concepts in different natural languages, e.g. several wordnets sharing the synsets from the English WordNet. However, *lemon* and LIME are also compatible with the approach to multilingual wordnets, in which each wordnet has its own set of synsets, while an inter-language index establishes a mapping between them. In the following excerpt, we define a `void:Linkset` providing `skos:exactMatch` mappings between two `ontolex:ConceptSets` (defined elsewhere):

```
:ItalianWN_EnglishWN_index a void:Linkset;
    void:subjectsTarget ex:ItalianWN;
    void:objectsTarget ex:EnglishWN;
    void:linkPredicate skos:exactMatch .
```

5.5   Describing Conceptualizations

A lime:Conceptualization is a dataset relating a set of lexical concepts to a lexicon, indicated by the properties lime:conceptualDataset and lime:lexiconDataset, respectively. In the representation of wordnets, it plays a role like that of a lime:LexicalizationSet for the ontology lexicalization. A different class has been introduced, since the association between lexical concepts and words is different from the lexicalization of ontology concepts.

In addition to the explicit references to the lexicon and the lexical concept set, a conceptualization holds a number of resuming metadata (see Requirement R5). The properties lime:lexicalEntries and lime:concepts hold the number of lexical entries and lexical concepts that have been associated, respectively.

5.6   Describing Lexical Link Sets

An interesting use of wordnets is to enrich an ontology with links to lexical concepts, which may provide a less ambiguous inter-lingua (than natural language, which has inherent lexical ambiguity) for the task of ontology matching.

To represent a collection of these links, we introduced lime:LexicalLinkset, which extends void:Linkset with additional metadata tailored to this specific type of linking. The properties lime:referenceDataset and lime:conceptual-Dataset clearly distinguish between the different roles that the linked datasets play from the perspective of the *lemon* model, whereas properties from the VoID vocabulary only deal with lower-level features, e.g. to which dataset the subjects of the link belong to. Similarly to the case of lime:LexicalizationSet, the property lime:partition references a lime:LexicalLinkset dealing with a given resource type. Due to the lack of space, we will not provide specific examples for the relevant metrics. However, they are analogous to the ones already discussed for lexicalization sets, expect for the fact they now refer to links rather than lexicalizations.

6   A Use-Case: Ontology Matching

Ontology matching is the task of finding a set of correspondences between a pair of input ontologies. Although ensemble strategies – combining different kinds of matching techniques based on terminology, structure, extension and models of the compared resources – dominate evaluation campaigns, lexical comparison [2] is the basic step providing the initial "anchors" for further analysis performed through those techniques. While matchers can certainly find out how and in which languages labels are expressed by analyzing the data to determine the matching techniques to be applied, descriptive summaries of the linguistic characteristics of the ontologies in question would save computation time, making this information directly accessible.

We focus here on the activities that a coordinator needs to perform beforehand in order to define a successful mediation strategy. Linguistic metadata have been shown to be useful in support coordination activities in a semi-automatic process [39].

LIME metadata about the input ontologies allows the coordinator to estimate their level of linguistic compatibility, which in turn indicates how easily they can be matched. If the coordinator finds at least one pair of lexicalizations that sufficiently cover the ontologies, then it may use them to perform the match. When multiple lexicalizations exist, the coordinator may exclude those that do not sufficiently cover the input ontologies, or it could assign different weights to the scores computed with respect to each of them. Similarly, a coordinator may consider whether the input ontologies have been enriched with links to lexical concepts found in the same wordnet, which provide a less ambiguous inter-lingua than natural language (see Sect. 5.6).

The explicit linguistic metadata about the input ontologies allow the coordinator to reason upon them, and determine an appropriate matching strategy by applying some heuristics. The greatest benefit of an explicit metadata vocabulary is that it supports access to previously unknown information. Indeed, using LIME it would be possible to locate relevant data from remote repositories.

Such metadata aggregation would benefit from the protocols that VoID specifies to support the independent publication of dataset descriptions in a predictable way. The fact that LIME is an extension of VoID entails that the same protocols may support harvesting of LIME metadata. Moreover, the same services that aggregate and make available VoID descriptions in general should also support LIME metadata as well.

7 Conclusions and Future Work

We presented LIME, a vocabulary developed in the context of the Ontolex group, providing metadata terms specifically relevant to *lemon*. The publication of such metadata alongside the corresponding datasets intends to foster their discoverability, understandability and exploitability. LIME provides metadata terms related to the core module of *lemon*. Future work will probably include development of extensions dealing with other *lemon* modules. A question for future work is how to include aspects related to the quality of linguistic resources as metadata.

The URI of the LIME ontology is: http://www.w3.org/ns/lemon/lime and it is currently available at:

   https://github.com/cimiano/ontolex/blob/master/Ontologies/lime.owl.

Acknowledgements. This research has been partially supported by the EU funded project SemaGrow (http://www.semagrow.eu/) under grant agreement no: 318497 and by the EU funded project LIDER (http://www.lider-project.eu).

References

1. Cimiano, P., Buitelaar, P., McCrae, J., Sintek, M.: LexInfo: a declarative model for the lexicon-ontology interface. Web Seman. Sci. Serv. Agents World Wide Web 9(1), 29–51 (2011)
2. Pazienza, M.T., Sguera, S., Stellato, A.: Let's talk about our "being": a linguistic-based ontology framework for coordinating agents. Appl. Ontology Spec. Issue Formal Ontol. Commun. Agents 2(3–4), 305–332 (2007)

3. Unger, C., Freitas, A., Cimiano, P.: An introduction to question answering over linked data. In: Koubarakis, M., Stamou, G., Stoilos, G., Horrocks, I., Kolaitis, P., Lausen, G., Weikum, G. (eds.) Reasoning Web. LNCS, vol. 8714, pp. 100–140. Springer, Heidelberg (2014)
4. Atzeni, P., Basili, R., Hansen, D.H., Missier, P., Paggio, P., Pazienza, M.T., Zanzotto, F.M.: Ontology-based question answering in a federation of university sites: the moses case study. In: Meziane, F., Métais, E. (eds.) NLDB 2004. LNCS, vol. 3136, pp. 413–420. Springer, Heidelberg (2004)
5. Basili, R., Vindigni, M., Zanzotto, F.M.: Integrating ontological and linguistic knowledge for conceptual information extraction. In: IEEE/WIC International Conference on Web Intelligence, Washington (2003)
6. Cimiano, P.: Ontology Learning and Population from Text Algorithms, Evaluation and Applications XXVIII. Springer, Heidelberg (2006)
7. Bouayad-Agha, N., Casamayor, G., Wanner, L.: Natural language generation in the context of the semantic web. Seman. Web 5(6), 493–513 (2014)
8. Bontcheva, K., Wilks, Y.: Automatic report generation from ontologies: the MIAKT approach. In: Meziane, F., Métais, E. (eds.) NLDB 2004. LNCS, vol. 3136, pp. 324–335. Springer, Heidelberg (2004)
9. Galanis, D., Androutsopoulos, I.: Generating multilingual descriptions from linguistically annotated OWL ontologies: the NaturalOWL system. In: Proceedings of the Eleventh European Workshop on Natural Language Generation, Stroudsburg, pp. 143–146 (2007)
10. Pazienza, M.T., Stellato, A., Turbati, A.: Linguistic watermark 3.0: an RDF framework and a software library for bridging language and ontologies in the semantic web. In: 5th Italian Semantic Web Workshop on Semantic Web Applications and Perspectives (SWAP 2008), FAO-UN, Rome, Italy, 15–17 December 2008
11. Oltramari, A., Stellato, A.: Enriching ontologies with linguistic content: an evaluation framework. In: The Role of OntoLex Resources in Building the Infrastructure of Web 3.0: Vision and Practice (OntoLex 2008), Marrakech, Morocco, 31 May 2008
12. Cimiano, P., Haase, P., Herold, M., Mantel, M., Buitelaar, P.: LexOnto: a model for ontology lexicons for ontology-based NLP. In: Proceedings of the OntoLex 2007 Workshop (held in conjunction with ISWC 2007) (2007)
13. Buitelaar, P., Declerck, T., Frank, A., Racioppa, S., Kiesel, M., Sintek, M., Engel, R., Romanelli, M., Sonntag, D., Loos, B., Micelli, V., Porzel, R., Cimiano, P.: LingInfo: design and applications of a model for the integration of linguistic information in ontologies. In: OntoLex 2006, Genoa, Italy (2006)
14. Montiel-Ponsoda, E., Aguado-de-Cea, G., Gómez-Pérez, A., Peters, W.: Enriching ontologies with multilingual information. Nat. Lang. Eng. 17, 283–309 (2011)
15. McCrae, J., Aguado-de-Cea, G., Buitelaar, P., Cimiano, P., Declerck, T., Gómez-Pérez, A., Gracia, J., Hollink, L., Montiel-Ponsoda, E., Spohr, D., Wunner, T.: Interchanging lexical resources on the Semantic Web. Lang. Resour. Eval. 46(4), 701–719 (2012)
16. Chiarcos, C., McCrae, J., Cimiano, P., Fellbaum, C.: Towards open data for linguistics: linguistic linked data. In: Oltramari, A., Vossen, P., Qin, L., Hovy, E. (eds.) New Trends of Research in Ontologies and Lexical Resources, pp. 7–25. Springer, Heidelberg (2013). doi:10.1007/978-3-642-31782-8_2
17. McCrae, J., Fellbaum, C., Cimiano, P.: Publishing and linking wordnet using lemon and RDF. In: Proceedings of the 3rd Workshop on Linked Data in Linguistics, Reykjavik, Iceland (2014)
18. Miller, G.: WordNet: a lexical database for english. Commun. ACM 38(11), 39–41 (1995)
19. Fellbaum, C.: WordNet: An Electronic Lexical Database. WordNet Pointers, MIT Press, Cambridge (1998)

20. Jain, P., Hitzler, P., Yeh, P., Verma, K., Sheth, A.: Linked data is merely more data. In: AAAI Spring Symposium: Linked Data Meets Artificial Intelligence (2010)
21. Alexander, K., Cyganiak, R., Hausenblas, M., Zhao, J.: Describing linked datasets with the VoID vocabulary (W3C Interest Group Note). In: World Wide Web Consortium (W3C). http://www.w3.org/TR/void/. Accessed 3 March 2011
22. Auer, S., Demter, J., Martin, M., Lehmann, J.: LODStats – an extensible framework for high-performance dataset analytics. In: ten Teije, A., Völker, J., Handschuh, S., Stuckenschmidt, H., d'Acquin, M., Nikolov, A., Aussenac-Gilles, N., Hernandez, N. (eds.) EKAW 2012. LNCS, vol. 7603, pp. 353–362. Springer, Heidelberg (2012). doi:10.1007/978-3-642-33876-2_31
23. W3C: data catalog vocabulary (DCAT). In: World Wide Web Consortium (W3C). http://www.w3.org/TR/vocab-dcat/. Accessed 16 Jan 2014
24. Bird, S., Simons, G.: Extending dublin core metadata to support the description and discovery of language resources. Comput. Humanit. 37(4), 375–388 (2003)
25. Lagoze, C., Van de Sompel, H.: The open archives initiative: building a low-barrier interoperability framework. In: Proceedings of the 1st ACM/IEEE-CS Joint Conference on Digital Libraries, New York, pp. 54–62 (2001)
26. Calzolari, N., Del Gratta, R., Francopoulo, G., Mariani, J., Rubino, F., Russo, I., Soria, C.: The LRE map. Harmonising community descriptions of resources. In: Proceedings of the Eighth International Conference on Language Resources and Evaluation (LREC 2012), Istanbul, Turkey, pp. 1084–1089 (2012)
27. Piperidis, S.: The META-SHARE language resources sharing infrastructure: principles, challenges, solutions. In: Proceedings of the Eighth International Conference on Language, Istanbul, Turkey, pp. 36–42 (2012)
28. Fiorelli, M., Pazienza, M.T., Stellato, A.: LIME: towards a metadata module for ontolex. In: 2nd Workshop on Linked Data in Linguistics: Representing and Linking Lexicons, Terminologies and Other Language Data, Pisa, Italy (2013)
29. Borin, L., Dannélls, D., Forsberg, M., McCrae, J.: Representing swedish lexical resources in RDF with lemon. In: Proceedings of the ISWC 2014 Posters & Demonstrations Track a Track Within the 13th International Semantic Web Conference (ISWC 2014), Riva del Garda, Italy, pp. 329–332 (2014)
30. Ehrmann, M., Cecconi, F., Vannella, D., McCrae, J., Cimiano, P., Navigli, R.: Representing multilingual data as linked data: the case of BabelNet 2.0. In: Proceedings of the Ninth International Conference on Language Resources and Evaluation (LREC-2014), Reykjavik, Iceland, 26–31 May 2014, pp. 401–408 (2014)
31. Eckle-Kohler, J., McCrae, J., Chiarcos, C.: LemonUby - a large, interlinked syntactically-rich lexical resources for ontologies. Semantic Web Journal (2015, accepted)
32. Sérasset, G.: Dbnary: wiktionary as a LMF based multilingual RDF network. In: Proceedings of the Eighth International Conference on Language Resources and Evaluation (LREC-2012), Istanbul, Turkey, 23–25 May 2012, pp. 2466-2472 (2012)
33. Buitelaar, P.: Ontology-based semantic lexicons: mapping between terms and object descriptions. In: Huang, C.-R., Calzolari, N., Gangemi, A., Lenci, A., Oltramari, A., Prevot, L. (eds.) Ontology and the Lexicon: A Natural Language Processing Perspective. Cambridge University Press, Cambridge (2010)
34. Cimiano, P., McCrae, J., Buitelaar, P., Montiel-Ponsoda, E.: On the role of senses in the ontology-lexicon. In: Oltramari, A., Vossen, P., Qin, L., Hovy, E. (eds.) New Trends of Research in Ontologies and Lexical Resources, pp. 43–62. Springer, Heidelberg (2013)
35. Evans, V.: Lexical concepts, cognitive models and meaning-construction. Cogn. Linguist. 17(4), 491–534 (2006)
36. Cimiano, P., Unger, C., McCrae, J.: Ontology-based interpretation of natural language. Synth. Lect. Hum. Lang. Technol. 7(2), 1–178 (2014)

37. Pazienza, M.T., Stellato, A.: An environment for semi-automatic annotation of ontological knowledge with linguistic content. In: Sure, Y., Domingue, J. (eds.) ESWC 2006. LNCS, vol. 4011, pp. 442–456. Springer, Heidelberg (2006)
38. ISO, International organization for standardization: language codes - ISO 639. In: ISO, International Organization for Standardization. http://www.iso.org/iso/home/standards/language_codes.htm
39. Fiorelli, M., Pazienza, M.T., Stellato, A.: A meta-data driven platform for semi-automatic configuration of ontology mediators. In: Calzolari, N., Choukri, K., Declerck, T., Loftsson, H., Maegaard, B., Mariani, J., Moreno, A., Odijk, J., Piperidis, S. (eds.) Proceedings of the Ninth International Conference on Language Resources and Evaluation (LREC 2014), Reykjavik, Iceland, May 2014

Learning a Cross-Lingual Semantic Representation of Relations Expressed in Text

Achim Rettinger$^{(\boxtimes)}$, Artem Schumilin, Steffen Thoma, and Basil Ell

Karlsruhe Institute of Technology (KIT), Karlsruhe, Germany
{rettinger,steffen.thoma,basil.ell}@kit.edu
artem.schumilin@student.kit.edu

Abstract. Learning cross-lingual semantic representations of relations from textual data is useful for tasks like cross-lingual information retrieval and question answering. So far, research has been mainly focused on cross-lingual entity linking, which is confined to linking between phrases in a text document and their corresponding entities in a knowledge base but cannot link to relations. In this paper, we present an approach for inducing clusters of semantically related relations expressed in text, where relation clusters (i) can be extracted from text of different languages, (ii) are embedded in a semantic representation of the context, and (iii) can be linked across languages to properties in a knowledge base. This is achieved by combining multi-lingual semantic role labeling (SRL) with cross-lingual entity linking followed by spectral clustering of the annotated SRL graphs. With our initial implementation we learned a cross-lingual lexicon of relation expressions from English and Spanish Wikipedia articles. To demonstrate its usefulness we apply it to cross-lingual question answering over linked data.

Keywords: Unsupervised relation extraction · Cross-lingual relation clustering · Relation linking

1 Motivation

Due to the variability of natural language, a relation can be expressed in a wide variety of ways. When counting how often a certain pattern is used to express a relation (e.g. which movie is starring which actor), the distribution has a very long tail: frequently used patterns make up only a small fraction; the majority of expressions use rare patterns (see Welty et al., [18]). While it would be possible to manually create patterns for a small set of languages, this would be a tedious task, results would not necessarily be correct, and coverage would most likely be far from optimal due to the size of the long tail. Thus, automatically extracting a set of syntactical variants of relations from text corpora would ease this task considerably.

However, there are numerous challenges associated to automating this task. It is essential to capture the context in which such a pattern applies. Typically, all of the information conveyed in a sentence is crucial to disambiguate the

© Springer International Publishing Switzerland 2015
F. Gandon et al. (Eds.): ESWC 2015, LNCS 9088, pp. 337–352, 2015.
DOI: 10.1007/978-3-319-18818-8_21

meaning of a relation expressed in text. Thus, a rich meaning representation is needed that goes beyond simple patterns consisting of named entity pairs and the string in-between them. Furthermore, semantically related relations need to be detected, grouped and linked to existing formalized knowledge. The latter is essential, if the meaning of the learned representations need to be related to human conceptualizations of knowledge, like questions answering over linked data. Finally, another dimension of complexity arises when we also consider the variability of natural language across different languages (e.g., English and Spanish). Then, finding patterns, aligning semantically related ones across languages, and linking them to one existing formal knowledge representations requires the learning of a cross-lingual semantic representation of relations expressed in text of different languages.

Unsupervised learning of distributional semantic representations from textual data has received increasing attention in recent years [10], since such representations have shown to be useful for solving tasks like document comparison, information retrieval and question answering. However, research has focused almost exclusively on the syntactic level and on single languages. At the same time, there has been progress in the area of cross-lingual entity disambiguation and linking, but this work is mostly confined to (named) entities and does not extend to other expressions in text, like the phrases indicating the relations between entities. What is missing so far is a representation that links linguistic variations of semantically related and contextualized textual elements across languages to their corresponding relation in a knowledge base.

In this paper, we present the first approach to unsupervised clustering of semantically related and cross-lingual relations expressed in text. This is achieved by combining multi-lingual semantic role labeling (SRL) with cross-lingual entity linking followed by spectral clustering of the resulting annotated SRL graphs. The resulting cross-lingual semantic representation of relations is, whenever possible, linked to English DBpedia properties, and enables e.g., to extend the schema with new properties, or to support cross-lingual question answering over linked data systems.

In our initial implementation we built a cross-lingual library of relation expressions from English and Spanish Wikipedia articles containing 25,000 SRL graphs with 2000 annotations to DBpedia entities. To demonstrate the usefulness of this novel language resource we show its performance on the Multilingual Question Answering over Linked Data challenge (QALD-4)[1]. Our results show that we can clearly outperform baseline approaches in respect to correctly linking (English) DBpedia properties in the SPARQL queries, specifically in a cross-lingual setting where the question to be answered is provided in Spanish.

In summary, the main contributions of our proposed approach to extract, cluster and link contextualized relation expressions in text are the following:

- Relation expressions can be extracted from text of different languages and are not restricted to a predefined set of relations (as defined by DBpedia).

---

[1] http://greententacle.techfak.uni-bielefeld.de/~cunger/qald/index.php?x=task1&q=4.

- Extracted expressions are embedded in a semantic graph, describing the context this expression appears in.
- Semantically related relation expressions and their associated context are disambiguated and clustered across languages.
- If existing, relation clusters are linked to their corresponding property in the English DBpedia.

In the remainder of this paper we first discuss related work, before introducing our approach to learning a cross-lingual semantic representation of grounded relations (Sects. 3, 4, 5 and 6). In Sect. 7 we evaluate our initial implementation on the QALD-4 benchmark and conclude in Sect. 8.

2   Related Work

Lewis and Steedman [7] present an approach to learning clusters of semantically equivalent English and French binary relations between referring expressions. Similar to us, a cluster is a language-independent semantic representation that can be applied to a variety of tasks such as translation, relation extraction, summarization, question answering, and information retrieval. The main difference is that we perform clustering on Semantic Role Label (SRL) graphs – thus operating on an abstract meaning representation - instead of binary syntactic relations. A meaning representation is more language-independent than a syntactic representation (like string patterns or dependency trees) since it abstracts from grammatical variations of different languages. This facilitates the learning of cross-lingual and language-independent semantic representations. This basic difference applies to almost all of the remaining approaches listed in this section, like Lin and Pantel (DIRT, [8]), who learn textual inference rules such as ("X wrote Y", "X is the author of Y") from dependency-parsed sentences by building groups of similar dependency paths.

An additional difference of related approaches like [5,11,14,16,17] is their dependency on preexisting knowledge base properties. In contrast, our approach does not start from a predefined set of knowledge base property for which we learn textual representations, but instead derives clusters of textual expressions via Semantic Role Labeling first for which we then try to find a corresponding relation in the KB. Thus, our approach is not confined to finding relations preexisting in a knowledge base. Newly identified relations could even be used for extending the ontology. This, however, would be contribution to ontology learning and is out of the scope of this paper. The approaches restricted to preexisting KB relations (and shallow parsing) are discussed in more detail now. Walter et al. (M-ATOLL, [17]) learn dependency paths as natural language expressions for KB relations. They begin with a relation from DBpedia, retrieve triples for this relation and search within a text corpus for sentences where the two arguments of the relation can be found within a sentence. The sentence is dependency-parsed and, given a set of six dependency patterns, a pattern matches the dependency tree. Mahendra et al. ([11]) learn textual expressions of DBpedia relations from

Wikipedia articles. Given a relation, triples are retrieved and sentences are identified where the two arguments of the relation can be found within a sentence. The longest common substring between the entities in sentences collected for a relation is learned as the relation's textual expression. Vila et al. (WRPA, [16]) learn English and Spanish paraphrases from Wikipedia for four pre-specified relations. Textual triples are derived using data from an article's infobox and its name. The string between the arguments of a relation within a sentence is extracted and generalized and regular expressions are created. Gerber and Ngonga Ngomo (BOA, [5]) language-independently learn textual expressions of DBpedia relations from Wikipedia by regarding the strings between a relation's arguments within sentences. Nakashole et al. (PATTY, [14]) learn textual expressions of KB relations from dependency-parsed or POS-tagged English sentences. Textual expressions are sequences of words, POS-tags, wildcards, and ontological types.

In contrast to the work just mentioned, there are a few approaches that leverage a semantic representation. Grounded Unsupervised Semantic Parsing by Poon (GUSP, see [15]) translates natural-language questions to database queries via a learned probabilistic grammar. However, GUSP is not cross-lingual. Similarly, Exner and Nugues [4] learn mappings from PropBank to DBpedia based on Semantic Role Labeling. Relations in Wikipedia articles are detected via SRL, named entities are identified and linked to DBpedia and use these links to ground PropBank relations to DBpedia. Again, this is not cross-lingual.

To the best of our knowledge, our approach is the only one that (i) extracts potentially novel relations and (ii) where possible, links to preexisting relation in a KB and (iii) does this across languages by exploiting a language-independent semantic representation rather than a syntactic one.

3   A Pipeline for Learning a Cross-Lingual Semantic Representations of Grounded Relations

Our pipeline, as shown in Fig. 1, consists of three major stages.

In the first stage (see Sect. 4), the multi-lingual text documents are transformed and processed by Semantic Role Labeling (SRL). In our evaluation we use Wikipedia articles as input data, but any text that produces valid SRL graphs is feasible. Please note, to construct a cross-lingual representation a multi-lingual comparable corpus covering similar topics is advisable. However, there is no need for an aligned or parallel corpus. SRL produces semantic graphs of frames with predicates and associated semantic role-argument pairs. In parallel, we apply cross-lingual entity linking to the same text documents. This detects entity mentions in multi-lingual text and annotates the corresponding mention strings with the entity URI originating exclusively from the English DBpedia. After that, we combine and align the output of both, SRL and entity linking in order to extract a cross-lingual SRL graphs. The only remaining language-dependent elements in a cross-lingual SRL graph are the predicate nodes.

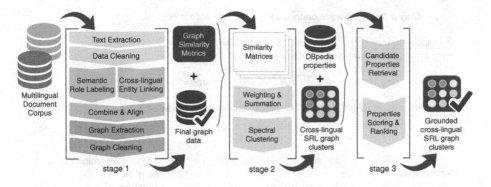

Fig. 1. Schematic summary of the processing pipeline.

The next stage performs relational learning of cross-lingual clusters (Sect. 5) on the previously acquired annotated SRL graphs. The similarity metrics that we define in Sect. 5.1 are central to this stage of the pipeline.

In the subsequent third stage, the obtained clusters are linked to DBpedia properties. Section 6 describes this procedure in greater detail. As a result we get cross-lingual clusters of annotated SRL graphs, i.e. textual relation expressions, augmented with a ranked set of DBpedia properties. Ultimately, these grounded clusters of relation expressions are evaluated in the task of property linking on multi-lingual questions of the QALD-4 dataset.

4   Extracting and Annotating SRL Graphs

Multi-lingual Semantic Role Labeling is performed on the input text independently for every language. SRL is accomplished by means of shallow and deep linguistic processing as described in [9]. The result of this processing step is a semantic graph consisting of semantic frames with predicates and their arguments. Each semantic frame is represented as a tree with the predicate as the root and its arguments as the leaf nodes. The edges are given by the semantic roles of the predicate arguments (cmp. Fig. 2).

SRL graphs are directed, node and edge labelled graphs describing the content of a whole document. Several predicates appear in one graph, so one sub-tree per predicate is extracted for clustering (the predicate being the root of the tree), resulting in a few trees per sentence and many trees per document. Trees from one document contain partially duplicated information. Formally, an SRL graph is a set of triples $t = (p, r, v)$ where the predicate p belongs to a set of SRL predicates ($p \in P_{SRL}$), the role r belongs to a set of SRL roles ($r \in R_{SRL}$), and v is either a string value or an SRL predicate ($v \in P_{SRL} \cup String$). We consider a frame as valid, if it has at least two non-frame arguments. Such a constraint reduces the number of usable frames, which, in turn is compensated by the large amount of the raw textual data.

Only a few cults were banned *by the Roman authorities...*

```
<frame displayName="ban.01" ID="F541" sentenceID="57" tokenID="57.6" >
    <argument displayName="cult" role="A1:Theme" id="W544" />
    <argument displayName="imperial_roman" role="A0:Agent" id="E1" />
    <argument displayName="be.00" role="AM-ADV"  frame="true" id="F542" />
    <descriptions>
        <description URI="00796392-v" displayName="ban" knowledgeBase="WordNet-3.0" />
    </descriptions>
</frame>

<DetectedTopic URL="http://dbpedia.org/resource/Cult_(religious_practice)" mention="cults"
    displayName="Cult (religious practice)" from="7064" to="7069" weight="0.01" \>
<DetectedTopic URL="http://dbpedia.org/resource/Roman_Empire" mention="Roman authorities"
    displayName="Roman Empire" from="7089" to="7106" weight="0.393" \>
```

Fig. 2. Example sentence with corresponding partial XML outputs produced by SRL (*frame* element) and the cross-lingual entity linking tool (*DetectedTopic* elements).

The example in Fig. 2 demonstrates the operation of the SRL pipeline, beginning with an example sentence for which the semantic frame is obtained. To achieve cross-lingual SRL graphs role labels of non-English SRL graphs are mapped to their corresponding English role labels. Whenever possible SRL predicates from all languages are linked to English wordnet synsets. That's not always possible since not every phrase of a predicate in an extracted SRL graph is mentioned in WordNet, specifically for non-English languages.

The next step towards generating cross-lingual SRL graphs is cross-lingual entity linking to the English DBpedia. This language-independent representation of the predicate arguments provides additional cross-lingual context for the subsequent predicate cluster analysis.

We treat this step as a replaceable black-box component by using the approach described in [19]. Reference [19] relies on linkage information in different Wikipedia language versions (language links, hyper links, disambiguation pages, ...) plus a statistical cross-lingual text comparison function, trained on a comparable corpora. The cross-lingual nature of our analysis is achieved by mapping text mentions in both languages to the English-language DBpedia URIs. The bottom part of Fig. 2 is a sample of the annotation output for the above example sentence. Annotations that correspond to SRL arguments are enclosed in *URL* attributes of *DetectedTopic* elements.

The intermediate results of both, the SRL and annotation steps finally need to be combined in order to extract the actual graphs. Figure 3 contains an example of four sentences along with the extracted cross-lingual SRL graphs from English and Spanish sentences. The graph vertices show the SRL predicate and argument mention strings along with DBpedia URIs (`dbr` namespace http:// dbpedia.org/resource/) and Wordnet-IDs. Edge labels specify the semantic role. Obviously, the graphs on the top and on the bottom are more similar to each other compared to the graphs on the level and right, respectively. Thus, cross-lingual SRL graphs are similar regarding the content, not the language.

Spanish sentence 1:
En mayo de 1937 el Deutschland estaba **atracado** en el *puerto* de Palma, en Mallorca, junto con otros *barcos* de guerra neutrales de las armadas británica e italiana.

English sentence 2:
In *May* 1937, the *ship* was **docked** in the *port* of Palma on the *island* of Majorca, along with several other neutral warships, including vessels from the British and Italian navies.

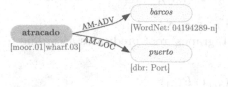

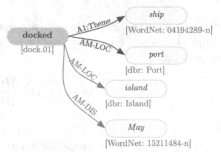

Spanish sentence 3:
Los problemas en sus motores obligaron a una serie de reparaciones que culminaron en una revisión completa a fines de 1943, tras lo que el *barco* **permaneció** en el *Mar Báltico*.

English sentence 4:
Engine problems forced a series of repairs culminating in a complete overhaul at the end of 1943, after which the *ship* **remained** in the *Baltic*.

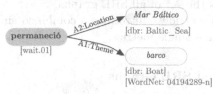

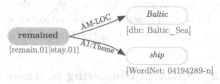

Fig. 3. Cross-lingual SRL graphs extracted from English and Spanish sentences.

5 Learning a Cross-Lingual Semantic Representation of Relation Expressions

For the purpose of clustering a set of cross-lingual SRL graphs we introduce a set of metrics specifying a semantic distance of SRL graphs (see Sect. 5.1). Section 5.2 discusses the spectral clustering algorithm.

5.1 Constructing Similarity Matrices of Annotated SRL Graphs

Goal of this step is to construct a similarity matrix, specifying the pair-wise similarity of all SRL graphs. We tried three different graph-similarity metrics m_1, m_2, m_3.

Formally, a cross-lingual SRL graph is an SRL graph where v is either a string value, an SRL predicate, or a unique identifier ($v \in P_{SRL} \cup String \cup \mathcal{U}$). $g(p)$ denotes the graph with predicate p as the root SRL predicate. $m_1 : G \times G \to \{1; 0\}$ compares the SRL graphs' root predicates according to their names, e.g. exist.01 vs. meet.02:

$$m_1(g_i, g_j) := \begin{cases} 1 & , p(g_i) = p(g_j) \\ 0 & , else \end{cases} \tag{1}$$

$m_2 : G \times G \to [1; 0]$ compares two SRL graphs' root predicates according to their annotated role values:

$$m_2(g_i, g_j) := \frac{|A(g_i) \cap A(g_j)|}{|A(g_i) \cup A(g_j)|} \tag{2}$$

where $A(g_k) := \{v \mid \exists r \in R_{SRL} : (p(g_k), r, v) \in g_k \wedge v \in \mathcal{U}\}$.

$m_3 : G \times G \to [1; 0]$ compares two SRL graphs' root predicates according to their role labels:

$$m_3(g_i, g_j) := \frac{|B(g_i) \cap B(g_j)|}{|B(g_i) \cup B(g_j)|} \tag{3}$$

where $B(g_k) := \{r \mid \exists v \in P_{SRL} \cup String \cup \mathcal{U} : (p(g_k), r, v) \in g_k\}$.

Now, given the set of cross-lingual SRL graphs $\{g_1, ...g_n\}$ and given the three SRL predicate similarity metrics, we can construct three SRL predicate similarity matrices. Each SRL predicate similarity metric is applied for pairwise comparison of two (annotated) SRL graphs' root predicates. The root predicate p of an (annotated) SRL graph g, denoted by $p(g)$, is the predicate for which no triple $(p_2, r, p) \in g$ exists with $p \neq p_2$. G denotes the set of all SRL graphs.

Based on a separate evaluation of each metric we introduce a combined similarity metric as a weighted sum of the three single metrics.

5.2   Spectral Clustering of Annotated SRL Graphs

Spectral Clustering uses the spectrum of a matrix derived from distances between different instances. Using the spectrum of a matrix has been successfully used in many computer vision applications [12] and is also applicable for similarity matrices. As input a similarity matrix S derived from one metric or a weighted combination of several metrics is given. As a first step the Laplacian matrix L is built by subtracting the similarity matrix S from the diagonal matrix D which contains the sum of each row on the diagonal (respectively column since S is symmetric) (Eq. 4).

$$L_{ij} = D_{ij} - S_{ij} = \begin{cases} \sum_m S_{im} - S_{ij} = \sum_m S_{mj} - S_{ij} & \text{if } i = j \\ -S_{ij} & \text{otherwise} \end{cases} \tag{4}$$

For building k clusters, the second up to the $k + 1$ smallest eigenvalue and corresponding eigenvector of the Laplacian matrix are calculated. Afterwards the actual clustering starts with running the k-means algorithm on the eigenvectors which finally results in a clustering for the instances of S.

To enforce the learning of cross-lingual clusters, we introduce the weighting matrix W which is used to weight the mono- and cross-lingual relations in the similarity matrix S (Eq. 5). While setting the monolingual weight $w_{monolingual}$ to zero, forces the construction of only cross-lingual clusters, we received better results by setting $w_{monolingual} > 0$. This can be intuitively understood as we get more clean clusters when we don't force cross-lingual relations into every cluster, as there is no guarantee that a matching cross-lingual relation even exists. Finally the weighted matrix S^*, the result of the product W and S (Eq. 6), is given as input to the previously described spectral clustering algorithm.

$$W_{ij} = \begin{cases} w_{monolingual} & \text{if i and j are monolingual} \\ 1 & \text{if i and j are crosslingual} \end{cases} \quad (5)$$

$$S^*_{ij} = W_{ij} \cdot S_{ij} \quad (6)$$

6 Linking Annotated SRL Graph Clusters to DBpedia Properties

In order to find potential links of the obtained clusters to DBpedia properties, we exploit the SRL graphs' argument structure as well as the DBpedia entity URIs provided by cross-lingual entity linking. The origin of possible candidates is limited to the DBpedia ontology[2] and infobox[3] properties.

Acquisition of Candidate Properties. For a given annotated SRL graph we retrieve a list of candidate properties by querying DBpedia for the in- and outbound properties associated with its arguments' entities. Consequently, the candidate properties of an entire predicate cluster are determined by the union of the individual graphs' candidate lists. Several specific properties, such as the Wikipedia-related structural properties (e.g. wikiPageID, wikiPageRevisionID etc.) are excluded from the candidate list.

Scoring of Candidate Properties. After the construction of the candidate list, the contained properties are scored. The purpose behind this is to determine a ranking of properties by their relevance with respect to a given cluster. In principle, several different scoring approaches are applicable to the underlying problem. For example, a relative normalized frequency score of property p_i w.r.t. cluster C_j calculated as

$$S^{rnf}(p_i, C_j) = \frac{relative\ frequency\ of\ p_i\ in\ C_j}{relative\ frequency\ of\ p_i\ over\ all\ clusters}$$

is appropriate to reflect the importance as well as the exclusiveness of property i for cluster j. However, our experiments determined the absolute frequency score of a property within a cluster to be the best performing measure.

Algorithm 1 shows the structure of the complete grounding algorithm in a simplified form. This algorithm is similar to the approach by Exner and Nugues [4].

---

[2] URI namespace http://dbpedia.org/ontology/.
[3] URI namespace: http://dbpedia.org/property/.

Algorithm 1. Algorithm that computes a ranked set of DBpedia properties for a given relation cluster.

Input: SRL graph cluster c
$result \leftarrow \emptyset$
for all $p \in \{p^{KB} \mid \exists g \in c : \exists(p^{SRL}, r, e) \in g : (\exists o : (e, p^{KB}, o) \in KB \vee \exists s : (s, p^{KB}, e) \in KB)\}$ **do**
     $result \leftarrow result \cup (p, |\{(s, p, o) \in KB \mid \exists g \in c : (p^{SRL}, r, e) \in g : e \in \mathcal{R} \wedge (s = e \vee o = e)\}|)$
end for
Return: result

7 Evaluation on Cross-Lingual Relation Linking for Question Answering over Linked Data

We make use of the evaluation data set provided by the Multi-lingual Question Answering over Linked Data challenge (task 1 of QALD-4). The data set contains 200 questions (12 out of 200 are out-of-scope w.r.t DBpedia knowledge base) in multiple languages as well as corresponding gold-standard SPARQL queries against DBpedia.

To evaluate the quality of our results, we conducted property linking experiments. We deliberately concentrate on the sub-task of property linking to avoid distortion of the performance by various pre- and post-processing steps of a full QA-system. Linking the properties necessary for constructing the SPARQL query constitutes an important step of a question answering system such as QAKiS [1], SemSearch [6], ORAKEL [2], FREyA [3], and TcruziKB [13] which generate SPARQL queries based on user input.

7.1 Linking Properties in the QALD Challenge

First, we generated compatible data representation from the QALD-4 question sentences by sending them through stage 1 of our processing pipeline (see Sect. 3). Hereby we obtained cross-lingual SRL graphs for English and Spanish questions.

Next, using our similarity metrics and the previously learned grounded clusters, we classified each individual SRL graph of the questions set and determined its target cluster. Consequently, each SRL graph of the questions set was assigned DBpedia properties according to the groundings of its associated target cluster. This way, for each question, our approach linked properties, which were finally evaluated against the gold-standard properties of the QALD-4 training dataset.

7.2 Data Set and Baselines

We employed Wikipedia as the source of multi-lingual text documents in the English (EN, Wikipedia dump version 2013.04.03) and Spanish (ES, Wikipedia dump version 2012.05.15) language. Over 23,000,000 cross-lingual annotated

Table 1. Key statistics of the data sets used for our experiments.

	Dataset 1: "long articles"		Dataset 2: "short articles"	
	English	Spanish	English	Spanish
# documents	29	29	1,063	1,063
# extracted graphs	10,421	14,864	13,009	12,402
# mentioned DBpedia entities	2,065		13,870	
# unique DBpedia entities	1,379		6,300	

SRL graphs were extracted from more than 300,000 pairs of language link-connected English and Spanish Wikipedia articles.

In order to get an initial assessment of our approach we conducted our experiments on two samples of the original data. Table 1 provides an overview of the key dataset statistics. Dataset 1 consists of a random sample of long Wikipedia article pairs, which together sum up to approximately 25,000 SRL graph instances. The second sample with a similar number of graphs was derived from randomly selected short article pairs in order to provide a wider coverage of different topics and corresponding DBpedia entities.

Baseline 1: String Similarity-Based Property Linking. This first naïve baseline links properties based on string similarity between the question tokens and DBpedia property labels. Given a question from the QALD-4 training dataset, we firstly obtain the question tokens using the Penn treebank-trained tokenizer. In the next step, each token is assigned the one DBpedia property with the highest string similarity between its label and the token string. String similarity is measured by means of the normalized Damerau-Levenshtein distance. For each token, the one property with the highest label similarity enters the candidate set. Finally, the identified candidate properties are evaluated against the QALD-4 gold-standard properties. Because the vast majority of property labels are of English origin, we could not apply this baseline to Spanish QALD-4 data.

Baseline 2: Entity-Based Property Linking. Baseline 2 takes a more sophisticated approach to finding good candidate properties. For this baseline, we first use the set of entities associated with a given question for linking of candidate properties exactly the same way as we perform grounding of cross-lingual SRL graph clusters (Sect. 5.1). In the next step, the list of candidate properties is pruned by thresholding the normalized Damerau-Levenshtein similarity of their labels to the question tokens. Again, this will have negative effect on the performance for Spanish-language questions for the same reasons as discussed in Sect. 7.2. We report results for two variations of this baseline, which differ in the mode of entity retrieval for a given question: In the first case, entities are collected from the cross-lingual annotated SRL graphs, while in the second case we obtain the entities directly from the output of the entity linking tool.

Table 2. Performance of Baseline 2 without and with SRL graph extraction.

		String similarity threshold					
		0.4	0.5	0.6	0.7	0.8	0.9
WITHOUT SRL	precision EN [%]	2.2	5.0	11.3	19.3	21.9	21.6
	precision ES [%]	0.7	1.9	5.0	6.3	12.5	21.4
	F1-measure EN [%]	4.1	8.4	15.7	22.6	23.2	22.3
	F1-measure ES [%]	1.4	2.9	6.0	6.8	14.3	22.0
WITH SRL	precision EN [%]	3.2	6.7	16.8	24.3	23.5	22.5
	precision ES [%]	0.7	1.9	5.6	3.2	10.0	0.0
	F1-measure EN [%]	5.4	9.7	19.2	26.5	24.5	22.5
	F1-measure ES [%]	1.2	2.5	6.2	3.1	10.5	0.0

7.3   Evaluation Results

Baseline 1: Results. A naïve selection of candidate properties based solely on string similarity between the question tokens and property labels shows poor overall performance on the English-language QALD-4 questions:

precision: 2.15 %
recall: 10.68 %
F1-measure: 3.58 %

As discussed in Sect. 7.2, this baseline is limited to English-language questions.

Baseline 2: Results. The top part of Table 2 shows the performance of Baseline 2 in the case *without* SRL graph extraction.

Due to the cross-lingual nature of property linking through our grounding algorithm, there is a clear performance increase for Spanish-language questions. It is also notable that the behaviour of the performance measure is consistent over all string similarity thresholds for both languages. The bottom part of Table 2 shows Baseline 2 results with SRL graph extraction. Here, we see a small but consistent performance increase for the English language over Baseline 2 without SRL. This observation supports our assumption that the inclusion of the semantic structure of annotated arguments as provided by Semantic Role Labeling does improve performance.

Results with Grounded Cross-Lingual SRL Graph Clusters. The evaluation of our approach was conducted on the previously described (Table 1) experimental datasets and a variety of different clustering configurations with respect to different similarity matrices as well as different internal parameter sets of the spectral clustering algorithm.

Table 3. Best performing grounded clusters configurations for QALD-4 questions.

Lang.	Clustering configuration				Performance [%]		
	Metric	#clusters	#eigenvectors	$w_{monolingual}$	Precision	Recall	F1
ES	m2	500	100	0.0	30.19	28.57	29.36
ES	m2	200	100	0.0	30.05	28.44	29.22
ES	m2	100	50	0.0	30.05	28.19	29.09
ES	m2	200	50	0.0	29.77	28.19	28.96
EN	m2	200	50	0.0	29.52	27.24	28.33
EN	m2	100	50	0.0	29.44	27.09	28.22
EN	m2	200	100	0.0	29.13	26.91	27.97
EN	m2	10	50	0.0	28.99	26.74	27.82

Table 4. Best performing results for "short articles" vs "long articles".

Lang.	Clustering configuration				Performance [%]		
	dataset	# clusters	# eigenvectors	$w_{monolingual}$	Precision	Recall	F1
EN	2 (short)	200	100	0.0	27.09	26.25	26.67
EN	2 (short)	200	50	0.0	24.12	23.85	23.98
ES	2 (short)	200	100	0.0	28.70	27.47	28.07
ES	2 (short)	200	50	0.0	27.68	26.50	27.07
EN	1 (long)	200	100	0.0	21.30	21.00	21.15
EN	1 (long)	200	100	0.0	20.38	20.19	20.28
ES	1 (long)	200	50	0.0	21.33	20.87	21.10
ES	1 (long)	200	50	0.0	18.98	18.64	18.81

Table 3 reports the results of several top performing configurations. It is notable that across languages and different parameter sets, the completely cross-lingual, entity-focused metric m_2 outperforms the other configurations, which supports the basic idea of our approach. In addition to this, we observe a consistent improvement over our baselines for English, and even more so for the Spanish language.

To investigate the effect of input data and parameter choice on the quality of results, we conducted further experiments, which involved grounded clusters computed on a weighted sum of all metrics with cross-lingual constraints. In particular, we demonstrate the effect of the short- versus long-articles dataset, i.e. the impact of more diverse input data. Table 4 shows results of this comparison. Obviously, shorter and more concise articles seem to produce SRL graphs with more meaningful clusters. It would be interesting to evaluate whether co-reference resolution would improve the performance for longer articles.

Another aspect of interest is the effect of the number of Eigenvectors within the spectral clustering algorithm. This parameter greatly increases the computational

Table 5. Best performing results in respect to number of eigenvectors.

Lang.	Clustering configuration				Performance [%]		
	Dataset	#clusters	#eigenvectors	$w_{monolingual}$	Precision	Recall	F1
EN	2 (short)	500	500	0.5	27.65	27.15	27.04
EN	2 (short)	200	200	0.5	27.23	26.87	27.05
ES	2 (short)	200	500	0.5	29.09	27.35	28.19
ES	2 (short)	200	300	0.5	29.09	27.35	28.19
EN	2 (short)	200	50	0.5	25.00	24.56	24.77
EN	2 (short)	500	50	0.5	21.58	21.49	21.53
ES	2 (short)	200	50	0.5	18.02	17.94	17.98
ES	2 (short)	500	50	0.5	13.24	13.24	13.24

resources needed to compute the clustering. But our experimental results also clearly show an advantage of a high number of Eigenvectors (Table 5).

Both experiments revealed that more input data as well as higher-dimensional clustering has the potential to further improve the performance of our approach. Another incentive for scaling those dimensions is to cover the long tail of relation expressions. Still, we would argue that this limited evaluation clearly demonstrates the benefits of our approach, since we outperform Baseline 2 by about 6 % and Baseline 2 is comparable to what is used in most of the related work. That shows a big potential to improve those QA systems.

8   Conclusion and Future Work

This paper introduces an approach to unsupervised learning of a cross-lingual semantic representation of relations expressed in text. To the best of our knowledge this is the first meaning representation induced from text that is (i) cross-lingual, (ii) builds on semantic instead of shallow syntactic features, and (iii) generalizes over relation expressions. The resulting clusters of semantically related relation graphs can be linked to DBpedia properties and thus support tasks like question answering over linked data. Our results show that we can clearly outperform baseline approaches on the sub-task of property linking.

Directions for future work include, learning the semantic representation from more documents. Our current implementation serves as a strong proof-of-concept, but does not yet cover the long tail of relation expressions sufficiently. Including all Wikipedia articles resulting in millions of graphs is merely an engineering challenge, only the clustering step would need to be adjusted. In addition, we would like to assess the potential of our approach to discover novel relation-types (and their instantiations) to the knowledge base.

Acknowledgments. The research leading to these results has received funding from the European Union Seventh Framework Programme (FP7/2007-2013) under grant agreement no. 611346.

References

1. Cabrio, E., Cojan, J., Aprosio, A.P., Magnini, B., Lavelli, A., Qakis, F.G.: an open domain qa system based on relational patterns. In: Proceedings of the 11th International Semantic Web Conference (ISWC 2012), demo paper (2012)
2. Cimiano, P., Haase, P., Heizmann, J., Mantel, M., Studer, R.: Towards portable natural language interfaces to knowledge bases - the case of the ORAKEL system. Data Knowl. Eng. **65**(2), 325–354 (2008)
3. Damljanovic, D., Agatonovic, M., Cunningham, H.: FREyA: an interactive way of querying linked data using natural language. In: García-Castro, R., Fensel, D., Antoniou, G. (eds.) ESWC 2011. LNCS, vol. 7117, pp. 125–138. Springer, Heidelberg (2012)
4. Exner, P., Nugues, P.: Ontology matching: from propbank to DBpedia. In: SLTC 2012, The Fourth Swedish Language Technology Conference, pp. 67–68 (2012)
5. Gerber, D., Ngomo, A.-C.N.: Extracting multilingual natural-language patterns for RDF predicates. In: ten Teije, A., Völker, J., Handschuh, S., Stuckenschmidt, H., d'Acquin, M., Nikolov, A., Aussenac-Gilles, N., Hernandez, N. (eds.) EKAW 2012. LNCS, vol. 7603, pp. 87–96. Springer, Heidelberg (2012)
6. Lei, Y., Uren, V.S., Motta, E.: SemSearch: a search engine for the semantic web. In: Staab, S., Svátek, V. (eds.) EKAW 2006. LNCS (LNAI), vol. 4248, pp. 238–245. Springer, Heidelberg (2006)
7. Lewis, M., Steedman, M.: Unsupervised induction of cross-lingual semantic relations. In: EMNLP, pp. 681–692 (2013)
8. Lin, D., Pantel, P.: Dirt - discovery of inference rules from text. In: Proceedings of the Seventh ACM SIGKDD International Conference on Knowledge Discovery and Data Mining, KDD 2001, pp. 323–328. ACM (2001)
9. Lluís, X., Carreras, X., Màrquez, L.: Joint arc-factored parsing of syntactic and semantic dependencies. Trans. Assoc. Comput. Linguist. **1**, 219–230 (2013)
10. Madhyastha, P.S., Carreras Pérez, X., Quattoni, A.: Learning task-specific bilexical embeddings. In: Proceedings of COLING-2014 (2014)
11. Mahendra, R., Wanzare, L., Bernardi, R., Lavelli, A., Magnini, B.: Acquiring relational patterns from wikipedia: a case study. In: Proceedings of the 5th Language and Technology Conference (2011)
12. Malik, J., Belongie, S., Leung, T., Shi, J.: Contour and texture analysis for image segmentation. Int. J. Comput. Vis. **43**(1), 7–27 (2001)
13. Mendes, P.N., McKnight, B., Sheth, A.P., Kissinger, J.C.: TcruziKB: enabling complex queries for genomic data exploration. In: Proceedings of the 2008 IEEE International Conference on Semantic Computing, ICSC 2008, pp. 432–439 (2008)
14. Nakashole, N., Weikum, G., Suchanek, F.: Patty: a taxonomy of relational patterns with semantic types. In: EMNLP-CoNLL 2012, pp. 1135–1145 (2012)
15. Poon, H.: Grounded unsupervised semantic parsing. In: ACL (1), pp. 933–943. Citeseer (2013)
16. Vila, M., Rodríguez, H., Mart'i, A.M.: Wrpa: a system for relational paraphrase acquisition from wikipedia. Procesamiento del Lenguaje Nat. **45**, 11–19 (2010)

17. Walter, S., Unger, C., Cimiano, P.: M-ATOLL: a framework for the lexicalization of ontologies in multiple languages. In: Mika, P., Tudorache, T., Bernstein, A., Welty, C., Knoblock, C., Vrandečić, D., Groth, P., Noy, N., Janowicz, K., Goble, C. (eds.) ISWC 2014, Part I. LNCS, vol. 8796, pp. 472–486. Springer, Heidelberg (2014)
18. Welty, C., Fan, J., Gondek, D., Schlaikjer, A.: Large scale relation detection. In: Proceedings of the NAACL HLT 2010 First International Workshop on Formalisms and Methodology for Learning by Reading, FAM-LbR 2010, pp. 24–33 (2010)
19. Zhang, L., Rettinger, A.: X-lisa: cross-lingual semantic annotation. PVLDB **7**(13), 1693–1696 (2014)

HAWK – Hybrid Question Answering Using Linked Data

Ricardo Usbeck[1]([✉]), Axel-Cyrille Ngonga Ngomo[1], Lorenz Bühmann[1], and Christina Unger[2]

[1] University of Leipzig, Leipzig, Germany
{usbeck,ngonga}@informatik.uni-leipzig.de
[2] University of Bielefeld, Bielefeld, Germany
cunger@cit-ec.uni-bielefeld.de

Abstract. The decentral architecture behind the Web has led to pieces of information being distributed across data sources with varying structure. Hence, answering complex questions often requires combining information from structured and unstructured data sources. We present HAWK, a novel entity search approach for Hybrid Question Answering based on combining Linked Data and textual data. The approach uses predicate-argument representations of questions to derive equivalent combinations of SPARQL query fragments and text queries. These are executed so as to integrate the results of the text queries into SPARQL and thus generate a formal interpretation of the query. We present a thorough evaluation of the framework, including an analysis of the influence of entity annotation tools on the generation process of the hybrid queries and a study of the overall accuracy of the system. Our results show that HAWK achieves 0.68 respectively 0.61 F-measure within the training respectively test phases on the Question Answering over Linked Data (QALD-4) hybrid query benchmark.

1 Introduction

Recent advances in question answering (QA) over Linked Data provide end users with more and more sophisticated tools for querying linked data by allowing users to express their information need in natural language [17,19,20]. This allows access to the wealth of structured data available on the Semantic Web also to non-experts. However, a lot of information is still available only in textual form, both on the Document Web and in the form of labels and abstracts in Linked Data sources [9]. Therefore, a considerable number of questions can only be answered by using hybrid question answering approaches, which can find and combine information stored in both structured and textual data sources [22].

In this paper, we present HAWK, the (to best of our knowledge) first full-fledged hybrid QA framework for entity search over Linked Data and textual data. Given a textual input query q, HAWK implements an 8-step pipeline, which comprises (1) part-of-speech tagging, (2) detecting entities in q, (3) dependency parsing and (4) applying linguistic pruning heuristics for an in-depth analysis of

© Springer International Publishing Switzerland 2015
F. Gandon et al. (Eds.): ESWC 2015, LNCS 9088, pp. 353–368, 2015.
DOI: 10.1007/978-3-319-18818-8_22

the natural language input. The results of these first four steps is a predicate-argument graph annotated with resources from the Linked Data Web. HAWK then (5) assign semantic meaning to nodes and (6) generates basic triple patterns for each component of the input query with respect to a multitude of features. This deductive linking of triples results in a set of SPARQL queries containing text operators as well as triple patterns. In order to reduce operational costs, (7) HAWK discards queries using several rules, e.g., by discarding not connected query graphs. Finally, (8) queries are ranked using extensible feature vectors and cosine similarity.

Our main contributions can be summarized as follows:

- We present the first QA framework tackling hybrid question answering;
- HAWK analyses input queries based on predicate-argument trees to deeply understand and match semantic resources;
- Our framework is generic as it does not rely on templates. It is thus inherently able to cover a wide variety of natural language questions.
- The modular architecture of HAWK allows simple exchanging of pipeline parts to enhance testing and deployment;
- Our evaluation suggests that HAWK is able to achieve F-measures of 0.61 on rather small training datasets.

The rest of the paper is structured as follows: Afterwards, our methodology is explained in detail in Sect. 2. HAWK's performance and the influence of entity annotation systems is evaluated in Sect. 3. Section 4 discusses related work. Finally, we conclude in Sect. 5. Additional information can be found at our project home page http://aksw.org/Projects/HAWK.html.

2 Method

In the following, we describe the architecture and methodology of HAWK. We explain our approach by using the following running example: Which recipients of the Victoria Cross died in the Battle of Arnhem? While this question cannot be answered by using solely DBpedia or Wikipedia abstracts, combining knowledge from DBpedia and Wikipedia abstracts allows deriving an answer to this question. More specifically, DBpedia allows to retrieve all recipients of the Victoria Cross using the triple pattern ?uri dbo:award dbr:Victoria_Cross.

In order to find out whether the returned resources died in the Battle of Arnhem, the free text abstract of those resources need to be checked. For example, the abstract for John Hollington Grayburn contains the following information: 'he went into action in the Battle of Arnhem [...] but was killed after standing up in full view of a German tank'.

Figure 1 gives an overview of the architecture of HAWK. In the following we describe the depicted steps in more detail.

2.1 POS-Tagging, Segmentation

A large number of frameworks have been developed for these purposes over the last years. We rely on *clearNLP* [3] which is based on transition-based dependency

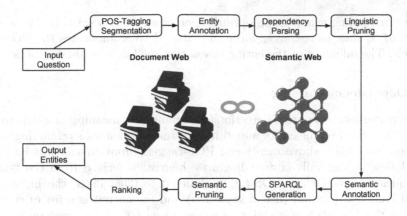

Fig. 1. Architectural overview of HAWK.

parsing and sophisticated segmentation algorithm. Regarding our running example the following POS-tags are generated: Which(WDT) recipients(NNS) of(IN) the(DT) Victoria(NNP) Cross(NNP) died(VBN) in(IN) the(DT) Battle(NNP) of(IN) Arnhem(NNP)?(PUNCT).

2.2 Entity Annotation

HAWK identifies named entities and tries to link them to semantic entities from the underlying knowledge base, in our case DBpedia 3.9, via well-established entity annotation tools, also called entity tagging tools:

- **Wikipedia Miner** [14] is based on different facts like prior probabilities, context relatedness and quality, which are then combined and tuned using a classifier.
- **DBpedia Spotlight** [13] was published in 2011. This tool combines named entity recognition and disambiguation based on DBpedia.
- **TagMe 2** [6] is based on a directory of links, pages and an inlink graph from Wikipedia. The approach recognizes entities by matching terms with Wikipedia link texts and disambiguates the match using the in-link graph and the page dataset.
- **FOX** [18] has been introduced 2014 as an ensemble learning-based approach combining several state-of-the-art named entity recognition approaches. The FOX framework outperforms the current state of the art entity recognizers and relies on the entity linking tool AGDISTIS [23].

Additionally, we implemented two artificial spotters for evaluation:

- **Union** is a spotter that combines the result sets of the above introduced spotters and returns thus a superset of all spotters.
- **Optimal** will spot all entities from the gold standard to be able to ignore spotting influences in the following steps of the pipeline.

For our running example, an optimal spotter identifies Victoria_Cross and Battle_of_Arnhem as resources form DBpedia. HAWK annotates the POS-tag ADD to it. The influence of the entity annotation module is evaluated in Sect. 3.

2.3 Dependency Parsing

HAWK performs noun phrase detection for semantically meaningful word groups not yet recognized by the entity annotation system also known as chunking. This detection reuses the above mentioned POS-tagger. Input tokens will be combined following manually-crafted linguistic heuristics derived from the benchmark questions, and their POS-tag is changed to CNN. Thus, the input is a natural language question (list of keywords) and the output is a list of chunks, see Algorithm 1. HAWK's modular structure allows for an easy exchange of the POS-tagger or dependency parser.

Algorithm 1. Algorithm for combining noun phrases

Data: Tokenized question (*list*) with Part-of-Speech-tags (POS-tags)
subsequence = ();
for $t \in [0, |list|]$ **do**
    token = list.get(t);
    if *subsequence* = $\emptyset$ **then**
     | **if** $pos(t) \in$ (CD|JJ|NN(.)*|RB(.)*) **then** subsequence.add(token);
    else
        if $t + 1 < |list| \wedge pos(t) \in$ (IN) $\wedge pos(t + 1) \in$ ((W)?DT) **then**
         | **if** *subsequence.size*() $>= 2$ **then** combine(subsequence);
         | subsequence = ();
        else if $pos(t - 1) \in$ (NNS) $\wedge pos(t) \in$ (NNP(S)?) **then**
         | **if** *subsequence.size*() > 2 **then** combine(subsequence);
         | subsequence = ();
        else if $!pos(t - 1) \in$ (JJ|HYPH) $\wedge (pos(t) \in$ (VB|WDT|IN))) **then**
         | **if** *subsequence.size*() > 1 **then** combine(subsequence);
         | subsequence = ();
        else if $pos(t) \in$ (NN(.)*|RB|CD|CC|JJ|DT|IN|PRP|HYPH|VBN)
        then
         | subsequence.add(token)
        else
         | subsequence = ();
    end
end

Subsequently, in order to capture linguistic and semantic relations, HAWK parses the query using dependency parsing and semantic role labeling [3]. The dependency parser is given the chunked question. The generated predicate-argument tree is directed, acyclic, and all its nodes contain their POS-tags as well as their labels, see Fig. 2.

2.4   Linguistic Pruning

The natural language input can contain tokens that are meaningless for retrieving the target information or even introduce noise in the process. HAWK therefore prunes nodes from the predicate-argument tree based on their POS-tags, e.g., deleting all DET nodes, interrogative phrases such as Give me or List, and auxiliary tokens such as did. Algorithm 2 details the algorithm for removing nodes. Figure 3 depicts the predicate-argument tree obtained for our running example after pruning.

Algorithm 2. Algorithm for pruning noisy nodes

Data: Dependency-argument tree with Part-of-Speech-tags
Queue queue = [tree.getRoot()];
while *queue*! = ∅ **do**
  node = queue.poll();
  if *pos(node)* ∈ (WDT|POS|WP\$|PRP\$|RB|PRP|DT|IN|PDT) **then**
    | tree.remove(node);
  end
  queue.add(node.getChildren());
end
if *root.label* == (*"Give"*) **then**
  for *childNode* ∈ *root.getChildren*() **do**
    | **if** *childNode* == *"me"* **then** tree.remove(childNode);
  end
end
if *root.label* ∈ { *"List"*, *"Give"* } **then** tree.remove(root);

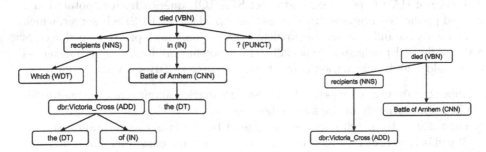

Fig. 2. Predicate-argument tree for the example question 'Which recipients of the Victoria Cross died in the Battle of Arnhem?'

Fig. 3. Tree after pruning. Argument edges are ordered from left to right.

2.5   Semantic Annotation

After linguistic pruning, HAWK annotates each node in the tree with possible concepts from the knowledge base and its underlying ontology. To this end, our framework uses information about possible verbalizations of ontology concepts, based on both `rdfs:label` information from the ontology itself and (if available) verbalization information contained in lexica. In general, such lexica offer a range of lexical variants beyond the labels present in DBpedia. For example, for the property `spouse`, the DBpedia English lexicon[1] provides the noun entries 'wife' and 'husband' as well as the verb entry 'to marry'.

HAWK now tries to match each node label to a class or property from the DBpedia ontology using fuzzy string matching. Moreover, HAWK follows intuitions used in [19] to lower the number of annotations avoiding additional computational effort. In particular, we consider the POS-tag of nodes to determine the type of the target reference:

- nouns correspond to object type properties and classes
- verbs correspond to object type properties
- question words (e.g., `who` or `where`) correspond to classes (e.g., `Person` or `Place`).

Afterwards, HAWK ranks properties according to their prominence score in the knowledge base and returns only the top n properties. If the search does not retrieve any annotations, we additionally ask the lemmata of the node label and repeat the above described process to increase recall.

Considering our running example,the nodes `died` (VB) will be annotated with `dbo:deathplace` and `dbo:deathdate` and the node `recipients` (NNS) with `dbo:award`. After this step, either a node is annotated with a reference from the knowledge base or it will be lead to a full-text lookup to be resolved to a knowledge base resource as explained in the following section.

2.6   Generating SPARQL Queries

The core of HAWK is the generation of SPARQL queries from annotated and pruned predicate-argument trees. It uses an Apache Jena FUSEKI[2] server, which implements the full-text search predicate `text:query` on a-priori defined literals over configured predicates. Especially, the following predicates were indexed as they yield a high information content with respect to DBpedia 3.9:

- `dbpedia:abstract` for general interest information about a resource not modelled appropriately in the knowledge base
- `rdfs:label` to match resources not found by the entity annotation system
- `dbpedia:redirect` to identify common synonyms, e.g., 'first man in space' pointing to http://dbpedia.org/resource/Yuri_Gagarin
- `dc:subject` for linking top-level categories like 'assassin' to resources like http://dbpedia.org/resource/James_Earl_Ray.

Currently, HAWK resolves full-text information either by using exact matches of node labels or fuzzy matches on each non-stopword token of a label; Table 1 depicts the two possibilities for the running example.

---

[1] https://github.com/cunger/lemon.dbpedia.
[2] http://jena.apache.org/documentation/serving_data/.

Table 1. Examples for full-text query types.

Query type	Query syntax	Node label
Exact	`?var text:query ('Battle of Arnhem')`	Battle of Arnhem
Fuzzy	`?var text:query ('Battle~1 AND Arnhem~1')`	Battle of Arnhem

Table 2. Generated triple patterns for running example.

Node type	Query fragment
CNN	`?proj text:query ('Battle of Arnhem')`
	`?const text:query ('Battle of Arnhem')`
Verb	`?proj dbo:deathPlace ?const`
	`?const dbo:deathPlace ?proj`

To capture the full semantics of an input question, HAWK traverses the predicated-argument tree in a pre-order walk to reflect the empirical observation that (i) related information are situated close to each other in the tree and (ii) information are more restrictive from left to right. This breadth-first search visits each node and generates several *possible triple patterns* based on the number of annotations and the POS-tag itself. That is, for each node a set of SPARQL query patterns is generated following the rules depicted in Table 3 w.r.t. ontology type information, e.g., a variable bound to the class `Place` will not have an outgoing predicate `birthPlace`.

Using this approach allows HAWK to be independent of SPARQL templates and to work on natural language input of any length and complexity. Each pattern contains at least one variable from a pre-defined set of variables, i.e., `?proj` for the resource projection variable, `?const` for resources covering constraints related to the projection variable as well as a variety of variables for predicates to inspect the surrounding of elements in the knowledge base graph. Table 2 shows generated triple patterns for parts of the example query.

During this process, each iteration of the traversal appends the generated patterns to each of the already existing SPARQL queries. This combinatorial effort results in covering every possible SPARQL graph pattern given the predicate-argument tree.

2.7 Semantic Pruning of SPARQL Queries

Producing the n-fold-cross-product of possible pattern combinations generates a huge number of SPARQL queries, most of which are semantically senseless,e.g., a city that has a birth date. To effectively handle this large set of queries and reduce the computational effort, HAWK implements various methods for pruning:

- **#textfilter:** HAWK can safely assume that SPARQL queries containing full-text lookups over more than one variable or containing more than two node labels do not yield semantically senseful information and thus discards such queries.

Table 3. Triple patterns for generating SPARQL queries while traversal.

Node POS-tag and non-empty annotations	Query fragment
VB(.)*	`?proj Annotation ?const.`
VB(.)*	`?const Annotation ?proj.`
VB(.)*	`?const ?proot ?proj.`
NN(.)*|WRB	`?proj Annotation ?const.`
NN(.)*|WRB	`?const Annotation ?proj.`
NN(.)*|WRB	`?proj a Annotation.`
NN(.)*|WRB	`?const a Annotation.`
NN(.)*|WRB	`?const text:query (node label)`
WP	`?const a Annotation.`
WP	`?proj a Annotation.`
In all cases	Add empty triple pattern
Node POS-tag and empty annotations	Query Fragment
CNN|NNP(.)*|JJ|CD	`?proj text:query (node label)`
CNN|NNP(.)*|JJ|CD	`?const text:query (node label)`
VB(.)*	`?proj text:query (node label)`
VB(.)*	`?const text:query (node label)`
ADD	`?proj ?pbridge nodeURI.`
ADD	`FILTER (?proj IN (nodeURI))`
ADD	`?proj text:query (node label)`
ADD	`?const text:query (node label)`
NN|NNS	`?proj text:query (node label)`
NN|NNS	`?const text:query (node label)`
In all cases	Add empty triple pattern

- **#unbound triple pattern:** SPARQL queries containing more than one triple pattern of the form `?varx ?vary ?varz` or one such triple pattern and only text searches, lead to a traversal of large parts of the knowledge base graph and high computational effort.
- **Unconnected query graph:** SPARQL query graphs which are not connected from cartesian products are pruned for the sake of runtime and their lack of semantics.
- **Cyclic triple:** Queries containing edges of the form `?s <http://xyz> ?o. ?o <http://xyz> ?s` or `?s <http://xyz> ?o. ?s <http://abc> ?o` are also removed.
- **Missing projection variable:** The before mentioned traversal and SPARQL generation process can produce SPARQL queries without triple patterns containing the projection variable. These queries are also removed from the set of queries.

- **Disjointness:** Also SPARQL queries with triple patterns violating disjointness statements are discarded:
  - ?s a cls . ?s p ?o . if cls and domain of p are disjoint
  - ?o a cls . ?s p ?o . if cls and range of p are disjoint
  - ?s p1 ?o1 . ?s p2 ?o2 . if domain of p1 and p2 are disjoint
  - ?s1 p1 ?o . ?s2 p2 ?o . if range of p1 and p2 are disjoint
  - ?s p1 ?o . ?s p2 ?o . if p1 and p2 are disjoint.

  Due to lack of explicit disjointness statements in many knowledge bases, we (heuristically) assume that classes and properties that are not related via subsumption hierarchy are disjoint.

Although semantic pruning drastically reduces the amount of queries, it often does not result in only one query. HAWK thus requires a final ranking step before sending the SPARQL query to the target triple store.

2.8 Ranking

HAWK ranks queries using supervised training based on the gold standard answer set from the QALD-4 benchmark. In the *training phase*, all generated queries are run against the underlying SPARQL endpoint. Comparing the results to the gold standard answer set, HAWK stores all queries resulting with the same high F-measure. Afterwards the stored queries are used to calculate an average feature vector comprising simple features mimicking a centroid-based cosine ranking. HAWK's ranking calculation comprises the following components:

- **NR_OF_TERMS** calculates the number of nodes used to form the full-text query part as described in Sect. 2.6.
- **NR_OF_CONSTRAINTS** counts the amount of triple patterns per SPARQL query.
- **NR_OF_TYPES** sums the amount of patterns of the form ?var rdf:type cls.
- **PREDICATES** generates a vector containing an entry for each predicate used in the SPARQL query.

While running the *test phase* of HAWK, the cosine similarity between each SPARQL query using the above mentioned features and the average feature vector of training queries is calculated. Moreover, HAWK determines the target cardinality x, i.e., LIMIT x, of each query using the indicated cardinality of the first seen POS-tag of the input query, e.g., the POS-tag NNS demands the plural while NN demands the singular case and thus leads to different x. The performance of this ranking approach is evaluated in Sect. 3.

3 Evaluation

3.1 Benchmark

We evaluate HAWK against the QALD [21] benchmark. QALD has been used widely to evaluate question answering systems, e.g., TBSL, SINA, FREyA or

QAKiS, which are presented in Sect. 4. In the recent fourth installment of QALD, hybrid questions on structured and unstructured data became a part of the benchmark. To evaluate HAWK, we focus on this hybrid training dataset comprising 25 questions, 17 out of which are entity searches using only DBpedia type information, no aggregation process and require only SELECT-queries. The available test dataset comprises only 10 question with 6 entity searches and linguistic structures that are completely different from the training dataset. Before evaluation, we had to curate the benchmark datasets regarding, among others, incorrect grammar, typological errors, duplicate resources in the answer set. The cleaned datasets can be found in our source code repository.[3] Without this correction HAWK's f-measure shrinks to nearly zero for questions containing failures. To the best of our knowledge there is no other published approach on hybrid question answering.

3.2 Influence of the Entity Annotation System

First, we evaluated the influence of the applied entity annotation systems to the overall ability to produce correct answers. Thus, HAWK has been run using DBpedia Spotlight, TagMe, Fox and Wikipedia Miner. Additionally, an optimal entity annotator derived from the gold standard as well as an union of all entity annotation results was analysed.

Our results suggest that HAWK is able to retrieve correct answers with an F-measure of 0.68 using FOX as entity annotation system and assuming an optimal ranking. Furthermore, the optimal ranker is only able to achieve an F-measure of 0.58 since HAWK can cope better with missing annotation results and is tuned towards retrieving full-text information. Against intuition, the Union annotator is the worst annotation system. Merging all annotation results in queries consisting solely of semantic resources eliminating the possibility to match ontology properties and classes to important parts of the query, e.g., matching the word author to resource rather than to a property prevents HAWK from generating the correct SPARQL query. Thus, the Union annotator achieves only an F-measure of 0.10.[4]

3.3 Influence of the Ranking Method

Next, evaluating the effectiveness of the feature-based ranking has to include an in-depth analysis of the contribution of each feature to the overall result. Thus, we calculated the power set of the set of features and evaluated each feature group using the F-measure reached by the top n queries. Figures 4 and 5 show the F-measure@N for all query result sets of size N from all 17 questions.

Delving deeper into this analysis, we find:

- Although **NR_OF_TERMS** produces the largest sum of F-measures as a single feature, **NR_OF_CONSTRAINTS** achieves a higher F-measure as

---

[3] https://github.com/AKSW/hawk/tree/master/resources.

[4] Details on this evaluation can be found in the supplement on our project homepage.

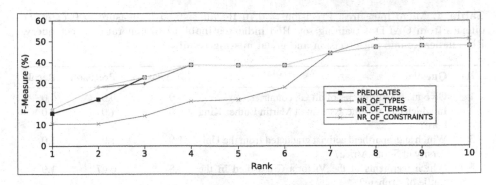

Fig. 4. F-measures on training dataset using $N = [1, \ldots, 10]$ and one feature.

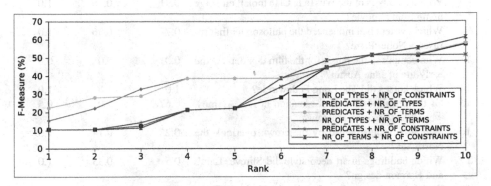

Fig. 5. F-measures on training dataset using $N = [1, \ldots, 10]$ and two features.

soon as $N = 7$ due to the larger number of needed constraints with respect to the query length.

– The highest mass of F-measure reaches the pair **PREDICATES, NR_OF_TERMS** with an F-measure of 0.58 at $N = 10$. However, HAWK is able to achieve a higher F-measure of 0.61 at $N = 10$ using **NR_OF_TERMS, NR_OF_CONSTRAINTS**.
– We only regard the top-10-ranked queries. The correct queries belonged to the top-n queries as shown in Table 4.
– The combination of three or all four features does not lead to an improvement.

HAWK generates up to 15000 SPARQL queries per question containing more than one query generating the correct answer. We consider ranking the resulting SPARQL queries most challenging with respect to the fact that an ideal ranking can lead to F-measures up to 0.72 at $N = 1$.

3.4 Error Analysis

In the following, we analyze error sources in HAWK based on the training queries failing to reach a higher F-measure. Table 4 shows for each entity search question from the training dataset its evaluation results.

Table 4. Micro measures: Precision = 0.70 Recall = 0.85 F-measure = 0.72 at 17 queries from QALD 4 training set. Red indicates inability to generate correct query, Blue indicates missing precision and green missing recall.

ID	Question	F-measure	Precision	Recall
1	Give me the currencies of all G8 countries.	0.0	0.0	0.0
2	In which city was the assassin of Martin Luther King born?	1.0	1.0	1.0
3	Which anti-apartheid activist graduated from the University of South Africa?	1.0	1.0	1.0
5	Which recipients of the Victoria Cross died in the Battle of Arnhem?	0.8	0.67	1.0
6	Where did the first man in space die?	1.0	1.0	1.0
8	Which members of the Wu-Tang Clan took their stage name from a movie?	0.31	0.18	1.0
9	Which writers had influenced the philosopher that refused a Nobel Prize?	0.71	0.56	1.0
11	Who composed the music for the film that depicts the early life of Jane Austin?	0.0	0.0	0.0
14	Which horses did The Long Fellow ride?	1.0	1.0	1.0
15	Of the people that died of radiation in Los Alamos, whose death was an accident?	0.67	1.0	0.5
16	Which buildings owned by the crown overlook the North Sea?	0.25	0.14	1.0
17	Which buildings in art deco style did Shreve, Lamb and Harmon design?	0.5	0.33	1.0
18	Which birds are protected under the National Parks and Wildlife Act?	1.0	1.0	1.0
19	Which country did the first known photographer of snowflakes come from?	1.0	1.0	1.0
20	List all the battles fought by the lover of Cleopatra.	1.0	1.0	1.0
22	Which actress starring in the TV series Friends owns the production company Coquette Productions?	1.0	1.0	1.0
23	Dakar is the capital of which country member of the African Union?	1.0	1.0	1.0

- **Entity Annotation:** Queries 1, 11 and 15 cannot be answered by HAWK due to failing entity annotation. None of the tested annotation tools was able to either find the resources Jane_T._Austion nor G8 or Los_Alamos. Without matching entity annotations a full-text search retrieves too many matches for reaching high precision values on limited result set.
- **Missing type information:** some of the resources of the gold standard do not have appropriate type information leading to a high amount of queries that need to be ranked correctly.
- **Query structure:** Queries like 11 or 15 inherit complex query structures leading to a multitude of interpretations while generating the SPARQL query graph.

4   Related Work

Hybrid question answering is related to the fields of hybrid search and question answering over structured data. In the following, we thus give a brief overview of the state of the art in these two areas of research.

First, we present hybrid search approaches which use a combination of structured as well as unstructured data to satisfy an user's information need. Semplore [25] is the first known hybrid search engine by IBM. It combines existing information retrieval index structures and functions to index RDF data as well as textual data. Semplore focuses on scalable algorithms and is evaluated on an early QALD dataset. Bhagdev et al. [1] describe an approach to hybrid search combining keyword searches, Semantic Web inferencing and querying. The proposed K-Search outperforms both keyword search and pure semantic search strategies. Additionally, an user study reveals the acceptance of the Hybrid Search paradigm by end users. A personalized hybrid search implementing a hotel search service as use case is presented in [24]. By combining rule-based personal knowledge inference over subjective data, such as expensive locations, and reasoning, the personalized hybrid search has been proven to return a smaller amount of data thus resulting in more precise answers. Unfortunately, the paper does not present any qualitative evaluation and it lacks source code and test data for reproducibility. All presented approaches fail to answer natural-language questions. Besides keyword-based search queries, some search engines already understand natural language questions. Question answering is more difficult than keyword-based searches since retrieval algorithms need to understand complex grammatical constructs.

Second, we explain several QA approaches in the following. Schlaefer et al. [16] describe *Ephyra*, an open-source question answering system and its extension with factoid and list questions via semantic technologies. Using Wordnet as well as an answer type classifier to combine statistical, fuzzy models and previously developed, manually refined rules. The disadvantage of this system lies in the hand-coded answer type hierarchy. Cimiano et al. [4] developed *ORAKEL* to work on structured knowledge bases. The system is capable of adjusting its natural language interface using a refinement process on unanswered questions. Using F-logic and SPARQL as transformation objects for natural language user queries it fails to make use of Semantic Web technologies such entity disambiguation. Lopez et al. [11] introduce *PowerAqua*, another open source system, which is agnostic of the underlying yet heterogeneous sets of knowledge bases. It detects on-the-fly the needed ontologies to answer a certain question, maps the users query to Semantic Web vocabulary and composes the retrieved (fragment-) information to an answer. However, PowerAqua is outperformed by TBSL (see below) in terms of accuracy w.r.t. the state-of-the-art QALD 3 benchmark. Damljanovic et al. [5] present *FREyA* to tackle ambiguity problems when using natural language interfaces. Many ontologies in the Semantic Web contain hard to map relations, e.g., questions starting with 'How long...' can be disambiguated to a time or a distance. By incorporating user feedback and syntactic analysis FREyA is able to learn the users query formulation preferences increasing the systems question answering precision. Cabrio et al. [2] present a demo of *QAKiS*, an agnostic QA system grounded in ontology-relation matches. The relation matches are based on surface forms extracted from Wikipedia to enforce a wide variety of context matches, e.g., a relation birthplace(person, place) can be explicated by X was born in Y or Y is the birthplace of X. Unfortunately, QAKiS matches only one relation per query and moreover relies on basic heuristics which do not account for the variety of natural language in general. Unger et al. [20] describe *Pythia*, a question answering system based on two steps. First, it uses a domain-independent representation of a query such as verbs, determiners and wh-words. Second, Pythia is based on a domain-dependent, ontology-based interface to transform queries into F-logic. Unfortunately, Pythia does not scale for larger domains since manual mapping of ontology terms via LexInfo is required. Moreover, Unger et al. [19] present a manually curated, template-based approach, dubbed *TBSL*, to match a question against a specific SPARQL query. Combining natural language processing capabilities with Linked Data leads to good benchmark results on the QALD-3 benchmark (see below). TBSL cannot be used to a wider variety of natural language questions due to its limited repertoire of 22 templates. Shekarpour et al. [17] develop *SINA* a keyword and natural language query search engine which is aware of the underlying semantics of a keyword query. The system is based on Hidden Markov Models for choosing the correct dataset to query. *Treo* [8] emphasis the connection between the semantic matching of input queries and the semantic distributions underlying knowledge bases. The tool provides an entity search, a semantic relatedness measure, and a search based on spreading activation. Recently, Peng et al. [15] describe an approach for hybrid QA mapping keywords as well as resource candidates to modified SPARQL queries. Due to its novelty we were not able to compare it to HAWK.

Several industry-driven QA-related projects have emerged over the last years. For example, DeepQA of IBM Watson [7], which was able to win the Jeopardy! challenge against human experts. Further, KAIST's Exobrain[5] project aims to learn from large amounts of data while ensuring a natural interaction with end users. However, it is yet limited to Korean for the moment.

The field HAWK refers to is hybrid question answering for the Semantic Web, i.e., QA based on hybrid data (RDF and textual data). To the best of our knowledge, none of the previous works has addressed this question so far. For further insights please refer to [10,12] which present surveys on existing question answering approaches.

5 Conclusion

In this paper, we presented HAWK, the first hybrid QA system for the Web of Data. We showed that by using a generic approach to generate SPARQL queries out of predicate-argument structures, HAWK is able to achieve up to 0.68 F-measure on the QALD-4 benchmark. Our work on HAWK however also revealed several open research questions, of which the most important lies in

---

[5] http://exobrain.kr/.

finding the correct ranking approach to map a predicate-argument tree to a possible interpretation. So far, our experiments reveal that the mere finding of the right features for this endeavor remains a challenging problem. We thus aim to apply an automatic feature engineering approach from deep learning in future works to automatically generate the correct ranking function. Moreover, we aim to integrate HAWK in domain-specific information systems where the more specialized context will most probably lead to higher F-measures. Additionally, we will assess the impact of full-text components over regular LD components for QA, partake in the creation of larger benchmarks (we are working on QALD-5) and aim towards multilingual, schema-agnostic queries. Negations within questions and improved ranking will also be considered. Finally, several components of the HAWK pipeline are computationally very complex. Finding more time-efficient algorithms for these steps will be addressed in future works.

Acknowledgments. This work has been supported by the ESF, the Free State of Saxony and the FP7 project GeoKnow (GA No. 318159).

References

1. Bhagdev, R., Chapman, S., Ciravegna, F., Lanfranchi, V., Petrelli, D.: Hybrid search: Effectively combining keywords and semantic searches. In: Bechhofer, S., Hauswirth, M., Hoffmann, J., Koubarakis, M. (eds.) ESWC 2008. LNCS, vol. 5021, pp. 554–568. Springer, Heidelberg (2008)
2. Cabrio, E., Cojan, J., Gandon, F., Hallili, A.: Querying multilingual DBpedia with QAKiS. In: Cimiano, P., Fernández, M., Lopez, V., Schlobach, S., Völker, J. (eds.) ESWC 2013. LNCS, vol. 7955, pp. 194–198. Springer, Heidelberg (2013)
3. Choi, J.D., Palmer, M.: Getting the most out of transition-based dependency parsing. In: ACL, pp. 687–692 (2011)
4. Cimiano, P., Haase, P., Heizmann, J., Mantel, M., Studer, R.: Towards portable natural language interfaces to knowledge bases - The case of the ORAKEL system. Data Knowl. Eng. **65**(2), 325–354 (2008)
5. Damljanovic, D., Agatonovic, M., Cunningham, H., Bontcheva, K.: Improving habitability of natural language interfaces for querying ontologies with feedback and clarification dialogues. J. Web Semant. **19**, 1–21 (2013)
6. Ferragina, P., Scaiella, U.: Fast and Accurate Annotation of Short Texts with Wikipedia Pages. IEEE software (2012)
7. Ferrucci, D.A., et al.: Building watson: An overview of the DeepQA project. AI Mag. **31**(3), 59–79 (2010)
8. Freitas, A., Oliveira, J.G., Curry, E., O'Riain, S., da Silva, J.C.P.: Treo: combining entity-search, spreading activation and semantic relatedness for querying linked data. In: 1st Workshop on Question Answering over Linked Data (QALD-1) (2011)
9. Gerber, D., Hellmann, S., Bühmann, L., Soru, T., Usbeck, R., Ngonga Ngomo, A.-C.: Real-Time RDF extraction from unstructured data streams. In: Alani, H., Kagal, L., Fokoue, A., Groth, P., Biemann, C., Parreira, J.X., Aroyo, L., Noy, N., Welty, C., Janowicz, K. (eds.) ISWC 2013, Part I. LNCS, vol. 8218, pp. 135–150. Springer, Heidelberg (2013)

10. Kolomiyets, O., Moens, M.-F.: A survey on question answering technology from an information retrieval perspective. Inf. Sci. **181**(24), 5412–5434 (2011)
11. Lopez, V., Fernández, M., Motta, E., Stieler, N.: PowerAqua: Supporting users in querying and exploring the semantic web. Semant. Web J. **3**, 249–265 (2012)
12. Lopez, V., Uren, V.S., Sabou, M., Motta, E.: Is question answering fit for the semantic web?: A survey. Semant. Web J. **2**(2), 125–155 (2011)
13. Mendes, P.N., Jakob, M., Garcia-Silva, A., Bizer, C.: DBpedia spotlight: Shedding light on the web of documents. In: I-Semantics (2011)
14. Milne, D., Witten, I.H.: Learning to link with wikipedia. In: 17th ACM CIKM (2008)
15. Peng, P., Zou, L., Zhao, D.: On the marriage of SPARQL and keywords. CoRR, abs/1411.6335 (2014)
16. Schlaefer, N., Ko, J., Betteridge, J., Sautter, G., Pathak, M., Nyberg, E.: Semantic Extensions of the Ephyra QA System for TREC (2007)
17. Shekarpour, S., Marx, E., Ngomo, A.-C.N., Auer, S.: Sina: Semantic interpretation of user queries for question answering on interlinked data. J. Web Semant. **30**(3), 39–51 (2014)
18. Speck, R., Ngomo, A.-C.N.: Ensemble learning for named entity recognition. In: Mika, P., Tudorache, T., Bernstein, A., Welty, C., Knoblock, C., Vrandečić, D., Groth, P., Noy, N., Janowicz, K., Goble, C. (eds.) ISWC 2014, Part I. LNCS, vol. 8796, pp. 519–534. Springer, Heidelberg (2014)
19. Unger, C., Bühmann, L., Lehmann, J., Ngomo, A.N., Gerber, D., Cimiano, P.: Template-based question answering over RDF data. In: 21st WWW Conference, pp. 639–648 (2012)
20. Unger, C., Cimiano, P.: Pythia: Compositional meaning construction for ontology-based question answering on the semantic web. In: Muñoz, R., Montoyo, A., Métais, E. (eds.) NLDB 2011. LNCS, vol. 6716, pp. 153–160. Springer, Heidelberg (2011)
21. Unger, C., Forascu, C., Lopez, V., Ngomo, A.N., Cabrio, E., Cimiano, P., Walter, S.: Question answering over linked data (QALD-4). In: CLEF, pp. 1172–1180 (2014)
22. Usbeck, R.: Combining linked data and statistical information retrieval. In: Presutti, V., d'Amato, C., Gandon, F., d'Aquin, M., Staab, S., Tordai, A. (eds.) ESWC 2014. LNCS, vol. 8465, pp. 845–854. Springer, Heidelberg (2014)
23. Usbeck, R., Ngonga Ngomo, A.-C., Röder, M., Gerber, D., Coelho, S.A., Auer, S., Both, A.: AGDISTIS - Graph-based disambiguation of named entities using linked data. In: Mika, P., Tudorache, T., Bernstein, A., Welty, C., Knoblock, C., Vrandečić, D., Groth, P., Noy, N., Janowicz, K., Goble, C. (eds.) ISWC 2014, Part I. LNCS, vol. 8796, pp. 457–471. Springer, Heidelberg (2014)
24. Yoo, D.: Hybrid query processing for personalized information retrieval on the semantic web. Knowl. Base Syst. **27**, 211–218 (2012)
25. Zhang, L., Liu, Q., Zhang, J., Wang, H., Pan, Y., Yu, Y.: Semplore: An IR approach to scalable hybrid query of semantic web data. In: Aberer, K., Choi, K.-S., Noy, N., Allemang, D., Lee, K.-I., Nixon, L.J.B., Golbeck, J., Mika, P., Maynard, D., Mizoguchi, R., Schreiber, G., Cudré-Mauroux, P. (eds.) ASWC 2007 and ISWC 2007. LNCS, vol. 4825, pp. 652–665. Springer, Heidelberg (2007)

Machine Learning

Automating RDF Dataset Transformation and Enrichment

Mohamed Ahmed Sherif$^{(\boxtimes)}$, Axel-Cyrille Ngonga Ngomo, and Jens Lehmann

Department of Computer Science, University of Leipzig, 04109 Leipzig, Germany
{sherif,ngonga,lehmann}@informatik.uni-leipzig.de

Abstract. With the adoption of RDF across several domains, come growing requirements pertaining to the completeness and quality of RDF datasets. Currently, this problem is most commonly addressed by manually devising means of enriching an input dataset. The few tools that aim at supporting this endeavour usually focus on supporting the manual definition of enrichment pipelines. In this paper, we present a supervised learning approach based on a refinement operator for enriching RDF datasets. We show how we can use exemplary descriptions of enriched resources to generate accurate enrichment pipelines. We evaluate our approach against eight manually defined enrichment pipelines and show that our approach can learn accurate pipelines even when provided with a small number of training examples.

1 Introduction

Over the last years, the Linked Data principles have been used across academia and industry to publish and consume linked data [16]. With this adoption of Linked data come novel challenges pertaining to the integration of these datasets for dedicated applications such as tourism, question answering, enhanced reality and many more. Providing consolidated and integrated datasets for these applications demands the specification of data enrichment pipelines, which describe how data from different sources is to be integrated and altered so as to abide by the precepts of the application developer or data user. Currently, most developers implement customized pipelines by compiling sequences of tools manually and connecting them via customized scripts. While this approach most commonly leads to the expected results, it is time-demanding and resource-intensive. Moreover, the results of this effort can most commonly only be reused for new versions of the input data but cannot be ported easily to other datasets. Over the last years, a few frameworks for RDF data enrichment such as LDIF[1] and DEER[2] have been developed. The frameworks provide enrichment methods such as entity recognition [22], link discovery [15] and schema enrichment [4]. However, devising appropriate configurations for these tools can prove a difficult endeavour, as the tools require (1) choosing the right sequence of enrichment functions

---

[1] http://ldif.wbsg.de/.
[2] http://aksw.org/Projects/DEER.html.

© Springer International Publishing Switzerland 2015
F. Gandon et al. (Eds.): ESWC 2015, LNCS 9088, pp. 371–387, 2015.
DOI: 10.1007/978-3-319-18818-8_23

and (2) configuring these functions adequately. Both the first and second task can be tedious.

In this paper, we address this problem by presenting a supervised machine learning approach for the automatic detection of enrichment pipelines based on a refinement operator and self-configuration algorithms for enrichment functions. Our approach takes pairs of concise bounded descriptions (CBDs) of resources $\{(k_1, k_1') \ldots (k_n, k_n')\}$ as input, where k_i' is the enriched version of k_i. Based on these pairs, our approach can learn sequences of atomic enrichment functions that aim to generate each k_i' out of the corresponding k_i. The output of our approach is an enrichment pipeline that can be used on whole datasets to generate enriched versions.

Overall, we provide the following core contributions: (1) We define a supervised machine learning algorithm for learning dataset enrichment pipelines based on a refinement operator. (2) We provide self-configuration algorithms for five atomic enrichment steps. (3) We evaluate our approach on eight manually defined enrichment pipelines on real datasets.

2   Preliminaries

Enrichment: Let $\mathcal{K}$ be the set of all RDF knowledge bases. Let $K \in \mathcal{K}$ be a finite RDF knowledge base. K can be regarded as a set of triples $(s, p, o) \in (\mathcal{R} \cup \mathcal{B}) \times \mathcal{P} \times (\mathcal{R} \cup \mathcal{L} \cup \mathcal{B})$, where $\mathcal{R}$ is the set of all resources, $\mathcal{B}$ is the set of all blank nodes, $\mathcal{P}$ the set of all predicates and $\mathcal{L}$ the set of all literals. Given a knowledge base K, the idea behind *knowledge base enrichment* is to find an *enrichment pipeline* $M : \mathcal{K} \to \mathcal{K}$ that maps K to an enriched knowledge base K' with $K' = M(K)$. We define M as an ordered list of *atomic enrichment functions* $m \in \mathcal{M}$, where $\mathcal{M}$ is the set of all atomic enrichment functions. $2^{\mathcal{M}}$ is used to denote the power set of $\mathcal{M}$, i.e. the set of all enrichment pipelines. The order of elements in M determines the execution order, e.g. for an $M = (m_1, m_2, m_3)$ this means that m_1 will be executed first, then m_2, finally m_3. Formally,

$$M = \begin{cases} \phi & \text{if } K = K', \\ (m_1, \ldots, m_n), \text{where } m_i \in \mathcal{M}, 1 \leq i \leq n & \text{otherwise,} \end{cases} \quad (1)$$

where ϕ is the empty sequence. Moreover, we denote the number of elements of M with $|M|$. Considering that a knowledge base is simply a set of triples, the task of any atomic enrichment function is to (1) determine a set of triples Δ^+ to be added the source knowledge base and/or (2) determine a set of triples Δ^- to be deleted from the source knowledge base. Any other enrichment process can be defined in terms of Δ^+ and Δ^-, e.g. altering triples can be represented as combination of addition and deletion.

In this article we cover two problems: (1) how to create self-configurable atomic enrichment functions $m \in \mathcal{M}$ capable of enriching a dataset and (2) how to automatically generate an enrichment pipeline M. As a running example, we use the portion of *DrugBank* shown in Fig. 1. The goal of the enrichment here is

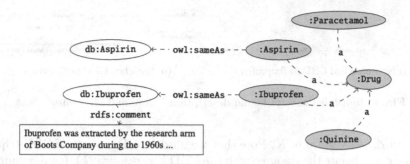

Fig. 1. RDF graph of the running example. Ellipses are RDF resources, literals are rectangular nodes. Gray nodes stand for resources in the input knowledge base while nodes with a white background are part of an external knowledge base.

to gather information about companies related to drugs for a market study. To this end, the `owl:sameAs` links to *DBpedia* (prefix `db`) need to be dereferenced. Their `rdfs:comment` then needs to be processed using an entity spotter that will help retrieve resources such as the `Boots Company`. Then, these resources need to be attached directly to the resources in the source knowledge base, e.g., by using the `:relatedCompany` property. Finally, all subjects need to be conformed under one subject authority (prefix `ex`).

Refinement Operators: Below, we give definitions of refinement operators and their properties. Refinement operators have traditionally been used, e.g. in [11], to traverse search spaces in structured machine learning problems. Their theoretical properties give an indication of how suitable they are within a learning algorithm in terms of accuracy and efficiency.

Definition 1 (Refinement Operator and Properties). *Given a quasi-ordered space $(S, \preccurlyeq)$ an upward refinement operator r is a mapping from S to 2^S such that $\forall s \in S : s' \in r(s) \Rightarrow s \preccurlyeq s'$. s' is then called a generalization of s. A pipeline $M_2 \in \mathcal{M}$ belongs to the refinement chain of $M_1 \in \mathcal{M}$ iff $\exists i \in \mathbb{N} : M_2 \in r^i(M_1)$, where $r^0(M) = M$ and $r^i(M) = r(r^{i-1}(M))$. A refinement operator r over the quasi-ordered space $(S, \preccurlyeq)$ can abide by the following criteria. r is finite iff $r(s)$ is finite for all $s \in S$. r is proper if $\forall s \in S, s' \in r(s) \Rightarrow s \neq s'$. r is complete if for all s and s', $s' \preccurlyeq s$ implies that there is a refinement chain between s and s'. A refinement operator r over the space $(S, \preccurlyeq)$ is redundant if two different refinement chains can exist between $s \in S$ and $s' \in S$.*

3   Knowledge Base Enrichment Refinement Operator

Our refinement operator expects the set of atomic enrichment functions $\mathcal{M}$ as input and returns an enrichment pipeline M as output. Each positive example $e \in \mathcal{E}$ is a pair of CBDs (k, k'), with $k \subseteq K$ and $k' \subseteq K'$, the K' stands

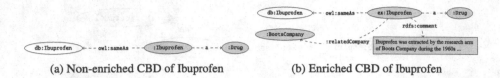

(a) Non-enriched CBD of Ibuprofen   (b) Enriched CBD of Ibuprofen

Fig. 2. Ibuprofen concise bound description before and after enrichment

for the enriched version of K. Note that we model CBDs as sets of RDF triples. Moreover, we denote the resource with the CBD k as $resource(k)$. For our running example, the set $\mathcal{E}$ could contain the pair shown in Fig. 2a as k and in Fig. 2b as k'.

The set of all first elements of the pairs contained in $\mathcal{E}$ is denoted $source(\mathcal{E})$. The set of all second elements is denoted $target(\mathcal{E})$. To compute the refinement pipeline M, we employ an upward refinement operator (which we dub ρ) over the space $2^{\mathcal{M}}$ of all enrichment pipelines. We write $M \supseteq M'$ when M' is a subsequence of M, i.e., $m'_i \in M' \rightarrow m'_i = m_i$, where m_i resp. m'_i is the ith element of M resp. M'.

Proposition 1 (Induced Quasi-Ordering). $\supseteq$ *induces a quasi-ordering over the set $2^{\mathcal{M}}$.*

Proof. The reflexivity of $\supseteq$ follows from each M being a subsequence of itself. The transitivity of $\supseteq$ follows from the transitivity of the subsequence relation. Note that $\supseteq$ is also antisymmetric. $\qquad\square$

We define our refinement operator over the space $(2^{\mathcal{M}}, \supseteq)$ as follows:

$$\rho(M) = \bigcup_{\forall m \in \mathcal{M}} M \mathbin{+\!\!+} m \qquad (\mathbin{+\!\!+} \text{ is the list append operator}) \qquad (2)$$

We define precision $P(M)$ and recall $R(M)$ achieved by an enrichment pipeline on $\mathcal{E}$ as

$$P(M) = \frac{\left| \bigcup\limits_{k \in source(\mathcal{E})} M(k) \bigcap \bigcup\limits_{k' \in target(\mathcal{E})} k' \right|}{\left| \bigcup\limits_{k \in source(\mathcal{E})} M(k) \right|}, R(M) = \frac{\left| \bigcup\limits_{k \in source(\mathcal{E})} M(k) \bigcap \bigcup\limits_{k' \in target(\mathcal{E})} k' \right|}{\left| \bigcup\limits_{k' \in target(\mathcal{E})} k' \right|}.$$

$$(3)$$

The F-measure $F(M)$ is then

$$F(M) = \frac{2P(M)R(M)}{P(M) + R(M)}. \qquad (4)$$

Using Fig. 2a from our running example as source and Fig. 2b as target with the CBD of :Iboprufen being the only positive example, an empty enrichment pipeline $M = \phi$ would have a precision of 1, a recall of $\frac{3}{4}$ and an F-measure of $\frac{6}{7}$. Having defined our refinement operator, we now show that ρ is finite, proper, complete and not redundant.

Proposition 2. *ρ is finite.*

Proof. This is a direct consequence of $\mathcal{M}$ being finite.   □

Proposition 3. *ρ is proper.*

Proof. As the quasi order is defined over subsequences, i.e. the space $(2^{\mathcal{M}}, \supseteq)$, and we have $|M'| = |M| + 1$ for any $M' \in \rho(M)$, ρ is trivially proper.   □

Proposition 4. *ρ is complete.*

Proof. Let M resp. M' be an enrichment pipeline of length n resp. n' with $M' \supseteq M$. Moreover, let m'_i be the ith element of M'. Per definition, $M \mathbin{+\mkern-8mu+} m'_{n+1} \in \rho(M)$. Hence, by applying ρ $n' - n$ times, we can generate M' from M. We can thus conclude that ρ is complete.   □

Proposition 5. *ρ is not redundant.*

Proof. ρ being redundant would mean that there are two refinement chains that lead to a single refinement pipeline M. As our operator is equivalent to the list append operation, it would be equivalent to stating that two different append sequences can lead to the same sequence. This is obviously not the case as each element of the list M is unique, leading to exactly one sequence that can generate M.   □

4   Learning Algorithm

The learning algorithm is inspired by refinement-based approaches from inductive logic programming. In these algorithms, a search tree is iteratively built up using heuristic search via a fitness function. We formally define a node N in a search tree to be a triple (M, f, s), where M is the *enrichment pipeline*, $f \in [0, 1]$ is the F-measure of M (see Eq. 4), and $s \in \{normal, dead\}$ is the status of the node. Given a search tree, the heuristic selects the fittest node in it, where fitness is based on both F-measure and complexity as defined below.

4.1   Approach

For the automatic generation of enrichment pipeline specifications, we created a learning algorithm based on the previously defined refinement operator. Once provided with training examples, the approach is fully automatic. The pseudocode of our algorithm is presented in Algorithm 4.1.

Our learning algorithm has two inputs: a set of positive examples $\mathcal{E}$ and a set of atomic enrichment operators $\mathcal{M}$. $\mathcal{E}$ contains pairs of (k, k') where each k contains a CBD of one resource from an arbitrary source knowledge base K and k' contains the CBD of the same resource after applying some manual enrichment. Given $\mathcal{E}$, the goal of our algorithm is to learn an enrichment pipeline M that maximizes $F(M)$ (see Eq. 4).

As shown in Algorithm 4.1, our approach starts by generating an empty refinement tree τ which contains only an empty root node. Using $\mathcal{E}$, the algorithm then accumulates all the original CBDs in k (SOURCE($\mathcal{E}$)). Using the same procedure, k' is accumulated from $\mathcal{E}$ as the knowledge base containing the enriched version of k (TARGET($\mathcal{E}$)). Until a termination criterion holds (see Sect. 4.3), the algorithm keeps expanding the most promising node (see Sect. 4.2). Finally, the algorithm ends by returning the best pipeline found in τ: (GetPipeline(GetMaxQualityNode(τ))).

Having a *most promising node* t at hand, the algorithm first applies our refinement operator (see Eq. 2) against the most promising enrichment pipeline M_{old} included in t to generate a set of atomic enrichment functions $\mathcal{M} \leftarrow \rho(M_{old})$. Consequently, using both k_{old} (as the knowledge base generated by applying M_{old} against k) and k', the algorithm applies the self configuration process of the current atomic enrichment function $m \leftarrow$ SELFCONFIG(m, k_{old}, k) to generate a set of parameters P (a detailed description for this process is found in Sect. 5). Afterwards, the algorithm runs m against k_{old} to generate the new enriched knowledge base $k_{new} \leftarrow m(k_{old}, P)$. A dead node $N \leftarrow$ CREATENODE(M, 0, *dead*) is created in two cases: (1) m is inapplicable to k_{old} (i.e., $P == null$) or (2) m does no enrichment at all (i.e., k_{new} is isomorphic[3] to k_{old}). Otherwise, the algorithm computes the F-measure f of the generated dataset k_{new}. M along with f are then used to generate a new search tree node $N \leftarrow$ CREATENODE(M, f, *normal*)). Finally, N is added as a child of t (ADDCHILD(t, N)).

4.2 Most Promising Node Selection

Here we describe the process of selecting the most promising node $t \in \tau$ as in GETMOSTPROMISINGNODE() subroutine in Algorithm 4.1. First, we define *node complexity* as linear combination of the node's children count and level. Formally,

Definition 2. (Node Complexity). *The complexity of a node $N = (M, f, s)$ in a refinement tree τ is a function $c: N \times \tau \rightarrow [0, 1]$, where $c(N, \tau) = \alpha \frac{|N_d|}{|\tau|} + \beta \frac{N_l}{\tau_d}$, $|N_d|$ is number of all N's descendant nodes, $|\tau|$ is the total number of nodes in τ, N_l is N's level, τ_d is τ's depth, α is the children penalty weight, β is the level penalty weight and $\alpha + \beta = 1$. Seeking for simplicity, we will use the $c(N)$ instead of $c(N, \tau)$ in the rest of this paper.*

We can then define the fitness $f(N)$ of a *normal* node N as the difference between its enrichment pipeline F-measure (Eq. 4) and weighted complexity. $f(N)$ is zero for *dead* nodes. Formally,

Definition 3. (Node Fitness). *Let $N = (M, f, s)$ be a node in a refinement tree τ, N's fitness is the function*

$$f(N) = \begin{cases} 0 & \text{if } s = \text{dead}, \\ F(M) - \omega \cdot c(N) & \text{if } s = \text{normal}. \end{cases} \tag{5}$$

---

[3] http://www.w3.org/TR/rdf11-concepts/.

where M is the enrichment pipeline contained in the node N, ω is the complexity weight and $0 \leq \omega \leq 1$.

Note, that we use the *complexity* of pipelines as second criterion, which makes the algorithm (1) more flexible in searching less explored areas of the search space, and (2) leads to simpler specification being preferred over more complex ones (Occam's razor [3]). The parameter ω can be used to control the trade-off between a greedy search ($\omega = 0$) and search strategies closer to breadth first search ($\omega > 0$). The fitness function can be defined independently of the core learning algorithm.

Consequently, the most promising node is the node with the maximum fitness through the whole refinement tree τ. Formally, the most promising node t is defined as $t = \arg\max_{\forall N \in \tau} f(N)$, where N is not a *dead* node. Note that if several nodes achieve a maximum fitness, the algorithm chooses the shortest node as it aims to generate the simplest enrichment pipeline possible.

Algorithm 4.1. ENRICHMENTPIPELINELEARNER($\mathcal{E}^+$, $\mathcal{M}$)

---

comment: initialize τ

$\tau \leftarrow$ CREATEROOTNODE()
$k \leftarrow$ SOURCE($\mathcal{E}$)
$k' \leftarrow$ TARGET($\mathcal{E}$)
repeat
⎧ **comment:** Expand most promising node of τ
⎪
⎪ $t \leftarrow$ GETMOSTPROMISINGNODE(τ)
⎪ $M_{old} \leftarrow$ GETPIPELINE(t)
⎪ $\mathcal{M} \leftarrow \rho(M_{old})$
⎪ **comment:** Create a child of t for each $m \in \mathcal{M}$
⎪
⎨ **for each** $m \in \mathcal{M}$
⎪   ⎧ $k_{old} \leftarrow M_{old}(k)$
⎪   ⎪ $P \leftarrow$ SELFCONFIG(m, k_{old}, k')
⎪   ⎪ $k_{new} \leftarrow m(k_{old}, P)$
⎪   ⎪ **if** $P == null$ **or** $k_{new} == k_{old}$
⎪   **do** ⎨   **then** $\{ N \leftarrow$ CREATENODE($M, 0, $ dead)
⎪   ⎪   **else** ⎧ $f \leftarrow$ F(m)
⎪   ⎪   ⎩ $N \leftarrow$ CREATENODE($M, f, $ normal)
⎩   ⎩ ADDCHILD(t, N)
until TERMINATIONCRITERIONHOLDS(τ)
return (GETPIPELINE(GETMAXQUALITYNODE(τ)))

4.3   Termination Criteria

The subroutine TERMINATIONCRITERIONHOLDS() in Algorithm 4.1 can check several termination criteria depending on configuration: (1) optimal enrichment pipeline found (i.e., a fixpoint is reached), (2) maximum number of iterations reached, (3) maximum number of refinement tree nodes reached, or a combination of the aforementioned criteria. Note that the termination criteria can be defined independently of the core learning algorithm.

5 Self-Configuration

To learn an appropriate specification from the input positive examples, we need to develop self-configuration approaches for each of our framework's atomic enrichment functions. The input for each of these self-configuration procedures is the same set of positive examples $\mathcal{E}$ provided to our pipeline learning algorithm (Algorithm 4.1). The goal of the self-configuration process of an enrichment function is to generate a set of parameters $P = \{(mp_1, v_1), \ldots, (mp_m, v_m)\}$ able to reflect $\mathcal{E}$ as well as possible. In cases when insufficient data is contained in $\mathcal{E}$ to carry out the self-configuration process, an empty list of parameters is returned to indicate inapplicability of the enrichment function.

5.1 Dereferencing Enrichment Functions

The idea behind the self-configuration process of the enrichment by *dereferencing* is to find the set of predicates D_p from the enriched CBDs that are missing from source CBDs. Formally, for each CBD pair (k, k') construct a set $D_p \subseteq \mathcal{P}$ as follows: $D_p = \{p' : (s', p', o') \in k'\}\backslash\{p : (s, p, o) \in k\}$. The dereferencing enrichment function will *dereference* the object of each triple of k_i given that this object is an external URI, i.e. all o in k_i with $(s, p, o) \in k_i$, $o \in \mathcal{R}$ and o is not in the local namespace of the dataset will be dereferenced. Dereferencing an object returns a set of triples. Those are filtered using the previously constructed property set D_p, i.e. when dereferencing o the enrichment function only retains triples with subject o and a predicate contained in D_p. The resulting set of triples is added to the input dataset.

We illustrate the process using our running example: In the first step, we compute the set $D_p = \{$:relatedCompany, rdfs:comment$\}$ which consists of the properties occurring in the target but not in the source CBD. In the second step, we collect the set of resources to dereference, which only consists of the element db:Ibuprofen. In the third step, we perform the actual dereferencing operation and retain triples for which the subject is db:Ibuprofen and the predicate is either :relatedCompany or rdfs:comment. In our example, no triples with predicate :relatedCompany exist, but we will find the desired triple (db:Ibuprofen, rdfs:comment, "Ibuprofen ..."), which is then added to the input dataset.

5.2 Linking Enrichment Function

The aim of *link discovery* is as follows: Given two sets $R_s \subseteq \mathcal{R}$ of source resources and $R_t \subseteq \mathcal{R}$ of target resources, we aim to discover links $L \subseteq R_s \times R_t$ such that for any $(s, t) \in L$ we have $\delta(s, t) \leq \theta$ where δ is a similarity function and θ a threshold value. The goal of the linking enrichment function is to learn so called *link specifications* including a similarity function δ and a threshold θ. To this aim, we rely on an unsupervised hierarchical search approach, which optimizes a target function akin to F-measure. The search space of all link specifications is split into a grid and the approach computes the objective function for all points in the grid. Thereafter, the region surrounding the point which achieves the highest score is selected as new search space. This approach is applied iteratively until a stopping condition (e.g., a maximal number of iterations) is reached. More details can be found at [18].

5.3 NLP Enrichment Function

The basic idea here is to enable the extraction of all possible named entity types. If this leads to the retrieval of too many entities, the unwanted predicates and resources can be discarded in a subsequent step. The self-configuration of the NLP enrichment function is parameter-free and relies on FOX [17]. The application of the NLP self configuration to our running example generates all possible entities included in the literal object of the `rdfs:comment` predicate. The result is a set of related named entities all of them related to our `ex:Iboprufen` object by the default predicate `fox:relatedTo` as shown Fig. 3a. In the following 2 sections we will see how our enrichment functions can refine some of the generated triples and delete others.

5.4 Conformation Enrichment Functions

The *conformation*-based enrichment currently allows for both *subject-authority-based conformation* and *predicate-based conformation*. The self-configuration process of *subject-authority-based conformation* starts by finding the most frequent subject authority rk in $source(\mathcal{E})$. Also, it finds the most frequent subject authority rk' in the target dataset $target(\mathcal{E})$. Then this self-configuration process generates the two parameters: (`sourceSubjectAuthority`, rk) and (`target SubjectAuthority`, rk'). After that, the self-configuration process replaces each subject authority rk in $source(\mathcal{E})$ by rk'.

Back to our running example, the authority self-conformation process generates the two parameters (`sourceSubjectAuthority`, `":"`) and (`targetSubject Authority`, `"ex:"`). Replacing each `":"` by `"ex:"` generates, in our example, the new conformed URI `"ex:Iboprufen"`.

We define two predicates $p_1, p_2 \in \mathcal{P}$ to be *interchangeable* (denoted $p_1 \leftrightarrows p_2$) if both of them have the same subject and object. Formally, $\forall p_1, p_2 \in \mathcal{P} : p_1 \leftrightarrows p_2 \iff \exists s, o \mid (s, p_1, o) \wedge (s, p_2, o)$.

The idea of the self-configuration process of the *predicate conformation* is to change each predicate in the source dataset to its *interchangeable* predicate in the target dataset. Formally, find all pairs $(p_1, p_2) \mid \exists s, p_1, o \in k \wedge \exists s, p_2, o \in k' \wedge (s, p_1, o) \in k \wedge (s, p_2, o) \in k'$. Then, for each pair (p_1, p_2) create two self-configuration parameters (`sourceProperty`, p_1) and (`targetProperty`, p_2). The predicate conformation will replace each occurrence of p_1 by p_2.

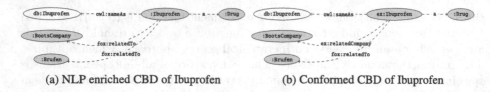

(a) NLP enriched CBD of Ibuprofen   (b) Conformed CBD of Ibuprofen

Fig. 3. Ibuprofen CBD after NLP and predicate conformation enrichment

In our example, let us suppose that we ran the NLP-based enrichment first then we got a set of related named entities all of them related to our `ex:Iboprufen` object by the default predicate `fox:relatedTo` as shown in Fig. 3a. Subsequently, applying the predicate conformation self-configuration will generate (`source Property`, `fox:relatedTo`) and (`targetProperty`, `ex:relatedCompany`) parameters. Consequently, the predicate conformation module will replace `fox:relatedTo` by `ex:relatedCompany` to generate Fig. 3b.

5.5 Filter Enrichment Function

The idea behind the self-configuration of *filter*-based enrichment is to preserve only valuable triples in the source CBDs k and discard any unnecessary triples so as to achieve a better match to k'. To this end, the self-configuration process starts by finding the intersection between source and target examples $I = \bigcup_{(k,k')\in\mathcal{E}} k\cap k'$. After that, it generates an enrichment function based on a SPARQL query which is only preserving predicates in I. Formally, the self-configuration results in the parameter set $P = \bigcup_{p\in K\cap K'\cap\mathcal{P}} p$.

Back to our running example, let us continue from the situation in the previous section (Fig. 3b). Performing the self-configuration of filters will generate $P = \{\texttt{fox:relatedTo}\}$. Actually applying the filter enrichment function will remove all unrelated triples containing the predicate `fox:relatedTo`. Figure 4 shows a graph representation for the whole learned pipeline for our running example.

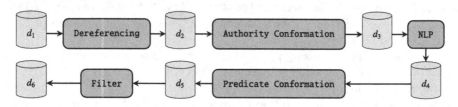

Fig. 4. Graph representation of the learned pipeline of our running example, where d_1 is the positive example source presented in Fig. 2a and d_6 is the positive example target presented in Fig. 2b.

6   Evaluation

The aim of our evaluation was to quantify how well our approach can automate the enrichment process. We thus assumed being given manually created training examples and having to reconstruct a possible enrichment pipeline to generate target CBDs from the source CBDs. In the following, we present our experimental setup including the pipelines and datasets used. Thereafter, we give an overview of our results, which we subsequently discuss in the final part of this section.

6.1   Experimental Setup

We used three publicly available datasets for our experiments:

1. From the biomedical domain, we chose *DrugBank*[4] as our first dataset. We chose this dataset because it is linked with many other datasets[5], from which we can extract enrichment data using our atomic enrichment functions. For our experiments we deployed a manual enrichment pipeline M_{manual}, in which we enrich the drug data found in *DrugBank* using abstracts dereferenced from *DBpedia*, then we conform both *DrugBank* and *DBpedia* source authority URIs to one unified URI. For *DrugBank* we manually deployed two experimental pipelines:

   - $M^1_{DrugBank} = (m_1, m_2)$, where m_1 is a dereferencing function that dereferences any `dbpedia-owl:abstract` from DBpedia and m_2 is an authority conformation function that conforms the *DBpedia* subject authority[6] to the target subject authority of *DrugBank*[7].
   - $M^2_{DrugBank} = M^1_{DrugBank} + m_3$, where m_3 is an authority conformation function that conforms *DrugBank*'s authority to the *Example* authority[8].

2. From the music domain, we chose the *Jamendo*[9] dataset. We selected this dataset as it contains a substantial amount of embedded information hidden in literal properties such as `mo:biography`. The goal of our enrichment process is to add a geospatial dimension to *Jamendo*, e.g., the location of a recording or place of birth of a musician. To this end, we deployed a manual enrichment pipeline, in which we enrich *Jamendo*'s music data by adding additional geospatial data found by applying the NLP enrichment function

---

[4] *DrugBank* is the Linked Data version of the DrugBank database, which is a repository of almost 5000 FDA-approved small molecule and biotech drugs, for RDF dump see http://wifo5-03.informatik.uni-mannheim.de/drugbank/drugbank_dump.nt.bz2.

[5] See http://datahub.io/dataset/fu-berlin-drugbank for complete list of linked dataset with *DrugBank*.

[6] http://dbpedia.org.

[7] http://wifo5-04.informatik.uni-mannheim.de/drugbank/resource/drugs.

[8] http://example.org.

[9] *Jamendo* contains a large collection of music related information about artists and recordings, for RDF dump see http://moustaki.org/resources/jamendo-rdf.tar.gz.

against `mo:biography`. For *Jamendo* we deploy manually one experimental pipeline:

– $M^1_{Jamendo} = \{m_4\}$, where m_4 is an NLP function that find *locations* in `mo:biography`.

3. From the multi-domain knowledge base *DBpedia* [12] we used the class `AdministrativeRegion` for our experiments. As DBpedia is a knowledge base with a large ontology, we build a set of five pipelines of increasing complexity:

– $M^1_{DBpedia} = \{m_5\}$, where m_5 is an authority conformation function that conforms the *DBpedia* subject authority to the *Example* target subject authority.

– $M^2_{DBpedia} = m_6 \mathbin{+\!\!+} M^1_{DBpedia}$, where m_6 is a dereferencing function that dereferences any `dbpedia-owl:ideology`.

– $M^3_{DBpedia} = M^2_{DBpedia} \mathbin{+\!\!+} m_7$, where m_7 is an NLP function that finds *all* named entities in `dbpedia-owl:abstract`.

– $M^4_{DBpedia} = M^3_{DBpedia} \mathbin{+\!\!+} m_8$, where m_8 is a filter function that filters for abstracts.

– $M^5_{DBpedia} = M^3_{DBpedia} \mathbin{+\!\!+} m_9$, where m_9 is a predicate conformation function that conforms the source predicate `dbpedia-owl:abstract` to the target predicate of `dcterms:abstract`.

Altogether, we manually generated a set of eight pipelines, which we then applied against their respective datasets. The evaluation protocol was as follows: Let M be one of the manually generated pipelines. We applied M to an input knowledge base K and generated an enriched knowledge base $K' = M(K)$. We then selected a set of resources in K and used the CBD pairs of selected resources and their enriched versions as examples E. E was then given as training data to our algorithm, which learned an enrichment pipeline M. We finally compared the triples in K' (which we used as reference dataset) with the triples in $M(S)$ to compute the precision, recall and F-measure achieved by our approach. All generated pipelines are available at the project web site[10].

All experiments were carried out on a 8-core PC running *OpenJDK* 64-Bit Server 1.6.0_27 on *Ubuntu* 12.04.2 LTS. The processors were 8 Hexa-core *AMD Opteron* 6128 clocked at 2.0 GHz. Unless stated otherwise, each experiment was assigned 6 GB of memory. As termination criteria for our experiments, we used (1) a maximum number of iterations of 10 or (2) an optimal enrichment pipeline found.

6.2   Results

We carried out two sets of experiments to evaluate our refinement based learning algorithm. In the first set of experiments, we tested the effect of the complexity weight ω to the search strategy of our algorithm. The results are presented in Table 1. In the second set of experiments, we test the effect of the number of positive examples $|\mathcal{E}|$ on the generated F-measure. Results are presented in Table 2.

---

[10] https://github.com/GeoKnow/DEER/tree/master/evaluations/pipeline_learner.

Configuration of the Search Strategy. We ran our approach with varying values of ω to determine the value to use throughout our experiments. This parameter is used for configuring the search strategy in the learning algorithm, in particular the bias towards simple pipelines. As shown in Sect. 4.2, this is achieved by multiplying ω with the node complexity and subtracting this as a penalty from the node fitness. To configure ω, we used the first pipeline $M^1_{DrugBank}$. The results suggest that setting ω to 0.75 leads to the best results in this particular experiment. We thus adopted this value for the other studies.

Table 1. Test of the effect of ω on the learning process using the *Drugbank* dataset, where $|\mathcal{E}| = 1$, M is the manually created pipeline, $|M|$ is the complexity of M, M' is the pipeline generated by our algorithm, and I_n is the number of iterations of the algorithm.

ω	$|M|$	$|M'|$	$|\tau|$	I_n	$P(M')$	$R(M')$	$F(M')$
0	3	1	61	10	1.0	0.99	0.99
0.25	3	1	61	10	1.0	0.99	0.99
0.50	3	1	61	10	1.0	0.99	0.99
0.75	3	3	25	4	1.0	1.0	1.0
1.0	3	1	61	10	1.0	0.99	0.99

Effect of Positive Examples. We measured the F-measure achieved by our approach on the datasets at hand. The results shown in Table 2 suggest that when faced with data as regular as that found in the datasets Drugbank, DBpedia and Jamendo, our approach really only needs a single example to be able to reconstruct the enrichment pipeline that was used. This result is particularly interesting, because we do not always generate the manually created reference pipeline described in the previous subsection. In many cases, our approach detects a different way to generate the same results. In most cases (71.4 %) the pipeline it learns is actually shorter than the manually created pipeline. However, in some cases (4.7 %) our algorithm generated a longer pipeline to emulate the manual configuration. As an example, in case of $M^1_{Jamendo}$ the manual configuration was just one enrichment function, i.e., NLP-based enrichment to find all *locations* in mo:biography. Our algorithm learns this single manually configured enrichment as (1) an NLP enrichment function that extracts all named entities types and then (2) a filter enrichment function that filters all non-location triples. Our results also suggest that our approach scales when using a small number of positive example as on average the learning time for one positive example was around 48 s.

7   Related Work

Linked Data enrichment is an important topic for all applications that rely on a large number of knowledge bases and necessitate a unified view on this data,

Table 2. Test of the effect of increasing number of positive examples in the learning process. For this experiment we set $\omega = 0.75$. M is the manually created pipeline, $|M|$ is the size of M, $T_{M(KB)}$ is the time for applying M to the entire dataset, M' is the pipeline generated by our algorithm, T_l is the learning time, $|\tau|$ is the size of the refinement tree τ, I_n is the number of iterations performed by the algorithm, and all times are in minutes.

M	$|\mathcal{E}|$	$|M|$	$T_{M(KB)}$	$|M'|$	$T_{M'(KB)}$	T_l	$|\tau|$	I_n	$P(M')$	$R(M')$	$F(M')$
$M^1_{DBpedia}$	1	1	0.2	1	1.6	1.3	7	1	1.0	1.0	1.0
	2	1	0.2	1	1.8	1.3	7	1	1.0	1.0	1.0
$M^2_{DBpedia}$	1	2	23.3	1	0.1	0.2	7	1	1.0	0.99	0.99
	2	2	15	2	17	0.3	55	9	0.99	1.0	0.99
$M^3_{DBpedia}$	1	3	14.7	3	15.2	6.1	55	9	1.0	0.99	0.99
	2	3	15	2	15.1	0.1	55	9	0.99	0.99	0.99
$M^4_{DBpedia}$	1	4	0.4	2	0.1	0.7	13	2	0.99	0.99	0.99
	2	4	0.6	2	0.3	0.9	13	2	0.99	1.0	0.99
$M^5_{DBpedia}$	1	5	22	2	0.1	0.7	13	2	1.0	1.0	1.0
	2	5	25.5	2	0.2	0.9	13	2	1.0	1.0	1.0
$M^1_{DrugBank}$	1	2	3.5	1	4.1	0.1	61	10	0.99	0.99	0.99
	2	2	3.6	1	3.4	0.1	61	10	0.99	0.99	0.99
$M^2_{DrugBank}$	1	3	25.2	1	0.1	0.1	61	10	1.0	0.99	0.99
	2	3	22.8	1	0.1	0.1	61	10	1.0	0.99	0.99
$M^1_{Jamendo}$	1	1	10.9	2	10.6	0.1	13	2	0.99	0.99	0.99
	2	1	10.4	2	10.4	0.1	7	1	0.99	0.99	0.99

e.g., Question Answering frameworks [13], Linked Education [6] and all forms of semantic mashups [9]. In recent work, several challenges and requirements to Linked Data consumption and integration have been pointed out [14]. For example, the R2R framework [2] addresses those by enabling the publish of mappings across knowledge bases that allow to map classes and defined the transformation of property values. While this framework supports a large number of transformations, it does not allow the automatic discovery of possible transformations. The Linked Data Integration Framework (LDIF) [21], whose goal is to support the integration of RDF data, builds upon R2R mappings and technologies such as SILK [10] and LDSpider[11]. The concept behind the framework is to enable users to create periodic integration jobs via simple XML configurations. Still these configurations have to be created manually. The same drawback holds for the Semantic Web Pipes[12] [20], which follows the idea of Yahoo Pipes[13] to enable the integration of data in formats such as RDF and XML. By using Semantic Web Pipes, users can efficiently create semantic mashups by using a number of

---

[11] http://code.google.com/p/ldspider/.
[12] http://pipes.deri.org/.
[13] http://pipes.yahoo.com/pipes/.

operators (such as getRDF, getXML, etc.) and connect these manually within a simple interface. KnoFuss [19] addresses data integration from the point of view of link discovery. It begins by detecting URIs that stand for the same real-world entity and either merging them together or linking them via owl:sameAs. In addition, it allows to monitor the interaction between instance and dataset matching (which is similar to ontology matching [7]). Fluid Operations' Information Workbench[14] allows to search through, manipulate and integrate datasets for purposes such as business intelligence. [5] describes a framework for semantic enrichment, ranking and integration of web videos, and [1] presents semantic enrichment framework of *Twitter* posts. Finally, [8] tackles the linked data enrichment problem for sensor data via an approach that sees enrichment as a process driven by situations of interest. To the best of our knowledge, the work we presented in this paper is the first generic approach tailored towards learning enrichment pipelines of Linked Data given a set of atomic enrichment functions.

8 Conclusions and Future Work

In this paper, we presented an approach for learning enrichment pipelines based on a refinement operator. To the best of our knowledge, this is the first approach for learning RDF based enrichment pipelines and could open up a new research area. We also presented means to self-configure atomic enrichment pipelines so as to find means to enrich datasets according to examples provided by an end user. We showed that our approach can easily reconstruct manually created enrichment pipelines, especially when given a prototypical example and when faced with regular datasets. Obviously, this does not mean that our approach will always achieve such high F-measures. What our results suggest is primarily that if a human uses an enrichment tool to enrich his/her dataset manually, then our approach can reconstruct the pipeline. This seems to hold even for relatively complex pipelines.

Although we achieved reasonable results in terms of scalability, we plan to further improve time efficiency by parallelising the algorithm on several CPUs as well as load balancing. The framework underlying this study supports directed acyclic graphs as enrichment specifications by allowing to split and merge datasets. In future work, we will thus extend our operator to deal with graphs in addition to sequences. Moreover, we will look at pro-active enrichment strategies as well as active learning.

References

1. Abel, F., Gao, Q., Houben, G.-J., Tao, K.: Semantic enrichment of twitter posts for user profile construction on the social web. In: Antoniou, G., Grobelnik, M., Simperl, E., Parsia, B., Plexousakis, D., De Leenheer, P., Pan, J. (eds.) ESWC 2011, Part II. LNCS, vol. 6644, pp. 375–389. Springer, Heidelberg (2011)

---

[14] http://www.fluidops.com/information-workbench/.

2. Bizer, C., Schultz, A.: The R2R framework: Publishing and discovering mappings on the web. In: Proceedings of the COLD (2010)
3. Blumer, A., Ehrenfeucht, A., Haussler, D., Warmuth, M.K.: Occam's razor. Inf. Process. Lett. **24**(6), 377–380 (1987)
4. Bühmann, L., Lehmann, J.: Pattern based knowledge base enrichment. In: Alani, H., Kagal, L., Fokoue, A., Groth, P., Biemann, C., Parreira, J.X., Aroyo, L., Noy, N., Welty, C., Janowicz, K. (eds.) ISWC 2013, Part I. LNCS, vol. 8218, pp. 33–48. Springer, Heidelberg (2013)
5. Choudhury, S., Breslin, J.G., Passant, A.: Enrichment and ranking of the youtube tag space and integration with the linked data cloud. Springer, Berlin (2009)
6. Dietze, S., Sanchez-Alonso, S., Ebner, H., Yu, H.Q., Giordano, D., Marenzi, I., Nunes, B.P.: Interlinking educational resources and the web of data: A survey of challenges and approaches. Progr. Electron. Libr. Inform. Syst. **47**(1), 60–91 (2013)
7. Euzenat, J., Shvaiko, P.: Ontology Matching. Springer, Heidelberg (DE) (2007)
8. Hasan, S., Curry, E., Banduk, M., O'Riain, S.: Toward situation awareness for the semantic sensor web: Complex event processing with dynamic linked data enrichment. Semantic Sensor Networks, p. 60 (2011)
9. Hoang, H.H., Cung, T.N.-P., Truong, D.K., Hwang, D., Jung, J.J.: Semantic information integration with linked data mashups approaches. Int. J. Distrib. Sens. Netw. **2012**, 12 (2014)
10. Isele, R., Bizer, C.: Learning linkage rules using genetic programming. In: Sixth International Ontology Matching Workshop (2011)
11. Lehmann, J., Hitzler, P.: Concept learning in description logics using refinement operators. Mach. Learn. J. **78**(1–2), 203–250 (2010)
12. Lehmann, J., Isele, R., Jakob, M., Jentzsch, A., Kontokostas, D., Mendes, P.N., Hellmann, S., Morsey, M., van Kleef, P., Auer, S., Bizer, C.: DBpedia—a large-scale, multilingual knowledge base extracted from wikipedia. Semant. Web J. (2014)
13. Lopez, V., Unger, C., Cimiano, P., Motta, E.: Evaluating question answering over linked data. Web Semant. Sci. Serv. Agents World Wide Web **21**, 3–13 (2013)
14. Millard, I., Glaser, H., Salvadores, M., Shadbolt, N.: Consuming multiple linked data sources: Challenges and experiences. In: COLD Workshop (2010)
15. Ngomo, A.-C.N.: On link discovery using a hybrid approach. J. Data Semant. **1**(4) 203–217, (December 2012)
16. Ngomo, A.-C.N., Auer, S., Lehmann, J., Zaveri, A.: Introduction to linked data and its lifecycle on the web. In: Koubarakis, M., Stamou, G., Stoilos, G., Horrocks, I., Kolaitis, P., Lausen, G., Weikum, G. (eds.) Reasoning Web. LNCS, vol. 8714, pp. 1–99. Springer, Heidelberg (2014)
17. Ngonga Ngomo, A.-C., Heino, N., Lyko, K., Speck, R., Kaltenböck, M.: SCMS—semantifying content management systems. In: Aroyo, L., Welty, C., Alani, H., Taylor, J., Bernstein, A., Kagal, L., Noy, N., Blomqvist, E. (eds.) ISWC 2011, Part II. LNCS, vol. 7032, pp. 189–204. Springer, Heidelberg (2011)
18. Ngomo, A.-C.N., Lyko, K.: Unsupervised learning of link specifications: deterministic vs. non-deterministic. In: Proceedings of the Ontology Matching Workshop (2013)
19. Nikolov, A., Uren, V., Motta, E., de Roeck, A.: Overcoming schema heterogeneity between linked semantic repositories to improve coreference resolution. In: Gómez-Pérez, A., Yu, Y., Ding, Y. (eds.) ASWC 2009. LNCS, vol. 5926, pp. 332–346. Springer, Heidelberg (2009)

20. Phuoc, D.L., Polleres, A., Hauswirth, M., Tummarello, G., Morbidoni, C.: Rapid prototyping of semantic mash-ups through semantic web pipes. In: WWW, pp. 581–590 (2009)
21. Schultz, A., Matteini, A., Isele, R., Bizer, C., Becker, C.: LDIF—linked data integration framework. In: COLD (2011)
22. Speck, R., Ngonga Ngomo, A.-C.: Ensemble learning for named entity recognition. In: Mika, P., Tudorache, T., Bernstein, A., Welty, C., Knoblock, C., Vrandečić, D., Groth, P., Noy, N., Janowicz, K., Goble, C. (eds.) ISWC 2014, Part I. LNCS, vol. 8796, pp. 519–534. Springer, Heidelberg (2014)

Semi-supervised Instance Matching
Using Boosted Classifiers

Mayank Kejriwal$^{(\boxtimes)}$ and Daniel P. Miranker

University of Texas at Austin, Austin, USA
{kejriwal,miranker}@cs.utexas.edu

Abstract. Instance matching concerns identifying pairs of instances that refer to the same underlying entity. Current state-of-the-art instance matchers use machine learning methods. Supervised learning systems achieve good performance by training on significant amounts of manually labeled samples. To alleviate the labeling effort, this paper presents a *minimally supervised* instance matching approach that is able to deliver competitive performance using only 2 % training data and little parameter tuning. As a first step, the classifier is trained in an ensemble setting using *boosting*. Iterative *semi-supervised learning* is used to improve the performance of the boosted classifier even further, by *re-training* it on the most confident samples labeled in the current iteration. Empirical evaluations on a suite of six publicly available benchmarks show that the proposed system outcompetes optimization-based minimally supervised approaches in 1–7 iterations. The system's average F-Measure is shown to be within 2.5 % of that of recent supervised systems that require more training samples for effective performance.

Keywords: Instance matching · Semi-supervised learning · Boosting

1 Introduction

Instance matching is the problem of matching pairs of instances that refer to the same *underlying* entity [24]. It is an important preprocessing step in knowledge discovery and data mining algorithms [6], and is documented to have numerous applications in the Semantic Web community [24].

Current state-of-the-art instance matchers use a variety of machine learning techniques to achieve effective performance [1,5,27]. Many of these systems are *supervised*, and require sets of manually annotated samples to train their classifiers. This manual effort can be expensive, especially in open communities.

In recent years, *minimally supervised* approaches have been devised to alleviate extensive labeling effort [15,16]. While such approaches perform reasonably in many cases, a comparative analysis shows that there is still a considerable gap between their performance and that of supervised systems [17]. An additional problem is that such systems require extensive parameter tuning, and the specification of a function called the *pseudo F-Measure* (PFM). Intuitively,

© Springer International Publishing Switzerland 2015
F. Gandon et al. (Eds.): ESWC 2015, LNCS 9088, pp. 388–402, 2015.
DOI: 10.1007/978-3-319-18818-8_24

the PFM serves as a proxy for the *true* F-Measure, with minimally supervised instance matchers heuristically attempting to optimize the PFM over unlabeled (or sparsely labeled) data instead of the true (unknown) F-Measure [18]. A recent study found the PFM to be uncorrelated (and even *negatively* correlated) with the true F-Measure in several cases [17], raising concerns about whether currently defined PFMs are appropriate proxies.

This paper presents a *minimally supervised* instance matching system that offers a practical compromise between the two paradigms above. The proposed system expects a few input *seed* training samples to bootstrap itself. To maximize its performance on unseen data, the system employs a *meta-classification* strategy called *boosting* [7]. Boosting is a machine learning method that relies on weighting several *base* machine learning classifiers to build an *ensemble classifier*. Ensemble classifiers use weighted majority voting to classify samples, which is shown to improve performance on many challenging tasks [7].

The ensemble classifier in this paper is used for *probabilistic* instance matching, where the classifier scores each instance pair according to its likelihood of being a matching pair. Given the low degree of supervision, the overall output is not expected to have high quality. Instead, the system uses a small percentage of the most confidently labeled instance pairs to iteratively *self-train* itself in a *semi-supervised* fashion. The intent is to improve performance with each iteration, with large gains anticipated in the initial iterations.

To the best of our knowledge, this is the first minimally supervised instance matching system that combines boosting methods with iterative semi-supervised learning to achieve effective performance. The ensemble classifier is trained using the *AdaBoost* algorithm [21], and with a choice of two base classifiers, *random forests* and *multilayer perceptrons* [12,23], both of which have been individually validated for instance matching [22,27].

Evaluations on six benchmark datasets show that, using just 2 % of the ground-truth (or 50 samples, whichever is less) for training, the proposed system with the multilayer perceptron as a base classifier outperforms, on average, state-of-the-art minimally supervised approaches, and performs competitively compared to fully supervised systems that use more training samples. Additionally, the best performance is consistently achieved within 1–7 semi-supervised iterations. The system is also shown not to require extensive parameter-tuning in order to achieve these benefits. Lastly, we show, through implementation, that the proposed system can be integrated seamlessly with state-of-the-art orthogonal components (e.g. *blocking*) that are required in a complete workflow.

2   Related Work

Instance matching is an extensively researched subject, and goes by many different names, including *record linkage, entity resolution, the merge-purge problem* and *data matching*, to name just a few [3,6,24]. A naïve instance matcher pairs every instance in the dataset with every other, and then scores the pair (as matching or non-matching) in an expensive *classification* phase [6]. The untenable quadratic complexity of this approach indicates a two-step workflow, with the first step designated as *blocking* [4]. Blocking places instances into (possibly over-lapping) clusters, either by *partitioning* the instance space in some manner [14], or by using an *inexpensive* clustering function called a *blocking key* [4,8]. Instances *sharing* a cluster are paired and classified, leading to savings.

State-of-the-art systems that focus on the blocking aspect of instance matching include Limes and MultiBlock [8,14], the latter being implemented in the *Silk* toolkit. Both these approaches depend on the link specification classifier being *known*. Section 3.1 describes why this supervised blocking approach is unsuitable for the present work. To the best of our knowledge, only two *classifier-agnostic* approaches have been proposed for schema-free RDF data. The first of these is the unsupervised *Attribute Clustering* (AC) algorithm, recently proposed by Papadakis et al. [20], and is used as the blocking module in this paper. Recently, a DNF (Disjunctive Normal Form) blocking scheme learner for RDF data was also proposed but is relatively more complex to implement [9,10].

The classification step has also been extensively researched, with a survey of existing systems provided by Scharffe et al. [24]. Popular examples of supervised systems include FEBRL [5] and Marlin [1]; for a comparative evaluation, we refer the reader to the work by Köpcke et al. [11]. To the best of our knowledge, the only work that has considered a multilayer perceptron is a supervised evaluation effort by Soru and Ngomo [27]. Also, we are only aware of one (supervised) work that has implemented boosting in an instance matching architecture [22]. In contrast to either effort, this paper proposes a *minimally supervised* instance matcher that simultaneously incorporates boosting and iterative semi-supervised learning to improve performance. For a full treatment on boosting, the reader is referred to the seminal work by Freund and Schapire [7]. The book by Chapelle et al. comprehensively covers semi-supervised learning [2].

As earlier mentioned, current minimally supervised approaches optimize a pseudo F-Measure (PFM) function [18], or perform *active learning* [15,16]. The proposed system is compared against these approaches in Sect. 4; they were also compared under different configuration settings in a recent evaluation effort [17]. Finally, two influential examples of *fully implemented* RDF-based instance matchers are RDF-AI and KnoFuss [19,25].

3   Approach

The schematic of the full instance matching system is illustrated in Fig. 1. Note that, while the dotted component (the classification step) in the figure consti-tutes the key innovation, it cannot be implemented in isolation. In addition to blocking, generating restriction sets (matching classes and properties between two files) is an important task in the schema-free RDF setting [15]. To maximize performance, we re-implement state-of-the-art pre-classification modules, with a preference for unsupervised, but empirically high-performing, approaches. Note that, in principle, a practitioner can always replace a module with their own. Experimentally, the modules below delivered good performance (Sect. 4).

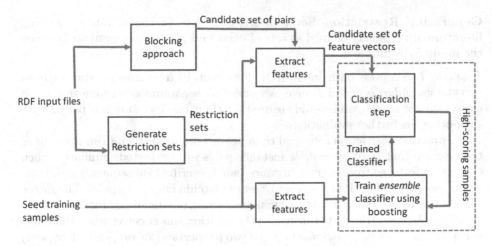

Fig. 1. The proposed instance matching system. The dotted component (the *classification step* of instance matching) is iteratively executed for a pre-defined number of self-training rounds, and constitutes the key innovation of the paper

3.1 Pre-classification Steps

Blocking Approach. Recall, from Sect. 2, that blocking is the first step of typical two-step instance matchers and can be thought of as a pre-processing clustering step that selects only a subset (of the Cartesian product of the full sets of instances) for further processing [4]. The goal is to avoid exhaustive pairwise comparisons of instances in the classification step. Let the set of instance pairs generated by the blocking step be denoted as the *candidate set*.

Blocking may generate the candidate set with or without the knowledge of the classifier (see Sect. 2). In a semi-supervised setting, the latter approach is advantageous. The main reason is that, since candidate set generation is independent of classification, it only needs to be executed *once*. Thus, only the classification step is subject to semi-supervised learning (the boundary of the dotted component in Fig. 1), leading to computational savings.

Given this rationale, this paper uses the recently proposed *trigrams-based Attribute Clustering* (AC) algorithm for the blocking approach [20]. The approach is *unsupervised* and performs well empirically. The AC algorithm works by grouping properties (or *attributes*) after computing the overlap between the properties' value-sets using a trigram-based similarity score. Two instances share a cluster if they share tokens in any two properties that were grouped together. The candidate set is generated from the clusters using a suitable blocking algorithm, several of which were evaluated in the original paper [20]. Experimentally, the *block purging* algorithm[1] was found to work well for the proposed system.

---

[1] Block purging eliminates clusters larger than a threshold value, with the premise that such clusters are the result of (non-discriminative) stop-word tokens [20].

Generating Restriction Sets. *Restriction sets* in the instance matching literature are typically defined as sets of *class* and *property alignments* between the input RDF files [15].

Example 1: Suppose both input RDF files contain interlinked instances from two classes, *Addresses* and *People*. A restriction set would determine that these classes do not match, and would ensure that their instances are not paired with each other for further evaluations.

In practice, restriction sets tend to improve both quality *and* run-time, since they ensure that only *compatible* instance pairs are evaluated. Similarly, when extracting features from a given instance pair (described subsequently), the system is more effective if it has access to a set of matching property pairs. The *Raven* system was one of the first instance matchers to automatically deduce restriction sets from the data [15]. Experimentally, the solution was effective when there was considerable *extensional overlap* between two properties (for property alignment) or instance sets (for class alignment), assumptions that were found to hold for the benchmarks in this paper. For more heterogeneous datasets, a sophisticated type-inference algorithm (e.g. *Typifier* [13]) may be a safer option.

Extracting Features. An instance matching classifier does not directly take an instance pair as input. Instead, the pair is first converted into a real-valued feature vector. Let a *feature extraction function* be defined as a function that accepts a pair of strings as input and outputs a real-valued number. Given a set G of such functions and a set Q of property alignments output by the restriction set generator, $|Q||G|$ features can be extracted for each compatible instance pair, by applying each function in G to the *property values* corresponding to an alignment in Q.

Example 2: Consider two independent datasets describing people and an alignment *(Home-Address, Residence)* between two of their respective properties. Given an instance pair (e_1, e_2) from the datasets, the simple feature extraction function *CommonToken* would compare their addresses and return 1 if they share a common token, and 0 otherwise.

The choice of G is an important determinant of overall instance matching performance [3]. Existing instance matchers typically include token-based and string-based functions as features [1,5]. Numeric features have also been found to improve performance, especially if dates and other numeric data regularly occur in the files [22]. A comprehensive text by Christen evaluated *phonetic* features, and found them to be quite effective [3]. Drawing on these efforts, we implement 28 feature extractors for the proposed system, including 2 numeric features, 8 string and token-based features, and 18 phonetic features. Many of these features are efficiently implemented in the FEBRL package [5]; more details and examples are provided on our project website [2].

---

[2] https://sites.google.com/a/utexas.edu/mayank-kejriwal/projects/
semi-supervised-im-using-boosting.

Algorithm 1. Classification step

Input: Seed training sets (comprising *feature vectors*) of positive and negative samples D and N resp., Candidate Set Γ, Base Classifier M, Iteration rounds *num*, Positive factors for positive and negative samples $factor_D$ and $factor_N$ resp.

Output: Ranked list L of pairs in Γ

1. Initialize list L of size $|\Gamma|$
2. Initialize $num_D := |D|$
3. Initialize $num_N := |N|$
4. Train classifier M with the *AdaBoost* ensemble method using D and N as training sets; let the trained classifier model be denoted as M'
5. Initialize *count* := 0
6. **while** *count* < *num* **do**
   Score each pair in Γ using M' and place pair in L
   Sort L in ascending order using the scores as sorting keys
   $num_D := num_D \times factor_D$
   $num_N := num_N \times factor_N$
   Repeat step 4 by using the first num_D elements in L as positive training examples, and last num_N elements in L as negative training examples
   count := *count* + 1
7. **end while**
8. **return** L

3.2 Classification Step

Algorithm 1 contains the pseudocode for the classification step. In addition to the base classifier M, the algorithm takes as arguments seed training sets of matching and non-matching instance pairs and the candidate set Γ, with each instance pair in these sets converted to a feature vector. Finally, three parameters (*num*, $factor_D$ and $factor_N$) are used to control semi-supervision and are subsequently described.

Freund and Schapire first described boosting as 'the general problem of producing a very accurate prediction rule by combining rough and moderately inaccurate rules-of-thumb' [7]. Thus, boosting is an ensemble-based method that seeks to train and combine several instances of a *base* classifier to obtain a final strong *ensemble* classifier. A popular implementation of a boosting algorithm, and the one used in this paper, is *AdaBoost* [21]. AdaBoost works by dynamically placing higher weights on training samples that are misclassified by the current classifier in each boosting round. The *committee* of classifiers thus trained are in turn weighted according to their overall performance on the training set, with the weighted committee constituting the *ensemble classifier*. During testing, the ensemble classifier scores a feature vector from the candidate set by computing an appropriately normalized weighted sum of scores.

To illustrate this process, suppose that a trained instance M' of the base classifier M is configured to output a confidence score $score(M')$ for a particular classification. Assuming that the ensemble classifier is a weighted committee of

m trained models, $w_1 M_1' + \ldots + w_m M_m'$, the confidence score of the ensemble classifier on a feature vector is $w_1 score(M_1') + \ldots + w_m score(M_m')$.

Once the ensemble classifier is trained, every feature vector in Γ is scored in this manner and the sorted list L is compiled. Note that, if the training sets are large enough, the parameters of the base classifier and also AdaBoost can be determined through grid-search and cross-validation. In the present task, the training sets are assumed to be small, typically of the order of 2 % of the ground-truth or 50 samples, whichever is less. In many benchmarks, 2 % of the ground-truth constituted fewer than even 10 training samples. In such situations, parameter tuning is viable. Instead, the goal is to achieve good generalization for reasonable *default* values of the parameters.

To accomplish this and avoid overfitting, Algorithm 1 employs *semi-supervised learning* to iteratively *self-train* the classifier on (previously) unlabeled samples for num iterations. It is also possible to devise alternate convergence choices, but this issue is left for future work. Concerning how many *more* samples the system should self-train on in each new iteration, Algorithm 1 uses the parameters $factor_D$ and $factor_N$ for this purpose. It is typical to set $factor_D = factor_N (= factor)$. In this paper, we adopt an *aggressive* strategy and set $factor = 2$. Intuitively, such a strategy leads to stable performance in only a few iterations, but risks introducing more noise into the system. $factor$ can also be used to set num, assuming that $x\%$ of the ground-truth was used for bootstrapping the system. Consider that, in the first self-training round, $factor * x\%$ (positive and negative) samples are used, followed by $factor^2 x\%$ in the next round (and so on). It is reasonable to assume that $factor^{num-1} x$ should not be allowed to exceed 100 %. Setting $x = factor = 2$ indicates[3] that $num \leq 7$.

In early experiments, we found $factor = 2$ (but with the caveat in the footnote) and $num = 7$ to yield a good compromise between noise and convergence, and assume these values in the rest of this work. A detailed analysis of alternate parameter settings is a topic for future work.

In summary, while boosting starts from a *weak classifier* and attempts to strengthen it by dynamically *re-weighting* the training set, semi-supervised learning starts from a *small training set* and attempts to *grow* it iteratively by exploiting confidence scores.

Note that the performance of boosting depends on the base classifier M. In this paper, we consider both *random forests* and *multilayer perceptrons* as base classifiers. A random forest is a committee of bootstrap-aggregated (or 'bagged') decision trees, and is known to make decision tree performance more robust on noisy data [12]. A multilayer perceptron (MLP) is a *feedforward artificial neural network* that can distinguish data that is not linearly separable, unlike the original perceptron model [23]. As Sect. 4 will illustrate, the two classifiers offer different tradeoffs. MLPs tend to perform better empirically on challenging tests, but take more time to train, even on small training sets. In contrast, random forests have fast training times, but may suffer from low performance on difficult test cases [27].

---

[3] Note that $2^7 = 128\,\%$. To prevent this extra source (28 %) of noise, the seventh iteration of Algorithm 1 sets $factor$ to $100/64 = 1.5625$. More generally, Algorithm 1 can be implemented to take x as a parameter, and to enforce $factor^{num-1} x \leq 100\,\%$.

The performance of semi-supervised learning depends both on the performance of the boosted classifiers and the number of incorrectly labeled samples in each of the self-training sets. If the system does not perform well initially, semi-supervision is likely to degrade performance further. The next section will show that, in many cases, semi-supervised learning and boosting can be used to offset each other's disadvantages. Semi-supervised learning helps to compensate for the overfitting problems often caused by boosting on small training sets [12], while boosting helps to compensate for the incorrect labels ('noise') introduced by semi-supervised learning.

4 Experiments

4.1 Data

Six benchmarks are used to evaluate the system. The first three, *Persons 1*, *Persons 2* and *Restaurants* were publicly released by the 2010 Instance Matching Evaluation Initiative (or IAEI), conducted as part of the annual Ontology Alignment Evaluation Initiative[4] (OAEI). These cases are 'easy' in that *supervised* systems have been shown to achieve over 95 % F-Measures on all of them [11]. This is not true of *minimally supervised* approaches, as Sect. 4.5 will demonstrate. For this reason, the three benchmarks provide an interesting test for the proposed (minimally supervised) system.

The other three real-world benchmarks are designated as *ACM-DBLP*, *Amazon-GoogleProducts* and *Abt-Buy*[5]. *ACM-DBLP* covers the bibliographic domain and is relatively clean, with 2617 and 2295 instances in the source and target respectively, and a ground-truth set of 2224 matching pairs. The other two datasets cover e-commerce instances and are known to be difficult even in supervised settings [11,27]. *Amazon-GoogleProducts* links 1363 source instances to 3226 target instances via 1300 matches, while *Abt-Buy* links 1081 source instances to 1092 target instances via 1097 matches.

The six described benchmarks were specifically chosen because, along with covering several domains, they enable comparing the proposed system to the *best* reported results of at least four other state-of-the-art approaches that were recently evaluated on them [11,17,27].

4.2 Implementation

Random forests, multilayer perceptrons and the AdaBoost algorithm are already implemented in the Java Weka API[6], which were used for these experiments.

---

[4] http://oaei.ontologymatching.org/2010/im/index.html. We did not use the 2014 IAEI benchmarks because, at the time of writing, their ground-truths were unavailable, and they were not evaluated by competing instance matching baselines.

[5] Available at http://dbs.uni-leipzig.de/en/research/projects/object_matching/fever/benchmark_datasets_for_entity_resolution.

[6] http://www.cs.waikato.ac.nz/ml/weka/.

Given the small size of the seed training set, Weka's default parameter values are used without any special tuning. Section 4.6 discusses this issue further. Finally, all programs were implemented serially in Java on a 32-bit Ubuntu machine with 3385 MB of RAM and a 2.40 GHz Intel 4700 MQ i7 processor.

4.3   Pre-classification Results

The re-implemented Raven restriction set generator was found to yield perfect class and property alignments for all the benchmarks. Similarly, the trigram-based Attribute Clustering blocking approach yielded perfect candidate set recall for the three IAEI benchmarks. On the real-world datasets, the approach was not able to achieve perfect recall, but still performed reasonably. Specifically, the *Abt-Buy* and *ACM-DBLP* candidate sets covered 95.44 % and 97.43 % of the ground-truth respectively. Recall on *Amazon-GoogleProducts* was the lowest (83.54 %) owing to the difficulty of the dataset. Note that this bounds the maximum recall that can be achieved by the classification step, which penalizes its maximum possible F-Measure. The next section discusses this issue further.

In terms of run-time, all pre-classification steps were found to execute in a total of less than 3.5 s for all the benchmarks. Similar to existing instance matchers, this time was negligible compared to classification time (Sect. 4.6).

4.4   Classification Metrics

The metrics, *precision*, *recall* and their $F_1 - Measure$, were used for evaluating performance. Denoting the set of returned results as R and the ground-truth as G, the precision is defined by the formula $|R \cap G|/|R|$, while the recall is defined by the formula $|R \cap G|/|G|$. The $F_1 - Measure$ (henceforth denoted simply as the *F-Measure*[7]) is given by *2*Precision*Recall/(Precision+Recall)* and quantifies precision-recall tradeoff.

The previous section noted that, on *Amazon-GoogleProducts* (and to a lesser extent, *Abt-Buy* and *ACM-DBLP*), candidate set recall was imperfect, which implies that the maximum achievable classification F-Measure is strictly below 100 %[8]. For these systems, the reported F-Measures are only *pessimistic* estimates, since it is improbable that the classifier would have labeled *all* of the missing (matching) pairs incorrectly. To realistically estimate the true F-Measure, we *re-weight* the pessimistic F-Measure F_p using the formula $100 * FM_p / FM_{max}$, where FM_{max} is the maximum possible F-Measure achievable under the current candidate set (e.g. 91.03 % on Amazon-GoogleProducts). Where applicable, both F-Measures (pessimistic and re-weighted) are reported.

---

[7] The general F-Measure formula is parametrized by a quantity, β. In the case of the $F_1 - Measure$, $\beta = 1$.

[8] For example, the maximum achievable classification F-Measure on *Amazon-GoogleProducts* is $2 * 83.54 * 100/(83.54 + 100) = 91.03 \%$, since maximum achievable recall is the candidate set recall, 83.54 %.

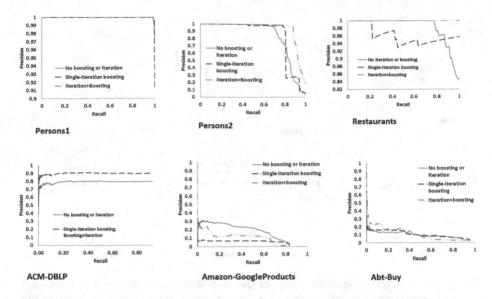

Fig. 2. The best precision-recall results of the proposed system (over seven iterations) against the two baselines, when using a random forest as the base classifier. On *Persons 1*, the three curves are *near*-coincidental, while in the case of *ACM-DBLP*, the best performance of the proposed system was achieved in the first iteration itself (hence, two curves *are* coincidental). Note the change in Y-axis scale for *Persons 1* and *Restaurants*

4.5   Classification Results

For both base classifiers (random forests and multilayer perceptrons), the precision-recall tradeoff offered by the proposed system is evaluated against two baselines. The first baseline is the base classifier itself, trained on the same samples as the proposed system, but without boosting or semi-supervised learning. The second baseline is similar to the first, except that boosting (but not semi-supervised learning) is used. For each benchmark, the precision of both baselines is plotted against the recall. Given that the proposed system is evaluated over seven iterations, we plot (for each benchmark) the precision-recall curve for the iteration in which the proposed system achieved the highest F-Measure.

Figure 2 shows the results for the random forest base classifier. On *Persons 1*, all three systems performed equally well, achieving nearly 100 % F-Measure. On both *Persons 2* and *Restaurant*, the proposed system either equals or outperforms the other two systems for all recall values. Interestingly, in the case of *Restaurants*, we note that although the second baseline (using just the boosted classifier) outperforms the first baseline in terms of the highest F-Measure achieved, the latter offers better tradeoff at *lower* recall values.

On the other three benchmarks, the differences between the systems are not as apparent. On *ACM-DBLP*, boosting affected performance positively, but semi-supervised learning did not, since the best (proposed) system performance was achieved in the first iteration itself. On *Amazon-GoogleProducts*, boosting

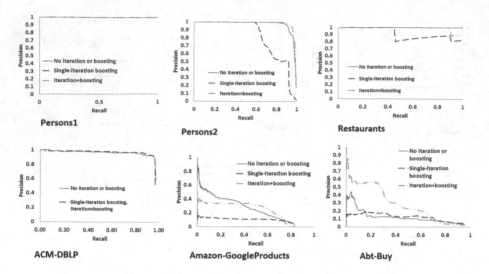

Fig. 3. The best precision-recall results of the proposed system (over seven iterations) against the two baselines, when using a multilayer perceptron as the base classifier. On *Persons 1*, the three curves are near-identical. Similar to Fig. 2, the best result of the proposed system, in the case of *ACM-DBLP*, was achieved in the first iteration

clearly degrades performance, but the semi-supervised learning is able to partially compensate for it. On *Abt-Buy*, the three systems are again nearly identical, but unlike on *Persons 1*, none of the systems perform well. As earlier noted in Sect. 4.1, both Abt-Buy and *Amazon-GoogleProducts* are challenging cases, since even supervised systems performed relatively poorly on them [11,27].

Figure 3 shows the results for the case where the base classifier is a multilayer perceptron (MLP). For the first four benchmarks, the findings are similar to those in Fig. 2, with an exception in the case of *Restaurants*, where the proposed system shows a slight dip at the end and the base classifier ends up with the best F-Measure (100 %). Otherwise, the highest F-measure is always achieved by the proposed system, an observation that is most apparent in the case of *Abt-Buy*. Another interesting finding is that the non semi-supervised boosted classifier consistently performs *worse* than the base classifier. We believe that this attests to the expressive strength of MLPs over random forests. Boosting the MLP makes it more prone to overfitting, but the semi-supervised learning compensates for it. As in the case of *Amazon-GoogleProducts* in Fig. 2, this illustrates the utility of combining both techniques with an expressive base classifier.

Comparison to Minimally Supervised Approaches. Table 1 lists the highest F-Measure scores achieved by the proposed system over the seven iterations that were conducted and compares it to three state-of-the-art minimally supervised approaches that were also evaluated on the six benchmarks. As noted earlier in Sect. 2, these approaches also seek to minimize supervision by optimizing a function called a pseudo F-Measure (PFM) in a variety of hypothesis spaces including

Table 1. A comparison of the highest F-Measures achieved by the proposed system (multilayer perceptron-based) to those of other minimally supervised approaches

Test Case	Linear	Boolean	Genetic	Proposed (pessimistic)	Proposed (re-weighted)
Persons1	**100.00 %**	99.50 %	**100.00 %**	**100.00 %**	**100.00 %**
Persons2	41.45 %	59.12 %	37.04 %	**97.19 %**	**97.19 %**
Restaurants	88.56 %	88.56 %	88.56 %	**94.68 %**	**94.68 %**
ACM-DBLP	**97.96 %**	97.46 %	97.71 %	93.42 %	94.65 %
Amazon-GP	**49.08 %**	39.97 %	43.11 %	39.13 %	42.98 %
Abt-Buy	**48.60 %**	37.66 %	45.08 %	36.27 %	37.14 %
Average	70.94 %	72.18 %	68.58 %	**76.78 %**	**77.77 %**

linear, boolean and *genetic* (Table 1). The *Raven* system attempts to optimize a user-provided PFM using linear and boolean classifiers and tuned parameter values [15], while *Eagle* exploits genetic algorithms [16]. For fairness, only the best results achieved by these systems are listed in Table 1. For the proposed system, the best results achieved with the multilayer perceptron as base classifier are shown, owing to its relatively superior performance[9]. The table show that, on average, even the pessimistic estimate exceeds the next best (the Raven boolean classifier) system performance by over 4.5 %. If the random forest-based classifier is used on *Restaurants*, the difference widens by about 1 % (see previous footnote).

Comparison to Supervised Approaches. Soru and Ngomo recently evaluated several base classifiers in a supervised setting using 10-fold cross validation [27]. We mentioned in Sect. 2 that that was the only work, to the best of our knowledge, that attempts using multilayer perceptrons for the instance matching task. Without ensemble methods or semi-supervised learning, the average highest F-Measure that was achieved on the six benchmark test cases was 79.25 %. If the re-weighted approach is assumed, the proposed system (multilayer perceptron-based) is within 1.5 % of this average, from the data in Table 1, and even the pessimistic approach is within 2.5 %. A similar finding applies when analyzing[10] the evaluations conducted by Köpcke et al. [11] on two other supervised SVM-based instance matching systems, FEBRL and Marlin [1,5].

FEBRL and Marlin were not tested on the IAEI benchmarks since they were originally designed to solve the *record linkage* problem for Relational Databases (RDBs) [1,5]. On the *ACM-DBLP* benchmark, the best configurations of both systems performed well, achieving near-perfect F-Measure scores. On *Amazon-GoogleProducts*, FEBRL achieved between 30–40 % F-Measure even when trained on 100 training samples, while the F-Measure achieved by the best configuration of Marlin (when trained on 100 samples) approached 50 %.

---

[9] The exception was *Restaurants* where the random forest achieved 100 % best FM.

[10] The reference for this claim is Fig. 3 (on page 6) of the original paper [11].

On *Abt-Buy*, FEBRL achieved about 20 % F-Measure after being trained on 100 samples, while Marlin achieved above 60 % F-Measure on its best configurations.

To conclude, the proposed system slightly outperforms FEBRL on the real-world benchmarks (despite being trained on only half the training set), but is outperformed by Marlin. The literature also indicates that these systems required careful selection of parameters and models, and do not include components for restriction set generation and unsupervised blocking. It is unclear if these systems can be adapted as instance matchers for schema-free RDF data.

4.6   Discussion

We conclude this section with a discussion of the run-times, as well as the dependence of the system on the parameter *num* (the number of iterations) in Algorithm 1. Although the multilayer perceptron (MLP) outperformed (by a large margin) the random forest base classifier for the more challenging test cases (*Amazon-GoogleProducts* and *Abt-Buy*), the difference was less severe on the other test cases. In the case of *Persons 2* and *Restaurants*, both methods performed equally well. The reason why this observation is important is because the MLP had much higher run-times than the random forest. On *Restaurants*, for example, the random forest-based system had run-times ranging from 2–5 s (for the entire classification step) depending on the iteration. The MLP-based system achieved run-times ranging from 17 s (for the first iteration) to almost 20 min (for the final iteration). Similar observations were noted for the other datasets[11]. This confirms earlier findings that the MLP can be slower by 1–2 orders of magnitude, and has a direct dependence on the size of the training set [27]. Given this disparity in run-times between the two classifiers, the random forest is clearly a better base classifier choice for the IAEI benchmarks, and considering only the slight performance penalty, *ACM-DBLP* as well.

Note that it was not always the case that the best performance was achieved in the last iteration. For *ACM-DBLP* in particular, Figs. 2 and 3 show that the best performance was achieved in the first iteration. On average, we found that the performance tended to peak on or before the *fifth* iteration[12], after which it slowly started declining. We hypothesize that this is due to the boosted classifier getting overfitted on the training data after a certain number of iterations. Future work will test this hypothesis through more evaluations.

Finally, note that the proposed classifier was only tested with default parameter settings, because the seed training sets were too small to perform grid-search or cross validation. Thus, it is reasonable to assume that the performance of the system can be improved even further if a good parameter-tuning methodology can be devised, without using an extensive validation set. We believe that this is an important issue for future work.

---

[11] Supplemental experimental results are noted on the project website (footnote 2).

[12] This corresponds to $2^5 = 32$ % of the ground-truth (assuming no re-training noise).

5 Conclusion and Future Work

This paper presented a minimally supervised instance matching system that combines semi-supervised learning with the AdaBoost algorithm to achieve effective performance. Using a multilayer perceptron as the base classifier with default parameter configurations, the system outperformed, on average, competing minimally supervised approaches by over 4.5 %. It also came within 2.5 % F-Measure (using a pessimistic estimate) of the performance of fully supervised approaches that use larger training sets and 10-fold cross-validation to achieve the same level of performance. Drawing on prior evaluations from the literature, the system was also found to be competitive with the state-of-the-art FEBRL instance matcher. Along with these results, the low run-times make the system a promising candidate for off-the-shelf schema-free RDF instance matching.

Future work will seek to efficiently apply the findings to large-scale datasets, which raises some new challenges, including the efficiency of semi-supervised methods and the large training times of multilayer perceptrons. Addressing these challenges is clearly important, especially for large-scale efforts such as Linked Open Data[13] [26].

References

1. Bilenko, M., Mooney, R. J.: Adaptive duplicate detection using learnable string similarity measures. In: Proceedings of the Ninth ACM SIGKDD International Conference on Knowledge Discovery and Data Mining, pp. 39–48. ACM (2003)
2. Chapelle, O., Schölkopf, B., Zien, A., et al.: Semi-supervised Learning, vol. 2. MIT Press, Cambridge (2006)
3. Christen, P.: Data Matching: Concepts and Techniques for Record Linkage, Entity Resolution, and Duplicate Detection. Springer, New York (2012)
4. Christen, P.: A survey of indexing techniques for scalable record linkage and deduplication. IEEE Trans. Knowl. Data Eng. 24(9), 1537–1555 (2012)
5. Christen, P., Churches, T., Hegland, M.: Febrl – a parallel open source data linkage system. In: Dai, H., Srikant, R., Zhang, C. (eds.) PAKDD 2004. LNCS (LNAI), vol. 3056, pp. 638–647. Springer, Heidelberg (2004)
6. Elmagarmid, A.K., Ipeirotis, P.G., Verykios, V.S.: Duplicate record detection: a survey. IEEE Trans. Knowl. Data Eng. 19(1), 1–16 (2007)
7. Freund, Y., Schapire, R.E.: A decision-theoretic generalization of on-line learning and an application to boosting. In: Vitányi, P.M.B. (ed.) EuroCOLT 1995. LNCS, vol. 904, pp. 23–37. Springer, Heidelberg (1995)
8. Isele, R., Jentzsch, A., Bizer, C.: Efficient multidimensional blocking for link discovery without losing recall. In: WebDB (2011)
9. Kejriwal, M., Miranker, D.P.: An unsupervised algorithm for learning blocking schemes. In: 2013 IEEE 13th International Conference on Data Mining (ICDM), pp. 340–349. IEEE (2013)
10. Kejriwal, M., Miranker, D.P.: A two-step blocking scheme learner for scalable link discovery. In: Ontology Matching, p. 49 (2014)

---

[13] linkeddata.org.

11. Köpcke, H., Thor, A., Rahm, E.: Evaluation of entity resolution approaches on real-world match problems. Proc. VLDB Endow. **3**(1–2), 484–493 (2010)
12. Liaw, A., Wiener, M.: Classification and regression by randomforest. R News **2**(3), 18–22 (2002)
13. Ma, Y., Tran, T., Bicer, V.: Typifier: inferring the type semantics of structured data. In: 2013 IEEE 29th International Conference on Data Engineering (ICDE), pp. 206–217. IEEE (2013)
14. Ngomo, A.-C.N.: A time-efficient hybrid approach to link discovery. In: Ontology Matching, p. 1 (2011)
15. Ngomo, A.-C.N., Lehmann, J., Auer, S., Höffner, K.: Raven-active learning of link specifications. In: Proceedings of the Sixth International Workshop on Ontology Matching, pp. 25–37. Citeseer (2011)
16. Ngomo, A.-C., Lyko, K.: EAGLE: efficient active learning of link specifications using genetic programming. In: Simperl, E., Cimiano, P., Polleres, A., Corcho, O., Presutti, V. (eds.) ESWC 2012. LNCS, vol. 7295, pp. 149–163. Springer, Heidelberg (2012)
17. Ngomo, A.-C.N., Lyko, K.: Unsupervised learning of link specifications: deterministic vs. non-deterministic. In: OM, pp. 25–36 (2013)
18. Nikolov, A., d'Aquin, M., Motta, E.: Unsupervised learning of link discovery configuration. In: Simperl, E., Cimiano, P., Polleres, A., Corcho, O., Presutti, V. (eds.) ESWC 2012. LNCS, vol. 7295, pp. 119–133. Springer, Heidelberg (2012)
19. Nikolov, A., Uren, V., Motta, E., De Roeck, A.: Handling instance coreferencing in the knofuss architecture (2008)
20. Papadakis, G., Ioannou, E., Palpanas, T., Nejdl, W., et al.: A blocking framework for entity resolution in highly heterogeneous information spaces. IEEE Trans. Knowl. Data Eng. **25**, 2665–2682 (2013)
21. Rätsch, G., Onoda, T., Müller, K.-R.: Soft margins for adaboost. Mach. Learn. **42**(3), 287–320 (2001)
22. Rong, S., Niu, X., Xiang, E.W., Wang, H., Yang, Q., Yu, Y.: A machine learning approach for instance matching based on similarity metrics. In: Cudré-Mauroux, P., Heflin, J., Sirin, E., Tudorache, T., Euzenat, J., Hauswirth, M., Parreira, J.X., Hendler, J., Schreiber, G., Bernstein, A., Blomqvist, E. (eds.) ISWC 2012, Part I. LNCS, vol. 7649, pp. 460–475. Springer, Heidelberg (2012)
23. Ruck, D.W., Rogers, S.K., Kabrisky, M., Oxley, M.E., Suter, B.W.: The multilayer perceptron as an approximation to a bayes optimal discriminant function. IEEE Trans. Neural Netw. **1**(4), 296–298 (1990)
24. Scharffe, F., Ferrara, A., Nikolov, A., et al.: Data linking for the semantic web. Int. J. Semant. Web Inf. Syst. **7**(3), 46–76 (2011)
25. Scharffe, F., Liu, Y., Zhou, C.: Rdf-ai: an architecture for rdf datasets matching, fusion and interlink. In: Proceedings of the IJCAI 2009 Workshop on Identity, Reference, and Knowledge Representation (IR-KR), Pasadena (2009)
26. Schmachtenberg, M., Bizer, C., Paulheim, H.: Adoption of the linked data best practices in different topical domains. In: Mika, P., Tudorache, T., Bernstein, A., Welty, C., Knoblock, C., Vrandečić, D., Groth, P., Noy, N., Janowicz, K., Goble, C. (eds.) ISWC 2014, Part I. LNCS, vol. 8796, pp. 245–260. Springer, Heidelberg (2014)
27. Soru, T., Ngomo, A.-C.N.: A comparison of supervised learning classifiers for link discovery. In: Proceedings of the 10th International Conference on Semantic Systems, pp. 41–44. ACM (2014)

Assigning Semantic Labels to Data Sources

S.K. Ramnandan[1]([✉]), Amol Mittal[2], Craig A. Knoblock[3], and Pedro Szekely[3]

[1] Indian Institute of Technology - Madras, Chennai, India
nandparikrish@gmail.com
[2] Indian Institute of Technology - Delhi, New Delhi, India
amolmittal.iitd@gmail.com
[3] University of Southern California, Los Angeles, USA
{knoblock,pszekely}@isi.edu

Abstract. There is a huge demand to be able to find and integrate heterogeneous data sources, which requires mapping the attributes of a source to the concepts and relationships defined in a domain ontology. In this paper, we present a new approach to find these mappings, which we call semantic labeling. Previous approaches map each data value individually, typically by learning a model based on features extracted from the data using supervised machine-learning techniques. Our approach differs from existing approaches in that we take a holistic view of the data values corresponding to a semantic label and use techniques that treat this data collectively, which makes it possible to capture characteristic properties of the values associated with a semantic label as a whole. Our approach supports both textual and numeric data and proposes the top k semantic labels along with their associated confidence scores. Our experiments show that the approach has higher label prediction accuracy, has lower time complexity, and is more scalable than existing systems.

Keywords: Semantic labeling · Source modeling

1 Introduction

Semantic labeling of a data source involves assigning a class or property in an ontology to each attribute of a data source. When the source is a table, the objective is to assign to each column in the table a class or property that specifies the semantics of the column. When the source is more complex, such as an XML or JSON file, the objective is to map each attribute of the source to a class or property that specifies its semantics. The goal of our work is to learn a

This research is was supported in part by IARPA via AFRL contract number FA8650-10-C-7058 and in part by DARPA via AFRL contract number FA8750-14-C-0240. The U.S. Government is authorized to reproduce and distribute reprints for Governmental purposes notwithstanding any copyright annotation thereon. The views and conclusions contained herein are those of the authors and should not be interpreted as necessarily representing the official policies or endorsements, either expressed or implied, of IARPA, DARPA, AFRL, or the U.S. Government.

© Springer International Publishing Switzerland 2015
F. Gandon et al. (Eds.): ESWC 2015, LNCS 9088, pp. 403–417, 2015.
DOI: 10.1007/978-3-319-18818-8_25

semantic labeling function from a set of sources that have been manually labeled. When presented with a new source, the learned semantic labeling function can automatically assign the semantic labels to each attribute of the new source.

We are interested in mapping diverse data sources with different schemas to a common ontology. Taheriyan et al. [14] explain that this involves two steps - assigning semantic labels (class or data property) from the ontology to each source attribute and determining the relationships between the labelled attributes using ontology properties. Our work focuses on the first step of learning the semantic labeling function from the data. To learn the mapping, we use the data rather than the attribute names, which can be quite cryptic as they are often abbreviated (e.g., fname rather than first-name). The challenge is that new sources rarely have the same set of values for an attribute as the sources that the system was trained on. Distinguishing numeric attributes is especially challenging. For example, *Humidity* and *ChanceOfSnow* are both percentages and are thus very similar.

The contribution of our work is a new algorithm for learning a semantic labeling function with the following properties:

- **Efficiency and Scalability**: evaluations show that our method is about 250 times faster than our previous method using Conditional Random Fields.
- **Coverage**: our method can effectively learn semantic labels for both text and numeric data and can handle noisy "mostly" numeric data where a fraction of values are not numbers.
- **Accuracy**: our comprehensive evaluation shows that our method improves the accuracy of competing approaches on a wide variety of sources.
- **Generality**: our method is ontology and schema agnostic and can learn a semantic labeling function with respect to any ontology or classification scheme that a user selects for their application.

We now formally define the problem of semantic labeling of data sources. A data source s is defined as a collection of ordered pairs $< \{a\}, \{v_a\} >$ where a denotes an attribute name (e.g. "Date of birth", "PIN Code" etc.) and $\{v_a\}$ denotes the set of data values corresponding to the attribute a (e.g., if a is "Date of birth", the set $\{v_a\}$ will have values like "02-10-1992", "Jan 1, 1950", etc.).

Input to our algorithm is a set of *labelled* data sources. Different data sources can have attributes that have different attribute names but map to the same semantic label. E.g., data source s_1 has an attribute "Population" and source s_2 has an attribute "Number of people" and both these attributes are assigned the same semantic label "populationTotal" from the given ontology. In our approach, the data values from these sources are normalized to a standard format. Multiple data sources are often mapped to the same ontology in many practical scenarios, e.g., museums map their data to a common cultural heritage ontology and universities map their data to a research networking ontology (e.g. vivoweb.org).

When we *combine* the labelled data sources, we get training data of the form $\{ (< \{a^1\}, \{v_i^1\} >, l^1), (< \{a^2\}, \{v_i^2\} >, l^2), \cdots, (< \{a^n\}, \{v_i^n\} >, l^n)\}$. Here, for each j, $\{a^j\}$ denotes the set of attribute names assigned to the semantic label l^j

and $\{v_i^j\}$ denotes union of the sets of corresponding data values. The goal is to learn the the *semantic labelling function* ϕ : $< \{a\}, \{v_i\} > \rightarrow l$.

To assign a semantic label to an attribute in a new data source, we take an ordered pair $< \{a\}, \{v_a\} >$ and use the semantic labelling function ϕ to predict its semantic label.

The rest of the paper is structured as follows: In Sect. 2, we describe our approach to semantic labelling. We describe how we handle textual and numeric data differently and how we combine the two to provide a robust technique capable of handling noise. In Sect. 3, we survey related work. In Sect. 4, we present the results of our experiments. Finally, in Sect. 5, we describe the future enhancements to our approach and conclude.

2   Approach

This section describes our approach for learning to label source attributes with semantic types using data sources that have already been aligned to an ontology. The training data consists of a set of semantic labels and each semantic label has a set of data values $v_i's$ and attribute names $a's$ associated with it. Our approach takes a holistic view by using techniques that capture characteristic properties associated with each semantic label as a whole rather than features from individual values. Given a new set of data values, the goal is to predict the top k candidate semantic labels along with confidence scores.

2.1   Textual Data

We define a *textual semantic label* as a semantic label associated with textual data values (e.g. title of a painting, department name, etc.). In our approach, the set of data values associated with each textual semantic label $\{v_i\}$ in the training data is treated as a *document*. Similarly, at prediction time, the new set of data values is treated as a *query* document.

We index the training documents to improve query time efficiency. Data values are first tokenized by space and punctuation, then normalized and then indexed. Normalizations include removal of blank spaces, stemming, removal of common stop words, etc. Each document has a vector space model representation where each dimension corresponds to a unigram token from the vocabulary of tokens extracted. We used Apache Lucene[1] for indexing and searching of documents.

The weight assigned to a term in a document vector is the product of its *term frequency* (TF) and *inverse document frequency* (IDF), called TF-IDF. For each term t in the document (or query) x, *term frequency* (TF) of t in x measures the number of occurrences of t in x and *inverse document frequency* (IDF) of t measures the inverse of the number of documents containing term t.

Remember that each training document in the index corresponds to a distinct semantic label. In order to suggest the top k candidate semantic labels for the set

---

[1] Apache Lucene: http://lucene.apache.org/core/.

of new data values at prediction time, we rank semantic labels in decreasing order of the cosine of the angle between the query document vector and each training document vector. The confidence score associated with a predicted semantic label is the corresponding *cosine similarity* between the documents' vectors.

The cosine similarity for a query document q and a training document d is

$$sim(q, d) = \frac{V(q) \times V(d)}{|V(q)| \times |V(d)|} \tag{1}$$

where $V(q)$ and $V(d)$ are the corresponding vector space model representations.

The idea behind using this approach stems from the fact that each semantic label has a characteristic set of tokens associated with it that can collectively help in identifying the correct semantic label. For example, if the data is about *dimensions of a painting*, data values typically look like "28 in. x 30 in." and hence, the presence of tokens like *x* and *in* strongly characterize this semantic label.

We call this approach the *TF-IDF-based cosine-similarity approach*. Though it seems quite simple, it results in higher prediction accuracy in terms of the mean reciprocal rank [3] and is extremely fast (low query time due to indexing) compared to existing approaches that extract features from each data value.

We also tried another similar approach in which the weight we assign to a term in a document vector is 1 if the term occurs in the document and 0 otherwise. Here, we rank semantic labels in decreasing order of the *Jaccard similarity* between the query document vector and the training document vector (corresponding to a semantic label). However, the TF-IDF cosine similarity approach proved to work better since the non-binary term weights are more informative and allows for a continuous degree of similarity between queries and documents.

2.2   Numeric Data

If the data values associated with a semantic label are numeric, instead of the TF-IDF-based approach, we analyse the distribution of numeric values corresponding to a semantic label. This arises from the simple intuition that the distribution of values in each semantic type is different. For example, the distribution of weights is likely to be different from the distribution of temperatures. In order to measure the similarity between distributions, we use *statistical hypothesis testing*.

The key output of statistical hypothesis testing used in our approach is the p-value. The p-value helps determine the statistical significance of the results of the hypothesis testing and is the probability of obtaining a test statistic at least as extreme as the one obtained using the sample data, assuming that the null hypothesis is true. Irrespective of the actual statistical hypothesis test used, the underlying idea is the same. The null hypothesis we are testing is that the two groups of data values are drawn from the same population (semantic label). A low p-value provides strong evidence against the null hypothesis while a large p-value provides weak evidence against the null hypothesis.

The training data consists of a set of numeric semantic labels and each semantic label has a sample of numeric data values. At prediction time, given a new set of numeric data values (query sample), we perform statistical hypothesis tests between the query sample and each sample in the training data corresponding to a distinct semantic label. We rank the semantic labels in descending order of the p-values returned by the statistical hypothesis tests performed and suggest the top k candidate semantic labels with the confidence scores as corresponding p-values.

We considered Welch's t-test [6] as our statistical hypothesis test. Given two samples of data, the t statistic is defined by:

$$t = \frac{\bar{X}_1 - \bar{X}_2}{\sqrt{\frac{s_1^2}{N_1} + \frac{s_2^2}{N_2}}} \tag{2}$$

where $\bar{X}_i$, s_i^2 and N_i are the sample mean, sample variance and sample size of the ith sample respectively. Welch's t-test does not assume that both samples of data have the same standard distribution. Once the t statistic is calculated, it uses the t distribution to test the null hypothesis that the two population means are equal (though the population variances may differ).

The problem with Welch's t-test is that it looks only at the *mean* of the population and not the complete distribution and hence does not match our need to test that the samples are drawn from the same distribution. Moreover, Welch's t-test expects the sample and population data to be approximately normal and expects the samples to have a similar number of data points. Most of the time, our problems fail to meet these expectations. To overcome this issue, we applied non-parametric tests to compare two samples of data.

We considered Mann-Whitney's U test [6], a non-parametric test of the null hypothesis that the two samples have the same distribution. It is more efficient than the t-test on non-normal distributions and does not expect the samples to have a similar number of data points. This test ranks all values from the two samples from low to high and then computes a p-value that depends on the difference between the mean ranks of the two samples. If you assume that the two samples are drawn from distributions with the same shape, then it can be viewed as a comparison of the medians of the two samples.

We also considered the two-sample Kolmogorov - Smirnov (KS) Test [6], a non-parametric test that tests if the two samples are drawn from the same distribution by comparing the cumulative distribution functions (CDF) of the two samples. Similar to the Mann-Whitney test, it does not assume normal distributions of the population and works well on samples with unequal sizes.

The KS test computes the D statistic which is the maximum vertical difference between the CDFs of the two samples and is given by

$$D_{N_1, N_2} = \sup_x |F_{1, N_1}(x) - F_{2, N_2}(x)| \tag{3}$$

where F_{1, N_1} and F_{2, N_2} are the cumulative distribution functions of sample 1 and sample 2 respectively. The p-value associated with the KS test determines the probability that the cumulative distribution functions of two samples that are randomly sampled from the same population are as far apart as observed with respect to the D statistic.

The KS test is slightly more powerful than the Mann-Whitney's U test in the sense that it cares only about the relative distribution of the data and the result does not change due to transformations applied to the data. Also, the KS test is more sensitive to differences in the shape of the distribution, variance, and median, while the Mann-Whitney's U test is more sensitive to changes in the median. The non-parametric Wilcoxon signed-rank test is intended for paired variates and hence is not applicable in our case of independent attribute values. Our experiments on numeric data show that the Kolmogorov-Smirnov test achieves the highest label prediction accuracy of the various statistical hypothesis tests.

2.3   Overall Approach

We now present our overall approach (called *SemanticTyper*) combining the approaches to textual and numeric data. For textual data, we use the *TF-IDF*-based approach and for numeric data, we use the *Kolmogorov-Smirnov* (KS) statistical hypothesis test.

Data sources are often noisy and contain attributes with a mixture of numeric and text data. It is challenging to decide whether it is actually a numeric column and the text values are noise (e.g., years with noise such as "1999–2000") or it is a column of textual data (e.g., database identifiers). The challenge is to determine a threshold for the amount of noise allowed in a numeric column.

In order to resolve this, we adopted the rule that in the training data, if for a semantic label the fraction of pure numeric data values is below 60 %, it is trained as textual data (and hence indexed as document). If the fraction of numeric values is above 80 %, it is trained as purely numeric data (its distribution is extracted to be used in KS test) after discarding textual data values. In the other case (if the fraction is between 60 % and 80 %), the data is trained as both textual and numeric data (it is both indexed as a document and its distribution is extracted to be used in KS test).

At the time of prediction, given a new set of data values, we again calculate the fraction of numeric values. If it is greater than 70 %, it is tested as numeric data (textual data values are discarded). Else, it is tested as textual data. The above numbers (60 %,70 %,80 %) were arrived at empirically by running a coarse grid over these values by varying them in steps of 5 % and choosing the values that resulted in highest average label prediction accuracy.

During one of the experiments, we observed that while training, the fraction of numeric data values corresponding to the "Postal Code" semantic label was 71 % and hence it was trained as both textual and numeric data. During prediction, the fraction of numeric data values was 50 % and was hence was tested as textual data. The TF-IDF-based approach was hence used and was successful in predicting the correct semantic label as the first candidate suggestion. This clearly illustrates the strength of our approach in handling noisy data.

3   Related Work

Goel et al. [5] describe an approach that uses a supervised machine learning technique based on Conditional Random Fields (CRF) for semantic labelling of data sources. They extract features from the data values after tokenizing and building a CRF graphical model to represent the latent structure of the data sources, such as the dependency between field labels and their token labels, dependency between neighboring tokens within a field, and dependency between labels of neighboring fields. They assign semantic labels to all fields in a tuple (corresponding to a row in the data source) and then combine the labels of the fields in a particular source attribute to assign a label to the attribute. However, there is a tradeoff between the amount of latent structure exploited and corresponding training time to generate the CRF models.

Limaye et al. [8] work on the problem of annotating tables on the Web with entity, type, and relationship labels. They propose a probabilistic graphical model to label table cells with *entities*, table columns with *types*, and pairs of table columns with *binary relations* simultaneously rather than making the labelling decisions separately for each. The task of assigning semantic labels to columns is achieved using two feature functions (among 5 in total) - one that looks at the dependency between the type of column and the entity of entries in that column and the other that looks at the dependency between the type of column and the column header text using textual similarity measures. Mulwad et al. [9] assigns candidate labels for each cell value using Wikitology, similar to Limaye's work in using a probabilistic graphical model to assign labels to individual cells.

The approaches described above rely on training a probabilistic graphical model to annotate columns with semantic types. They analyze entries in the column separately and do not use any statistical measures to extract characteristic properties of the column data as a whole. Further, training probabilistic graphical models is not scalable as the number of semantic labels in the ontology increases due to explosion of the search space. Unlike in a named entity extraction setting, dependency between labels of adjacent source attributes (used in [5]) is not of use in semantic labeling of data sources since the order of attributes in a data source is not consistent enough to improve the accuracy of the labelling.

Venetis et al. [15] present an approach to annotate tables on the Web by leveraging resources already on the Web. They extract an *isA database* from the Web that is of the form (instance, class) and subsequently, label a particular column with a particular class label if a substantial fraction of the cells in that column are labelled with that class label in the *isA database*. They look for explicit matches for cell contents from a column in the *isA database* to assign labels to the table cells individually and then use a maximum likelihood approach to predict a semantic label for the column.

Syed et al. [13] exploit a web of semantic data for interpreting tables. They use the table headings (whenever available) and the values stored in the table cells to infer a semantic model that can be further used to generate linked data. This is achieved through the development of Wikitology - a hybrid knowledge base of information extracted from Wikipedia and RDF data from DBpedia and other Linked Data sources.

An important aspect of the work by both Venetis et al. and Syed et al. is that they exploit a huge amount of data extracted from various sources. While having more data can be useful, it also restricts the approach to only those domains and ontologies where there is a large amount of extracted data. If we have a user defined ontology, it can be difficult to use the models from a general source, such as DBpedia. This is taken care in our approach where we learn the semantic labelling function from sources previously labeled using a given ontology. Sequeda et al. [11] address the problem of mapping relational tables to RDF, but generate IRIs based on predefined rules and do not learn mappings to labels in an existing ontology as we do.

A lot of work has been done in the related areas of schema and ontology matching [2, 4, 7, 10]. Schema matching takes two schemas as input and produces a mapping between semantically identical attributes. Schema and ontology matching can be viewed as the combination of semantic typing and relationship mapping and this paper focuses on the former. Stonebraker et al. [12] developed an approach to schema matching that uses a collection of four different *experts* whose results are combined to generate mappings between attributes. One of their experts uses TF-IDF based cosine similarity to compare columns of textual data and another uses the Welch's t-test to compare columns of numeric data. Our work, which draws on some of these ideas, formulated an overall combined approach which is highly scalable, applied it to the problem of semantic typing, performed detailed experiments and analysis to come up with a better performing statistical test (Kolmogorov-Smirnov), and demonstrated the effectiveness of the approach on a diverse range of datasets.

4   Evaluation

For our experiments, we used datasets from multiple domains: *museum, city, weather, phone directory* and *flight status*. There are three types of experiments based on the nature of semantic labels to be assigned in the data sources: purely textual, purely numeric, and mixture of textual and numeric labels. The datasets and code used in our experiments have been published online[2].

4.1   Data Sets

For evaluating our approach on *purely textual* labels, we used data from the *museum* domain consisting of 29 data sources in diverse formats from various art museums in the U.S. Semantic labels were assigned to the attributes in these data sources manually to the Europeana Data Model, an ontology of cultural heritage data.[3]

---

[2] https://github.com/usc-isi-i2/eswc-2015-semantic-typing.git.

[3] https://joinup.ec.europa.eu/catalogue/distribution/europeana-data-model-primer.

For evaluating our approach on collection of *purely numeric* labels, we identified 30 numeric data properties from the *City* class in DBpedia and extracted these properties for various cities in the world. Most of the data properties possess more than 17,000 data values. We split the data associated with each semantic label into 10 partitions and manually synthesized 10 data sources by combining one partition from each semantic label to create one data source.

For evaluating our overall approach on a mixture of textual and numeric labels, we used 52 data properties from the *City* class from DBpedia, 30 of which are the ones used in the numeric approach and the remaining 22 data properties contain textual data values. The interesting aspect of the data collected from DBpedia is that it is noisy in the sense that even semantic labels, which are supposed to contain numeric data values, often contain textual values since the data is often authored on Wikipedia by a diverse group of people. This is where our overall approach is effective in handling noise.

We also evaluated our overall approach on the *weather*, *phone directory*, and *flight status* domains, which contain closely related data extracted from separate Web sites and consist of a diverse mixture of textual and numeric semantic labels. The datasets corresponding to the above domains were used in the experiments of Ambite et al. [1].

4.2   Experimental Setup

As already explained, we are not only interested in the top-1 prediction but in the top-k predictions due to inherent similarity in many semantic labels. In our experiments, we took the value of k to be 4 since experiments showed that the correct prediction was included 97 % of the time using our approach. In each experiment, the evaluation metrics of interest are mean reciprocal rank (MRR) [3] and average training time. MRR is useful because we are interested in the rank at which the correct semantic label is predicted among the 4 predictions provided by the system. It helps analyse the ranking of predictions made by any semantic labeling approach using a single measure rather than having to analyse top-1 to top-4 prediction accuracies separately, which is a cumbersome task.

Suppose the data set consists of n sources $\{s_0, s_1, s_2..., s_{n-1}\}$. We perform n runs and average the results of these n runs to prevent cases in which the test data source is skewed in favor of our approach. In the ith run, we test our approach in labelling data source s_i. In order to understand how the number of labelled data sources in the training data affects our performance, in the ith run, we perform $n-1$ experiments. In the jth experiment (j running from 1 to $n-1$) in the ith run, we train on j data sources, specifically the j subsequent data sources starting from s_{i+1} (wrapping around 1 in a cyclical fashion), and test our approach on data source s_i. We obtain the MRR and training times for each experiment separately and average them over the n runs. Thus, we essentially perform $n(n-1)$ experiments.

For example in the museum dataset containing 29 data sources, in the 1st run, we test our approach on data source s_1 by performing 28 experiments. We train

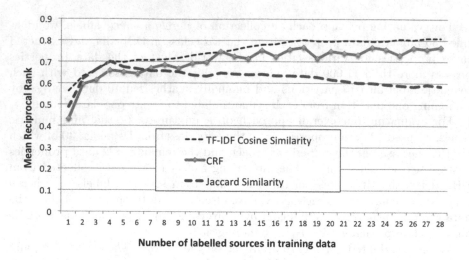

Fig. 1. Textual data from the museum domain

using only data source s_2 in experiment 1, data sources $\{s_2, s_3\}$ in experiment 2, $\cdots$ and data sources $\{s_2, s_3, \cdots, s_{29}\}$ in experiment 28.

There can be cases where a semantic label is absent in the training set but is present in the test set. In such a case, an ideal system is expected to identify this case and report that the semantic label in the test set is *absent* in the training set. If this is correctly identified, we assign a reciprocal rank of 1. Unlike previous approaches, the TF-IDF-based approach has the potential to identify this case if there is limited or no overlap in tokens between the test and training document. The KS-test gives a low p-value in such cases but identifying a suitable threshold for the KS-test will be addressed in future work.

4.3   Results: Textual Data

We used the 29 data sources from the museum domain to test our approach on textual data. Figure 1 shows the variation of MRR against the number of labelled data sources used in training for the three approaches on textual data: TF-IDF-based cosine similarity, a Jaccard-similarity-based approach (as explained in Sect. 3.1) and the Conditional Random Field (CRF)-based learning technique, which extracts features from data values individually [5].

As evident from Fig. 1, the TF-IDF-based cosine-similarity approach achieves higher MRR regardless of the number of labelled sources in the training data compared to the other two approaches. It reaches a maximum MRR of 0.81 when trained with 28 labelled data sources. It achieves an MRR of 0.56 when trained with 1 labelled data source, indicating that on the average, it predicts the correct semantic label in the second rank. The MRR steadily increases with the number of labelled data sources, attaining an MRR of 0.78 when trained with 16 labelled data sources itself. Beyond 16 data sources, we observe gradual increase in the MRR for the TF-IDF-based approach. When trained with 16 labelled data sources, the CRF-based approach and Jaccard similarity reach MRRs of 0.72 and 0.63 respectively.

Each point on the x-axis corresponds to the number of labelled training sources and the corresponding ordinate value is the average of the MRRs obtained in n experiments (each experiment corresponding to a distinct test data source). In order to ensure that the results we observed based on the average MRR are *statistically significant*, we ran a one-sided paired two-sample t-test between the TF-IDF-based approach and the other two approaches for the number of labelled training sources ranging from 1 to 28. We observe that for all points on the x-axis, we favour the alternative hypothesis that the population mean MRR for the TF-IDF-based approach is greater than that of either of the other two approaches with a 95 % confidence.

An interesting observation is that the Jaccard-similarity approach achieves an MRR comparable to the TF-IDF-based approach when the number of training data sources is less than 5, beyond which the performance of the Jaccard similarity approach starts declining monotonically and performs worse than the CRF-based technique thereafter. A possible explanation for this observation is that in the Jaccard similarity approach, the weights of tokens in the vector representation of documents representing semantic labels is binary indicating presence of terms. Hence, as the number of training data sources increases, a larger fraction of tokens in the vocabulary are present in each document and the binary weights are not informative enough resulting in the vector models of most documents giving close Jaccard similarities. Thus, the Jaccard similarity approach finds it more difficult to predict the correct semantic label at a higher rank as the number of training data sources increases.

4.4 Results: Numeric Data

We used the numeric data properties of the *City* class from DBpedia (divided into 10 data sources) to test our approach on numeric data. Figure 2 shows the variation of MRR against the number of training data sources used for approaches proposed by us in in Sect. 2.2, namely the Welch's t-test, the Mann-Whitney U test, and the Kolmogorov-Smirnov test. In addition to these three approaches, we also tested the TF-IDF-based approach (used for textual data) on this numeric data and compared the results with the existing CRF-based semantic labelling technique [5].

Figure 2 clearly shows that the Kolmogorov-Smirnov (KS)-test-based approach achieves much higher MRR than the other 4 approaches for all number of labelled data sources used in training. It reaches a maximum MRR of 0.879 when trained with 6 data sources and then saturates, retaining almost the same MRR for higher number of training data sources used. The maximum MRR scores achieved by other approaches is as follows: the Mann-Whitney U-test-based approach is 0.779, the t-test-based approach is 0.608, the TF-IDF-based approach is 0.715, and the CRF-based approach is 0.729.

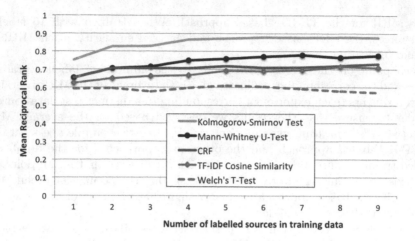

Fig. 2. Numeric data from DBPedia on the city domain

The interesting observation is that the Welch's t-test-based approach, which theoretically should perform better than the TF-IDF-based approach and the CRF-based approach on numeric data, actually does not perform better. This is possibly because the assumptions of the t-test that the distribution of the underlying population be Gaussian and that the two samples being compared have similar number of data points is violated. The curve for the t-test approach is decreasing with an increase in the number of training sources since the assumption of equal number of data points is violated to a greater extent as more data sources are included in the training.

We observe that the TF-IDF-based approach performs almost as well as the CRF-based technique, and that the KS-test and the Mann-Whitney-test-based approaches are clearly better suited to tackle numeric data with the KS-test-based approach achieved the highest MRR.

We ran a one-sided paired two-sample t-tests between the KS test and each of the other approaches to ensure the results are statistically significant. For each point on the x axis, we observed that we favour the alternative hypothesis that the population mean MRR for the KS test is greater than that of the other approaches with 95 % confidence.

4.5   Results: Overall Approach

First, we used the data extracted from DBpedia consisting of the 52 numeric & textual data properties of the *City* class to test our proposed overall approach (*Semantic Typer*). Figure 3(a) shows the variation of MRR with the number of training data sources. We compare our proposed overall approach against the CRF-based semantic labelling technique [5] and the TF-IDF-based approach.

As can be seen from the graph, *Semantic Typer* achieves an average increase of 0.09 and 0.12 in MRR compared to the CRF-based labelling technique and

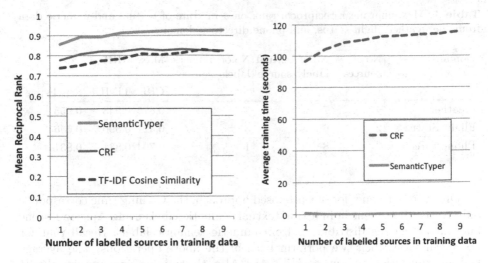

Fig. 3. (a) Mean reciprocal rank (b) Average training time for a mixture of textual and numeric data from DBPedia on the city domain

TF-IDF-based approach respectively. The maximum MRR achieved by *SemanticTyper* is 0.926, CRF-based technique is 0.823 and TF-IDF-based approach is 0.821.

For each point on the x-axis, we ran a one-sided two-sample t-tests. We reject the null hypothesis in favour of the alternative hypothesis that the population mean MRR achieved by *SemanticTyper* is greater than that of either of the other 2 approaches with 95 % confidence, showing that the differences are statistically significant.

We also compared our overall approach, (*SemanticTyper*), against the CRF-based approach and TF-IDF-based approach on the datasets from *weather*, *phone directory* and *flight status* domains [1]. In each of the 3 domains, *SemanticTyper* consistently achieved higher MRR as compared to CRF and TF-IDF-based approaches as we increased the number of labelled training sources (since the *phone directory* domain consists of mainly textual data, *SemanticTyper* reflects the TF-IDF-based approach). We present the maximum MRR achieved by the approaches in each domain in Table 1(we observe it occurs when training on all labelled data sources apart from the test source).

4.6 Training Time

For evaluation of the training time, we ran the CRF-based labelling technique [5] on the complete city dataset from DBpedia. As shown in Fig. 3(b), the training time increased linearly with the number of sources in the training data, starting from 96.6 s for 1 training data source to 115.6 s for 9 training data sources. The average training time was found to be 109.9 s.

Table 1. Maximum mean reciprocal rank on a mixture of textual and numeric data from the weather, flight status, and phone directory domains

Domain	No.of sources	No.of textual labels/source	No.of numeric labels/source	Max. MRR		
				CRF	TF-IDF	SemTyper
Weather	4	7	4	0.875	0.943	0.955
Flight Status	2	6	3	0.421	0.590	0.646
Phone Directory	3	8	1	0.704	0.831	0.831

On the other hand, for our proposed approach, the training time corresponds only to the time spent in indexing textual semantic labels using Apache Lucene and extracting the distribution from numeric semantic labels. Recall that for noisy semantic labels, we perform both of the above operations. The average training time using our approach is 0.45 s. Also, the training time remains almost constant even as more data sources are used for training. We do notice that there is a fixed header cost in training time in our approach due to connection establishment, I/O operations in indexing using Apache Lucene, though this is on the order of a tenth of a second.

Thus, we observe that the average training time of the CRF-based approach compared to our approach is about 250 times slower. This drastic drop in training time for our approach is possible because unlike the CRF-based approach, we are operating on the set of data values of a semantic label as a whole.

5   Conclusion and Future Work

This paper presents an integrated approach to the problem of mapping attributes of a data source to data properties defined in a domain ontology. Automating the semantic labeling process is crucial in constructing semantic descriptions of heterogeneous data sources prior to integrating them. Our approach called *SemanticTyper* is significantly different from approaches in past work in that we attempt to capture the distribution and hence characteristic properties of the data corresponding to a semantic label as a whole rather than extracting features from individual data values. It is evident from experimental results that our approach has much higher label prediction accuracy and is much more scalable in terms of training time than existing systems. Our approach makes no restrictions on the ontology from which data properties are to be assigned.

We plan to explore several directions in future work. First, the schema of a data source often contains metadata about attributes, such as attribute name, that can be helpful in assigning a semantic label to an attribute. For example, consider two semantic labels - *BirthDate* and *DeathDate*. The values of both semantic labels look very similar making it difficult to predict the correct semantic label as the first suggestion. But we can leverage the attribute name to differentiate between the two. Thus, we want to extend our approach to exploit the information contained in attribute names to improve the labelling. Second, in case of numeric data, many times instead of continuous real valued attributes (like rainfall or elevation), we have attributes that take only a set of discrete values (like age in years, number of states, etc.). So, the performance can be enhanced further by identifying these cases and then using more suitable statistical tests (e.g., the Mann-Whitney test). Third, we plan to explore alternative tokenization and word n-gram representations as well.

References

1. Ambite, J.L., Darbha, S., Goel, A., Knoblock, C.A., Lerman, K., Parundekar, R., Russ, T.: Automatically Constructing Semantic Web Services from Online Sources. In: Bernstein, A., Karger, D.R., Heath, T., Feigenbaum, L., Maynard, D., Motta, E., Thirunarayan, K. (eds.) ISWC 2009. LNCS, vol. 5823, pp. 17–32. Springer, Heidelberg (2009)
2. Cafarella, M.J., Halevy, A., Wang, D.Z., Wu, E., Zhang, Y.: Webtables: Exploring the power of tables on the web. Proc. VLDB Endow. **1**(1), 538–549 (2008)
3. Craswell, N.: Mean reciprocal rank. In: Liu, L., Zsu, M. (eds.) Encyclopedia of Database Systems, p. 1703. Springer, New York (2009)
4. Doan, A., Domingos, P., Halevy, A.: Learning to match schemas of data sources: a multistrategy approach. Mach. Learn. **50**(3), 279–301 (2003)
5. Goel, A., Knoblock, C.A., Lerman, K.: Exploiting structure within data for accurate labeling using conditional random fields. In: Proceedings of the 14th International Conference on Artificial Intelligence (ICAI) (2012)
6. Lehmann, E., Romano, J.: Testing Statistical Hypotheses. Springer Texts in Statistics. Springer, New York (2005)
7. Li, W.S., Clifton, C.: Semantic integration in heterogeneous databases using neural networks. In: Proceedings of the 20th International Conference on Very Large Data Bases (VLDB). pp. 1–12 (1994)
8. Limaye, G., Sarawagi, S., Chakrabarti, S.: Annotating and searching web tables using entities, types and relationships. PVLDB **3**(1), 1338–1347 (2010)
9. Mulwad, V., Finin, T., Joshi, A.: Semantic message passing for generating linked data from tables. In: Alani, H., et al. (eds.) ISWC 2013, Part I. LNCS, vol. 8218, pp. 363–378. Springer, Heidelberg (2013)
10. Noy, N.F.: Semantic integration: a survey of ontology-based approaches. SIGMOD Rec. **33**(4), 65–70 (2004)
11. Sequeda, J., Arenas, M., Miranker, D.P.: On directly mapping relational databases to RDF and OWL (extended version). CoRR abs/1202.3667 (2012)
12. Stonebraker, M., Bruckner, D., Ilyas, I., Beskales, G., Cherniack, M., Zdonik, S., Pagan, A., Xu, S.: Data curation at scale: the data tamer system. In: Proceedings of CIDR 2013 (2013)
13. Syed, Z., Finin, T., Mulwad, V., Joshi, A.: Exploiting a web of semantic data for interpreting tables. In: Proceedings of the Second Web Science Conference (2010)
14. Taheriyan, M., Knoblock, C.A., Szekely, P., Ambite, J.L.: A Scalable Approach to Learn Semantic Models of Structured Sources. In: Proceedings of the 8th IEEE International Conference on Semantic Computing (ICSC 2014) (2014)
15. Venetis, P., Halevy, A., Madhavan, J., Paşca, M., Shen, W., Wu, F., Miao, G., Wu, C.: Recovering semantics of tables on the web. Proc. VLDB Endow. **4**(9), 528–538 (2011)

Inductive Classification Through Evidence-Based Models and Their Ensembles

Giuseppe Rizzo[✉], Claudia d'Amato, Nicola Fanizzi, and Floriana Esposito

LACAM – Dipartimento di Informatica, Università degli Studi di Bari
"Aldo Moro", Bari, Italy
{giuseppe.rizzo,claudia.damato,nicola.fanizzi,floriana.esposito}@uniba.it

Abstract. In the context of Semantic Web, one of the most important issues related to the class-membership prediction task (through inductive models) on ontological knowledge bases concerns the imbalance of the training examples distribution, mostly due to the heterogeneous nature and the incompleteness of the knowledge bases. An ensemble learning approach has been proposed to cope with this problem. However, the majority voting procedure, exploited for deciding the membership, does not consider explicitly the uncertainty and the conflict among the classifiers of an ensemble model. Moving from this observation, we propose to integrate the Dempster-Shafer (DS) theory with ensemble learning. Specifically, we propose an algorithm for learning *Evidential Terminological Random Forest* models, an extension of Terminological Random Forests along with the DS theory. An empirical evaluation showed that: (i) the resulting models performs better for datasets with a lot of positive and negative examples and have a less conservative behavior than the voting-based forests; (ii) the new extension decreases the variance of the results.

1 Introduction

In the context of Semantic Web (SW), ontologies and the ability to perform reasoning on them, via deductive methods, play a key role. However, standards inference mechanisms have also shown their limitations due to the incompleteness of ontological knowledge bases deriving from the Open World Assumption (OWA). In order to overcome this problem, alternative forms of reasoning, such as *inductive reasoning*, have been adopted to perform various tasks such as concept retrieval and query answering [1,2]. These tasks have been cast as a classification problem, consisting in deciding the class-membership of an individual with respect to a query concept, to be solved through inductive learning methods that exploit statistical regularities in a knowledge base. The resulting models can be directly applied to the knowledge base or mixed with deductive reasoning capabilities [3]. Although the application of these methods has shown interesting results and the ability to induce assertional knowledge that is not logically derivable, these methods have also revealed some problems due to the aforementioned incompleteness. In general, the individuals that are positive and negative instances for a given concept may not be equally distributed. This skewness may be stronger when considering individuals whose membership cannot

© Springer International Publishing Switzerland 2015
F. Gandon et al. (Eds.): ESWC 2015, LNCS 9088, pp. 418–433, 2015.
DOI: 10.1007/978-3-319-18818-8_26

be assessed because of the OWA. This *class-imbalance* setting may affect the model, resulting with poor performances.

Various methods have been devised for tackling the problem, spanning from sampling methods to ensemble learning approaches [4]. Concerning the specific task of instance classification for inductive query answering on SW knowledge bases, we investigated on the usage of ensemble methods [5], where the resulting model is built by training a certain number of classifiers, called *weak learners*, and the predictions returned by each weak learner are combined by a rule standing for the *meta-learner*. Specifically, we proposed an algorithm for inducing *Terminological Random Forests* (TRFs) [5], an ensemble of *Terminological Decision Trees* (TDTs) [6]. The method extends *Random Forests* and *First Order Random Forests* [7,8] to the case of DL representation languages. When these models are employed, the membership for a test individual is decided according to a majority vote rule (although various strategies for combining predictions have been proposed [9–11]): each classifier returning a vote in favor of a class equally contributes to the final decision. In this way, some aspects are not considered explicitly, such as the uncertainty about the class label assignment and the disagreement that may exist among weak learners. The latter plays a crucial role for the performance of ensemble models [12]. In the specific case of TRFs, we noted that most misclassifications were related to those situations in which votes are distributed evenly with respect to the admissible labels.

A weighted voting procedure may be an alternative strategy to mitigate the problem, but it requires a criterion for setting the weights. In this sense, introducing a meta-learner which manipulates *soft predictions* of each classifier (i.e. a prediction with a confidence measure for each class value) rather than *hard predictions* (where a class value is returned) may be a solution. For TRFs, this can be done by considering the extension of TDT models based on the *Dempster-Shafer Theory* (DS) [13], which provides an explicit representation of ignorance and uncertainty (differently from the original version proposed in [6]). In machine learning, resorting to the DS operators is a well-known solution [14]. Most of the existing ensemble combination methods resort to a solution based on *decision templates*, which are obtained by organizing, for each classifier against each class, a mean vector (called *reference vector*). When these methods are employed, predictions are typically made by computing the similarity value between a decision profile of an unknown instance with the decision templates. Other approaches that does not require the computation of these matrices have been proposed [14]. However, all the methods consider a propositional representation. Additionally, none of them has been employed for predicting assertions on ontological knowledge bases.

The main contribution of the paper concerns the definition of a framework for the induction of *Evidential Terminological Random Forests* for ontological knowledge bases. This is an ensemble learning approach that employs Evidential TDTs (ETDTs) [13] and does not require the computation of decision templates, similarly to [14]. After the induction of the forest, a new individual is classified by combining, by means of the Dempster's rule [15], the available evidence on the membership coming from each tree.

The remainder of the paper is organized as follows: the next section recalls the basics of the Dempster-Shafer Theory; Sect. 3 presents the novel framework for evidential terminological random forests, while in Sect. 4, a preliminary empirical evaluation is described. Sect. 5 draws conclusions and illustrate perspectives for further developments.

2   Basics on the Dempster-Shafer Theory

The Dempster-Shafer Theory (DS) is basically an extension of the Bayesian subjective probability. In the DS, the *frame of discernment* is a set of exhaustive and mutually exclusive hypotheses $\Omega = \{\omega_1, \omega_2, \cdots, \omega_n\}$ about a domain. For instance, the frame of discernment for a classification problem could be the set of all admissible class values. Moving from this set, it is possible to define a Basic Belief Assignment (BBA) as follows:

Definition 1 (Basic Belief Assignment). *Given a frame of discernment* $\Omega = \{\omega_1, \omega_2, \ldots, \omega_n\}$. *A Basic Belief Assignment (BBA) is a function that defines a mapping* $m : 2^\Omega \rightarrow [0, 1]$ *such that:*

$$\sum_{A \in 2^\Omega} m(A) = 1 \qquad (1)$$

Given a piece of evidence, the value of a BBA m for a set A expresses a measure of belief exactly committed to A. This means that the value $m(A)$ does imply no further claims about any of its subsets. This means that when $A = \Omega$, a case of *total ignorance* occurs. Each element $A \in 2^\Omega$ for which $m(A) > 0$ is said to be a *focal element* for m. The function m can be used to define other functions, such as the belief and the plausibility function.

Definition 2 (Belief Function and Plausibility Function). *For a set* $A \subseteq \Omega$, *the belief in* A, *denoted* $Bel(A)$, *represents a measure of the total belief committed to* A *given the available evidence.*

$$\forall A, B \in 2^\Omega \quad Bel(A) = \sum_{B \subseteq A} m(B) \qquad (2)$$

The plausibility of A, *denoted* $Pl(A)$, *represents the amount of belief that could be placed in* A, *if further information became available.*

$$\forall A, B \in 2^\Omega \quad Pl(A) = \sum_{B \cap A \neq \emptyset} m(B) \qquad (3)$$

It can be proved that, knowing just one among m, Bel and Pl allows to derive all the other functions [16].

In the DS, various measures for quantifying the amount of uncertainty have been proposed, e.g. the *non-specificity measure* [17]. The latter can be regarded as a measure for representing the imprecision of a BBA function. This measure can be computed by the following equation:

$$Ns = \sum_{A \in 2^{\Omega}} m(A) \log(|A|) \tag{4}$$

It is easy to note that the non-specificity value is higher when the focal elements are larger subsets of Ω, for the elements of which no further claims can be made.

One of the most important aspects related to the DS is the availability of various operators for pooling evidence from different sources of information. One of them, called *Dempster's rule*, aggregates independent evidences defined within the same frame of discernment. Let m_1 and m_2 be two BBAs. The new BBA obtained by combining m_1 and m_2 using the rule of combination, m_{12}, can be expressed by the orthogonal sum of m_1 and m_2. Generally, the normalized version of the rule is used:

$$\forall A, B, C \subseteq \Omega \quad m_{12}(A) = m_1 \oplus m_2 = \frac{1}{1-c} \sum_{B \cap C = A} m_1(B) m_2(C) \tag{5}$$

where the conflict c can be computed as: $c = \sum_{B \cap C = \emptyset} m_1(B) m_2(C)$

In the DS, the independence of the available evidences is typically a strong constraint that can be relaxed by using further combinations rules, e.g. the *Dubois-Prade's rule* [18].

$$m_{12}(A) = \sum_{B \cup C = A} m_1(B) m_2(C) \tag{6}$$

Differently from the Dempster's rule, the latter considers the union between two sets of hypothesis rather than their intersection. As a result, the conflict between sources of information does not exists.

3   Evidence-Based Ensemble Learning for Description Logic

The TDT (and RF) learning approach is now recalled before introducing the method for the induction of an evidence-based versions of these classification models.

3.1   Class-Imbalance and Terminological Random Forests

In machine learning, the class-imbalance problem concerns the skewness of training data distribution. Considering a multilabel setting, where the number of class label is greater than 3, the problem usually occurs when the number of training instances belonging to the a particular class (the *majority class*) overwhelms the number of those belonging to the other classes (which represent the *majority class*). In order to tackle the problem, most common strategies based on sampling strategy have been proposed [19]. One of the simplest method is an under-sampling strategy that randomly discards instances belonging to the majority class in order to re-balance the dataset. However, this method causes a loss of information due to the possible discarding of useful examples required for inducing a quite predictive model. A Terminological Random Forest (TRF) is an ensemble model trained through a procedure that combines a random under-sampling strategy with the ensemble learning induction [5]. The main purpose for the induction of these models is to mitigate the loss of information mentioned above in the context of SW knowledge bases. A TRF is basically made up of a certain number of Terminological Decision Trees (TDTs) [6], where each of them is built by considering a (quasi-)balanced dataset. The ensemble model assigns the final class for a new individual by appealing to a majority vote procedure. Therefore each TDT returns an *hard prediction*: this means that each tree contributes equally to the decision concerning the class label, regardless its confidence about predictions. In order to consider also this kind of information and tackling sundry problems as the uncertainty about the class assignment (i.e. when the confidence about either a class or another one is approximately equals) and the disagreement between classifiers that may lead to misclassifications [5], we need to resort to other models for the ensemble approach, such as Evidential Terminological Decision Trees [13].

3.2   Evidential Terminological Decision Trees

In [13], it has been shown how the class-membership prediction task can be tackled by inducing Evidential Terminological Decision Trees (ETDTs), an extension of the TDTs [6] based on evidential reasoning. ETDTs are defined in a similar way of TDTs. However, unlike TDTs, each node contains a couple $\langle D, m \rangle$, where D is a DL concept description and m is BBA concerning the membership w.r.t. D, rather than the sole concept description. Practically, to learn an ETDT model, a set of concept descriptions is generated from the current node by resorting to the refinement operator, denoted by ρ. For each concept, a BBA is also computed by considering the positive, negative and uncertain instances w.r.t. the generated concept. Then the best description (and the corresponding BBA) is selected, i.e. the one having the smallest non-specificity measure value w.r.t. the previous level. In other words, this means that the description is the one having the most definite membership.

Figure 1 reports a simple example of ETDT used for predicting whether a car is to be sent back to the factory (SendBack) or can be repaired. We can observe that the root concept ∃hasPart.⊤ is progressively specialized. Additionally, the concepts installed into the intermediate nodes are characterized by a decreasingly non specificity measure value.

3.3   Evidential Terminological Random Forests

An Evidential Terminological Random Forest (ETRF) is an ensemble of ETDTs. We will focus on the procedures for producing an ETRF and for predicting

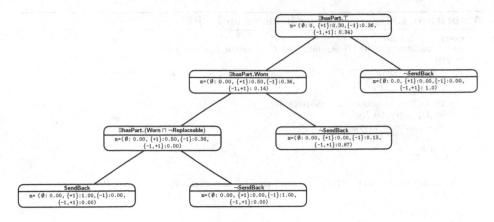

Fig. 1. A simple example of ETDT: each nodes contains a DL concept description and a BBA obtained by counting the instances that reach the node during the training phase

class-membership of input individuals exploiting an ETRF. Moving from the formulation of the concept learning problem proposed in [5], we will use the label set $\mathcal{L} = \{-1, +1\}$ as *frame of discernement* of the problem. The labels in $\mathcal{L}$ are usually used to denote, respectively, the cases of positive and negative membership w.r.t. a target concept C. However, in order to represent the uncertain-membership related to the Open World Assumption, we will employ the label set $\mathcal{L}' = 2^{\mathcal{L}} \setminus \{\emptyset\}$ and the singletons $\{+1\}$ and $\{-1\}$ to denote the positive and negative membership w.r.t. C while the case of uncertain-membership will be labeled by $\mathcal{L} = \{-1, +1\}$.

Growing ETRFs. Algorithm 1 describes the procedure for producing an ETRF. In order to do this, the target concept C, a training set $\mathsf{Tr} \subseteq \mathsf{Ind}(\mathcal{A})$ and the desired number of trees n are required. Tr may contain not only positive and negative examples but also instances with uncertain membership w.r.t. C. According to a bagging approach, the training individuals are sampled with replacement in order to obtain n subsets $\mathsf{D}_i \subseteq \mathsf{Tr}$, with $i = 1, \ldots, n$. In order to obtain D_is, it is possible to apply various sampling strategies although, in this work, we followed the approach proposed in [5]. Firstly, the initial data distribution is considered by adopting a stratified sampling w.r.t. the class-membership values in order to represent instances of the minority class. In the second phase, undersampling can be performed on the training set in order to obtain (quasi-)balanced D_i sets (i.e. with a class imbalance that will not affect much the training process). This means that if the majority class is the negative one, the exceeding part of the counterexamples is randomly discarded. In the dual case, positive instances are removed. In addition, the sampling procedure removes also all the uncertain instances. In Algorithm 1, the procedure that returns the sets D_i implementing this strategy is BALANCEDBOOTSTRAPSAMPLE. For each D_i, an ETDT T is built by means of a recursive strategy, as described in [13] which is implemented by the procedure

Algorithm 1. The routines for inducing an ETRF

```
 1  const: θ: threshold
 2  function INDUCEETRF(Tr : training set; C : concept; n ∈ N): TRF
 3  begin
 4    P̂r ← ESTIMATEPRIORS(Tr, C): {C prior membership probabability estimates}
 5    F ← ∅
 6    for i ← 1 to n
 7        Di ← BALANCEDBOOTSTRAPSAMPLE(Tr)
 8        let Di = ⟨Ps, Ns, Us⟩
 9        Ti ← INDUCEETDTREE(Di, C, P̂r);
10        F ← F ∪ {Ti}
11  return F
12  end
13
14  function INDUCEETDTREE(⟨Ps, Ns, Us⟩: training set; C:concept; m: BBA, P̂r: priors)
15  begin
16
17    T ← new ETDT
18    if |Ps| = 0 and |Ns| = 0 then
19        begin
20            if Pr(+1) ≥ Pr(−1) then {pre−defined constants wrt the whole training set}
21                T.root ← ⟨C, m⟩
22            else
23                T.root ← ⟨¬C, m⟩
24            return T
25        end
26    if (m({−1} ≃ 0) and (m({+1}) > θ) then
27        begin
28            T.root ← ⟨C, m⟩
29            return T
30        end
31    if (m({+1} ≃ 0) and (m({−1}) > θ) then
32        begin
33            T_root ← ⟨¬C, m⟩
34            return T
35        end
36    RS ← RANDOMSELECTION(ρ(D)) {random selection of specializations}
37    S ← ∅
38    for E ∈ RS {assignBBA for each candidate}
39        m′ ← COMPUTEBBA(E, ⟨Ps, Ns, Us⟩)
40        S ← S ∪ {⟨E, m′⟩}
41
42    ⟨E*, m*⟩ ← SELECTBESTCANDIDATE(S)
43    ⟨⟨Pˡ, Nˡ, Uˡ⟩, ⟨Pʳ, Nʳ, Uʳ⟩⟩ ← SPLIT(E*, ⟨Ps, Ns, Us⟩)
44    T.root ← ⟨E*, m*⟩
45    T.left ← INDUCEETDT(⟨Pˡ, Nˡ, Uˡ⟩, E*, P̂r)
46    T.right ← INDUCEETDT(⟨Pʳ, Nʳ, Uʳ⟩, E*, P̂r)
47  return T
48  end
```

INDUCEETDT). It distinguishes various cases. The first one uses prior probability (estimate) to cope with the lack of examples ($|Ps| = 0$ and $|Ns| = 0$). The second one sets the class label for a leaf node if it is sufficiently pure, i.e. no positive (resp. negative) example is found while most examples are negative (resp. positive). This purity condition is evaluated by considering the BBA m given as input for the algorithm ($m(\{-1\} \simeq 0$ and $m(\{+1\}) > \theta$, $m(\{+1\} \simeq 0$ and $m(\{-1\}) > \theta$). The values of a BBA function for the membership values are obtained by computing the number of positive, negative and uncertain-membership instances w.r.t. the current concept. Finally, the third (recursive) case concerns the availability of both

---

Algorithm 2. Class-membership prediction

```
 1  function CLASSIFYBYTRF(a : individual; F : TRF; C : target concept) : L
 2  begin
 3    M[] ← new array
 4    for each T ∈ F
 5      M[T] ← CLASSIFY(a, T)
 6
 7    m̄ ← ⊕ₘ∈M m   {pooling according to a combination rule}
 8
 9    for each l ∈ 2^L   {class assignement}
10      Compute Bel̄(l) from m̄
11
12    if (|Bel̄({−1}) − Bel̄({+1})| > ε ) then
13      return arg max_{l∈L'\{−1,+1}} Bel̄(l)
14    else
15      return L
16  end
17
18  function CLASSIFY(a, T): m̄
19  begin
20    L ← FINDLEAVES(a, T)   {list of BBA}
21    m̄ ← ⊕ₘ∈L m
22    return m̄
23  end
```

---

negative and positive examples. In this case, the current concept description D has to be specialized by means of an operator exploring the search space of downward refinements of D. Following the approach described in [5,8], the refinement step produces a set of candidate specializations $\rho(D)$ and a subset of them, namely RS, is then randomly selected (via function RANDOMSELECTION) by setting its cardinality according to the value returned by a function f applied to the cardinality of the set of specializations returned by the refinement operator (e.g. $\sqrt{|\rho(D)|}$). A BBA m' is then built for each candidate $E \in RS$. Again, the function can be obtained by counting the number of positive, negative and uncertain-membership instances). Then the best pair $\langle E^*, m^* \rangle \in S$ according to the non-specificity measure employed in [13] is determined by the SELECTBESTCANDIDATE procedure and finally installed in the current node. Specifically, the procedure tries to find the pair $\langle E^*, m^* \rangle$ having the smallest non-specificity measure value. After the assessment of the best pair E^*, the individuals are partitioned by the procedure SPLIT for the left or right branch according to the result of the instance-check w.r.t. E^*, maintaining the same group ($P^{l/r}, N^{l/r}$, or $U^{l/r}$). Note that a training example a is replicated in both children in case both $\mathcal{K} \not\models E^*(a)$ and $\mathcal{K} \not\models \neg E^*(a)$. The divide-and-conquer strategy is applied recursively until the instances routed to a node satisfy one of the stopping conditions discussed above.

Prediction. After an ETRF is produced, predictions can be made relying on the resulting classification model. The related procedure sketched in Algorithm 2 works as follows. Given the individual to be classified, for each tree T_i of the forest, the procedure CLASSIFY returns a BBA assigned to the leaves reached from the root in a path down the tree. Specifically, the algorithm traverses recursively the ETDT by performing an instance check w.r.t. the concept contained in each node that is reached: let $a \in \mathsf{Ind}(\mathcal{A})$ and D the concept installed in the current node, if $\mathcal{K} \models D(a)$ (resp. $\mathcal{K} \models \neg D(a)$) the left (resp. right) branch is followed. If neither $\mathcal{K} \not\models D(a)$ nor $\mathcal{K} \not\models \neg D(a)$ is verified, both branches are followed. After the exploration of a single ETDT, the list L may contain several BBAs. In this case, BBAs are pooled according to a combination rule as the Dubois-Prade's one [13]. The function CLASSIFY returns the combined BBA according to this rule (denoted by the symbol $\oplus$). After polling all trees, a set of BBAs deriving from the previous phase are exploited to decide the class label to the test individual a. Function CLASSIFYBYTRF takes an individual a and a forest F. Then, the algorithm iterates on the forest trees collecting the BBAs via function CLASSIFY. Then, the BBAs are pooled according to a further combination rule, which can be different from the one employed during the exploration of a single ETDT. Additionally, this combination rule should be also an associative operator [15]. In this way, the result should not be affected by the pooling order of the BBAs. In our experiments we combined these BBAs via Dempster's rules (denoted by the symbol $\oplus$ in the function CLASSIFYBYTRF). By using this rule, the disagreement between classifiers, which corresponds to the conflict exploited as normalization factor, is explicitly considered by the meta-learner. The final decision is then made according to the belief function value computed from the pooled BBAs $\overline{m}$. In this case, we aim to select the $l \in 2^{\mathcal{L}}$ which maximizes the value of the function. However, in order to cope with the monotonicity of belief function which can lead easily to return an unknown-membership as a final prediction, the meta-learner must compare the value for the positive and negative class label and it assign the unknown membership if their values are approximately equal. This is made by comparing the difference between belief function values w.r.t. a threshold ϵ.

4 Preliminary Experiments

The experimental evaluation aims at evaluating the effectiveness of the classification based on the ETRF models[1] and the improvement in terms of prediction w.r.t. TRFs. We provide the details of the experimental setup and present and discuss the outcomes.

4.1 Setup

Various Web ontologies have been considered in the experiments (see Table 1). They are available on TONES repository[2]. For each ontology of TONES, 15 query concepts have been randomly generated by combining (using the conjunction and disjunction operators or universal and existential restriction) 2 through 8 (primitive or defined) concepts of the ontology.

---

[1] The source code will be available at: https://github.com/Giuseppe-Rizzo/SWML Algorithms.

[2] http://www.inf.unibz.it/tones/index.php.

Table 1. Ontologies employed in the experiments

Ontology	DL Lang.	#Concepts	#Roles	#Individuals
BCO	$\mathcal{ALCHOF}(\mathcal{D})$	196	22	112
BioPax	$\mathcal{ALCIF}(\mathcal{D})$	74	70	323
NTN	$\mathcal{SHIF}(\mathcal{D})$	47	27	676
HD	$\mathcal{ALCIF}(\mathcal{D})$	1498	10	639

As in previous works [5,13], because of the limited population of the considered ontologies, all the individuals occurring in each ontology were employed as (training or test) examples.

A 10-fold cross validation design of the experiments was adopted so that the final results are averaged for each of the considered indices (see below). We compared our extensions with other tree-based classifiers: TDTs [6], TRFs [5] and ETDTs [13].

In order to learn each ETDTs by considering a balanced set of examples, a stratified sampling was required (see Sect. 3). Three stratified sampling rates related to the D_is were set in our experiments, namely 50 %, 70 % and 80 %.

Finally, forests with an increasing number of trees were induced, namely: 10, 20 and 30. For each tree in a forest, the number of randomly selected candidates was determined as the square root of candidate refinements: $\sqrt{|\,\rho(\cdot)\,|}$. We employed these settings for training both ETRFs and TRFs. As in previous works [5,6,13], to compare the predictions made using RFs against the ground truth assessed by a reasoner, the following indices were computed:

- *match* rate (M%), i.e. test individuals for which the inductive model and a reasoner agree on the membership (both $\{+1\}$, $\{-1\}$, or $\{-1,+1\}$);
- *commission* rate (C%) i.e. test cases where the determined memberships are opposite (i.e. $\{+1\}$ vs. $\{-1\}$ or viceversa);
- *omission* rate (O%), i.e. test cases for which the inductive method cannot determine a definite membership while the reasoner can ($\{-1,+1\}$ vs. $\{+1\}$ or $\{-1\}$);
- *induction* rate (I%). i.e. test cases where the inductive method can predict a definite membership while the reasoner cannot assess it ($\{+1\}$ or $\{-1\}$ vs. $\{-1,+1\}$).

4.2 Results

As regards the distribution of the instances w.r.t. the target concepts, we observed that negative instances outnumber the positive ones in BCO and Human Disease (HD). In the case of BCO this occurred for all concepts but one with a ratio between positive and negative instances of $1:20$. In the case of HD this kind of imbalance occurred for all the queries. Moreover, in the case of HD the number of instances with an uncertain-membership is very large (about 90 %). On the other hand, in the case of NTN, we noted the predominance of positive instances: for

Table 2. Results of experiments with TDTs and ETDTs models

Ontology index		TDT	ETDTs
Bco	M%	80.44 ± 11.01	90.31 ± 14.79
	C%	07.56 ± 08.08	01.86 ± 02.61
	O%	05.04 ± 04.28	00.00 ± 00.00
	I%	06.96 ± 05.97	07.83 ± 15.35
Biopax	M%	66.63 ± 14.60	87.00 ± 07.15
	C%	31.03 ± 12.95	11.57 ± 02.62
	O%	00.39 ± 00.61	00.00 ± 00.00
	I%	01.95 ± 07.13	01.43 ± 08.32
NTN	M%	68.85 ± 13.23	23.87 ± 26.18
	C%	00.37 ± 00.30	00.00 ± 00.00
	O%	09.51 ± 07.06	00.00 ± 00.00
	I%	21.27 ± 08.73	75.13 ± 26.18
HD	M%	58.31 ± 14.06	10.69 ± 01.47
	C%	00.44 ± 00.47	00.07 ± 00.17
	O%	05.51 ± 01.81	00.00 ± 00.00
	I%	35.74 ± 15.90	89.24 ± 01.46

Table 3. Comparison between TRFs and ETRF with sampling rate of 50 %

Ontology index		Sampling rate 50 %					
		TRF			ETRF		
		10 trees	20 trees	30 trees	10 trees	20 trees	30 trees
Bco	M%	86.27 ± 15.79	86.24 ± 15.94	86.26 ± 15.84	91.31 ± 06.35	91.31 ± 06.35	91.31 ± 06.35
	C%	02.47 ± 03.70	02.43 ± 03.70	02.84 ± 03.70	02.91 ± 02.45	02.91 ± 02.45	02.91 ± 02.45
	O%	01.90 ± 07.30	01.97 ± 07.55	01.92 ± 07.37	00.00 ± 00.00	00.00 ± 00.00	00.00 ± 00.00
	I%	09.36 ± 13.96	09.36 ± 13.96	09.36 ± 13.96	05.88 ± 06.49	05.88 ± 06.49	05.88 ± 06.49
Biopax	M%	75.30 ± 16.23	75.30 ± 16.23	75.30 ± 16.23	96.92 ± 08.07	96.79 ± 08.15	96.55 ± 08.15
	C%	18.74 ± 17.80	18.74 ± 17.80	18.74 ± 17.80	00.79 ± 01.22	00.91 ± 01.74	00.77 ± 01.74
	O%	00.00 ± 00.00	00.00 ± 00.00	00.00 ± 00.00	00.00 ± 00.00	00.00 ± 00.00	00.00 ± 00.00
	I%	01.97 ± 07.16	01.97 ± 07.16	01.97 ± 07.16	02.29 ± 08.13	02.30 ± 08.15	02.30 ± 08.15
NTN	M%	83.41 ± 07.85	83.42 ± 07.85	83.42 ± 07.85	05.38 ± 07.38	05.38 ± 07.38	05.38 ± 07.38
	C%	00.02 ± 00.04	00.02 ± 00.04	00.02 ± 00.04	06.58 ± 07.51	06.58 ± 07.51	06.58 ± 07.51
	O%	13.40 ± 10.17	13.40 ± 10.17	13.40 ± 10.17	00.00 ± 00.00	00.00 ± 00.00	00.00 ± 00.00
	I%	03.17 ± 04.65	03.16 ± 04.65	03.16 ± 04.65	88.05 ± 08.50	88.05 ± 08.50	88.05 ± 08.50
HD	M%	68.00 ± 16.98	68.00 ± 16.99	67.98 ± 16.99	10.29 ± 00.00	10.29 ± 00.01	10.29 ± 00.02
	C%	00.02 ± 00.05	00.02 ± 00.05	00.02 ± 00.05	00.26 ± 00.26	00.26 ± 00.27	00.26 ± 00.28
	O%	06.38 ± 02.03	06.38 ± 02.03	06.38 ± 02.03	00.00 ± 00.00	00.00 ± 00.00	00.00 ± 00.00
	I%	25.59 ± 18.98	25.59 ± 18.98	25.59 ± 18.98	89.24 ± 00.26	89.24 ± 00.26	89.24 ± 00.26

most concepts the ratio between positive and negative instances was 12 : 1 and a lot of uncertain-membership instances were found (again, over 90 %). A weaker imbalance could be noted with BioPax. For most query concepts the ratio between positive and negative instances was 1 : 5. In addition, for most query concepts, uncertain-membership instances lacked. This kind of instances were available only for 2 queries. The class distribution was balanced for three concepts only.

Tables 2, 3, 4 and 5 report the results of this empirical evaluation. On the other hand, Table 6 shows the differences between indexes for TRFs and ETRFs. In general, we can observe how ensemble methods perform better or, in the worst cases, have the same performance of a single classifiers approach for most ontologies. For example, when we compare ETRFs w.r.t. ETDTs, a significant improvement was obtained for BIOPAX (the match rate was around 96 % for ETRFs and 87 % for ETDTs). For BCO, there was a more limited improvement:

Table 4. Comparison between TRFs and ETRF with sampling rate of 70 %

Ontology index		Sampling rate 70 %					
		TRF			ETRF		
		10 trees	20 trees	30 trees	10 trees	20 trees	30 trees
Bco	M%	84.12 ± 18.27	85.70 ± 16.98	85.52 ± 17.09	91.31 ± 06.35	91.31 ± 06.35	91.31 ± 06.35
	C%	02.16 ± 03.09	02.32 ± 03.39	02.30 ± 03.38	02.91 ± 02.45	02.91 ± 02.45	02.91 ± 02.45
	O%	04.50 ± 12.59	02.65 ± 09.93	02.86 ± 10.04	00.00 ± 00.00	00.00 ± 00.00	00.00 ± 00.00
	I%	09.23 ± 13.99	09.33 ± 13.97	09.31 ± 13.91	05.88 ± 06.49	05.88 ± 06.49	05.88 ± 06.49
Biopax	M%	75.30 ± 16.23	75.30 ± 16.23	75.30 ± 16.23	96.65 ± 08.05	95.98 ± 08.13	96.55 ± 08.15
	C%	18.74 ± 17.80	18.74 ± 17.80	18.74 ± 17.80	01.07 ± 01.67	01.71 ± 02.50	00.77 ± 01.74
	O%	00.00 ± 00.00	00.00 ± 00.00	00.00 ± 00.00	00.00 ± 00.00	00.00 ± 00.00	00.00 ± 00.00
	I%	01.97 ± 07.16	01.97 ± 07.16	01.97 ± 07.16	02.28 ± 08.13	02.31 ± 08.17	02.30 ± 08.15
Ntn	M%	83.42 ± 07.85	83.42 ± 07.85	83.42 ± 07.85	05.50 ± 07.28	05.50 ± 07.28	05.50 ± 07.28
	C%	00.02 ± 00.04	00.02 ± 00.04	00.02 ± 00.04	06.52 ± 07.54	06.52 ± 07.54	06.52 ± 07.54
	O%	13.40 ± 10.17	13.40 ± 10.17	13.40 ± 10.17	00.00 ± 00.00	00.00 ± 00.00	00.00 ± 00.00
	I%	03.16 ± 04.65	03.16 ± 04.65	03.16 ± 04.65	87.99 ± 08.84	87.99 ± 08.84	87.99 ± 08.84
HD	M%	68.00 ± 16.98	68.00 ± 16.99	67.98 ± 16.99	10.29 ± 00.00	10.29 ± 00.01	10.29 ± 00.02
	C%	00.02 ± 00.05	00.02 ± 00.05	00.02 ± 00.05	00.26 ± 00.26	00.26 ± 00.27	00.26 ± 00.28
	O%	06.38 ± 02.03	06.38 ± 02.03	06.38 ± 02.03	00.00 ± 00.00	00.00 ± 00.00	00.00 ± 00.00
	I%	25.59 ± 18.98	25.59 ± 18.98	25.59 ± 18.98	89.24 ± 00.26	89.24 ± 00.26	89.24 ± 00.26

Table 5. Comparison between TRFs and ETRF with sampling rate of 80 %

Ontology index		Sampling rate 80 %					
		TRF			ETRF		
		10 trees	20 trees	30 trees	10 trees	20 trees	30 trees
Bco	M%	75.57 ± 24.28	81.27 ± 19.27	79.33 ± 22.41	91.31 ± 06.35	91.31 ± 06.35	91.31 ± 06.35
	C%	01.45 ± 01.77	01.89 ± 02.65	01.64 ± 02.36	02.91 ± 02.45	02.91 ± 02.45	02.91 ± 02.45
	O%	13.51 ± 22.19	08.05 ± 15.04	10.38 ± 19.28	00.00 ± 00.00	00.00 ± 00.00	00.00 ± 00.00
	I%	08.47 ± 14.07	08.65 ± 14.23	09.36 ± 13.96	05.88 ± 06.49	05.88 ± 06.49	05.88 ± 06.49
Biopax	M%	75.30 ± 16.23	75.30 ± 16.23	75.30 ± 16.23	95.47 ± 07.95	94.29 ± 08.96	96.55 ± 08.15
	C%	18.74 ± 17.80	18.74 ± 17.80	18.74 ± 17.80	02.24 ± 02.63	03.40 ± 05.54	00.77 ± 01.74
	O%	00.00 ± 00.00	00.00 ± 00.00	00.00 ± 00.00	00.00 ± 00.00	00.00 ± 00.00	00.00 ± 00.00
	I%	01.97 ± 07.16	01.97 ± 07.16	01.97 ± 07.16	02.29 ± 08.11	02.31 ± 08.17	02.30 ± 08.15
Ntn	M%	83.41 ± 07.85	83.42 ± 07.85	83.42 ± 07.85	05.50 ± 07.28	05.50 ± 07.28	05.50 ± 07.28
	C%	00.02 ± 00.04	00.02 ± 00.04	00.02 ± 00.04	06.52 ± 07.54	06.52 ± 07.54	06.52 ± 07.54
	O%	13.40 ± 10.17	13.40 ± 10.17	13.40 ± 10.17	00.00 ± 00.00	00.00 ± 00.00	00.00 ± 00.00
	I%	03.17 ± 04.65	03.16 ± 04.65	03.16 ± 04.65	87.99 ± 08.84	87.99 ± 08.84	87.99 ± 08.84
HD	M%	68.00 ± 16.98	68.00 ± 16.99	67.98 ± 16.99	10.29 ± 00.00	10.29 ± 00.01	10.29 ± 00.02
	C%	00.02 ± 00.05	00.02 ± 00.05	00.02 ± 00.05	00.26 ± 00.26	00.26 ± 00.27	00.26 ± 00.28
	O%	06.38 ± 02.03	06.38 ± 02.03	06.38 ± 02.03	00.00 ± 00.00	00.00 ± 00.00	00.00 ± 00.00
	I%	25.59 ± 18.98	25.59 ± 18.98	25.59 ± 18.98	89.24 ± 00.26	89.24 ± 00.26	89.24 ± 00.26

it was only around 1.31 % and it was likely due to the number of examples available in BCO. In this case, when ETRFs model were induced, there was a larger overlap between the ETDTs in the forests and the sole ETDT model employed in the single-classifier approach, i.e. the models were very similar to each other.

As regards the comparison between ETRFs and TRFs model, an improvement of match rate and a subsequent decrease of induction rate was observed for Bco. This improvement was around 6 % for match rate while it was of 3 % for the induction rate when a sampling rate of 50 % was employed. The improvement of match rate was larger when the sampling rate of 70 % and 80 % were employed. In this case, the addition of further instances lead to that the improvement of the predictiveness of the ETRFs. The ensemble of models proposed in this

Table 6. Differences between the results for TRFs and ETRFs model. The symbol •
is used to denote that a positive or negative difference that is in favor of ETRFs, while
the symbol ○ is used to denote a positive or negative difference that is in favor of TRFs

Ontology	Index	Sampling rate 50 %			Sampling rate 70 %			Sampling rate 80 %		
		10 trees	20 trees	30 trees	10 trees	20 trees	30 trees	10 trees	20 trees	30 trees
Bco	ΔM%	+05.04 •	+05.07 •	+05.05 •	+07.19 •	+05.61 •	+05.79 •	+15.74 •	+10.04 •	+11.98•
	ΔC%	+00.44 ○	+00.48 ○	+00.07 ○	+00.75 ○	+00.59 ○	+00.61 ○	+01.46 ○	+01.02 ○	+01.27○
	ΔO%	-01.90 •	-01.97 •	-01.92 •	-04.50 •	-02.65 •	-02.86 •	-13.51 •	-8.05 •	-10.38 •
	ΔI%	-03.48 •	-03.48 •	-03.48 •	-03.35 •	-03.45 •	-03.43 •	-02.59 •	-02.77 •	-03.48 •
BioPax	ΔM%	+21.62 •	+21.49 •	+21.25 •	+21.35 •	+20.68 •	+21.25 •	+20.17 •	+18.99 •	+21.25 •
	ΔC%	-17.95 •	-17.83 •	-17.97 •	-17.67 •	-17.03 •	-17.97 •	-16.50 •	-15.34 •	-17.97 •
	ΔO%	+00.00 •	+00.00 •	+00.00 •	+00.00 •	+00.00 •	+00.00 •	+00.00 •	+00.00 •	+00.00 •
	ΔI%	+00.32 ○	+00.33 ○	+00.33 ○	+00.31 ○	+00.34 ○	+00.33 ○	+00.32 ○	+00.34 ○	+00.33 ○
NTN	Δ M%	-78.03 ○	-78.04 ○	-78.04 ○	-77.92 ○	-77.92 ○	-77.92 ○	-77.91 ○	-77.92 ○	-77.92 ○
	ΔC%	+06.56 ○	+06.56 ○	+06.56 ○	+06.50 ○	+06.50 ○	+06.50 ○	+06.50 ○	+06.50 ○	+06.50 ○
	ΔO%	-13.40 •	-13.40 •	-13.40 •	-13.40 •	-13.40 •	-13.40 •	-13.40 •	-13.40 •	-13.40 •
	ΔI%	+84.88 ○	+84.89 ○	+84.89 ○	+84.83 ○	+84.83 ○	+84.83 ○	+84.82 ○	+84.83 ○	+84.83 ○
HD	ΔM%	-57.71 ○	-57.71 ○	-57.69 ○	-57.71 ○	-57.71 ○	-57.69 ○	-57.71 ○	-57.71 ○	-57.69 ○
	ΔC%	+00.24 ○	+00.24 ○	+00.24 ○	+00.24 ○	+00.24 ○	+00.24 ○	+00.24 ○	+00.24 ○	+00.24 ○
	ΔO%	-06.38 •	-06.38 •	-06.38 •	-06.38 •	-06.38 •	-06.38 •	-06.38 •	-06.38 •	-06.38 •
	ΔI%	+63.65 ○	+63.65 ○	+63.65 ○	+63.65 ○	+63.65 ○	+63.65 ○	+63.65 ○	+63.65 ○	+63.65 ○

paper showed a more conservative behavior w.r.t. the original version. It can be
noted that the increase of match rate was mainly due to uncertain-membership
instances that were not classified as induction cases, as a result of the values of
belief functions employed for making decisions. Another cause is related to the
lack of omission cases. In this case, the procedure for forcing the answer leads
to decide in favor of the correct class-membership value. Besides the value of
commission rate did not change in a significant way. The proposed extension is
also more stable in terms of standard deviation: for ETRFs, this value is lower
than the one obtained for TRFs.

With BioPax, we observed again the increase of the match and a significant
decrease of commission rate. Also the induction rate was larger with ETRFs than
with TRFs, likely due to the procedure for forcing the answer. As regards the experiments on HD and NTN ontology, we can observe, differently from the original version of TRFs, how the induction rate was very high when ETRFs were employed.
For the latter case, this result was mainly due to the original data distribution
that showed an overwhelming of uncertain instances. As previously mentioned,
they approximately represented about 50 % of the total number of instances in the
ABox of HD and about 90 % for NTN. TRFs showed a conservative behavior by
returning an unknown membership (due to uncertain results of the intermediate
tests during the exploration of trees [5]) which tends to preserve the matches with
the gold-standard membership also in case of uncertain membership. This explains
the high match rate observed in the experiments. After the induction of ETRFs,
the models showed a braver behavior also due to the forcing procedure. As a result,
it tends to more easily assign a positive or negative membership to a test instance
leading to the increase of the induction rate, with a value of about 89 % while omission cases missed. Induction cases represent new non-derivable knowledge that can
be potentially useful for ontology completion, their larger number suggest that the

result may be also due to the existing noise (also due to the employment of the entire ABox as dataset). This basically means that most induced assertions may be not definitely related to learned concepts, but they cannot considered as real errors like commission rate.

Similarly to our previous experiments proposed in [5], we observed also how the generated concept descriptions that were installed as node for each ETDT do not improve the quality of the splittings, similarly to the case of TDTs where the training was lead by the information gain criterion. This occurred for all the datasets that were considered here. In both cases, most instances were sent along a branch, while a small number of them were sent along the other one. This means that *small disjuncts problem* is a common problem both TRFs and ETRFs and neither the information gain nor the non-specificity measure can be considered as suitable measures for selecting the best concept description that is used to split instances during the training phase. A further remark concerns the predictiveness of the proposed method w.r.t. both the sampling methods and the number of trees in a forest. Also for ETRFs, the performance did not change significantly when a larger number of trees was set or when the algorithm resort to a larger stratified sampling rate. While in the former case the results are likely due to a weak diversification between ETDTs, in the latter case, the result was likely due to the availability of examples whose employment did not change the quality of splittings generated during the growth process. For ETRFs, similarly to TRF models, the refinement operator is still a bottleneck for learning phase: execution times spanned from few minutes to almost 10 h as the experiments proposed in [5]. However, when an intermediate test with an uncertain result was encountered, the exploration of alternative paths affected the efficiency of the proposed method.

5 Conclusion and Extensions

We have proposed an algorithm for inducing Evidential Terminological Random Forests, an extension of Terminological Random Forests devised to tackle the class-imbalance problem for learning predictive classification models for SW knowledge bases. As the original version, the algorithm combines a sampling approach with ensemble learning techniques. The resulting models combine predictions that are represented as basic belief functions rather than votes by exploiting combination rules in the context of the Dempster-Shafer Theory for making the final decision. In addition, a preliminary empirical evaluation with publicly available ontologies has been performed. The experiments have shown how the new classification model seems to be more predictive than the previous ones and it tends to assign a definite membership. Besides, the predictiveness of the model can be sufficiently tolerant to variation of the number of trees and the sampling rate. The standard deviation is also lower than the original TRFs. In the future, we plan to extend the method along various directions. One regards the choice of the refinement operator that may be applied in order to generate more discriminative intermediate tests. This plays a crucial role for the quality of the classifiers involved in the ensemble model in order to obtain quite predictive weak learners from both expressive and shallow ontologies extracted from the Linked Data cloud [20]. In order to cope with the latter case, the method could be parallelized in order to employ it as a nonstandard tool to reason over such datasets. Further ensemble techniques and novel rules for combining the answers of the weak learners could be employed. For example, weak learners can be induced from subsets of training instances generated by means of a procedure based on cross-validation rather than sampling with replacement. Finally, further investigations may concern the application of strategies aiming to optimize the ensemble, that is an important characteristic of such learning methods [12,21].

Acknowledgments. This work fulfills the objectives of the LOGIN "LOGistica INTegrata" (2012–2015) (PII INDUSTRY 2015), announcement "New Technologies for the Made in Italy".

References

1. Rettinger, A., Lösch, U., Tresp, V., d'Amato, C., Fanizzi, N.: Mining the semantic web - statistical learning for next generation knowledge bases. Data Min. Knowl. Discov. **24**, 613–662 (2012)
2. d'Amato, C., Fanizzi, N., Esposito, F.: Inductive learning for the semantic web: what does it buy? Semant. Web **1**, 53–59 (2010)
3. d'Amato, C., Fanizzi, N., Fazzinga, B., Gottlob, G., Lukasiewicz, T.: Ontology-based semantic search on the web and its combination with the power of inductive reasoning. Ann. Math. Artif. Intell. **65**, 83–121 (2012)
4. He, H., Ma, Y.: Imbalanced Learning: Foundations, Algorithms, and Applications, 1st edn. Wiley-IEEE Press, Hoboken (2013)
5. Rizzo, G., d'Amato, C., Fanizzi, N., Esposito, F.: Tackling the class-imbalance learning problem in semantic web knowledge bases. In: Janowicz, K., Schlobach, S., Lambrix, P., Hyvönen, E. (eds.) EKAW 2014. LNCS, vol. 8876, pp. 453–468. Springer, Heidelberg (2014)
6. Fanizzi, N., d'Amato, C., Esposito, F.: Induction of concepts in web ontologies through terminological decision trees. In: Balcázar, J.L., Bonchi, F., Gionis, A., Sebag, M. (eds.) ECML PKDD 2010, Part I. LNCS, vol. 6321, pp. 442–457. Springer, Heidelberg (2010)
7. Breiman, L.: Random forests. Mach. Learn. **45**, 5–32 (2001)
8. Assche, A.V., Vens, C., Blockeel, H., Dzeroski, S.: First order random forests: learning relational classifiers with complex aggregates. Mach. Learn. **64**, 149–182 (2006)
9. Kuncheva, L.: A theoretical study on six classifier fusion strategies. IEEE Trans. Pattern Anal. Mach. Intell. **24**, 281–286 (2002)
10. Xu, L., Krzyzak, A., Suen, C.: Methods of combining multiple classifiers and their applications to handwriting recognition. IEEE Trans. Syst. Man Cybern. **22**, 418–435 (1992)
11. Rogova, G.: Combining the results of several neural network classifiers. In: Yager, R., Liu, L. (eds.) Classic Works of the Dempster-Shafer Theory of Belief Functions. Studies in Fuzziness and Soft Computing, vol. 219, pp. 683–692. Springer, Heidelberg (2008)

12. Yin, X.C., Yang, C., Hao, H.W.: Learning to diversify via weighted kernels for classifier ensemble. CoRR abs/1406.1167 (2014)
13. Rizzo, G., d'Amato, C., Fanizzi, N., Esposito, F.: Towards evidence-based terminological decision trees. In: Laurent, A., Strauss, O., Bouchon-Meunier, B., Yager, R.R. (eds.) IPMU 2014, Part I. CCIS, vol. 442, pp. 36–45. Springer, Heidelberg (2014)
14. Bi, Y., Guan, J., Bell, D.: The combination of multiple classifiers using an evidential reasoning approach. Artif. Intell. **172**, 1731–1751 (2008)
15. Sentz, K., Ferson, S.: Combination of evidence in Dempster-Shafer theory. Technical report, SANDIA, SAND2002-0835 (2002)
16. Klir, J.: Uncertainty and Information. Wiley, Hoboken (2006)
17. Smarandache, F., Dezert, J.: An introduction to the DSm theory for the combination of paradoxical, uncertain, and imprecise sources of information. CoRR abs/cs/0608002 (2006)
18. Dubois, D., Prade, H.: On the combination of evidence in various mathematical frameworks. In: Flamm, J., Luisi, T. (eds.) Reliability Data Collection and Analysis. Eurocourses, vol. 3, pp. 213–241. Springer, The Netherlands (1992)
19. He, H., Garcia, E.A.: Learning from imbalanced data. IEEE Trans. Knowl. Data Eng. **21**, 1263–1284 (2009)
20. Heath, T., Bizer, C.: Linked Data: Evolving the Web into a Global Data Space. Synthesis Lectures on the Semantic Web. Morgan and Claypool Publishers, San Rafael (2011)
21. Fu, B., Wang, Z., Pan, R., Xu, G., Dolog, P.: An integrated pruning criterion for ensemble learning based on classification accuracy and diversity. In: Uden, L., Herrera, F., Bajo, J., Corchado, J.M. (eds.) 7th International Conference on KMO. AISC, vol. 172, pp. 47–58. Springer, Heidelberg (2013)

Mobile Web, Internet of Things and Semantic Streams

Standardized and Efficient RDF Encoding for Constrained Embedded Networks

Sebastian Käbisch$^{(\boxtimes)}$, Daniel Peintner, and Darko Anicic

Siemens AG, Corporate Technology, Munich, Germany
{Sebastian.Kaebisch,Daniel.Peintner.ext,Darko.Anicic}@siemens.com

Abstract. In the context of Web of Things (WoT), embedded networks have to face the challenge of getting ever more complex. The complexity arises as the number of interchanging heterogeneous devices and different hardware resource classes always increase. When it comes to the development and the use of embedded networks in the WoT domain, Semantic Web technologies are seen as one way to tackle this complexity. For example, properties and capabilities of embedded devices may be semantically described in order to enable an effective search over different classes of devices, semantic data integration may be deployed to integrate data produced by these devices, or embedded devices may be empowered to reason about semantic data in the context of WoT applications. Despite these possibilities, a wide adoption of Semantic Web or Linked Data technologies in the domain of embedded networks has not been established yet. One reason for this is an inefficient representation of semantic data. Serialisation formats of RDF data, such as for instance a plain-text XML, are not suitable for embedded devices. In this paper, we present an approach that enables constrained devices, such as microcontrollers with very limited hardware resources, to store and process semantic data. Our approach is based on the W3C Efficient XML Interchange (EXI) format. To show the applicability of the approach, we provide an EXI-based μRDF Store and show associated evaluation results.

Keywords: Web of Things (WoT) · Microcontroller · RDF · EXI · RDF store

1 Introduction

We are witnessing a new era of innovation which is taking place through the convergence of the physical and cyber world. This era is characterised with an emergence of technologies such as low-cost sensing, smart devices, advanced computing, powerful analytics, and the new levels of connectivity permitted by the Internet - all together often referred to as Internet of Things (IoT). Further integration of physical devices and the data they produce with the Web is also known as the Web of Things (WoT).

While it has a huge potential to change our lives in various aspects, WoT still faces a number of challenges such as for example identification and discovery of

© Springer International Publishing Switzerland 2015
F. Gandon et al. (Eds.): ESWC 2015, LNCS 9088, pp. 437–452, 2015.
DOI: 10.1007/978-3-319-18818-8_27

WoT devices and services, machine interpretation and integration of WoT data, automated interactions of WoT devices in a certain context and others.

Semantic Web (SW) technologies are seen as a good candidate to tackle these and other challenges in the realm of WoT. The W3C Resource Description Framework (RDF) [19] is a powerful data model that is used for conceptual descriptions and modelling of information in the Web. RDF expressions, provided in a form of subject-property-object triples, represent statements about (Web) resources. In the context of WoT, resources are physical 'things' (e.g., sensors, actuators, etc.) that are connected to the Web and can be in the same way described as a set of RDF statements. RDF descriptions, written in accordance to a certain schema or ontology, may later help in discovery of WoT devices with certain characteristics. This can reduce the time of building new applications significantly, as for example the semantic search can be used for this task. The data produced by selected devices may be easier integrated and processed, thereby creating a new information or an added-value service. A WoT device can also be easier integrated into a running system if both the device and the contextual information of the system are semantically described. Thanks to semantic reasoning, that enables the WoT device to find its role in the system, it also enables the device to demonstrate a plug&play functionality in an WoT environment.

Despite these few examples, a straight forward use of SW technologies in the context of Web of Things applications is not possible. Typical devices, associated with physical 'things', are very limited in terms of their capabilities (i.e., processing power, available memory, energy supply etc.). For example, WoT devices, such as sensors and actuators run by microcontrollers with only few kilo Bytes of RAM and ROM and have a slow processing unit (e.g., ARM Cortex-M3 microcontroller[1]), are not capable to store and process RDF triples serialized in formats such as plain-text RDF/XML.

In the recent of years there has been many efforts to find a format to compress huge sets of RDF triples (e.g., HDT [7] and RDSZ [8]). Although the compression results are respectful in terms of the decrease of the network traffic, these approaches however do not target very constrained devices such as microcontrollers. Two reasons hinder them in this goal, and those are memory usage and processing constrains, imposed by tiny devices such as for example ARM Cortex-M3 microcontroller.

Consequently, requirements related to an RDF serialization format for constrained devices, and at the same time, for the use of SW technologies in the realm of WoT, should fulfil the following aspects:

- **Low Memory Usage**: the memory used for semantic descriptions should be as small as possible and should always leave enough space for the actually run time procedure.
- **Small Message Size**: in embedded networks the bandwidth usage can be very critical, hence transferred messages should be kept small.
- **Type Awareness**: physical devices will mainly exchange physical values with certain characteristics (unit of measure, precision, sampling rate etc.), hence

---

[1] http://www.arm.com/products/processors/cortex-m/cortex-m3.php.

the data shall be represented in a type aware manner. Type awareness optimizes the overall processing and reduces the memory usage.
- **Simple Processing**: small embedded devices shall be enabled to read the content of semantic data in a high efficient and direct manner. For example, the overhead of a transformation of data should be avoided before the actual data content can be retrieved.
- **A Standardized Solution**: To avoid or reduce the development effort and costs such as found in proprietary solutions, a standardized approach for the use of semantics from powerful devices up to tiny constrained embedded devices, should be pursued.

This paper addresses all the above mentioned requirements and proposes an approach that relies on the technique of the standardized W3C's Efficient XML Interchange (EXI) format [17]. It makes the serialization of RDF data efficient and applicable, even for very constrained embedded devices.

The paper presents the following contributions and is organised as follows.

- We start to give an overview about related work in Sect. 2 and discuss its intricacy in terms of its applicability in the microcontroller environment.
- In Sect. 3 we introduce the W3C EXI format and our different proposals to serialize RDF-based data in a efficient manner.
- To show the applicability of our approach in the embedded domain, we have developed μRDF Store - a repository that stores and serializes semantic data in the EXI format. This work is detailed in Sect. 4.
- Finally, we present evaluation results showing the effectiveness of our approach to encode RDF with EXI. Further on, we prove its applicability to the constrained embedded domain such as the one with microcontrollers (Sect. 5).

2   Related Work

The related work in this topic can be parted into two main subjects, namely the effort of existing RDF compression approaches and the existing semantic repositories.

2.1   RDF Compressions

HDT and SHDT. Header-Dictionary-Triples (HDT) [7] is a well known binary format for publishing and exchanging of RDF data. The main idea behind the approach is to decompose an RDF document into a Header-Dictionary-Triples (HDT) format, and represent it in a compact manner, thereby decreasing the redundancy in an RDF graph. The HDT format consists of: a *Header*, a *Dictionary*, and *Triples*. The Header includes optional metadata that describes the RDF dataset. The Dictionary provides a vocabulary of the RDF terms, i.e., a catalogue where for each distinct term, a unique ID is assigned. This way, the dictionary contributes to the goal of compactness by replacing the long repeated strings in triples by short IDs. IDs can be used for indexing of RDF data too. The triples component comprises the pure structure of the underlying RDF graph, i.e., compactly encodes the set of triples while avoiding the noise produced by long labels and repetitions. In this way an original RDF triple can be expressed as three IDs, thereby replacing each element in a triple with the reference to the dictionary. An experimental evaluation of a concrete implementation from [7] shows that datasets in the HDT format can be compacted by more than fifteen times as compared to a naive representation. Specific compression techniques over HDT, such as for example Huffman [12] and PPM [3] encoding, may further improve these compression rates. However, this is also implemented at the expense of additional processing overhead which is not feasible to constrained embedded devices with very limited memory and processing capability (e.g., microcontroller ARM Cortex-M3).

Streaming HDT (SHDT) [10] further extends the original HDT format toward a format which is better suited for a streaming data. For big documents that cannot fit into memory, SHDT avoids full assembling of the dictionary before it starts writing triples, and does not need to collect all triples of a document to create the graph encoding. Instead, a document is assembled on-the-fly as a stream of chunks with sizes that depend on available memory. As such, the SHDT approach would be also more suitable for an embedded environment, since the implementation complexity and memory usage (no buffer for assembling the dictionary is required any more) is lower than with the native HDT approach. Unfortunately, HDT and SHDT are not compatible to each other. The incompatibility arises from the fact that SHDT can re-use IDs while encoding, and for the HDT format this is not the case.

In general, both approaches are focusing on encoding of RDF data represented as strings, and do not provide potentials for an effective data-type aware encoding. In our view, this is a very important issue. In embedded networks when it comes to a direct machine to machine (M2M) interaction, physical values are mostly typed (e.g., int, boolean, etc.). Using a string based representation of data types (as in RDF) would always lead to an additional processing overhead in type conversion on both sides, encoder's and decoder's side. In addition, there is a missing clarification about the trade-off between the dynamic RAM size of the directory and the message size.

RDSZ. The RDF Differential Stream compressor based on Zlib (RDSZ) [8] approach uses differential encoding to take compressional advantages of the structural similarities in an RDF stream with the general purpose stream compressor Zlib which implements the DEFLATE-algorithm [15]. The major focus is on avoidance of redundancy in the stream. However, this is done at the expense of additional data processing steps, that lead to the lost of the basic RDF triple structure of the produced stream. In addition, the proposed Zlib library is not applicable to small embedded devices such as microcontrollers.

ERI. Efficient RDF Interchange (ERI) [6] is based on RDSZ and an assumption that the structure of the data of RDF streams is predetermined. This structure is determined throughout *Presets* - an information set that identifies, among other things, predicates producing massive data repetitions. The Presets have to be shared forehand by encoder and decoder in order to take advantage of streamed repeated data. Further on, ERI produces an RDF stream as a continuous flow of blocks of triples where each block is modularized into sets of structural and value channels. For each channel standard compression approaches, such as Zlib, can be applied.

ERI is mainly focused on the compression of the size of RDF data with the goal of decreasing the network traffic. However, an implementation of this approach in the constrained embedded domain would be hard due to the necessary pre-determination of the Presets and their sharing by encoders and decoders, as well as the usage of compression techniques such as Zlib. Furthermore, this approach, similarly as previous approaches, also does not take the advantage of the type aware encoding into account.

RDF Thrift. The open source project RDF Binary using Apache Thrift[2] is a binary format for RDF. The approach defines basic encoding for RDF terms, and then builds formats for RDF graphs, RDF datasets and for SPARQL results. The main goal of RDF Thrift is to enable efficient processing and transfer of RDF data, using Apache Thrift[3] as a non-human-readable data format designed for efficient exchange of data between co-operating processes and interoperable across different programming languages.

2.2 Semantic Repositories

Conventional Stores. There exists a number of RDF repository implementations such as Apache Jena[4], Sesame[5], YARS[6] and many others[7]. For an extensive survey, see also [5]. As mentioned in the introduction section, these implementations have not been suited to run on constrained embedded devices as found in today's IoT/WoT applications.

In the remaining part of this section we give an overview of few RDF repositories that are working with various types of compact representations for RDF.

RDF HDT. An implementation of the earlier described HDT approach is available as an open source project[8]. It is a set of libraries that enable RDF data to be represented, indexed and queried in the HDT format. The project provides implementations in both C++ and Java, as well as an HDT integration with Apache Jena.

Wiselib TupleStore. An approach which addresses constrained devices is the Wiselib TupleStore [11]. To handle the string-based data of RDF triples, the Huffman compression [12] can be applied. This kind of RDF Store keeps a

---

[2] http://afs.github.io/rdf-thrift/.

[3] http://thrift.apache.org.

[4] http://jena.apache.org/.

[5] http://rdf4j.org/.

[6] http://sw.deri.org/2004/06/yars/.

[7] http://www.w3.org/wiki/SemanticWebTools#RDF_Triple_Store_Systems.

[8] http://www.rdfhdt.org.

collection of quadruples: subject, predicate, object, and a bit mask which defines to which RDF document the tuple belongs. In terms of serialization, TupleStore supports the SHDT approach as the serialization format (described above).

3   The W3C EXI Format for RDF

Recently the World Wide Web Consortium (W3C), home of XML, was faced with the drawbacks of plain-text XML representation, and hence created a working group called XML Binary Characterization (XBC) [9] to analyze the condition and possibilities of a binary XML format. This format was supposed to be compatible with the standardized plain-text XML format, as well as with the XML Infoset. The outcome was the W3C's Efficient XML Interchange (EXI) format, which gained recommendation status at the beginning of 2011 [17]. The EXI format uses a relatively simple grammar-driven approach that achieves very efficient encodings (EXI streams) for a broad range of use-cases. According to [2] the EXI representation is often over hundred times smaller than the one of XML. Based on the high compression ratio and the opportunity to obtain the typed data content directly from the EXI stream, XML-based messaging is feasible in the embedded domain too, even for very constrained devices [14]. Based on EXI's beneficial characteristics w.r.t. the embedded domain and constrained resources such as memory, processing capability, and bandwidth usage, EXI is getting established more and more in embedded industry applications such as in the domain of automotive industry (e.g., e-Mobility [13]) and smart grid application (e.g., Smart Energy Profile 2 [21]).

As noted above, EXI uses a grammar-driven approach to represent XML-based data in an efficient binary form and vice versa. Such a grammar is constructed according to a given XML Schema where each defined complex type is represented as a deterministic finite automaton (DFA). Moreover, EXI also has the capability to work schema-less, meaning that an EXI processor uses generic grammars provided by the EXI standard.

In the case of RDF/XML representation, it makes sense to use the schema-informed EXI mode given that we know the RDF *schema* and how RDF data looks like [20]: each RDF document starts with the *RDF* root element and nests the set of *Description* child elements to formulate triples. This enables one to formulate various RDF schemas and EXI grammar respectively which can be selected depending on the actual applications. Those kinds of variations will be discussed in the next subsections.

3.1   Generic RDF EXI Grammar

Figure 1 shows an excerpt of a sample EXI grammar (set of automaton) G that can be used for encoding and decoding generic RDF data. This grammar reflects an XML Schema that represents the RDF framework with the *RDF* root element and its embedded *Description* element for representing the triple information. It is worth noting that the *Root* grammar is a predefined grammar

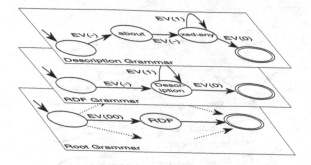

Fig. 1. Generic RDF EXI grammar

that occurs in each EXI grammar representation of arbitrary XML Schemas. It contains all entry points to all root elements in a given schema. Here, we highlight the context of the relevant RDF root element of the RDF XML framework. In general, each DFA contains one start state and one end state, which reflect the beginning and the end, respectively, of a complex type declaration. Transitions to the next state represent the sequential order of element and/or attribute declarations within a complex type. Optional definitions (e.g., *choice*, $minOccurs = '0'$, $maxOccurs = 'unbounded'$ etc.) are reflected by multiple transitions and assigned an event code (EV). For instance, the *Description* element is typically a reoccurring element in a RDF instance and consequently defined as a 'loop' in the XML Schema by $maxOccurs = 'unbounded'$ and reflected by the EXI grammar by the two transitions: one to the *Description* state again and one to the end state. For the signalization, a one bit event code is used and assigned to the transition (EV(1) for the *Description*; EV(0) for no further *Description*). Generally, the number of bits used for m transitions is determined by $\lceil log_2 m \rceil$. EV(-) on transitions indicates, no event code is required.

The *xsd:any* state represents the predicate and object description. This state indicates the generic part since the name of the predicate elements as well as the object values are application dependent.

An example RDF-XML snippet such as the following one:

```
<RDF>
  <Description about= 'temperature'>
    <type resource='sensor'/>
    <value>8.4</value>
  </Description>
  <Description about= 'humidity'>
    <type resource='sensor'/>
    <value>79.2</value>
    . . .
```

would be transformed into an:

00 'temperature' type resource 'sensor' value '8.4' 0 1 'humidity' 0 1 0 3 '79.2'...

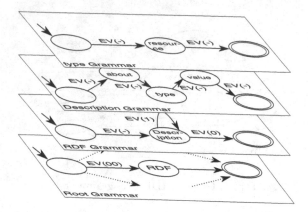

Fig. 2. Application specific RDF EXI grammar

EXI stream[9]. This sketches already how compact an EXI can become compared to the XML counterpart. Blue color indicates the bit-based event codes to navigate the EXI grammar for encoding (and decoding). Green indicates the values of the attributes (e.g., *about* attribute with 'temperature' and 'humidity') and elements (e.g., *value* element with '8.4' and '9'). Generally, EXI is a type-aware coder that provides efficient coding mechanisms for the most common data types (e.g., int, float, enumerations, etc.). For the sake of simplicity, the values are shown in human readable form in the sample EXI stream. Nevertheless, in the case of the float-based value of the temperature context, EXI would only spend two bytes to represent the value '8.4'. The orange content represents the *predicate* elements which are not schema known and covered by the *xsd:any* deceleration. The EXI coding mechanism for that case is based on the following idea: by the first occurrence of an unknown element or attribute the name is provided in the EXI stream (e.g., value). Internally, the string-based name is memorized and an associated unique ID is assigned. That said, for any other appearance of the same string this ID is used instead.

3.2   Application-Specific RDF EXI Grammar

To avoid the usage of such a generic approach that associates, e.g., unknown predicate element names, one can define an XML Schema or EXI grammar respectively. It make sense to follow this approach if the ontology and the context of the semantic description is already known and can be reflected in a schema definition. This can include, e.g., all data and object properties, classes, and possible data value ranges. For example, let us assume there is an ontology for an embedded device that is only intended to serve temperature and humidity values as conducted in the XML snippet above. To represent this semantic requirement, the EXI grammar which is shown in Fig. 2 can be derived. Compared to the grammar shown in Fig. 1 the *Description* automaton is more concrete by the

---

[9] For the sake of convenience, namespaces will be omitted in the paper.

type and a *value* state between the *about* attribute state and the end state. Applying this to the XML snippet above we would get

```
00 'temperature' 0 '8.4' 1 'humidity' 0 '79.2'..
```

as EXI stream. It can be immediately seen, this results in a more compact representation since the knowledge about the type, resource, and the value element is already mapped to the grammar, and does not need to be represented in the EXI stream any longer. In addition, since the ontology provides the definition of all classes relevant for the stream, we can define an enumeration list of all class names within the XML Schema. EXI will only use the enumeration value for association, as previously shown for the red 0 (='sensor').

As mentioned before, embedded devices from the industrial automation domain will mainly exchange physical values. String-based values are rare. Therefore we propose to use the W3C EXI Profile for limiting the usage of dynamic memory [4]. This enables us to operate without value string tables. In the case of reoccurring value strings (e.g., 'temperature' and 'humidity'), those strings will be simply handled as *new* strings (given that the possible number of string entries is set to zero).

4   μRDF Store with EXI

In this section we will explain the use of different EXI grammar approaches to efficiently represent and store RDF data in a semantic repository. For this purpose we have implemented a triple store called μRDF Store. To interact and to operate with the μRDF Store, we use a REST-based interface based on the IETF Constrained Application Protocol (CoAP) [18]. Our approach can be compared to RDF Provider of the Wiselib TupleStore [11] (see also Sect. 2.2). In contrast to this, our approach is based on the standardized coding mechanism inherited from the W3C EXI format. The mechanism and the format are used both, to efficiently serialize and to store the data in the RDF repository.

The fundamental concept and the use of the two different grammar variants of our μRDF store are shown in Fig. 3. They both use the same REST-based communication component, implemented with the IETF CoAP approach. So far, we have implemented three CoAP resources to manipulatable data in the μRDF store: *addTriples* to add new or update existing triples, *searchTriples* to enable graph pattern matching, and *deleteTriples* to remove triples from the semantic repository. To serialize the full content of the μRDF store, one can use the *searchTriples* resource with the search pattern (*,*,*). All requested patterns will be answered by an RDF/XML-based document, which is encoded by the EXI format and the underlying EXI grammar, respectively.

The use of the generic grammar and concrete grammar approach in the μRDF store will be explained in the following subsections.

4.1   μRDF Store with Generic Grammar

Apart from the used generic grammar, different string tables can be used to manage unknown element/attributes names (from properties) and string-based values

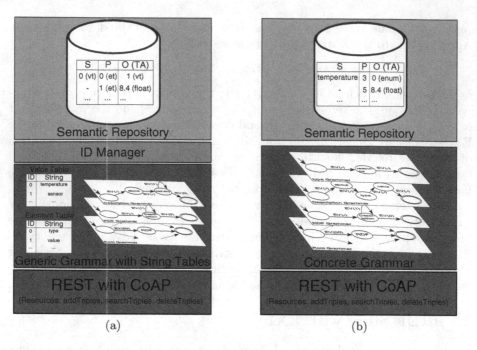

Fig. 3. μRDF using the (a) generic grammar approach with a value table (vt) and an element table (et) and (b) the concrete grammar approach.

(see Sect. 3.1). More precisely, if there is a PUT request on the *addTriples* resource, with a payload of an RDF-based message encoded by EXI (mime-type=EXI), the encoded subject names (provided by the *about* attribute withing the *Description* element) and string-based values of the objects will be affiliated in the value table. Property element names (nested in the RDF Description element) will be managed in the element table. For instance, the EXI snippet below

00 'temperature' type resource 'sensor' ...

identifies the triple with the subject 'temperature' and assigns the ID value 0 throw the value table, predicate 'type' that is assigned by the ID 0 throw the element table, and the object 'sensor' by the ID 1 throw the value table (see also Sect. 3.1). These IDs are used in the semantic repository to represent the triple's subject, property, and object. Based on our running example, the IDs (0,0,1) in the repository corresponds to (temperature, type, sensor).

The *ID Manager* component is mainly used to achieve consistency between the string tables and the repository. This is necessary when triples are deleted from the repository (via the *deleteTriples* resource).

The great advantage of the generic approach is that no requester (e.g., a client) of the μRDF Store service needs to have a pre-knowledge of the content of the semantic repository in order to decode the (result) of an RDF graph. This is possible thanks to the relative generic EXI grammar approach, combined with the EXI's default coding mechanism [17]. The downside of this, is that

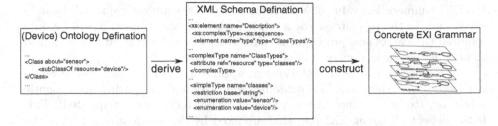

Fig. 4. Grammar construction based on an ontology and XML Schema definition.

more memory has to be available to handle the string based values within the string-tables, as well as to have relatively higher number of string representations within the RDF-based serialized messages (see Sect. 3.1). The next subsection explains how we can overcome this issue by using a concrete EXI grammar.

4.2 µRDF Store with Concrete Grammar

String tables, as used in the generic approach, are not necessary in the concrete grammar approach. This is justified by the fact that almost all triple graph structures are known from a defined ontology (see Sect. 3.2) and can be reflected within the EXI grammar. To create such a grammar, we follow processing steps shown in Fig. 4. That is, we assume a WoT device operates in a concrete context that is described by an ontology. Based on its content, an XML Schema definition is constructed. The schema reflects the RDF/XML basic structure, as well as possible property structures with data type definitions. Following our running example, we will have a class *sensor* in the ontology. A typical individual triple can be (temperature, type, sensor). Thus, the RDF/XML Schema definition will embed and define the *type* element within the *Description* declaration. This, in turn, via the complexType *ClassType*, will declare a list of possible object value assignments for the attribute *resource* (see type *classes*) that are based on all known classes of the (device) ontology (sensor, device, etc.). Based on such an XML Schema definition, an EXI grammar is constructed. The encoding and decoding mechanism of the grammar is described by the EXI standard [17]. The grammar includes an ID resolution (an integer value) of all element/attribute names and possible object value assignments (e.g., sensor). More precisely, each state will have a unique EXI ID representation, which can be used to identify particular elements/attributes. Thus the usage of the string-based representation is not further required.

The semantic repository will use these IDs to represent triples. This will be true for the properties and, if so, string-based values. E.g., the EXI snipped

00 'temperature' 0 ...

will be represented as (temperature, 3, 0) in the repository (see Fig. 3 and Sect. 3.2). Thereby, the temperature value will be saved as a string, the property entry *type* is represented by the EXI ID 3, and the object value is represented as the EXI enumeration value 0. Note that an unknown subject value will be only saved once in the repository. For a triple with a known subject, it will be only required to save its new property and the value. The subject itself will be linked to an existing subject entry.

An ID manager as used in the generic approach is not necessary since we do not have to put the effort in synchronization of string tables with the semantic repository (to prevent inconsistency to occur when a deletion is requested). This is the benefit of having EXI IDs, that are fixed by the pre-determination of the EXI grammar and based on the XML Schema which was structured based on a (device) ontology. Consequently, this will also reduce the number of strings in the RDF-based serialized messages. The downside of this approach is that the requester of the uRDF Store service needs the same EXI grammar to read the (result) RDF graph message.

It should be also noted that a complex ontology can, at the same time, lead to complex XML Schema, and respectively to complex EXI grammars. To tackle this challenge, in [14] we have presented an approach where we can further optimize the EXI grammar. The technique is called the context-based grammar optimization. It removes EXI grammar fragments (states and transitions) that are not needed for a particular context implementation. For example, an ontology that is defined for building automation scenarios will contain information, among others, such as for sensors and actuators. A constrained embedded device, that operates only a temperature and a humidity sensor, do not really need the EXI grammar definition that is intended to actuator-based devices. Consequentially, these grammar fragments can be omitted then.

5   Evaluation

EXI is known to reach a high compression rate and to be a very fast coding mechanism at the same time (see e.g., [2] and [14]). In this section we will evaluate the applicability of the presented μRDF Store. An RDF/XML-based serialization/de-serialization with the standardized EXI format will be presented. Tests are run in the embedded domain. We will focus on the compactness of representation of RDF-based documents, and required memory. Both generic and concrete grammars will be considered.

5.1   Dataset, Target Platform, and Implementation

As a dataset we use an ontology which was motivated by scenarios from a public-funded ITEA Project, called 'Building as a Service' (BaaS)[10]. Among others, this ontology defines concepts related to sensors in a building (extended from the W3C Semantic Sensor Network (SSN) ontology [16]), as well as concepts related to locations (e.g., location of a sensor in a building). Our triple sets are relatively small (20, 40, 60, 80, and 100 triples). This is justified with the fact that a tiny device such as a temperature sensor can be described with such a moderate semantic description, and has no resources to store more triples.

---

[10] http://www.baas-itea2.eu.

As a target platform we have selected the well known ARM Cortex-M3 micro-controller with following specification: 72 MHz CPU, 64 kBytes of RAM, and 256 kBytes of Flash memory.

Our generic μRDF Store implementation is written in C and uses a CoAP-based Web service interface for interaction with the store. For our μRDF Store that operates on concrete grammars, we have used our code generation approach [14]. To evaluate the alternative serialization formats, we have used implementations from the HDT and Thrift approaches (see Sect. 2).

5.2 Compactness

Figure 5 shows the resulting size as a percentage of the original plain-text RDF/XML document size (= 100 %). The diagram compares the RDF serialization in following formats: EXI generic, EXI concrete, HDT, and Thrift. The X-axis represents the number of triples that were serialized, and shows the document size (in bytes) when the triples are represented in a plain-text RDF/XML format. As can be seen, EXI serializations reach the best compactness results in all test cases. Especially, the approach is very effective if we use the concrete grammar for the RDF serialization. For this case, we have achieved results which are up to 15 times smaller than the equivalent RDF/XML representation. This is one of the key strengths of the EXI-based approach, which also in a concrete deployment leads to a less network traffic. Furthermore, the opportunity arises to pack a complete message in one or only few data packages that are provided by a constrained network protocol. For instance, the IETF IPv6 over Low power Wireless Personal Area Networks (6LoWPAN) [1] protocol provides only a payload between 81 and 102 bytes (depending on the configuration). Consequently, to transport 20 triples the equivalent concrete EXI representation (=78 bytes) would need only one 6LoWPAN package.

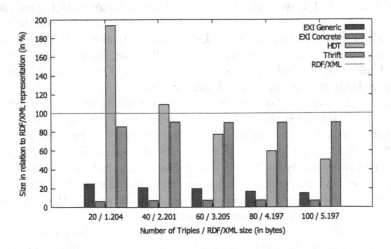

Fig. 5. RDF serialization size

Table 1. Memory usage on ARM Cortex-M3 (in Bytes)

	Generic		Concrete	
#Triples	ROM	RAM	ROM	RAM
20	36521	3422	31957	2398
40	36521	4958	31957	2654
60	36521	6366	31957	2910
80	36521	7902	31957	3294
100	36521	9310	31957	3550

Because of the dictionary that is carried in each RDF document (see Sect. 2), HDT will perform better than RDF/XML when the number of triples is (relatively) big. In our case this is true starting with the triple set of 60. Comparing the 100 triple test set, HDT is still 3 times bigger compared to the generic approach and 7 times bigger compared to the concrete variant. The serialization results of Thrift are always better then RDF/XML and better than HDT in cases of data sets with 20 and 40 triple. However, they are still not as good as results with the EXI serializations (in average 7 times bigger compared to the generic, and 12 times bigger compared to the concrete EXI approach).

5.3   Code Footprint

An important property in order to successfully realize a semantic repository is the memory usage. As already mentioned, constrained embedded devices such as microcontrollers are heavily restricted in this issue.

For evaluating the memory usage we compiled the μRDF Store as presented in Sect. 4 for an ARM Cortex-M3 microcontroller. Table 1 shows the result of the ROM and RAM usage compiled for the different amount of triples (20, 40, 60, 80, and 100) and μRDF Store variants (basic and concrete). Even though the generic μRDF Store variant is able to keep as many triples as RAM is available on the microcontroller, we defined an upper limit of triples which are to be expected (or really needed) for a particular use case. This makes it also easier to compare both variants in terms of memory usage.

The code footprint (ROM) of the concrete variant is around 5 KBytes less compared to the generic variant. This is the advantage of not having implemented an ID manager and the string tables that are needed by the generic variants. Here, the code footprint (ROM) of the generic and concrete μRDF Store is for all triple test cases the same. This is based on the fact that both operate always on their same EXI grammar: The generic one operates on the generic RDF framework grammar and the concrete variant on the grammar that was derived from the ontology and XML Schema respectively (see Sect. 4.2).

The main difference is in the RAM size. The most impact can be seen at the generic approach where the used RAM usage increases rapidly in relation to the number of used triples. This is justified by the needed string tables that are used by EXI to keep unknown element/attribute names and string-based object values to assign an EXI ID which is then used in the semantic repository. The concrete μRDF Store is able to use and operate directly on the EXI IDs since all possible variants are already pre-determined at the time of grammar generation. Consequently, less RAM has to be used, e.g., to save 100 triple in the repository. Compared to the generic variant, almost 3 times more RAM usage is needed to manage the same triple set.

5.4 Summary

The evaluation results showed that we can significantly reduce the RDF representation size by applying the EXI format as serialization format. Furthermore, this approach is also efficiently applicable to constrained devices such as microcontrollers for implementing, e.g., a semantic repository.

6 Conclusion and Future Work

The W3C standard RDF serialization formats incur high cost in parsing, processing and storing RDF data. This issue becomes especially apparent when RDF data needs to be handled by constrained embedded devices, and it significantly hinders usage of Semantic Technologies in the domain of Web of Things applications. In this paper we have proposed an approach to tackle this issue. The approach is based on the Efficient XML Interchange (EXI) Format – a W3C standard binary format for XML. We have adapted the EXI approach to make it applicable for RDF too. We have proposed a generic RDF EXI grammar, as well as an application specific one. We have implemented the proposed grammars and compared our implementation to state of the art implementations. It is worth noting that our approach is not only efficient but also established on a W3C standard, which is an important feature when it comes to the deployment of the technology in industry settings.

In the future, we will enable RDF EXI data to be queried with a SPARQL-like language and reasoned with an inference engine, adapted for the embedded domain.

References

1. Bormann, C., Mulligan, G.: Ipv6 over low power wpan (6lowpan) (2009). http://datatracker.ietf.org/wg/6lowpan/charter/
2. Bournez, C.: Efficient XML Interchange Evaluation. W3C Working Draft, 7 April 2009. http://www.w3.org/TR/exi-evaluation/
3. Cleary, J.G., Witten, I.H.: Data compression using adaptive coding and partial string matching. IEEE Trans. Commun. **32**(4), 396–402 (1984)
4. Fablet, Y., Peintner, D.: Efficient XML Interchange (EXI) Profile for limiting usage of dynamic memory. W3C Recommendation, 09 September 2014. http://www.w3.org/TR/exi-profile/

5. Faye, D.C., Curé, O., Blin, G.: A survey of RDF storage approaches. Revue Africaine de la Recherche en Informatique et Mathématiques Appliquées **15**(1), 25 (2012)
6. Fernández, J.D., Llaves, A., Corcho, O.: Efficient RDF interchange (ERI) format for RDF data streams. In: Mika, P., Tudorache, T., Bernstein, A., Welty, C., Knoblock, C., Vrandečić, D., Groth, P., Noy, N., Janowicz, K., Goble, C. (eds.) ISWC 2014, Part II. LNCS, vol. 8797, pp. 244–259. Springer, Heidelberg (2014)
7. Fernández, J.D., Martínez-Prieto, M.A., Gutiérrez, C., Polleres, A., Arias, M.: Binary RDF representation for publication and exchange. Web Semant.: Sci., Serv. Agents World Wide Web **19**, 22–41 (2013)
8. Fernández, N., Arias, J., Sánchez, L., Fuentes-Lorenzo, D., Corcho, Ó.: RDSZ: an approach for lossless RDF stream compression. In: Presutti, V., d'Amato, C., Gandon, F., d'Aquin, M., Staab, S., Tordai, A. (eds.) ESWC 2014. LNCS, vol. 8465, pp. 52–67. Springer, Heidelberg (2014)
9. Goldman, O., Lenkov, D.: XML binary characterization. World Wide Web Consortium, Note NOTE-xbc-characterization-20050331, March 2005. http://www.w3.org/TR/2005/NOTE-xbc-characterization-20050331
10. Hasemann, H., Kröller, A., Pagel, M.: RDF provisioning for the internet of things. In: 3rd IEEE International Conference on the Internet of Things, IOT 2012, Wuxi, Jiangsu Province, China, October 24–26, 2012, pp. 143–150 (2012)
11. Hasemann, H., Kröller, A., Pagel, M.: The wiselib tuplestore: a modular RDF database for the internet of things. CoRR, abs/1402.7228 (2014)
12. Huffman, D.A.: A method for the construction of minimum-redundancy codes. Proc. Inst. Radio Eng. **40**(9), 1098–1101 (1952)
13. ISO/IEC. Iso/iec dis 15118–2: Road vehicles - vehicle to grid communication interface - part 2: Network and application protocol requirements (2012)
14. Käbisch, S., Peintner, D., Heuer, J., Kosch, H.: Optimized XML-based web service generation for service communication in restricted embedded environments. In: 16th IEEE International Conference on Emerging Technologies and Factory Automation (2011)
15. Katz, P.W.: String searcher, and compressor using same, September 24 1991. US Patent 5,051,745
16. Henson, C., Lefort, L., Taylor, K.: W3c semantic sensor network incubator group (SSN-XG). W3C XG, W3C (2011). http://www.w3.org/2005/Incubator/ssn/
17. Schneider, J., Kamiya, T., Peintner, D., Kyusakov, R.: Efficient XML Interchange (EXI) Format 1.0 (Second Edition). W3C Recommendation, W3C, February 2014. http://www.w3.org/TR/2014/REC-exi-20140211/
18. Shelby, Z., Hartke, K., Bormann, C.: Constrained application protocol (coap). Technical report, IETF (2013). http://datatracker.ietf.org/doc/draft-ietf-core-coap/
19. W3C. RDF 1.1 Concepts and Abstract Syntax (2014). http://www.w3.org/TR/2014/REC-rdf11-concepts-20140225/
20. W3C. RDF 1.1 XML syntax (2014)
21. ZigBee. Smart Energy Profile 2 (SEP 2) (2013). http://www.zigbee.org/

Services, Web APIs, and the Web of Things

SPSC: Efficient Composition of Semantic Services in Unstructured P2P Networks

Xiaoqi Cao$^{(\boxtimes)}$, Patrick Kapahnke, and Matthias Klusch

German Research Center for Artificial Intelligence (DFKI), Saarbrücken, Germany
{Xiaoqi.Cao,Patrick.Kapahnke,Klusch}@dfki.de

Abstract. The problem of automated semantic peer-to-peer (P2P) service composition has been addressed in cross-disciplinary research of semantic web and P2P computing. Solutions for semantic web service composition in structured P2P networks benefit from the underlying distributed global index but at the cost of network traffic overhead for its maintenance. Current solutions to service composition in unstructured P2P networks with selective flooding can be more robust against changes but suffer from redundant messaging, lack of efficient semantics-empowered search heuristics and proven soundness. In this paper, we present a novel approach, called SPSC, for efficient semantic service composition planning in unstructured P2P networks. SPSC peers conduct a guarded heuristics-based composition to jointly plan complex workflows of semantic services in OWL-S. The semantic service query branching method based on local observations by peers about the semantic overlay alleviates the problem of reaching dead-ends in the not fully observable and heuristically pruned search space. We theoretically prove that the SPSC approach is sound and provide a lower bound of its completeness. Finally, our experimental evaluation shows that SPSC achieves high cumulative recall with relatively low traffic overhead.

Keywords: Semantic services · Workflow composition · P2P computing

1 Introduction

In the past decade, the challenge of automated centralized and decentralized composition of semantic web services in OWL-S, SAWSDL or WSML[1] has attracted considerable interest and development of various solutions in the semantic web and P2P community [21]. In fact, there are quite sophisticated AI planning based tools for centralized composition of semantic services such as OWLS-Xplan [14] for OWL-S services [19]. Unlike web service composition, the automated composition of semantic web services by use of AI planning techniques is inherently supported by their formally grounded semantic descriptions. However, these semantic service composition planners cannot be used for a distributed composition of semantic services for collaborative applications in P2P settings. In these cases, any service composition approach has to cope with the

---

[1] For an introduction to semantic web services, we refer to, for example, [16].

© Springer International Publishing Switzerland 2015
F. Gandon et al. (Eds.): ESWC 2015, LNCS 9088, pp. 455–470, 2015.
DOI: 10.1007/978-3-319-18818-8_28

lack of a global service directory or dynamic changes of the set of service pro-
sumers and the availability of semantic services to be found and composed for
jointly accomplishing a given task.

For example, approaches to semantic web service composition in structured
or hybrid P2P networks such as [9, 20, 24] benefit from a distributed, semantics-
empowered index, but at the cost of traffic overhead for its maintenance in
dynamic environments. On the other hand, current solutions for semantic service
composition in unstructured P2P networks can be more robust against changes
but suffer from redundant messaging, lack of efficient semantics-empowered
search heuristics and proven soundness of the distributed composition by the
peers. There are a few solutions for this problem. For example, PM4SWS [10, 11]
applies classical flooding which causes heavy network traffic for on-line query
answering. Relying on state transition gossiping and query/network status analysis, SCComp [6–8] enables selective flooding, but still has the risk of one peer
receiving duplicated messages with the same sub-goal. AntAgt [3, 4, 23] yields
less network traffic by applying a walker-based query routing strategy, but suffers
from its dependence on user specified query plan templates. It does not perform
fully automated service composition. Besides, none of the current approaches
also takes non-functional factors such as quality of service (QoS) and composition plan length into account for the automated semantic services composition.

To this end, we present SPSC (Semantic P2P Service Composition Planning)
for automated and efficient QoS-aware composition of OWL-S services in unstructured P2P networks. The joint generation of complex service workflows by SPSC
peers basically relies on (a) the local matching of the semantic input/output/
preconditions/effects (IOPE) of OWL-S services with variable bindings, and (b)
the memorization of potentially useful services. As a result, SPSC peers jointly
explore a heuristically pruned search space using a walker-based query branching strategy, which mitigates the risk of failure due to dead-ends. SPSC is robust
against network and service dynamics. In contrast to other approaches to the same
problem, we also theoretically prove that SPSC is sound and has a reasonable
lower bound of completeness with respect to the solution existence. Finally, our
preliminary experimental evaluation revealed that SPSC achieves high cumulative
recall with low traffic overhead.

In Sect. 2, we provide preliminaries required to understand the SPSC approach which is detailed in Sect. 3. We then analyze the completeness of SPSC
and prove its soundness in Sect. 4, followed by experimental results in Sect. 5.
A discussion of related work is in Sect. 6 before we conclude in Sect. 7.

2   Preliminaries

In unstructured P2P networks, peers have no global view on network topology or
services provided by other peers. A peer p maintains its limited domain knowledge in its local knowledge base, including an OWL ontology O_p and a set of
predicates A_p, based on a shared primitive term vocabulary V. Each $\alpha \in A_p$ is
the first order logic interpretation of a concept or property in O_p [1]. Each peer

can provide atomic OWL-S services. Besides input (I), output (O), precondition (P) and effect (E), each service has its provider peer id *pid* and a QoS value $qos \in [0,1]$, indicating the overall service availability. Each IO parameter contains a variable $?x$ and its concept type $X \in O_p$. P/E is a CNF formula over predicates in A_p and IO variables. Denote S_p the set of services known by p.

Example 1: Service $S9$ (cf. Fig. 1) represents an industrial production process, which consumes some *Material* $?m$ and *Softener* $?so$ to produce *Product* $?pro$. Its precondition $P_9 = tempLargerThan$ $(?m, 60) \wedge qualityNotBad(?m) \wedge speedEq(?so, 5)$, requires the temperature of $?m$ to be larger than 60, an adequate quality of $?m$ and the softener $?so$ to be added at speed 5. The effect $E_9 = shaped(?pro)$ ensures that, after the execution, $?pro$ is shaped. ∎

In context of SPSC, a request R is defined analogously to a service, containing IOPE, but without QoS and *pid*. We assume that a request can typically not be solved by one atomic service, but a composition, i.e. a *workflow*. Such a workflow includes parameter bindings to make up data flows.

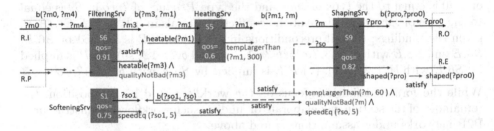

Fig. 1. An example workflow with parameter bindings (Color figure online).

Definition 1: *Service parameter binding* $b(?x, ?y)$.
A binding $b(?x, ?y)$ of service parameters $?x$ and $?y$ of services S and respectively S' is a tuple $\langle ?x, ?y, \varphi \rangle$ where φ is a substitution $\{?x \mapsto ?z, ?y \mapsto ?z\}$. ∎

That is, if an output $?x$ of $S.O$ is bound to an input $?y$ of $S'.I$, the data of $?x$ can be transmitted to $?y$ and used by S' as input, which is modeled by introducing the common substitute $?z$.

Definition 2: *Workflow* wf.
A workflow is an orchestration of semantic services constructed to fulfill a request R. It consists of a set of services and a set of parameter bindings defining the data flow among them. Start and end of wf are defined according to R. The side starting with $R.I$ and $R.P$ (ending with $R.O$ and $R.E$) is called the left side $L(wf)$ (right side $R(wf)$) of wf. wf is *correct* wrt. R (satisfies R), iff:

(i) All inputs of services $S \in wf$ are bound to outputs of other services in wf or $R.I$.
(ii) The overall IO signature of wf plugs into request R:

(a) $\forall S \in wf, ?x : X \in S.I : \exists S' \in (wf \backslash \{S\}) \cup \{R\}, ?x' : X' \in S'.I : X' \sqsubseteq X$;

(b) $\forall ?y' : Y' \in R.O : \exists S \in wf, ?y : Y \in S.O : Y \sqsubseteq Y'$.

(iii) With parameter bindings, no conflicting literals is in $(\bigcup_{S \text{ in } wf} S.E) \cup R.P$;

(iv) With parameter bindings, preconditions of all services in wf are satisfied: $\forall S \in wf : \exists \mathbb{S} \subseteq wf : (\bigwedge_{S' \in \mathbb{S}} S'.E) \wedge R.P \implies S.P$;

(v) $R.E$ can be implied by wf: $\bigwedge_{S \text{ in } wf} S.E \implies R.E$. ∎

Example 2: Figure 1 shows a correct workflow wf wrt. (satisfying) R: $R.I = \{?m0 : Material\}$, $R.O = \{?pro0 : Product\}$, $R.P = true$ and $R.E = shaped$ $(?pro0)$. R asks for some service that produces a shaped product using its source material. IO (PE) are illustrated with black (red) arrows. Parameter bindings (implications) are shown as blue dashed (solid) arrows. In brief, wf specifies the following procedure: a source material $?m0$ is applied to a filtering process to assure some quality requirements. Then it is heated and shaped with additional softener into a product. wf is correct wrt. R because: (i) each input of any service in wf has been bound to an output of another service in wf. E.g. the binding between $?m4$ and $?m0$; (ii) wf plugs into R, because the type $Material$ of $?m0$ is equal to the type of $?m4$, and the type $Product$ of $?pro$ in $S9$ is equal to the type of $?pro0$; (iii) there are no conflicting literals in $(\bigcup_{S \text{ in } wf} S.E) \cup R.P$, given the bindings; (iv) all preconditions in wf hold: $S9.P$ is implied by $S6.E$, $S5.E$ and $S1.E$ with $b(?m3, ?m1)$, $b(?m1, ?m)$ and $b(?so1, ?so)$; $S5.P$ is implied by $S6.E$ with $b(?m3, ?m1)$. (v) $R.E$ is implied by $S9.E$ with $b(?pro, ?pro0)$. ∎

While the former definitions focus on the workflows and its composition, the remainder of the section will elaborate on finding such workflows in unstructured P2P networks under assumptions stated above.

Definition 3: *Distributed stateless semantic service composition problem.*
The distributed stateless semantic service composition problem is a tuple $\langle \mathcal{N}, \mathcal{S}, R, wf \rangle$. Given request R, the goal is to construct a correct workflow wf satisfying R. wf is collaboratively composed by peers in an unstructured P2P network $\mathcal{N}$ based on their services $\mathcal{S}$. ∎

In SPSC, a request R to the network is delegated to a walker-based query. Besides R, a query contains auxiliary fields required by the proposed algorithm.

Definition 4: *Semantic query (abbr. query) q for a request R.*
$q = \langle R, path, psug, TTL, wf, Tb, h \rangle$, where R is the request; $path$ is a sequence of peer IDs that q has traversed; $psug$ is a path suggestion for this query; TTL is the time-to-live value of this query; wf is the workflow (initialized as empty) answering to R; Tb is the memo table (initialized as empty), which will be used by the memorization strategy (cf. Sect. 3.2); h ($h \in [0, 1]$) is the current guard value of wf (initialized as 0). ∎

3   Distributed Semantic Service Composition

SPSC mainly builds on three aspects: local observations of peers, guarded composition and query routing.

Local Observations of Peers: In SPSC, any peer p is allowed to observe the entire content of a received query q while it is backtracking. Any unknown service in $q.wf$ is added to $\mathcal{S}_p$ for later use. Once knowing about (not providing) S, p is called a *service signature maintainer of* S. Besides, p updates its local view on the network topology based on the observed query path and path suggestion.

Guarded Composition: A query q in SPSC is an epidemic walker with TTL limitation. A workflow wf is built collaboratively by peers on the query path using a bidirectional chaining approach. On receiving q on its forward journey, a peer p executes the local composition process (cf. Algorithm 1) based on its local knowledge about services. Once wf is correct or TTL=0, p makes q backtrack.

For composition, p locally checks whether each $S \in \mathcal{S}_p$ can be chained to the left or right side of wf. A chaining score (cf. Sect. 3.1) is computed to measure the chaining quality. If it is larger than a threshold (cf. Sect. 3.2), p considers S to be potentially useful and temporarily adds it to wf, yielding a new workflow wf'. In order to protect wf from arbitrary augmentation, a guard value h' wrt. wf' is computed. If h' is larger than the original guard value recorded in q, S is treated as a useful service wrt. wf, and wf' will be fixed. Then, p replaces $q.h$ with h'. In cases that S can **(a)** be chained but without incrementing the guard value, or **(b)** not be chained into a workflow at all, p applies memorization strategy for carrying the potentially useful service in q. For **(a)**, p adds S into the memo table of q; for **(b)**, p adds S into the memo table with a rate r_m (cf. Eq. 2). If an alternative service S' (cf. Sect. 3.1) of a candidate service $S \in wf$ is found, p issues a sub-query with a new workflow wf^* using S' instead of S.

Query Routing: p routes q, after the local composition process. Instead of an immediate neighbor, p suggests a path for routing q, based on its local knowledge. The suggested path traverses multiple key peers and its total inverse importance score per traffic cost is minimized, under TTL limit (cf. Eq. 3). Once formed, such a path is set to $q.psug$ (cf. Def.4) and q is routed to the first peer on $q.psug$.

3.1 Chaining Between Two Services

On receiving a query, each peer checks whether a known service can be chained to the left or right side of the current workflow. In particular, to chain service S' after S, the following has to be considered: (i) to what extent can the variables of $S.O$ be accepted by $S'.I$, and (ii) to what extent can the effect $S.E$ imply $S'.P$. For this, the peer computes chaining scores $ch_{IO}(S, S')$ at IO and $ch_{PE}(S, S')$ at PE levels. On top of this, the overall score $ch(S, S')$ is computed:

$$ch(S, S') = \tfrac{1}{2}(ch_{IO}(S, S') + ch_{PE}(S, S')) \cdot df(ch_{IO}(S, S'), ch_{PE}(S, S')); \qquad (1)$$
$$df(t, t') = min\{\tfrac{t}{t'}, \tfrac{t'}{t}\}, t, t' \in (0, 1].$$

This valuation considers IO and PE equally, while it further adjusts the overall outcome by including a difference factor $df(\cdot, \cdot)$. This ensures that low quality results with large discrepancy between $ch_{IO}(S, S')$ and $ch_{PE}(S, S')$ are downgraded and possibly filtered out later. To compute $ch(S, S')$, $ch_{IO}(S, S')$ is considered first.

This step determines which parameter in $S.O$ can be used by which parameter in $S'.I$ and yields a set of parameter bindings. By applying the substitutions $\{?z \mapsto ?x,\ ?z \mapsto ?y\}$ of bound parameters $?x \in S.O$ and $?y \in S'.I$, the $S.E$ and $S'.P$ formulas are adapted, in order to compute $ch_{PE}(S, S')$ afterwards. SPSC concerns IO before PE, because the latter with all possible parameter bindings would introduce a large computational overhead.

IO Chaining Score. For each concept Y of each variable $?y \in S'.I$, this process tries to find its best subsumee from the set of variable/concept pairs $(?x : X)$ of $S.O$. Such a subsumee yields the largest concept subsumption similarity score (such as [17]), compared to the others in $S.O$ and additionally exceeds a binding threshold $\beta \in (0, 1]$. Once found, a binding is created. Given the bindings, $ch_{IO}(S, S') = \frac{|M|}{|S'.I|}$, where $M \subseteq S'.I$ is the set of bound parameters in $S'.I$.

PE Chaining Score. The first step is to apply the substitutions of the bindings above to $S.E$ and $S'.P$. Subsequently, the implication $S.E \to cl$ is checked using θ-subsumption [18], for each clause cl in $S'.P$ that does not contain unbound variables. Let SC be the set of satisfied clauses in $S'.P$, $|S'.P|$ the total number of clauses $S'.P$: $ch_{PE}(S, S') = \frac{|SC|}{|S'.P|}$. If there exists a contradiction in $(\bigcup_{S \text{ in } wf} S.E) \cup R.P$ given the variable substitutions, $ch_{PE}(S, S')$ is set to 0.

Algorithm 1. $queryProcess(q)$.   **Input**: query q;   **Output**: void.

1: **if** q is being forwarded
2:     $q.TTL \leftarrow q.TTL - 1$;
3:     **for** each $S \in S_p$ **do** {
4:         $ch \leftarrow$ bidirectional chaining S into $q.wf$;
5:         compute the new guard value h';
6:         **if** $h' > q.h$
7:             **if** the workflow of q is *correct*, **break**;   **else** update $q.Tb$;
8:             $q.h \leftarrow h'$; **goto** line 3;
9:         **else if** $(ch > \theta$ and $h' \leq q.h)$ add S into memo table $q.Tb$; **goto** line 3;
10:         **else** add S into $q.Tb$ with the rate $r_m(S)$; }
11:     **if** $q.wf$ is *correct* **or** $q.TTL = 0$, make q backtrack;
12:     **else**, make a path suggestion for q and route q;
13:     **if** $q.wf$ is not correct **and** $q.TTL > 0$
14:         **for** each candidate service S in $q.wf$ **do** {
15:             $S_{pred} \leftarrow findAlternativePredecessorServices(S, wf)$;
16:             **for** each $S' \in S_{pred}$ **do** {
17:                 $q' \leftarrow createSubQuery(q, \{S'\})$; **if** $q'.wf$ is new, $queryProcess(q')$;}
18:             $S_{succ} \leftarrow findAlternativeSuccessorServices(S, wf)$;
19:             **for** each subset $S'_{succ} \in 2^{(S_{succ} \cup S)} \setminus \{S\}$ **do** {
20:                 $q' \leftarrow createSubQuery(q, S'_{succ})$; **if** $q'.wf$ is new, $queryProcess(q')$;} }
21:     **endif**
22: **else** q is backtracking, update the local observation;
23:     **if** p is not the requester peer of q, force q to backtrack;

3.2 Semantic Composition of Services

Guarded Composition: Each query q in SPSC is a TTL-restricted epidemic walker starting from the requester peer. The workflow is collaboratively constructed by peers on the query path by means of bidirectional chaining. On receiving q, each peer p executes $queryProcess(q)$ (cf. Algorithm 1). Workflow constructions takes places while q is being forwarded. For each $S \in S_p$, p considers to chain S to both $L(wf)$ and $R(wf)$ (line 4). For this, it computes $ch(L(wf), S)$ and $ch(S, R(wf))$, where the output of $L(wf)$ (input of $R(wf)$) contains all unbound outputs (inputs) of services currently in $L(wf)$ ($R(wf)$). If either $ch(L(wf), S)$ or $ch(S, R(wf))$ is larger than the chaining threshold $\theta \in (0,1]$, S will be regarded as *candidate service*. p temporarily makes the hypothesis that S has been chained to wf, which results in a new hypothetical workflow wf'. Subsequently, p computes the guard value h' (line 5), which is the chaining score (cf. Eq. 1) of $L(wf')$ and $R(wf')$: $h' = ch(L(wf'), R(wf'))$. If $h' > q.h$, S is treated as *useful service* for constructing the workflow and wf' is fixed. $q.h$ is replaced with h' (line 8). In case that two observed services have the same IOPE signature but different QoS values, the one with higher quality is used.

Memorization Strategy: A query q can encounter some service S that **(a)** can be chained to one side but without increasing the guard value or **(b)** can not be temporarily chained to any side at all. S potentially would work as a key predecessor/successor of other useful services at later steps. Please note, that this situation is considerably different from what is typically assumed for centralized AI planners such as [14] which can fully observe the problem space. In the P2P setting considered for SPSC however, this case may appear frequently. To avoid missing S, a memorization strategy is introduced to carry over information about those potentially useful services. For this, the memo table Tb (cf. Definition 4) is used. Each row in Tb corresponds to a candidate service. It contains 3 entries: (1) the profile of S; (2) a side flag in $\{L, R, null\}$, which indicates whether S can be chained at the left, right or none of the both sides of the workflow; (3) a pointer that references another service S' in this table, if S can be chained to S' as a direct predecessor or successor. The pointer is $null$, if the service of this row can not be chained to any side or its direct predecessor/successor has not been determined yet. The memorization strategy is as follows: In case **(a)**, p adds S to $q.Tb$; sets the side flag; and sets the pointer to the direct predecessor/successor (line 9). In case **(b)**, p adds S to $q.Tb$ based on the usefulness rate $r_m(S)$ of S ($r_m(S) \in [0,1]$, cf. Eq. 2) (line 10).

Apart from the cases (a) and (b), when the chaining of a useful service S^* leads to an increment of guard value, the memo table can also be updated by removing predecessor and successor services of S^*. This can happen, when they do not have unbound inputs or unsatisfied preconditions, due to their chaining with S^*. p checks this and updates the memo table if needed (line 8).

To estimate the potential usefulness of an un-chainable service S wrt. wf, $r_m(S)$ is computed by each peer locally, based on a set Q_S of observed queries in the past. Let $a(S)$ $(a'(S))$ be the number of (correct) workflows that use S; $b(S)$ $(b'(S))$ be the number of (correct) workflows that do not use S.

$$r_m(S) = \begin{cases} \omega & \text{, if } a'(S) = 0; \\ \frac{a'(S)}{a(S)+1} \cdot (1 - \frac{b'(S)}{b(S)+1}), & \text{otherwise.} \end{cases} \quad (2)$$

$\frac{a'(S)}{a(S)+1}$ $(\frac{b'(S)}{b(S)+1})$ is the statistical positive (negative) influence of treating (ignoring) S as candidate. ω $(\omega \in [0,1], \omega \in \mathbb{R})$ is the default memorization rate. To choose Q_S, one option is to collect all the observed queries. It is easy to be applied, but rather inaccurate due to irrelevant queries. Another option is to consider only the queries similar to q by applying service matchmakers, like iSeM [15]. It yields better accuracy, but some computational overhead. A compromise is to consider the relevant queries observed in a time window.

Query Branching with Alternative Service: Let S_1 and S_2 be two different services. If they can be chained to the same side of another service S with the bindings that contain the same subset of variables in $S.O$ $(S.I)$, S_1 and S_2 are called *alternative successors (predecessors)* wrt. S. For example, $S10$ (*ShapingSrv1*) is an alternative predecessor service to the *shapingSrv* (cf. Fig. 1) wrt. $R.O$: $I_{10} = (Material\ ?m)$; $O_{10} = (Product\ ?pro)$; $P_{10} = tempLargerThan(?m, 200) \wedge qualityNotBad\ (?m)$; $E_{10} = shaped(?pro)$. Both of $S9$ and $S10$ can be chained to $R.O$ with bindings on the same subset $\{Product\ ?pro0\}$ of variables.

If a peer p can not find a correct solution locally, p tries to find the alternative predecessor $(\mathcal{S}_{pred})$ / successor $(\mathcal{S}_{succ})$ services (lines 15 and 18) for each hypothetically chained candidate service S in memo table. On top of this, p determines the possible sub-queries. For each $S' \in \mathcal{S}_{pred}$, p creates a sub-query q', in order to investigate the possible workflow with S' (line 17): p initializes q' as a copy of q. Then, it replaces S with S' in $q'.Tb$ and unchains those candidate services that depend on S. Further, p computes $q'.h$ by Eq. 1. Finally, p executes $queryProcess(q')$, if $q'.wf$ has not been processed by p before. If there exists a non-empty set $\mathcal{S}_{succ}$ of alternative successor services of S wrt. a service S^* in wf, the services in any subset of $\mathcal{S}_{succ}$ can be chained to $S^*.O$ at the same time by sharing the data of bound variables. Namely, after the execution of S^*, all services in $\mathcal{S}_{succ}$ have chance to be executed in one workflow. In this case, p will issue (line 20) one sub-query for each element in the power set $2^{\mathcal{S}_{succ} \cup S} \backslash \{S\}$. E.g. if $\mathcal{S}_{succ} = \{S'\}$, p issues the sub-queries for $\{S'\}$ and $\{S, S'\}$.

3.3   Query Routing

A query q is forwarded, if its workflow wf is *not correct* and $q.TTL > 0$. For this, p computes a path suggestion (PS) containing a sequence of key peers, for which the total inverse importance score per traffic cost is minimized, under the TTL limit. (line 13 in Algorithm 1). A key peer is either (1) the provider of a memorized candidate service S in wf, or (2) the signature maintainer peer p_m of S. From p_m, a peer $p^* \in q.path$ got to know S and p^* is the first one (compared with the others in $q.path$) that uses S for the building of wf. The reason to consider key peers is that they have higher chances of knowing about other services chain-able to S. The creation of PS is modeled as a relaxed variant of the travelling salesman problem (Eq. 3): (i) no distinct return journey is needed; (ii) a peer can be traversed by a (sub-)query multiple times, if needed to reach key peers.

$$\textbf{minimize}: \sum_{p' \in P_{key}} w(p'', q, p'); \quad \textbf{s.t.}: \sum_{p'_i, \ p'_{i+1}} L(p'_i, p'_{i+1}) \leq q.TTL.$$
$$w(p'', q, p') = \frac{L(p'', p')}{sr(p', S)}; \qquad sr(p', S) = r_m(S) \cdot \frac{qos(S)}{\lceil wf_H \rceil + 1 - dep(S)}. \tag{3}$$

where P_{key} is the set of key peers and $p'' \in \{p\} \cup P_{key}$; $w(p'', q, p')$ is the inverse importance score per traffic cost of a key peer p', if q is suggested to reach p' from p''; $L(p'_i, p'_{i+1})$ is the length of the shortest path between the i-the and the $(i+1)$-th key peers in PS; $sr(p', S)$ is the importance score of S wrt. wf, which is determined by the historical usefulness rate value $r_m(S)$ and the stability factor of wf. The latter is estimated based on the service quality and the dependency relations between S and its predecessors or successors. $|wf_H|$ is the total number of hypothetically chained candidate services; the dependency factor $dep(S)$ is the number of the necessary predecessors/successors of S in Tb.

Inspired by the closest neighbor heuristics [13], p computes an approximately optimal PS in a greedy manner. Based on p's local knowledge about the network topology, p iteratively selects the current best key peer p'_{best} that yields the minimal $w(p''_{last}, q, p'_{best})$. p''_{last} is either the last key peer or p in current PS. After each iteration, p concatenates the shortest path $p''_{last} \rightarrow p'_{best}$ to the tail of current PS, considering TTL limitation. When p receives q and $q.psug \neq empty$, p recomputes it if p has made contribution to the building of workflow, i.e. $q.Tb$ has been updated by p; otherwise, p routes q according to $q.psug$. p routes q to a random neighbor, if $q.psug$ is empty and p is not able to suggest a path for q.

4   Theoretical Analysis

Lower Bound of Completeness wrt. Plan Existence. Let $F \in \mathbb{N}^+$ be the initial TTL value of each query. In unstructured P2P, approaches for solving a query q can only be incomplete in any case, given that there is no guarantee that peers knowing about services required for the solution can be traversed before TTL is exceeded. Therefore, the following analysis is focused on solvable cases, which are characterized as follows: in a connected unstructured P2P network with N peers, all services S required for the correct solution to $q.R$ are known by a set P ($|P| \leq F$) of peers that can be traversed in F hops from q's requester. The collaborative composition process is modeled by a finite Markov process. Let v $(1 - v)$ be the probability of q being (not) forwarded to a peer in P. Once $q.wf$ is correct (final state), q is not forwarded anymore with probability 1. If $|P| \leq F$, the probability Pr of reaching the final state within F hops is: $Pr = \sum_{j=|P|+1}^{F} \binom{j-1}{|P|-1} \cdot v^{|P|} \cdot (1 - v)^{j-|P|} + v^{|P|}$; otherwise, $Pr = 0$.

In the worst case, $|P| = F$ and each $p \in P$ knows at least one service in S. This yields the generic lower bound $v^{|P|}$. By memorization strategy and peers observation, a request then can be solved by less than $|P|$ peers. Namely, $v = \frac{n_S^{(t)} \cdot dg}{N} \cdot \frac{1}{dg} = \frac{n_S^{(t)}}{N}$ increases over queries. $n_S^{(t)}$ is the total number of peers that know S after the t-th query; dg is the maximum peer connectivity; ω^* is the average memorization rate wrt. a service $S \in \mathcal{S}$. The propagation of the signature of S can be modeled by a recursive function (cf. Eq. 4) with $n_S^{(0)} = 1$:

$$n_S^{(t)} = n_S^{(t-1)} + \frac{F^2}{N^2}\omega^* \cdot n_S^{(t-1)} \cdot (N - n_S^{(t-1)}), \tag{4}$$

We investigate the following: (**1**) Will all N peers eventually know about S or not? (**2**) How fast will the epidemic process converge? For (**1**), it holds that $n_S^{(\infty)} = N$ and moreover $v \to 1$ for $t \to \infty$; For (**2**), the right-hand part $(N - n_S^{(t-1)})$ of Eq. 4 will eventually reach some fixed $\varepsilon > 0$, allowing for the following substitution: $n_S^{(t)} = n_S^{(0)} \cdot (1 + \frac{F^2\omega^*\varepsilon}{N^2})^t$. This indicates that $n_S^{(t)}$ converges *sublinearly* to N with the rate $(1 + \frac{F^2\omega^*\varepsilon}{N^2})$.

Proof of Correctness. The correctness of SPSC consists of two aspects: (1) correctness of the guard heuristics and (2) correctness of the collaborative composition. Intuitively, (1) means that a correct workflow is achieved when its guard value equals to 1 (Theorem 4.1), while (2) indicates that the guard value of a workflow is monotonically increasing during the distributed composition process and reaches 1 within a lower bound (Theorem 4.2).

Theorem 4.1. *A workflow wf is correct, if $h = 1$.*

Proof: We prove this by contradiction. Assuming that $h = 1$, but wf is not correct, it follows that at least one criteria in Def. 4 is not satisfied. By Eq. 1, the violation of any criterion leads to $h < 1$. Contradiction.   ∎

Lemma 4.1. *The guard value of a (sub-)query q is monotonically increasing during the entire query processing on all its traversed peers.*

Proof: According to Algorithm 1, no peer decreases the guard value by its local composition process. During query routing, no process changes the guard value. ∎

Inspired by the Floyd-Hoare theory [2] and Polyhedral Compilation Foundations lecture notes[2] of the UCLA, we reduce the joint composition of SPSC into a loop algorithm, and prove the correctness of it. Consider the whole P2P network as a huge computer containing lots of processing units (peers). A query is a task that is processed by peers in turn until TTL=0 or it is resolved (correct workflow composed). Each unit (peer) executes Algorithm 1 on receiving the query. This corresponds to an iteration. Following [2], we prove the preservation of evidencing invariants: (**a**): h of each (sub-)query q is monotonically increasing. This means that the joint composition process leads any intermediate partial solution (workflow) strictly towards a better follow-up step; (**b**): No alternative branch is missed. This indicates that all possible workflow options will be investigated.

---

[2] http://www.cs.ucla.edu/~pouchet/lectures/doc/888.11.algo.6.pdf.

Theorem 4.2. *SPSC is correct: Given a query, SPSC returns a correct solution with lower bound probability, if that solution exists within Fhops.*

Proof: Initialization: $q.h$ is initialized with 0. Before the composition starts, h is not decreasing. The workflow container is empty. Hence, no alternative can be missed. **Maintenance:** By Lemma 4.1, $q.h$ is monotonically increasing during local composition. Moreover, Algorithm 1 ensures that it checks all alternative services for each service in wf. No alternative service is missed at p. **Termination:** The entire process terminates, if $q.TTL = 0$ or $h = 1$. At this time, h is not smaller than its initial value. No alternative service for each service in wf has been missed, as no one was missed in each iteration. Overall, $q.h$ is not decreasing and has a lower bound probability to reach 1 ($q.wf$ is correct). ∎

Complexities. Denote $\mathbf{N}$ ($\mathbf{E}$): the total number of peers (edges) in an unstructured P2P network; $\mathbf{m_1}$: the number of primitive terms in V; $\mathbf{m_2}$ ($\mathbf{m_3}$): the maximum number of PE predicates (IO parameters) in a service; $\mathbf{l_{ch}}$: the complexity for computing service chaining score: $l_{ch} = l_{bp} + l_{sat}$, where $l_{bp} = \mathcal{O}(m_3^2 \cdot m_1^{m_1})$ is the complexity for determining parameter bindings; $l_{sat} = \mathcal{O}(|O_p|^{m_3} \cdot m_2)$ is the complexity for checking whether a service effect is satisfied [18], where $|O_p|$ is the number of concepts in a peer's local ontology. $\mathcal{O}(m_1^{m_1})$ is the cost for measuring concept similarity; $\mathbf{n}$: the number of services a peer can know about; $\mathbf{F}$: the initial value of query TTL; $\mathbf{l_{sp}} = \mathcal{O}(E + N log N)$: the cost for computing a shortest path [5]; $\mathbf{L}$: the number of services in a workflow.

Computational complexity. In Algorithm 1, p attempts to chain local services exhaustively to the current workflow. This yields the worst case complexity $\mathcal{O}(n^n \cdot l_{ch})$. p also checks alternative services for each candidate service in wf yielding the process of up to $L \cdot 2^n$ sub-queries. Thus, the complexity of local composition is $\mathcal{O}(L \cdot 2^n \cdot n^n \cdot l_{ch} + n^n \cdot l_{ch}) \sim \mathcal{O}(L \cdot (2n)^n \cdot l_{ch})$. To suggest a routing path, p computes the $w(\cdot, \cdot, \cdot)$ value (cf. Eq. 3) for each candidate service S. $r_m(S)$ is computed in $\mathcal{O}(1)$ incrementally. The actual workflow size and dependencies can be computed in $\mathcal{O}(L)$. For augmenting a suggested path, p selects the best key peer. This costs at most $\mathcal{O}(L^2 \cdot l_{sp})$. Further, there can be at most F augmentations. Overall, the computation complexity for path suggestion at p is $\mathcal{O}(L^2 \cdot F \cdot l_{sp})$.

Traffic complexity. For a query, p issues $\mathcal{O}(L \cdot 2^n)$ sub-queries at most, of which each inherits the current TTL value. Thus, the total number of forwarding messages of a query is $2 \cdot \sum_{j=0}^{F-1}((L \cdot 2^n + 1)^j) \sim \mathcal{O}((L \cdot 2^n + 1)^F)$.

Robustness. Unstructured P2P networks are ad hoc environments. SPSC handles the dynamics of the network topology and services. The arrival of a new service provider or the addition of a new service S matters, if the provider peer p in the meanwhile processes a query q. In this case, p performs the local composition process against S. If q is backtracking, p issues a sub-query q from itself when S can work as an alternative service. The departure of a service provider or the deletion of a service can cause in incorrect path suggestions. In SPSC, peers react passively in this situation, without extra message exchange. If a departure event is detected (messaging timeout) by another peer p' with routing q, p'

deletes the reference of S from $\mathcal{S}_{p'}$ and $q.wf$. Subsequently, p' recomputes $q.psug$. Service signature update is treated as a sequence of deletion and addition.

5 Experimental Evaluation

Settings. Based on our P2P framework[3], we simulated random graph (RG) and random power law graph (RPLG) based unstructured P2P networks with 1000 peers. Their average connectivity degrees are 10.295 and 4.457, respectively. To enable large scale evaluation, we disabled peer IP-based communication and simulated this by using global data structures and function calls. The initial query TTL is 10. $\theta = 0.3$ and $\beta = 1.0$. To the best of our knowledge, no test collection is suited for stateless composition of semantic services with IOPE. The IPC 2011[4] test collection is well-known in stateful AI planning. However, the factual representations of initial and goal states of IPC queries are not suitable for applying SPSC. The WSC[5] test bed supports only IO but not PE. Therefore, we developed a preliminary test collection[6] with 40 IOPE semantic services and 7 requests. Each request is labeled with one or two correct solutions with different groups of services. The service and query distributions are random. The experiments has been done on a PC with Core i7 CPU (2.80 GHz), 8 GB RAM.

Evaluation Measures. Let Q be the set of issued queries. $EC_{m,q} \in \{0,1\}$ means whether (or not) there exists a set of services at remote peers reachable within m hops from the requester. $C_{m,q} \in \{0,1\}$ means whether (or not) a correct solution of q has been composed within m hops. We check: **(1) CRE$_m$**: average cumulative recall within distance m: $CRE_m = \frac{1}{|Q|} \sum_{q \in Q} \frac{C_{m,q}}{EC_{m,q}}$. $\frac{C_{m,q}}{EC_{m,q}}$ is 0, if $EC_{m,q} = 0$. **(2) QUR**: average QoS rate of resolved queries. Besides the services in the test collection with their pre-defined QoS, another copy of them with 50 % lower QoS has been deployed. Let $rtqu_q$ be the run time quality of a resolved query q, defined as the average quality of all services used in the result workflow, and $exqu_q$ the average quality of the optimal solution wrt. service quality (100 % QoS). $QUR = \frac{1}{|Q|} \sum_{q \in Q} \frac{rtqu_q}{exqu_q}$. **(3) #M**: average number of forwarded messages per query. **(4)** average traffic load size (in KB) of query. **(5)** total number of forward messages of each peer. **(6) AQRT**: average query response time.

Cumulative Recall and Workflow Quality. We compare the average cumulative recall after 1000 queries using different memorization rates ω, in RG and RPLG networks (cf Fig. 2a and b). Baseline results for composition without memorization and without guard value mechanism are also shown. As can be seen, SPSC with memorization largely outperforms the baselines, which either are not able to keep track of potentially useful services, or perform arbitrary chaining. In addition, SPSC achieves 10 % $\sim$ 20 % higher cumulative recall in RG compared to RPLG, as the latter may contain islands, while the RG does not.

---

[3] http://sourceforge.net/p/mymedia-peer/code/HEAD/tree/trunk/.

[4] http://www.plg.inf.uc3m.es/ipc2011-deterministic/Resources.html.

[5] http://www.ws-challenge.org/.

[6] http://sourceforge.net/projects/mymedia-peer/files/.

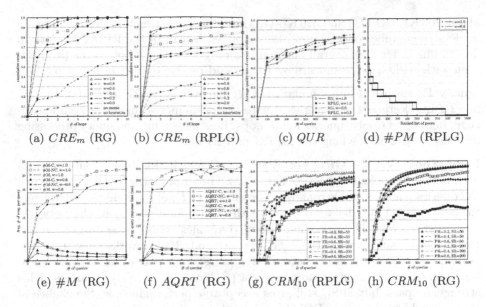

(a) CRE_m (RG)   (b) CRE_m (RPLG)   (c) QUR (d) $\#PM$ (RPLG)

(e) $\#M$ (RG)   (f) $AQRT$ (RG)   (g) CRM_{10} (RPLG)   (h) CRM_{10} (RG)

Fig. 2. Experimental evaluation results of SPSC with different settings.

For both configurations, it holds that higher ω values yield better recall. In RG, more than 90 % of queries are resolved before their TTL limit is reached. Particularly, the correct solutions for at least 90 % of the queries are composed at early hops already when the memorization rate was relatively high ($\omega \geq 0.6$). This indicates that necessary services for resolving requests are propagated effectively and path suggestions support proper routing. Further, we check the system evolution speed with the CRE_{10} value (CRE at 10th hop) over time. After about (200) 500 queries, more than (60 %) 80 % requests are correctly resolved. This evidences the effectiveness of peer local observation and memorization mechanism. SPSC query routing also effectively considers QoS (cf. Fig. 2c) as a criterium for path suggestions, ultimately leading to an increase of QUR over time.

Network Traffic Overhead. The average number of messages per query $\#M$ decreases as the number of queries increases, and converges to a value less than 3 for RG (cf. Fig. 2e) and 2 for RPLG. The number of messages for successful queries $\#M_C$ also decreases similarly, since the knowledge about services from observations at peers is enriched over time. The number of messages for unresolved queries $\#M_{NC}$ is large and increases over time. However, the $\#M$ values imply that query branching occurs more rarely, since queries are solved in a few hops. Overall, SPSC in RG costs larger network traffic than with RPLG, since peers in RG have similar connectivity, while in RPLG, some "backbone" peers are better connected. They are easier to observe queries and hence obtain more knowledge to solve queries. Investigation of the traffic load size per query shows results in line with the previous observations. The average size of resolved queries was 60 KB (RPLG) and 75 KB (RG), while for unresolved queries, messages of about 200 KB (RPLG) and 620 KB (RG) size have been sent on average. Fig. 2d depicts the number of messages received at each peer of the RPLG network in descending order. The overall maximum is only 13 without bottleneck problem, even with RPLG, as peers learn over time and resolve queries in few hops.

Query Response Time. Similar to $\#M$, the overall AQRT in RG (cf. Fig. 2f) and RPLG decreases over queries, due to the peers increasingly observed knowledge, helping to resolve queries in few hops. Less messaging and query processing decrease AQRT in the long run for RG and RPLG.

Robustness. We test CRE_{10} of SPSC in RG and RPLG based configurations with network topology dynamics. For this, we programmatically force, after each SR queries (called a stable round), a percentage (FR) of randomly selected peers to leave off and the departed peers in the last round to re-join the network. System starts with all peers online and no dynamics event occurs during a stable round. The results with RPLG (cf. Fig. 2g) and RG networks show that the system can recover given the network dynamics, since peer observation helps to repair the semantic overlay. More frequent (SR) or heavier (FR) dynamics yields stronger impact, but SPSC still gives acceptable performance, as the chance of losing "backbone" peers in RPLG is relatively small given the random selection. To test SPSC performance with service dynamics, we programmatically force a percentage (PR) of randomly selected peers to forget all their knowledge about services after each stable round. The results with RG (cf. Fig. 2h) and RPLG show that the system can recover under service dynamics. The impact is stronger, if dynamics is more frequent or heavier.

6 Related Work

PM4SWS [10,11] performs IO-level semantic service composition. Each peer records observed compositions in a lookup table. Given a query, if no correct solution found in the table, it tries to chain a known service to the current workflow. Using the classic flooding, it can cause in immense network traffics. In contrast, SPSC peer issues sub-queries for only the new partial solutions.

In [6–8], Furno et al. present the probabilistic flooding-based stateful service composition method SCComp. Peers route queries to a set of selected helpful neighbors to resolve the sub-goals. Once a sub-goal has been resolved, extra transitive messages are sent for re-constructing the overall solution. Despite the selective flooding, network traffic can still be heavy, since a peer still has chance to receive duplicate queries with the same sub-goal. In contrast, SPSC uses walker-based routing with search space pruning and memorization strategy. SCComp needs extra messages to adapt to network dynamics, but SPSC does not.

AntAgt [3,4,23] utilizes an ant-inspired and agend-based approach. Peers maintain co-use matrices that contain pairs of classified reusable services observed in historical plans. A composition task is assumed to be pre-configured in terms of a set of key classes, forming a workflow template. Give a query, a peer selects its local services matching some keys and forward queries to another peer for the remaining keys. SPSC does not depend on plan templates but actually finds work-flows at runtime. Similar efforts [12, 22] also rely on design phase.

Approaches based on (semi-)structured overlay, e.g. DHT [20, 24] or super peers [9], can assure certain completeness. However, to adapt to the network dynamics, approaches in this kind cost large traffics to maintain overlay. Using super peers introduces bottlenecks and single points of failure. In contrast, SPSC operates unstructured and does not require additional coordination effort.

7 Conclusion

The presented SPSC approach solves the problem of efficient and distributed OWL-S service composition planning in unstructured P2P networks. In con-trast to related work, it mitigates composition failures caused by dead-ends and prunes the search space for efficient joint composition through heuristics-based semantics-empowered memorization and query branching. SPSC has been theo-retically proven to be sound with reasonable lower bound of completeness. The experiments revealed its high cumulative recall with low network traffic over-head, and robustness to dynamic changes.

Acknowledgment. This work is supported by the German ministry for education and research (BMBF) in the projects Collaborate3D and Inversiv under grant numbers 01IW1102 and 01IW14004.

References

1. Baader, F.: The Description Logic Handbook: Theory, Implementation, and Appli-cations. Cambridge University Press, New York (2003)
2. Floyd, R.W.: Assigning meanings to programs. Mathematical Aspects of Computer Science, vol. 1, pp. 19–32. American Mathematical Society, Providence (1967)
3. Forestiero, A., Mastroianni, C., Papadakis, H., Fragopoulou, P., Troisi, A., Zimeo, E.: A scalable architecture for discovery and planning in P2P service networks. In: Gorlatch, S., Fragopoulou, P., Priol, T. (eds.) Grid Computing, pp. 97–108. Springer, New York (2008)
4. Forestiero, A.; Mastroianni, C.; Papuzzo, G.; Spezzano, G.: A proximity-based self-organizing framework for service composition and discovery. In: Proceedings of the 10th International Symposium on Cluster, Cloud and Grid Computing, pp. 428–437. IEEE (2010)
5. Fredman, M.L., Tarjan, R.E.: Fibonacci heaps and their uses in improved network optimization algorithms. J. ACM **34**(3), 596–615 (1987). ACM
6. Furno, A., Zimeo, E.: Efficient cooperative discovery of service compositions in unstructured P2P networks. In: Proceedings of the 21st Euromicro International Conference on Parallel, Distributed and Network-Based Processing (PDNBP), pp. 58–67. IEEE (2013)
7. Furno, A., Zimeo, E.: Gossip strategies for service composition. In: Euromicro International Conference on Parallel, Distributed and Network-Based Processing, pp. 27–35. IEEE (2014)

8. Furno, A., Zimeo, E.: Self-scaling cooperative discovery of service compositions in unstructured P2P networks. J. Parallel Distrib. Comput. **74**(10), 2994–3025 (2014). Elsevier
9. Galatopoullos, D.G., Kalofonos, D.N., Manolakos, E.S.: A P2P SOA enabling group collaboration through service composition. In: Proceedings of the 5th International Conference on Pervasive Services, pp. 111–120. ACM (2008)
10. Gharzouli, M., Boufaida, M.: PM4SWS: A P2P model for semantic web services discovery and composition. J. Adv. Inf. Technol. **2**(1), 15–26 (2011). Acadamy Publisher
11. Gharzouli, M., Boufaida, M.: A generic P2P collaborative strategie for discovering and composing semantic web services. In: Proceedings of the 4th International Conference on Internet and Web Applications and Services, pp. 449–454. Venice/Mestre, Italy (2009)
12. Gu, X., Nahrstedt, K.: Distributed multimedia service composition with statistical QoS assurances. IEEE Trans. Multimedia **8**(1), 141–151 (2006). IEEE
13. Johnson, D.S., McGeoch, L.A.: The traveling salesman problem: a case study in local optimization. Local Search Comb. Optim. **1**, 215–310 (1997)
14. Klusch, M., Gerber, A., Schmidt, M.: Semantic web service composition planning with OWLS-XPlan. In: AAAI Fall Symposium on Semantic Web and Agents (2005)
15. Klusch, M., Kapahnke, P.: The iSeM matchmaker: a flexible approach for adaptive hybrid semantic service selection. Web Semant. **15**, 1–14 (2012). Elsevier
16. Klusch, M.: Semantic web service description. In: Schumacher, M., Helin, H., Schuldt, H. (eds.) CASCOM - Intelligent Service Coordination in the Semantic Web, Chap. 3, Springer, New York (2008)
17. Li, Y., Bandar, Z.A., McLean, D.: An approach for measuring semantic similarity between words using multiple information sources. EEE Trans. Knowl. Data Eng. **15**(4), 871–882 (2003). IEEE
18. Maloberti, J., Sebag, M.: Fast theta-subsumption with constraint satisfaction algorithms. Mach. Learn. **22**(2), 137–174 (2004). Springer
19. Martin, D. et al.: OWL-S: Semantic markup for web services (2004). http://www.w3.org/Submission/OWL-S/
20. Qin, P., Liu, R.: Search and combination of semantic web services based on chord. Comput. Knowl. Technol. **6**(28), 7936–7938 (2010)
21. Staab, S., Stuckenschmidt, H.: Semantic Web and Peer-to-Peer. Springer, New York (2006)
22. Tao, F., LaiLi, Y., Xu, L., Zhang, L.: FC-PACO-RM: a parallel method for service composition optimal-selection in cloud manufacturing system. IEEE Trans. Industr. Inf. **9**(4), 2023–2033 (2013). IEEE
23. Zimeo, E., Troisi, A., Papadakis, H., Fragopoulou, P., Forestiero, A., Mastroianni, C.: Cooperative self-composition and discovery of grid services in P2P networks. Parallel Process. Lett. **18**(3), 329–346 (2008). World Scientific
24. Zhu, Z., Hu, Y., Lan, R., Wu, W., Li, Z.: A P2P-based semantic web services composition architecture. In: Proceeding of ICEBE, pp. 403–408. IEEE (2009)

Linked Data-as-a-Service: The Semantic Web Redeployed

Laurens Rietveld[1](✉), Ruben Verborgh[2], Wouter Beek[1](✉),
Miel Vander Sande[2], and Stefan Schlobach[1](✉)

[1] Department of Computer Science, VU University Amsterdam,
Amsterdam, The Netherlands
{laurens.rietveld,w.g.j.beek,stefan.schlobach}@vu.nl
[2] Ghent University – IMinds, Ghent, Belgium
{ruben.verborgh,miel.vandersande}@ugent.be

Abstract. Ad-hoc querying is crucial to access information from Linked
Data, yet publishing queryable RDF datasets on the Web is not a trivial
exercise. The most compelling argument to support this claim is that the
Web contains hundreds of thousands of data documents, while only 260
queryable SPARQL endpoints are provided. Even worse, the SPARQL
endpoints we *do* have are often unstable, may not comply with the standards, and may differ in supported features. In other words, hosting
data online is easy, but publishing Linked Data via a queryable API
such as SPARQL appears to be too difficult. As a consequence, in practice, there is no single uniform way to query the LOD Cloud today. In
this paper, we therefore combine a large-scale Linked Data publication
project (LOD Laundromat) with a low-cost server-side interface (Triple
Pattern Fragments), in order to bridge the gap between the Web of
downloadable data documents and the Web of live queryable data. The
result is a repeatable, low-cost, open-source data publication process.
To demonstrate its applicability, we made over 650,000 data documents
available as data APIs, consisting of 30 billion triples.

Keywords: API · Data publishing · Web Services · Linked Data

1 Introduction

In 2001 the Semantic Web promised to provide a distributed and heterogeneous
data space, like the traditional Web, that could at the same time be used as a
machine-readable Web Services platform [4]. Data publishers would open up their
knowledge for potentially unanticipated reuse by data consumers. Intelligent
agents would navigate this worldwide and heterogeneous data space in order to
perform intelligent tasks. In 2015 this promise remains largely unmet.

When we look at empirical data about the rudimentary infrastructure of the
Semantic Web today, we see multiple problems: Millions of data documents exist

This work was supported by the Dutch national program COMMIT.

F. Gandon et al. (Eds.): ESWC 2015, LNCS 9088, pp. 471–487, 2015.
DOI: 10.1007/978-3-319-18818-8_29

that potentially contain information that is relevant for intelligent agents. However, only a tiny percentage of these data documents can be straightforwardly used by software clients. Typically, online data sources cannot be consistently queried over a prolonged period of time, so that no commercial Web Service would dare to depend on general query endpoint availability and consistency. In practice, Semantic Web applications run locally on self-deployed and centralized triple-stores housing data that has been integrated and cleaned for a specific application or purpose. Meanwhile, the universally accessible and automatically navigable online Linked Open Data (LOD) Cloud remains structurally disjointed, unreliable, and — as a result — largely unused for building the next generation of large-scale Web solutions.

The problem here is *sustainability*. While it is technically possible to publish data in a standards-compliant way, many data publishers are unable to do so. While it is technically possible to pose structured live queries against a large dataset, this is prohibitively expensive in terms of both engineering effort and hardware support.

Take for instance the concept of federation, in which a query is evaluated against multiple datasets at the same time. According to the original promise of the Semantic Web federation is crucial, since it allows an automated agent to make intelligent decisions based on an array of knowledge sources that are both distributed and heterogeneous. In practice, however, federation is extremely difficult [19] since most datasets do not have a live query endpoint; the few query endpoints that do exist often have low availability; the few available live query endpoints sometimes implement constrained APIs which makes it difficult to guarantee that queries are answered in a consistent way.

We have performed a redeployment of the LOD Cloud that makes the Semantic Web queryable on an unprecedented scale, while retaining its originally defined properties of openness and heterogeneity. We provide an architecture plus working implementation which allows queries that span a large number of heterogeneous datasets to be performed. The working implementation consists of a full-scale and continuously updating copy of the LOD Cloud as it exists today. This complementary copy can be queried by intelligent agents, while guaranteeing that an answer will be established consistently and reliably. We call this complementary copy *Linked Data-as-a-Service* (LDaaS).

LDaaS was created by tightly combining two existing state-of-the-art approaches: the LOD Laundromat and Linked Data Fragments. While the integration itself is straightforward, we show that its consistent execution delivers a system that is able to meet a wide-spanning array of requirements that have not been met before in both width and depth.

This paper is organized as follows: Sect. 2 given an overview of the core concepts and related work. Section 3 details the motivation behind LDaaS. Section 4 specifies the architecture and design of LDaaS, which we evaluate in Sect. 5. We conclude in Sect. 6.

2 Core Concepts and Related Work

2.1 Web Interfaces to RDF Data

In order to characterize the many possibilities for hosting Linked Datasets on the Web, *Linked Data Fragments* (LDF)[26] was introduced as a uniform view on all possible Web APIs to Linked Data. The common characteristic of all interfaces is that, in one way or another, they offer specific parts of a dataset. Consequently, by analyzing the parts offered by an interface, we can analyze the interface itself. Each such part is called a *Linked Data Fragment*, consisting of:

- **data:** the triples of the dataset that match an interface-specific *selector*;
- **metadata:** triples that describe the fragment;
- **controls:** hyperlinks and/or hypermedia forms that lead to other fragments.

The choices made for each of those elements influence the functional and non-functional properties of an interface. This includes the effort of a server to generate fragments, the cacheability of those fragments, the availability and performance of query execution, and the party responsible for executing those queries.

Using this conceptual framework, we will now discuss several interfaces.

Data Dumps. File-based datasets are conceptually the most simple APIs: the *data* consists of all triples of the dataset. They are possibly combined into a compressed archive and published at a single URL. Sometimes the archive contains *metadata*, but *controls*—with the possible exception of HTTP URIs in RDF triples—are not present. Query execution on these file-based datasets is entirely the responsibility of the client; obtaining up-to-date query results requires re-downloading the entire dataset periodically or upon change.

Linked Data Documents. By organizing triples by subject, Linked Data Documents allow to *dereference* the URL of entities. A document's *data* consists of triples related to the entity (usually triples where the subject or object is that entity). It might contain *metadata* triples about the document (e.g. creator, date) and its *controls* are the URLs of other entities, which can be dereferenced in turn. Linked Data Documents provide a fast way to collect the authoritative information about a particular entity and they are cache-friendly, but predicate- or object-based queries are practically infeasible.

SPARQL Endpoints. The SPARQL query language [13] allows to express very precise selections of triples in RDF datasets. A SPARQL endpoint [10] allows the execution of SPARQL queries on a dataset through HTTP. A fragment's *data* consists of triples matching the query (assuming the CONSTRUCT form); the *metadata* and *control* sets are empty. Query execution is performed entirely by the server, and because each client can ask highly individualized requests, the cacheability of SPARQL fragments is quite low. This, combined with complexity of SPARQL query execution, likely contributes to the low availability of public SPARQL endpoints [1,7]. To mitigate this, many endpoints restrict usage, by reducing the allowed query execution time, limiting the number of rows that can be returned or sorted, or not supporting more expensive SPARQL features [7].

Triple Pattern Fragments. The Triple Pattern Fragments (TPF) API [25] has been designed to minimize server processing, while at the same time enabling efficient live querying on the client side. A fragment's *data* consists of all triples that match a specific triple pattern, and can possibly be paged. Each fragment (page) contains the estimated total number of matches, to allow for query planning, and contains hypermedia controls to find all other Triple Pattern Fragments of the same dataset. The controls ensure each fragment is *self-describing*: just like regular webpages do for humans, fragments describes in a machine-interpretable way what the possible actions are and how clients can perform them. Consequently, clients can use the interface without needing the specification. Complex SPARQL queries are decomposed by clients into Triple Pattern Fragments. Since requests are less granular, fragments are more likely to be reused across clients, improving the benefits of caching [25]. Because of the decreased complexity, the server does not necessarily require a triple-store to generate its fragments.

Other Specific APIs. Several APIs with custom fragments types have been proposed, including the Linked Data Platform [24], the SPARQL Graph Store Protocol [20], and other HTTP interfaces such as the Linked Data API [17] and Restpark [18]. In contrast to Triple Pattern Fragments, the fragments offered by these APIs are not self-describing: clients require an implementation of the corresponding specification in order to use the API, unlike the typically self-explanatory resources on the human Web. Furthermore, no query engines for these interfaces have been implemented to date.

2.2   Existing Approaches to Linked Data-as-a-Service

Large Linked Datasets. The Billion Triple Challenge[1] is a collection of crawled Linked Data that is publicly available and that is often used in Big Data research. It is crawled from the LOD Cloud [5] and consists of 1.4 billion triples. It includes large RDF datasets, as well as data in RDFa and Microformats. However, this dataset is not a complete crawl of the LOD Cloud (nor does it aim to be), as datasets from several catalogs are missing. Additionally, the latest version of this dataset dates back to 2012.

Freebase [6] publishes 1.9 billion triples, taken from manual user input and existing RDF and Microformat datasets. Access to Freebase is possible through an API, through a (non-SPARQL) structured query language, and as a complete dump of N-Triples. However, these dumps include many non-conforming, syntactically incorrect triples.

---

[1] See http://km.aifb.kit.edu/projects/btc-2012/.

Large-Scale Linked Data Indexes. In order to make Linked Data available through a centralized interface, Sindice [21], active from 2007 to 2014, crawled Linked Data resources, including RDF, RDFa and Microformats. Datasets were imported on a per-instance and manual opt-in basis. Raw data versions cannot be downloaded and access is granted through a customized API.

LODCache[2], provided by OpenLink, similarly crawls the Web for Linked Data, but does not make data dumps available. Its SPARQL endpoint suffers from issues such as low availability, presumably related to its enormous size of more than 50 billion triples. There is no transparent procedure to include data manually or automatically. Given the focus on size, its main purpose is likely to showcase the scalability of the Virtuoso triple-store, rather than providing a sustainable model for Linked Data consumption on the Web. Other initiatives, such as Europeana [14], aggregate data from specific content domains, and allow queries through customized APIs.

Finally, DyLDO [16] is a long-term experiment to monitor the dynamics of a core set of 80 thousand Linked Data documents on a weekly basis. Each week's crawl is published as an N-Quads file. This work provides interesting insight in how Linked Data evolves over time. It is not possible to easily select triples from a *single* dataset, and not all datasets belonging to the Linked Data Cloud are included. Another form of incompleteness stems from the fact that the crawl is based on URI dereferencing, not guaranteeing datasets are included in their entirety.

LOD Laundromat. The LOD Laundromat [3] crawls the Linked Data Cloud, and re-publishes any Linked Dataset it finds, in a canonical, standards-compliant, compressed, N-Triples or N-Quads format. The goal of LOD Laundromat is not that of a primary publication platform. Instead, it is a complementary approach to existing efforts, to publish siblings of existing idiosyncratic datasets. The collection of datasets that it comprises is continuously being extended, both in an automated fashion as well as a manual fashion: anyone can add their dataset URL to the LOD Laundromat[3], where their dataset will be cleaned and re-published. Human data consumers are able to navigate a large collection of high-quality datasets, and download the corresponding clean data. Additionally, machine processors are able to easily load very large amounts of real-world data, by selecting clean data documents through a SPARQL query.

Dydra. Dydra[4] is a cloud-based RDF graph database, which allows users without hosting capabilities to publish RDF graphs on the Web. Via their Web interface, Dydra provides a SPARQL endpoint, the option to configure permissions, and other graph management features. However, access to Dydra is limited: free access is severely restricted, and there are no public pay plans for paid services.

---

[2] See http://lod.openlinksw.com/.
[3] See http://lodlaundromat.org/basket.
[4] See http://dydra.com.

3 Motivation

In this section, we motivate why there is a need for an alternative deployment of the Semantic Web, and why we opt for a Linked Data-as-a-Service approach.

3.1 Canonical Form

One of the biggest hurdles towards Web-scale live querying is that — at the moment — Semantic Web datasets cannot all be queried in the same, uniform way (Problem 1).

Problem 1. *In practice, there is no single, uniform way in which the LOD Cloud can be queried today.*

First of all, most Semantic Web datasets that are available online are data dumps [9,15], which implies that they cannot be queried live. In order to perform structured queries on such datasets, one has to download the data dumps and deploy them locally. Secondly, many data dumps that are available online are not fully standards-compliant [2,15]. This makes the aforementioned local deployment relatively difficult, since it requires the use of tools that can cope with archive errors, HTTP errors, multiple syntax formats, syntax errors, etc. Thirdly, not all datasets that *can* be queried live use a standardized query language (such as SPARQL). Indeed, some require a data consumer to formulate a query in a dedicated query language or to use a custom API. Fourthly, most custom APIs are not self-describing, making it relatively difficult for a machine processor to create such queries on the fly. Fifthly, most online datasets that can be queried live and that are using standardized query languages such as SPARQL are imposing restrictions on queries that can be expressed and results that can be returned [1,7]. Finally, different SPARQL endpoints impose *different* restrictions [7]. This makes it difficult for a data consumer to predict whether, and if so how, a query will be answered. The latter point is especially relevant in the case of federated querying (see Sect. 3.4), where sub-queries are evaluated against multiple endpoints with potentially heterogeneous implementations.

For the last decade or so, Problem 1 has been approached by creating standards, formulating guidelines, and building tools. In addition, Semantic Web evangelists have tried to educate and convince data producers to follow those guidelines and use those tools. This may still be the long-term solution. However, we observe that this approach has been taken for over a decade, yet leading to the heterogeneous deployment described above. We therefore introduce the complementary Solution 1 that allows all Semantic Web data to be queried live in a uniform way and machine-accessible way.

Solution 1. *Allow all Semantic Web documents to be queried through a uniform interface that is standards-compatible and self-descriptive.*

3.2 Scalability and Availability

After the first 14 years of Semantic Web deployment there are at least millions of data documents [8,12] but only 260 live query endpoints [7]. Even though the number of endpoints is growing over time [1,7], at the current growth rate, the gap between data dumps and live queryable data will only increase (Problem 2). The number of query endpoints remains relatively low compared to the number of datasets, and many of the endpoints that do exist suffer from limited availability [7].

Problem 2. *Existing deployment techniques do not suffice to close the gap between the Web of downloadable data documents and the Web of live queryable data.*

Several causes contribute to Problem 2. Firstly, it is difficult to deploy Semantic Web data, since this currently requires a complicated stack of software products. Secondly, existing query endpoints perform most calculations on the server-side, resulting in a relatively high cost and thus a negative incentive for the data publisher. Thirdly, in the presence of dedicated query languages, custom APIs, and restricted SPARQL endpoints, some have advocated to avoid SPARQL endpoints altogether, recommending the more flexible data dumps instead, thereby giving up on live querying. Solution 2 addresses these causes.

Solution 2. *Strike a balance between server- and client-side processing, and automatically deploy all Semantic Web data as live query endpoints. If clients desire more flexibility, they can download the full data dumps as well.*

3.3 Linked Data-as-a-Service

Even though software solutions exist to facilitate an easy deployment of various Web-related services such as email, chat, file sharing, etc., in practice users gravitate towards centralized online deployments (e.g., Google and Microsoft mail, Facebook chat, Dropbox file sharing). We observe similar effects in the (lack of) popularization of Semantic Web technologies (Problem 3). Even though multiple software solutions exist for creating, storing, and deploying Semantic Web services (e.g., RDF parsers, triple-stores, SPARQL endpoints), empirical observations indicate that the deployment of such services with existing solutions has been problematic [15]. As a consequence, live querying of Semantic Web data has not yet taken off in the same way as other Web-related tasks have.

Problem 3. *Even though a technology stack for publishing Semantic Web data exists today, there is currently no simplified Web Service that does the same thing on a Web-scale.*

While technologies exist that make it possible to publish a live query endpoint over Semantic Web data, there is currently no simplified Web *Service* that allows data to be deployed on a very large scale. Under the assumption that take-up of traditional Web Services is an indicator of future take-up of Semantic Web

Services (an assumption that cannot be proven, only argued for), it follows that many data publishers may prefer a simplified Web Service to at least perform some of the data publishing tasks (Solution 3).

Solution 3. *Provide a service to take care of the tasks that have proven to be problematic for data publishers, having an effective cost model for servicing a high number of data consumers.*

3.4 Federation

In a federated query, sub-queries are evaluated by different query endpoints. For example, one may be interested in who happens to know a given person by querying a collection of HTML files that contain FOAF profiles in RDFa. At present, querying multiple endpoints is problematic (Problem 4), because of the cumulating unavailability of individual endpoints, as well as the heterogeneity of interfaces to Linked Data.

Problem 4. *On the current deployment of the Semantic Web it is difficult to query across multiple datasets.*

Given the heterogeneous nature of today's Semantic Web deployment (Sect. 3.1), there are no LOD Cloud-wide guarantees as to whether, and if so how, sub-queries will be evaluated by different endpoints. In addition, properties of datasets (i.e., metadata descriptions) may be relevant for deciding algorithmically which datasets to query in a federated context. Several initiatives exist that seek to describe datasets in terms of Linked Data (e.g., VoID, VoID-ext, Bio2RDF metrics, etc.). However, such metadata descriptions are often not available, and oftentimes do not contain enough metadata in order to make efficient query federation possible.

Solution 4. *Allow federated queries to be evaluated across multiple datasets. Allow metadata descriptions to be used in order to determine which datasets to query.*

4   Workflow and Architectural Design

The scale of the LOD Cloud requires a low-cost data publishing workflow. Therefore, the LOD Laundromat service is designed as a (re)publishing platform for data dumps, i.e. data files. As detailed in Sect. 2.1, data dumps are the most simple API that can be offered. To allow structured live querying, while still maintaining technical and economical scalability, we have integrated the low-cost TPF API.

We first discuss the publishing workflow supported by the combination of the LOD Laundromat and Triple Pattern Fragments. We then elaborate on the architectural design of their integration, and how we improved both approaches to keep LDaaS scalable.

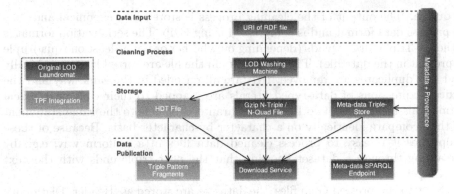

Fig. 1. LOD Laundromat (re)-publishing workflow

4.1 Re-Publishing Workflow

Figure 1 shows the re-publishing workflow of the LOD Laundromat (already presented in [3]), extended with the Triple Pattern Fragment API. Here, we see how the LOD Laundromat (1) takes a reference to an online RDF document as input, (2) cleans the data in the LOD Washing Machine, (3) stores several representations of the data, and publishes the data through several APIs. Below, we discuss each step of the workflow in detail.

Data Input. The LOD Laundromat maintains a collection of Linked Data seed points, called the LOD Basket[5]. The seed points are Web locations from which generally non-standards compliant or 'dirty' data can be downloaded.

Cleaning Process. The LOD Washing Machine[6] is the module of the LOD Laundromat that takes 'dirty' data documents from the LOD Basket and tries to download them. Potential HTTP errors are stored as part of the data document's metadata description that is generated by the LOD Washing Machine. Data documents that occur in archives are recursively unpacked. Once fully unpacked, the serialization format of the data document is determined heuristically based on the file extension (if any), the value of the `Content-Type` HTTP header (if present), and a lenient parse of the first chunk of the data file. All standard RDF 1.1 serialization formats are supported: N-Quads, N-Triples, RDFa, RDF/XML, TriG, and Turtle. Once the serialization format has been guessed, the document is parsed. Since many data documents contain syntax errors[7], only compliant triples are retained. Every warning is stored as metadata of the resultant dataset in order to make the cleaning process transparent. As a final step, VoID descriptions that occur within a document that is being cleaned are added to the LOD Basket for future cleaning.

---

[5] See http://lodlaundromat.org/basket.

[6] See https://github.com/LODLaundry/llWashingMachine.

[7] For an indication, see http://lodlaundromat.org/visualizations/.

Storage. The output of the cleaning process is stored in a canonical and easy to process data format and is compressed using Gzip. The serialization format is either N-Triples or N-Quads (depending on whether or not at least one quadruple is present in the data file). The statements in the file are sorted lexicographically and any duplicates are removed. IRIs are all encoded in the same way and the lexical expressions of data-typed literals are mapped to their canonical lexical form. This means that two lines are guaranteed to denote the same statement iff they compare identically on a character-by-character basis. Because of these properties it is easy to process cleaned data files in a uniform way, e.g., by streaming through a dataset knowing that the next triple ends with the next newline character.

Next to compressed Gzip files, the datasets are stored as 'Header, Dictionary Triples' (HDT) files as well. HDT files are compressed, indexed files, in a binary serialization format. HDT files are suitable for browsing and querying RDF data without requiring to decompression and/or ingestion into a triple-store [11].

Besides the cleaned data files, LOD Laundromat uses a triple-store which disseminates the metadata obtained during the cleaning process. The triple-store also contains metrics about the structural properties of each cleaned data document[8].

Data Publication. The LOD Wardrobe[9] module provides several APIs to access the data generated by the LOD Laundromat.

The first API supports complete control over the data: the HDT and cleaned compressed N-Triples/N-Quads files are available for download. An RDF dump of the LOD Laundromat metadata is available for download as well. The HDT files allows users to download datasets and either query them directly on the command-line (via triple-pattern queries), or to publish these via a Triple Pattern Fragment API. The low-level access to the compressed N-Triples/N-Quads files allow bulk processing of such files, particularly considering the advantages that come with this canonical format: streamed processing of a sorted set of statements.

The TPF API provides access via triple pattern queries, and uses HDT files as storage type. This low-cost API, discussed in Sect. 2, enables structured querying on the crawled datasets.

Finally, the third API is a SPARQL endpoint, which provides SPARQL access to the metadata triple-store. The combination of this API with the previous two is powerful: the SPARQL endpoint enables finding datasets based on structural properties such as the in-degree, out-degree, serialization format, etc. Based on the query results, the user can access the datasets by either downloading the Gzip or HDT files, or accessing the Triple Pattern Fragments API.

---

[8] Under submission: "LOD in a Box: The C-LOD Meta-Dataset". See http://www.semantic-web-journal.net/content/lod-box-c-lod-meta-dataset.

[9] See http://lodlaundromat.org/wardrobe/.

4.2   LDaaS Architectural Design

The architecture for crawling cleaning Linked Data is described in [3], where the architecture of TPF is described in [25]. Below we discuss the measures we took to combine both systems, and the improvements we made to the scalability of LDaaS.

TPF Horizontal Scalability. The HDT library can read and query HDT files that are larger than main memory by loading them as *memory-mapped files*. This means the file is mapped byte-by-byte to pages of virtual memory of the application, and regions of the file are swapped in and out by the operating system as needed. This is not horizontally scalable though: although this approach works for 30–40 large datasets, in practice, processes with hundreds or thousands of memory-mapped files tend to become unstable.

Therefore, we extended the TPF architecture with an alternative strategy in which only very large HDT files ($\geq 10\,GB$) are mapped to memory. In order to query the remaining majority of smaller files, an out-of-process approach is used. When an HTTP request arrives, the server spawns an external process that briefly loads the corresponding HDT file, queries the requested triple pattern, and closes it again. While this involves a larger delay than if the file were mapped to the server process, the overhead is limited for such smaller files because of the efficient HDT index format, and it guarantees the server process' stability. The few large files are still memory-mapped, because spawning new processes for them would result in a noticeably longer delay.

HDT File Generation. The original LOD Laundromat architecture creates and serves clean compressed Gzipped N-Quads and N-Triples files. To support the use of a TPF API, we extended this implementation by generating HDT files as well. The HDT files are automatically generated based on the clean compressed Gzipped N-Quads and N-Triples files. Because the latest implementation of HDT does not support named graphs, the N-Quads files are processed as regular triples, without the specified graph.

Adding TPF Datasets Efficiently. Datasets crawled by the LOD Laundromat should become available via the TPF API in a timely manner. The original TPF API applies several 'sanity checks' on the data documents before hosting them. However, with 650,000 documents in the configuration file, this process requires minutes of processing time. Because the LOD Laundromat pipeline guarantees 'sane' HDT files, we avoid this issue by extending the TPF API with an optimized loading procedure which disables these sanity checks. As a result, re-loading the configuration whenever a new dataset is cleaned, requires seconds instead of minutes.

5   Evaluation

We use the architecture described in the previous section to present a working implementation where we publish the LOD Cloud via Triple Pattern Fragments. In this section, we evaluate this deployment and validate the solutions from Sect. 3.

Solution 1: Allow all Semantic Web documents to be queried through a uniform interface that is standards-compatible and self-descriptive.

Solution 1 is evaluated analytically. Currently, 650,950 datasets (29,547,904, 444 triples) are hosted as live query endpoints. Although this does not include all existing Semantic Web data, these numbers show that our approach can realistically be applied on Web scale (see Solution 3 for usage numbers).

Since the Triple Pattern Fragments APIs are generated for all data in the LOD Wardrobe, data queryable by LDaaS inherits the completeness and *data* standards-compliance properties of the LOD Laundromat (see [3] for these compliance properties). *Query* standards-compliance — on the other hand — is attained only partially, since the server-centric paradigm of the SPARQL specification is purposefully deviated from in the current approach in order to fulfill Solution 2.[10] This primarily involves those parts of the SPARQL standard that require the Closed World Assumption (something the authors consider to be at odds with the basic tenets of Semantic Web philosophy) and common data manipulation functions that can be easily implemented by a client (e.g., sorting a list, calculating a maximum value).

The Linked Data FragmentsAPI is self-descriptive, employing the Hydra vocabulary for hypermedia-driven Web APIs.[11] Hydra descriptions allow machine processors to detect the capabilities of the query endpoints in an automated way. In addition, the LDaaS query endpoints do not impose restrictions on the number of operations that may be performed or the number of results that can be retrieved. This allows full data graphs to be traversed by machine processors. Also, pagination is implemented in a reliable way, as opposed to SPARQL endpoints which cannot guarantee consistency with shifting LIMIT and OFFSET statements.

Finally, uniformity is guaranteed on two-levels: data and interface. The former leverages the LOD Laundromat infrastructure (validated in [3]) as an enabler for homogeneous deployment strategies. Thus, when an agent is able to process one data document, it is also able to query 600K+ data documents. The latter denotes that through Triple Pattern Fragments, processing queries only relies on HTTP, the uniform interface of the Web. Queries are processed in exactly the same way by all endpoints, in contrast to the traditional Semantic Web deployment where different endpoints implement different standards, versions or features.

---

[10] Even though there is a client-side rewriter that allows SPARQL queries to be performed against an LDF server backend, the standards-compliance of this rewriter is not assessed in this paper.

[11] See http://www.hydra-cg.com/spec/latest/core/.

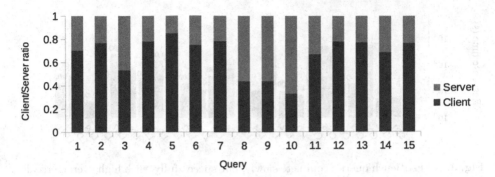

Fig. 2. Processing time is shared between client and server.

Solution 2: Strike a balance between server- and client-side processing, and automatically deploy all Semantic Web data as live query endpoints. If clients desire more flexibility, they can download the full data dumps as well.

The SPARQL protocol relies on servers to do the heavy lifting: the complete computational processing is performed on the server, and the client is only responsible for sending the request and receiving the SPARQL results. The TPF API, used by LDaaS, takes a different approach. Executing SPARQL queries on the TPF API requires the client to perform joins between triple patterns, and e.g. apply filters or aggregations. As a result, the computational processing is shared between the client and the server, putting less strain on the server.

To quantify this balancing act between server and client-side processing of LDaaS, we evaluated a set of queries from the SP^{2}B benchmark, on a (synthetic) dataset of 10 million triples[12], added to the LOD Laundromat. We measure the client-side and server-side processing time, both running on the same hardware, and excluding network latency. The results, shown in Fig. 2, confirm that the computation is shared between client and server. More specifically, the client does most of the processing for the majority of these SP^{2}B SPARQL queries.

Solution 3: Provide a service to take care of the tasks that have proven to be problematic for data publishers, having an effective cost model for servicing a high number of data consumers.

Apart from facilitating common tasks (cleaning, ingesting, publishing), the LOD Laundromat operates under a different cost model than public SPARQL endpoints. In the month prior to submission, the LOD Laundromat served more than 700 users who downloaded 175,000 documents and who issued more than 35,000 TPF API requests.

We consider the hardware costs of disk space and RAM usage below.

Disk space. Currently, 650,950 datasets (29,547,904,444 triples) are hosted as Triple Pattern Fragments. The required storage is 265 GB in the compressed

---

[12] Experiments showed that these results do not differ greatly between SP^{2}B datasets of different sizes.

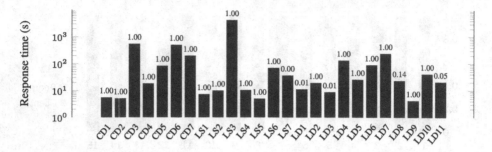

Fig. 3. All FedBench queries complete slowly, but successfully, with high average recall (shown on top of each bar) when ran on the deployed LDaaS.

HDT format, or on average 0.41 MB per dataset or 8.97 bytes per triple. The disk space used to store the equivalent gzip-compressed N-Triples (or N-Quads) files is 193 GB (0.30 MB per dataset or 6.53 bytes per triple). Such compressed archives do not allow for efficient triple-pattern queries, which the HDT files can handle at high speed.

Memory usage. The TPF server consists of 10 independent worker processes. Because JavaScript is single-threaded, it does not have a concurrency policy for memory access, so each worker needs its own space to allocate resources such as the metadata for each of the 650,950 datasets. However, no further RAM is required for querying or other tasks, since they are performed directly on the HDT files. We have allocated 4 GB per worker process, which was experimentally shown to be sufficient, bringing the total to 40 GB of RAM.

Solution 4: Allow federated queries to be evaluated across multiple datasets. Allow metadata descriptions to be used in order to determine which datasets to query.

Finally, we ran FedBench [23] to test the employability of the resulting TPF interfaces for answering federated SPARQL queries. A total of 9 datasets[13], excluding the isolated SP²B dataset, were added to the LOD Laundromat, completing our publishing workflow. Also, we extended the existing TPF client to distribute each fragment request to a predefined list of interfaces and aggregate the results.

We executed the *Cross Domain (CD)*, *Linked Data (LD)*, and *Life Science (LS)* query sets in three runs, directly on http://ldf.lodlaundromat.org from a desktop computer on an external high-speed university network. Figure 3 shows the average execution time for each query with the number of returned results. All queries were successfully completed with an average result recall of 0.81, which confirms the ability to evaluate federated queries. The imperfect recall is a result of an occasional request timeout in queries (LS7, LD1, LD3, LD8, LD11), which, due to limitations of the current implementation, can drop potential

---

[13] https://code.google.com/p/fbench/wiki/Datasets.

results. Next, general execution time is magnitudes slower compared to state-of-the-art SPARQL Endpoint federation systems [22]. However, this is expected considering *(a)* the LDF paradigm which sacrifices query performance for low server cost, and *(b)* the greedy implementation where the set of sent HTTP requests is a naive Cartesian product between the set of fragments and the datasets.Nevertheless, several queries (LD9, LS5, CD2, CD1, LS1, LD3, LS2) complete within 10 s, which is promising for future development in this area.

6 Conclusion

After the first 14 years of Semantic Web deployment the promise of a single distributed and heterogeneous data-space remains largely unfulfilled. Although RDF-based data exists in ever-increasing quantities, large-scale usage by intelligent software clients is not yet a reality. In this paper we have identified and analyzed the main problems that contribute to this lack of usage. Although this list is probably not exhaustive, we selected four pressing problems based on empirical evidence and related work: *(a)* no single uniform way exists to query the LOD cloud; *(b)* there exists a gap between the Web of downloadable data documents and the Web of live queryable data; *(c)* despite the available technology stack, no simplified Web service offers the same functionality on a Web-scale; *(d)* querying across multiple datasets on the current Semantic Web is difficult.

In order to address these issues, we formulated corresponding sustainable solutions, which we proposed and implemented as a redeployment architecture for the Linked Open Data cloud. By combining a large-scale Linked Data publication project (LOD Laundromat) with a low-cost server-side interface (Triple Pattern Fragments), we were able to realize this with minimal engineering.

In doing so, we *(a)* closed the API gap by providing low-cost structured query capabilities to otherwise static datasets; *(b)* did so via a uniform, self-descriptive, and standards-compatible interface; *(c)* enabled in turn federated queries across a multitude of datasets, and *(d)* provide a service for publishers to use. More important than the deployment we provide is the wide applicability of the open source technology stack, whose architecture is detailed in this paper. In contrast to centralized approaches such as the LOD Cache, which focuses on a single centralized database of everything, our approach of one low-cost interface per dataset works in a Web context with multiple servers. It enables querying over multiple datasets by providing clients with the resources needed to perform federation themselves, rather than seizing server-side control of this costly task. To increase accessibility even more, our future work involves disseminating the graph information of N-Quads files via the API as well, and providing an uniform, self-describing API containing all dataset summarizations, in order to improve the discoverability.

As a result of the approach introduced in this paper, we can now provide live queryable access to a large amount of datasets that could previously only be reliably published as data dumps. While it is possible that the current Semantic Web path will eventually lead there, it is worthwhile—and necessary—to explore tio1 assmtpgn_se

alternative stacks already today. Given the solutions it brings to the current Semantic Web problems, we conclude that the technology stack introduced in this paper enables a Semantic Web that is not only technologically, but also economically scalable.

References

1. Auer, S., Demter, J., Martin, M., Lehmann, J.: LODStats – an extensible framework for high-performance dataset analytics. In: ten Teije, A., Völker, J., Handschuh, S., Stuckenschmidt, H., d'Acquin, M., Nikolov, A., Aussenac-Gilles, N., Hernandez, N. (eds.) EKAW 2012. LNCS, vol. 7603, pp. 353–362. Springer, Heidelberg (2012)
2. Beek, W., Groth, P., Schlobach, S., Hoekstra, R.: A web observatory for the machine processability of structured data on the web. In: Proceedings of the 2014 ACM Conference on Web Science, pp. 249–250. ACM (2014)
3. Beek, W., Rietveld, L., Bazoobandi, H.R., Wielemaker, J., Schlobach, S.: LOD laundromat: a uniform way of publishing other people's dirty data. In: Mika, P., et al. (eds.) ISWC 2014, Part I. LNCS, vol. 8796, pp. 213–228. Springer, Heidelberg (2014)
4. Berners-Lee, T., Hendler, J., Lassila, O., et al.: The semantic web. Sci. Am. **284**(5), 28–37 (2001)
5. Bizer, C., Heath, T., Berners-Lee, T.: Linked data - the story so far. Int. J. Seman. Web Inf. Syst. **5**(3), 1–22 (2009)
6. Bollacker, K., Evans, C., Paritosh, P., Sturge, T., Taylor, J.: Freebase: a collaboratively created graph database for structuring human knowledge. In: Proceedings of the 2008 ACM SIGMOD International Conference on Management of Data. ACM (2008)
7. Buil-Aranda, C., Hogan, A., Umbrich, J., Vandenbussche, P.-Y.: SPARQL web-querying infrastructure: ready for action? In: Alani, H., et al. (eds.) ISWC 2013, Part II. LNCS, vol. 8219, pp. 277–293. Springer, Heidelberg (2013)
8. Cheng, G., Gong, S., Qu, Y.: An empirical study of vocabulary relatedness and its application to recommender systems. In: Aroyo, L., Welty, C., Alani, H., Taylor, J., Bernstein, A., Kagal, L., Noy, N., Blomqvist, E. (eds.) ISWC 2011, Part I. LNCS, vol. 7031, pp. 98–113. Springer, Heidelberg (2011)
9. Ermilov, I., Martin, M., Lehmann, J., Auer, S.: Linked open data statistics: collection and exploitation. In: Klinov, P., Mouromtsev, D. (eds.) KESW 2013. CCIS, vol. 394, pp. 242–249. Springer, Heidelberg (2013)
10. Feigenbaum, L., Williams, G.T., Clark, K.G., Torres, E.: SPARQL 1.1 protocol. Recommendation, W3C, March 2013. http://www.w3.org/TR/sparql11-protocol/
11. Fernández, J.D., Martínez-Prieto, M.A., Gutiérrez, C., Polleres, A., Arias, M.: Binary RDF representation for publication and exchange (HDT). Web Semant. Sci. Serv. Agents World Wide Web **19**, 22–41 (2013)
12. Ge, W., Chen, J., Hu, W., Qu, Y.: Object link structure in the semantic web. In: Aroyo, L., Antoniou, G., Hyvönen, E., ten Teije, A., Stuckenschmidt, H., Cabral, L., Tudorache, T. (eds.) ESWC 2010, Part II. LNCS, vol. 6089, pp. 257–271. Springer, Heidelberg (2010)
13. Harris, S., Seaborne, A.: SPARQL 1.1 query language. Recommendation, W3C, March 2013. http://www.w3.org/TR/sparql11-query/

14. Haslhofer, B., Isaac, A.: data.europeana.eu: The Europeana linked open data pilot. In: International Conference on Dublin Core and Metadata Applications. pp. 94–104 (2011)
15. Hogan, A., Umbrich, J., Harth, A., Cyganiak, R., Polleres, A., Decker, S.: An empirical survey of linked data conformance. Web Semant. Sci. Serv. Agents World Wide Web 14, 14–44 (2012)
16. Käfer, T., Abdelrahman, A., Umbrich, J., O'Byrne, P., Hogan, A.: Observing linked data dynamics. In: Cimiano, P., Corcho, O., Presutti, V., Hollink, L., Rudolph, S. (eds.) ESWC 2013. LNCS, vol. 7882, pp. 213–227. Springer, Heidelberg (2013)
17. Linked Data API. https://code.google.com/p/linked-data-api/
18. Matteis, L.: Restpark: Minimal RESTful API for retrieving RDF triples (2013). http://lmatteis.github.io/restpark/restpark.pdf
19. Millard, I., Glaser, H., Salvadores, M., Shadbolt, N.: Consuming multiple linked data sources: challenges and experiences. In: First International Workshop on Consuming Linked Data (COLD 2010), November 2010, Event Dates: 2010-11-07
20. Ogbuji, C.: SPARQL 1.1 Graph Store HTTP Protocol. Recommendation,W3C, March 2013. http://www.w3.org/TR/sparql11-http-rdf-update/
21. Oren, E., Delbru, R., Catasta, M., Cyganiak, R., Stenzhorn, H., Tummarello, G.: Sindice.com: a document-oriented lookup index for open linked data. Int. J. Metadata Semant. Ontol. 3(1), 37–52 (2008)
22. Saleem, M., Khan, Y., Hasnain, A., Ermilov, I., Ngomo, A.-C.N.: A fine-grained evaluation of SPARQL endpoint federation systems. Seman. Web J. 6(3) (2015)
23. Schmidt, M., Görlitz, O., Haase, P., Ladwig, G., Schwarte, A., Tran, T.: FedBench: a benchmark suite for federated semantic data query processing. In: Aroyo, L., Welty, C., Alani, H., Taylor, J., Bernstein, A., Kagal, L., Noy, N., Blomqvist, E. (eds.) ISWC 2011, Part I. LNCS, vol. 7031, pp. 585–600. Springer, Heidelberg (2011)
24. Speicher, S., Arwe, J., Malhotra, A.: Linked Data Platform 1.0.Candidate recommendation, W3C, June 2014. http://www.w3.org/TR/2014/CR-ldp-20140619/
25. Verborgh, R., et al.: Querying datasets on the web with high availability. In: Mika, P., et al. (eds.) ISWC 2014, Part I. LNCS, vol. 8796, pp. 180–196. Springer, Heidelberg (2014)
26. Verborgh, R., Vander Sande, M., Colpaert, P., Coppens, S., Mannens, E., Van de Walle, R.: Web-scale querying through linked data fragments. In: Proceedings of the 7th Workshop on Linked Data on the Web, April 2014

Cognition and Semantic Web

Gagg: A Graph Aggregation Operator

Fadi Maali$^{(\boxtimes)}$, Stéphane Campinas, and Stefan Decker

Insight Centre for Data Analytics, National University of Ireland, Galway, Ireland
{fadi.maali,stephane.campinas,stefan.Decker}@insight-centre.org

Abstract. Graph aggregation is an important operation when studying graphs and has been applied in many fields. The heterogeneity,
fine-granularity and semantic richness of RDF graphs introduce unique
requirements when aggregating the data. In this work, we propose *Gagg*,
an RDF graph aggregation operator that is both expressive and flexible.
We provide a formal definition of Gagg on top of SPARQL Algebra, define
its operational semantics and describe an algorithm to answer graph
aggregation queries. Our evaluation results show significant improvements in performance compared to plain-SPARQL graph aggregation.

1 Introduction

With the increasing adoption of graph data in various domains, the importance of
graph measures and algorithms is growing. Graph traversal, centrality measures,
and graph aggregation are being used to analyse social [31], transportation [2]
and biological networks [23,27]. This paper focuses on graph aggregation.

Graph aggregation condenses a large graph into a structurally similar but
smaller graph by collapsing vertices and edges. Graph aggregation was applied
to the Web graph to group Web pages by their domains in order to efficiently
compute PageRank scores [6]. Similarly, [11] proposed ranking RDF datasets
by aggregating their resources. In biological network studies, example usages of
graph aggregation include enhancing data visualisation [19] and studying transcriptional regulatory networks [12]. Graph aggregation is also used to provide
business intelligence on top of graph data [5,8,28,33]. Furthermore, many measures in social network analysis [14] and in bibliometrics [15,17] are also based
on aggregating the underlying graphs.

RDF, the data model underlying the Semantic Web, is a graph data model
that is used in bio-informatics[1], social networks [24], bibliography [13,26], etc.
Therefore, graph aggregation is one of the tools used to analyse RDF data. In
addition to the examples mentioned before, aggregating RDF graphs has been
also used to induce schemas [7,20,21], produce descriptive statistics [1,3,22] and
build indices [18,25].

While there exists a number of systems to aggregate graph data [8,30,32,33],
these systems do not provide the expressivity necessary to handle RDF data. The
heterogeneity, fine-granularity and semantic richness of RDF graphs introduce

---

[1] http://www.ebi.ac.uk/about/news/press-releases/RDF-platform.

© Springer International Publishing Switzerland 2015
F. Gandon et al. (Eds.): ESWC 2015, LNCS 9088, pp. 491–504, 2015.
DOI: 10.1007/978-3-319-18818-8_30

unique requirements when aggregating the data. For instance, Fig. 2 shows an example bibliographic RDF data describing some papers and their authors. One might be interested in studying co-authorship structure between authors or at a more coarse-grained level, between organisations (Fig. 3a). Similarly, one might choose to aggregate the data to study the structure of citation between authors, organisations or conferences (Fig. 3c). Such expressivity cannot be achieved by existing tools, proposed mainly in the field of graph databases, because the dimensions of aggregation and the relationship (e.g., co-authorship) is not explicitly defined in the original data.

Furthermore, all graph aggregation operators have been defined as separate operators. Hence, these operators cannot make use of the expressivity and optimisation techniques already built in existing data models such as relational or SPARQL algebra. Moreover, this necessitates transforming the data and loading it into different systems.

In this paper, we define *Gagg*, an RDF graph aggregation operator for RDF data that is both expressive and flexible. We provide a formal definition of Gagg based on existing SPARQL operators (Sect. 3) and devise an algorithm for efficient evaluation of Gagg expressions (Sect. 4). Furthermore, we demonstrate the expressivity and efficiency of Gagg in our evaluation (Sect. 5).

Aggregation of RDF graphs can be achieved using existing SPARQL 1.1 [16] operators. An aggregated graph requires a complicated single SPARQL query (a combination of sub-queries, CONSTRUCT and GROUP BY operators) or a series of SPARQL queries to aggregate nodes and edges (as done in [22] for instance). Such queries become complicated and verbose and therefore hard to write, debug and optimise. Having graph aggregation as a first-class operator simplifies query writing and optimisation. Moreover, our evaluation results show that Gagg can run up to orders of magnitudes faster than a monolithic SPARQL query and about 3 times faster than a series of fine tuned queries.

2   Related Work

On-Line Analytical Processing [9] (OLAP) has been first proposed as a way for people to analyse multi-dimensional data. Several works aim at analysing graph data using the OLAP paradigm. The Graph Cube [33] paper considers only simple graphs, while we target more complex graphs that are possible with the RDF graph model. The work in [8] proposes the aggregation of graph which changes the topology of the graph. However, we allow a more flexible definition of the aggregation dimensions in our approach. In this work, we introduce the graph aggregation as a graph operator that is anchored into graph algebra, allowing the graph aggregation to be part of a wider graph analysis flow.

The challenge of graph analysis has been studied within the Semantic Web community as well. The RDF Analytics [10] paper introduces an analytical schema over the data. This schema allows then to write analytical queries over the data, abstracting from the actual structure of the data. However, unlike Gagg this approach does not generate a graph as the analytical query output, thus preventing the use of the aggregated graph as the input of other graph operations.

The analysis of graph data under an aggregated form is investigated in several works [5,28] with an application oriented towards business logic.

The process of graph summarisation which represents a graph with a smaller graph that is homomorphic to the original graph is investigated in [7,30,32]. Such works apply a Gagg-like operation over the data. Therefore, the Gagg operator can be used to alleviate the cost of performing such operations.

3   Model

Gagg is defined in two-steps as shown in Fig. 1. Firstly, nodes and edges in the original graph G are grouped together in an intermediate graph that we call the *grouped graph*. Secondly, the grouped graph is reduced into an *aggregated graph*.

The first step is based on a set of dimensions that defines how nodes and edges are grouped together. For example, in Fig. 2 the resources :a1 and :a2 are grouped together when aggregating authors by the organisation they are member of. As we detail later, we use SPARQL operators as a flexible and powerful way to define grouping criteria.

The second step condenses the grouped graph into the final aggregated graph. This operation is done by what we call a *graph reduce function*. A template similar to that of SPARQL construct is used by the graph reduce function to structure the final results. In this template, typical aggregate functions such as sum and count, can be applied to the nodes and edges in the grouped graph. It is worth pointing out that the grouped graph is not an RDF graph as its nodes represent sets of resources, while the aggregated graph is an RDF graph that can be used as input for further processing.

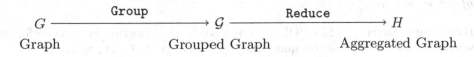

Fig. 1. Operational flow of the graph aggregation

3.1   Preliminaries

We present in this section the fundamental concepts used throughout the paper.

Definition 1 (Data Graph). *A* data graph G *defined over a set of terms* $\mathcal{T}$ *is a tuple* $G = \langle V, A, l_V \rangle$, *where* V *is a set of nodes,* $A \subseteq V \times \mathcal{T} \times V$ *is the set of labelled edges, and* $l_V : V \mapsto \mathcal{T}$ *is a node labelling function. The* l_V *function is an injection, meaning that each node has a unique label.*

We assume the existence of a set of variables $\mathcal{X}$ which symbols are not part of the set of labels $\mathcal{T}$, i.e., $\mathcal{X} \cap \mathcal{T} = \emptyset$. A query is expressed as a set of patterns that are matched against the graph data. A *triple pattern* is the atomic element for building a graph query, which matches an edge of the graph.

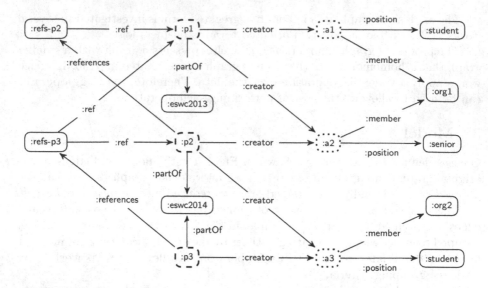

Fig. 2. Bibliographic network inspired from [29]. Dashed nodes represent papers, and dotted nodes the authors.

Definition 2 (Triple Pattern). *A triple pattern (s, p, o) is a triple where any of the three components can be either a variable or a term, i.e., the triplet $(s, p, o) \in (\mathcal{T} \bigcup \mathcal{X}) \times (\mathcal{T} \bigcup \mathcal{X}) \times (\mathcal{T} \bigcup \mathcal{X})$.*

Definition 3 (Basic Graph Pattern). *A basic graph pattern (BGP) is a set of triple patterns.*

Basic graph patterns in SPARQL represent conjunctive queries. From hencefor-ward, we use the conjunctive query notation[2] $q(\bar{x}) := t_1, \cdots, t_n$ where $t_1, \cdots, t_n$ are triple patterns and therefore $\{t_1, \cdots, t_n\}$ is a BGP.

We denote by $Var(q)$ the set of variables occurring in the query q. The *query head* variables $\bar{x}$ are called *distinguished variables*, and are a subset of the variables occurring in $t_1, \cdots, t_n$, i.e., we have $\bar{x} \subseteq Var(q)$.

We denote with $q(G)$ the set of solutions of q on G. For the evaluation of a query q against a graph G, we refer the reader to the W3C Recommendation [16].

Definition 4 (Join Query). *Let $q_1, \cdots, q_n$ be basic graph patterns which non-distinguished variables are pairwise disjoints. We call the query $q(\bar{x}) := q_1(\bar{x}_1) \wedge \cdots \wedge q_n(\bar{x}_n)$ a join query of $q_1, \cdots, q_n$, where $\bar{x} \subseteq \bar{x}_1 \cup \cdots \cup \bar{x}_n$.*

A join query combines multiple BGPs and joins them based on their shared distinguished variables.

---

[2] We reuse here some of the notations and definitions from [10].

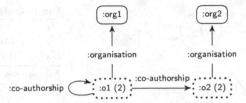

(a) Aggregation of people by the organisation, counting the number of papers authored by the organisation. The edges *:co-authorship* link organisations by the papers they authored.

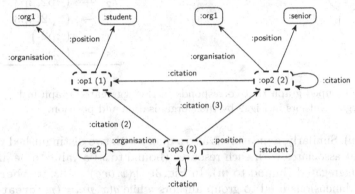

(b) Aggregation of people by their organisation and position, counting the number of their papers. The edge *:citation* represents an author citing an other via a paper.

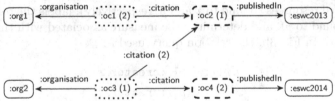

(c) Aggregation of people by their organisation and papers by their conference. We count the number of authors in an organisation, and the number of papers in a conference. The edge *:citation* represents a link from an organisation to a conference, where an author cited a paper from a particular conference.

Fig. 3. Summary graphs of the data in Fig. 2. The number within parenthesis report a count statistics of the aggregated data.

3.2   Graph Aggregation Operator

We build on the definitions introduced before to define a graph aggregation operator. In particular, dimensions used for aggregation, measures that are to be aggregated, and the relations between nodes in the graph are all expressed as queries. A *dimension* is a query with two distinguished variables $q(x, v)$ that defines how resources (bound to x) are grouped based on associated values

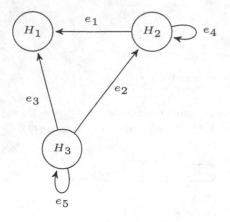

Dimensions	
$H_1 \rightarrow$	(:org1, :student)
$H_2 \rightarrow$	(:org2, :student)
$H_3 \rightarrow$	(:org1, :senior)

Measures	
$H_1 \rightarrow$	(:p1)
$H_2 \rightarrow$	(:p2, :p3)
$H_3 \rightarrow$	(:p2, :p3)
$e_1 \rightarrow$	(:p2)
$e_2 \rightarrow$	(:p2, :p3, :p3)
$e_3 \rightarrow$	(:p2, :p3)
$e_4 \rightarrow$	(:p2)
$e_5 \rightarrow$	(:p3)

Fig. 4. The grouped graph that corresponds to the aggregated graph in Fig. 3b. This graph aggregate authors in Fig. 2 by their organisation and position.

(bound to v). Similarly, a measure is also a query with two distinguished variables $q(x, m)$ that associates with each resource (bound to x) a value to be measured and later aggregated (bound to m). In Fig. 3b, $q(x, org) := (x, :\texttt{member}, org)$ is one of the dimensions used to group authors while $q(x, p) := (p, :\texttt{creator}, x)$ is the measure associated with each node as we are counting the papers written by each author.

A relation query is a query with four distinguished variables $q(x, p, y, m)$ that defines related resources (bound to x and y, respectively), labels the relation (via the value bound to p), and determines the measure associated with this relation (bound to m). In Fig. 3b, the relation query used is:

$$q(x, :\texttt{cite}, y, p1) := (p1, :\texttt{creator}, x) \wedge$$
$$(p2, :\texttt{creator}, y) \wedge$$
$$(p1, :\texttt{references}, refs) \wedge$$
$$(refs, :\texttt{ref}, p2)$$

Notice that $p1$ is used as a measure since we are interested in counting the papers. Additionally, the relation is bound to the constant value :cite to give it a readable name[3].

Definition 5 (Grouped Graph). *A grouped graph is a graph* $(\mathcal{V}, \mathcal{A}, l_{\mathcal{V}})$ *with two associated functions: dimensions* $: \mathcal{V} \rightarrow 2^{\mathcal{T}}$ *and measures* $: \mathcal{V} \cup \mathcal{A} \rightarrow 2^{\mathcal{T}}$.

Figure 4 shows an example grouped graph with its associated *dimensions* and *measures* functions.

---

[3] For the sake of simplicity, we slightly violated conjunctive query notation by using a constant in the header.

Definition 6 (Graph Reduce Function). *A graph reduce function f is a function that maps a grouped graph into a data graph.*

We are now ready to provide a definition of the Graph Aggregation Query.

Definition 7 (Graph Aggregation Query). *A graph aggregation query is a tuple $Q = (D, M, E, N, R, f)$ such that:*

- *R is a relation query with distinguished variables x, p, y, o;*
- *D is a set of dimensions such that for each dimension $d \in D$ the distinguished variables of d are x, v_d for some unique variable v_d;*
- *E is a set of dimensions such that for each dimension $c \in E$ the distinguished variables of c are y, v_c for some unique variable v_c;*
- *two measure queries M and N with distinguished variables x, m and y, n, respectively;*
- *a graph reduce function f.*

In the definition above, R is meant to define related nodes in the typical form of (subject, predicate, object) with an associated measure. D and E are the set of dimensions to group the subjects and objects defined by R. While the dimensions for subjects and objects can be the same, Fig. 3c depicts an example where it is beneficial to group subjects and object by different dimensions. Finally, M and N are the measures for subject and object nodes.

3.3   Operational Semantics

A grouped graph $\mathcal{G} = (\mathcal{V}, \mathcal{A}, l_{\mathcal{V}})$ is the result of grouping a data graph $G = (V, A, l_V)$ according to the graph aggregation query $Q = (D, M, E, N, R, f)$ if the following holds:

1. $w \in \mathcal{V}$ and $dimensions(w) = d$ iff $\exists (r, d) \in D(G)$ or $(r, d) \in E(G)$[4]. In this case we say that the node r in the original graph *maps to* the node w in the grouped graph and denote this as $r \mapsto w$;
2. $(u, p, v) \in \mathcal{A}$ and $o \in measures((u, p, v))$ iff $\exists (r, p, s, o) \in R(G)$ such that $r \mapsto u$ and $s \mapsto v$;
3. For all $u \in \mathcal{V}$; $a \in measures(u)$ iff $(r, a) \in M(G)$ or $(r, a) \in N(G)$ and $r \mapsto u$.

4   Answering Graph Aggregation Queries

The evaluation of a graph aggregation query is performed in three steps: (1) building a *binding table* that is the solution of the queries defined by the dimensions, relation and measures; (2) building a grouped graph from the binding table; and (3) applying the *reduce function* over the grouped graph to achieve the final results.

---

[4] $q(G)$ is the solution of query q against graph G. We extend the notion here to a set of queries where the result is the join query as defined before.

4.1 Binding Table

Evaluating a query in SPARQL results in a binding table as detailed in [16]. The first step to answer a graph aggregation query $\mathcal{Q}$ is to combine and evaluate the query:

$$q(x, p, y, o, v_D, m, v_E, n) := q_R(x, p, y, o) \wedge q_D(x, v_D) \wedge$$
$$q_M(x, m) \wedge q_E(y, v_E) \wedge q_N(y, n)$$

The result is a binding table $\mathfrak{B}$ which is a set of rows. If r is a row in $\mathfrak{B}$ and x is a variable, we use $r[x]$ to refer to the value bound with the variable x in r. Delegating the evaluation of the binding table exploits the best practices and optimisation techniques already built in existing SPARQL engines.

4.2 Building the Grouped Graph

Algorithm 1 describes how starting from the binding table resulting from the previous step, a grouped graph compatible with the defined operational semantics can be built. The function GetGroupNode(v) creates a node corresponding to the dimensions values v, updates the *dimensions* mapping of $\mathcal{G}$ and adds the created node to $\mathcal{V}$. If a node corresponding to the dimension values already exists in $\mathcal{V}$, the function just returns the node. The GetGroupNode function needs some hash structure that maps dimension values to nodes and keeps the measures associated with each node and edge. Assuming that this data structure fits in memory, the complexity of GetGroupNode is $O(1)$. Consequently, Algorithm 1 has a complexity of $O(|\mathfrak{B}|)$ as it scans the binding table only once.

4.3 Applying the Graph Reduce Function

The graph reduce function applies an aggregate function on the set of measures and restructure the grouped graph. One possible way to express a graph reduce function is to base it on a template similar to the one used in CONSTRUCT queries in SPARQL.

5 Evaluation

In this section, we discuss the expressivity of the Gagg operator and present an experimental performance comparison with plain SPARQL queries.

5.1 Expressivity

We have used Gagg to express type summary as defined in [7] and to reproduce VoID statistics similar to the results provided by previous systems [1,22]. Furthermore, Gagg was applied to bibliographic data to compute a number of

---

Algorithm 1. Aggregated graph creation from the table of bindings

Data: The binding table $\mathfrak{B}$ and the graph aggregation query
$(D, q_M(x, m), E, q_N(x, n), q_R(x, p, y, o), f)$
Result: The grouped graph $\mathcal{G} = \langle \mathcal{V}, \mathcal{A}, l_{\mathcal{V}}, dimensions, measures \rangle$.

1 **for** $r \in \mathfrak{B}$ **do** // For each row in the binding table
    // Retrieve grouped nodes corresponding to the dimensions
2 | $u \leftarrow$ GetGroupNode($r[D]$)
3 | $v \leftarrow$ GetGroupNode($r[E]$)
    | // create an edge
4 | $e \leftarrow (u, r[p], v)$
5 | $\mathcal{A} \overset{\cup}{\leftarrow} e$
    | // Add measures
6 | $measures(u) \overset{\cup}{\leftarrow} r[m]$
7 | $measures(v) \overset{\cup}{\leftarrow} r[n]$
8 | $measures(e) \overset{\cup}{\leftarrow} r[o]$
9 **end**

---

bibliometrics as shown in the next subsection. Finally, we have used Gagg to aggregate the LOD Cloud[5]. As this data is available in RDF[6] we were able to generate different versions of the LOD diagram by aggregating datasets by their topic, license, publisher, etc. Gagg is expressive enough to aggregate datasets and count them or sum their triples counts[7]. Similarly, it can count the number of linksets and sum the number of interlinking triples. This provided views over the LOD cloud from a variety of perspectives.

5.2   Performance Evaluation

We extended the query algebra in Apache Jena[8] with the Gagg operator. The implementation builds the intermediate graph and then apply aggregate functions whose implementations are re-used from Jena. We compare the performance of the usage of Gagg to that of standard SPARQL. In particular, we report the average running time of four approaches[9]:

reduced provides incomplete results as it aggregates only the relationships and not the subjects and objects. This is included as a *baseline* to quantify the extra time needed by the other approaches to get the full results.

---

[5] http://lod-cloud.net/.

[6] http://lod-cloud.net/data/void.ttl.

[7] The scripts to generate the aggregated graphs of the LOD Cloud diagram are available at https://github.com/fadmaa/rdf-graph-aggregation.

[8] https://jena.apache.org/ version 2.12.0.

[9] We report the SPARQL queries of the approaches at https://github.com/fadmaa/rdf-graph-aggregation.

fullSparql builds the aggregated graph using one CONSTRUCT SPARQL query. This query contains three sub-queries such that the first one defines the relationship, the second aggregates and counts subjects and the final one aggregates and counts objects.

3Sparqls uses three separate CONSTRUCT SPARQL queries to build the aggregated graph. Similar to the fullSPARQL approach, one query defines the relationship and the other two queries aggregate subjects and objects. Notice that these queries need to rely to some characteristics of the data or some hashing function to assure that the results of the three queries use the same identifiers for the aggregated nodes. Therefore, writing these queries was relatively hard. The final result is the union of the three graphs resulted from the queries, however, to prevent introducing extra penalty on the running time, the values we report do not include the time needed to union the three results.

Gagg uses the Gagg operator.

We used JUnitBenchmarks[10] to run the evaluation. JUnitBenchmarks performs JVM warm-up phases and repeat the execution multiple times to enhance the reliability of the reported times. The evaluation was run on a 4 core machine running Linux (3.18.1-3) at 2.60 GHz with 8 Gb of RAM. The JAVA version is 1.7.0_71.

We experimented with BSBM [4] and SP2B [29] datasets, varying the sizes of data. Two set of queries are used to perform two tasks: building a type summary and calculating some bibliometrics-based summary.

Type Summary. For this graph aggregation query, all resources in the RDF data are grouped by their types (i.e., the values of `rdf:type`) and all relations between resources are grouped. The summary reports the number of instances per type and the number of relations of each type that exists between instances of two classes. This type of statistics are the ones reported in VoID statistics and in the RDF graph summary in [7].

In the corresponding Gagg operators, the set of dimensions of subjects and objects is $(?x, \texttt{rdf:type}, ?t)$ and the relation ship query is $(?x, ?p, ?y)$.

Bibliometrics. We report on three graph aggregation queries that were evaluated on top of SP^2B data:

co-authorship gets the graph structure of co-authorship. Nodes in the summary graph represent authors along with the number of papers they published while edges represent co-authorship between them along with the counts.

citation gets the graph structure of author citation. Nodes in the summary graph represent authors along with the number of papers they authored while edges represent citation across authors along with their counts.

---

[10] http://labs.carrotsearch.com/junit-benchmarks.html.

conf-citation gets the graph structure of citation among papers grouped by the conference they are published in. Nodes in the summary graph represent conferences along with the number of papers published in each while edges represent citation across conferences along with their counts.

5.3 Discussion

The average running times to compute the Type Summary queries are reported in Table 1 while the average running times of the bibliometrics queries are shown in Table 2. Entries marked with N/A failed to finish as the machine ran out of memory or the execution took too long.

In general fullSparql approach showed the worst performance among the tested approaches. This is not surprising giving that dimensions and measures are evaluated three times in the fullSparql because results need to be aggregated along different dimensions each time, i.e., for subject, object and relation. Results of the three sub-queries of fullSparql also need to be joined together. In particular, the dramatic growth in the TypeSummary queries is due to the need for joining the results of the three sub-queries before aggregation. Because we are interested in aggregating all relations in the graph to compute a type summary, the sub-queries are not selective and produce large intermediary results. This is an extra overhead cost that both Gagg and 3Sparqls approaches avoid. In comparison to fullSparql, Gagg achieved up to two orders of magnitude improvement in response time.

The performance improvement of Gagg of about a 2.5 factor in comparison to 3Sparqls is reasonable. Gagg builds and scans the binding table once instead of three times. Nonetheless, it still performs the three aggregations.

Finally, in comparison to the reduced approach, the overhead that Gagg adds to achieve the full aggregated graphs is small. We remind that this approach gives incomplete results, since it does not aggregate the subject and object resources.

Table 1. Average running times of type summary queries.

dataset-size (# triples)	fullSparql (s)	3Sparqls (s)	reduced (s)	Gagg (s)
bsbm-5K	0.08	0.06	0.01	0.03
bsbm-190K	9.84	1.25	0.42	0.55
bsbm-370K	31.88	2.82	1.00	1.13
bsbm-1.8M	454.07	13.48	4.37	5.61

(a) BSBM

dataset-size (# triples)	fullSparql (s)	3Sparqls (s)	reduced (s)	Gagg (s)
sp2b-50K	0.42	0.22	0.08	0.09
sp2b-100K	0.84	0.44	0.15	0.16
sp2b-500K	4.75	2.19	0.75	0.84
sp2b-1M	10.32	4.84	1.56	1.8

(b) SP^{2}B

Table 2. Average running times of bibliometrics queries on the SP^{2}B data.

dataset-size (# triples)	fullSparql (s)	3Sparqls (s)	reduced (s)	Gagg (s)
sp2b-50K	3.93	0.18	0.053	0.09
sp2b-100K	4.05	0.20	0.05	0.08
sp2b-500K	4.02	0.18	0.05	0.08
sp2b-1M	N/A	6.80	1.04	2.62

(a) Co-authorship

dataset-size (# triples)	fullSparql (s)	3Sparqls (s)	reduced (s)	Gagg (s)
sp2b-50K	1.15	1.02	0.32	0.07
sp2b-100K	4.89	4.29	1.44	0.09
sp2b-500K	94.06	86.39	29.41	0.18

(b) Citation

dataset-size (# triples)	fullSparql (s)	3Sparqls (s)	reduced (s)	Gagg (s)
sp2b-50K	0.14	0.17	0.05	0.06
sp2b-100K	0.67	0.68	0.22	0.23
sp2b-500K	N/A	29.31	9.7814	9.8091

(c) Conf-citation

6   Conclusion

We introduce in this work an operator called *Gagg* for aggregating graph data. We defined the operator as a two-steps processing, where the graph is first grouped based on some dimensions, which is then reduced into an aggregated graph. The aggregated graph exhibits groups of dimensions and relations between such groups, as well as statistics associated to the groups and links. Our definition of the operator is formally anchored in the RDF algebra, making it possible to be composed with other graph operations. The actual aggregation of the graph can be fully customised by a user via the use of BGP queries. We showed in our evaluation that the graph aggregation Gagg improves significantly the performance of plain-SPARQL graph aggregation.

In future work, we plan to refine the formalisation of the Gagg operator to include (a) multi-valued dimensions; and (b) missing data, especially for the definition of dimensions. We plan also to investigate optimisations of graph queries using the Gagg operator. Moreover, providing a distributed implementation of Gagg might be an interesting direction to pursue.

Acknowledgements. Fadi Maali is funded by the Irish Research Council, Embark Postgraduate Scholarship Scheme. This publication has emanated from research supported in part by a research grant from Science Foundation Ireland (SFI) under Grant Number SFI/12/RC/2289.

References

1. Auer, S., Demter, J., Martin, M., Lehmann, J.: LODStats – An extensible framework for high-performance dataset analytics. In: ten Teije, A., Völker, J., Handschuh, S., Stuckenschmidt, H., d'Acquin, M., Nikolov, A., Aussenac-Gilles, N., Hernandez, N. (eds.) EKAW 2012. LNCS, vol. 7603, pp. 353–362. Springer, Heidelberg (2012)
2. Barrett, C., Jacob, R., Marathe, M.: Formal-language-constrained path problems. SIAM J. Comput. **30**(3), 809–837 (2000)
3. Böhm, C., Lorey, J., Naumann, F.: Creating VoID descriptions for web-scale data. Web Semantics: Science, Services and Agents on the World Wide Web **9**(3), 339–345 (2011)
4. Bizer, C., Schultz, A.: The Berlin Sparql Benchmark. Int. J. Seman. Web Inf. Syst. (IJSWIS) **5**(2), 1–24 (2009)
5. Bleco, D., Kotidis, Y.: Business intelligence on complex graph data. In: Proceedings of the 2012 Joint EDBT/ICDT Workshops, EDBT-ICDT 2012. ACM (2012)
6. Broder, A.Z., Lempel, R., Maghoul, F., Pedersen, J.O.: Efficient pagerank approximation via graph aggregation. Inf. Retrieval **9**(2), 123–138 (2006)
7. Campinas, S., Perry, T., Ceccarelli, D., Delbru, R., Tummarello, G.: Introducing RDF graph summary with application to assisted SPARQL formulation. In: Hameurlain, A., Tjoa, A.M., Wagner, R. (eds.) DEXA Workshops. IEEE Computer Society (2012)
8. Chen, C., Yan, X., Zhu, F., Han, J., Yu, P.S.: Graph OLAP: towards online analytical processing on graphs. In: Eighth International Conference on Data Mining (ICDM 2008). IEEE (2008)
9. Codd, E.F., Codd, S.B., Salley, C.T.: Providing OLAP. On-Line Analytical Processing) to User-Analysts, An IT Mandate. E. F. Codd and Associates (1993)
10. Colazzo, D., Goasdoué, F., Manolescu, I., Roatiş, A.: RDF analytics: lenses over semantic graphs. In: 23rd International Conference on World Wide Web, WWW 2014, International World Wide Web Conferences Steering Committee (2014)
11. Delbru, R., Toupikov, N., Catasta, M., Tummarello, G., Decker, S.: Hierarchical link analysis for ranking web data. In: Aroyo, L., Antoniou, G., Hyvönen, E., ten Teije, A., Stuckenschmidt, H., Cabral, L., Tudorache, T. (eds.) ESWC 2010, Part II. LNCS, vol. 6089, pp. 225–239. Springer, Heidelberg (2010)
12. Dobrin, R., Beg, Q.K., Barabási, A.L., Oltvai, Z.N.: Aggregation of topological motifs in the escherichia coli transcriptional regulatory network. BMC Bioinform. **5**(1), 10 (2004)
13. Fernandez, M., d'Aquin, M., Motta, E.: Linking data across universities: an integrated video lectures dataset. In: Aroyo, L., Welty, C., Alani, H., Taylor, J., Bernstein, A., Kagal, L., Noy, N., Blomqvist, E. (eds.) ISWC 2011, Part II. LNCS, vol. 7032, pp. 49–64. Springer, Heidelberg (2011)
14. Freeman, L.C.: A set of measures of centrality based on betweenness. Sociometry **40**, 35–41 (1977)
15. Georgieva-Trifonova, T.: Warehousing and OLAP analysis of bibliographic data. Intell. Inf. Manage. **3**(5), 190–197 (2011)
16. Harris, S., Seaborne, A.: SPARQL 1.1 Query Language (2013). http://www.w3.org/TR/sparql11-query/ (Accessed 18 December 2014)
17. Jakawat, W., Favre, C., Loudcher, S.: OLAP on information networks: a new framework for dealing with bibliographic data. In: Catania, B., Cerquitelli, T., Chiusano, S., Guerrini, G., Kämpf, M., Kemper, A., Novikov, B., Palpanas, T., Pokorny, J., Vakali, A. (eds.) New Trends in Databases and Information Systems. AISC, vol. 241, pp. 361–370. Springer, Heidelberg (2014)

18. Kaushik, R., Bohannon, P., Naughton, J.F., Korth, H.F.: Covering indexes for branching path queries. In: ACM SIGMOD International Conference on Management of Data. ACM (2002)
19. Kazemzadeh, L., Kamdar, M.R., Beyan, O.D., Decker, S., Barry, F.: LinkedPPI: enabling intuitive, integrative protein-protein interaction discovery. In: 4th Workshop on Linked Science, ISWC 2014 Workshop (2014)
20. Khatchadourian, S., Consens, M.P.: ExpLOD: summary-based exploration of interlinking and rdf usage in the linked open data cloud. In: Aroyo, L., Antoniou, G., Hyvönen, E., ten Teije, A., Stuckenschmidt, H., Cabral, L., Tudorache, T. (eds.) ESWC 2010, Part II. LNCS, vol. 6089, pp. 272–287. Springer, Heidelberg (2010)
21. Li, H.: Data profiling for semantic web data. In: Wang, F.L., Lei, J., Gong, Z., Luo, X. (eds.) WISM 2012. LNCS, vol. 7529, pp. 472–479. Springer, Heidelberg (2012). http://dx.doi.org/10.1007/978-3-642-33469-6_59
22. Mäkelä, E.: Aether – generating and viewing extended VoID statistical descriptions of RDF datasets. In: Presutti, V., Blomqvist, E., Troncy, R., Sack, H., Papadakis, I., Tordai, A. (eds.) ESWC Satellite Events 2014. LNCS, vol. 8798, pp. 429–433. Springer, Heidelberg (2014)
23. Mason, O., Verwoerd, M.H.A.: Graph theory and networks in biology. Syst. Biol. IET 1(2), 89–119 (2007)
24. Mendes, P.N., Passant, A., Kapanipathi, P.: Twarql: tapping into the wisdom of the crowd. In: Proceedings of the 6th International Conference on Semantic Systems. ACM (2010)
25. Milo, T.: Index structures for path expressions. In: Beeri, C., Bruneman, P. (eds.) ICDT 1999. LNCS, vol. 1540, pp. 277–295. Springer, Heidelberg (1998)
26. Möller, K., Heath, T., Handschuh, S., Domingue, J.: Recipes for semantic web dog food — The ESWC and ISWC metadata projects. In: Aberer, K., Choi, K.-S., Noy, N., Allemang, D., Lee, K.-I., Nixon, L.J.B., Golbeck, J., Mika, P., Maynard, D., Mizoguchi, R., Schreiber, G., Cudré-Mauroux, P. (eds.) ASWC 2007 and ISWC 2007. LNCS, vol. 4825, pp. 802–815. Springer, Heidelberg (2007)
27. Pavlopoulos, G., Secrier, M., Moschopoulos, C., Soldatos, T., Kossida, S., Aerts, J., Schneider, R., Bagos, P.: Using graph theory to analyze biological networks. BioData Mining 4(1) (2011). http://dx.doi.org/10.1186/1756-0381-4-10
28. Petermann, A., Junghanns, M., Muller, R., Rahm, E.: BIIIG: enabling business intelligence with integrated instance graphs. In: 30th International Conference on Data Engineering Workshops (ICDEW). IEEE (2014)
29. Schmidt, M., Hornung, T., Meier, M., Pinkel, C., Lausen, G.: SP2Bench: A SPARQL performance benchmark. In: Semantic Web Information Management. Springer, Heidelberg (2010)
30. Tian, Y., Hankins, R.A., Patel, J.M.: Efficient aggregation for graph summarization. In: ACM SIGMOD International Conference on Management of Data, SIGMOD 2008. ACM (2008)
31. Wasserman, S.: Social Network Analysis: Methods and Applications, vol. 8. Cambridge University Press, Cambridge (1994)
32. Zhang, N., Tian, Y., Patel, J.M.: Discovery-driven graph summarization. In: 26th International Conference on Data Engineering (ICDE). IEEE (2010)
33. Zhao, P., Li, X., Xin, D., Han, J.: Graph Cube: on warehousing and OLAP multidimensional networks. In: ACM SIGMOD International Conference on Management of Data, SIGMOD 2011. ACM (2011)

FrameBase: Representing N-Ary Relations Using Semantic Frames

Jacobo Rouces[1]([✉]), Gerard de Melo[2], and Katja Hose[1]

[1] Aalborg University, Aalborg, Denmark
jrg@es.aau.dk, khose@cs.aau.dk
[2] Tsinghua University, Beijing, China
gdm@demelo.org

Abstract. Large-scale knowledge graphs such as those in the Linked Data cloud are typically represented as subject-predicate-object triples. However, many facts about the world involve more than two entities. While n-ary relations can be converted to triples in a number of ways, unfortunately, the structurally different choices made in different knowledge sources significantly impede our ability to connect them. They also make it impossible to query the data concisely and without prior knowledge of each individual source. We present FrameBase, a wide-coverage knowledge-base schema that uses linguistic frames to seamlessly represent and query n-ary relations from other knowledge bases, at different levels of granularity connected by logical entailment. It also opens possibilities to draw on natural language processing techniques for querying and data mining.

1 Introduction

Over the past few years, large-scale knowledge bases (KBs) have grown to play an important role on the Web. Many institutions rely on Linked Data principles to publish their data using Semantic Web standards [2]. These KBs are mostly based on simple subject-predicate-object (SPO) triples, as defined by the RDF model [15]. Such triples are convenient to process and can be visualized as entity networks with labeled edges.

Whereas triple representations work straightforwardly for relations involving two entities, many interesting facts relate more than just two participants – a problem that has gained renewed attention in several recent papers [13,22] as well as in the current W3C proposal to add roles to schema.org [1]. For a birth event, for instance, one may wish to capture not just the time but also the location and parents. For an actress starring in a movie, the name of the portrayed character may be relevant. Such facts naturally correspond to n-ary relations. In order to capture them as triples, several different representation schemes have been proposed. Table 1 shows some possibilities of expressing that an entity John was married in 1964, some of which also include additional information such as the name of the bride. We will discuss these representations in more detail later in Sect. 2.

© Springer International Publishing Switzerland 2015
F. Gandon et al. (Eds.): ESWC 2015, LNCS 9088, pp. 505–521, 2015.
DOI: 10.1007/978-3-319-18818-8_31

Table 1. Triple representations of n-ary relations

Direct Binary Relation

John	marriedOnDate	1964	.

RDF Reification

John	marries	Mary	.
s	type	Statement	.
s	subject	John	.
s	property	marries	.
s	object	Mary	.
s	time	1964	.

Subproperties

p	subPropertyOf	Marriage	.
John	p	Mary	.
p	time	1964	.

Neo-Davidsonian (Specific Roles)

e	type	Marriage	.
e	groom	John	.
e	bride	Mary	.
e	time	1964	.

Neo-Davidsonian (General Roles)

e	type	Marriage	.
e	agent	John	.
e	agent	Mary	.
e	time	1964	.

As the example shows, this sort of semantic heterogeneity leads to significant data integration challenges. One KB might use a simple binary property between two entities, whereas another may instead choose a more complex representation that accommodates additional arguments. The representations can easily be so at odds with each other that no particular mapping between entities could bridge the differences. There are entities at each side that have no counterpart at the other. This leads to several challenging problems:

1. When **linking data**, there are currently no mechanisms to connect KBs with different modeling choices. Predicates exist to link equivalent classes, instances, or properties, but not for connecting the different patterns, as explained above. Existing work on ontology and KB alignment [3] is limited to finding aliases.
2. When **querying**, the query must be built in a way that fits the particular modeling choices made for the respective KB. Otherwise, the recall may be as low as zero [26]. Even worse, when we don't have a single coherent KB but a set of different KBs, there is no simple query (as could be formulated on a single given schema) that will have a high recall across all KBs.
3. When **natural language interfaces** to KBs are queried, state-of-the-art systems typically attempt to map verbs and predicate phrases to RDF predicates [33]. This approach, however, cannot be applied when the KB fails to provide a compatible binary relation.

FrameBase. To address these problems, we have created FrameBase, a broad-coverage schema that can homogeneously integrate other KBs and has strong connections to natural language. It overcomes the above-mentioned forms of heterogeneity – by sticking to a specific modeling choice general enough to subsume the others (neo-Davidsonian representation) – together with a large vocabulary for events and roles. This vocabulary is reusable and based on an extensible hierarchy. We also develop a mechanism to convert back and forth between the new

Table 2. Triple Overhead. n is the number of participants in an event, and k the number of pairs that are relevant to be linked by direct binary relations. The first column indicates the total number of triples that can be materialized. The second column excludes direct binary relationships, which can be inferred unambiguously by the inference system in the last column. In the case of RDF reification, this inference could be accomplished by a rule creating the triple from its reification triples. In the case of neo-Davidsonian representation, we use rules of a different form (described later in Sect. 5). In both cases, each rule is a definite clause, i.e. a disjunction of logical atoms with only one negated, which is the consequent when the clause is written as an implication. The third column indicates the number of triples needed to connect entities that represent the same event, which is a phenomenon that arises when using RDF reification or subproperties.

	All triples	Core	Linking event	Reasoning
RDF Reification	$(n+4)k$	$(n+3)k$	$+k(k-1)$	One definite clause
Subproperties	$(n+2)k$	$(n+1)k$	$+k(k-1)$	RDFS
Neo-Davidsonian	$1+n+k$	$1+n$	$+0$	Several def. clauses

representation and direct binary relations, using a vocabulary of binary relations automatically generated from linguistic annotations. These are more concise and can be used when only two arguments are relevant.

This paper is structured as follows. After analyzing the state of the art in Sect. 2, an overview of FrameBase is given in Sect. 3. Section 4 explains how we construct the FrameBase schema, while Sect. 5 presents our representation conversion mechanism. Section 6 provides a qualitative evaluation, and Sect. 7 concludes the paper with an outlook to future work.

2 State of the Art

In this section, we review related work and conduct a thorough analysis of existing approaches for modeling n-ary relations, which are synthesized in Table 1. In Table 2, we provide a detailed comparison of their space efficiency, which has consequences with regards to their applicability for large-scale KBs.

2.1 Direct Binary Relations

A common way to represent n-ary facts is to simply decompose them directly into binary relations between two participants [8]. But in doing so, important information may be lost. For instance, given a triple with property `wasMarriedOnDate` and two triples with `gotMarriedTo`, we cannot be sure to which marriage the given time span applies.

2.2 RDF Reification

The RDF standard proposes RDF reification [15], which introduces a new identifier (IRI) for a statement and then describes the original RDF statement using three new triples with `subject`, `predicate`, and `object` properties. Subsequently, arbitrary properties of the statement can be captured by adding further triples about it.

In the different versions of YAGO [16], RDF reification is used to attach additional information to the event represented by the original RDF triple (evoked by its property) – as in the *RDF Reification* example in Table 1. This has the advantage that both the original triple as well as the reified triple can be present in the KB and queries that do not require the additional information can still use the original binary relation directly. However, this also has several drawbacks:

- Formally, the event represented by a triple and the triple as a statement are different entities with different properties. For instance, an institution may endorse the triple as a statement without endorsing the marriage. Using RDF reification, both are represented by the same RDF resource identifier, which conceptually is meant to be unambiguous. This is a potential source of confusion and inconsistency.
- The number of triples increases by a factor of 4. For each triple `S P O`, one has to add `T a rdf:Statement`, `T rdf:subject S`, `T rdf:predicate P`, and `T rdf:object O`. These do not add any new information themselves but are merely a prerequisite for then being able to extend the original binary relation to an n-ary relation by subsequently adding more triples with `T` as subject.
- The advantage of being able to include the original non-reified triple only applies for the primary binary relation, and not for the other $\frac{n(n-1)}{2} - 1$ ones that can be formed (not counting inverses). Some of these may be rare or irrelevant, but others may be important and are indeed used in YAGO (e.g. `bornAtPlace`, `bornOnDate`).
- The choice of the primary pair of entities and their binary relation (John and Mary in Table 1) is arbitrary, and a third party willing to query the KB cannot replicate the choice independently. If their choice is different, they will not obtain any results. A possible solution, which is actually implemented in YAGO2s, is to include the triples for the other pairs and reify them, too, but this adds yet another factor of overhead, besides data redundancy that would complicate updates.
- When two or more different events share the same values for the primary pair of arguments, they will share the same triple, but require separate reifications, producing non-unique triple identifiers. For example, if there are two flight connections between Paris and London with different airlines, the triple `Paris isConnectedTo London` will be reified twice, with two different triple identifiers.

If the triplestore implementation makes use of quads (http://www.w3.org/TR/n-quads/), the 4-fold overhead can be avoided (though the underlying storage needs a new column), but the other disadvantages still remain. Quad-based singleton named graphs [15] could be used instead of RDF reification, the problems being the same.

2.3 Subproperties

A recent proposal [22] aims to solve some of the issues with RDF reification by instead declaring a subproperty of the original property in the primary pair, and using this subproperty as the subject for the other arguments of the n-ary relation. This is shown in the *Subproperties* example in Table 1.

While the approach enables us to use RDFS reasoning to obtain the triple with the parent property that relates two of the participants, and also reduces the overhead of RDF reification, it still suffers from the problems mentioned above related to the existence of a primary pair. For one, the non-reified binary relationships for the other pairs cannot be inferred from that subproperty.

2.4 Neo-Davidsonian Representations

Another approach, and the one that we will adapt for FrameBase, is to make use of so-called neo-Davidsonian representations [18, p. 600f.]. This means that we first define an entity that represents the event or situation (also referred to as a *frame*) underlying the n-ary relation. Then, this entity is connected to each of the n arguments by means of a property describing the *semantic role* [13,23].

Note that the process of converting from the binary representation to the neo-Davidsonian one is also called reification, but this is different from *RDF reification* as discussed earlier. In RDF reification, an entity is defined that stands for a whole triple so that additional triples can be used to describe the reified triple as a unit that represents a statement. However, in the context of event semantics, reification is used to denote the process by which an entity is defined that refers to the event, process, situation, or more generally, frame, evoked by a property or binary relation. Having done this, additional information about it can then easily be added. Both kinds of reification have in common that a new entity is defined to refer to something that before was not explicitly represented by an entity in the KB, but in one case it is a RDF statement while in the other it is an event.

Advantages. Table 2 compares the neo-Davidsonian approach to the alternatives. These require a lot more triples when several direct binary relations need to be included. In the worst case, $k = \frac{n(n-1)}{2}$ despite discounting reciprocal relations, but even if not all of these relations are relevant, connecting all agents and possibly patients to all other elements would be relevant, which would easily satisfy $k > n$.

Semantic Heterogeneity. Unfortunately, there are different ways of using the neo-Davidsonian approach, with different levels of granularity for the events and the semantic roles, from a very small set of abstract generic ones [28] to more specific ones [4].

The Simple Event Model (SEM) Ontology [32] falls within the category of neo-Davidsonian representation with general roles (see Table 1). It defines four very general entities, *Event*, *Actor*, *Place*, and *Time*. It also establishes a framework for creating more specific ones by extending these, but it does not provide these extensions, nor ways to integrate existing KBs in a way that would solve the problem of semantic heterogeneity. Similarly, LODE (Linking Open Descriptions of Events) [28] specifies only very general concepts such as the four just mentioned.

Freebase [4] is a KB built both from tapping on existing structured sources and via collaborative editing. Although it uses its own formalisms, there are official and third-party translations to RDF. Freebase makes use of so-called *mediators* (also called *compound value types*, CVTs) as a way to merge multiple values into a single value, similar to a `struct` datatype in C. There are around 1,870 composite value types in Freebase (1,036 with more than one instance) and around 14 million composite value instances. While CVTs do not represent frames or events per se, from a structural perspective, they can be regarded as isomorphic to a neo-Davidsonian representation with specific roles (see Table 1). However, Freebase places a number of restrictions on CVTs. For instance, they cannot be nested, and there is no hierarchy or network of them that would for example relate a purchasing event to a getting event.

There is ongoing work to add the modeling of semantic roles to schema.org [1]. Schema.org is an effort sponsored by Google, Yahoo, and Microsoft to establish common standards for semantic markup in Web pages. Currently, the new roles pattern proposal is just a proposed model without a proper role inventory, and schema.org merely targets a small restricted number of domains.

FrameNet [11,27] is a well-known resource in natural language processing (NLP) that defines over 1,000 *frames* with participants (so-called *frame elements*). For example, the verb *to buy* and the noun *acquisition* are assumed to evoke a commercial transaction frame, with frame elements for the seller, the buyer, the goods, and so on.

Previous work has proposed general patterns for using FrameNet in knowledge representation [12] and converted FrameNet to RDF [24], proposing a way to generate schemas from FrameNet. Similarly, the FRED system [25] for building semantic representations from natural language can be configured to use FrameNet.

3 System Overview

As we have seen, there are a number of different representations used in KBs. In this paper, we use the linguistic resources FrameNet [11] and WordNet [9] to fully develop an extensive schema for large-scale knowledge representation and integration. The schema is composed of an expressive neo-Davidsonian level that draws on a large common inventory of frames, together with a more concise level of direct binary relations, which is connected to the former by means of inference rules.

3.1 FrameNet-Based Representation

The use of FrameNet is motivated by the following considerations.

- FrameNet has a long history and aims at descriptions of arbitrary natural language. It thus provides a relatively large and growing inventory of frames and roles, with a broad coverage of numerous different domains.
- FrameNet comes with a large collection of English sentences annotated with frame and frame element labels. This data led to the task of automatic *semantic role labeling* (SRL) [14] of text, now one of the standard tasks in NLP. This strong connection to natural language facilitates question answering and related tasks.
- While FrameNet's lexicon and annotations cover the English language, its frame inventory is abstract enough to be adopted for languages as different as Spanish and Japanese [29]. This also makes it much more suitable as a basis for knowledge representation than language-specific syntax-oriented SRL resources such as PropBank [19].
- FrameNet provides an reasonable level of granularity for the phenomena that humans care to describe. From a theoretical perspective, there is no universally appropriate single level of reification. Any frame element might be reified on its own, and any two elements of a frame could be connected directly by a predicate. Using FrameNet, we strike a well-motivated balance, at a point that is granular enough to constitute a model for natural language semantics. As we will explain in Sect. 5, we also provide a second level of representation, less expressive but more concise, based on the direct binary predicates between frame elements.

3.2   Overview

For creating the FrameBase schema using FrameNet, we take the following steps, which will be further explained in Sect. 4.

a) **FrameNet–WordNet Mapping.** First, we create a high-precision mapping between FrameNet and another well-known lexical resource called Word-Net [9], which will be used to enrich the lexical coverage and relations of the FrameBase schema.
b) **Schema Induction.** We use FrameNet, WordNet, and the mapping to create an RDFS schema for FrameBase that has very wide coverage and is extensible. The schema exploits semantic relations from these components (e.g., synonymy, hyponymy, and perspectivization) to transform the original resources for our lightweight RDFS model.
c) **Automatic Reification–Dereification Mechanism.** We create reification–dereification rules in the form of definite clauses that allow the KB to be queried independently of whether a frame is reified or not, and that may also be used to reduce overhead in the KB.

4   FrameBase Schema Creation

4.1   FrameNet–WordNet Mapping

While FrameNet [11,27] is the largest high-quality inventory of semantic frame descriptions and their participants, WordNet [9] is the most well-known resource

capturing meanings of words in a lexical network, covering for example nouns
and named entities missing in FrameNet. WordNet, for instance, serves as the
backbone of YAGO's ontology. We propose a novel way of mapping the two
resources, which later enables us to integrate both of them into our schema.

WordNet contains synsets, which are sets of sense-disambiguated synony-
mous words with a given part of speech (POS), such as noun or verb. FrameNet
contains lexical units (LUs), which are also POS-annotated words associated to
frames. Because of the semantics of the containing frame, lexical units are also
disambiguated to a certain extent, though not with the same granularity as in
WordNet. Our objective is to map synsets and lexical units with the same meaning, so we can later use this to enrich our FrameNet-based schema with relations
and annotations from WordNet.

We choose to map each lexical unit to one and only one synset. While there
are some lexical units that could be mapped to more than one synset, this will
favor precision, which is desirable for the purpose of obtaining a clean knowledge
base. The only cases where this model would be detrimental to precision are those
where lexical units do not have any associated synset, but these are few and most
can easily be avoided by omitting lexical units with parts of speech not covered
in WordNet, such as prepositions.

Our choice allows us to model the mapping as a function $S(l|a, b)$ from lexical
units to synsets as in (1). S_l stands for the synsets that have the same lexical label
and POS as the lexical unit l, μ_L and μ_G are the lexical and gloss (definition)
overlap, respectively, f yields the corpus frequency of the synset, and a and b
are parameters for a linear combination (the third parameter can be omitted
because of the argmax function).

$$S(l|a,b) = \underset{s \in S_l}{\operatorname{argmax}} \; \mu_L(l, s) + a \cdot \mu_G(l, s) + b \cdot f(s) \qquad (1)$$

The lexical overlap μ_L of a lexical unit l and a synset s is the size of the intersection between the POS-annotated words from the lexical units in the same
frame as l and the POS-annotated words in s and its neighborhood. We define
the neighborhood as the synsets connected by a selection of lexical and semantic
pointers such as "See also", "Similar to", "Antonym", "Attribute" and "Derivationally related". This expansion is useful to reduce sparsity and better match
the sets with those generated for the lexical units, which due to the different
semantics of frames and synsets, may already include these related words.

The gloss overlap μ_G is the size of the intersection between the set of words
in the definition of the lexical unit and the gloss of the synset. For preprocessing
these, we rely on the CoreNLP library [31] to clean XML tags, tokenize, POS-
label, and lemmatize the text, and we filter out all words except nouns and
verbs.

We trained a and b with a greedy search over several randomized seeds,
obtaining optimal values $a = 5, b = 0.13$.

4.2 Schema Induction

We model frames as classes whose instances are the particular events. The frame elements of each frame are properties whose domain is that frame. We create a class hierarchy of frames as follows.

1. **General Frames:** FrameNet's frame inheritance and perspectivization relations are modeled as class subsumption between frames, by means of two specific properties that inherit from `rdfs:subClassOf`, so that both remain distinguishable but contribute to the hierarchy and allow RDFS inference. We additionally declared a top frame for the hierarchy. Inheritance between frame element properties is modeled with a direct subproperty relation.

   Thus, under this model, an instance of the *Commerce_sell* frame with a certain *Commerce_sell-Buyer* x, is also an instance of the *Giving* frame and x is the *Giving-Recipient*, because the first frame inherits from the latter. Likewise, it is also an instance of *Transfer* and x is the *Transfer-Recipient*, because *Giving* is a perspective on *Transfer*.

2. **Leaf Nodes:** Since FrameNet's original frame inventory is coarse-grained and different lexical units like *construction* and *to glue* evoke the same frame, we generate what has occasionally been called a *microframe* model: We transform FrameNet such that every lexical unit is treated as evoking its own separate fine-grained frame, which is made a subclass of the more coarse-grained original FrameNet frame.

3. **Intermediate Nodes:** The microframe nodes are very fine-grained, e.g. distinguishing *buy* from *acquire*, while some original frames from FrameNet are very coarse-grained, as mentioned above. For instance, various kinship relationships such as *mother*, *sister-in-law*, etc. are lumped together. This wide range of lexical units may stand in various lexical-semantic relationships without these being indicated, including synonymy, antonymy, or nominalization. The only characteristic they have in common is that, by definition, they evoke a similar kind of situation. Overall, neither the fine-grained nor the coarse-grained levels are ideal for knowledge representation purposes.

   We address this by providing a novel intermediate level composed of *synset-microframes* that group equivalent *LU-microframes* together. For this, we generate a set of directly equivalent synset-microframes for each LU-microframe, and we declare `owl:equivalentClass` predicates between these pairs. This is the only predicate we use that needs inference beyond pure RDFS, but we also include a pair of reciprocal `rdfs:subClassOf`, which is semantically equivalent and leaves the possibility of using any out-of-the-box RDFS inference engine. The clusters are thus defined as the resulting equivalence classes over the set of all microframes.

   These clusters are built in several steps. First, for a given LU, we get the corresponding synsets from the FrameNet–WordNet mapping in Sect. 4.1. In the case of our mapping, the set has no more than one element, but in the general case it could have more. Then, we expand that set by adding all other synsets related by lexical relations reflecting cross-POS morphological transformations: "Derivationally related", "Derived from Adjective", "Participle" and "Pertainym". In general, these lexical relations do not necessarily imply any close semantics (e.g., *create/make – creature/animal*), but when restricted to synsets all tied to the same FrameNet frame, such cases are normally factored out. The goal of using the lexical relations is linking cross-POS LUs that evoke the same specific situation with a different syntactic form, such as nominalizations (*produce–production*), non-finite verb forms (*produce–produced*), adjectivization, or adverbization.

We also use names, definitions and glosses in FrameNet and WordNet to create text annotations for our schema. We attach lexical forms with `rdfs:label` and definitions and glosses from FrameNet and WordNet with `rdfs:comment`.

5 Automatic Reification–Dereification Mechanism

While frames are convenient for representational purposes, users wishing to query the knowledge base benefit from binary predicates between pairs of frame elements. For example, for a birth event, binary predicates like `bornInPlace` and `bornOnDate` can facilitate querying by offering a more compact and simple representation.

We thus present a novel mechanism to seamlessly convert between frame representations and DBPs. This mechanism can also allow us to avoid materializing frame instances when only two frame elements are needed.

We generate *dereification rules* of the following form:

`?s BinaryPredicate ?o ← ?f a Frame,    ?f FE1 ?s,    ?f FE2 ?o`

Additionally, for each dereification rule there is a converse reification rule so that one can go back from binary predicates to the frame representation. Each direct binary predicate (DBP) has only one set of possible frame and frame elements associated, and therefore chaining reification and dereification rules is an idempotent operation.

We build the reification–dereification rules automatically using the annotations of English sentences given for different LUs in FrameNet, namely the grammatical functions (GFs) and phrase types (PTs) [27] associated with different frame elements in the example sentences of each lexical unit.

For verb-based microframes, FrameNet provides three kinds of GF labels: External Argument (Ext), Object (Obj), and Dependent (Dep). Some of the PT labels that can be found are N, NP, Obj, PPinterrog [27]. We create dereified binary predicates for the pairs of frame elements whose syntactic annotations for some sentence satisfy the creation rules below, using the GF and grammatical PT labels. We list the creation rules below, and add some examples of reification–dereification rules associated to the DBPs created by some of them. The postfixes "-s" and "-o" indicate the data associated to the FEs that fill the first and second arguments of the DBP, or equivalently, the subject and the object of the resulting RDF triple.

- Create DBP with name "ConjugateThirdPersSing(LU)"   if
    (GF-s EQUALS Ext) & (GF-o EQUALS Obj) &
    (PT-o IN { N, NP, Obj, PPinterrog, Sinterrog, QUO, Sfin, Sub, VPing })

Examples of obtained resulting DBPs and reification-dereification rules:

?S :dereif-Forming_relationships-divorces ?O

$\leftrightarrow$ $\begin{cases} \text{?R a :frame-Forming\_relationships-divorce.v ,} \\ \text{?R :fe-Forming\_relationships-Partner\_1 ?S ,} \\ \text{?R :fe-Forming\_relationships-Partner\_2 ?O .} \end{cases}$

?S :dereif-Win_prize-wins ?O

$\leftrightarrow$ $\begin{cases} \text{?R a :frame-Win\_prize-win.v ,} \\ \text{?R :fe-Win\_prize-Competitor ?S ,} \\ \text{?R :fe-Win\_prize-Prize ?O .} \end{cases}$

- Create DBP with name "is ConjugatePastParticiple(LU) by"   if
    (GF-s EQUALS Obj) & (GF-o EQUALS Subj) &
    (PT-o IN { N, NP, Obj, PPinterrog, Sinterrog, QUO, Sfin, Sub, VPing })
- Create DBP with name "ConjugateThirdPersSing(LU) Prep"   if
    (GF-s EQUALS Ext) & (GF-o EQUALS Dep) & (PT-o EQUALS PP(Prep))

Examples of obtained resulting DBPs and reification-dereification rules:

?S :dereif-Creating-createsFrom ?O

$\leftrightarrow$ $\begin{cases} \text{?R a :frame-Creating-create.v ,} \\ \text{?R :fe-Creating-Creator ?S ,} \\ \text{?R :fe-Creating-Components ?O .} \end{cases}$

?S :dereif-Win_prize-winsAt ?O

$\leftrightarrow$ $\begin{cases} \text{?R a :frame-Win\_prize-win.v ,} \\ \text{?R :fe-Win\_prize-Competitor ?S ,} \\ \text{?R :fe-Win\_prize-Venue ?O .} \end{cases}$

For some FEs in this and the next rule, we assign a specific preposition, like "at" for Time *and "in" for* Place*. For example:*

?S :dereif-Destroying-destroysAtTime ?O

$\leftrightarrow$ $\begin{cases} \text{?R a :frame-Destroying-destroy.v ,} \\ \text{?R :fe-Destroying-Cause ?S ,} \\ \text{?R :fe-Destroying-Time ?O .} \end{cases}$

?S :dereif-Intentionally_create-establishesInPlace ?O

$\leftrightarrow$ $\begin{cases} \text{?R a :frame-Intentionally\_create-establish.v ,} \\ \text{?R :fe-Intentionally\_create-Creator ?S ,} \\ \text{?R :fe-Intentionally\_create-Place ?O .} \end{cases}$

- Create DBP with name "is ConjugatePastParticiple(LU) Prep"   if
    (GF-s EQUALS Obj) & (GF-o EQUALS Dep) & (PT-o EQUALS PP(Prep))

By using the grammatical subject as subject of the triple, we avoid rules defining certain kinds of DBPs that would be rarely useful, like those connecting the time and place, or the place and the cause.

There is no explicit syntactic annotation in FrameNet to indicate if the example sentences are in passive form. We used two different heuristics for detecting this. One draws on the POS annotations available in FrameNet, and decides that

a sentence is in passive iff the target (LU) verb is conjugated as a past participle, and there is a conjugated form of the verb *to be* in a prior position, without
another verb in between. The other heuristic uses the Stanford Parser [20]. Both
heuristics make type I and II mistakes differently, so we discarded the cases
where they disagree, and for the ones that they agree that they are passive, we
created the rules inverting the Ext/Obj GFs.

We restrict ourselves to verb-based microframes, because the process above
is more difficult and error-prone with nouns. However, the synset-microframe
clustering of our schema already makes many of the morphosemantic variations
of a verb, including nominalizations, logically equivalent.

With the rules obtained with the process above, the same DBP can be associated to different pairs of frame elements in a given LU-microframe, owing to
different senses or syntactic frames for a given verb (for example the transitive
and intransitive frames for *smuggle*). This would conflate different senses, and if
the reification and the dereification directions of the rules were chained, it would
logically entail different pairs of frame elements, which would not be sound. Furthermore, a given pair of frame elements can also produce different DBPs. To
achieve the idempotency mentioned earlier, we use the Kuhn–Munkres algorithm
to obtain a one-to-one assignment, using as weights the number of annotated
example sentences for a DBP and a pair of frame elements, because the patterns
with more example sentences are usually more intuitive. The cubic complexity
of the algorithm is not a concern because each frame leads to a separate graph
on which we can operate independently.

We have implemented the reification-dereification rules as SPARQL CON-
STRUCT queries, due to SPARQL's prominence as a standard query language
for KBs. These can be used to materialize the DBPs into the KB. Other options
would be possible, such as using a general-purpose inference engine that can
handle propositional clauses, like the Rubrik reasoner in Jena [5].

6   Evaluation

We now evaluate the quality of the results and show some example queries.

6.1   FrameNet–WordNet Alignment

To evaluate the created schema, we first compared our FrameNet–WordNet mapping to the MapNet gold standard [30]. MapNet uses older versions of FrameNet
and WordNet, so that we had to apply mappings from WordNet 1.6 to 3.0 [7],
removing those with a confidence lower than one. For mapping FrameNet 1.3 to
1.5, we removed the few LUs that are not contained in the new version. Table 3
compares the results against state-of-the-art approaches and the scores that they
report on the MapNet gold standard. As expected, our approach achieves high
precision, while still maintaining good recall. We use 5-fold cross-validation for
our results.

Table 3. Comparison of our FrameNet–WordNet mapping to state-of-the-art approaches in terms of precision, recall, F1, and accuracy

	Prec	Rec	F1	Acc
SVM Polyn. kernel 1 [30]	0.761	0.613	0.679	—
SVM Polyn. kernel 2 [30]	0.794	0.569	0.663	—
SSI-Dijkstra [21]	0.78	0.63	0.69	—
SSI-Dijkstra+ [21]	0.76	0.74	0.75	—
Neighborhoods [10]	—	—	—	0.772
Our mapping	0.789	0.709	0.746	0.864

6.2 Schema Induction

The FrameBase schema is based on FrameNet and WordNet and our mappings between the two resources. It provides 19,376 frames, including 11,939 LU-microframes and 6,418 synset-microframes, all with lexical labels. A total of 18,357 microframes are clustered into 8,145 logical clusters, which are the sets of microframes whose elements are linked by a logical equivalence relation. The size of the schema is 250,407 triples.

We have obtained an average precision of $87.55\% \pm 6.18\%$ with a 95% Wilson confidence interval. The evaluation showed a small change of nuance for $31.15\% \pm 9.38\%$ of the correct pairs – most of these are caused by our choice to use semantic pointers such as "Similar to", which could be removed if we desire very fine-grained distinctions of microframes. The precision has been calculated from a random sample of 100 intra-cluster pairs that have been independently annotated by two of the authors. We have obtained the linear weighted Cohen's Kappa over the three-valued combination of the two variables with which we annotate each cluster pair, obtaining a value of 0.23 over a maximum of 0.87. We obtained the scores with a random annotator.

In addition to the number of frames, the FrameBase schema provides a vocabulary of frame elements that goes well beyond the knowledge currently included in most KBs, in particular beyond time and location. This additional knowledge is routinely conveyed in natural language, and we believe that using a schema that provides for it paves the way to include it in KBs, either manually or automatically.

6.3 Reification–Derefication Rules

We also provide 14,930 reification–dereification rules for the same number of direct binary predicates, with both human-readable IRIs and lexical labels. We obtained an average precision of $86.59\% \pm 6.41\%$, and $76.13\% \pm 8.65\%$ of the correct rules were found easily readable. We consider a rule to be not easily readable if the name of the direct binary predicate contains a frame element whose meaning is not obvious for a layman reader, or if it contains a preposition that is appropriate for some but not all possible objects, or it is not appropriate for the frame element in the name. For this evaluation, we followed the same annotation methodology as for the intra-cluster pairs, obtaining a Cohen's kappa of 0.39 over a maximum of 0.54.

6.4   Knowledge Base Integration and Querying

Knowledge from other KBs such as Freebase can be integrated using *integration rules*, which can also be implemented as SPARQL CONSTRUCT queries. The two examples below were created manually.

```
CONSTRUCT {
  _:e a framebase:frame-People_by_jurisdiction-citizen.n .
  _:e framebase:fe-People_by_jurisdiction-Person ?person .
  _:e framebase:fe-People_by_jurisdiction-Jurisdiction ?country .
} WHERE {
  ?person freebase:people.person.nationality ?country . }
```

```
CONSTRUCT {
  _:e a framebase:frame-Leadership-leader.n .
  _:e framebase:fe-Leadership-Leader ?o1 .
  _:e framebase:fe-Leadership-Governed ?o2 .
  _:e framebase:fe-Leadership-Role ?o3 .
  _:e framebase:fe-Leadership-Type ?o4 .
  _:timePeriod a framebase:frame-Timespan-period.n .
  _:timePeriod framebase:fe-Timespan-Start ?o5 .
  _:timePeriod framebase:fe-Timespan-End ?o6 .
} WHERE {
  ?cvti a freebase:organization.leadership .
  OPTIONAL { ?cvti freebase:organization.leadership.person ?o1 .}
  OPTIONAL { ?cvti ...:organization.leadership.organization ?o2 .}
  OPTIONAL { ?cvti freebase:organization.leadership.role ?o3 .}
  OPTIONAL { ?cvti freebase:organization.leadership.title ?o4 .}
  OPTIONAL { ?cvti freebase:organization.leadership.from ?o5 .}
  OPTIONAL { ?cvti freebase:organization.leadership.to ?o6 .} }
```

FrameBase facilitates novel forms of queries. The following query, for instance, uses reified patterns to find the heads of the World Bank. Note that the clusters implemented in RDFS allow searching for the noun *head* (from the leadership frame), although the integration rule above only produced an instance of `fmbs:frame-Leadership-leader.n`. The results in Table 4 show example instances seamlessly integrated into our FrameBase schema from both Freebase (rows 1–3, extracted from the second example integration rule above) and YAGO2s (rows 4–5, extracted with a similar integration rule made for YAGO2s).

```
SELECT DISTINCT ?leader ?role WHERE {
  ?lumfi a fmbs:frame-Leadership-head.n .
```

Table 4. Results from the query

?leader	?role
fb:m/0h_ds2s 'Caroline Anstey'	fb:m/04t64n 'Managing Director'
fb:m/0d_dq5 'Mahmoud Mohieldin'	fb:m/04t64n 'Managing Director'
fb:m/047cdkk 'Sri Mulyani Indrawati'	fb:m/01yc02 'Chief Operating Officer'
yago:Jim_Yong_Kim	–
yago:Robert_Zoellick	–

```
?lumfi fmbs:fe-Leadership-Governed ?worldBank.
?lumfi fmbs:fe-Leadership-Leader ?leader .
VALUES ?worldBank {yago:World_Bank freebase:m.02vk52z}
OPTIONAL{ ?lumfi fmbs:fe-Leadership-Role ?role } }
```

Alternatively, a direct binary predicate from the dereification rules can be used
to obtain the same non-optional results, as illustrated in the query below. Either
leads or *heads* can be used because the LU-microframes for these verbs are in
the same cluster as the nouns *leader* and *head*, and there is a dereification rule
between the *Leader* and *Governed* frame elements for both.

```
SELECT DISTINCT ?leader WHERE {
    ?leader fmbs:dereif-Leadership-heads ?worldBank.
    VALUES ?worldBank {yago:World_Bank freebase:m.02vk52z} }
```

FrameBase can also be applied with natural language processing tools for question answering and data mining. For example, given the question "Who has
been the head of the World_Bank", the SRL tool SEMAFOR [6] successfully
extracts the frame *Leadership* with lexical unit *head.noun* and frame elements
Governed and *Leader*. Based on this, and after a named entity disambiguator
like AIDA [17] matches World_Bank to the entities in the KBs, the structured
query can easily be built. Moreover, the same procedure can also be used to
integrate new knowledge from a text into the KB, like FRED [25] does.

7   Conclusion

FrameBase is a novel approach for connecting knowledge from different heterogeneous sources to decades of work from the NLP community. Events can be
described in very different ways across different knowledge bases. Our framework not only provides an efficient model to describe n-ary relations, but also
integrates and transforms FrameNet and WordNet to yield a broad-coverage
inventory of frames. Additionally, linguistic annotations in FrameNet such as
the ones used to create the reification–dereification rules can also be used to
generate natural language, for instance, for summarizing a portion of a KB for
non-technical users.

Regarding future lines of work, we are currently completing the integration of the instance data from YAGO2s and Freebase into the FrameBase schema, using integration rules such as the examples in Sect. 6.4, but automatically generated. This will lead to the first large-scale FrameNet-based KB. Given FrameBase's close connection to natural language, we also intend to study methods for better adapting semantic role labeling tools to question answering [6]. We are also investigating the ways that FrameBase enables for querying multiple KBs simultaneously with on-the-fly data integration.

Please refer to http://framebase.org for information on using FrameBase.

Acknowledgments. This research was partially funded by the European Union Seventh Framework Programme (FP7/2007-2013) under grant agreement No. FP7-SEC-2012-312651 (ePOOLICE project). as well as China 973 Program Grants 2011CBA00300, 2011CBA00301, and NSFC Grants 61033001, 61361136003, 20141330245.

References

1. Roles in Schema.org. Technical report, W3C (2014). http://www.w3.org/wiki/WebSchemas/RolesPattern
2. Bizer, C., Heath, T., Berners-Lee, T.: Linked data-the story so far. IJSWIS **5**(3), 1–22 (2009)
3. Böhm, C., de Melo, G., Naumann, F., Weikum, G.: LINDA: distributed web-of-data-scale entity matching. In: CIKM 2012, pp. 2104–2108 (2012)
4. Bollacker, K., Evans, C., Paritosh, P., Sturge, T., Taylor, J.: Freebase: a collaboratively created graph database for structuring human knowledge. In: SIGDATA, pp. 1247–1250 (2008)
5. Carroll, J.J., Dickinson, I., Dollin, C., Reynolds, D., Seaborne, A., Wilkinson, K.: Jena: implementing the semantic web recommendations. In: WWW 2004 (2004)
6. Das, D., Chen, D., Martins, A.F.T., Schneider, N., Smith, N.A.: Frame-semantic parsing. Comput. Linguist. **40**(1), 9–56 (2014)
7. Daudé, J., Padró, L., Rigau, G.: Mapping wordnets using structural information. In: ACL (2000)
8. Del Corro, L., Gemulla, R.: Clausie: clause-based open information extraction. In: WWW 2013 (2013)
9. Fellbaum, C. (ed.): WordNet: An Electronic Lexical Database. The MIT Press, Cambridge (1998)
10. Ferrández, O., Ellsworth, M., Munoz, R., Baker, C.F.: Aligning framenet and wordnet based on semantic neighborhoods. In: LREC 2010 (2010)
11. Fillmore, C.J., Johnson, C.R., Petruck, M.R.: Background to framenet. Int. J. Lexicography **16**(3), 235–250 (2003)
12. Gangemi, A., Presutti, V.: Towards a pattern science for the semantic web. Semant. Web **1**(1), 61–68 (2010)
13. Gangemi, A., Presutti, V.: A multi-dimensional comparison of ontology design patterns for representing n-ary relations. In: van Emde Boas, P., Groen, F.C.A., Italiano, G.F., Nawrocki, J., Sack, H. (eds.) SOFSEM 2013. LNCS, vol. 7741, pp. 86–105. Springer, Heidelberg (2013)
14. Gildea, D., Jurafsky, D.: Automatic labeling of semantic roles. Comput. Linguist. **28**(3), 245–288 (2002)

15. Hayes, P., Patel-Schneider, P.: RDF 1.1 semantics. Technical report, W3C (2014). http://www.w3.org/TR/rdf11-mt/
16. Hoffart, J., Suchanek, F.M., Berberich, K., Weikum, G.: YAGO2: a spatially and temporally enhanced knowledge base from wikipedia. Artif. Intell. **194**, 28–61 (2013)
17. Hoffart, J., Yosef, M.A., Bordino, I., Fürstenau, H., Pinkal, M., Spaniol, M., Taneva, B., Thater, S., Weikum, G.: Robust disambiguation of named entities in text. In: EMNLP 2011, pp. 782–792 (2011)
18. Jurafsky, D., Martin, J.H.: Speech and Language Processing. Pearson Prentice Hall, Englewood Cliff (2009)
19. Kingsbury, P., Palmer, M.: From TreeBank to PropBank. In: LREC 2002 (2002)
20. Klein, D., Manning, C.D.: Accurate unlexicalized parsing. In: ACL 2003, pp. 423–430 (2003)
21. Laparra, E., Rigau, G., Cuadros, M.: Exploring the integration of WordNet and FrameNet. In: GWC 2010 (2010)
22. Nguyen, V., Bodenreider, O., Sheth, A.: Don't like RDF reification?: making statements about statements using singleton property. In: WWW 2014 (2014)
23. Noy, N., Rector, A.: Defining N-ary Relations on The Semantic Web. W3C Working Group Note, W3C Consortium, April 2006. http://www.w3.org/TR/swbp-n-aryRelations/
24. Nuzzolese, A.G., Gangemi, A., Presutti, V.: Gathering lexical linked data and knowledge patterns from FrameNet. In: K-CAP 2011, pp. 41–48 (2011)
25. Presutti, V., Draicchio, F., Gangemi, A.: Knowledge extraction based on discourse representation theory and linguistic frames. In: ten Teije, A., Völker, J., Handschuh, S., Stuckenschmidt, H., d'Acquin, M., Nikolov, A., Aussenac-Gilles, N., Hernandez, N. (eds.) EKAW 2012. LNCS, vol. 7603, pp. 114–129. Springer, Heidelberg (2012)
26. Rouces, J.: Enhancing recall in semantic querying. In: SCAI 2013, vol. 257, p. 291 (2013)
27. Ruppenhofer, J., Ellsworth, M., Petruck, M.R., Johnson, C.R., Scheffczyk, J.: FrameNet II: Extended Theory and Practice. ICSI, Berkeley (2006)
28. Shaw, R., Troncy, R., Hardman, L.: LODE: linking open descriptions of events. In: Gómez-Pérez, A., Yu, Y., Ding, Y. (eds.) ASWC 2009. LNCS, vol. 5926, pp. 153–167. Springer, Heidelberg (2009)
29. Subirats, C.: Spanish FrameNet: a frame-semantic analysis of the spanish lexicon. In: Boas, H.C. (ed.) Multilingual FrameNets in Computational Lexicography Methods and Applications. Mouton de Gruyter, New York (2009)
30. Tonelli, S., Pighin, D.: New Features for FrameNet: WordNet Mapping. In: CoNLL 2009, pp. 219–227 (2009)
31. Toutanova, K., Klein, D., Manning, C.D., Singer, Y.: Feature-rich part-of-speech tagging with a cyclic dependency network. In: HTL-NAACL 2003 (2003)
32. Van Hage, W.R., Malaisé, V., Segers, R., Hollink, L., Schreiber, G.: Design and use of the Simple Event Model (SEM). Web Semant. Sci. Serv. Agents World Wide Web **9**(2), 128–136 (2011)
33. Yahya, M., Berberich, K., Elbassuoni, S., Ramanath, M., Tresp, V., Weikum, G.: Natural language questions for the web of data. In: EMNLP-CoNLL 2012 (2012)

Human Computation
and Crowdsourcing

Towards Hybrid NER: A Study of Content and Crowdsourcing-Related Performance Factors

Oluwaseyi Feyisetan[✉], Markus Luczak-Roesch, Elena Simperl,
Ramine Tinati, and Nigel Shadbolt

University of Southampton, Southampton, UK
oof1v13@soton.ac.uk
http://www.sociam.org

Abstract. This paper explores the factors that influence the human component in hybrid approaches to named entity recognition (NER) in microblogs, which combine state-of-the-art automatic techniques with human and crowd computing. We identify a set of content and crowdsourcing-related features (number of entities in a post, types of entities, skipped true-positive posts, average time spent to complete the tasks, and interaction with the user interface) and analyse their impact on the accuracy of the results and the timeliness of their delivery. Using Crowd-Flower and a simple, custom built gamified NER tool we run experiments on three datasets from related literature and a fourth newly annotated corpus. Our findings show that crowd workers are adept at recognizing people, locations, and implicitly identified entities within shorter microposts. We expect them to lead to the design of more advanced NER pipelines, informing the way in which tweets are chosen to be outsourced or processed by automatic tools. Experimental results are published as JSON-LD for further use by the research community.

Keywords: Crowdsourcing · Human computation · Named entity recognition · Microposts

1 Introduction

Information extraction is a central component of the Web of Data vision [2]. An important task in this context is the identification of named entities - the people, places, organisations, and dates referred to in text documents - and their mapping to Linked Data URIs [20]. State-of-the-art technology in entity recognition achieves near-human performance for many types of unstructured sources, and most impressively so for well-formed, closed-domain documents such as news articles or scientific publications written in English [14,15]. It has been less successful so far in processing social media content such as microblogs, known for its compact, idiosyncratic style [6]. Human computation and crowdsourcing offer an effective way to tackle these limitations [19], alongside increasingly sophisticated algorithms capitalising on the availability of huge data samples and open knowledge bases such as DBpedia and Freebase [17].

© Springer International Publishing Switzerland 2015
F. Gandon et al. (Eds.): ESWC 2015, LNCS 9088, pp. 525–540, 2015.
DOI: 10.1007/978-3-319-18818-8_32

However, such hybrid approaches to NER (named entity recognition) [6] are far from being the norm. While the technology to define and deploy them is on its way - for instance, tools such as GATE already offer built-in human computation capabilities [18] - little is known about the overall performance of crowd-machine NER workflows and the factors that affect them. Besides various experiments reporting on task design, spam detection, and quality assurance aspects (e.g., [7,19,24]), at the moment we can only guess what features of a micropost, crowd contributor, or microtask platform will have an impact on the success of crowdsourced NER. The situation is comparable to the early stages of information extraction; once the strengths and weaknesses of particular methods and techniques had been extensively studied and understood, the research can then focus on overcoming real issues, propose principled approaches, and significantly advance the state of the art.

This paper is a first in-depth study that examines the factors which influence the performance of the crowd in hybrid NER approaches for microposts. We identify a set of content and crowdsourcing-related features (number of entities in a post, types of entities, skipped true-positive posts, average time spent to complete the tasks, and interaction with the user interface) and analyse their impact on the accuracy of the results and the timeliness of their delivery. We run experiments on three datasets from related literature and a fourth newly annotated corpus using CrowdFlower and our own game-with-a-purpose (GWAP) [21] called Wordsmith.[1]

An analysis of the results reveals that shorter tweets with fewer entities tend to be more amenable to microtask crowdsourcing. This applies in particular to those cases in which the text refers to single people or places entities, even more so when these have been subject to recent news or public debate on social media. Though recommended by some crowdsourcing researchers and platforms, the use of the miscellaneous as a NER category seems to confuse the contributors. However, they are well suited to identify a whole range of entities that were not explicitly targeted by the requester, from people who are less famous to partial, overlapping and what we call *"implicitly named entities"*.

The remainder of this paper is structured as follows: we first discuss the related literature in context of the annotation of micropost data, and review existing proposals to add human and crowd computing features to the task. In Sect. 3 we introduce the research questions and describe the methods, experimental set-up, and data used to address them. We then present our results based on the experiment conducted, and finally discuss the core findings. We expect them to lead to the design of more advanced NER pipelines, informing the way in which tweets are chosen to be outsourced or processed by automatic tools. The results of our experiments are published as JSON-LD for further use by the research community.[2]

---

[1] http://seyi.feyisetan.com/wordsmith.

[2] Download available at https://webobservatory.soton.ac.uk/wo/dataset#54bd90e6c 3d6d73408eb0b88.

2 Preliminaries and Related Work

Several approaches have been applied to build tools for entity extraction, using rules, machine learning, or both [13]. An analysis of the state of the art in named entity recognition and linking on microposts is available in [6]. The authors also discuss a number of factors that affect precision and recall in current technology - current limitations tend to be attributed to the manner of text e.g., vocabulary words, typographic errors, abbreviations and inconsistent capitalisation, see also [8,16].

Crowdsourcing has been previously used to annotate named entities in micropost data [10]. In this study, Finin et al. used CrowdFlower and Amazon's Mechanical Turk as platforms. Crowd workers were asked to identify person (PER), location (LOC) and organisation (ORG) entities. Each task unit consisted of 5 tweets with one gold standard question, with 95 % of the tweets annotated at least twice. The corpus consisted of 4, 400 tweets and 400 gold questions. A review of the results of [10] was carried out and reported in [11]. They observed annotations that showed lack of understanding of context e.g., *china* tagged as LOC when it referred to *porcelain*. They also highlighted the issue of entity drift wherein entities are prevalent in a dataset due to temporal popularity in social media. This adds to the difficulty of named entity recognition [6].

A similar approach has been used to carry out NER tasks on other types of data. Lawson et al. [12] annotated 20, 000 emails using Mechanical Turk. The workers were also required to annotate person (PER), location (LOC), and organisation (ORG) entities. By incorporating a bonus system based on entities found and inter-annotator agreement, they were able to improve their result quality considerably. The results were used to build statistical models for automatic NER algorithms. An application in the medical domain is discussed in [23]. The crowd workers were required to identify and annotate medical conditions, medications, and laboratory tests in a corpus of 35, 385 files. They used a custom interface (just as we do with Wordsmith) and incorporated a bonus system for entities found. Reference [5] proposed a hybrid crowd-machine workflow to identify entities from text and connect them to the Linked Open Data cloud, including a probabilistic component that decides which text to be sent to the crowd for further examination. Other examples of similar systems are [4,18]. Reference [18] also discussed some guidelines for crowdsourced corpus annotation (including number of workers per task, reward system, task quality approach, etc.), elicited from a comparative study.

Compared to the works cited earlier, we perform a quantitative analysis based on controlled experiments designed specifically for the purpose of exploring performance as a function of content and crowdsourcing features. The primary aim of our research is not to implement a new NER framework, but rather to understand how to design better hybrid data processing workflows, with NER as a prominent scenario in which crowdsourcing and human computation could achieve significant impact. In this context the Wordsmith game is seen as a means to outsource different types of data-centric tasks to a crowd and study their behavior, including purpose-built features for quality assurance, spam detection, and personalized interfaces and incentives.

3   Research Questions and Experiment Design

Our basic assumption was that *particular types of microposts will be more amenable to crowdsourcing than others*. Based on this premise, we identified two related research hypotheses, for which we investigated three research questions:

[H1.] Specific features of microposts affect the accuracy and speed of crowdsourced entity annotation.

RQ1.1. How do the following features impact the ability of non-expert crowd contributors to recognize entities in microposts: (a) the number of entities in the micropost; (b) the type of entities in the microposts; (c) the length of micropost text?

[H2.] We can understand crowd worker preferences for NER tasks.

RQ2.1. Can we understand crowd workers preferences based on (a) the number of skipped tweets (which contained entities that could have been annotated); (b) the precision of answers; (c) the amount of time spent to complete the task; (d) the worker interface interaction (via a heatmap)?
RQ2.2. How do these four worker-related dimensions correlate with the content features from RQ1.1?

To address these research questions we ran a series of experiments using Crowd-Flower and our custom-built Wordsmith platform. We used CrowdFlower to seek help from, select, and remunerate microtask workers; each CrowdFlower job included a link to our GWAP, which is where the NER tasks were carried out. Wordsmith was used to gather insight into the features that affect a worker's speed and accuracy in annotating microposts with named entities of four types: people, locations, organisations, and miscellaneous. We describe the game in more detail in Sect. 4

Research data. We took three datasets from related literature, which were also reviewed by [6]. They evaluated NER tools on these corpora, while we are evaluating crowd performance. The choice of datasets ensures that our findings apply to hybrid NER workflow, in which human and machine intelligence would be seamlessly integrated and only a subset of microposts would be subject to crowd-sourcing. The key challenge in these scenarios is to optimize the overall performance by having an informed way to trade-off costs, delays in delivery, and non-deterministic (read, difficult to predict) human behavior for an increase in accuracy. By using the same evaluation benchmarks we make sure we establish a baseline for comparison that allows us not only to learn more about the factors affecting crowd performance, but also about the best ways to combine human and machine capabilities.The three datasets are:

(1) the *Ritter* corpus by [16] which consists of 2, 400 tweets. The tweets were randomly sampled, however the sampling method and original dataset size are unknown. It is estimated that the tweets were harvested around September 2010

(given the publication date and information from [6]). The dataset includes, but does not annotate Twitter @*usernames* which they argued were unambiguous and trivial to identify. The dataset consists of ten entity types.

(2) the *Finin* corpus by [10] consists of 441 tweets which was the gold standard for a crowdsourcing annotation exercise. The dataset includes and annotates Twitter @*usernames*. The dataset annotates only 3 entity types: person, organisation and location. Miscellaneous entity types are not annotated. It is not stated how the corpus was created, however our investigation puts the corpus between August to September 2008.

(3) the Making Sense of Microposts 2013 Concept Extraction Challenge dataset by [3], which includes training, test, and gold data; for our experiments we used the gold subset comprising 1450 tweets. The dataset does not include (and hence, does not annotate) Twitter @*usernames* and #*hashtags*.

We also created and ran an experiment using our own dataset. In previous work of ours we reported on an approach for automatic extraction of named entities with Linked Data URIs on a set of 1.4 billion tweets [8]. From the entire corpus of six billion tweets, we sampled out $3,380$ English ones using *reservoir sampling*. This refers to a family of randomized algorithms for selecting samples of k items (e.g., 20 tweets per day) from a list S (or in our case, 169 days or 6 months from January 2014 to June 2014) of n items (for our dataset, over $30million$ tweets per day), where n is either a very large or an unknown number. In creating this fourth gold standard corpus, we used the NERD ontology [17] to create our annotations, e.g., a school and musical band are both sub-class-of **nerd:Organisation**, but a restaurant and museum, are sub-class-of **nerd:Location**.

The four datasets contain social media content from different time periods (2008, 2010, 2013, 2014) and have been created using varied selection and sampling methods, making the results highly susceptible to entity drift [11]. Furthermore, all four used different entity classification schemes, which we normalized using the mappings from [6]. Table 1 characterizes the data sets along the features we hypothesize might influence crowdsourcing effectivity.

Experimental conditions. We performed one experiment for each dataset, which adds up to $7,665$ tweets. For each tweet we asked the crowd to identify four types of entities (people, locations, organisations, and miscellaneous). We elicited answers from a total of 767 CrowdFlower workers, with three assignments to each task. Each CrowdFlower job referred the workers to a Wordsmith-based task consisting of multiple tweets to be annotated. Each job was awarded 0.05 USD with no bonus. We will discuss these choices in the next section.

Results and methods of analysis. The outcome of the experiments were a set of tweets annotated with entities according to the four categories mentioned earlier. We measured the execution time and compared the accuracy of the crowd inputs against the four benchmarks. By using a number of descriptive statistics to analyse the accuracy of the users performing the task, we were able to compare the precision, recall, F1 scores for entities found within and between the

Table 1. The four datasets used in our experiments

Dataset overview				
Metric	Finin	Ritter	MSM2013	Wordsmith
Corpus size	441	2,400	1,450	3,380
Avg. Tweet length	98.84	102.05	88.82	97.56
Avg. @usernames	0.1746	0.5564	0.00	0.5467
Avg. #hashtags	0.0226	0.1942	0.00	0.2870
No. PER entities	169	449	1,126	2,001
No. ORG entities	162	220	236	390
No. LOC entities	165	373	100	296
No. MISC entities	0	441	95	405
#hashtags annotated	NO	NO	NO	YES
@usernames annotated	YES	NO	NO	YES

four datasets, as well as aggregate the performance of users in order to identify a number of distinguishing behavioural characteristics related NER tasks. Our outcomes are discussed in-light of existing studies in respects to the performance of the crowd and hybrid NER workflows. For each annotation, we measured data points based on mouse movements every 10 ms. Each point had an x and y coordinate value which was normalized based on the worker's screen resolution. These data points were used to generate the heatmaps for our user interface analysis. For each annotation, we also recorded the time between when the worker views the tweet to when the entity details are submitted.

4   Crowdsourcing Approach

Crowdsourcing platform: Wordsmith. As noted earlier, we developed a bespoke human computation platform called *Wordsmith* to crowdsource NER tasks. The platform is designed as a GWAP and sources workers from CrowdFlower. A custom design approach was chosen in order to cater for an advanced entity recognition experience, which could not be obtained using CrowdFlower's default templates and markup language (CML). In addition, Wordsmith allowed us to set up and carry out the different experiments introduced in Sect. 3.

The main interface of Wordsmith is shown in Fig. 1. It consists of three sections. The annotation area is at the center of the screen with sidebars for additional information. The tweet under consideration is presented at the top of the screen with each text token presented as a highlight-able span. The instruction to *'click on a word or phrase'* is positioned above the tweet, with the option to skip the current tweet below it. Custom interfaces in literature included radio buttons by [10] and span selections by [4,12,22]. We opted for a click-and-drag approach in order to fit all the annotation components on the screen (as opposed to [10]) and to cut down the extra type verification step by [4]. By clicking on a tweet

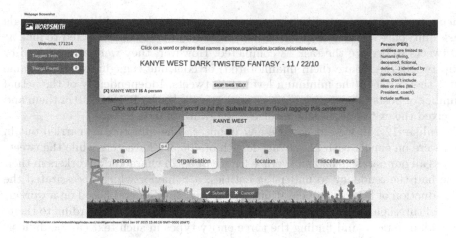

Fig. 1. Wordsmith interface

token(s) the user is presented with a list of connector elements representing the entity text and the entity types. Contextual information is provided in line to guide the user in making the connection to the appropriate entity type. When the type is selected, the type definition is displayed on the right hand side. The left sidebar gives an overview of the number of tweets the user has processed, and the total number of entities found. Once the worker has annotated 10 tweets, an *exit code* appears within the left side bar. This is a mechanism used to signal task completion in CrowdFlower, as we will explain in more detail later.

Recruitment. We sourced the workers for our bespoke system from CrowdFlower. Each worker was invited to engage with a task as shown in Fig. 2, which redirected him/her to Wordsmith. After annotating 10 tweets via the game, the worker was presented with an exit code, which was used to complete the CrowdFlower job. We recruited *Level 2 contributors*, which are top contributors who account for 36 % of all monthly judgements on the CrowdFlower platform [9]. Since we were not using expert annotators, we set the judgement count at 3 answers per unit i.e.,

Identifying Things in Tweets

Instructions ▾

You are required to click here to go to the tagging page:
Type in your Crowdflower ID and tag 10 (TEN) tweets
Only tag tweets you are sure of, if you are unsure, click the SKIP button

Enter the Exit Code here (required)
You would get the exit code after tagging 10 tweets

Fig. 2. CrowdFlower interface

each tweet was annotated by three workers. Each worker could take on a single task unit; once starting annotating in WordSmith, they were expected to look at 10 tweets to declare the task as completed. However, they were also allowed to skip tweets (i.e., leave them unannotated) or continue engaging with the game after they reached the minimum level of 10 tweets. Independently of the actual number of posts tagged with entities, once the worker had viewed 10 of them and received the exit code, he/she receives the reward of 0.05 \$.

Unlike [12,23], we did not use any bonuses. The annotations carried out in [12] were on emails with an average length of 405.39 characters while the tweets across all our datasets had an average length of 98.24 characters. Workers in their case had the tendency to under-tag entities, a behavior which necessitated the introduction of bonus compensations which were limited and based on a worker-agreed threshold. The tasks in [23] use biomedical text, which according to them, '[is] full of jargon, and finding the three entity types in such text can be difficult for non-expert annotators'. Thus, improving recall in these annotation tasks, as opposed to shortened and more familiar text, would warrant a bonus system.

Input data and task model. Each task unit refers to N tweets. Each tweet contains $x = \{0, ..., n\}$ entities. The worker's objective is to decide if the current tweet contains an entity and correctly annotate the tweet with their associated entity types. The entity types were person (PER), location (LOC), organisation (ORG), and miscellaneous (MISC). We chose our entity types based on the types mentioned in the literature of the associated datasets we used. Our task instructions encouraged workers to skip annotations they were not sure of. As we used Wordsmith as task interface, it was also possible for people to continue playing the game and contribute more, though this did not influence the payment. We report on models with adaptive rewards elsewhere [9]; note that the focus here is not on incentives engineering, but on learning about content and crowd characteristics that impact performance. To assign the total set of 7, 665 tweets to tasks, we put them into random bins of 10 tweets, and each bin was completed by three workers.

Annotation guidelines. In each task unit, workers were required to decide whether a tweet contained entities and annotate them. We adopted the annotation guidelines from [10] for person (PER), organisation (ORG) and location (LOC) entity types. We also included a fourth miscellaneous (MISC) type, based on the guidelines from [16]. Instructions were presented at the start of the CrowdFlower job, at the start via the Wordsmith interface and inline during annotation. Whenever a worker is annotating a word (or phrase), the definition of the currently selected entity type is displayed in a side bar.

Output data and quality assurance. Workers were allowed to skip tweets and each tweet was covered by one CrowdFlower job viewed by three workers. Hence, the resulting entity-annotated micropost corpus consisted of all 7, 665 tweets, each with at most three annotations referring to people, places, organisations, and miscellaneous. Each worker had two gold questions presented to them to assess their understanding of the task and their proficiency with the annotation interface. Each gold question tweet consisted of two of the entity types that were to be annotated. The first tweet was presented at the beginning, e.g., *'do you know that Barack Obama is the president of USA'* while the second tweet was presented after the worker had annotated five tweets, e.g., *'my iPhone was made by Apple'*. The workers are allowed to proceed only if they correctly annotate these two tweets.

5   Results

5.1   Analysis of Micropost Features

The first set of results in Table 2 shows precision, recall and F1 values for the four entity types for all four datasets. We also include a confusion matrix highlighting the entity mismatching types e.g., assigning *Cleveland* as location when it refers to the basketball team. The low performance values for the Ritter dataset can be attributed in part to the annotation schema (just as in [6]). For example, the Ritter gold corpus assigns the same entity type *musicartist* to single musicians and group bands. More significantly, the dataset does not annotate Twitter *@usernames* and *#hashtags*. Considering that most *@usernames* identify people and organisations, and the corpus contained 0.55 *@usernames* per tweet (as shown in Table 1), it is not surprising that scores are rather low. The result also shows high precision and low confusion in annotating location entities, while the greatest ambiguities come from annotating miscellaneous ones.

The results for the Finin dataset show higher F1 scores across the board when compared to the Ritter experiments. The dataset did not consider any MISC annotations and although it includes *@usernames* and *@hashtags*, only the *@usernames* are annotated. Here again, the best scores were in the identification of people and places. For the MSM2013 dataset the results show the highest precision and recall scores in identifying PER entities. However, it is important to note that this dataset (as shown in Table 1) contained, on average, the shortest tweets (88 characters). In addition, the URLs, *@usernames* and *#hastags* were anonymized as _URL_, _MENTION_ and _HASHTAG_, hence the ambiguity arising from manually annotating those types was removed. Furthermore, the corpus had a disproportionately high number of PER entities (1, 126 vs. just 100 locations). It also consisted largely of clean, clearly described, properly capitalised tweets, which could have contributed to the precision. Consistent with the results above, the highest scores were in identifying PER and LOC entities while the lowest one was for those entities classified as miscellaneous.

Our own *Wordsmith dataset* achieved the highest precision and recall values in identifying people and places. Again, crowd workers had trouble classifying entities as MISC and significant noise hindered the annotation of ORG instances. A number of ORG entities were misidentified as PER and an equally high number of MISC examples were wrongly identified as ORG. The Wordsmith dataset consisted of a high number of *@usernames* (0.55 per tweet) and the highest concentration of *#hashtags* (0.28 per tweet).

Table 2. *Experiment results* - Named entity recognition on the four datasets.

Ritter dataset

Worker annotations				Confusion matrix (vs gold)			
Entity type	Precision	Recall	F1 score	PER	ORG	LOC	MISC
Person	42.93	**69.19**	52.98	765	7	26	20
Organisation	28.75	39.57	33.30	10	140	62	88
Location	**67.06**	50.07	**57.33**	9	9	751	22
Miscellaneous	20.04	20.23	20.13	15	46	29	217

Finin dataset

Worker annotations				Confusion matrix (vs gold)			
Entity type	Precision	Recall	F1 score	PER	ORG	LOC	MISC
Person	**68.42**	58.96	**63.34**	78	1	7	-
Organisation	50.94	27.84	36.00	1	27	5	-
Location	66.14	**60.71**	63.31	1	4	84	-
Miscellaneous	-	-	-	-	-	-	-

MSM2013 dataset

Worker annotations				Confusion matrix (vs gold)			
Entity type	Precision	Recall	F1 score	PER	ORG	LOC	MISC
Person	**87.21**	**86.61**	**86.91**	3,828	25	8	7
Organisation	43.27	38.77	40.90	16	299	13	28
Location	60.57	67.29	63.75	13	21	321	5
Miscellaneous	10.44	29.11	15.37	12	82	5	91

Wordsmith dataset

Worker annotations				Confusion matrix (vs gold)			
Entity type	Precision	Recall	F1 score	PER	ORG	LOC	MISC
Person	**79.23**	71.41	**75.12**	5,230	34	29	32
Organisation	61.07	53.46	57.01	93	811	30	46
Location	72.01	**72.91**	71.26	25	58	1,078	8
Miscellaneous	27.07	47.43	34.47	50	113	12	718

5.2   Analysis of Behavioral Features of Crowd Workers

The results on the skipped true-positive tweets are presented in Fig. 4. It contains the distribution of the entities present in the posts that were left unannotated in each dataset according to the gold standard. On average across all four experiments, people tend to avoid recognizing organisations, but were more keen in identifying locations. Disambiguating between the two remained challenging across all datasets as evidenced in the confusion matrices in Table 2. Identifying locations such as *London* was a trivial task for contributors, however, entities such as museums, shopping malls, and restaurants were alternately annotated as either

Finin Dataset   Ritter Dataset

MSM2013 Dataset   Wordsmith Dataset

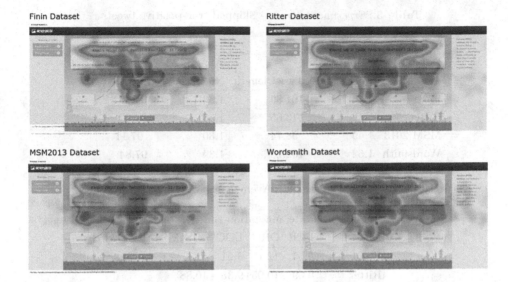

Fig. 3. Wordsmith Heatmaps across the 4 datasets

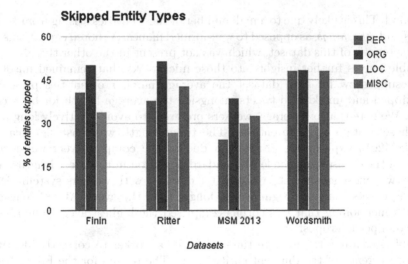

Fig. 4. Skipped tweets

LOC or ORG. Disambiguating tech organisations was not trivial either - that is, distinguishing entities such as Facebook, Instagram, or Youtube as Web applications or independent companies without much context. In the MSM2013 dataset, person entities were least skipped due to the features of the dataset discussed earlier (e.g., clear text definition, consistent capitalisation etc.). In the Wordsmith dataset, however, PER, ORG, and MISC entity tweets were skipped with equal

Table 3. *Experiment results* - Skipped true-positive tweets

Skipped tweets				
Dataset	Skipped		Annotated	
	No. entities	Tweet length	No. entities	Tweet length
Finin	1.56	101.39	1.33	94.82
Ritter	1.42	113.05	1.35	104.22
MSM 2013	1.49	98.74	1.30	97.11
Wordsmith	1.62	102.22	1.39	97.84

Table 4. *Experiment results* - Average accurate annotation time

Average accurate annotation time (seconds)				
Dataset	PER	ORG	LOC	MISC
Finin	9.54	12.15	8.91	-
Ritter	9.69	10.05	9.35	10.88
MSM 2013	9.54	10.77	8.70	10.35
Wordsmith	8.06	8.50	9.56	9.48

likelihood. This is likely due to a high number of these entities arising from *@usernames* and *#hashtags*, as opposed to well-formed names. As noted earlier, this was a characteristic of this dataset, which was not present in the other three.

Table 3 gives further insight into those microtasks that remained unsolved. The results show for each dataset the average number of entities present in the skipped and un-skipped tweets, alongside the average length for both categories. We note that on average, workers preferred to avoid relatively long posts and those containing more entities. The tweet length was least significant in the MSM2013 experiment, once again due to the comparatively well-formed nature of the dataset and the least standard deviation in the tweet lengths. This feature was most significant in the Ritter dataset, with workers systematically skipping tweets that were significantly longer than the average tweet length; it is worth mentioning that this corpus comprised the highest average number of characters per micropost.

Table 4 contains the average time taken for a worker to correctly identify a single occurrence of the different entity types. The results for the Finin, Ritter and MSM2013 datasets consistently show the shortest time needed corresponds to locations, followed by person entities. In the Wordsmith dataset, workers correctly identified people instances in the shortest time overall, however, much longer times were taken to identify places. As discussed earlier, this can be attributed also to entities arising from *@usernames* and *#hashtags*. The other datasets either exclude this or do not annotate it in their gold standards.

Figure 3 shows the result of our datapoint captures via heatmaps. The results show mouse movements concentrated horizontally along the length of the tweet text area. Much activity is also around the screen center where the entity text appears after it is clicked. The heatmaps then diverge in the lower parts of the screen which indicate which entity types were tagged. From a larger image of the interface in Fig. 1, we can reconcile the mouse movements to point predominantly to "PERSON" and "LOCATION" entities in proportions which are consistent with the individual numbers presented in Table 2.

6 Discussion and Conclusion

In this final section we assimilate our results into a number of key themes and discuss their implications on the prospect of hybrid NER approaches that combine automatic tools with human and crowd computing.

Crowds can identify people and places, but more expertise is needed to classify miscellaneous entities. Our analysis clearly showed that microtask workers are best at spotting locations, followed by people, and finally with a slightly larger gap, organisations. When no clear instructions are given, that is, when the entity should be classified as MISC, the accuracy suffers dramatically. Assigning entities as organisations seems to be cognitively more complex than persons and places, probably because it involves disambiguating their purpose in context e.g., universities, restaurants, museums, shopping malls. Many of these entities could also be ambiguously interpreted as products, brands, or even locations, which also raises the question of more refined models to capture diverse viewpoints in annotation gold standards [1].

Crowds perform best on recent data, but remember people. All four analyzed datasets stem from different time periods (Ritter from 2008, Finin from 2010, MSM from 2013, and Wordsmith from 2014). Most significantly one can see that there is a consistent increase of the F1 score the more recent the dataset is, even if the difference is only a couple of months as between the MSM and the Wordsmith cases. We interpret that the more timely the data, the better the performance of crowd workers, possibly due to the fact that newer datasets are more likely to refer to entities that gained public visibility in media and on social networks in recent times and that people remember and recognize easily. This concept known as entity drift was also highlighted by [6, 11]. The only exception for this is the PER entity type, which was the most accurate result for the MSM dataset.

Partial annotations and annotation overlap. The experiments showed a high share of partial annotations by the workers. For example, workers annotated *london fashion week* as *london* and *zune hd* as *zune*. Other partial annotations stemmed from identifying a person's full name, e.g., *Antoine De Saint Exupery* was tagged by all three annotators as *Antoine De Saint*. Overlapping entities occurred when a text could refer to multiple nested entities e.g., *berlin university museum* referring to the university and the museum and *LPGA HealthSouth Inaugural Golf Tournament* which was identified as an organisation and an event.

These findings call for richer gold standards, but also for more advanced means to assess the quality of crowd results to reward partial answers. Such phenomena could also signal the need for more sophisticated microtask workflows, possibly highlighting partially recognized entities to acquire new knowledge in a more targeted fashion, or by asking the crowd in a separate experiment to choose among overlaps or partial solutions.

Spotting implicitly named entities thanks to human reasoning. Our analysis revealed a notable number of entities that were not in the gold standard, but were picked up by the crowd. A manual inspection of these entities in combination with some basic text mining has shown that the largest set of these entities suggest that human users tend to spot unnamed entities (e.g., *prison* or *car*), partial entities (e.g., *apollo* versus *the apollo*), overlapping entities (e.g., *london fashion week* versus *london*), and hashtags (e.g., *#WorldCup2014*). However, the most interesting class of entities which were not in the gold standard but were annotated by the crowd are what we call *implicitly named entities*. Examples such as *hair salon, last stop, in store*, or *bus stop* show that the crowd is good at spotting phrases that refer to real named entities implicitly depending on the context of the post's author or a person or event this one refers to. In many cases, the implicit entities found are contextualised within the micropost message, e.g., *I'll get off at the stop after Waterloo*. This opens up interesting directions for future analysis that focus only on those implicit entities together with features describing their context in order to infer the actual named entity in a human-machine way. By combining text mining and content analysis techniques, it may be possible to derive new meaning from corpora such as those used within this study.

Closing the entity linking loop for the non-famous. Crowd workers have shown good performance in annotating entities that were left out by the gold standards and presented four characteristic classes of such entities (unnamed entities, partial entities, overlapping entities, and hashtags). We observe a fifth class that human participants mark as entities, which refer to non-famous, less well-known people, locations, and organisations (e.g., the name of a person who is not a celebrity). This is an important finding for hybrid entity extraction and linking pipelines, which can benefit from the capability to generate new URIs for yet publicly unknown entities.

Wide search, but centred spot. Our heatmap analysis shows that we had a very wide view along the text axis, and a consistent pattern that the likelihood of annotating in the center is higher even though they seem to search over the entire width of the text field. This correlates with statistics about the average position of the first annotation, which is higher than for the gold standard. This might mean that people are more likely to miss out on annotating entities on the left and right edges of the interface. A resolution could be to centralize the textbox and make it less wide hence constraining the worker's field of vision as opposed to [10] where workers were required to observe vertically to target entities. We cannot fully substantiate this claim yet and reserve this for further work due to the responsive nature of the interface which would have presented the annotation text slightly different on varying screen resolutions and with screen resizings.

Concluding remarks and future work. In this paper we have experimented with a novel approach to finding entities within micropost datasets using crowdsourced methods. Our experiments, conducted on four different micropost datasets, have revealed a number of crowd characteristics with respect to their performance and behaviour of identifying different types of entities. In terms of the wider impact of our study, we consider that our findings will be useful for streamlining and improving hybrid NER workflows, offering an approach that allows corpora to be divided up between machine- and human-led workforces, depending on the types and number of entities to be identified or the length of the tweets. Future work in this area includes devising automated approaches to determining when best to select human or machine capabilities, and also examining *implicitly named entities* in order to develop methods to identify and derive message-related context and meaning.

References

1. Aroyo, L., Welty, C.: Crowd truth: harnessing disagreement in crowdsourcing a relation extraction gold standard. In: WebSci2013. ACM (2013)
2. Auer, S., Bizer, C., Kobilarov, G., Lehmann, J., Cyganiak, R., Ives, Z.G.: DBpedia: a nucleus for a web of open data. In: Aberer, K., et al. (eds.) ISWC/ASWC 2007. LNCS, vol. 4825, pp. 722–735. Springer, Heidelberg (2007)
3. Basave, A.E.C., Varga, A., Rowe, M., Stankovic, M., Dadzie, A.: Making sense of microposts (# msm2013) concept extraction challenge. In: # MSM, pp. 1–15 (2013)
4. Braunschweig, K., Thiele, M., Eberius, J., Lehner, W.: Enhancing named entity extraction by effectively incorporating the crowd. In: BTW Workshops 2013, pp. 181–195 (2013)
5. Demartini, G., Difallah, D.E., Cudré-Mauroux, P.: Zencrowd: leveraging probabilistic reasoning and crowdsourcing techniques for large-scale entity linking. In: Proceedings of the 21st International Conference on World Wide Web, pp. 469–478. ACM (2012)
6. Derczynski, L., Maynard, D., Rizzo, G., van Erp, M., Gorrell, G., Troncy, R., Petrak, J., Bontcheva, K.: Analysis of named entity recognition and linking for tweets. Inf. Process. Manag. **51**(2), 32–49 (2015)
7. Difallah, D.E., Demartini, G., Cudré-Mauroux, P.: Mechanical cheat: spamming schemes and adversarial techniques on crowdsourcing platforms. In: CrowdSearch, pp. 26–30 (2012)
8. Feyisetan, O., Simperl, E., Tinati, R., Luczak-Roesch, M., Shadbolt, N.: Quick-and-clean extraction of linked data entities from microblogs. In: Proceedings of the 10th International Conference on Semantic Systems, SEM 2014, pp. 5–12. ACM (2014)
9. Feyisetan, O., Simperl, E., Van Kleek, M.: Improving paid microtasks through gamification and adaptive furtherance incentives. In: Proceedings of the 24th International Conference on World Wide Web. International World Wide Web Conferences Steering Committee (2015)

10. Finin, T., Murnane, W., Karandikar, A., Keller, N., Martineau, J., Dredze, M.: Annotating named entities in twitter data with crowdsourcing. In: Proceedings of the NAACL HLT 2010 Workshop on Creating Speech and Language Data with Amazon's Mechanical Turk, pp. 80–88. Association for Computational Linguistics (2010)
11. Fromreide, H., Hovy, D., Søgaard, A.: Crowdsourcing and annotating NER for Twitter #drift. European language resources distribution agency (2014)
12. Lawson, N., Eustice, K., Perkowitz, M., Yetisgen-Yildiz, M.: Annotating large email datasets for named entity recognition with mechanical turk. In: Proceedings of the NAACL HLT 2010 Workshop on Creating Speech and Language Data with Amazon's Mechanical Turk, pp. 71–79. Association for Computational Linguistics (2010)
13. Liu, X., Zhang, S., Wei, F., Zhou, M.: Recognizing named entities in tweets. In: Proceedings of the 49th Annual Meeting of the Association for Computational Linguistics: Human Language Technologies, vol. 1, pp. 359–367. ACL (2011)
14. Marrero, M., Sanchez-Cuadrado, S., Lara, J.M., Andreadakis, G.: Evaluation of named entity extraction systems. Adv. Comput. Linguist. Res. Comput. Sci. **41**, 47–58 (2009)
15. Nadeau, D., Sekine, S.: A survey of named entity recognition and classification. Lingvisticae Investigationes **30**(1), 3–26 (2007)
16. Ritter, A., Clark, S., Etzioni, O., et al.: Named entity recognition in tweets: an experimental study. In: Proceedings of the Conference on Empirical Methods in Natural Language Processing, pp. 1524–1534. Association for Computational Linguistics (2011)
17. Rizzo, G., Troncy, R.: Nerd: evaluating named entity recognition tools in the web of data (2011)
18. Sabou, M., Bontcheva, K., Derczynski, L., Scharl, A.: Corpus annotation through crowdsourcing: Towards best practice guidelines. In: Proceedings of LREC (2014)
19. Snow, R., O'Connor, B., Jurafsky, D., Ng, A.Y.: Cheap and fast–but is it good?: evaluating non-expert annotations for natural language tasks. In: Proceedings of the Conference on Empirical Methods in Natural Language Processing, pp. 254–263. Association for Computational Linguistics (2008)
20. Usbeck, R., Ngonga Ngomo, A.-C., Röder, M., Gerber, D., Coelho, S.A., Auer, S., Both, A.: AGDISTIS - graph-based disambiguation of named entities using linked data. In: Mika, P., et al. (eds.) ISWC 2014, Part I. LNCS, vol. 8796, pp. 457–471. Springer, Heidelberg (2014)
21. von Ahn, L., Dabbish, L.: Designing games with a purpose. Commun. ACM **51**(8), 58–67 (2008)
22. Voyer, R., Nygaard, V., Fitzgerald, W., Copperman, H.: A hybrid model for annotating named entity training corpora. In: Proceedings of the Fourth Linguistic Annotation Workshop, pp. 243–246. Association for Computational Linguistics (2010)
23. Yetisgen-Yildiz, M., Solti, I., Xia, F., Halgrim, S.R.: Preliminary experience with amazon's mechanical turk for annotating medical named entities. In: Proceedings of the NAACL HLT 2010 Workshop on Creating Speech and Language Data with Amazon's Mechanical Turk, pp. 180–183. Association for Computational Linguistics (2010)
24. Yuen, M., King, I., Leung, K.: A survey of crowdsourcing systems. In: 2011 IEEE Third International Conference on Privacy, Security, Risk and Trust (Passat) and 2011 IEEE Third International Conference on Social Computing (SocialCom), pp. 766–773. IEEE (2011)

Ranking Entities in the Age of Two Webs, an Application to Semantic Snippets

Mazen Alsarem[1], Pierre-Edouard Portier[1]([✉]), Sylvie Calabretto[1], and Harald Kosch[2]

[1] Université de Lyon, CNRS INSA de Lyon, LIRIS, UMR5205,
69621 Lyon, France
pierre-edouard.portier@insa-lyon.fr
[2] Universität Passau,
Innstr. 43, 94032 Passau, Germany

Abstract. The advances of the Linked Open Data (LOD) initiative are giving rise to a more structured Web of data. Indeed, a few datasets act as hubs (e.g., DBpedia) connecting many other datasets. They also made possible new Web services for entity detection inside plain text (e.g., DBpedia Spotlight), thus allowing for new applications that can benefit from a combination of the Web of documents and the Web of data. To ease the emergence of these new applications, we propose a query-biased algorithm (LDRANK) for the ranking of web of data resources with associated textual data. Our algorithm combines link analysis with dimensionality reduction. We use crowdsourcing for building a publicly available and reusable dataset for the evaluation of query-biased ranking of Web of data resources detected in Web pages. We show that, on this dataset, LDRANK outperforms the state of the art. Finally, we use this algorithm for the construction of semantic snippets of which we evaluate the usefulness with a crowdsourcing-based approach.

1 Introduction

In this work, we introduce LDRANK (see Sect. 4), an efficient query-biased and context-aware ranking algorithm that applies to the resources of a LOD graph. When combined with the automatic annotation of resources in Web pages (e.g. through DBpedia Spotlight [21]), LDRANK offers the opportunity to build useful semantic snippet that can apply to any Web page regardless of its provenance (see Sect. 5). In this introduction, we provide the background information from which the necessity for this new algorithm will appear.

On the web of documents links are indications of a relationship between information carried by the documents. Although these indications are coarse-grained, they revealed themselves as essential for the most-effective ranking algorithms (PageRank [23], HITS [16], SALSA [20]).

On the web of data, links are fine-grained explicit relationships between resources (i.e., URI for things of the phenomenal world, be they mental or physical). The vast majority of the existing ranking strategies for the web of data (see [25] and [15] for recent surveys) are relying on adaptations of PageRank.

© Springer International Publishing Switzerland 2015
F. Gandon et al. (Eds.): ESWC 2015, LNCS 9088, pp. 541–555, 2015.
DOI: 10.1007/978-3-319-18818-8_33

The modifications made to adapt the PageRank algorithm to the web of data are necessary due to the high heterogeneity of both the provenance of the datasets and the types of the relationships. Otherwise, there are also a few experiments with learning-to-rank approaches applied to the web of data (e.g., [6]). These techniques depend on the availability of relevance judgments for training (although indirect measures of correlated quantities can sometimes be used, e.g. the number of visits agents made to a resource).

In order to manage the aforementioned intrinsic heterogeneity of the web of data, the Linked Open Data (LOD) initiative promotes simple principles for publishing resources in a way conducive to a web of linked data with shared knowledge expressed in a common formalism (RDF) and accessible through a common interface (HTTP). As a key use-case, DBpedia has been used in conjunction with NLP strategies in order to associate resources with their surface forms in a text document. The main current applications for this use-case are: DBpedia Spotlight [21], AlchemyAPI[1] (similar to DBpedia Spotlight, but finds resources in various LOD datasets and thus includes a coreference resolution step), OpenCalais (see Footnote 1), SemanticAPI from Ontos (see Footnote 1), ZenCrowd [7].

In this context, we address the problem of ranking resources that come from the automatic annotation of a Web page selected by a web search engine in response to a user query. The main challenge is to make good use of the knowledge given by the query and the Web page's text in order to palliate the sparsity and heterogeneity of the graph of resources. We propose an algorithm, LDRANK, and we compare it to other modified PageRank algorithms. Moreover, we apply it to the construction of semantic snippets[2]. A snippet is an excerpt from a Web page determined at query-time and used to express how a Web page may be relevant to the query. A semantic snippet is meant to improve the process of matching the ranked Web pages presented within a Search Engine Result Page (SERP) with the user's mental model of her information need. It achieves this objective by making apparent the relationships existing between the information need and the more relevant resources present in the Web page.

In Sect. 2 we introduce the related works about enhanced snippets for the web of documents and for the web of data. In Sect. 3, we describe the construction of a dataset for the evaluation query-biased entity ranking algorithms. In Sect. 4 we present the LDRANK algorithm and its evaluation. In Sect. 5, we introduce ENsEN, the software system we developed to provide semantic snippets. In Sect. 6 we present the results of an evaluation of the usefulness of ENsEN.

2   Related Works

We first mention works that generate snippets for native RDF documents. Ge et al. [11], and Penin et al. [24] focus on the generation of snippets for ontology search. Bai et al. [2] generate snippets for a semantic web search engine.

---

[1] www.alchemyapi.com; www.opencalais.com; www.ontos.com.

[2] http://liris.cnrs.fr/drim/projects/ensen/: live demo, source code, technical report, datasets.

In [24], the authors first identify a topic thanks to an off-line hierarchical clustering algorithm. Next, they compute a list of RDF sentences (i.e. sets of connected RDF statements) semantically close to the topic. Finally, they rank the selected RDF statements by considering both structural properties of the RDF graph and lexical features of the terms present in the ontology (by way of a Wordnet-based similarity measure).

In [11], the authors first transform the RDF graph into a term association graph in which each edge is associated with a set of RDF sentences. Their objective is to produce a compact representation of the relationships existing between the terms of the query. These relationships are to be found in the RDF graph. To do this, they decompose the term association graph into maximum r-radius components in order to avoid long distance relations between query terms. Next, they search sub-snippets in these components (i.e. connected subgraphs that link some of the query-terms). Finally, they select some of the sub-snippets to form the final snippet.

In [2], the authors first assign a topic to the RDF document (they use a property such as *p:primaryTopic* if it exists, otherwise they rely on a heuristic based on the comparison of the URI of the candidates topic-nodes with the text of the URL of the RDF document). Next they design a ranking algorithm for RDF statements. Particularly, they introduce the notions of *correlative* (e.g. `foaf:surname` and `foaf:family_name`) and *exclusive* (e.g. `foaf:name` and `foaf:surname`) properties. Finally, they use this ranking algorithm to give the user a set of relationships between the query-related statements and the topic-related statements.

To sum up, we agree with Ge *et al.* [11] that the main benefit of possessing highly structured data from an RDF graph is the possibility to find non-trivial relationships among the query terms themselves, and also between the query terms and the main concepts of the document. Moreover, we agree with Penin *et al.* [24] and Bai *et al.* [2] about the necessity to design a ranking algorithm for RDF statements that considers both the structure of the RDF graph and lexical properties of the textual data. However, we find ourselves in an inverted situation with genuine text extracted from classical Web pages, and RDF graphs automatically generated from these Web pages.

Indeed, LOD resources can either come from: (i) a LOD dataset (e.g. by way of SPARQL queries), (ii) semantic annotations embedded in a Web page (i.e., by using RDFa, Microdata, or Microformats[3]), or (iii) automatic association of resources with surface forms of the Web page by way of NLP strategies (e.g. DBpedia Spotlight [21], ZenCrowd [7],...). Among the approaches that offer to enhance the snippets of a SERP by using the web of data [12] [26], none rely on automatic annotation: they use only embedded annotations. Haas *et al.* [12] employed structured metadata (i.e. RDFa and several microformats) and information extraction techniques (i.e. handwritten or machine-learned wrappers designed for the top host names e.g., en.wikipedia.org, youtube.com,...) to enhance the SERP

---

[3] www.w3.org/TR/xhtml-rdfa-primer/; microformats.org/; www.w3.org/TR/microdata/.

with multimedia elements, key-value pairs and interactive features. By combining metadata authored by the documents' publishers with structured data extracted by ad-hoc wrappers designed for a few top host names, they are able to build enhanced snippets for many results of a SERP. They chose not to use the LOD graph to avoid the problem of the transfer of trust between the Web of documents and the Web of Data. Indeed, they argue that the quality of the editorial processes that produce the Web of Data from the Web of documents (e.g. the transformation from Wikipedia to DBPedia) cannot be controlled. Therefore, from their point of view, making use of the LOD graph for enhancing snippets would introduce too much noise. Also, Google Rich Snippet (GRS) [26] is a similar initiative that relies exclusively on structured metadata authored by the Web pages' publishers.

Moreover, a study made in 2012 [4] on the over 40 million websites of the Common Crawl corpus[4] shows that 5.64 % of the websites contained embedded structured data. However, nearly 50 % of the top 10,000 websites of the Alexa list of popular websites[5] had structured data. Moreover, the authors of the study say that: "The topics of the data [...] seem to be largely determined by the major consumers the data is targeted at: Google, Facebook, Yahoo!, and Bing". Therefore, there is still a clear need for a high quality process that, given a document relevant to a Web search query, can select the most relevant resources among those automatically discovered within the document (e.g., through state of the art NLP algorithms), and this, whatever the document's provenance may be. An efficient algorithm for ranking the resources of a LOD graph while taking into account their textual context could serve this purpose.

However, most of the existing approaches that can be used to rank the resources of graphs coming from the Web of data are not well adapted to this task. Thus, OntologyRank [8] (used by Swoogle) introduces a modified version of PageRank with a teleportation matrix that takes into account the types of the links between ontologies. Similarly, PopRank [22] offers a modified PageRank that considers the different types of predicates between resources. RareRank [28] introduces a modified PageRank with a teleportation matrix that takes into account topical relationships between resources as available from ontologies. The approach introduced in [9] modifies the teleportation matrix by taking into account the ranking of the Web pages within which the resources were discovered. Since this approach can be applied to our context, we include it to our evaluations (see Sect. 4.6). Finally, TRank [27] addresses the task of ranking entity types given an initial entity and its textual context.

Given this context, we introduce LDRANK, a query-biased and context-aware ranking algorithm for LOD resources. Moreover, we apply LDRANK to the construction of generic semantic snippets that can apply to any Web page. In the next section, we introduce how we built a dataset through crowdsourced relevance judgments to evaluate our algorithm, LDRANK.

---

[4] http://commoncrawl.org.

[5] http://www.alexa.com/topsites.

3 Dataset for Evaluating Query-Biased Ranking of LOD Resources

We are interested in query-biased algorithms for the ranking of resources in sparse and heterogeneous LOD graphs associated with a textual context. To our knowledge, there is no evaluation dataset suited to this context (this can be verified for example through a recent survey [25]). Therefore, we used a crowd-sourcing approach for making our evaluation dataset (freely available online[6]). We now describe how this dataset was obtained.

3.1 Data Collection

We took randomly 30 queries from the "Yahoo! Search Query Tiny Sample" offered by Yahoo! Webscope[7]. We submitted the queries to the Google search engine and we kept the top-5 Web pages for each query. For each one of the 150 HTML Web pages, we extracted its main raw textual content by applying the algorithm proposed by Kohlschtter, Fankhauser, and Nejdl [17]. On average, the text we kept for each Web page is made of 467 words. We applied DBpedia Spotlight [21] on these texts to detect resources. There are on average 81 detected resources by Web page.

3.2 Microtasks Generation

Considering the length of our texts, the task of evaluating all the annotations of a Web page would be too demanding. Therefore, we divide this task into smaller "microtasks". A microtask will consist in scoring the relevance of the annotations of a single sentence. We split the text of a Web page into sentences with the ICU BreakIterator algorithm[8]. There are on average 22 sentences by document. Moreover, if a sentence contains more than 10 annotated resources, the work will be split over multiple microtasks. We used the CrowdFlower[9] crowdsourcing platform. It distributes work to contributors in the U.S. and 153 other countries while maintaining quality and controlling costs. It has a global pool of 5 million contributors. A microtask is called a job by CrowdFlower. The design of a job is specified in CML, a markup language provided by CrowdFlower. For each job, we give the worker a short list of instructions about how to complete the job (we tested many formulations until finding a suitable one understood by all workers). We provide the worker with a topic made of a title (the query) and a short text (the sentence). For each resource in the sentence, there is a question asking the worker to evaluate the correctness and the relevance of the annotation. We used the ordinal scale proposed by Järvelin and Kekäläinen when they introduced the DCG graded relevance [13]: irrelevant (0), marginally relevant (1), fairly relevant

---

[6] http://liris.cnrs.fr/drim/projects/ensen/.

[7] http://webscope.sandbox.yahoo.com/catalog.php?datatype=l.

[8] http://icu-project.org/apiref/icu4c/classicu_1_1BreakIterator.html.

[9] http://www.crowdflower.com/.

(2), and highly relevant (3). Each question is associated with a small text that describe the resource (viz. the beginning of its DBpedia abstract). Each job was given to 10 workers. Therefore, for each job we have 10 judgments. Each job was paid $.01.

3.3 Quality Control

We only accepted workers that had completed over a hundred questions across a variety of job types and had an high overall accuracy. Workers had a maximum of 30 min to provide an answer. Workers had to spend at least 10 s on the job before giving an answer. We measured the agreement between workers with the Krippendorff's alpha coefficient [18]. This coefficient uses by default a binary distance to compare answers, but other distances can be used. To take into account the fact that we used an ordinal scale encoding both correctness and relevance, we used the following symmetric distance: $d(0,1) = 0.5$; $d(0,2) = 0.75$; $d(0,3) = 1$; $d(1,2) = 0.25$; $d(1;3) = 0.5$; $d(2;3) = 0.25$; $d(x,x) = 0$. With these parameters, we obtained an alpha of 0.22. According to Landis and Koch's scale [19], this can be considered a fair agreement (the scale was designed for Fleiss' kappa, but the Krippendorff's alpha is in most ways compatible with the kappa). However, by comparison with existing works that applied crowdsourcing to an information retrieval context, we cannot be satisfied with an alpha of 0.22. For example, Jeong et al. [14] obtained a Fleiss' kappa of 0.41 (i.e. moderate agreement) for a crowd-powered socially embedded search engine. However, Alonso, Marshall, and Najork [1] obtained a Krippendorff's alpha between 0.03 and 0.19 for a more subjective task: deciding if a tweet is or is not interesting. To improve the quality of our dataset, we found the workers that often disagreed with the majority. In fact, by removing the workers that disagree with the majority in more than 41.2 % of the cases, we obtained a Krippendorff's alpha of 0.46. Then, 96.5 % of the jobs are done by at least 3 workers, 66 % of the jobs are done by at least 5 workers, and we have only 0.7 % of the jobs done by only 1 worker.

3.4 Aggregation of the Results

We used majority voting for aggregating the results within each sentence. We used two different methods to break ties : (i) the maximum of the mean of the workers' trust (a metric provided by CrowdFlower), or (ii) the highest value. We discovered later that these two choices result in very similar outcomes when the dataset is used to compare ranking algorithms. We used the same majority voting strategy to aggregate the results at the level of a Web page.

In the next section, we introduce LDRANK, a query-biased ranking algorithm for LOD resources. The dataset we just described will be used in Sect. 4.6 to evaluate LDRANK and to compare it to the state of the art.

4   LDRANK, a Query-Biased Ranking Algorithm for LOD Resources

4.1   Context

We introduce LDRANK (Linked Data Ranking Algorithm), a quey-biased algorithm for ranking the resources of a RDF graph. We suppose that the resources were discovered in a Web page found by a Web search engine in answer to a user's query.

In our experiments, the resources are detected in the Web page by DBpedia Spotlight [21]. From this set of resources and through queries to a DBpedia SPARQL endpoint, we obtain a graph by finding all the relationships between the resources. To each resource, we associate a text obtained by merging its DBpedia abstract and windows of text (300 characters) from the Web page centered on the surface forms associated with the resource. We remove the empty words and we apply stemming[10] to this text.

LDRANK is adapted by design to such sparse graphs of LOD resources detected in a Web page. First, LDRANK uses the explicit structure of the graph through a PageRank-like algorithm; second, it uses the implicit relationships that can be inferred from the text associated with the resources through an original variation of the Singular Value Decomposition (SVD); and third, it takes into account the ranking of the Web pages where the resources were found thanks to a scoring function first introduced by Fafalios and Tzitzikas [9].

More precisely, the SVD-based textual analysis and the exploitation of the ranking obtained from a Web search engine result page, each produce a different probability vector expressing some prior knowledge (or belief) about the importance of the resources (see Sects. 4.2 and 4.3). Next, these probability vectors are combined through a consensual linear opinion aggregation strategy first introduced by Carvalho and Larson [5] (see Sect. 4.4). Finally, we use this combined prior knowledge to influence the convergence of a PageRank-like algorithm towards a stable probability distribution corresponding to the final ranking of the resources (see Sect. 4.5).

4.2   Prior Knowledge Based on a Web Search Engine Result Page

Algorithm H (Hit Score). This algorithm computes a probability vector (*hitdistrib*) that represents prior knowledge about the importance of the resources based on the rank of the Web pages in which they were detected. This strategy was first introduced by Fafalios and Tzitzikas [9].

H1. $A \leftarrow$ the list of the top Web pages ranked by a Web search engine.
H2. $E \leftarrow$ the set of detected resources.
H3. $docs(e) \equiv$ the documents of A containing the detected resources e.
H4. $rank(a) \equiv$ the rank of document a in A.

---

[10] http://snowball.tartarus.org.

H5. $hitscore(e) \equiv \sum_{a \in docs(e)} (size(A) + 1) - rank(a)$

H6. $hitdistrib[e] \leftarrow hitscore(e) / \sum_{e' \in E} hitscore(e')$

H7. [*End.*] ∎

4.3 Prior Knowledge Based on a Latent Analysis of Textual Data

Algorithm S (Linked Data Iterative SVD). This algorithm computes a probability vector (*svddistrib*) that represents prior knowledge about the importance
of the resources based on the textual data associated to them.

S1. [*Initial matrix.*] $R \leftarrow$ the sparse resource-stem matrix (i.e., resources in
rows, stems in columns) in Compressed Column Storage (CCS) format[11].

S2. [*Initial important resources.*] $info\_need \leftarrow$ a set of resources made of
the union of the resources detected in the text of the query and the
one resource with the best hitscore (for the case when no resources were
detected in the query). We assume that these resources are likely to be
close to the information need of the user.

S3. [*First SVD.*] $(U, S, V^T) \leftarrow svdLAS2A(R, nb\_dim)$ Compute the singular
value decomposition (SVD) of R at rank $k = nb\_dim$. Since R is very
sparse, we use the *las2* algorithm developed by Michael W. Berry [3] to
compute the decomposition: $R_k = U_k S_k V_k^T$ with U_k and V_k orthogonal,
S_k diagonal, such that $\|R - R_k\|_F$ is minimized (i.e. from the perspective
of the Frobenius norm, R_k is the best rank-k approximation of R).

S4. [*Resources' coordinates in the reduced space.*] $SUT \leftarrow SU^T$ In the new
k-dimensional space, this operation scales the coordinates of the resources
(i.e. the rows of U) by their corresponding factor in S. This is done by the
matrix product: SU^T. Thus, we obtain the coordinates of the resources in
the reduced space (i.e. the columns of SUT).

S5. $prev\_norms \leftarrow$ euclidean norms of the resources in the reduced space.

S6. [*Updated matrix.*] $R' \leftarrow R$ where the rows corresponding to the resources
of $info\_need$ have been multiplied by the parameter *stress* (since R is in
CCS format, it is more convenient to do this operation on the transpose
of R).

S7. [*Second SVD.*] $(U', S', V'^T) \leftarrow svdLAS2A(R', nb\_dim)$

S8. [*Updated resources' coordinates in the reduced space.*] $SUT' \leftarrow S'U'^T$

S9. $norms \leftarrow$ updated euclidean norm of the resources in the reduced space.

S10. [*Drift of the resources away from the origin of the reduced space.*]
$svdscore(e) \equiv norms[e] - prev\_norms[e]$.

S11. $svddistrib[e] \leftarrow svdscore(e) / \sum_{e'} svdscore(e')$

S12. [*End.*] ∎

We shall now introduce the essential property of the SVD on which relies
Algorithm S. For a strong dimensional reduction (i.e. for small values of k), the
transformation $S_k U^T$ tends to place resources that were orthogonal to many

---

[11] http://netlib.org/linalg/html_templates/node92.html.

other resources in the row space of R near the origin of the k-dimensional result-ing space. Indeed, as we said above, the SVD can be seen as an optimization algorithm, and to minimize the error due to the impossibility for a resource to be orthogonal to more than k non co-linear resources, this resource should be placed as close to the origin as possible for its dot product with other resources to remain small. A similar argument can be used to show that resources co-linear to many other resources in the row space of R will also tend to be near the origin of the k-dimensional space.

Algorithm S uses this property for ranking the resources by their impor-tance relatively to the user's information need. In R' the resources that are believed to be close to the information need are given artificially more impor-tance. Therefore, resources having interesting relationships with the resources artificially pushed away from the origin will also move away from the origin. By "interesting", we mean different from the relationships they maintain with much of the other resources (cf. the geometric argument developed above about the SVD seen as an optimization algorithm).

We obtained the best experimental results with a reduction to the 1 dimen-sional line (i.e. with $nb\_dim = 1$ in steps S3 and S7 of Algorithm S), and with a stress factor (step S6 of Algorithm S) of 1000.0.

4.4 Belief Aggregation Strategy

We consider $hitdistrib$ (from Algorithm H), $svddistrib$ (from Algorithm S), and the equiprobable distribution ($equidistrib$) as three experts' beliefs (or prior knowledge) about the importance of the resources. To aggregate these beliefs, we apply Carvalho and Larson [5] consensual linear opinion pool algorithm. It is an iterative algorithm where at each step expert i re-evaluates its distribution as a linear combination of the distributions of all the experts. The weight asso-ciated by expert i to the distribution of expert j is proportional to the distance between the two distributions. The authors define this distance such that the process converges towards a consensus. We will refer to this resulting consensual probability vector by the name $finaldistrib$.

4.5 LDRANK

The PageRank [23] algorithm transforms the adjacency matrix (M) of a net-work of Web pages into a matrix H which is both stochastic (i.e., each row of H sums to 1) and primitive (i.e., $\exists k$ s.t. $H^k > 0$), thus assuring the existence of a stationary vector (i.e., the positive eigenvector corresponding to the eigen-value 1). This stationary vector is a probability vector that can been interpreted as representing the importance of each Web page. Moreover, it can be computed efficiently with the power iteration algorithm by taking into account the sparsity of the stochastic matrix.

In the original version of the PageRank algorithm, no assumption is made about the probability of importance of the Web pages before the link analysis takes place. In other words: first, the matrix M is transformed into a stochastic matrix S by replacing each null row by the equiprobable distribution ($equidistrib$); second, the matrix S is transformed into a primitive matrix H by a linear combination with the so-called teleportation matrix (T): $H = \alpha S + (1 - \alpha)T$ where each row of T is the equiprobable distribution ($equidistrib$).

In algorithm LDRANK, instead of using the equiprobable distribution, we use the consensual distribution ($finaldistrib$) introduced above in Sect. 4.4. We obtained the best experimental results for $0.6 \leq \alpha \leq 0.8$. Moreover, we set at $1E - 10$ the value of the convergence threshold controlling the termination of the power iteration method that computes the stationary vector.

LDRANK is available online under an open-source license[12].

4.6 LDRANK Evaluation

We compared four ranking strategies, each one of them is based on a different source of prior knowledge used to inform a PageRank-like algorithm: unmodified PageRank i.e., prior knowledge about the importance of the resources is modeled by an equiprobable distribution (we name this strategy EQUI); PageRank modified with the hitscore prior knowledge introduced in Sect. 4.2 and due to Fafalios and Tzitzikas [9] (named HIT); PageRank modified with our new SVD-based prior knowledge introduced in Sect. 4.3 (named SVD); and PageRank modified with a consensual mixture of the three previous sources of prior knowledge (named LDRANK).

In order to compare the four strategies (EQUI, HIT, SVD and LDRANK), we used the NDCG (Normalized Discounted Cumulative Gain) metric. The DCG (Discounted Cumulative Gain) at rank r is defined as: $DCG_r = rel_1 + \sum_{i=1}^{r} \frac{rel_i}{log_2 i}$. NDCG at rank r is DCG at rank r normalized by the ideal ranking at rank r. The construction of the dataset used for the evaluation was introduced in Sect. 3.

The results are presented in Fig. 1. We can see that the SVD and HIT strategies obtain similar performances. However, they are clearly outperformed by their consensual combination. Moreover, since we systematically took into account the sparsity of the data, we obtain good execution time performances (see Fig. 2). The SVD strategy takes more time than the HIT strategy since it needs to compute the SVD. The additional time spent by the combined strategy is due to the time necessary to converge towards a consensus. Finally, we did similar experiments by considering the edges of the graph bidirectional. The relative performance and accuracy of the algorithms were similar, but the absolute NDCG scores were slightly better.

It should be noted that through these experiments, beside introducing a new efficient ranking strategy based on an original use of the SVD dimensionality reduction, we are also offering evidence that different strategies based on a modification of the teleportation matrix of the PageRank algorithm can profitably be combined when considered as concurrent sources of prior knowledge about the importance of the resources.

---

[12] Source code available online under an opensource license http://liris.cnrs.fr/drim/projects/ensen/.

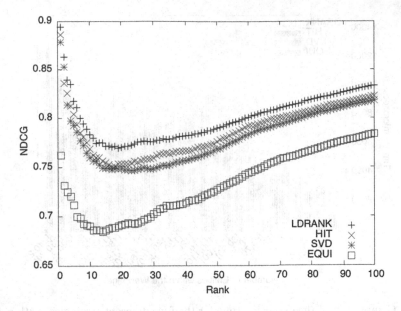

Fig. 1. Comparison of the NDCG scores for the four different strategies

5   Overview of ENsEN

In order to better convince the reader of the usefulness and efficiency of
LDRANK, we used it at the core of ENsEN (Enhanced Search Engine): a software system that enhances a SERP with semantic snippets (a live demonstration is available online, see a previous footnote for the URL). Given the query,
we obtain the SERP (we used Google for our experiments). For each result of
the SERP, we use DBpedia Spotlight to obtain a set of DBpedia resources.
In the same way, we find resources from the terms of the query. From this set
of resources and through queries to a DBpedia SPARQL endpoint, we obtain a
graph by finding all the relationships between the resources. To each resource, we
associate a text obtained by merging its DBpedia's abstract and windows of text
from the Web page centered on the surface forms associated with the resource.
With as input the graph, its associated text, and the resources extracted from
the query, we execute LDRANK and we obtain a ranking of the resources. The
top-ranked resources (viz. "main-resources") are displayed on the snippet. From
a DBpedia SPARQL endpoint, we do a 1-hop extension of the main-resources
in order to increase the number of triples among which we will then search for
the more important ones. To do this, we build a 3-way tensor from the extended
graph: each predicate corresponds to an horizontal slice that represents the adjacency matrix for the restriction of the graph to this predicate. We compute the
PARAFAC decomposition of the tensor into a sum of factors (rank-one three-
way tensors) and interpret it in manner similar to [10]: for each main-resource,
we select the factors to which it contributes the most (as a subject or as an

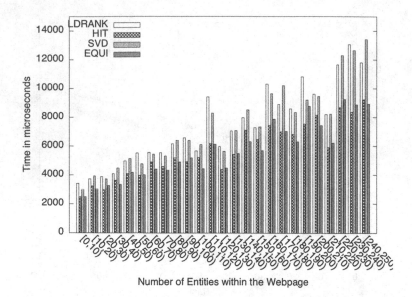

Fig. 2. Comparison of the execution time for the four different strategies (with processor: 2.9 GHz Intel Core i7, and memory: 8 GB 1600 MHz DDR3)

object), and for each one of these factors we select the triples with the best ranked predicates. Thus, we associate to each main-resource a set of triples that will appear within its description. Finally, we used a machine learning approach to select short excerpts of the Web page to be part of the description of each main-resource. In the context of this paper, for lack of space, we cannot describe this process but full details are available in an online technical report (see a previous footnote for the URL).

6   Crowdsourcing-Based User Evaluation

We selected randomly 10 tasks from the "Yahoo! Answers Query To Questions" dataset[13]. Each task was made of three questions on a common topic. To each task corresponds a job on the CrowdFlower platform. Each job was priced $0.20. We collected 20 judgments for each task. Half of the workers was asked to use our system, and the other half used Google. In order to control that a worker answered the task by using our system, we generated a code that the worker had to copy and paste into her answer. The correctness results are shown on Fig. 3. Only complete answers were considered correct. We also monitored the time spent to answer the tasks (see Fig. 4). Thus, ENsEN is clearly beneficial to its users in terms of usefulness.

---

[13] http://webscope.sandbox.yahoo.com/catalog.php?datatype=l.

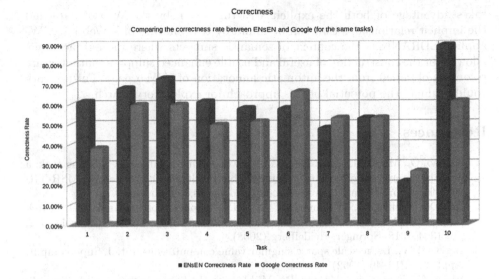

Fig. 3. Average number of correct answers

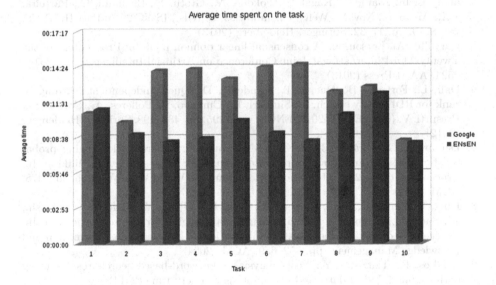

Fig. 4. Time spent for answering the tasks

7 Conclusion

We proposed a new algorithm, LDRANK, for ranking the resources of a sparse
LOD RDF graph given the knowledge of a user's information need expressed
as a query made of keywords. These kind of graphs appear in particular as
the result of the automatic detection of resources in a Web page. LDRANK

takes advantage of both the explicit structure given by the Web of data and the implicit relationships that can be found by text analysis of a Web page. We applied LDRANK in the context of semantic snippets where its high accuracy allowed for the construction of useful and usable enhanced snippets that integrate resources obtained from the automatic annotation of a Web page. Future work could evaluate the potential of this approach for exploratory search.

References

1. Alonso, O., Marshall, C., Najork, M.: Crowdsourcing a subjective labeling task: a human-centered framework to ensure reliable results. Technical report, MSR-TR-2014-91. http://research.microsoft.com/apps/pubs/default.aspx
2. Bai, X., Delbru, R., Tummarello, G.: RDF snippets for semantic web search engines. In: Meersman, R., Tari, Z. (eds.) OTM 2008, Part II. LNCS, vol. 5332, pp. 1304–1318. Springer, Heidelberg (2008)
3. Berry, M.W.: Large-scale sparse singular value computations. Int. J. Supercomput. Appl. **6**(1), 13–49 (1992)
4. Bizer, C., Eckert, K., Meusel, R., Mühleisen, H., Schuhmacher, M., Völker, J.: Deployment of RDFa, microdata, and microformats on the web – a quantitative analysis. In: Alani, H., Kagal, L., Fokoue, A., Groth, P., Biemann, C., Parreira, J.X., Aroyo, L., Noy, N., Welty, C., Janowicz, K. (eds.) ISWC 2013, Part II. LNCS, vol. 8219, pp. 17–32. Springer, Heidelberg (2013)
5. Carvalho, A., Larson, K.: A consensual linear opinion pool. In: Proceedings of the Twenty-Third international Joint Conference on Artificial Intelligence, pp. 2518–2524. AAAI Press (2013)
6. Dali, L., Fortuna, B., Duc, T.T., Mladenić, D.: Query-independent learning to rank for RDF entity search. In: Simperl, E., Cimiano, P., Polleres, A., Corcho, O., Presutti, V. (eds.) ESWC 2012. LNCS, vol. 7295, pp. 484–498. Springer, Heidelberg (2012)
7. Demartini, G., Difallah, D.E., Cudré-Mauroux, P.: Zencrowd: leveraging probabilistic reasoning and crowdsourcing techniques for large-scale entity linking. In: Proceedings of the 21st International Conference on World Wide Web, pp. 469–478. ACM (2012)
8. Ding, L., Finin, T., Joshi, A., Pan, R., Cost, R.S., Peng, Y., Reddivari, P., Doshi, V., Sachs, J.: Swoogle: a search and metadata engine for the semantic web. In: Proceedings of the Thirteenth ACM International Conference on Information and Knowledge Management, pp. 652–659. ACM (2004)
9. Fafalios, P., Tzitzikas, Y.: Post-analysis of keyword-based search results using entity mining, linked data, and link analysis at query time (2014)
10. Franz, T., Schultz, A., Sizov, S., Staab, S.: Triplerank: ranking semantic web data by tensor decomposition. In: Bernstein, A., Karger, D.R., Heath, T., Feigenbaum, L., Maynard, D., Motta, E., Thirunarayan, K. (eds.) ISWC 2009. LNCS, vol. 5823, pp. 213–228. Springer, Heidelberg (2009)
11. Ge, W., Cheng, G., Li, H., Qu, Y.: Incorporating compactness to generate term-association view snippets for ontology search. Inf. Process. Manage. **49**, 513–528 (2013)
12. Haas, K., Mika, P., Tarjan, P., Blanco, R.: Enhanced results for web search. In: Proceedings of the 34th International ACM SIGIR Conference on Research and Development in Information Retrieval, pp. 725–734. ACM (2011)

13. Järvelin, K., Kekäläinen, J.: Ir evaluation methods for retrieving highly relevant documents. In: Proceedings of the 23rd Annual International ACM SIGIR Conference on Research and Development in Information Retrieval, pp. 41–48. ACM (2000)

14. Jeong, J.W., Morris, M.R., Teevan, J., Liebling, D.J.: A crowd-powered socially embedded search engine. In: ICWSM (2013)

15. Jindal, V., Bawa, S., Batra, S.: A review of ranking approaches for semantic search on web. Inf. Process. Manage. **50**(2), 416–425 (2014)

16. Kleinberg, J.M.: Authoritative sources in a hyperlinked environment. J. ACM (JACM) **46**(5), 604–632 (1999)

17. Kohlschütter, C., Fankhauser, P., Nejdl, W.: Boilerplate detection using shallow text features. In: Proceedings of the Third ACM International Conference on Web search and Data Mining, pp. 441–450. ACM (2010)

18. Krippendorff, K.: Content analysis: An introduction to Its Methodology. Sage, Thousand Oaks (2012)

19. Landis, J.R., Koch, G.G.: The measurement of observer agreement for categorical data. Biometrics **33**, 159–174 (1977)

20. Lempel, R., Moran, S.: Salsa: the stochastic approach for link-structure analysis. ACM Trans. Inf. Syst. (TOIS) **19**(2), 131–160 (2001)

21. Mendes, P.N., Jakob, M., García-Silva, A., Bizer, C.: Dbpedia spotlight: shedding light on the web of documents. In: Proceedings of the 7th International Conference on Semantic Systems, pp. 1–8. I-Semantics 2011, ACM (2011)

22. Nie, Z., Zhang, Y., Wen, J.R., Ma, W.Y.: Object-level ranking: bringing order to web objects. In: Proceedings of the 14th International Conference on World Wide Web, pp. 567–574. ACM (2005)

23. Page, L., Brin, S., Motwani, R., Winograd, T.: The pagerank citation ranking: bringing order to the web (1999)

24. Penin, T., Wang, H., Tran, T., Yu, Y.: Snippet generation for semantic web search engines. In: Domingue, J., Anutariya, C. (eds.) ASWC 2008. LNCS, vol. 5367, pp. 493–507. Springer, Heidelberg (2008)

25. Roa-Valverde, A.J., Sicilia, M.A.: A survey of approaches for ranking on the web of data. Inf. Retrieval **17**, 1–31 (2014)

26. Steiner, T., Troncy, R., Hausenblas, M.: How google is using linked data today and vision for tomorrow. In: Proceedings of Linked Data in the Future Internet 700 (2010)

27. Tonon, A., Catasta, M., Demartini, G., Cudré-Mauroux, P., Aberer, K.: TRank: ranking entity types using the web of data. In: Alani, H., Kagal, L., Fokoue, A., Groth, P., Biemann, C., Parreira, J.X., Aroyo, L., Noy, N., Welty, C., Janowicz, K. (eds.) ISWC 2013, Part I. LNCS, vol. 8218, pp. 640–656. Springer, Heidelberg (2013)

28. Wei, W., Barnaghi, P., Bargiela, A.: Rational research model for ranking semantic entities. Inf. Sci. **181**(13), 2823–2840 (2011)

In-Use and Industrial Track

Troubleshooting and Optimizing Named Entity Resolution Systems in the Industry

Panos Alexopoulos$^{(\boxtimes)}$, Ronald Denaux, and Jose Manuel Gomez-Perez

Expert System Iberia, Madrid, Spain
{palexopoulos,rdenaux,jmgomez}@expertsystem.com

Abstract. Named Entity Resolution (NER) is an information extraction task that involves detecting mentions of named entities within texts and mapping them to their corresponding entities in a given knowledge resource. Systems and frameworks for performing NER have been developed both by the academia and the industry with different features and capabilities. Nevertheless, what all approaches have in common is that their satisfactory performance in a given scenario does not constitute a trustworthy predictor of their performance in a different one, the reason being the scenario's different characteristics (target entities, input texts, domain knowledge etc.). With that in mind, in this paper we describe a metric-based Diagnostic Framework that can be used to identify the causes behind the low performance of NER systems in industrial settings and take appropriate actions to increase it.

1 Introduction

Information Extraction (IE) involves the automatic extraction of structured information from texts, such as entities and their relations, in an effort to make the information of these texts more amenable to applications related to Question Answering, Information Access and the Semantic Web. In turn, Named Entity Resolution (NER) is an IE subtask that involves detecting mentions of named entities within texts (e.g. people, organizations or locations) and mapping them to their corresponding entities in a given knowledge source. The typical problem in this task is ambiguity, i.e. the situation that arises when a term may refer to multiple different entities. For example, the term "Tripoli" may refer, among others, to the capital of Libya or to the city of Tripoli in Greece. Deciding which reference is the correct one is the primary challenge for NER systems.

In the last years, systems and frameworks for performing NER have been developed both by the academia and the industry with different features and capabilities [1,5–8,10,15]. These systems typically vary in a number of dimensions, including the type of background domain knowledge they utilize (annotated corpora, thesauri, ontologies etc.), the algorithms they apply, and their customization capabilities, i.e., the ability provided to the user to change key parameters of the system so as to adapt it to his/her particular domain and/or application scenario. Moreover, the effectiveness of several NER systems has been

© Springer International Publishing Switzerland 2015
F. Gandon et al. (Eds.): ESWC 2015, LNCS 9088, pp. 559–574, 2015.
DOI: 10.1007/978-3-319-18818-8_34

empirically measured and reported in their respective scientific publications as well as in dedicated evaluation papers [4,14].

In our opinion, the most interesting aspect of these evaluations is not so much the absolute precision and recall scores that each system achieves but rather the volatility of these scores as the characteristics of the problem (texts to be analyzed, available domain knowledge etc.) change. For example, in [6] the effectiveness of the AIDA NER system is found to be 83 % on the AIDA-YAGO2 dataset and 62 % on Reuters-21578. Similarly, in [10], the effectiveness of DBPedia Spotlight is found to be 81 % when applied on a set of 155,000 wikilink samples and 56 % on a set of 35 paragraphs from New York Times documents. In another paper [15] Spotlight achieves an F1 score of 34 % on the AIDA/CO-NLL-TestB dataset (created in [6]). Finally, the AGDISTIS system [15] scores 76 % on the AQUAINT dataset (created in [12]), 60 % on the AIDA/CO-NLL-TestB dataset and 31 % on the IITB dataset (created in [9]).

What these scores illustrate is that **a NER system's satisfactory performance in a given scenario does not constitute a trustworthy predictor of its performance in a different one**. Or, to put it differently, it's always likely that the system will perform poorly when the scenario's characteristics change. This is an important ramification for developers of NER solutions in the industry as commercial clients typically expect a high and consistent performance from the systems they pay for. Thus, a question that naturally arises is the following: **If in a given NER scenario the system's effectiveness is found to be low, what can be done in order to increase it?**

In an effort to answer this question we describe in this paper a **NER Diagnostic Framework** that consists of a set of metrics that quantify particular aspects of both the problem and the solution applied in a given scenario (such as for example the quality of the system's knowledge base). The idea is that via the calculation and interpretation of these metrics, NER developers are able to identify the most likely causes of their system's low performance and act on this information in order to increase it. In this paper we describe in detail the framework's metrics and we provide illustrative examples of their application and usefulness in a number of concrete cases.

The structure of the rest of the paper is as follows. In the next section we provide a high-level view of the way NER systems work and we use this view in order to identify the potential reasons why such systems might not be effective. In Sect. 3 we define a set of metrics that can be used to troubleshoot a NER system, i.e., to determine (i) which of these reasons and to what extent apply in a given scenario and (ii) the necessary actions for dealing with these reasons and reducing their effect. Section 4, in turn, describes how the application of the diagnostic framework enabled us to achieve significantly increased NER effectiveness in two different cases. Finally, in Sects. 5 and 6 we make a critical discussion of our work, summarize its key aspects and outline the potential directions it could take in the future.

2   NER Systems and Their Effectiveness

2.1   Anatomy of a NER System

As suggested in the introduction, a NER system detects mentions of entities in texts and maps them unambiguously to their corresponding entities in a given knowledge resource. To do that, the system typically utilizes four types of input (Fig. 1):

1. A set of texts on which NER is to be performed.
2. A set of target entities which are to be detected and disambiguated.
3. An entity thesaurus where each entity is associated to a unique identifier and a set of potential surface forms.
4. Some knowledge resource to serve as contextual evidence for the disambiguation of ambiguous entity mentions in the texts.

The latter input is derived from the strong contextual hypothesis of Miller and Charles [11] according to which terms with similar meanings are often used in similar contexts. For a given entity, such a context usually consists of (i) the words that "surround" the entity in some reference text [3,10] and/or (ii) the entities that are related to this entity in some knowledge graph [6,8,15]. Thus, for example, a disambiguation context for the entity "Larry Page" could be entities like "Google" and "PageRank" whereas for the entity "Jimmy Page" entities like "Led Zeppelin" and "Hard Rock". Consequently, knowledge resources that contain such contexts (and thus used by NER systems) are texts that are already annotated with these entities (e.g., wikipedia articles) as well as entity-related knowledge graphs (e.g., DBPedia[1] or YAGO[2]). Given these inputs, a NER system works in two steps:

- **Step 1:** The entity thesaurus and some NLP framework (e.g., GATE[3]) are used to extract from the texts terms that possibly refer to entities. The result is a set of terms, each associated to a set of candidate entities.
- **Step 2:** The contextual evidence knowledge resource is used to determine for each term the most probable entity it refers to (disambiguation).

In the second step, when the evidence knowledge resource consists of annotated texts, disambiguation is performed by calculating the similarity between the term's textual context in the input text and the contexts of its candidate entities in the annotated texts. When the contextual evidence is a knowledge graph then graph-related measures are employed to determine the similarity between the graph formed by the entities found within the ambiguous term's textual context and the sub-graphs formed by each candidate entity's "neighbor" entities. In all cases, the candidate entity with the most similar context is assumed to be the correct one.

---

[1] http://dbpedia.org.

[2] www.mpi-inf.mpg.de/yago-naga/yago/.

[3] http://gate.ac.uk/.

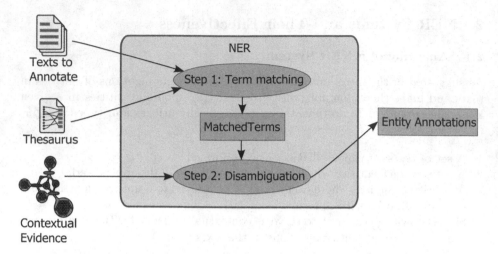

Fig. 1. Anatomy of a NER system, including inputs, processing steps and output.

2.2 When NER Effectiveness is Low and Why

Effectiveness of NER systems is typically measured in terms of *precision* and *recall*. Precision is determined by the fraction of correctly resolved terms (i.e., terms for which the entity with the highest confidence is the correct one) to the total number of detected terms (i.e., terms with at least one associated entity). Recall, on the other hand, is determined by the fraction of correctly resolved terms to the total number of existing entity mentions in the input texts. Thus, a NER system has **low precision** if the input texts do not really contain (most of) the system-assigned entities. This usually happens when:

- There is a **high degree of ambiguity**, i.e., many entities from the thesaurus are (wrongly) associated to many text terms.
- The **contextual knowledge is inadequate** to correctly fulfil the disambiguation of terms. For example, if a text contains the term "Page" as a reference to the entity "Jimmy Page" and the contextual evidence knowledge resource has no information about this entity, then the disambiguation will most likely fail.

On the other hand, a NER system has **low recall** when it fails to detect entities in the texts that are actually there. This may happen in two cases:

- When the **thesaurus is incomplete** by not containing either several of the target entities or adequate surface forms for them (e.g., the thesaurus may not associate the surface form "Red Devils" to the football team of Manchester United).
- When the system, in order to be confident about a term's disambiguated meaning, requires a certain minimum amount of contextual evidence to be found in the input texts but fails to do so. This failure may be due to the **lack of evidence** in the evidence knowledge resource and/or the texts themselves.

Obviously, the above analysis is still too abstract to be of much use; therefore our approach for troubleshooting a NER system when precision and/or recall are found to be low involves using concrete metrics to make terms like "high ambiguity" and "adequate evidence" more precise and determine the extent to which they apply in the scenario at hand.

3 Metric-based Diagnosis of NER Systems

3.1 Ambiguity Metrics

In the previous section, we mentioned that one reason for low NER precision is high ambiguity, i.e., the wrong association of many target entities to terms in the text. This may happen when many target entities can be mixed (i.e., confused) with:

- **Common lexical terms** that are not really entities. For example, if the target entities are companies then the location services company "Factual" can be easily mixed in a text with the namesake common adjective. For the purposes of this paper we call this phenomenon **Lexical Ambiguity**.
- **Other target entities.** For example, if the target entities are locations then the city of Tripoli in Greece may be mixed with Tripoli in Libya. For the purposes of this paper we call this phenomenon **Target Entity Ambiguity**.
- **Non-target entities** from the contextual evidence knowledge graph. For example, if the target entities are football teams and the knowledge graph contains also locations then the *team of Barcelona* may be mixed with the *city of Barcelona*. For the purposes of this paper we call this phenomenon **Knowledge Graph Ambiguity**.
- **Entities from other domains**, not included in the thesaurus nor in the evidence knowledge graph. For example, if the target entities are companies then the telecom company Orange may be mixed with the namesake fruit. For the purposes of this paper we call this phenomenon **Global Ambiguity**.

In order to identify which of these four ambiguity types and to what extent characterize a given NER scenario, we work as follows. First, we consider a representative sample of the texts that we are supposed to perform NER on and we manually annotate them with target entities as well as non-target entities from the contextual evidence knowledge graph. Subsequently, we perform the same task in an automatic way by using the NER system *without any disambiguation* (i.e., we perform only step 1 of the process described in Sect. 2.1). Having done that we may measure the different types of ambiguity as follows:

- **Lexical Ambiguity:** We measure this as the percentage of terms which (i) are common lexical terms rather than entities in the text, (ii) have not been manually annotated with any target entity and (iii) have been wrongly mapped by the system to one or more target entities.

- **Target Entity Ambiguity:** We measure this as the percentage of terms which (i) have been annotated with a target entity and (ii) have been mapped by the system to this target entity but also to other target entities.
- **Knowledge Graph Ambiguity:** We measure this in two complementary ways. First, as the percentage of terms which (i) have been manually annotated with a target entity and (ii) have been mapped by the system to this target entity but also to other non-target entities. For the purposes of this paper we call this KGA_1. Second, as the percentage of terms which (i) have been manually annotated with a non-target entity and (ii) have been mapped by the system to this entity but also to other target entities. For the purposes of this paper we call this KGA_2.
- **Global Ambiguity:** We measure this as the percentage of terms which (i) are not common lexical terms but actual entities in the texts, (ii) have not been manually annotated with any entity and (iii) have been mapped by the system to one or more target entities.

All the above percentages are calculated over the total number of terms the NER system has detected in the texts. Also, please note that the above ambiguity types and metrics are not meant to replace any existing formal ambiguity classification frameworks [2]; they are merely informal tools which, as we will show in subsequent sections, we have found to be very useful in analyzing NER scenarios.

3.2 Evidence Adequacy Metrics

Complementary to high ambiguity, a second reason for low NER effectiveness is the inadequacy of the contextual knowledge applied as disambiguation evidence (step 2 of the process described in Sect. 2.1). When this knowledge has the form of a knowledge graph, then by adequacy we practically mean two things:

1. How rich is the knowledge graph in terms of relation/attribute values for its entities. As suggested in Sect. 2.1, these values are used as contextual disambiguation evidence, therefore if many entities lack them, their disambiguation will probably fail. For example, if we want to disambiguate film mentions in texts, a potential evidence could be the actors that played in them. If this relation is poorly populated in the knowledge graph, then the latter may be inadequate for the particular task.
2. How prevalent is the contextual evidence provided by the knowledge graph in the input texts. Even if the knowledge graph is rich, it won't help if the texts do not contain the evidence it provides. Considering the film example, even if we know all the film's actors, this knowledge will not be useful if films and their actors do not co-occur in the texts.

Knowledge graph richness can be measured in many ways, depending on the desired level of detail. Some metrics we have found useful are the following:

- **The percentage of target entities with no related entities at all.** If this number is high then the knowledge graph is practically useless for the disambiguation of the particular entities.
- **The average number of entities a target entity is related to.** If this number is lower than expected (e.g., if films are related in average to only 1 or 2 entities when they are typically expected to be related to several actors, directors, producers, characters etc.) then the knowledge graph might not be as useful as it could.
- **The average number of entities a target entity is related to via a specific relation.** If this number is lower than expected then this relation cannot really contribute to the disambiguation task even if it is expected to do so. For example, if the "hasActor" relation for films is poorly populated (e.g., only one or two actors per film) then the NER system is practically not able to use any actor mentions in the texts as film disambiguation evidence.

The above metrics can be easily calculated by merely querying the knowledge graph. On the other hand, in order to measure the prevalence of the graph's contextual evidence in the input texts we use both the texts and the graph. In particular, we consider again the representative sample of input texts that we used for measuring ambiguity in the previous section and which we have already manually annotated with target entities as well as non-target entities from the contextual evidence knowledge graph. Then, for each pair of a target and non-target entity in the annotated texts, we derive from the knowledge graph the relation(s) and/or the relation paths (up to a certain length) through which the entities are linked. This allows us to calculate the following:

- **The percentage of target entities for which there is at least one evidential entity in the texts.** If this number is low then obviously the knowledge graph is not useful for the given texts.
- **The average number of evidential entities a target entity is related to in the texts.** If this number is too low then again the knowledge graph is not appropriate for the given text.
- **The percentage of target entities for which there is at least one evidential entity in the texts via a specific relation or relation path.** If this number is low then this particular relation is not useful for the given texts.
- **The average number of evidential entities a target entity is related to in the texts via a specific relation (or relation path).** Again, this number allows to assess the relative usefulness of the graph's relations for the disambiguation task.

Please note that the definition of metrics for the adequacy of text-based evidence knowledge resources (i.e., entity annotated texts) has been left out of this paper's scope and will be addressed in future work. The reason for that is that we haven't used so much this kind of evidential knowledge in the NER scenarios we have come against so far.

3.3 Acting on the Metrics

As suggested in the introduction, the ultimate goal of the metrics is to enable practitioners to improve the unsatisfactory effectiveness of a NER system in a given scenario. For that, in this section, we map the potential values of these metrics to concrete actions that may achieve this goal.

For starters, if the Lexical Ambiguity of the entities is considerable then the word sense disambiguation (WSD) capabilities of the linguistic analysis component of the NER system need to be enhanced. Depending on the existing capabilities of the system and the extent of the problem, these enhancements can range from simple heuristics (e.g., that a company mention in a text typically starts with a capital letter) to complete implementations of WSD frameworks [13].

On the other hand, if Global Ambiguity is found to be high, then it may be that many of the input texts are not really related to the domain of the target entities. For example, if NER is performed on news articles in order to detect mentions of films (with e.g., LinkedMDB[4] as an evidence knowledge graph) and most of these articles are not relevant to the cinema domain, then it's quite likely that many non-film entities will be mistaken for films. To remedy this situation one could possibly expand the evidence knowledge graph so as to include all the domains the input texts are about; nevertheless this can be quite difficult and resource-intensive to achieve. Another, more practical approach, would be to use a domain/topic classifier in order to filter out the non-relevant texts and apply the NER process only to the relevant ones. Intuitively, this will boost precision even if some level of recall is sacrificed.

The next metric that can lead to action is the Knowledge Graph Ambiguity, i.e. the ambiguity between target entities and entities from the evidence knowledge graph. As suggested in Sect. 3.1 we measure this by means of two different percentages, i.e., the percentage of text target entities that may be confused with evidential ones (KGA_1) and the percentage of text evidential entities that may be confused with target ones (KGA_2). If KGA_1 is found to be high and KGA_2 low, then what is most probably needed is the pruning of the evidence knowledge graph in order to remove parts of it that are not so essential but can still cause noise.

To show why pruning may be necessary assume that we perform NER in a set of film reviews, targeting mentions of actors and using DBPedia as an evidence knowledge graph. Since DBPedia contains many person entities that are not actors, it is quite likely that many actor mentions in the texts will be mistaken for other persons (e.g., the actor Roger Moore could be mistaken with the namesake computer scientist). A high KGA_1 score would clearly illustrate this. On the other hand, since the input texts are primarily about films, the probability that the term "Roger Moore" actually refers to the computer scientist rather than the actor is low. Again, a low KGA_2 would make this obvious. Thus, if we were to remove from the knowledge graph all the non-actor person entities, we would most likely increase precision by allowing the NER system to focus only on the disambiguation of actor entities.

---

[4] http://data.linkedmdb.org.

Pruning the knowledge graph may be also helpful when the latter contains misleading evidential relations. For example, consider an excerpt from a contemporary football match description saying that "Ronaldo scored two goals for Real Madrid". To disambiguate the term "Ronaldo" in this text using DBpedia, the only contextual evidence that can be used is the entity "Real Madrid". Yet, there are two players with that name that are semantically related to it, namely Cristiano Ronaldo (current player) and Ronaldo Luis Nazario de Lima (former player). Thus, if both relations are considered then the term will not be disambiguated. Yet, the fact that the text describes a contemporary football match suggests that, in general, the relation between a team and its former players is not expected to appear in it. Thus, for such texts, it would make sense to ignore this relation in order to achieve more accurate disambiguation.

The pruning of the knowledge graph in the above cases can be done in two stages. In the first stage, the entities (and their relations) that are not related (directly or indirectly) to the target entities could be discarded. In the second stage, the removed entities would include those that are related to the target entities but via relations that are not prevalent in the texts. For the latter, the third knowledge graph prevalence metric of Sect. 3.2 could be used, namely the average number of evidential entities a target entity is related to in the texts via a specific relation. The pruning should start from the relations with the lowest score.

Of course, this whole exercise is meaningful only if the evidence knowledge graph has some highly prevalent relations to retain after the pruning. If that's not the case, then the ideal action would be to change/expand the knowledge graph with different relations than the ones it already has and which are most likely to appear in the texts. If that's not possible, an alternative action that could be performed in case of low graph prevalence would be the reduction of the minimum evidence threshold that the system uses in the disambiguation phase, provided however that Target Entity Ambiguity and Knowledge Graph Ambiguity are also low. This action would potentially increase recall (since much less non-ambiguous entities for which little evidence has been found in the text would be rejected by the system) without decreasing much precision (since for the few entities that are ambiguous there was not much evidence to use in the first place).

Finally, if the richness of the knowledge graph is low, the obvious thing to do would be to enrich it. Since that may not be always possible due to lack of resources, the relation prevalence metric could also be used here in order to select to enrich only the most useful relations.

Table 1 summarizes the key points of the above analysis by providing a map between observed metric values, problem diagnosis and recommended action(s). In all cases, it should be made clear that the whole framework we are describing here is characterized by some degree of inexactness, meaning that there's always a possibility that (i) a diagnosis is wrong even if the metrics support it and (ii) that the execution of a recommended action fails to improve NER effectiveness even if the diagnosis is relatively accurate. For that, every time an action is taken, precision and recall of the NER process needs to be re-measured in order to verify that the system actually performs better. The re-measurement should be done every time with a new test set so as to ensure that our actions have not introduced any bias to the process.

4   Framework Application Cases

In this section we describe two cases where the application of the paper's diagnostic framework helped us to significantly increase the (initially low) effectiveness of Knowledge Tagger, our in-house developed NER system. Knowledge Tagger uses primarily ontological knowledge graphs as disambiguation evidence.

4.1   Case 1: Resolving Players in Football Texts

In this case we had to semantically annotate a set of textual descriptions of football match highlights from the Spanish Liga, like the following: *"It's the 70th minute of the game and after a magnificent pass by Pedro, Messi managed to beat Claudio Bravo. Barcelona now leads 1-0 against Real."*. The descriptions were used as metadata of videos showing these highlights and our goal was to determine, in an unambiguous way, which were the players mentioned in each video. The annotated descriptions were then to be used as part of a semantic search application where users could retrieve videos that showed their favorite player, with much higher accuracy.

Our first attempt towards performing this task involved using Knowledge Tagger with DBPedia as both an entity thesaurus (as it included all football players we were interested in) and an evidential knowledge graph. The result of this was a precision of 60% and a recall of 55%, measured against a manually annotated set of 100 texts. For comparison purposes, we also applied the AIDA NER system (that uses the YAGO knowledge graph) on the same texts and we got similar figures (precision 62% and recall 58%).

To diagnose the reasons for this rather mediocre performance, we calculated the metrics of Sect. 3 using a 100 text diagnostics dataset. As shown in Table 2, the main types of ambiguity that characterized our case were Target Entity Ambiguity (several players with similar names) and Knowledge Graph Ambiguity (several players sharing similar names with other DBPedia entities). In particular, KGA_1 (actual players mixed with non-players) was high while KGA_2 (actual non-players mixed with players) was low. This was rather expected as the input texts were very domain specific and thus unlikely to contain many person entities that are not footballers.

Given these metric values, we went on to prune the knowledge graph (as suggested in Sect. 3.3) by removing most of the non-football related entities as well as several player relations that had no evidential value. To determine the latter we calculated the text prevalence of the player relations in the knowledge graph (see Sect. 3.2). As Table 3 shows, the most prevalent (and thus useful for

Table 1. Metric values and actions

Metric value	Diagnosis	Action
High Lexical Ambiguity	The NER system cannot perform well enough Word Sense Disambiguation	Improve the linguistic analysis component of the NER system
High Global Ambiguity	Many of the input texts are not really related to the domain of the target entities	Use a domain/topic classifier in order to filter out the non-relevant texts and apply the NER process only to the relevant ones
High KGA_1 and low KGA_2	The evidence knowledge graph may contain several non-target entities that hamper the disambiguation process rather than helping it	Prune the evidence knowledge graph in order to remove non-essential, noisy entities
Low Knowledge Graph Richness	Knowledge Graph is not adequate as disambiguation evidence	Enrich the knowledge graph starting from the most prevalent relations
High Knowledge Graph Richness but low Text Prevalence	Knowledge Graph is not adequate as disambiguation evidence	Change or expand the knowledge graph with entities that are more likely to appear in the texts
Low Knowledge Graph Text Prevalence and Low Target Entity Ambiguity and Knowledge Graph Ambiguity	The system's minimum evidence threshold is too high	Decrease the threshold

disambiguation) relations were those between players and the their current team, current co-players and current managers; so we kept those and discarded the rest.

Then we applied again Knowledge Tagger but with the pruned knowledge graph and this time precision and recall were found to be 82 % and 80 % respectively. Thus, our framework managed to provide a fairly accurate diagnosis for the initially mediocre effectiveness of our NER system in the particular case (i.e., that the knowledge graph was bigger than needed) and point us to an action (the pruning of the graph) that actually increased this effectiveness.

4.2 Case 2: Resolving Companies in News Articles

In this case our task was to detect and disambiguate mentions of technology startups within news articles coming from a variety of news sources (newspapers, blogs, specialized websites like techcrunch etc.). For that, we had at our disposal a thesaurus of 4000 company entities as well as a custom-built knowledge graph that contained useful knowledge about each company like its founders, investors, competitors and business areas. Running Knowledge Tagger with this knowledge graph as disambiguation evidence gave us a precision of 35 % and a recall of 50 %, both of which of course were rather low.

To identify the underlying reasons for this low effectiveness, we applied again our diagnostic framework, starting with the identification of the ambiguity types

Table 2. Ambiguity metric values for football case

Metric	Value
Lexical Ambiguity	1 %
Target Entity Ambiguity	30 %
KGA_1	56 %
KGA_2	4 %
Global Ambiguity	2 %

Table 3. Text prevalence of knowledge graph relations and relation paths in the football case

Relation	Prevalence
Relation between soccer players and their current club	85 %
Relation path between players and their current co-players	95 %
Relation path between players and their current managers	75 %
Relation between players and their nationality	10 %
Relation between players and their place of birth	2 %
Relation between players and their spouse	0 %

we were up against. As Table 4 shows, contrary to the football case, our main problem in this scenario was not the ambiguity between startups and/or other related entities in the knowledge graph but the global ambiguity, i.e., the ambiguity between startups and entities outside our domain. A posteriori, this was somewhat expected as the news we were analyzing were not necessarily related to startups or technology. Moreover, there was a considerable lexical ambiguity as several companies had names like "Factual", "Collective" and "Prime".

Given the high global ambiguity, we built and applied, as suggested by our framework, a simple binary classifier to filter out news articles that were not related to our domain. The classifier was based on the multinomial Naive Bayes algorithm and was trained on a set of 400 news articles (200 within the domain and 200 outside), achieving an accuracy of 90 %. Running Knowledge Tagger only on the classified as domain-specific news articles resulted in a substantially increased precision of 72 % while recall stayed roughly the same (52 %). At the same time, in order to deal with the considerable lexical ambiguity, we incorporated to the linguistic analysis component of our system (which is based on GATE) some heuristic rules like, for example, the rule that text terms that refer to startups should start with a capital letter. This increased precision to 78 % and recall to 57 %.

To see if any more improvements were possible, we measured the knowledge graph's prevalence in the texts which turned out to be low. In fact, almost 40 % of the texts contained no evidential entities at all while most of the graph's relations had small prevalence (see Table 5). Based on this fact and the low

Table 4. Ambiguity metric values for companies case

Metric	Value
Lexical Ambiguity	10 %
Target Entity Ambiguity	4 %
KGA_1	4 %
KGA_2	3 %
Global Ambiguity	40 %

Table 5. Text prevalence of knowledge graph relations and relation paths in the companies case

Relation	Prevalence
Relation between companies and the business areas they are active in	50 %
Relation between companies and their founders	40 %
Relation between companies and their competitors	35 %
Relation between companies and their CEO	20 %
Relation between companies and their investors	15 %
Relation between companies and their CFO or CMO	6 %

scores for Target Entity and Knowledge Graph Ambiguity, we ran Knowledge Tagger again but with a reduced minimum evidence threshold; this increased recall to 62 %. Thus, again, our diagnostic framework proved quite useful in determining the underlying causes of our NER's ineffectiveness and guiding us to the appropriate remedial actions.

5 Discussion

The framework we have presented in this paper has been derived from the experiences we had in building NER solutions for actual commercial clients and the two application cases (and their examples/datasets) that we have described reflect exactly those experiences. That is why the quantitative results we report are from our own NER system rather than other systems. These cases may not be covering all possible situations, but they do illustrate how different two NER scenarios may be.

Regarding the level of automation, the framework is applied as follows: First, a diagnostic set of texts is manually created. Second, all metrics are automatically calculated and shown to the user. Third, the metrics are manually interpreted by the user using the guidelines of Sect. 3.3. Thus, our currently implemented system supports the calculation and (basic) visualization of the metrics. The automation of the metrics interpretation is left as future work as it requires a more formal definition of both the metrics and the diagnostic rules (e.g., the definition of "lower than expected" or the comparison of the different metrics).

Given that, the main effort one needs to invest in applying the framework involves the manual annotation of the texts and the execution of the remedial actions the metrics will suggest (e.g., the graph's pruning). In the first use case we described in this paper (football), the application of our framework took us about a week as the texts were short, the domain rather small (Spanish league only) and the pruning of the graph easily done by a few SPARQL queries. The second case (startups) was more demanding (around 3 weeks) as we had to deal with longer texts and enhance Knowledge Tagger with better word sense disambiguation and domain filtering capabilities. Of course, these estimations cannot be considered as any kind of benchmark.

A key insight that one can derive from our framework regarding NER effectiveness is that evidential knowledge should not be applied in a blind manner; in some cases more knowledge may be required (see knowledge graph expansion/enrichment actions in Table 1) but in other cases less knowledge is actually better (see knowledge graph pruning actions in Table 1 as well as the case in Sect. 4.1). In other words, it's not so much the amount of knowledge that counts but its appropriateness to the particular scenario. Our metrics facilitate the assessment of this appropriateness and thus the selection of the optimal knowledge. A second insight is that it's not always necessary to have the optimal evidential knowledge in order to get a satisfactory effectiveness; as the second case in Sect. 4.2 showed, domain filtering and better lexical matching rules were enough to increase NER precision to an acceptable level. Again, the framework's metrics are crucial in recognizing such situations.

Of course, it has to be noted that our framework is rather informal and not necessarily applicable to all NER systems. It is based on insights we have extracted from studying and using existing NER systems (including our own) in real-world scenarios and it's primarily targeted to practitioners that do not have necessarily deep knowledge of NER algorithms and theoretical frameworks, but still need to have some control over their systems' performance.

6   Conclusions and Future Work

In this In-Use paper we have considered the task of Named Entity Resolution and we have defined a Diagnostics Framework for troubleshooting and optimizing corresponding systems in industrial scenarios. Our motivation for this work has been the empirical fact that a NER system's satisfactory performance in a given scenario does not constitute a trustworthy predictor of its performance in different settings. As industrial clients typically expect a high and consistent performance from the NER solutions they pay for, our framework helps NER system developers and consultants identify the reasons why their system performs unsatisfactorily in a given scenario and take appropriate actions to increase performance.

In defining our framework we have first identified the main factors that affect NER effectiveness; two of these are (i) the level of ambiguity that characterizes the scenario's entities and (ii) the adequacy of the contextual evidence applied for disambiguation. Then we have defined metrics and processes for quantifying these factors and we have linked the values of these metrics to specific actions (see Table 1) that, as Sect. 4 shows, are able to increase NER effectiveness.

As the Diagnostics Framework is currently implemented as part of our own NER system (Knowledge Tagger), our immediate future work will focus on implementing it in a more generic way so that different systems could make use of it. A key feature of such an implementation will be the comprehensive and intuitive visualization of the metrics so that the framework's users can easily interpret their values. Moreover, we intend to extend the framework with metrics for measuring the evidential adequacy of textual knowledge resources as well as any other metrics that we may find useful. Finally, in the longer term, we intend to investigate whether and in what way could this metric-based optimization of NER systems be performed fully automatically, i.e., having the system itself rather than human users interpret the metrics and take up the corresponding actions.

References

1. Alexopoulos, P., Villazon-Terrazas, B., Gomez-Perez, J.M.: Knowledge tagger: customizable semantic entity resolution using ontological evidence. In: Lohmann, S. (ed.) I-SEMANTICS (Posters & Demos). CEUR Workshop Proceedings, vol. 1026, pp. 16–19. CEUR-WS.org (2013)
2. Bos, J.: A survey of computational semantics: representation, inference and knowledge in wide-coverage text understanding. Lang. Linguist. Compass 5(6), 336–366 (2011)
3. Ferragina, P., Scaiella, U.: TAGME: on-the-fly annotation of short text fragments (by Wikipedia Entities). In: Proceedings of the 19th ACM International Conference on Information and Knowledge Management, CIKM 2010, pp. 1625–1628. ACM, New York (2010)
4. Gangemi, A.: A comparison of knowledge extraction tools for the semantic web. In: Cimiano, P., Corcho, O., Presutti, V., Hollink, L., Rudolph, S. (eds.) ESWC 2013. LNCS, vol. 7882, pp. 351–366. Springer, Heidelberg (2013)
5. Hassell, J., Aleman-Meza, B., Arpinar, I.B.: Ontology-driven automatic entity disambiguation in unstructured text. In: Cruz, I., Decker, S., Allemang, D., Preist, C., Schwabe, D., Mika, P., Uschold, M., Aroyo, L.M. (eds.) ISWC 2006. LNCS, vol. 4273, pp. 44–57. Springer, Heidelberg (2006)
6. Hoffart, J., Yosef, M.A., Bordino, I., Fürstenau, H., Pinkal, M., Spaniol, M., Taneva, B., Thater, S., Weikum, G.: Robust disambiguation of named entities in text. In: Proceedings of the Conference on Empirical Methods in Natural Language Processing, EMNLP 2011, pp. 782–792. Association for Computational Linguistics, Stroudsburg (2011)
7. Kemmerer, S., Grossmann, B., Müller, C., Adolphs, P., Ehrig, H.: The neofonie NERD system at the ERD challenge 2014. In: Proceedings of the First International Workshop on Entity Recognition, ERD 2014, pp. 83–88. ACM, New York (2014)
8. Kleb, J., Abecker, A.: Entity reference resolution via spreading activation on RDF-graphs. In: Aroyo, L., Antoniou, G., Hyvönen, E., ten Teije, A., Stuckenschmidt, H., Cabral, L., Tudorache, T. (eds.) ESWC 2010, Part I. LNCS, vol. 6088, pp. 152–166. Springer, Heidelberg (2010)

9. Kulkarni, S., Singh, A., Ramakrishnan, G., Chakrabarti, S.: Collective annotation of wikipedia entities in web text. In: Proceedings of the 15th ACM SIGKDD International Conference on Knowledge Discovery and Data Mining, KDD 2009, pp. 457–466. ACM, New York (2009)
10. Mendes, P.N., Jakob, M., García-Silva, A., Bizer, C.: Dbpedia spotlight: shedding light on the web of documents. In: Proceedings of the 7th International Conference on Semantic Systems, I-Semantics 2011, pp. 1–8. ACM, New York (2011)
11. Miller, G.A., Charles, W.G.: Contextual correlates of semantic similarity. Lang. Cogn. Process. **6**(1), 1–28 (1991)
12. Milne, D., Witten, I.H.: Learning to link with wikipedia. In: Proceedings of the 17th ACM Conference on Information and Knowledge Management, CIKM 2008, pp. 509–518. ACM, New York (2008)
13. Navigli, R.: Word sense disambiguation: a survey. ACM Comput. Surv. **41**(2), 10:1–10:69 (2009)
14. Rizzo, G., Troncy, R.: NERD: a framework for evaluating named entity recognition tools in the Web of data. In ISWC 2011: 10th International Semantic Web Conference, Bonn, Germany, 23–27 October 2011
15. Usbeck, R., Ngonga Ngomo, A.-C., Röder, M., Gerber, D., Coelho, S.A., Auer, S., Both, A.: AGDISTIS - graph-based disambiguation of named entities using linked data. In: Mika, P., et al. (eds.) ISWC 2014, Part I. LNCS, vol. 8796, pp. 457–471. Springer, Heidelberg (2014)

Using Ontologies for Modeling Virtual Reality Scenarios

Mauro Dragoni[1]([⊠]), Chiara Ghidini[1], Paolo Busetta[2], Mauro Fruet[2], and Matteo Pedrotti[2]

[1] FBK–IRST, Trento, Italy
{dragoni,ghidini}@fbk.eu
[2] Delta Informatica, Trento, Italy
{paolo.busetta,mauro.fruet,matteo.pedrotti}@deltainformatica.eu

Abstract. Serious games with 3D interfaces are Virtual Reality (VR) systems that are becoming common for the training of military and emergency teams. A platform for the development of serious games should allow the addition of semantics to the virtual environment and the modularization of the artificial intelligence controlling the behaviors of non-playing characters in order to support a productive end-user development environment. In this paper, we report the ontology design activity performed in the context of the PRESTO project aiming to realize a conceptual model able to abstract the developers from the graphical and geometrical properties of the entities in the virtual reality, as well as the behavioral models associated to the non-playing characters. The feasibility of the proposed solution has been validated through real-world examples and discussed with the actors using the modeled ontologies in every day practical activities.

1 Introduction

Serious games with 3D interfaces are a branch of VR systems and are often used for the training of military personnel (in individual as well as team coordination danger situations) and, more recently, for the training of civilian professionals (firefighters, medical personnel, etc.) in emergency situations using tools such as VBS3[1] and XVR[2].

A crucial step towards the adoption of VR for training is the ability to configure scenarios for a specific training session at reduced costs and complexity. By looking at state of the art technologies, it is already possible to do so for physical landscapes, physical phenomena, and crowds (including their behaviors), and trainers and system integrators can assemble and customize serious game products for a specific scenario using commercial products and libraries that need to be (easily) adapted to the specific landscapes and needs of the clients.

Not so advanced is the technology for enriching the scenarios with non playing characters, that is, those characters (people, animals, vehicles, small teams,

---

[1] https://www.bisimulations.com/.
[2] http://futureshield.com/xvr-esemble.shtml.

© Springer International Publishing Switzerland 2015
F. Gandon et al. (Eds.): ESWC 2015, LNCS 9088, pp. 575–590, 2015.
DOI: 10.1007/978-3-319-18818-8_35

and so on) directly involved in game playing in collaboration with (or in opposition to) human players, but whose behavior is entirely animated in an artificial manner. Here the problem is (at least) twofold. A first problem is the lack of configuration environments for trainers and system integrators to complement the "physical landscape" with descriptions of the non playing characters at a high level. As an example, an environment that makes possible the configuration of a scenario for fire emergency training in a hospital ward that contains, in addition to the physical reconstruction of the ward building and of the fire, a set of non playing characters composed of three nurses, of which one expert, one doctor from another ward who is not familiar with the safety procedures of the ward, and eight patients among which a child and a blind patient. A second problem is the lack of algorithms for the generation/selection of realistic and plausible behaviors for non playing characters, able to adapt themselves to the evolution of the game. While this is not a problem for entertainment games, it is a serious problem for serious games as it has the effect of discouraging and disengaging the trainee, so that it is not uncommon the recruitment of experts to impersonate additional characters (such as team mates, enemies, victims, dogs, injured people, and so on) in the simulation, making it more complex and expensive.

Current attempts to the programming of non playing characters rely on ad hoc specifications/implementations of their behaviors done by VR developers. Thus, a specific behavior (e.g., a function emulating a panicking reaction) is hardwired to a specific item (e.g., the element "Caucasian_boy_17" of a VR such as XVR) directly in the code. This generates a number of problems typical of ad hoc, low level solutions: the solution is scarcely reusable, it often depends on the specific knowledge of the code of a specific developer, and is cumbersome to modify, since every change required by the trainer has to be communicated to the developers and directly implemented in the code in a case by case manner. The existence of high level specifications of non playing characters and modular behaviors, described in a manner that is independent from the specific VR, and available for both trainers and developers, would be an important step towards the definition of reusable, flexible, and therefore cheaper, scenarios that include non playing characters.

In this paper, we focus on the experience of using Semantic Web techniques, and in particular lightweight ontologies, for the high level description of the artificial entities (including characters) and their behaviors in gaming in order to uncouple the description of scenarios performed by the trainers from their physical implementation in charge to the developers. Differently from a number of works in literature that often uses ontologies for a detailed description of the geometrical properties of space and objects, the focus of our work is on the description of the entities of a VR scenario from the cognitive point of views of the trainers and the developers alike, in a way that is semantically well founded and independent of a specific game or scenario [1], and with the goal of fostering clarity, reuse, and mutual understanding [2].

The outcome of such an experience is a shared vocabulary, presented in Sect. 3, grounded in the foundational ontology DOLCE that helps in identifying the basic entities of a VR scenario, together with their mappings to items of a specific VR implementation (such as XVR). An evaluation of the usefulness of such a shared vocabulary in a real-world use case (the PRESTO project described in Sect. 2) is presented in Sect. 5, while a discussion concerning lessons learned about the feasibility of the proposed system is reported in Sect. 6.

To the best of our knowledge, the construction and evaluation of the ontology presented in this paper provides a first experience towards the description of a virtual world from a cognitive level that can highlight the potential and criticality of using Semantic Web techniques, and existing ontologies, to describe a VR from a cognitive point of view and can provide the basis for further developments.

2 The PRESTO Project

The objective of PRESTO (Plausible Representation of Emergency Scenarios for Training Operations) research project is the creation of a system for the customization of serious games scenarios based on virtual reality. The advantage of this system, compared to the state of the art, resides in the richness and the ease of defining the behavior of artificial characters in simulated scenarios, and on the execution engines able to manage cognitive behaviors, actions, and perceptions within a virtual reality environment. One of the main outcome of the project is the possibility of specifying procedures, psychological profiles, and other factors that influence the behavior of individuals and/or small groups in any role (emergency teams, victims, observers, terrorists, criminals, etc.) and to build scenarios, for instance a car accident, in which part or all of the people involved are simulated by artificial characters. To this end, the system has to include an environment for building the training scenarios by the VR trainer, tools for the specification of cognitive and perceptual models used for augmenting psychological profiles of non-player characters, and execution engines able to manage cognitive behaviors, actions, and perceptions within a virtual reality environment.

The system can be used, for example, for training safety personnel, for the verification and the optimization of operational procedures, and for the analysis of work environments. The system has been tested in a pilot use case selected in a specific application domain of large interest in both commercial and research fields: training for emergency management within close environments (such as fires, evacuations, overload of users due to external factors such great disasters scale, etc.). The pilot has been be conducted in collaboration with the Health Services of the Trentino local government (APSS).

The open problems addressed by this project may be summarized as follows:

1. the perception of the virtual environment by an artificial character and the execution of its models and procedures must be able to adapt to the context, to its history and status (fatigue, emotions, intake of stimulants such as caffeine or depressants such as alcohol) and must maintain a level of variability (i.e. in the accuracy of the vision, the rate of reaction, in the choices among alternatives) such that the behavior is plausible but not trivially predictable;

2. the representation of procedures and patterns of behavior must be independent of one specific usage scenario and accessible to training specialists (i.e.
   industrial safety or civil protection) rather than just a computer, in an environment facilitating the definition and configuration of training scenarios by
   such specialists.

The first open problem relates to aspects such as the usage of a BDI (Beliefs-
Desire-Intention) multi-agent system with cognitive extensions, CoJACK [3], as
the artificial intelligent engine for the generation/selection of behaviors in serious
games [4], that go beyond the scope of this paper.

What we present in this work, instead, is the experience of using Semantic
Web techniques, and in particular lightweight ontologies, to contribute to the
second open problem, that is the development of a programming environment for
serious game platforms thanks to end-user development tools [5] and the ability
to mix and match scenario components (including behavioral components) taken
off-the-shelf from a market place.

3 PRESTO Ontology Design

The development of programming environment for the high level description
of artificial entities (including characters) and their behaviors in scenarios of
serious games requires the ability to represent a wide range of entities that *exist*
in the (artificial) world. The approach taken in PRESTO is to use ontologies
to represent this knowledge, in a way that is semantically well specified and
independent of a specific game or scenario [1].

The construction of the PRESTO ontology therefore is driven by typical questions that arise when building ontological representations of a domain, that is:

- "What are the entities that exist, or can be said to exist, in a Virtual Reality
  scenario?"
- "How can such entities be grouped, related within a hierarchy, and subdivided
  according to similarities and differences?"

Differently from Ontology in philosophy, where these questions are motivated
from the need to investigate the nature and essence of being, we have looked
at these questions from the pragmatic point of view of computer science, where
ontologies and taxonomic representations have been widely proposed and used
to provide important conceptual modeling tools for a range of technologies, such
as database schemas, knowledge-based systems, and semantic lexicons [2] with
the aim of fostering clarity, reuse, and mutual understanding.

A serious problem we had to face in PRESTO was the lack-of/limited-availability
of training experts and software developers, and the broad scope of items and behaviors that can occur in an arbitrary scenario of VR, that can range from terror-
ist attacks in a war zone, to a road accidents in a motorway, to a fire alarm in a
nuclear plant or hospital and so on. Because of that reason, building everything
from the ground up by relying on domain experts and using one of the state of
the art ontology engineering methodologies such as METHONTOLOGY [6] was
deemed unfeasible. Thus the process followed in PRESTO has been driven by an

attempt to: (1) maximize the reuse of already existing knowledge and (2) revise and select this knowledge with the help of experts by means of more traditional ontology engineering approaches such as the one mentioned above. The choice of already existing knowledge has lead us to consider the following two sources:

- state of the art foundational ontologies which provide a first ontological characterization of the entities that exist in the (VR) world; and
- the concrete items (such as people, tools, vehicles, and so on) that come with virtual reality environments and can be used to populate scenarios.

Our choices for the PRESTO project were the upper level ontology DOLCE (Descriptive Ontology for Linguistic and Cognitive Engineering) [7], and the classification of elements provided by XVR. DOLCE was chosen as this ontology not only provides one of the most known upper level ontologies in literature but it is also built with a strong cognitive bias, as it takes into account the ontological categories that underlie natural language and human common sense. This cognitive perspective was considered appropriate for the description of an artificial world that needs to be plausible from a human perspective. The decision to use the classification of elements provided by XVR was due to the extensive range of item available in their libraries (approximatively one thousand elements describing mainly human characters, vehicles, road related elements, and artifacts like parts of buildings) and the popularity of XVR as virtual reality platform.

The construction of the first version of the ontology of PRESTO was therefore performed by following a middle-out approach, which combined the reuse and adaptation of the conceptual characterization of top-level entities provided by DOLCE and the description of extremely concrete entities provided by the XVR environment. More in detail,

- we performed an analysis and review of the conceptual entities contained in DOLCE-lite [7] together with the Virtual Reality experts (both trainers and developers) and selected the ones referring to concepts than needed to be described in a VR scenario; this analysis has originated the top part of the PRESTO ontology described in Sect. 4.1.
- we performed a similar analysis and review of the XVR items, together with their classifications, in order to select general concepts (e.g., vehicle, building, and so on) that refer to general VR scenarios; this analysis has originated the middle part of the PRESTO ontology described in Sect. 4.2.
- as a third step we have injected (mapped) the specific XVR items into the ontology, thus linking the domain independent, virtual reality platform independent ontology to the specific libraries of a specific platform, as described in Sect. 4.3.

A reader could ask now why we didn't simply/mainly rely on the XVR classification in order to produce the, so called, PRESTO ontology. The reason is twofold: first of all, the XVR classification mainly concerns with objects. It provides therefore a good source of knowledge for entities "that are" (in DOLCE called Endurants), but a more limited source of knowledge on entities "that happen" (in DOLCE called Perdurants). Second, the XVR libraries contain objects described at an extremely detailed level whose encoding and classification resembles more to a Directory structures built to facilitate the selection of libraries rather than a well thought is-a hierarchy and therefore presents a number of problems that prevent its usage 'as such'. In the following, we review the most common problems we found in the categorization of the XVR items:

– Concepts names are used to encode different types of information. For instance the concept name "Caucasian_male_in_suit_34" is used to identify a person of Caucasian race, dressed in suit and of 34 years of age. Encoding the information on race, age, and so on via e.g., appropriate roles enables the definition of classes such as e.g., "Caucasian_person", "young adult", "male" and so on and the automatic classification (and retrieval) of XVR item via reasoning.
– The terminology used to describe concepts is not always informative enough: for instance, it is difficult to understand the meaning of the entity "HLO_ assistant" from its label and description and to understand whether this item may suggest a type of "assistant" that may be useful in several scenarios and could therefore be worth adding to the ontology.
– The level of abstraction at which elements are described varies greatly. For instance the library containing police personnel items classifies, an the same hierarchical level the general concept of "Police_Officer" and the rather specific concept of "Sniper_green_camouflage".
– the criteria for the classification is not always clear: for instance, the "BTP_ officer" (British Transport Police) concept is not a subclass of "Police_Officer".
– Certain general criteria of classification are not present in all the libraries. As an example, the general concept "Adult_Male" should be a general concept used for the classification of male characters. Nonetheless, it is present in e.g., the library of "Environment_humans" (that is, the library that describes generic characters) and is not present in e.g., the libraries of "Rescue_humans" and "Victims" (that is, the libraries of characters impersonating rescuers and victims, respectively).
– Unclear classification: for instance, in the XVR original classification a "sign" is a "road_object", and a "danger_sign" is an "incident_object". By considering that no relations are defined between the entities "sign" and "danger_sign", it is not possible to infer any relation between "danger_sign" and "road_object".
– Duplication of concept names: for instance, the label "police_services" is used to describe both human police characters in the library "environment_human", and police vehicles, in the library "rescue_vehicle".

In the next section we provide an overview of the PRESTO ontology and of its top-level, middle level and XVR specific components in detail.

4   The PRESTO Ontology

As introduced in Sect. 3, the PRESTO ontology[3] is composed of three parts: (i) a top level part constructed with the help of DOLCE; (ii) a middle level describing

---

[3] The current version of the PRESTO ontology cannot be published due to copyrights constraints. A preliminary version, from which it is possible to observe the rational used for modeling it, may be found here: https://shell-static.fbk.eu/resources/ ontologies/CorePresto.owl.

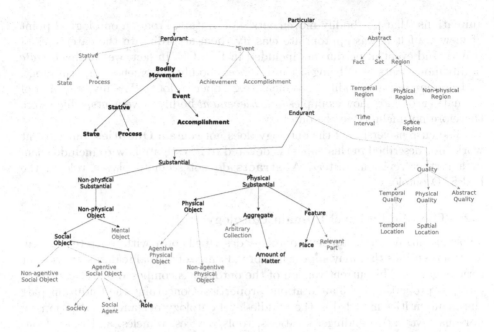

Fig. 1. The top-level PRESTO ontology.

general entities that can occur in a VR scenario, and (iii) a specific set of entities representing objects and "behaviors" available in a concrete VR.

4.1   The Top-Level Ontology: DOLCE Entities

Figure 1 shows the taxonomy of DOLCE entities taken from [7] revised and customised to the needs of PRESTO.

Entities in gray where not included in the PRESTO ontology, while entities in boldface where added specifically for PRESTO.

Among the first level of entities we selected **Endurants** and **Perdurants**: endurants are indeed useful to describe the big number of physical and non-physical objects that can occur in a serious game, including avatars, vehicles, tools, animals, roles and so on; perdurants are instead useful to describe what happens in a scenario. Concerning endurants the diagram in Fig. 1 shows the ones we selected to be included in PRESTO; note that we did not include the distinction between agentive and non-agentive physical objects because of an explicit requirement by the PRESTO developers. In fact, they require the possibility to treat every object in a VR as an agentive one for the sake of simplicity[4]. While perdurants can be useful in a VR to describe a broad set of "things that happen", in the current version of the ontology they were mainly used to describe

---

[4] A typical example is vehicle, which the developers prefer to treat as an agentive objective, rather than a non agentive object driven by an agent, for the sake of simplicity of the code.

animations (that is, "bodily_movements") of avatars. From an ontological point of view we felt it was appropriate classify them according to the categories of stative and eventful perdurants included in DOLCE. In fact, we can have *state* bodily movements (e.g., being sitting), *process* bodily movements (e.g., running), and *accomplishment* bodily movement (e.g., open a door). The investigation of animations did not show examples of *achievement* bodily movements, which were therefore not included in the ontology.

The current version of the ontology does not contain **Qualities**, but current work (not described in this paper) is devoted to investigate how to include them in a further revision. Instead **Abstracts** do not seem to play a role in the PRESTO ontology.

4.2 The Middle-Level Domain Ontology

This part augments the top level ontology described above with concrete, but still abstract, entities that may appear in a broad range of virtual reality scenarios for serious games. The current version of the ontology is composed of 311 concepts, 5 object properties and 3 annotations properties. Concerning the Endurant part the main entities modeled in the middle-level ontology pertain classifications of persons (avatars), buildings, locations, tools/devices, vehicles, and roles. Concerning perdurants the ontology contains concepts describing *state*, *process* and *accomplishment* bodily movement. An excerpt of the middle-level ontology can be seen in Fig. 2.

4.3 Injecting the Bottom-Level Ontology

The linking of the bottom-level ontology, representing the classification scheme used for organizing the items contained in the 3D-library, is not a trivial task.

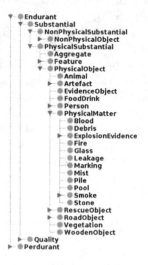

Fig. 2. The middle-level PRESTO ontology.

Indeed, the correct alignment of these levels enables the transparency of the system with respect to the actual content of the 3D-library.

While the creation of the top and middle-level of the PRESTO ontology is meant to create a stable knowledge source, the definition of the alignments with the bottom-level elements is an activity that has to be done every time a new 3D-library is plugged into the system.

To ease this injection we decided to accomplish it in two separate steps: (i) an automatic definition of alignments by using an ontology alignment tool and (ii) a manual refinement of the alignments before using the complete ontology in the production stage.

The output of the alignment task is the linking between the abstract concepts contained in the middle PRESTO ontology and the concrete items contained in the underlying 3D-library implemented in the system. Indeed, such alignments allow the access to the entire set of items defined in the 3D-library and that are physically used for building the virtual reality scenario.

For sake of clarification about the alignment process works, let's consider the following example. In the middle-level of the ontology we have defined the concept "Tent" representing a general tent that may be used for building a virtual reality scenario. By plugging, for example, the XVR library, we need to find an alignment between the entity "Tent" and the specific tent items contained in XVR, such as "Decontamination_Tent_Zone_1", "Family_tent_blue", "Treatment_Area", and so on. To do that, as first step, we execute the Alignment API library [8]: for the entity "Tent", the XVR item identified in the 3D-library and aligned with it is "Tents". Such an alignment, classifies the bottom-level ontology "Decontamination_Tent_Zone_1", "Decontamination_Tent_Zone_2", "Decontamination_Tent_Zone_3", "Family_tent_blue", "Family_tent_orange", "Festival_tent", and "Treatment_Area" as children of the concept "Tents". As a consequence, all these elements can be retrieved and used at run time to produce a specific scenario which requires the presence of a tent, while the scenario can still be described using the abstract term "tent". Also, the same high level scenario may be easily adapted to the usage of other 3D-libraries, simply by exploiting the (different) mappings of such libraries with the middle level "Tents" concept.

In some cases the automatic alignment we used fails: for example, the middle-level entity "Weapon" is automatically aligned with the bottom-level entity "Baton" instead of being aligned with the bottom-level entity "Service-weapon". In these cases, a manual refinement of the generated alignments was done afterwards for pruning wrong axioms.

By considering the XVR use case, the automatic alignment procedure allowed a time-effort reduction, with respect of doing everything manually, of around 65 % in the definition of the alignment between the middle-level and the bottom-level ontologies, thus showing the potential of using ontology mapping technologies in the concrete scenario of virtual reality libraries.

5   PRESTO Ontology in Action

In this section, we present how the PRESTO ontology has been applied in the development process of virtual reality scenarios. We will start with a brief description of the virtual reality environment used in the PRESTO project, the XVR 3D-library. Then, we will present code samples showing how the ontology has been exploited in practice for development purposes and how it has been used in the definition of agent behavioral scripts.

5.1 XVR 3D-Library

XVR is a virtual reality training software used to educate and train operational and tactical safety and security professionals.

One of the most important features of XVR is that the trainer can build an incident scenario and has full control over the course of events in the scenario during the exercise. He can also give feedback, for instance by role-playing the control room or other rescue staff. The trainer, for example, is able (i) to respond to the student's decisions by activating events in the virtual scenario, (ii) decide to condense time and jump to a next phase in the incident, (iii) to ask the student to assess the new situation and respond appropriately, and (iv) to use his full experience and creativity to influence the scenario during an exercise to optimize his learning objectives.

The XVR engine includes an extensive 3D-model database, the XVR library. The XVR library contains dozens of 3D environments and hundreds of virtual objects such as rescue professionals, people, victims, vehicles, wrecks, fires, leaks, and countless other objects. Such objects may be "static" and they cannot be changed over time, or "dynamic" such as adjustable fires or an adjustable explosion range as well as victims to which triage can be applied. These adjustable objects allow the trainer to make changes to the scenario (without the students noticing) so the scenario changes dynamically over time.

From the technical point of view, the XVR library is integrated as extension of Unity3D that is a framework developed for making the creation of video games more easy. It contains a complete game development ecosystem: (i) a powerful rendering engine fully integrated with a complete set of tools and workflows for creating interactive 3D and 2D content; (ii) multi-platform publishing; and (iii) thousands of ready-made assets. For independent developers, Unity's democratizing ecosystem smashes the time and cost barriers to creating games. From the development point of view, Unity3D provides a set of APIs[5] that can be used for software development.

XVR provides enhanced APIs allowing the control of specific feature of the XVR items that, otherwise, would not be possible with the classic Unity3D APIs (for example the power of fire extinguishers, or escalator movements). Besides this, the XVR library inherits the all functionalities of the Unity3D engine.

5.2 Ontology Enhanced Development

Below, it is possible to observe some examples about how the use of the ontology allows to work by maintaining a high level of abstraction and transparency with respect to the underlying 3D-library used by the system.

---

[5] http://docs.unity3d.com/ScriptReference/.

```
 1:    IPhysicalEntity entity = (IPhysicalEntity) scene.GetEntity(id.as_string());
 2:    if(entity.getModel().equals("asset_object_int_chair"))
 3:    {
 4:      currentDistance = agentPosition.Distance((Vector) position.as_object());
 5:      if (currentDistance < minDistance)
 6:      {
 7:        seat = entity;
 8:        minDistance = currentDistance;
 9:      }
10:    }
11:  }
```

Algorithm 1. Usage of the Unity3D API without the PRESTO ontology.

```
 1:    IEntity entity = scene.GetEntity(id.as_string());
 2:    if(ontology.IsA(entity, CorePresto.seatable))
 3:    {
 4:      currentDistance = agentPosition.Distance((Vector) position.as_object());
 5:      if (currentDistance < minDistance)
 6:      {
 7:        seat = entity;
 8:        minDistance = currentDistance;
 9:      }
10:    }
11:  }
```

Algorithm 2. Usage of the Unity3D API with the PRESTO ontology.

These first two source code examples show the difference in using, or not, the PRESTO ontology in the development process. Algorithm 1 shows a branch of code where a Model-Based Object Creation strategy, concerning in the direct access to the objects contained in the 3D-library, has been used. On the contrary, Algorithm 2, shows how the Ontology-Enhanced Object Creation strategy helps in the abstraction for accessing the elements defined in the virtual reality scenario. The main difference can be seen at line 2 of both algorithms: while in Algorithm 1, the model name of the entity to check is hard-coded in the source code, in Algorithm 2 the type of the entity is checked by invoking the API in charge of mapping the type of the current entity with the concepts defined in the PRESTO ontology.

The second set of examples, shown below, concerns the definition of scripts used for describing the behavior of the characters that are placed in the virtual reality scenario. Briefly, such characters, based on the values of some parameters or based on the "situation" of the scenario, have to act in a certain way. This way of acting is described by some behavioral models like the ones proposed below.

Script 1 shows an example of the assignment of the goal "GoToLocation", to all elements placed in the scenario referring to the concept "http://www.Presto/UnityItems#Robot". In this case, the entities placed in the virtual reality scenarios are linked through the use of the ontological concepts.

```
<scenes>
  <scene name="Mech approaching">
    <updateAgent concept="http://Presto/UnityItems#Robot">
      <role>BOT</role>
      <behaviouralModel>Interpreter:Robot</behaviouralModel>
      <goal>GoToLocation</goal>
    </updateAgent>
  </scene>
</scenes>
```

Script 1. Example of behavioral model developed with the support of the PRESTO ontology.

The equivalent version, where the name of instances are used instead of the name of concepts, is presented in Script 2. The problem here is that the name of the instances to which the goal has to be applied is completely specified within the behavioral model. This way, the developer has to specify, before to know how the scenario has been composed, the entire list of entities placed in it.

```
<scenes>
  <scene name="Mech approaching">
    <updateAgent name="Mech1">
      <role>BOT</role>
      <behaviouralModel>Interpreter:Robot</behaviouralModel>
      <goal>GoToLocation</goal>
    </updateAgent>
    <updateAgent name="Mech2">
      <role>BOT</role>
      <behaviouralModel>Interpreter:Robot</behaviouralModel>
      <goal>GoToLocation</goal>
    </updateAgent>
    <updateAgent name="Mech3">
      <role>BOT</role>
      <behaviouralModel>Interpreter:Robot</behaviouralModel>
      <goal>GoToLocation</goal>
    </updateAgent>
  </scene>
</scenes>
```

Script 2. Example of behavioral model without using the PRESTO ontology.

6   Lessons Learned

In the previous sections, we presented which are the goals of the PRESTO project and we explained how and why the use of ontologies simplifies the development of virtual reality scenarios, as well as, improves the re-usability of the source code when the developed software is plugged to different underlying 3D-libraries.

In this Section, we sum up the experience of the PRESTO project by reporting which aspects have been perceived as advantages by the people actively involved in the project and, on the contrary, which ones have been considered as criticalities that need to be analyzed more in details for future perspectives.

The evaluation of the usefulness and effectiveness of the proposed ontology-based system has been conducted by interviewing developers and modelers concerning the usability of the proposed system with respect to previous version of the platform where ontologies were not adopted. From the research point of view, the two questions that we want to answer are:

RQ1: "Is the use of an ontology-based system useful for simplifying the development of virtual reality scenario?"

RQ2: "Is the use of an ontology-based system enough for managing the behavior of the characters deployed in the scenario?"

Below, we report the outcomes of the discussions about the most important aspects done with both the developers and the modelers involved in the project.

Code Re-usability. The high level of code re-usability observed by the developers was the most perceived advantage of the proposed system. As described in Sect. 5, the use of the ontology allows to develop the structure of virtual reality scenario, as well as, characters behavioral models, by abstracting the references to the physical entities. This way, the implementation remains completely independent by the libraries used for modeling the actual 3D-element or for defining ad-hoc behavioral models.

The result is that every time a new classification scheme, describing the content of a 3D-library or a set a behavioral models, is plugged to the system, the effort requested for migrating the source code to the new libraries is strongly reduced. The industrial nature of the project make this aspect the most important one, especially from the business point of view by considering the economical saving in using the proposed technology.

Development Effort. The second point, that is directly connected with the previous one, is related to the effort saved by the developer during his work. In particular, there are two aspects that have been highlighted:

- speed-up the development process: by using a "fixed" set of concepts, "fixed" in the sense that the set of concepts remains the same independently by the 3D-library used, developers do not need to learn, every time a new library is plugged to the system, the classification scheme of the items or of the behavioral models contained in the plugged library.
- developer knowledge limited to part of the ontology structure: as direct consequence of the aspect presented above, by using the ontology, the developer is not demanded to know what has been modeled "under" the middle-level. This because the alignment between the middle and the bottom levels of the ontology is delegated to the modeler; therefore, the developer does not have to know the entire structure of ontology, but his knowledge may be limited to the top and middle levels. Indeed, the developer expresses each reference to entities by using exclusively the concept contained in the middle-level of the ontology without knowing any detail related to the physical description of the 3D-items, as well as, of the behavioral models.

Criticalities. Besides the positive consideration described above, the discussions with all the people involved in the project rose some criticalities during the usage of the platform. The first criticality is related to evaluation of the effort needed for maintaining the ontology by plugging new classification schemes when needed with respect to the hard-coding of the entities in the source code. The rose issue concerns that the plug of a new classification scheme to the ontology requires the accomplishment of two tasks: (i) the transformation of the 3D-items (or behavioral models) classification scheme to a bottom-level ontology and (ii) the definition of the alignments between the entities modeled in the middle-level to the plugged ones. About the first task, the effort for completing it may vary based on the quality of the classification scheme. In Sect. 3, as example of the difficulties that might be found in such an activity, we presented which were the issues detected in adapting the XVR classification schema. Instead, concerning the alignment task, we discussed, always in Sect. 3, how the use of automatic ontology alignment tools may help in reducing the effort needed for completing the plug of a new classification scheme to the ontology. On the other hand, by having the entity labels hard-coded in the software, the work of migrating the code from one library to another is unsafer unless to find some development solutions that, by the way, would request an effort comparable, if not higher, with the plug of a new classification scheme.

The second criticality concerns the management of ambiguities when the plugged classification schemes are richer with respect to the vocabulary modeled in the middle-level ontology. The risk is that during the development of a scenario, the developer, through the ontology, is not able to access to all items contained in the 3D-library. However, by considering that in the use cases addressed until now in the project this event did not happen, the resolution of this weak point has been demanded as future work for the next version of the system.

Finally, by summing-up all the collected observations, we may positively answer to both research questions. We may state that the use of the ontology made the development process easier with respect of the hard coding alternative. The same perception has been reported also for what concerns the management of the behavioral models.

7   Related Work and Conclusion

In this paper, we focused on the experience of using Semantic Web techniques, and in particular lightweight ontologies, for the description of the artificial entities and their behaviors in gaming with the aim of uncoupling the description of virtual reality scenarios from their physical implementation in charge to the developers.

With respect to the literature, where ontologies are often used for a detailed description of the geometrical properties of space and objects [9], we focused more on how the description of the entities of a VR scenario can be easily represented and managed from the practical point of view. Indeed, the literature addressed such problems only marginally by focusing mainly on the use of ontologies for managing the representation of virtual reality scenarios themselves [10,11], even if in some cases a clear target domain, like the management of information related to disasters [12], is took into account. Also the description of character behaviors have been supported by using ontologies for different purposes like as support for UML-based descriptions [13] or as a "core" set of structural behavioral concepts for describing BDI-MAS architectures [14].

However, all these works do not take into account issues concerning the practical implementations of flexible systems for building virtual reality scenarios. The proposed solution demonstrated the viability of using Semantic Web technologies for abstracting the development of virtual reality scenarios either from the point of view of the 3D-design and from the modeling of character behaviors.

References

1. Gruber, T.R.: Toward principles for the design of ontologies used for knowledge sharing? Int. J. Hum. Comput. Stud. **43**(5–6), 907–928 (1995)
2. Guarino, N., Welty, C.: Identity and subsumption. In: Green, R., Bean, C.A., Myaeng, S.H. (eds.) The Semantics of Relationships: an Interdisciplinary Perspective, vol. 3. Kluwer, Dordrecht (2001)
3. Ritter, F.E., Bittner, J.L., Kase, S.E., Evertsz, R., Pedrotti, M., Busetta, P.: CoJACK: a high-level cognitive architecture with demonstrations of moderators, variability, and implications for situation awareness. Biol. Inspired Cogn. Archit. **1**, 2–13 (2012)
4. Evertsz, R., Pedrotti, M., Busetta, P., Acar, H., Ritter, F.: Populating VBS2 with realistic virtual actors. In: Conference on Behavior Representation in Modeling & Simulation (BRIMS), Sundance Resort, Utah, 30 March–2 April 2009
5. Paternò, F.: End user development: survey of an emerging field for empowering people. ISRN Software Engineering **2013**, 1–11 (2013)
6. Fernández-López, M., Gómez-Pérez, A., Juristo, N.: Methontology: from ontological art towards ontological engineering. In: Proceedings Symposium on Ontological Engineering of AAAI (1997)
7. Gangemi, A., Guarino, N., Masolo, C., Oltramari, A., Schneider, L.: Sweetening ontologies with DOLCE. In: Gómez-Pérez, A., Benjamins, V.R. (eds.) EKAW 2002. LNCS (LNAI), vol. 2473, p. 166. Springer, Heidelberg (2002)
8. David, J., Euzenat, J., Scharffe, F., dos Santos, C.T.: The alignment API 4.0. Semant. Web **2**(1), 3–10 (2011)
9. Chu, Y.L., Li, T.Y.: Realizing semantic virtual environments with ontology and pluggable procedures. In: Lanyi, C.S. (ed.) Applications of Virtual Reality. InTech, Rijeka (2012)
10. Bille, W., Pellens, B., Kleinermann, F., Troyer, O.D.: Intelligent modelling of virtual worlds using domain ontologies. In: Delgado-Mata, C., Ibáñez, J. (eds.) Intelligent Virtual Environments and Virtual Agents, Proceedings of the IVEVA 2004 Workshop, ITESM Campus Ciudad de Mexico, Mexico City, D.F., Mexico, 27 April 2004. CEUR Workshop Proceedings, vol. 97. CEUR-WS.org (2004)
11. Xuesong, W., Mingquan, Z., Yachun, F.: Building VR learning environment: an ontology based approach. In: First International Workshop on Education Technology and Computer Science, ETCS 2009, vol. 3, pp. 160–165, March 2009

12. Babitski, G., Probst, F., Hoffmann, J., Oberle, D.: Ontology design for information integration in disaster management. In: Fischer, S., Maehle, E., Reischuk, R. (eds.) Informatik 2009: Im Focus das Leben, Beiträge der 39. Jahrestagung der Gesellschaft für Informatik e.V. (GI), Lübeck, 28 September–2 October 2009. Proceedings LNI, vol. 154, pp. 3120–3134. GI (2009)
13. Bock, C., Odell, J.: Ontological behavior modeling. J. Object Technol. **10**(3), 1–36 (2011)
14. Faulkner, S., Kolp, M.: Ontological basis for agent ADL. In: Eder, J., Welzer, T., (eds.) The 15th Conference on Advanced Information Systems Engineering (CAiSE 2003), Klagenfurt/Velden, Austria, pp. 16–20, June 2003. CAiSE Forum, Short Paper Proceedings, Information Systems for a Connected Society. CEUR Workshop Proceedings, vol. 74. CEUR-WS.org (2003)

Supporting Open Collaboration in Science Through Explicit and Linked Semantic Description of Processes

Yolanda Gil[1(⊠)], Felix Michel[1], Varun Ratnakar[1], Jordan Read[2],
Matheus Hauder[3], Christopher Duffy[4], Paul Hanson[5],
and Hilary Dugan[5]

[1] Information Sciences Institute, University of Southern California,
Marina del Rey, CA 90292, USA
{gil,felixm,varunr}@isi.edu
[2] Center for Integrated Data Analytics, U.S. Geological Survey,
Middleton, WI 53562, USA
jread@usgs.gov
[3] Software Engineering for Business Information Systems,
Technical University Munich, Munich 85748, Germany
hauder@in.tum.de
[4] Civil and Environmental Engineering, Penn State University,
University Park, PA 16801, USA
cxd11@psu.edu
[5] Center for Limnology, University of Wisconsin, Madison, WI 53706, USA
{pchanson,hdugan}@wisc.edu

Abstract. The Web was originally developed to support collaboration in science. Although scientists benefit from many forms of collaboration on the Web (e.g., blogs, wikis, forums, code sharing, etc.), most collaborative projects are coordinated over email, phone calls, and in-person meetings. Our goal is to develop a collaborative infrastructure for scientists to work on complex science questions that require multi-disciplinary contributions to gather and analyze data, that cannot occur without significant coordination to synthesize findings, and that grow organically to accommodate new contributors as needed as the work evolves over time. Our approach is to develop an organic data science framework based on a task-centered organization of the collaboration, includes principles from social sciences for successful on-line communities, and exposes an open science process. Our approach is implemented as an extension of a semantic wiki platform, and captures formal representations of task decomposition structures, relations between tasks and users, and other properties of tasks, data, and other relevant science objects. All these entities are captured through the semantic wiki user interface, represented as semantic web objects, and exported as linked data.

Keywords: Semantic MediaWiki · Open data science · Organic Data Science

© Springer International Publishing Switzerland 2015
F. Gandon et al. (Eds.): ESWC 2015, LNCS 9088, pp. 591–605, 2015.
DOI: 10.1007/978-3-319-18818-8_36

1   Introduction

The Web was originally developed to support scientific collaboration. Today, scientific collaboration over the Web takes many forms, including blogs, wikis, forums, code repositories, etc. These collaboration frameworks, like the Web, are used beyond science and are often originally developed outside of a science context.

We are interested in supporting scientific collaborations where joint work occurs on a concrete problem of interest, with many participants, and over a long period of time. Although the Web may be used to share information, there is no explicit support for the shared tasks involved. These tasks are discussed through email, phone calls, and occasional face-to-face meetings. We focus on scientific collaborations that revolve around complex science questions that require:

- *multi-disciplinary contributions*, so that the participants belong to different communities with diverse practices and approaches
- *significant coordination*, where ideas, models, software and data need to be discussed and integrated to address the shared science goals
- *unanticipated participants*, so that the collaboration needs to grow over time and include new contributors that may bring in new skills, or data

Such scientific collaborations do occur but are not very common. Unfortunately, they take a significant amount of effort to pull together and to sustain for the usually long period of time required to solve the science questions. Our goal is to develop a collaborative software platform that supports such scientific collaborations, and ultimately make them significantly more efficient and commonplace. Some scientific collaborations revolve around sharing instruments (e.g., the Large Hadron Collider), others focus on a shared database (e.g., the Sloan Sky Digital Survey), and others form around a shared software base (e.g., SciPy). In contrast, our focus is on collaborations where participants jointly pursue a shared scientific question.

We are developing a new approach to on-line collaboration that we call *Organic Data Science*. Our approach enables users to create tasks, exposes how they are being addressed, and facilitates other users to join in solving any task.

Our Organic Data Science framework is implemented as an extension of a semantic wiki, in particular the Semantic MediaWiki platform [1]. Users can add properties to tasks as needed, and can describe any entity of interest to the collaboration (datasets, software, papers, etc.) using semantic properties of the wiki. Semantic wikis provide an easy-to-use interface where users can define structured properties, which are then represented in RDF. The framework is still under development, and it evolves to accommodate user feedback and to incorporate new collaboration features.

There is a wide range of approaches that have been explored for collaboration, although they have not had much adoption in science practice [2]. There is also a significant body of work on studying on-line communities [3], notably on Wikipedia. Our work builds on the social design principles uncovered by this research.

The main contributions of this work are: (1) the design of the framework so it can capture structured information about scientific tasks and associated entities, (2) the implementation of the framework as an extension of a semantic wiki platform, and (3) the integration of the framework with other systems through the use of linked data.

This paper begins with an overview of the framework and the kinds of information captured to make the science process open. We then discuss the overall architecture and implementation of the system. After an overview of related work, we present some preliminary data on the use of the framework, and conclusions and future work.

2 The Organic Data Science Framework

Our approach is to expose science processes declaratively to support the formation of ad hoc groups to work on tasks of interest, to enable anyone to contribute to tasks that match their interests, and to advertise ongoing work to potential newcomers. Science processes describe the what, who, when, and how of the activities pursued by the collaboration. This section describes the Organic Data Science framework, focusing on how semantic representations are used. We use examples from an ongoing collaboration that is using this framework to study the age of water in an ecosystem,[1] but have anonymized the examples by using fictitious names.

The framework incorporates principles from studies of successful on-line communities, which we describe elsewhere [4].

2.1 Representing Tasks

Every task has its own page, and therefore a unique URL, which gives users a way to refer to the task from any other pages in the site as well as outside of it. Subtasks can be created that will be linked to the parent task, resulting in a hierarchical task structure. Task pages follow a pre-defined structure that is automatically presented to the user when a new task is created.

Figure 1 illustrates the representation of a task. On the left, the task is highlighted in the context of all its parent tasks as well as other top-level tasks. On the right, the subtasks are shown at the top. The bottom right shows metadata properties of tasks. As in any wiki page, text can be included to describe the task. Following the text, there is a space where users can define additional structured properties. Each task has an icon to the left that indicates progress on the task.

Task Metadata. Task metadata are major semantic properties of the task. We created a tabular interface to enter semantic properties. All task metadata is stored in the wiki as semantic properties of the task page.

We distinguish between *pre-defined metadata* and *dynamically-defined metadata*. *Pre-defined metadata* are properties of tasks that the system will use to assist users to manage tasks. *Dynamically-defined metadata* allow users to create new properties on the fly that help group tasks with domain-specific features, for example tasks that are related to calibration of models or outreach tasks.

Pre-defined metadata can be *required* or *optional*. Required metadata includes the start date, target date, task owner, task type (high, medium, and low level), and a

---

[1] http://www.organicdatascience.org/ageofwater/.

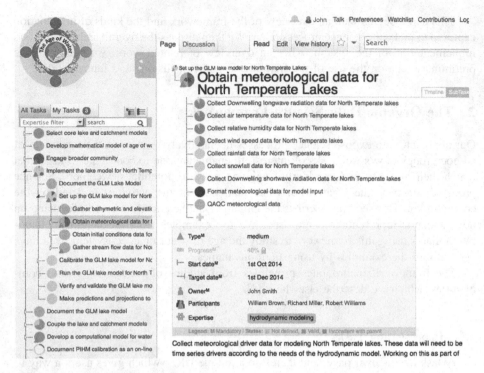

Fig. 1. Organic Data Science: describing tasks.

user-provided estimate of the progress to date. Tasks whose required metadata is incomplete have special status in the system and are highlighted differently in the interface to alert users of their missing metadata. Optional task metadata includes the task participants and the task expertise indicating the kind of background or knowledge required to participate in the task.

An important aspect of the framework is tracking the contributions of each user. This allows the system to show who can be credited for the content of each page.

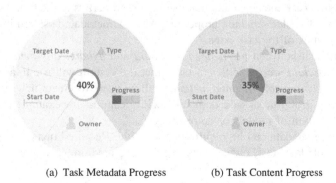

(a) Task Metadata Progress   (b) Task Content Progress

Fig. 2. Conceptual task state estimation.

Task Status. The system uses metadata properties to estimate the progress and status of tasks. Tasks that have a type indicated as high-level are assumed to have a high degree of abstraction and high uncertainty in the estimation of the task completion, such as the major tasks at the project level. Medium-level tasks are those that have a medium uncertainty in estimation of the task completion, such as activities within the project that are decomposed into several subtasks. Low-level tasks are those that have a low uncertainty in estimation of the task completion, such as small well-defined tasks that can be accomplished in a short time period.

The user selects the task type, which is indicated in the interface with different tones of green in the task icon. High-level task are colored in lighter green and lower-level tasks in darker green. The progress to date for low-level tasks is provided manually by their owners or participants, since the tasks have small duration. The progress of high-level and medium-level tasks is calculated by the system.

The progress of a medium-level task is calculated as an average of the progress of its subtasks. For high-level tasks, we assume a linear progress based on the start and target date in relation to today's date. This is because we assume that high-level tasks may have subtasks that have not been specified yet. To provide simple user feedback, metadata properties are shown in different colors to indicate their state: metadata properties that are not yet specified are shown in gray, valid properties in green, and properties that are inconsistent with properties of the parent task in yellow.

Figure 2 illustrates how the system uses the task metadata to generate the task state. The left side of the figure shows an example of a task whose required metadata is incomplete, where the Task State shows the percentage of required metadata that has been provided by users inside of a ring that shows that percentage in green. The side right of the figure shows an example of a task where users have provided all required metadata. Their status is represented by a pie chart showing the progress metadata property value in green. Different shades of green are used to express the task type, with lighter green indicating higher-level tasks.

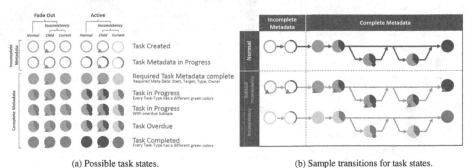

(a) Possible task states.   (b) Sample transitions for task states.

Fig. 3. Task states and sample task state transitions.

Figure 3(a) illustrates all possible task state icons. The left columns show the task state for tasks which are faded out in the interface (shown just to provide context but do not match a search filter). Overdue tasks are indicated with an orange pie chart. A small orange point indicates that at least one subtask is overdue. This helps users identify overdue subtasks. Yellow icons indicate inconsistent tasks, which may be caused by move actions, for example if their start date is before the start date of a parent task. The yellow triangles indicate an inconsistent subtask. Note that yellow and orange colors were also used to indicate overdue and inconsistent tasks.

Figure 3(b) illustrates some sample transitions for task states. For example, the first line shows a typical task that has no metadata when it is created, then required metadata is added but no work has been done in the actual task, and then progress in the task grows until completion although in some cases a subtask or the task itself can be behind schedule. The task state is shown in three different sizes depending on the location in the interface. Large size icons include the progress as a percentage, and are used for the currently opened task as well as in the user pages.

Task Cloning. We have found that often times the same task is done by several people with their own data. To support this, we have created a task cloning facility that takes a task tree and create personalized versions for a set of users. An example is shown in Fig. 4. The group held a workshop that had more than 50 participants, with the goal that each should be able to run a particular hydrological model with their own data. Several general tasks were created which documented what needed to be done in terms of installing software and prepare the data. The system then created personalized versions of those tasks for each workshop participant. This capability enabled the workshop organizers to track where each person was in the process. Each participant could annotate in their own page the particular problems that they were running into.

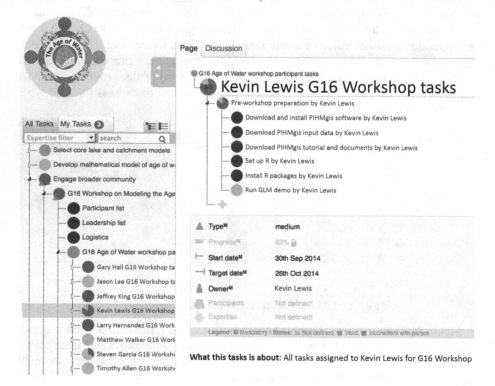

Fig. 4. Cloning tasks for several users to track their individual progress.

2.2   Representing Users

The system automatically creates a page for each user with an account on the wiki.

Figure 5 shows an example of a user page (broken into two pieces to fit the space). The system shows in that page the tasks that the user is owner or participant in, and organizes them according to whether the task is ongoing, upcoming, or completed based on the start and end dates. To do this, the semantic properties of the task are used. The system also retrieves all the expertise involved in the tasks that the user is contributing to, and shows it above the tasks.

The system also shows the most recent contributions made by that user to the different pages of the wiki (top right of Fig. 5). This is important to highlight the areas of the collaborative work that each user is working on. In addition, users can see their work recognized. The system also displays a scoreboard of credits in the front page of the wiki.

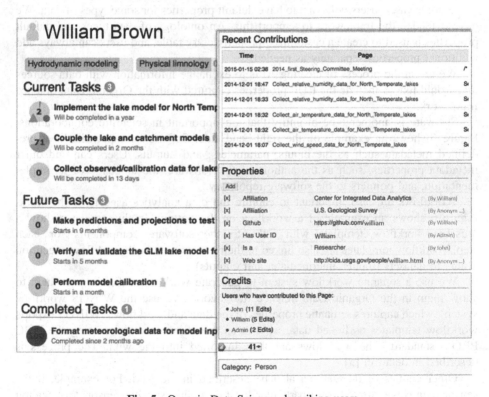

Fig. 5. Organic Data Science: describing users.

User pages can also have metadata properties. This is shown on the bottom right of Fig. 5. Properties can be added by other users, as is the case here. Credits are then shown to acknowledge all users that have edited the user page.

2.3   Representing Data, Software, Workflows, and Other Entities of Interest

Like tasks and people, any other entities of interest in the collaboration can be created to have their own page and associated URL. The most common entities are data, software components, and workflows, and we have created a pre-defined structure that is automatically presented to the user when a new entity is created.

Data is an important entity in a scientific collaboration. Figure 6 shows an example of a dataset description on the left. Datasets can have a type, in this case it is sensor data, and can have metadata properties. Users can add any metadata properties that suit their purposes in using the data. There are two major types of data. *User-described data* is stored in existing repositories external to the wiki. Users then just add a pointer (URL) to the dataset, and simply describe its metadata properties. *User-provided data* is uploaded to the wiki by users, and also described with metadata properties. This distinction enables seamless integration with external data sources.

In some cases, users will want to have default properties for some types of data. We have extended the framework to support this. An ontology of data types and default properties is used to create a customized property entry table, and users can always add additional properties separately as needed.

We are in the process of creating APIs to exchange information with data sources that would like to include the RDF properties captured with the Organic Data Science framework.

Software is another type of entity that are important in scientific collaborations. Figure 6 shows an example on the right-hand side. Software components have pre-defined metadata such as the inputs, parameters, and outputs. Users can add other metadata properties, such as the authors of the software, the language of its implementation, and pointers to the software repository.

Workflows are also important to capture the data analytics aspects of the work. Figure 6 shows an example of a workflow on the bottom. In this case, we show a reusable workflow template with links to the software components for each step. Workflow templates are also linked to their executions. Each workflow execution points to datasets (inputs, intermediate, and outputs).

We use a separate workflow system to generate workflows, then import them to show them in the Organic Data Science framework. We use the WINGS workflow system, which captures semantic properties of the data and workflows. WINGS exports workflow templates as linked data, as well as workflow executions using the W3C PROV standard. The workflows are then imported into the wiki. The process is described in detail in [5].

Other entities of interest can also be described in the wiki. For example, if the sensor data was collected for a particular location with a specific sensor, the location and the sensor can be described in detail through semantic properties.

2.4   Queries

All the semantic properties are stored in the wiki framework as RDF assertions. Semantic properties are queried in two important ways.

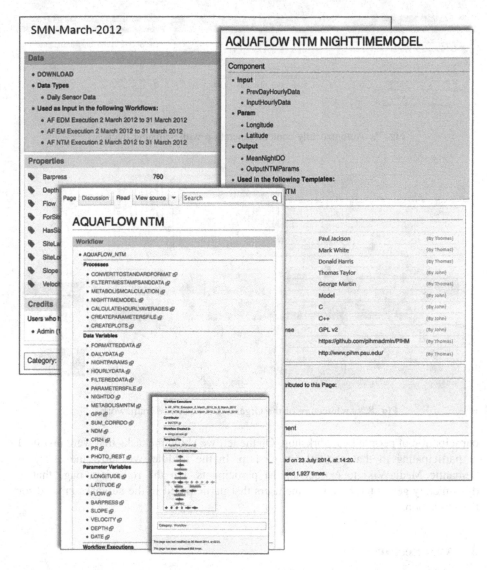

Fig. 6. Organic Data Science: describing datasets, software components, and workflows.

Semantic properties are queried by the system to assist users in managing tasks. We described in Sect. 2.1 how task properties are used to generate the status icons of tasks. They are also used by the system to generate much of the content of the user pages, as we described in Sect. 2.2.

Semantic properties are also used to generate wiki page content. Semantic MediaWiki offers a query language that can be embedded in a wiki page to dynamically generate content.

Figure 7 illustrates how the metadata properties of the task are used in queries. In this case, a dynamically-defined property "participant-of" was added to indicate the

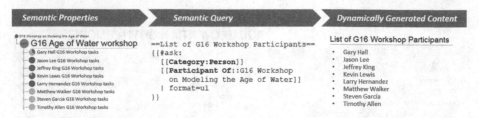

Fig. 7. Automatically content generation with semantic queries.

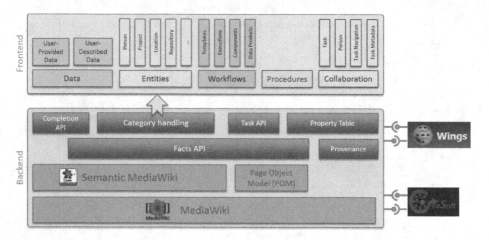

Fig. 8. Architecture of the Organic Data Science framework.

participation of people in a workshop. On the left we show the tasks that were involved in participating in that particular workshop. In the middle, we show the query in Semantic MediaWiki to extract all the participants. On the right is a page that is dynamically generated based on the users that participated in the subtasks created for the workshop.

3 Architecture

This section describes the architecture of the Organic Data Science Framework. A high-level overview of the architecture is shown in Fig. 8. The Organic Data Science Framework is implemented as a set of extensions of the Semantic MediaWiki and MediaWiki platforms. We also use the Page Object Model (POM) extension of MediaWiki,[2] which supports the manipulation of the content of the wiki pages. These three existing components, which provide underlying infrastructure, are shown in dark grey at the bottom of the figure. The rest of the components in the figure are the extensions that comprise the Organic Data Science Framework.

---

[2] http://www.mediawiki.org/wiki/Extension:Page_Object_Model.

We developed an extension to assert and retrieve assertions in the wiki, which is the Facts API. This enables easy access to the semantic properties regardless of how specific properties are handled in Semantic MediaWiki.

The Provenance extension handles attribution for each assertion in the system. Each semantic property is annotated according to the user that asserted it. This provenance information can be queried to generate the credit shown in the different pages.

The Completion API extension enables the system to offer users completions of the properties as they are typing, based on the properties that already exist in the system. This encourages users to adopt properties that others have already created, fostering agreement and normalization of property names. The Task API extension is customized to handle information about tasks. It manages the task-subtask tree, generates the status icons, and tracks task deadlines to generate user alerts.

Finally, the Category Handling extension manages the generation of different pages that are displayed to the user, depending on the category of the page. We described in Sect. 2 different categories of entities, such as tasks, users, data, etc. We have developed other categories at the request of users that are not discussed above, including procedures and data repositories. The representation of a person can be different, for example to distinguish someone who is part of the collaboration and should have a page as described in Sect. 2.2 from a person who has developed some software of interest but is not part of the collaboration.

The Organic Data Science framework can interact with external systems through the use of Semantic Web representations. We discussed above the integration with the WINGS workflow system.[3] Other external systems that we plan to integrate into the Organic Data Science framework include data repositories, software repositories, collaboration networks, and publication repositories.

The Organic Data Science Framework software is open source and is released on GitHub under an Apache 2.0 license.[4]

The Organic Data Science Framework can be set up for different communities. If communities choose to do so, they can make decisions to split the site into separate sites. Each site can point to others as URIs, enabling a looser form of collaboration. We have set up a special site for training new users. Each user is given a set of personalized training tasks, generated with the Task Cloning facility described in Sect. 2.1. Users are trained first to contribute to existing tasks, which is very simple training and takes 20–30 min. They are then trained to create new tasks and manage them, which is more advanced and requires another 20–30 min.

4 Use of the Organic Data Science Framework

The major use of our framework is by a community of hydrologists and limnologists that are studying the age of water in an ecosystem while collaborating with us to develop the Organic Data Science framework.

---

[3] http://www.wings-workflows.org/.

[4] https://github.com/IKCAP/organicdatascience.

Figure 9 illustrates the evolution of the collaboration graphs generated from the task metadata properties that link tasks and users. Each user is a node in the graph, with the links indicating whether two users have a task in common where they are owner or participant. The thickness of the link indicates how many tasks two users have in common. The graph on the left illustrates that many users collaborate with several others in different sets of tasks. It also shows that two different sub communities were being formed in practice (top and bottom areas of the graph), and the group agreed to split the work into two separate sites whose collaboration graphs are shown on the right of the figure.

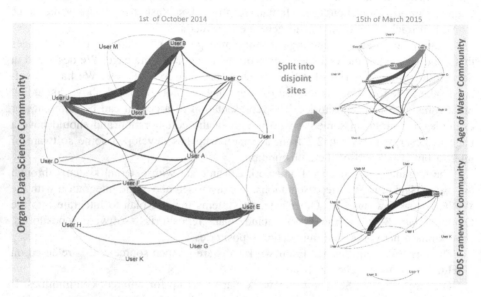

Fig. 9. Evolution of the Organic Data Science collaboration graph.

Several other science collaborations are starting to use the wiki:

- A water metabolism working group.[5] Some of its participants attended a workshop where the Organic Data Science framework was being used. They found the framework useful and are just starting to train new users. They decided to start a new top-level task within the age of water site, since they intend to share some datasets and software with the age of water research group. This group poses new challenges in terms of maintaining their identity while being part of a larger site with many other activities that are irrelevant to them.
- The ENIGMA consortium for neuroimaging genetics.[6] This consortium includes more than 70 institutions that collaborate to do joint neuroscience studies. The institutions keep their data locally, but they all agree to the method and software to

---

[5] http://www.gleon.org/research/working-groups/lake-metabolism.

[6] http://enigma.ini.usc.edu/publications/the-enigma-consortium-in-review/.

be used to analyze their data. They organize themselves into working groups, each group studies a particular disease (e.g., autism) and cohort (e.g., children). A major driver for them is to use the Organic Data Science wiki to track what institutions participate in what study, the characteristics of their datasets, and the point person in that institution for each particular study. The Task Cloning capability is particularly useful here, as is the description of data and workflows. A requirement of this group is that some information needs to remain private.

- The GPF group publishing a special issue of a journal. This is a group of geoscientists preparing articles that follow a similar format in that they publish explicitly all datasets, software, and workflows used to generate the results in the paper. The site is being used to coordinate the activities involved in tracking the status of each paper, and to compare the approaches in different papers.
- The iSamples collaboration for cataloging field science samples in geosciences. There are many catalogs of geosciences samples, and this group wishes to create a meta-catalog that will enable scientists to find an appropriate catalog to deposit their samples. An interesting challenge in this collaboration is creating structured descriptions of the curation procedures for each catalog.

All of the above collaborations are in their initial stages. Each collaboration has chosen a few selected people who have started to populate their site. Each also has specific extensions or customizations that they would like to see in the wiki. Many of the extensions described in Sect. 3 are useful for several of these wikis.

Table 1 shows some data for scientific collaboration groups. The vast majority of defined RDF-Triples are pre-defined metadata properties, as we have not yet emphasized the creation of dynamically defined properties when we train new users. As the site grows in content, we expect that these properties will be most useful in organizing information and exposing other thematic dimensions for tasks, people, and other resources in the site. At the moment, we have only trained a few selected users to create new semantic properties.

Table 1. Highlights of communities using the Organic Data Science framework.

Community	# Pages	# Tasks	# Tasks with completed metadata	Avg. of task completion rates	# Registered users	# RDF triples
Age of water	759	380	350	43.95 %	53	2475
ENIGMA	204	80	2	2.50 %	6	299
GPF	239	168	168	26.19 %	32	1536
ODS Framework	417	77	61	77.92 %	19	681
ODS training	1,235	1115	1112	99.64 %	36	9219

We hope to create an ecosystem of developers of the Organic Data Science framework that will contribute to the existing extensions, create new ones, and share their codes so further collaborations can customize the design of their sites.

5 Related Work

Bry et al. [6] give a detailed overview of semantic wikis and a thorough comparison of semantic wiki frameworks. Semantic wikis have been used for scientific collaborations. Most of them are used to track particular entities, such as genes[7] or mutations.[8] The CSDMS wiki[9] is used to describe science software, and could be integrated as an external software repository.

Shared workflow repositories (e.g., [7]) allow scientists to collaborate by reusing computational methods, but do not include semantic properties for workflow tasks.

Some Web collaboration tools are also centered on coordinating tasks. For example, software development tools support issue tracking and task formulation. A major difference is that our framework is driven by science goals from the start, where each task addresses some aspect of a science goal and can result in scientific objects (software, datasets, etc.) that can be described as semantic objects in their own right.

6 Conclusions

This paper has presented the Organic Data Science framework, a new approach for scientific collaboration that opens the science process and exposes information about shared tasks, participants, and other relevant entities. The framework enables scientists to formulate new tasks and contribute to tasks posed by others. The framework is currently in use by a community, and is beginning to be used by others.

There are many areas of future work. Setting up the framework for new communities is a non-trivial process. The software installation is easy, but a site has to be carefully managed to jumpstart the contributions. We are investigating mechanisms to document this process and facilitate the initial stages. We continue to explore different requirements for supporting scientific collaborations in a variety of contexts.

Acknowledgments. We gratefully acknowledge funding from the US National Science Foundation under grant IIS-1344272.

References

1. Krötzsch, M., Vrandecic, D., Völkel, M., Haller, H., Studer, R.: Semantic Wikipedia. J. Web Semant. **5**(4), 251–261 (2007)
2. Introne, J., Laubacher, R., Olson, G.M., Malone, T.W.: Solving wicked social problems with socio-computational systems. KI-Künstliche Intell. **27**(1), 45–52 (2013)
3. Kraut, R.E., Resnick, P.: Building Successful Online Communities: Evidence-Based Social Design. MIT Press, Cambridge (2011)

---

[7] http://en.wikipedia.org/wiki/Portal:Gene_Wiki.
[8] http://www.snpedia.com/.
[9] http://csdms.colorado.edu/.

4. Michel, F., Gil, Y., Hauder, M.: A virtual crowdsourcing community for open collaboration in science processes. In: Americas Conference on Information Systems (AMCIS) (2015)
5. Garijo, D., Gil, Y., Corcho, O.: Towards workflow ecosystems through semantic and standard representations. In: Proceedings of the Ninth Workshop on Workflows in Support of Large-Scale Science (WORKS), held in conjunction with the IEEE ACM International Conference on High-Performance Computing (SC) (2014)
6. Bry, F., Schaffert, S., Vrandečić, D., Weiand, K.: Semantic Wikis: approaches, applications, and perspectives. In: Eiter, T., Krennwallner, T. (eds.) Reasoning Web 2012. LNCS, vol. 7487, pp. 329–369. Springer, Heidelberg (2012)
7. De Roure, D., Goble, C.A., Stevens, R.: The design and realisation of the myExperiment virtual research environment for social sharing of workflows. Future Gener. Comput. Syst. **25** (5), 561–567 (2009)

Crowdmapping Digital Social Innovation with Linked Data

Harry Halpin[1]([✉]) and Francesca Bria[2]

[1] World Wide Web Consortium/MIT, 32 Vassar Street, Cambridge, MA 02139, USA
hhalpin@w3.org
[2] Nesta, 1 Plough Place, London EC4A 1DE, UK
francesca.bria@nesta.org.uk

Abstract. The European Commission recently became interested in mapping digital social innovation in Europe. In order to understand this rapidly developing if little known area, a visual and interactive survey was made in order to crowd-source a map of digital social innovation, available at http://digitalsocial.eu. Over 900 organizations participated, and Linked Data was used as the backend with a number of valuable advantages. The data was processed using SPARQL and network analysis, and a number of concrete policy recommendations resulted from the analysis.

Keywords: Digital social innovation · Linked data · Crowdsourcing · Policy

1 Introduction

In order to understand the emerging field of digital social innovation (DSI), the DigitalSocial.eu website[1] was created to crowdsource a map of organizations and projects involved in digital social innovation.[2] This crowd-sourced map is a part of a larger study by the European Commission to create new data-driven policy in order to support social innovation throughout Europe. The back-end of the crowd-mapping website was a triple-store that exposed the data as both Linked Data and a SPARQL endpoint, with sophisticated visualizations being dynamically generated "on the fly" from the RDF data to allow the inspection of network of digital social innovation. Using SPARQL and network analysis, a number of detailed questions from the European Commission could then be answered about the current structure of digital social innovation. So far, 967 organizations working on DSI in Europe were mapped as of January 18th 2015, including 609 projects between the organizations, with more organizations being added dynamically to the data-set every day. This is one of the first studies to

---

[1] http://digitalsocial.EU.

[2] This work was funded by the European Commission via the DSI contract and the DCENT EC project. More information on the DCENT project is here: http://dcentproject.eu/.

© Springer International Publishing Switzerland 2015
F. Gandon et al. (Eds.): ESWC 2015, LNCS 9088, pp. 606–620, 2015.
DOI: 10.1007/978-3-319-18818-8_37

show off the power in Linked Data to create *data-driven policy* via the use of semantic technologies to bootstrap a data-set, increase the scope of a survey, and so help structure a complex data analysis. By allowing diverse sets of flexible data to be inter-connected and combined, and then having new data being added with a focused crowd-sourcing survey campaign, a large set of empirical data could be boot-strapped easily on an entirely new topic.

To summarize, our contributions are:

1. Defining the emerging field of digital social innovation.
2. A website based on RDF that crowd-mapped a large data-set about digital social innovation in Europe where semantic technologies were a crucial advantage.
3. A detailed network analysis of digital social innovation in Europe.
4. Data-driven policy recommendations to the European Commission that were driven by the analysis of the collected data.

2   What Is Digital Social Innovation?

The new field of "Digital Social Innovation" (DSI) has emerged over the last few years, pointing to radically new ways of organizing many of the essentials of life from money and health to democracy and education. We tentatively defined Digital Social Innovation (DSI) as "a type of social and collaborative innovation in which innovators, users and communities collaborate using digital technologies to co-create knowledge and solutions for a wide range of social needs and at a scale and speed that was unimaginable before the rise of the Internet."[3] To provide some intuition, communities as diverse as fablabs, hackerspaces, and community wifi networks are part of this new trend.

This definition has a number of different elements to be clarified. Innovation in general is any change to the process of production, consumption, or distribution of commodities necessary for the social reproduction of society. Innovation is first and foremost a collective process undertaken by a large number of actors. Innovation is no longer seen as a linear step-by-step process in which research activities or technology pushes automatically lead to innovation and the commercialization of new products, but rather as a complex, dynamic, and interdependent process involving different stakeholders, including "bottom-up" communities that connect over the Web. Some innovations involve big discontinuities - 'radical' or 'disruptive' innovations - and others involve continuous small 'incremental' innovations [5]. In particular, social and institutional change, called "social innovation," often takes place as gradual and incremental change outside of revolutionary periods. Yet it is precisely social innovation that seems to be desperately needed in an era where many governments and services are viewed as ineffective or failed. As innovation happens as part of larger collective process,

---

[3] DSI Interim Report: http://content.digitalsocial.eu/wp-content/uploads/2014/09/FINAL-2ND-INTERIM-STUDY-REPORT.pdf.

mapping the social networks of innovators and their users who then co-produce the innovation is crucial.

Second, while we can demarcate the study insofar as the definition of digital social innovation to focus on "digital" technologies that scale using the Web, we still have a very wide range of possible areas DSI can be applied to, from health to democracy. After all, today almost all facets of life are touched by digital technologies. While many areas of focus in digital social innovation are still emergent, some are growing very fast, and others are quite marginal. In order to narrow our study somewhat, we will focus on innovation where the digital aspect of scaling depends on bringing together a community of innovation over the Web, which would simply not be possible in the era before the Web. Simply put, this eliminates from our study organizations for social innovation that do not use the Web or organizations that do not depend crucially on the Web for their scaling.

Note in terms of using the internet to "scale" we want to distinguish between two levels: (1) the level of the technical networking infrastructure itself provided by the Internet and (2) the level of online services built on top of these networks on the Web. Metcalfe's Law, (i.e. that the value of the network is in proportion to the number of members squared, so that the value of the network goes up for all users the more users are added) clearly applies to the value of technical networks given by examples such as widespread smartphone usage. One open question for DSI is that we can also scale social innovation via services using the Web, and thus we need to pay close attention to the structural dynamics of the social network of DSI that should be understood.

What forms of digital social innovation are emerging? What are their characteristics and needs? How they can scale? What role can the European Commission play in this context? These are some of the over-arching questions that this research is trying to answer. The general thesis the European Commission-funded study on digital social innovation is that it provides a new path out of the larger economic crisis that is neither reliant on traditional business models or austerity measures in the public sector, but that the power of innovation over the Web can allow people to self-organize in order to solve their myriad problems. Yet until now, digital social innovation has been almost entirely invisible to policy makers and has had none of the extensive support that has gone into digital technologies for the military, government, or business. Yet DSI has the potential to contribute to three of the most important challenges facing Europe: reinventing public services, often in less costly ways; reinventing community, and how people collaborate together; and reinventing business in ways that are better aligned with human needs. The evidence gathered here enables us to recommend how best to combine research, strategy, and policy for DSI in relation to the Digital Agenda for Europe and under the Horizon 2020 Work Programme, and in particular, but not limited to, the Collective Awareness Platforms (CAPS) Programme.[4]

---

[4] http://ec.europa.eu/digital-agenda/en/collective-awareness-platforms-sustainability-and-social-innovation.

We identified six primary domains of digital social innovation. (1) *The Collaborative Economy*: the rise of digital marketplaces for people to transact and share skills, assets and money is fast becoming a key economic trend that enables people to share skills, knowledge, food, clothes, housing and so on. The Collaborative economy has been documented by organizations like Couchsurfing and OuiShare.[5] (2) *New ways of sensing* is a vibrant ecosystem of makers is developing across Europe and globally. Low-cost home 3D manufacturing tools (3D printers, CNC (computer numeric control) machines), free CAD/CAM software like Blender, 123D or Sketchup and open source designs are now giving innovators better access to the enabling infrastructures, products, skills and capabilities they need to enhance collaborative making. (3) *Open democracy* strives to create opportunities for all members of a population to make meaningful contributions to political decision-making. Organizations and projects pioneering open democracy, large-scale feedback, and citizen participation through crowdsourcing legislation such as Open Ministry or Liquid Feedback are transforming the traditional models of representative democracy. (4) *Awareness networks*, including cities including Vienna and Santander, are transforming governments, businesses and society by pioneering new practices in open data and open sensor networks that are changing the provision and delivery of public services. (5) *Open Access* exploits the power of open data, open APIs, and citizen science to provide citizens better public services, with projects like CitySDK defining interoperable interfaces for city-scale applications. (6) In terms of *funding and incubation*, as has been the case with the support for innovative businesses, social innovations often need support in the early idea stages to refine their business models and grow their venture. Incubators like Nesta typically support innovators in exchange for equity, at pre-seed or seed stage. There are nearly 100 incubators/accelerators in Europe.

In terms of methods, we identified four primary methods. *Open networks* includes wireless sensor networks, community (bottom-up) networking (such as Freifunk and Guifi), and privacy-aware open networks as well as hardware such as Arduino. *Open data* includes how governments and other large organizations and companies that hold or generate data about society can release their data to enable citizens to hold government to account for what it spends, the contracts it gives, and the assets it holds. The Linked Data community is a prime example. *Open knowledge* covers the variety of ways in which citizens can use online services and platforms for mass scale social collaboration. Ordinary people today use blogs, wikis, social networks and hundreds of other collaborative platforms to manage their daily lives, solve social challenges, and to participate in e-campaigns, crowdfunding, and the like. *Open hardware* consists of hardware whose blueprints are made publicly available so that anyone can study, modify, distribute, make, extend, and sell the design or hardware based on that design.

---

[5] Note that DSI entities with proper names such as Ouishare mentioned are defined in the DSI case study document: http://content.digitalsocial.eu/wp-content/uploads/2014/05/DSI-report-casestudies.pdf.

The work by organization like Raspberry Pi and Arduino illustrates the potential in open hardware.

3   Crowd-Mapping with Linked Data

As DSI is a relatively new field of study, there is little existing knowledge on who the digital social innovators are; what types of activities they are involved in and how they are using digital tools to achieve a social impact. Therefore, the first task of European Commission was to look in more detail at the different types of organizations involved with DSI, and the activities these organizations are involved in. This led to the creation of a formal vocabulary to capture the characteristics of DSI organizations, which was formalized as an RDF(S) vocabulary, as can be browsed[6] along with various necessary pieces of data such as name, address, size (number of employees), and so on. The DSI ontology is available also for re-use.[7] It crucially depends on inter-linking with other vocabularies such as the Datacube vocabulary[8] and FOAF. In particular, we needed to capture the following characteristics for each DSI organization (where the categories for each role are given in parenthesis):

1. A typology of organizations (government and public sector organizations, businesses, academia and research organizations, social enterprises, charities and foundations; and grassroots communities);
2. The way these organizations are supporting DSI (undertaking research, delivering a service, organizing networking events and festivals, etc.);
3. The main technological trends the organizations and their activities fit under (open data, open networks, open knowledge, open hardware);
4. The area of society the organizations and their activities operate and seek an impact in: The DSI field does not have fixed boundaries; it cuts across all sectors (the public sector, private sector, third sector and social movements) and cuts across domains as diverse as (1) health, wellbeing and inclusion; (2) innovative socio-economic models (3) energy and environment; (4) participation and open governance, (5) science, culture and education; and (6) public services.

In order to understand the DSI landscape, large amounts of technical work was needed in order to build the foundations for a solid map. First, a number of diverse data-sets already collected about digital social innovation needed to be transformed into a common format, in particular data from traditional Excel spreadsheets and SQL databases. Yet this data often was incomplete and partial in terms of the kinds of information we needed for our study. Also, we considered that as we began our study, we would want to capture increasingly large amounts of data as well as perhaps pruning unnecessary or under-utilized categories.

---

[6] http://data.digitalsocial.eu/data/organizations-and-activities.
[7] http://xmlns.com/foaf/spec/.
[8] http://www.w3.org/TR/vocab-data-cube/.

Lastly, we wanted to do complex and open-ended data analysis over our data on-line before commencing the final offline data analysis. While SQL databases were considered, their inability to deal with dynamic schemas easily, and the difficulty of querying traditional "NoSQL" databases is well-known. In this regard, Semantic Web technologies were considered the best fit, as they easily coped with incomplete data, dynamic schemas, and complex querying via SPARQL. We then used off-the-shelf standards such as RDB2RDF and CSV2RDF[9] to convert existing data over to RDF, and where possible supplemented the data for well-known organizations with RDF-compatible data from DBPedia and OpenStreetMaps.[10]

Pre-existing data on DSI rarely captured the relationships, in particular the social network of which DSI actors were working with what other actors on particular DSI projects. For example, the city of Helsinki was working with both international networks like Open Knowledge Foundation as well as national groups like Open Ministry, and European-level groups like "Code for Europe," to open their data. Thus, we thought that the social networks of DSI actors would naturally map onto RDF's network-like data structure, and we could use a survey to both add new DSI organizations as well as gather information about their collaborative projects. While a graph database would have allowed a similar analysis, it would not have allowed data to be added 'on the fly' without manual intervention but only via the survey. In order to gather this data, we created a RDF-backed website, built using Ruby on Rails, that combined a Sesame-based native RDF backend that was initially structured according to our DSI RDF(S) vocabulary and seeded with Nesta's information as transformed to RDF. This allowed us to create a "map" by projecting the RDF data with geolocation information onto our own instance of OpenStreetMaps, which then could present the social network of DSI actors visually. An example of this is shown in Fig. 1. When new visitors came to the website, they were asked to "Get on the Map" by filling out a simple survey that fit their organization and projects into the various categories presented earlier. When they listed partners in projects, we asked for contact information in order to get in touch with partners.

4 Semantics for Surveys

One crucial question is what advantages does Semantic Web technologies provide for this kind of survey-based data collection? When the work was first started, the initial group of contacts came from Nesta's pre-existing DSI work, which led to a map of 32 organizations that were studied using traditional case-study based methodology. From the case-study methodology, an initial RDF(S) vocabulary and online survey was created that was sent to contacts found from Nesta and partners (Waag Society, IRI, ESADE Business School) contacts database, converting them to use RDF using the aforementioned semantic pipeline. Starting in October 2014, this traditional online survey-making work continued till May

---

[9] http://data-gov.tw.rpi.edu/ws/csv2rdf.html.
[10] http://wiki.openstreetmap.org/wiki/OSM_Semantic_Network.

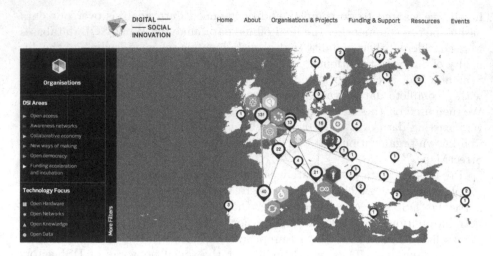

Fig. 1. Screenshot of RDF-backed DSI map

2014. This led to a total of 32 case studies from the contacts of the 8 original organizations, and increase of 300.25 %. However, only "friends of friends" of our partners were being added to the data-set.

We embedded our RDF data-set and interlinked with existing data via named entity recognition [6] and then sent the results to DBPedia Lookup.[11] This allowed the discovery of organizations, names, and e-mails in the data-set via SPARQL queries. This was then interlinked via missing geographical areas using LinkedGeoData[12] (based on OpenStreetMaps) via pre-made DBPedia mappings in order to analyze the geographic distribution of organizations in the data to determine organizations that were missing. Although we could not check the precision of Edinburgh LT Named Entity Recognition system on this particular data-set, the accuracy over a 100 entity sample was 97 %. Furthermore, an initial categorization of DSI into nine areas of society impacted was made, which took advantage of the schema-less nature of RDF to see what kinds of DSI were missing. Then the survey was closely linked into the new schema, and outreach was done to these geographic areas, domains, and organizations via names and contacts discovered in the larger interlinked data-set. Outreach with the semantic-enabled survey far surpassed the non-enriched survey, as the number of organizations in the data-set grew to 581 by August 2014. This was an increase of 480 %, in comparison with the increase of 300.25 % without semantic technologies.

After the initial burst of activity, we added four new categories of DSI to the schema to help guide the outreach. However, at this point we had reached the limit of using semantics to help pull new organizations in and so had reached the

---

[11] https://github.com/dbpedia/lookup.
[12] http://linkedgeodata.org.

limit of our data-set, so we mapped 967 DSI organizations and 609 collaborative projects as of January 2015 (an increase of only 166.44 %). From our domains (given that a single organization could be in more than one category), there were 412 open knowledge, 269 open networks, 258 open data, and 105 open hardware projects. In terms of areas of society impacted, there were 254 organizations focusing on education, 251 on democracy, 164 on arts, 163 on health, 162 on employment, 138 on neighborhood regeneration, 130 on the environment, and 110 on science, and 104 on finances.

5 Network Analysis

We have hypothesized that the success of DSI is located in the social structure of the larger network of social innovation. Social networks are formally defined as set of nodes (or network members) that are tied by one or more types of relations. In the case of the DSI social network collected in this study, the nodes in a graph are organizations, and the edges represent joint projects. The results of this analysis have informed the recommendations on a policy. The data-set and resulting policy changes are needed for the EC to knit the map of DSI actors into a coherent single integrated EC DSI network, and thus achieve the "critical mass" necessary to harness the collective intelligence of DSI organizations to solve large-scale European social problems. At the time of our data analysis,[13] there are a total of 930 organizations with a total of 588 shared projects in the DSI data-sets. This data-set likely fairly represents the empirical phenomena at hand with two caveats (1) It has a bias towards English speakers as the survey was not translated into other European languages, and (2) as outreach was directed by the partners it reflects their social networks likely more in-depth than disconnected social networks. However, it is a large sample and thus worth exploring in detail. A number of questions were determined by the European Commission, which we then answered with a combination of SPARQL, network analysis tools such as Gephi,[14] and custom scripts written in Python and Perl.

In the DSI data-set, nodes (also called vertices) are organizations and shared projects are edges (also called links) between nodes. Although the edges are directed in the native RDF data-structure, we assume that if an organization included another organizations in its project and the aforementioned project did not, that was an oversight of the latter project, not an error on the behalf of the former. Thus, the edges are undirected. In this paper, we do not provide detailed mathematical definitions of the common network analysis constructs used but quick qualitative definitions, as quantitative definitions can be found in final report.[15]

---

[13] Nov. 13th 2014.

[14] http://gephi.github.io/.

[15] http://content.digitalsocial.eu/wp-content/uploads/2014/05/DSI-report_final_19. 05.2014.pdf.

5.1   What Is the Distribution of Social Innovation Across Europe?

Is social innovation done by a few large actors or evenly distributed between various actors? The answer is social innovation in Europe is currently done often by a few large actors in concert with a large mass of smaller organizations, but the majority of social innovation actors in Europe are disconnected from these networks.

In order to determine this, for all the organizations we mapped their degree, which is for a given node (organization) the number of connections (links) it has with other nodes (organizations). There are 243 organizations with connections to other organizations (26 %). The average number of connections per organization is almost 3 organizations. There are a few organizations that are hyper-connected "hubs," including the Waag Society, Nesta, Fondazione Mondo Digitale, and Institute for Network Cultures.

5.2   What Communities of Social Innovation Exist in Europe?

A community exists when a network is partitioned in such a manner that nodes within a community are more densely interconnected than those outside of the network. The clustering coefficient is way to understand this quantitatively. A triplet consists of three nodes that are connected by either via two nodes (a straight line) or three links undirected, where a triangle is defined by three closed triplets, where each node a triangle is part of a triplet. The global clustering coefficient is the number of triangles over the total number of triplets. This measure gives an indication of the clustering in the whole network. The global clustering coefficient of the DSI network is 0.875 with undirected links.

Modularity is the fraction of number of the edges that fall within a given community minus the expected fraction of the number if edges were distributed at random. The modularity of the DSI network is .65, where modularity is the percentage of the connections that fall within the given community minus the expected such links if they were random [7]. There are approximately 115 distinct disconnected communities of social innovation (measured in terms of connected components that are connected to each other but not connected to anyone else). Although there is one large pan-European network, there are also many smaller communities do not have connections to the larger cross-European digital social innovation "super-community." The vast amount of disconnected communities is visualized in Fig. 2.

Communities can also be automatically identified are mostly small by optimizing around modularity [1]. The results are given in Fig. 3, where a few large communities stand out from each other. These inter-connected communities only count for 28 % of the total amount of connected DSI activities. The largest community (green 10.29 %) is focused around open hardware and open networks and includes organizations such as iMinds, Fairphone, the City of Amsterdam, and FabLab Barcelona, despite it being the smallest category of DSI methods. Its most interconnected member is the Waag Society, and there is a large focus on awareness networks and new ways of making. The collaborative economy

Fig. 2. Connected and dis-connected communities in the DSI network.

and open knowledge is the specialty of the second largest but also more scattered community (red - 7.41 %), consisting of ESADE, IRI, European Institute for Participatory Media, and the Institute for Network Cultures. A third large communities is grouped around Nesta (blue - 5.35 %) and is focused on funding, acceleration, and open democracy, although it has a very diverse technology focus, containing groups such as Open Ministry, Nominet, and Mozilla. Open data for open access is the last large community (purple 4.95 %), with a centre on FutureEverything, but also containing Open Knowledge and its local chapters as well and city councils working on open data such as that of Salford. Interestingly, although the open hardware network is the smallest overall, it is the most highly-interconnected and intermixed with open networks. Open knowledge is the most popular technological focus of DSI but it also the most spread out and disconnected. Other communities, such as those around open data, are developing connected communities. Nonetheless, the vast majority of communities are not interconnected.

5.3 Which Organizations Currently Bridge the Various Communities?

How can we determine which organizations act as crucial "bridges" between different organizations in DSI? This can be measured by using betweenness centrality, where the centrality of an organization is measured by counting the number of times a node occurs as a shortest number of links between any other nodes [3]. Betweenness centrality is equal to the number of shortest paths from all nodes to all others that pass through that node. The betweenness centrality was done using Brandes' algorithm [3]. It also calculated the total network diameter of 7

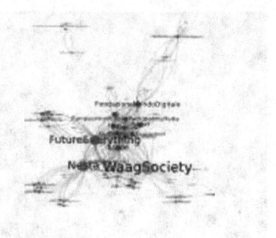

Fig. 3. DSI organizations in automatically discovered (colored) communities

and average path of 2.75. By this metric, these central organizations are: Waag Society, Nesta, Future Everything, Fondiazione Mondo Digitale, Kreater Social Innovation Agency, Forum Virium Helsinki, Swirrl, Open Knowledge Finland, IRI, BettterPlaceLab, Alfamicro, Amsterdam Smart City, Alfamicro, European Institute for Participatory Media, and ESADE. Each bridging of these organizations brings over 70 organizations together using the shortest possible number of links.

Who connects the diverse DSI communities, such as those of open data, open knowledge, open hardware, and open networks? What is more interesting than just being well-connected is whether an organization bridges diverse parts of the network with the greatest connectivity. Even if a organization is not central and so has only a few links, it may be these few important links that connect communities of well-connected organizations. Eigenvector centrality is a measure of reach (or influence) of a node in the network, and is thus important to quantify this idea of bridging diverse communities. It differs from betweenness centrality insofar as links to heavily ranked nodes contribute more, and so is closely related to the well-known Google Pageranking algorithm. If we look at the this kind of centrality, we see that a number of new organizations are crucial in bridging diverse communities (over .6 eigenvector centrality) outside of the original list of central organizations bubble up to the top: Institute of Network Cultures, iDROPSzw, Elva Community Engagement, Arduino, and Fing. To encourage cross-hybridization of different kinds of social innovation, special effort should be made by the European Commission to strengthen these digital crucial connectors between diverse DSI communities. Interdisciplinary European projects that force diverse communities to work together would strengthen the overall resilience of DSI in Europe by combining open hardware, open data, open knowledge, and open networks.

5.4   What Are the Conditions for Scaling DSI?

Successful actors in DSI have managed to leverage large networks using the Web in order to accomplish innovation at scale by the network effect. We can define scale in terms of scale-free, namely that the distribution of DSI should undergo the phase shift typical of complex systems from a disconnected network to a highly interconnected and self-similar small world network, where communities are clustered. This scale free network is often seen in organically developing ecosystems and is thought to be a sign of efficiency and resilience [2]. Note that power-laws have an important property called "scale invariance," which means that when scaling the network by a constant (i.e. multiplies the original power-law relation by the constant) only causes proportionate scaling of the function itself, which shows the underlying distribution is stable.

We used a set of techniques that test to see if a power-law existed in our data using the Kolmogorov-Smirnov distance (a non-parametric information-theoretic measure of the similarity between distance) on a set of simulated data of a power-law and the actual data. We used techniques outlined by Clauset et al. [4] to find a power-law possibly after $x = 3$ with and an α of 3.13. and a σ (standard deviation) of .19. We found a Kolmogorov-Smirnov statistic D of .1004. There was a p-value of less than .01. When tested rigorously, a power-law was indeed a strongly better fit ($p < 0.01$) than an alternative distribution without such a long-tail, such as the exponential distribution [4]. An exponential distribution does not have the majority of its strength in the long tail. However, the power law appears truncated, so that the power-law behavior may only actually apply to organizations with above 3 connections. Figure 4 shows the comparison between the power law distribution and the exponential function of the DSI network.

The reason digital social innovation has not yet scaled is because the long tail of smaller European DSI Networks is still heavily disconnected, with 687 organizations out of 930 (74%) have no links to other organizations! Many of these organizations are also in countries without much support, such as Eastern Europe. If we want a single scaling European DSI network, an additional magnitude more of links (approximately 350 links) is needed to gather all the disconnected organizations to a single European network. This is probably too many connections that can be made via traditional European projects, but via a recommendation system a future version of the Digital Social Innovation website could introduce innovators to both other local innovators and innovators sharing similar interests across Europe to boot-strap these connections. By connecting the currently isolated innovators, we should be able to achieve the necessary phase shift so that the scaling power of the heavily interconnected innovators is replicated across Europe by currently isolated innovators and communities. Globally, we are already interested outside of Europe (such as Harvard Ash Center) to re-use the ontology and eventually link data-sets.

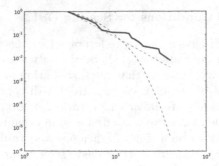

Fig. 4. Comparing the power law distribution (red) to exponential distribution (green) against the real actual network data (blue) (Color figure online).

6 Data-Driven Policy Recommendations

Based on the data, a number of recommendations were made to the European Commission. The full report, with much more detail, is available online.[16] In order to implement future DSI policy goals and strategies, several tools and instruments have to be deployed. Although most policy influencing DSI will be at national, regional and local levels, it is clear the European Commission has an important role in networking these new actors in the field due to vast disparities in connections. Rather than through traditional networking events, the European Commission can then use the network data to find the small disconnected communities and introduce them based on national and sector-specific networking i.e. around health, money, and education.

Crowdfunding is a promising collaborative approach for such bottom-up networks in comparison to traditional European large-scale research projects, which are often too "heavy-weight" and require larger networks than most of the DSI organizations in Europe have. However, while traditionally crowdfunding depends on individuals donating funding, there is no reason why crowd-funded projects cannot receive in-kind funding from the public sector or have their general structure be replicated using traditional research funding. The European Commission should start promoting more of these crowdfunding tools for DSI, involving users in choosing the best projects to be funded in a bottom-up fashion, as part of their funding allocations already in place for ICT research and development programmes in. Note that the CHEST project has already begun in this fashion using a traditional EC-funded project structure to start a crowd-sourcing campaign.[17] Another example is the 'European Social Innovation Challenge that in 2013, the European Commission launched in memory of Diogo Vasconcelos, to encourage new social innovations from all over Europe. The Competition invited Europeans to come up with new solutions to reduce unemployment with the three winning projects will be awarded financial support. By leaning on the

---

[16] http://content.digitalsocial.eu.

[17] http://chest-project.eu.

large DSI networks already existing around funding and acceleration, progress could be made quickly, but care needs to be taken to help disconnected DSI organizations. Given the large network of DSI on open hardware, more focus on how open hardware is necessary for trusted local hardware would be of use. More work is needed in opening public sector information, as the smaller but still substantial DSI communities focused on open data.

Open knowledge is comparatively doing better than open data in terms of DSI, and copyright reform is necessary to ensure its growth. The European Commission recently published its 'Report on the responses to the Public Consultation on the Review of the EU Copyright Rules.' This report summarizes the responses (over 11,000) that the Commission received in response to the copyright consultation held between December 2013 and March 2014. The results show conflicting positions between citizens and institutional users on one side and corporate rights holders on the other. Such patterns in public policy consultations show that stakeholders involvement is crucial, and that the Commission should take advantage of the increased user involvement in open knowledge, in particular to channel energy towards DSI.

Perhaps one of the largest recommended changes is, given the large number of DSI organizations in Europe, is to open public procurement to these organizations. In January 2014, the European Parliament adopted new procurement directives on PPI (Public procurement of innovative solutions) featuring increased flexibility and simplification on the procedures to follow, negotiations and time limits; clearer conditions on how to establish collaborative or joint procurement; and the creation of innovation partnerships. A review of procedures in public procurement is needed in order to include actors from grassroots DSI communities in procurement.

Lastly, the preservation of net neutrality to allow DSI organizations to use the Web to scale their services. It is a crucial to define and make public how network operators manage traffic volumes and restrict applications usage. Not only does net neutrality protect the freedom of expression and freedom of information online, it reasserts the principle of fair competition and guarantees that users may freely choose between services online, and thus is crucial to help DSI actors reach scale. Otherwise, large existing organizations that may not be as innovative could lock out smaller DSI actors rather than working with them collaboratively. One final note is that we may even eventually see DSI applied to policy-making directly. For example, Tim Berners-Lee (the inventor of the Web) is advocating for a sort of Magna Carta for the Web to establish basic rights and freedoms where the Magna Carta for all Web users could be directly crowd-sourced from the Web itself, engaging effectively in multi-stakeholder processes.

7   Conclusion and Next Steps

The DSI works shows how Linked Data can be used to combine traditional sources of data with survey-collected data in order to create a crowd-mapped data-set around new and innovative areas like digital social innovation. Through the website digitalsocial.eu, we have shown how visualizations and mapping can make Linked Data comprehensible by policy-makers. Through our network analysis how the various characteristics of DSI can be both understood structurally and how this understanding can produce concrete policy-level recommendations.

As a site digitalsocial.eu is still active, and but it is not in general interactive enough to get existing organizations to up-date their activities. For this to be the case, there would have to be concrete benefits. One idea is to tie new funding initiatives either directly or indirectly (via announcements) to the site. If recommender algorithms could be combined with the community clustering algorithms already used, we could effectively create a "LinkedIn" of DSI that directed new and existing organizations to like-minded organizations for partnership in projects and applications for funding. Combined with appropriate internationalization and reach outside of Europe, Linked Data could provide the infrastructure for growth of digital social innovation not only in Europe, but in the entire world.

References

1. Blondel, V., Guillaume, J.-L., Lambiotte, R., Lefebvre, E.: Fast unfolding of communities in large networks. J. Stat. Mech.: Theory Exp. **10**, 1000 (2008)
2. Boisot, M., McKelvey, B.: Connectivity, extremes, and power laws: towards a power-law science of organizational effectiveness. J. Manag. Inq. **20**(2), 119–133 (2011)
3. Brandes, U.: A faster algorithm for betweenness centrality. J. Math. Sociol. **25**(2), 163–177 (2001)
4. Clauset, A., Shalizi, C., Newman, M.: Power-law distributions in empirical data. SIAM Rev. **54**(4), 661–703 (2009)
5. Freeman, C., Soete, L.: The Economics of Industrial Innovation, 3rd edn. MIT Press, Cambridge (1997)
6. Mikheev, A., Moens, M., Grover, C.: Named entity recognition without gazetteers. In: Proceedings of the Ninth Conference on European Chapter of the Association for Computational Linguistics, EACL 1999, pp. 1–8. Association for Computational Linguistics, Stroudsburg (1999)
7. Newman, M.: Modularity and community structure in networks. Proc. Nat. Acad. Sci. U.S.A. **103**(23), 8577–8696 (2006)

Desperately Searching for Travel Offers? Formulate Better Queries with Some Help from Linked Data

Chun Lu[1,2(✉)], Milan Stankovic[1,2], and Philippe Laublet[2]

[1] Sépage, 27 rue du Chemin Vert, 75011 Paris, France
{chun,milstan}@sepage.fr
[2] STIH, Université Paris-Sorbonne, 28 rue Serpente, 75006 Paris, France
philippe.laublet@paris-sorbonne.fr

Abstract. Various studies have reported on inefficiencies of existing travel search engines, and user frustration generated through hours of searching and browsing, often with no satisfactory results. Not only do the users fail to find the right offer in the myriad of websites, but they end up browsing through many offers that do not correspond to their criteria. The Semantic Web framework is a reasonable candidate to improve this. In this paper, we present a semantic travel offer search system named "RE-ONE (Relevance Engine-One)". We especially highlight its ability to help users formulate better search queries. An example of a permitted query is *in Croatia at the seaside where there is Vegetarian Restaurant*. We conducted two experiments to evaluate the Query Auto-completion mechanism. The results showed that our system outperforms the Google Custom Search baseline. Queries freely conducted in RE-ONE are shown to be 63.4 % longer in terms of number of words and 27 % richer in terms of number of search criteria. RE-ONE supports better users' query formulation process by giving suggestions in greater accordance with users' idea flow.

Keywords: Semantic search · Travel search · Linked data · Query Auto-completion

1 Introduction

The sector of e-tourism is today in lightning growth. According to Google 2013 Traveler [16], the Web is the source of inspiration for 61 % of people and the source of a travel planning for 80 %. Search is the primary entry point to the travel-related information online. 58 % of leisure travelers and 64 % of business travelers always start their travel booking and planning process with search. However, 68 % begin searching online without having a clear travel destination in mind. Consumers spend up to 45 days and conduct 38 visits to travel sites before booking [5]. In the sample session of the study, the user switched frequently among retail sites, travel sites, weather sites, generalist search engine sites, social media sites etc. Users have to interact with vast amounts of information by doing lots of browsing and searching before finding relevant travel offers, and being able to verify if those meet their criteria. Obviously, existing systems do not support users well in expressing their needs and finding what they want

© Springer International Publishing Switzerland 2015
F. Gandon et al. (Eds.): ESWC 2015, LNCS 9088, pp. 621–636, 2015.
DOI: 10.1007/978-3-319-18818-8_38

if users end up spending so much time and doing so much manual verification (on external sites) for offers took into consideration. Our motivation is to develop an efficient search system to accelerate the travel offer finding with the following hypotheses:

- By guiding the user during the query formulation process in an intelligent way, we can make the user formulate longer and richer queries, that will yield more satisfactory results in comparison to commonly used Query Auto-completion systems such as our baseline Google Custom Search.
- By leveraging Semantic Web graphs and external sources (information not present in the travel offer's presentation), we can improve the user's ability to check if a travel offer satisfies his/her criteria, thus reducing the need to crosscheck information on multiple other sites. Users would thus use novel criteria directly in the search bar so that information access becomes more direct and quicker.

The main contributions from this paper are three fold:

- a travel destination-centered data graph gathering sources from RDF databases, social media websites and web services
- a pattern-based method to verbalize the semantic data graph in a controlled language
- a Query Auto-completion mechanism to guide users during the query formulation process perceived to be in great accordance with users' idea flow.

The remainder of the paper is organized as follows. In Sect. 2, we present some related work. In Sect. 3, we present our system named RE-ONE (Relevance Engine-One). In Sect. 4, we present the conducted experiments. In Sect. 5, we conclude the paper.

2 State of the Art

In this part, we relate our system to some academic and industrial contributions.

2.1 Why Semantic Web Framework?

The traditional full-text search approach is widely used by frameworks and services such as Google Search[1], Apache Solr[2], Lucene[3], ElasticSearch[4] etc. This approach is not efficient enough for the travel offer search. We highlight here two main weak points.

Firstly, the spectrum of search possibilities depends on words in the stored documents and indexes mainly generated from them. If an information is not described in

---

[1] https://www.google.com/.

[2] http://lucene.apache.org/solr/.

[3] http://lucene.apache.org/core/.

[4] http://www.elasticsearch.org/.

the documents, users can difficultly find documents with it. It is often the case in the travel search context. Because a travel can be associated to so many things that they cannot all be mentioned in the documents. For example, in a travel offer, the destinations are Hyères, le Lavandou etc., which are situated in the department of Var in France. But if this information is not mentioned in the presentation, full-text search systems would not find this offer given a very legitimate query like "Var" or "in the Var" or "in the department of Var".

Secondly, they deliver documents containing the words in the search query but not satisfying the criteria carried by the words. For example, for the query "travel in Paris", full-text search systems would find all offers having the word "Paris" in the presentation, even if Paris is the departure city.

The Semantic Web framework is a reasonable candidate to address these two weak points for two reasons. Firstly, a big amount of data about travel destinations is available on the Web. Many of them are already structured according to Semantic Web standards and can be found on RDF databases like DBpedia. Other data can be easily structured according to the same standards. These data can be used as additional indexes to enlarge the spectrum of search possibilities. Secondly, search systems based on Semantic Web framework deliver documents satisfying the criteria carried by the words in the search query. Given the same query "travel in Paris", with an appropriate ontology, semantic search systems like [2, 3, 6–8, 11, 15] would understand that the user is searching for offers that have Paris as destination. This accelerates the access to relevant information and saves users' time.

For these reasons, we decided to use Semantic Web framework to try to solve the travel search problem in a new way, building our travel offer search system that we could plug into existing travel websites and provide an advanced, more intelligent, search solution.

2.2   Search Over Linked Data

Keyword search is the most popular technique for querying data with loose structure on the Web. Its success comes from the flexibility it provides to the user to retrieve information from a data source without mastering a complex query language (e.g., XQuery, SPARQL) and without knowing the structure of the data source [7]. In [3], the authors proposed a method for effective and efficient entity search over RDF data. They described an adaptation of the BM25F ranking function for RDF data. In [8], the authors presented a semantic search system that provides the user with a capability to query Semantic Web information using natural language, by means of *PowerAqua* [11] and complements the specific answers retrieved during the Question Answering process with a ranked list of documents from the Web. *PowerAqua* is a natural language interface to ontologies. Natural language interfaces are systems which allow users to express their search queries in some natural language and retrieve answers from given ontological databases. *PowerAqua* can be coupled with multiple heterogeneous RDF databases but most of such systems can only be coupled with one RDF database. These systems often face the habitability problem that refers to how easily, naturally and effectively users can use the language to express themselves within the constraints imposed by the system [6].

FREyA [6] uses two methods for improving the habitability: feedback and clarification dialogues. The system models feedback by showing the user how the query is interpreted, thus suggesting repair through query reformulation. Clarification dialogues are used to control the query interpretations generated by the systems. *GINO* [2] allows users to edit and query ontologies in a language akin to English. It uses a small static grammar, which it dynamically extends with elements from the loaded ontologies. *AGGREGO SEARCH* [15] is similar to *GINO*. It offers a keyword-based query solution. It suggests grammatical connectors from natural languages during the query formulation step in order to specify the meaning of each keyword, thus leading to a complete and explicit definition of the intent of the search.

In the travel context, search systems face also another challenge: users do not know what to search and their queries are very short. Making the user express his/her needs in a more expressive way is a declared need. While the approaches may be well adapted for the query disambiguation or interpretation task, this need is not really addressed.

In [12], the authors presented a number of methods and their implementation in an online tool for mining type-based query context information, i.e. query prefixes and postfixes that are common to a class of entities, while uncommon to other entities outside of their class. Postulating that these context words represent aspects of entities that search engine users are interested in, they proceeded to investigate on the case of Wikipedia the extent to which this schema of information needs matches the schema of available structured data. They found that at least for the most common context words the overlap is very low as the most common queries are not specific enough to be answered by factual data. They indicated that a promising direction of research is the investigation of how search engines might assist users in formulating more precise queries. This is exactly what we are trying to achieve in travel.

We developed a Query Auto-completion mechanism. Users are assisted during the whole query formulation process. Similar to *GINO and AGGREGO SEARCH*, our vocabularies come from the considered RDF database. There are two main differences. The first difference is that, in those systems, vocabularies are used almost directly with no extensive adaptation to the use-case, and vocabularies used in RDF databases are not always very natural and explicit. For example, on DBpedia, the rdfs:label value of the property dbpedia-owl:country is country. If we use this vocabulary directly, a segment of query would be: "country France", while the natural way to say it is: "in France". *AGGREGO SEARCH* enriched vocabularies with additional logical connectors like "and" and some tool words like "of". However, this enrichment does not make its use enough natural. We used a pattern-based method to verbalize our semantic data graph in a controlled language. The second difference is that the suggestions in those systems are not ranked. All possible terms are suggested in the order of appearance in the considered RDF database. Our system contains an approach to rank criteria suggestions in a way leading the user to compose queries more likely to yield satisfactory results.

2.3   Linked Data Applied in Travel Context

In [14], the authors pointed out some issues that hampered the automatic access and reuse of data sets about travel statistical indicators: (i) by them being offered as data dumps in non-semantic encodings; (ii) by them assuming some implicit knowledge that is necessary to build applications (e.g., that a city is situated in a certain country) and (iii) by the use of incompatible ways to measure the same indicator without formally specifying the assumptions behind the measurement technique. They explored the use of linked data technologies to solve these issues by triplifying the content of a broadly used data source of European tourism statistics. They built a prototype system using the data to support tourism decision makers in their activities of combining and comparing statistical indicators.

In [9], the authors presented an application for exploiting, managing and organizing Linked Data in the domain of news and blogs about travelling. The system makes use of several heterogeneous datasets to help users to plan future trips, and relies on the Open Provenance Model for modeling the provenance information of the resources. This system can be considered mostly a visualization tool. The scenario on the top of which was developed the application was related to the general context of travelling, where travelers want to share, read and reuse experiences in blogs and online news items.

These two papers demonstrated the benefits of using Linked Data in the travel domain. But we have different concerns, [14] is interested in statistical indicators, [9] in travel experience visualization, and RE-ONE in travel offer search.

2.4   Industrial Travel Search Systems

Kayak[5] represents the type of tools where users need to type the exact destination to find corresponding offers. It is not effective enough in the considered scenario. On *TripTuner*,[6] users do not search with words but by adjusting six criteria sliders. The number of criteria is very limited and the criteria are the same for all users no matter what they search for.

Find my carrots[7] and *Zap Travel*[8] claim to be semantic-based travel search engines. Users can type queries in controlled natural languages. We observed some proposed query examples and found some notable points. Some queries are too long for the contained information. For example *"What cities can I visit in Europe that are good for nightlife?"*, *"I want to go to Los Angeles, CA from Bangalore with my wife, 10 year old son and 5 year old daughter next sunday and return 10 days later"*. Users' willingness to type such queries is uncertain and the systems do not give a sufficient support in formulating them. *Zap Travel* ignores or changes the semantics of important elements

---

[5] http://www.kayak.com/.

[6] http://triptuner.com/.

[7] http://www.findmycarrots.com/.

[8] http://www.zaptravel.com/.

in users' queries. For example, in *"I want to go golfing in California"*, "golfing" is ignored, in *"Somewhere warm"*, "warm" is interpreted as "beach". Such systems thus, generate other frustrations (such as inaccuracy of results with regards to criteria etc.) while trying to solve the travel search problem.

2.5   Other Industrial Search Systems

Facebook Graph Search[9] is a semantic search system introduced by Facebook in March 2013 which allows users to search in a English-based controlled natural language within the Facebook Social Graph. Some query examples are *"Photos of my friends in New York"*, *"Photos I like"*, *"People who like Cycling and live in Seattle, Washinton"*, *"Cities my family visited"*. However, *Facebook Graph Search* does not provide any travel search feature.

Yahoo Knowledge Graph is a knowledge base used by Yahoo to enhance its search engine's results with semantic-search information gathered from a wide variety of sources.

IBM Watson[10] is an artificially intelligent computer system capable of answering questions posed in natural language, developed in IBM's DeepQA project. The sources of information for Watson include encyclopedias, dictionaries, thesauri, newswire articles, and literary works. Watson also used databases, taxonomies, and ontologies. Specifically, DBPedia, WordNet, and Yago were used.

Wolfram Alpha[11] is a computational knowledge engine. It uses built-in knowledge curated by human experts to compute on the fly a specific answer and analysis for every query. The long-term goal is to make all systematic knowledge computable and broadly accessible.

Google Search provides a platform called *Google Custom Search* that allows web developers to feature specialized information in web searches, refine and categorize queries and create customized search engines, based on *Google Search*. Many actors in the sector of the e-tourism install Google Custom Search on their websites. *Google Custom Search* provides no special feature for travel-related content. It indexes from and searched in the custom website's documents. The search quality depends strongly on the documents which are different on every website.

3   System RE-ONE

In this part, we present five aspects of our system: travel destination-centered semantic data graph, data graph verbalization, travel offer catalogue annotation, Query Auto-completion, search results ranking.

---

[9] https://www.facebook.com/about/graphsearch.

[10] http://en.wikipedia.org/wiki/Watson_%28computer%29.

[11] http://www.wolframalpha.com/.

3.1 Travel Destination-Centered Semantic Data Graph

Travel destinations are very important in travel offers. However, they are not always well described in travel offers' presentations. This can limit considerably the spectrum of search possibilities. This problem can be addressed by leveraging the Semantic graph of DBpedia where travel destinations are linked to other relevant information.

In this paper, travel destinations that we consider are cities. On DBpedia, we did not find a class of which the instances are all the cities in the world. The class *dbpedia-owl:City* exists, but its instances are not complete, for example, *dbpedia: Paris* is not an instance of it. The most appropriate class is *dbpedia-owl:Settlement*, even though some instances are countries, districts or other types. So our travel destinations are instances of the class *dbpedia-owl:Settlement*. This class is linked with a big number of object properties and datatype properties. Many of them are not interesting in the travel context. For example, *dbpedia-owl:inseeCode* which links to a numerical indexing code used by the French National Institute for Statistics and Economic Studies (INSEE) to identify various entities, *foaf:homepage* which links to the homepage of something, *dbpedia-owl:subdivisions* which links to the number of subdivisions etc. Some of them do not have clear semantics. For example, *dbpprop:alt*, *dbpprop:align* etc. We did a manual selection of properties which might be interesting. So far, the selected properties are the following: *dbpedia-owl:country*, *rdfs:label*, *dbpedia-owl:location*, *dcterms:subject*. We isolated the selected classes and properties and we created a travel destination-centered semantic data graph.

The information that we retrieved from DBpedia can only cover a part of users' search needs. As [5] shows, users consult diverse types of websites to gather information when they do travel search. To simplify users' search task, we included in our data graph these types of information that are now manually crosschecked by users on multiple sites. They are: points of interest, coastal or not, and weather.

Foursquare has a very rich taxonomy of points of interest categories[12]. We did a manual selection of categories that are relevant to travel search and representative to travel destinations. We did not consider categories like "Professional", "Office", "School", "Residence" etc. Via its API, we retrieved for each of our destination, if it exists in Foursquare, the points of interest that belong to the selected categories and are located in it. As to if a travel destination is coastal or not, we calculated this information with data retrieved via the API of *Bing Maps*[13]. We retrieved monthly average temperatures of our travel destinations via the API of *World Weather Online*[14].

Thus, we created a travel destination-centered semantic data graph gathering sources from DBpedia, social media websites and web services. Figure 1 shows its structure.

---

[12] https://developer.foursquare.com/categorytree.

[13] http://msdn.microsoft.com/en-us/library/dd877180.aspx.

[14] http://www.worldweatheronline.com/.

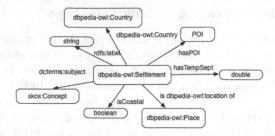

Fig. 1. Main structure of the travel destination-centered data graph

3.2 Data Graph Verbalization

We used a pattern-based method to verbalize the (property, object) couples of the triples in the data graph. Here are the patterns.

(Property, object) couples	Verbalization pattern
dbpedia-owl:country, dbpedia-owl:Country	in + country's label
is dbpedia-owl:location of, dbpedia-owl:Place	where is located + place's label
rdfs:label, datatype value	in + value
dcterms:subject, skos:Concept	Concept's label
hasTempSept, datatype value	where it is hot/moderate/cold in September
hasPOI, POI	where there is + POI's category
isCoastal, datatype value	at the seaside

After the verbalization process, each instance of the class *dbpedia-owl:Settlement* is associated with a certain number of semantic tags written in a controlled language. Figure 2 is a result excerpt for the city of Nice.

Fig. 2. Example illustrating the pattern-based data graph verbalization

3.3 Travel Offer Catalogue Annotation

Given a travel offer catalogue, an annotation task is conducted. An offer initially retrieved from a particular travel catalogue, is often a structured data entry containing travel destinations, dates, prices as structured data, and a URL containing textual and multimedia information. Offers are processed individually. Only two elements are considered and analysed: the travel destinations and the URL.

Each offer is first assigned all semantic tags that are associated with its travel destinations. Then we used a Named Entity extractor called "Dandelion" [13] to analyze the textual content in the URL and to extract DBpedia concepts. The semantic tags and the labels of extracted concepts constitute together the offer's indexes. As we can see in Fig. 3 below, each offer of the catalogue is annotated with a certain number of indexes. Indexes can be unique to one offer or common to several offers (index 3).

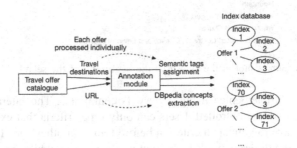

Fig. 3. Travel offer catalogue annotation workflow.

3.4 Query Auto-Completion

In [1], we can find a short explanation of the autocomplete algorithm of *Google Search*: autocomplete predictions are automatically generated by an algorithm without any human involvement, based on a number of objective factors, including how often past users have searched for a term. The algorithm automatically detects and excludes a small set of search terms. But it is designed to reflect the diversity of our users' searches and content on the web. So just like the web, the search terms shown may seem strange or surprising. Except for this, we did not have access to a more detailed explanation about their algorithm.

Our Query Auto-completion mechanism is different. In order to maximize the chances of satisfactory searches, our approach is not based on how often past users have searched for a term but on how a criterion is relevant to find offers corresponding to it. We define a criterion as an attribute of an offer allowing direct verification whether the offer has it or not. A criterion can contain one or several words. A criterion can be expressed in different forms: keywords or in a natural language, for example, "seafood restaurant", "where there is a seafood restaurant", "where I can find a seafood restaurant", "with a seafood restaurant" are all different forms of the same criterion.

Indexes generated in Sect. 3.3 can be considered as criteria. Knowing all criteria that allow to find offers in a catalogue, we can calculate, for each criterion, the number of offers that can be found with it. Criteria are then ranked by this number in descending order. At the beginning of the search session, users are suggested 8 criteria which are the best ranked criteria of each type of information (data graph & extracted DBpedia concept) (Fig. 4).

It is important to note that the systems reinforces the diversity of suggestion types so that the users can, from the very start, get to know broadly what are the types of search criteria that can be searched. The users are subtly informed of the constraints imposed by the system.

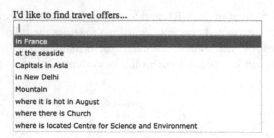

Fig. 4. Screenshot of the system at the beginning of the search session.

The system is implemented using jQuery Tokeninput[15]. The interaction between the system and users are controlled. Users can only type criteria that exist in the index database. Users have to validate a criterion before typing another one. The suggestions are generated in two different modes. The first mode is active while the user is typing a word. The suggestions are in this case calculated with regards to the highest string similarity with the text being typed by the user. We used the Levenshtein distance as our string metric. The other mode is active when one or more criteria are validated and the user is idle, then the system proposes additional criteria suggestions while taking into account the criteria already validated. In the two modes, the ranking of suggestions is performed in a way that maximizes the probability of preforming a successful query on a given website catalogue, and that favors the diversity of proposed criteria types.

$$rank(c, Q) = p("c + Q") \tag{1}$$

The system searches in the offers that correspond to the validated criteria (remaining offers) all available criteria (that are not yet validated). Available criteria are ranked according to the formula (1). The rank of a criterion c (for instance "in Slovenia"), provided that c is one of the available criteria, not included in the validated ones that constitute the current query Q, is proportional to the probability of finding an offer in the catalogue that corresponds to the extended query: Q + c, in which criterion c is added to the already validated criteria. An essential part of the process is making sure that proposed criteria are diverse: a step made possible by the use of semantic data graphs in which offer properties are typed in a hierarchical way. We display one criterion (the best-ranked) from each type of information as much as possible (if the type is still present in the available criteria. For example, "at the seaside" is the only criterion of its type, if it is validated, it will not be suggested again.), while preserving the order of appearance in order of the best ranked ones.

3.5   Search Results Ranking

We did not implement a specific search results ranking method. Because in our case, all retrieved results correspond to the query and are of the same importance. For example,

---

[15] http://loopj.com/jquery-tokeninput/.

for the query "in Croatia at the seaside", all found offers are in Croatia and at the seaside. When a search query is submitted, the system searches for offers that correspond to all the criteria. Search results are now ranked by the profitability index defined by catalogue providers.

4 Evaluation

In this section, we describe two experiments conducted to test our research hypotheses.

4.1 Experiment Data

Our experiments are conducted using the travel offer catalogue provided by a French tour operator. The catalogue counts 956 travel offers. The travel destinations are numerous and cover more than 150 countries.

4.2 Baseline

The baseline that we compare with is the Google Custom Search installed on the website of the French tour-operator. This tool is a good candidate for baseline for two reasons. Firstly, it is the personalized version of the most used search engine in the United States [3] and it is widely used by travel websites. Secondly, we have full access to the catalogue, this allowed us to compare the two systems with the same data.

4.3 Metrics

The following metrics have been used:

- *average number of words per query*
- *average number of criteria per query*
- *provenance of criteria.*

We used the *average number of words per query* because the travel website owners told us about the limits they encounter with short queries in terms of providing personalized and optimal user experience. But it is an objective measure as there is no human judgment involved, the fact that different systems propose criteria in different forms, and according to different algorithms, the difference observed in the number of words is not sufficient to conclude that one or the other system provides better support in query formulation process. For this reason, we were interested in the *average number of criteria per query*, which should not be influenced by the form in which the two systems present their suggestions, but only by their capacity to suggest a criterion that the user would actually consider adding to his/her query. In addition to these metrics, we were interested in the qualification of criteria used, in terms of their provenance (user thought-of, or suggested by the system), expressed on the following scale from option 1 (criterion formulated by the user and not suggested by the system) to option 5 (criterion suggested by the system that user hasn't thought of himself).

1. *It is a criterion that I already had in mind and it was not in the suggestions.*
2. *It is a criterion that I already had in mind and it was also in the suggestions.*
3. *It is a criterion that I did not have in mind. It was in the suggestions. It is relevant. But I coud have thought about it.*
4. *It is a criterion that I did not have in mind. It was in the suggestions. It is relevant. It is surprising and I coud not have thought about it.*
5. *It is a criterion that I did not have in mind. Some suggestions inspired me and helped me find this criterion.*

4.4   Two Conducted Experiments

The website of the tour-operator is only in French. The Google Custom Search is also performed in French. We developed a French version of RE-ONE. Vocabularies and the pattern-based verbalization method are translated and adapted to French. We asked 34 people to participate in the evaluation. They are all French citizens or French speakers. They have between 23 and 35 years old. They are used to doing travel search on the Web.

The duration of the offers in the test catalogue is very varied, from 1 day to 71 days. We are thus exposed to the risk of people manifesting different behavior and using different criteria for long and short trip searches. In order to avoid bias, we thus divided our users into two groups: A to whom we gave the task of searching for short (1–4 days) trips that correspond to (extended) weekend trips and B to whom we gave the task of searching for long (5 and more days) trips that correspond to longer holidays. Both groups used both our system and the baseline system.

Firstly, participants put themselves into the scenario of searching for the next travel. They identify clearly a concrete possible next occasion for travel in their agendas, and imagine the concrete usual context of looking for places to go on that occasion. At this very early stage they do not yet have a precise destination. They turn to the search systems to find offers. Secondly, Participants performed their search twice, once in RE-ONE and once in the baseline system. To avoid possible bias due to the order of use of the systems, we made half of the users search in RE-ONE first and the other half search in the baseline system first. Thirdly, participants splitted the queries into criteria and chose for each criterion the most suitable option from the scale introduced in Sect. 4.3. They are well informed of our definition of criterion introduced in Sect. 3.4 and are given some splitting examples. In spite of this process, this task remains a potential source of subjectivity or error. To avoid bias, we ran a verification phase after the experiment, in which 3 independent reviewers were asked to verify, for each query-to-criteria split performed by the users in the study, if the split was performed according to our definition. Only splits that 2 or 3 reviewers approved were taken into account in further measurement. Finally this review phase required the elimination of only 2 queries.

4.5   First Experiment: Searching for a Short Trip

In the first group which performed a search for a short trip, a significant difference in average word number was observed between the systems: 2.06 ± 1.14 in the baseline system and 5.76 ± 3.46 in RE-ONE. The difference was significant according to T-test (p-value < 0.001). A smaller, but still significant (p-value < 0.05) difference was observed in the number of criteria: 1.59 ± 0.78 in the baseline system and 2.12 ± 0.8 in RE-ONE. Both metrics are consistent and allow us to conclude about the positive impact of our system in terms of assistance in query formulation; queries conducted in RE-ONE were in average 64.2 % longer and 25 % richer than that in the baseline system. The following table is a part of users' queries for the short trip search that are translated literally by us from French to English. The same user carried out the two queries of each row (Fig. 5).

RE-ONE	The baseline system
Church New art	Church
Northern Europe North Cape	Europe
Cross-country skiing in Coroico	Cross-country skiing France
Volcanic island Porto-Novo Ribera Grande	Island of Malta

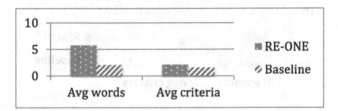

Fig. 5. Average number of words and criteria per query statistics in the first experiment.

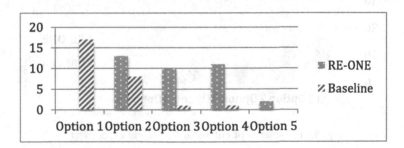

Fig. 6. Provenance of criteria statistics in the first experiment.

Figure 6 allows us to observe the difference in criteria provenance, on our scale option 1–option 5, options closer to one being closer to user's own ideas, and options closer to 5 being closer criteria attributable to the systems' assistance. We see that the distribution of criteria provenance for RE-ONE is stronger in options attributing the presence of criteria in final queries to the system's assistance, while queries formulated in the baseline system are richer in criteria thought-of by the user.

4.6   Second Experiment: Search for a Long Trip

Similarly to the first experiment, in the case of long trip search, a significant (t-test p-value < 0.05) was observed in the average number of words per query 2.65 ± 1.37 for the baseline system and 7.06 ± 5.4 for RE-ONE. For the number of criteria, again a slightly smaller but significant (p-value < 0.05) difference was created: 1.59 ± 0.62 for the baseline system and 2.24 ± 0.9 for RE-ONE. In other words, queries conducted in RE-ONE were in average 62.5 % longer and 29 % richer than those in the baseline system. The following table is a part of users' queries for the long trip search (Fig. 7).

RE-ONE	The baseline system
Seafood Culture Salvador Dali	Seafood
Summer where there is a historical site	Summer historical
South-East Asia Hô-Chi-Minh City	South-East Asia travel
Trek in New Zealand	Linguistic stay

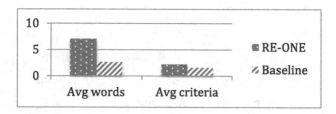

Fig. 7. Average number of words and criteria per query statistics in the second experiment.

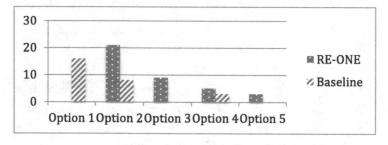

Fig. 8. Provenance of criteria in the second experiment

Looking at the provenance of criteria, again we can conclude the superiority of RE-ONE over the baseline in terms of the presence of criteria attributable to the system's assistance (Fig. 8).

4.7   General Discussion

In both experiments, RE-ONE outperforms the the baseline system baseline, and that according to all metrics that we used. In average, queries conducted in RE-ONE are

63.4 % longer and 27 % richer than that in the baseline system. As regards to supporting users' query formulation process, RE-ONE also shows a clear advantage.

While the interaction seems smoother in the baseline system as users can type whatever they like, if the user starts typing a term that is not suggested, then the baseline system is not able to do suggestions afterwards. This explains the big number of criteria that correspond to option 1. Since RE-ONE is a controlled system, users can only type search criteria that exist in our known indexes. This is why there is 0 criterion corresponding to option 1. We were interested in the effect of this constraint. We examined the logs of the experiments, we calculated the number of times that users could not type what he/she had in mind and then typed another criterion. There were in total 8 times for the short trip search and 11 times for the long trip search. The number is much smaller than the baseline in both experiments. The results for the other four options show that the suggestions of RE-ONE are always in greater accordance with users' idea flow, and able to suggest criteria of added value with regards to users own ideas, which end up being accepted and constituting the final queries. It is especially when looking at options qualifying the criteria as external to what the user had in mind (options 3–5) that RE-ONE shows great superiority with regards to the baseline.

We have thus demonstrated the ability of our system, combining travel offers with external information from semantic graphs to provide effective assistance in travel search query formulation.

5 Conclusions

In this paper, we presented RE-ONE, a semantic travel offer search system. We highlighted its ability to help users formulate better queries. This is made possible by leveraging the semantic graph containing sources from RDF databases, social media websites and web services. As for the evaluation, 34 people participated in two experiments, half of them simulated a short trip search, the other half a long trip search. The data is the travel offer catalogue provided by a French tour-operator. Our system outperforms the Google Custom Search baseline in both experiments leading users to formulate longer and richer queries. We provide better support by giving relevant (accepted by the users) suggestions in great accordance with users' idea flow.

In spite of good evaluation results, we still find some weak points to be improved in a future work. Firstly, we can enrich the data graph with other properties on DBpedia or other external sources. Secondly, the quality of DBpedia concepts extraction is not good enough. We can find some strange concepts like "A40 autoroute". Thirdly, some concepts are well extracted but not relevant to travel like "Laborer". We need to find a method to remove automatically concepts that are poorly extracted or not relevant. Fourthly, we can reduce the lexical constraints and provide more flexibility to users. Fifthly, we can develop a personalization module to analyze users' search behavior and to do some adaptations.

In today's technology-rich world, users are confronted with vast amounts of data and spend much effort interacting with them. As we showed in this paper, we are convinced that Semantic Web technologies can provide a solid support in users' query formulation process.

References

1. Autocomplete. https://support.google.com/websearch/answer/106230?hl=en. Accessed 4 Nov 2014
2. Bernstein, A., Kaufmann, E.: GINO - a guided input natural language ontology editor. In: Cruz, I., Decker, S., Allemang, D., Preist, C., Schwabe, D., Mika, P., Uschold, M., Aroyo, L.M. (eds.) ISWC 2006. LNCS, vol. 4273, pp. 144–157. Springer, Heidelberg (2006)
3. Blanco, R., Mika, P., Vigna, S.: Effective and efficient entity search in RDF data. In: Aroyo, L., Welty, C., Alani, H., Taylor, J., Bernstein, A., Kagal, L., Noy, N., Blomqvist, E. (eds.) ISWC 2011, Part I. LNCS, vol. 7031, pp. 83–97. Springer, Heidelberg (2011)
4. comScore Releases October 2014 U.S. Desktop Search Engine Rankings. http://www.comscore.com/fre/Insights/Market-Rankings/comScore-Releases-October-2014-US-Desktop-Search-Engine-Rankings. Accessed 29 Dec 2014
5. Custom Research: Exploring the Traveler's Path to Purchase. http://info.advertising.expedia.com/path-to-purchase. Accessed 28 Aug 2014
6. Damljanović, D., Agatonović, M., Cunningham, H., Bontcheva, K.: Improving habitability of natural language interfaces for querying ontologies with feedback and clarification dialogues. Web Semant. Sci. Serv. Agents World Wide Web **19**, 1–21 (2013)
7. Dass, A., Aksoy, C., Dimitriou, A., Theodoratos, D.: Exploiting semantic result clustering to support keyword search on linked data. In: Benatallah, B., Bestavros, A., Manolopoulos, Y., Vakali, A., Zhang, Y. (eds.) WISE 2014, Part I. LNCS, vol. 8786, pp. 448–463. Springer, Heidelberg (2014)
8. Fernandez, M., Lopez, V., Sabou, M., Uren, V., Vallet, D., Motta, E., Castells, P.: Semantic search meets the web. In: Proceedings of the IEEE International Conference on Semantic Computing, pp. 253–260 (2008)
9. Garijo, D., Villazón-Terrazas, B., Corcho, Ó.: A provenance-aware linked data application for trip management and organization. In: I-SEMANTICS 2011, pp. 224–226
10. Introducing Graph Search. https://www.facebook.com/about/graphsearch. Accessed 4 Apr 2014
11. Lopez, V., Fernández, M., Motta, E., Stieler, N.: PowerAqua: supporting users in querying and exploring the semantic web. Semant. Web **3**(3), 249–265 (2012)
12. Meij, E., Mika, P., Zaragoza, H.: Investigating the demand side of semantic search through query log analysis. In: Proceedings of the Workshop on Semantic Search at the 18th International World Wide Web Conference (2009)
13. Parmesan, S., Scaiella, U., Barbera, M., Tarasova, T.: Dandelion: from raw data to dataGEMs for developers. In: Proceedings of the ISWC Developers Workshop 2014, Riva del Garda, Italy, pp. 1–6, October 2014
14. Sabou, M., Brasoveanu, A., Arsal, I.: Supporting tourism decision making with linked data. In: I-SEMANTICS 2012, pp. 201–204
15. Smits, G., Pivert, O., Jaudoin, H., Paulus, F.: AGGREGO SEARCH: interactive keyword query construction. In: EDBT, pp. 636–639 (2014)
16. The 2013 Traveler. http://www.thinkwithgoogle.com/research-studies/2013-traveler.html. Accessed 28 Aug 2014

Towards the Russian Linked Culture Cloud: Data Enrichment and Publishing

Dmitry Mouromtsev[1]([✉]), Peter Haase[1,2], Eugene Cherny[1,3], Dmitry Pavlov[1,4], Alexey Andreev[1], and Anna Spiridonova[1]

[1] ITMO University, St. petersburg, Russia
mouromtsev@mail.ifmo.ru, aandreyev13@gmail.com, spiranna@list.ru
[2] metaphacts GmbH, Walldorf, Germany
ph@metaphacts.com
[3] Åbo Akademi University, Turku, Finland
eugene.cherny@niuitmo.ru
[4] Vismart Ltd., St. Petersburg, Russia
dmitry.pavlov@vismart.biz

Abstract. In this paper we present an architecture and approach to publishing open linked data in the cultural heritage domain. We demonstrate our approach for building a system both for data publishing and consumption and show how user benefits can be achieved with semantic technologies. For domain knowledge representation the CIDOC-CRM ontology is used. As a main source of trusted data, we use the data of the web portal of the Russian Museum. For data enrichment we selected DBpedia and the published Linked Data of the British Museum. The evaluation shows the potential of semantic applications for data publishing in contextual environment, semantic search, visualization and automated enrichment according to needs and expectations of art experts and regular museum visitors.

Keywords: Semantic web · Semantic data publishing · CIDOC-CRM · Open data · Cultural heritage

1   Introduction

The smooth and natural transfer of cultural heritage is the key factor for the preservation of national identity, which is crucial in the era of rapid globalization. At the same time the traditional mechanisms of heritage transfer from generation to generation nowadays undergo a serious change and experience a great challenge as the digital era unfolds before our own eyes. The digital era prompts developers of content and applications to use a new language of communication and a new channel to deliver the information to the consumer. Thus, cultural heritage transfer can strongly benefit from the digital movement to make it more exciting, personal and vivid. Although in order to make sure that the cultural heritage is being preserved, the digitization of content is not enough whilst adequate representation of the data starts to play a decisive role.

© Springer International Publishing Switzerland 2015
F. Gandon et al. (Eds.): ESWC 2015, LNCS 9088, pp. 637–651, 2015.
DOI: 10.1007/978-3-319-18818-8_39

Progress has been made in this direction by introducing the digitization of the art works and creating large structured storage of digitized artifacts. The second step was made by creating user applications with digital data: It included establishment of large museum portals, the launch of mobile applications of various kinds and features. Some of the museums have already placed their digital collections in the open data cloud, thus opening it for querying and integration [1]. To back this trend up all the vital infrastructure was created. Of particular importance in this context is CIDOC-CRM - a Conceptual Reference Model providing definitions and a formal structure for describing the implicit and explicit concepts and relationships used in the cultural heritage domain.

In this paper, we report on the results of the first steps towards the Russian Linked Culture Cloud making the heritage data available, including the publication as Linked Data as well as through end user applications. Our long-term goal is to build the overall Russian Linked Culture Cloud by integrating data from many providers like museums and other institutions and having a powerful user interface and a set of practical tools for data acquisition, modification and publishing. The pilot project was started in cooperation with the Russian Museum in St. Petersburg, which holds the largest collection of Russian art in the world. The primary goal of our research was to demonstrate the applicability and benefits of usage of semantic data to tackle the challenges of cultural heritage transfer in the digital era. The system is meant to deliver benefits to two different target groups: the museum art experts and museum visitors. These two groups greatly differ in their needs, but the system covers the interests of both of them.

Taking into account the needs of potential users we managed to set forth the following objectives:

- *Simplified integration of external data.* While the initial effort on making the internal data open and available might look like a significant investment at the start, in the long run it holds big promises with numerous benefits achieved through integration with external data. Our challenge was to make this process easier for organizations by means of providing the mechanisms suitable for simplified acquisition of data from open sources via various APIs or by crawling and further structuring the data including smooth integration into existing data models.
- *Dealing with quality of external data.* The first challenge is directly related to the second one. Integration of external data must be accompanied with validation methodology, quality assessment, purification of acquired external data. The system must be able to perform this task easily.
- *Flexibility of data presentation.* The third challenge is to demonstrate how the employed semantic technologies can enhance the end user experience while interacting with the data. The data presentation should be adjusting in real-time to the user preferences, interests expressed either explicitly in his profile or indirectly by his actions and interaction track with system.
- *Richer representation.* Among our potential users will be the art experts that need the deeper representation of information more or less ready for analysis.

The examples of such representations might be the timelines of events and art object creation dates, the graph depicting the popularity of art movements, the maps of traces of artists and so on. Creation of such forms of visualisations involves a deep domain knowledge, clear understanding of users needs and a thorough scenario of user interaction, which altogether makes a complicated goal to achieve.

The project is still in rapid development and contributors are welcome. For collaboration we use GitHub repository: https://github.com/ailabitmo/Culture-Cloud-Datasets, in which one can learn the technical details of the data transformation process.

2 Overview of the System

In this section we present an overview of the created system. It has been built using the *metaphacts Knowledge Graph Workbench*[1], a platform for the development of semantic applications. The system architecture diagram is depicted in the Fig. 1.

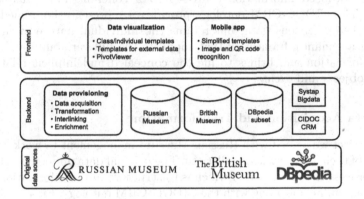

Fig. 1. Architecture of the System

Using the data provisioning services of platform, the original data sources have been transformed, interlinked, enriched and finally ingested into a triple store (a Systap Blazegraph[2] database), holding the integrated Linked Data graph. As described in detail in the subsequent section, Russian Museum relational data was transformed to RDF, represented using the CIDOC-CRM ontology. Where possible, links to DBpedia have been generated. The British Museum thesauri were used as genre and artwork type taxonomies. The resulting data in the triple store is published via a SPARQL endpoint, accessible at http://culturecloud.ru/sparql.

---

[1] http://www.metaphacts.com/.
[2] http://www.blazegraph.com/.

Using additional backend services of the platform, e.g. visualization, search and exploration services, two applications have been built: a web application and a mobile app, as described in detail in Sect. 4. The applications are accessible at http://culturecloud.ru/ On the frontend side we made use of the rich templating mechanism of the platform and created templates for the relevant CIDOC-CRM classes to visualize artworks and authors. Each template also includes data from linked DBpedia entities. The main purpose of the mobile application is to provide museum visitors with additional information about art objects. It has the ability to recognize the artwork by making photo of it or by scanning a QR code. Special simplified templates were developed for this use case.

3   Publishing/Creation

3.1   Ontology Model

We created and published the museum data according to the CIDOC-CRM ontology [3]. CIDOC-CRM serves as a basis for mediation of cultural heritage information and to provide the semantic 'glue' needed to transform todays disparate, localised information sources into a coherent and valuable global resource. The CIDOC-CRM ontology provides a representation aimed at harmonizing heterogeneous data, but retains the individual nature of the data - providing a semantic framework that supports the full variability and richness of the information and brings to life the concealed and implicit relationships between objects and events.

3.2   Data Acquisition and Transformation

In this project we agreed with Russian Museum management to work with data from one of their sites: www.rmgallery.ru. The original data undergoes a transformation process the main goal of which is to structure initial information into an RDF data graph conforming with the CIDOC-CRM ontology. Figure 2 shows an example of the initial data representation in RDF and interlinking, as discussed in the next section.

CIDOC-CRM is an event-centric model. The central part of semantic representation is the event of production of some object *crm:E12_Production*. It connects all other entities that are relevant to it: A creator is connected with the *crm:P14_carried_out_by* property, an artwork is connected with the *crm:P108_has_produced* property, creation time is connected with the *crm:P4_has_time_span* property. The artwork is represented as an instance of class *crm:E22_Man-Made_Object* (Fig. 3).While not shown in the diagrams, the person's biography and artwork description are associated with *crm:E21_Person* and *crm:E22_Man-Made_Object* respectively via the *crm:P4_has_note* property.

All textual information in the dataset (names, titles, descriptions, etc.) were placed in two languages annotated with the corresponding language tag.

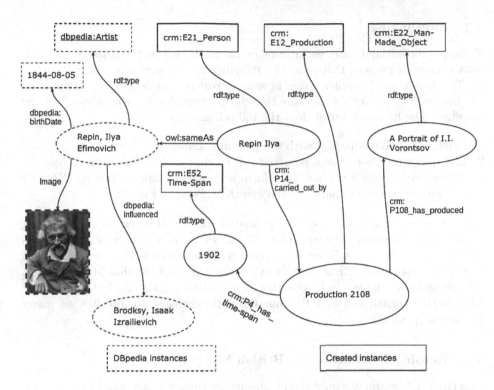

Fig. 2. Example of initial data representation and interlinking

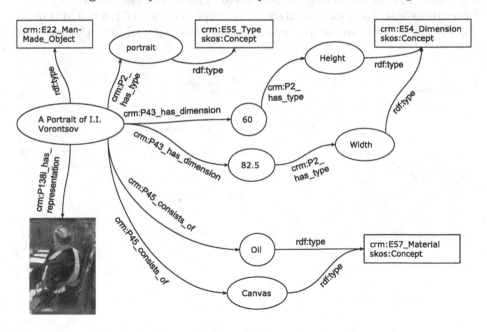

Fig. 3. Artwork representation example

3.3 Interlinking

To enrich the initial dataset we interlinked the authors from the Russian Museum data with persons from DBPedia. The interlinking was performed in two stages.

The first stage is implemented in semi-automatic mode: a Ruby script asks to choose from one of the options that script provides for the person's name matches. The first-step script does the following:

1. Query the Wikipedia API with the person's name.
2. List query results on the screen and ask to choose the most suitable one.
3. When user selects a variant, transform a chosen Wikipedia link to DBpedia one and create owl:sameAs for the *crm:E21_Person* (Fig. 2).

The second stage is carried out in automated mode and based on simple string comparison of person's initials. First of all, we extract names of the persons with type *dbpedia:Artist*. Then we transform all names to initials and performed a string comparison with names of the persons from the Russian Museum data. The second stage proves to be effective as it is shown in the Table 2. We worked with both international and Russian DBpedia datasets to interlink as many authors as possible.

3.4 Reusing Thesauri of the British Museum

The British Museum has published high-quality thesauri that could be used with any museum, thus we decided to reuse them. The thesauri are based on SKOS. Every thesaurus object has the skos:Concept type and one of CIDOC-CRM more specific type. For example, the material "oil" has types of *skos:Concept* and

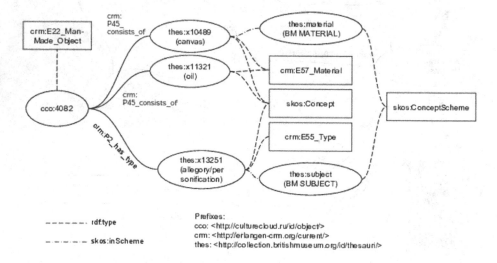

Fig. 4. Usage example of The British Museum thesauri

crm:E57_Material and is part of "BM MATERIAL" concept scheme. The "allegory/personification" subject has types *skos:Concept* and *crm:E55_Type* and is part of "BM SUBJECT" concept scheme. We used the latter for describing the genre of the artworks. Figure 4 shows an example of the usage.

For some genres there were no appropriate entities in British Museum dataset (illustration, caricature, theatrical scenery), for these we created additional instances following the exact same scheme.

3.5   Annotating Unstructured Text with DBpedia Spotlight

We have two pieces of unstructured data in the Russian Museum dataset: artwork descriptions and author biographies. We decided to contextualize this information with DBpedia Spotlight[3]. It identifies for DBpedia entities in the text and returns a text annotated with links to DBpedia resources. We replaced all initial textual information with the annotated one and added all entities in the annotation to our dataset as triples (*Entity, cc : hasAnnotation, DBpediaEntity*), where *Entity* is either an artwork or an author and *DBpediaEntity* is the DBpedia resource associated with the text by Spotlight (Fig. 5).

Links in unstructured text provide additional ways for site visitor to explore existing information, besides links to the semantic entities created at transformation and enrichment stages.

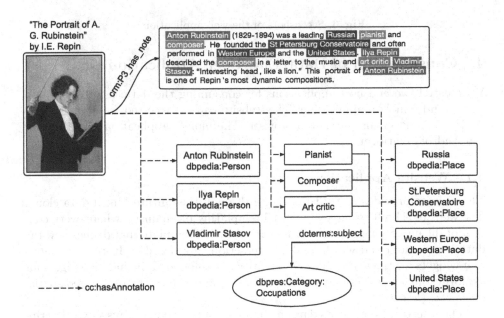

Fig. 5. Example of text annotated with DBpedia Spotlight (persons highlighted with orange, places with blue and occupations with green) (Color figure online)

---

[3] http://dbpedia-spotlight.github.io/.

644   D. Mouromtsev et al.

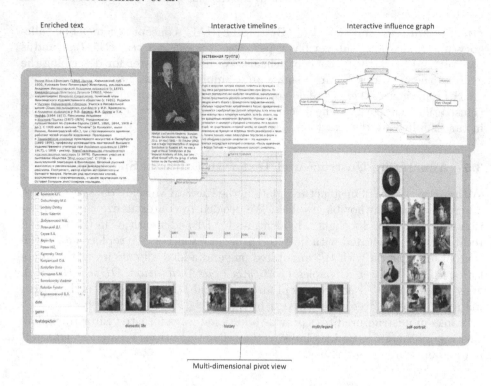

Enriched text   Interactive timelines   Interactive influence graph

Multi-dimensional pivot view

Fig. 6. Sceenshots of the web application

4   Consumption of Data/End User Application

We created two end user applications for consuming the data: a website application and a mobile application. The website can be accessed from any mobile device or desktop computer web browser. The mobile application is created for the Android platform.

4.1   Website Application

The website provides a way to navigate through the culture linked data cloud. The website is built using a wiki-based templating mechanism, where every concept of the underlying ontology is associated with a template that defines how the data is presented and which kind of interactions are possible. In the templates, rich widgets for the various data modalities are embedded, including widgets for exploring image collections, timelines for temporal data, maps for geo-spatial data, etc. (Fig. 6).

The website also presents data in a number of traditional ways - text descriptions and illustrations of art works, hyperlinks connecting the web pages and so on. At the same time the system allows the integration of more effective tools for data presentation, which provide a brighter use experience and prove to be more fruitful in a process of data exploration. Some of the widgets include:

Enriched text. Enriched text is a paragraph where some toponyms, people names and dates are linked against the semantic descriptions of external sources, in our case DBpedia and the British Museum. When the user clicks the link the article opens on this same site. This delivers the additional context directly to the user and keeps him on site, while in other systems he would be forced to leave the original resource.

Interactive timelines. A Timeline widget enables additional visual demonstration of how long the process took place or in what sequence the things were occurring. For instance, our system employs timelines when we demonstrate the artists lifetimes in relation with the art movement to which they all belong. The other use case for timelines is to place the art objects on artists life span to display his periods of activity and inactivity. This provides a means to learn and discover the facts rather than reading the paragraphs of simple text.

Interactive influence graph. The graph of influences illustrates the influences of one artist on another. From this graph many intriguing conclusions could be made: who was the most influential artist in his time, who stands aside in the cultural art process, etc. The end-user can use such graph for finding other artist that can interest him based on the artists that he already knows. The art experts can construct the more complicated graphs showing the connections between artists, art movements, countries, art school, etc.

Multi-dimensional Pivot widget. The Pivot widget allows to visually explore the data by sorting and filtering it in multiple dimensions. For instance, one can select the artists of 1890s that worked in the genres of portrait and sort their artworks by artists names. This is another exciting and interactive way to learn the content and make fascinating discoveries along the way. It is quite obvious that such tool can be of a great help and simplify the routine work when selecting the artworks for catalogues or when constructing the new exhibition.

Semantic search. A search widget has been implemented that allows to visually construct structured, semantic queries against the fundamental relationships of the CIDOC-CRM ontology. The search widget provides auto-suggestions for search terms utilizing an entity index along with a suggestion of relationships that are applicable to a selected entity.

4.2   Mobile Application

The mobile applications is intended to make the visit to the museum more informative. It is done by enabling automatic identification of art work by taking snapshot with a mobile device (accuracy about 80 percent). When the artwork is identified, the mobile app brings additional annotation about it and its creator. Visitors can also rate the artwork and the rating will be shared across the social network so that the user's friends can receive recommendation based on user's ratings of what to see in the museum (We use the most popular social network in Russia - http://www.vk.com).

Hence the key features of application are:

- Artwork recognition by photo.
- Provision of information about the artwork.
- Ranking of artworks and sharing user rating across the social network.
- Delivery of user-tailored recommendations for customized museum visits.

The information is presented to the user in highly customized form, individually and deliberately sorted and filtered.

4.3   Added Value for End-User

We divided the beneficiaries of our system into two major categories: Art Experts and Museum Visitors. The current state of the system already provides to the organizations e.g. museums an easy and a cheap way to maintain their website and develop information materials. As a result the number of visitors is growing. Such result is achieved due to the nature of semantic technologies, which enables simplified integration of external data sources. Secondly, the data model itself is more transparent and obvious to the experts with no technical background, which leads to easier support of such model. Then, new data acquired to expand the existing system could be integrated from the data providers and thereafter queried like internal with the reference to the internal data model. Finally, displaying external data on-site ensures the user does not leave and teaches him to have a single entry-point to all art-related content.

As for the regular visitors, the system brings them the art-related information in a more interactive, exciting and thought-provoking way. By interacting with widgets the user makes his own trajectory through the site content with regard to his own preferences and interests. The user does not consume the information in a traditional way by going from one link to another, but, more or less, makes his own unique exploration path through the materials, utilizing all the interactive tools. The other important aspect of the system for the common museum visitor is the presence of social features. Now people can follow their friends' paths through museum, share their impressions of art with others and learn more from whom they trust. This process is simplified by the automatic artwork recognition feature implemented in the mobile application allowing users instantly to learn more about the painting by taking a picture of it from their Android device.

5   Evaluation

5.1   Source Data and Evaluation Details

In our system we used three different sources of data:

- Original data from Russian Museum[4] provides basic information about artworks and authors.

---

[4] http://rmgallery.ru/.

- The British Museum thesauri[5] were used for describing genres of artworks.
- DBpedia[6] was used for adding information about authors, such as date of birth and death, artistic movement author belongs to, persons who influenced author, etc.
- Associated Spotlight annotations were placed in the related section of the authors and artworks pages.

For assessing the data quality we have created more specialized versions of several metrics listed in [5]. Our main goal was to find out how successful was the enrichment of the original dataset. A detailed description of all metrics is presented in the following section.

5.2 Metrics Description

In this section we will describe metrics we used to assess quality of the resulting dataset. We split all metrics into three different categories:

1. General dataset metrics describe the volume of data we collected. These metrics consists of VoID statistics metrics (number of triples, classes, properties, entities, distinct subjects and distinct objects) and quantity of the main entities from www.rmgallery.ru (authors and artworks).
2. Original dataset metrics describe completeness of the data from www.rmgallery.ru. It shows how many artworks entities have specific information (annotation/description, size, genre, creation time) and how many of author entities have the biography information.
3. Interlinking metrics describe how much additional information we gathered by interlinking the original data with DBpedia. The first part of these metrics describes how many owl:sameAs links were created for authors and specifies how many of them were obtained using Wikipedia search or syntactical approaches. We also have counted the number of links to the international and Russian DBpedia. The second part of interlinking metrics depicts how many authors were complemented with specific information from DBpedia (birth/ death date, birth/date place, art movement author considered to belong to, influenced and influenced by information).

One special note should be taken regarding a trust assessment. We did not develop objective computable metrics for that task, thus we presented subjective evaluation of provenance in the next section.

5.3 Evaluation Results

Available information about artworks and authors was transformed to the semantic form and we have the following statistics about its completeness: more than 90 % of entities has dimension, genre, creation time and author bio information and

---

Table 1. Evaluation of general and original dataset metrics (percentage of total number of artworks or authors)

General metrics		Original dataset metrics	
Triples	50795	Artwork descriptions	68 % (628)
Classes	15	Artwork dimension	99 % (911)
Properties	23	Artwork genre	94 % (863)
Entities	8068	Artwork creation time	96 % (887)
Distinct subjects	8081	Author's bio	98 % (260)
Distinct objects	13861		
Artworks	921		
Authors	265		

68 % of artworks has descriptions. 85 % of authors were interlinked with DBpedia which allowed us to enrich 60 % of author pages with birth-death dates.

A comparison of the general and original dataset metrics (Table 1) unveils incompleteness in the Russian Museum data, as not all artworks or authors have additional information, such as genre, dimension, etc. This probably could be related to human element in curated museum data.

The results of interlinking metrics (Table 2) were in line with our expectations. Decrease of the added information number correlates to increase of the obtaining information difficulty. For example, birth and death dates are probably the most easy to find information about authors, but to find the information about art movement or persons who influenced the author one probably should look up the specialized literature.

The original data is poor in terms of coverage and incompleteness (rather than inconsistency) and lack of semantics. The value of the interlining is not only in the number (volume) of direct links, but in the rich additional data that provides context. The link generation algorithms have been manually tuned, as part of this the generated links have been manually validated. The improvement of the enrichment quality is based on a continuous cycle. The basic metrics allow to manage this process and evaluate results of adding new datasets (for example we are working on adding [7]).

DBpedia Spotlight Annotations. The annotations of originally unstructured text from the Russian Museum data gives us a good use case for the end user, as they can observe a dataset while reading information about artworks.

But raw annotations are mostly unusable to perform computational reasoning over data they add, as we do not know how exactly annotations are connected to the text. For example Spotlight added annotation "Finland" to the description of Repin's painting "What an Expanse!". But in this form it is impossible to understand that Repin was inspired by some places in Finland.

---

[7] http://www.wikiart.org.

Table 2. Evaluation of interlinking metrics (percentage of total number of *interlinked* authors)

Total number of interlinked authors	226 of 265 (85%)
incl. at the first stage	40% (90)
incl. at the second stage	60% (136)
incl. with International DBpedia	81% (183)
incl. with Russian DBpedia	80% (181)
Number of authors enriched with	
birth date	60% (136)
death date	60% (137)
birth place	22% (50)
death place	20% (46)
art movement	13% (30)
"influenced"	4% (9)
"influenced by"	4% (8)

In our case DBpedia Spotlight is a good solution for providing a light-weight contextualization. But to make annotations usable in meaningful dataset queries, predicates describing how exactly annotations are related to the text and entities would be needed.

6   Related Work

In the cultural heritage domain, Linked Data and Semantic Web technologies have been successfully applied to publish and interlink heterogeneous, semantically rich data. Great amounts of cultural heritage data have been published in national and international portals, such as Europeana[8]. As of today, a number of different ontologies and metadata schemes are used for the representation of the data. CIDOC-CRM is the prevailing model when it comes to the representation of semantically rich cultural heritage data [2]. For example, the British Museum has published their complete data collection as Linked Open Data based on CIDOC-CRM[9]. Notable other sites that have published large collections based on CIDOC-CRM include Claros[10] and the Arches project[11]. The ResearchSpace project[12] is developing a collaborative environment for humanities and cultural heritage research using CIDOC-CRM.

---

[8] http://www.europeana.eu.
[9] http://collection.britishmuseum.org.
[10] http://www.clarosnet.org/XDB/ASP/clarosHome/.
[11] http://www.getty.edu/conservation/our_projects/field_projects/arches/.
[12] http://www.researchspace.org.

On the data consumptions side, new applications based on the semantically rich data have been developed that enable new forms of user experience. These range from supporting semantic search in portals to mobile applications. E.g., the SMARTMUSEUM [4] system utilizes an ontology-based representation of content descriptions as a basis for context-aware, on-site access to cultural heritage in a mobile scenario. Applying context reasoning and recommendation algorithms provide users with recommendations for sites, such as museums or buildings of architectural interest, and objects on those sites, such as sculptures or other works of art, and provides explanatory descriptions and multimedia content associated with individual objects. In comparison to the related solutions our project stands out as being an external service to heritage owners, which provides interlinking and search/representation facilities to end-users and third-party applications.

7   Conclusions

In this paper we described a system for semantic publishing, enrichment, search and visualisation of cultural heritage data as a first step towards a Russian Linked Culture Cloud. The system is based on the metaphacts Knowledge Graph Workbench. As a main source of data at the initial step the virtual gallery of the Russian Museum was selected. For transformation and representation of data CIDOC-CRM Ontology was used with extended thesauri from the British Museum repository. Data enrichment is done by DBpedia. We also used the DBpedia Spotlight API to annotate and extract data from unstructured text in the initial data source (annotations, biography and so on).

The performed analyses of user benefits revealed a high demand on the flexible and extensible representation models for building applications that allow to get access to digital cultural heritage. Our system illustrates potentials of semantic technologies for creation of such solutions including semantic search and visualizations both for art experts and regular museum visitors.

One of the features we achieved is to make data deliverable to end users more informative in comparison with any data source provisioning our system. For example, the initial Russian Museum dataset does not contain much information about authors. Interlinking with external sources allowed us to show user additional information about authors, such as date of birth or person they influenced.

Our evaluations show that the enrichment of the limited original dataset was quite successful and automation of this process is efficient.

Future work. Some problems raised during the project progress require additional research and further development. The most challenging problems are:

- Expand the number of data sources especially of raw data from heritage institutions. It could require extending thesauri and the CIDOC-CRM ontology in term of new kind of terms and classes.

- Support of collaborative work and contradicting facts representation in the domain ontology for art experts knowledge modelling. This will make the system more natural for the cultural heritage area. On these topics we intend to synergize with the work performed in the ResearchSpace project on argumentation and belief.
- Collecting the user statistics for tracking users trajectory through the site content and analytics of preferences and interests. Such data will allow to build an efficient recommender system.
- Developing a solution for the automated quality assessment of data sources and its trust ranking.

Acknowledgements. This work was partially financially supported by Government of Russian Federation, Grant 074-U01.

References

1. Hyvnen, E.: Publishing and Using Cultural Heritage Linked Data on the Semantic Web. Synthesis Lectures on Semantic Web: Theory and Technology. Morgan & Claypool, Palo Alto (2012). Available as paperback and ebook (9781608459988)
2. Oldman, D., Doerr, M., de Jong, G., Norton, B., Wikman, T.: Realizing lessons of the last 20 years: a manifesto for data provisioning and aggregation services for the digital humanities (A position paper). D-Lib Mag. **20**(7/8), 6 (2014). http://dx.doi.org/10.1045/july2014-oldman
3. Oldman, D., CRM Labs.: The CIDOC conceptual reference model (CIDOC CRM): Primer (2014). http://www.cidoc-crm.org/docs/CRMPrimer_v1.1.pdf
4. Ruotsalo, T., Haav, K., Stoyanov, A., Roche, S., Fani, E., Deliai, R., Mäkelä, E., Kauppinen, T., Hyvönen, E.: SMARTMUSEUM: a mobile recommender system for the web of data. J. Web Sem. **20**, 50–67 (2013). http://dx.doi.org/10.1016/j.websem.2013.03.001
5. Zaveri, A., Rula, A., Maurino, A., Pietrobon, R., Lehmann, J., Auer, S.: Quality assessment for linked data: A survey. Submitted to Semantic Web Journal (2014)

From Symptoms to Diseases – Creating the Missing Link

Heiner Oberkampf[1,2]([✉]), Turan Gojayev[1,3], Sonja Zillner[1,4],
Dietlind Zühlke[5], Sören Auer[3,5], and Matthias Hammon[6]

[1] Siemens AG, Corporate Technology, Munich, Germany
[2] Software Methodologies for Distributed Systems,
University of Augsburg, Augsburg, Germany
heiner.oberkampf@gmail.com
[3] Institute for Applied Computer Science, University of Bonn, Bonn, Germany
[4] School of International Business and Entrepreneurship,
Steinbeis University, Berlin, Germany
[5] Fraunhofer Institute for Intelligent Analysis and Information Systems,
Sankt Augustin, Germany
[6] Department of Radiology, University Hospital Erlangen, Erlangen, Germany

Abstract. A wealth of biomedical datasets is meanwhile published as
Linked Open Data. Each of these datasets has a particular focus, such as
providing information on diseases or symptoms of a certain kind. Hence,
a comprehensive view can only be provided by integrating information
from various datasets. Although, links between diseases and symptoms
can be found, these links are far too sparse to enable practical applications such as a disease-centric access to clinical reports that are annotated with symptom information. For this purpose, we build a model
of disease-symptom relations. Utilizing existing ontology mappings, we
propagate semantic type information for *disease* and *symptom* across
ontologies. Then entities of the same semantic type from different ontologies are clustered and object properties between entities are mapped to
cluster-level relations. The effectiveness of our approach is demonstrated
by integrating all available disease-symptom relations from different biomedical ontologies resulting in a significantly increased linkage between
datasets.

1 Introduction

A wealth of biomedical datasets is meanwhile published as Linked Open Data.
Examples include ontologies of the *Unified Medical Language System* (UMLS),
the *Human Disease Ontology* (DO), *Symptom Ontology* (SYMP) or *DBpedia*.
Each of these datasets has a particular focus, such as providing information on
diseases or symptoms of a certain kind. Hence, a comprehensive view on diseases
and symptoms can only be provided by integrating information from various
datasets. Although, links between the datasets can be found, we learned that
these links are far too sparse to enable practical knowledge-based applications.
In our use scenario, we want to extract a disease-symptom knowledge model

F. Gandon et al. (Eds.): ESWC 2015, LNCS 9088, pp. 652–667, 2015.
DOI: 10.1007/978-3-319-18818-8_40

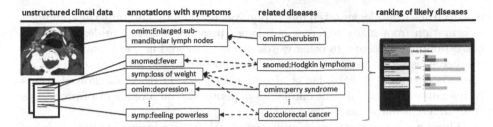

Fig. 1. Disease-centric view on patient data.

from publicly available biomedical data to extend our application described in [11] and Sect. 2, where we rank likely diseases based on semantic annotations of clinical images and reports. This allows a disease-centric access on unstructured clinical as shown in Fig. 1. To build a model of such disease-symptom relations, we need to integrate entities of semantic type *disease* and their relations to entities of type *symptom* from different ontologies.

The *BioPortal* [21], being the world's largest ontology repository for biomedicine, contains more than 400 different ontologies and more than 6 million entities that define a wide range of concepts. Even though the BioPortal provides lexical information (labels, definitions etc.), comprehensive mappings between semantic types or properties are frequently missing. Thus it is not possible to directly access all diseases defined in different ontologies from BioPortal. In particular, it is not possible to extract a diseases-symptom graph needed for our application scenario.

In the following we use the term *entity* to refer to a concrete class or instance defined in one ontology or dataset. This abstraction is necessary since knowledge representation differs across repositories and domains: e.g. in DBpedia `dbp:Lymphoma` is an instance of `dbp:Disease`, while in biomedical ontologies lymphoma is commonly represented as a subclass of disease. As described below, the UMLS defines 133 *semantic types* to represent important high level categories such as disease, symptom, organism or anatomical structure. We follow that approach and use an annotation property to uniformly refer to the *semantic type* of an entity (e.g. `radlex:Hodgkin_lymphoma disy:semanticType disy:Disease`). We use the term *concept* to describe the abstracted meaning on a conceptual level without reference to any concrete implementation, such as some particular ontology. E.g. the entities `radlex:Hodgkin_lymphoma`, `do:Hodgkin's lymphoma` and `omim:Hodgkin disease` represent the same disease concept *Hodgkin lymphoma*. Again, we follow the UMLS approach where Concept Unique Identifiers are used to integrate entities of different ontologies on the conceptual level.

As in our use-case scenario, in many application contexts only certain parts of the available knowledge are relevant. For example, one would like to query only data about entities of specific semantic types (in our case *disease* and *symptom*) – but across many different resources. Or, only relations between entities of two specific semantic types are of interest. Querying across multiple resources is essential since ontologies often model one specific domain and only the combined information from many different ontologies provides a complete description of corresponding concepts. In other words one is interested in queries over different resources based on semantic types. This kind of queries, however, depends on the existence of a global schema of semantic types. Further, integrated access to information from different ontologies depends also on alignment of properties from different ontologies.

There are several attempts and partial solutions addressing these requirements (cf. Sect. 6): Firstly, there has been much work on algorithms for ontology matching, i.e. mapping of entities and schemas from one ontology to another. An overview of the state of the art in this area is given by [18]. The matching methods are mostly based on *strings* (labels, definitions, comments etc.) and *structure* (relations between entities). With schema mappings one can federate queries over different resources by translating the query from a global schema to local schemas. Another possibility is to integrate data into a new repository where all data is mapped to a common schema. In this scenario, lexical information such as labels and textual definitions are often mapped to a common vocabulary such as *Dublin Core* or *SKOS*.

Even though there are various mapping algorithms and correspondingly mapping resources available, semantic types (i.e. meta descriptions) are still not globally aligned. Thus it is difficult to retrieve all entities of a certain semantic type from different ontologies or knowledge repositories. Further, it is even more difficult to query across different resources since most of them use their own schema. Without knowing the different schemas one cannot query and integrate information correctly. Thus it is currently not possible to do a semantic search or filtering over heterogeneous resources to extract all available knowledge for a given application scenario. There are several reasons for the absence of globally aligned semantic types and object properties: Firstly, there is no agreed target schema for semantic types or object properties (as SKOS is for certain data properties). Secondly, object properties are used in different contexts, often without clear domain and range specification and vague semantics. Thirdly, in property URIs and labels different abbreviations and IDs are used, preventing automatic mapping techniques.

In this work we describe an approach to propagate semantic types from an initial set of entities to other ontologies by using existing ontology mappings. Then, entities that have the same semantic type are clustered, which provides the basis for integrated access to information across different ontologies. Aligned semantic types allow us to manually map relations that are used between entities of two different semantic types in a context-sensitive manner. Finally, the entity level relations are mapped to cluster-level relations and represented in a cluster graph. We demonstrate the feasibility of our approach in our medical application scenario where we propagate the semantic types *disease* and *symptom* in order to harmonize available knowledge about their correlations.

The remainder of the paper is organized as follows: In the next Sect. 2 we detail our application scenario. Then we describe the resources used for the application scenario of diseases and symptoms in Sect. 3. We outline our approach for semantic type based integration and present the actual realization in Sect. 4. Evaluation results are summarized in Sect. 5, before we discuss related work in Sect. 6 and conclude in Sect. 7.

2   Application Scenario

As described in [11] clinical patient data from many different resources such as medical images, reports and laboratory results, provide the basis for clinical decision making (diagnosis, treatment evaluation and planning). However, the enormous volume and complexity of this mostly unstructured data, prevents clinical staff to get the full use of the data by reviewing it all. Here, semantic annotations can be used to make the data better accessible, e.g. in a search application (see e.g. [17]). The problem, however, is that annotations capture only *descriptive* information of the report's content, i.e. the observations made, the findings discovered, the various symptoms identified. That is, annotations simply represent the content as it is. In a diagnosis process, however, the clinician would like to search for *all symptoms* related to some specific disease such as *Hodgkin lymphoma*. To make this kind of search possible a knowledge model containing the relation between diseases and symptoms is necessary (cf. Fig. 1). Without such a model, a search for Hodgkin lymphoma indicating findings is only possible through a search for specific symptoms as e.g. *lymph node enlargement, feeling powerless* etc. assuming that the clinician is informed about likely symptoms of a disease. However, clinicians are usually experts in one particular domain, leading to a lack of prior knowledge about the interrelations of symptoms and diseases in case certain diseases are no longer in the scope of their expertise. In other words, there is a clear danger that the information about the relevance of identified symptoms remains overlooked or misinterpreted, leading to non-appropriate treatments, etc. Thus, the relevance-based highlighting of information about clinical observations in the context of likely diseases supports clinicians to improve their treatment decisions. In [12] we used a manually created disease-symptom model to show that it can be used to infer a ranking of likely diseases based on annotations of unstructured clinical data. The general idea is to match the patient's symptom information with the typical symptoms of diseases defined in the knowledge model.

Instead of creating such a knowledge model manually, this work aims to explore and reuse knowledge about disease-symptom relations from existing LOD resources. This, however, bears a significant integration effort. Firstly, disease and symptom entities need to be identified in different resources. Secondly, relations between these entities need to be aligned. The most important resources used for this domain-specific application scenario are described in the following section. For other domains one would need to select other resources.

3   Employed Ontology Resources

BioPortal - Biomedical Ontology Repository [21] provides public access to more than 400 ontologies and 6 million entities in those ontologies. It tends to be the most comprehensive repository of ontologies in the biomedical domain. Ontologies in BioPortal cover various fields of biomedicine such as diseases, phenotypes, clinical observations and findings, genes, proteins etc. The data on BioPortal consists of three essential parts (for details we refer to [10,14,15]):

- **Ontologies:** The main part of data in BioPortal is the repository of ontologies that are uploaded by users. To ease querying over different ontologies the BioPortal has mapped some properties for lexical information to a common schema by defining subproperty relations.
- **Metadata:** A specifically designed ontology is used to store metadata of ontologies such as version, creators, reviews, mappings, views etc. [10].
- **Mappings:** Ontology mappings are relations between entities of different ontologies that denote similarity (or equivalence) of two entities. A mapping specifies at least a target entity, target ontology, source entity, source ontology and a relation type (e.g. `skos:exactMatch`, `skos:closeMatch`, `skos:related Match`, `owl:sameAs`, `rdfs:seeAlso`). In total the BioPortal contains six different mapping resources. Most relevant for this work are lexical mappings (LOOM [5]), created by a software, based on the similarity notion between preferred labels or preferred and alternative labels and the mappings created by UMLS CUIs. An example of a LOOM mapping is given in Fig. 2. All mappings are available through a REST-full API[1] and a SPARQL endpoint [15]. They can be used without preprocessing.

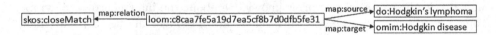

Fig. 2. Example of a LOOM mapping between an entity from Disease Ontology and one from Online Mendelian Inheritance in Man Ontology.

Unified Medical Language System (UMLS) is a system for integrating major vocabularies and standards from the biomedical domain, such as *SNOMED CT*, *MeSH*, ICD and others. UMLS consists of three main components: Metathesaurus, Semantic Network and SPECIALIST lexicon. The *Metathesaurus* is a vocabulary that contains 1 million unique biomedical concepts with 5 million labels from more than 100 terminologies, classification systems and thesauri, and more than 17 million relationships between concepts. Each concept is given a permanent *concept unique identifier* (CUI) whose role is to link similar entities from different vocabularies or ontologies. The *Semantic Network* provides a categorization (called *semantic types*) of the concepts that appear in Metathesaurus and also relationships that can be used between concepts of different semantic types. In total there are 133 semantic types (e.g. organism, anatomical structure, clinical findings, disease or syndrome etc.) and 54 semantic relationships defined in the Semantic Network. Each concept of the Metathesaurus has at least one semantic type assigned. For our application scenario the semantic types

---

[1] http://data.bioontology.org/.

disease or syndrome (T047) and *sign or symptom* (T184) are most relevant. The semantic type *finding* (T033), which is a supertype of *sign or symptom* is also relevant, however out of scope for this work.

Human Disease Ontology (DO) represents a comprehensive knowledge base of inherited, developmental and acquired diseases [16]. Currently it contains 8681 disease, 2260 of which have a textual definition. DO integrates medical vocabularies through the usage of cross-mappings to other ontologies, such as MeSH, ICD, NCI's thesaurus, SNOMED CT or OMIM. DO is part of the Open Biomedical and Biological Ontologies (OBO) Foundry [19] and utilized for disease annotation by major biomedical databases such as Array Express, NIF or IEDB.

Symptom Ontology (SYMP) is an OBO Foundry ontology and contains 936 symptom entities, where symptom is defined as 'a perceived change in function, sensation or appearance reported by a patient indicative of a disease'. SYMP is organized primarily by body regions with a branch for general symptoms.

4   Approach and Realization

The rationale of our approach is to utilize existing mappings to integrate information about entities of the same semantic type from different ontologies and to align relations between different semantic types. The approach consists of the following five steps as shown in Fig. 3:

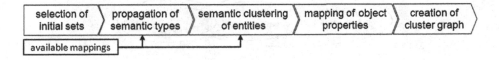

Fig. 3. The five steps of our approach.

1. **Selection of Initial Sets:** For each semantic type of interest one has to define a set of initial entities as representatives of that semantic type.
2. **Propagation of Semantic Types:** Use mappings to assign a semantic type to entities for which no corresponding semantic type has yet been assigned.
3. **Clustering of Entities:** Use mappings to create clusters of entities from the same semantic type. To preserve distinctions made by the original ontologies, we require that a cluster never contains two entities from the same ontology.
4. **Mapping of Object Properties:** Having two sets of entities with different semantic type we can analyse all relations between them that are defined in the source ontologies. Since the number distinct object properties used between entities of two different semantic types is small enough, we can manually map them to cluster level relations.
5. **Creation of Cluster Graph:** The cluster information as well as the entity-level relations are integrated into a final cluster graph. Further, the entity-level relations are mapped to cluster-level relations to allow integrated access and aggregation of available information from entity-level on cluster-level.

Selection of Initial Sets. To propagate semantic types across ontologies of the BioPortal, we first select initial sets of entities for which the corresponding semantic types are defined:

1. **Initial disease set** consists of all entities of DO and those entities of UMLS ontologies with semantic type *disease or syndrome* (in total 153,223 distinct entities from 18 ontologies).
2. **Initial symptom set** consists of all entities of SYMP and those entities of UMLS ontologies with semantic type *sign or symptom* (in total 14,971 distinct entities from 18 ontologies).

We noted that in the case of diseases and symptoms the initial sets actually overlap as shown in Fig. 4. In total 471 entities occur in the intersection of the initial sets. Since the entities of DO and SYMP are disjoint, this means that those entities must be defined in some of the UMLS ontologies as disease *and* symptom. However, according to our clinical expert, in general a distinction between disease and symptom should be possible and thus we consider that the overlap is due to wrong assignment of semantic types. Indeed our clinical expert could manually classify most of the entities in question as either disease (189 entities, e.g. *migraine*) or symptom (234 entities, e.g. *dry mouth*), however 48 entities are both (e.g. *eating disorder*)[2]. As a result the overlap is very small in comparison to the large number of disease and symptom entities, so that it can be tolerated.

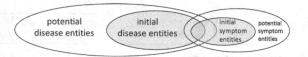

Fig. 4. The initial set of diseases and symptoms with potential entities obtained through mappings. The shown overlaps were resolved in subsequent steps.

Propagation of Semantic Types. With the initial sets for diseases and symptoms at hand, we use the existing mappings on BioPortal to retrieve more entities of the same semantic types. Here we assume that entities being mapped to each other via at least one existing mapping are semantically similar. This semantic equivalence information is reused within our approach by propagating the semantic type information of the entities of the initial set to each of their mapped entities: An entity is in the set of *potential* diseases if there is a mapping to some entity of the initial disease set (for symptoms respectively). In total this results in 247,683 entities from 219 ontologies for diseases and 34,088 entities from 161 ontologies for symptoms. However, as shown in Fig. 4, the resulting sets again overlap. To determine a single semantic type for entities in the overlap we proceed as follows: Firstly, being in an initial set is more relevant than being in

---

[2] Complete classification results are available at http://goo.gl/CFgFVx.

a potential set. Secondly, for entities in the intersection of potential disease and potential symptom sets (7,531 entities), the classification is based on the number of mappings to entities of the different initial sets. That is, if for a corresponding entity there are more mappings to entities of the set of initial diseases than to entities of the set of initial symptoms, then the entity gets assigned the semantic type disease. Else it gets assigned the semantic type symptom. After separation, we are left with 240,264 disease entities and 23,642 symptom entities.

Clustering of Entities. From the previous step we obtained a large set of entities of semantic type disease and also one for symptoms. However, this does not imply that all of these entities are about different diseases (symptoms respectively). Our assumption is, that many of those entities cover the same semantic concept and thus can be clustered. For instance, there are multiple entities describing the semantic concept *Hodgkin lymphoma*: snomed:Hodgkin_lymphoma, omim:Hodgkin_disease, radlex:Hodgkin_lymphoma, do:Hodgkin's_lymphoma etc. Again, we use established ontology mappings to identify clusters of entities describing the same semantic concept. In the context of the set of disease and symptom entities only the mappings UMLS_CUI and LOOM from BioPortal are relevant, i.e. have corresponding entities as source or target.

For both semantic types the set of entities together with mappings represent an undirected graph. A natural way to cluster this graph would be to simply take the maximally connected components. This approach, however, creates some very big clusters: The largest connected component of the disease graph contains around 70,000 entities if we consider all mappings and even around 33,000 if we consider only mappings from UMLS_CUI *or* LOOM. Even though big clusters are not problematic per se, these very big clusters indicate that the *quality* of the mappings is not fine-grained enough: A cluster with about 70,000 entities from about 250 ontologies contains many entities that represent different concepts. Our pragmatic solution to work with the available mappings, avoiding these large clusters, is to put at most one entity from each ontology in one cluster. Thereby we keep distinctions of concepts made by the different ontologies. Here we assume that each disease or symptom is not represented by more than one entity in the same ontology. Obviously this constraint limits the cluster size to the number of ontologies. The number of clusters as well as their maximal size using different mappings are given in Table 1. Although this approach avoids the creation of big clusters, we note that since our clusters are disjoint, this also creates many clusters of very small sizes. E.g. mappings X1-Y1 and X1-Y2 where X1 is from one ontology and Y1 and Y2 are from another ontology results in clusters {X1,Y1} and {Y2}. As a result the number 1-entity clusters almost doubles in comparison to the case where one takes maximally connected components as clusters. As shown in Table 1 LOOM (covering all BioPortal ontologies) is better in the direct comparison to UMLS using the adapted approach, however it is even better to exploit both mappings for increased coherence of the resulting graph.

Table 1. Number of clusters and maximum cluster sizes with different mappings.

(a) Disease Graph

	UMLS	LOOM	All
clusters	167,970	113,165	102,990
max cluster size	20	53	64
1-entity-clusters	135,313	70,820	62,562

(b) Symptom Graph

	UMLS	LOOM	All
clusters	16,416	13,000	11,530
max cluster size	18	53	57
1-entity-clusters	13,243	9,491	8,010

Mapping of Object Properties. The initial motivation for this work was the identification of disease-symptom *relationships* and their retrieval from different ontologies in BioPortal. More than 2,600 distinct properties are used in BioPortal ontologies. Moreover, some of the property names consist of just a URI, which makes it difficult to answer the question, whether a property is used to connect diseases and symptoms, or not. Having large sets of entities for diseases and symptoms we are able to extract disease-symptom relations from BioPortal in a focused way: We iterate over the ontologies and select triples from each ontology, where the subject is an entity from our disease set and the object is an entity of our symptom set (or the other way around). With this procedure we find 33 distinct properties from diseases to symptoms and 42 distinct properties from symptoms to diseases. However, most of the found properties represent *structural* relationships between disease and symptom entities. The most frequently used relation between disease and symptom entities is rdfs:subClassOf and we also find is-a or sibling relationships. These relations are also found between entities of the initial sets thus it is not due to wrong propagation of semantic types. This means, that in existing ontologies of the BioPortal, entities of semantic type disease and symptom are not fully separated by hierarchical structuring. Even though we did not expect to see subclass relationships between entities of different semantic types, we note that in comparison to the size of the overall set of entities the number of these structural relations is very small.

Regarding the disease-symptom relations denoting *correlations*, we found has_manifestation, manifestation_of from OMIM, related_to from MED-LINEPLUS and cause_of from SNOMED CT. has_manifestation is an inverse property of manifestation_of and thus connects the same entities. We declare these properties as subproperty of a common relation hasSymptom and include this information in our data model as shown in Fig. 5. Thus, relations between entities are mapped to relations between clusters.

Creation of the Cluster Graph. We create a model that integrates disease and symptom information, as well as the information about their relations. First of all, we store all disease and symptom URIs as entities and assign the corresponding semantic type by an annotation property disy:semanticType.

We use a property sourceOntology for each entity to show in which ontology it occurs. One entity URI might occur in one, as well as in many different ontologies. To represent the mappings between entities, we use the mapping sources as

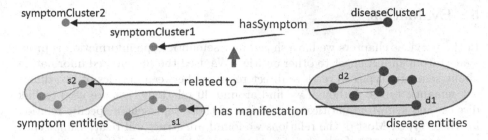

Fig. 5. Mapping entity-level relations to cluster-level relations.

a property. Also we define these properties as a subproperty of `skos:exactMatch` to make it possible to query the mappings without discriminating their sources. For each entity we store the preferred labels as strings using `skos:prefLabel`. We also select a preferred label for each cluster based on the frequency of preferred labels of the contained entities. In case of multiple labels occurring with the same frequency, we select the longest among them. One entity might have one or more preferred labels. Together with these properties, we also put the subclass information into our data model. We store the subclass relationships among disease entities, among symptom entities and between disease and symptom entities. As described in the previous subsection we create cluster-level relations if there is at least one relation between corresponding entities. We represent this information through a `hasSymptom` property between the corresponding disease clusters and symptom clusters. That is, a property such as `has_manifestation` between disease and symptom entities is mapped to `hasSymptom` between the corresponding disease and symptom clusters. In the context of other semantic types the relation could be mapped to another property. That is, the *context* of the semantic types provides the basis for the mapping of the relation. This context-specific mapping is important since domain and range of properties are often not defined or too high level. An example representation of the cluster graph is shown in Fig. 6. With the cluster graph one can now retrieve all disease symptom relations and also different labels of one disease or symptom concept.

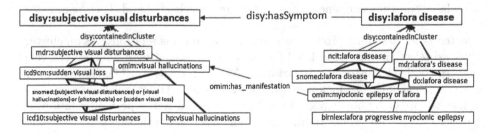

Fig. 6. The disease-symptom cluster graph model with LOOM mappings.

5   Evaluation

In the previous chapters we have shown how semantic type information is propagated from an initial set to other entities. We used the propagated information about semantic types to retrieve direct relations between entities of two different semantic types. Although we find around 40 relations that are used to link disease and symptom entities, only a few of those represent a specific relation for these types. Most of the relations we found are structural relationships such as `rdfs:subClassOf`. Only the object properties `has_manifestation` and from OMIM, `related_to` from MEDLINEPLUS and `cause_of` from SNOMED CT represent a specific disease-symptom relationship. Since we extended the relations between entities by relations on cluster-level, the evaluation of our results is also on cluster-level: Firstly, we evaluate the quality of the clusters itself and secondly we evaluate the cluster-level relations.

Clusters. To evaluate the correctness of the clusters we check, whether all entities of one cluster represent the same concept shown by the cluster preferred label. Thus for each semantic type, we have randomly selected 100 clusters which contain more than one entity and asked our clinical expert to examine the preferred labels of all entities in those selected clusters.

The evaluated disease clusters contained up to 28 entities and up to 15 different labels. For 91 out of 100 clusters all entities were about the same disease and 9 clusters contain one or more entity that are not about the same disease as the one shown by the cluster preferred label. E.g. a cluster 'bladder diverticula' correctly contained entities with label 'diverticulum of bladder' but falsely also entities with label 'bladder diverticulitis' and 'diverticulitis of bladder'. A diverticulitis however is not the same as a diverticulum since it describes an inflammation of diverticula what indicates a condition that needs to be treated, whereas diverticula are usually asymptomatic and no therapeutic measures are necessary. In average the 9 incorrect clusters contained about 25 % wrong entities.

The evaluated symptom clusters contained up to 36 entities and up to 18 different labels. For 86 out of 100 clusters were correct and 14 clusters contained entities that did not fit to the cluster. E.g. a symptom cluster with label 'neck pain' correctly contained entities with label 'cervicalgia' but falsely also entities with label 'pressionsanguine', 'blood pressure', 'backache' and 'back pain'.

Cluster-Level Relations. To evaluate diseases-symptoms relationships on cluster-level we select the preferred label for the clusters linked by a `hasSymptom` relation. In total the cluster graph contains 2,531 such relations. The clinical expert evaluated 500 of them which were randomly selected. All 500 relations were evaluated as correct by our expert. Even though we did not expect all relations to be correct, one can expect similar result for other semantic types as well: Since clusters are created based on established mappings which are based on similarity (or even equivalence) the cluster and also the cluster label does represent the same concept as the contained entities. Thus if we have a relation between two entities the relation is likely to hold on cluster level as well. Only if the clusters are incorrect *and* selected preferred cluster does not represent the entity that participates in the entity level relation (e.g. has_manifestation from OMIM) then the cluster-level relation would be false. As shown in Fig. 6, the cluster preferred label might be different to the label of the entities participating in the entity level relation. The advantage of cluster-level aggregation, is that relations defined in different ontologies can be easily combined as shown in Fig. 5. Between two clusters we have at most one entity link. In the cluster graph disease clusters have up to 10 hasSymptom links to other symptom clusters. Since the entity level links are mainly from OMIM, we note that the overall *link rate* does not improve a lot. However, trough clusters, we enhance the total number of links significantly: Initially 1,114 distinct disease entities were related to 345 distinct symptom entities. Now 5,960 distinct disease entities are related to 3,615 distinct symptom entities from many different ontologies.

6   Related Work

As argued in [8] there is a strong need for a 'semantically linked data', that overcomes current difficulties in querying which is mainly due to the heterogeneity of schemas used by different datasets. Much work has been published on algorithms for ontology matching, i.e. mapping of entities such as classes, instances and properties from one ontology to another. Matching methods are mostly based on *strings* (labels, definitions etc.) and *structure* (relations between entities) - for an overview we refer to [18]. E.g. the system BLOOMS+ [7] finds schema level links between LOD data sets, utilizing the Wikipedia category hierarchy. Each class of an input ontology is represented by a subtree of this hierarchy and the matching is then based on a tree-comparison. The output is a set of equivalentClass and subClassOf mappings between classes of different ontologies. BLOOMS+ is evaluated against manually created mappings used by the FactForge[3] application and outperforms existing solutions.

The authors of [22] propose a semi-automatic Framework for InTegrating ONtologies (FITON) to reduce the semantic heterogeneity of different ontologies by retrieving core ontology entities such as top level classes and frequently used properties which are then aligned. FITON utilizes sameAs relations between instances to match classes and properties, which is similar to our approach. Additionally, they use machine learning techniques in a subsequent step to retrieve core ontology entities necessary to describe instances in order to allows more easy querying. They also attempt to define domain and range for properties.

The authors of [13] describe an *extensional* approach to generate alignments between ontologies. That is, they use information about the instances (i.e. the extension) of classes and mappings on instance level (owl:sameAs) to create alignments of different ontologies by subsumption relations between the corresponding classes. Since they combine classes and properties of two ontologies they obtain a richer representation for both. Thus they allow users to describe and query one data set in terms of an ontology used by another dataset.

---

[3] http://factforge.net/.

In contrast to the approaches mentioned above which mainly map classes of two ontologies, we assign global semantic types to entities from many different ontologies by *using* existing mappings of entities (which can be classes or instances). Our approach builds on top of existing mapping solutions to enable queries across different resources based on global semantic types. I.e. our main goal is not to have related entities mapped to each other, but rather to *extract* available knowledge about relations between entities of different semantic types. This use-case driven approach is different from general ontology alignment.

Regarding our specific application scenario, the UMLS [3,4] was the most important resource. Since the UMLS Semantic Network defines semantic types for all entities of its member ontologies it was not difficult to obtain a good initial set of disease and symptom entities. Further the UMLS CUIs provided a significant mapping resource. Thus, our work can be seen as an attempt to extend the scope of the UMLS semantic types to other ontologies and datasets of the LOD. linkedlifedata[4] provides integrated 'access to 25 public biomedical databases' by creating a distributed graph model with specific types such as drugs, clinical trials, proteins, genes and many more. They also provide semantic filters for UMLS ontologies however corresponding object properties are not aligned. The BioPortal [21] maps certain data and annotation properties to SKOS vocabulary, so users can easily retrieve textual definitions and labels from different ontologies. In summary existing repositories provide only a partial solution, since there are many more ontologies available than those of the UMLS. Even though the BioPortal or linkedlifedata provide mappings of lexical information, mappings for general object properties are missing. The Bio2RDF repository [1] is the largest linked network of life science data. To allow and simplify federated queries across different resources specific types and relations are mapped to the Semanticscience Integrated Ontology [2]. The OBO Foundry [19] promotes the coordinated evolution of ontologies by providing a set of basic properties that are used by many ontologies. That is, the reuse of properties and entities right from the start is encouraged so that a later mapping is not necessary. Especially the OBO ontologies DO as well as the SYMP are good resources and would be valuable for our application scenario if they were linked. The authors of [9] try to relate DO and SYMP, but assume that one can already get symptoms for a selected disease from a health website or server, or a database and as a result they have symptoms only for 11 diseases. The Generic Human Disease Ontology (GHDO) [6] is a model with four dimensions: diseases, symptoms, causes and treatments. For each disease, different treatments and symptoms can be specified. Nonetheless, there was no such ontology published from the proposed model. Yet in another work [20], an ontology model for storing disease and symptom relationships is proposed, but the actual work and results are left for future. In summary existing disease-symptom graphs are either very small [6,9,20] or were created manually [12]. Our approach creates the disease-symptom graph automatically with little expert input.

---

[4] http://linkedlifedata.com/.

7   Conclusion

We presented an approach that utilizes existing mapping resources to propagate semantic type information from an initial set to entities of other ontologies. This allows to analyse and map existing relations between two different semantic types as shown along the disease symptom application scenario. As a result we have a clear picture of the amount and quality of available disease-symptom knowledge. We could show that context specific schema integration is feasible and that our approach leads to significantly more links between datasets. To the best of our knowledge there is no work that aligns properties in a context specific way respecting the semantic type of the entities connected by the mapped properties. The representation in a cluster graph allows us to query disease symptom information from a large set of ontologies in an integrated way. Additionally to usage of the results for our disease-ranking application the knowledge model can be used as a starting point for several applications: For instance, one could use the textual definitions of different disease entities contained in one cluster for extraction of additional disease information. Or symptom information can be extracted by annotating textual definitions of diseases with entities of the symptom graph leading to even more links between diseases and symptoms. In future work we want to apply the approach to other semantic types such as clinical findings to cover more annotations of unstructured clinical data which have relations to diseases. One can also include other resources such as the human phenotype annotations of OMIM diseases into the disease graph.

The overall approach proved to be useful however there are several steps of the approach that can be improved to further enhance the quality of the output. For instance, the propagation of semantic type information could be enhanced by including more mappings and by weighting the information during propagation of semantic types. In this work we included only one mapping step, but one could also go further steps to retrieve more entities. Similarly the clustering algorithm can be enhanced: Here, one could weight different mapping sources and maximize the clustering coefficient for each cluster to avoid path-like clusters.

Acknowledgements. This research has been supported in part by the KDI project, which is funded by the German Federal Ministry of Economics and Technology under grant number 01MT14001 and by the EU FP7 Diachron project (GA 601043).

References

1. Callahan, A., Cruz-Toledo, J., Ansell, P., Dumontier, M.: Bio2RDF release 2: improved coverage, interoperability and provenance of life science linked data. In: Cimiano, P., Corcho, O., Presutti, V., Hollink, L., Rudolph, S. (eds.) ESWC 2013. LNCS, vol. 7882, pp. 200–212. Springer, Heidelberg (2013)
2. Callahan, A., Cruz-Toledo, J., Dumontier, M.: Ontology-based querying with Bio2RDF's linked open data. J. Biomed. Semant. 4(S1), 1–13 (2013)
3. Campbell, K.E., Oliver, D.E., Spackman, K.A., Shortliffe, E.H.: Representing thoughts, words, and things in the UMLS. J. Am. Med. Inform. Assoc.: JAMIA 5(5), 421–431 (1998)

4. Lindberg, B.H.D., McCray, A.: The unified medical language system. Methods Inf. Med. **32**(4), 281–291 (1993)
5. Ghazvinian, A.: Creating mappings for ontologies in biomedicine: simple methods work. AMIA Annu. Symp. Proc. **2009**, 198–202 (2009)
6. Hadzic, M., Chang, E.: Ontology-based multi-agent systems support human disease study and control. In: Czap, H., Unland, R., Branki, C. (eds.) SOAS. Frontiers in Artificial Intelligence and Applications, vol. 135, pp. 129–141. IOS Press, Amsterdam (2005)
7. Jain, P., Yeh, P.Z., Verma, K., Vasquez, R.G., Damova, M., Hitzler, P., Sheth, A.P.: Contextual ontology alignment of lod with an upper ontology: a case study with proton. In: Antoniou, G., Grobelnik, M., Simperl, E., Parsia, B., Plexousakis, D., De Leenheer, P., Pan, J. (eds.) ESWC 2011, Part I. LNCS, vol. 6643, pp. 80–92. Springer, Heidelberg (2011)
8. Jain, P., Hitzler, P., Yeh, P.Z., Verma, K., Sheth, A.P.: Linked Data is Merely More Data. Linked Data Meets Artificial Intelligence. Technical report SS-10-07, AAAI Press, pp. 82–86 (2010)
9. Mohammed, O., Benlamri, R., Fong, S.: Building a diseases symptoms ontology for medical diagnosis: an integrative approach. In: International Conference on Future Generation Communication Technology (FGCT), pp. 104–108, Dec. 2012
10. Noy, N.F., Dorf, M., Griffith, N., Nyulas, C., Musen, M.A.: Harnessing the power of the community in a library of biomedical ontologies. In: Workshop on Semantic Web Applications in Scientific Discourse (2009)
11. Oberkampf, H., Zillner, S., Bauer, B., Hammon, M.: Interpreting patient data using medical background knowledge. In: 3rd International Conference on Biomedical Ontology (ICBO 2012), KR-MED Series, Graz, Austria. CEUR-WS.org, Austria (2012)
12. Oberkampf, H., Zillner, S., Bauer, B., Hammon, M.: Towards a ranking of likely diseases in terms of precision and recall. In: 1st International Workshop on Artificial Intelligence and NetMedicine at ECAI 2012, pp. 11–20 (2012)
13. Parundekar, R., Knoblock, C.A., Ambite, J.L.: Discovering concept coverings in ontologies of linked data sources. In: Cudré-Mauroux, P., Heflin, J., Sirin, E., Tudorache, T., Euzenat, J., Hauswirth, M., Parreira, J.X., Hendler, J., Schreiber, G., Bernstein, A., Blomqvist, E. (eds.) ISWC 2012, Part I. LNCS, vol. 7649, pp. 427–443. Springer, Heidelberg (2012)
14. Salvadores, M., Alexander, P.R., Musen, M.A., Noy, N.F.: Bioportal as a dataset of linked biomedical ontologies and terminologies in rdf. Semant. Web **4**(3), 277–284 (2013)
15. Salvadores, M., Horridge, M., Alexander, P.R., Fergerson, R.W., Musen, M.A., Noy, N.F.: Using SPARQL to query BioPortal ontologies and metadata. In: Cudré-Mauroux, P., Heflin, J., Sirin, E., Tudorache, T., Euzenat, J., Hauswirth, M., Parreira, J.X., Hendler, J., Schreiber, G., Bernstein, A., Blomqvist, E. (eds.) ISWC 2012, Part II. LNCS, vol. 7650, pp. 180–195. Springer, Heidelberg (2012)
16. Schriml, L.M., Arze, C., Nadendla, S., Chang, Y.-W.W., Mazaitis, M., Felix, V., Feng, G., Kibbe, W.A.: Disease Ontology: a backbone for disease semantic integration. Nucleic Acids Res. **40**(Database issue), D940–D946 (2012)
17. Seifert, S., et al.: Semantic Annotation of Medical Images. In: SPIE, Medical Imaging: Advanced PACS-based Imaging Informatics and Therapeutic Applications (2010)
18. Shvaiko, P.: Ontology matching: state of the art and future challenges. IEEE Trans. Knowl. Data Eng. **25**(1), 158–176 (2013)

19. Smith, B., et al.: The OBO Foundry: coordinated evolution of ontologies to support biomedical data integration. Nat. Biotechnol. **25**(11), 1251–1252 (2007)
20. Thirugnanam, M., Ramaiah, M., Pattabiraman, V., Sivakumar, R.: Ontology based disease information system. Procedia Eng. **38**, 3235–3241 (2012)
21. Whetzel, P., et al.: Bioportal: enhanced functionality via new web services from the national center for biomedical ontology to access and use ontologies in software applications. Nucleic Acids Res. **39**(suppl 2), W541–W545 (2011)
22. Zhao, L., Ichise, R.: Ontology integration for linked data. J. Data Semant. **3**(4), 237–254 (2014)

Using Semantic Web Technologies for Enterprise Architecture Analysis

Maximilian Osenberg[1,2,3,4], Melanie Langermeier[4(✉)], and Bernhard Bauer[4]

[1] Elite Graduate Program Software Engineering, Technical University Munich,
Munich, Germany
[2] Elite Graduate Program Software Engineering, Ludwigs-Maximilian-University,
Munich, Germany
[3] Elite Graduate Program Software Engineering, University of Augsburg,
Augsburg, Germany
[4] Software Methodologies for Distributed Systems, University of Augsburg,
Augsburg, Germany
{osenberg,langermeier,bauer}@ds-lab.org

Abstract. Enterprise Architecture (EA) models are established means for decision makers in organizations. They describe the business processes, the application landscape and IT infrastructure as well as the relationships between those layers. Current research focuses merely on frameworks, modeling and documentation approaches for EA. But once these models are established, methods for their analysis are rare. In this paper we propose the use of semantic web technologies in order to represent the EA and perform analyses. We present an approach how to transform an existing EA model into an ontology. Using this knowledge base, simple questions can be answered with the query language SPARQL. The major benefits of semantic web technologies can be found, when defining and applying more complex analyses. Change impact analysis is important to estimate the effects and costs of a change to an EA model element. To show the benefits of semantic web technologies for EA, we implemented an approach to change impact analysis and executed it within a case study.

1 Introduction

Today's organizations have to deal with the complexity of large IT landscapes together with fast changing business architectures. Enterprise architecture (EA) models are used to capture the IT infrastructure elements, the used applications as well as the business processes. Especially the relationships between the elements are of major interest in order to understand the organizations' structure. The domain of Enterprise Architecture Management (EAM) captures the process of assessing the current EA of an organization as well as defining and implementing a target architecture [12]. Thus, EAM is a mean for incorporating changes throughout the whole organization as well as for driving optimizations of the architecture, especially the alignment of business and IT. The optimization of the business processes itself is dealt within the domain of Business Process Re-engineering.

© Springer International Publishing Switzerland 2015
F. Gandon et al. (Eds.): ESWC 2015, LNCS 9088, pp. 668–682, 2015.
DOI: 10.1007/978-3-319-18818-8_41

Current methods and tools in the EA domain provide means to calculate specific key performance indicators and visualize the results in an EA model e.g. an architecture diagram can be annotated in a way, that application systems running out of support shortly are colored red (see [18]). But combining this fact with other ones, e.g. the rate of business critical processes supported by the application, or the availability of a successor application bears challenges. A vital question in this context is also the effect of a specific change. The change in one element can cause ripple effects throughout the whole organization. Those indirect effects of a change are not always obvious, but can cause severe costs for a project. Especially since EA models are typically very large, humans cannot capture these effects easily. Change impact analysis is used to calculate the affected elements and thus provide the enterprise architect further information, whether a change should be implemented or not. Current implementations of more complex analyses and measures are highly dependent on the used meta model. Since every organization has its own, customized EA meta model, re-using existing analysis methods is not trivial.

In this paper we propose the use of semantic web technologies to represent EA models and to perform analyses on them. We reuse an existing formalization in order to transform an EA model into an ontology (Sect. 3.1). Then we show how simple measures and reports can be defined using SPARQL and reasoning. In order to implement more complex analyses in a flexible way, we propose to solely define their semantics and finally integrate them in an existing EA ontology (Sect. 3.2). The applicability of our approach is shown through the implementation of a change impact analysis (Sect. 4) and its execution in a case study (Sect. 5).

2   Foundations and Related Work

EA models are used to document the organization, its components and the relationship between those. Thus they provide a mean to capture and understand the complex dependencies between the business and the supporting IT infrastructure [11]. An EA model is documented using an organization specific set of concepts and relationships between those. Typical examples for concepts are *business processes*, *application components* and *infrastructure components* as well as *use* and *realize* relationships between those. Existing EA frameworks, like the Zachman framework [27] or TOGAF [22] propose different approaches for the documentation. There is no common standard for EA models. The actual used meta model is, in most cases, an adaption of an existing framework, tailored to the specific needs of the organization. This leads to a high variety of meta models used in organizations and is a major challenge, when defining methods and techniques to gain value from the EA model. Current research focuses on the development of EA frameworks as well as modeling and documentation approaches. EA analysis is not the main focus and thus not much work exists [16,17]. Existing approaches rely on techniques like XML [3] or a probabilistic extension of OCL [7]. In practice, reporting and measure calculation in the domain of EA is often performed using SQL databases but also with Excel sheets. In [19] SPARQL was proposed for analyzing an

EA, as it allows to perform different kinds of analyses with different complexities using the same technology. These approaches have in common that they are dependent on the underlying meta model, the adaption to a different one requires much effort. Despite for analysis purposes, semantic web technologies are also proposed for other reasons in EAM: Chen et al. present a method to integrate data from several sources into one EA repository using semantic web technologies [1]. Their goal is to automate the time-consuming documentation process through the use of semantic web technologies. In [5] a formalization of the TOGAF meta model using ontologies is presented in order to improve the quality and consistency of an EA model. The use of semantic web technologies is more common in the domain of business process analysis. E.g. [4] propose their use to integrate static and procedural domain knowledge as well as execution data in order to analyze them.

EA models can also be utilized to determine the potential impact of a change to one or more model elements. De Boer et al. describe in [2] an informal approach to change impact analysis in ArchiMate models. ArchiMate [23] is a modeling language for enterprise architectures, based on the TOGAF standard [22]. They start by considering a change to be either a *modification, extension* or *deletion* (or none). A *modification* is a change that modifies existing functionality, whereas an *extension* is a change that preserves existing functionality and adds new functionality (e.g. changing the signature of a method in contrast to adding a new method to an existing class); a *deletion* is a change that removes a whole component [2]. When calculating the impact of a change, starting from the first component to be changed, all components in the EA model are visited iteratively – comparable to a depth-first-search – and are annotated with how they need to be changed. The type of the relation determines how a relation between two components behaves towards a change. An example for such a propagation rule is given in the following for the relation type *access* that exists between two components A and B (e.g. application A accesses a data store B):

- In case of a change starting from A:
  - If A is **deleted**, it has no impact on B, because B doesn't depend on A.
  - If A is **extended** (or modified) this may change the way, the data stored in B is handled and thus requires an extension (or modification) of B.
- In case of a change starting from B:
  - If B is **deleted**, the object A can no longer access B. This does not mean that A needs to be changed, but that the access relation of A is lost. This has to be signaled to the user, so he can either link the access relation of A with another data object or delete A or its access relation.
  - If B is **extended**, it still provides the functionality it did before the change happened. Thus, A is not subject to change.
  - If B is **modified**, the data or the way data in B is accessed, has changed. Thus, A has to modified too.

Aier and Kurpjuweit provide an approach for change impact analysis by calculating the transitive closure of the relationships [9]. Therefore they use a relational composition operator to define the implicit relations between objects.

This composition operator must only allow compositions of relation types, which mean a dependency of objects in the context of change impact analysis. Since the authors focus on dependency analysis in general, they do not provide a differentiation between different change types. Further change impact analysis approaches are based on probability distributions [6,21]. Those methods are based on change probabilities, whom establishment requires a high workload. Thus if this information is not available, those methods are not the best approach. Change impact analysis is also supported in current EA tools. It is typically implemented as a report that determines a hard coded set of elements, e.g. all applications supporting a specific process and the related organization units (e.g. [18]). Another approach to determine the impact provided by EA tools are visualizations, e.g. using an interactive hierarchy graph (e.g. [14]) or through highlighting affected elements with colors (e.g. [18]). Thereby the tools do not differ between specific change types out of the box. Additionally the impact is rarely determined in a transitive way, thus ripple effects are not considered directly.

3   Applying Semantic Web Technologies to EA

We propose the use of semantic web technologies for the representation of an EA and to perform analysis on them. The transformation of an existing EA model into an ontology is described in Sect. 3.1. Methods for their analysis are presented in Sect. 3.2. Despite existing ones, we present a method for the execution of complex analysis in different EA models.

3.1   From Formal Description to EA Ontology

We present our method for transformation along the meta model shown in Fig. 1. The meta model is based on ArchiMate [23] and belongs to the case study used for the evaluation. Nevertheless our method can be applied to any other EA meta model as well. A *Role* is a structural concept that can "do" things (e.g. an employee or a customer of a company). A *Process* is usually executed by a *Role* if (in the model) there exists an *assign* relationship between these two concepts. A *Service* provides functionality that is *realized* by a *Component* (e.g. a software application). A *Service* can be *used* by either a *Role*, an *Application* or a *Process*. A *DataObject* (e.g. a database system or a part of a database) can be *accessed* manipulatively. Note that every relation type t has a corresponding t^{-1} which does not exist in Fig. 1 due to clarity.

According to Aier and Kurpjuweit [9] an EA meta model can be formalized as tuple $M = (C, T, R)$, where C is a set of *concepts*, T is a set of *relation types* with $\forall t \in T : \exists t^{-1} \in T : (t^{-1})^{-1} \in T$, and $R \subseteq C \times C \times T$ is the set of relations that can exist between two *concepts*.

An EA model is described as tuple $A = (E, T^*, Q, F)$, where E is a set of *objects*, being an instance of a *concept*, T^* is the transitive closure of the *relation types* T, $Q \subseteq E \times E \times T^*$ is a set of relations that exist between two *objects*, and $F_e: E \rightarrow C$ is a function that returns the *concept* of an *object*.

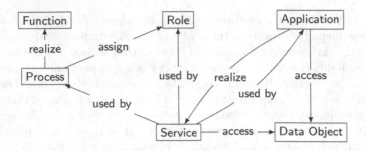

Fig. 1. EA meta model of the case study

For a *model* A to be a correct instance of a *meta model* M we will require the following condition to be fulfilled: $\forall (e_1, e_2, t) \in Q : (F_c(e_1), F_c(e_2), t) \in R$ Applying this formalization to our example, we get six different concepts and four different relations (with their inverse):

$C = \{Role, Application, Function, DataObject, Process, Service\}$
$T = \{use, usedBy, access, accessedBy, realize, realizedBy, assign,$
    $assignedBy\}$
$R = \{(Application, Service, realize), (Service, Application, realizedBy),$
    $(Role, Service, use), (Service, Role, usedBy), ...\}$

Due to space limitations we do not list all triples of R here. Consider Fig. 1 for the other triples. The integration of this formalism in real applications is not straightforward. Additionally, to benefit from deduction and SPARQL [26] we translated it into an OWL2 ontology [15]. Given a meta model $M = (C, T, R)$ we first create an `owl:Class` for each c $\in C$. However, all classes have to be marked disjoint to each other, as components in a EA model can only be instance of one class (see definition of F_e). For each relation type $t \in T$ of the meta model, we create an `owl:ObjectProperty`. Every object property has to be linked with its corresponding inverse through the `owl:inverseOf` annotation. Finally the set of triples R is represented using the `rdfs:domain` and `rdfs:range` information. The primary idea is to set the domain c1 and range c2 of a object property o according to the triple $(c1, c2, o) \in R$. However, in EA it is possible to use one relationship type for several pairs of classes. These are the relationships $t \in T$ with $|\{(c_1, c_2)|(c_1, c_2, t) \in R\}| > 1$. In our example *usedBy* is used for the relation between *Service* and *Process* but also between *Service* and *Application*. According to [20] we decided to solve this problem with superclasses in order to have the reasoner work correctly. For the *usedBy* relationship, this would indicate a new superclass *ServiceUser*. For the relation types *access* and *realize* the same procedure will be applied. At least we have to implement the EA Model (E, T^*, Q, F) in the ontology. For each $e \in E$ an individual $\mathcal{I}$ will be created. Using the `rdf:type` assertion the respective type F_e is assigned to $\mathcal{I}$. For each relationship $(e_1, e_2, t) \in Q$ an object property assertion with relation type $t \in T$ is defined between the corresponding individuals for e_1 and e_2.

3.2   Analyzing the Enterprise Architecture

Having transformed an EA model into an ontology, semantic web technologies can be employed to gain benefits from the modeled information. The easiest way is the deduction of implicit knowledge using the reasoning capabilities. Often relationships are only modeled in one direction. A typical example is the *usedBy* relationship. For every application, the used services are known and modeled in the EA. But from the perspective of a service, not all applications that use it are known. In this case the inverse of each relationship can be deduced and provides further knowledge about the EA. Especially the *users* of a service are getting important, when it comes to decision about potential changes.

Using semantic web technologies it is possible to realize existing methods for the deduction of implicit dependencies. For example the composition operation proposed by [9] or the relation composition proposed by [24]. Such a relationship composition can be used for dependency analysis as proposed by the former authors, but also for generating landscape maps. A landscape map is a matrix that is used to visualize dependencies between EA elements [25]. Such a matrix is a common mean for EA management.

Another widespread method for EAM is the definition of reports and the calculation of specific measures. Reports can e.g. be a list of all applications assigned to a specific organization unit or all processes that use applications hosted on a specific server. [13] proposes a catalog of key performance indicators for EA management, including e.g. the *Application criticality ranking*. This measure is calculated using the following definition: *The number of applications with criticality rating available divided by the total number of applications.* Assuming that the required information for a report or measure is modeled in the EA, the calculation of those using SPARQL [26] is straightforward. Since it is a minor effort to define such SPARQL queries, it is no problem to specify them individually for each organization.

The re-implementation effort of an analysis increases with the complexity of the calculation routine. Examples for more complex analyses are the performance and cost analysis proposed by [8] or the different analyses proposed in [16]. These analyses are dependent on a specific meta model and adapting them to an existing EA initiative requires much effort. We propose the combination of SPARQL and reasoning for the specification of more complex analyses to enable their execution in an existing EA model with slight adaption effort. Therefore, the concepts required to perform the analysis have to be defined in an own *analysis ontology*. This ontology is the foundation for the specification of the analysis, either using SPARQL or through respective assertions in the ontology (and deduction). For the execution of the analysis in an existing EA model the *analysis ontology* has to be imported. It is also possible to import both the EA and the analysis ontology in a new one. Using mapping constructs like class, property and data equivalency or subclass definitions the analysis concepts are mapped to the EA concepts. Running the reasoner infers the axioms that are required to execute the analysis in the EA model. The former defined analysis can now be executed without further adaptions.

4   Implementation of Change Impact Analysis

The generic approach in the previous section for the definition and adaption of complex analysis is now applied to change impact analysis. The foundation for the implementation of change impact analysis is the informal specification provided by de Boer et al. [2]. First we specify the required analysis semantics in an ontology and show how it can be integrated in an EA ontology (Sect. 4.1). Then we present an implementation approach using SPARQL in order to determine the effects of a change (Sect. 4.2). A second implementation approach uses the ability of the reasoner to deduce the change type of an element from the change semantics of the relationship (Sect. 4.3). We implemented both approaches using the ontology editor Protégé[1]. We did not implement a stand-alone application. As reasoner we used HermiT. The SPARQL queries were stored in a text file and executed in Protégé to execute the change impact analysis.

4.1   Defining and Integrating Change Semantics

The EA ontology created in Sect. 3.1 contains the EA relevant semantics. Defining the analysis based on this knowledge makes it difficult to execute it on other EA models with a different meta model. Therefore we define the required knowledge to perform change impact analysis in a separate ontology. This ontology contains information about the change semantics, i.e. concepts that indicate how changes made to a component affect the components that are in a relationship with it.

De Boer et al. define the change semantics in an EA model based on the type of change and the type of the relationship [2]. They differentiate between the change types *modification, extension, deletion* and *no change* (see Sect. 2). Depending on the type of relationship such a change will be *propagated* or *not propagated* along the relationship. It is also possible that a change is only *signaled* to the user, who has to decide about the actual propagation. The *signaling* is used, when the propagation is dependent from further aspects and not only the relationship type. For example the deletion of a service does not definitely imply the deletion of the realizing application. Nevertheless, there may be demand for action, which will be signaled to the user. According to these considerations, we know, how a change in the objects A resp. B will go through the model. If e.g. B has been changed, we have to – comparable to a depth first search – check all the relationships that link B with other objects for changes. If there is a relationship that propagates the change, for this element the same review has to be done. For each of the change types, we create a new `owl: ObjectProperty`. These are: *extensionPropagatingAssociation, modificationPropagatingAssociation, deletionPropagatingAssociation* and *deletionSignallingAssociation*. In order to use these change semantics in a specific EA ontology, the change concepts and the EA concepts have to be mapped to each other. All relation types $t \in T$ are defined as specializations of the type of changes they propagate. E.g. the relation A *realized by* B, will always propagate a respective change in B.

---

[1] A free, open-source ontology editor and framework. See http://protege.stanford.edu/.

Fig. 2. Hierarchical structure of the ObjectProperties according to their behavior towards a change.

Fig. 3. ObjectProperties that have been inferred by the reasoner for the individual "CustomerInformationServices"

Following the object property *realizedBy* is a `owl:subPropertyOf` *extensionPropagatingAssociation*, *modificationPropagatingAssociation* and *deletionPropagatingAssociation*. The reasoner enables the deduction of the type of change propagation of a specific relationship, since the superior relation always applies implicitly. I.e consider an arbitrary object property p, the set of its superior object properties P_s (i.e. p is specialization of each $p_s \in P_s$) and two individuals $\mathcal{A}$ and $\mathcal{B}$:

$$\forall p_s \in P_s : \left(\mathcal{A} \xrightarrow{p} \mathcal{B} \right) \implies \left(\mathcal{A} \xrightarrow{p_s} \mathcal{B} \right) \tag{1}$$

An example structure of ObjectProperties can be found in Fig. 2. The inferred assertions by the reasoner for a specific ObjectProperty are shown in Fig. 3.

4.2 Impact Analysis with SPARQL

According to de Boer et al. [2], we want to perform a step-by-step analysis of our EA ontology. Given an individual $\mathcal{I}$ that is changing and the type of the change (extension, modification, deletion) we can calculate the impact of the change as described in pseudo code in Listing 1.1, with

- `changed_element` is the URI of the individual $\mathcal{I}$ that causes change analysis with change type c.

- Properties(c) is a function that maps a change type to its corresponding set of object properties.[2]
- Visited are the individuals of the ontology that have been visited. Initially Visited = ∅.
- Result ⊆ $I \times O$ is a set of tuples that contain an individual of the ontology and the object property of the relationship that has been found.
- ToBeVisited is the set of individuals that remain to be visited (initially it only contains changed_element).
- p is the individual that is currently being visited.
- S is the result of the SPARQL query.

Listing 1.1. Ontology-based dependency analysis in pseudo code.

```
1  BEGIN DependencyAnalysis
2
3      ToBeVisited = {changed_element}.
4      Visited = { }.
5      Result = { }.
6
7      WHILE ToBeVisited IS NOT EMPTY.
8          p = ToBeVisited.getElement().
9
10         FOREACH property IN Properties(c)
11             S := SELECT ?object
12                 WHERE{ p my:property ?object }.
13
14             FOREACH s IN S.
15                 INSERT TUPLE(s, property) INTO Result
16                     IF NOT EXISTS.
17             ENDFOREACH.
18
19             INSERT DISTINCT (S MINUS (Visited INTERSECT S))
20                 INTO ToBeVisited IF NOT EXISTS.
21
22             DELETE p FROM ToBeVisited.
23             INSERT p INTO Visited.
24         END FOREACH.
25
26     ENDWHILE.
27     RETURN Result.
28 END.
```

First we assign one of the individuals of the set ToBeVisited to p (l. 8). Then for each object property property, that needs to be considered for the change type c, we query the individuals that are related to p via property using SPARQL (ll. 10–12). The query result is stored into the set S. The individuals in S are added to the Result set (ll. 14–17), including the object property type property. Each element of S, that is not yet in the set Visited, is added to the set ToBeVisited (ll. 19, 20). Finally we remove p from ToBeVisited and store it in Visited (ll. 22, 23). We repeat these steps until there are no more individuals in ToBeVisited. All individuals that are affected by the change are now in the Result set, including their respective change propagation type. Therewith we can decide whether the individual is really affected, or – in case of a deletion – only needs to be signaled to the user.

---

[2] e.g. Change type *extension* is mapped to {extensionPropagatingAssociation} and *deletion* is mapped to {deletionPropagatingAssociation, deletionSignallingAssociation}.

According to Table 1 there are several cases, where there is only a signal for a possible impact propagated. Considering the following scenario:

$$\mathcal{I}_0 \xrightarrow{o_0} \mathcal{I}_1 \xrightarrow{o_1} \ldots \xrightarrow{o_{m-1}} \mathcal{I}_m \xrightarrow{o_m} \mathcal{I}_{m+1} \xrightarrow{o_{m+1}} \ldots \xrightarrow{o_{n-1}} \mathcal{I}_n \qquad (2)$$

with $\forall i \in \{0, 1, ..., n\} : \nexists \mathcal{K} \in I : \mathcal{K} \xrightarrow{o} \mathcal{I}_i \wedge \mathcal{K} \neq \mathcal{I}_{i-1}$.

We assume that all relations o_i in the chain trigger only a signal about a potential change to the user and furthermore, that for all individuals with index $< m$ the user already decided that they should be changed, however for $\mathcal{I}_m$, the user decided that it is not affected by the change. Then all individuals with index $> m$ do not have to be signaled to the user (except when they could be affected by the change through other individuals). In order to realize this behavior in our algorithm Listing 1.1 we need to ask the user after line 8, whether p should be changed or not – in case that c is signaling for all (p, c) ∈ Result. If the user decides, that p does not need to be changed, then all tuples with p at their left position need to be removed from Result and p also needs to be removed from ToBeVisited. The algorithm can then continue with line 7.

4.3 Impact Analysis with Defined Classes

As second alternative we propose the use of reasoning capabilities to deduce the effect of a change from the available information. Therefore we extend the analysis ontology with the classes *DeletedComponent*, *DeletionSignaledComponent*, *ExtendedComponent* and *ModifiedComponent*. In order to represent the external change that triggers the analysis, we add three data properties, *isDeleted*, *isExtended* and *isModified*. If an individual $\mathcal{I}$ of the ontology is affected by the change, the reasoner should deduce that it is instance of the respective change class. Given two individuals $\mathcal{I}_1$ and $\mathcal{I}_2$ with the relationship $\mathcal{I}_2 \xrightarrow{extension Propagating Association} \mathcal{I}_1$, the reasoner should deduce, that if $\mathcal{I}_2$ is extended, also $\mathcal{I}_1$ has to be extended (indicated by the assertion owl:type :ExtendedComponent). To enable this deduction, we add inverse object properties for all kinds of change propagating properties. In the example this is the *extensionReceivingAssociation*. Additionally also a *modificationReceivingAssociaten*, *deletionSignalReceveivingAssociation* and a *deletionReceivingAssociation* are added. Each of them is enriched with the assertion about the respective inverse propagating object property. For each change class we are now able to specify an equivalent class expression. Those class definitions are shown in Listing 1.2 using the Manchester OWL Syntax. For the class *ExtendedComponent* this says: An individual that has owl:type :ModelingComponent and that has an :extensionReceivingAssociation with another :ExtendedComponent has also the type :ExtendedComponent. Additionally an individual is member of this class, if it is annotated with the data propery :isExtended true. The expressions for the classes *DeletedComponent* and *ModifiedComponent* are defined in the same way using the corresponding receiving object property. An individual is a member of the class *DeletionSignaledComponent*, if owl:type: ModelingComponent can be inferred and if it has a: deletionSignalReceivingAssociation from a :DeletedComponent. If the user decides that a *DeletionSignaledComponent* needs to be deleted, he has to assign the *isDeleted* data property to it. This way, it is ensured that the *DeletionSignaledComponents* are kept minimal, and further assertions are only made if the user decides about the deletion.

Listing 1.2. Class definitions in Manchester OWL Syntax

```
 1  Class: cs:ModifiedComponent
 2      EquivalentTo:
 3          ((cs:modificationReceivingAssociation some cs:ModifiedComponent)
 4          or (cs:isModified some {true}))
 5
 6  Class: cs:ExtendedComponent
 7      EquivalentTo:
 8          ((cs:extensionReceivingAssociation some cs:ExtendedComponent)
 9          or (cs:isExtended some {true}))
10
11  Class: cs:DeletedComponent
12      EquivalentTo:
13          ((cs:deletionReceivingAssociation some cs:deletedComponent)
14          or (cs:isDeleted some {true}))
15
16
17  Class: cs:DeletionSignaledComponent
18      EquivalentTo:
19          (cs:deletionSignalReceivingAssociation some cs:deletedComponent)
```

For the execution of this analysis in a specific EA model, the relationship types t of the EA ontology have to be mapped to the respective change propagation properties (analog to the procedure in Sect. 4.2. The change receiving properties can be deduced from this information by the reasoner. After asserting the actual change using the data properties, the reasoner can be synchronized and deduces the membership of the individuals in the four change classes. The result can be retrieved with a simple SPARQL query.

5   Case Study

We evaluated our approach using the PEIS (Personal Environmental Information System) case study from the ENVIROFI project[3]. A description of the use case can be found in [10]. This case study is a good representative to validate our approach. Since the meta model is based on ArchiMate, a popular EA modeling technique, the typical EA elements and dependencies are covered. Additionally the size of the use case is large enough to be able to test the propagation of change effects, whereas humans can still retrieve the actual effect of a change to be able to compare the results. An overview of the EA model of PEIS is shown in Fig. 4. The meta model for PEIS was already introduced in Sect. 3.1 in Fig. 1. According to the method proposed in Sect. 3.1 we manually transformed the EA model into an ontology. Using the reasoning capabilities we inferred the return directions of each relationship. As expected, reports like the number of uses of an application can be defined in a fast and easy way using SPARQL. Finally we applied our approaches proposed in Sects. 4.2 and 4.3 to the PEIS use case.

---

[3] Environmental Observation Web and its Service Applications within the Future Internet: www.envirofi.eu.

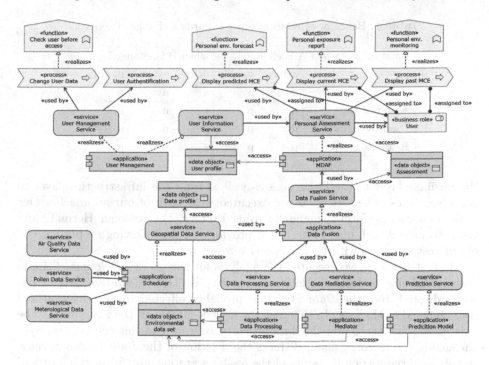

Fig. 4. EA model of the PEIS use case

Table 1 contains an overview over the different relation types and the change semantics we assigned to them. The left part of the table defines the change semantic in the original direction, e.g. for A accesses B; the inverse relationship is defined in the right part of the table. For a relation $r\colon A \xrightarrow{r} B$ from component A to component B, the change semantic is defined in Table 1 with:

- **p** means that the change is **propagated** (modification is propagated as modification, deletion as deletion and extension as extension) to the associated component,
- **n** means that the change is **not propagated** and
- **s** means that the change is **signaled** to the user, who has to decide whether or not the change shall be propagated.

If there is a change propagation, we added the respective *subObjectProperty* assertion. For example, for the relation $A \xrightarrow{access} B$ only a modification and an extension is propagated. Following the assertion `:access owl:subPropertyOf :extensionPropagatingAssociation` and the assertion `:access owl:sub-PropertyOf :modificationPropagatingAssociation` have to be added. This is done for all cells in Table 1.

For the evaluation of the change impact analysis we defined several test cases. Every test case contains a specific change to a component as well as the components that we expect to be affected by the change. The test cases are defined in manner, that every change type and every change propagation type is covered at least once. We also considered testing the change propagation from

Table 1. Behavior of relation types towards a change $A \xrightarrow{r} B$.

Relation r	when A is changed			when B is changed		
	delete	extend	modify	delete	extend	modify
Access	n	n	n	s	n	p
Assigned to	s	p	p	s	n	n
Used by	s	n	p	s	n	n
Realizes	p	p	p	s	n	p

the business layer to the lower ones as well as from the infrastructure layer to the upper ones. The test cases are executed with both of our approaches Our evaluation was performed manually using Protégé, the reasoner HermiT, and the textual SPARQL query interface it provides. In the following we present two of our test scenarios with their respective results.

As first test case we executed the analysis for the change *Deletion of Application Mediator* and got the following result: The *Data Mediation Service* has to be deleted, too; the *Data Fusion* is probably affected by the deletion and thus signaled to the user. In this case the user decides that *Data Fusion* is to be deleted too, he has to add the data property *isDeleted* to this component. Synchronizing the reasoner again deduces the deletion of the *Data Fusion Service*. In this case the retrieved results of the analysis are meaningful to the user and a good approximation of the potential change effect.

The second test case encompasses the *Modification of Personal Assessment Service*. This change is propagated to the processes *Display predicted, current* and *past MCE* as well as their realizing functions. Also the *User* is affected by the modification. But also in the other direction the change is propagated to the realizing application *MDAF*. In this case the result set is greater than in the previous scenario. This might indicate that a change in this service can have a high impact on the business outcome, especially since many elements from the business layer are affected. However, it may also indicate that the used change impact rules in Table 1 are too weak and thus the result set is too large.

Summarizing, we observed that the results of an test case are identical for both approaches. We also realized that we had a strong match between the components that we had expected and the results returned by the approaches. In both cases it is meaningful to compare the calculated impact with the actual impact and if required, adapt the change impact rules. Nevertheless we were able to execute the change impact analysis on the PEIS EA model with only restricted amount of effort for the integration of the analysis semantics.

6   Conclusion

In this paper we proposed semantic web technologies for the enterprise architecture domain. We specified how to transform an EA model into an ontology and outlined how to add value to those data. Simple reports and measures can be directly implemented using SPARQL individually for each EA initiative. Due to the higher effort for more complex analysis, there is a need for methods to re-use the analysis definitions. We propose the separate definition of an *analysis ontology* and an *EA ontology*. The *EA ontology* contains the organization specific definition of EA concepts and their relationships as well as the concrete instance elements. The *analysis ontology* describes analysis specific concepts, which are used for the specification of the actual analysis. In order to execute an analysis on an *EA ontology*, the analysis concepts have to be mapped to the *EA ontology*.

We demonstrated the use of semantic web technologies in the EA domain using the PEIS case study. The EA, formerly not modeled in an ontology, was transformed into an OWL2 ontology. Typical EA reports and measures could be re-built using SPARQL queries very quickly. As complex analysis we redefined an existing specification of change impact analysis. We integrated the defined analysis concepts in the established EA ontology and executed the analysis. Although the definition of the analysis ontology and the execution specification was time consuming, the integration into the EA model and the final execution was slight. Through an iterative refinement of the mapping, the precision of the analysis results could be improved.

References

1. Chen, W., Hess, C., Langermeier, M., Stuelpnagel, J., Diefenthaler, P.: Semantic enterprise architecture management. In: Proceedings of the 15th International Conference on Enterprise Information Systems (2013)
2. de Boer, F., Bonsangue, M., Groenewegen, L.P.J, Stam, A.W., Stevens, S., Van Der Torre, L.: Change impact analysis of enterprise architectures. In: IEEE International Conference on Information Reuse and Integration, pp. 177–181 (2005)
3. de Boer, F.S., Bonsangue, M.M., Jacob, J., Stam, A., Van der Torre, L.: Enterprise architecture analysis with XML. In: Proceedings of the 38th Annual Hawaii International Conference on System Sciences, HICSS 2005. IEEE (2005)
4. Di Francescomarino, C., Corcoglioniti, F., Dragoni, M., Bertoli, P., Tiella, R., Ghidini, C., Nori, M., Pistore, M.: Semantic-based process analysis. In: Mika, P., Tudorache, T., Bernstein, A., Welty, C., Knoblock, C., Vrandečić, D., Groth, P., Noy, N., Janowicz, K., Goble, C. (eds.) ISWC 2014, Part II. LNCS, vol. 8797, pp. 228–243. Springer, Heidelberg (2014)
5. Gerber, A., Kotz, P., van der Merwe, A.: Towards the formalisation of the TOGAF content metamodel using ontologies. In: Proceedings of the 12th International Conference on Enterprise Information Systems (ICEIS 2010) (2010)
6. Holschke, O., Närman, P., Flores, W.R., Eriksson, E., Schönherr, M.: Using enterprise architecture models and bayesian belief networks for failure impact analysis. In: Feuerlicht, G., Lamersdorf, W. (eds.) ICSOC 2008. LNCS, vol. 5472, pp. 339–350. Springer, Heidelberg (2009)
7. Johnson, P., Ullberg, J., Buschle, M., Franke, U., Shahzad, K.: P^{2}AMF: predictive, probabilistic architecture modeling framework. In: van Sinderen, M., Oude Luttighuis, P., Folmer, E., Bosems, S. (eds.) IWEI 2013. LNBIP, vol. 144, pp. 104–117. Springer, Heidelberg (2013)
8. Jonkers, H., Iacob, M.-E.: Performance and cost analysis of service-oriented enterprise architectures. In: Gunasekaran, A. (ed.) Global Implications of Modern Enterprise Information Systems: Technologies and Applications. IGI Global, Hershey (2009)

9. Kurpjuweit, S., Aier, S.: Ein allgemeiner Ansatz zur Ableitung von Abhängigkeitsanalysen auf Unternehmensarchitekturmodellen. In: Wirtschaftsinformatik (1), pp. 129–138. Citeseer (2009)
10. Langermeier, M.: A model-driven approach for open distributed systems. Technical report 2013–03, University of Augsburg (2013)
11. Lankhorst, M.: Enterprise Architecture at Work. Springer-Verlag Berlin and Heidelberg GmbH & Co. KG, Berlin (2012)
12. Lucke, C., Krell, S., Lechner, U.: Critical issues in enterprise architecting - a literature review. In: Proceedings of the 16th Americas Conference on Information Systems (2010)
13. Matthes, F., Monahov, I., Schneider, A., Schulz, C.: EAM KPI catalog v 1.0. Technical report, Technical University Munich (2012)
14. MID GmbH. MID Innovator for Enterprise Architects (2015). http://www.mid.de/produkte/innovator-enterprise-modeling.html. Accessed 15 January 2015
15. Motik, B., Patel-Schneider, P.F., Parsia, B.: OWL 2 Web Ontology Language: Structural Specification and Functional-Style Syntax, 2nd edn. (2012). http://www.w3.org/TR/owl2-syntax. Accessed 13 January 2015
16. Närman, P., Buschle, M., Ekstedt, M.: An enterprise architecture framework for multi-attribute information systems analysis. Softw. Syst. Model. 13(3), 1085–1116 (2014)
17. Niemann, K.: From Enterprise Architecture to IT Governance. Springer, Heidelberg (2006)
18. Software AG. Alfabet Enterprise Architecture Management (2015). http://www.softwareag.com/corporate/products/aris_alfabet/ea/overview/default.asp. Accessed 15 January 2015
19. Sunkle, S., Kulkarni, V., Roychoudhury, S.: Analyzing enterprise models using enterprise architecture-based ontology. In: Moreira, A., Schätz, B., Gray, J., Vallecillo, A., Clarke, P. (eds.) MODELS 2013. LNCS, vol. 8107, pp. 622–638. Springer, Heidelberg (2013)
20. Russ, T.: (protege-owl) Specifying domain and range in object properties (2010). https://mailman.stanford.edu/pipermail/protege-owl/2010-November/015509.html. Accessed 07 January 2015
21. Tang, A., Nicholson, A., Jin, Y., Han, J.: Using bayesian belief networks for change impact analysis in architecture design. J. Syst. Softw. 80(1), 127–148 (2007)
22. The Open Group. TOGAF Version 9.1. Van Haren Publishing (2011)
23. The Open Group. ArchiMate 2.0 specification: Open Group Standard. Van Haren Publishing (2012)
24. van Buuren, R., Jonkers, H., Iacob, M.-E., Strating, P.: Composition of relations in enterprise architecture models. In: Ehrig, H., Engels, G., Parisi-Presicce, F., Rozenberg, G. (eds.) ICGT 2004. LNCS, vol. 3256, pp. 39–53. Springer, Heidelberg (2004)
25. van der Torre, L.W.N., Lankhorst, M.M., ter Doest, H., Campschroer, J.T.P., Arbab, F.: Landscape maps for enterprise architectures. In: Martinez, F.H., Pohl, K. (eds.) CAiSE 2006. LNCS, vol. 4001, pp. 351–366. Springer, Heidelberg (2006)
26. W3C SPARQL Working Group. SPARQL 1.1 Overview (2013). http://www.w3.org/TR/sparql11-overview. Accessed 13 January 2015
27. Zachman, J.A.: A framework for information architecture. IBM Syst. J. 26(3), 276–295 (1987)

PADTUN - Using Semantic Technologies in Tunnel Diagnosis and Maintenance Domain

Dhavalkumar Thakker[1](✉), Vania Dimitrova[1], Anthony G. Cohn[1], and Joaquin Valdes[2]

[1] University of Leeds, Leeds LS2 9JT, UK
{D.Thakker,V.G.Dimitrova,A.G.Cohn}@leeds.ac.uk
[2] SNCF, 6 Av François Mitterrand, 93574 La Plaine St Denis Cedex, France
Joaquin.VALDES@sncf.fr

Abstract. A Decision Support System (DSS) in tunnelling domain deals with identifying pathologies based on disorders present in various tunnel portions and contextual factors affecting a tunnel. Another key area in diagnosing pathologies is to identify regions of interest (ROI). In practice, tunnel experts intuitively abstract regions of interest by selecting tunnel portions that are susceptible to the same types of pathologies with some distance approximation. This complex diagnosis process is often subjective and poorly scales across cases and transport structures. In this paper, we introduce PADTUN system, a working prototype of a DSS in tunnelling domain using semantic technologies. Ontologies are developed and used to capture tacit knowledge from tunnel experts. Tunnel inspection data are annotated with ontologies to take advantage of inferring capabilities offered by semantic technologies. In addition, an intelligent mechanism is developed to exploit abstraction and inference capabilities to identify ROI. PADTUN is developed in real-world settings offered by the NeTTUN EU Project and is applied in a tunnel diagnosis use case with Société Nationale des Chemins de Fer Français (SNCF), France. We show how the use of semantic technologies allows addressing the complex issues of pathology and ROI inferencing and matching experts' expectations of decision support.

Keywords: Tunnel diagnosis · ROI inferencing using semantics · Tunnel ontology

1 Introduction

Organisations managing a large inheritance of old tunnels and underground structures are confronted with the need to guarantee the full safety of use while optimising their overall maintenance costs. This is particularly critical in railway tunnels, for example, in France, the mean age of railway tunnels is 124 years, with 80 % of them over 100 years of age. For the maintenance of tunnels, diagnosing pathologies is an important reasoning task. Tunnel experts carry out periodic tunnel inspections leading to the **evaluation of a tunnel's global conditions by identification of main pathologies based on possible causes in the form of disorders and diagnosis influencing factors** [1]. This is a complex process, prone to subjectivity and poorly scales across cases and domains. To address this problem in the EU project NeTTUN (nettun.org), a DSS

© Springer International Publishing Switzerland 2015
F. Gandon et al. (Eds.): ESWC 2015, LNCS 9088, pp. 683–698, 2015.
DOI: 10.1007/978-3-319-18818-8_42

called PADTUN, is being developed involving tunnel experts and knowledge engineers. Pathology Assessment and Diagnosis of TUNnels (PADTUN) system is applied in a tunnel diagnosis use case with the French national railway, SNCF.

For tunnel diagnosis, **in addition to inferring possible pathologies in individual tunnel portions**, it is also important to consider spatial elements, such **as inferring continuous tunnel portions (called here 'regions of interest(ROI)')** with similar types of pathologies. The key challenge is **to develop an aggregation mechanism to group together individual portions in larger regions of interest** based on a similarity of pathologies. This abstraction is extremely important for efficiency reasons. For example, a two kilometre tunnels with ten meter portions will have 200 portions for tunnel experts to inspect. Hence, an appropriate aggregation resulting in regions of interest and ultimately reducing the number of individual portions to inspect, will facilitate and improve the efficiency of the diagnosis process. The prime driver for building PADTUN is to capture the tacit knowledge required for successful completion of these tasks in order to preserve the knowledge and expertise of very few experts in such organisations. Although the cost of performing these tasks well is very small, maintenance operations and the impact of a tunnel malfunction can be costly and catastrophic.

The PADTUN system is a novel DSS for tunnel diagnosis and maintenance using semantic technologies. PADTUN **assists tunnel experts in making decisions about a tunnel's condition with respect to its disorders and diagnosis influencing factors.** PADTUN also allows **reviewing regions of interest with similar pathologies.** The use of semantics is a very fitting proposition in developing DSS [2]. For example, one of the prominent areas where semantics has been applied is, in making domain knowledge required for making decisions explicit [3]. In our work, PADTUN ontologies are developed and used to model tacit knowledge from tunnel experts. These ontologies capture the existing decision process concerning maintenance of tunnels and provide a context model for automated decision support. The PADTUN ontologies are **the first ever ontologies** developed for **the domain of tunnel diagnosis and maintenance**. Another prominent aspect, where semantics are utilised as part of PADTUN development, is fulfilling the requirement of the DSS and decision maker to have access to heterogeneous data. The unique feature of semantic technologies in enabling the fusion of heterogeneous data has been employed in a number of projects [4]. In PADTUN development, heterogeneous data, providing contextual information are annotated with ontologies to take advantage of the inferring capabilities offered by semantic technologies. We use semantics even further and utilise PADTUN ontologies for calculating homogeneous portions in order to identify regions of interest. In particular, semantics plays a key role in detecting continuity by considering semantic similarity between pathologies represented as concepts. With this work, we contribute to semantic web research by applying semantic technologies in urban and infrastructure planning and maintenance, a domain that is starting to receive attention from the semantic web community [5].

Section 2 outlines the technical architecture of the PADTUN system. The two main components of this architecture are described in the following two sections. We carried out an initial evaluation of the system. The evaluation details are described in Sect. 5. We conclude by discussing the findings and outlining the future work.

2 Pathology Assessment and Diagnosis of Tunnels (PADTUN)

Figure 1 depicts the integrated view of the PADTUN system. PADTUN is designed using three-tier architecture consisting of layers for interface, application and data.

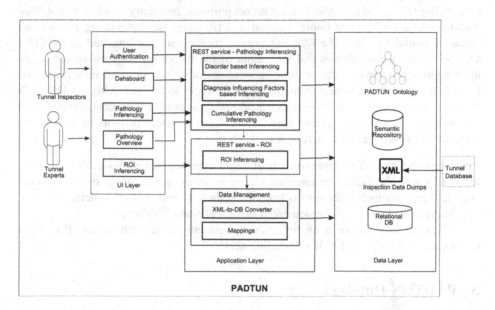

Fig. 1. PADTUN system architecture

Data Layer. Infrastructure managers, including SNCF, own and manage inspection databases of tunnels that record the provenance of data related to inspections and any repairs. This data contains information about any disorders diagnosed during inspections and contextual factors. In the case of PADTUN, this inspection data is made available from SNCF's internal system as XML dumps.

In order for the system to work, PADTUN requires domain-specific knowledge. Encoding and specifying such knowledge in ontologies is one of the main contributions of this paper. The PADTUN ontologies are designed in consultation with the tunnel experts in the project and by extensively reviewing literature on the subject. These ontologies codify knowledge about tunnel disorders, diagnosis influencing factors, lining materials and pathologies. PADTUN ontologies are described in more detail in Sect. 3. The data layer also contains a semantic repository that allows storing the ontologies and performing reasoning. OWLIM was chosen due to scalability reasons [6] as the system is required to reason over a large number of tunnels and inspection data. The system also contains a relational database in the form of MySQL to store inspection and result data for caching purpose.

Processing layer. PADTUN consists of an intelligent processing layer built on a data layer that suggests pathologies per portion and regions of interest, together with explanations.

Three components are included as part of the processing layer. The pathology inferencing component implemented as RESTful service utilises the ontologies and infers a list of pathologies when provided with disorders, lining material and diagnosis influencing factors details for individual tunnel portions. Internally, it infers pathologies based on (i) disorders and lining material and (ii) diagnosis influencing factors and creates a cumulative list. The ROI inferencing component, implemented as RESTful service utilises the ontologies and the output of the pathology inferencing service to infer regions of interest. Both of these services are described in detail in Sect. 4. The Data management component contains business logic to convert XML to DB with the help of a converter, and stores the inspection data as per the new schema dictated by the ontology. In order to achieve conversion, the component consists of a mapping between the schema and the ontologies.

Presentation Layer. This layer consists of a user interface that allows decision makers to interact with the DSS. The interface allows users to upload tunnel inspection data and view and manipulate the results from the pathology and ROI inferencing services. The interface component is implemented using PHP and JavaScript.

Following sections focus on the main component of the architecture, PADTUN ontologies, pathology and ROI inferencing services.

3   PADTUN Ontologies

PADTUN ontologies are developed using METHONTOLOGY [10] methodology. NeTTUN use cases helped us to define scope and purpose of the ontologies and provided a reasonably well-defined target.

Scope & Purpose. The ontologies need to capture the existing decision process concerning the diagnosis of tunnels, to provide a context model for automated decision support. This conceptual model should include disorders observed during the inspections, tunnel common pathologies and diagnosis influencing factors. This knowledge also needs to be classified and linked, in order to identify associations of disorders and diagnosis influencing factors with pathologies.

Knowledge Sources. The ontologies are designed based on the knowledge of experts within the NeTTUN project. To ensure a wide range of use and generality, extensive literature in the area [1, 7–9] has been consulted.

3.1   Conceptualisation

This activity requires that the domain knowledge is structured in a conceptual model describing the problem and its solution in terms of a domain [10]. We used a number of methods for knowledge elicitation including expert interviews, brainstorming sessions using tools such as IHMC Concept Maps to facilitate the conceptualisation process. Initial conceptualisation focused on the elicitation of the top-level ontology concepts.

Top Level Concepts. Several tunnel type classifications were considered. For instance, tunnels can be classified regarding their operational use, construction method, age and other characteristics. The proposed classification regarding the PADTUN scope is based on an elementary part of a tunnel, an atomic portion, called here *tunnel portion*. A *tunnel portion* can be defined as "an elementary part of the tunnel with all the necessary elements that enable a diagnosis to be made" [1, 8]. In this respect, a tunnel portion presents a geology, a geometry, and structural characteristics such as lining and repair features.

A *tunnel portion* is derived from larger tunnel stretches. Because the scope of the ontologies is maintenance, these larger tunnel stretches have been defined as *Tunnel Inspection Stretch*, corresponding to tunnel lengths where an inspection has been carried out. This *Tunnel Inspection Stretch* has one location and has been inspected at least once. Further, within a *Tunnel Inspection Stretch*, and regarding *Geology*, one or more *Tunnel Geo Stretch* can be identified, each one characterized by one single *geology*. This conceptualisation is presented in a concept map in Fig. 2.

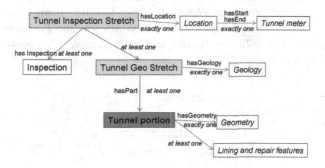

Fig. 2. Concept map with the top level concepts related to tunnel

Pathologies. A *pathology* is a problem that causes *tunnel disorders*; it is also the link between the disorders and its causes. *Pathologies* provoke tunnel degradation, which manifests itself in a combination of disorders, often more than one. Considering tunnel experts' interviews and literature on the subject, the most common pathologies have been identified and classified according to these degradation processes. These were collected from the experts as a knowledge glossary [10, 11].

Tunnel disorders. Disorders are disturbances in the expected quality level of a tunnel, being subjected to evolution. Disorders are also symptoms of pathologies. A classification of disorders was collected from the experts as a knowledge glossary. The associations between disorders and pathologies were provided as a table (see Fig. 3). There were in total 227 such associations provided by the experts.

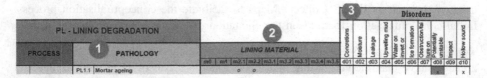

Fig. 3. Shows the association between pathologies and disorders with (1) *mortar ageing* pathology as an example. (2) shows the coded list of lining material that has to be present to manifest *mortar ageing* (3) shows the disorders i.e. "potentially unstable" (structure) that has to be present to manifest mortar ageing. The coloured cell signifies the *typicality* of such disorder for this pathology.

Diagnosis Influencing factors. Factors representing all elements influencing tunnel degradation, which are considered by the expert(s) when making decisions. The associations between pathologies and diagnosis influencing factors were provided as a Table. There were in total 78 associations provided by the experts.

3.2 Conceptual Model

The conceptualisation of the domain was converted into OWL ontologies [12]. Figure 4 shows the upper ontology of *Tunnel* with linkages to other major concepts from the domain model such as *Tunnel Types, Tunnel Geo Stretch,* and *Pathology*. The upper level also captures that a *Tunnel Portion* can have *disorders, diagnosis influencing factors, lining materials.*

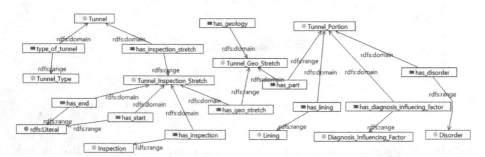

Fig. 4. PADTUN upper ontology.

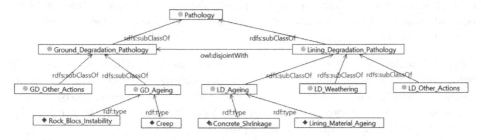

Fig. 5. Partial representation of pathologies classification based on degradation types.

Figure 5 shows the representation of pathologies and instances based on degradation types. Regarding the causes of the degradation (the origin of the problem), two general groups of pathologies were identified distinguishing based on its origin. They were *ground degradation pathologies* (if pathologies occur underground) and lining degradation pathologies (if pathologies occur with lining) [7, 8]. Figure 6 depicts how an association between a disorder and a pathology is represented in the ontology. This example shows how the rule provided by the experts in a table (see Fig. 3) is represented in the ontology. Similarly, Fig. 7 illustrates an association between a pathology and a diagnosis influencing factor and other contextual information such as the level of influence.

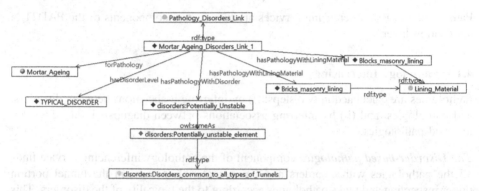

Fig. 6. Association between a pathology & a disorder (ontological representation of Fig. 3)

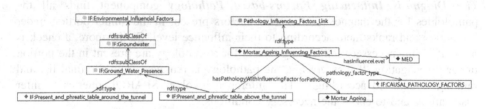

Fig. 7. Showing an association between a pathology and a diagnosis influencing factor.

To facilitate the evolution of the PADTUN ontologies, they were developed as a group of smaller but interlinked modular ontologies [13]. Table 1 presents a summary of the ontological features of the PADTUN ontologies with size, expressivity [14], and complexity of the core knowledge captured by axioms. In particular, PADTUN ontologies utilise OWL features such as sameAs, disojointWith, and equivalentClass. The PADTUN ontologies are available from here[1].

---

[1] http://imash.leeds.ac.uk/ontologies/nettun/request/.

Table 1. PADTUN ontologies features

Feature	Value
No of classes	125
No of properties	49
No of individuals	590
No of axioms	3981
DL expressivity	ALEHO

4 Pathology and ROI Inferencing Service

Pathology and ROI inferencing services are two central components of the PADTUN application layer.

4.1 Pathology Inferencing

Pathologies are calculated in two steps: (i) by inferring associations between disorders, and pathologies; and (ii) by inferring associations between diagnosis influencing factors and pathologies.

The Disorder-based pathologies component of the pathology inferencing service finds all the pathologies with disorders and lining materials present in the tunnel portion under inspection and ranks pathologies according to the typicality of the disorders. This inference involves SPARQL queries[2] to infer associations.

The Diagnosis Influencing Factors-based Pathology component finds all the pathologies for the diagnosis influencing factors present in the tunnel portion under inspection and ranks them according to their influence level. Furthermore, a check is made if all the necessary influencing factors for a pathology are present in the portion under investigation. If they are not, the pathology is removed from the final list and ranking is adjusted accordingly. This inference involves SPARQL queries to infer associations and to check the necessary conditions.

The pseudo code of these two components is presented below. The weights (m and n in the pseudo code) were set by series of interaction with the experts. The values m = 4 and n = 1 were found to be the best according to experts' judgement based on three tunnels. We validated this further with seven tunnels and the values were found to be suitable without further adjustments.

The Cumulative pathologies component combines the results of the previous two components by aggregating the score of pathologies in both the lists (*disorder-based pathology list* & *influencing factor-based pathology list*).

---

[2] Sample SPARQL queries are available at: http://imash.leeds.ac.uk/papers/eswc2015/appendix.

```
Disorder-based Pathologies

read disorders, lining materials for a tunnel portion, m, n; m =
points awarded for typical disorders, n= points awarded for normal
disorders
for each disorder in disorders
   for each lining material in lining materials
      find pathologies, disorder level with given disorder and
lining material
      store pathology, disorder level in a pathology list 1
   end for each
end for each
for each pathology in pathology list 1
   if disorder level = TYPICAL
   then
         score = score + m;
      store pathology, score in disorder-based pathology        list
   else
         score = score + n;
      store pathology, score in a disorder-based pathology list
   end if
end for each
sort disorder-based pathology list on score in descending order

Diagnosis Influencing Factors-based Pathology

read diagnosis influencing factors list 1 for a tunnel portion m, n;
m = points awarded for high influencing factors, n= points awarded
for medium influencing factors
for each diagnosis influencing factor in diagnosis influencing fac-
tors list 1
      find pathologies, influence level with given diagnosis influenc-
ing factor
      store pathology, influence level in pathology list 1
end for each
for each pathology in pathology list 1
if influence level = HIGH
   then score = score + m;
         store pathology, score in pathology list 2
else if influence level = MED
   then score = score + n;
         store pathology, score in pathology list 2
end if
end for each
for each pathology in pathology list 2
find necessary influencing factors for pathology and
   store in influencing factors list 2
if subset (influencing factors list 2, influencing factors list 1)
   then add pathology in influencing factor-based pathology list
else
   do nothing
end if
end for each
sort influencing factor-based pathology list on score in descending
order
```

4.2   Regions of Interest (ROI) Inferencing Service

One of the decision support aspects of the PADTUN is to identify regions of interest concerning pathologies. In practice, tunnel experts intuitively abstract regions of interest and in doing so aggregate tunnel portions that are susceptible to the same types of pathologies with some distance approximation. However, it was not clear from the outset how the experts themselves infer ROIs once pathologies per portion were identified. Hence, a mock-up of several possible alternatives was presented to the experts in order to identify the best way of inferring ROIs. We here present the logical formalism for these alternative ways to define and calculate ROIs.

Let's say Top n ranked pathologies per individual portion of a tunnel are denoted by observation, obs(P). Then a region of interest R is a continuous homogeneous portion of the tunnel consisting of a set of individual tunnel portions (P). The granularity of continuity is determined by how big gap (n) between adjacent tunnel portions is allowed.

In addition, homogeneity in an ROI can be determined by the validity of a logical expression $\Phi(X)$ that is applied to portions X of a Tunnel. The aggregation predicate $R_{\Phi,n}(X)$ is

$$R_{\Phi,n}(X) \equiv \forall(x_i \in X) \, \exists (x_j \in X) \left[x_i \neq x_j \wedge \Phi(\{x_i, x_j\}) \wedge \mathrm{dist}(x_i, x_j) \leq n\right]$$

Where, $\Phi(X)$ is one the following predicates which specifies different possible conditions as to when two tunnel portions can be aggregated:

Portions with (Approximately) Equal Observations ($\Phi_=$, $\Phi_\approx$). Observations under consideration are deemed '*equal*' when they share the same pathologies. For two portions p_1 and p_2, $\Phi_=$ is defined as: $\Phi_=(\{p_1, p_2\}) \equiv obs(p_1) = obs(p_2)$. Observations are '*approximately equal*' if all their pathologies are semantically similar:

$$\Phi_\approx(\{p_1, p_2\}) \equiv [\forall(o_1 \in obs(p_1) \rightarrow \exists(o_2 \in obs(p_1)) \; similar \; (o_1, o_2)] \wedge$$
$$[\forall(o_2 \in obs(p_2) \rightarrow \exists(o_1 \in obs(p_2)) \; similar \; (o_1, o_2)]$$

Portions with (Approximately) Incorporating Observations ($\Phi_\subseteq$, $\Phi_{\subseteq}$). One observation '*incorporates*' another observation if it contains all the pathologies that the other observation has, i.e. $\Phi_\subseteq (\{p_1, p_2\}) \equiv (obs(p_1) \cap obs(p_2)) \in \{obs(p_1), obs(p_2)\}$. Also, one observation is a '*approximately incorporating*' another observation if there exists some set of concepts in one that are semantically similar to another so that one set of observations contain all the observations that the other observation has, i.e.

$$\Phi_{\subseteq}(\{p_1, p_2\}) \equiv [\forall(o_1 \in obs(p_1) \rightarrow \exists(o_2 \in obs(p_2)) \; similar(o_1, o_2)]$$

Portions with (Approximately) Overlapping Observations ($\Phi_\cap$, $\Phi_{\cap}$). One observation '*overlaps*' another observation if it contains only some pathologies that the other one has and vice versa: $\Phi_\cap(\{p_1, p_2\}) \equiv (obs(p_1) \cap obs(p_2)) \neq \emptyset \wedge \neg \, \Phi_\subseteq(\{p_1, p_2\})$. Also, one observation '*approximately overlaps*' another observation if it contains some concepts (e.g. disorders) that are semantically similar to the concepts from the other observation and vice versa is also true, i.e.

$$\Phi_{\overline{\cap}}(\{p_1, p_2\}) \equiv [\exists(o_1 \in obs(p_1)\ \exists(o_2 \in obs(p_1))\ similar(o_1, o_2)] \wedge$$
$$[\forall\ (o_2 \in obs(p_2) \rightarrow \exists(o_1 \in obs(p_2))\ [similar(o_1, o_2)]] \wedge \neg\ \Phi_{\in}(\{p_1, p_2\})$$

Portions with the Same Classification (Φ_C). Two observations belongs to the *same classification* if they both contain pathologies belonging to the same ontology class.

$$\Phi_C(\{p_1, p_2\}) \equiv (obs(p_1) \in C \wedge obs(p_2)) \in C).$$

Example. Consider a tunnel (see Fig. 8) with ten tunnel portions. The observations consisting of pathologies on each of these ten portions are given in the figure with $O = \{d_i, ..., d_n\}$; where d_1 = *Mortar Ageing*; d_2 = *Dissolution*; d_3 = *Creep*; d_4 = *Faults Degradation*; d_5 = *Rock Weathering* and d_6 = *Swelling*. It is also given that d_2 and d_6 are semantically similar, i.e. similar (d_2, d_6). A domain expert can then tailor what he would like to view as region of interest by manipulating two criteria from the aggregation function: (i) allowed gap(n) and (ii) predicate ($\Phi(X)$) to use. Figure 8 shows various ROIs under different selections. For example, when the selection is $n = 1$ and the predicate for portions with equal observations ($\Phi_=$) is selected (first row, Fig. 8), the resultant eight ROIs are: $\{\{p_1, p_2\}, \{p_3\}, \{p_5\}, \{p_6\}, \{p_7\}, \{p_8\}, \{p_9\}, \{p_{10}\}\}$.

A different selection (last row, Fig. 8), by keeping $n = 1$ but changing the predicate to R_{Φ_C} reduces number of ROIs to one, i.e. $\{\{p_5, p_6, p_7, p_8\}\}$. Each portion in this ROI belongs to the *Ground Degradation Pathology* class from the PADTUN ontology. The ontological representation of this portion is depicted in Fig. 9.

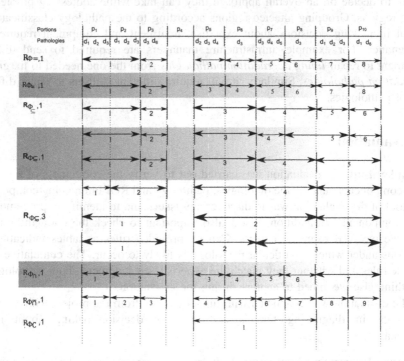

Fig. 8. Result of various selections of aggregation predicates and gap. Resultant ROIs are numbered and shown as aggregation of individual portions.

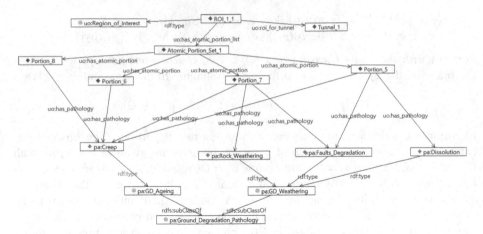

Fig. 9. Ontological representation of one of the resultant ROIs (selection: $n = 1$ and R_{Φ_C}).

Finalising Aggregation Function(s) to Implement. Experts were shown a mock-up of ROIs with different selections (above). The aggregation function *Portions with the same classification (R_{Φ_C})* was deemed to be most useful for decision-making and was implemented for the final version of the ROI inferencing service. Detecting regions with portions that have pathologies belonging to the same classification helps decision makers to decide on an overall approach they can take while addressing problematic tunnel regions. Grouping affected regions according to the pathology classification is helpful in making decisions about expertise, treatment and equipment required for maintenance. For example, infrastructure managers are required to send different equipment to repair *lining degradation pathologies* from the one needed to fix *ground degradation pathologies*. Similarly, it will require different skillsets to repair different type of pathologies.

5   Evaluation

Overall Set-up. An evaluation was carried out to verify the correctness of the PAD-TUN components, namely the ontologies, pathology and ROI Inferencing components. The goal of the evaluation was to discover any issues and to identify improvements in these components. In addition, it was also important to check the correctness of the input we received from the experts. Experts provided rules as tables indicating the situations under which a particular pathology is likely to occur. The cumulative effect of these rules and whether they match the experts' tacit judgment about pathologies is something else we aimed to capture during the evaluation.

The evaluation was conducted with tunnel experts from the project with extensive experience in diagnosing tunnels and strategic decision-making about tunnel maintenance.

Pathology Inferencing Evaluation & Results. Figure 10 shows the partial interface for the pathology inferencing component of the PADTUN system. The columns "rank" and "pathology" shows the rank of the pathology. The "disorders" column shows the disorders that were present in the tunnel portion under investigation and contributed to manifesting this pathology. The colour coding shows whether the disorders are typical disorders for the pathology.

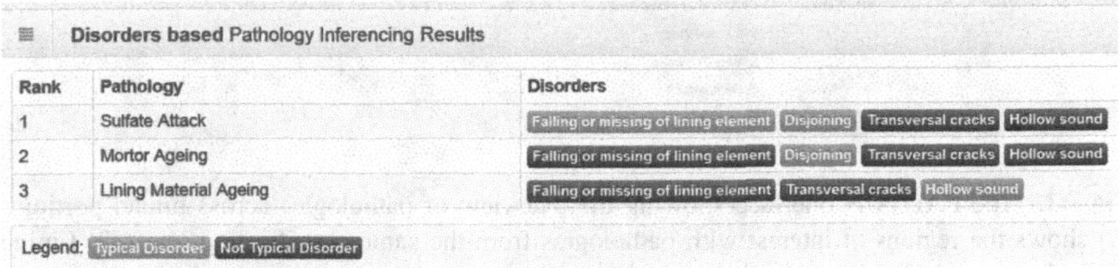

Disorders based Pathology Inferencing Results

Rank	Pathology	Disorders
1	Sulfate Attack	Falling or missing of lining element Disjoining Transversal cracks Hollow sound
2	Mortor Ageing	Falling or missing of lining element Disjoining Transversal cracks Hollow sound
3	Lining Material Ageing	Falling or missing of lining element Transversal cracks Hollow sound

Legend: Typical Disorder Not Typical Disorder

Fig. 10. The PADTUN interface for the pathology inferencing service. It shows results of "disorders-based pathology inferencing" on a tunnel portion.

For this evaluation, 41 portions of 3 tunnels were selected by consulting the experts. The aim was to select tunnel portions with a good variety of disorders. The experts were provided the output of the pathology inferencing service as part of the interface (Fig. 10). They were asked to comment on individual (disorder and diagnosis influencing factors based) pathology inferencing and cumulative pathology inferencing results.

The experts approved the presence of the pathologies and their ranking in all the test cases for the individual (disorder and diagnosis influencing factors based) pathology inferencing. However, during discussions it became evident that although they agreed with the individual inferencing they were not satisfied with the cumulative calculations. We discovered that the pathologies were correctly calculated based on disorders and diagnosis influencing factors and according to the rules encoded. However, in their tacit calculations, experts always expected a pathology to be present in both the lists for them to consider the pathology in the cumulative list. As a result of this exercise, this cumulative list rule was added to the ontology and to the pathology inferencing service. This scenario highlights the need of domain expert involvement in testing ontologies and the resultant benefit in terms of ongoing knowledge expansion.

ROI Inferencing Evaluation & Results. A gold standard consisting of 3 tunnels and respective ROIs was collected from tunnel experts. These three tunnels have a different number of portions. The tunnel 1 is one of the smallest tunnels with 19 portions but a higher number of pathologies. The tunnel 2 has 35 portions with some portions without any pathology. The tunnel 3 has 42 portions and a good mix of lining disorders and pathologies. The evaluation included these 96 portions. For each of these tunnels, experts provided ROIs based on pathology classification. For example:

"Portions 1 to 3 in tunnel 1 have pathologies from Lining Degradation classification; Portions 1 to 19 in tunnel 1 have pathologies from Lining Ageing degradation classification."

Fig. 11. The PADTUN interface showing the overview of pathologies across tunnel portions. (1) shows the regions of interest with pathologies from the same classification, e.g., (2) Lining Degradation and (3) Lining Ageing.

Figure 11 depicts the PADTUN interface showing the overview of pathologies across tunnel portions and highlighting ROIs.

The output of the ROI Inferencing was compared with the gold standard using traditional IR approach of precision, recall and F-Measure [15]. True positives (*tp* - exact matches from the system list and gold standard), false positives (*fp* - the system indicated ROIs that were not in the expert list), true negatives (*tn*- possible ROIs that were not present in either of the lists) and false negatives (*fn*- a region that was not present in the system list but was present in the gold standard) were calculated.

The result is summarised in Table 2. Three configurations of the ROI inferencing service are considered. In the first one, for a classification to be considered at least one pathology from the classification has to be in the top three ranks. The second configuration is more restrictive and expects at the least two pathologies from a classification in the top three ranks for the classification to be considered. In the final

Table 2. Precision, recall and F-Measure results for the ROI inferencing component; (left) considering ROIs with at least one pathology from a classification in the top 3 ranks; (middle) considering ROIs with min 2 pathologies from a classification in the top 3 ranks; (right) considering ROIs with at least three portions.

	Min 1 pathology				Min 2 pathologies				Min 3 portions as ROI			
Tunnel	tp	fp	tn	fn	tp	fp	tn	fn	tp	fp	tn	fn
#1	2	3	0	0	2	1	0	0	2	1	0	0
#2	4	6	1	0	4	2	1	0	4	0	1	0
#3	7	2	0	3	8	0	0	2	7	2	0	3
Total	13	11	1	3	14	3	1	2	13	3	1	3
Precision	0.54				0.82				0.81			
Recall	0.81				0.87				0.81			
F-Measure	0.65				0.84				0.81			

configuration, if any ROI has three or fewer portions then the ROI is discarded from the analysis ensuring that ROIs contain a substantial number of portions for the analysis.

The configuration with the rule that at least two pathologies of a classification need to be present in an ROI achieved the highest result in all three criteria. F-Measure was 84 %. Under an interpretation of the agreement between expert list and system list of ROIs, this is considered to be "an almost perfect agreement" [16]. The configuration restricting cut-off number of portions per ROI achieved similar performance. The least restrictive configuration fared worst with 54 % precision.

6 Conclusions and Future Work

In this paper, we have demonstrated the application of semantic web technologies in a new domain of tunnel diagnosis and maintenance. A DSS system, PADTUN, is presented that supports tunnel experts with decision-making about diagnosing pathologies and detecting continuous portions with similar pathology spread. This was only possible with semantic web technologies as the aggregation mechanism requires semantic reasoning over pathology classification. Use of semantic technologies makes the framework flexible where the domain experts can select larger and more granular portions with different configuration including selecting portions with similar pathologies in top ranks and ignoring short gaps. This flexibility allows us to work with the experts to select an ideal configuration, which is in our plans for immediate future work.

Acknowledgements. This work is part of the NeTTUN project, funded by the EC 7th Framework under Grant Agreement 280712.

References

1. UIC, Union International des Chemins de Fer (UIC) Draft report - Assessment of Tunnels (2009)
2. Blomqvist, E.: The use of Semantic Web technologies for decision support–a survey. Semant. Web **5**(3), 177–201 (2014)
3. Power, D.J., Sharda, R.: Model-driven decision support systems: concepts and research directions. Decis. Support Syst. **43**(3), 1044–1061 (2007)
4. Lécué, F., Schumann, A., Sbodio, M.L.: Applying semantic web technologies for diagnosing road traffic congestions. In: Cudré-Mauroux, P., Heflin, J., Sirin, E., Tudorache, T., Euzenat, J., Hauswirth, M., Parreira, J.X., Hendler, J., Schreiber, G., Bernstein, A., Blomqvist, E. (eds.) ISWC 2012, Part II. LNCS, vol. 7650, pp. 114–130. Springer, Heidelberg (2012)
5. Lécué, F., Tucker, R., Tallevi-Diotallevi, S., Nair, R., Gkoufas, Y., Liguori, G., Borioni, M., Rademaker, A., Barbosa, L.: Semantic traffic diagnosis with STAR-CITY: architecture and lessons learned from deployment in Dublin, Bologna, Miami and Rio. In: Mika, P., Tudorache, T., Bernstein, A., Welty, C., Knoblock, C., Vrandečić, D., Groth, P., Noy, N., Janowicz, K., Goble, C. (eds.) ISWC 2014, Part II. LNCS, vol. 8797, pp. 292–307. Springer, Heidelberg (2014)

6. Thakker, D., Osman, T., Gohil, S., Lakin, P.: A pragmatic approach to semantic repositories benchmarking. In: Aroyo, L., Antoniou, G., Hyvönen, E., ten Teije, A., Stuckenschmidt, H., Cabral, L., Tudorache, T. (eds.) ESWC 2010, Part I. LNCS, vol. 6088, pp. 379–393. Springer, Heidelberg (2010)
7. Sandrone, F., Labiouse, V.: Analysis of the evolution of road tunnels equilibrium conditions with a convergence–confinement approach. Rock Mech. Rock Eng. **43**(2), 201–218 (2010)
8. SNCF, IN 1256 Surveillance des ouvrages souterrains (2008)
9. UIC Assessment of tunnels UIC Draft Report. International Union on Railways Publication (2013)
10. Fernández-López, M., Gómez-Pérez, A., Juristo, N.: Methontology: from ontological art towards ontological engineering. In: Spring Symposium on Ontological Engineering of AAAI (1997)
11. Uschold, M.: Building ontologies: towards a unified methodology. AIAI TR (1996)
12. McGuinness, D.L., Van Harmelen, F.: OWL web ontology language overview. W3C Recommendation **10**(10), 2004 (2004)
13. Stuckenschmidt, H., Parent, C., Spaccapietra, S.: Modular Ontologies: Concepts, Theories and Techniques for Knowledge Modularization. LNCS, vol. 5445. Springer, Heidelberg (2009)
14. Horrocks, I., Sattler, U., Tobies, S.: Practical reasoning for very expressive description logics. Log. J. IGPL **8**(3), 239–263 (2000)
15. Powers, D.M.: Evaluation: from precision, recall and F-measure to ROC, informedness, markedness and correlation. J. Mach. Learn. Technol. **2**, 37–63 (2011)
16. Landis, J.R., Koch, G.G.: The measurement of observer agreement for categorical data. Biometrics **33**, 159–174 (1977)

PhD Symposium

Crowdsourcing Disagreement for Collecting Semantic Annotation

Anca Dumitrache(✉)

VU University Amsterdam, Amsterdam, The Netherlands
anca.dumitrache@vu.nl

Abstract. This paper proposes an approach to gathering semantic annotation, which rejects the notion that human interpretation can have a
single ground truth, and is instead based on the observation that disagreement between annotators can signal ambiguity in the input text,
as well as how the annotation task has been designed. The purpose of
this research is to investigate whether disagreement-aware crowdsourcing is a scalable approach to gather semantic annotation across various
tasks and domains. We propose a methodology for answering this question that involves, for each task and domain: defining the crowdsourcing
setup, experimental data collection, and evaluating both the setup and
the results. We present initial results for the task of medical relation
extraction, and propose an evaluation plan for crowdsourcing semantic
annotation for several tasks and domains.

Keywords: Crowdsourcing · Human computation · Ground truth ·
Natural language processing · Semantic annotation · Semantic ambiguity

1 Introduction/Motivation

As knowledge available on the Web expands, information extraction methods
have become invaluable for facilitating data navigation and populating the Semantic Web. Gathering semantic data in the form of entities and relations
between existing datasets, is central to information extraction systems (i.e. the
task of machine learning for most analytics). Human-annotated gold standard, or
ground truth, is used for training, testing, and evaluation of information extraction components. The traditional approach to gathering this data is to employ
experts to perform annotation tasks.

However, such an annotation process can be both expensive, and time consuming [1], due to the costs associated with working with domain experts.
Furthermore, experts might prove difficult to find for broad, open domains
(e.g. sentiment analysis). This presents a challenge for extending information
extraction methods, and concurrently Semantic Web systems into new domains.
Human annotation is needed to solve this problem, but the process of gathering
this data is not scalable at the level of the large datasets currently available on

© Springer International Publishing Switzerland 2015
F. Gandon et al. (Eds.): ESWC 2015, LNCS 9088, pp. 701–710, 2015.
DOI: 10.1007/978-3-319-18818-8_43

the Web. Efficiently integrating human knowledge with automated procedures is necessary for tackling this issue [28].

IBM is facing this problem when adapting the question-answering system Watson [12] to new domains. To compete in the Jeopardy TV quiz show, Watson was trained on publicly available datasets, taxonomies, and ontologies. Adapting the system to the medical domain, however, requires large amounts of human-annotated data, as medical resources on the Web are not so readily available.

Furthermore, unlike the Jeopardy setup, where one correct answer exists for every question, the medical domain is more ambiguous – it is often the case that doctors disagree on the same diagnosis. The traditional approach to gathering annotation is based on restrictive annotation guidelines, and often results in over-generalized observations, as well as a loss of ambiguity inherent to language [1], thus becoming unsuitable for use in training information extraction systems.

Being cheaper and more scalable, crowdsourcing is a possible alternative to using dedicated annotators. Crowdsourcing also allows for collecting enough annotations per task in order to represent the diversity inherent in language. By employing a large crowd to collect semantic annotations, it becomes possible to observe inter-annotator disagreement. Previous research in crowdsourcing medical relation extraction [2,3] has shown that disagreement can be an informative, useful property, and its analysis can result in reduced time, lower cost, better scalability, and better quality human-annotated data.

This paper describes a PhD project within the context of CrowdTruth, a larger initiative investigating how disagreement-aware crowdsourcing can be used to collect annotations for text, videos, and images. Building on previous success-ful results [2,3], this paper aims to explore the question of how crowdsourcing can be employed as a tool for collecting semantic annotation. Specifically, we analyze the role of disagreement, and whether its analysis can be used to improve the quality of existing semantic ground truth. We propose a methodology to crowd-source a series of semantic annotation tasks (e.g. relation extraction, sentiment analysis), with the purpose of demonstrating that disagreement can be a task and domain-independent indicator of semantic ambiguity.

2   State of the Art

Crowdsourcing for collecting semantic annotation has been used before in a **variety of tasks and domains**: medical entity extraction [13,27], clustering and disambiguation [19], relation extraction [18], and ontology evaluation [20]. However, most of these approaches rely on the assumption that one universal gold standard must exist for every task. Disagreement between annotators is discarded by either restricting annotator guidelines, or picking one answer that reflects some consensus usually through using majority vote. The number of annotators per task is kept low, typically between one and three workers, also in the interest of eliminating disagreement.

There exists some research on the impact of ambiguity on crowdsourcing annotation. In assessing the OAEI benchmark, [9] found that disagreement between annotators (both crowd and expert) is an indicator for inherent uncertainty in the domain knowledge, and that current benchmarks in ontology alignment and evaluation are not designed to model this uncertainty. Reference [22] found similar results for the task of crowdsourced POS tagging – most inter-annotator disagreement was indicative of debatable cases in linguistic theory, rather than faulty annotation. In our approach, we use the crowd to collect semantic annotation, and harness inter-annotator disagreement as an inherent feature of semantic interpretation.

There is extensive literature on how to **measure crowdsourcing results**. Of particular interest are ways of identifying spam workers [8,15,16], and analyzing workers' performance for quality control and optimization of the crowdsourcing processes [23]. However, these approaches rely on a series of faulty assumptions about ground truth quality [5]: (1) that there exists a single, universally constant truth, (2) that this truth can be found through agreement between annotators, (3) that high agreement means high quality, and (4) that disagreement needs to be eliminated. Consequently, most crowdsourcing metrics attempt to measure the quality of the workers, without accounting for the ambiguity in the input text, and the clarity of the annotation task. Human annotation is a process of semantic interpretation, often described using the triangle of reference [17] linking: sign (input text), interpreter (worker), referent (annotation). Ambiguity for one aspect will propagate in the triangle – an unclear sentence will cause more disagreement between workers. Therefore, we design metrics to harness disagreement for each of the three aspects of the triangle, measuring the quality of the worker, as well as the ambiguity of the text and the task.

Evaluating crowd performance with existing benchmarks has been performed for a variety of tasks and domains. Reference [27] show that the crowd can perform just as well as experts in medical entity extraction. Reference [24] prove the crowd can match the experts for another five annotation tasks: affect recognition, word similarity, recognizing textual entailment, event temporal ordering, and word sense disambiguation. Our approach mainly targets a crowd of lay workers, and we evaluate the results through comparison with existing gold standards, annotated by experts or automatically collected.

More knowledge-intensive tasks have proved difficult for the crowd to solve. Reference [21] show that tagging flowers with their botanical names could not be performed by a crowd of lay people. In these cases, nichesourcing [10], or employing crowds of experts to perform the annotations, can combine the advantages of using a crowd with the domain knowledge of experts. We define a generalizable methodology for crowdsourcing that we can then use to run nichesourcing experiments.

3   Problem Statement

Based on the issues we identified in Sect. 2, we define our main research question: *is disagreement-aware crowdsourcing a scalable approach to gather semantic annotation across various tasks and domains?* This can be broken down into several sub-questions:

1. How to measure disagreement in a crowdsourcing setup for semantic annotation? The triangle of reference [17] indicates disagreement holds different
   meanings for each of its three concepts, and therefore we need to define separate metrics that capture disagreement and use it to measure:
   (a) the ambiguity of an input *text unit*;
   (b) the clarity of an *annotation*;
   (c) the quality of a *worker*.
2. How is disagreement present in crowdsourcing across different domains and
   tasks related to semantic annotation? We investigate this by applying our
   disagreement metrics to crowdsourcing data and performing a comparative
   analysis across:
   (a) tasks: *text annotation* (entity extraction, relation extraction, relation
       direction), *alignment* (passage alignment, ontology alignment).
   (b) domains: requiring *expertise* (medical domain), requiring *no expertise*
       (open domain, sentiment analysis).
3. How does crowdsourcing compare to existing gold standard baselines? Factors
   to consider here are:
   (a) *implementation costs:* Is crowdsourcing cheaper, less time-consuming,
       more scalable than the usual gold standard approaches?
   (b) *quality of data:* Is crowdsourcing data more reliable than traditional
       ground truth data?

4 Research Methodology and Approach

To answer the research questions defined in Sect. 3, we aim to perform a series of
crowdsourcing experiments across several types of annotation tasks, in a variety
of domains. To conduct each of these experiments, we define a methodology
consisting of three steps (Fig. 1).

The initial step in our approach consists of **defining the crowdsourcing
setup**. We first *identify suitable data*, in the form of raw text together with
available annotation, to perform our experiments. Suitable in this context refers

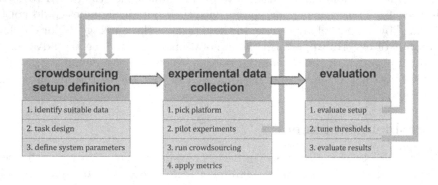

Fig. 1. Research methodology steps.

to data that (a) has some degree of complexity that makes it difficult to automatically extract annotation and (b) contains subjective opinion that could be interpreted in different ways by the crowd. Based on these features, we identified several candidate datasets:

- *Wikipedia medical sentences*: relations and entities can be automatically collected with distant supervision [26] and the UMLS vocabulary of medical terms [7], but the data contains noise and requires human input for correction;
- *Wikipedia open domain sentences*: relations and entities can be automatically collected with distant supervision [6] using DBpedia entities, also produces noisy data;
- *Twitter statuses*: contain a variety of subjective opinions on current events, that can be retrieved based on hashtags.

Next, we perform the *task design*, where we break down the annotation task into a workflow of independent micro-tasks that can be performed by the workers. The task design needs to structure the crowd annotations in a way that can be quantified by the disagreement metrics. When possible, the crowd will be asked to pick an answer from a given vocabulary (i.e. common medical relations, open domain relations, sentiments). For entity extraction, however, the goal is to crowdsource the vocabulary itself, so the workers are allowed to pick any combination of words in the input text. Entity clustering is then employed to reduce the noise in the answer set. To ensure that the data can be measured using our metrics, we aggregate the crowd answers into answer vectors per task.

We then *define the system parameters*. The metrics for measuring disagreement are defined at this step. The first to define is the sentence-annotation score – making use of the answer vectors introduced in the task design, it computes the likelihood that a given annotation exists in one input sentence. Based on it, we define metrics to harness disagreement at the level of the worker (to differentiate spammers from quality workers that nevertheless diverge from the majority), unit (to find unclear input data), and annotation (to find ambiguity in the annotation design). Also part of the system parameters are the settings for running the task: (1) how much *time* will the workers have to solve it, (2) how much the *payment* will be, and (3) the *number of workers* that will be solving one task.

The second step in our methodology is the **experimental data collection**. Here we *decide on the crowdsourcing platform* to run our experiments. Two established options exist: CrowdFlower[1] gives access to a larger workforce with less possibility to interact with the workers, whereas Amazon Mechanical Turk[2] has a smaller workforce with whom the task creators can communicate directly, thus creating a community of returning workers. To overcome these weaknesses and have an environment tailored to our crowdsourcing tasks, we also work at creating our own platform, through which we will be able to target

---

[1] http://CrowdFlower.com.
[2] http://MTurk.com.

a specific crowd that possesses domain expertise, for the purpose of nichesourcing experiments.

Next we perform several *pilot experiments* on a small sample of the data, for the purpose of tuning the crowdsourcing setup defined in the previous step of the methodology. According to these results, we adjust the task design, as well as the system parameters (e.g. worker pay, thresholds for detecting spam etc.). This enables us to *run the crowdsourcing tasks* on the entirety of the data. Finally, we *apply the metrics* to the data we collected, an use them to identify and remove spam workers, ambiguous input and unclear annotations.

The final step in our methodology is to perform an **evaluation**. First, we *evaluate the setup*, and *tune the thresholds* of the system parameters, to determine whether the task design and system parameters performed well. Overwhelming agreement or disagreement between workers serve an indicator for bad selection of data, or faulty crowdsourcing setup, meaning that the corresponding steps in the methodology need to be repeated.

The quality of the data is measured by *evaluating the results* in comparison with existing baselines for semantic annotation. In knowledge-intensive domains, the baseline refers to gold standard expert annotation, whereas in cases where no domain knowledge is required, we can compare also to data that is automatically collected. Evaluation is done in two ways: (1) directly, by studying the overlap between crowd data and baseline and identifying the features of data units where baseline and crowd disagree, and (2) using machine learning, by training and testing a model for information extraction (i.e. relation extraction, named entity recognition, sentiment analysis) with both crowd and baseline data.

5   Evaluation Plan

We evaluate our methodology by **instantiating with a specific task and domain**, with the goal of outlining an answer for the second two research sub-questions: (1) defining disagreement-aware metrics, and (3) comparing to an existing baseline (Sect. 3). Based on the IBM Watson use case described in Sect. 1, we define a setup for the task of *medical relation extraction*. The purpose of this experiment is to evaluate crowdsourced semantic relation data in comparison with ground truth generated by medical experts, in the context of training a relation extraction classifier for IBM Watson. The results are detailed in Sect. 6.

The next step will be to **perform the same annotation task** (i.e. semantic relation extraction) **in other domains**, for the purpose of answering part of research sub-question (2) observing how our setup performs cross-domain, while also refining the answers for research sub-questions (1) and (3). As the previous experiment was based in a knowledge-intensive domain, we investigate next the open domain, using a different text corpus with the *DBpedia* vocabulary for identifying both terms and relations. For comparison purposes, the task design and workflow, as well as the metrics for harnessing disagreement are the same.

Consequently, we plan to **analyze other semantic annotation tasks** in the same domains. The purpose of these experiments is to analyze how semantic disagreement is present cross-task, also as part of research sub-question (1). For the medical domain, we analyze crowdsourced *named entity recognition for medical terms*. For the open domain, we plan to perform sentiment analysis tasks over *Twitter* data. We are also planning to investigate semantic alignment tasks, such as passage alignment and ontology alignment. For knowledge-intensive tasks and domains, we plan to perform *nichesourcing* experiments involving crowds of experts. Specifically, we target the medical community through our own gamified crowdsourcing platform [11].

Finally, we will perform a **review across all experiments** that we investigated. The purpose is to identify the features of disagreement in crowdsourced annotation data that are independent of task and domain. We also investigate to what extent our methodology is generalizable for any combination of semantic annotation task and domain. The results of this analysis will then be used to answer our main research question on whether disagreement-aware crowdsourcing is a scalable approach to gather semantic annotation.

6   Preliminary Results

For the first set of experiments part of the evaluation plan (Sect. 5) – performing crowdsourced relation extraction over medical text – we designed a workflow of crowdsourcing tasks performing named entity correction, relation extraction, and relation direction (example templates in Fig. 2). We ran these tasks on both CrowdFlower and Amazon Mechanical Turk, collecting crowd judgments for around 2,000 medical sentences.

Fig. 2. Tasks on CrowdFlower (from left to right: entity correction, relation extraction)

To process these results and answer research sub-question (1) (Sect. 3), we modeled the crowd answers as vectors, and defined a set of metrics based on cosine similarity. The metrics are used to harness disagreement, and measure the quality of crowd workers, ambiguity of medical sentences, and the clarity of medical relations employed. Results on a series of pilot experiments have been published [4,25], using this setup on a restricted set of medical sentences, where the crowd results were manually evaluated against expert judgments. This thesis aims to build on these initial experiments by exploring how disagreement is present in large datasets, across a variety of tasks and domains, and analyze how it can be used to build a better ground truth for semantic annotation.

The aim is to develop a scalable, semi-automated method for collecting semantic annotation with crowdsourcing.

We have published work on CrowdTruth [14], our framework for crowdsourcing ground truth data. CrowdTruth connects with both Amazon Mechanical Turk and CrowdFlower for launching and monitoring tasks, and implements the disagreement metrics for a live analysis of the results from the crowd. We are also developing a gamified platform, Dr. Detective [11], targeting medical experts for nichesourcing tasks such as extracting entities related to a given diagnosis.

Currently, we are investigating the usefulness of crowdsourced data in training and evaluating a machine learning model, in order to answer research subquestion (3). We train a medical relation extraction classifier [26] using both crowd results and expert judgments in a cross-validation experiment, and compare the results of the evaluation for each dataset using accuracy and F1 score. In a paper that is currently in submission, we prove that, in training the model, crowdsourced data from the lay crowd, that has been weighted with disagreement scores, performs just as well as gold standard data from medical experts.

7   Conclusions

In this paper, we explored how crowdsourcing can be used to collect semantic annotation. We proposed an approach rejecting the notion that human interpretation can have a single ground truth, and is instead based on the observation that disagreement between annotators can signal ambiguity in the input text, as well as how the annotation task has been designed. In order to analyze this hypothesis, we defined three research questions: (1) how to measure disagreement in a crowdsourcing setup for semantic annotation, (2) how is disagreement present in crowdsourcing across different domains and tasks for semantic annotation, and (3) how does crowdsourcing compare to the existing gold standard.

We defined a three-step methodology for answering these questions: (1) defining the crowdsourcing setup, (2) experimental data collection, (3) evaluating both the setup and the results. As preliminary work, we presented the Crowd-Truth platform for crowdsourcing tasks with disagreement metrics, and the results of an experiment comparing the crowd against experts for medical relation extraction. As part of our evaluation plan, we will extend our work by performing relation extraction experiments in the open domain, as well as implementing other annotation tasks (sentiment analysis, ontology alignment). To answer our research question, we will perform a comparative analysis of our results across tasks and domains, identifying the generalizable characteristics of disagreement in crowdsourced annotation.

Acknowledgments. We thank Lora Aroyo and Chris Welty for helping develop this research plan, Abraham Bernstein for help with editing the paper, Robert-Jan Sips, Anthony Levas and Chang Wang for assistance with performing the experimental work.

References

1. Aroyo, L., Welty, C.: Harnessing disagreement for event semantics. In: 11th International Semantic Web Conference Proceedings of the 2nd International Workshop on Detection, Representation, and Exploitation of Events in the Semantic Web (DeRiVE 2012), p. 31 (2012)
2. Aroyo, L., Welty, C.: Crowd truth: harnessing disagreement in crowdsourcing a relation extraction gold standard. In: WebSci2013. ACM (2013)
3. Aroyo, L., Welty, C.: Measuring crowd truth for medical relation extraction. In: AAAI 2013 Fall Symposium on Semantics for Big Data (2013)
4. Aroyo, L., Welty, C.: The three sides of crowdtruth. J. Hum. Comput. **1**, 31–34 (2014)
5. Aroyo, L., Welty, C.: Truth Is a Lie: 7 Myths about Human Computation. AI Magazine (2014) (in press)
6. Augenstein, I.: Joint information extraction from the web using linked data. In: Mika, P. (ed.) ISWC 2014, Part II. LNCS, vol. 8797, pp. 505–512. Springer, Heidelberg (2014)
7. Bodenreider, O.: The unified medical language system (UMLS): integrating biomedical terminology. Nucleic Acids Res. **32**(suppl 1), D267–D270 (2004)
8. Bozzon, A., Brambilla, M., Ceri, S., Mauri, A.: Reactive crowdsourcing. In: Proceedings of the 22nd International Conference on World Wide Web WWW 2013, International World Wide Web Conferences Steering Committee, Republic and Canton of Geneva, Switzerland, pp. 153–164. (2013). http://dl.acm.org/citation.cfm?id=2488388.2488403
9. Cheatham, M., Hitzler, P.: Conference v2.0: an uncertain version of the OAEI conference benchmark. In: Mika, P. (ed.) ISWC 2014, Part II. LNCS, vol. 8797, pp. 33–48. Springer, Heidelberg (2014)
10. de Boer, V., Hildebrand, M., Aroyo, L., de Leenheer, P., Dijkshoorn, C., Tesfa, B., Schreiber, G.: Nichesourcing: harnessing the power of crowds of experts. In: ten Teije, A. (ed.) EKAW 2012. LNCS, vol. 7603, pp. 16–20. Springer, Heidelberg (2012)
11. Dumitrache, A., Aroyo, L., Welty, C., Sips, R.J., Levas, A.: "Dr. detective": combining gamification techniques and crowdsourcing to create a gold standard in medical text. In: 12th International Semantic Web Conference Proceedings of the 1st International Workshop on Crowdsourcing the Semantic Web (CrowdSem 2013) (2013)
12. Ferrucci, D., Brown, E., Chu-Carroll, J., Fan, J., Gondek, D., Kalyanpur, A.A., Lally, A., Murdock, J.W., Nyberg, E., Prager, J., Schlaefer, N., Welty, C.: Building watson: an overview of the deepqa project. AI Mag. **31**, 59–79 (2010)
13. Finin, T., Murnane, W., Karandikar, A., Keller, N., Martineau, J., Dredze, M.: Annotating named entities in twitter data with crowdsourcing. In: Proceedings of the NAACL HLT CSLDAMT 2010, pp. 80–88. Association for Computational Linguistics (2010)
14. Inel, O., et al.: CrowdTruth: machine-human computation framework for harnessing disagreement in gathering annotated data. In: Mika, P. (ed.) ISWC 2014, Part II. LNCS, vol. 8797, pp. 486–504. Springer, Heidelberg (2014)
15. Ipeirotis, P.G., Provost, F., Wang, J.: Quality management on amazon mechanical turk. In: HCOMP 2010 Proceedings of the ACM SIGKDD Workshop on Human Computation. pp. 64–67. ACM, New York (2010). http://doi.acm.org/10.1145/1837885.1837906

16. Kittur, A., Chi, E.H., Suh, B.: Crowdsourcing user studies with mechanical turk. In: CHI 2008 Proceedings of the SIGCHI Conference on Human Factors in Computing Systems, pp. 453–456. ACM, New York (2008). http://doi.acm.org/10.1145/1357054.1357127

17. Knowlton, J.Q.: On the definition of "picture". AV Commun. Rev. **14**(2), 157–183 (1966)

18. Kondreddi, S.K., Triantafillou, P., Weikum, G.: Combining information extraction and human computing for crowdsourced knowledge acquisition. In: 2014 IEEE 30th International Conference on Data Engineering (ICDE), pp. 988–999. IEEE (2014)

19. Lee, J., Cho, H., Park, J.W., Cha, Y.R., Hwang, S.W., Nie, Z., Wen, J.R.: Hybrid entity clustering using crowds and data. The VLDB J. **22**(5), 711–726 (2013). http://dx.doi.org/10.1007/s00778-013-0328-8

20. Noy, N.F., Mortensen, J., Musen, M.A., Alexander, P.R.: Mechanical turk as an ontology engineer?: using microtasks as a component of an ontology-engineering workflow. In: Proceedings of the 5th Annual ACM Web Science Conference, pp. 262–271. ACM (2013)

21. Oosterman, J., Nottamkandath, A., Dijkshoorn, C., Bozzon, A., Houben, G.J., Aroyo, L.: Crowdsourcing knowledge-intensive tasks in cultural heritage. In: WebSci 2014 Proceedings of the 2014 ACM Conference on Web Science, pp. 267–268. ACM, New York (2014). http://doi.acm.org/10.1145/2615569.2615644

22. Plank, B., Hovy, D., Søgaard, A.: Linguistically debatable or just plain wrong? In: Proceedings of the 52nd Annual Meeting of the Association for Computational Linguistics (Volume 2: Short Papers), pp. 507–511. Association for Computational Linguistics, Baltimore, June 2014. http://www.aclweb.org/anthology/P/P14/P14-2083

23. Singer, Y., Mittal, M.: Pricing mechanisms for crowdsourcing markets. In: WWW 2013 Proceedings of the 22nd International Conference on World Wide Web, pp. 1157–1166. International World Wide Web Conferences Steering Committee, Republic and Canton of Geneva, Switzerland (2013). http://dl.acm.org/citation.cfm?id=2488388.2488489

24. Snow, R., O'Connor, B., Jurafsky, D., Ng, A.Y.: Cheap and fast–but is it good?: evaluating non-expert annotations for natural language tasks. In: EMNLP 2008 Proceedings of the Conference on Empirical Methods in Natural Language Processing, pp. 254–263. Association for Computational Linguistics, Stroudsburg (2008). http://dl.acm.org/citation.cfm?id=1613715.1613751

25. Soberón, G., Aroyo, L., Welty, C., Inel, O., Lin, H., Overmeen, M.: Measuring crowd truth: disagreement metrics combined with worker behavior filters. In: 12th International Semantic Web Conference on Proceedings of the 1st International Workshop on Crowdsourcing the Semantic Web (CrowdSem 2013) (2013)

26. Wang, C., Fan, J.: Medical relation extraction with manifold models. In: Proceedings of the 52nd Annual Meeting of the Association for Computational Linguistics (Volume 1: Long Papers), pp. 828–838. Association for Computational Linguistics (2014). http://aclweb.org/anthology/P14-1078

27. Zhai, H., Lingren, T., Deleger, L., Li, Q., Kaiser, M., Stoutenborough, L., Solti, I.: Web 2.0-based crowdsourcing for high-quality gold standard development in clinical natural language processing. J. Med. Internet Res. **15**(4), e73 (2013)

28. Zhong, N., Ma, J.H., Huang, R.H., Liu, J.M., Yao, Y.Y., Zhang, Y.X., Chen, J.H.: Research challenges and perspectives on wisdom web of things (w2t). J. Supercomput. **64**(3), 862–882 (2013)

Ontology Change in Ontology-Based Information Integration Systems

Fajar Juang Ekaputra[(✉)]

Institute of Software Technology CDL-Flex, Vienna University of Technology,
Favoritenstrasse 9-11/188, 1040 Vienna, Austria
fajar.ekaputra@tuwien.ac.at

Abstract. Ontology change is an important part of the Semantic Web field that
helps researchers and practitioners to deal with changes performed in ontologies.
Ontology change is especially important in Ontology-Based Information Integration (OBII) systems, where several ontologies are interrelated and therefore,
changes raise various complexities and implications, such as modifications of
ontology mappings and change propagation. Current approaches to ontology
change mainly focus on a single ontology and therefore do not properly address
the constraints specific to OBII systems. To address the challenge of ontology
change in OBII contexts, we plan to adapt successful techniques proposed both
by Semantic Web and Model-Driven Engineering communities. We discuss the
research goals, methods, and evaluation options to address this challenge. Real-
world case studies are used for the development and evaluation of the proposed
methods.

Keywords: Ontology change · Ontology evolution · Ontology versioning ·
Ontology-Based information integration · Model-Driven engineering

1 Context and Motivation

The notion of using ontologies for information integration has been applied for around
two decades [1]. Wache et al. have reviewed various approaches for Ontology-Based
Information integration (OBII) that use ontologies to integrate information from multiple heterogeneous sources [2], while Calvanese et al. explain typical components of
an OBII consisting of a shared (common) ontology, a number of local ontologies, and
mappings between the local and common ontologies [3].

Such an integration raises issues on how to maintain the integrated system, i.e., how
to manage the ontology change within the system. Ontology change support is an
important requirement of an OBII system, especially in a software-intensive system
such as business information and industrial automation [4] where change support is
often needed to deal with changes in ontology schemas (i.e., T-Box) and data (i.e.,
A-Box). These changes have to be validated, applied and propagated to all relevant

F.J. Ekaputra—Christian Doppler Research Laboratory "Software Engineering Integration for
Flexible Automation Systems"; http://cdl.ifs.tuwien.ac.at.

© Springer International Publishing Switzerland 2015
F. Gandon et al. (Eds.): ESWC 2015, LNCS 9088, pp. 711–720, 2015.
DOI: 10.1007/978-3-319-18818-8_44

parts of the system to ensure its consistency. "**Ontology Change**", as described by Flouris et al. [5], refers to "the problem of deciding the modifications to perform upon ontologies in response to a certain need for a change as well as the implementation of these modifications and the management of their effects in depending data, services, applications, agents or other elements". In the OBII context, we define "change propagation" as part of ontology change process that deals with the management of the ontology change effects.

The current approaches to deal with ontology change from the Semantic Web community are mostly focused on a single ontology and therefore these approaches are not sufficient to support ontology changes in an OBII system that consist of multiple heterogeneous ontologies with complex mappings. Also, the Model-Driven Engineering (MDE) community has proposed the notion of model co-evolution for expressing composite changes within a model and for propagating these changes to re-establish global consistency [6, 7]. As part of our research, we aim to investigate whether and how MDE co-evolution approach could be adapted to ontology change in the OBII settings.

In our research, we plan to address the gap of ontology change support in OBII systems by identifying, defining and developing the required mechanisms and methods, while studying and adapting appropriate approaches both from Semantic Web and MDE communities. As the first step towards that goal, we have studied the literatures from both communities and identified requirements for ontology change within OBII systems from two case studies: (1) **Power Plant Design** from the Industrial Automation System (IAS) domain and (2) **Integration System for Scholarly Data** of the domain of Empirical Software Engineering (EMSE). These initial requirements from the case studies will be discussed within Sect. 5.

The rest of the paper is structured as follows: Sub-Sect. 1.1 illustrates an OBII problem setting example. Section 2 defines the state of the art in ontology change and model evolution. Section 3 provides the problem statement and motivates the research contribution. Section 4 derives the research approach and Sect. 5 shows the preliminary results. We introduce our evaluation plan in Sect. 6, and conclude the paper in Sect. 7.

1.1   An Ontology-Based Information Integration System Example

As an illustrating OBII system example, let us take a look on the case of information integration in a modern power-plant planning from the IAS domain. Figure 1 shows the simplified representation of the system that mainly consists of the following three elements (marked with the corresponding numbers in the figure):

(1) **Local Ontologies** represent the data from the different tools and domains involved in a power plant system engineering. In the example, the local ontologies come from mechanical, electrical and software engineering.

(2) **The Common Ontology** represents the aggregation of important concepts (e.g., signal and CPU) of local ontologies from the perspective of the system stakeholders. In the example, the common ontology is the global ontology of the power-plant.

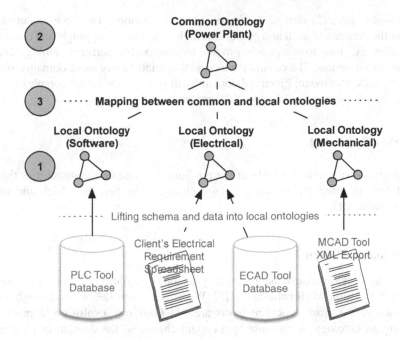

Fig. 1. Components of IAS power-plant design system

(3) **Mapping between Common and Local Ontologies** represent the semantic overlaps between local and common ontologies.

In the setting shown in Fig. 1, the *mechanical* engineers will use their domain-specific tool like MCAD[1] to design the machinery. In parallel, *electrical* engineers use their specialized tool such as *EPlan*[2] to design the wiring for each machine and the connections between machines. There are also *Programmable Logic Controller* (PLC) software components to support the production automation, created by *software* engineers. In between the process, clients will provide feedback to the engineers regarding their adjustment of requirements.

Since the specific tools from each domain are typically proprietary, the means to exchange data are limited to tool data export (e.g., spreadsheet, XML) or database views. Ideally, the exported data or database views would be lifted into local ontology and then be mapped with the global ontology, in line with the principles of the Global-as-View approach [8]. The mapping between local and global ontologies may be not straightforward, e.g., concatenation or computation of two attributes values in local ontology will be mapped to one attribute value in the global ontology. Important challenges in such environment are: (1) change process identification, i.e., to identify the necessary change processes for performing ontology changes within the environment, e.g., change propagation, where changes in one element should be propagated to

---

[1] http://www.solidworks.com/sw/products/3d-cad/packages.htm.

[2] http://www.eplanusa.com/us/solutions/electrical-engineering/eplan-electric-p8/.

relevant ontologies; (2) change detection and representation, i.e., how to detect and represent the changes of local and global ontologies with their mappings; and (3) change tool support, i.e., how to adequately provide tool support to perform ontology change within the environment. The common concepts that relate two or more domains, such as Signal and CPU (Software, Electrical domain) will provide additional complexity since a change in one domain could affect different parts of the system.

2   State of the Art

In this section, we revisit the state of the art from two research communities that are relevant for our research, namely ontology change from Semantic Web and model evolution from MDE.

2.1   Ontology Change

Flouris et al. provide an excellent summary of many ontology change terms that are used in the Semantic Web community [5]. We refer to their definition throughout our work. Two of the most important terms are: (1) **Ontology evolution**, a process of modifying an ontology in response to a certain change in the domain or its conceptualization, and (2) **Ontology versioning**, an ability to handle an evolving ontology by creating and managing different variants/versions of this ontology.

Change Process. Recent work from Zablith et al. [9] has summarized major ontology evolution process approaches [10–14]. They proposed five steps for the ontology evolution process: (1) Detecting Evolution Need, (2) Suggesting Changes, (3) Validating Changes, (4) Assessing Impact, and (5) Managing Changes. These processes are designed with the focus on the changes in an ontology schema. A closer approach to our research comes from Papavassiliou et al. They take into account changes both in the ontology schema and data [15]. However, these approaches mainly consider changes in a single ontology instead of in the context of OBII systems, which presents the challenge of complex changes and its propagation across the system. We identify this as a gap and we plan to include the solution as part of our ontology change process definition.

Change Detection and Representation. A major requirement for the ontology change in OBII is the ability to detect low-level (i.e., addition and deletion of triples) changes and high-level (e.g., concept move and deletion) changes between different ontology versions [15] and represent them in a machine readable formats for future analytics, while considers their effects on the change propagation process. To address change detection between two ontology versions, the use of heuristics algorithms [16], structural differences [15, 17], and OWL reasoning [18] have been proposed and evaluated. To support the change detection mechanism, approaches for change representation as change ontologies [11, 19] and change languages [20] have also been proposed. Similar to ontology change process, the approaches in this area are typically focused on detecting changes of a single ontology. In our research, we aim to build on the state of the art of ontology change detection and representation to detect and represent low-level changes and selected sets of high-level changes of OBII system ontologies and their complex mappings.

Change Tool Support. To provide tool support for ontology change, an initial set of requirements that focused on ontology evolution was introduced by Stojanovic and Motik for the KAON tool [21]. In the similar timeframe, *PrompDiff* change detection algorithm was integrated into *Protégé* tool [16]. Later on, Noy et al. introduced support for different scenarios of ontology editing in *Protégé*, providing background support for storing ontology metadata using CHAO vocabulary [11]. The latest addition to the impressive set of *Protégé* ontology change support tools is the *Protégé* versioning server,[3] which is based on the previously proposed architecture client-server architecture [22]. An interesting line of work comes from the adaptation of distributed versioning systems, *SemVersion* [23] and *R&Wbase* [24], which provide support for ontology versioning similar to source code versioning systems. However, the aforementioned tools are mainly designed to work with a single ontology and therefore, they do not fully address important requirements of an OBII system, such as change propagation to provide global consistency across the system.

2.2 Model Evolution

The evolution aspects of MDE are getting more attention with the growing importance of modeling in software development [25]. Various tools for supporting model refactoring have been proposed in the literature [26, 27]. Unlike change in ontologies, which focused primarily on single ontology scenarios, MDE research has a richer set of approaches in the area of model co-evolution [6, 7] and model change analysis (e.g., composite change detection [28] and change sequence identification [29]). However, these approaches have not been studied in the context of OBII. As part of our research, we will investigate whether and how co-evolution and change analysis algorithms could be adapted to ontology change in OBII settings.

3 Problem Statement and Contribution

In order to address the challenge explained in Sect. 1, we identify the main research question (RQ) of our work as follow: *"Which mechanisms and methods are required to cope with ontology change in an Ontology-Based Information Integration (OBII) system, where ontologies are used as means for data integration for heterogeneous data sources?"*

This main research question is refined into smaller research questions as follows:

---

[3] http://protegewiki.stanford.edu/wiki/Protege_5_Development_Environment.

RQ1: What kinds of ontology changes, process and analysis are required in an OBII system? What are the specific characteristics of ontology change in such a system? The research question aims for the identification and description of ontology change types (e.g., mapping changes), change processes (e.g., change propagation), and change analytics (e.g., detection of complex composite changes) that are needed in an OBII system. The answer to the question should be based on a comprehensive interpretation of an OBII system from the ontology change perspective.

RQ2: What methods and techniques can solve problems caused by ontology change in an OBII system? Do model co-evolution methods from MDE provide relevant solution alternatives? In order to solve the challenge identified in the RQ2 while consider the specific characteristic that answer RQ1, what kind of methods and techniques are necessary? Are the current available techniques and technologies from both the Semantic Web and the MDE communities able to address the requirements? We expect that the answer for this research questions could also useful in more general environments as alternative to the current state of the art.

4 Research Methodology and Approach

Within this research we strive to solve how to deal with ontology change within OBII system. The proposed research will be developed within the design science methodology, using the regulative cycle as conceptual framework and, specifically, following the guidelines provided by Wieringa in [30]. At the moment, we are in the first phase, focusing on gathering the requirements and conducting the literature study, to provide a solid ground for further steps.

- **The first phase in this methodology is the problem investigation**, focusing on the analysis of the problems that this research should confront as well on the properties that a good design solution should have. We have done preliminary literature studies and interviews with domain experts from two application domains. We have to look into the data and identify sets of changes that often happen in the system, e.g., frequent instance changes and change propagation over an OBII system. Next, we are planning do a comprehensive literature research on ontology change and related fields (e.g., MDE model co-evolution and MDE change detection algorithms). The goal of this phase is to define a set of requirements and the associated evaluation metrics that will be used throughout the research.
- **The second phase is the solution design**. This phase explores the possibility of applying or adapting the currently available approach to design a good solution. The process includes the realization of manual and alternative approaches to address the challenges, including those coming from the MDE community and evaluating the feasibility of those approaches. Based on requirements, literature studies, and manual approach realizations results, the goal of this phase is to create a solution design as a conceptual framework that will define the required ontology changes, processes, and analytics necessary for the OBII context.
- **The third phase is the solution design validation**. This phase aimed to check the solution design against the previously identified requirements and gather feedbacks

for the proposed approach before the implementation phase. We plan to involve relevant researchers for checking the logical feasibility of our approach, while providing the experts in our application domains with a conceptual prototype of our solution (e.g., scenario, persona) to collect and analyze their feedbacks.

- **The fourth phase is the implementation of the solution**. In this phase, we plan to realise the solution design within the selected application domains by implementing the prototype according to our solution design and the case study scenario definition.
- **The fifth phase evaluates the solution in the selected scenarios**. This phase aims to find out how well the solution approach worked in real-world settings. The validation process will be carried out as case-studies in selected application domains.

5 Preliminary Results

In order to capture the requirements for ontology change in OBII systems, we have conducted semi-structured interviews (according to [31]) with domain experts from two different application domains, IAS and EMSE, as mentioned in Sect. 1. We analyzed the interview results and take into account the current state of the art in the research.

From IAS domain experts, we learned that they deal with daily updates of instance changes and three to four data model changes per year. They would like to be able to store versions for instance and ontology changes, and to be able to query the ontology change history within a selected time period. We sum up the requirements from IAS domain as follows:

- Ontology evolution and change propagation.
- Ontology versioning
- Query across changed data and metadata/analytics of changes.
- System scalability (to millions of data instances)

From EMSE domain experts, we learned that, in spite of slight differences, the core issues for ontology change are similar to the IAS domain. They have less frequent changes compared to the IAS. Additionally, the contribution for the knowledge changes are less structured and dependent to the EMSE community activity. The requirements from EMSE community can be summarized as follows:

- Ontology versioning.
- Query across changed data and metadata for concept tracing
- (Semi-)automated query updates based on data model changes (as typical domain experts are not familiar with Semantic Web technology).
- (Semi-)automated ontology debugging support
- Ontology mapping across different instances of EMSE knowledge bases.

6 Evaluation Plan

We plan to base our evaluation approach on two case studies in the domains of IAS and EMSE. We will follow the case-study-based evaluation presented in [32] to validate our approach. Following the research methodology that we have defined in Sect. 4, we plan two separate evaluations in our research.

- **Evaluation of the solution design.** Within this step, we will validate our design with the stakeholders, including relevant scientific researchers and application domain experts. The evaluation goal is to provide a clear view on how the solution design will answer the set of stated requirements and the associated evaluation metrics.
- **Evaluation of the solution implementation.** The purpose of this evaluation is to validate whether the proposed solution works better in addressing the requirement of ontology change of an OBII system compared to the alternative solutions. We plan to build our implementation according to our solution design and use the evaluation metrics for comparison with solution implementation alternatives. Afterwards, we plan to do user studies to check the solution implementation in real-world settings according to our application domain case studies.

7 Conclusions

In this work, we have provided an overview on the research plan for addressing challenges of ontology change of an OBII system. We positioned our work within the state of the art, explained the problem statement and our planned contribution, and proposed an approach to address the challenges.

As part of the research, we are currently in close cooperation with stakeholders from the domains of our two planned case studies. This advantage allows us to receive better feedback regarding the requirements and to take more informed and better decisions regarding the design and development of our solution. These success factors are likely lead us to get better results. We hope that our research will bring advantages to both research communities and industry partners.

Acknowledgements. This work was supported by the Christian Doppler Forschungsgesellschaft, the Federal Ministry of Economy, Family and Youth, Österreichischer Austauschdienst (ÖAD) and the National Foundation for Research, Technology and Development, Austria. I want to thank my supervisors, Prof. Stefan Biffl, Dr. Estefanía Serral, and Dr. Marta Sabou, the ESWC mentor, Prof. Steffen Staab, and anonymous reviewers for their helpful comments and feedbacks to improve this paper.

References

1. Uschold, M., Gruninger, M.: Ontologies: principles, methods and applications. Knowl. Eng. Rev. **11**, 93–136 (1996)
2. Wache, H., Voegele, T., Visser, U., Stuckenschmidt, H., Schuster, G., Neumann, H., Hübner, S.: Ontology-based integration of information-a survey of existing approaches. In: IJCAI 2001 Workshop: Ontologies and Information Sharing, pp. 108–117 (2001)
3. Calvanese, D., De Giacomo, G., Lenzerini, M.: Ontology of integration and integration of ontologies. In: International Description Logics Workshop, p. 2 (2001)
4. Moser, T., Biffl, S.: Semantic tool interoperability for engineering manufacturing systems. In: Proceedings of 15th IEEE International Conference on Emerging Techonologies and Factory Automation (ETFA 2010), pp. 1–8 (2010)

5. Flouris, G., Manakanatas, D., Kondylakis, H., Plexousakis, D., Antoniou, G.: Ontology change: classification and survey. Knowl. Eng. Rev. **23**, 117–152 (2008)
6. Cicchetti, A., Di Ruscio, D.: Automating co-evolution in model-driven engineering. In: Enterprise Distributed Object Computing Conference, pp. 222–231 (2008)
7. Wimmer, M., Moreno, N., Vallecillo, A.: Viewpoint co-evolution through coarse-grained changes and coupled transformations. In: Furia, C.A., Nanz, S. (eds.) TOOLS 2012. LNCS, vol. 7304, pp. 336–352. Springer, Heidelberg (2012)
8. Ullman, J.D.: Information integration using logical views. Theor. Comput. Sci. **239**, 189–210 (2000)
9. Zablith, F., Antoniou, G., D'Aquin, M., Flouris, G., Kondylakis, H., Motta, E., Plexousakis, D., Sabou, M.: Ontology evolution: a process-centric survey. Knowl. Eng. Rev. **30**, 45–75 (2015)
10. Klein, M., Noy, N.: A component-based framework for ontology evolution. In: Proceedings of IJCAI (2003)
11. Noy, N.F., Chugh, A., Liu, W., Musen, M.A.: A framework for ontology evolution in collaborative environments. In: Cruz, I., Decker, S., Allemang, D., Preist, C., Schwabe, D., Mika, P., Uschold, M., Aroyo, L.M. (eds.) ISWC 2006. LNCS, vol. 4273, pp. 544–558. Springer, Heidelberg (2006)
12. Zablith, F.: Evolva: a comprehensive approach to ontology evolution. In: Aroyo, L., Traverso, P., Ciravegna, F., Cimiano, P., Heath, T., Hyvönen, E., Mizoguchi, R., Oren, E., Sabou, M., Simperl, E. (eds.) ESWC 2009. LNCS, vol. 5554, pp. 944–948. Springer, Heidelberg (2009)
13. Vrandecic, D., Pinto, S., Tempich, C., Sure, Y.: The DILIGENT knowledge processes. J. Knowl. Manag. **9**, 85–96 (2005)
14. Stojanovic, L.: Methods and tools for ontology evolution (2004). http://d-nb.info/1001606787/34/
15. Papavassiliou, V., Flouris, G., Fundulaki, I., Kotzinos, D., Christophides, V.: On detecting high-level changes in RDF/S KBs. In: Bernstein, A., Karger, D.R., Heath, T., Feigenbaum, L., Maynard, D., Motta, E., Thirunarayan, K. (eds.) ISWC 2009. LNCS, vol. 5823, pp. 473–488. Springer, Heidelberg (2009)
16. Noy, N., Musen, M.: Promptdiff: a fixed-point algorithm for comparing ontology versions. In: AAAI/IAAI (2002)
17. Redmond, T., Noy, N.: Computing the changes between ontologies. In: Joint Workshop on Knowledge Evolution and Ontology Dynamics, pp. 1–14 (2011)
18. Gröner, G., Silva Parreiras, F., Staab, S.: Semantic recognition of ontology refactoring. In: Patel-Schneider, P.F., Pan, Y., Hitzler, P., Mika, P., Zhang, L., Pan, J.Z., Horrocks, I., Glimm, B. (eds.) ISWC 2010, Part I. LNCS, vol. 6496, pp. 273–288. Springer, Heidelberg (2010)
19. Palma, R., Haase, P., Corcho, O., Gómez-Pérez, A.: Change representation for OWL 2 ontologies (2009)
20. Papavassiliou, V., Flouris, G., Fundulaki, I., Kotzinos, D., Christophides, V.: Formalizing high-level change detection for RDF/S KBs. Technical report TR-398, FORTH-ICS (2009). http://users.ics.forth.gr/ ∼ fgeo/Publications/TR398.pdf
21. Stojanovic, L., Motik, B.: Ontology evolution within ontology editors. In: Proceedings of OntoWeb-SIG3 Work (2002)
22. Redmond, T., Smith, M., Drummond, N., Tudorache, T.: Managing change: an ontology version control system. In: OWLED (2008)
23. Völkel, M., Groza, T.: SemVersion: an RDF-based ontology versioning system. In: Proceedings of the IADIS International Conference WWW/Internet, p. 44 (2006)

24. Vander Sande, M., Colpaert, P., Verborgh, R., Coppens, S., Mannens, E., Van de Walle, R.: R & Wbase: git for triples. In: Linked Data on the Web Workshop (2013)
25. France, R., Rumpe, B.: Model-driven development of complex software: a research roadmap. In: International Conference on Software Engineering: Future of Software Engineering (2007)
26. Moha, N., Gueheneuc, Y.: DECOR: a method for the specification and detection of code and design smells. Trans. Softw. Eng. **36**, 20–36 (2009)
27. Liu, H., Yang, L., Niu, Z., Ma, Z., Shao, W.: Facilitating software refactoring with appropriate resolution order of bad smells. In: ESEC/FSE, pp. 265–268 (2009)
28. Langer, P., Wimmer, M.: A posteriori operation detection in evolving software models. J. Syst. Softw. **86**, 551–566 (2013)
29. ben Fadhel, A., Kessentini, M.: Search-based detection of high-level model changes. In: ICSM, pp. 212–221 (2012)
30. Wieringa, R.: Design science as nested problem solving. In: Proceedings of the 4th International Conference on Design Science Research in Information Systems and Technology, p. 1. ACM Press, New York (2009)
31. Gray, D.E.: Doing Research in the Real World. SAGE Publications, London (2009)
32. Runeson, P., Höst, M., Rainer, A., Regnell, B.: Case Study Research in Software Engineering: Guidelines and Examples. Wiley, Hoboken (2012)

Creating Learning Material from Web Resources

Katrin Krieger[✉]

Faculty of Computer Science, Knowledge-based Systems
and Document Processing Research Group, Otto-von-Guericke-University
Magdeburg, Magdeburg, Germany
`katrin.krieger@ovgu.de`

Abstract. We observed that learners use general Web resources as learning material. In order to overcome problems such as distraction and abandonment of a given learning task, we want to integrate these Web resources into Web-based learning systems and make them available as learning material within the learning context. We present an approach to generating learning material from Web resources that extracts a semantic fingerprint for these resources, obtains educational objectives, and publishes the learning material as Linked Data.

1   Problem Statement

Technology-enhanced learning (TEL), especially Web-based learning, has become a fundamental part in education over the last decades. E-Learning platforms provide access to electronic learning material, accompany in-class lectures in blended learning scenarios or offer assessment facilities for formal and informal testing. Whole courses are held online, whether as qualification training, school education in sparsely populated areas or as courses dealing with special topics, letting remotely located experts teach students all over the world. TEL has torn down barriers in time and space, enabling students to learn where and whenever they want.

Our research focuses on a blended learning scenario. Students attend both lectures and tutorial classes. The provision of learning material such as slides and scripts and the assignment of homework are handled via a learning management system (LMS). The LMS allows students to upload their programming homework via a website; it also checks the completed assignments and gives immediate feedback through e-assessment functionality[1].

In in our setting, we teach undergraduate students, who form a heterogeneous group with respect to previous knowledge and skills. Therefore, it is essential that each learner gets support in terms of additional assistance and feedback.

When students solve their homework assignments, they have to apply the theoretical input from the lecture to practical problems. This is a scenario, where they have to focus on the given task, thus a more directed approach to problem solving – in contrast to exploratory or inquiry-based learning – is reasonable.

Experience has shown that students having difficulty in an e-assessment session not only rely on the learning materials provided for the course, but search

---

[1] c.f. eduComponents, http://wdok.cs.uni-magdeburg.de/educomponents.

© Springer International Publishing Switzerland 2015
F. Gandon et al. (Eds.): ESWC 2015, LNCS 9088, pp. 721–730, 2015.
DOI: 10.1007/978-3-319-18818-8_45

the Web for additional materials that might be helpful. This interrupts their e-assessment session and might lead to distraction and even abandonment of the assigned task [10].

In general, learners seem to use conventional Web resources[2] as learning material. Our idea is to provide learning material in e-learning contexts that has been integrated from such general Web resources. We will analyze, how general Web resources can be linked to e-learning environments and develop a method to automatically integrate appropriate Web resources into the recent learning context of the LMS.

Our strategy is to offer learners additional learning material, which they can access immediately instead of interrupting the e-assessment session and turn to a Web search engine. Web resources will be automatically integrated into the recent learning context and presented as additional learning material in a didactical meaningful way.

2   Hypotheses

Learners use Web resources as learning material in educational contexts. Hence, we propose the following **hypotheses**:

1. It is possible to judge (automatically) whether the content of a Web resource is relevant with respect to a learning context or not.
2. Web resources carry data that can be used to derive information describing educational and didactical characteristics.
3. If a Web resource can be automatically structured and augmented with metadata as presumed, it is possible to integrate this Web resource into learning contexts in technology enhanced learning (TEL) systems such as LMS.

3   Research Question

The hypotheses stated previously lead to the **central research question** for this dissertation project:

> How can Web resources be structured and enriched with metadata such that they can be linked to e-learning contexts and act as learning material?

4   Approach

The hypotheses stated in Sect. 2 identify three aspects that have to be taken into consideration when we want to automatically create learning material that can be integrated into Web-based LMS:

---

[2] Artifacts found on the Web - documents, slides, videos, audio files, etc. will be referred to as Web resources throughout this paper.

1. The Web resource has to match the learning context. That means that the learning context and the Web resource have to be semantically closely related. Helpful learning material uses the same terms and definitions as the learning context. Hence, we have to take care that we generate a sufficiently accurate description of the content of the Web resource. This description can then be used to judge whether the resource is a candidate to act as learning material in a particular context.
2. The Web resource has to be augmented with educational metadata such that it can be integrated into the LMS in a didactical meaningful way. This educational metadata is about different pedagogical dimensions that can be used to filter and sort the learning material, enabling the learner to chose a material that might be the most suitable for his personal needs.
3. We want to close the gap between the e-learning environment and the Web. We want to help the learner to stay focused on his task and offer additional learning material that can be immediately accessed. This means that we need a seamless integration of the created learning material into our Web-based LMS. The de-facto standard for data integration on the Web is Linked Data. Therefore we will make the learning material with its semantic and educational description available as Linked Data - as so-called *Linked Learning Items (LLI)*.

In the following subsections we will go into detail about how these aspects will be addressed.

4.1 Overall Process

In order to create learning material from Web resources, we have to define a process that takes a Web document as input and produces a Linked Learning Item as output. This process contains three stages that correspond with the aspects identified above.

We designed a REST-based framework with interchangeable services which realize the three aspects: create a semantic description of the input Web resource, extract educational metadata, and deliver the resulting LLI.

4.2 Semantic Fingerprint

To create a semantic description of the content of a Web resource that helps judging whether this resource is relevant as learning material in certain learning contexts, we will generate a structure we call *semantic fingerprint*. This fingerprint will be a graph-like structure, containing ontological concepts as vertices and relations between these concepts as edges.

A semantic fingerprint is generated in an iterative process:

1. Keywords are extracted from the resource. This set of keywords $K = \{k_1, \ldots, k_n\}$ is the input for the following steps.

2. Graph nodes are created by mapping each keyword, that has been extracted from the resource, to a number of concepts: $C = \bigcup_{i=1}^{n} C_i$ for $C_i = \{c_1, c_2, \ldots, c_{|C_i|}\}$

   Each keyword k is mapped to a set with a certain number of concepts c. This is done by querying DBpedia's SPARQL endpoint for concepts that match the given keyword.

   At the end of this step, the graph contains only nodes, but no edges: $SF = (C, \emptyset)$.

   This set of nodes consists of relevant as well as irrelevant nodes, because mapping keywords to concepts will return also concepts, that have the same or similar label but represent different concepts. These irrelevant concepts will be removed later from the graph.

3. To determine connections between the nodes C we try to find paths between those nodes. We expand every node and look for neighboring concepts C_e, i.e. we perform a breadth first search. This is done by querying DBpedia's SPARQL endpoint for concepts that have a relation with the given concept.

   Further connections can be found with reasoning over the graph to reveal implicit relationships. The feasibility of applying other approaches like OWL API or the OWL entailment regime has to be investigated.

   Furthermore we will analyze how semantic relationships that are included in the text of the Web resource, but not in the ontology, could be extracted and added to the graph (e.g., with approaches from natural language processing, such as latent semantic analysis).

   This step introduces more nodes to the graph as well as semantic relationships as edges. The result is a graph $SF = (C \cup C_e, E)$ containing all concepts C, that can be mapped to the resource's keywords, neighboring nodes C_e, as well as their relationships.

4. The graph is cleaned by removing irrelevant edges and concepts. The result of this step is a graph consisting of several connected subgraphs. Each subgraph contains concepts about different topics, that are not semantically related. To identify irrelevant relations we use a number of heuristics.

5. We identify all connected subgraphs in the graph.

6. The semantically most relevant subgraph is chosen as the semantic fingerprint for the resource $SF = (C', E')$.

4.3   Educational Metadata

To enable an appropriate didactical representation of the LLI we need to describe it with educational metadata.

We have inspected and analyzed existing standard vocabularies and efforts (c.f. Sect. 8.2). The selection of educational metadata vocabularies for this project depends on two factors: the usefulness for the description within the LLI, i.e. it is useful for filtering and sorting; and the availability of data that can be automatically extracted or generated.

We identified several fields from the educational categories of the *Learning Objects Metadata standard*[3] (LOM) that will serve as educational metadata fields for the LLIs:

- interactivity type
- learning resource type
- semantic density
- description

The *interactivity type* can have the values *active, expositive, and mixed* and describes the level of interaction a learner can have with the learning resource. We will derive the value for this field from the type of the Web resource. When we know, that the resource is a video, we can conclude that this is an "expositive" resource.

The *learning resource type* can have a number of predefined values: *exercise, simulation, questionnaire, diagram, figure, graph, index, slide, table, narrative text, exam, experiment, problem statement, self assessment, and lecture.* We also want to derive the value from the Web resource type as well as from its content format.

Semantic density describes the degree of conciseness of a learning resource. We will exploit the semantic fingerprint to obtain a value for this field which can have the values *very low, low, medium, high, very high.* The size and shape of the semantic fingerprint might give insights about the semantic density. How we can derive a value for semantic density from the semantic fingerprint has still to be investigated.

The *description* is an open text element. The value can be obtained from the resource's title or its content description. We have made some experiments with Web 2.0 portals such as StackOverflow[4]. These portals offer APIs which enable and easy access on such data programmatically.

4.4 Publication as Linked Data

For a seamless integration of the Web resource along with its semantical and educational description we will deliver the learning material as an LLI. An LLI is a data object conform to Linked Data standards that enable a Web-based integration of the data as well as the possibility to share the LLI with others, e.g., in . A serialization of the LLI as JSON-LD[5] is planned.

5 Evaluation Plan

5.1 Hypothesis #1

"It is possible to judge (automatically) whether the content of a Web resource is relevant with respect to a learning context or not."

---

[3] http://ltsc.ieee.org.
[4] http://www.stackoverflow.com.
[5] http://json-ld.org/.

A semantic fingerprint has certain desired properties:

P1: Concepts in the fingerprint are distinct and unambiguous. That means, that the fingerprint should contain only concepts, that describe the resource content as clearly as possible. Concepts, that refer to homonyms or polysems of keywords do not belong to the fingerprint and would only add noise.

P2: Concepts in the semantic fingerprint are connected through relations. A semantic fingerprint is a completely connected graph. Concepts, that are semantically related, are connected through an edge.

P3: Resources, that have semantically similar contents will yield similar fingerprints. This means, that those fingerprints contain common concepts and relations or other particular substructures in the graph.

P4: A semantic fingerprint covers all essential concepts that belong to the resource. Thus, all keywords from the resource that belong to a certain topic or area should relate to at least one concept in the resulting fingerprint.

Since we explicitly add relationship edges to the fingerprint during the generation process and remove such nodes, that are not connected to the graph, property P2 is always met. To show that our approach generates semantic fingerprints, that carry the desired properties P1, P3 and P4, as well as to demonstrate the robustness of the method, we will conduct an evaluation.

The first stage is a quantitative analysis where we examine the influence of the keywords on the generated fingerprints. In the second stage of the evaluation we let human reviewers rate the quality of the semantic fingerprints. Some first findings are shown in Sect. 6.

5.2   Hypothesis #2

"Web resources carry data that can be used to derive information describing educational and didactical characteristics."

The LLIs contain a description with educational metadata. This description includes fields for the different dimensions of such data, such as *interactivity type*, *difficulty*, or *learning resource type*. The approach to extract and generate the values for these elements can be considered successful when we find values for all elements. The quality of the collected educational metadata in terms of helpfulness and suitability in a learning context will be evaluated with human probands which will include learners as well as instructors. We plan to let at least 5 learners and 5 instructors rate the educational metadata of 20 LLIs with a questionnaire.

5.3   Hypothesis #3

"If a Web resource can be automatically structured and augmented with meta- data as presumed, it is possible to integrate this Web resource into learning contexts in technology enhanced learning (TEL) systems such as LMS."

The LLIs are data objects that are compliant to the Linked Data principles. By adhering to these very principles throughout development and implementation we can make sure that the LLIs can be integrated into Web-based systems such as LMS. No formal evaluation is needed.

6   Preliminary Results

We have developed and implemented a REST-based Web service that will generate a Linked Learning Item from a Web resource.

An HTTP-based client can send a document or document context to the Web service. The Web service will compute the semantic fingerprint and educational metadata. It will return this data as an LLI. To generate the semantic fingerprint the Web service queries connectors to APIs of knowledge bases such as Freebase, DBpedia, or Wordnet, to match keywords from the resource to ontological concepts and discover relations between those concepts (see Sect. 4). Another component within the Web service will extract and generate values for the educational metadata. For testing purposes we implemented different connectors to Web 2.0 platforms such as Slideshare[6] and StackOverflow as well as a connector that indexes the content of lecture slides. We can query these connectors to get Web resources for which we then compute the LLI. Please note that these connectors do not belong to the core of the Web Service and have been developed only for the development of the LLI method.

Furthermore, we have developed an approach to create semantic fingerprints from Web resources and conducted an initial evaluation[7]. The evaluation revealed, that the size of the generated keyword list for a given document is crucial. Hence, the keyword extraction algorithm that will be used in conjunction with the fingerprint generation process should rather return more keywords than trying to prefilter them. Since the fingerprint generation process will eliminate irrelevant concepts it is not necessary to filter the keyword list. It should be preferred to create the fingerprint with a higher number of keywords.

7   Relevancy

The dissertation will contribute to several research fields since it concerns technology enhanced learning (TEL), Linked Data and the Semantic Web. We will inspect different methods and processes from these fields and analyze their usefulness for the solution of the stated problem. A combination of techniques will be deployed and tested to automatically augment Web resources with educationally relevant metadata and deliver an LLI.

The practical impact of this dissertation project will be as follows:

1. *Learners* will benefit from our new method while working with an LMS. They will be provided with new learning material that can be delivered instantaneously, e.g., during an e-assessment session. They can fully focus on solving

---

[6] http://slideshare.net.
[7] This work has been submitted as a conference article to COMPSAC 2015.

problems, because they will be supported with additional learning material within the system. They do not need to interrupt their session to consult a search engine for further information on the subject.

2. *Instructors* will benefit from a decreased workload for the creation of electronic learning material since additional learning material can be automatically created. The new method could be used in an authoring tool as a kind of recommendation service. During the creation of a course or assignment, the authoring tool could automatically fetch Linked Learning Items that match the recent learning context and offer them for integration as additional learning material.

3. *The Linked Data community*, especially the Linked Education community[8], will benefit from an important real-world application that turns legacy Web data into Linked Data-compliant data that can be integrated into Web-based e-learning environments.

8 Related Work

8.1 Semantic Fingerprints – Building Structured Data

With the Semantic Web and Linked Open Data developing quickly, there are various approaches to automatically map entities from unstructured text to LD entities and detect relations between those entities.

LODifier [1] uses Named Entity Recognition (NER) and maps the named entities to DBpedia URIs. However, in contrast to our approach, the detection of relations between such entities is done by means of statistical parsers and discourse representation structures. To disambiguate concept mappings, the authors use Wordnet mapping tools. The resulting structure is converted into an output format which is conform to RDF standards. References [2,7] follow a similar approach, but do not work on completely unstructured text. These methods are based on partially labeled data and therefore demand manual annotation as a preprocessing step, which is not necessary in our method. Reference [11] describes an approach to build semantic networks from plain text and Wikipedia pages, that relies only on linguistic tools and uses no other structured data as resource.

Reference [6] describes another approach to build ontologies from natural language texts by combining Discourse Representation Theory, linguistic frame semantics, and ontology design patterns.

We will look into combining our purely Linked Data-driven approach with linguistic tools used in [1,6,11] in order to create a more accurate semantic representation as the semantic fingerprint.

Web documents, or HTML documents in particular, carry a structure, that can be exploited for generating structured data.

Rowe describes in [8] a method for turning legacy Web pages about scientists and faculty staff into Linked Data utilizing the document object model (DOM) and Hidden Markov Models to build RDF triples and link those facts to the Web of Data.

---

[8] http://linkededucation.wordpress.com/.

SparqPlug also exploits the DOM of a legacy webpage to build Linked Data models. SPARQL queries are executed over an RDF model that has been created from the DOM in order to extract relevant data [3].

So far, we have not taken the exploitation of the HTML structure into account, but approaches like SparqPlug could be included into our precess to prestructure Web documents. This preprocessing step might be valuable when we extract keywords or concepts, respectively, that serve as input for the semantic fingerprint creation process.

8.2 Educational Metadata

There have been efforts to structure and formalize electronic learning material as so called Learning Objects (LO). These are pieces of digital learning content along with metadata containing a structured semantic description. The LOs reside in Learning Object repositories where users can lookup, re-use, and share those objects. The idea – in analogy to software components – was to build libraries with reusable learning material that can be assembled into a new LO, e.g. a course about computer graphics containing pieces of content from mathematics, physics, and computer science. This was meant to ease the re-use of already existent electronic learning material and the creation of new material as a mashup from other learning resources.

In order to create Web-based learning material that is ontologically annotated, there is a need for standard ontologies that cover different aspects of teaching and learning. Besides standard domain ontologies dealing with knowledge about particular domains, ontologies about pedagogical knowledge, e.g., curriculum sequencing, student modelling, grading and other pedagogical issues are required [4].

PASER [5] is a system for automatically synthesizing curricula for online courses. AI planning and Semantic Web technologies are used to combine appropriate learning objects into personalized online lectures. This approach includes different metadata standards such as LOM, content packing, educational objectives and learner related information. PASER employs an ontology for maintaining a hierarchy of competencies.

SIEG [9] is a system that creates learning objects for a certain e-learning application automatically from ontologies. These domain ontologies are deployed for different courses, such as WordNet is used to create learning objects about english grammar, or YAGO is used for learning objects about history. The resulting learning objects store triples, such that they can be used for learning facts.

Both approaches build on already existing educational metadata which is used to create the respective learning object. To our knowledge, there is no work on extracting and deriving educational metadata from unannotated documents yet.

Acknowledgements. I would like to express my gratitude to my Ph.D. advisor Prof. Dr. Dietmar Rösner for continuous support and encouragement. Likewise, I want to thank Prof. Sebastian Rudolph and the anonymous reviewers for their time and substantial feedback.

References

1. Augenstein, I., Padó, S., Rudolph, S.: LODifier: generating linked data from unstructured text. In: Simperl, E., Cimiano, P., Polleres, A., Corcho, O., Presutti, V. (eds.) ESWC 2012. LNCS, vol. 7295, pp. 210–224. Springer, Heidelberg (2012)
2. Byrne, K., Klein, E.: Automatic extraction of archaeological events from text. In: Proceedings of Computer Applications and Quantitative Methods in Archaeology, pp. 1–16 (2010)
3. Coetzee, P., Heath, T., Motta, E.: Sparqplug: generating linked data from legacy HTML, SPARQL and the DOM. In: Bizer, C., Heath, T., Idehen, K., Berners-Lee, T. (eds.) Proceedings of the WWW 2008 Workshop on Linked Data on the Web. CEUR Workshop Proceedings, vol. 369. CEUR-WS.org (2008)
4. Devedžić, V.: Education and the semantic web. Int. J. Artif. Intell. Educ. **14**, 39–65 (2004)
5. Kontopoulos, E., Vrakas, D., Kokkoras, F., Bassiliades, N., Vlahavas, I.: An ontology-based planning system for e-course generation. Expert Syst. Appl. **35**(1), 398–406 (2008)
6. Presutti, V., Draicchio, F., Gangemi, A.: Knowledge extraction based on discourse representation theory and linguistic frames. In: ten Teije, A., et al. (eds.) EKAW 2012. LNCS, vol. 7603, pp. 114–129. Springer, Heidelberg (2012)
7. Ramakrishnan, C., Kochut, K.J., Sheth, A.P.: A framework for schema-driven relationship discovery from unstructured text. In: Cruz, I., et al. (eds.) ISWC 2006. LNCS, vol. 4273, pp. 583–596. Springer, Heidelberg (2006)
8. Rowe, M.: Data.dcs: converting legacy data into linked data. In: Bizer, C., Heath, T., Berners-Lee, T., Hausenblas, M. (eds.) Proceedings of the WWW 2010 Workshop on Linked Data on the Web (LDOW 2010), vol. 628, April 2010
9. Soto, A., Hernández, J.A.F., de los Angeles Buenabad Arias, M, Diez, G.: Using ontologies to generate learning objects automatically. In: Gelbukh, A., Mendoza, M.G., Alcántara, O.H. (eds.) Proceedings of the 1st Workshop on Intelligent Learning Environments WILE 2009 (2009)
10. Winter, J., Cotton, D., Gavin, J., Yorke, J.: Effective e-learning? Multi-tasking, distractions and boundary management by graduate students in an online environment. Res. Learn. Technol. J. Assoc. Learn. Technol. (ALT) **18**(1), 71–83 (2010)
11. Wojtinnek, P.R., Völker, J., Pulman, S.: Building semantic networks from plain text and wikipedia with application to semantic relatedness and noun compound paraphrasing. Int. J. Seman. Comput. (IJSC) **6**(1), 67–91 (2012). Special Issue on Semantic Knowledge Representation

The Design and Implementation of Semantic Web-Based Architecture for Augmented Reality Browser

Tamás Matuszka$^{(\boxtimes)}$

Eötvös Loránd University, Budapest, Hungary
tomintt@inf.elte.hu

Abstract. Due to the proliferation of smartphones, Augmented Reality applications have become more widespread nowadays. Augmented Reality browsers have especially enjoyed wide popularity within these applications. The physical environment could be extended by location-aware additional information using these browsers. At present, typically a specific data source is used by the current Augmented Reality browsers, even if there is an enormous amount of available data sources. The Semantic Web could help to bridge this problem. The goal of this work is to combine Augmented Reality and Semantic Web technologies in order to enhance the existing mobile Augmented Reality browsers using Semantic Web technologies. For this purpose, we utilize the advantages of the Semantic Web technologies such as data integration, unified data model as well as publicly available semantic data sources, among other things.

Keywords: Mobile semantic web · Augmented reality · Data integration · Ontology

1 Introduction

Smartphones have become an accepted part of our everyday life nowadays. With their help, many regular activities are much easier. The spread of mobile phones has facilitated the proliferation of Augmented Reality (AR) applications as well. Augmented Reality allows to extend the user's surrounding environment with computer generated virtual elements [3]. One type of Augmented Reality, called marker-based AR, uses images for this purpose. For example, when a user looks at a picture of a newspaper via mobile phone, then a three-dimensional model can be displayed on the top of the picture. Another type of Augmented Reality, namely location-based AR, is able to superimpose location-aware additional information about Points of Interests (POI-s) on the real-life view of the user. Points of Interest could be, for instance, monument, statue, museum. The position of the user can be determined easily by means of the built-in sensors of smartphones. A typical example is when the user looks around with the mobile phone and can see the icons which represent restaurants located nearby. Thus, the users can find interesting places and can get additional information about

© Springer International Publishing Switzerland 2015
F. Gandon et al. (Eds.): ESWC 2015, LNCS 9088, pp. 731–739, 2015.
DOI: 10.1007/978-3-319-18818-8_46

them, even if these are not in the field of view. Augmented Reality browsers can be used, among other things, for this purpose. These applications combine the traditional Augmented Reality application with Internet browsing.

Currently, the existing Augmented Reality browsers use only one data source while a huge amount of information has become publicly available on the Internet. We have realized that the combination of the Semantic Web offered possibilities with the Augmented Reality may result in more advanced AR browsers in terms of the richness of data provision. The benefits of Semantic Web technologies in the field of data integration can be used for merging data from heterogeneous sources. Currently, an enormous amount of publicly data source can be found on Linked Open Data cloud [4] in semantically represented format. Several data sources have spatial attributes. As a result, this information can also serve as a data source for an Augmented Reality browser. Due to the unified data model provided by Semantic Web technologies, the data from different sources will be stored in a common data format. Therefore, the browser does not have to deal with the data coming from different sources during the information processing.

The integration of geographic databases can play a particularly important role for location-based augmented reality browsers. The implementation of our proposed system is considered an improvement of the current Augmented Reality browsers. For this purpose, the examination and possible further extensions of the existing ontologies are needed. Several browsers have been developed in order to browse the publicly available semantic datasets. Nevertheless, relatively few of them are native mobile applications. Our proposed system is considered as a type of a visual interface to the Linked Open Data. In this way, it contributes to the development of Mobile Semantic Web.

The structure of the paper is as follows: after the introductory Sect. 1, we outline the State of the Art in Sect. 2. Section 3 deals with the problem statement and novel contributions. Thereafter, the research methodology and the proposed approach are described in Sect. 4. Then, the intermediate result and remaining work are presented in Sect. 5 while Sect. 6 describes our evaluation plan. Finally, the conclusions are described in Sect. 7.

2   Problem Statement and Contributions

This research relies on the hypothesis that the existing mobile Augmented Reality browsers can be enhanced using Semantic Web technologies in terms of the richness of data provisioning and additional practical functions. Our proposed approach allows us to use arbitrary geographic data sources, as opposed to the currently existing browsers. One possible scenario is the following. The user is in a foreign city and she does not know what interesting places are nearby. It would be great if she could somehow find out what kind of places are in the near, which she is interested in. Of course, she can ask somebody, but the asked person may not know every place in the city. It would be good if she could reach a database, from which she could get a lot of information about her environment and can visualize the data in a convenient way with her mobile phone. The problem raises a number of research questions.

1. What are the challenges of integrating geographic POI datasets? In detail: how can static databases used by AR applications be connected and extended by semantic datasets?
   The proposed approach should be able to integrate data on the fly from arbitrary geographic data sources in a unified manner. In addition, the appearing difficulties during the integration (see details in Sect. 4) should be handled by the system. The proposed solution has to ensure the use of semantic datasets located in the Linked Open Data cloud. As a result, it becomes possible to combine the currently used data with semantic datasets.
2. (a) What kind of architecture is suitable for a semantically enriched Augmented Reality browser?
   (b) How can we model the POI data sources in order to ensure the appropriate generality?
   Here, generality means that the proposed approach should be able to use arbitrary data sources which contain Points of Interests. To ensure this, an appropriate architecture is needed that enables an efficient and scalable implementation. The effectiveness means in our case that the system is able to add datasets on the fly to an augmented reality browser. In addition, the development of an appropriate information model is required. Since the data come from different sources, therefore, the same properties may appear under different names in distinct datasets. For example, the name of a POI is identified by *rdfs:label* property while the name of the same POI is stored by a *name* attribute in a second database. These mappings can be well described by an ontology. Thus, the examination and extension of ontologies created for this purpose are needed.
3. How can we extend the recent Augmented Reality browsers with new functionalities?
   Data enrichment can serve as a possible step in the further development of Augmented Reality browsers. However, in addition to the existing functions, with the implementation of quite different features can be enhanced the popularity of Augmented Reality browsers.
4. Can our system be used in new application fields?
   It is important to know what are the possible application areas of the newly implemented approach. The implementation of the above-mentioned unique functions may result in new application fields beyond the recent ones.

3   State of the Art

In the past few years, some commercial and open source Augmented Reality browsers have been published (for instance, Layar[1], Mixare[2], Wikitude[3]).

---

[1] https://www.layar.com/.

[2] http://www.mixare.org/.

[3] http://www.wikitude.com/.

These applications use only one data source and the openly available datasets are not used. Wikitude is built on Augmented Reality Markup Language (ARML)[4], Mixare and Layar use hidden and proprietary data structures [28].

Recently, some papers have been published aiming to utilize the advantages of the combination of the Semantic Web and Augmented Reality in the field of AR browsing. Martín-Serrano, Hervás, and Bravo present a tourism Android application that is using Web 3.0 technology tools in order to extract data from various data sources with the help of publicly available services on the Internet [15]. This approach can be seen as a possible answer to the research question 4. FOAF ontology [8] was used for determining the user's context. Furthermore, Semantic Web Rule Language (SWRL) [13] served as a basis of a recommendation system that provides new places to the users using rule-based inferences. Braun, Scherp, and Staab describe a mobile application called csxPOI (collaborative, semantic, and context-aware points-of-interest) in [7]. The users are able to collaboratively create, share and modify Points of Interests using this application. As usual, the Points of Interests represent real physical places. The properties of such places are stored in a collaboratively created ontology. This solution is related to the research question 2(b). However, whereas our approach is proposed to use multiple data sources, their solution is based on POI-s created by the users. Van Aart et al. in [27] explore the characteristics of location-aware smartphones for browsing and searching cultural heritage information. Their application determines the location of the user based on GPS coordinates and creates a user context from the combination of nearby locations, local historic events, etc. The authors combine two types of knowledge. The first one is general knowledge (for example, about geolocations and point of interests stored in Geonames and DBpedia). The second one is specialized knowledge about cultural heritage. The issue raised by the research question 2(a) is solved in the following way. The authors proposed a three-tier architecture: LOD resources as a data layer, a reasoning layer, and an AR-based user interaction layer.

The management of data from different sources is the task of data integration, which is an intensively researched area [9,20,21]. The Semantic Web technologies can be used for this purpose as well. Currently, one of the most preferred data integration methods is the ontology-based data integration. This method is responsible for defining the scheme and it helps to avoid the semantic problems [23]. In our case, geographic data sources (including POI-s) are used, therefore, these specific properties should be also considered. Harth and Gil describe their geospatial dataset integration method in [12]. The data come from Linked Open Data, similarly to the our proposed approach. The authors presented the Neo-Geo [22] integration vocabulary to model two datasets. This vocabulary can be seen as a partial solution to the research question 1. The authors describe the integration of data only from the LOD while, in our case, the integration of other data sources are also needed.

In conclusion, it can be seen that there are existing solutions for some subproblems. However, in the best of our knowledge, there is no complex solution which

---

can integrate arbitrary geographic data sources (including POI-s) in order to provide richer data than the existing solutions to an Augmented Reality browser.

4   Research Methodology and Approach

The main aim of this work is to design and implement a semantically enhanced Augmented Reality browser framework by answering the issues raised in Sect. 2. To achieve our goal, we may not necessarily invent a new approach but rather combine existing methods and adapt as well as extend them to our own purposes.

The first step of the research is the design and implementation of the module which enables the data integration. The task can be divided into subproblems. The selection of a specific set of data sources that are used by the prototype is needed. Thereafter, the schema matching [25] should be performed that gets two schemas as input and generates semantically correct schema mappings between them. This requires the examination of the literature and the preparation of possible enhancements. Another similarly important problem is the entity resolution (also known as deduplication) [6,26]. This method is responsible for the identification and merging of the same real-world entities. After reviewing the existing solutions, our aim is to adopt them in case of such datasets that contain Points of Interests, if necessary, to develop new solutions. We propose to use for this purpose density-based clustering on POI-s as well as performing string similarity metrics on POI names.

In order to have efficient and scalable operation of the system, it is essential to construct a well-designed architecture. Our proposal offers a three-tier architecture. The first layer is the data layer, which includes a variety of data sources, such as relational databases, NoSQL databases or semantic datasets located in Linked Open Data cloud. The second layer is the middleware, which is responsible for the integration of data, the schema matching as well as performing the entity resolution. It is also responsible for providing the data to the client in a unified manner. This can be achieved by web services. The last layer is the lightweight client, in our case it is a smartphone with Android operating system. This part of the architecture communicates with the middleware. It is also important to create a unified data model for the reasons mentioned in Sect. 2. After we reviewed several spatial ontologies, we propose to use and extend the ontology of LinkedGeoNames [1] as the information model. Our proposed approach produces the integrated data in RDF format [14]. Due to this solution, the integrated data can easily be queried by SPARQL [24] queries, regardless of the POI-s origin. They come from different sources and the data sources use different data storage methods.

The next step is the investigation of the functionality of current Augmented Reality browsers. Then, we try to identify possible potential new functions. The current AR browsers display only a static content corresponding to a specific POI during the browsing. This method could be more dynamic when the POI is used as a search term and the Linked Open Data cloud is served as a data source. The resulting semantic content can be further browsed through on the links. Therefore, our proposed approach can be seen as a combination of an Augmented Reality browser and a semantic browser. The system described so far is considered to be static in the sense that users cannot add new POI-s to the data sources. The proposed approach should provide this method as well. For this purpose, the investigation of performance of spatial databases in terms of insertion time and query time is needed. The system can recommend POI-s based on their corresponding information and the user's context using rule-based inferences. For example, the user wants to go to a cinema. In that case, the system would recommend cinemas based on the starting time and the current time. For this purpose, Semantic Web Rule Language (SWRL) or SPARQL can be used.

5   Intermediate Results

We give a solution to the research question 1 and research question 2(a) in [16]. As we mentioned in Sect. 4, it should be selected a subset of data sources that are used by the prototype during the data integration. We have chosen five datasets, including social networks (Facebook, Foursquare), semantic datasets (DBpedia [5], LinkedGeoData [1]) as well as Google. In the case of Facebook, Foursquare, and Google, the public API-s were used while SPARQL queries were sent to the public endpoints of semantic datasets. Due to the general implementation, the system can be extended by arbitrary data source that contains Point of Interests. For this purpose, only the implementation of the parser of the new data source is needed, no other modifications are required during the integration process. We have determined the common schema pairwise using COMA++ [2]. The problem of entity resolution was solved by a two-step solution. The first step is a density-based clustering algorithm (we have chosen the DBSCAN algorithm [11]), which determines the POI-s belonging to the common cluster based on their coordinates. In this way, the possible same entities are determined. However, this solution is not yet sufficient for the unique identification. Hence, the name of the POI-s belonging to the common cluster were compared with two string similarity metrics. If the value of the comparison exceeds an empirically determined threshold, then the probability that the two POI-s are same entities is quite large. The integrated data will be available in RDF format and it can be accessed via web services. We have implemented our integration system as a middleware, which provides web services that are accessible via REST API.

In [16], we have created an information model as well, which is related to the research question 2(b). We have extended the ontology of LinkedGeoData by the appropriate classes and properties. The goal of LinkedGeoData is to add a spatial dimension to the Semantic Web. The spatial data is collected by the OpenStreetMap[5] project and it is available in RDF format. Furthermore, the extended ontology includes the mappings resulted by the schema matching. In addition, we wanted to provide the filtering of the POI-s by categories, thus these categories were also selected from this ontology. In order to map the different

---

[5] http://www.openstreetmap.org.

names of the categories to the ones stored in our ontology, it was necessary to create some data properties (for example, *inFoursquare*). For provenance reasons, we have created a *Datasource* class and derived the classes of the corresponding data sources from this class. The origin of a POI can be determined by means of these classes. The Protege editor was used for editing the above- mentioned OWL ontology.

In [17], we present a Linked Data-driven mobile Augmented Reality browser. The users can navigate and collect local-aware information by means of this solution. A sensor-based tracking approach was combined with RDF processing of related geographical data. The used data come from semantically represented data source from the Linked Open Data. Henceforth, we improved our prototype, it communicates with the above-mentioned data integration middleware and acquires the underlying data from there. In addition, we do not want to restrict the users only to the use of existing Points of Interests, but we may want to allow them to create new ones as well. For this purpose, we want to know, which spatial database is the most effective in terms of insertion and query time of POI-s. In [18], we implemented a benchmarking application which can be used for this purpose. In addition, we measured the performance of several relational and semantic databases. As we mentioned in Sect. 4, it could be more dynamic when the POI is used as a search term and the Linked Open Data cloud is served as a data source. In [19], we describe a Linked Data-driven mobile semantic web browser. Federated datasets can be browsed by means of this Android application. The client finds the list of resources for the desired keyword. Thereafter, the associated data can be displayed and filtered. Furthermore, due to the interconnectivity, the total federated dataset will become browsable.

In the remainder of this Ph.D. project, our focus lies on the following components. The integration of our semantic browser into the prototype of our Augmented Reality browser is needed. In addition, we want to find additional functionalities and application areas as well as we will implement and evaluate the rule-based recommendation system. In order to validate the work, we have to carry out a more in-depth evaluation of the proposed approach.

6   Evaluation Plan

In the evaluation method of the entity resolution part of data integration system we aim to use well-known evaluation metrics to count the number of correctly identified same entities. We will use the following standard concepts: true positive, true negative, false positive, false negative, precision, recall and accuracy. Furthermore, we want to measure the number of the resulted POI-s of several queries separately and collectively (i.e. the result of our proposed integration system). The fundamental assumption was that the given result after data integration will be much wider than separately.

We will perform usability test and user evaluations of our Augmented Reality browser based on the evaluation methods described in [10]. Different measures will be observed regarding, for example, the performance of spatial databases, the running time of the semantic browser part of our proposal.

7   Conclusion

In this work an approach which combines Semantic Web technologies and Augmented Reality is proposed. It is designed to enhance the existing mobile Augmented Reality browsers in terms of richness of data provisioning and additional practical functions. For this purpose, the existing data integration methods and Augmented Reality browser approaches were reviewed. The utilization of Semantic Web technologies, such as OWL, RDF, SPARQL was proposed to achieve the goal of this research. Preliminary results were described, namely the details of the proposed data integration system, a prototype implementation of a client and a mobile semantic browser as well as a plan for the future was established. The proposed approach is regarded as an improvement of the current Augmented Reality browsers as well as a type of a visual interface to the Linked Open Data. In this way, it could contribute to the development of Mobile Semantic Web as well.

Acknowledgments. This work was partially supported by the European Union and the European Social Fund through project FuturICT.hu (grant no.: TAMOP-4.2.2.C-11/1/KONV-2012-0013). The author is grateful to his supervising professor Dr. Attila Kiss for helpful discussion, advices and comments.

References

1. Auer, S., Lehmann, J., Hellmann, S.: Linkedgeodata: adding a spatial dimension to the web of data. In: Bernstein, A., Karger, D.R., Heath, T., Feigenbaum, L., Maynard, D., Motta, E., Thirunarayan, K. (eds.) ISWC 2009. LNCS, vol. 5823, pp. 731–746. Springer, Heidelberg (2009)
2. Aumueller, D., Do, H.H., Massmann, S., Rahm, E.: Schema and ontology matching with COMA++. In: Proceedings of the 2005 ACM SIGMOD international conference on management of data, pp. 906–908. ACM (2005)
3. Azuma, R.T.: A survey of augmented reality. Presence 6(4), 355–385 (1997)
4. Bizer, C., Jentzsch, A., Cyganiak, R.: State of the LOD Cloud. http://wifo5-03.informatik.uni-mannheim.de/lodcloud/state/
5. Bizer, C., Lehmann, J., Kobilarov, G., Auer, S., Becker, C., Cyganiak, R., Hellmann, S.: DBpedia-a crystallization point for the web of data. Web Semant. Sci. Serv. Agents World Wide Web 7(3), 154–165 (2009)
6. Benjelloun, O., Garcia-Molina, H., Menestrina, D., Su, Q., Whang, S.E., Widom, J.: Swoosh: a generic approach to entity resolution. VLDB J. Int. J. Very Large Data Bases 18(1), 255–276 (2009)
7. Braun, M., Scherp, A., Staab, S.: Collaborative creation of semantic points of interest as linked data on the mobile phone (2007)
8. Brickley, D., Miller, L.: FOAF vocabulary specification 0.98. Namespace Document, 9
9. Duong, T.H., Jo, G., Jung, J.J., Nguyen, N.T.: Complexity analysis of ontology integration methodologies: a comparative study. J. UCS 15(4), 877–897 (2009)
10. Dünser, A., Billinghurst, M.: Evaluating augmented reality systems. In: Furht, B. (ed.) Handbook of Augmented Reality, pp. 289–307. Springer, New York (2011)

11. Ester, M., Kriegel, H.P., Sander, J., Xu, X.: A density-based algorithm for discovering clusters in large spatial databases with noise. In: KDD, vol. 96, pp. 226–231 (1996)
12. Harth, A., Gil, Y.: Geospatial data integration with linked data and provenance tracking. In: W3C/OGC Linking Geospatial Data Workshop (2014)
13. Horrocks, I., Patel-Schneider, P., Boley, H., Tabet, S., Grosof, B., Dean, M.: SWRL: A Semantic Web Rule Language Combining OWL and RuleML (2011). http://www.w3.org/Submission/SWRL/
14. Klyne, G., Carroll, J.J.: Resource description framework (RDF): Concepts and Abstract Syntax (2006)
15. Martín-Serrano, D., Hervás, R., Bravo, J.: Telemaco: context-aware system for tourism guiding based on web 3.0 technology. In: 1st Workshop on Contextual Computing and Ambient Intelligence in Tourism, Riviera Maya, Mexico (2011)
16. Matuszka, T., Kiss, A.: Geodint: towards semantic web-based geographic data integration. In: Nguyen, N.T., Attachoo, B., Trawiński, B., Somboonviwat, K. (eds.) ACIIDS 2014, Part I. LNCS, vol. 8397, pp. 191–200. Springer, Heidelberg (2014)
17. Matuszka, T., Kámán, S., Kiss, A.: A semantically enriched augmented reality browser. In: Shumaker, R., Lackey, S. (eds.) VAMR 2014, Part I. LNCS, vol. 8525, pp. 375–384. Springer, Heidelberg (2014)
18. Matuszka T., Kiss A.: Experimental evaluation of some geodata management systems. In: 9th IEEE International Conference on Computer Engineering and Systems, pp. 92–98. Cairo (2014)
19. Matuszka, T., Gombos, G., Kiss, A.: mSWB: towards a mobile semantic web browser. In: Awan, I., Younas, M., Franch, X., Quer, C. (eds.) MobiWIS 2014. LNCS, vol. 8640, pp. 165–175. Springer, Heidelberg (2014)
20. Micsik, A., Turbucz, S., Tóth, Z.: Exploring publication metadata graphs with the LODmilla browser and editor. Int. J. Digit. Libr. **15**, 1–10 (2014)
21. Nguyen, N.T.: A method for ontology conflict resolution and integration on relation level. Cybern. Syst. Int. J. **38**(8), 781–797 (2007)
22. Norton, B., Vilches, L.M., Len, A.D., Goodwin, J., Stadler, C., Anand, S.S., Harries, D., Villazn-Terrazas, B., Atemezing, G.A.: NeoGeo vocabulary specification - madrid edn., Salas, J.M., Harth, A. (eds.). http://geovocab.org/doc/neogeo/
23. Noy, N.F.: Semantic integration: a survey of ontology-based approaches. ACM Sigmod Rec. **33**(4), 65–70 (2004)
24. Prud'Hommeaux, E., Seaborne, A.: SPARQL query language for RDF. W3C recommendation, 15 (2008)
25. Rahm, E., Bernstein, P.A.: A survey of approaches to automatic schema matching. VLDB J. **10**(4), 334–350 (2001)
26. Sidló, C.I.: Generic entity resolution in relational databases. In: Grundspenkis, J., Morzy, T., Vossen, G. (eds.) ADBIS 2009. LNCS, vol. 5739, pp. 59–73. Springer, Heidelberg (2009)
27. van Aart, C., Wielinga, B., van Hage, W.R.: Mobile cultural heritage guide: location-aware semantic search. In: Cimiano, P., Pinto, H.S. (eds.) EKAW 2010. LNCS, vol. 6317, pp. 257–271. Springer, Heidelberg (2010)
28. Zander, S., Chiu, C., Sageder, G.: A computational model for the integration of linked data in mobile augmented reality applications. In: Proceedings of the 8th International Conference on Semantic Systems, pp. 133–140. ACM (2012)

Information Extraction for Learning Expressive Ontologies

Giulio Petrucci[1,2]([✉])

[1] Fondazione Bruno Kessler, Via Sommarive, 18, 38123 Trento, Italy
[2] University of Trento, Via Sommarive, 14, 38123 Trento, Italy
petrucci@fbk.eu

Abstract. Ontologies are used to represent knowledge in a formal and unambiguous way, facilitating its reuse and sharing among people and computer systems. A large amount of knowledge is traditionally available in unstructured text sources and manually encoding their content into a formal representation is costly and time-consuming. Several methods have been proposed to support ontology engineers in the ontology building process, but they mostly turned out to be inadequate for building rich and expressive ontologies. We propose some concrete research directions for designing an effective methodology for semi-supervised ontology learning. This methodology will integrate a new axiom extraction technique which exploits several features of the text corpus.

1 Introduction

According to a widely accepted definition, an Ontology is *a formal representation of a shared conceptualization* (see [15]): dealing with a formal and explicit representation of a commonly agreed understanding of a domain, can help to overcome the problem of ambiguity in knowledge representation and sharing. In the Semantic Web scenario, ontolgies provide the conceptual scheme for metadata carrying the explicit data semantics, endowing machines with the capability to interpret data unambiguously and perform reasoning over them.

Several approaches, known as *Ontology Learning*, have been proposed along the years to facilitate the encoding of knowledge from large textual sources, which are massively available, into ontologies. Such approaches still experience some severe limitations, specially trying to extract complex and expressive formalizations like axioms.

The intended contribution of our work is twofold. First, we aim to provide a novel automatic technique, capable to abstract the formulation of OWL DL axioms from large text corpora. Second, we intend to combine such technique together with other state-of-the-art methods in a full methodology that will support the ontology engineer in the axiom extraction process, reducing its cost.

The paper is structured as follows. In Sect. 2 we will depict the State of the Art in Ontology Learning. In Sect. 3 we state our research problem and the contribution we want to give. In Sect. 4 we will describe our research methodology. In Sect. 5 we present our preliminary results. In Sect. 6 we present our evaluation plan. Finally, Sect. 7 concludes the paper.

© Springer International Publishing Switzerland 2015
F. Gandon et al. (Eds.): ESWC 2015, LNCS 9088, pp. 740–750, 2015.
DOI: 10.1007/978-3-319-18818-8_47

2   State of the Art

Human knowledge is often carried by large unstructured textual sources. Building an ontology from such sources can be resource-intensive and time consuming. To support ontology engineers in such process, several approaches have been proposed, known as *Ontology Learning* (see [7]), which build upon well-established techniques from Natural Language Processing, Machine Learning, Information Retrieval, Knowledge Acquisition and Ontology Engineering. The various tasks relevant in the Ontology Learning process and their mutual dependencies have been organized in the *Ontology Learning Layer Cake* (see Fig. 1), a conceptual sketch of a generic ontology learning layered architecture in which each layer is associated with a task and its output is the input for the one on the top of it.

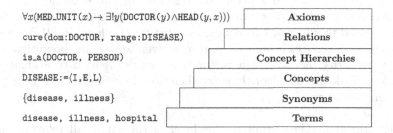

$\forall x(\text{MED\_UNIT}(x) \rightarrow \exists! y(\text{DOCTOR}(y) \land \text{HEAD}(y, x)))$	**Axioms**
cure(dom:DOCTOR, range:DISEASE)	**Relations**
is_a(DOCTOR, PERSON)	**Concept Hierarchies**
DISEASE:=⟨I,E,L⟩	**Concepts**
{disease, illness}	**Synonyms**
disease, illness, hospital	**Terms**

Fig. 1. The Ontology Learning Layer Cake

Recently, the ontology engineering community has been pursuing the ambitious goal to extract increasingly complex information ranging from terms, to relations, to hierarchies, and finally to axioms. Even if the fully automatic acquisition of knowledge by machines is still a long term goal, several automatic and semi-automatic techniques, along with several ready-to-use tools, have been proposed for each layer of the cake.

Term Extraction. The goal of this task is to identify all the relevant terms in the text corpus. Frequency based criteria or metrics from Information Retrieval (TF, TF-IDF, TIM-DRM) are used in [8,13,18,20,30,37], together with the C-value/NC-value metric from Computational Linguistics. Linguistic features are exploited in [18,30,33] while a combined approach is presented in [44]: extracted terms are connected as nodes in a graph structure, ranked and filtered on the basis of metrics from Graph Theory (Betweenness, Centrality, ecc) or Information Retrieval and finally selected according to some voting schemes (Majority, Intersection, ecc). In [40] a machine learning based approach has been shown capable to adapt to different domains with a reduced training effort.

Synonym Extraction. In order to group together terms with similar meaning, the well known *distributional hypothesis* is largely exploited as in [8,29,33]. Other

Text Mining clustering techniques are used in [13] while external resources as WordNet[1] are used in [30].

Concept Learning. At this layer, concepts must be induced in an intensional way. Clustering algorithms and Latent Semantic Indexing (LSI) are used in [13] while in [33] sets of terms considered synonyms are casted into new concepts named after the more occurring term. WordNet Domains and other resources are used in [36] to associate the newly extracted keyphrases with existing concepts. Context similarity in [8,29] induces concepts definition over sets of terms.

Concept Hierarchy. The goal of this task is to learn taxonomic relations over extracted concepts. Lexico-syntactic patterns from [17] are used in [8,44]. The approach presented in [35] uses syntactic features to train a binary classifier to predict if two nouns are in a taxonomic relation. In [33] taxonomy is induced with a hierarchical clustering process while in [29] a complex context similarity measure is used to add new concepts in an existing ontology. In [21,37] a graph with concepts as vertices is built via pattern-driven web search operations, while in [14] a similarity metric over a vector space model is used to evaluate term relatedness. Task-specific algorithms are then used in order to turn these graphs into taxonomic trees.

Relation Learning. The output of this layer is the set of all relations among concepts and individuals, eventually organized in a hierarchical order. Linguistic patterns and metrics from Graph Theory are used in [44]. Linguistic patterns are used also in [18] in order to detect verb-based relations. In [29], context similarity is taken as an evidence of a generic conceptual relation. Statistical significance of co-occurrence is used in [32] in order to predict a relation between two terms. In [9], patterns expressed in an *ad hoc* formalism are used to detect instances of known relations. Syntactic features are used in [8] in order to detect general relations, while a combination of a set of patterns together with WordNet is used for mereological relations. The assumption of an intrinsic redundancy in large corpora is exploited in [16] in order to apply graph mutual reinforcement between a set of relation lexico-syntactic patterns and corresponding matching instances. Iterative approaches are followed in [1,5,42] starting from a small hand-crafted set of patterns, matching textual relation instances are used to extend the pattern set. Parse tree feature spaces are used in [6] in order to train tree kernel based classifiers which can predict occurrences of predefined relations. Hand-crafted rules are used in [2] in order to label a set of examples which will be used to train a classifier. This semi-supervised approach has been extended in [11] with POS-tags patterns acting as syntactic constrains and a large dictionary of relation acting as a lexical constraint, in order to improve the extractions quality. A pairwise vector space clustering is used in [34] in order to detect recurring patterns and identify relation instances. A clustering technique is used also in [26] in order to detect generic relations for given type signatures. Ontological

---

[1] http://wordnet.princeton.edu/.

resources like Freebase,[2] YAGO[3] and Wikipedia[4] infoboxes are exploited in [25, 27,28,41] as sources of evidence in order to match textual relation instances from which different types of features are extracted to train classifiers or cluster instances.

Axiom Learning. The last layer addresses the problem of axioms learning. The usage of lexico-syntactic patterns has been exploited in [39] for generating formal class description from definitional sentences. This approach has been followed in [38] in order to detect disjointness among classes using external lexical resources, underlying ontologies and Pointwise Mutual Information (PMI) relying on the Web as a source of evidence. A radically different approach is presented in [31] where Discourse Representation Theory (DRT, see [19]) is used in order to represent the content of a single document in formal structures called Discourse Representation Structures (DRSs). Those structures are then mapped to OWL constructs applying a set of translation rules and exploiting several external lexical (FrameNet[5] and VerbNet[6]) and ontological (FOAF,[7] DBpedia,[8] Dolce+DnS Ultralite[9]) resources. The translation from DRSs to OWL constructs relies on a set of *Ontology Design Patterns* (ODPs). An ODP is *"a reusable successful solution to a recurrent modeling problem*[10]*"* and can be seen as a sort of template to be used in some particular and recurring situations. Acting as constraints, they are supposed to ensure quality for the final ontology construction. In [22], an system for the extraction of $\mathcal{EL}$++ concepts definitions from text is presented. Text fragments involving concepts from the SNOMED CT[11] ontology are matched and their lexical and ontological features are used to train a maximum entropy classifier in order to predict the axiom describing the involved entities. Users can provide their feedback, helping the system to correct the underlying model.

3   Problem Statement and Contribution

Reasoning-based applications can infer new knowledge beyond what explicitly stated in the domain representation they rely on. Their power of reasoning depends on the expressivity of such representation: an ontology provided with complex TBox axioms can act as a valuable support for the representation and the evaluation of a deep knowledge about the domain it represents.

Automatic learning of expressive TBox axioms is a complex task. From a linguistic point of view, conjunctions, negations and disjunctions are difficult

---

[2] http://www.freebase.com.
[3] www.mpi-inf.mpg.de/yago-naga/yago/.
[4] https://www.wikipedia.org/.
[5] https://framenet.icsi.berkeley.edu/fndrupal/.
[6] http://verbs.colorado.edu/~mpalmer/projects/verbnet.html.
[7] http://www.foaf-project.org/.
[8] http://dbpedia.org.
[9] http://www.ontologydesignpatterns.org/ont/dul/DUL.owl.
[10] http://ontologydesignpatterns.org/wiki/Main_Page.
[11] http://www.ihtsdo.org/snomed-ct/.

to parse and interpret. The same is for detecting local contexts for universal quantifications. Statistical relevance based metrics could be misleading as definitional sentences can appear infrequently in the corpus and the knowledge to be encoded in a single axiom can be spread across several sentences.

State-of-the-art methods and tools capable to handle large text corpora still appear to be more suitable to support the construction of light-weight ontologies. On the other hand, axiom extraction methods are intended to work in a sentence-by-sentence translation modality, with constraints on the structure of the sentence or the particular domain of interest. As a consequence, ontology learning from large text corpora still remains a heavily manual process which can end up having unsustainable costs. Therefore, we state our research problem in the form of the following question:

> How can semi-supervised techniques significantly help to extract relevant expressive axioms from a large domain text corpus and therefore minimize human intervention in the process of ontology building?

Answering this question, the first contribution we aim to give is the design of **an automatic technique to extract TBox axioms from large text corpora**. Our target axioms are those that can be expressed through OWL DL constructs. Each text corpus is assumed to have some inner coherence about some domain. As in [43], we focus on corpora from which a significant amount of ontological statements (definitions of concepts, their relations, ecc) rather than factual statements can be extracted – like encyclopedic texts, textbooks or specifications. Setting this research goal, we hypothesize that statistical, linguistic and semantic features of such text corpora can be exploited to train a system capable to detect textual occurrences of axioms.

The second contribution is the organization of our new axiom extraction technique and other state-of-the-art methods together with human activities into a fully-fledged **methodology**, outlined in Fig. 2. The initial input is a text corpus and the final output is a set of axioms which are intended to be expressive conceptualization of the knowledge originally contained in the input corpus. The four phases are:

1. **Light-Weight Extraction (LE)**: state-of-the-art methods are used to extract concepts, relations and concept hierarchies from the corpus.
2. **User Selection (US)**: the ontology engineer can select a subset of the ontology elements produced by the previous phase or add new ones that may have been missed. This interaction validates the knowledge extracted so far and highlights what the engineer considers as more relevant.
3. **Axioms Extraction (AE)**: the user can select a relation, concept or a pair of concepts and the system will provide all the hypotheses of axioms involving them, along with some textual evidence if possible. Hypotheses will be ranked according to how much the system is *confident* that the single axiom actually holds in the corpus.
4. **User Feedback (UF)**: the user can express a judgment about the correctness of the axiom hypotheses suggested by the previous phase, in order to remove uncertainty.

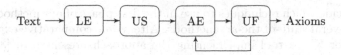

Fig. 2. An outline for the proposed methodology

4 Research Methodology and Approach

In order to train a system capable to learn axioms from text, we first need to identify which features of the text corpus must be exploited. As shown in Sect. 2, several approaches relying on lexico-syntactic features and deep linguistic analysis of sentences have been proposed. With some ongoing experiments we are investigating the possibility to combine them with statistical relevance based ones as in [30,44]. As definitory sentences could be strong points of evidence for axioms holding in the text, we want to exploit them as well with deeper linguistic analysis techniques, as in [31,37]. Some preliminary studies have been performed using the BPMN 1.1 specification[12] as the input text corpus and a corresponding ontology, manually developed by an ontology engineer.

Starting from this, we plan to build a set of training examples: the inputs is a text corpus and the expected output is a set of axioms actually holding according to the corpus content. We have started investigating some available ontologies to extract axioms from them and build our expected outputs. Usually, they are not supplied with a corresponding text corpus so that we will have to build it by ourselves harvesting the web or some other large document repositories. Our idea is to train our system with these examples assuming that the system can *scale* to other corpora maintaining an acceptable performance level, in a sort of domain adaptation fashion. The approaches presented in [24] for keyphrases extraction and in [12] for taxonomy induction exploited the same intuition. We want to extend this investigation to the axiom extraction problem.

Our target ontology language is OWL DL. We plan to develop our system in an iterative way, having different type of constructs as target for each step. So far, we have planned to proceed according to the following hypothesis of work:

1. Atomic Negation, Concept Intersection, Inverse Properties, Nominals
2. Complex Concept Negation, Role Hierarchy, Cardinality Restrictions
3. Universal Restrictions, Limited Existential Quantification

5 Preliminary Results

During the first year of our work we focused on reviewing the State of the Art and performing some exploratory activities. We outlined the preliminary version of our methodology on the main idea of alternating manual and automatic tasks. In

---

[12] http://www.omg.org/spec/BPMN/1.1/.

order to decide which techniques to use in the first phase of our methodology, we analyzed several state-of-the-art methods. After some comparative experiments, we opted for KX, a tool implementing the approach presented in [30] for the term extraction task, as it turned out giving the best performance. We still have to investigate further in order to decide which relation extraction and concept hierarchy induction techniques to be adopted.

We tested several NLP tools over the BPMN 1.1 specification in order to get a rough idea of their behavior. We performed deep syntactic analysis with Mate-tools (see [3]) and with the Stanford Core NLP toolkit (see [23]) which has been extended with a plugin (still under development) that annotates the shortest path parse tree fragment (as in [6,41]) between pairs of relevant concepts spotted by KX: such paths could be easily analyzed in order to check how they can be useful for our work. We used SEMAFOR (see [10]) in order to extract all the occurrences of the semantic frames collected in FrameNet. We also tried to use Boxer (see [4]) to extract a deep semantic representation of the text based on DRSs, which have the interesting property of being equivalent to First-Order Logic formulae.

Recently we started building our training set according to analogous experiences in literature. In [29], the OpenCyc ontology is exploited for the domains of *Fisheries and Aquaculture* and *Economy and Finance*. The Aquatic Sciences and Fisheries Abstract (ASFA) thesaurus[13] has been used as a corpus for the former, while the the Harvey Glossary[14] for the latter. In [37] the Economy and Finance corpus has been extended with scientific journal or conference papers about the topic. The Economist also provide a related glossary.[15] In the same work, authors followed the same procedure to build a corpus for the domain of *Artificial Intelligence*, but no valuable ontology seems to be available. The BioPortal[16] project provides a large repository of ontologies for the biomedical domain. Several corpora for such domain[17] are available as it has been explored in depth by the NLP research community. However, as it comprises a large variety of different topics, finding suitable corpus/ontology pairs may not be straightforward.

During the last weeks, further explorations suggested us the opportunity to deepen some topics from the distributed compositional semantics field in order to deal with linguistic issues in axiom detection.

6   Evaluation Plan

Our axiom extraction technique will be evaluated according to its capacity of correctly identify axioms actually holding in the input text corpus. We plan to continuously evaluate it using the axioms contained in out training set ontologies

---

[13] http://www4.fao.org/asfa/asfa.htm.
[14] http://biz.yahoo.com/glossary.
[15] http://www.economist.com/economics-a-to-z.
[16] http://bioportal.bioontology.org/ontologies.
[17] e.g. http://www2.informatik.hu-berlin.de/~hakenber/links/benchmarks.html.

as the gold standard. Well-known metrics like Precision and Recall could be used in a quite straightforward way in this scenario.

Later, we plan to involve some human assessors in order to judge some axioms, maybe verbalized, as actually holding in the text corpus or not. Our idea is to involve more human assessors and measure the quality of the judgment using some inter-annotator agreement metric.

The final evaluation phase will focus on the effectiveness of our methodology in term of cost reduction. Starting from the same specification we will build again the BPMN ontology using our methodology. This will allow us to compare both the correctness of the extracted axioms and the time spent for this task with the ones of the corresponding hand-made ontology.

7 Conclusions

Several approaches have been proposed to support ontology engineers in the tasks of building ontologies from large textual corpora. Looking at state-of-the-art techniques for semi-automatic ontology engineering, despite the progress made so far, they are not able to give significant support in rich and expressive ontology building so that their cost can become unaffordable. To overcome this limitation, we want to design a new axiom extraction technique to be integrated into a a semi-automatic methodology together with other state-of-the-art methods. We hypothesize that available large textual and knowledge sources can be used to train a domain-independent system capable of providing a human actor some hypotheses about axioms holding among concepts in the knowledge contained in a text corpus. We also outline an evaluation process, involving both automatic evaluation against a gold standard and human assessment in order to evaluate relevance and correctness of the extracted axioms together with the effectiveness of our methodology in term of human effort reduction.

References

1. Agichtein, E., Gravano, L.: Snowball: extracting relations from large plain-text collections. In: Proceedings of the Fifth ACM Conference on Digital Libraries (2000)
2. Banko, M., Cafarella, M.J., Soderland, S., Broadhead, M., Etzioni, O.: Open information extraction from the web. In: Proceedings of the 20th International Joint Conference on Artificial Intelligence, pp. 2670–2676 (2007)
3. Bohnet, B.: Very high accuracy and fast dependency parsing is not a contradiction. In: Proceedings of the 23rd International Conference on Computational Linguistics, pp. 89–97 (2010)
4. Bos, J.: Wide-coverage semantic analysis with boxer. In: Proceedings of the 2008 Conference on Semantics in Text Processing, pp. 277–286 (2008)
5. Brin, S.: Extracting patterns and relations from the World Wide Web. In: Atzeni, P., Mendelzon, A.O., Mecca, G. (eds.) WebDB 1998. LNCS, vol. 1590, pp. 172–183. Springer, Heidelberg (1999)

6. Bunescu, R.C., Mooney, R.J.: A shortest path dependency kernel for relation extraction. In: Proceedings of the Conference on Human Language Technology and Empirical Methods in Natural Language Processing, pp. 724–731 (2005)
7. Cimiano, P., Mädche, A., Staab, S., Völker, J.: Handbook on ontologies. In: Staab, S., Studer, R. (eds.) Ontology learning. International Handbooks on Information Systems, pp. 245–267. Springer, Heidelberg (2009)
8. Cimiano, P., Völker, J.: Text2Onto. In: Montoyo, A., Muñoz, R., Métais, E. (eds.) NLDB 2005. LNCS, vol. 3513, pp. 227–238. Springer, Heidelberg (2005)
9. Dahab, M.Y., Hassan, H.A., Rafea, A.: TextOntoEx: automatic ontology construction from natural english text. Expert Syst. Appl. **34**(2), 1474–1480 (2008)
10. Das, D., Schneider, N., Chen, D., Smith, N.A.: Probabilistic frame-semantic parsing. In: Human Language Technologies: The 2010 Annual Conference of the North American Chapter of the ACL, pp. 948–956 (2010)
11. Etzioni, O., Fader, A., Christensen, J., Soderland, S., Mausam, M.: Open information extraction: the second generation. In: Proceedings of the 22nd International Joint Conference on Artificial Intelligence, vol. 11, pp. 3–10 (2011)
12. Fallucchi, F., Pazienza, M.T., Zanzotto, F.M.: Generic ontology learners on application domains. In: Proceedings of the International Conference on Language Resources and Evaluation (2010)
13. Fortuna, B., Grobelnik, M., Mladenic, D.: OntoGen: semi-automatic ontology editor. In: Smith, M.J., Salvendy, G. (eds.) HCII 2007. LNCS, vol. 4558, pp. 309–318. Springer, Heidelberg (2007)
14. Fountain, T., Lapata, M.: Taxonomy induction using hierarchical random graphs. In: Proceedings of the 2012 Confrence of the North American Chapter of the ACL: Human Language Technologies, pp. 466–476 (2012)
15. Guarino, N., Oberle, D., Staab, S.: What is an ontology? In: Staab, S., Studer, R. (eds.) Handbook on Ontologies. International Handbooks on Information Systems, pp. 1–17. Springer, Heidelberg (2009)
16. Hassan, H., Hassan, A., Emam, O.: Unsupervised information extraction approach using graph mutual reinforcement. In: Proceedings of the 2006 Conference on Empirical Methods in Natural Language Processing, pp. 501–508 (2006)
17. Hearst, M.A.: Automatic acquisition of hyponyms from large text corpora. In: Proceedings of the 14th Conference on Computational linguistics, vol. 2, pp. 539–545 (1992)
18. Jiang, X., Tan, A.H.: Mining ontological knowledge from domain-specific text documents. In: Proceedings of the Fifth IEEE International Conference on Data Mining, pp. 665–668 (2005)
19. Kamp, H., Reyle, U.: From Discourse to Logic. Studies in Linguistics and Philosophy, vol. 42. Springer, Netherlands (1993)
20. Kang, Y.B., Haghighi, P.D., Burstein, F.: CFinder: an intelligent key concept finder from text for ontology development. Expert Syst. Appl. **41**(9), 4494–4504 (2014)
21. Kozareva, Z., Hovy, E.: A semi-supervised method to learn and construct taxonomies using the web. In: Proceedings of the 2010 Conference on Empirical Methods in Natural Language Processing, pp. 1110–1118 (2010)
22. Ma, Y., Syamsiyah, A.: A hybrid approach to learn description logic based biomedical ontology from texts. In: ISWC 2014 Proceeding (2014)
23. Manning, C.D., Surdeanu, M., Bauer, J., Finkel, J.R., Bethard, S., McClosky, D.: The stanford coreNLP natural language processing toolkit. In: Proceedings of the 52nd Annual Meeting of the ACL, pp. 55–60 (2014)

24. Medelyan, O., Witten, I.H.: Domain-independent automatic keyphrase indexing with small training sets. JASIST **59**(7), 1026–1040 (2008)
25. Mintz, M., Bills, S., Snow, R., Jurafsky, D.: Distant supervision for relation extraction without labeled data. In: Proceedings of the Joint Conference of the 47th Annual Meeting of the ACL and the 4th International Joint Conference on Natural Language Processing of the AFNLP, vol. 2, pp. 1003–1011 (2009)
26. Mohamed, T.P., Hruschka, Jr., E.R., Mitchell, T.M.: Discovering relations between noun categories. In: Proceedings of the Conference on Empirical Methods in Natural Language Processing, pp. 1447–1455 (2011)
27. Moro, A., Navigli, R.: Integrating syntactic and semantic analysis into the open information extraction paradigm. In: Proceedings of the Twenty-Third International Joint Conference on Artificial Intelligence, pp. 2148–2154 (2013)
28. Nakashole, N., Weikum, G., Suchanek, F.: Patty: A taxonomy of relational patterns with semantic types. In: Proceedings of the 2012 Joint Conference on Empirical Methods in Natural Language Processing and Computational Natural Language Learning, pp. 1135–1145 (2012)
29. Novalija, I., Mladenic, D., Bradesko, L.: Ontoplus: text-driven ontology extension using ontology content, structure and co-occurrence information. Knowl.-Based Syst. **24**(8), 1261–1276 (2011)
30. Pianta, E., Tonelli, S.: KX: a flexible system for keyphrase extraction. In: Proceedings of the 5th International Workshop on Semantic Evaluation. pp. 170–173 (2010)
31. Presutti, V., Draicchio, F., Gangemi, A.: Knowledge extraction based on discourse representation theory and linguistic frames. In: ten Teije, A., Völker, J., Handschuh, S., Stuckenschmidt, H., d'Acquin, M., Nikolov, A., Aussenac-Gilles, N., Hernandez, N. (eds.) EKAW 2012. LNCS, vol. 7603, pp. 114–129. Springer, Heidelberg (2012)
32. Schutz, A., Buitelaar, P.: *RelExt*: A tool for relation extraction from text in ontology extension. In: Gil, Y., Motta, E., Benjamins, V.R., Musen, M.A. (eds.) ISWC 2005. LNCS, vol. 3729, pp. 593–606. Springer, Heidelberg (2005)
33. Shih, C.W., Chen, M.Y., Chu, H.C., Chen, Y.M.: Enhancement of domain ontology construction using a crystallizing approach. Expert Syst. Appl. **38**(6), 7544–7557 (2011)
34. Shinyama, Y., Sekine, S.: Preemptive information extraction using unrestricted relation discovery. In: Proceedings of the Main Conference on Human Language Technology Conference of the North American Chapter of the ACL, pp. 304–311 (2006)
35. Snow, R., Jurafsky, D., Ng, A.Y.: Semantic taxonomy induction from heterogenous evidence. In: Proceedings of 21st International Conference on Computational Linguistics and 44th Annual Meeting of the ACL (2006)
36. Tonelli, S., Rospocher, M., Pianta, E., Serafini, L.: Boosting collaborative ontology building with key-concept extraction. In: 2011 Fifth IEEE International Conference on Semantic Computing (ICSC), pp. 316–319 (2011)
37. Velardi, P., Faralli, S., Navigli, R.: Ontolearn reloaded: a graph-based algorithm for taxonomy induction. Comput. Linguist. **39**(3), 665–707 (2013)
38. Völker, J., Haase, P., Hitzler, P.: Learning expressive ontologies. In: Proceedings of the 2008 conference on Ontology Learning and Population: Bridging the Gap between Text and Knowledge, pp. 45–69. IOS Press, Amsterdam (2008)
39. Völker, J., Hitzler, P., Cimiano, P.: Acquisition of OWL DL Axioms from Lexical Resources. In: Franconi, E., Kifer, M., May, W. (eds.) ESWC 2007. LNCS, vol. 4519, pp. 670–685. Springer, Heidelberg (2007)

40. Witten, I.H., Paynter, G.W., Frank, E., Gutwin, C., Nevill-Manning, C.G.: KEA: Practical automatic keyphrase extraction. In: Proceedings of the Fourth ACM Conference on Digital Libraries, pp. 254–255 (1999)
41. Wu, F., Weld, D.S.: Open information extraction using wikipedia. In: Proceedings of the 48th Annual Meeting of the ACL, pp. 118–127 (2010)
42. Zhu, J., Nie, Z., Liu, X., Zhang, B., Wen, J.R.: Statsnowball: a statistical approach to extracting entity relationships. In: Proceedings of the 18th International Conference on World Wide Web, pp. 101–110 (2009)
43. Zouaq, A., Gasevic, D., Hatala, M.: Towards open ontology learning and filtering. Inf. Syst. **36**(7), 1064–1081 (2011)
44. Zouaq, A., Gasevic, D., Hatala, M.: Linguistic patterns for information extraction in ontocmaps. In: Proceedings of the 3rd Workshop on Ontology Patterns (2012)

A Scalable Adaptive Method for Complex Reasoning Over Semantic Data Streams

Thu-Le Pham[✉]

Insight Centre for Data Analytics, National University of Ireland Galway,
Galway, Ireland
thule.pham@insight-centre.org

Abstract. Data streams are the infinite sequences of data elements that are being generated by companies, social network, mobile phones, smart homes, public transport vehicles and other modern infrastructures. Current stream processing solutions can handle streams of data to timely produce new results but they lack the complex reasoning capacities that are required to go from data to actionable knowledge. Conversely, engines that can perform such complex reasoning tasks, are mostly designed to work on static data. The main aim of my research proposal is to provide a solution to perform complex reasoning on dynamic semantic information in a scalable way. At its core, this requires a solution which combines advantages of both stream processing and reasoning research areas, and has flexible heuristics for adaptation of the stream reasoning processes in order to enhance scalability.

Keywords: Stream reasoning · Stream processing · Non-monotonic reasoning · Multi-context systems

1   Introduction

The ever growing advance of the Internet and Sensor technology has brought new challenges evoked by the explosion of highly dynamic data. Large volumes of data are continuously produced from various sources, and published at a speed which exceeds by far our current methods and infrastructure for processing it. An infographic from analytics software provider Domo[1], attempts to quantify just how much data is generated in one minute online. It has been estimated that in 2013 every minute on the Internet 200 million emails were sent, 4 million queries were submitted in Google, and 2.5 million pieces of content were posted on Facebook.These numbers do not include the volumes of data coming from sensors and Internet of Things (IoT) devices. We refer to each of these dynamic data flows as a data stream.

More specifically, data streams are defined as sequences of time-varying data elements [4]. They occur in various modern applications such as environment monitoring, traffic management, space situational awareness, and so on. These

---

[1] http://www.domo.com/learn/data-never-sleeps-2.

© Springer International Publishing Switzerland 2015
F. Gandon et al. (Eds.): ESWC 2015, LNCS 9088, pp. 751–759, 2015.
DOI: 10.1007/978-3-319-18818-8_48

real applications face several challenges because the data they need to process is massive, ordered, can be incomplete, heterogeneous, and noisy. In addition to that, they have to provide timely response, therefore time delay becomes a key evaluation metric. Advances on Semantic Web & Linked Data research and standards have already provided formats and technologies for representing and sharing knowledge on the Web. In the last few years, Semantic Web technologies such as RDF, OWL, SPARQL have provided mechanisms for processing semantic data streams. However these solutions can not exhibit complex reasoning capabilities such as the ability of managing defaults, common-sense, preferences, recursion, and non-determinism. Conversely, logic-based non-monotonic reasoners can perform such tasks but are suitable for data that changes in low volumes at low frequency. Therefore, there is a clear need for design and implementation of new approaches to enable complex reasoning for web data streams.

The concept of "stream reasoning", as defined in [13], is considered as the application of reasoning techniques to data streams. Stream reasoning is described as "an unexplored yet high- impact research area and a new multidisciplinary approach that can provide the abstractions, foundations, methods, and tools required to integrate data streams, the Semantic Web, and reasoning systems" [13]. A variety of concrete applications highlight clearly the important need for stream reasoning technologies, such as Urban Computing [4] (i.e., the application of pervasive computing to urban environment), Smart Cities (i.e., the application of processing and understanding the information relevant for the life of a city and use it to make the city run better, faster, and cheaper) [11], and so on. Stream reasoning is definitely considered as a research area that can have a huge impact on quality of life.

From the analysis of several application scenarios, the authors in [11] extracted the key challenges for stream reasoning systems. These are challenges that we will consider in our approach on stream reasoning for the Semantic Web:

- Integration: data in most scenarios comes from multiple sources with various data types. This raises issues of representing and combining heterogeneous data under processing. Moreover, stream reasoning systems also use domain knowledge in reasoning. This background knowledge is mainly static and time-independent. This integration is challenging because retrieving and analysing large volumes of dynamic data and static knowledge during stream reasoning can be particularly expensive with current technologies.
- Scalability: the scalability is typically evaluated on two aspects. They are computational complexity (i.e., the ability to perform more complex tasks) and input size (i.e., the ability to process a larger input). It is essential that the reasoning process is scalable regarding both aspects.
- Expressivity: all scenarios aim at deriving high level knowledge from large volumes of low level knowledge. Expressivity of a reasoner is known to be inversely related to its performance - the more expressive reasoner is, the longer it takes to perform reasoning.

The overall purpose of this PhD proposal is to critically investigate how to perform complex reasoning on data streams maintaining scalability. We refer to scalability as to the ability to provide answers in an acceptable time when the throughput increases and the reasoning gets computationally intensive. We will explore a heuristic-based stream reasoning approach for the (dynamic) web of data, where query processing and non-monotonic reasoning can be adapted to continuously improve the expressivity versus scalability trade-off.

The combination is based on the principle of having a 2-tier approach (Fig. 1) where:

- Query processing is used to filter semantic data elements. We plan to use RDF stream query processing engines such as C-SPARQL [2], CQELS [10].
- Non-monotonic reasoning is used for computationally intensive tasks. In this proposal, we use Answer Set Programming (ASP) [9] over non-ground programs for the reasoning component.

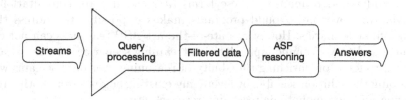

Fig. 1. 2-tier approach

2   State of the Art

There are various existing approaches aiming to perform reasoning over data streams [5]. In stream processing, the existing solutions are divided into two categories: (1) Data Stream Management Systems and (2) Complex Event Processing [11]. The former approach has some well-known engines such as CQELS and C-SPARQL that have ability to process continuously low-level data streams at high rate. The later approach considers observable raw data as primitive events and expresses composite events by some specific operators. These approaches do not manage incomplete information and do not perform complex reasoning tasks.

In the knowledge representation and reasoning community, recent works have been proposed, which attempt toward scalable reasoning using the MapReduce framework. The authors in [1] focus on distributed methods for non-monotonic rule-based reasoning. Their current works perform parallel defeasible reasoning under the assumption of stratification which imposed a severe limitation considering the range of allowed rule set and ASP is still beyond this work. Other attempts focus on extending the well established declarative complex reasoning framework of ASP with dynamic data. M. Gebser et al. [9] proposed modelling approaches for continuous stream reasoning based on reactive ASP, utilizing time-decaying logic programs to capture sliding window data in a natural way.

This is a first step towards gearing ASP to continuous reasoning tasks. However, these approaches still mainly process on low changing data and relatively smaller data sizes. Do et al. [6] also utilize ASP in their stream reasoning system and the approach is based on the DLV system [8], which does not deal with continuous and window-based reasoning over data stream within the reasoner. A similar approach is proposed in [12], where the authors present the StreamRule framework, which combines a stream processing engine and a non-monotonic reasoner. Despite some preliminary investigations, no detailed evaluation is currently available to assess the performance of StreamRule.

3   Problem Statement and Contributions

Most of the real-time applications mentioned in Sect. 1 require dealing with incomplete and noisy input streams, inconsistency, defaults, qualitative preferences, and non-determinism. These forms of reasoning are computationally intensive. ASP over non-ground programs makes it possible to address these cases in offline scenarios. However, state-of-the-art ASP reasoners can not cope with huge and very dynamic input data in streaming scenarios. In this research, we intend to focus on enriching the ability of reasoning over data streams while still keeping the solution scalable by leveraging existing engines from both stream processing and non-monotonic reasoning research areas.

We will extend the approach in [12], which combines CQELS in stream query processing for data on the Web with ASP-based engines. We rely on the following assumptions: (i) that not all dynamic data streams are relevant for complex reasoning tasks, (ii) we consider semantically annotated RDF streams as input, (iii) the dynamic stream is dynamically changing in size, rate, and accuracy. The query processing engine will be used for filtering and aggregating input data in order to provide less amount of higher-level data for the reasoner. However, we want to have a better way to integrate these two components than as a pipeline. Therefore, the questions we want to target are the followings:

a. *Is there a correlation between streaming rate, reasoning complexity, and window size which can help designing heuristics to increase the performance of a 2-tier stream reasoning framework?*

   We observed that current implementation of StreamRule as a pipeline can cause a bottleneck for the reasoning component. Therefore, the non-monotonic reasoner needs to return results faster than the inputs arrive from the stream query component. We want to study the relationship between streaming rate, reasoning complexity, and window size which can be used to design heuristics that improve the performance of the stream reasoning system.

b. *How can we integrate the semantic of stream processing with the semantic of answer set programming?*

   We can bridge the gap between stream processing and reasoning by integrating latest advances from both these research areas. Combining them as a pipeline is a simple way to have a stream reasoning system which can deal with complex reasoning tasks on top of query processing. However, this method can not help in managing the information flow between two different semantics. Therefore, it requires an expressive framework which can help to combine them in a better way.

c. *How can we resolve inconsistency raised in a heterogeneous distributed system?*

One of the issues which arises easily in heterogeneous and distributed systems is inconsistency. The heterogeneous and distributed data coming from noisy streams can cause conflicts within a knowledge domain. Moreover, inconsistency may happen when the system exchanges information across different knowledge domains. This makes it necessary to develop a method for handling inconsistency.

4 Research Methodology and Approach

In order to answer the above research questions, our approach unfolds in the following phases:

a. Correlation between streaming rate, reasoning complexity, and window size:
   Steaming rate, reasoning complexity, and window size are among the main features which can affect the performance of our stream reasoning system. This step deals with the identification of relationships between these features. For example, a correlation exists between logical window size and streaming rate: faster streams are more likely to produce query matches, so they require smaller window sizes, unless the speed of the reasoning process is increased by faster hardware. In order to discover such correlations, we intend to follow these steps:
   - Identify classes of reasoning tasks and their complexity, including a qualitative and quantitative analysis where possible.
   - For each reasoning task, we conduct experiments on StreamRule to observe the behaviour of each component in the system. This observation can be help to discover the correlation which then can be translated into a heuristic.
   - Study how different combinations of heuristics can affect the performance of the system.
   The contribution of this work in stream reasoning is to help designing an adaptation mechanism for enhancing the scalability of the system. In other words, it can help to address the trade-off between complexity and scalability in dynamic environment.

b. Integration of the semantics of stream processing with the semantics of Answer Set Programming:
   Given the latest advances of both stream processing and reasoning research areas, this step aims to find an expressive representation which can capture different logics (standard RDF/SPARQL semantics for stream processing and Stable Model semantics for ASP reasoning) in a system. We intend to consider an instance of Multi-Context System (MSC) [3] for this task. MCS is a

powerful method for many application scenarios where heterogeneity of logics and inter-contextual information exchange are essential. The basic idea is to leave the diverse logics and knowledge bases (called *contexts* or *nodes*) untouched, and to equip each context with a collection of so-called bridge rules in order to model the necessary information flow among contexts. The contexts themselves may be heterogeneous in the sense that they can use different logical languages and different inference systems. Moreover, MCS are capable of integrating "typical" monotonic knowledge representation logics like description logics or temporal logics, and non-monotonic logics like default logic and ASP. From this view point, we consider our state-of-the-art stream processing engine and reasoner as contexts, namely:

- A query processing context: this context connects the whole system to the real world by receiving data streams and reduces the enormous volume of data via stream query pattern matching.
- A non-monotonic reasoning context: this context analyses information obtained from the query processing context, extracts high level knowledge, and performs complex reasoning.

These two contexts can exchange information via a set of bridge rules. The efficient query processing context can reduce the irrelevant data from input streams and the bridge rules can control the useful information flow from the stream processing context to the reasoning context. Moreover, in order to enable the ability of adaptation of the system, we will add a context which is called "control context" to the framework (see (Fig. 2)). This element contains meta-knowledge about query processing and reasoning context and controls their behaviour. The heuristics designed in step (a) can help to develop this control component.

c. A mechanism for managing consistency in reasoning:

MCS can enable integration at a general level between different formalisms. However, due to its distributed nature, information exchange can have unforeseen effects, and in particular cause a system to be inconsistent. To tackle this issue, we aim to analyse inconsistencies in our system, in order to understand where and why such inconsistencies occur, and how they can be managed. This will allow to specify how to handle inconsistencies and to extend the system with a consistency management mechanism. This mechanism can be improved by:

- Extending the definition of equilibrium of MCS for capturing the dynamic property of data streams.
- Exploiting the relationships between SPARQL 1.1. and ASP.
- Imposing different kinds of preferences on the notions of diagnosis and explanation introduced in [7].
- Establishing concrete consistency management procedures for analysis.

5   Initial Investigation

In our initial investigation, we have conducted an experiment for better understanding the nature of the correlation between (event-based) window size and

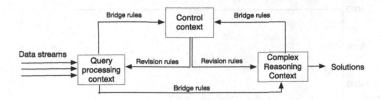

Fig. 2. Conceptual framework

streaming rate (research question a). This experiment mainly focused on the performance of ASP reasoning with different streaming rates. We used the state-of-the-art ASP reasoner clingo 4.3.0[2] and Java 7. The experiment were conducted on a machine running Debian GNU/Linux 6.0.10, containing 8-cores of 2.13 GHz processor and 64 GB RAM.

The ASP rule set we used for this experiment includes 10 rules which have 2 negation-as-failure rules. We executed the ASP reasoner with various amount of input data (events) from 100 to 50000. The trend line of the processing time is illustrated in (Fig. 3). This type of trend line shows that given a unit of time, for some of certain streaming rates, there is a corresponding (event-based) window size which can help to reduce the processing time of the system to less than the unit of time. For example, given a unit of time is 1 s and a streaming rate 20000 events/second, if we feed all 20000 events to the reasoner, it will take 1232 ms for processing. However, if we divide 20000 events into 10 groups of 2000 events and stream these groups to the reasoner, it will take 720 ms for processing whole 20000 events.

Based on the above experiment, we can find an optimal window size for a given streaming rate for a particular ASP program for reducing the processing time of the system. However, this conclusion holds iff there is no dependency between input events for the reasoning component. This assumption can not be applied for many real scenarios and move investigation is required to understand how we can relax this assumption. Therefore, the next steps will be: (i) study how to relax this assumption to still find an optimal window for a given streaming rate, (ii) investigate correlation with different windows and complexity levels of reasoning.

6   Evaluation Plan

An evaluation plan is an important step to observe the efficiency of our stream reasoning approach and compare it with similar solutions. At this very initial stage of my PhD, I foresee to conduct two evaluations:

– **System Evaluation:** In order to evaluate our system, we will provide the formal proof of soundness and completeness of the formalism using MCS,

---

[2] http://sourceforge.net/projects/potassco/files/clingo/4.3.0/.

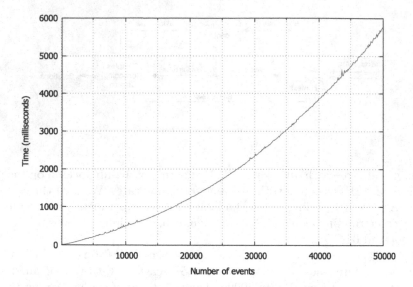

Fig. 3. Offline processing time

including the consistency check for the theoretical evaluation. In the experimental evaluation, we consider these following metrics:

- Complexity, expressed in the number of rules and types of rules within a logic program.
- Dataset size, expressed in the number of facts in the input.
- Latency, as the time required from receiving input data in the stream query processor to providing the output as answer sets.

We will analyse a list of reasoning tasks which are in different complexity levels. This step can be based on real scenarios from the EU project CityPulse [3]. Moreover, we can collect real data streams from this project for designing evaluation. We will conduct experiments with different combinations of heuristics for testing the performance of our system.

– **Comparison:** It is important to provide the baseline for comparing our system with existing systems. We want to set up a benchmark which should be sufficiently generic for a fair comparison. Three mentioned metrics and the benchmark can be used to enable the comparison with other methods.

7   Conclusion

In this paper, we have described the emerging challenges of stream reasoning for the web of data, identified questions in this area we want to tackle, and also proposed a methodology and an approach to target them. We also have presented the initial investigation of the correlation between streaming rate and window-size, and a tentative evaluation plan for testing our approach. The goal of my

---
[3] http://www.ict-citypulse.eu/.

PhD is to enable complex reasoning on data streams so that we can bridge the gap between stream processing and stream reasoning and enable a new market of applications to be built on Semantic Web streams. In relation to this work, we are aware of relate activities on RDF stream processing standards[4] and ASP-based stream reasoning [5,6]. This work is partially supported by "CityPulse: real-time IoT stream processing and large-scale analytics for smart city applications".

References

1. Antoniou, G., Batsakis, S., Tachmazidis, I.: Large-scale reasoning with (semantic) data. In: Proceedings of the 4th International Conference on Web Intelligence, Mining and Semantics (WIMS14), p. 1. ACM (2014)
2. Barbieri, D.F., Braga, D., Ceri, S., Grossniklaus, M.: An execution environment for c-sparql queries. In: Proceedings of the 13th International Conference on Extending Database Technology, pp. 441–452. ACM (2010)
3. Brewka, G., Ellmauthaler, S., Pührer, J.: Multi-context systems for reactive reasoning in dynamic environments. In: Proceedings of the International Workshop on Reactive Concepts in Knowledge Representation (ReactKnow), pp. 23–30 (2014)
4. Della Valle, E., Ceri, S., Barbieri, D.F., Braga, D., Campi, A.: A First Step Towards Stream Reasoning. In: Domingue, J., Fensel, D., Traverso, P. (eds.) FIS 2008. LNCS, vol. 5468, pp. 72–81. Springer, Heidelberg (2009)
5. Della Valle, E., Schlobach, S., Krötzsch, M., Bozzon, A., Ceri, S., Horrocks, I.: Order matters! harnessing a world of orderings for reasoning over massive data. Semant. Web 4(2), 219–231 (2013)
6. Do, T.M., Loke, S.W., Liu, F.: Answer set programming for stream reasoning. In: Butz, C., Lingras, P. (eds.) Canadian AI 2011. LNCS, vol. 6657, pp. 104–109. Springer, Heidelberg (2011)
7. Eiter, T., Fink, M., Schüller, P., Weinzierl, A.: Finding explanations of inconsistency in multi-context systems. Artif. Intell. 216, 233–274 (2014)
8. Eiter, T., Ianni, G., Schindlauer, R., Tompits, H.: DLV-HEX: Dealing with semantic web under answer-set programming. In: Proceedings of ISWC (2005)
9. Gebser, M., Grote, T., Kaminski, R., Obermeier, P., Sabuncu, O., Schaub, T.: Answer set programming for stream reasoning. CoRR, abs/1301.1392 (2013)
10. Le-Phuoc, D., Dao-Tran, M., Xavier Parreira, J., Hauswirth, M.: A native and adaptive approach for unified processing of linked streams and linked data. In: Aroyo, L., Welty, C., Alani, H., Taylor, J., Bernstein, A., Kagal, L., Noy, N., Blomqvist, E. (eds.) ISWC 2011, Part I. LNCS, vol. 7031, pp. 370–388. Springer, Heidelberg (2011)
11. Margara, A., Urbani, J., van Harmelen, F., Bal, H.: Streaming the web: reasoning over dynamic data. Web Semant.: Sci. Serv. Agents on the World Wide Web 25, 24–44 (2014)
12. Mileo, A., Abdelrahman, A., Policarpio, S., Hauswirth, M.: Streamrule: a non-monotonic stream reasoning system for the semantic web. In: Faber, W., Lembo, D. (eds.) RR 2013. LNCS, vol. 7994, pp. 247–252. Springer, Heidelberg (2013)
13. Valle, E.D., Ceri, S., van Harmelen, F., Fensel, D.: It's a streaming world! reasoning upon rapidly changing information. IEEE Intell. Syst. 24(6), 83–89 (2009)

---

[4] https://www.w3.org/.
[5] http://www.kr.tuwien.ac.at/research/projects/dhsr/.
[6] http://potassco.sourceforge.net.

Sequential Decision Making with Medical Interpretation Algorithms in the Semantic Web

Patrick Philipp[(✉)]

Institutes AIFB, KSRI, Karlsruhe Institute of Technology (KIT), Karlsruhe, Germany
patrick.philipp@kit.edu

Abstract. Supporting physicians in their daily work with state-of-the art technology is an important ongoing undertaking. If a radiologist wants to see the tumour region of a headscan of a new patient, a system needs to build a workflow of several interpretation algorithms all processing the image in one or the other way. If a lot of such interpretation algorithms are available, the system needs to select viable candidates, choose the optimal interpretation algorithms for the current patient and finally execute them correctly on the right data. We work towards developing such a system by using RDF and OWL to annotate interpretation algorithms and data, executing interpretation algorithms on a data-driven and declarative basis and integrating so-called meta components. These let us flexibly decide which interpretation algorithms to execute in order to optimally solve the current task.

Keywords: Sequential decision making · Linked APIs · Data-driven and declarative framework

1 Introduction

Supporting physicians in their daily work with state-of-the art technology is an important ongoing undertaking. Technical experts are, therefore, developing interpretation algorithms to, for instance, automatically process medical images. To help radiologists assess the development of tumour patients, a tumour progression mapping (TPM) is beneficial. The brain has to be stripped out of a patient's headscan, registered with respect to prior headscans of the patient and normalized until a final interpretation algorithm can generate a TPM. These interpretation algorithms need to be fed with the correct data and executed in correct order. In addition, there might be several interpretation algorithms available for one subtasks (e.g. for segmenting the brain) which might not all perform 'optimally'. Above all, as the state-of-the-art in image processing evolves, new interpretation algorithms might need to be taken into account for this task.

Besides TPM generation, there are numerous other complex tasks to support physicians. We divide them into pre-surgical, intra-surgical and post-surgical tasks and give an abstract and incomplete overview in Table 1.

These tasks are complex because they either need rich function classes to solve them, comprise numerous subtasks or both. Interpretation algorithms, such

© Springer International Publishing Switzerland 2015
F. Gandon et al. (Eds.): ESWC 2015, LNCS 9088, pp. 760–771, 2015.
DOI: 10.1007/978-3-319-18818-8_49

Table 1. Complex medical task classification.

Pre-surgical	Intra-surgical	Post-surgical
Diagnosis	Interpreting sensor outputs	Health stability estimation
Treatment proposition	Risk analysis	Further treatment proposition

as image processors, might be important in all three phases. We work towards a system able to solve numerous different complex tasks by choosing among a large pool of interpretation algorithms. We, therefore, propose a semantic framework for sequential decision making. Interpretation algorithms are annotated with semantic concepts formalized in RDF and OWL, wrapped as Linked APIs and integrated into a data-driven, declarative workflow. We use so-called *meta components* to choose among interpretation algorithms for a given task. A central open problem deals with how and to what degree we can leverage semantic descriptions for optimally solving complex tasks.

2 State of the Art

In this section, we give an overview of research related to our setting. The section is divided into two parts. First, we depict research about (semantic-) workflow systems, as we need to enable workflows of interpretation algorithms to solve complex tasks. The second part deals with decision making within these workflows. We have to find eligible interpretation algorithms to reach a goal and then choose the optimal candidate.

2.1 Workflow Systems

The work centered around semantic workflows [5] aims to enable the automatic composition of components in large-scale distributed environments. Generic semantic descriptions support combining algorithms and enable formalizing ensembles of learners. Therefore, conditions and constraints need to be specified. The framework also automatically matches components and data sources based on user requests.

Taverna [8] is a another scientific workflow system supporting process prototyping by creating generic service interfaces and thus easing the integration of new components. Semantic descriptions are being used to better capture the view of the scientists. Taverna is able to integrate data from distributed sources and automate the workflow creation process for users.

Wood et al. [16] create abstract workflows as domain models which are formalized using OWL and enable dynamic instantiation of real processes. These models can the be automatically converted into more specific workflows resulting in OWL individuals. The components can be reused in another context or process, and one can share abstract representations across the Web through OWL classes.

All of the above approaches develop abstractions of interfaces between workflow components in terms of meta data. Ontologies and taxonomies are, therefore, used to represent central structures for workflows. While some approaches use OWL to generate meta-data, we try to model a low amount of axioms and keep the approach flexible. We use this flexibility and incorporate decision making strategies, as will be discussed in the subsequent section.

2.2 Decision Making for Workflows

In our setting, we need to decide among $2, \ldots, n$ interpretation algorithms for a subtask and build a workflow of $1, \ldots, m$ interpretation algorithms to solve a complex task. We, therefore, distinguish between *meta learning* and *planning* approaches from the literature and will further classify our setting in Sect. 3.

Planning. Automatic orchestration of analytical workflows has been studied by Beygelzimer et al. [2]. The system essentially uses a planner, a leaner and a large (structured-) knowledge base to solve complex tasks. A large amount of potential workflows are taken into account to answer a user specified query with the optimal choice. The decision process comprises complex learning and planning approaches, and entails exploring large possible feature spaces. Lastly, atomic actions are lifted with semantic annotations to better adapt to user queries. Although our goal equals automatically orchestrating workflows, we also want to enable have multiple possibly situation-dependent learners, as there might not be a generic solution.

Markov Decision Processes (MDP) are often employed to learn workflows. Applications to the health care sector comprise the work of Sahba et al. [11]. They use MDPs to model segmentation algorithms for transrectal ultrasound images and to optimize the prevalent parameters. Besides, Gao et al. [3] used MDPs to enable the composition of web services described with Web Service Definition Language (WSDL). The goal is to optimize decisions in terms of web service availability and runtime. We, in contrast, deal with possibly heterogeneous interpretation algorithms in one single workflow. We need to capture important features to optimally choose them in correct situations. This also distinguishes our work from optimizing for availability or runtime.

Meta Learning. Besides optimizing workflows, one can use ensemble learning strategies to choose between two competing candidate interpretation algorithms. A prominent strategy is the multiplicative weights method [1] (e.g. used in boosting). Here, candidates are combined based on their performance on training sets. The method was already applied to decision trees with patient factors (e.g. by Moon et al. [7]) to combine predictions. We, however, focus on the interplay of such strategies with available semantics for interpretation algorithms and data. We, thus, want to enable to use such sophisticated ensemble learners within our framework if they are well-suited for the current (sub-) task.

3 Problem Statement and Contributions

Let X be the set of all tasks, Y the set of all abstract tasks and A the set of all available interpretation algorithms. Let further S be the set of *abstract states* defined by a subset of objects O, literals L and relations R. We denote, for simplicity, F_{s_k} as the set of features of a state s_k (i.e. a subset of $O \times R \times O$ and $O \times R \times L$). A grounded state $g(s_k)$ depicts an instance of s_k in nature. The set A_{s_k} defines the subset of applicable interpretation algorithms in s_k which is known to some degree. We, thus, assume that an interpretation algorithm $a_i \in A$ can be defined by a subset of features of F in a similar way as states $s_k \in S$. Knowing A_{s_k} depends on how we define features $f \in F$ for s_k and a_i. Let $T(s, a, s')$ be the transition function for some state s and interpretation algorithm a ending in s'. Our knowledge of $T(s, a, s')$, again, depends on the available features for s, a and s'. $T(g(s), a, g(s'))$ is not known and requires further knowledge to be approximated. A task $x(g(s_k), (s_K))$ is a function defined on a grounded start state $g(s_k)$ and an abstract goal state s_K. Reaching an unknown grounded goal state $g(s_K)$ takes 1 to n state transitions $(g(s), a, g(s'))$. To solve $x(g(s_k), (s_K))$, we need to find a sequence of interpretation algorithms a_i ending in the unknown grounded goal state $g(s_K)$ with high probability. An abstract task $y(g(s_k), (s_K))$ is defined similarly and we need to find any sequence $a_1, \ldots, a_n$ to get from $g(s_k)$ to s_K. Our setting is much related to a Markov Decision Process (MDP) (S, A, T, R, γ) with R, in addition, being the reward function for state, interpretation algorithm pairs (s, a) and γ the discount factor. The latter regulates the influence of future interpretation algorithms a_i taken in future steps s_k on the value estimations of current states and actions. Defining $R(s, a)$ for $x(g(s_k), (s_K))$ is not straightforward as $g(s_K)$ is unknown. An absorbing state with $R(s_k, a_i) = 0$ can be artificially modelled to denote the goal s_K.

We define **abstract planning** as trying to solve an *abstract task* $y(g(s_k), (s_K))$. Here, we ignore that multiple interpretation algorithms a_i might be available for s_k. **Meta learning** considers $|A_{s_k}| > 1$ and tries to solve a subtask $x_i(g(s_k), s_K)$ to find the optimal a_i for $g(s_k)$. **Planning** deals with solving $x(g(s_k), s_K)$ with known T and R, and planning-related **learning** considers T, R unknown and tries to approximate them (as, for instance, is done in model-based reinforcement learning).

We disclosed the following **challenges** for sequential decision making with medical interpretation algorithms:

(a) Interpretation algorithm might be developed by different researchers from different institutions. We need a common (meta-) representation to integrate the interpretation algorithms and the data they consume.

(b) Interpretation algorithms need to be quickly and concurrently accessible if numerous complex tasks have to be solved for different endusers.

(c) We need to reduce the effort to manually define procedures to solve complex tasks in order to quickly integrate new interpretation algorithms and use them if they perform better.

(d) To handle heterogeneous and competing interpretation algorithms, we need meta components with potentially different (degrees of-) specialisation (e.g. some might only deal with continuous outcomes, others with discrete ones; some might leverage groundings, others abstract levels).

(e) It is unclear which information we need to incorporate into our decision making. Investigating the connection between (abstract-) planning and (meta-) learning problems and (meta-) representations of interpretation algorithms is, thus, important.

(f) For physicians to use the system, they have to trust the proposed solutions.

Based on these challenges, we see the following **contributions** of our work:

(i) We formalize the problem setting and introduce a framework for interpretation algorithms and meta components to automatically solve complex medical tasks.

(ii) We develop meta components to conduct abstract planning and meta learning, and disclose further challenges for planning and planning-related learning.

(iii) We are analysing the interplay between semantics (for meta components, interpretation algorithms and data) and added value for solving complex medical tasks.

(iv) We started to investigate the issue of 'trust' and try to give accurate confidence estimates for solutions.

4   Research Methodology and Approach

An overview of our approach is illustrated in Fig. 1. Based on this abstract representation of our ideas, we will focus on three different parts in this section. We, first, describe our research methodology for developing data-driven, declarative workflows to enable sequential decision making for complex medical tasks by explaining the illustrated components. We, then, dwell on meta component scenarios in part two and three - (abstract-) planning and (meta-) learning - and explain their interfaces within the framework.

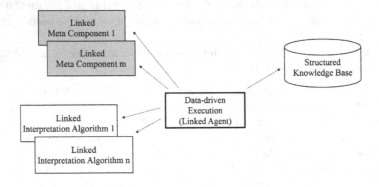

Fig. 1. A schematic overview of our approach.

4.1   Data-Driven, Declarative Workflows

To integrate interpretation algorithms and make them easily accessible, we build on Linked APIs [12] and Linked Data-Fu [13]. These concepts help us to tackle challenges (a) and (b), and build a foundation for challenge (c).

Linked APIs describe a class of RESTful services which are extended with descriptions inspired by the Semantic Web. In our approach, we define important information about interpretation algorithms in terms of a description based on RDF and OWL, and publish RDF wrappers of interpretation algorithms persistently on the Web. We will refer to them as *Linked interpretation algorithms*. To have a central and controlled vocabulary, we developed ontologies for both data types and interpretation algorithms and are working on formalizing evaluation metrics. Besides non-functional requirements (e.g. contributors, textual descriptions or example requests and responses), we model functional aspects of the interpretation algorithms. Here, it remains open how to model the inputs and outputs, and their respective pre- and postconditions to optimally leverage interpretation algorithms for (abstract-) planning and (meta-) learning (challenge (d), see Sect. 6 for a short discussion).

To execute Linked interpretation algorithms, we use the Linked Data-Fu Engine [14]. It enables virtual data integration of distributed data sources to properly execute Linked interpretation algorithms. This is crucial as we have different kinds of information/knowledge relevant for solving complex tasks. **Knowledge from experts** helps estimating the interpretation algorithms' performances on data sets. It highly influences the initial belief about the applicability of interpretation algorithms. As the system gathers more evidence, beliefs might be challenged. **Evidence-based knowledge from other sources** (i.e. other researchers and published papers) essentially comprises domain knowledge as well, but might be subjective and hard to validate. **Statistics-based knowledge** is gathered by testing the interpretation algorithms on training samples and keeping track of their performances on new data.

We automatically generate rules for Linked Data-Fu based on preconditions of interpretation algorithms. The term *Linked agent* is used to denote a Linked Data-Fu instance with access to Linked interpretation algorithms, to a structured (and distributed-) knowledge base and to *meta components*. The latter extend the data-driven, declarative workflows with strategies (of arbitrary complexity) to choose Linked interpretation algorithms for solving a complex task. The Linked agent can, then, easily execute the proper worfklows based on a subset of chosen Linked interpretation algorithms. Figure 2 visualizes the interactions of the Linked agent for using abstract planning and meta learning components. The meta components are only called if the current state s_k matches their preconditions, which is one step towards solving challenge (d). The next section deals with our endeavours to develop such meta components and to extend them to the pure planning and learning scenarios.

4.2   (Abstract-) Planning and Planning-Related Learning

As defined in Sect. 3, we are trying to solve an abstract task $y(g(s_k), (s_K))$ with abstract planning. We, therefore, use the MDP formulation and only evaluate

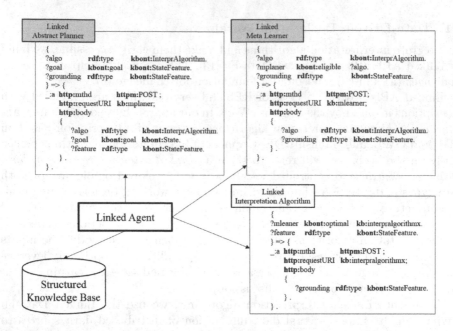

Fig. 2. Components of the framework with general rules.

Linked interpretation algorithms on a concept level based on the grounded start state $g(s_k)$. We model a finite MDP by using the pre- and postconditions of Linked interpretation algorithms as states s_k with local scopes, i.e. we only consider preconditions of states s_k for transitions, and assume to know the state features F_{s_k}. The transition probabilities T are defined in Eq. 1 and make up a $S \times (A+1) \times S$ matrix by adding a dummy interpretation algorithm pointing to the goal state, when the latter was reached. The reward function R is a $S \times (A+1)$ matrix and shifts all rewards to the dummy interpretation algorithm (see Eq. 2). By using any strategy to solve the MDP (e.g. value iteration), we find eligible Linked interpretation algorithms to solve the task.

$$T(s, a, s') = \begin{cases} t_{sas'} = \frac{1}{|A_{s_k}|} & \exists(s, a, s') \text{ based on } F_s \text{ and } F_{s'} \\ t_{sas'} = 0 & \text{otherwise} \end{cases} \tag{1}$$

$$R(s, a) = \begin{cases} r_{sa} = 1 & \text{if } a \text{ equals dummy algorithm and } s \text{ equals goal} \\ r_{sa} = 0 & \text{otherwise} \end{cases} \tag{2}$$

Based on this first simple case, we can model and solve more complex workflows with unsure or stochastic transitions between states and might be able to tackle the case where pre- and postconditions do not exactly match. However, besides abstract tasks, we need to solve $x(g(s_k), (s_K))$ based on the grounded states $g(s_k)$ resulting from executing Linked interpretation algorithms in a workflow. This is a different scenario, as we have to assess the quality of results in terms of different evaluation criteria. Moreover, T and R might be unknown for numerous states and Linked interpretation algorithms, and we need to learn them with planning-related learning approaches. See Sect. 6 for our next steps towards solving $x(g(s_k), (s_K))$.

4.3   Meta Learning

In the meta learning setting, we try to solve $x_i(g(s_k), s_K))$. We approach this problem setting by investigating ensemble learning strategies and extend them by incorporating semantics. A first meta learner might assess the expected performance of a Linked interpretation algorithm for classification based on training samples close to the grounded state $g(s_k)$. We train the Linked interpretation algorithms (if possible in terms of their preconditions) on a subset of samples and predict on the remaining ones (i.e. we cross-validate). The heuristic repeats the process until all training samples have been assessed and derives the probability for a new grounded state $g(s_k)$ based on its performance on similar instances. We can use any similarity function to derive these similar instances (i.e. nearest neighbours). The heuristic is summarized in Algorithm 1.

Algorithm 1. Majority Heuristic given Linked interpretation algorithms L, number of neighbours to consider k, state s_k, cut t

---
1: $N \leftarrow$ nearestNeighbours($g(s_k)$, k)
2: $T \leftarrow$ set of training samples cut into t subsets
3: **for all** $t \in T$ **do**
4:     **for all** $l \in L$ **do**
5:         train(l, T without t) //if possible
6:         updatePerformanceTable(l, t)
7: **for all** $l \in L$ **do**
8:     $w_l \leftarrow$ estimatePerformance(l, N)
9: **for all** $p \in P$ **do**
10:    $H(p) \leftarrow \sum_{l \in L} w_l \mathbf{1}[h_l(g(s_k)) = p]$
11: $h^* \leftarrow \arg\max_{p \in P} H(p)$
12: **return** h^*

---

5   Preliminary Results

We applied the approach to two medical scenarios - image processing for tumour progression mappings (TPM) and sensor interpretation to recognize surgical phases - and evaluated them in terms of correctness, time consumption and effect of meta components. Figure 3 illustrates the shared architecture comprising a structured knowledge base integrated via a Semantic MediaWiki (SMW), several Linked interpretation algorithms, the Linked agent and two Linked meta components.

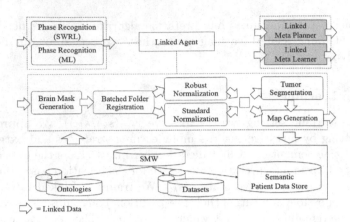

Fig. 3. The semantic framework for medical sequential decision making (extended based on [9]).

5.1   Tumour Progression Mapping and Abstract Planning

As discussed in Sect. 1, a TPM supports radiologists in assessing the development of a patient when treated for brain tumours. The available Linked interpretation algorithm are listed in Fig. 3. Listing 1.1 comprises the preconditions to generate a brain mask, which takes as input a headscan and two reference images. The image ontology is available in the knowledge base (**kbont** namespace). We evaluated the correct functioning and time consumption in [4,10], and modelled the scenario as finite MDP, as explained in Sect. 4.2. We, therefore, added Linked interpretation algorithms for sensor interpretation to test if only goal-oriented Linked interpretation algorithms were chosen. The MDP consisted of 9 states according to possible transitions we derived based on modelled pre- and postconditions of the interpretation algorithms. When applying value iteration to solve the MDP with T, R following Eqs. 1 and 2, we derived $V = < 0.32805. 0.3645, 0.405. 0.405, 0.45, 0.45, 1.00, 0, 0 >$ after 6 iterations with discount factor 0.9. The starting state was a grounding for 'Brain Mask Generation' and the goal state was the generated TPM. V gives us the estimated values of states s_k and assigns 0 to states related to sensor interpreters. We, thus, do not have to execute them to reach the goal state 'TPM'.

```
?headscan            rdf:type       kbont:Headscan;
                     dc:format      "image/nrrd".

?brainAtlasImage     rdf:type       kbont:BrainAtlasImage;
                     dc:format      "image/mha".

?brainAtlasMask      rdf:type       kbont:BrainAtlasMask;
                     dc:format      "image/mha".
```

Listing 1.1. Preconditions of the brain mask generation step (namespaces are omitted)

5.2   Surgical Phase Recognition and Meta Learning

In surgical phase recognition, one tries to predict the phase of the ongoing surgery based on sensor outputs. Based on this phase, one could visualize risk structures and, thereby, support the surgeon. We wrapped two phase recognizers as Linked interpretation algorithms. 'SWRL' uses rules formalized with the Semantic Web Rule Language to predict the phase, and 'ML' uses machine-learning and can be trained with annotated surgeries. We evaluated the correct functioning and time consumption in [9] and integrated the meta learning heuristic (see Algorithm 1) into the architecture. Table 2 summarizes the results. The meta learner was able to provide stable and sometimes better results than the single Linked interpretation algorithms.

Table 2. Performance evaluation of phase recognition algorithms and meta learner in 5 different surgeries.

Algorithm	Surgery 1	Surgery 2	Surgery 3	Surgery 4	Surgery 5
ML–based	0.91	0.66	0.90	0.45	0.64
SWRL	0.93	0.78	0.89	0.81	0.72
Linked meta learner	0.93	0.78	0.92	0.78	0.72

6   Evaluation Plan

Our research approach and preliminary results showed that our framework is able to solve first complex tasks. The next step to systematically approach challenge (e) is to explore the effect of feature selection on the meta leaning case and the planning-related learning case. We, here, study the interplay between semantics and meta components to be able to assess how fine-grained the pre- and postconditions for Linked interpretation algorithms need to be. Hence, we need to find out how much semantics we need to confidently learn transition probabilities $T(s, a, s')$ and the rewards $R(s, a)$ associated with taking interpretation algorithm a in state s.

We, also, want to better leverage semantics in the (abstract-) planning case. We only modelled a flat image structure for the TPM scenario which restricts generalization and flexibility. We will, therefore, investigate relational MDPs [15] and try to better capture the semantics of Linked interpretation algorithms when modelling the MDP. This might enable to better generalize to new unknown states s_k if their features F_{s_k} have been sufficiently explored before. Generalization, in turn, helps to solve the pure planning case $x(g(s_k), g(s_K))$.

We will focus on giving confidence estimates for the performance of meta components on new states s_k. We aim to extend our abstract planning (and pure planning-) approach with learners of the 'Knows what it knows' (KWIK) framework [6] and give theoretical justifications for the framework's performance (challenge (f)).

7   Conclusions

Solving complex tasks with heterogeneous Linked interpretation algorithms depicts a diverse problem setting and imposes interesting challenges. The medical domain exhibits sufficient complexity for investigating this problem and provides scenarios for sequential decision making under uncertainty. We, first, formalized the setting and disclosed the necessity of semantics, a data-driven and declarative execution and meta components. We, then, proposed a framework which enables to easily incorporate Linked meta components as well as new Linked interpretation algorithms, and to automatically solve complex tasks (contribution (i)). Lastly, we presented first conceptual and practical results for the meta learning and abstract planning cases (contribution (ii)). We work towards extending the capabilities of the meta components and especially investigate their interplay with semantics (longterm contribution (iii)). As trust is an important issue for endusers of the framework, we aim to give exact and transparent confidence estimates for the generated solutions (longterm contribution (iv)).

References

1. Arora, S., Hazan, E., Kale, S.: The multiplicative weights update method: a meta-algorithm and applications. Theor. Comput. **8**(1), 121–164 (2012)
2. Beygelzimer, A., Riabov, A., Sow, D., Turaga, D., Udrea, O.: Big data exploration via automated orchestration of analytic workflows. In: ICAC, pp. 153–158. USENIX, San Jose (2013)
3. Gao, A., Yang, D., Tang, S., Zhang, M.: Web service composition using markov decision processes. In: Fan, W., Wu, Z., Yang, J. (eds.) WAIM 2005. LNCS, vol. 3739, pp. 308–319. Springer, Heidelberg (2005)
4. Gemmeke, P., Maleshkova, M., Philipp, P., Götz, M., Weber, C., Kämpgen, B.: Using linked data and web apis for automating the pre-processing of medical images. In: COLD (ISWC) (2014)
5. Gil, Y., Gonzalez-Calero, P., Kim, J., Moody, J., Ratnakar, V.: A semantic framework for automatic generation of computational workflows using distributed data and component catalogues. Exp. Theor. AI **23**(4), 389–467 (2011)
6. Li, L., Littman, M., Walsh, T., Strehl, A.: Knows what it knows: a framework for self-aware learning. ML **82**(3), 399–443 (2011)
7. Moon, H., Ahn, H., Kodell, R., Baek, S., Lin, C., Chen, J.: Ensemble methods for classification of patients for personalized medicine with high-dimensional data. AI Med. **41**(3), 197–207 (2007)
8. Oinn, T., Greenwood, M., Addis, M., Alpdemir, M., Ferris, J., Glover, K., Goble, C., Goderis, A., Hull, D., Marvin, D., Li, P., Lord, P., Pocock, M., Senger, M., Stevens, R., Wipat, A., Wroe, C.: Taverna: Lessons in creating a workflow environment for the life sciences: research articles. Concurr. Comput. Pract. Exper. **18**(10), 1067–1100 (2006)
9. Philipp, P., Katic, D., Maleshkova, M., Rettinger, A., Speidel, S., Wekerle, A., Kämpgen, B., Kenngott, H., Studer, R., Dillmann, R., Müller, B.: Towards cognitive pipelines of medical assistance algorithms. In: CARS (2015)

10. Philipp, P., Maleshkova, M., Götz, M., Weber, C., Kämpgen, B., Zelzer, S., Maier-Hein, K., Klauß, M., Rettinger, A.: Automatisierung von vorverarbeitungsschritten für medizinische bilddaten mit semantischen technologien. In: BVM, pp. 263–268. Springer (2015)
11. Sahba, F., Tizhoosh, H., Salama, M.: Application of reinforcement learning for segmentation of transrectal ultrasound images. BMC Med. Imaging **8**(1), 8 (2008)
12. Speiser, S., Harth, A.: Integrating linked data and services with linked data services. In: Antoniou, G., Grobelnik, M., Simperl, E., Parsia, B., Plexousakis, D., De Leenheer, P., Pan, J. (eds.) ESWC 2011, Part I. LNCS, vol. 6643, pp. 170–184. Springer, Heidelberg (2011)
13. Stadtmüller, S., Norton, B.: Scalable discovery of linked apis. Metadata Semant. Ontol. **8**(2), 95–105 (2013)
14. Stadtmüller, S., Speiser, S., Harth, A., Studer, R.: Data-fu: a language and an interpreter for interaction with read/write linked data. In: WWW, pp. 1225–1236 (2013)
15. van Otterlo, M.: The logic of adaptive behavior: knowledge representation and algorithms for adaptive sequential decision making under uncertainty in first-order and relational domains, vol. 192. Ios Press (2009)
16. Wood, I., Vandervalk, B., McCarthy, L., Wilkinson, M.D.: OWL-DL domainmodels as abstract workflows. In: Margaria, T., Steffen, B. (eds.) ISoLA 2012, Part II. LNCS, vol. 7610, pp. 56–66. Springer, Heidelberg (2012)

Towards Linked Open Data Enabled Data Mining

Strategies for Feature Generation, Propositionalization, Selection, and Consolidation

Petar Ristoski[(✉)]

University of Mannheim, Mannheim, Germany
petar.ristoski@informatik.uni-mannheim.de

Abstract. Background knowledge from Linked Open Data sources can be used to improve the results of a data mining problem at hand: predictive models can become more accurate, and descriptive models can reveal more interesting findings. However, collecting and integrating background knowledge is a tedious manual work. In this paper we propose a set of desiderata, and identify the challenges for developing a framework for unsupervised generation of data mining features from Linked Data.

Keywords: Linked Open Data · Data mining · Feature generation

1 Introduction

Knowledge discovery is defined as "a non-trivial process of identifying valid, novel, potentially useful, and ultimately understandable patterns in data" [9]. As such, data mining and knowledge discovery are typically considered knowledge intensive tasks. Thus, knowledge plays a crucial role here. Knowledge can be (a) in the primary data itself, (b) in external data, which has to be included with the problem first, or (c) in the data analyst's mind only.

The latter two cases are interesting opportunities to enhance the value of the knowledge discovery processes. Consider the following case: a dataset consists of countries in Europe and some economic and social indicators. An analyst dealing with such data on a regular basis will know that some of the countries are part of the European Union, while others are not. Thus, she may add an additional variable EU_Member to the dataset, which may lead to new insights (e.g., certain patterns holding for EU member states only).

In that example, knowledge has been added to the data from the analyst's mind, but it might equally well have been contained in some exterior source of knowledge. However, collecting and integrating large amounts of background knowledge can be a labor intensive task. Moreover, in most cases, only a small fraction of that background knowledge will be actually used in the data mining model itself, but it is hard to pinpoint the relevant parts in advance. Furthermore, variables involved in unexpected findings are easily overseen, since assumptions

F. Gandon et al. (Eds.): ESWC 2015, LNCS 9088, pp. 772–782, 2015.
DOI: 10.1007/978-3-319-18818-8_50

about interrelations in the application domain lead the user when selecting additional attributes, i.e., she will be subject to a selection bias. To overcome these shortcomings, Linked Open Data represents a valuable source of background knowledge.

Linked Open Data (LOD) is an open, interlinked collection of datasets in machine-interpretable form, built on W3C standards as RDF[1], and SPARQL[2]. Currently the LOD cloud consist of about $1,000$ datasets covering various domains [1,25], making it a valuable source for background knowledge in data mining.

Figure 1 gives an overview of a general LOD-enabled knowledge discovery process. Given a set of local data (such as a relational database), the first step is to link the data to the corresponding LOD concepts from the chosen LOD dataset. After the links are set, outgoing links to external LOD datasets can be explored. In the next step, various techniques for data consolidation and cleansing are applied. Next, transformations

link   combine   cleanse   transform   analyze   interpret

Fig. 1. LOD-enabled knowledge discovery process

on the collected data need to be performed in order to represent the data in a way that it can be processed with any arbitrary data analysis algorithms. After the data transformation is done, a suitable data mining algorithm is applied on the data. In the final step, the results of the data mining process are presented to the user.

In this proposal we focus on the second, third and fourth step of the LOD-enabled knowledge discovery pipeline. Moreover, we propose a framework for automated unsupervised generation of data mining features from LOD. Such a framework should be able to find useful and relevant data mining features, which can be used in any arbitrary predictive or descriptive data mining model, aiming to increase the model's performances.

2   Problem Statement and Contributions

To develop a scalable framework for unsupervised generation of data mining features from LOD, we will need to address the following working domains:

Feature Generation. Most data mining algorithms work with a propositional *feature vector* representation of the data, i.e., each instance is represented as a vector of features $\langle f_1, f_2, ..., f_n \rangle$, where the features are either binary (i.e., $f_i \in \{true, false\}$), numerical (i.e., $f_i \in \mathbb{R}$), or nominal (i.e., $f_i \in S$, where S is a finite set of symbols). Linked Open Data, however, comes in the form of *graphs*, connecting resources with types and relations, backed by a schema or ontology.

---

[1] W3C. RDF. http://www.w3.org/TR/2004/REC-rdf-concepts-20040210/, 2004.

[2] W3C. SPARQL Query Language for RDF. http://www.w3.org/TR/rdf-sparql-query/, 2008.

Thus, for accessing LOD with existing data mining tools, transformations have to be performed, which create propositional features from the graphs in LOD, i.e., a process called *propositionalization* [14].

Defining an appropriate set of features for a data mining problem at hand is still much of an art. However, it is also a step of key importance for the successful use of data mining. Therefore, we define requirements the feature generation framework needs to fulfill:

(i) Given a data mining task, and an input data mining dataset, with the corresponding $1 : 1$ or $1 : m$ (common in text mining) mappings of the local instances to LOD entities, the framework should be able to generate features from any given LOD source that are highly relevant for the given data mining task, where the task is predictive or descriptive.

(ii) Beside setting basic parameters, the feature generation should be performed without user interaction, i.e., unsupervised and automated.

(iii) The generated feature set should be optimal, i.e., the goal is to generate minimal feature set that maximizes the learning model's performances, and minimizes the cost of the feature generation process itself. For creating such optimal feature set, two paradigms exist: *minimal representation*, and *maximal between-class separability*. The minimal representation implies that the instances in the input dataset should be represented with as simple feature set as possible that fully describes all target concepts, e.g., Occam's razor approach. To provide a good generalization such approaches should appropriately address the *bias-variance dilemma*, i.e., the generated features should be general enough to keep the variance low, but relevant enough to keep the bias low. The second paradigm, mainly applicable in classifiers design, relates to generating feature set that guarantees *maximal between-class separability* for a given data set, and thus help building better learning models.

(iv) Although the input dataset contains only links to one LOD dataset, the framework should be able to find useful features from multiple LOD sources by exploring links (such as *owl:sameAs*).

(v) When designing such a framework, scalability should be taken in mind, as the size of many LOD datasets is rather large, e.g., DBpedia 2014[3] contains about 3 billion triples.

(vi) The framework should comply with various standards for publishing and consuming LOD, e.g., the data can be served via SPARQL endpoint, RDF dumps, or URI dereferencing.

Propositionalization Strategies. When generating data mining features from graph-based data, different propositionalization strategies can be used. For example, the standard binary or numerical representation can be used, or more sophisticated representation strategies that use some graph characteristics might be introduced. Our hypothesis is that the strategy of creating features may have an influence on the data mining result. For example, proximity-based algorithms like k-NN will behave differently depending on the strategy used to create numerical features, as the strategy has a direct influence on most distance functions.

---

[3] http://dbpedia.org/About.

Feature Selection. Although the optimal feature generation approach would not require the use of feature selection step afterwards, in some cases the feature selection step might be desirable. For example, the complexity of the feature generation approach can be reduced by allowing it to generate features with more flexible constraints, which will be later processed by the feature selection algorithm. In feature vectors generated from LOD we can often observe relations between the features, which in most of the cases are explicitly expressed in the LOD schema, or can be inferred using appropriate reasoning approaches. If those relations are not properly explored during the feature generation step, it can be done in the feature selection step to reduce the feature space, which will allow us to remove correlated, contradictory, and repetitive features.

Feature Consolidation. When creating features from multiple LOD sources, often a single semantic feature can be found in multiple LOD source represented with different properties. For example, the area of a country in DBpedia is represented with the property *db:areaTotal*, while in YAGO[4] using the property *yago:hasArea*. The problem of aligning properties, as well as instances and classes, in ontologies is addressed by *ontology matching* techniques [7]. Using such techniques, we can find correspondences between features in multiple LOD sources, which then can be fused into a single feature using data fusion techniques [2]. Such a fusion can provide a feature that would mitigate missing values and single errors for individual sources, leading to only one high-value feature.

The initial contributions of the proposal can be summarized as follows: (i) A framework for automated unsupervised generation of data mining features from LOD, from single or (ii) multiple LOD sources. (iii) Novel propositionalization strategies for generating features from LOD, and analysis on their effect on the performances of the data mining models. (iv) Novel feature selection and consolidation methodologies that can be applied on features generated from LOD.

3   State of the Art

Feature Generation. In the recent past, a few approaches for generating data mining features from Linked Open Data have been proposed. Many of those approaches are supervised, i.e., they let the user formulate SPARQL queries, and a fully automatic feature generation is not possible. LiDDM [12] is an integrated system for data mining on the semantic web, allowing the users to declare SPARQL queries for retrieving features from LOD that can be used in different machine learning techniques. Similar approach has been used in the RapidMiner[5] semweb plugin [13], which preprocesses RDF data in a way that it can be further processed directly in RapidMiner. Cheng et al. [4] proposes an approach for automated feature generation after the user has specified the type of features. To do so, similar like the previous approaches, the users have to specify the SPARQL query, which makes this approach supervised rather than unsupervised.

---

[4] www.mpi-inf.mpg.de/yago-naga/yago.
[5] http://www.rapidminer.com/.

Mynarz et al. [17] have considered using user specified SPARQL queries in combination with SPARQL aggregates.

FeGeLOD [18] is the first fully automatic unsupervised approach for enriching data with features that are derived from LOD. In this work six different unsupervised feature generation strategies are proposed, by exploring specific or generic relations.

A similar problem is handled by *Kernel functions*, which compute the distance between two data instances, by counting common substructures in the graphs of the instances, i.e. walks, paths and threes. In the past, many graph kernels have been proposed that are tailored towards specific application [10], or towards specific semantic representation [8]. Only several approaches are general enough to be applied on any given RDF data, regardless the data mining task. Lösch et al. [15] introduce two general RDF graph kernels, based on intersection graphs and intersection trees. Later, the intersection tree path kernel was simplified by Vries et al. [6]. In another work, Vries et al. [5] introduce an approximation of the state-of-the-art Weisfeiler-Lehman graph kernel algorithm aimed at improving the computation time of the kernel when applied to RDF.

Furthermore, Tiddi et al. [27] introduced the *Dedalo* framework that traverses LOD to find commonalities that form explanations for items of a cluster. Given a supervised data mining task, such an approach could be easily adapted and used as feature generation approach.

Propositionalization Strategies. Even though several approaches have been proposed for creating propositional features from LOD, usually the resulting features are binary, or numerical aggregates using SPARQL COUNT constructs. Furthermore, none of them provide evaluation of the model performances when using different propositionalization strategies.

Feature Selection. Feature selection is a very important and well studied problem in the literature [3]. The objective is to identify features that are correlated with or predictive of the class label. Standard feature selection methods tend to select the features that have the highest relevance score without exploiting the semantic relations between the features in the feature space. Therefore, such methods are not appropriate to be applied on feature sets generated from LOD.

While there are a lot of state-of-the-art approaches for feature selection in a standard feature space [3], only few approaches for feature selection in a feature space extracted from structured knowledge bases are proposed in the literature. Jeong et al. [11] propose the *TSEL* method using a semantic hierarchy of features based on WordNet relations. The algorithm tries to find the most representative and most effective features from the complete feature space, based on the *lift* measure, and χ^2. Wang et al. [28] propose an k-NN based *bottom-up hill climbing* search algorithm to find an optimal subset of concepts for document representation. Lu et al. [16] describe a *greedy top-down* search strategy, based on the nodes' information gain ratio, trying to select a mixture of concepts from different levels of the hierarchy.

Feature Consolidation. To the best of our knowledge, there is no proposed approach in the literature for generating and consolidating data mining features from multiple LOD sources.

4 Research Methodology and Approach

Feature Generation. So far, we have implemented and extended the approaches initially presented in the FeGeLOD system [18]. For a given input dataset containing the entities and the corresponding LOD entity URIs, the following strategies for feature generation may be used: (i) Generating feature for each direct data property of an entity in the dataset. (ii) Features for specific relations of an entity, e.g. *dcterms:subject* in DBpedia. This approach allows to further explore the relation to a user specified length, e.g., one can follow the *skos:broader* relation for an already extracted *dcterms:subject* from DBpedia. (iii) Features for each incoming or outgoing relation of an entity. (iv) Feature for each incoming or outgoing relation of an entity including the value of the relation. (v) Feature for each incoming or outgoing relation of an entity, including the related types, i.e., they are concerned with qualified relations

Furthermore, we implemented approaches for generating features based on graph sub-structures using graph kernels: the *Weisfeiler-Lehman Kernel* [5], and the *Intersection Tree Path Kernel* [6,15].

These approaches are rather trivial and simplistic. As shown in the evaluation, using these approaches we are able to generate useful feature vectors that improve the performances of the learning model in unsupervised environment. However, the generated feature vectors are rather large and contain many irrelevant features.

Propositionalization Strategies. In this phase we have only considered some of the trivial propositionalization strategies: (i) *Binary*, indicating the presence of a given feature. (ii) *Count*, specifying the exact number of appearances of the feature. (iii) *Relative Count*, specifying the relative number of appearances of the feature. (iv) *TF-IDF*, calculated using the standard TF-IDF equation.

More sophisticated propositionalization strategies might be developed. For example, the target variable from the local dataset can be used for developing supervised weighting approaches, as used in some text mining application. Furthermore, we can use the graph properties for calculating feature weights, e.g., the fan-in and fan-out values of the graph nodes can give a better representation of the popularity of the resources included in the features, which might be a good indicator of the feature's relevance for the data mining task. More sophisticated popularity scores can be calculated using some of the standard graph ranking algorithms, e.g., PageRank and HITS.

Feature Selection. We have introduced an approach [24] that exploits hierarchies for feature selection in combination with standard metrics, such as *information gain* and *correlation*. The core idea of the approach is to identify features with similar relevance, and select the most valuable abstract features, i.e. features from as high as possible levels of the hierarchy, without losing predictive power. To measure the similarity of relevance between two nodes, we use the standard correlation and information gain measure. The approach is implemented in two steps, i.e., initial selection and pruning. In the first step, we try to identify, and filter out the ranges of nodes with similar relevance in each branch of the hierarchy. In the second step we try to select only the most valuable features from the previously reduced set.

Feature Consolidation. To identify features that represent the same information retrieved from multiple LOD sources, we have implemented an approach that relies on the probabilistic algorithm for ontology matching PARIS [26]. The approach outputs all discovered properties correspondences, which then can be resolved using different conflict resolution strategies [2], e.g., majority voting, average, etc. New fusion strategies can be developed based on the provenance information, e.g., if building a learning model in the movies domain, information retrieved from movies specific LOD sources (like LinkedMDB[6]) should be more accurate and extensive than cross-domain LOD sources (like DBpedia).

5   Evaluation Plan

To evaluate the feature generation framework, the feature selection and consolidation, and the propositionalization strategies, we need to collect significant number of datasets that cover different application domains, and can be used in different data mining tasks and different data mining algorithms. We consider two types of dataset for evaluation. First, datasets that already contain initial data mining features and a target variable. Such datasets could be easily collected from some of the popular machine learning repositories, like the UCI ML Repository[7]. The initial features of such datasets could be used for building models using state-of-the-art methods, which will serve as baselines for evaluating the performances of the learning models built on the enriched datasets with LOD features. An example for such a dataset is the *Auto MPG* dataset[8], which captures different characteristics of cars (such as cyclinders, horsepower, etc.), and the target is to predict the fuel consumption.

The second category of datasets are so called "empty datasets", which contain only the instances and one or more target variables. An example for such a dataset is the Mercer quality of living dataset[9], which contains a list of cities and their quality of living as numerical value (the target variable).

To evaluate the performances of a given data mining model, performance function p is used. In different data mining tasks different performance functions are used, e.g., accuracy is used for classification; root mean squared error for

---

[6] http://www.linkedmdb.org/.
[7] http://archive.ics.uci.edu/ml/index.html.
[8] http://archive.ics.uci.edu/ml/datasets/Auto+MPG.
[9] http://across.co.nz/qualityofliving.htm.

regression; support and confidence for association rules; purity and entropy for clustering, etc. Then, the evaluation for each of the given data mining tasks can be easily performed just by using the corresponding performance function on the model built on the enriched dataset.

For supervised data mining tasks where gold standard is available, the evaluation can be performed using some of the standard evaluation techniques, e.g. cross-validation. However, in unsupervised data mining tasks, like rule learning or clustering, in many cases the validity of the discovered patterns and hypothesis cannot be trivially and uniformly decided. Therefore, a user study may need to be conducted, where humans can decide the validity of the discovered hypothesis. For example, the ratings could be acquired using services like Amazon Mechanical Turk[10] or CrowdFlower[11].

As the feature generation complexity may rise very fast, as well as the number of generated features, a second evaluation metric should be introduced. Such a metric should be able to measure the trade-off between the feature generation complexity, the learning model training runtime on the enriched dataset, and the model performances.

To evaluate the performances of the feature selection approaches we introduce the *feature space compression* measure, which is defined as: $c(V') := 1 - \frac{|V'|}{|V|}$, where V is the original feature space, V' is the filtered feature space, and $V' \subseteq V$. Since there is a trade-off between the feature set and the performances, an overall target function is, e.g., the harmonic mean of p and c[12].

To evaluate the feature consolidation approaches we can collect some existing datasets that are commonly used for evaluation in the ontology matching community, or generate new ones. Once the gold standard is defined, standard evaluation metrics may be used, e.g., precision, recall and F-measure. To evaluate the model performances on the reduced feature space, again we use the model performance function p.

6   Intermediate Results

In this section we present some initial results of the approaches described in this proposal. The approaches are implemented in the RapidMiner Linked Open Data extension[13] [19,20], which represents an integral part of this thesis. The RapidMiner LOD extension supports the user in all steps of the LOD-enabled knowledge discovery process. The extension is publicly available, and has been successfully used in several applications.

Feature Generation. The initial feature generation strategies from the FeGeLOD framework have been evaluated in several prior publications. In [20,22]

---

[10] https://www.mturk.com.

[11] http://www.crowdflower.com/.

[12] Note that the value for p might need to be normalized first, depending on the used metric.

[13] http://dws.informatik.uni-mannheim.de/en/research/rapidminer-lod-extension.

we have shown that features generated from LOD can help finding useful explanations for interpreting statistical data. In [21] several LOD sources were used to generate features that can be used in books recommender systems. More extensive evaluation of the strategies was performed in [19,23]. The evaluation on the Cities and the Auto MPG datasets is extended and presented here.

We use the Cities dataset for classification (the target variable was discretized into high, medium, and low) using three classification methods. The Auto MPG dataset is used for the task of regression, also using three regression methods. The instances of both datasets were first linked to the corresponding resource in DBpedia, and then the following feature sets were generated: direct types (rdf:type), categories (dcterms:subject), incoming relations (rel in), outgoing relations (rel out), combination of both, outgoing relations including values (rel-vals out), incoming relations including values (rel-vals in), numerical values, and dataset generated using the Weisfeiler-Lehman graph kernel algorithm (WLK).

Table 1 depicts the size and the results for each feature set, except for the incoming relations values set, which is rather large to be evaluated. We can notice that the features generated from LOD lead to RMSE five times smaller than the original data. From the results we can notice that the results differ for different feature sets, and different algorithms, but in almost all cases the features generated using the kernel feature generation strategy

Table 1. Classification accuracy results for the Cities dataset, and RMSE results for the Auto MPG dataset.

Dataset Set/Method	#Att.	Cities			#Att.	Auto MPG		
		NB	KNN	C4.5		LR	M5	KNN
original	0	/	/	/	8	3.35	2.85	4.02
types	721	55.71	56.17	59.05	264	3.84	2.83	3.57
categories	999	59.52	44.35	58.96	308	4.47	2.9	3.62
rel in	1,304	60.41	58.46	60.35	227	3.84	2.9	3.61
rel out	1,081	47.62	60.0	56.71	370	3.79	3.1	3.6
rel in & out	2,385	59.44	58.57	56.47	597	3.92	3.0	3.57
rel-vals out	3,091	53.68	49.98	61.82	1,497	2.87	1.83	1.50
numerics	774	46.29	34.48	49.98	185	4.32	3.47	2.98
WLK	48,373	64.55	52.36	71.26	26,687	3.05	1.69	0.74

lead to the best results. However, the complexity for generating the kernel functions is by three orders of magnitude higher than any other strategy. Additionally, the number of features generated with the kernel strategy is 20 to 40 times higher than any other strategy, which also greatly affects the runtime for building the learning models. Therefore, a near optimal trade-off between the feature generation complexity, the size of the dataset and the learning model performances should be found.

Propositionalization Strategies. In [23] we performed an evaluation on different propositionalization strategies on three different data-mining tasks, i.e., classification, regression and outlier detection, using three different data mining algorithms for each task. The evaluation was performed for binary, numerical, relative count and TF-IDF vector representation, on five different feature sets. The evaluation showed that the propositionalization strategy have major impact on the data mining results, however we were not able to come with a general recommendation for a strategy, as it depends on the given data mining task, the given dataset, and the data mining algorithm to be used.

Feature Selection. In [24] we have performed initial evaluation of the feature selection approach in hierarchical feature spaces, on both synthetic and real world dataset, using three algorithms for classification. Using the approach, we were able to achieve feature space compression up to 95 %, without decreasing the model's performances, or in some cases increasing it. The evaluation has shown that the approach outperforms standard feature selection techniques as well as recent approaches which explore hierarchies.

Feature Consolidation. In [20] we have shown that, for example, the value for the population of a country can be found in 10 different sources within the LOD cloud, which using the matching and fusion approach were merged into a single feature without missing values.

7 Conclusion

In this work we have identified the challenges, and set the initial bases for developing a scalable framework for automatic and unsupervised feature generation from LOD that can be used in any arbitrary data mining algorithms. We believe that such a framework will be of a great value in the data preparation step of the knowledge discovery process, by reducing the time needed for data transformation and manipulation, with as little as possible user interaction.

Acknowledgements. This thesis is supervised by prof. Dr. Heiko Paulheim. The work presented in this paper has been partly funded by the German Research Foundation (DFG) under grant number PA 2373/1-1 (Mine@LOD).

References

1. Bizer, C., Heath, T., Berners-Lee, T.: Linked data - the story so far. IJSWIS **5**, 1–22 (2009)
2. Bleiholder, J., Naumann, F.: Data fusion. ACM Comput. Surv. **41**(1), 1–41 (2008)
3. Blum, A.L., Langley, P.: Selection of relevant features and examples in machine learning. Artif. intell. **97**, 245–271 (1997)
4. Cheng, W., Kasneci, G., Graepel, T., Stern, D., Herbrich, R.: Automated feature generation from structured knowledge. In: CIKM (2011)
5. de Vries, G.K.D.: A fast approximation of the Weisfeiler-Lehman graph kernel for RDF data. In: Blockeel, H., Kersting, K., Nijssen, S., Železný, F. (eds.) ECML PKDD 2013, Part I. LNCS, vol. 8188, pp. 606–621. Springer, Heidelberg (2013)
6. de Vries, G.K.D., de Rooij, S.: A fast and simple graph kernel for RDF. In: DMLOD (2013)
7. Euzenat, J., Shvaiko, P.: Ontology Matching. Springer, New York (2007)
8. Fanizzi, N., d'Amato, C.: A declarative kernel for $\mathcal{ALC}$ concept descriptions. In: Esposito, F., Raś, Z.W., Malerba, D., Semeraro, G. (eds.) ISMIS 2006. LNCS (LNAI), vol. 4203, pp. 322–331. Springer, Heidelberg (2006)
9. Fayyad, U.M., Piatetsky-Shapiro, G., Smyth, P.: Advances in Knowledge Discovery and Data Mining. AAAI Press, Cambridge (1996)
10. Huang, Y., Tresp, V., Nickel, M., Kriegel, H.-P.: A scalable approach for statistical learning in semantic graphs. Semant. Web **5**, 5–22 (2014)

11. Jeong, Y., Myaeng, S.-H.: Feature selection using a semantic hierarchy for event recognition and type classification. In: International Joint Conference on Natural Language Processing (2013)
12. Kappara, V.N.P., Ichise, R., Vyas, O.P.: Liddm: a data mining system for linked data. In: LDOW (2011)
13. Khan, M.A., Grimnes, G.A., Dengel, A.: Two pre-processing operators for improved learning from semanticweb data. In: RCOMM (2010)
14. Kramer, S., Lavrač, N., Flach, P.: Propositionalization approaches to relational data mining. In: Džeroski, S., Lavrač, N. (eds.) Relational Data Mining, pp. 262–291. Springer, New York (2001)
15. Lösch, U., Bloehdorn, S., Rettinger, A.: Graph kernels for RDF data. In: Simperl, E., Cimiano, P., Polleres, A., Corcho, O., Presutti, V. (eds.) ESWC 2012. LNCS, vol. 7295, pp. 134–148. Springer, Heidelberg (2012)
16. Lu, S., Ye, Y., Tsui, R.: Domain ontology-based feature reduction for high dimensional drug data and its application to 30-day heart failure readmission prediction. In: Collaboratecom, pp. 478–484 (2013)
17. Mynarz, J., Svátek, V.: Towards a benchmark for LOD-enhanced knowledge discovery from structured data. In: The Second International Workshop on Knowledge Discovery and Data Mining Meets Linked Open Data (2013)
18. Paulheim, H., Fürnkranz, J.: Unsupervised generation of data mining features from linked open data. In: WCWIMS (2012)
19. Paulheim, H., Ristoski, P., Mitichkin, E., Bizer, C.: Data mining with background knowledge from the web. In: RapidMiner World (2014)
20. Ristoski, P., Bizer, C., Paulheim, H.: Mining the web of linked data with rapidminer. In: Semantic Web Challenge at ISWC (2014)
21. Ristoski, P., Loza Mencía, E., Paulheim, H.: A hybrid multi-strategy recommender system using linked open data. In: Presutti, V., et al. (eds.) SemWebEval 2014. CCIS, vol. 475, pp. 150–156. Springer, Heidelberg (2014)
22. Ristoski, P., Paulheim, H.: Analyzing statistics with background knowledge from linked open data. In: Workshop on Semantic Statistics (2013)
23. Ristoski, P., Paulheim, H.: A comparison of propositionalization strategies for creating features from linked open data. In: LD4KD (2014)
24. Ristoski, P., Paulheim, H.: Feature selection in hierarchical feature spaces. In: Džeroski, S., Panov, P., Kocev, D., Todorovski, L. (eds.) DS 2014. LNCS, vol. 8777, pp. 288–300. Springer, Heidelberg (2014)
25. Schmachtenberg, M., Bizer, C., Paulheim, H.: Adoption of the linked data best practices in different topical domains. In: Mika, P., Tudorache, T., Bernstein, A., Welty, C., Knoblock, C., Vrandečić, D., Groth, P., Noy, N., Janowicz, K., Goble, C. (eds.) ISWC 2014, Part I. LNCS, vol. 8796, pp. 245–260. Springer, Heidelberg (2014)
26. Suchanek, F.M., Abiteboul, S., Senellart, P.: PARIS: probabilistic alignment of relations, instances, and schema. PVLDB 5(3), 157–168 (2011)
27. Tiddi, I., d'Aquin, M., Motta, E.: Dedalo: looking for clusters explanations in a labyrinth of linked data. In: Presutti, V., d'Amato, C., Gandon, F., d'Aquin, M., Staab, S., Tordai, A. (eds.) ESWC 2014. LNCS, vol. 8465, pp. 333–348. Springer, Heidelberg (2014)
28. Wang, B.B., Mckay, R.I.B., Abbass, H.A., Barlow, M.: A comparative study for domain ontology guided feature extraction. In: ACSC (2003)

Semantic Support for Recording Laboratory Experimental Metadata: A Study in Food Chemistry

Dena Tahvildari[✉]

Business Web and Media Group, Vrije University of Amsterdam,
Boelelaan, 1081 Amsterdam, The Netherlands
d.tahvildari@vu.nl

1 Introduction and Research Objective

A fundamental principle of scientific enquiry is to create proper documentation of data and methods during experimental research [1, 5]. Providing the context of observations is essential for the understanding their meaning and for the reproduction of the experiment. Proper annotation also increases the likelihood of data being found and re-used by the same or other researchers [2]. Good scientific practice in the laboratory requires that lab reports describe the sequence of experimental activities executed in the lab. Moreover, method descriptions should include detailed information on the materials and equipment, analytical methods, parameter settings, lab conditions, failures and other details that facilitate reproduction of an experiment. This calls for adding descriptions (metadata) to research data and methods [3]. Most researchers consider the task of describing experimental details to be essential, but at the seen as time consuming and distracting from the 'real research'. As a consequence, the documentation is often suboptimal.

Laboratory research is typically recorded in laboratory notebooks; they are indispensable sources for writing the laboratory methodological reports. Researchers are comfortable with paper notebooks and they are accepted as authoritative information sources and as legal documents. Paper lab notebooks offer simplicity and flexibility, but besides the risk of loss and deterioration they do not allow the information to be searched, shared and processed computationally [9, 28, 29]. Moreover, they cannot provide tooling for more efficient and effective recordings. The availability of computational environments for collecting and analyzing experimental data and the definition of digital formats for data have created persuasive incentives for the transition from paper to electronic lab notes. Powerful computing infrastructures have become a necessity to keep pace with the expanding volume of data and to retain control of the results. However, a survey by Downing et al., 2008 in the chemistry lab at Cambridge Imperial College, shows that most researchers make their notes on paper. In addition, they keep data on disparate systems that are linked to specific equipment. Moreover, researchers do not use any standards for writing descriptions of the experiments. They preserve the resulting documents on a variety of computing platforms and systems. These files are in many cases not interpretable for others because of the quality of the

F. Gandon et al. (Eds.): ESWC 2015, LNCS 9088, pp. 783–794, 2015.
DOI: 10.1007/978-3-319-18818-8_51

descriptions [4]. This leads to data loss and confusion for scientists who need to understand the experimental results and interpret how they were created.

It is evident that the current documentation practices in the lab are no longer efficient in the digital era. Digital recording will allow new ways to support this process. In particular, the use of semantic metadata will enable machines to interpret and integrate data generated by different sources (equipment, people, and repositories) in various formats. Our hypothesis is that the presence of vocabularies for annotating the context of a lab experiment, in return can contribute to an efficient and effective experimental documentation process. This line of reasoning is the main motivation in our research. The objective of the research is:

> *"to explore if and how the documentation task undertaken by scientists could be improved through the use of an ontology-based metadata capture supporting tool in the laboratory."*

The documentation task should be easy and efficient, but at the same time deliver high quality recordings. There is also a debate both inside and outside the scientific communities over the lack of reproducibility of experiments.

In this study, we first identify quality criteria in the domain for experimental documentation, starting with method descriptions found in literature. We evaluate in detail the methods reporting in a comprehensive set of laboratory experiments that should enable valid reproduction, integration and comparison of research procedures. In our work we focus on Food Chemistry, assuming that the outcomes will be valuable for other domains as well. Second, we define indicators to measure the efficiency of the documentation task as performed in the lab. We develop vocabularies to formally describe the domain knowledge. Finally, given the developed models and defined metrics we design a prototype tool that supposedly will assist researchers in efficiently producing high-quality lab notes. We will set up an intervention study to evaluate the tool and underlying hypothesis in the context of a Food Chemistry research group.

2   Related Work

The related work presented in this section concerns different domains within computer science studies, which are selected for the purpose of our research; (1) the domain of metadata quality, (2) the field of description logic/ontology engineering, and (3) the field of scientific workflow management systems.

1. In the literature research metadata is defined as *"the data record that contains structured information about some resources. It describes, explains, locates, or otherwise makes it easier to retrieve, use, or manage an information resource [5]."* In science, creating a high-quality metadata for research resources is important. The presence of metadata, if created accurately, can lead to the provision of more accurate methodological reports. Several research initiatives related with scientific metadata quality have been conducted [6–8, 11–14]. These efforts approach the subject from diverse perspectives, trying to cover most of its different aspects.

Najjar, Ternier & Duval 2003, performed a statistical analysis on a sample of metadata records from various repositories and evaluate the usage of the standard [9].

Also, Crystal et al., 2005 reports on a study that investigated the ability of resource authors to create acceptable – quality metadata in an organizational setting using manual evaluation by experts [10].

Andy Brass, 2014 and his research team conducted a research on the quality of methods reporting in parasitology experiments. They defined a checklist of essential parameters that should be reported in methodology sections of scientific articles. They scored the number of those parameters that are reported for each publication. Interesting aspect of their research is that they used bibliometric parameters (impact factors, citation rate and h-index) to look for association between journal and author status and the quality of method reporting [38]. Their results indicate that the *"bibliometric parameters were not correlated with the quality of method reporting"* (Spearman's rank correlation coefficient < -0.5; $p > 0.05$). They concluded that the quality of methods reporting in experimental parasitology is a source of concern and it has not enhanced over time, despite their being evidence that most of the assessed parameters do influence the results. They proposed set of parameters to be used as guidelines to improve the quality of the reporting of experimental infection models as a requirement for comparing datasets.

Finally, some initiatives, such as the Minimum Information About a Microarray Experiment (MIAME) [39] and the Minimum Information About a Proteomics Experiment (MIAPE) [40], have been used by several journals such as the Journal of Proteomics, as a condition for publication.

2. Ontologies have been presented as a possible solution for expressing metadata. They satisfy metadata requirements and are capable of representing the specific semantics of each research domain. In the biomedical domain, the ontology for Biomedical Investigation (OBI) helps to model the design of investigations, including the protocols, materials used, instruments used, the data generated and the types of analysis performed on them [15, 17]. OBI is an extension of the Basic Formal Ontology (BFO)[1] as the upper-level ontology as a means to describe general entities that do not belong to a specific problem domain. Therefore, all OBI classes are a subclass of some BFO class. The ontology has the scope of modeling all biomedical investigations and as such contains ontology terms for aspects such as:

- Biological material – such as plasma,
- Instrument – such as DNA microarray, and centrifuge,
- Actions of an experiment and sub steps of the experiment such as electrophoresis material separation,
- Data processing - for example Principle Component Analysis.

Biomedical experimental processes involve numerous sub-processes, involving experimental materials such as organisms, and cell cultures. These experimental materials are represented as subclasses of the BFO class material entity. OBI uses BFO's material entity as the basis for defining physical elements. To assess the use of OBI for annotation they used it in an automated functional genomics investigation with Robot Scientist [31]. The robot requires a complete and precise description of all

---

[1] http://ifomis.uni-saarland.de/bfo/.

experimental actions, and this use case demonstrates how OBI was able to provide elements of such a description. The general ontology of scientific experiments EXPO [16], also intends to formally describe the domain-independent knowledge about planning, actions and analysis of scientific experiments. EXPO formalized the generic concepts of experimental design such as Methodology and results representation and it links the SUMO (the Suggested Upper Merged Ontology) with subject-specific ontologies of experiments. EXPO is expressed in the OWL-DL.[2] This ontology has the class expo:Experimental_protocol and describes some of its properties, expo: has_applicability, expo:has_goal, expo:has_plan. The level of granularity makes EXPO unwieldy for usage in an operational data management workflow. The last vocabulary, which can be relevant to our research, is OM (Ontology of units of Measure and related concepts). Haijo Rijgersberg et al., 2009, developed OM to facilitate a transparent exchange and process of quantitative information [18]. OM is expressed in OWL. They have designed applications to test the usefulness of OM and its services. First, a web application that checks for the consistency in dimension and unit of formulas. Second, an add-in Microsoft Excel that assists in data annotation and unit conversion [19].

The existing ontologies, in particular OBI, could be applicable in our approach for developing vocabularies in the food chemistry domain. We intend to design vocabularies by building upon the existing ontologies using OWLstandards.

One of the main areas that the description logic-based ontology can be helpful is its use development time activity. The idea is that, using ontologies, we can have hierarchy of the domain knowledge assembled in the system, and it can identify the existing inconsistent, and incoherence in the descriptions. Also, we can use ontology as a mechanism that can provide metadata suggestions for researchers (decision support tool).

3. Jeremy Frey, 2004 is one of the pioneers in the domain of laboratory automation, who specifically investigates the use of semantic technologies in laboratory data capture and re-use for chemical labs [23–25, 27]. Also, one of the most relevant references in this field is the paper by Hughes et al. (2004) [27]. They have developed an innovative human-centered system, which captures the process of a chemistry experiment from plan to execution. This system comprises an electronic lab book, which has been successfully trialed in a synthetic organic chemistry laboratory, and a flexible back-end storage system (using RDF technologies). They took the "design-by-analogy" research approach in a close collaboration with chemists to develop the "MyteaExperiment" planner [27]. Similarly, LabTrove is a social network system to facilitate the association of the data to the proposed scientific elements at the point of creation (annotation at source) rather than by annotating the data with commentary after the experiment has taken place [34]. The LabTrove application was designed to help researchers to share their experimental plans, thoughts, observations and achievements with the wider online community in a semantically rich and extensible manner. Using the application, scientists will no longer have to print out data results to insert into conventional lab books; instead, results will be logically associated with the experiment and therefore they become accessible as desired. And the last knowledge management

---

[2] http://www.w3.org/TR/owl-guide/.

application related to our work is Tiffany [30], which is specifically designed for laboratory studies. Tiffany model is a refinement of the W3C PROV-O[3] model for provenance, combining the ability to trace back the workflow with extra information, which is useful for researchers, such as the type of activity and the research question being investigated. Tiffany is used at Wageningen UR to help food domain researchers in giving structure to their research workflow and facilitate:

- Good archiving.
- Re-use.
- Knowledge transfer.
- Serendipity.

LabTrove and Tiffany are the main workflow management systems that we consider to study in detail to check for their applicability to our approach. Finally, an inspiring reference that could help us in understanding the laboratory life, which is considered as a reference to laboratory scientists' behavior, is the work done by the eminent French philosopher Bruno Latour. He observed the laboratory scientists within the period of two years and described the process that scientists undertake for conducting an experiment and developing scientific facts in the laboratory [37]. This source could help us to get insight on the behavioral features of laboratory scientists, which could be a valuable knowledge in the application design phase.

3 Research Problem and Research Questions

The problem statement that motivates our research is:

"Inefficiencies in capturing the context of the experimental procedures by laboratory scientists within the physical lab lead to the poor documentation of the research process and ultimately result in the provision of inadequate methodological reports."

The problem is rooted in several factors. First, there are factors such as motivation and gratification for describing experimental methods in detail. Although documentation is an integral part of scientific research, it is a labor intensive and cumbersome activity for scientists. Researchers are reluctant to allocate time to record, sufficiently annotate and share the context of observations in the lab. Secondly, in many cases, researchers simply do not know what kind of information is valuable for recording; for example, are room lighting and room temperature important information to be recorded? There is no single approach to do this, it varies from one experiment to the other and depends on the intended use of the recordings. For example, a SOP (Standard Operation Procedure) will be used as a well-defined detailed description for potentially many (unknown) users, whereas a simple 'Friday afternoon trial' will only be have to be understood by a small number of researchers. Another source of additional effort by the researcher is the fact that many laboratory instruments are not yet integrated into a digitized workflow of a lab researcher, especially in academic research institutes and

---

[3] http://www.w3.org/TR/prov-o/.

universities. Therefore, often researchers have to enter and transfer data and the associated descriptions more than once – from equipment measurements to their notebook, from their notebooks into digital formats and files, from personal computers to institutional repositories, etc.

The problem has costly impact on (1) the reproducibility, and (2) the traceability of laboratory data and methods.

We propose the following research question to address the above problem.

"Do semantic technologies and their applications contribute to the efficiency of the documentation task and improve the quality of experimental metadata provided by the laboratory researchers in the domain of Food Chemistry?"

To answer the main research question, we propose the following sub research questions:

RQ1 – What are quality criteria for experimental methodological reports?

RQ2 – What are the influencing variables that stimulate reproducibility of the laboratory experimental procedure?

RQ3 – What are measurable indicators for the efficiency of the documentation task in the lab?

RQ4 – Which ontologies are required to annotate the context of experimental methods in the domain of food chemistry?

RQ5 – Which ontology-based supporting tools can help laboratory researchers in annotating their experimental data and methods in an efficient and effective way?

4   Scope of the Research

In this research we only focus on improving the documentation task within the environment of physical laboratory or as what the domain scientists name it the "wet lab".

We are aware of the fact that we need to make a clear choice for the user of our applications, because it affects our choices when conducting experiments. We assume that the primary users of our software are human researchers (Robot Scientist is out of the scope of this research), who work in the academic institute of food sciences. We consider that they have the background knowledge and the expertise of working in the lab. We specifically, target the doctoral students, technicians and senior researchers from the food chemistry domain.

Stimulating the "**exact reproducibility of findings**" is not the main focus of our research. However, we argue that improving quality the methodological reporting could influence some acceptable levels of "**reproducibility of the experimental procedures**" in lab experiment.

Finally, in creating metadata quality criteria, we are completely aware that it is not feasible to identify all the information from the context of the lab, since the big amount of knowledge in the lab is categorized as tacit knowledge. Within this context, elicitation and measurement of tacit knowledge in laboratory environments are concepts that we take into consideration in our approach.

5 Research Methodology

For each of the research questions, we explore the literature to find theories, techniques and best practices developed for the same or other domains. To define quality criteria for method descriptions we consult the literature and make interviews with scientists in the field, initially open but gradually more specific. We use computational text analysis tools to detect the characteristics of method descriptions in food chemistry publications. The combined findings from these investigations help us to propose quality indicators. Given the theoretical framework and the development of a coding schema (ontology), we refine our propositions through structured interviews within a larger number of scientists. In parallel, we use text analysis techniques to analyze the content of method sections in published articles in the domain. We are interested to find the most frequent and co-occurring words in the corpus and classify terms in several topics. This phase is the initial step in understanding the domain knowledge that is used when describing methods and for defining supporting vocabularies. The concepts and vocabularies will be used at the later stage of the research in tools.

Our present dataset for text analysis is a corpus containing 241 method sections from 9 different scientific journals in food chemistry domain that are published in the period of 2000 to 2014. We used the Python programming language for pre-processing the sections. We did our analysis using R-Studio programming language. Next, we consult the domain experts in food chemistry. We ask them to (1) to give general quality criteria they use for judging method descriptions, depending on the intended use, (2) to comment on the quality of a number of specific method descriptions given to them and (3) comment on the results from the text analysis (term frequency analysis and topic models) as representations of method descriptions in general. Based on these results, we aim to develop quality criteria, which then will be evaluated through an experiment with scientists. An option here is that we select a number of method sections that score either very low or very high on our quality indicators, and have the researchers classify all sections as well.

For RQ3 we interview and observe researchers, in order to identify efficiency criteria for the documentation task, for example the time needed for the task of associating metadata experimental data.

For RQ4 we take the NeOn methodology to develop vocabularies. The review of NeOn methodology reported in the work by Garcia et al., 2011 [26, 32]. The steps are:

1. Preparation,
2. Conceptualization,
3. Knowledge acquisition and Domain Analysis,
4. Semantic analysis,
5. Building ontology and validation,
6. Evaluation.

We use the ontology development tool ROC + in order to allow food chemists to setup the initial vocabularies and verify these by checking automatically generated annotations of the selected method sections [33].

Finally, for RQ5, we design and build an ontology-based application that aims to support experimental scientists in creating high-quality method descriptions, through software engineering techniques. To accomplish this goal we first need to identify the commonly used applications in the workflow of scientists. In this way we can design an application that can be integrated into the present way of working and contribute to the efficiency. By separating aspects that are specific for the food chemistry domain from general design decision we aim to gain insight that is applicable to experimental science in general.

6 Preliminary Findings (RQ1)

Through a bottom-up approach we analyzed our data to learn about the domain, the structure of the method descriptions, terminology used, and the nature of experiments in food chemistry. For this, we first manually reviewed the method descriptions of a few numbers of papers to get a basic understanding of the field. We focused our analysis on identifying necessary and sufficient information for reporting methods. Moreover, we tried to define categories to classify the knowledge into concepts such as equipment, reagent, and actions. This helps us to compare our categorization with terminology used by researchers. We used NVivo software for qualitative data analysis because of the unstructured nature of our dataset. In addition to manual analysis, we used Natural Language Processing techniques such as term frequency analysis and topic modeling in R to learn more about underlying meanings in the text. From our inspections, we detected the workflow aspects in method descriptions. The sequence of actions was implicit and was dependent on the requirements of the respective journals. However, we could find commonalities in the structure of these descriptions as most of them had an input-output structure. From the manual analysis, we identified that two main elements are visible in these workflows, (1) experimental actions and (2) experimental objects.

Actions in the descriptions were usually presented by verbs; most of the experimental actions were described implicitly and accurate information (metadata) for implementing the action was not always available. For instance, structures such as "*Transfer approximately 9 mL oxalic acid solution*" or "*Use dry cuvettes to mix and read on a spectrophotometer at 440 nm against CHM solvent*" repeatedly occurred in our dataset. Domain experts are usually required in order to interpret the information in the descriptions. The results from the term frequency analysis and topic modeling are available at https://gist.github.com/denatahvildari. We will communicate these results with the domain scientists to be able to analyze them.

7 Research Evaluation Plan

The overall evaluation of the research will be accomplished through using the ontology in applications and assessing the results in real-life experiments (application-based evaluation). We will setup intervention studies with scientists to assess how well the ontology-based tools improve the efficiency of the documentation task and improvement in providing qualified methodological reports. To evaluate the ontologies as such, we will follow the practice introduced by Gomez-Perez et al. [22], which suggest the following assessment criteria (this method is also used and reported in [26]):

1. Consistency.
2. Completeness.
3. Conciseness.

Further more, to determine the usefulness of the representations, the important question is to find out if the representations (ontologies) are sufficient. For example, through an experiment we can evaluate the sufficiency of ontologies by asking researchers to create methodology description using the representations. Afterwards, we ask other researcher to reproduce the experimental process using the previous protocol, and create another description. If we can show that the two descriptions about the same experiment are equivalent, the validity of the ontologies can be tested.

The validation of the proposed tooling is that, other researchers can use the information of high-quality descriptions to replicate an experimental setup. To measure this, we aim to set up an experiment. For example, we take two groups of researchers. We ask researchers in one group to conduct an experiment and write down laboratory method reports while using metadata indications that we previously identified. Next, we ask other researchers from the other group use these information sources and try to set up the experiment. We then measure and discuss the success of the reproduction task based on the expertise and the levels of accomplishments in completing the reproducibility.

8 Discussion

In this research we aim to design tool to help researchers to record their experimental metadata in an efficient way. We argue that by designing ontology-based metadata record applications for the context of the lab, we contribute to the development of electronic laboratory notebooks and in return we promote the provision of the high methodological reporting. Ultimately, with having sufficient information about the experimental procedure the reproducibility could positively be influenced. However, inspired by the research by Vasilevsky et al. 2013, we agree on the point that the "identifiability of the research resources" [36] in a specific research domain is a prime necessity. Otherwise, the successful reproducibility cannot be achieved. They conducted a research to investigate the "identifiability" of the resources in biomedical research domain from publications. Based on their result, 54 % of the research resources in this domain are not uniquely identifiable in research publication. However, they didn't check whether adding identifability was enough to get reproducibility. We assume, through our approach, we find other variables in addition to resource identifiability that could affect the scientific reproducibility such as "the experimenter's awareness about the domain metadata".

Another point for discussion in our research comes from the observation by Drummond, 2009 [35]. He argues that reproducibility is different than replicability; his claim is: *"reproducibility requires changes, while replicability avoids them"* [35]. He further argues that scientific replication does not worth all the great deal of extra work incurred by the researcher. His article points at a valid point that in any case, the full replication of the previous experiment is not achievable, since the experiment is being carried out by another researcher, in another laboratory, with different equipment. He concludes that reproducibility covers a wide rang and replication falls at one end of this range. We argue that replicability is the exact repetition of an experiment to obtain the same results; while reproducibility is the repetition of an experiment with small adjustment and modification, e.g. changes that will unavoidably occur when undertaking the same experiment in different laboratories. Our main interest in this research is to identify the variables that stimulate the reproduction of the "lab experimental processes" not the "results". Our main statement is that if results are replicable but the experimental process is not reproducible, they may be of little value because they are likely to be characterized to the precise conditions used in an experiment (for example, the use of a scarce sample or equipment, that only certain laboratories are authorized to work with). The information reported in the material and methods section of an article plays a fundamental role in achieving this aim.

We think that even the weakest version of reproduction has some values. Fore example, among laboratory researchers, the term "technical reproducibility" is a very well known one. The term indicates that every laboratory experiment should be carried out in duplications to be checked for the validity of the procedure – researchers calculate the coefficient of variation of the duplicated experiments. If this ratio is greater that 10 %, they need to re-do the experiment. This, in fact emphasizes on the value of reproducibility, comparability and their prerequisites. Despite the extra effort involved in the documentation task, we claim that if researchers are aware of essential metadata of their domain, and if they are equipped with efficient tools that support them at the development time, at least the "technical reproducibility" is achievable.

We know that achieving general agreement on standards, particularly metadata vocabularies, is a challenge in most of the disciplines. We also think that a solution for defining lab metadata is much more than just a technical challenge. Motivating scientists to use terms from controlled vocabularies by providing tools that use those terms is not straightforward.

Acknowledgement. This PhD research is a joint project between the Computer Science Department of Vrije University of Amsterdam and the Wageningen UR. The author acknowledges the help of Prof. Jan Top in shaping and writing the manuscript and appreciates the insights from Prof. Guus Schreiber and Prof. Bijan Parsia.

References

1. Baranova, A., Campagna, S.R., Chen, R., et al.: Toward more transparent and reproducible omics studies through a common metadata checklist and data publications. Omics: A J. Integr. Biol. **18**(1), 10–14 (2014)
2. Agosti, M., Ferro, N., Frommholz, I., Thiel, U.: Annotations in digital libraries and collaboratories – facets, models and usage. In: Heery, R., Lyon, L. (eds.) ECDL 2004. LNCS, vol. 3232, pp. 244–255. Springer, Heidelberg (2004)
3. World Health Organization. Handbook: good laboratory practice (GLP): quality practices for regulated non-clinical research and development. World Health Organization (2010)

4. Downing, J., Murray-Rust, P., Tonge, A.P., Morgan, P., Rzepa, H., Cotterill, F., Day, N., Harvey, M.: SPECTRa: the deposition and validation of primary chemistry research data in digital repositories. J. Chem. Inf. Model. **48**(8), 1571–1581 (2008)
5. Jones, M.B., Berkley, C., Bojilova, J., Schildhauer, M.: Managing scientific metadata. Internet Comput. **5**(5), 59–68 (2001)
6. Moulaison, H., Felicity D.: Metadata quality in digital repositories (2014)
7. Park, J.-R.: Metadata quality in digital repositories: A survey of the current state of the art. Cataloging Classif. Q. **47**(3–4), 213–228 (2009)
8. Robertson, R.J.: Metadata quality: implications for library and information science professionals. Libr. Rev. **54**(5), 295–300 (2005)
9. Najjar, J., Stefaan, T., Duval, E.: The actual use of metadata in ARIADNE: an empirical analysis. In: Proceedings of the 3rd Annual ARIADNE Conference, pp. 1–6 (2003)
10. Abe, C., Greenberg, J.: Usability of a metadata creation application for resource authors. Libr. Inf. Sci. Res. **27**(2), 177–189 (2005)
11. Mitchell, E.T.: Metadata literacy: an analysis of metadata awareness in college students. Ph. D. dissertation, University of North Carolina at Chapel Hill (2009)
12. Dushay, N., Hillmann, D.I.: Analyzing metadata for effective use and re-use. In: DCMI Metadata Conference and Workshop, Seattle, USA (2003)
13. Moen, W.E., Stewart, E.I., McClure, C.L.: The role of content analysis in evaluating metadata for the U.S. government information locator service (gils): Results from an exploratory study (1997). <http://www.unt.edu/wmoen/publications/GILSMDContentAnalysis.htm>. Accessed March 2013
14. Hughes, G., Mills, H., De Roure, D., Frey, J.G., Moreau, L., Smith, G., Zaluska, E., et al.: The semantic smart laboratory: a system for supporting the chemical escientist. Org. Biomol. chem. **2**(22), 3284–3293 (2004)
15. Brinkman, R., Courtot, M., Derom, D., Fostel, J.M., He, Y., Lord, P.W., Malone, J., et al.: Modeling biomedical experimental processes with OBI. J. Biomed. Semant. **1**(S-1), S7 (2010)
16. Soldatova, L.N., et al.: An ontology of scientific experiments. J. R. Soc. Interface **3**(11), 795–803 (2006)
17. Courtot, M., et al.: The OWL of Biomedical Investigations in OWLED Workshop in the International Semantic Web Conference (ISWC), Karlsruhe, Germany (2008)
18. Rijgersberg, H., Top, J., Meinders, M.: Semantic support for quantitative research processes. IEEE Intell. Syst. **24**(1), 37–46 (2009)
19. Rijgersberg, H., van Assem, M., Top, J.: Ontology of units of measure and related concepts. Semant. Web **4**(1), 3–13 (2013)
20. Suarez-Figuera, M.C.: Ontology Engineering in a Networked World, Xii, p. 444. Springer, Berlin (2012)
21. Garcia-Castro, A.: Developing Ontologies in the Biological Domain in Institute for Molecular Bioscience, p. 275, University of Queensland, Queensland (2007)
22. Gomez-Perez, A.: Evaluation and assessment of knowledge sharing technology. In: Mars, N. J.I. (ed.) Towards Very Large Knowledge Bases: Knowledge Building & Knowledge Sharing, pp. 289–296. IOS Press, Amsterdam (1995)
23. Coles, S.J., Frey, J.G., Bird, C.L., Whitby, R.J., Day, A.E.: First steps towards semantic descriptions of electronic laboratory notebook records. J. Cheminform. **5**(1), 52 (2013)
24. Frey, J.G.: Curation of laboratory experimental data as part of the overall data lifecycle. Int. J. Digit. Curation **3**(1), 44–62 (2008)
25. Frey, J.G.: The value of the semantic web in the laboratory. Drug Discov. Today **14**(11), 552–561 (2009)

26. Alexander, G., Giraldo, Olga., Garcia, J.: Annotating experimental records using ontologies. In: International Conference on Biomedical Ontology, Buffalo, NY, USA (2011)
27. Hughes, G., Mills, H., Smith, G., Frey, J., et al.: Making tea: iterative design through analogy. In: Proceedings of the 5th Conference on Designing Interactive Systems: Processes, Practices, Methods, and Techniques, pp. 49–58. ACM (2004)
28. Klokmose, C.N., Zander, P.O.: Rethinking laboratory notebooks. In: E. Kolker, V. Ozdemir, L. Martens,W. Hancock, G. Anderson, N. Anderson, S. Aynacioglu (2010)
29. Nussbeck, S.Y., Weil, P., Menzel, J., Marzec, B., Lorberg, K., Schwappach, B.: The laboratory notebook in the 21st century. EMBO reports (2014)
30. Top,.J., Broekstra, J.: Tiffany: sharing and managing knowledge in food science. Keynote in ISMICK, Brazil (2008)
31. Soldatova, L., et al.: An ontology for a Robot Scientist. Bioinformatics (Special issue for ISMB) 22(14), –e471 (2006)
32. Suárez-Figueroa, M.C.: NeOn Methodology for building ontology networks: specification, scheduling and reuse. Diss. Informatica (2010)
33. Koenderink, N.J.J.P., van Assem, M., Hulzebos, J., Broekstra, J., Top, J.L.: ROC: a method for proto-ontology construction by domain experts. In: Domingue, J., Anutariya, C. (eds.) ASWC 2008. LNCS, vol. 5367, pp. 152–166. Springer, Heidelberg (2008)
34. Milsted, A.J., et al.: LabTrove: a lightweight, web based, laboratory "Blog" as a route towards a marked up record of work in bioscience research laboratory. PloS one 8(7), e67460 (2013)
35. Drummond, C.: Replicability is not reproducibility: nor is it good science (2009)
36. Vasilevsky, N.A., Brush, M.H., Paddock, H., Ponting, L., Tripathy, S.J., LaRocca, G.M., Haendel, M.A.: On the reproducibility of science: unique identification of research resources in the biomedical literature. PeerJ 1, e148 (2013)
37. Latour, B., Woolgar, S.: Laboratory Life: The Construction of Scientific Facts. Princeton University Press, Princeton (2013)
38. Flórez-Vargas, O., Bramhall, M., Noyes, H., Cruickshank, S., Stevens, R., Brass, A.: The quality of methods reporting in parasitology experiments. PLoS ONE 9(7), e101131 (2014)
39. Brazma, A., Hingamp, P., Quackenbush, J., Sherlock, G., Spellman, P., Stoeckert, C., Vingron, M.: Minimum information about a microarray experiment (MIAME)—toward standards for microarray data. Nat. Genet. 29(4), 365–371 (2001)
40. Taylor, C.F., Paton, N.W., Lilley, K.S., Binz, P.A., Julian, R.K., Jones, A.R., Hermjakob, H.: The minimum information about a proteomics experiment (MIAPE). Nat. Biotechnol. 25 (8), 887–893 (2007)

Exploiting Semantics from Ontologies to Enhance Accuracy of Similarity Measures

Ignacio Traverso-Ribón[✉]

FZI Research Center for Information Technology, Karlsruhe, Germany
traverso@fzi.de

Abstract. Precisely determining semantic similarity between entities becomes a building block for data mining tasks, and existing approaches tackle this problem by mainly considering ontology-based annotations to decide relatedness. Nevertheless, because semantic similarity measures usually rely on the ontology class hierarchy and blindly treat ontology facts, they may erroneously assign high values of similarity to dissimilar entities. We propose ColorSim, a similarity measure that considers semantics of OWL2 annotations, e.g., relationship types, and implicit facts and their inferring processes, to accurately compute the relatedness of two ontology annotated entities. We compare ColorSim with state-of-the-art approaches and report on preliminary experimental results that suggest the benefits of exploiting knowledge encoded in the ontologies to measure similarity.

Keywords: Ontology annotated entities · Semantic similarity · Pattern discovery

1 Introduction and Motivation

Semantic Web initiatives have facilitated the definition of ontologies and large linked datasets, as well as the encoding of domain knowledge by annotating datasets with terms from ontologies. Ontology-based annotations induce annotation graphs or heterogeneous information networks where nodes represent entities or annotations, and links correspond to relationships among entities. Annotations encode domain knowledge required to precisely compute similarity between annotated concepts. Figure 1 presents *therapeutical targets HER1* and *HER2* and annotations from the Gene Ontology (GO)[1]. These annotations explicitly describe properties of *HER1* and *HER2*, and state-of-the-art similarity measures like AnnSim [13] or DiShIn [4], decide relatedness between *HER1* and *HER2* in terms of the similarity of these annotations. However, because annotations correspond to terms in an ontology, they can be of different types or be related through different relationships. Additionally, these annotations can be also used to perform reasoning tasks that infer new implicit annotations. In case semantic similarity measures do not consider this information, inaccurate

---

[1] Annotations extracted from Uniprot-GOA http://www.ebi.ac.uk/GOA.

© Springer International Publishing Switzerland 2015
F. Gandon et al. (Eds.): ESWC 2015, LNCS 9088, pp. 795–805, 2015.
DOI: 10.1007/978-3-319-18818-8_52

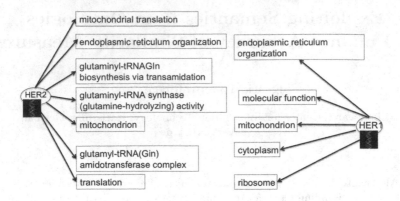

Fig. 1. Annotations in GO of genes HER1 and HER2

similarity values can be assigned. Our research aims at exploiting all this knowledge to precisely decide relatedness, and defining a novel similarity measure named ColorSim which is able to: (*i*) distinguish the *types of the relationships* in the annotation graphs; and (*ii*) consider *implicit relationships* and compare them in terms of the *justifications* that support these inferences. Further, we devise an efficient and scalable implementation of ColorSim and will implement a framework for link prediction and domain pattern discovery that will exploit the properties of ColorSim. For a preliminary evaluation of our approach, we use the online tool Collaborative Evaluation of Semantic Similarity Measures (CESSM) [18] to study the quality of ColorSim on a dataset composed of pairs of proteins from UniProt [2]. We compare ColorSim with respect to three domain-specific similarity measures: Sequence Similarity (SeqSim) [22], ECC [5], and Pfam [18], and eleven state-of-the-art semantic similarity measures. Experimental results suggest that ColorSim exhibits high correlation with domain-specific measures, and is competitive with similarity measures that consider both information content and structural characteristics of the compared annotations. We plan to extend our study for analyzing the impact of ColorSim on link prediction and pattern discovery in the Life Sciences domain, e.g., drug-target interaction collections [2,16] and GO annotated families of genes [13]; as well as in the e-learning domain, e.g., for the recommendation of learning objects annotated with the Pedagogical Ontology (PO) developed in the INTUITEL[3] project.

2   Related Work

We have identified the following similarity measures that are able to deal with heterogeneous information networks: (*i*) Taxonomic-based, (*ii*) Meta-Path-based, (*iii*) Neighborhood-based, (*iv*) Annotation-based, and (*v*) Information Content-based similarity measures.

---

[2] http://www.uniprot.org/.
[3] http://www.intuitel.eu.

Taxonomic-Based Similarity Measures: Taxonomic-based similarity measures decide relatedness in terms of the topology of the ontology and usually consider only the *is-a* relationship. D_{ps} [15] and D_{tax} [1] are state-of-the-art taxonomic similarity measures that assign *higher* similarity values to pairs of nodes that are at *greater* depth in the taxonomy and closer to their *lowest common ancestor*, i.e., similarity is defined in terms of the *deepest common ancestor* of these two nodes in the ontology. Usually, they do not consider any kind of semantics; therefore, relationship types or implicit facts may not be taken into account.

Meta-Path Based Similarity Measures: Meta-path-based similarity measures compute relatedness in terms of the sub-graphs of an original information network that satisfies a *meta-path* expression. A *meta-path* is a path expression on the nodes and edges of the information network, and characterizes a set of paths. The intuition behind meta-path-based similarity measures is that, the more linked two concepts are by paths that satisfy the input meta-path, the more similar they are. PathSim [23] and HeteSim [20] are meta-path-based similarity measures that compute relatedness based on this idea. These similarity measures are not designed to deal with ontologies, and the semantics that describe the terms used to annotate the concepts in the information network is not considered by these measures. Therefore, they only take into account links that are explicitly defined in the information network, omitting implicit facts and their corresponding justifications.

Neighborhood Based Similarity Measures: Neighborhood based similarity measures define relatedness of two concepts in terms of the similarity of their neighbors. SimRank [7] extends PageRank [12] to compute relatedness between graph related concepts. However, SimRank is not designed to deal with ontologies; thus, it does not differentiate between link types, their semantics, and implicit facts, i.e., all the neighbors are considered in the same way, regardless of the type of the relationships that connect them.

Information Content Based Similarity Measures: Information Content measures show how informative is a concept in a certain corpus. It is calculated with the following formula: $IC(x) = -\log\left(\frac{freq(x)}{N}\right)$, where *freq*$(x)$ is the number of times the concept x appears in the corpus, and N is the size of the corpus; therefore, more frequently used concepts are seen as less informative. The main work in this area is the similarity measure presented by Resnik et al. [19], which defines relatedness between two concepts as the Information Content of the most informative common ancestor. Further, Jiang and Conrath [8], and Lin [11] rely on this idea. Couto et al. refines with GraSM [3] and DiShIn [4] the similarity measure of Resnik defining the disjunctive common ancestors of two concepts; the similarity is defined by the average of the Information Content of all the disjunctive common ancestors. The Information Content-based similarity measures are designed to calculate the similarity between words in a thesaurus; therefore, they only consider the topology of the taxonomy.

Annotation-Based Similarity Measures: *AnnSim* [13] is an annotation-based similarity measure that determines relatedness of two entities in terms of the similarity of their annotations. To compute the similarity of annotations, *AnnSim* combines properties of path- and topological-based similarity measures like D_{tax} and Dice coefficients, and does not consider any additional semantics represented in the corresponding ontology. Contrary to existing approaches, ColorSim considers *semantics* as a *first-class citizen*, and exploits this knowledge during the computation of relatedness between ontology-based annotated entities.

3   Problem Statement and Contributions

We hypothesize that semantics encoded in ontologies possess valuable information that have to be considered to determine relatedness. Our first research goal addresses the challenges of defining a semantic similarity measure able to differentiate between relationship types and exploit their semantics; then, we plan to develop a framework that relies on this measure to enhance data mining tasks. Our research questions (*RQ*) are the following: (*RQ1*) What is the improvement of considering semantics during the computation of similarity between two annotated concepts?; (*RQ2*) How can semantic similarity measures efficiently scale up to large datasets and be computed in real-time applications?; and (*RQ3*) What is the impact of expressive semantic similarity measures on data mining tasks, e.g., to discover domain patterns between annotated concepts?.

Existing similarity measures are not able to fully exploit information about relationship types or their properties. Therefore, our first research goal is to propose a novel semantic similarity measure. We rely on OWL2 as vocabulary to describe concepts and relationships, and the axioms that describe their semantics; further, an OWL2 reasoner is assumed to infer implicit facts. Figure 2(a) presents a taxonomy of relationships in the Gene Ontology (GO). Relationship taxonomies can refine a neighborhood-based similarity approach assuming that not only the neighbors of a concept influence in the similarity measure, but also the relationship type used to infer that this concept is a neighbor. For example, if we have four concepts A, B, C, and D, all of them identical in terms of taxonomy-based similarity, but related through the following relationships: (*i*) A *part_of* D; (*ii*) B *negatively_regulates* D; and (*iii*) C *positively_regulates* D. Since *negatively_regulates* and *positively_regulates* are more similar according to the taxonomy (See Fig. 2(a)), both B and C must be more similar than A and B, or A and C.

Additionally, existing semantic similarity measures do not take into account implicit facts. The description of the relationships in the datasets of the Linking Open Data (LOD) cloud, includes a set of semantic properties specified with OWL2, e.g., *transitivity*, *reflexivity*, *ObjectPropertyChain*, or *symmetry*, which allow the reasoner to infer new implicit relationships between two concepts. To illustrate, consider the following properties of GO relationships: (*i*) *hasPart* is the inverse of *partOf*; and (*ii*) *regulates* is transitive over *partOf* by means of

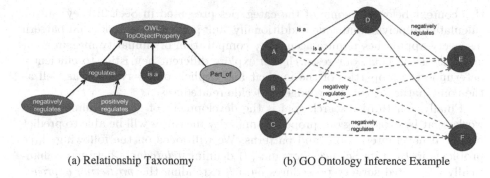

(a) Relationship Taxonomy   (b) GO Ontology Inference Example

Fig. 2. Differences according to the knowledge encoded in GO

an *ObjectPropertyChain* axiom. Additionally, relationships are transitive over the *is-a* relationship in OWL2. Although considering implicit relationships is a step forward in comparison with the-state-of-the art, this is not enough for computing accurate values of similarity. We consider that not only the final inference is relevant to calculate the similarity, but also the followed *derivation route* to reach this inference. This *route* is provided by OWL2 reasoners as a set of axioms that supports the final inference. Figure 2(b) illustrates implicit relationships according to the semantics encoded in GO using dashed arrows. The reasoner infers that A, B, and C *negatively regulate* E and F. A and B share the justification, while the justification for C is different. The justification for A and B is based on the fact that the property *negatively_regulates* is transitive over the *is-a* relationship, while the justification for C relies on the transitivity of *negatively_regulates*. Further, the same implicit relationship may have more than one justification. For example, the implicit relationship *negatively_regulates* in Fig. 3(a) can be inferred by applying: (*a*) *transitivity* over *negatively_regulates*, or (*b*) *transitivity* over the *is-a* relationship.

Our second research goal is to provide a framework able to efficiently compute ColorSim on real-time and to scale up to large datasets. Currently, Web based recommendation systems are based on similarity measures that have to be calculated in real-time to satisfy users' requests. Similarity measures used in

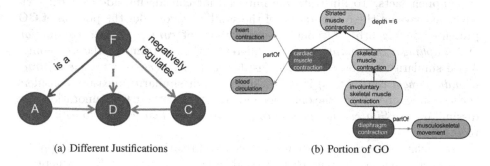

(a) Different Justifications   (b) Portion of GO

Fig. 3. Examples of implicit facts in GO (dashed arrows)

this context belong to some of the categories presented in Sect. 2; they can be calculated in polynomial time. Additionally, link prediction and domain pattern discovery approaches require accurately computation of similarity measures for large datasets. Thus, our research will explore different heuristics to efficiently determine the properties of the implicit and explicit ontology facts, as well as the combination of this knowledge to decide relatedness.

Finally, our third research goal is the development of graph mining frameworks that by exploiting our proposed similarity measures will be able to predict potential novel interactions and patterns. We will focus on the following three problems in the Life Sciences domain: (*1*) defining *relatedness* between semantically annotated surgery procedures [9]; (*2*) extending the *predicting approach* proposed by Palma et al. [14] to suggest new interactions between drugs and targets; and (*3*) analyzing and enhancing the *quality* of computationally inferred Gene Ontology annotations [21].

4   Proposed Approach and Research Methodology

We aim at enhancing semantic similarity measures with semantics from ontologies, e.g., relationship types, implicit facts and their corresponding justifications, and thus, improve tasks of link prediction, pattern discovery, and recommendations. We propose ColorSim, a semantic similarity measure that computes relatedness between two entities E_1 and E_2 annotated with ontology terms. ColorSim assigns values of similarity to E_1 and E_2 close to 1.0, if their corresponding annotation sets A_1 and A_2, are highly similar, i.e., similarity depends on how good is the matching between the annotations in A_1 and A_2. To compute this matching, sets A_1 and A_2 are represented as a weighted bipartite graph $WBG = (A_1 \cup A_2, WE)$, where WE is a set of the weighted edges in the Cartesian product of A_1 and A_2, and an edge weight corresponds to the similarity between annotations $a_1 \in A_1$ and $a_2 \in A_2$ connected by the edge.

The novelty of our approach relies on the computation of the similarity between a_1 and a_2. ColorSim considers not only the *class hierarchy* of the ontology to decide the relatedness between a_1 and a_2, but also takes into account the explicit and implicit neighbors, the type of the relationships that supports the inference of these neighbors, and the reasoning processes performed to infer the implicit facts. To illustrate the impact that considering additional knowledge can have on the computation of the similarity, consider the portion of GO presented in Fig. 3(b). Although the neighbors of *cardiac muscle contraction* and *diaphragm contraction* are very different either in terms of the taxonomy-based similarity and based on their justifications, D_{tax}(*cardiac muscle contraction, diaphragm contraction*) is *0.75*. Contrary, our similarity measure considers the semantics encoded in the ontology and detects that these two annotations are dissimilar, i.e., *Sim(cardiac muscle contraction, diaphragm contraction)* is equal to *0.135*.

We define for each annotation a_i, a set R_i of relationships where a_i appears as subject. Each element in R_i is a quadruple $t = (a_i, a_j, r_{ij}, E_{ij})$, where r_{ij}

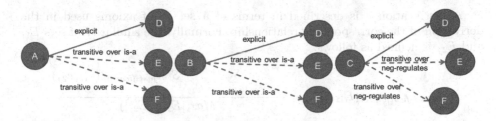

Fig. 4. Neighborhoods of nodes in Fig. 2(b). Solid and dashed arrows represent explicit and implicit relationships, respectively. Implicit relationships are labelled with the axioms used to derive the relation.

is a relationship type such that there is an out-going link from a_i to a_j in the ontology, and E_{ij} is a set composed of the justifications that support the inference of r_{ij}, whenever r_{ij} is an implicit fact. Figure 4 illustrates neighborhoods of nodes where the same relationships are inferred using different justifications. Quadruples represent the association between two nodes through an explicit or implicit relationship, e.g., $t_1 = (A, E, neg\text{-}regulates, \{transitive\ over\ is\text{-}a\})$ is an example of a quadruple where the relationship *neg-regulates* is implicit and inferred by using the axiom *transitive over is-a*. Based on the knowledge represented in quadruples, we compute the similarity $Sim(a_1, a_2)$ as follows:

$$Sim(a_1, a_2) = \frac{\sum\limits_{(t_{1i}, t_{2j}) \in R_1 \times R_2} Sim_{relationship}(t_{1i}, t_{2j})}{Max(|R_1|, |R_2|)}$$

where

- R_1 and R_2 are the relationships sets of a_1 and a_2, respectively;
- quadruples $t_{1i} = (a_1, a_i, r_{1i}, E_{1i})$ and $t_{2j} = (a_2, a_j, r_{2j}, E_{2j})$ belong to the Cartesian product of $R_1 \times R_2$; and
- $Sim_{relationship}(t_{1i}, t_{2j})$ is defined as a triangular norm tN[4] that combines the values of similarity of the justifications of r_{1i}, r_{2j} with the taxonomy-based similarity of t_{1i} and t_{2j}.

The $Sim_{relationship}(t_{1i}, t_{2j})$ is defined as follows:

$$Sim_{relationship}(t_{1i}, t_{2j}) = tN(Sim_D(t_{1i}, t_{2j}), Sim_{justificationSet}(E_{1i}, E_{2j}))$$

where,

- The taxonomic similarity of t_{1i} and t_{2j}, $Sim_D(t_{1i}, t_{2j})$, corresponds to a triangular norm that combines three taxonomic similarities: $D_{tax}(a_1, a_2)$, $D_{tax}(a_i, a_j)$, and $D_{tax}(r_{1i}, r_{2j})$; and
- $Sim_{justificationSet}(E_{1i}, E_{2j})$ is a similarity measure that determines the relatedness of the justification sets E_{1i} and E_{2j} based on the similarity of the justifications in the Cartesian product of E_{1i} and E_{2j}.

---

[4] For this ontology we used the *Product TN* for $Sim_{relationship}$ and Sim_D.

A justification e is described in terms of a set X of axioms used in the derivation of the corresponding relationship. Formally, the similarity of sets E_{1i} and E_{2j} is defined as follows:

$$Sim_{justificationSet}(E_{1i}, E_{2j}) = \frac{\sum\limits_{(e_{1i}, e_{2j}) \in (E_{1i} \times E_{2j})} Sim_{justification}(e_{1i}, e_{2j})}{Max(|E_{1i}|, |E_{2j}|)}$$

where,

– $Sim_{justification}(e_{1i}, e_{2j})$ is defined as the similarity of the sets X_{1i}, X_{2j} of axioms of e_{1i}, e_{2j}, i.e., $Sim_{justification}(e_{1i}, e_{2j}) = Sim_{axiomSet}(X_{1i}, X_{2j})$
– the similarity of two sets of axioms, $Sim_{axiomSet}(X_{1i}, X_{2j})$, is defined in terms of the type of the axioms.

Currently, we consider four types of OWL2 axioms: *subClassOf*, *subPropertyOf*, *ObjectPropertyChain*, and *TransitiveProperty*. Further, we provide a different definition of similarity for each axiom, and the similarity between different axioms is 0.0.

Based on the definition of the similarity $Sim(a_1, a_2)$ between two annotations a_1 and a_2, we compute the *1-to-1 maximal weighted bipartite graph matching* between two sets of annotations. Given two annotation sets A_1 and A_2, let $MWBG = (A_1 \cup A_2, WEr)$ be the *1-to-1 maximal weighted bipartite graph matching* for a weighted bipartite graph $WBG = (A_1 \cup A_2, WE)$, where $WEr \subseteq WE$, *ColorSim* on *MWBG* is as follows:

$$ColorSim(MWBG) = \frac{\sum\limits_{(a_1, a_2) \in WEr} Sim(a_1, a_2)}{Max(|A_1|, |A_2|)}$$

5   Preliminary Results

We use the CESSM Collaborative Evaluation of GO-based Semantic Similarity Measures [18] to evaluate ColorSim on a dataset composed of pairs of proteins from UniProt. These proteins are annotated with GO terms separated into the GO hierarchies of biological process (BP), molecular function (MF), and cellular component (CC). GO and UniProt are both from August 2008. CESSM implements eleven semantic similarity measures; some of them are measures specifically developed for the GO ontology while others are general measures. We evaluated ColorSim with the provided dataset and compared our results w.r.t. the other measures and the three gold standards. Figures 5(a) and 5(b) report the results of ColorSim produced by the CESSM tool. The correlation between ColorSim and SeqSim is higher than 0.72; its behavior is very similar to simGIC (GI) [17] and simUI (UI) [6], two similarity measures specific for GO. Table 1 shows the correlations of ColorSin and state-of-the-art measures w.r.t. three gold standard measures: ECC, Pfam, and SeqSim. ColorSim is the sixth best with ECC, the first with Pfam, and the fourth with SeqSim. Further, ColorSim is the

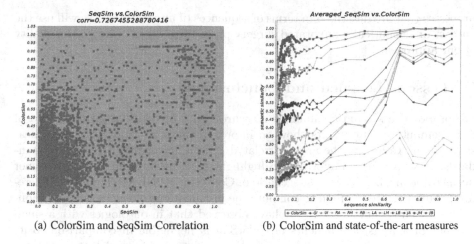

(a) ColorSim and SeqSim Correlation   (b) ColorSim and state-of-the-art measures

Fig. 5. Correlation between SeqSim and ColorSim

Table 1. Correlation with three baseline similarity measures: ECC, Pfam, and SeqSim

Similarity	GI	UI	RA	RM	RB	LA	LM	LB	JA	JM	JB	ColorSim
ECC	**0.398**	**0.402**	0.302	0.308	**0.444**	0.304	0.313	**0.435**	0.193	0.254	**0.371**	**0.369**
Pfam	0.455	0.451	0.323	0.263	0.459	0.287	0,206	0.373	0.173	0.165	0.332	**0.499**
SeqSim	**0.774**	**0.730**	0.407	0.303	**0.740**	0.341	0.254	0.637	0.216	0.235	0.586	**0.726**

domain-independent measure with the highest correlation. The Pearson's correlation of ColorSim with SeqSim is 0.726 while the state-of-the-art annotation similarity measure AnnSim has a correlation of 0.65 with SeqSim in the same dataset. Both measures rely on the GO annotations to compute similarity. However, AnnSim is based on D_{tax}, and it only considers the class hierarchy of the ontology and may assign high values of similarity to dissimilar proteins which also have low values of SeqSim. Contrary, ColorSim is able to distinguish the relationships that relate the neighbors of two annotations and the axioms used to infer the implicit facts. Thus, ColorSim can assign more accurate values of similarity and exhibits a better correlation with baseline similarity measures.

6 Evaluation Plan

We will develop an implementation of ColorSim able to efficiently scale up to large datasets. The evaluation of our approach will be conducted on different biomedical datasets that represent associations between drugs and targets [2,16], and genes and GO terms [13]; as well as PO annotated learning objects. We also plan to enhance the link prediction approach proposed by Palma et al. [14] with the properties of ColorSim and study the impact that these new features have on link prediction. Finally, we will extend ColorSim to consider order between the annotations of two entities; this feature will allow to detect relatedness between processes that are described in terms of sequences of annotations. We will use the dataset of semantically annotated surgery procedures [9] to evaluate the quality of our approach.

7   Lessons Learned and Conclusions

We proposed a semantic similarity measure aware of relationship types and of their semantics. Our results show an improvement w.r.t. state-of-the-art measures, being ColorSim the most correlated generic measure with the gold standards. However, it is important to highlight that because an OWL2 reasoner needs to be invoked, the worst scenario of ColorSim is 2NEXP-Time [10]. Therefore, heuristics are required to compute the justifications of the implicit relationships efficiently. Furthermore, we have observed that in ontologies with a small number of axioms, the benefits of ColorSim is negligible in comparison to its computational cost. Thus, we need to develop strategies to detect conditions that benefit the computation of the implicit relationships and their respective justifications. The study of these computational issues and the development of a graph mining framework that exploit the benefits of ColorSim, are part of our future work.

Acknowledgments. This work was supported by the German Ministry of Economy and Energy within the TIGRESS project (Ref. KF2076928MS3) and the EU's 7th Framework Programme FP7-ICT-2011.8 (INTUITEL, Grant 318496). I thank Maria-Esther Vidal (mvidal@ldc.usb.ve) for her guidance and insights.

References

1. Benik, J., Chang, C., Raschid, L., Vidal, M.-E., Palma, G., Thor, A.: Finding cross genome patterns in annotation graphs. In: Bodenreider, O., Rance, B. (eds.) DILS 2012. LNCS, vol. 7348, pp. 21–36. Springer, Heidelberg (2012)
2. Bleakley, K., Yamanishi, Y.: Supervised prediction of drug-target interactions using bipartite local models. Bioinformatics **25**(18), 2397–2403 (2009)
3. Couto, F.M., Silva, M.J., Coutinho, P.M.: Semantic similarity over the gene ontology: family correlation and selecting disjunctive ancestors. In Proceedings of the 14th ACM International Conference on Information and Knowledge Management, CIKM 2005, pp. 343–344. ACM, New York (2005)
4. Couto, F.M., Silva, M.J., et al.: Disjunctive shared information between ontology concepts: application to gene ontology. J. Biomed. Semant. **2**, 5 (2011)
5. Devos, D., Valencia, A.: Practical limits of function prediction. Proteins: Struct. Funct. Bioinf. **41**(1), 98–107 (2000)
6. Guo, X., Liu, R., Shriver, C.D., Hu, H., Liebman, M.N.: Assessing semantic similarity measures for the characterization of human regulatory pathways. Bioinformatics **22**(8), 967–973 (2006)
7. Jeh, G., Widom, J.: Simrank: a measure of structural-context similarity. In: Proceedings of the Eighth ACM SIGKDD International Conference on Knowledge Discovery and Data Mining, pp. 538–543. ACM (2002)
8. Jiang, J.J., Conrath, D.W.: Semantic similarity based on corpus statistics and lexical taxonomy. CoRR, cmp-lg/9709008 (1997)

9. Katić, D., Wekerle, A.-L., Gärtner, F., Kenngott, H., Müller-Stich, B.P., Dill-mann, R., Speidel, S.: Knowledge-driven formalization of laparoscopic surgeries for rule-based intraoperative context-aware assistance. In: Stoyanov, D., Collins, D.L., Sakuma, I., Abolmaesumi, P., Jannin, P. (eds.) IPCAI 2014. LNCS, vol. 8498, pp. 158–167. Springer, Heidelberg (2014)

10. Kazakov, Y.: SRIQ and SROIQ are harder than SHOIQ. In: DL 2008 (2008)

11. Lin, D.: An information-theoretic definition of similarity. In: ICML, vol. 98 (1998)

12. Page, L., Brin, S., Motwani, R., Winograd, T.: The PageRank citation ranking: Bringing order to the web (1999)

13. Palma, G., Vidal, M.-E., Haag, E., Raschid, L., Thor, A.: Measuring relatedness between scientific entities in annotation datasets. In: Proceedings of the International Conference on Bioinformatics, Computational Biology and Biomedical Informatics (2013)

14. Palma, G., Vidal, M.-E., Raschid, L.: Drug-target interaction prediction using semantic similarity and edge partitioning. In: Mika, P., Tudorache, T., Bernstein, A., Welty, C., Knoblock, C., Vrandečić, D., Groth, P., Noy, N., Janowicz, K., Goble, C. (eds.) ISWC 2014, Part I. LNCS, vol. 8796, pp. 131–146. Springer, Heidelberg (2014)

15. Pekar, V., Staab, S.: Taxonomy learning: factoring the structure of a taxonomy into a semantic classification decision. In: Proceedings of the 19th ICCL, vol. 1, pp. 1–7. Association for Computational Linguistics (2002)

16. Perlman, L., Gottlieb, A., Atias, N., Ruppin, E., Sharan, R.: Combining drug and gene similarity measures for drug-target elucidation. J. Comput. Biol. 18(2), 133–145 (2011)

17. Pesquita, C., Faria, D., Bastos, H., Falcão, A., Couto, F.: Evaluating gobased semantic similarity measures. In: Proceedings of the 10th Annual Bio-Ontologies Meeting, vol. 2007, pp. 37–40 (2007)

18. Pesquita, C., Pessoa, D., Faria, D., Couto, F.: Cessm: collaborative evaluation of semantic similarity measures. Jornadas en bioinformatica 157, 1–5 (2009)

19. Resnik, P.: Using information content to evaluate semantic similarity in a taxonomy. arXiv preprint cmp-lg/9511007 (1995)

20. Shi, C., Kong, X., Huang, Y., Yu, P.S., Wu, B.: Hetesim: A general framework for relevance measure in heterogeneous networks. arXiv preprint (2013). http://arxiv.org/abs/1309.7393arXiv:1309.7393

21. Škunca, N., Altenhoff, A., Dessimoz, C.: Quality of computationally inferred gene ontology annotations. PLoS Comput. Biol. 8(5), e1002533 (2012)

22. Smith, T., Waterman, M.: Identification of common molecular subsequences. J. Mol. Biol. 147(1), 195–197 (1981)

23. Sun, Y., Han, J., Yan, X., Yu, P.S., Wu, T.: Pathsim: Meta path-based top-k similarity search in heterogeneous information networks. In: VLDB 2011 (2011)

e-Document Standards as Background Knowledge in Context-Based Ontology Matching

Audun Vennesland[✉]

Norwegian University of Science and Technology, Trondheim, Norway
audun.vennesland@idi.ntnu.no

Abstract. Ontology matching is the process of finding correspondence between heterogeneous ontologies and consequently support semantic interoperability between different information systems. Using contextual information relative to the ontologies being matched is referred to as context-based ontology matching and is considered one promising direction of improving the matching performance. This PhD investigates how such contextual information, often residing in disparate sources and represented by different formats, can be optimally represented to ontology matching systems and how these systems best can employ this context to produce accurate and correct correspondences. Currently we are investigating how the international e-Document standard Universal Business Language from the transport logistics domain can provide useful context when matching domain ontologies for this particular domain. Early evaluation tests and analysis of the results suggest that the current version of the Universal Business Language ontology does not impact on the matching results and that further reconfiguration and enhancements are needed.

1 Introduction

The use of external context as input to identifying correspondence between heterogenous ontologies is seen as a promising approach within ontology matching [1,2] and is referred to as context-based ontology matching. When two ontologies are to be matched, they often lack a common ground on which comparisons can be based. In context-based ontology matching the intention is to establish such a common ground using the relations between the ontologies being matched and their environment represented by external resources [3].

Often the external resources are represented by formal or less formal ontologies [4,5] or other sources of context. However, the quality of the external sources varies [6], something which threatens the validity of the identified alignments. Moreover, even if the application of semantic technologies is mature in some domains the use of semantic technologies is still limited in many other domains and formalized context is difficult to come by. A survey among ontology matching practitioners [2] states that integration of domain knowledge into alignment techniques is a significant challenge. Hence, investigation of other and reliable sources of context as well as improved techniques for exploiting such context is required.

© Springer International Publishing Switzerland 2015
F. Gandon et al. (Eds.): ESWC 2015, LNCS 9088, pp. 806–816, 2015.
DOI: 10.1007/978-3-319-18818-8_53

e-Documents standards specify through message specifications (including XSD schemas), business process descriptions, narratives, instance data and other material how information should be exchanged electronically.

Our approach is to identify appropriate methods for transforming such contextual information into a more formal representation, investigate how it can be optimally employed by ontology matchers, and evaluate its impact on the ontology matching process. e-Document standards is selected as a case based on their inherent qualities (presumably quality assured and sustainable information, mixture of domain-specific and more generic information elements, a combination of structured and unstructured formats, and the availability of proper instance data).

2   State of the Art

2.1   Context-Based Ontology Matching

Ontology matching is the process of identifying correspondences (alignments) between heterogeneous ontologies that enable the information systems applying the ontologies to interpret data being communicated among them. Euzenat and Shvaiko [3] distinguishes between *element-level techniques* and *structure-level techniques*. Element-level techniques focuses on the ontology entities (or instances of them) themselves while disregarding their relations with other entities (or instances of them). Examples of such techniques are *string-based similarity* measures (which might identify correspondences based on name similarity), *language-based techniques* (e.g. using NLP and lexical resources to capture conceptual similarity and hence correspondence between entities not necessarily having the same name) and *informal- or formal resource-based techniques* which employs external sources, either formal ones such as ontologies or informal sources such as web sites or documents, to improve the matching operation. Structure-level techniques on the other hand analyze how entities (or their instances) appear together in a structure. Some examples of structure-level techniques are *graph-based techniques* (such as the use of graph algorithms to identify similar neighboring entities and relations and thereby calculate correspondence), *model-based techniques* (e.g. the use of description logic reasoning in order to identify correspondence on the basis of semantic interpretation) and *instance-based techniques* (for example using statistical methods to compare sets of class instances to identify correspondence between these classes).

Context-based ontology matching uses external resources in order to help establish a common ground (contextualization) between the ontologies to be matched and is considered a promising approach [1,2]. These external resources can be formal or informal. Formal resources are typically ontological structures using a formal language such as OWL or RDF. Different levels of ontological structures have previously been applied to aid the ontology matching task, including the use of upper-level ontologies [4], a combination of many ontologies [5], use of less formal resources such as WordNet [7], and use of informal resources such as web sites to identify correspondences [8].

According to [9] the use of external context can be categorized into three use cases: (i) using the external context as a reference (e.g. using linguistic resources to find synonyms that can help establish similarity among entities), (ii) as an oracle (i.e. replacing the human expert when validating suggested alignments from the matching operation by querying external background knowledge) or (iii) as a mediator (i.e. mapping entities from the source and target ontologies to an intermediate ontology and thereby identify correspondence).

2.2 e-Document Standards

Useful contextual information resides in e-Document standards (a.k.a. business document standards or e-business standards) and associated material. Although this work initially focuses on standards related to the transport logistics domain similar standards developed using similar processes and in close cooperation between standards developing organizations and domain experts exist in other domains. Some examples are general trade [10,11], public and private procurement [12], food and agriculture [13], manufacturing, and consumer electronics. So even though the focus initially is on a specific domain, the approach should be generalizable to other domains also.

In the work so far we have focused on OASIS UBL (Universal Business Language). UBL is an OASIS standard providing a library of e-Documents and information elements for the procurement and transport logistics domains. In the most recent version of the standard (version 2.1) the library consists of 698 classes (elements) with attributes and associations, encompassing both domain specific and more generic elements. The entire library is represented in XSD schemas.

Figure 1, which represents an excerpt from the UBL library, exemplifies some of the possible context data available in the XSD schemas. In this particular example, which have been compressed for the sake of brevity, we see the TransportMeans complex type, the element JourneyID, which represents a property of TransportMeans (denoted by the cbc prefix) and the element OwnerParty, which represents an association from TransportMeans (denoted by the cac prefix). In addition to the hierarchical structure the schema also includes element definitions, alternative business terms, cardinalities, and data type definition.

Besides the data represented by the XSD schemas, the standard provides XML instances for all e-Documents included in the standards, offering an opportunity to apply instance-based matching techniques.

3   Problem Statement and Contributions

The use of contextual information is claimed to improve ontology matching operations and many state of the art ontology matchers utilize different types of external sources as support in their matching operations. A preliminary literature review suggests that few research endeavors have focused on identifying exactly which features are attractive w.r.t. expressing context and how these features should

```
<xsd:complexType name="TransportMeansType">
  <xsd:annotation>
    <xsd:documentation>
      <ccts:Component>
        <ccts:Definition>A class to describe a particular vehicle or vessel used for
          the conveyance of goods or persons.</ccts:Definition>
        <ccts:ObjectClass>Transport Means</ccts:ObjectClass>
        <ccts:AlternativeBusinessTerms>Conveyance</ccts:AlternativeBusinessTerms>
      </ccts:Component>
    </xsd:documentation>
  </xsd:annotation>
  <xsd:sequence>
    <xsd:element ref="cbc:JourneyID" minOccurs="0" maxOccurs="1">
      <xsd:annotation>
        <xsd:documentation>
          <ccts:Component>
            <ccts:Definition>An identifier for the regular service schedule of this
              means of transport.</ccts:Definition>
            <ccts:Cardinality>0..1</ccts:Cardinality>
            <ccts:ObjectClass>Transport Means</ccts:ObjectClass>
            <ccts:PropertyTerm>Journey Identifier</ccts:PropertyTerm>
            <ccts:DataType>Identifier. Type</ccts:DataType>
            <ccts:AlternativeBusinessTerms>Voyage Number, Scheduled Conveyance
              Identifier (WCO ID 205), Flight Number</ccts:AlternativeBusinessTerms>
          </ccts:Component>
        </xsd:documentation>
      </xsd:annotation>
    </xsd:element>
    <xsd:element ref="cac:OwnerParty" minOccurs="0" maxOccurs="1">
      <xsd:annotation>
        <xsd:documentation>
          <ccts:Component>
            <ccts:Definition>The party that owns this means of
              transport.</ccts:Definition>
            <ccts:Cardinality>0..1</ccts:Cardinality>
            <ccts:ObjectClass>Transport Means</ccts:ObjectClass>
            <ccts:PropertyTerm>Party</ccts:PropertyTerm>
          </ccts:Component>
        </xsd:documentation>
      </xsd:annotation>
    </xsd:element>
```

Fig. 1. Relevant information from the UBL XSD schema

be optimally represented or modeled in order to support the matching process. Furthermore, the ontology matching systems are apparently very often targeting the (bio) medical domain, and although some of them also performs well in other tracks of the OAEI benchmark campaign, preliminary analysis suggest that their performance, and the underlying matching strategies, are to some degree domain dependent (see preliminary evaluation results in Sect. 6.2).

On this basis we have devised the following research questions:

RQ1: Which external sources of context can positively impact on the ontology matching performance?
RQ2: How should this external context be modeled in order to maximize its exploitation potential in ontology matching?
RQ3: Which ontology matching strategies are best suited for exploiting such context?

4   Research Approach

The approach in this PhD can be best characterized as a mixed-strategy design [14]. On the one hand we follow a fixed design introducing an experimental strategy where we measure the effect of manipulating the variables involved, evaluate the effect of this manipulation, and analyze why the result became as it did. On the other hand we use a flexible design in the sense that the overall process is highly exploratory and that we in the end seek to establish some theories describing why this happened given the available data and the processing performed on them. The e-Document standards represents a case study, and presumingly these standards possess context that can positively contribute to improved ontology matching results. But this is also influenced by how the context data is processed by the ontology matchers (and the choice of algorithms employed).

The experimental strategy followed is illustrated in Fig. 2. The contextual information source is transformed to a formal representation. Using this formal representation as background knowledge, the experiment takes two ontologies as input and identifies correspondences among them using an ontology matcher. The resulting alignment from the matching operation is compared against a reference alignment holding the "true" set of correspondences among the ontologies and evaluated on the basis of commonly accepted metrics (precision, recall and F-measure). The evaluation results are then analyzed and if required the external context and/or the ontology matcher is reconfigured before the next iteration in the experiment cycle.

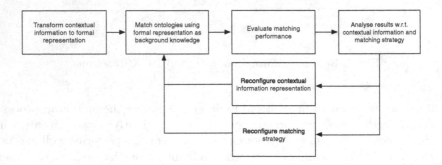

Fig. 2. Overall process

5   Preliminary Results

An initial development following the approach described in the previous chapter has been performed. The following developments are basically prerequisites for further investigation of the research questions defined in Sect. 3.

1. **Transform contextual information to formal representation:** XSLT (eXtensible Stylesheet Language Transformation) was used to transform data from UBL XSD schemas to an OWL ontology. This work extends the generic xsd2owl method [15] to fit with the characteristics of the UBL standard as well as other relevant e-Document standards in order to be generalizable to other settings.

2. **Match ontologies using formal representation (background knowledge):** The resulting OWL ontology from the previous step was used as background knowledge to support the ontology matching using an existing ontology matching system. In this initial setup we used the AgreementMakerLight (AML) ontology matcher [16,17].
3. **Evaluate matching performance and analyse results:** We manually developed a reference alignment holding the correct set of correspondences between the ontologies to be matched. This reference alignment was used as a baseline to compare the alignment from the ontology matching operation against. Currently this reference alignment is developed by the author and must be validated by domain experts. The evaluation measures used were precision, recall and F-measure (see Sect. 6 for more details about the evaluation).

Before reaching the next steps in the experiment cycle (Reconfigure contextual information representation and Reconfigure matching strategy) described in Sect. 4 a careful analysis of the evaluation scores must be conducted. This analysis must encompass an examination of the AML (and possibly other candidate ontology matchers) and how this matcher treats contextual information, the suitability (heterogeneity) of the to-be-matched ontologies, a verification of the correctness of the reference alignment, and an analysis of the UBL ontology and how this potentially could be enriched with additional semantics as well as data from supplementary material associated with the UBL 2.1 standard.

The generated UBL ontology is quite large, counting 1338 classes, 821 object properties and 1314 data properties. In addition to these declarations the ontology contains the following axioms: Sub Class, Object Property Domain, Object Property Range, Data Property Domain, Data Property Range, Functional Object Properties, and Functional Data Properties.

Figures 3, 4 and 5 shows the structures used by the three involved ontologies for describing the means of transport used in a transport logistics operation. As can be seen the structures are quite similar (as perceived by humans), but the naming conventions differ.

A difference between the generated UBL ontology and the other two is that while the Common Framework and LogiCO ontologies use sub class relations between classes, the relations between these entities in the UBL ontology are represented as object properties (as indicated by the dotted associations). As the UBL XSD schemas do not differentiate between associations representing what conceptually could be interpreted as sub classes (e.g. that MaritimeTransportMeans could be a sub class of TransportMeans) and other associations (e.g. that there is an association from TransportMeans to the MeasurementDimension element that enable a specification of the dimensions of the TransportMeans) we have treated these associations as object properties rather than identified those that are true sub class relations.

6   Preliminary Evaluation

Two ontologies from the transport logistics domain is being matched using an open source ontology matching system. The matching is performed both on

Fig. 3. Vehicle structure in the Com-   Fig. 4. Means of transport structure
mon Framework ontology   in the LogiCO ontology

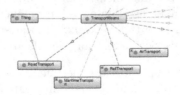

Fig. 5. Transport means structure in the UBL ontology

classes and properties, but only equivalence correspondences are identified. The
ontologies to be matched are the LogiCO ontology [18] and the Common Framework ontology. The LogiCO ontology contains 153 classes, 96 properties and 14
individuals. The Common Framework ontology contains 331 classes, 283 properties and 1384 individuals. The Common Framework ontology imports the PRO-
TON upper-layer ontology [19] for modeling generic concepts while LogiCO relies
on DOLCE+DNS Ultralite [20].

In this first evaluation we are using the AgreementMakerLight ontology
matching system. Although AML is primarily focused on matching ontologies
for the biomedical domain it was chosen as an evaluation testbed since it spe-
cializes in the use of background knowledge, it is easy to reconfigure and extend,
and has received top scores in the latest OAEI benchmarks which also includes
matching ontologies outside of the biomedical domain [21].

6.1   Evaluation Scenarios

The following evaluation scenarios are run:

1. A comparative evaluation of one ontology matching operation including
   the two ontologies where one run is using the constructed ontology from
   e-Document standards and the other run is performed without any context
   information
2. A comparative evaluation of one ontology matching operation including the
   two evaluation ontologies using other sources of contextual information (e.g.
   WordNet)

The evaluation measures applied are precision, recall and F-measure. Precision
measures the ratio of correctly found correspondences over the total number of

found correspondences. Recall measures the ratio of correctly found correspondences over the total number of expected correspondences. F-measure represents the harmonic mean of precision and recall and balances the importance of the other two evaluation measures [3].

6.2 Preliminary Evaluation Results

With a very limited verification of the UBL ontology and the reference alignment, the first evaluation run showed, as illustrated in Fig. 6, that when matching the two ontologies with no background knowledge using the default confidence level of 0.6 the precision was 77.1 %, the recall 57 % and the F-measure 66 %. The confidence level basically states that the ontology matcher trusts with 60 % certainty or above that the identified correspondence is correct.

When matching also the properties, this significantly decreased the scores with a precision of only 6.2 %, a recall of 57.1 % and an F-measure of 11.2 %. The highest scores were achieved when tuning the confidence degree from the default .6 to .9. When matching classes only this yielded a precision of 100 %, a recall of 52.4 % and an F-measure of 68.8 %.

When using the current version of the UBL ontology as background knowledge this did not influence the results at all, leaving the precision, recall and F-measure measures as they were when no background knowledge was employed. This was the case regardless of confidence level setting.

We also made an attempt using WordNet as contextual support in order to see how this compared to using the UBL ontology as background knowledge. When matching only the classes this produced the same scores as with the UBL ontology. When including the properties this actually lowered the scores resulting in a precision of 10.7 %, a recall of 33.9 % and an F-measure of 16.3 %.

These results indicatively show that the classes of the two ontologies are to some extent homogeneous, but that the properties of the two ontologies are very differently structured and named. Examining the resulting alignment from the matching operation manually we see that all identified correspondences are all exact string matches (e.g. 'Train' = 'Train'), while other (humanly) intuitive correspondences (e.g. 'CoordinateSystemName' vs. 'GeoCoordinateSystem') have

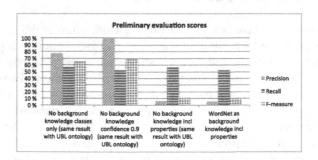

Fig. 6. Preliminary evaluation scores

not been captured by the matching system. Another observation is that the entities imported from the upper-layer ontologies being used (DOLCE+DNS Ultralite in the LogiCO ontology and PROTON in Common Framework ontology) are correctly matched. These entities are typically generic elements such as 'object' and 'event'.

When examining the three ontologies more in-depth we observe that if the ontology matching had utilized the object properties of the UBL ontology as anchors and from this derived that two classes using the same object property as anchors corresponds to each other the results could improve. An example of this is the 'TransportMeans' entity in the LogiCO ontology vs the 'Vehicle' entity in the Common Framework ontology (see Figs. 3, 4 and 5). The UBL ontology, similar to the LogiCO ontology, specifies the 'TransportMeans' class. In the UBL ontology this class has an object property 'hasAirTransport'. The range of this object property is the class 'AirTransport'. Further this 'AirTransport' class has an object property called 'hasAircraftID'. In the Common Framework ontology there is a class 'Aircraft' which is a sub class to 'Vehicle'. It should be possible to derive a correspondence between the 'Aircraft' class in the Common Framework ontology and the 'hasAircraftID' object property in the UBL ontology and hence that 'Vehicle' corresponds to 'TransportMeans' in the UBL ontology. Following this trail a correspondence between 'Vehicle' in the Common Framework ontology and 'TransportMeans' in the LogiCO ontology could be deduced.

Being preliminary work there are some obvious threats to both validity and reliability. We need to investigate more in-depth the matching techniques used by the matching system and possibly investigate how different techniques perform with the current setup. Further, the reference alignment should be more thoroughly assessed by domain expertise from the transport logistics domain. Such an assessment is planned, but not performed yet. Last but not least, the UBL ontology requires further validation and enrichment in order to make sure that the domain knowledge possessed by the standard is appropriately maintained in full scale. Primary candidate enhancements are to include the element definitions from the UBL XSD schemas (see Fig. 1 depicting among other things the element definitions) and instance data to see how this affects the evaluation scores.

7   Conclusions and Future Work

This PhD investigates how contextual information, often residing in disparate sources and represented by different formats, can be optimally represented to ontology matching systems and how these systems best can exploit this context to produce accurate and correct alignments. Using the Universal Business Language as a case, we have investigated how international e-Document standards in the transport logistics domain can provide background knowledge to support the matching of domain ontologies for this particular domain. The current developments include prerequisite artifacts required for performing the rest of the study. Early evaluation tests involving two ontologies from the transport logistics domain suggest that using the current version of the generated UBL ontology as background knowledge does not influence the matching performance and that several reconfigurations and enhancements are required. However, manual analysis of the two ontologies being matched and the developed UBL ontology suggest that the UBL standard can provide useful context to support a matching between the two transport logistics ontologies. Further work include a deeper analysis of the evaluation results, domain expertise assessment of the UBL ontology developed and the reference alignment, a more in-depth investigation of the ontology matcher being used in the evaluation and enriching the UBL ontology using additional contextual information from the UBL standard.

References

1. Shvaiko, P., Euzenat, J.: Ontology matching: state of the art and future challenges. IEEE Trans. Knowl. Data Eng. **25**(1), 158–176 (2013)
2. Otero-Cerdeira, L., Rodríguez-Martínez, F.J., Gómez-Rodríguez, A.: Ontology matching: a literature review. Expert Syst. Appl. **42**(2), 949–971 (2015)
3. Euzenat, J., Shvaiko, P., et al.: Ontology Matching. Springer, Heidelberg (2013)
4. Mascardi, V., Locoro, A., Rosso, P.: Automatic ontology matching via upper ontologies: a systematic evaluation. IEEE Trans. Knowl. Data Eng. **22**(5), 609–623 (2010)
5. Locoro, A., David, J., Euzenat, J.: Context-based matching: design of a flexible framework and experiment. J. Data Semant. **3**(1), 25–46 (2013)
6. Thayasivam, U., Doshi, P.: On the utility of WordNet for ontology alignment: is it really worth it? In: Proceedings of the Fifth IEEE International Conference on Semantic Computing (ICSC), pp.267–274. IEEE (2011)
7. Jean-Mary, Y.R., Shironoshita, E.P., Kabuka, M.R.: Ontology matching with semantic verification. Web Semant. Sci. Serv. Agents World Wide Web **7**(3), 235–251 (2009)
8. Paulheim, H., Hertling, S.: WeSeE-match results for OAEI 2013. In: Proceedings of the ISWC Workshop OM-2013, pp.197–202 (2013)
9. Chen, X.: Exploiting BioPortal as background knowledge in ontology alignment. Master thesis, Miami University (2014)
10. GS1 Global: GS1 XML Business Message Standards (BMS) (2014)
11. UN/CEFACT: Core Components Technical Specification - Part 8 of the ebXML Framework. Technical report (2003)
12. CEN BII/WS: CEN BII (CEN Workshop on Business Interoperability Interfaces for Public Procurement in Europe) (2015)
13. KTBL: About AgroXML (2012)
14. Robson, C.: Real World Research, 3rd edn. Wiley, Chichester (2011)
15. García, R., Celma, O.: Semantic integration and retrieval of multimedia metadata. In: Proceedings of the 5th International Workshop on Knowledge Markup and Semantic Annotation, pp. 69–80 (2005)
16. Faria, D., Pesquita, C., Santos, E., Cruz, I.F., Couto, F.M.: AgreementMakerLight: a scalable automated ontology matching system. In: Proceedings from the 10th International Conference on Data Integration in the Life Sciences (DILS 2014), July 2014
17. Faria, D., Martins, C., Nanavaty, A., Taheri, A., Pesquita, C., Santos, E., Cruz, I.F., Couto, F.M.: AgreementMakerLight Results for OAEI 2014 (2014)

18. Daniele, L., Pires, L.F.: An ontological approach to logistics. In: Enterprise Interoperability: Research and Applications in Service-Oriented Ecosystem (Proceedings of the 5th International IFIP Working Conference IWIE 2013). Wiley (2014)
19. Damova, M., Kiryakov, A., Simov, K., Petrov, S.: Mapping the central LOD ontologies to PROTON upper-level ontology. In: Proceedings of the Fifth International Workshop on Ontology Matching (OM-2010), pp.61–72 (2010)
20. Mascardi, V., Cordì, V., Rosso, P.: A Comparison of Upper Ontologies (Technical report DISI-TR-06-21). Technical report, University of Geova, Italy (2007)
21. Dragisic, Z., Eckert, K., Euzenat, J., Faria, D., Ferrara, A., Granada, R., Ivanova, V.: Results of the ontology alignment evaluation initiative 2014. In: Proceedings of the 9th International Workshop on Ontology Matching Collocated with the 13th International Semantic Web Conference (ISWC 2014) (2014)

Semantics-Enabled User Interest Mining

Fattane Zarrinkalam$^{(\boxtimes)}$

Department of Computer Engineering,
Ferdowsi University of Mashhad, Mashhad, Iran
fattane.zarrinkalam@stu-mail.um.ac.ir

Abstract. Microblogging services such as Twitter allow users to express their feelings and views in real-time through microposts. This provides a wealth of information both collectively and individually that can be effectively mined so as to facilitate personalization, recommendation and customized search. A fundamental task with this respect would be to extract users' interests. This has been mainly done using probabilistic models that rely on measures such as frequency of co-occurrence of important phrases, which forgoes the underlying semantics of the phrases in favor of highlighting the role of syntactical repetition of content. Some recent works have considered the role of semantics by using knowledge bases such as DBPedia and Freebase. However, they limit the topics of interest to be a set of individual concepts extracted from the microposts in isolation, i.e. without considering the relationships of the microposts to each other or to other users. This proposal seeks to further build on these works by introducing a definition of topical interest, which enables the identification of more specific and semantically complex topics involving multiple interrelated concepts. Based on this definition, methods will be introduced for the detection of both explicitly observed and implicitly implied user interests, in addition to the identification of user interest shifts based on the temporal clues.

Keywords: #eswcphd2015zarrinkalam · User interest detection · Microblogging service · Semantics-enabled

1 Introduction

With the emergence and the growing popularity of microblogging services like Twitter, many users extensively use microposts to express their feelings and views about different topics. This has made microblogging services a source of implicit and explicit information for user interest identification [1, 2]. This has the potential to contribute to different application areas such as filtering twitter streams [3, 4], news recommendation [5] and user community identification [6], among others.

When processing microposts for the identification and extraction of user interests, traditional keyword-based methods, which are often proposed for processing formal and large documents, are less effective on microposts, due to the short length, noisiness and informality of the content [7, 8]. A potential approach for addressing these issues is to consider the underlying semantics of microposts. To this end, recent works have proposed to utilize external knowledge bases (such as DBpedia) to link the terms in the microposts to the relevant concepts described in those knowledge bases. Since these

© Springer International Publishing Switzerland 2015
F. Gandon et al. (Eds.): ESWC 2015, LNCS 9088, pp. 817–828, 2015.
DOI: 10.1007/978-3-319-18818-8_54

knowledge bases represent the concepts and their relationships, these links provide a way of inferring underlying semantics of the microposts [8–10]. We intend to further build on this approach. The following example provides the basis for this proposal as it distinguishes its contributions from the state of the art.

Motivating Example. Each February, Tim Hortons, a well-known Canadian chain restaurant holds a campaign called *Roll Up the Rim to Win*. A customer can try his luck by buying a paper cup of coffee and unrolling the rim of the cup after finishing his drink, to determine whether he has won a prize, where the greatest one is a Toyota Camry. During the time when the campaign is being held, many users tweet about this event. These tweets contain terms for which a related DBpedia concept, e.g. *Tim Hortons*, *Toyota Camry*, *Roll Up* and *Coffee,* can be identified. These DBpedia concepts can be used to provide semantic information for the corresponding tweets. It is easy to see that a meaningful topic of interest for this example needs to be constructed using a collection of concepts. However, existing works usually represent each interest using one single concept. Therefore, two DBpedia concepts *Tim Hortons* and *Toyota Camry* are considered as two distinct interests. In other words, these approaches cannot infer that a user is interested in a more specific topic, which is actually a combination of multiple related concepts. Further, they often confine users' interests to a set of pre-defined concepts (e.g. a subset of DBpedia concepts) and therefore interests to recent events such as *Tim Hortons* campaign that are not among that set cannot be discovered on the fly.

This proposal will address these shortcomings by proposing a framework that considers the semantics of microposts with due consideration given to social network structure and the temporal aspects of social content. Our framework is composed of three main components: (1) The extraction of the so-called *topics* in a given time interval, which are built through conjunction of multiple semantic concepts. For instance, during the February, conjunction of DBpedia concepts *Tim Hortons*, *Toyota Camry*, *Roll Up* and *Coffee* might be considered to be a topic of interest. (2) Interest detection for each individual user as it pertains to the extracted *topics*, whether it be explicitly observed or implicitly implied; (3) The temporal modeling of each user's interest shifts with regards to extracted topics.

The rest of the proposal is organized as follows. Section 2 briefly reviews the related work. The problem statement and contributions are presented in Sect. 3, and the proposed approach is introduced in Sect. 4. Section 5 outlines an evaluation plan, and finally, Sect. 6 concludes the proposal.

2 Background Literature

There are three different types of information available on social networks, which have been used in the literature for extracting user interests: (1) User-generated textual contents, such as Twitter posts (*content-based*), (2) Social network structure that shows the relationships between users (*network structure-based*), and (3) Temporal factors that represent the dynamic nature of user interests (*temporal*).

2.1 Content-Based Approaches

There are different approaches for extracting users' interest through the analysis of the user generated textual content. In the *Bag of Words* approach, users' interests are represented as a set of terms extracted from the users' contents [2, 11, 12]. For example, Yang et al. [11] have used a weighted term vector for modeling user interests, and applied cosine similarity for measuring the similarity of users.

Topic Modeling approach provides a probabilistic model for the term frequency occurrences in documents of a given corpus. As a matter of fact this approach forms topics by extracting groups of co-occurring terms and views each document as a mixture of various topics [13]. Latent Dirichlet Allocation (LDA), as a well-known topic modeling method, is frequently used for interest detection [14–16]. For example, Weng et al. [16] have created a single document from the collection of a user's tweets, and then have discovered the topics by running LDA over this document.

Since the *Bag of Words* and *Topic Model* approaches focus on terms without considering their semantic and the relationship between them, they cannot utilize underlying semantics of textual content. Furthermore, these approaches assume that a single document contains rich information, as a result they may not perform so well on short, noisy and informal texts like twitter posts [7–9]. To address these issues, there is another line of work for extracting user interests from microposts through representing user interests as a *Bag of Concepts*. Usually, external knowledge bases such as DBpedia/Wikipedia, Freebase and Yago are used as a source for extracting the candidate concepts. Since these knowledge bases represent the concepts and their relationships, they provide a way of inferring underlying semantics of the content [8–10]. For example, Michelson and Macskassy [8] have proposed Twopics which first extracts a set of Wikipedia entities from a user's tweets and then identifies the high-level interests of the user by traversing and analyzing the Wikipedia categories of the extracted entities. Kapanipathi et al. [3] have modeled users' interests by annotating their tweets with DBPedia concepts, and have used these annotations to filter tweets based on the users' interests. Abel et al. [17] have proposed to enrich twitter messages by linking them to related news articles and then extracting the entities mentioned in the enriched messages as the users' interests. Kapanipathi et al. [9] have introduced two kinds of interests for a user: (1) weighted primitive interests, which is bag of concepts extracted from the entities mentioned in the user's tweets and (2) implicit interests extracted by mapping primitive interests to Wikipedia category hierarchy using a spreading activation algorithm.

2.2 Network Structure-Based Approaches

The social connections of the users are another kind of information that can be used for user interest extraction from social networks [4, 14, 19, 20]. The social connections are usually modeled as a graph in which nodes are users and edges represent their connections. Theory of Homophily [18] is followed by most of the works in this category and it refers to the tendency of users to connect to users with common interests or preferences. For example, Mislove et al. [19] have used this theory to infer missing information and interests of a user based on the information provided by her neighbors. Pennacchiotti et al. [4] have extracted the interests of a user by using tweets of the neighboring users in addition to her own tweets. Wang et al. [14] have extended the Homophily theory by proposing a specific link structure assumption under which local link structures between two nodes are consi-dered to be an indicator of node similarity. For example, if two users share many followers, they are likely to be similar in terms of topical interests.

2.3 Temporal Approaches

Temporal aspects are also considered in some works to infer user interests from social networks [1, 5, 21]. For example Abel et al. [5, 21] have shown that a user's interests change over time and are influenced by public trends. They have modeled user interests in a given timestamp as a set of weighted concepts which are entities or hashtags extracted from the user's tweets in that timestamp. For calculating the weight of each concept, the tweets with shorter temporal distance to the given timestamp are assigned greater weight since they are considered to be more important. The authors have also shown that considering temporal dynamics of the user interests can improve the performance of a personalized news recommender system.

2.4 Discussion

Several interesting works have been performed on extracting users' topical interests from microbloging services. However, the current works struggle with at least one of the following limitations:

- In most studies [1–3, 5, 8–10, 14, 17], each topic of interest is considered to be represented by a single concept. Therefore, it is not possible to infer more specific topics which are only expressible by combining multiple related concepts. Using these approaches, for instance, given a tweet *"Tim Hortons RRRoll Up Replay Game: Tim Hortons RRRoll Up Replay Game Prizes: (1): 2015 Toyota Camry XSE"*, may identify *Tim Hortons* and *Toyota Camry* as two distinct topics. The user might not be too interested in *Toyota Camry* as a general topic, but is rather interested in a campaign which includes *Toyota Camry* and *Tim Hortons* together.
- In most studies [1, 3, 5, 8–10, 14, 17], semantic topics of interest are confined to a set of predefined concepts, e.g. only Wikipedia categories, and it is not possible to identify emerging topical interests which are not yet in this predefined initial set. For instance, when an event like *Tim Hortons campaign* appears for the first time, it might rapidly show itself as a topic in the tweets just after a few minutes, but can take much longer to have a Wikipedia page created for it.
- Most of the current works [1, 3, 8–10, 14] do not consider the context of the microposts to extract users' interests. In other words, these works overlook the fact that users usually make an implicit assumption that the readers are aware of the context in which the post is being made. So, understanding the underlying semantics of a post may require consideration of the relationships of posts to each other or to other users. For example, a user might have replied to many tweets related to *Tim Hortons campaign*, without mentioning any of the buzzwords.

- There are some works that consider the temporal aspects for identification of the users' interests [1, 5, 21]. However, they generally do not take into account identification of the user's interest shifts during time, while this is valuable and it can provide valuable insight about the evolution of the users' behavior and distinguishing between his short-term and long-term interests. For instance, knowledge about the interest shifts makes it possible to distinguish between a community of users who show interest in *Tim Hortons* only each February during the campaign and a community of users who follow this topic throughout the year.

3   Problem Statement and Contributions

This proposal seeks to address the limitations discussed in the previous section by proposing a framework that views the content of a social network as a temporal graph. This graph is composed of three heterogeneous vertice types representing (i) individual users, (ii) social contents such as microposts, and (iii) semantic concepts. More specifically, this proposal pursues the following three main contributions:

- We propose to model user interests through a collection of topical interest. We consider each topical interest a conjunction of several coherent semantic concepts. To globally identify so-called *topics* in a given time interval from the social network graph as defined in Sect. 4.1, a concept graph is built in which the vertices represent the semantic concepts extracted from the microposts published in that interval, and the edges indicate semantic relatedness between each two concepts (Sect. 4.2). Each topic is considered to be a cluster in this graph which includes a set of sufficiently related concepts in that time interval. This has the added benefit that each detected interest does not necessarily need to be from amongst a set of predefined concepts, and also, it makes it possible to define semantically complex topics which involve multiple concepts as opposed to single terms or concepts;
- We view a specific user's interests as a set of topics identified from the social network. This set includes explicitly observed interests of the user and also the implicitly implied interests. For a user, the explicit interests are identified from the concepts he has explicitly mentioned in his microposts, with due consideration given to the relationships of microposts to each other or to other users. The implicit interests are the topics that the user is expected to be interested in, and these topics are identified based on the interests of the communities the user is a member of. The proposed framework includes a component for identifying these communities, and based on the identified communities, the implicit interests of the users are determined.
- We further postulate that a user's topical interests can differ and/or evolve based on different time intervals, which refer to as user interest shift. We will propose methods that will be able to accurately model and predict user interest shifts.

4 Proposed Approach

This section describes the underlying representation model of the proposed framework, along with its technical contributions.

4.1 Representation Model

The proposed framework is designed around viewing the data of a microbloging service as a heterogeneous graph with three types of vertices: (1) User vertices representing the individual users. (2) Content vertices representing the contents published by the users. (3) Concept vertices representing the underlying semantics of social contents. Further, the edges of the graph include instances of the different types of relationships between the users, social contents and concepts. It is important to note that in the model not only vertices of the same type can be interconnected, but also different vertices types can be connected to each other.

For instance, in the case of Twitter, as shown in Fig. 1, content vertices include the tweets and the Web pages mentioned in each tweet. Concept vertices can be DBpedia concepts that can be derived directly from the tweets or indirectly from the content of the Web pages mentioned in the tweets. Furthermore, some relationships that can be used include: Follow relation between two users, relation between a user and the tweets she has made or retweeted or marked as 'Favorite', relation between a tweet and the Web pages linked in the tweet, relation between a tweet and the concepts associated with that tweet and others.

The amount of information shown in the network graph of Fig. 1 is readily available in Microblogging services, except for the concept vertices and their associated relationships. These concepts can be extracted using existing systems such as TAGME [22] and DBpedia Spotlight [23] which can be used to annotate a textual content with the resources in Wikipedia/DBpedia. For example, for a given tweet "*Tim Hortons roll up the rim abuses my love for coffee AND gambling*", DBpedia Spotlight identifies three links to DBpedia: *Tim Hortons* is linked to the DBpedia concept represented in "http://dbpedia.org/resource/Tim_Hortons"; *Coffee* is linked to "http://dbpedia.org/page/Coffee" and *Gambling* is linked to "http://dbpedia.org/page/Gambling". The weighted edges between any two concept vertices represent the semantic relatedness of those concepts. This relatedness value generally, not in a specific time interval, can be computed using a Wikipedia-based measure, which for instance computes the relatedness by link structure analysis techniques over wikipedia pages.

To consider the fact that the user interests are not static and they change over time, it is required to represent the network graph as a temporal graph. We will use one of the existing techniques [24, 25] which enable efficient storage and retrieval of temporal graphs and allow retrieving specific snapshots of the network graph. In our proposed approach, time is divided into fixed length intervals and a snapshot of the network graph is retrieved for each time interval $[t_{k-1}, t_k]$. This snapshot includes the users of the social network at time t_k, the contents added to the network during the corresponding time interval, and the concepts associated with these contents.

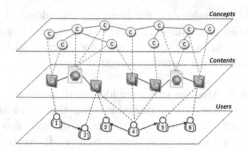

Fig. 1. Representation model

4.2 Concrete Contributions

The proposed framework includes three main contributions which rely on the foundations of the representation model described above. Next, these contributions are described.

Complex Semantic Topic Extraction. The goal of this component is to identify the so-called *topics*, which are modeled by clusters of concepts that are interrelated on the network graph (shown in Fig. 2). To identify these topics for each time interval, it is required to measure the semantic relatedness of the identified concepts in that time interval. Since the semantic relatedness between two concepts changes over time [26], by relying only on the static nature of knowledge bases like DBpedia it is not possible to consider the temporal issues effectively. For instance, computing the relatedness of *Tim Hortons* and *Toyota Camry* based on DBpedia link structure analysis results in the same small value both in February and August. But these concepts may appear so frequently in the users' microposts in February, due to the *Tim Hortones campaign*.

There are some works that seek to address temporal issues by utilizing the dynamics of the social network for computing relatedness of the concepts in a timely manner [26, 27]. However, they compute the relatedness of two concepts in a specific time interval only based on the co-occurrence of those concepts in the microposts published in that time interval. In contrast, we are seeking to provide improvement over these works by considering valuable information reflected in the 3-layer representation model of the network graph. A potential method is discussed as follows.

The relatedness of two concepts $C1$ and $C2$ at a given time interval can be calculated based on how similar are the content vertices associated with $C1$ to the content vertices associated with $C2$. Following the idea of SimRank measure [28], similarity of two content vertices $C1'$ and $C2'$ can then be computed based on the similarity of the content (user) vertices associated with $C1'$ to the content (user) vertices associated with $C2'$. Likewise, similarity of the user vertices can be computed based on the similarity of their associated users and contents.

The overall relatedness of two concepts in a time interval can therefore be computed as a weighted sum of two relatedness values, i.e. the temporal relatedness computed by the method described in the previous paragraph, and the static DBpedia-based relatedness. The weight values are expected to be obtained experimentally.

The computed relatedness values of the concepts are added to the network graph corresponding to a given time interval, in terms of weighted edges between the concepts. Finally, as illustrated in Fig. 2, the topics are determined by applying a graph-based clustering method on the resulting weighted graph.

User Interest Detection. After the topics are identified and modeled from the network graph, individual user's interests are modeled as a function of the identified topics. Our goal is to identify both *explicitly* expressed interests and also *implicitly* inferred interests of each user. To identify explicitly observed interests, we would need to measure the interest of each user against each topic of interest based on the content vertices associated with that user. The basic idea is that the more frequently the concepts of a topic are mentioned in the contents of a user, the more interested the user may be in that topic. We are going to augment this idea with using context information of the user contents. For instance, it is possible that a user has replied to a tweet which is much related to *Tim Hortons campaign*, but the reply itself does not mention any of the concepts associated with this topic. The simple idea mentioned above is unable to see the fact that the reply tweet is also related to that topic, and therefore does not notice the user's interest in the topic.

In order to identify implicitly inferred relations of users to identified topics, it is interesting to extract user-topic communities. As illustrated in Fig. 3, each of these communities include the largest set of mutually similar-enough topics along with the users interested in those topics. To identify these communities, we would need to measure the similarity between each pair of topics. This can be performed by measuring similarity of each topic to a set of predefined high-level topics that can be extracted from existing knowledge bases (e.g. the high-level DBPedia categories). Having the user-topic communities created, the implicitly implied interests of a user can be determined as the topics belonging to the communities in which the user resides in.

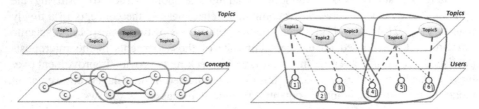

Fig. 2. Topic extraction   **Fig. 3.** User-topic communities

Interest Shift Detection. In order to address the interest shift aspect of user interest detection, the identified interests of a user in several consecutive time intervals are monitored. This helps in differentiating between the short-term and the long-term interests of the user. Further, by considering similarity and relatedness of the topic of interests of a user in different intervals, it is possible to model the evolution of the user's behaviour over different topics, i.e. how his interests are attenuated against some topics and focused on some other ones.

One possible way of analyzing interest shift of a user, is port his topics of interest for different time intervals to a set of points in the *2D* space. Knowing that a user is interested in a set of *m* topics T_k at time interval *k*, and a set of *n* topics T_{k+1} at time interval *k+1*, it is possible to build a matrix *m×n* representing distances between each pair of topics *(T_i, T_j)* where $T_i \in T_k$ and $T_j \in T_{k+1}$. This matrix can be computed based on using our topic similarity measure introduced in the previous section. The distance matrix can then be transformed to a set of points in the *2D* space, using Multidimensional Scaling (MDS) methods. Having the topics of interests ported to the *2D* space, it is possible to devise algorithms for identifying user interest shifts by comparing the position of the user's topics of interest in different time intervals.

5 Evaluation Plan

In order to evaluate the proposed methods, we need to first collect a dataset of real-world social network users. Due to widespread use of Twitter and accessibility of its data, a dataset will be created using Twitter data. Since our method is designed to provide improvement over *Bag of Concepts* approach, we are going to compare it with the state of the art works like [5, 8, 9]. Our evaluation plan includes two main approaches: a user study, and an application-based study.

User Study. As it is acknowledged in different works [1, 9], the most reliable and precise way of evaluating the results of interest detection for a user is to ask the same user to verify the results. Then, the user's feedback can be used for measuring quality of the proposed interest detection method. However, User study is costly and its validity is subject to different types of threats which are hard to address in reality. As a result, we will conduct an application-based study to complement the user study.

Application-based. It is possible to evaluate the proposed method by investigating how it affects the performance of an application which works on the basis of the user interests. Similar to [5], we are going to use news recommender application for this purpose. First, a ground truth is built by collecting, for each user, the news articles from BBC or CNN to which the user has explicitly linked in his tweets (or retweets) in a given time interval. Then, a news recommendation algorithm will be used that is able to recommend news articles based on the user's interests identified by our method. By comparing the recommended news with the ones in the ground truth, it is possible to evaluate quality of the recommendations, and therefore determine how successfully the interests have been identified. Traditional Information Retrieval (IR) metrics like P@K and Mean Reciprocal Rank (MRR) can be used for this step.

It must be noted that since our main goal is not to propose a news recommender system, a simple recommender algorithm, like the one used in [5], will be used for this application based evaluation scenario. An additional point is that, instead of using the prepared ground truth, it is also possible to ask the users to judge the recommendations.

The plan described above, evaluates the quality of the proposed interest detection method. However, in order to investigate the importance of the proposed interest shift detection method, a possible approach is to use it for measuring user similarity.

The idea is that considering similarity of the interest shifts of two users is a more accurate way of measuring those users' similarity, compared to simply considering the users' interests at one time interval. If this idea turns out to be valid, then the results of the interest shift detection can contribute to applications that require measuring similarity of the users, for instance content recommenders that employ the collaborative filtering method and hence need to compare users for finding the neighboring users of a specific user.

6   Conclusions

User interest modeling is the basis and core of many services such as recommendation and customization. Due to the popularity of microblogging services like Twitter and the fact that they are considered as a source of implicit and explicit information about the users' interests, recently, user interest detection from microblogging services has been the subject of many researches. We would like to propose a new framework to extract user interests as semantically complex topics composed of multiple interrelated concepts. This framework views data of a microblogging service as a temporal graph with three types of vertices: *(i)* individual users connections; *(ii)* social contents like microposts; and *(iii)* semantic concepts that represent the underlying semantics of the contents. This framework supports the identification of both the observed interests and implicitly implied interests of the user, with due consideration given to the fact that a user's topics of interest may change with time. It is expected that the proposed framework can address shortcomings of the current interest detection approaches that are based on a more limited notion of topical interest. Further, the proposed approach is expected to be able to improve quality of the applications which work on the basis of user interests.

References

1. Budak, C., Kannan, A., Agrawal, R., Pedersen, J.: Inferring user interests from microblogs. Technical Report, MSR-TR-2014-68 (2014)
2. Shin, Y., Ryo, C., Park, J.: Automatic extraction of persistent topics from social text streams. World Wide Web **17**(6), 1395–1420 (2013). Springer
3. Kapanipathi, P., Orlandi, F., Sheth, A., Passant, A.: Personalized filtering of the twitter stream. In: SPIM Workshop at ISWC 2011, pp. 6–13. CEUR-WS (2011)
4. Pennacchiotti, M., Silvestri, F., Vahabi, H., Venturini, R.: Making your interests follow you on twitter. In: 21st ACM International Conference on Information and knowledge management (CIKM 2012), pp. 165–174. ACM (2012)
5. Abel, F., Gao, Q., Houben, G.-J., Tao, K.: Analyzing user modeling on twitter for personalized news recommendations. In: Konstan, J.A., Conejo, R., Marzo, J.L., Oliver, N. (eds.) UMAP 2011. LNCS, vol. 6787, pp. 1–12. Springer, Heidelberg (2011)
6. Palsetia, D., Patwary, M.M., Agrawal, A., Choudhary, A.: Excavating social circles via user interests. J. Soc. Netw. Anal. Min. **4**(1), 1–12 (2014). Springer

7. Sriram, B., Fuhry, D., Demir, E., Ferhatosmanoglu, H., Demirbas, M.: Short text classification in twitter to improve information filtering. In: 33rd International ACM SIGIR Conference on Research and Development in Information Retrieval, pp. 841–842. ACM, (2010)

8. Michelson, M., Macskassy, S.A.: Discovering users' topics of interest on twitter: a first look. In: 4th Workshop on Analytics for Noisy Unstructured Text Data, pp. 73–80 (2010)

9. Kapanipathi, P., Jain, P., Venkataramani, C., Sheth, A.: User interests identification on twitter using a hierarchical knowledge base. In: Presutti, V., d'Amato, C., Gandon, F., d'Aquin, M., Staab, S., Tordai, A. (eds.) ESWC 2014. LNCS, vol. 8465, pp. 99–113. Springer, Heidelberg (2014)

10. Lu, C., Lam, W., Zhang, Y.: Twitter user modeling and tweets recommendation based on wikipedia concept graph. In: The AAAI 2012 Workshop on Intelligent Techniques for Web Personalization and Recommender Systems (2012)

11. Yang, L., Sun, T., Zhang, M., Davison, B.D.: We know what @you #tag: does the dual role affect hashtag adoption?. In: 21th International Conference on World Wide Web (WWW, 2012), pp. 261–270. ACM (2012)

12. Chen, J., Narin, R., Nelson, L., Bernstein, M., Chi, E.: Short and tweet: experiments on recommending content from information streams. In: 28th international conference on Human factors in Computing Systems (CHI '10), pp. 1185–1194. ACM (2010)

13. Blei, D.: Probabilistic topic models. Commun. ACM **55**(4), 77–84 (2012)

14. Wang, J., Zhao, W.X., He, Y., Li, X.: Infer user interests via link structure regularization. ACM Trans. Intell. Syst. Technol. (TIST) - Special Issue on Linking Social Granularity and Functions **5**(2), 23 (2014). ACM

15. Ramage, D., Dumais, S., Liebling, D.: Characterizing microblogs with topic models. In: 4th International AAAI Conference on Weblogs and Social Media, pp. 130–137 (2010)

16. Weng, J., Lim, E.P., Jiang, J., He, Q.: TwitterRank: finding topic-sensitive influential twitterers. In: 3rd ACM International Conference on Web Search and Data Mining (WSDM 2010), pp. 261–270. ACM (2010)

17. Abel, F., Gao, Q., Houben, G.-J., Tao, K.: Semantic enrichment of twitter posts for user profile construction on the social web. In: Antoniou, G., Grobelnik, M., Simperl, E., Parsia, B., Plexousakis, D., De Leenheer, P., Pan, J. (eds.) ESWC 2011, Part II. LNCS, vol. 6644, pp. 375–389. Springer, Heidelberg (2011)

18. McPherson, M., Smith-Lovin, L., Cook, J.M.: Birds of a feather: homophily in social networks. Annu. Rev. Sociol. **27**(1), 415–444 (2001)

19. Mislove, A., Viswanath, B., Gummadi, K.P., Druschel, P.: You are who you know: inferring user profiles in online social networks. In: 3th ACM International Conference on Web search and Data Mining (WSDM 2010), pp. 251–260. ACM (2010)

20. Abbasi, M.A., Tang, J., Liu, H.: Scalable learning of users' preferences using networked data. In: 25th ACM Conference on Hypertext and Social Media, pp. 4–12. ACM (2014)

21. Abel, F., Gao, Q., Houben, G.J., Tao, K.: Analyzing temporal dynamics in twitter profiles for personalized recommendations in the social web. In: 3rd International Web Science Conference (WebSci 2011), ACM (2011)

22. Ferragina, P., Scaiella, U.: Fast and accurate annotation of short texts with wikipedia pages. J. IEEE Softw. **29**(1), 70–75 (2012). IEEE

23. Mendes, P.N., Jakob, M., Garc´ıa-Silva, A., Bizer, C.: DBpedia spotlight: shedding light on the web of documents. In: I-Semantics 2011, pp. 1–8. ACM (2011)

24. Khurana, U., Deshpande, A.: Efficient snapshot retrieval over historical graph data. In: The IEEE International Conference on Data Engineering, pp. 997–1008. IEEE (2013)

25. Han, W., Miao, Y., Li, K., Wu, M., Yang, F., Zhou, L., Prabhakaran, V., Chen, W., Chen, E.: Chronos: a graph engine for temporal graph analysis. In: EuroSys. ACM (2014)
26. Milikic, N., Jovanovic, J., Stankovic, M.: Discovering the dynamics of terms semantic relatedness through twitter. In: 1st Workshop on #MSM 2011 (2011)
27. Celik, I., Abel, F., Houben, G.-J.: Learning Semantic relationships between entities in twitter. In: Auer, S., Diaz, O., Papadopoulos, G.A. (eds.) ICWE 2011. LNCS, vol. 6757, pp. 167–181. Springer, Heidelberg (2011)
28. Jeh, G., Widom, J.: SimRank: a measure of structural-context similarity. In: 8th ACM SIGKDD International Conference on Knowledge Discovery and Data Mining (KDD'02), pp. 538–543. ACM (2002)

Author Index

Printed in the United States
By Bookmasters